Independently produced by Tom Riker & Harvey Rottenberg at Gardener's Catalogue Studio, New York City, designed by John Krausz.

THE GARDENER'S CATALOGUE

FOOD GARDENS

FOOD GARDENS continues in the tradition of THE GARDENER'S CATALOGUE, providing accurate "how-to-do-it", "where-to-find-it" information for gardeners.

From seed selection, through harvest and storage, the book provides the know-how to grow your own vegetables, fruits, herbs, nuts, berries and mushrooms, in almost every region of the United States and Canada.

We have designed FOOD GARDENS to help beginners, as well as to introduce new ideas and sources to people who have been growing food for years.

The most up-to-date articles have been contributed by recognized experts in their fields. Whether you cultivate acres or just a little window box, they provide clear, detailed answers to all your questions.

We have selected articles, by internationally reknowned horticulturists, from popular gardening magazines that flourished near the turn of the century. The techniques they describe are still valid today, and should prove extremely helpful to modern gardeners.

The lovingly rendered plants and animals, the beautiful old farm buildings and fantastic machines that illustrate FOOD GARDENS are reproductions of rare woodcuts from the 1700's, engravings from gardening texts of the following century and steel and copper plates that were originally printed in antique seed catalogues.

We wish to share these remarkable pieces of art with you, since they show a kind of skill and workmanship that has almost disappeared in the last seventy-five years.

By thoughtfully blending the old and the new, we hope to show the continuity of gardening crafts as they've been developed through centuries. We seek to preserve the best the past has to offer and encourage the adoption of innovative, ecologically sound practices that are being developed today.

As more and more people turn to small gardens as a source for wholesome, nutritious, good-tasting food, we hope FOOD GARDENS will be their guide to intelligent action.

PUBLISHED BY
WILLIAM MORROW & COMPANY, INC.
NEW YORK, NEW YORK

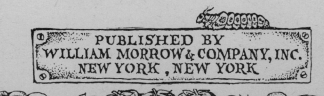

Our special thanks to

James J. Anding	W. E. Larmie
Robert G. Askew	M. B. Linn
Richard A. Ashley	Lowell F. Locke
James A. Beutel	Alan A. MacNab
Delores Bonander	Charles Marr
J. D. Butler	Verna Mikesh
L. V. Busch	Martin Miller
Munns A. Caldwells	P. A. Minges
Jack Cooper	N. F. Oebker
J. W. Courter	R. G. Platt
F. P. Cuthbert Jr.	W. J. Reid Jr.
Stewart Dallyn	Roscoe Randell
Malcolm Dana	Ashby M. Rhodes
Hubert Davis	A. D. Rizzi
Richard Delano	William A. Roberts
Carl Dietz	Reed S. Roberts
G. A. Duncan	D. P. Rogers
Harold V. Eck	Jean Roth
Robert E. Fletcher	Earl Scholz
Peter A. Ferretti	Vladimir G. Shatak
Pell E. Gates	Raymond Sheldrake Jr.
S. G. Gesell	M. C. Shurtleff
Christine Groppe	W. E. Splittstoesser
Robert E. Gough	James M. Stanley
R. A. Hayden	Allen K. Stoner
R. W. Hepler	H. H. Thornberry
R. C. Herner	Daniel R. Tompkins
Neal Holland	L. D. Topoleski
W. A. Huelsen	Orrin C. Turnquist
Arthur E. Hutchins	J. S. Vandemark
B. J. Jacobsen	E. K. Wade
Elbert R. Jaycox	J. N. Walker
Hunter Johnson Jr.	Robert E. Wester
Roy W. Judd Jr.	Llewelyn Williams
A. N. Kasimatis	L. Williams
Claude L. King	Frank Winter
Aron Kinrus	John A. Wott
George Klingbeil	William P. Wye
George F. Knowlton	George York
Jay S. Koths	
C. F. Koval	

for their expert contributions in the fields of
Horticulture, Agriculture, Viticulture, Pomology,
Floriculture, Plant Pathology, Entomology,
Agronomy, Botany, Agricultural Engineering,
and Garden Crafts.

Thanks to our expert Canadian contributors; INFORMATION CANADA and
The Winnipeg Horticultural Society, publishers of "The Prairie Garden",
PO Box 517, Winnipeg, Manitoba, R3C2J3.

And authors:
W. Andrews
P. J. Peters
H. F. Harp
David R. Ediger

THE GARDENER'S CATALOGUE PEOPLE

THE GARDENER'S CATALOGUE was conceived and is produced independently by Harvey Rottenberg and Tom Riker.

FOOD GARDENS was edited and organized by Tom, whose years of experience as a Horticulturist and Garden Designer made this book possible. The Horticultural and Botanical Archive illustrations were chosen by Tom, an expert in the field of archive art.

Harvey was the project's producer and wrote the original material in cooperation with Tom.

The book and cover were designed by John Krausz, art director for the original GARDENER'S CATALOGUE.

John designed our Logo, acted as his own production man, and, with Karl Bruning, devised the image-retrieval method used. Karl was the project's camera man and darkroom specialist.

Michael Edstrom executed the cover design, hand-lettering almost every element and re-working the drawing from the original catalogue, as well as doing the boardwork and the technical illustrations on page 56 and pages 289-290.

Susan Olshan acted as associate producer and handled information retrieval. June Elliott was editorial and production assistant.

Lars Skattebol once again supplied his editorial and technical know-how.

"The World in a Bottle," the borders on pages 1 and 3, as well as other illustrations are by Barbara Remington (Brem).

Our thanks go to 3-Way Typo, who did the headlines, Metro-Giant for their prompt and accurate photostat service, and David Easter, who made the almost 5,000 little lines necessary for the printer, Webcrafters Inc. of Madison, Wisconsin to line the pages up.

COPYRIGHT © 1975 by Tom Riker and Harvey Rottenberg

Grateful acknowledgment is made for permission to reprint previously published material as follows:

Page 6, "The Hoax Is on Us" from *The American Food Scandal* by William Robbins. Copyright © 1974 by William Robbins. Reprinted by permission of William Morrow & Company, Inc.

Page 108, "For the Long Haul—Plant Root Crops" by Maurice Franz; reprinted from *Organic Gardening and Farming*. Copyright 1975 by Rodale Press, Inc.

Page 143, "Potherbs or Greens for the Maritimes" by E. W. Chipman. © Information Canada, Ottawa, 1974. Reprinted by permission of Canada Department of Agriculture.

Pages 182-183, "Fruit Tree Grades" and "Small Fruits" reprinted from *American Standards for Nursery Stock*. Copyright © 1973 by American Association of Nurserymen, Inc.

Page 186, "Canadian Apples" reprinted from *Apples*. © Information Canada, Ottawa, 1973. Reprinted by permission of Canada Department of Agriculture.

Pages 244-247, lists reprinted from *Handbook for Greenhouse Gardeners* edited by Elvin McDonald. Copyright 1971 by Lord & Burnham.

Page 249, photograph from *The Terrace Gardener's Handbook* by Linda Yang; foreword by Elizabeth Scholtz; drawings by Sue Gardener. Copyright © 1975 by Linda Yang. Reproduced by permission of Doubleday & Company, Inc.

Pages 279-280, "How To Grow Vegetables In Your Apartment" by Nadine Zamichow, reprinted from *Wisdoms Child*. © 1975 by City Pennysavers, Inc.

Pages 288-289, first published under the title "Blooming Cactus and Succulents as Houseplants Under Full-Spectrum Lights" by Dr. George Milstein. © 1975 by Duro-Lite Lamps, Inc.

Page 318, "Poisonous Plants—The Case for the Guilty Garden" by Robert F. Lederer. Copyright © 1972 by The American Association of Nurserymen.

Printed in the United States of America.

1 2 3 4 5 79 78 77 76 75

Library of Congress Catalog Card Number: 75-27155

ISBN 0-688-07963-6 (pbk.)

FOOD GARDENS

TABLE OF CONTENTS

FOOD GARDENS IS AN IMPORTANT GARDENING TOOL

We don't mean to suggest that books can replace the first-hand knowledge you get from working the soil. But, FOOD GARDENS and the original GARDENER'S CATALOGUE are both very important gardening tools.

We call them tools because the information and sources you will find in the books help you to plan successful gardens. They are best used in combination.

First, we offer the best "how-to" instructions we can gather from the horticultural industry, government agencies, publishers, schools of agriculture, testing stations, botanical institutions and gardeners, everywhere in the world.

Then we provide long lists of suppliers, where you may buy seeds, nursery stock, greenhouse equipment, and anything else you might need to garden—indoors, outdoors, or underglass.

Our bibliographies, suggested reading lists, and book reviews allow you to dig deeper and find other books which discuss subjects in detail that are merely outlined in our books.

Helpful horticultural organizations are featured to supply sources for even more information and good advice.

Though GARDENER'S CATALOGUE books present a staggering amount of data, what we have gathered, so far, is only a fraction of the abundance of good information available to gardeners today. The material available ranges from the simplest directions for laymen, through technical instruction for space-age professional growers.

Much of it costs little or nothing at all. You will notice, for example, that most of the articles we have selected came from the United States Department of Agriculture, the Department of Interior, state extension services and land-grant colleges. As part of their function, these organizations are specifically chartered to encourage and provide accurate advice to gardeners. The people who staff them are paid with our tax dollars. So we should not hesitate to write or call them for help.

The answer to a problem that is plaguing your garden, may be on your county agent's desk. You'll never know, unless you get in touch.

Since we personally favor organic growing methods, and most official government and industry sources follow a go-slow policy as far as recommending the removal of questionable chemicals from our gardens, we have stressed organic gardening instructions by leading authorities in that field, as well as consumer and ecology organizations that will help you live and garden safely.

We have provided the tool. It is up to you to make use of it. Experiment with our growing instructions. Send for some catalogues and do some comparison shopping in local nurseries and garden centers. Get involved with your local botanical gardens. Join a horticultural society.

You will find, the more deeply you become involved in gardening, the more important GARDENER'S CATALOGUE books will become as tools for you.

FEEDBACK, KEEP THOSE CARDS AND LETTERS COMING

Every one of your cards and letters has helped us plan this volume and future works from THE GARDENER'S CATALOGUE.

Keep them coming and we will continue to make The Catalogue a backyard fence we can all gossip over to exchange gardening news and ideas.

Gathering and presenting all the material for FOOD GARDENS involved even more concentrated effort than preparing the original GARDENER'S CATALOGUE, though feedback from our readers was immensely helpful.

We still have not done business directly with all the suppliers listed in either book. Nor have we seen or read all the books and magazines available to gardeners.

It is still important that you let us know how the dealers we list treat you. Also continue to let us know about any gardening goodies, books, or sources for product and information we may have left out.

Remember to include the Title, Author, Publisher and date of publication of any information or literature you send our way. When recommending products include the brand name as well as the address or the manufacturer or distributor.

Your comments and criticism proved the best information is still in the heads and hands of our fellow gardeners. Let's keep hearing about your problems and successes. We would like to keep seeing any anecdote or bit of gardening lore you wish to share.

If THE GARDENER'S CATALOGUE is to remain the most important gardening tool since the watering can, we need your continuing advice. Keep us sharp. Stay in touch.

Our address is FOOD GARDENS, c/o THE GARDENER'S CATALOGUE, P.O. Box 3302, New York, N.Y. 10001.

Remember to include your name and address when you write. Let us know if you move after you've written. Then, someday you may open a GARDENER'S CATALOGUE publication and find your name and material featured alongside some of the most important horticultural writers in the world.

All correspondence received by us will be deemed our property. We reserve the right to edit and publish all the material we receive.

THERE IS STILL NOTHING FOR SALE IN THE GARDENER'S CATALOGUE EXCEPT MORE GARDENER'S CATALOGUES

Your letters indicated feelings were pretty well divided about seeing merchandise offered directly through THE GARDENER'S CATALOGUE. Though a sizeable majority was excited by the idea, enough people were opposed to give us second thoughts.

The main objections were aesthetic—some people are offended by promotional material—and moral—some people felt offering things for sale would weaken our consumer-advocacy position.

The first set of objections concerned us more than the second. Anything we offer would have to pass vigorous quality standards.

Our friends in the industry still insist that a catalogue ought to sell something. And, they've offered to let our readers in on very good deals on items ranging from seeds to home greenhouses.

Once again, we've decided to leave it up to you. Let us known what you think. If enough of our readers really want to see approved gardening material for sale in these pages we will arrange it in our next edition.

YOU CAN GARDEN EVEN IF YOU DON'T OWN LAND

Gardens For All, Inc.
P. O. box 2302
Norwalk, Conn. 06852

Gardens For All is a non-profit, federally tax-exempt educational and counseling organization. It is helping thousands of families all over the United States who don't have the know-how or the place to garden, to find their very own productive vegetable garden plot and reap the joys and rewards of growing their own vegetables.

This is done through a new concept called "Community Gardens" which has proved overwhelmingly successful.

A Community Garden is simply a good-sized piece of land which is lying idle at the moment, usually made available by a local church, business, service organization or township. It is divided into many standard-sized garden plots (about 25' x 30' each) and apportioned out to interested persons so that they can have their own personal vegetable garden.

It's as simple as that.

Gardens For All, Inc., in the past three years has helped organize Community Gardens in many, many towns. Among them are

BURLINGTON, VERMONT

In Burlington, the number of families involved in community gardening has grown from 15 to 750 in four years. The township, churches and schools have provided the land. Gardens For All provided the leadership.

ARLINGTON COUNTRY, VIRGINIA

Last year a combination of senior citizens and young married couples started a community garden in Arlington County with the help of Gardens For All's procedural manual. They reported that by following the organizational materials supplied by Gardens For All "to a T," the program was so successful that this year they will double its size from 75 to 150 gardening plots.

FEEDBACK FEEDBACK FEEDBACK FEEDBACK FEEDBACK FEEDBACK FEEDBACK FEEDBACK FEEDBACK FEEDBACK FEEDBACK FEEDBACK FEED
FEEDBACK FEEDBACK FEEDBACK FEEDBACK FEEDBACK FEEDBACK FEEDBACK FEEDBACK FEEDBACK FEEDBACK FEEDBACK FEEDBACK FEED

Many readers wrote, ". . . what do the code letters in the Cactus and Succulent section of the original GARDENER'S CATALOGUE mean?"

CODE
C - Cacti   R - Retail
S - Succulents   W - Wholesale
MO - Mail Order   P - Phytosanitary Certificate
L - List available   (furnished on request)

". . . where can I send for the Bee and Honey books listed on page 208 of THE GARDENER'S CATALOGUE?"

The books should be available on special order by local booksellers. In general the best Beekeeping information is available from the AMERICAN BEE JOURNAL, HAMILTON, ILLINOIS, 62341 and GLEANINGS IN BEE CULTURE, MEDINA, OHIO, 44256. They will probably be able to help if your bookstore fails.

". . . how can I grow the huge amorphophallus titanum pictured on page 185 of THE GARDENER'S CATALOGUE?"

Unless you have a well-controlled greenhouse situation or live in the tropics you cannot bring amorphophallus into bloom. The specimen pictured in our book was grown from a 113 pound corm. The bloom is not a true flower, but an inflorescence. Once it is coaxed into blossom, the "phallus" remains erect for about four days before it droops over and is enclosed again by the plant's petals, at which point fertilization occurs. Just as a side note, when this rare plant was brought into bloom in Germany in 1895, riots occurred as masses thronged to see it.

". . . several of the companies you mention only do business with wholesale customers."

These companies were listed to help people who buy cooperatively in large quantities and others considering going into the plant business. If your order is too small for them to handle, they should refer you to local retailers who handle their products.

". . . do you know any good sources for mailorder gardening books?"

The American Garden Guild, 245 Park Avenue, New York, N.Y. 10017 is a good source. Garden Way Publications, Dept. 121z, Charlotte, Vermont, 05445 is another good source for books by mail. An amazing garden cart is also available from Garden Way Research, Dept. 122z, at the same address. And, Garden Way Mfg. Co., 102 Second & Ninth Ave., Troy, N. Y., 12180, supplies a great rototiller.

". . . where can I get a dibble?"

Several dibbles appear in this volume. They are merely pointed sticks used to make holes in the ground for seeds and seedlings. You may make one by sharpening an old wooden tool handle. Or, you may make a multiple dibble by drilling a series of equally spaced holes in a straight line on a 1 x 4 inch board of any convenient length and gluing a snugly fitting pointed dowel in each hole. Spacing will be determined by the requirements of each crop.

Dear Sirs:
I have purchased THE GARDENER'S CATALOGUE, a enjoy it very much. I feel I should tell you that many of th cactus people you list have a charge for their catalogs. Also I tell you with deep regret that the Davis Cactus Garden ha closed, due to the death of Mr. Davis.
One item I missed in your Catalogue is a source for hop plants or seeds. I have been looking for Brewer's Gold for a long time with no success. If you could inform me of a sou for the seeds or plants, I would be most grateful.
Thank you and MORE
Jon Svibruck
Phila. Pa.

Well Sweep Herb Farm, 317 Mt. Bethel Rd., Port Murray, N. J. 07865 is a source of rare plants such as ginseng, golde seal & hops.

Dear Proprietors,
The Old Farmer's Almanac contains a lot of informatio useful to people who grow things. And for people who sto what they grow, too. The Almanac also has a lot to say about the weather—weather forecasting, regional average dates of the first killing frosts, rainy day amusements, average growing seasons, long-range weather forecasts, wir and barometer tables, and lists of meteor showers—among other things.
If you got just a few little green growin' critters or a whole herd of salad-on-the-hoof, you'll find it reading of interesting and useful nature.
Pax, Semper,
Crash Karuzas
Wheat Ridge, Colorado

PUBLIC INTEREST CONSUMER ACTION GROUPS

During the last few years concerned citizens and professionals have banded together to insure that the quality of our lives is not damaged by irresponsible individuals, governments or industries.

The Center for Science in the Public Interest (CSPI) is an off-shoot of Ralph Nader's Center for the Study of Responsive Law. The work of this group is typical of the efforts being made on our behalf by many public-interest and consumer groups across the country these days.

We have reprinted the editorial below from NUTRITION ACTION, the CSPI Food Project Newsletter.

A subscription costs only $10 and will help this organization do more work to help us in our fight for a better life. CSPI welcomes inquiries and ideas from any interested individual or group.

STAMP OUT FOOD FADDISM

A narrow matted row of strawberries.

Listening to many health professionals, food company representatives, and government officials, one would think that food faddism is the major food problem in the United States. People dying of scurvy from eating only brown rice, going broke from buying only organically grown food, being hospitalized from over-dosing on wheat germ and liver—this is the specter of food faddism that many believe threatens the American public.

Food faddism is indeed a serious problem. But we have to recognize that the guru of food faddism is not Adelle Davis, but Betty Crocker. The true food faddists are not those who eat raw broccoli, wheat germ, and yogurt, but those who start the day on Breakfast Squares, gulp down bottle after bottle of soda pop, and snack on candy and Twinkies.

Food faddism is promoted from birth. Sugar is a major ingredient in baby food desserts. Then come the artificially-flavored and colored breakfast cereals loaded with sugar, followed by soda pop and hot dogs. Meat marbled with fat and alcoholic beverages dominate the diets of many middle-aged people. And, of course, white bread is standard fare throughout life.

This diet—high in fat, sugar, cholesterol, and refined grains—is the prescription for illness; it can contribute to obesity, tooth decay, heart diseases, intestinal cancer, and diabetes. And these diseases are, in fact, America's major health problems. So if any diet should be considered faddist, it is the standard one. Our far-out diet—almost 20% refined sugar and 45% fat—is new to human experience and foreign to all other animal life.

People who shop in health food stores, on the other hand, are probably more nutrition-conscious than most of the population. A few really go off the deep end, for instance, those who have died of scurvy. A few are messianic and boring. Some are more vocal and concerned than the rest of us about the harmful effects of the insecticides, herbicides, and other chemicals that growers and distributors have found useful. Nevertheless, their diets are generally low in fat and sugar, and relatively rich in whole grains, legumes, fruits, and nuts.

It is incredible that people who eat a junk food diet constitute the norm, while individuals whose diets resemble those of our great-grandparents are labeled deviants. It is outrageous that food companies encourage people to eat an unwholesome diet, and that the government health agencies do nothing to reverse the trend. Health professionals should decry food faddism, but should make sure that they are referring to the most dangerous and wide-spread form.

Center for Science in the Public Interest
1779 Church Street, N.W., Washington, D. C. 20036

CONSUMERS UNION

Consumers Union (CU) is a group that helps the public.

Their magazine, CONSUMER REPORTS, regularly issues ratings on consumer goods and services which are based on laboratory and controlled-use tests as well as expert judgements of purchased samples.

In the past five years CU has tested and reported on a few gardening products: pruning saws, compost grinders, hoses, lawn seed and electric hedge cutters.

The organization is very responsive to requests from its readers. So, if you wish to see more gardening supplies tested by this impartial, non-profit group, we suggest you write and let them know.

Subscriptions are available from CONSUMER REPORTS, P. O. Box 1000, Orangeburg, New York, 10962.

A NATIONAL ASSOCIATION OF GARDENERS

The special needs and desires of America's Gardeners have been ignored long enough. We are 33-million strong and we spend an estimated $10 billion a year tending our gardens. With that kind of strength you would think it is time our voices were heard loud and clear and the work we do to feed ourselves and improve the general environment was materially encouraged and rewarded. The recent storm of bombast and press releases heralding the start of the government's WIN garden program passed quickly into a void of bureaucratic do-nothingism.

Gardeners deserve a better shake. But, nothing will be done for us until we make our strength felt by the policy makers.

Therefore we are pleased to announce the formation of a Founders Committee for a National Association of Gardeners. We encourage all our readers to raise their voices and lend a hand in the formation of the new association. Every one of your ideas and suggestions will help determine the group's direction. If you wish to get involved or have any questions write:

Founders Committee for a National Association of Gardeners
c/o The Gardener's Catalogue Food Project
GPO Box 3302
New York, N. Y. 10001

GARDENER'S CATALOGUE GIFTS

Many of your letters asked us to forward copies of the Catalogue to family and friends whose gardens are spread out all across the country.

We love to help out. It creates a more direct link between you and us, and the plant lover that receives your gift.

But, to do this, we must put the books in costly padded packages, mail them, and do a bit of bookkeeping each time. So, we must ask you to chip in one dollar for postage, packaging and handling, if you want us to continue forwarding your gift packages from THE GARDENER'S CATALOGUE studio.

Send $7.95 for each gift copy of THE GARDENER'S CATALOGUE or FOOD GARDENS you want us to forward to
Gardener's Catalogue Gifts
G.P.O. Box 3302
New York, New York 10001

FEEDBACK FEEDBACK FEEDBACK FEEDBACK FEEDBACK FEEDBACK FEEDBACK FEEDBACK FEEDBACK FEEDBACK FEEDBACK FEEDBACK FEEDBACK
FEEDBACK FEEDBACK FEEDBACK FEEDBACK FEEDBACK FEEDBACK FEEDBACK FEEDBACK FEEDBACK FEEDBACK FEEDBACK FEEDBACK FEEDBACK

SCOVIL HOE CO.
Higganum, Conn. 06441, U.S.A.

Scovil Hoes are forged from a single piece of high carbon steel. They are scientifically tempered to hold a cutting edge and will not shatter on rocks.

For more than 185 years, the name Scovil has meant quality and rugged construction. All Scovil products are fully guaranteed.

S. A. Mitchell, Jr. of the Scovil Hoe Company sent this for your consideration. While Scovil's prices are high, they do give you quality for your money.

SCOVIL HOE CO.
Higganum, Conn. 06441, U.S.A.

Gentlemen,
I received a copy of THE GARDENER'S CATALOGUE as a gift for Christmas.

At a casual glance I notice cuts of people in mid 1800 garb and some cuts of machinery and methods even older.

Please advise if this is a comic book or is it intended to be instructive. I would appreciate a response.
Yours truly,
Howard G. Robinson
Fair Lawn, N. J.

Yes to both questions. Aside from their beauty and charm, the illustrations are intended to be informative and to show the development and continuity of gardening craft through the years. Current technical illustrations are available from most of the sources we include in our books. Our object is to make our readers aware of these sources so that they can exploit them themselves.

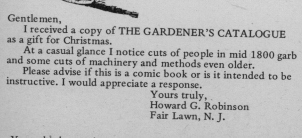

Dear All:
"Where are the apples of yesteryear?" At Southmeadow Fruit Gardens, 2363 Tilbury Place, Birmingham, Michigan 48009. Plus Peaches (Early & late Crawfords), pears, grapes, etc. etc. etc. A fantastic source! It is to be hoped that in sharing this address I'm not cutting off my nose to spite my face as I plan to start ordering from them this spring and it will be at least a 10 year plan to get all I want. Can you conceive of 60 different varieties of apples—29 pears—22 peaches—56 grapes? They have 26 of the apples you enumerate in your list. An exciting shopping list. Do not read it if you have no land on which to plant. Frustrating!

May I please know who is responsible for the engravings —etchings—whatever that look like old time pictures? Are they actually from old catalogues, or contemporary work made to look antique? I've been looking for similar material in drawings about the size of your catalogue pages, preferably in black & white that I can tint and use in a specific project. I need either separately or together —violets, lilacs, roses etc.

Thank you muchly,
Mrs. Ralph E. Johnson
Richland, Wash.

Thanks for a good source. Most of the illustrations you are interested in come from old seed catalogues and horticultural books. The ones that come from collectors and dealers tend to be very costly. But, we've made lots of inexpensive finds, poking around antique shops, uncatalogued library stacks and dusty bookstore basements. We were pleased to hear that many readers used THE GARDENER'S CATALOGUE as a coloring book and others used selected illustrations as applique patterns.

5

MORE FEEDBACK ON PAGE 319-320

THE AMERICAN FOOD SCANDAL

Why You Can't Eat Well On What You Earn

William Robbins

William Morrow & Company, Inc., New York, 1974

The Hoax Is On Us

One of the oldest propaganda tricks is the technique of the big lie. The theory is that, if people are told the lie often and emphatically, enough of them will believe to make the trick successful. The theory is obviously true.

For it has helped to perpetrate a hoax of mammoth proportions on the American people. It is a hoax that is a composite of many deceptions, and it robs American families daily of millions of dollars of the money that they spend, knowingly and unknowingly, for their food.

Abetted by government agencies, the businesses that form the nation's food-supply chain are the authors and beneficiaries of the deceptions. They are a vast complex, of infinite variety, including corporations that produce and corporations that process and sell, as well as conglomerates that have a hand on each link of the chain that runs from field to supermarket. They include also the industries that serve and supply the others. They are an amorphous mass, grouped under the mongrel name of agribusiness but unified by the common goal of taking all that they can from consumers. They have been outrageously successful.

The food industry, or agribusiness—the terms are almost interchangeable—has succeeded partly because it has been one of the world's most skillful practitioners of the technique of the big lie. Americans, we are told, are blessed with better food at lower costs than anyone in any other country. So we are told by the industry, which is the world's largest concentration of financial power. We are told so by the industry's lobbyists, who compose the most potent political force in Washington. And their message is chorused by Congressmen and bureaucrats in the national capital who guard the industry's interests and do its bidding.

We have been told the big lie so often that few skeptics are left among us, and even fewer raise the pertinent questions.

Better than what? Our food is grown, processed and impregnated with chemicals, with hardly a passing thought from the industry about their effect on the consumer's health and little show of concern when an ingredient, after long use, turns out to be carcinogenic. We have been robbed of variety by stores and distributors and of taste by nearly every hand that touches our food.

"Let them eat the Delicious," say the buying officials of the supermarkets if we want apples. And where are the Rome Beauties, the Northern Spies, the Grimes Goldens, the Baldwins and Yellow Newtons of yesteryear? Their delightful flavors, like the tart sweetness of a fresh blackberry or the exotic tang of a ripe persimmon, have been sacrificed to a mythical god of efficiency, and our children may never know the riches of which they have been robbed.

Our tomatoes have become hard, grainy and tasteless because government researchers, serving agribusiness rather than the consumer, breed them for toughness rather than quality. And, as our supply system has been corrupted, those hard tomatoes, developed primarily to withstand the steel fingers of mechanical harvesters, are picked green and reddened with a gas spray while being shipped over vast distances. In the stores we get the same dry, pulpy, boxed-and-shipped vegetables whatever the season and whatever juicy and tasty varieties might be offered by small local farmers.

And how can we believe that our costs are lower when we are bled by hidden costs, both financial and social? We have paid billions in subsidies to wealthy farmers and giant agribusiness corporations and billions more because their prices were artificially supported by the Government. And we pay additional billions to be bombarded by advertising messages designed to persuade us that worse is really better.

Our food costs also include the billions spent for unnecessary processing that diminishes both quality and taste, for extravagant packaging and for preparation of "convenience" foods that offer us the flavor of cardboard, often with less time saved than we would achieve with a pan and a can opener.

The hidden costs include, in addition, hundreds of millions of dollars in extra taxes. Consumers must pay more because of tax dodges that let farming corporations pay less, while wealthy absentee investors in farming schemes often pay no tax at all. We pay, as another hidden part of our food bills, the billions in welfare

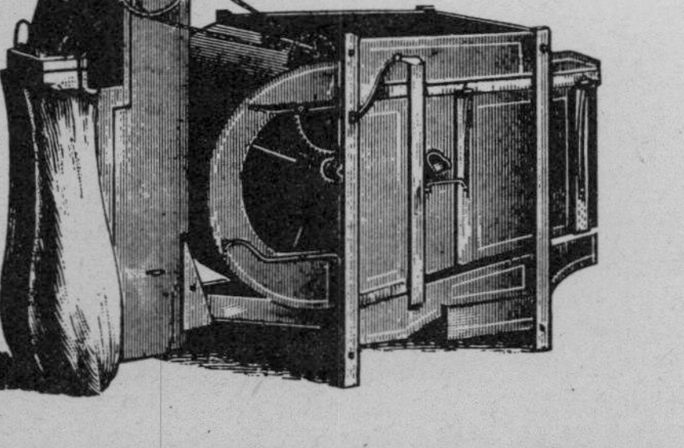

costs brought on as small farmers and farm workers are driven from their fields. And still higher and more devastating are the social costs of our desolated rural villages and country lanes, left behind by the dispossessed people who crowd our slums.

Oh no, we are told, what is meant is that Americans pay at the food counters a smaller percentage of their income—less than 16 percent—for food than other nations do. That, too, is deception. Again the pertinent questions: Which Americans? The poor? A family of four at the poverty level—among the most tragic victims and easiest marks for advertising frauds—spends nearly half its earnings for a meager subsistence. The average wage-earner? That family of four, if it moved up to the median tax bracket, would pay nearly a third of its income for food, and if it should advance to the relatively higher income average of suburbanites, it would still pay over 25 percent. Only among families with relatively high incomes do we reach a level where less than a fifth of spendable earnings goes for food.

The government and industry claims rang more hollow than ever in 1972 and 1973 when soaring costs virtually eliminated meats from the diets of low-income families. The resulting loss of food value came at a time when, according to a report by a Senate committee on "Hunger—1973," twelve million Americans were still malnourished.

Poorer families in 1973 were forced to seek substitutes for such old standbys as hamburger and hot dogs, and red meat was cut from the federal surplus-food programs long depended upon by the needy, the schools and other institutions.

In the twelve-month period ended at midyear the cost of the roast in a roast beef dinner rose nearly 22 percent. Buying by families seeking a cheaper alternative drove the cost of the chicken in chicken dinners up nearly 29 percent, and eggs, cheese, fish and other main dishes were climbing at similar rates.

These were high prices for the consumer to pay for a combination of industry practices and governmental actions that included politically motivated restraints on production and poorly managed export programs.

But the industry, and its hucksters, should never be allowed to dodge the issue of real costs with its specious equation of cash-register prices and some mythical average of total personal income, which lumps the wealthy in with the poor. The relatively little that a wealthy man must pay does not ease the strain on families of moderate income. And any accurate assessment must include the hidden costs. All of us long ago could have got tax relief—ranging from a few hard-earned dollars for the poor to thousands upon thousands for the well-to-do—had it not been for the subsidies and tax advantages that have become a form of welfare for the wealthy farmers and farming corporations, and if not for their jobless victims and the costs of helping them survive in their newfound urban squalor.

A new farm program passed in 1973 may reduce the subsidies and it has some other advantages over previous legislation, but it also insures that the cost of food will never again fall below the high levels that were reached in 1972, whether those costs are paid through prices or taxes.

The principal advantage is that price guarantees to farmers, provided in the program, help to restrain scarcity-induced inflation because they encourage growers to produce as much as they can.

But the problems in our food-supply system amount to more than the situation as it exists today, shot through though it is with waste and inequities and laced though it is with deception and outright fraud. Bigger problems threaten our not-so-distant future. Until recently, despite the needless costs, food has been a better buy than, for example, our automobiles or the gasoline that speeds them relentlessly toward the junkyards.

For those are products of industries in which trends toward shared monopolies-oligopolies, as the economists call them—have run their course. They are products, like many others, of industries in which prices for an entire segment of the economy are "administered," that is, dictated by the executives of the strongest company rather than by the forces of competition. Because a few companies control the market in follow-the-leader fashion, our cars can be sold for style rather than durability, to be changed when the buyers of one fashion must be tempted with another.

Forces in the food industry have already quietly accumulated the power of similar shared monopolies, and they are displaying their strength. Two companies share the production of soup, for example; four control the cereal shelves; one company is dominant in cheese. Trends point toward a similar leverage in other phases of processing, as well as in production, marketing and retailing. And in food the forces of control grasp more than a luxury. They seize on our most vital necessity. In the taste, purity and variety of food, they capture an essential element in the quality of life. The iron hand of control reaches for our throats.

And that is not strange, for the prize is great. The American food industry is the largest in the world. It is a $150-billion-a-year industry, bigger than automobiles, steel, oil or even the defense establishment.

The National Commission on Food Marketing, in an excellent but largely unnoticed study in 1966, analyzed the gathering forces and reported to Congress and the President on present and potential effects on the consuming public. Control of the food supply, from processing to the retail counter, the commission found, was passing into the hands of ever fewer and larger companies. Competition was declining, and a live-and-let-live attitude prevailed among the surviving corporations and conglomerates as they pursued their common goal of carving up the consumer's dollar. The less competition, the higher the price. And monopolistic positions in product lines were protected by heavy advertising that both increased consumers' costs and barred competing brands from the grocery shelves.

The National Commission on Food Marketing was created by Congress, and its members were appointed by the President of the United States, the President pro tempore of the Senate and the Speaker of the House. Its final report, "Food from Farmer to Consumer," was a summary of ten book-length technical studies. Staffs for the work were drawn from several government agencies, but none contributed so extensively as the Federal Trade Commission, which wrote a key study, "The Structure of Food Manufacturing."

Yet after the temporary National Commission's landmark report, the effort to systematically assess the trends was dismantled. Since then no board-based, concerted attempt has been made to curb or reverse the movement toward shared monopo'·· that was found.

Against a background of much foot-dragging on the part of politically appointed commissioners of the F.T.C., what progress has been made has been largely the result of initiatives from dedicated staff directors and economists within the agency. Guidelines have been drawn to curb mergers of retailers with annual sales of more than $100-million, but no effort has been made to roll back concentration of power that already exists or even to slow its expansion through the proliferation of a chain's supermarkets in areas where the company already has a big share of monopolistic power.

Attacks on overwhelming market power have been largely piecemeal, taking the form of individual suits by the F.T.C. or the Justice Department against prominent mergers or flagrant violations of antitrust law.

Lacking an adequate budget and often the freedom to carry the attack, many staff economists of the F.T.C. have grown discouraged, the more so because they also are barred by government-protected corporate secrecy from vital information on the state of competition in the economy.

Many people, including economists who should know better, have felt that the consumer was offered some protection by the simple nature of food production. Farming, the first link in the food-supply chain, was the freest form of competition in the American society. Productive resources were fragmented among millions of free and independent farmers.

But what farmers had was a freedom to commit economic suicide, and they have been doing that in large numbers. Processors long ago gained a foothold by growing on their own lands much of the produce needed to fill their cans. Now other national corporations and conglomerates are moving massively into food production and the so-called independent farmers are falling like wheatstraws before a scythe. Trends now in motion, unless checked, will finally give agribusiness control of that last bastion of free competition.

Statics understate the forces that are at work. By 1969, when the Department of Agriculture made its most recent study, corporations were said to have gained control of only 1 percent of the nation's farms. But that 1 percent represented an amalgamation of what were once many other farms, the end result of the merging of small farms into ever larger production units. Those corporate farms, although only 1 percent of the total number, owned 7 percent of all farmland and produced more than 8 percent of all cash income from farming, the Agriculture Department says. Still, according to the department, many of those corporate enterprises are only family farms organized as corporations. A subsequent review of census figures confirmed the basic conclusions, the department has said.

But some caution is necessary when dealing with Department of Agriculture statements. Top officials at the agency have long been apologists for agribusiness, from where most of them come and to which they hope to return, at far higher salaries. Agriculture officials tend to regard the fading of the family farm as an inevitable trend and to disregard their own mandate to protect it. And these men seem even to regard the trend as a phenomenon eminently to be desired, despite proof that the family-size farm can be more efficient than vast operations structured in layer upon layer of administrators and supervisors.

Even the department's statistics have been thrown into question by a follow-up study led by a rural economist, Professor Richard Rodefeld of Michigan State University. In heavily documented testimony before a Senate monopoly subcommittee, he said that he and a group of other researchers had found glaring inaccuracies in the department's basic data for Wisconsin, with understatement of corporate holdings ranging up to 216 percent.

But even if Agriculture Department figures were accepted as accurate, they are misleading. What they do not make clear is that the corporate invasion of farming has focused largely on the most strategic sections of the country, where control can pay off in the highest cash earnings. What is clear is that the number of farms is rapidly declining and that the independent farmer is a threatened species.

Since World War II, the number of farms has dropped by half, from over six million to fewer than three million. Until 1972, when abnormal influences temporarily slowed the trend, more than two thousand independent farmers a week were leaving their farms and the land was usually swallowed up by larger and wealtheir farmers and farming corporations. The pattern of the future is one often seen now: Once a large but independent farmer assembles neighboring acreage enough to be attractive to a corporatio he in turn is swallowed up. If the trends continue, within a decade large national corporations can control the output of the nation's farms and dictate prices along the food chain, from the land to the grocery counter.

They will be able to accomplish that not only by the acreage they own but also by other production which they control. For the corporations that enter farming today often rent more land than they own. Further, they often control through contracts with once-independent farmers far more land than they farm with their own hired manage About 75 percent of vegetables sold for processing are now grown under contracts with food-manufacturing corporati

More and more farmers are surrendering their independence in return for the semblance of security to be found in a contract with a corporation. It is only a semblance, for farmer after farmer has found himself in debt to his corporate client and headed toward bankruptcy. In such cases, the corporation is often only too glad to relieve him of the problems of landownership.

What all this means for the consumer of tomorrow is indicated by what it already has brought him today. He may, on Thanksgiving Day, as a witness at a Senate hearin testified, bow his head to his deity, but the immediate sou of his fare is more worldly. Describing a Thanksgiving dinner of 1971, the witness said: "The Smithfield ham comes from ITT, the turkey is a product of Greyhound Corporation, the lettuce comes from Dow Chemical Comp the potatoes are provided by the Boeing Company and Te neco brought the fresh fruits and vegetables. The applesau is made available by American Brands, while both Coca-C and Royal Crown Cola have provided the fruit juices."

The thanksgiver cannot, however, find the cost of his dinner a matter for rejoicing.

BASICS

Gardening is a universal hobby. A vegetable garden can provide nourishing food, healthful exercise and profitable leisure for persons of all ages.

Vegetable plants, like other living, growing things, have certain requirements. They need a good soil and plenty of plant food, water and sunlight. They must also be protected from their enemies. The successful gardener knows these requirements and fulfills them with care and at the proper time.

CHOOSE THE RIGHT PLACE

The size of the vegetable garden will vary with space available, size of the family, and the methods of cultivation and crop arrangement. Reduce the work of preparing the soil and controlling weeds by using as small an area as possible.

Avoid planting on sloping areas where practicable but if excessive water runoff and soil erosion are problems, run rows across the slope. Otherwise the direction of rows is not important; whether rows run north and south or east and west will make little difference in the growth and yield of crops.

Vegetables grow best in full sunlight in a loose, fertile, well-drained soil which has plenty of organic matter. Choose a level spot well away from trees and shrubs; stay at least 50 feet from black walnut trees to avoid walnut wilt on tomato.

A fence around the vegetable garden may be helpful but has several disadvantages. Fence rows waste soil and harbor weeds and certain insects and diseases; a fence may also be a nuisance if you use power tools for soil preparation. If you fence the farm vegetable garden, temporary end sections are suggested. These may be moved to one side while you plow, fertilize, disc and level the soil.

MAKE A GARDEN PLAN

Plan your home garden carefully. Use extra care to get as much as possible from the space available. When space is plentiful, as on the farm, plan for the proper amounts and variety for continuous harvest during the growing season and extra amounts for out-of-season use. Planning can also help save time and labor. Finish the plan by early February to make sure you get good seeds of the best cultivars (varieties) so you can start plants for transplanting on time.

Check family likes and dislikes and consider the space before deciding on the crops and varieties you grow. The suggested amounts assume that the family freezes, cans and stores vegetables for out-of-season use, thus keeping food purchases to a minimum.

The suggested Plan for a Small Home Garden, 20 x 50 feet, shows what you may do even on a limited area by careful planning and intensive cropping. The same kind of planning also will help save time and increase returns in a larger garden.

Arrange crops carefully. Your aim should be to grow the desired vegetables in the smallest space. You will need to control weeds and more total space means more weeds; less space, fewer weeds.

A garden plan on paper is essential. Before starting the plan, get the dimensions of the garden. Place perennial crops such as asparagus, rhubarb and winter onions along one side or at one end of the garden. These crops stay in the same place for several years and should be placed where they will not be in the way or damaged at soil preparation time. Plant these perennial crops in rows, well away from the fence or edge of the garden. Allow enough space between rows and between plants for good growth and easy care. Make certain, too, that the area is completely free of quackgrass before planting these perennial crops.

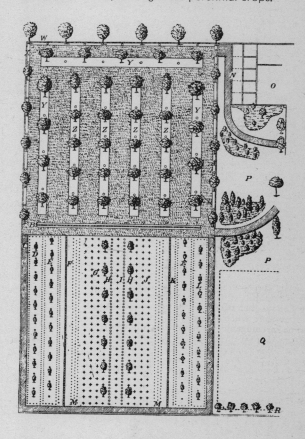

SHORT ROWS ARE BETTER

Short rows across the garden have many advantages. For many crops a 20-feet row at any one planting is enough. If you need more, plant extra rows. Sweet corn will pollinate better when two or more rows are planted together. Short rows with several planted at the same time are especially helpful with this crop.

Cultivating the backache.

Long rows often mean more than one crop in each row. This makes gardening somewhat more difficult because crops are planted at different times, grow at different rates, and need different amounts of space. Short rows in gardening, like short lines in reading, are more interesting and less tiring.

"The Vegetable Garden"
O.B. Combs and John Schoenemann
University of Wisconsin
Cooperative Extension Program

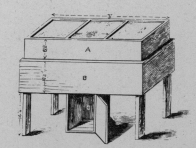

PRACTICE INTENSIVE CROPPING

Intensive cropping (using all the garden all the time) saves space and labor. You can plant crops which grow fast and are used quickly between rows of slower growing crops or in the same row before planting crops that you start later or that grow slower and stay in the garden longer.

Early radish and spinach, for example, may be planted in the same row before late beet, late carrot, Chinese cabbage, cucumber or tomato. When you grow tomatoes this way, the plants are often set in the row before the early crop is all harvested. Cucumbers, if transplanted or seeded in hills, may be planted in the same way.

Early, quick-growing crops like radish and spinach, as well as early beet, carrot, pea and leaf lettuce also may be planted between rows of cucumber, pumpkin, squash, tomato or late planted sweet corn. Likewise, head lettuce plants may be set between plants of early cabbage, early cauliflower, or tomato or ahead of late cabbage plants.

The three principal methods of intensive cropping are shown in the suggested plan.

In row 2, for example, two crops are grown in the same row (early spinach followed by late carrot). The late carrots are planted as soon as the early spinach is harvested.

In row 7, two crops are grown together in the same row (head lettuce and early cabbage). Plants of both crops are set in the garden at the same time but the head lettuce is harvested before the cabbage needs the space. Turnip is seeded in this row after the lettuce and cabbage are both harvested.

In row 12, a double row of a short-season crop (pea) is grown between two rows (rows 11 and 13) of a long season crop (tomato). The peas are planted early and are through producing before the tomatoes need the space. As indicated, early spinach may also be grown in each of the tomato rows.

With intensive cropping, then, all space is used by crops throughout the growing season.

Intensive cropping takes more fertilizer and water. Fertilizer is relatively inexpensive and careful weeding, thinning, and mulching will help retain moisture. Except on very light soils, intensive cropping may be done without artificial watering.

PLANT ACCORDING TO PLAN

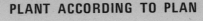

A finished garden plan like the one shown on this page will show (1) what crops are to be grown, (2) the number of different plantings of each crop, (3) the time and location of each planting and (4) the distance to plant each row from one end of the garden. A list of the crops to be planted, the seeds and plants needed and a planting schedule follow the plan. Except where specified, cultivars may be selected from the list on pages 6 to 8. Seeds and plants needed for larger or smaller gardens may be determined from information in the Planting Guide.

With this information, you can plant your home garden quickly and accurately. Locate each row when its planting time arrives simply by measuring the distance shown on the plan from one end of the garden. Or if you prefer, locate and mark both ends of the rows with numbered stakes as soon as the soil is ready for planting.

SEEDS AND PLANTS NEEDED FOR THE 20 x 50 FOOT GARDEN

BEAN	
Bush green	4 ounces
Bush wax	2 ounces
Pole	3 ounces
BEET	1/2 ounce
CABBAGE	
Early	1 packet or 13 plants
Late	1 packet or 10 plants
CARROT	1/8 ounce
CAULIFLOWER	1 packet or 13 plants
CHARD	1 packet
CHINESE CABBAGE	1 packet
CUCUMBER	1 packet
LETTUCE	
Buttercrunch (head)	1 packet or 47 plants
Salad Bowl (leaf)	1 packet

ONION	
Seeds or Plants	1 packet or 80 plants
Sets	1 pound
PARSLEY	1 packet or 2 plants
PARSNIP	1 packet
PEA	1 3/4 pounds
PEPPER	1 packet or 3 plants
RADISH	
Cavalier	1/2 ounce
Cherry Bell	3/4 ounce
White Icicle	3/4 ounce
SPINACH	1 1/4 ounces
SWEET CORN	4 ounces
TOMATO	1 packet or 12 to 18 plants
TURNIP	1 packet

PLANTING SCHEDULE

A planting schedule on paper will help you get everything in on time. Here is a schedule for the 20 x 50 garden. The planting dates are about right for the southern part of the state, but the weather may change them somewhat. Plant about one week later in central and two weeks later in northern Wisconsin.

APRIL 15
Chard, radish and parsnip in row 1.
Onion (seed) in row 4.
Pea in rows 8 and 10.
Radish in rows 9, 15 and 16.
Spinach in rows 11 and 13.
Beet in row 20.
Carrot in row 22.
Onion (sets) in row 24.
Leaf lettuce in row 26.

MAY 1
Parsley in row 1 (plants).
Spinach in rows 2 and 17.
Onion in row 4 (if plants are used).
Cauliflower and head lettuce plants in row 5.
Head lettuce plants in row 6.
Cabbage and head lettuce plants in row 7.
Radish in rows 21 and 23.

MAY 10
Radish in rows 3 and 30.
Pea in rows 12 and 14.
Bean in rows 18 and 19.
Sweet corn in rows 25, 27 and 29.
Spinach in row 28.

MAY 20
Tomato in rows 11 and 13.

JUNE 1
Pepper in row 1.
Cucumber in row 9.

JUNE 10
Sweet corn in rows 21 and 23.

JUNE 15
Pole bean in rows 15 and 16.

JULY 1
Carrot in rows 2 and 3.
Cabbage in row 6.
Bean in row 17.

JULY 10
Chinese cabbage in row 5.
Beet in row 30.

AUGUST 1
Turnip in rows 7 and 20.

AUGUST 10
Radish in rows 25 and 26.
Leaf lettuce in rows 28 and 29.

AUGUST 20
Radish in row 27.

Spanish or Vernon Hoe

PLAN FOR A SMALL VEGETABLE GARDEN (20 x 50 FEET)

ROW	FT. FROM END OF GARDEN	CROP(S)	SUGGESTIONS FOR PLANTING
1	1' 6"	Parsley, Chard, Cavalier Radishes and Parsnips, Peppers	Parsley plants first 2 feet of row; chard next 3 feet; seed radish and parsnip together 7 feet; 3 pepper plants
2	3' 6"	Spinach, Late Carrot	Carrots follow spinach.
3	5' 0"	Cavalier Radish, Late Carrot	Carrots follow radishes.
4	6' 3"	Onion	Seed and thin or set plants 3 inches apart.
5	8' 3"	Cauliflower, Buttercrunch Head Lettuce (plants), Chinese Cabbage	Cauliflower interplanted with early lettuce plants and followed by Chinese cabbage.
6	10' 3"	Buttercrunch Head Lettuce (plants), Late Cabbage (plants)	Lettuce interplanted with cabbage.
7	12' 3"	Early Cabbage, Head Lettuce (plants), Turnip	Cabbage interplanted with early lettuce plants and followed by turnip.
8	14' 0"	Pea	Two rows, 6 inches apart.
9	15' 9"	Cavalier Radish, Cucumber	Radishes followed by cucumbers.
10	17' 6"	Pea	Two rows, 6 inches apart.
11	19' 9"	Spinach, Tomato (plants)	Spinach followed by tomatoes. Set tomato plants in spinach row as spinach is harvested, 2 feet apart if staked, 3 feet unstaked.
12	22' 0"	Pea	Two rows, 6 inches apart.
13	24' 3"	Spinach	Spinach followed by tomatoes as in row 11.
14	26' 6"	Pea	Two rows 6 inches apart.
15	28' 0"	White Icicle Radish, Kentucky Wonder Pole Bean	Radishes followed by beans.
16	29' 0"	Cherry Bell Radish, Kentucky Wonder Pole Bean	Radishes followed by beans.
17	31' 0"	Spinach, Green Bush Bean	Spinach followed by beans.
18	32' 6"	Wax Bush Bean	
19	34' 0"	Green Bush Bean	
20	35' 6"	Early Beet, Turnip	Beets followed by turnips.
21	36' 9"	Cavalier Radish, Sweet Corn	Radishes followed by corn.
22	38' 0"	Early Carrot	
23	39' 3"	White Icicle Radishes, Sweet Corn	Radishes followed by corn
24	40' 6"	Onion (sets)	
25	41' 9"	Sweet Corn, Cherry Bell Radish	Corn followed by radishes.
26	43' 0"	Leaf Lettuce, Cherry Bell Radish	Lettuce followed by radishes.
27	44' 3"	Sweet Corn, Cherry Bell Radish	Corn followed by radishes.
28	45' 6"	Spinach, Fall Leaf Lettuce	Spinach followed by lettuce.
29	46' 9"	Sweet Corn, Fall Leaf Lettuce	Corn followed by lettuce.
30	48' 6"	White Icicle Radish, Late Beet	

AMERICAN WONDER PEA.

SEEDS AND PLANTS

Use only the very best seeds you can get. The price may or may not indicate the seed's quality. Good seed is inexpensive in the long run; poor seed is costly at any price. Saving seeds from most crops in the home vegetable garden is not advised. Commercial seedsmen, with their special knowledge and efficient methods, are able to furnish superior seeds at reasonable prices. Home-saved seeds sometimes carry disease, and in certain crops may become badly mixed through crossing. Seeds from hybrid cultivars will not breed true to the original hybrid.

WATER MELONS (FIELD OF).

ZEA MAYS (INDIAN CORN).

STORE LEFT-OVER SEEDS CAREFULLY

Unused seeds should be stored in a closed container in a cool, dry place. Good quality vegetable seeds generally will sprout very well even the third season, except onion, parsley, parsnip and sweet corn. Seeds of other common vegetables, if sown somewhat thicker, may be used until they are from three to four years old. Discard any questionable seeds or test them well ahead of planting time.

STARTING WITH PLANTS

Certain vegetables are commonly grown from plants started indoors. Do this to get earlier crops, longer harvest, and sometimes better quality.

Using well-grown plants for transplanting is especially helpful with early broccoli, cabbage, cauliflower and head lettuce. These vegetables grow best during spring and early summer when the weather is cooler and there is more rain.

Vegetables most commonly transplanted include broccoli, cabbage, cauliflower, celery, eggplant, head lettuce, onion, parsley, pepper, sweet potato and tomato. Other crops sometimes grown from transplants include brussels sprouts, cucumber, muskmelon, okra, pumpkin, squash and watermelon.

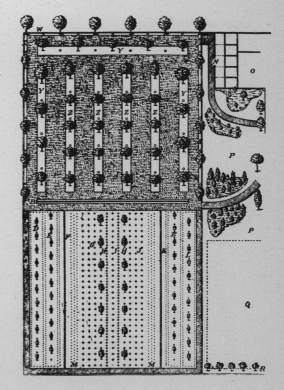

AGRICULTURAL HAND IMPLEMENTS.

WHERE TO GET PLANTS

You can grow vegetable plants at home or purchase them. If you buy plants locally or order from a catalog seedsman, try to get only those free from insects and diseases and of the desired cultivars. Place your order early with the local grower or with the catalog seedsman. In all cases be sure the cultivar you desire and the general date you will set the plants in the garden are clearly understood.

GROWING PLANTS AT HOME

With proper care, you can grow vigorous, healthy vegetable plants at home. See the Planting Guide for the time to sow seeds for transplanting.

You can grow plants in the house, in a hotbed, in a cold frame, or in a combination of house and cold frame or hotbed and cold frame. A hotbed is a small, covered structure with some form of artificial heat. A cold frame is similar without artificial heat. Hotbeds may be heated with electricity. A covered window-well heated with air from a warm basement, is one type of hotbed. A cold frame protects plants by trapping heat from the sun during the day and holding it overnight.

Equal parts of good garden soil, peat or compost and perlite makes a good growing mixture. Place the soil mixture in which you sow the seeds in plastic trays with separate compartments, small boxes, flats, plant bands, flower pots, berry boxes or other containers; or you may place it directly in a hotbed or cold frame. Commercial soil mixtures which contain added fertilizer and are generally free from damping-off organisms are available at garden centers.

Small boxes, fiber or plastic trays or wooden flats are used most often for starting vegetable plants because they are convenient, low in price and easy to get or to make. Cubes, discs or pots made from peat also may be used, especially for starting cucum-

ber, melon, pumpkin and squash, because the roots of these plants should not be disturbed at transplanting time. Bring soil for the mixture inside during late fall so it will be on hand and in suitable condition at seeding time.

Control Damping-Off. Plants growing indoors are subject to damping-off or seedling rot, unless started in a disease-free growing mixture. This disease is favored by overwatering, too much heat, not enough space or too little light. Damping-off may be largely avoided by (1) using clean plant growing mixture, (2) seed treatment, and (3) careful watering. Only by furnishing proper heat, light, space, water and moderate fertility and by avoiding seedling rot, can you grow vigorous, healthy plants indoors.

How to Grow Plants. Secure one or more plastic or fiber trays with or without compartments, wooden boxes or flats about 2½ or 3 inches deep, large enough to be practical yet small enough for easy handling when filled with growing mixture. The wooden flat commonly used by greenhouse plant growers is about 2 3/4 inches deep, 14 inches wide and 20 inches long. Smaller boxes, about 2½ x 10 x 12 inches, or plastic trays will be more useful for the home gardener. The average gardener will need at least three such containers: one for starting broccoli, head lettuce, cabbage and cauliflower, another for starting eggplant, and a third for tomato and pepper. If you grow celery and onion plants, you will need two or more containers. Use these same containers (or larger ones of about the same depth) if you lift the small seedlings and reset them shortly after they sprout. Narrow cracks or small holes in the bottom of containers are necessary for good drainage. A single sheet of newspaper will keep the soil from falling through cracks in wooden boxes. Fill each container with clean, moderately fertile growing mixture, making it level and firm.

Place seeds in trenches 1½ to 2 inches apart and about ¼ to ½ inch deep or place on the surface in pots or compartments and cover to about the same depth. You can make trenches easily and in even depth with a piece of thin board rounded on one edge and just long enough to reach across the inside of the container. Sow the seeds fairly thinly: eight to ten per inch (or two in each compartment) for most crops, and cover with more grow-

LARGE FLAG OR LONDON LEEK.

ing mixture. Water thoroughly by placing the container in a shallow pan so that water soaks in from the bottom; if you add water from the top, place a cloth over the container to prevent washing. Cover the container with a piece of window glass, cloth, paper or other material to prevent drying and set in a warm place (about 75-80 degrees F) until the seeds begin to sprout. As soon as seedlings begin to appear, take off the cover and shift the container to a cooler place (about 65-70 degrees) where there is plenty of light. Water only when needed to keep seedlings from wilting.

Thin Out or Move Seedlings. When seedlings (except onion) are large enough to be handled, (or as soon as the first true leaves start to grow), thin them carefully or lift and reset them in slightly moist growing mixture in other containers, or place them directly in a hotbed or cold frame. Leave onion seedlings in the original container until time for planting outdoors; clip the tops back to about 3 inches to keep them from falling over and becoming crooked. Space shifted seedlings carefully at least 2 x 2 inches apart, and water them.

As the weather turns warm, take seedlings growing indoors outside at least part of the day. You can leave them outside all the time as soon as danger of freezing is past. The covering of hotbeds or cold frames should be partly or entirely taken off as the weather becomes warmer.

Plant Protectors. If you use plant protectors, place them carefully over the hill when you sow the seeds or set the plants, but take them off or tear open the top as soon as the seedlings need more light and ventilation and the danger of frost is past. Protectors are sometimes placed over hills of early seeded cucumbers, melons, pumpkins and squashes or over tomato and pepper plants.

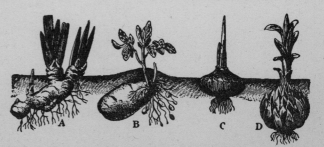

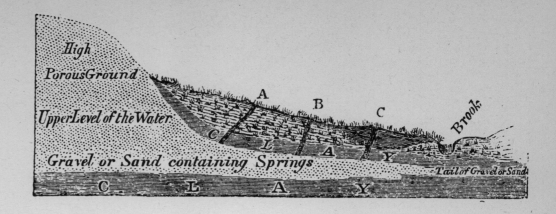

THE GARDEN SOIL

A good garden soil is deep, loose, fertile, well-drained, slightly acid and has a lot of organic matter (decayed plant and animal material). Because most garden soils fail to meet one or more of these requirements, the good gardener is always trying to better his soil.

Garden soils range from being almost pure sand to the more nearly ideal sandy loams to the silt loams and clays. Each has its good and bad features.

Sandy soils are easier to work, but they are generally very low in organic matter and so are not able to hold moisture and plant foods well. Adding organic material is your first step toward improving a sandy soil.

Heavier soils, such as the silt loams and especially the clays, usually hold water well enough but are harder to manage. Many of the heavier soils have too much water due to poor drainage. Better drainage (either by surface ditching or tiling or the use of raised beds) will prove helpful to these soils. The heavier, wetter soils also warm up more slowly in the spring. Adding organic matter helps improve heavier soils by making more space between the soil particles, improving drainage and generally making them much easier to handle. Fall plowing will also help.

To keep heavier soils in best condition, they should be worked only when a bit dry. Working them when they are too wet causes packing and forms clods. The age-old test of firming a small amount of soil in the hand is a good way to tell when a soil is dry enough to be worked. If the firmed soil does not crumble easily when gently pressed, it is too wet to work.

ECLIPSE GANG PLOW.

ORGANIC MATTER FOR THE GARDEN

Garden soils must be well supplied with plant food if they are to yield good crops of high quality vegetables. Humus (decayed plant material), supplies some of these plant foods. Humus also gives heavier, "hard-to-work" soils looser texture and sandy soils more ability to hold water and nutrients for plant use.

Most garden soils are low in humus because they have been cultivated for a long time. When humus is used up and not replaced, soils become hard, dry out easily and produce poor crops.

To build up the humus supply in garden soils use partially rotted barnyard manure, compost or other organic materials or green manure crops. If barnyard manure is available, add a uniform covering to a depth of 2 or 3 inches (10-20 tons per acre) each year.

Compost is primarily decaying plant materials. You can make it by piling plant refuse—plants from the garden, hay, straw, leaves, etc.—in shallow layers with small amounts of garden soil and commercial fertilizer sprinkled between. The pile should have a slight depression at the top so that it will stay moist; mixing once or twice during the season will hasten decay.

Compost started in early summer generally will be ready for use by late fall. Spread and plow or spade it into the soil as you would barnyard manure.

Another method for supplying organic matter to the garden soil is by growing a green manure crop. You can sow winter rye in your garden as you harvest vegetable crops in fall. This will help add humus when turned under the following spring. Rye for this purpose should be seeded by mid-September at the rate of 2 to 3 pounds per 1000 square feet. Add a moderate amount of a complete commercial fertilizer to the rye cover crop before plowing or spading and turn under as soon as the soil can be worked in spring.

FERTILIZING THE SOIL

Even when you add manure or other organic materials to the soil, an application of 1000 to 1500 pounds an acre (about 25 to 30 pounds to 1000 square feet) of a complete commercial fertilizer such as 6-6-18, 5-10-30, 5-20-20 or 6-24-24 mixture, is needed for best results in the average vegetable garden. (The first number in a fertilizer mixture stands for the proportion of nitrogen, the second for phosphorus and the third for potassium—three commonly needed soil elements.) If you don't have suitable organic matter, use a commercial fertilizer with more nitrogen such as 10-10-10 or 12-12-12 at about the same rate.

A dependable soil test will tell the actual fertilizer, lime and organic matter needs of your soil. Most vegetables grow best in a slightly acid soil, so do not add lime unless a soil test indicates otherwise.

Manures (especially fresh manures), composts and other organic materials preferably should be spread and plowed or spaded into the soil in late fall. Then, in the spring, spread any commercial fertilizer evenly over the garden and disc or rake it into the soil. If you turn the soil in the spring, manure or other organic materials and about two-thirds of the commercial fertilizer may be spread evenly and plowed or spaded into the soil together. Apply only well rotted manure or compost in the spring. Spread the remainder of the commercial fertilizer and disc or rake in after plowing. It is generally more practical to spread (broadcast) all fertilizers or other materials used to improve a home garden. Side-dressing (putting fertilizer along the row to the side of the plants) with 33-0-0 or 20-10-5 later in the season on leafy vegetables and

on fruiting vegetables like pepper, sweet corn and tomato will be helpful, especially on sandy and sandy loam soils. If you apply commercial fertilizers at planting time, you may place small amounts in bands beside the row or around plants or hills; or it may be dissolved in water and added as a liquid. Don't let dry fertilizer touch seeds or plant roots.

Liquid fertilizers are sometimes applied as "starter solutions" at planting time and for "side-dressing" later in the season. Special materials may be used or you can make a good mixture by dissolving 1 pound of a complete, water-soluble commercial fertilizer (such as 8-32-16) in 5 gallons of water. Water plants at transplanting time with about ½ pint of this liquid for each plant. Be sure that the fertilizer is dissolved and the solution is well mixed to avoid burning.

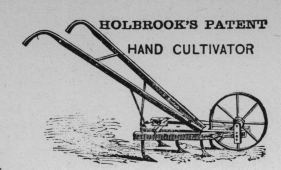

HOLBROOK'S PATENT
HAND CULTIVATOR

PREPARING THE SOIL

Unless there is serious danger of erosion, it is best to plow or spade most garden soils in the fall. Fall turning helps keep the soil in good condition and permits it to dry out and warm up earlier in spring. Fall turning also saves time during the spring rush and helps get rid of certain insects and diseases which live over winter in or on the soil.

Farm gardens and many larger gardens in towns and cities are plowed and prepared for planting with power tools. It is then fairly easy to get a fine, loose, level, weed-free seedbed. If you don;t use power tools, prepare the garden soil with a spade or spading fork and a rake. Spading takes more work but may be just as good if done right. In the average garden, which is cropped each season, a spading fork is a convenient tool for turning the soil. For turning under sod, heavy applications of manure or other organic matter, a long-handled spade is more useful.

WOODEN WHEELBARROW.

No matter how you prepare the soil, be sure that all manures or other refuse are completely covered. The soil should never be handled when too wet. The depth to plow or spade will vary with the soil. It might be well to vary the depth slightly from season to season. Most garden soils will produce well when worked to a depth of 6 to 8 inches.

Good garden soils—especially the lighter soils and even heavy soils if well supplied with organic matter—need not be prepared completely each season. Deep, thorough preparation every second season is often enough. In seasons when normal plowing or spading is not done, loosen the surface enough with hoe, rake or wheel hoe for easy seeding and transplanting. Normal, shallow cultivation after that will keep the soil free of weeds and in good physical condition.

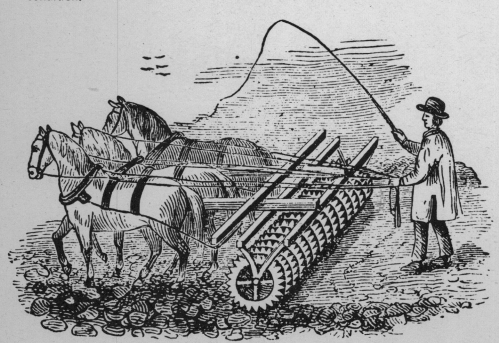

Crosskill's Clod-crusher.

TOOLS AND EQUIPMENT

The right tools save time and work; they make gardening easier and more enjoyable. You need only a few tools if you choose them carefully and use them in the right way and at the right time.

For Preparing the Soil. When farm and urban gardens are plowed and readied for planting with power tools, it is fairly easy to get a fine, loose, level seedbed. If you don't use power tools, prepare the soil with a spade or a spading fork and a rake. Using a fork and rake is more work, but it is effective if well done. A spading fork is a useful tool for turning the soil, but if you turn under sod or organic materials, a long-handled spade may work better.

For Seeding. You will need a hoe, a rake, a garden line with a sharpened stick at each end, and a measuring tape or yardstick at seeding time.

Use a hoe to loosen soil, open trenches and cover weeds.

A rake will be useful to smooth the soil and cover seeds.

A garden line drawn tightly just above the soil will help you establish straight rows.

A measuring tape or yardstick is needed to properly space rows and plants.

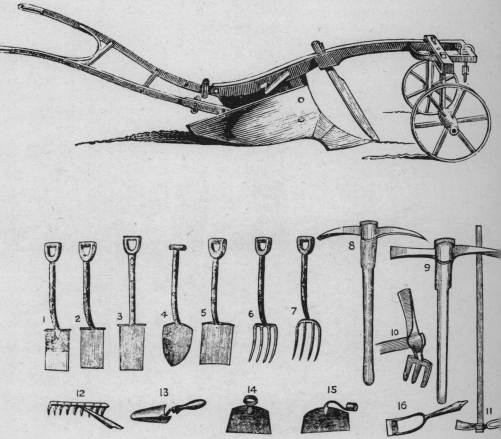

TOOLS USED IN CONNECTION WITH THE SOIL.

References: 1, No. 3 spade; 2, No. 2 spade; 3, lifting spade; 4, diamond-mouthed shovel; 5, square-mouthed shovel; 6, four-pronged digging fork; 7, dung fork; 8, pick-mattock; 9, mattock; 10, draw or Canterbury hoe; 11, pickfork; 12, iron rake; 13, trowel; 14, draw hoe; 15, swan-neck hoe; 16, Dutch hoe.

For Setting Plants. Most tools used in seeding may also be used when setting plants. Use either a hoe or trowel to make holes and trenches in which plants are set. A putty knife comes in handy when separating and moving plants growing in boxes or cold frames. The trowel and putty knife should both be strong and fairly narrow.

For Killing Weeds. A rake—one with straight teeth—is especially useful when weed seeds are just sprouting or when weeds are tiny. A properly made wheel hoe is an excellent weed control tool. If handled the right way, a wheel hoe—especially one with a thin cutting blade—will clean out weeds quickly and with very little work. Wheel hoes with teeth are harder to push, not as good for killing weeds, and may damage crop roots by deep cultivation.

For Pest Control. You may apply chemicals to control insect pests with either a duster or sprayer. Dusting may be more convenient in the average garden, but spraying often gives better coverage.

Take Care of Tools. Clean your tools after each day's use and keep them in a dry place. A wooden scraper or putty knife will remove soil from metal parts. Soil may also be removed by washing if you dry metal parts thoroughly. If tools get rusty, soak rusted parts in kerosene for a few hours and scour them with a wire brush or oiled rag dipped in fine sand.

Keep tool handles smooth by using fine sand paper from time to time. Keep hoe blades fairly sharp.

Garden tools should be thoroughly cleaned and stored in a dry place over winter.

PLANTING THE GARDEN

If good seeds are sown right and at the proper time, they will sprout quickly and evenly. Seeds need a warm, moist soil and plenty of air for quick sprouting.

The Planting Guide gives the approximate dates on which you can make first plantings at Madison (or in the southern one-third of Wisconsin). Gardeners living in the central one-third will generally plant about one week later and those in the north should wait about 10 more days. The type of soil, drainage, and the degree and direction of slope of the garden will also affect actual outdoor seeding dates. Sandy soils or other well-drained soils, especially those sloping to the south, generally dry out and warm up faster in spring.

Do Not Sow Too Deeply. The Planting Guide also tells how deep and how thick to plant seeds. You can sow seeds more deeply in late spring when the soil is warmer than in early spring when it is cold. Vegetable seeds, especially the smaller ones, are often

planted deeper and thicker than they need to be. If you use only good "live" seeds and plant them more carefully, you will need fewer seeds and less thinning.

Lima bean, beet and spinach, as well as seeds started indoors, may be treated with thiram or captan to control damping-off.

The strip of soil where each row is planted should be smooth, loose and free from clods and weeds. Freshly prepared soil will generally need only a light raking. Later in the season or on less desirable soils, you may need a hoe, hand cultivator, or wheel hoe to loosen the soil before smoothing it with a rake. Make seed trenches to an even depth with the corner of a hoe blade or with the end of a hoe handle. Use the hoe blade when making deeper trenches for bean, onion sets or plants, pea, potato and sweet corn; the end of the hoe handle is convenient for making shallow trenches for small-seeded vegetables.

Drop large seeds from your fingers; small seeds may be planted right from the seed packet. Mechanical seeders generally are not practical in the small home garden.

Plant the seeds evenly and cover snugly with moist soil. Use the back of a rake or hoe to cover the seeds. When you use a rake, you can firm the soil tightly about the seeds while leaving the surface fairly loose.

How to Seed in Dry Soil. Sometimes, especially when beet, carrot, Chinese cabbage, turnip and other vegetables are sown in July or early August for fall harvest, the soil will be very dry. You may soak larger seeds, such as pea, pumpkin, squash and sweet corn, in water for an hour or so before planting. Even with these seeds but especially with smaller seeds, it will help to fill the seed trench with water and let it soak into the soil before planting. Careful covering with fine soil should bring fast sprouting.

Covering rows which have been freshly seeded during dry weather with a mulch of lawn clippings or other material will help to hold moisture. Paper or boards also may be used, but the covering must come off at the very first sign of sprouting so the seedlings can get plenty of light.

Plant in Drills. Seeds of certain vegetables, such as vine crops, are sometimes planted in separate hills instead of drills (single seeds spaced along the row). However, in a well kept garden, yields are better when the seeds are planted, properly spaced, in drills.

The only time to consider planting vegetables in raised ridges or beds is when the soil is very heavy and poorly drained.

HOW TO SET PLANTS

Vegetable plants must be carefully set at the right time to grow well. The Planting Guide tells the dates on which early plants may be set in the garden at Madison.

Follow the Planting Guide for depth of planting—but remember that the kind of plant and the type, dampness and warmth of the soil make a difference.

Plants growing in pots, flats or other containers or in hotbeds or cold frames should be watered heavily an hour or more before transplanting time. If you do this, you won't need to water as you set the plants. All plants except onions should be taken out carefully with a block of soil attached to protect the roots.

Late afternoon or cloudy days are the best times for transplanting. You can also reduce wilting by taking off one or two lower leaves from plants like cabbage, broccoli, cauliflower, head lettuce, eggplant, pepper and tomato. Roots must stay on all transplants. You may "trench in" very tall tomato plants so the tops are only a few inches above the ground. Don't remove the tip of the plant or fruiting will be seriously delayed.

As when seeding, planting beside a tight line will mean straight rows. In a deep, loose, freshly prepared soil, you can make holes with a trowel or hoe.

HOLBROOK'S PATENT
REGULATOR SEED DRILL.

Transplanting slows plant growth. The rate at which a healthy plant will recover and start rapid growth will depend upon the care with which you transplant it. The following method is suggested for plants that have moist soil on their roots. Remove the dry surface soil from the spot where you will set the plant, open the hole, set in the plant, firm moist soil snugly about the roots and finish filling the hole with loose soil, leaving loose soil in a slight hollow around the stem.

Plants with little or no soil on their roots—especially if they have been pulled for some time—should be watered at transplanting time. A good way is to fill the fresh opened hole or trench with water, place the plant in the water, allow the water to soak into the soil, firm moist soil about the wet roots and finish filling the hole with loose soil. Do not press soil firmly against plant stems. Watering the surface after the plant is set is likely to cause the soil to bake and crack and much of the water will evaporate.

Sowing Fiddle

The trench in which you set onion or celery seedlings may be filled with water which you allow to soak into the soil before the roots are covered. You can then set the plants quite rapidly by placing the seedlings, properly spaced, against one side of the trench and pressing soil from the other side firmly against their roots with the back of a hoe or rake.

DRAG HOE OR PICKFORK.

WEED CONTROL

Easy, effective weed control is largely a question of proper timing. Weeds are easiest to control just as their seeds are germinating and before the young seedlings are established. At this stage, a careful stirring of the soil, so the top inch or so may dry out rapidly will generally control weeds. If you do this at intervals of about a week, and as soon after each rain as the soil is dry enough to be worked, weeds will not be a serious problem. Once the weeds get a foothold, control means hard work. If allowed to grow, weeds crowd and shade vegetables and rob them of water and plant foods.

Weeding Tools. Weed control tools are numerous and varied. If used at the right time, a straight-toothed rake is effective. A properly made, blade-type wheel hoe is faster, equally effective and easy to handle if used correctly. Well sharpened hoes used at a shallow angle are effective but relatively slow. Weeding tools with three to five tines, designed to tear up the soil 2 or 3 inches deep, often seriously injure shallow crop roots and are not very effective in weed control. Deep tillage also brings new weed seeds to the upper soil where they will germinate readily. Soils kept in good cropping condition do not need deep cultivation. The most effective weeding is shallow, thorough and timely.

 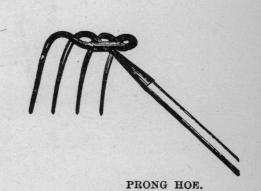

SCUFFLE HOE.   PRONG HOE.

Never permit weeds to go to seed either in or around the edges of the garden. Special care is needed to keep weeds from seeding, especially late in the season when you cultivate less frequently.

Chemical Weeding is Not Practical in Home Gardens. The chemicals commonly used by commercial vegetable growers are generally impractical in the home garden. Most vegetables are easily injured by 2, 4-D. If used near the garden, it should be applied carefully to weeds only and with a separate sprayer. Do not spray when wind might blow the material to vegetable crops or other sensitive plants.

Thinning. Vegetable seeds are often sown thicker than the plants are to grow to ensure an even stand. Some thinning, therefore, is needed so plants can grow fast and evenly. Most crops should be thinned soon after sprouting. One of the most common garden mistakes is failure to thin early and space plants properly.

You should thin all crops (except beets for greens, chard, leaf lettuce, mustard, onions from sets, spinach and turnips for greens) when germination is complete or by the time the first true leaves appear. You may delay thinning with the crops listed because you will be eating the plants taken out. Early thinning is especially important with beets for roots, carrots, Chinese cabbage, endive, head lettuce from seed, onions from seed, leek from seed, parsnips, radishes, rutabagas, salsify, and turnips for roots.

Mulching. Mulching the garden soil with straw, hay, lawn clippings or other material is an effective way to check weeds. Make certain that mulching materials are reasonably free of weed seeds, especially perennial weeds like quackgrass. Use enough mulch to cover all the soil to a depth of 2 inches or more and put the mulch close to the plants.

Mulching around tomatoes is especially beneficial. It helps to keep the fruit clean by keeping it off the ground. Mulching also helps check blossom-end rot by holding a higher and more even supply of moisture in the soil.

You may also cover the soil with black plastic sheets instead of hay, straw or lawn clippings to keep down seeds. Black plastic mulches work especially well on cucumber, melon, squash and tomato; clear plastic will not stop weed growth as the weeds often grow underneath the material.

14

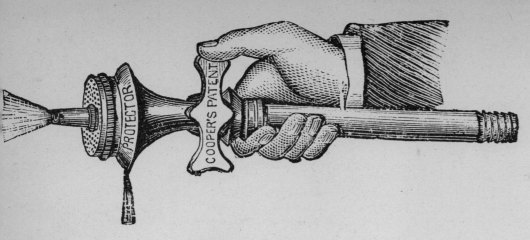

SOIL TREATMENT

Treating the soil with diazinon (Spectracide) will help control wire-worms, root maggots and white grubs. After you prepare the soil for planting, sprinkle about 11.5 pounds of 2% granules evenly over each 1000 square feet of garden area. Mix well with the upper 6 inches of the soil before planting the garden.

DUST OR SPRAY GROWING PLANTS

Damage from insect pests will vary from year to year. Watch for the first signs of trouble so you will have time to prevent serious losses.

The safest insecticides to use on vegetable crops are those containing rotenone, pyrethrins, malathion, or carbaryl. Malathion and carbaryl are good "all-purpose" insecticides.

WATERING THE GARDEN

Wise handling of garden soil to help it hold rain water is often a better and cheaper plan than watering it. In most seasons there is enough rain, but it does not always come at the right time. Here are some things you can do to hold rain water in the soil where plants can get it:

Keep a good supply of organic matter in the form of well-rotted manure or compost in the soil—this will hold water.

Keep down the weeds—don't let them even get a start or they will use water that should go to the crop plants.

Thin out the crop plants that aren't needed—they will use water too.

If you water your vegetable garden, remember that a heavy, even watering now and then is better than many light waterings. Use a hose and a good quality lawn sprinkler.

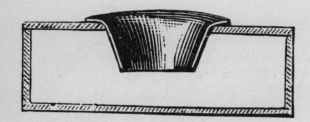

TRAP FOR EAR-WIGS.

PREVENT INSECT DAMAGE

A clean-up of all garden plants in fall or early spring will help control some garden insects. Insecticides should be used for treating the soil and for spraying or dusting plants.

You will need a good duster or sprayer. Follow label directions carefully when using any pest control materials.

CONTROL PLANT DISEASES

All diseased garden refuse, such as plant stalks, leaves and roots, should be put in a compost pile, plowed under in the fall or burned.

Strong, healthy plants will grow only on well drained soil that has enough "balanced fertility."

Damping-off seedlings in the seed flat or in the garden may be avoided by treating seeds before sowing with a seed protectant such as thiram or captan (75% wettable powders).

Late blight on tomato may cause serious damage, especially during cool, wet seasons. Spray or dust with maneb or zineb at weekly intervals, starting when the first tomato fruits are about the size of walnuts. These same materials will also be helpful in preventing losses from tomato leaf diseases such as Septoria, anthracnose and early blight.

Cabbage yellows disease stays a long time in garden soil. Use resistant varieties such as Badger Market, Wisconsin Golden Acre, Marion Market, Globe, Wisconsin All Seasons, Wisconsin Ballhead, Red Hollander and Badger Ballhead.

Injury to tomato roots from deep cultivation may cause blossom-end rot. Cultivate very shallow or use straw or other mulch soon after you set plants in the garden to keep down weeds so no cultivation is needed.

Subsoil plowing in the furrow of a common plow.

VIEW OF A SEED FIELD OF ONIONS.

ORGANIC GARDENING

Organic gardening, to the organic foods enthusiast, implies the growing of food plants on soils with high levels of organic matter supplied from animal manures, crop residues, composts or green manure crops and without supplementary mineral elements except those from natural mineral fertilizers obtained from naturally occurring deposits. It is presumed that any attempt to control diseases, insects and nematodes will be by use of resistant cultivars, other biological means, cultural practices or with naturally occurring pesticides obtained from plants. Weeds will be controlled by mulching or other cultural practices; no synthetic fertilizers, pesticides or herbicides are to be used

There are many ways in which organic matter, in various stages of decomposition, improves soils for plant growth. Organic materials also provide, after complete decomposition, substantial portions of the mineral elements needed by plants. Additional mineral elements are needed, however, for more nearly balanced plant growth and higher yields, especially on sandy oils, peat and muck soils and mineral soils which have been cropped for long periods. These mineral elements can be supplied more economically by using commercial fertilizers when the kinds and amounts are determined by soil tests. Research has shown that mineral elements used by plants enter the plant through the roots in water solution. Regardless of their original conditions or origin, therefore—natural or synthetic, organic or inorganic—mineral elements taken from the soil by plants must be in or reduced to an inorganic, water soluble form before they can move into and be used by the plant in the food manufacturing process.

Unfortunately, germ plasm carrying resistance to plant diseases and nematodes is presently known for far too few crops and diseases. Genetic resistance to insects is presently known for even fewer crops and insects; genetic resistance as a possible control for weeds is still, at best, in the exploratory stage. Furthermore, present knowledge indicates that genetic resistance often involves the presence in the resistant plant of special chemicals which actually account, in one way or another, for the resistance. These may be

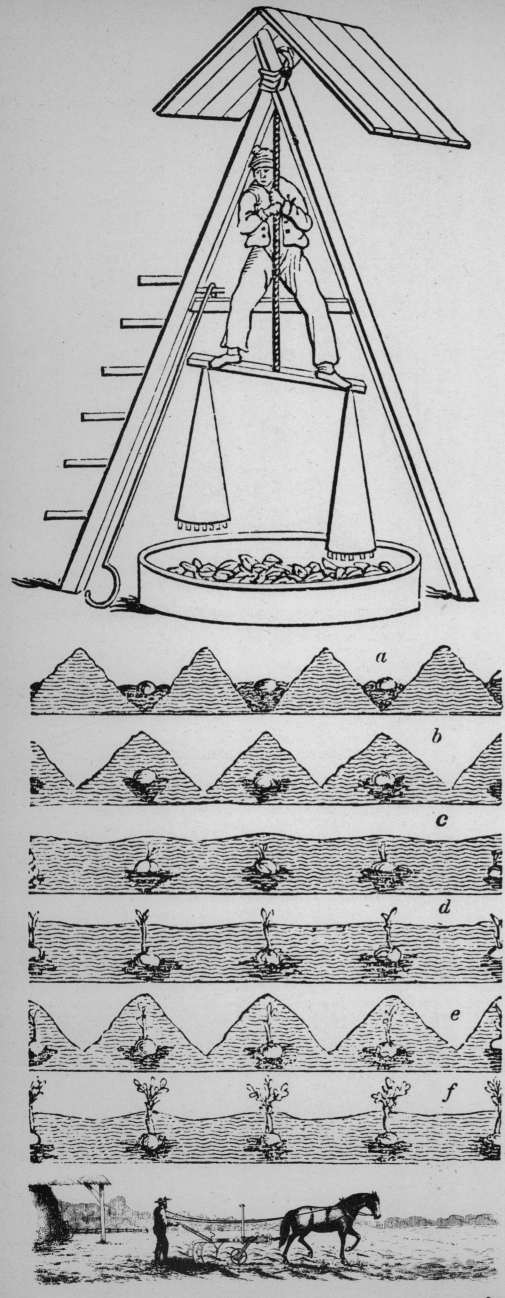

naturally occurring chemicals and, therefore, acceptable to the organic foods enthusiast, but there is no scientific evidence to indicate that a plant, or an animal for that matter, reacts any differently to a naturally occurring chemical than it does to the same chemical which has been synthesized in a laboratory. Likewise, there is no evidence to indicate that the nutritional value of foods produced by plants from inorganic or synthetic fertilizers is any different from that produced from organic or naturally occurring mineral fertilizers.

It is clear to all who are familiar with plant growth requirements and current food production problems that a total abandonment of all inorganic and synthetic chemicals, whether fertilizers, pesticides, or herbicides currently used in the production of food crops, is neither consistent with our knowledge of plant physiology and soil science nor with our knowledge of human nutrition and our total food needs.

PRINCIPLES OF ORGANIC GARDENING

ORGANIC GARDENING CAN BE SUCCESSFUL IF YOU FOLLOW SOUND PRINCIPLES

J.S. Vandemark, W.E. Splittstoesser, and Roscoe Randell
Illinois Research
University of Illinois Agricultural Experiment Station

Many home gardeners are taking up organic gardening, or gardening without chemicals for weed and pest control. But this does not mean gardening with neglect. For successful organic gardening, you need to control weeds, insects, and diseases; and you need to follow other established gardening practices.

PROVIDING NUTRIENTS

First of all, the soil must have adequate nutrients. To supply some of these nutrients, you can work undecomposed organic material (such as leaves, grass clippings, peat moss, straw or hay) into the soil. Bacteria and tiny fungi will break down this material into nutrients that plants can use. But these bacteria and fungi are heavy users of nutrients themselves, so your garden will need another natural source of nutrients, such as compost, manure, sewage sludge, steamed bonemeal, rock phosphate, muriate of potash, or hard wood ashes. Since organic matter will tend to make the soil slightly acid, a little ground-up agricultural limestone or marl may be needed.

PLANTING AND GENERAL CARE

Be sure to plant at the proper time. Plant in rows, leaving adequate space between plants. If you start with seed, thin the plants to the proper spacing after they have emerged. Use fresh commercial seed that is free of disease.

As soon as the seedlings can be identified, remove the weeds and grass by very shallow hoeing. Weeds not only compete with your garden plants for fertility, water, sunlight, and space, but may also harbor insects and diseases.

The space between the vegetable rows can be filled in with a mulch of undecomposed organic matter such as straw, leaves, grass clippings, or sawdust. The mulch will help control weeds and save water, and will eventually decay into humus.

Mulches, stakes, cages, or other training methods on plants should be used wherever feasible, especially for tomatoes. If tomato fruit comes in contact with the soil it is susceptible to various fruit rots.

To avoid soil compaction, do not work the soil when it is wet and sticky. Do not walk through the garden when it is damp as this will spread plant disease. Avoid watering plants in the evening. If the soil surface stays damp all night, disease organisms can thrive.

INSECT CONTROL

Some crops can be grown with little or no danger from disease or insect pests. These include radishes, lettuce, onions, leeks, shallots, chives, beets, chard, mustard, Chinese cabbage, parsnips, salsify, peas, spinach, sweet potatoes, turnips, and most herbs. Tomatoes can be grown if you hand-pick the tomato hornworms.

By paying attention to timing, you can also grow sweet corn without chemicals. If you plant corn about the middle of May, it will usually silk after June 15 and before mid-July, when there is little risk of serious earworm infestation.

Biological control is effective against some insects. This is the use of living organisms to reduce the number of damaging insects below a level of economic importance.

Bacillus thuringiensis, a microbial preparation, is available in several commercial formulations. It controls cabbageworms, tomato hornworms and fruitworms, webworms, and bagworms. With this type of biological control, you can successfully grow green beans, cabbage, kale, collards, brussels sprouts, broccoli, and cauliflower.

Lady beetles are sometimes released in gardens as a means of biological control. Although their preferred food is aphids, they will also eat eggs of several other insects. However, they do not kill grubs, Japanese beetles, or caterpillars. And if there is not an ample supply of live aphids on the plants when the beetles are released, they will eat each other or leave the area.

Praying mantid egg masses are also sometimes used. But mantids are poor searchers for food, usually waiting for their prey to come to them. They prefer grasshoppers, crickets, bees, wasps, and flies, and so may destroy beneficial insects.

Some crops are difficult to grow organically. Striped cucumber bugs spread bacterial wilt among cucumber, muskmelon, pumpkin, and summer squash plants. And flea beetles devour eggplant with gusto.

Despite organic precautions against insects, pest epidemics may become a threat. An insecticide is then needed to reduce the pest population to a tolerable level. Insecticides of vegetable origin such as pyrethrins, rotenone, and nicotine, may be used. Also, many man-made insecticides are both safer and more effective than botanical insecticides.

For more information, consult your County Extension Adviser, or the Extension Specialist in Vegetable Crops.

A SMALL CHEAP BARN.

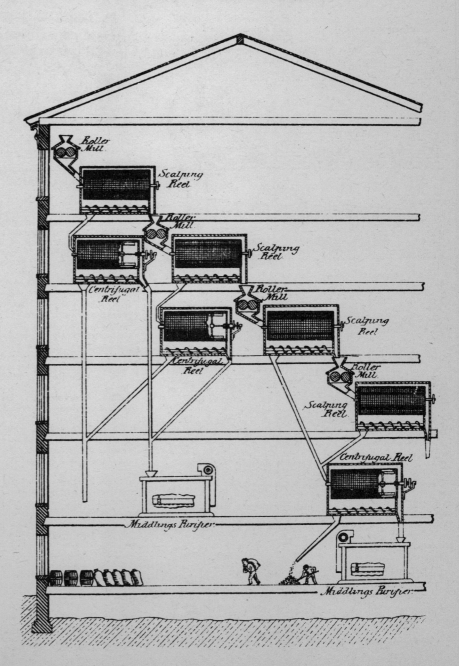

17

ORGANIC GARDENING EXPLAINED

James C. McCullagh
Rodale Press

A couple of years ago an American food scientist, M. Salomon, made the following statement:

"The organically grown food idea is not new but our cultural responses are such that the concept takes on a whole new dimension leading to special diets, a kind of mysticism, a certain fear of anything chemical or artificial, and in the extreme may find expression in ancient religious practices and a questioning and a turning against the establishment." (QUALITAS PLANTARUM, vol. 23, 1974.)

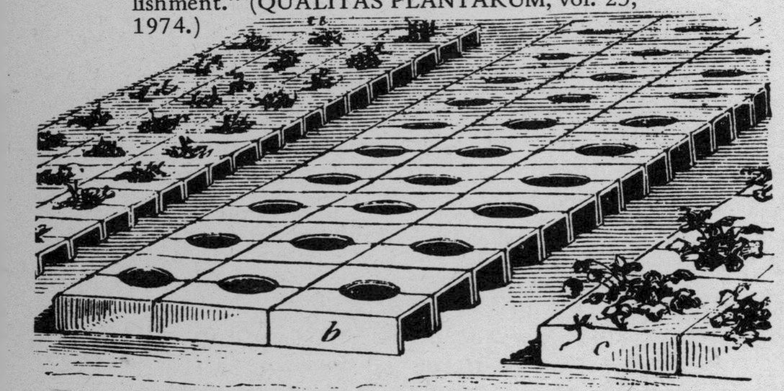

ROBERTS' MODE OF GROWING STRAWBERRIES.

Mr. Salomon notwithstanding, it is too often the food scientist and the scientific community in general that place the organic movement under the rubric of MYSTICISM and distort the true territory and the true definitions of organically grown and processed foods. Organic gardeners and farmers and consumers of such products (as well as many state governments), as will be shown, understand precisely the full dimensions of the terminology dealing with organics.

A recent report entitled, "Let's Take a Look at Organic Gardening," produced by the Cooperative Extension Service at Ohio State University is typical of the attacks which confuse the entire organic issue. The report boldly states that "No official definitions are available" for the term "organic foods," which, as will be shown, is not the case at all.

And in an interesting manifestation of convoluted logic, the author states: "Food habits and dietary patterns are changing. More meals are eaten outside the home. The trend is shifting from traditional food toward a more primitive way of eating." If eating highly processed food at the thousands of fast food chains across America is a movement toward primitive eating habits, we wonder what our ancestors ate.

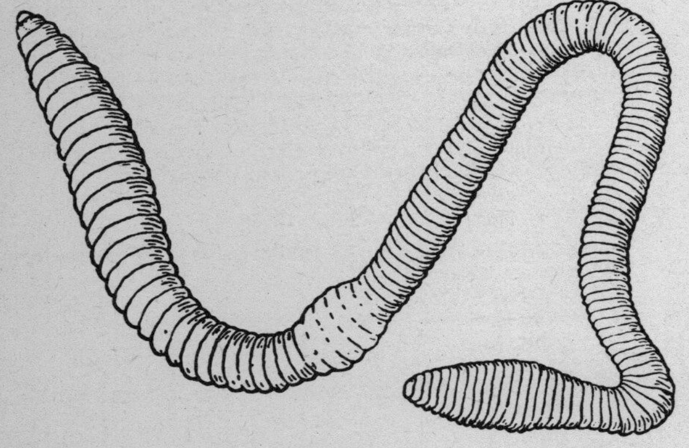

Earthworm

Most disturbing is that the report appears to place organic foods in the same nutritional basket with the Macrobiotic Diet, the Mucusless Diet, and the variety of vegetarian diets. Although organic foods may be a part of a number of diets, to infer that such foods represent just another bizarre diet, to use the language of the report, is misrepresentation at its best.

The sum total of this type of journalistic distortion is that it gives readers the impression that organic practices and organic foods are CULTISH and FADDISH. The fundamental question raised deals with the very objectivity of science. Has science been truly objective in its dealings with the organic movement? Dr. Julius Kaikow, professor Emeritus of the City University of New York, for one, thinks not. He has reported his opinion of a Symposium entitled "Food Supply and the Organic Food Myth," held at the 1974 meeting of the American Association for the Advancement of Science, in THE SOIL AND HEALTH FOUNDATION NEWS. Dr. Kaikow says "The very wording of the title expresses malicious bias. From the titles of the individual papers, just what will be discussed is perfectly predictable. Who is going to represent the other side? The concept of organic food is going to be given more than a black eye, and the philosophy of organic agriculture will not only be presented, it will undoubtedly be misrepresented. In effect, as I see it, a 'kangaroo court' is going to be convened and conducted.

"The organic philosophy is based on the concept that what is taken from the soil must be returned to it, otherwise the soil eventually becomes sterile. It is a concept that there exists a symbiotic relationship between food-producing areas and food-consuming areas. The crops sent to market carry off with them vast quantities of soil nutrients. These nutrients must be returned in order to maintain the productivity of the soil. Application of chemical fertilizers alone is not the answer. Such fertilizers have their limitations. Generally, in order to keep up production, more and more fertilizer must be applied each year. Moreover, such treatment destroys the structure of the soil, making it more susceptible to erosion, both by water and wind. Also, food quality suffers. Humus, derived from garbage (not plain refuse), sewage sludge, and manure, can firstly replenish much of this depletion and restore structure and tilth, thus permitting the soil to hold on to moisture more readily, and secondly to lessen the possibility of nutrients being leached by percolating ground water. For mineral additives, the organic school advocates the use of rock powders rather than chemical fertilizers. Superphosphate, for instance, is soluble in the laboratory, but ground phosphate rock is not. But the fact is that because of humic acids resulting from decomposing organic matter and from dissolved carbon dioxide in the ground water, phosphate rock has proven to be not only soluble, but longer lasting in the soil. Too much chemical fertilizer can be harmful to the soil and its microorganisms. The rock powders provide the same nutrients and do not harm the soil. Properly made compost provides not only nitrogen, but also trace elements. Furthermore, it acts as a buffer to heavy metals, where present."

"To categorize organic agriculture (of which organic food is a product), as a myth or a fad," Kaikow asserts, "is mere unwarranted castigation."

OFFICIAL DEFINITIONS OF ORGANIC

Much of the scientific community would have us believe that there is no consensus (just confusion) among organic practitioners as to the meanings of organically-grown and processed foods. The national record reveals that there is, indeed, a growing consensus among consumers, farmers, and governments as to a comprehensive meaning for organically grown and processed foods.

In 1971, Rodale Press Inc. developed a pilot certification program for organic farmers, which has since been adopted as a basis for certification by groups of organic farmers and consumers in many states. Regional groups are now active in 18 states, helping to certify, inspect, market and distribute organically-produced crops in every area of the country. The standards established by way of the pilot certification program have been applied conscientiously by each of these grower-consumer organizations, and the resultant flow of organic food products, buyer confidence, and increased farm production has benefited many people and communities.

Farm markets and roadside stand operations have been spurred in dozens of states, including Maine, where the Extension Service has worked cooperatively with the Maine Organic Farmers and Gardeners Association; and North Carolina, Georgia, and Virginia, where the Rural Advancement Fund has aided unemployed urban residents and depressed farm-area people in returning to land, growing crops organically and getting them to markets and distributors.

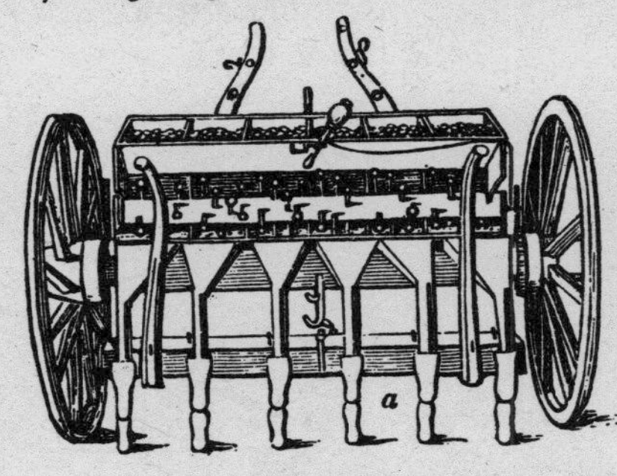

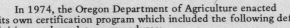

In 1974, the Oregon Department of Agriculture enacted its own certification program which included the following definitions and regulatory procedures:

"Organically-grown is food which has been grown without synthetic pesticides, fertilizers or chemicals; in soil in which the humus content is increased only by the addition of natural matter and in soil which the mineral content is increased only by the application of natural mineral fertilizers or other natural matter. There is also a definition for organically processed foods: food organically grown which in the processing has not been treated with preservatives, artificial coloring, artificial flavoring, or any other artificial or synthetic additive. In addition, the regulations establish as acceptable the labeling of meat and poultry products and by-products as 'produced in an organic environment' when the animal is maintained in an area in which the grasses, feeds and water supplies are free from intentional application of synthetic pesticides or chemicals; and when no artificial growth stimulants, hormones, drugs or antibiotics are administered to the animal unless prescribed by a veterinarian for treatment of a specific disease, and that in no event administered within 90 days of slaughter of the animal."

The new regulations place foods labeled as organically-grown, organically-processed or grown in an organic environment under the state's food labeling and advertising laws. If labels claim the food to be certified, a reproduction of the certificate, including the name and address of the person or organization issuing the certificate, must be available at the retail store upon demand of agriculture department inspectors.

Irvin Mann, Jr., Oregon's former State Director of Agriculture, said "We established criterion for producing and labeling food as 'organically grown' so that people will know what they are purchasing." Mann strongly criticized the Food and Drug Administration position on organically-grown foods: "Organic farmers are organizing and policing themselves and certifying themselves. They are doing this on a very realistic basis. The certification can be easily checked without abnormal expenditures. . . What the FDA forgets is this—whether you believe or do not believe that there is such a thing as 'organically-grown' foods is beside the point. What is involved and is in point is that several million people in the United States believe such a thing and wish to purchase such a thing on an honest basis. The Oregon approach is far from perfect but it is an attempt to deal with this widespread attitude on the part of a lot of Americans. That is what I think government is supposed to do to be responsive."

Kenneth E. Carl, Dairy and Consumer Service Director in the Oregon Department of Agriculture, is the man who has administered the organic food program in the state since the regulation became effective. He reported that "Both consumers and industry people have let us know that they are glad to see organically-grown foods made available for purchase this way, and they are eager to see the organic food movement make progress." Carl also indicated that inquiries from several other states have continued at a surprising rate, all asking for information and guidance in following Oregon's successful program in order to initiate their own.

"Of course people today recognize what natural and organically-grown foods are," said the Oregon Consumer Service Director. Attempting to deny or obscure that fact, he agreed, is like burying your head in the sand. "It is far better to help assure the availability, growing and confident marketing of organic foods by assisting with a direct, positive program such as this state has launched." Mr. Carl concluded by suggesting that a comparable federal program would be a highly desirable step.

In Wisconsin, Leon Kass of Elkhorn has indicated that his 54-acre truck farm has become a "test site" as a part of the state's move to pass similar legislation on organic food growing, marketing, and labeling. The Pennsylvania Department of Agriculture reports its survey of farmers, supermarket and health food store retailers has shown an increasing demand for organic foods ranging from grains to meats.

In New Hampshire, the Department of Agriculture prepared an organic foods bill that gives the Department the means of identifying and regulating "New Hampshire organically-grown produce." The New Hampshire bill passed both houses in June, 1973, and the governor signed it.

State Senator William J. Goodman has introduced a bill in Annapolis that would put Maryland among the ranks of states with organic food certification programs. Introduced on March 7, 1974, the Organic Farm Bill S.B. 960 calls for the certification of organic food producers, and the encouragement of additional organic farms in Maryland. An organic farm product is defined by the bill as "any agricultural, horticultural, vegetable, or fruit product of the soil, including livestock, meats, marine food products, poultry, eggs, dairy products, seeds and nuts, honey, and every product of the farm, forest, orchard, garden, or water, including canned, frozen, dried, pickled products that have been grown without being subjected to pesticides, herbicides, synthetic fertilizers or other synthetic substances; in soil in which the humus content is increased only by the addition of natural mineral fertilizers or other natural matter."

"Organic farming has become a viable and valuable industry," said Senator Goodman, explaining his sponsorship of the bill. "Contrary to many who would write off the organic farmer as an old-fashioned crackpot or consider those who buy organic foods as fools, organic farmers are using some of the most sophisticated methods available for pest control, soil conservation and nutrient recycling, and at the same time, organic farmers are presently getting a higher energy output-input ratio than many non-organic farmers."

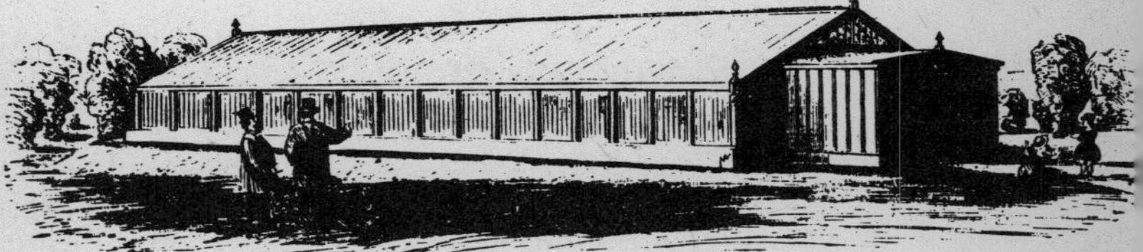

Nationally, New York Congressman Edward Koch introduced a bill into the U.S. House of Representatives on May 11, 1972 to "amend the Federal Food, Drug, and Cosmetic Act to regulate the advertising and distribution of organically-grown and processed foods." Representative Koch told his fellow Congressmen: "There is a need for a Federal inspection and certification program that would assure consumers that they are getting organically-grown food when they buy it. . . . Organically-grown food is a legal commodity, in strong demand, and should be available to those who want it."

"There is now a significant and growing sector of the American public showing interest in organically-grown foods. Organic food can no longer be considered a fad; indeed, it has quite a history in this country. . . The sales of food represented as organically-grown may reach several hundred million dollars this year, and this legislation is needed to protect the legitimate interests of both producers and consumers, and I urge you to support it."

Senator Alan Cranston of California presented a similar bill in the Senate. "I believe that the potential impact of this legislation can be much broader in scope than simply regulating the distribution, labeling and advertising of organic foods," he said. "It focuses attention on the positive environmental advantage of farming by the organic method. It also provides farming to smaller farming units at a time when small farmers are being forced off the land by large-scale mechanized agriculture."

"Environmentally speaking, I believe that the organic farming method is superior to modern farming methods," Senator Cranston continued. "The organic method is based on respect for the soil—respect which views the soil as a long-term source—and requires considerable care of the soil. It repudiates the need for pesticides and artificial fertilizers, relying instead on the additions of organic matter and natural mineral fertilizers to replenish the soil and on the use of predator insects to control harmful plant pests."

Co-sponsoring Cranston's measure, Senator Charles Percy of Illinois said, "This bill, for the first time, defines the terms 'organically-processed' and 'organically grown.' Organically processed foods are products which in their processing have not been treated with preservatives, hormones, antibiotics, or synthetic additives of any kind. Organically-grown items are foods which have been grown in soil whose humus content is increased by the addition of organic matter. . . Strong and effective legislation is needed in this area not only to protect the consumer of organic food products, but the legitimate producer and processor as well."

Unmistakably, people everywhere, in all walks of life, who constitute a significant minority, know what organically-grown food is. Millions now choose to raise their own by that method and to buy it grown organically. Similarly, a number of state and local governments has legislated official definitions of these fundamental terms. Accordingly, there should

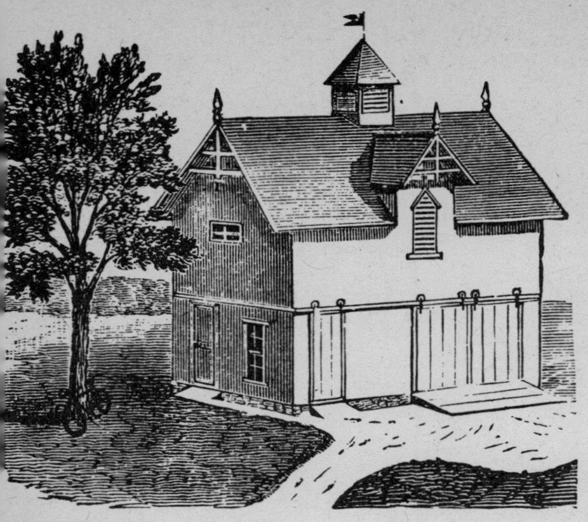

be absolutely no confusion in any part of society or government as to the full and complete definitions of organically-grown and organically-processed foods.

DANGERS OF INTENSIVE FARMING

As many people are beginning to realize, intensely-farmed land just cannot keep on supplying the amounts of zinc, manganese, iron, copper, and other trace minerals necessary to prevent dietary deficiencies. An increased awareness of the indispensability of micronutrients for maintaining the health of man, animals and plants has been evident in recent years. Prolonged cultivation of land and modern agricultural practices, such as double cropping, use of high-yielding hybrids and heavy application of concentrated fertilizers have resulted in a reduced supply of many of these elements. In fact, there are instances of reduced yield as well as quality of agricultural products, and there is an increasing demand for knowledge relating to the use of these essential elements in agriculture (PLANT NUTRIENT SURVEY, U. of Georgia Expt. Sta, Res. Report 102, May 1971).

It is generally concluded by scientists that the mineral quality of the soil influences the mineral balance of foods grown on that soil. Tomatoes, for example, varied more than double the amount of phosphorus in the highest to lowest comparison. They showed differences of nearly three times the potassium content, five times that of calcium, more than six of sodium, boron and cobalt, 12 times more magnesium, 53 times the copper, 68 of manganese and 1,938 more iron in the highest to lowest samples (Bear, F.E., et al., SOIL SCI. SOC. PROC., 13, 1948).

It has been observed that corn from fertile soil had a higher protein content and was a better hog feed than corn from the poor though highly-fertilized soil (Kohnke & Vestal, SOIL SCI. SOC. PROC. 13, 1948).

A report by Dr. Homer T. Hopkins of the U.S. Food and Drug Administration on the question of soils and fertilizers in relation to the quantity and chemical composition of foods and plant origin was submitted on June 11, 1965, to Dr. Phillip L. Harris, Director, Division of Nutrition. While working for the USDA previously, Dr. Hopkins had conducted studies of the mineral elements in fresh vegetables from different geographic areas and found that there was considerable divergence. He reviewed the literature on this subject for Dr. Harris and concluded that the statement that "the nutritional values of our crops are not significantly affected by either the soil or kind of fertilizer used" could not be defended. (FDA, DHEW, 2nd Nat'l Congress on Medical Quackery, Washington, D.C., Oct. 25-26, 1963).

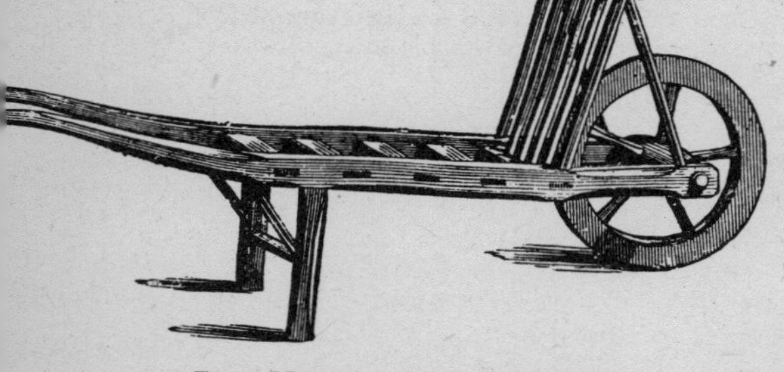

FLAT MARKET-GARDEN BARROW.

Dr. Hopkins cited the following as the basis for his conclusions: application of 40 tons of barnyard manure to potato soils on Long Island, N.Y. resulted in doubling the iron content of potatoes grown there. Composition of roughages may be affected greatly by the amount of plant food in the soil. Hypomagnesemia, or grass tetany, occurred in animals fed on grasslands heavily fertilized with potassium fertilizer. The chemical composition of forages may be altered by fertilization of soil. Application of a plant nutrient for soils in greater quantities than those required for maximum yield response usually resulted in luxury (excessive) consumption of the nutrient by the plant. Further, it has been demonstrated that the amounts of trace elements added to the soil as "contaminants" in chemical fertilizer supplying nitrogen, phosphorus and potassium are inconsequential.

HEALTH HAZARDS OF EXCESS NITRATES AND PESTICIDES

Over the past decade there has been a significant trend in the increased use of nitrogen-containing chemical fertilizers. The results of this trend have been: 1) an increase in the nitrogen compounds entering lakes and rivers, with the subsequent fouling of both recreational and municipal water supply facilities; and 2) an increase in the nitrate content of plant material (Bodiphala & Ormrod, CAN. INST. FOOD TECHNOL J. No. 1, 1971; WALL STREET JOURNAL, Nov. 10, 1971).

In a recent study, the use of fertilizer nitrogen in excess of 50 pounds per acre caused nitrate accumulation in red and icicle radishes, turnip roots, kale and leaves of turnips and mustard. (For example, 250 pounds per acre of 20-20-20 is equivalent to 50 pounds nitrate per acre. The usual application recommendation is 500 pounds per acre, or 100 pounds nitrate per acre. In general, applications of high nitrogen will decrease the calcium and phosphorous content of plants.

Public concern has been aroused over the possible health hazard of high levels of nitrates found in some foods, particularly the dangers of these foods in infant diets. The term "nitrate toxicity" as commonly used actually results from nitrate which is produced following the reduction of nitrate to nitrite by microbial action either prior to ingestion or within the gastrointestinal tract. The nitrate content of the food is thus only an index of the amount of nitrite which might be formed. Both nitrate and nitrite freely traverse the gastrointestinal wall into the blood stream. Nitrite—but not nitrate—oxidizes the ferrous iron of the red blood pigment hemoglobin and causes methemoglobinemia (reduced availability of oxygen to the tissue (Wright and Davidson, ADV. IN AGRON, 16, 1964).

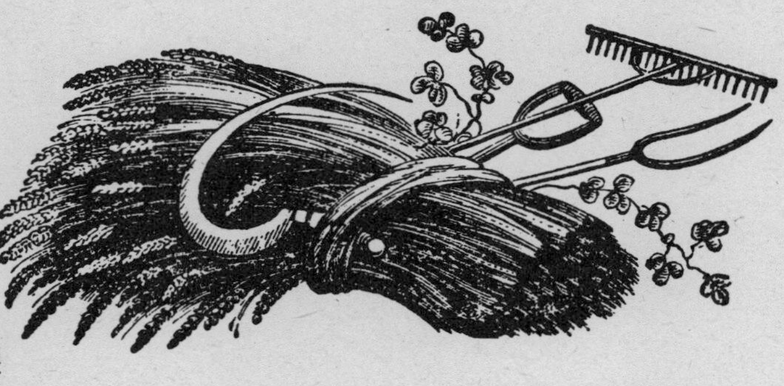

Nitrates can interfere with normal iodine metabolism of the thyroid gland and result in a reduction in the liver storage of vitamin A.

But there is also something insidious about the increased reliance on and use of nitrogen fertilizers. Werner Schuphan, who has spent a good deal of his professional career studying this problem, notes that "Increasing amounts of N-fertilizer generally results in higher contents of water thus lowering the contents of crude fibre. Therefore, tenderness and/or juciness in vegetables—desired criterion in market quality—may counteract with the desired nutritional criterion. That is: Getting a marked decrease in transit time of the stool through the alimentary canal by presence of sufficient amount of crude fibre."

Schuphan also discovered that the contents of potassium in spinach, lettuce, and cauliflower decrease due to the high application of N-fertilizer. The result is a marked, undesirable increase in the potassium-sodium ratio. And high dietary sodium, in numerous medical reports, has been linked to hypertension. (QUALITAS PLANTARUM, No. 23, 1973.)

In a subsequent issue of the same international nutrition journal (No. 25, 1974) Schuphan writes: "In seven years' trials with leafy vegetables a strong antagonistic behavior in minerals has been found following an increased supply in nitrogen. Contents of potassium, calcium, and phosphorus decreased strongly; contents of sodium and of Nitrate-N increased considerably. . ."

"In addition," he continues, "it is worth mentioning that crops which have received heavy amounts . . . of nitrogen, often suffer from undesired side effects. Storage qualities may be impaired (potatoes, carrots) and a decrease in flavor may occur. Crops are often less resistant to plant pests. Consequently they need more pesticides, and thus potentially may accumulate more toxic residues of pesticides and/or of their metabolites. This results in a lowering of the nutritive and hygienic value of the products."

Clearly, the use (and overuse) of nitrogen-containing chemical fertilizers holds genuine health, environmental, and ecological risks.

HEALTH, BIOLOGICAL, AND ENVIRONMENTAL ADVANTAGES OF ORGANIC FOODS

It is well-known that the addition of organic matter to the soil improves its water-holding capacity, increases its drought resistance and reduces the activity and movement of the pesticides. The effect of organic matter in the soil serves as an important reserve source of certain nutrients for plants and in many cases it helps to keep important nutrients available to the plant.

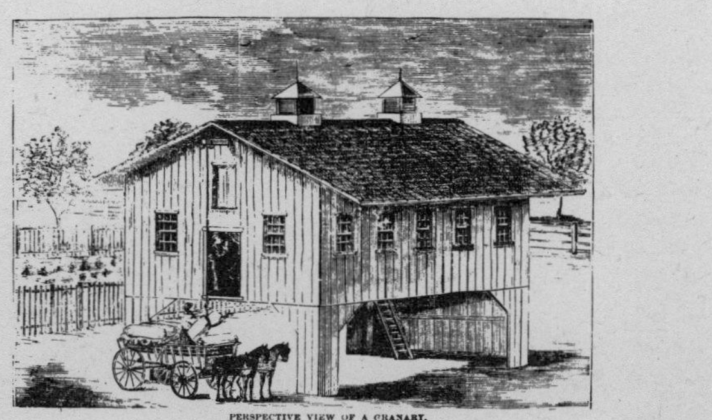

PERSPECTIVE VIEW OF A GRANARY.

The importance of organic matter and its effects on available nutrients has been demonstrated by Brown and Smith who found increases in both calcium and phosphorus content in turnip greens as the organic matter of the soil increased. (AGRON. J., 58, 1966). The results of an extensive and comprehensive experiment demonstrated a highly significant positive relationship between soil organic matter and iron content of turnip greens. (Belson, KC., MICH. ST. U. CENTENNIAL SYMPOSIUM ON NUTRITION OF PLANTS, ANIMALS, MAN, 1955).

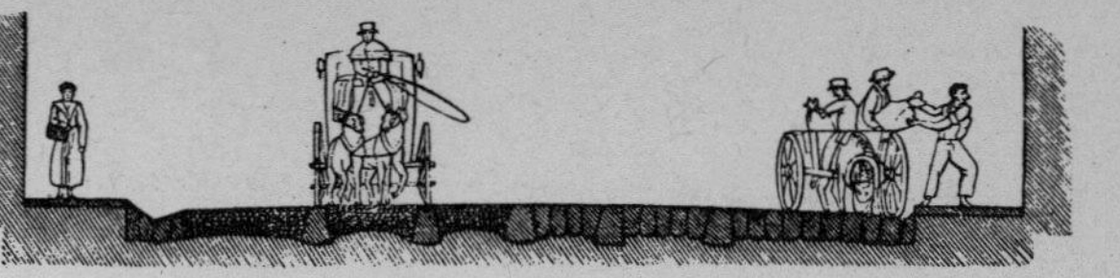

Organic fertilizer significantly increased the iron content of spinach in a study conducted at Kansas State University. Using feedlot manure as the sole nutrient source, W. S. Peavy and J. K. Gritiz found that the natural fertilizer produced a more iron-rich crop, compared to the chemical fertilizers. "Our results likely came from decomposing organic fertilizer forming organic acids that caused iron to chelate into forms more readily absorbed by the plants," the pair reported in the JOURNAL OF THE AMERICAN SOCIETY OF HORTICULTURAL SCIENCE (97, 1972).

Perhaps the most valuable and comprehensive account of the benefits of organic fertilizers is the massive twelve year study (1960-1972) undertaken by Werner Schuphan and recently published in QUALITAS PLANTARUM (23, 1974). In experimenting with a variety of crops in particular soils Schuphan attempted to assess the relative nutritional advantages of organic and NPK fertilizers.

According to his highly convincing data, "The most convincing facts are much higher contents of minerals—except of sodium—due to organic fertilizing. Potassium and iron show the greatest increases, in savoy as magnesium and cabbage. Contents of sodium, except in potatoes, are markedly decreased." (It should be noted that from a health and nutrition point of view, LOW SODIUM is very desirable.)

"The most surprising result," Schuphan continues, "is the behavior of nitrate-N in spinach. Organic manuring . . . results in extremely low contents in nitrate-N. No hazards to health whatsoever could be expected when such a low-nitrate Spinach were fed to infants."

The author also discovered that plants provided abundantly with nitrogen are attacked by aphids, small sluggish insects that suck the juice of plants, above the norm. "On the other hand plants manured organically are less or even not at all affected by aphids. It is well-known that organically grown plants have a more solid collenchymatous thickening-system increasing the mechanical strength of cell walls and a decreased water content in plants tissues both favouring a protective effect against aphids. In all likelihood, both criteria—lower content of free amino acids and more collenchymatous thickening in organically grown plants—might provide greater protection against aphids in cultivated plants."

Schuphan was also interested in the biological value of protein. There had been some evidence raised earlier (1954) that the biological value of the protein in spinach decreased due to heavy nitrogen supply. The author wanted to know the reason for this decrease. His argument follows: "We could elucidate significantly that methionine plays a key role in limiting the biological value of protein; thus a decrease, due to high N-fertilization, of this S-containing methionine—important to metabolic processes in plants (transmethylating)—gives rise to a very distinct decrease in the biological value of proteins."

Field reports led Schuphan to conclude that the contents of methionine are distinctly higher after organic manuring. "We may come to the conclusion," he writes, "that organic manuring favours unequivocally one of the most important essential amino acids, the S-containing methionine."

Schuphan makes it clear that there are some losses of yield with organic techniques. In his opinion, "These losses in yield the organic farmer must bear at his own expense, unless the nutritive value of his organically grown crops would rise to such an extent that low yield would be financially compensated by a higher price for his crops. That the consumer would benefit by a higher biological value" of organic fertilizers "is beyond question, as confirmed by the data based on twelve years' chemical investigations."

Crops manured with organic fertilizers have in comparison with NPK crops showed:

a) Dry Matter—+23%
b) Relative Protein—+18%
c) Ascorbic Acid—+28%
d) Total sugars—+19%
e) Methionine—+23% (determined in potatoes and spinach only)
f) Minerals
 /Potassium (K)—+18%
 /Calcium (Ca)—+10%
 /Phosphorus (P)—+13%
 /Iron (Fe)—77% (determined in spinach only)
 /Magnesium (Mg)—plus or minus 0%

Given the thoroughness of Schuphan's investigation over more than a decade, there can be no doubting the biological (and therefore nutritional) value of organically grown foods. Admittedly the yield is greater for those crops produced with chemical fertilizers. Nonetheless, because the standard farm crops have not provided nutritional health for many people in the last few decades, we might suggest that Quality is becoming far more important than Quantity. And with the application of new forms of biological pest controls and more effort in the area of nitrogen fixation, there is every reason to believe the yield of the organic garden and farm could be significantly increased.

THE ONLY SOLUTION

In addition to all the compelling scientific evidence, the organic gardener and farmer have always possessed a primitive, empirical sense about the quality and worth of their products. They KNOW that organic vegetables, fruits, grains, meats, poultry, and eggs taste far better than the plasticized products of giant agribusiness. This is a truth dictated by the senses which, though dulled by the mechanical world, are man's best barometer.

Professor Kaikow writes that "organic farming is the only hope left for the small family farm, where the land is part of the life of the producing family." We might go farther than that and say organic farming, which is the quintessence of good ecology, is the only viable solution for a country who daily insults her land, her water, and her future.

PRACTICES OF ORGANIC GARDENING

Extension Agent's Guide to Organic Gardening
Agricultural and Home Economics Extension Service
Pennsylvania State University

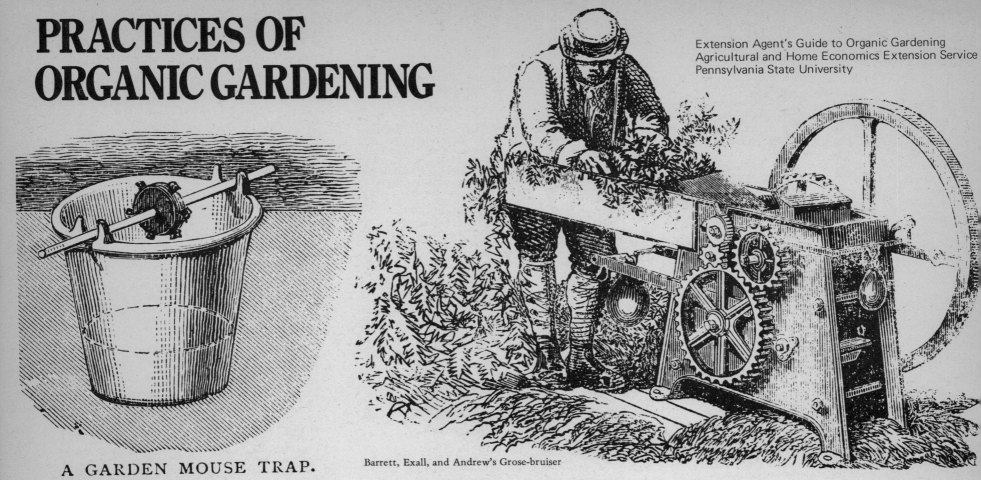

A GARDEN MOUSE TRAP.

Barrett, Exall, and Andrew's Grose-bruiser

INTRODUCTION

Increased interest in organic gardening is evident today. Reasons for this interest vary. Some organic gardeners think organically produced food is safer, tastes better, is more nutritious, is less complex to produce, or is less expensive to produce than food produced by conventional agricultural methods; some gardeners may gain satisfaction from the "back to nature" challenge.

The committee that put together the information in this publication did not attempt to define "organic gardening". Each person has his or her own concept of the subject, so a rigid definition would add little to the enclosed material. In general, we are working on the premise that organic gardening is the growing of crops with the addition of humus and "natural fertilizers" and without the use of "man-made fertilizers" and pesticides.

This publication is intended to provide information and answer questions most often asked by home gardeners who are interested in organic gardening.

Subject matter prepared by: Cultural Practices—Robert F. Fletcher, Peter A. Ferretti and R. W. Hepler; Plant Pathology—Alan A. MacNab; Entomology—S. G. Gesell.

GARDEN SOIL MANAGEMENT

Knowledge of garden soils and how to manage them is necessary if a garden is to be productive. Vegetables need full sunlight, as well as favorable amounts of moisture and plant food. They cannot compete with trees or other plants for sunlight, moisture, or nutrients. When planning a garden, avoid the vicinity of large trees, even though the vegetables would not be shaded to any great extent.

1. Nature of Garden Soils

Ideal garden soil is fertile, deep, friable, well-drained, and high in organic matter. Heavy clay soils are late in drying out and are difficult to cultivate and work properly. Extremely sandy soils may lack organic matter and may dry out too rapidly between water applications. The best soil is between these two extremes. The exact type of soil, however, is not as important if it is well-drained, adequately supplied with organic matter, and retains moisture.

2. Soil Preparation

Thorough soil preparation is needed for growing garden crops. The purpose in turning up soil and giving it various pulverizing treatments is to separate soil particles, to allow air to come in contact with as many particles as possible, and thereby to provide a favorable medium for roots. Soil must contain air to produce crops; also beneficial soil bacteria cannot live without it. Poorly drained soil has few air spaces and, therefore, it is unproductive.

The deeper the soil is prepared, the greater is its capacity for holding air and moisture. Soil should be plowed or spaded to a septh of at least 8 or 9 inches, provided the subsoil is not turned up.

Fall-plowing or spading is desirable if coarse organic material, heavy sod or a heavy coat of manure is to be turned under. Organic matter decomposes during fall and early spring. This results in better soil conditions for early crops. Fall-plowed ground left in the rough over winter dries out quickly so that the seedbed may be prepared and the garden planted early in the spring. Gardens should not be dug up and planted until the soil has sufficiently dried. Soil, when pressed tightly in the hand, should readily crumble when released; if it forms a compact, muddy mass, it is too wet to be worked. Heavy clay soils which are worked when they are wet, lose their crumbly texture, they become hard, compact, lumpy and, consequently, unproductive. Several seasons of careful handling are often required to restore such a soil to normal condition and production.

The tilth, or physical condition, of the seedbed at planting time is important. Each soil has characteristics which determine the tilth best suited for planting. No soil should be worked to a fineness that will permit sealing-over during rains. Some heavy garden soils should be left comparatively rough and cloddy to promote aeration and water penetration and reduce crusting of the soil surface.

Heavy soils low in organic matter, and soils containing large amounts of very fine clay, tend to harden and crust readily. Clay soils are resistant to changes in their structure; however, a small garden may be improved by applications of coarse sand, cinders, or coal ashes. An inch or two of either coarse sand, cinders, or coal ashes can be worked into the top-soil in any one year. They improve drainage rate and workability of clay soils, but are of limited value compared to organic matter.

A garden rotary tilling machine is an excellent means by which soil admendments (mentioned in previous paragraph) and organic materials can be incorporated into the garden soil. The best finishing or smoothing tool for the small garden is the iron rake. It is an excellent pulverizer and leveler. Rake stones and bits of rubbish to one side before planting.

3. Organic Matter for Soil Improvement

Organic matter effectively improves soil structure. When organic matter decays, humus is formed. The spongy texture of organic matter, when incorporated into soil, acts to:

a. Increase the water holding capacity of the soil and hold apart the tiny particles of a clay soil so they can drain out excess water more readily.

b. Provide clay soil with needed pore space, which lets in the air essential to good plant growth.

c. Prevent tiny particles of clay soil from cementing themselves together, thus making the soil mellower and, therefore, more easily penetrated by plant roots.

d. Fill in excess pore space of sandy soil, thus slowing down the drainage rate and increasing the water-holding capacity.

e. Regulate soil temperature.

f. Release nitrogen and other nutrients for plant use through the process of decay.

g. Increase the cation exchange capacity of the soil so that soils can hold and release more nutrients.

h. Buffer soils to reduce stresses on plant growth.

i. Promote growth of microorganisms which help condition soil.

Organic matter or humus may be added to garden soils in the form of manure, compost, peat moss, peat-humus, spent mushroom, and sawdust. Organic matter can be produced in the form of winter cover crops, green manure crops, or sod when the land is not used for gardening. A legume grass mixture is an effective green manure crop for improving soil.

It is a good practice to rotate location of the garden every few years when space is available and manure and other organic materials are scarce. This will help improve condition of the soil; it will also prevent plant diseases.

Organic materials used alone seldom supply a balanced source of plant nutrients. Most organic materials are low in phosphorus. Also decaying straw, leaves, and particularly sawdust, often temporarily deplete the soil of available nitrogen.

Cropping is intensive in most home gardens; two or three crops are sometimes grown each year. Garden soils which receive no organic material, are slowly depleted of organic matter and physical condition of the soil deteriorates.

Organic material could be supplied by plowing under green manure crops, cattle manure, sheep and poultry manure, fall cover crops, sawdust, spent mushroom compost, compost, or sewage sludge. Each of these is discussed below.

Green manure or "soil-building" crops should be planted on soils that lack tilth and are low in organic matter, before planting vegetables. For quicker results, 12 to 15 pounds of complete fertilizer, such as 5-10-5, should be applied to each 1,000 square feet before seeding the green manure or sod crop. This is equivalent to 0.75 - 1.50 - 0.75 lbs. of nitrogen-phosphate-potash per 1000 sq. ft. whether supplied from organic or inorganic fertilizers.

Fall cover crops, such as annual rye or ryegrass, should be seeded just after the last cultivation. They utilize excess nutrients, especially nitrogen, that might otherwise be lost by leaching before the next growing season. The green crop should be turned under the following spring, preferably before the "grass" is knee-high. Seed 1 to 2 pounds of annual ryegrass, or 3 or 4 pounds of annual rye per 1000 square feet. Seed ryegrass by September 15 in central Pennsylvania; rye may be seeded later. Good coverage and growth results from early planting. Little advantage can be gained from a seeding of a cover crop later than October 1, if spring crops are to be planted early.

In addition to adding organic matter and reducing

leaching losses, cover crops protect soil from erosion. Cover crop roots improve soil structure by their penetrating and loosening action through their secretions.

Animal manures are a source of plant nutrients and considered as a soil amendment. It also aids in soil aeration and provides nutrients for the microorganisms living in the soil. Microorganisms, actively decomposing organic matter, help improve soil structure.

Cattle manure is best applied in fall and winter and plowed under. Soils vary greatly in fertility, but it is safe to assume an application of barnyard manure at the rate of 50 to 100 pounds to 100 square feet is desirable. Use of a phosphate material in addition to manure will give a better balance of plant nutrients. Spade or work the manure well into the soil as soon as possible after spreading. This practice will conserve nutrients, aid decomposition and minimize odors, flies or other objectionable conditions.

Poultry and sheep manures are very concentrated and must be used cautiously. Broadcast and spade under or rototill in before planting, at the rate of 1 pound per 10 square feet.

Sawdust can be used to advantage. Three practical ways of utilizing sawdust are: in compost, as a mulch, and by direct application to the soil. An average application to the soil would be about 3 to 4 bushels of sawdust to each 100 square feet of garden area or 30 to 40 bushels to each 1000 square feet of garden space.

Usually acidity caused by applying sawdust to soil is of minor importance. Where soils are not already well supplied with lime, it usually is a good practice to add a little lime with the sawdust. If soil acidity is a factor, use about 3/4 to 1 pound of ground limestone to each bushel of sawdust.

Any injurious effects from the use of sawdust, however, are likely to be due to nitrogen deficiency rather than to acidity. Regardless of how sawdust is used, apply to the soil about 25 pounds of actual nitrogen per ton of sawdust. For 1 bushel of dry sawdust, this means about 1 pound of nitrate of soda, 0.8 pound of ammonium sulphate, or 0.5 pound of ammonium nitrate. Use nitrogen in at least two applications. It is suggested that about half the nitrogen be applied with the sawdust and the balance put on in one or more additional applications during the growing season.

Spent mushroom compost is a good source of organic matter for conditioning a garden soil. It is usually high in phosphorus. For garden soils low in organic matter, 2 to 4 inches may be spaded into the soil.

Compost is composed largely of decaying plant materials. Where other forms of organic matter are not available, build a compost pile near the garden to supply humus or rotted organic matter. Composting is a dual-good activity. Not only are you disposing of plant residues but in a way it helps keep our environment clean and you're also developing a useful material.

4. Sewage Sludge

a. Two types of sewage sludge are available to the gardener. These are:

Digested sludge: product given primary treatment by anearobic digestion but not heat-treated. Digested sludge is usually of relatively low quality as a fertilizer compared with products from an activated system. Digested sludges are often available without cost or at a low price. For the home gardener it is recommended that digested sludge be applied to bare land in the fall and lightly dug in, or composted with garden refuse. Digested sludge is not suggested for direct application to soils that will sustain a crop in that season.

Dried activated sludge: product made from sewage freed from grit and coarse solids, and aerated after being inoculated with microorganisms. The resulting flocculated organic matter is withdrawn from the tanks, filtered, dried in rotary kilns, ground and screened. Dried activated sludge, properly heat treated, normally commands a good price. Activated sludges are widely used as fertilizers for lawns and golf courses. Heat treated sludges are normally safe for use from a sanitary standpoint.

Milorganite, Hu-Actnite, Chicagrow, and Nitroganic are the trade names for materials produced in Milwaukee, Houston, Chicago, and Pasadena, respectively.

b. Nutrient content of sewage sludge:

The nutrient content of sewage sludge is variable. The following figures show the range within which most sludges will fall.

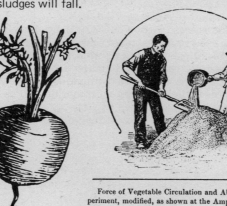

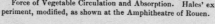

Force of Vegetable Circulation and Absorption. Hales' experiment, modified, as shown at the Amphitheatre of Rouen.

MINERAL NUTRIENT VALUE OF ORGANIC MATERIALS

Organic Materials

Animal Tankage (dry): 7, 10, 0.5, Medium
Bone Meal (raw): 2 to 6, 15 to 27, 0, Slow
Bone Meal (steamed): 0.7 to 4.0, 18 to 34, 0, Slow Medium
Castor Pomace: 5, 1.8, 1, Slow
Cocoa Shell Meal: 2.5, 1.0, 2.5, Slow
Compost (not fortified): 1.5 to 3.5, 0.5 to 1.0, 1.0 to 2.0, Slow
Cottonseed Meal (dry): 6, 2.5, 1.7, Slow Med.
Dried Blood (dry): 12, 1.5, .57, Medium Rapid
Fertrell-Blue Label: 1, 1, 1, Slow
Fertrell-Gold Label: 2, 2, 2, Slow
Fertrell-Super: 3, 2, 3, Slow
Fertrell-Super "N": 4, 3, 4, Slow
Fish Meal (dry): 10, 4, 0, Slow
Fish Scrap (dry): 3.5 to 12, 1 to 12, 0.8 to 1.6, Slow
Garbage Tankage (dry): 2.7, 3, 1, Very Slow
Guano (Bat): 5.7, 8.6, 2, Medium
Guano (Peru): 12.5, 11.2, 2.4, Medium
Kelp [2]: .9, .5, 4 to 13, Slow
Manure [3] (fresh)
Cattle: .25, .15, .25, Medium
Horse: .3, .15, .5, Medium
Sheep: .6, .33, .75, Medium
Swine: .3, .3, .3, Medium
Poultry (75% water): 1.5, 1, .5, Medium Rapid
Poultry (50% water): 2, 2, 1.0, Medium Rapid
Poultry (30% water): 3, 2.5, 1.5, Medium Rapid
Poultry (15% water): 6, 4, 3, Medium Rapid
Marl: 0, 2, 4.5, Very Slow
Milorganite (dry): 5, 2 to 5, 2, Medium
Mushroom Compost: 0.4 to 0.7, 57 to 62, 0.5 to 1.5, Slow
Peat and Muck: 1.5 to 3.0, 0.25 to 0.5, 0.5 to 1.0, Very Slow
Sawdust: 4, 2, 4, Very Slow
Sewage Sludge (Activated, dry): 2 to 6, 3 to 7, 0 to 1, Medium
Sewage Sludge (Digested): 1 to 3, ½ to 4, 0 to ½, Slow
Soybean Meal (dry): 6.7, 1.6, 2.3, Slow Medium
Tanbark [4]: 0. 1.5, 2, Very Slow
Tobacco Stems (dry): 2, .7, 6.0, Slow
Urea [5]: 42 to 46, 0, 0, Rapid
Wood Ashes [6]: 0, 1 to 2, 3 to 7, Rapid

scovery of the Transpiration of Plants. Muschenbroeck's experiment.

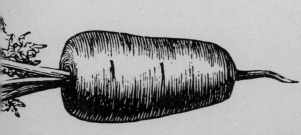

C. Rate of application for sewage sludge

Broadcasting at the rate of 5 to 7 pounds per 100 square feet is suggested. At these rates little if any fertilizer is needed on soils with average or above average fertility level. On soils low in available phosphorus and potassium, a light supplement of phosphate and potash or a fertilizer with a 0-1-2 ratio, such as 0-15-30 or 0-10-20, usually will be needed.

Untreated or raw sewage or improperly treated sewage sludge should not be applied to garden soil as a fertilizer or a soil conditioner.

EXTERIOR OF A GRAIN BIN.

Some of the materials may not be available because of of restricted sources.

1 The percentage of plant nutrients is highly variable and with some materials mean percentages are listed.

2 Contains common salt, sodium carbonates, sodium and potassium sulfates.

3 Plant nutrients available during year of application. Varies with amount of straw and method of storage.

4 Contains calcium.

5 Urea is an organic compound, but since it is synthetic, it is doubtful that most organic gardeners would consider it acceptable.

6 Potash content depends on the tree species burned. Wood ashes are alkaline, containing approximately 32% CaO.

LIMING THE GARDEN SOIL

1. Why Apply Lime?

It is generally true that vegetable crops grow best on slightly acid soils. Adding lime to soils not only reduces acidity but, in general, improves the physical condition or structure of certain heavy clay soils.

Most vegetables require at least moderate amounts of lime in soil to neutralize acid conditions and supply adequate amounts of available calcium for direct nutritional purposes. Also, the calcium content of soil greatly influences the availability of other plant nutrients. The chances of having a calcium problem in a well-managed garden soil are rare.

The only reliable way of finding your soil's pH and calcium needs is by a soil test. If calcium is needed but raising the pH is undesirable, substitute twice the amount of agricultural gypsum for the lime. Usually a soil that grows good red clover is suitable for vegetable production. In terms of pH value (a standard measurement of soil acidity) this means a pH level between 6.2 and 6.8.

Liming an acid soil is the first step in realizing its crop producing potential. When lime is needed, apply it several months ahead of planting time. It is a good practice to apply lime material in the fall after harvest. This is especially true where lime is badly needed to correct soil acidity before spring plantings.

2. How to Apply Lime

Regardless of how lime is applied, work it thoroughly into the soil. The more completely lime is mixed with soil, the more quickly its value is realized. Nutritional deficiencies sometimes occur in vegetable seedlings when lime is applied and not thoroughly worked into soil. The kind of lime applied has no particular influence on the final effect. Both ground limestone and hydrated lime are equally effective in reducing soil acidity when applied in equivalent amounts. About 30 pounds of hydrated lime are equivalent to 45 pounds of ground limestone. Hydrated lime acts more quickly, but ground limestone has a more lasting effect and is cheaper. On soils likely to be deficient in magnesium, the use of dolomitic ground limestone is suggested.

3. How Much Lime?

It takes relatively little lime to raise the pH of a sandy soil one full point on the pH scale, but more lime is required with a heavy soil well supplied with organic matter. The higher the organic matter and clay contents, the greater is the amount of lime required to correct the pH. After applying the required amount of lime, do not expect the pH to change quickly. Once a soil is brought to a desirable pH, 45 pounds of ground limestone per 1000 square feet every 4 or 5 years usually keeps it in good range. Where larger amounts are used and applied oftener, nutritional deficiencies sometimes will occur.

4. How to Apply Heavy Rates

For best results, apply all lime recommended by your soil test. Where large applications are made to extremely acid soils, it is important to distribute lime throughout the plow depth. For applications up to 2 tons per acre (9 pounds per 100 square feet), plow down or broadcast lime after plowing. With applications of 3 tons per acre (14 pounds per 100 square feet), it is desirable to plow down half and add the other half after plowing. With applications of 4 tons or more per acre (18 pounds per 100 square feet), it is very important that half be plowed down and the remainder applied after plowing to avoid over-liming injury.

The limestone used to enrich the quality of compost is another means of maintaining the proper calcium level in garden soils.

5. Will Lime and Fertilizer Promote Earthworms and Microorganisms?

a. **Earthworms:** At low pH values, the earthworm population in soils is greatly reduced and, in extreme cases, may be almost entirely eliminated. When such soils are limed and fertilized, larger crops are produced and the soil organic matter is increased because of the increased quantities of plant residues returned to the soil. These residues supply nutrients for earth worms. By incorporating organic matter and maintaining a high level of fertility by liming and fertilizing, the number of earthworms can be kept at a high level.

When organic debris and insulative cover are given to the earthworm during the winter, they prosper even if the land is tilled every year. Earthworm population growth is limited most by a lack of fertilizer, water,

and an adequate insulating cover during the winter.

b. **Microorganisms:** Research experiments show conclusively that supply soils with lime and fertilizer at recommended rates usually causes an enormous increase in the population of bacteria. Such minerals are a source of food for bacteria as well as plants. Prof. L. R. Frederick, Iowa State University, applied excessive rates of inorganic fertilizers and even under these conditions, numbers and activity of soil microbes were seldom reduced and the total weight of microbes in the soil actually increased.

MAKING COMPOST OR SYNTHETIC MANURE

1. How Does One Make a Compost Pile?

First, check local ordinances to make sure composting is permitted in your community. If permitted, avoid placing the pile in an area seen by the public. In addition, care must be taken to keep the pile from becoming a home for rats and other rodents. Bad odors can be minimized by using calcium cyanamide as a disinfectant. It can be sprinkled over the layers as you are building the compost pile.

Compost piles can be made with or without enclosures, above ground or in a pit. Enclosures can be made of concrete blocks, rough lumber, wire or snow fence. One widely practiced procedure for pit composting which does not necessitate any special equipment is as follows:

Build a pile in a shallow pit that is about one foot deep. The soil from the pit can be piled around the edges so that the depth is actually greater than one foot. The pit should be at least 4 to 6 feet in width and about 10 feet in length. Spread a layer of plant material about 6 inches deep in the bottom of this pit. This layer is moistened with water and sprinkled with lime and fertilizer. A small amount of garden soil can also be applied, if available, or a small amount of old stable manure can be used. Additional layers of the plant materials, a small amount of the soil or manure, lime, and fertilizers are applied until the pile is 4 to 6 feet high. In this manner, 7 to 8 layers of plant materials can be applied. Each layer should be moistened with water. Care is needed to avoid an excess of water in order to prevent any leaching of soluble fertilizers. Straw, old hay, and other materials that do not compact readily should be tramped down after each fresh layer is added.

Normally, one ton of air-dry plant residues will yield from 2 to 3 tons of moist compost. During the rotting process the compost pile should be turned at least once, preferably twice. If only one turning is contemplated, a suitable time is 45 to 50 days after the pile is constructed. If two turnings can be made, one should be approximately 30 days and the second 70 days after the pile is built. When turning take care to place the materials from the top and sides of the pile toward the center, and apply additional water if needed.

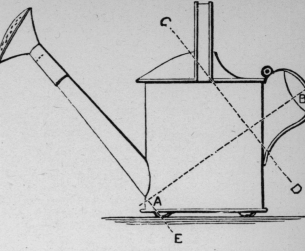

CONSTRUCTION OF WATER PO'

Influence of Insects upon the Fecundation of Flowers.

Willdenow's experiment on the

Common Birthwort: *Aristolochia Clematitis* (Linnæus).

(*Frontispiece.*) THE "ECHO FARM" BARN, LITCHFIELD, CONN.

2. Do Compost Activators Help?

The general conclusion is that these products do little to speed up the composting process. Crop wastes naturally contain all the microbes that are needed for decomposition, and they quickly establish themselves under proper conditions of moisture and ventilation. Bacteria derive their energy from nitrogenous materials, so it is essential that nitrogen be present in sufficient amounts. Natural or synthetic manure or a small amount of fertile soil will serve the same purpose. Fertilizer will speed up composting more than anything.

3. Application of Lime and Fertilizer

The addition of lime and fertilizer to the compost pile accelerates decomposition and improves the quality of the product. One ton of straw, leaves, old hay, or cornstalks will make a pile about 500 cubic feet. The dimensions of the pile can be adjusted in accordance with the available space.

4. Use of Chemical or Organic Materials Between Layers

The following materials should be applied between the layers when the pile is built:

Chemical Fertilizers
36 lbs. Ammonium Nitrate
or
60 lbs. Ammonium Sulfate
30 lbs. 20% Superphosphate
60 lbs. Ground Limestone

Where Organic Materials are Preferred to Chemicals
110 lbs. Dried Blood Meal
55 lbs. Bone Meal (Steamed)
60 lbs. Ground Limestone

5. Small Compost Units

Many home gardeners may feel that they do not have sufficient organic wastes at any one time to build a pile as previously described. A small pile, however, can be started with whatever materials are available. Compost piles may be developed as a continuous process. As additional organic materials become available, pile them on one end and take composted or rotted materials off the other end.

A small pile can be built on the open ground or in a bin made of rough boards, a snow fence, or stakes and chicken wire. Wire and snow fence are relatively inexpensive and can be opened easily to add material or remove compost. A layer of strong plastic film inside the fence helps hasten decomposition especially during prolonged dry periods.

In starting the pile, part of the organic materials are spread out in a layer to a depth of about 6 inches. A commercial fertilizer such as 5-10-5, 5-10-10 or its equivalent should be spread on each layer at the rate of one-half pound, or one cupful, to each 10 square feet. Also, spread ground limestone on each layer at the one-half pound rate. Sprinkling a few shovelsful of garden soil and manure over each layer is a desired practice. The soil and manure prevent blowing and help speed decomposition by compacting the pile, increasing the microorganisms, and helping to hold moisture. Each 6-inch layer of organic materials, lime,

fertilizer, garden soil and manure should be thoroughly moistened but not to the extent that the lime and fertilizer are leached. Additional layers are built in this way until all plant refuse is used up. One should build the pile with a flat top which slants towards the center to catch rainfall.

In order to speed decomposition as much as possible, one should chop or shred coarse materials as fine as possible—less than ½ inch, if practical. Turning and mixing the materials at least once during the summer will not only aide decomposition, but also will result in a more uniform compost.

6. How Much Compost to Use

When materials have decomposed so that they break apart readily, spread them evenly over the garden before the soil is plowed or spaded. The usual practice is to spread and spade compost into the soil in the same way as for barnyard manure. Applications of 500 to 1000 pounds to each 1000 square feet can be used to advantage. Three to four bushels can be applied to an area 10 feet by 10 feet, or 100 square feet. Clay soils may need heavier applications than a silt-loam. Long-season crops may benefit more than short-seasoned ones.

7. What Types of Material Can I Compost?

Leaves from deciduous trees and shrubs, marsh hay, lawn clippings (without weed killers), sawdust, straw, cornstalks and miscellaneous plants and plant parts from the vegetable and flower garden can be composted

8. What Can't Be Added to Compost Piles?

Do not use garbage containing metals, glass, meat, bones, grease, eggs, cheese or animal wastes. Avoid materials known to be infested with diseases. However, it should be pointed out that when properly prepared and thoroughly decayed, most non-spore and non-viral organisms will be killed by the temperatures produced in decomposition. Decomposition of residues is similar to the burning of fuel. In both cases heat is released. The heat inside a properly constructed compost pile may rise to 150 degrees or even 175 degrees F. So, if the pile is not kept sufficiently moist, the compost may become fire-fanged. When the pile is turned, care should be taken to return the outside layers of the pile to the centers so that the disease organisms, insects, and weed seeds surviving in the outer layers will also be subject to the destroying action of the heat.

Absorption by the Leaves.   Mariotte's experiment.

9. What Is Trench Composting?

Trench composting is similar to pit composting—just the shape is different. Pits are often 6 feet square and 18 inches deep whereas trench sizes can vary with the space available and the equipment for digging (hand shovel, rototiller, or plow). Both are filled with layers of 6 to 12 inches of fresh organic matter and topped with 1 inch layers of soil. Fertilizer and lime can be added to speed decomposition. The excavated soil can be used in the compost and the earthen sides help keep the compost moist.

Where space is a problem, home gardeners may want to experiment by locating the trench so that when it is completed, it can be topped with a few inches of mulch and used for a garden path.

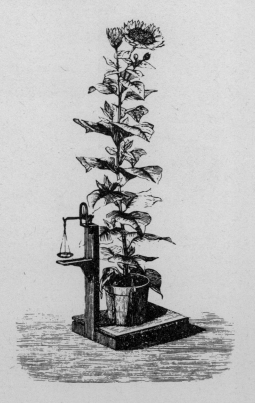

Transpiration in Plants.   Guettard's experiment.

10. Is It a Good Practice to Cover the Compost Pile With Sheets of Plastic?

Usually not. However, any cover applied when air temperatures are low in the winter will tend to maintain decomposition by helping to keep the pile warm.

In addition, if the compost pile is covered with sheets of plastic it will not catch rainfall or it might be difficult to add water. The compost pile should be watered as often as necessary to maintain a high moisture content, which promotes decomposition.

It is essential that the compost pile be well ventilated so that there is a sufficient exchange of gases between the atmosphere and the interior of the compost pile. The organisms which break down the plant and animal residues are aerobic, i.e., they must have oxygen from the atmosphere to carry on their life activities.

The problem of burning in a compost pile is important. Burning in a sense is due to build-up of anaerobic organisms which may produce ammonium toxicity in a compost pile. The heating occurs whenever there is a lack of aeration.

11. How Does One Prevent Flies and Rodents From Infesting a Compost Pile?

Grass and leaf compost piles may be breeding sites for some kinds of flies, and a refuge for rats or mice. The addition of fruit, vegetable, and meat scraps from the table increases the attraction and breeding of flies and offers rodents food as well as refuge.

Construction of a relatively fly-free and rodent-free compost pile is not practical. The 64 mesh wire screening needed to keep out the smallest flies would have to be covered with stronger, ¼-inch mesh hardware cloth to keep out rodents. In addition, the pit would need a 2-foot deep concrete foundation with an outward L-shaped projection from the base. This 2-foot extension would discourage tunneling by rodents. Rodents can be controlled with locked self-feeder bait boxes using an anticoagulant rodenticide.

FERTILIZERS

1. Natural (popularly called organic) vs. Man-made (often called inorganic or synthetic): Which is better to supply nutrients?

Both forms can be equally good. Organic materials are broken down by bacteria into inorganic, water-soluble forms. Plants cannot tell whether elements entered the soil solution from organic matter, inorganic fertilizer, or the weathering of soil.

2. Organic Fertilizers

Organic fertilizers handled and used in their natural moist form, include all kinds of animal manures and compost made with manures and other plant or animal products. Organic commercial fertilizers include dried and pulverized manures, bone meal, slaughter-house tankage, blood meal, dried and ground sewage sludge, cottonseed meal, and soybean meal.

The dried bloods, bone meal, cottonseed or linseed meal and tankage are more useful and valuable as live-stock feed than as fertilizer. From a practical conservation point of view, these waste products should be first used as feed and the manure then recycled and used as fertilizer. Bone meal consists mostly of calcium phosphate and used mainly as a source of phosphorus. The phosphorus in raw bone meal is only slowly available.

3. What Are the Advantages of Organic Fertilizers?

Organic fertilizers are less caustic and will cause less burning of plants (than inorganic fertilizers) if used in large applications. The organic materials are more slowly available to plants, which means that they are available to the plant for a longer time and are less likely to be lost from the soil.

Organic fertilizers may act as soil amendments. The advantages of organic matter as a soil amendment were discussed earlier. However, so little is applied with most types of organic fertilizers that the benefits are very slight or non-existent.

Effect of growing Plants on a horizontally rotating Wheel.

4. What Are the Disadvantages of Organic Fertilizers?

Organic fertilizers are more expensive than inorganic types. Many organic materials are low in nitrogen and other plant nutrients and some need composting before being incorporated into or used on soils. The nutrients in organic fertilizers are in an insoluble form, and are only made available to plants as the material decays in the soil. When organic materials that are low in nitrogen are added to the soil, the plants and the decomposing material compete for the soil nitrogen. This competition sometimes adversely affects plant growth.

Organic materials alone are not balanced sources of plant nutrients and their analysis in terms of the three major nutrients is generally low.

5. Inorganic Fertilizers

Inorganic fertilizers include various mineral salts which contain plant nutrients in combination with other elements. They all have certain characteristics quite strongly in contrast with organic fertilizers.

Fertilizers are needed to replenish mineral nutrients depleted from a soil. Nitrogen, phosphorus, and potassium are the three major elements, out of which 15 are essential, that are removed from soil in quantity by crops. These three are the nutrients most likely to need replenishing and are the chief ingredients of fertilizer.

Except where heavy applications of manure are made, a mixed fertilizer containing the three necessary elements—nitrogen, phosphorus, and potassium—will best fit garden needs. Various analyses suitable general garden use are 5-10-5, 5-10-10, 8-16-8, and 8-24-8. Special high water-soluble, high phosphate materials such as 11-52-17 and 10-55-10 are also available and highly recommended for starter solutions for transplants.

There are also unmixed fertilizers which carry only one element. Most important of these unmixed materials usually would be nitrogen and phosphate carriers. Nitrogen carriers vary from 16 to 45 per-cent nitrogen.

Phosphate fertilizers carry only phosphorus, which promotes flower, fruit, and seed development. It also serves to stiffen up the stem growth and stimulates root growth. Superphosphate usually is applied to manure to give a better balance of nutrients for the plant: 100 pounds to each ton of horse or cow manure and 100 pounds to each half-ton of sheep manure.

Potassium (potash in fertilizer) contributes heavily to the growth of root crops. It also has a stimulating effect on plant vigor and health.

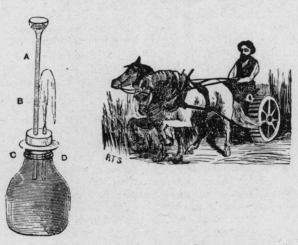

PRINCIPLE OF THE FOUNTAIN EXPLAINED.

Bulles d'oxygène

Eau et gaz carbonique en dissolution

6. What Are the Advantages of Inorganic Fertilizers?

Nutrients in inorganic fertilizers are in soluble form, quickly available to plants rather than long-lasting. Analysis of chemical fertilizers is relatively high in terms of nutrients they contain; thus only a small amount is added to the soil to provide the needed nutrients. Inorganic fertilizers are usually more economical.

7. What Are the Disadvantages of Inorganic Fertilizers?

Since relatively small amounts of inorganic fertilizers are needed to provide adequate plant nutrients, gardeners tend to apply too much fertilizer. Soluble nutrients, in concentrated solution, are caustic to growing plants and will cause injury. Some nutrients in inorganic fertilizers are very soluble and move with the soil water, and so can be lost from the plant root zone by leaching.

Garden Carrots

PLANT NUTRIENTS AND CROP PRODUCTION

1. At One Time All Farmers Were "Organic Farmers"

Prior to the introduction of mineral fertilizers, all farmers were "organic farmers." Legumes, barnyard manure and composts were the only sources of additional nutrients. Organic materials and natural fertilizers are still used to provide nutrients to green plants, but often supplemented by inorganic fertilizers according to soil test results. Nitrogen is supplied to succeeding crops by growing a vigorous crop of legumes (such as alfalfa and red clover) that are either plowed under for green manure or used for livestock feed. Barnyard manure—or for small plots, compost and other organic wastes—provide nitrogen, phosphorus and potassium and other nutrients.

2. The "Conventional Farmer"

While plants can be grown by using the "organic method" the modern farmer and commercial gardener cannot afford to use these materials alone. The average farmer cannot cover large acreages with composts because of both cost and unavailability. Even the modern livestock farmer can only return animal manures and incorporate green manure to part of his acreage. Many farmers do not have a source of animal manure at all. Thus, these farmers must maintain and improve organic matter by using appropriate soil management and cultural practices.

Although farmers use legumes, green cover-crops, manures and limestone, they do not provide the proper nutrient balance and fertility levels when used alone.

A SELF-FEEDING CORN CRIB.

3. Balance and Imbalance of Soil Nutrients

Soil nutrients can be present in unbalanced amounts through the use of organic fertilizers just as well as through use of inorganic ones. However, for each crop to achieve maximum yield and quality, a specific balance among elements is necessary. Most organic materials are unbalanced as such. The additional use of other plant nutrients is necessary to correct these imbalances and is needed to increase the yields for today's population and standard of living.

4. Does the Nutritional Value of Organically Produced Foods Differ From Those Grown With Synthetic Fertilizers?

The assumption that organically grown foods are nutritionally superior to those grown with chemical fertilizers is not well founded. There is no sound basis for such a concept. In fact, it is known that plants grown hydroponically will produce vegetables and fruits as nutritious as those grown by other methods. As you know in hydroponics 100% chemical-mineral salts are added to water in which the plant roots grow without the aid of soil.

Various experiments have been conducted to compare the effects of "organic" and "inorganic" sources of nutrient elements on nutritional factors of plant and animal products. Results in California and Florida showed little to no difference in Vitamin C content of oranges whether fed by nutrient solutions, farm manure, or natural soil. Other studies have shown that the content of calcium, phosphorus, iron, and copper in fruits is influenced only slightly by fertilizer treatments. At the Citrus Experiment Station in Riverside, California, fertilization has improved fruit quality factors such as size, appearance and palatability. However, there was no scientific evidence that such effects were related to the origin of the nutrients or the presence or absence of organic matter.

A 25-year test at Cornell University summarized by K. C. Beeson reported "the Vitamin C and carotene content of seedling rye on plots receiving large quantities of manure was the same as that of rye from plots fertilized with chemical fertilizer for the same period. Similarly, the Vitamin C, iron and copper were the same in potatoes grown on manured soil as those grown on soil treated with chemicals." Dr. O. A. Lorenz, Professor of Vegetable Crops at the University of California, states: "Animal feeding tests indicate that plants grown in nutrient solutions without organic matter, or in soil supplied with inorganic nutrients, are fully as nutritious as those grown with organic matter."

The most concentrated use of commercial fertilizers in the world is in the Netherlands. The rates used there

EARTH-WORMS.

ment in the composition found in the edible portion.

6. Will Lime and Fertilizer Promote Earthworms and Microorganisms?

Yes! Careful experiments show conclusively that soils supplied with lime and fertilizer at recommended rates usually cause an enormous increase in bacterial populations since minerals supply food for bacteria as well as plants. Prof. L. R. Federick, Iowa State University, applied inorganic fertilizers at excessive rates per acre. Even under these conditions, numbers and activity of soil microbes were seldom reduced and the total weight of microbes in the soil actually increased. Research also indicates that the organic material returned to the soil when fertilizing for maximum yields increased the soil organic matter because of the increased quantities of plant residues returned to the soil. By increasing crop yields and soil tilth, the fertilizers also increase the earthworm population. When organic debris and insulative cover are given to earthworms during the winter, they prosper even if the land is tilled every year. Earthworm population growth is limited most by a lack of fertilizer, water, and an adequate insulating cover during the winter.

1. Natural Deposits

Natural deposits of material such as limestone and marl are useable as a lime material to correct soil pH. Material such as greensand granite, sodium nitrate, and rock phosphate are also useable as a fertilizer. Natural deposit materials must be pulverized to a useable fineness. The only change that is made in the material is the fineness obtained by grinding. The value of these materials depends on the quickness of availability which is often governed by particle size—the finer, the most available.

Raw rock phosphate, even though from high grade minerals and finely ground, has been quite ineffective on alkaline soils due to low solubility and exceedingly slow reaction time. Raw rock phosphate is useful in reinforcing farm manure, compost piles, and is fairly effective on very acid soils. Soils low in phosphorus may need 6 to 8 tons to meet plant requirements for phosphorus. However, the phosphorus may be beneficial to plants in subsequent seasons following application.

Naturally occurring deposits of potasssium salts such as granite and greensand are available commercially. But again, the amount of available nutrients they supply is very low and tons of these materials must be applied per acre to equal several hundred pounds of muriate of potash.

2. What Is Greensand?

Greensand is a sandy deposit containing the greenish mineral, glauconite. Glauconite is a hydrated salt of iron and potassium silicate. It contains about 6% potash (K_2O) and is used as a source of potassium. The potassium is very slowly soluble. This slow solubility plus the rather low potash content necessitates large applications of this material when used as a fertilizer. Thus, greensand is not considered an economical source of potassium where large acreages are involved. Where cost is not a factor, and where large amounts of greensand are applied, its low solubility may prove beneficial because fertilizer burn is less likely.

re several times higher than the rates used in the United States. However, no ill effects have been noted when the fertilizers have been used as recommended.

The Dutch produce the highest yields of crops and also have the highest standard of public health in the world. This certainly indicates that food grown with the proper chemical fertilizer should not be harmful.

5. Do Cultural Practices and Environmental Conditions Influence Nutrient Content of Plants?

The nutrient content of edible plants is mostly under genetic control. A specific tomato variety or sweet corn variety, for example, is more nutritious than another because the variety is different, not because the soil or the fertilizer is different. Environmental factors such as light, temperature and available moisture have also been shown to affect plant composition. Minor effects have even been shown with various fertilization practices with certain vegetables. Even so, the major influence appears to be the total amount of yield of nutrients harvested per given area of garden rather than the improve-

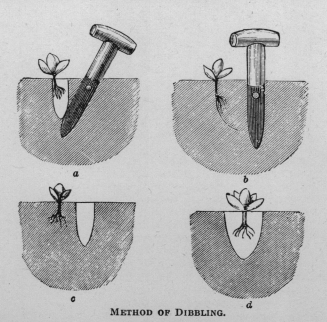

METHOD OF DIBBLING.

Adventitious roots upon a trunk. Duhamel's experiment.

3. What Is Granite Meal?

Granite meal or dust consists of ground up granite, an igneous rock, which has been used as a fertilizer source of potassium. The minerals containing potassium in granite are the K-feldspars and micas. In addition to these, granite is composed of the following minerals: amphiboles, pyroxenes and quartz. Quartz is by far the most abundant mineral in granite. Some granites also contain apatite which is a phosphorus-containing mineral.

The potash content of granite varies from 3 to 5% K_2O and, as with other silicate salts of potassium (e.g., greensand), the potash minerals in granite are very slowly soluble. Field studies have shown that it requires approximately 12 times the amount of potash in the form of granite meal to equal the potassium supplying power of potassium chloride (muriate of potash, 60% K_2O) or, 9 times equal to

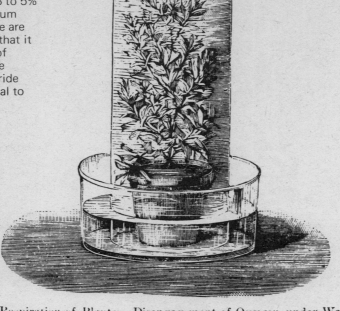

Respiration of Plants. Disengagement of Oxygen under Water.

that of potassium sulfate (at least 48% K_2O). This means that in order to get the same plant response from these two potash sources, it would take about 5 to 10 tons of granite meal per acre to equal several hundreds pounds of muriate of potash or sulfate.

4. Is Dried Blood a Fertilizer? How Much Does It Cost?

Dried blood is a specialty fertilizer which contains approximately 12 percent nitrogen (N), 2 percent phosphate (P_2O_5) and 0.5 percent potash (K_2O). It may be either red or black depending on the process used to remove water during drying. The availability of nitrogen in dried blood is about the same as that in processed sewage sludge (e.g. milorganite), cottonseed meal or soybean meal. It is considerably less than in urea (natural or commercial forms) or certain mineral sources of nitrogen such as ammonium nitrate and ammonium sulfate.

The average cost of nitrogen in dried blood is about $2.00 per pound, which is about 4 to 5 times more than a pound of nitrogen in milorganite and approximately 18 times the cost of a pound of nitrogen in urea.

5. What is Seaweed?

Any plant that grows in the sea can be called a seaweed. However, seaweed is generally considered to mean one of the larger brown or red algae. The giant kelp found in the Pacific and off the coasts of Ireland, Scotland, and Brittany is one type of brown algae.

During World War I, giant kelp was harvested to make fertilizer and explosives. Kelp contains about 20 to 25% potassium chloride. It also contains common salt, sodium carbonates, sodium and potassium sulfates and potassium or sodium iodide and trace elements. However, there are no experimental results indicating its value as a fertilizer. Also, because of its chemical composition, heavy applications should be avoided because of soluble-salt injury. Two brands of seaweed are available in quantity in the United States: Sea-Gro on the west coast and Algit nationwide. Before kelp becomes an animal feed supplement or a soil additive, it must be dried, desalted and ground. Prices vary according to area and method of processing. Kelp meal costs more per ton than many so-called mineral feeds.

VIEW OF A CONVENIENT DUCK HOUSE.

MULCHING VEGETABLES AND SMALL FRUITS

1. What Is a Mulch?

Broadly speaking, a mulch is any substance applied to the soil surface which protects the roots of plants from extremes in temperature or drought, or keeps fruits clean. A specific mulching material is selected because of particular properties which cause it to create a more favorable environment for a certain plant. Although substantial increases in production often result from the use of mulch, equivalent or reduced yield may also occur under some circumstances. Such factors as the crop, time of year, soil type, rainfall, and soil and air temperatures can all influence a plant's response to mulching. Remember, better growth and higher yields will only result when mulches improve the environment in which a plant is growing.

Mulches generally fall into two broad categories— (1) organic and (2) synthetic or man-made.

2. Organic Mulches

A partial listing of organic mulches might include straw, speltz, salt hay, cocoa hulls, peanut hulls, chopped cornstalks, ground corncobs, pine needles, broomsedge, sundangrass, grass clippings, leaf mold, composts, old newspapers or paper pulp, sawdust, bark scrapings, and well-rotted stable manures. Chicken manure (unless specially ashed) would be excluded as a mulch since it burns plants too easily.

Because organic mulches are usually bulky, hard to handle, unavailable in quantity, and often require considerable hand labor for application, these materials are mostly used by home gardeners. Except for commercial strawberry and blueberry growers, organic mulches are used only on a limited scale by commercial growers.

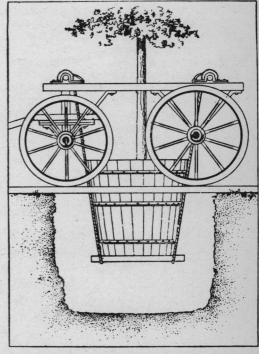

Side Elevation of Transplanting Machine for Trees of large size. The mass is raised by means of iron crowbars which fit into sockets in the rollers around which the lifting-ropes are wound.

Organic mulches return organic matter and plant nutrients (especially trace elements) to the soil and improve soil tilth (structure) as they decompose. Because most organic materials usually contain insufficient nitrogen to replace what is used up by the microorganisms causing its decomposition, available nitrogen in the soil may be depleted. Some additional nitrogen should therefore be provided to replace amounts used in decomposition.

3. Synthetic Mulches

Synthetic mulches include kraft paper, polyethylene and kraft paper-polyethylene combinations, wax-coated papers, aluminum and steel foils alone or in combination with paper or polyethylene, and asphalt spray emulsions. Because synthetic mulches are easily adapted to mechanization, may be designed for individual crop situations, and may be produced in quantity at low cost, they are expected to become even more common in specialized agricultural production.

New techniques in fabricating mulches are resulting in improved and more specialized mulches which possess light-reflecting or light-absorbing coatings, strip combinations, controlled disintegration, and color fading.

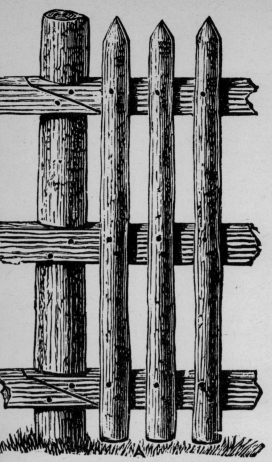

LARCH AND SCOTCH FIR PARK PALING.

Combustion of the Vapors of Bastard Dittany

4. Mulching Commercial Vegetables and Small Fruits

As stated earlier, organic row mulch is commercially important in Pennsylvania for strawberries and blueberries only.

Synthetic row mulch offers potential commercial use in Pennsylvania for early market tomatoes, muskmelons, summer squash, pepper, eggplant, and slicing cucumbers. Under special market situations, the mulching of sweet corn, watermelon, pumpkins, squash, and gourds may also be justified.

5. Mulching Home Garden Vegetables and Small Fruits

Since costs, labor, and mechanization are not limiting factors for most home gardeners, most vegetables and small fruits can be mulched with either organic or synthetic materials.

The white butterfly that lays the eggs for the cabbage-worm.

6. Mulching Objectives

a) A mulch will:

1) Conserve moisture and maintain uniform moisture.

2) Help keep weeds down.

3) Help prevent erosion.

4) Help prevent soil from packing and crusting.

5) Keep fruits from direct contact with the soil, thus minimizing many fruit rots.

6) Affect soil temperatures: porous mulches generally reduce soil temperatures and most non-permeable mulches increase soil temperatures. Highly reflective, non-permeable mulches such as aluminum foils and papers, however, are exceptions—they tend to reduce soil temperatures.

b) Before mulching, remove all weeds and condition the soil for best plant growth.

c) If porous mulches such as straw, salt hay, leaves, pine needles, sawdust, ground corncobs or cornstalks, grass clippings, leaf mold, composts, or peat moss are used, it may be necessary to irrigate periodically during the season.

d) If non-permeable mulches such as black polyethylene, kraft paper and aluminum are used, be sure adequate moisture is available before applying the material.

e) In rainy seasons, mulching may be harmful, because it helps keep the soil too wet for adequate aeration.

f) Black polyethylene mulch prevents evaporation from the covered area, thus conserving the moisture for plant use. The increased plant growth on mulched plots results in greater water loss as the plant transpires. Consequently, on lighter, well-drained soil during extremely dry seasons, irrigation is more necessary on polyethylene mulched crops than on non-mulched cultivated crops.

g) Regular black polyethylene does not break down or distintegrate, so remove it at the end of the season. In some cases it might be used a second year. The plastic strips can be destroyed by burning them after they are removed from the garden.

THE CHERRY CLACK.

h) After certain mulch materials have served their purpose, turn them under for organic matter. Do this in the fall or at least several weeks before further planting.

i) To aid and speed up decomposition, nitrogen should be broadcast on the mulch just prior to turning.

7. Soil Temperature (Mulches)

Mulches may either increase or decrease soil temperatures. A loose dry material such as straw or wood chips can act as an insulation and protect against high temperatures. Soil temperatures under black paper or plastic often will be higher than on unmulched soil. Highly reflective mulches such as white paper or aluminum foil can actually reduce soil temperatures by reflecting the sun's rays. Thus, such materials can be undesirable for early production of warm-season crops, but may benefit late summer planting of such crops as Zucchini squash or cool-season crops such as lettuce.

ORGANIC PEST CONTROLS

PASSING AN OBSTRUCTION.

YARD TO PORTABLE PIGPEN.

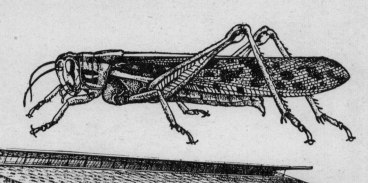

UNDERWOOD'S WASP-CATCHER.

Extension Agent's Guide to Organic Gardening
Agricultural and Home Economics Extension Service
Pennsylvania State University

Robert F. Fletcher, Peter A. Ferretti, R.W. Hepler, Alan A. MacNab and S.G. Gesell

INSECT CONTROL METHODS FOR ORGANIC GARDENERS

It is usually necessary to use a variety of methods to obtain satisfactory control of the many insect pests of the home garden. Since insect control methods often vary in their effectiveness, the gardener may wish to select alternative methods. The number of different methods that can be used to reduce insect pests are numerous and many home gardeners have their own "pet" methods that work well for them but may not be satisfactory for others.

1. Resistant Plant Materials—Where possible, use plant species or varieties that are resistant or at least tolerant to certain insects. What varieties of vegetables grow well in your area? Before buying seeds or plants, check with your neighbors and friends to see what varieties they are partial to. Your seed dealer and nurseryman can also offer tips on potential problems with certain varieties or plant materials. You can avoid problems by not planting roses, raspberries, or grapes if you are in an area heavily infested with Japanese beetles.

2. Cultural Methods—There are numerous things that can be done to reduce insect populations. Wait until the soil is warm enough for corn and bean seeds to germinate quickly. This will help in reducing maggot damage. Destruction of weeds and old corn stalks is an aid in cutting down corn borer populations. Rotate your crops to different sites in the garden each year. Keep weeds and grass out of the garden since such plants attract cutworms, webworms, corn borer, etc.

Another type of cultural control of pests is that of companion planting. We can find no hard data to prove or disprove the value of companion plantings. Following is a partial list of some of the "suggested" companion plantings that we have seen in print at various times:

a. Interplant beans with rosemary to control Mexican bean beetle.

b. Interplant cabbage with thyme to control imported cabbage worms.

c. Interplant carrots with onions or chives to control rust fly and nematodes.

d. Interplant cucumbers with radish or nasturtiums to control cucumber beetles.

e. Interplant cauliflower and other cole crops with mint.

f. Interplant eggplant with catnip to repel flea beetles.

g. Interplant potatoes with deadnettle to repel Colorado potato beetles.

h. Interplant raspberries with tansy to repel Japanese beetles.

i. Interplant roses with chives to repel aphids.

j. Interplant tomatoes with basil to deter the tomato hornworm.

Please bear in mind that these are only some of the many different combinations that have been suggested and we have no definite information on the effectiveness of any of them.

3. Mechanical Methods—The producer with a relatively few plants to protect can readily put to use a number of effective and very practical control methods. You can use preventative devices such as paper collars wrapped around the stems of transplants to ward off attack from cutworms of "hot caps" over cucurbit seedlings to keep off the striped cucumber beetles. Berry bushes and small fruit trees can be covered with mesh as a barrier to birds and Japanese beetles. Also used to prevent female canker worm moths from crawling up tree trunks are sticky barriers that actually trap and hold the insects.

Aphids can be repelled by placing sheets of aluminum foil on the soil under the plants. See the section on mulches for a discussion on the use of aluminum foil.

Several types of traps can be used in the garden. Slugs can be trapped under boards laid on the ground. The slugs can then be destroyed. Black light traps will collect a wide variety of insects of which some will be pests. Traps are a reasonably good tool for monitoring the species in the area but usually have little impact in protecting the garden. Another trap for slugs that has rapidly gained popularity involves placing small pans or cups in the soil so the lip of the cup is about even with the soil level and then bait the cups by filling them with stale beer—any brand of beer will suffice. Check the cups frequently to fish out the dead slugs and replenish beer.

Hand picking of pests and destruction of egg masses offers quick and positive results that can be employed by all home gardeners. This method is hard to beat if you can recognize the eggs and injurious stages of the pest species and have only a small number of plants to examine. Beating beetles into a can holding a small amount of kerosene or oil has been employed for many years.

4. Biological Control Methods—What is biological control? It is the direct or indirect use of living organisms to reduce the number of damaging insects below a level of economic importance. From this definition, we can readily see that biological control is nothing new but one of the oldest of our pest control methods.

Living organisms that control insect populations can be divided into three categories: parasites, predators, and pathogens.

Parasites normally complete their life cycle on or in a single host and at the expense of that host. Parasites are smaller than their host and one host often supports a number of parasites. Parasitism may or may not result in the death of the host. The population of a parasite can develop at a faster rate than the host.

Predators usually require a succession of hosts of the same or different species to complete their development. Predators are usually larger than their prey. Populations of predators usually develop slowly with the supply of food being a limited factor.

A PORTABLE PIGPEN.

TRAP FOR WASPS AND FLIES IN OPEN AIR.

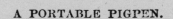

A NEAT PIGEON HOUSE.

Pathogens include the bacteria, fungi, and viruses that are the causative organisms of diseases of insects.

Parasites and predators exert greatest impact or control when a pest population has stabilized or is relatively low. Their affect on an expanding pest population is usually barely noticeable. Pathogens seem to be most effective when pest populations are at a high level; this is especially true with insect virus pathogens. This phenomenon is now evident with the gypsy moth infestation in Pennsylvania. Although parasites that attack gypsy moth eggs and pupae are well established, they cannot keep up with the rapidly increasing host population.

There are several distinct advantages in favor of biological control: (a) once established it is relatively permanent; (b) undesirable side effects are few as compared to those associated with chemical control; (c) the cost can be modest compared to numerous treatments each year with chemicals.

There are also a number of disadvantages associated with biological control that must be resolved before it can be utilized with numerous successes: (a) suitable control organisms are not known for many pest species; (b) suitable environmental situations for the control organism must be available; (c) host pests must be in large enough numbers to support the control organisms which means that some damage from the pest species should be expected; (d) most control organisms are not adaptable to manipulation.

There are three basic methods of increasing the efficiency of biological control organisms: (a) Conservation involves protecting the natural enemies in the area. There are numerous ways to aid the beneficial organisms including reduced use of pesticides that are particularly harmful to predators and parasites and maintain a reservoir of host pests so parasites and predators can continue to develop. (b) Introduction involves searching for natural enemies, and when found, they can be introduced into new areas. Odds of a new parasite becoming established in a new locality may approach 50 percent. However, establishment does not guarantee effectiveness—there are more failures than successes. (c) Augmentation requires the collection, rearing, and then the release of biocontrol agents. This method is similar to a conventional application of a pesticide but uses living organisms instead of chemicals.

Two microbial insecticides are available for general use. Bacillus thuringiensis is available in several commercial formulations and is effective against the larvae of a number of moths and butterflies. Bacillus popilliae (milky spore disease for Japanese beetle grubs) has been used with limited success for many years.

What about buying lady beetles and Praying Mantids?

Lady beetles—the species of lady beetle most likely to be available for sale is the convergent lady beetle, and its preferred host is aphids, but it will also eat eggs of a number of other insects. Lady beetles simply do not kill grubs, Japanese beetles, caterpillars, etc. If there is not an ample supply of live aphids on the grounds when the beetles are released, they disperse and leave the area. Normally, the majority of the beetles will leave the area anyway, food or no food being present.

Praying Mantid egg masses are sometimes available for sale. Chinese Mantid egg packets contain approximately 200 individual eggs. Mantids are predators and immediately upon hatching, the first food in sight is a brother or sister—few nymphs survive the first week of their life. Mantid casualty is also quite high during molting. Mantids are poor searchers for food—they usually wait for their prey to come to them. This has a tremendous influence on the kinds of insects they capture and kill. Their food preferences are grasshoppers, crickets, bees, wasps, and flies. Individual mantids may destroy more beneficial pollinating insects than destructive insects.

Take advantage of the native biological organisms in your area. Chances are fairly good that most of the effective biological organisms known to attack pest species are established in your area. They are, however, seldom present in sufficient numbers to quickly suppress a pest population. This is particularly true in the early part of the summer.

5. Chemical Control—In spite of the best laid plans for insect pest control, pest epidemics will develop to threaten one or more crops. Rather than lose the crop, an insecticide can be used to bring the pest population down to a tolerable level. Insecticides should be used only when necessary and always in accordance with the label directions. The choice of insecticides should be limited to those that exhibit moderately low human and animal toxicity so they can safely be used on food crops and in residential surroundings. Insecticides must also possesss another essential characteristic—the ability to degrade or break down into non-toxic substances soon after application so as not to adversely affect our ecosystem or contribute to environmental pollution. They must also do one more important thing—reduce the numbers of the pest.

Here are some pros and cons of botanical, natural, and man-made insecticides:

Numerous arguments have been proposed favoring botanical and natural insecticides over man-made insecticides. Supposedly botanicals and natural insecticides are less toxic and degrade faster than man-made insecticides and cause no problem to the ecosystem.

Comments will be made on five botanical, one natural and three man-made insecticides. The toxicity will be given as the lethal dosage necessary to kill 50 percent of white rats in the test under standardized conditions. These toxicity values are expressed in terms of a single dosage in milligrams of insecticide per kilograms of body weight. The nine insecticides fall within three groups of toxicity.

Group 2—Moderate Toxicity. Acute oral LD_{50} from 50-500 mg/kg. From 1 teaspoon to 1 ounce of technical insecticide may be lethal to a 150 pound man. Must carry word Warning on the label.

Group 3—Low Toxicity. Acute oral LD_{50} from 500-5,000 mg/kg. From 1 ounce to one pint of technical insecticide may be lethal to a 150 pound man. Must carry word Caution on the label.

Group 4—Relatively Non-Toxic. Acute oral LD_{50} from 5,000 to 15,000 mg/kg. From 1 pint to 2 pints of technical insecticide may be lethal to a 150 pounds man. No caution word is needed on the label.

The following are not recommendations but informational only:

A. Carbaryl Man-made Oral LD50: 540/mg/kg.
B. Diatomaceous earth Natural Oral LD50; no data.
C. Malathion Man-made Oral LD50; 1188 mg/kg.
D. Nicotine Botanical Oral LD50; 65 mg/kg.
E. Methoxychlor Man-made Oral LD50; 5000 mg/kg.
F. Pyrethrins Botanical Oral LD50; 1345 mg/kg.
G. Rotenone Botanical Oral LD50; 83 mg/kg.
H. Ryania Botanical Oral LD50; 1200 mg/kg.
I. Sabadilla Botanical Oral LD50; 4000 mg/kg.

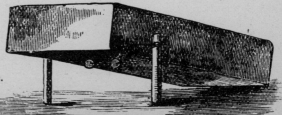

Brick as a Trap for Mice.

Compost — How and Why

DAVID R. EDIGER

Liquid-manure and Water Cart (Reeves & Son, Westbury, Wilts)

In the past decade, the topic of waste recycling has enjoyed a vastly increased popularity amongst many sectors of the population. The object of recycling is, of course, to divert discarded materials from the waste stream into some form of reutilization process. To many people, recycling consists only of depositing bundled newspaper and flattened tin cans at the neighborhood recycling depot. The rest of the process then becomes somebody else's responsibility.

Anyone with a rudimentary knowledge of natural systems knows that the concept of recycling is by no means a new innovation. Nature has been efficiently recycling its own wastes since the earth began. Animal wastes which fall on the ground are decomposed by natural biological processes. The decomposed wastes are then assimilated into the soil where they aid in replenishing the nutrients required for proper soil fertility. The same general process also applies to dead plant and animal matter. Efficient recycling of soil nutrients is essential if the soil is to keep up its role in sustaining life on this planet. The fact that the soil cover on all land areas of the earth averages only seven inches stresses the need for the recycling of essential nutrients.

Farmers and backyard gardeners have been aware of the benefits of composting for many years. The main purpose of this article is to outline the processes involved in composting and to provide some suggestions on proper composting procedure.

Process

One source defines composting as "a biochemical degradation of organic wastes to a sanitary, nuisance-free humus like material". While this definition is reasonably accurate, it tends to oversimplify the processes which occur during composting. Raw organic matter is considered to be unstable in that it is subject to attack by micro-organisms. These micro-organisms may include bacteria, fungi and moulds. During decomposition, complex organic compounds are broken down into simpler forms which can then be recycled into the soil structure.

During composting, living organisms feed upon the organic material and develop cell protoplasm from nitrogen, phosphorus, carbon and other nutrients. When organic material is decomposed in the presence of oxygen, the process is termed "aerobic". The aerobic process is most desirable in that it takes place more rapidly and results in a less offensive compost pile. Anaerobic conditions, which occur in the absence of oxygen, result in a lower decomposition efficiency and odors produced by gases such as methane and hydrogen sulfide.

Composting

Composting takes place essentially in four stages. The first is known as the mesophilic stage because mesophilic (intermediate) bacteria are the most active organisms in the decomposition process. During this stage the simple carbohydrates such as sugars and starches are broken down. Due to fact that mesophilic bacteria give off heat during the decomposition process, the temperature of the compost pile will rise to approximately 105°F.

As the temperature of the pile reaches 105°F, the activity of the mesophilic bacteria decreases, and the decomposition process is taken over by thermophilic (heat-lowing) organisms. During the thermophilic stage, the temperature of the compost pile should rise to 140°F — 160°F. It is in this stage that the major decomposition activity takes place. The high temperature will be maintained as long as there is a high level of bacterial activity. Once the majority of the organic material has been digested, the population of thermophilic organisms will decrease and the temperature of the compost pile will show a corresponding decrease. Figure I shows a typical temperature curve for a properly established compost pile.

After the thermophilic activity has subsided, the cooling-off period commences. During this phase the less readily degradable materials, such as cellulose and lignin, are attacked by the mesophiles. Due to the decreased level of decomposition activity, the temperature of the compost pile will continue to drop during this stage. The cooling-off stage also allows for final digestion of intermediate decomposition products, such as the oxidation of nitrite and nitrate.

The final or maturing stages begins when the temperature approaches normal outdoor conditions. Due to the slow reaction rate during this stage no significant temperature fluctuations occur. The maturing phase finishes off all the incomplete digestion processes, and produces the final compost.

Although numerous factors must be considered in determining the length of time required for complete composting, the following schedule would be roughly applicable at optimum conditions.

TABLE I DURATION OF COMPOSTING STAGES	
Stage	Time Required (days)
Mesophilic	3 - 6
Thermophilic	10 - 15
Cooling-off	10 - 30
Maturing	0 - 90 (depending on application of finished product)

Factors Affecting Compost Pile

There are many factors which can affect the operation of a compost pile and the quality of the finished product. One of the most important factors is the ratio of carbon to nitrogen in the raw organic material being used in the compost pile. Micro-organisms involved in composting require more carbon than nitrogen in order to complete the digestion process. If too much carbon, or not enough nitrogen is present, the composting process becomes more time consuming and less efficient. In some cases, the application of a nitrogen-deficient compost will result in the humus "robbing" nitrogen from the soil. Most studies have indicated an optimum carbon-nitrogen ratio, often written as C/N, of 30:1, or more simply, 30. Table II gives the C/N figures for some of the materials often applied to a compost pile.

TABLE II C/N VALUES FOR COMPOSTABLE MATERIALS		
Material	%N	C/N
Grass Clippings	2.4	19
Raw Garbage	2.15	25
Meat Scraps	5.10	—
Tomato	3.3	12
Turnip Tops	2.3	19
Whole Carrot	1.6	27
Potato Tops	1.5	25
Whole Turnip	1.0	44
Sawdust	0.11	511
Newspaper	Nil	—

Moisture Level

The moisture level in the compost pile is another important consideration; since water serves as a means of transportation for nutrients and soluble gas within the pile. If the moisture level is too low, the matabolic activity of the micro-organisms is decreased, and complete decomposition may not be attained. On the other hand, too much moisture may result in water filling up the void spaces between the organic particles. This will promote anaerobic decomposition, and all of its accompanying problems. Most experts recommend a moisture content of 50-60% for natural aerobic composting.

The temperature curve shown in Figure I is another significant factor. Although it is highly unlikely that actual composting conditions will produce a smooth, continuous curve, the general pattern should be evident. A sustained temperature of 140°F or higher is necessary for two reasons. First, the thermophilic bacteria are most active in this temperature range and hence will provide a more complete degree of decomposition. Secondly, high temperatures will ensure the destruction of undesirable elements such as weed seeds, fly eggs, and disease causing organisms. In order to ensure complete destruction, the temperature of the compost pile should remain above 140°F for approximately seven days. These high temperatures only occur during aerobic digestion, and thereby stress the need for avoiding anaerobic conditions, which occur in a lower temperature range.

Your Garden

To this point, you may be wondering how all this technical information relates to your garden. Indeed, to some of you it may be about as useful as last week's news. Many people, however, have been ardent advocates of composting for years without really understanding the details of the digestion process. Of all the forms of crop raising, the backyard garden puts the most intense demands on each square foot of soil. Because of this fact, garden soil requires the greatest degree of maintenance to ensure proper growing conditions.

Humus (organic) content in soil is a necessary component for proper plant growth. When the soil is intensely cultivated, it tends to lose this organic content and becomes infertile. When this point is reached, no

quantity of chemical fertilizers can restore the original conditions. When compost is applied to the soil, it essentially replaces the lost humus. Compost aids the soil in the following ways:

a) It aids in aggregation of small soil particles, to produce a soil structure with proper water-holding capabilities. When the humus content is low, the soil takes on a sand-like formation which will not hold water and is subject to erosion action.

b) It aids in nutrient exchange, i.e. it holds phosphorus and nitrogen in a form that is available to higher plants. These forms are relatively insoluble thereby increasing the chances of nutrient leaching from the soil.

c) Apart from phosphorus, nitrogen and potash, compost also contains trace elements necessary for optimum plant growth and decreased susceptibility to disease.

From the above points, it is apparent that finished compost could more aptly be described as a soil conditioner than a fertilizer. Application of good compost to the soil is preferable to applying chemical fertilizers, in that compost aids the existing natural systems as opposed to imposing an artificial set of conditions.

How To Start a Compost Pile

The only step remaining here is to describe how all this data can be translated into a working situation. Compost begins with a pile of raw organic waste matter. When selecting the materials to be included in the pile, consideration must be given to factors such as C/N and moisture content. If a material is included with C/N value substantially above 30, it should be balanced by a material with a low C/N ratio. Similarly, if very wet materials are included, a compensating quantity of dry material should be added. It is rather difficult to ascertain whether the moisture content is actually in the range of 50%. The pile should, however, appear damp if the moisture content is within the proper range.

In order to ensure complete decomposition, the material for the compost pile should be cut into pieces approximately 2 to 3 inches in size. This will allow adequate surface area for attack by micro-organisms. However, if the material is cut too small, it restricts the flow of air through the pile and will promote anaerobic conditions. After the materials have been cut up, blending may be necessary if the various components have substantially different C/N ratios and moisture contents. This is easily accomplished when the materials are being piled.

Size and Shape

The size and shape of the actual compost pile is also an important aspect. The pile must be self-insulating to the extent that it can maintain the high temperatures required in the thermophilic phase. In order to accomplish this, the pile should take on a profile approximately like that of a coal pile. A height of at least three feet is considered essential to limit heat and moisture loss. The material should be piled loosely enough to allow air passage through the pile.

Once the pile has been placed, the decomposition process will begin almost immediately. From this point temperature measurements should be made daily to assess the activity of the pile. A marked upward trend in temperatures curve should be noticed within the first two to three days. The peak of the temperature curve should be reached in six to eight days, and

this temperature should then be maintained for four or five days. Temperature readings should be made approximately half way between the outer surface and the center of the pile. Failure of the pile to reach temperatures of 140°F, or better, indicate that either the pile has gone anaerobic or the moisture content has dropped below acceptable.

Turning the pile at appropriate intervals is necessary to achieve proper decomposition. When the pile is turned, it should be done in such a way that it is essentially turned inside-out, i.e. the material from the centre of the pile moves to the outside and vice versa. Since the most active decomposition takes place at the centre of the pile, turning ensures that all materials are subjected to this higher rate digestion. Since the pile tends to settle, turning also loosens the particles and maintains adequate aeration for aerobic conditions. If the temperature of the pile drops unexpectedly, it may be due to excessive moisture loss. This is easily rectified by spraying the pile briefly with a garden hose. Care must be taken, however, not to saturate the pile. The intervals for turning the pile will be deter-

mined from the temperature. Through the mesophilic stage, turning is not required, as the population of micro-organisms must first be allowed to reach adequate proportions. During the peak of the thermophilic stage, the pile should be turned two or three times. Two turns should be sufficient in the cooling-off range. Once the pile has returned to near ambient conditions, it should be matured for a month or more. One turn may be required half way through the maturing period. Figure I shows the points on the temperature curve where the pile should be turned for optimum digestion efficiency.

If all these steps are taken, the finished product should have the texture and aroma of fresh humus. A final shredding may be necessary if the compost pile contained a high percentage of coarse fibred material.

Composting is a practice which can be beneficial both to your garden and to your environment in general. It is hoped that the information in this article may help to improve the quality of your compost. Don't forget to tell your friends and neighbors.

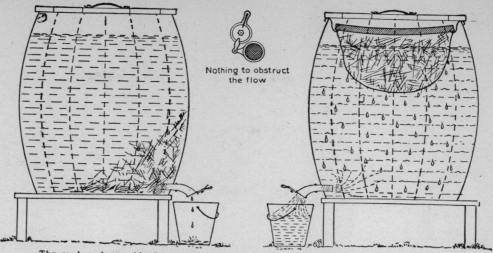

The gardener's stand-by for getting succulent crops in hot weather—a barrel of liquid manure.
The old way: If you dump the manure into the barrel it will clog the spigot and you will have to stir it
The new way: Suspend it in a bag at the top and you have the solution ready for use all the time

Hubert Davis
University of Kentucky
College of Agriculture
Cooperative Extension Service

MAKING COMPOST

Most homeowners are faced with the disposal of leaves, grass clippings, and other organic materials. Usually, these are burned or carted off by the city sanitation department. This year, save yourself unnecessary bills and gain a valuable organic source as well by using these organic residues to build a compost pile. Your garden will benefit from compost. It improves the soil and makes the finest plants grow even better.

What to Use

Compost is easy to make. All you need is raw organic matter, soil, and fertilizer. Leaves, grass clippings, weeds, garden refuse, and manure are excellent organic materials to use. Special additives don't help. Fertilizer will speed up composting more than anything.

How to Build A Compost Pile

Build the compost pile in an out-of-the-way section of your back lawn or in the corner of a vegetable garden. The best location is a shady spot; however, do not build directly under a tree because the tree's roots may grow into the pile. Make an open-end bin or box to hold the compost. It can be 3 to 5 feet wide, 2 to 4 feet high, and any length. You can build the box of wire fencing supported by post, or it may be constructed of boards or masonry materials.

To make the compost pile, alternate layers of raw organic material, fertilizer, and soil. Start with organic matter—6 inches deep, if the material is fairly solid, or 12 inches deep if it is loose. Add water if the material is dry. Next add fertilizer—for general-use compost, add 10-10-10 or 10-6-4 analysis fertilizer at the rate of 1½ cups per bushel of compact organic matter, or 5-10-5 at the rate of 2½ cups per bushel. Also add 2/3 cup of ground dolomitic limestone per bushel or organic matter. If making compost for acid-loving plants such as azaleas, rhododendrons, or holly, fertilize with 3/4 cup of ammonium sulfate or ½ cup of ammonium nitrate and omit the dolomitic limestone.

After you fertilize, add a 1-inch layer of soil. Continue to alternate layers of organic matter, fertilizer, and soil, as described, until the pile is 3 to 4 feet high. The pile should be slightly lower in the center for ease of watering. Complete with a layer of soil on the top and sides.

Care

Keep your compost moist but not soggy. No offensive odors should exist, providing the pile is kept moist and a layer of soil is on the top and sides. It is not necessary to turn or mix the pile if it has been built in the manner described above. Allow it to stand undisturbed for one full summer before it is used. For a continuous compost supply, make more than one pile.

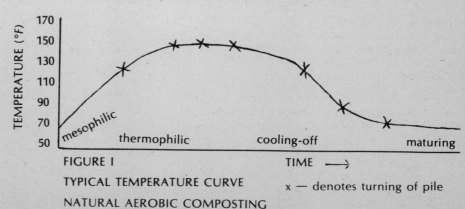

FIGURE I
TYPICAL TEMPERATURE CURVE
NATURAL AEROBIC COMPOSTING
TIME →
x — denotes turning of pile

LIME AND FERTILIZER

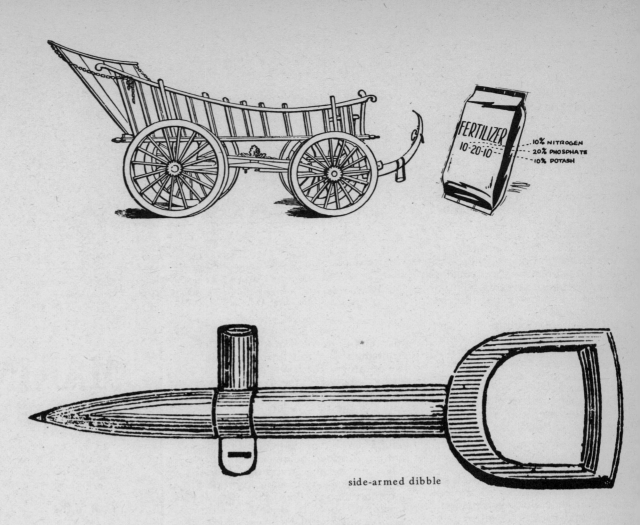

WARNER'S PATENT AQUAJECT.

Cooperative Extension Service
College of Agriculture and Natural Resources
The University of Connecticut at Storrs

By Richard A. Ashley
Extension Horticulturist

The application of the correct amount of lime and fertilizer materials (commercial fertilizers and manures) is essential if optimum growth in the home vegetable garden is to be obtained. The best way to determine what materials and the correct quantities to use is to have your soil tested every year.

Have Your Soil Tested

The University of Connecticut offers a complete soil testing service without charge. Contact your county Extension agent or write to the following address for a soil sample mailing kit:

Soil Testing Laboratory
Box U-102
The University of Connecticut
Storrs, Connecticut 06268

A kit will be sent to you containing a plastic mailing bag for the sample plus instructions on how to take soil samples. Instructions are printed on the back of the information sheet enclosed in the kit. Taking proper samples is extremely important. Poor sampling techniques will mean poor test results, hence improper recommendations for your crops. Fill out the information sheet completely. This will insure good recommendations based on the crop to be grown and on the previous fertility program.

After the tests are completed, the results will be mailed directly to you with recommendations for amounts of lime and fertilizer for the crop to be grown.

Liming

Because of continual weathering and use, Connecticut soils become more and more acid (sour) unless lime is applied periodically as a sweetening agent. Soil acidity is reported in a pH scale of 1 to 14 with a pH of 7 being neutral. A pH below 7 indicates an acid soil condition. Most vegetables grow best at a pH of from 6.0 to 6.5. Some Connecticut soils have a pH as low as 4.0 which is 100 times more acid than a soil of pH 6.0. Poor growth results if the soil is too acid.

A pH between 7 and 14 indicates a soil that is basic in nature. This pH condition does not normally exist in Connecticut soils and usually occurs only if too much lime has been applied. Over liming will result in poor crop yield or even death of a crop.

There are generally three types of lime available for the home garden: finely ground limestone, dolomitic limestone, and hydrated lime. Finely ground limestone and dolomitic limestone have about the same neutralizing power. However, the dolomitic contains magnesium carbonate and thus is a source of magnesium. Generally, the dolomitic form will be recommended.

Hydrated lime is manufactured from ground limestone by heating the limestone to drive off the carbon dioxide. This form of lime acts faster and is stronger than the ground or dolomitic limestones. However, hydrated lime can cause problems if not handled carefully and should not be used unless specifically recommended by the specialist evaluating your soil test results. Apply only the amount of lime recommended.

When applying lime spread it uniformly over the area that is to be treated. Work the lime into the soil with a rototiller or harrow if possible. If this equipment is not available or the area is too small for the equipment to be practical, rake in the lime as thoroughly as possible.

Fall liming is preferred. A second period when lime can be applied is in the early spring. Hydrated lime, or products containing hydrated lime, should not be applied with fertilizer applications.

Commercial Fertilizers

There are many brands and analyses of fertilizers on the market today. However, most vegetable garden recommendations will be made using a "complete" fertilizer with an analysis of either 5-10-10, 5-10-5, or 10-10-10. The term "complete" means that the fertilizer contains nitrogen (N), phosphate (P_2O_5), and potash (K_2O). The numbers refer to the percentage of each of these nutrients that are present in the fertilizer. The first number *always* refers to amount of nitrogen, i.e. a 5-10-10 fertilizer contains 5% nitrogen. The second number is always for the amount of phosphate, i.e. a 5-10-10 contains 10% phosphate (P_2O_5). The last number refers to the amount of potassium present, i.e. a 5-10-10 contains 10% potash (K_2O). Superphosphate is a material that is not a complete fertilizer since the analysis is 0-20-0. This material contains no nitrogen, 20% phosphate (P_2O_5), and no potassium.

If a fertilizer material other than that recommended by the specialist is used, it should contain all three of the major elements listed above. Secondly, base the rate of addition on the amount of nitrogen present. For example, if the specialist recommended 30 pounds of 5-10-10 per 1000-square feet, and the gardener used 15-10-10, the amount of the latter material to apply is 10 pounds per 1000-square feet. This is based on the fact that the specialist recommended a material containing percent nitrogen and the fertilizer that was used contains three times as much. Hence, the amount to apply should be reduced by three times. In most cases it is best to use the materials recommended.

Most commercial fertilizers can be stored from one season to the next. The place of storage should be cool and dry to prevent caking and/or hardening of the fertilizer in the bag.

Applying Fertilizers

Many home gardens are not properly fertilized. Soil tests of Connecticut vegetable gardens have shown great range in amounts of nutrients available to the plant. Many people do not apply enough fertilizer and in this way fail to obtain top production from their garden. The cost of fertilizer is very low in comparison to the cost of seed, plants, and labor that goes into making a successful garden. When the recommended amounts of fertilizers are used, the cost will be minimal.

Yet, some gardeners believe that if a little fertilizer does some good, a lot will do even more good. This is like taking two aspirin for a headache and then deciding to take a whole bottle at once to keep the headache from returning. Too much fertilizer will stunt and even kill plants. Apply only the recommended amounts.

One of the most important things to know when applying fertilizers is the size of the garden. Most recommendations are generally based on an area of 1000-square feet. A garden 40' x 25' contains 1000-square feet. If 30 lbs. of 5-10-10 per 1000-square feet is recommended and the garden contains 1500-square feet, the amount to apply to the entire garden is 45 lbs. of 5-10-10. This is because the garden is half again as large as the 1000-square feet used for the recommendation. Likewise, if the garden contains 300 square feet the amount should be reduced to 10 lbs. of 5-10-10, since the area to be covered is about one third that of the 1000-square feet area on which the recommendation is based.

It is best to broadcast the fertilizer over the entire area of the garden. A lawn spreader may be used for this purpose if the garden surface is not too rough. Rototill or disc under the fertilizer. If the garden is small, spade first and then apply the fertilizer. Rake in the fertilizer.

As the season progresses, certain crops such as sweet corn benefit from a sidedressing of fertilizer. Spread the recommended amount of fertilizer in a band next to the plants. Keep the fertilizer off the foliage as it will cause burning. Rake the fertilizer in lightly. Deep cultivation will cut off roots and reduce yield.

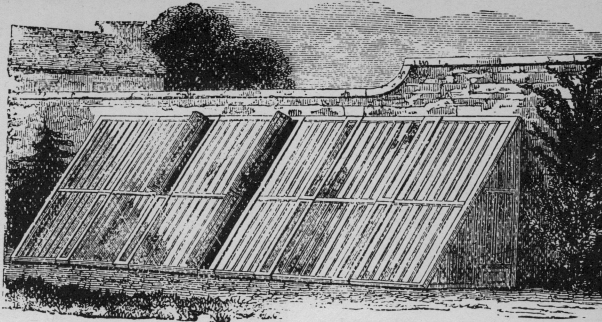

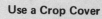

Fusiform Root.

Foliaceous Sepals,

Hop

Use a Crop Cover

After the first killing frost in the fall, plant the cover crop. This crop is beneficial, since it reduces winter erosion and leaching of the soil. Also, when the cover crop is plowed under in the spring most of the benefits of manure are achieved.

If possible, plant a rye or oats cover crop by the end of September. Oats will winter kill and will be easier to turn under in the spring. Use rye if the seeding date is later than October 7.

The following rates of rye or oats are recommended:

Sowing Date	Pounds/per 1000 sq. ft.
September	2
October*	3
November	3½

Oats should not be planted after October 7.

You should work the garden soil lightly by rototilling, discing or scratching vigorously with a rake. Broadcast the seed and cover it lightly by raking or dragging. You may sow an oat or rye cover crop between the rows of hardy vegetables, such as beets and carrots.

Turn under the cover crop as early in the spring as you can work the ground. This will allow time for the cover crop to break down before you plant your garden. If the cover crop is turned under too close to planting time, your garden plants may turn yellow and grow slowly as the decaying cover crop plants compete with the plants for the available plant nutrients.

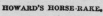

HOWARD'S HORSE-RAKE.

Hybrid Raspberry—Mahdi.

MULCHES FOR YOUR GARDEN

By the Soil Conservation Service

TEST FOR DRAINAGE IN SANDY SOIL.

References: *a*, test pit 4 ft. deep; *b*, 1 ft. of worked soil; *c*. "pan"; *d*, uncultivated soil; *e*, wet soil *f*, hard soil containing iron; *g*, clay; *h*, level of stagnant water. Dotted line represents drain.

USING A MULCH in your flower or vegetable garden may well be your most valuable garden practice. A good mulch can reduce soil blowing and washing, suppress weeds, keep the soil moist and cool, and add organic matter to the soil.

Grass clippings, sawdust, straw, and compost make excellent mulches. And they are easy to apply. Simply spread a 3- to 6-inch layer of one of these organic materials on the soil surface around your plants, making certain you do not cover the plants. Keeping the layer deep enough to do the job is important too. This means that you will need to add more mulching material over the old layers to get all the benefits of mulching.

Mulching with grass clippings is a good way to dispose of some of your clippings. But you may need to mix them with other mulch materials to keep them from packing down and preventing water from entering the soil.

Sawdust makes a better mulch if it is well rotted, or if you add 1 to 2 cups of ammonium sulfate or sodium nitrate to each bushel of fresh sawdust before applying the mulch. Weed-free straw is excellent but loose straw can be a fire hazard and, to some, it may be unsightly.

Compost is probably the best mulch you can use. And you can make it yourself from leftover plant materials from your garden. (See centerspread for suggestions on how to make compost.)

Mulches prevent loss of moisture from the soil by evaporation. Moisture moves by capillary action to the surface and evaporates if the soil is not covered by a mulch. Sun and wind hasten this loss of moisture.

You can reduce evaporation and control weeds by stirring the soil an inch or so deep but plant roots cannot develop in this soil layer. A layer of organic material on the surface gives the same benefits and allows normal plant-root development.

Energy from falling raindrops is dissipated on a mulched soil. The result is less soil erosion and less soil compaction.

Mulches suppress weeds, thus saving you a lot of work. An occasional weed may poke through the mulch but it is easily pulled out.

Mulches keep the soil from getting hot under intense sunlight. Many plants, including those in vegetable and flower gardens, need a cool surface soil.

Mulches, especially grass clippings and compost, add organic matter to the soil and furnish food for earthworms, which are valuable in aerating the soil. The organic matter helps to keep the soil crumbly and easy to work. Farmers call this good tilth. At the end of the growing season, the mulch can be worked into the soil to supply organic matter the following year.

If you use a mulch around perennials in the winter, remove it in the spring to let the soil thaw out and warm up.

Many organic materials, such as straw and autumn leaves, are rich in carbohydrates and low in nitrogen. Usually, you will find it beneficial to add nitrogen fertilizer to the material before applying it as a mulch. One to two cups of fertilizer high in nitrogen (ammonium sulfate) for each bushel of organic material is about right. To avoid burning the plants, do not let the fertilizer touch them.

To provide a source for one of the best mulches, every gardener should have a compost bin—preferably two—for making compost from organic materials. You can make the bins yourself by attaching ordinary wire fence or boards to solid posts or open brickwork. Each bin should be 4 to 6 feet high, 3 to 5 feet wide, and any convenient length. And one side of each should be removable for convenience in building up the compost material and for taking it out. In late fall, a temporary piece of wire fence may be used to increase the height about 2 feet. After the material settles in March, the piece of fence can be removed.

Compost is not only an excellent mulch but it is also a good fertilizer and soil conditioner when it is worked into the soil.

Leaves, grass clippings, stems and stalks from harvested vegetables, corn husks, pea

Two bins permit turning compost by moving it from one bin to the other.

hulls, and fine twigs are good materials for composting. You should always compost leaves before using them as a mulch. Raw leaves are flat and may keep water from entering the soil. Avoid using any diseased plants.

The ideal way to make compost is to use two bins. Fill one with alternate layers of organic material 6 to 12 inches thick and of garden soil about 1 inch thick. To each layer of organic material, add chemicals at the following rate:

Chemical	Rate in cups per bushel of organic material [1]
Method 1:	
Ammonium sulfate	1
or	
Ammonium nitrate	½
Ground dolomitic limestone [2]	⅔
or	
Wood ashes [2]	1½
Superphosphate	½
Magnesium sulfate (epsom salts) [3]	[4] 1/16
Method 2:	
Mixed fertilizer 5-10-5	3
Ground dolomitic limestone [2]	⅔

[1] Packed tightly with your hands.

[2] For acid compost (for azaleas and rhododendrons), omit lime, limestone, and wood ashes.

[3] Add epsom salts only if dolomitic limestone is unavailable and ordinary limestone is used (at same rate).

[4] Equivalent to 1 tablespoonful. (For more information, see USDA Leaflet 307, How Much Fertilizer Should I Use?)

Be sure to moisten the organic material thoroughly. Repeat this layering process until the bin is full or you run out of organic material. Pack the material tightly around the edges but only lightly in the center so that this area settles more than the edges and the water does not run off.

After 3 to 4 months of moderate to warm weather, commonly in June, begin turning the material by moving it from the first bin into the second one. Before turning, it is a good idea to move the material added the previous fall from the edges, which dry out first, to the center.

In areas that have cool frosty winters, compost made from leaves in November and December can be turned the following May or June.

GARDENING ON THE CONTOUR

By the Soil Conservation Service, U.S.D.A.

Does rainwater from your neighbor's property drain onto your garden? Is your garden on a slope so that water rushes off and is lost to the plants, taking soil with it? Is your garden on a steep slope where you want to plant perennials, shurbs, or azaleas? If so, you should think seriously of planting on the contour or perhaps building a terrace.

A contoured or terraced garden does not erode. Because water is channeled across the slope instead of down, the soil absorbs more rainwater and is less susceptible to drought. Contouring not only controls erosion but distributes water evenly. This pays off in better yields and higher quality vegetables or flowers.

To contour your garden, follow the natural lay of the land. It does not require special skill or equipment to find the contour line. A level can be improvised from materials on hand—an efficient device can be made from an ordinary carpenter's level mounted on a 2 by 4. To determine a level line begin about the center of the slope. Lay the 2 by 4 along the slope and move one end up or down until the bubble on the level is centered; mark the spot with a stake. Repeat this process across the slope to establish the contour guide line. Plant the rows of vegetables or flowers parallel to this line.

As you cultivate the garden, leave small channels between the rows to collect and hold the moisture so that it soaks into the soil.

If water from your neighbor's property drains onto your garden or if your garden is on a slope so that rainwater washes away the soil, a diversion terrace can divert the flow of water effectively. A terrace is simply a ridge with a shallow channel on the upper side. You can build it with a hoe and spade. Or, if your garden is large enough, you may use a garden tractor or larger equipment. Give the terrace a slight grade so that water does not stand in the channel but flows off gently. This water should flow onto a grassed area to prevent erosion. Make the terrace high enough to carry all the water that is intercepted. Make it wide enough so that you can work over it easily and so that it blends in with the natural shape of the land.

If your garden is on a fairly steep slope, consider building rock terraces. Unless you use rock terraces, the plants will lack moisture. Water runs off without soaking in, and even watering with a hose has little effect.

Beginning just below the top of the slope, place flat stones on edge in the soil to make small benches 2 to 4 feet wide, depending on the slope. Each bench should slant slightly toward the original slope. The water that is caught and held on these slopes will supply moisture to the plants. Because the water is held in check, no erosion occurs.

This kind of terrace requires a lot of stones and a lot of work in a large area, but it works well on short slopes. Slightly irregular stones are more attractive than bricks or blocks, which are pushed out of line easily by frost action.

For additional information see the local representative of the Soil Conservation Service, U.S. Department of Agriculture.

Approximate Composition of Fertilizer Materials

Material	Nitrogen (N)	Phosphoric acid (P_2O_5)	Potash (K_2O)
		percent	
Chemical			
Ureaform	30.0–40.0	...	...
Ammonium nitrate	33.5	...	...
Ammonium sulfate	20.5	...	...
Nitrate of soda	16.0	...	...
Urea	42.0–46.0	...	...
Superphosphate	...	16.0–20.0	...
Muriate of potash	...	...	48.0–62.0
Triple superphosphate	...	46.0	...
Organic			
Bonemeal, steamed	2.0	22.0	...
Garbage tankage	1.5	2.0	.7
Sewerage sludge	2.0	1.4	.8
Sewerage sludge, activated	6.0	3.0	.1
Tankage, animal	9.0	6.0	...
Tankage, processed	7.0	1.0	.1
Horse manure, fresh	.6	.3	.5
Cow manure, fresh	.5	.2	.5
Cow manure, dried	1.3	.9	.8
Hen manure, fresh	1.1	0.9	.5
Hen manure, dried, with litter	2.8	2.8	1.5
Wood ashes	...	.8	5.0
Cottonseed meal	6.0	3.0	1.0

Characteristics of Mulching Materials

Characteristics	Sawdust	Straw	Manure	Black paper	Black polyethylene
Longevity	Decomposes about ¼"-¾" per year	Not more than one year	Not more than one year	One growing season or less	Two or more years
Water retention (reduction of surface evaporation)	Good	Poor	Poor-fair	Good	Good (impervious to water)
Heat absorption	Poor	Poor	Poor	Good	Good
Soil heat retention	Fair	Poor	Fair	Good	Good
Weed control	Fair	Poor	Poor	Good	Excellent
Water penetration	Good	Good	Good	Fair-poor	None
Fertilizer value	Poor	Poor	Good	None	None
Extra nutrients needed for decomposition	Nitrogen	Nitrogen	None	None	None
Toxic qualities	Usually none	None	Possibility, if applied too heavily	If oil, tar, or creosote impregnated	None
Incidence of rotted fruit over nonmulched plants	Lower	Unknown (probably lower)	Unknown	Lower	Lower
Cleanliness of fruit	Good	Good	Poor	Excellent	Excellent
Durability (can it be walked on?)	Good	Poor	Poor	Poor	Good
Effect on soil structure	Poor	Good	Good	Unknown	Excellent
Appearance of mulch	Good	Poor	Poor	Good	Good

Experiment to show the Downward Tendency of Growth in Roots even when illuminated from below.

INSECTICIDES FOR ORGANIC GARDENERS

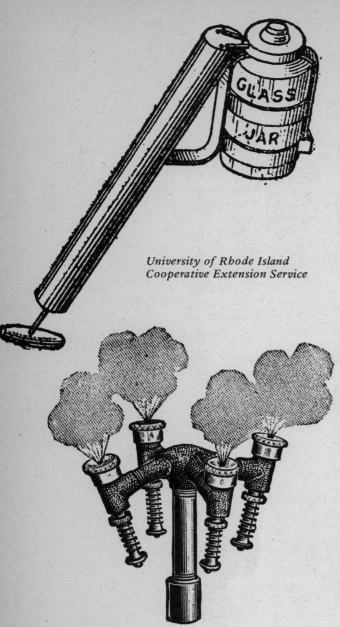

*University of Rhode Island
Cooperative Extension Service*

" Vermorel " Four-discharge Nozzle.

The following is a list of substances frequently used or recommended by organic gardeners, although purists do not rely on any pesticides. Instead they pay meticulous attention to horticultural and non-chemical control methods, taking pains not to disturb their crop's environment.

Users of pesticides should read the directions on the labels carefully. Pay particular attention to possible hazards, the concentration and amount of pesticides to use, the days to harvest and the possibility of pesticide injury to the plant (phytotoxicity).

NICOTINE
Nicotine is an alkaloid derived from plants in genus Nicotiana and is well known as a greenhouse insecticide. It is usually found as a 40 percent alkaloid formulation; used as a fumigant, dust or spray, and can be used on many crops and ornamentals.
Pest Controlled. Aphids, thrips and mealy bugs.
Environmental Impact. It is highly to moderately toxic to man, especially if inhaled; has a rapid breakdown (little residual effect), is not harmful to bees and most beneficial insects.

RYANIA
Ryania is a botanical derived from Ryania speciosa roots and stems, is a contact and stomach poison, and is not commonly found.
Pests Controlled. Cranberry fruit worms, European corn borers and caterpillars (codling moth) on apple.
Environmental Impact. Slightly toxic to mammals.

MILKY SPORE DISEASE
Milky spore is a bacterial disease that takes about three years to become effective but once effective the bacteria resist heat, cold, dryness, and moisture. The disease remains in the soil for a long time and is spread to adjacent areas by birds and other predators of the grubs.
Pests Controlled. Specifically for Japanese beetle grubs.
Environmental Impact. Harmless to other organisms.

ROTENONE
Rotenone is a non-phytotoxic botanical derived from derris or cuberoots. It is primarily a contact insecticide but also acts as a stomach poison and inactivates an enzyme system causing death from lack of oxygen. It is registered for most fruits and vegetables.
Pests Controlled. Aphids, cabbageworms, Colorado potato beetles, asparagus beetles, ants, bedbugs, cucumber beetles, cockroaches, European corn borers, bean beetles, fleas, flea beetles, Japanese beetles, lice, greenhouse white flies, houseflies, pepper maggots, rose chafers and squash bugs. It has some acaricidal (kills spiders and mites) action.
Environmental Impact. It is moderately toxic to man, extremely toxic to fish and other cold blooded animals, and is reported highly toxic to swine. The hazard to birds and wildlife is low. It has a short residual life, usually less than one week; is not compatible with alkaline materials; and is broken down in the presence of light and alkali to less toxic insecticidal compounds. It has a low environmental pollution level.

OILS
Most frequently used oil is petroleum (60 to 70 second superior oil) but oils derived from plants and animals are also used. Toxicity may be due to suffocation of eggs and insects or to the toxic properties of oil.
Do not use when frost is anticipated, but for best results use immediately before bud break when weather is dry, mild and sunny. Do not use on Douglas fir, blue spruce, sugar maple, Japanese maple, beech, birch, hickory, walnut or butternut.
Pests Controlled. Some aphids, mealy bugs, pear psylla, some armored scales, soft scales, and white flies.
Environmental Impact. It is safe to man and animals and exempt from tolerances on food. It may be toxic to some plants.

SABADILLA
Sabadilla is derived from seeds of Schoenocaulon officinale, but is not readily available. Alkali and heat treatment enhance its insecticidal activity.
Pests controlled. True bugs such as cinch, harlequin, squash, and stink bug, and also thrips when used in sugar bait.
Environmental Impact. There is slight toxicity to mammals but it can cause irritation to eyes and respiratory tract. It has rapid breakdown in the presence of light.

BACILLUS THURINGIENSIS
This is a bacterial disease that produces a poison in the gut of certain lepidoptera larvae.
Pests Controlled. Many lepidoptera (caterpillars); cabbage loopers, hornworms, cankerworms, gypsy moths, and tent caterpillars.
Environmental Impact. It is harmless to mammals and soil organisms, and is exempt from residue tolerances on food.

PYRETHRUM
Pyrethrum is a botanical derived from certain dried flower heads in the genus Chrysanthemum and comes in dust or liquid formulation. It is a contact insecticide with rapid knockdown that affects the nervous system of the insect. It can be used on most fruits and vegetables.
Pests Controlled. Ants, aphids, asparagus beetles, cabbage loopers, cheesemites, crickets, fleabeetles, flies, fruit flies, gnats, horseflies, leafhoppers, leafrollers, psyllids, roaches, spiders, sodwebworms, wasps and ticks.
Environmental Impact. It is slightly toxic to man, not hazardous to birds and other wildlife with extremely low toxicity to mammals. It is nontoxic when used on pets (dogs, cats, birds), and can be used in food areas. There is a broad spectrum of insecticidal activity, and lack of persistence and biomagnification in the food chain. Because it irritates insects, it acts as a flushing agent, making them leave their hiding places. There is rapid breakdown when exposed to sunlight and alkali.

APHIS BRUSHES.

DUSTING

BELLOWS.

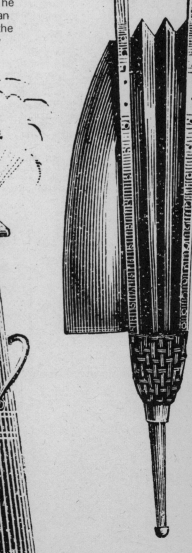

TEBB'S UNIVERSAL

FUMIGATOR.

IRON DEFICIENCIES IN PLANTS

How to control it in yards and gardens

By Lowell F. Locke and Harold V. Eck of the Agricultural Research Service, U.S.D.A.

Iron is an essential element for plant growth. Hence, all plants are susceptible to iron deficiency. Where the amount of iron available to plants does not meet their minimum needs, the plants fall into a diseased condition called iron chlorosis.

Iron chlorosis may occur anywhere in the United States, but is most likely to occur west of 100 degrees longitude (roughly the western half of the country) and on the sandier soils of the southeastern part of the country.

Soil areas that produce chlorotic plants range from a few square feet to many acres in size.

ECHEVERIA AGAVOIDES.

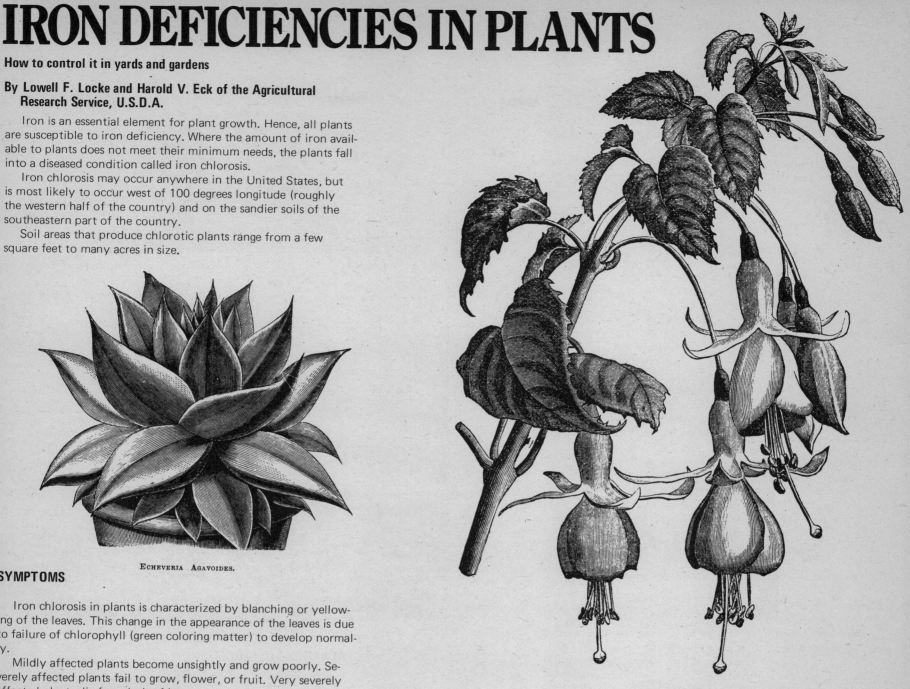

FUCHSIA—"DAY DREAM."

SYMPTOMS

Iron chlorosis in plants is characterized by blanching or yellowing of the leaves. This change in the appearance of the leaves is due to failure of chlorophyll (green coloring matter) to develop normally.

Mildly affected plants become unsightly and grow poorly. Severely affected plants fail to grow, flower, or fruit. Very severely affected plants die from lack of iron.

In deciduous (leaf-shedding) plants, areas between leaf veins become light green, yellow, or white. The greater the iron deficiency, the paler the areas. The leaf veins ordinarily remain green. In very severe cases, the edges of leaves—or entire leaves—turn brown, and the plants often die.

In conifers, needles turn yellow; then, if the deficiency is severe, they turn brown and die.

Occasionally only a part of a plant is affected.

CAUSES

Iron chlorosis occurs in susceptible plants wherever and whenever iron is not available to them.

The condition is often due to high pH, which makes it possible for other elements to interfere with the absorption of iron, rather than to lack of iron in the soil. It occurs most often on soils that are high in lime. Thus it is more prevalent in the arid West than in the humid East, since high-lime soils occur naturally in arid areas.

But iron chlorosis is not limited to naturally occurring high-lime soils. It may be caused by actual deficiency of iron, or by application of excessive amounts of lime or phosphate to certain soils. It may be caused by overirrigation, poor drainage, bicarbonate in the soil or in irrigation water, and high levels of certain heavy metals in the soil (for example, manganese, copper, and zinc).

PLANTS AFFECTED

Iron chlorosis affects trees, shrubs, vines, field crops, flowers, grasses, and many types of vegetables. In the Western States and in four adjoining States (Texas, Oklahoma, Kansas, and Nebraska), it has been observed in more than 250 species and varieties of plants.

Species of plants, and varieties of the same species, vary in their susceptibility to iron chlorosis. For example, sorghums show chlorosis where wheat does not—but if the iron deficiency becomes great enough, wheat will show chlorosis also.

CONTROL

If overirrigation or poor drainage is a possible cause of iron chlorosis, it should be corrected. Otherwise, the disease is controlled by furnishing soluble iron to plants, either through the soil or through the foliage of the plants.

Two principal types of iron-containing compounds used to furnish iron to plants are:

1. Iron chelates.
2. Inorganic compounds containing iron in soluble form. Ferrous sulfate (also called copperas) is such a compound.

You can buy iron chelates and ferrous sulfate at stores that sell garden supplies and fertilizer.

Iron Chelates.—Iron chelates are organic compounds containing iron. The iron remains available to plants when the chelates are placed in the soil.

The iron in chelates costs much more per pound than the iron in ferrous sulfate, but the amount of chelates required for control of chlorosis is much smaller than the required amount of ferrous sulfate, and the cost of treatment with chelates need not be greater.

Iron chelates are marked under various trade names and in various formulations. Some are applied to soil, others to foliage. Some of those intended for application to soil are for high-lime soils, and some are for iron-deficient soils.

If you decide to use an iron chelate, get one that has been formulated for your particular conditions and purposes, and follow the directions on the package.

Ferrous Sulfate.—Ferrous sulfate and similar compounds that contain inorganic iron furnish soluble iron to plants. However, when they are applied to the soil, much of the applied iron becomes unavailable to plants. Consequently, applications must be much in excess of amounts actually required by the plants. The iron is made unavailable by the same factors that cause iron chlorosis initially (high pH, interfering elements, etc.).

The sections that follow ("Treating Soil" and "Treating Foliage") refer to treatment with ferrous sulfate.

TREATING SOIL

Soil treatment is discussed below under the headings "Trees," "Shrubs and Vines," "Flowers and vegetables," and "Lawns." Each section contains information that will enable you to determine the number of gallons of ferrous sulfate solution that you will need.

For trees, shrubs, vines, flowers, and vegetables, the solution is prepared by dissolving ferrous sulfate in water at the rate of 1 pounds of the chemical per gallon of water. Thus, if you find that you need 25 gallons of solution, you will know that you need 25 pounds of ferrous sulfate. For lawns, the procedure is different and is explained in the section on lawns.

Trees

Before treating the soil in which a tree is growing, determine how much ferrous sulfate you will need. A convenient way to do this is to measure the diameter of the periphery of the tree at the drip line. If the treatment is to be made while the tree is dormant, you will need 1 gallon of ferrous sulfate solution for each foot of the diameter of the periphery. For example, if the diameter is 25 feet, you will need 25 gallons of solution. If the treatment is to be made during the growing season, you will need ½ gallon of ferrous sulfate solution for each foot of the diameter of the periphery.

After obtaining the necessary amount of ferrous sulfate and preparing the solution, proceed as follows:

Dig holes around the periphery at intervals of about 3 feet. Dig each hole deep enough to hold a gallon of liquid.

Pour 1 gallon of ferrous sulfate solution (½ gallon if treatment is made during the growing season) in each hole; let it soak away.

Fill each hole with water once or twice; let it soak away. Refill the holes with soil.

The summer after treating the soil, watch for symptoms of chlorosis. If chlorosis persists, take these additional steps:

Spray the foliage once or twice to gain temporary improvement.

Repeat the soil treatment when the trees are again dormant.

Shrubs and Vines

Dig a trench 4 to 6 inches deep around each shrub or vine, or dig four holes 6 to 8 inches deep.

In digging a trench, follow the periphery, or drip line, of the plant, but keep the trench at least 1 foot from the base of the plant.

In digging holes, place them at equal intervals around the periphery, but at least 1 foot from the base of the plant.

The amount of ferrous sulfate needed by a shrub or vine ranges from 2 to 5 gallons. The amount needed by a particular plant depends on the size of the plant.

Pour the solution in the trench or holes. After it has soaked away, fill the trench or holes with water once or twice, and let it soak away. Refill the trench or holes with soil.

Flowers and Vegetables

To treat the soil in which large flowers (annual and perennial) and vegetables are growing singly, dig a trench 2 to 3 inches deep around each plant; keep it at least 1 foot from the base of the plant. Pour 1 gallon of ferrous sulfate solution in the trench. After it has soaked away, fill the trench with water once or twice, and let it soak away. Refill the trench with soil.

To treat the soil in which flowers (annual and perennial) and vegetables are growing in rows, dig trenches 2 to 3 inches deep on both sides of each row and about 6 inches from the base of the plants. Pour ferrous sulfate solution in the trenches at the rate of 1 gallon per 10 feet of row—½ gallon each side of the row. The rest of the treatment is the same as for plants growing singly.

If either of these treatment is not fully effective, repeat it in 2 weeks.

Lawns

Choose between (a) applying ferrous sulfate in solution and (b) applying it in dry form, then watering it in.

First Method.—Dissolve ferrous sulfate in water at the rate of 1 pound of the chemical to 25 gallons of water. (A stronger solution could burn the grass.) Apply at the rate of 12½ gallons of solution to 100 square feet of lawn.

Second Method.—Spread dry ferrous sulfate on the grass when the grass is dry; spread it evenly by hand or with a fertilizer spreader. Apply at the rate of ½ pound of the chemical to 100 square feet of lawn. Give the lawn a good watering immediately after the application; this is necessary to keep the chemical from browning the grass.

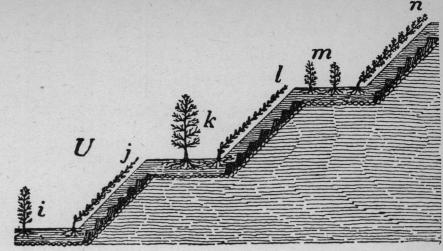

PLANTING FRUIT ON TERRACES

TREATING FOLIAGE

Quick but short-lived results are obtained by spraying ferrous sulfate solution on the foliage of plants affected with iron chlorosis. The amount required is much smaller than that required for application to the soil. However, if chlorosis is severe, frequent applications to foliage are required to keep plants green and healthy.

Preparing Spray

To prepare 50 gallons of spray—

Dissolve 2 pounds of ferrous sulfate in 50 gallons of water (A stronger solution would burn some plant varieties.)

Add 2 cups of a mild household detergent. The detergent acts as a wetting agent and increases the effectiveness of the spray.)

To prepare 3 gallons of spray, dissolve 2 ounces of ferrous sulfate in 3 gallons of water and add 2 tablespoons of detergent.

Applying Spray

Spray treatments can begin any time during the growing season but are most effective when started early in the season.

Thoroughly wet the foliage of the plants with spray. If you spray large trees, you will need a good power sprayer. A compressed-air sprayer is recommended for treating other plants.

Several treatment are necessary during a season. Spray at 2- to 4-week intervals until symptoms disappear; then spray whenever symptoms reappear.

If spray solution gets on flowers, it may stain and ruin them. To prevent this, direct the spray away from flowers, or spray when plants are not in bloom.

Early Spraying of Annual Plants

It is not necessary to wait until symptoms of iron chlorosis appear before spraying annual plants with ferrous sulfate solution.

If you know that annual plants of a particular species, planted in a particular area or plot, are likely to develop chlorosis, spray them within 10 days after they emerge from the soil. Repeat the treatment within 2 weeks. If chlorosis develops, spray chlorotic areas again; repeat in 2 weeks if necessary. This procedure prevents stunting of plants, and it prevents reductions in yield that would result from iron deficiency.

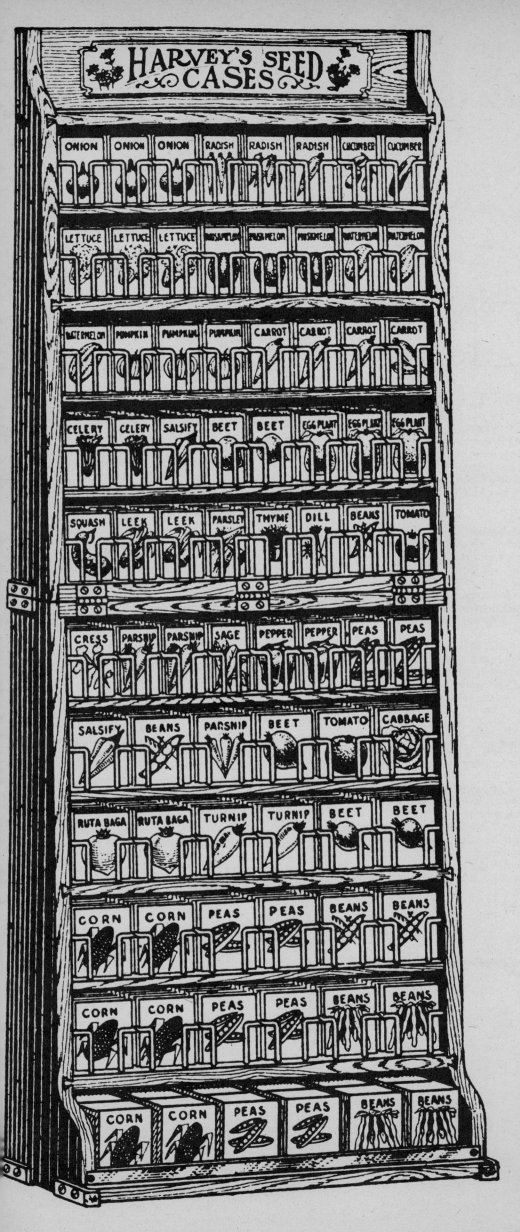

SEEDS TRANSPLANTS HOTBEDS & COLDFRAMES

END VIEW OF LEAN TO SEEDLING HOUSE.
a Ventilators. *b* Fibre-bed for plunging seed pans. *c* Small frame for special seeds. *d* Water tank, at opposite end to door, projecting for convenience of dipping seed pans. *e* Flow pipe. *f* Return pipe. *g* Perforated kiln tile staging. *h* Iron strap bars to carry kiln tiles.
(ABOVE) FRONTAL VIEW OF. HOUSE.
a Ventilators at varying levels.

TRUTH IN SEED LABELING

U.S. Department of Agriculture
Agricultural Marketing Service
Grain Division

Because of the Federal Seed Act, seed buying need not be hit or miss. The labels required on all seed moving across State lines give you most of the information you need to start a successful planting. Labels required by the Act show:

Name of kind and variety—So the buyer can choose the variety best suited for his needs.

Seed purity—The percentage of each kind or variety of seed and the amount of weed seeds and other unwanted matter in the seed.

Germination—The percentage of the seeds which are expected to grow into normal plants under ideal conditions.

PROTECTION AGAINST MISLABELED SEED

The Federal Seed Act helps protect the farmer, marketer, and consumer from mislabeled seed.

It was passed by Congress in 1939 to give this truth-in-labeling protection to farmers and other buyers of agricultural and vegetable seeds. The U.S. Department of Agriculture's Agricultural Marketing Service administers and enforces the law with the help of State seed agencies in each of the 50 States.

All States have seed laws requiring truthful labeling of seed offered for sale. The Federal Seed Act complements these laws by regulating seed moving between the States as well as seed imported into the United States.

To assure correct labeling, seed technologists examine samples of vegetable and agricultural seeds to determine what kinds of seed are in the container, how much of each kind, the number of weed seeds, and the percentage of inert matter (such as dirt and stones). They grow samples to determine the percentage of seeds that are expected to produce normal plants. All this information and more must be on the label.

By requiring truthful labeling and by prohibiting false advertising, the Federal Seed Act enables you to make an intelligent selection based on fact—not fiction.

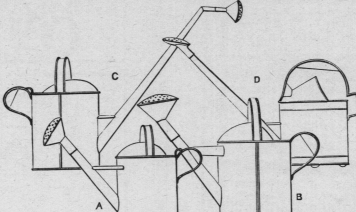

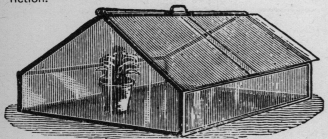

FRAZER'S NEW "IMPROVED" HAND LIGHT.

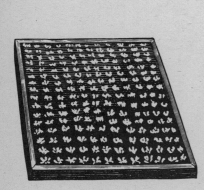

HOW TO READ THE LABEL

Purity

You don't have to guess at the contents of a seed container. The Act requires detailed labels on all farm and grass seed. Labels must indicate the percentage of each kind of seed present in excess of 5 percent. The percentages of other crop seeds, weed seeds, and inert matter (chaff, dirt, stones) must also be indicated.

Noxious-Weed Seeds

Some weed seeds are particularly harmful in certain areas. Each State has a list of seeds which it considers "noxious," or harmful. The Federal Seed Act requires all farm and grass seed shipped into the State to be labeled to show the name and number per unit of weight of these seeds present. If they are present, they may not exceed the limits set by the State.

Origin

Certain seeds (alfalfa, red clover, white clover, and field corn other than hybrids) which are grown in one area may not grow well in other areas. So the label must show the State or country of origin of these seeds. In this way you can select seed suited to your locality.

Germination

Germination rate tells you what percentage of the seeds is expected to produce normal plants under ideal conditions. A rate of 85 percent, for example, means that 85 out of every 100 pure seeds—given ideal care and growing conditions—will develop adequately.

It's wise to check seed labels to see when the seed was tested for germination. Seed loses its ability to grow or develop as it becomes older—especially in warm, humid areas. Because of this, it must have been tested within 6 months before it leaves the State. In most States, it must have been tested within 9 months before sale.

Hermetically sealed seed may be shipped interstate

for a longer period of time after testing—24 months—if it is packaged as required under the Federal Seed Act.

Vegetable Seed

The vegetable seeds you buy—for gardening or truck farming—require less labeling information than other agricultural and lawn seeds. Only the kind and name of the variety must be shown on containers of 1 pound or less if the seed is above a certain germination standard. (If labels on farm seeds don't list the variety name, they must say "Variety—Not Stated.") Also, vegetable seeds in containers of 1 pound or less with a germination rate below certain standards established by rules under the Federal Seed Act must be plainly marked "Below Standard" and must show the percentage of germination and the date of the germination test. Vegetable seed in containers of more than 1 pound must always show the germination percentage and the date of test.

Imported Seed

USDA and the U.S. Department of the Treasury enforce the foreign commerce provisions of the Federal Seed Act to insure that imported seed is of at least minimum quality. Each lot of seed to be imported into the United States is sampled at the port of entry by customs inspectors. The sample is sent to one of the four Federal Seed laboratories for testing, to make sure it meets the minimum standards of the Act before the seed lot is permitted to enter this country.

VIOLATIONS

To determine whether seed is correctly labeled, State seed inspectors visit seed stores and routinely draw samples for testing by State and Federal seed laboratories.

Seed officials also examine seed catalogues and other seed advertisements to guard against false or misleading statements.

Violators may be prosecuted either in criminal proceedings or in civil suits. The seed may be seized by Federal courts and required to be relabeled, destroyed, or used for other purposes. Warning notices are sent to shippers for minor violations.

FOOD GARDEN PLANTING TABLE

LOUIS THE THIRTEENTH'S OLD CASTLE AT VERSAILLES, WITH THE ORANGERY.

Quantity of seed and number of plants required for 100 feet of row, depths of planting, and distances apart for rows and plants

United States Department of Agriculture

Crop	Requirement for 100 feet of row		Depth for planting seed	Distance apart		Plants in the row
	Seed	Plants		Rows		
				Horse- or tractor-cultivated	Hand-cultivated	
			Inches	*Feet*		
Asparagus	1 ounce	75	1 –1½	4 –5	1½ to 2 feet	18 inches.
Beans:						
Lima, bush	½ pound		1 –1½	2½–3	2 feet	3 to 4 inches.
Lima, pole	½ pound		1 –1½	3 –4	3 feet	3 to 4 feet.
Snap, bush	½ pound		1 –1½	2½–3	2 feet	3 to 4 inches.
Snap, pole	4 ounces		1 –1½	3 –4	2 feet	3 feet.
Beet	2 ounces		1	2 –2½	14 to 16 inches	2 to 3 inches.
Broccoli:						
Heading	1 packet	50– 75	½	2½–3	2 to 2½ feet	14 to 24 inches.
Sprouting	1 packet	50– 75	½	2½–3	2 to 2½ feet	14 to 24 inches.
Brussels sprouts	1 packet	50– 75	½	2½–3	2 to 2½ feet	14 to 24 inches.
Cabbage	1 packet	50– 75	½	2½–3	2 to 2½ feet	14 to 24 inches.
Cabbage, Chinese	1 packet		½	2 –2½	18 to 24 inches	8 to 12 inches.
Carrot	1 packet		½	2 –2½	14 to 16 inches	2 to 3 inches.
Cauliflower	1 packet	50– 75	½	2½–3	2 to 2½ feet	14 to 24 inches.
Celeriac	1 packet	200–250	⅛	2½–3	18 to 24 inches	4 to 6 inches.
Celery	1 packet	200–250	⅛	2½–3	18 to 24 inches	4 to 6 inches.
Chard	2 ounces		1	2 –2½	18 to 24 inches	6 inches.
Chervil	1 packet		½	2 –2½	14 to 16 inches	2 to 3 inches.
Chicory, witloof	1 packet		½	2 –2½	18 to 24 inches	6 to 8 inches.
Chives	1 packet		½	2½–3	14 to 16 inches	In clusters.
Collards	1 packet		½	3 –3½	18 to 24 inches	18 to 24 inches.
Cornsalad	1 packet		½	2½–3	14 to 16 inches	1 foot.
Corn, sweet	2 ounces		2	3 –3½	2 to 3 feet	Drills, 14 to 16 inches; hills, 2½ to 3 feet.
Cress Upland	1 packet		⅛– ¼	2 –2½	14 to 16 inches	2 to 3 inches.
Cucumber	1 packet		½	6 –7	6 to 7 feet	Drills, 3 feet; hills, 6 feet.
Dasheen	5 to 6 pounds	50	2 –3	3½–4	3½ to 4 feet	2 feet.
Eggplant	1 packet	50	½	3	2 to 2½ feet	3 feet.
Endive	1 packet		½	2½–3	18 to 24 inches	12 inches.
Fennel, Florence	1 packet		½	2½–3	18 to 24 inches	4 to 6 inches.
Garlic	1 pound		1 –2	2½–3	14 to 16 inches	2 to 3 inches.
Horseradish	Cuttings	50–75	2	3 –4	2 to 2½ feet	18 to 24 inches.
Kale	1 packet		½	2½–3	18 to 24 inches	12 to 15 inches.
Kohlrabi	1 packet		½	2½–3	14 to 16 inches	5 to 6 inches.
Leek	1 packet		½–1	2½–3	14 to 16 inches	2 to 3 inches.
Lettuce, head	1 packet	100	½	2½–3	14 to 16 inches	12 to 15 inches.
Lettuce, leaf	1 packet		½	2½–3	14 to 16 inches	6 inches.
Muskmelon	1 packet		1	6 –7	6 to 7 feet	Hills, 6 feet.
Mustard	1 packet		½	2½–3	14 to 16 inches	12 inches.
Okra	2 ounces		1 –1½	3 –3½	3 to 3½ feet	2 feet.
Onion:						
Plants		400	1 –2	2 –2½	14 to 16 inches	2 to 3 inches.
Seed	1 packet		½–1	2 –2½	14 to 16 inches	2 to 3 inches.
Sets	1 pound		1 –2	2 –2½	14 to 16 inches	2 to 3 inches.
Parsley	1 packet		⅛	2 –2½	14 to 16 inches	4 to 6 inches.
Parsley, turnip-rooted	1 packet		⅛– ¼	2 –2½	14 to 16 inches	2 to 3 inches.
Parsnip	1 packet		½	2 –2½	18 to 24 inches	2 to 3 inches.
Peas	½ pound		2 –3	2 –4	1½ to 3 feet	1 inch.
Pepper	1 packet	50–70	½	3 –4	2 to 3 feet	18 to 24 inches.
Physalis	1 packet		½	2 –2½	1½ to 2 feet	12 to 18 inches.
Potato	5 to 6 pounds, tubers		4	2½–3	2 to 2½ feet	10 to 18 inches.
Pumpkin	1 ounce		1 –2	5 –8	5 to 8 feet	3 to 4 feet.
Radish	1 ounce		½	2 –2½	14 to 16 inches	1 inch.
Rhubarb		25–35		3 –4	3 to 4 feet	3 to 4 feet.
Salsify	1 ounce		½	2 –2½	18 to 26 inches	2 to 3 inches.
Shallots	1 pound (cloves)		1 –2	2 –2½	12 to 18 inches	2 to 3 inches.
Sorrel	1 packet		½	2 –2½	18 to 24 inches	5 to 8 inches.
Soybean	½ to 1 pound		1 –1½	2½–3	24 to 30 inches	3 inches.
Spinach	1 ounce		½	2 –2½	14 to 16 inches	3 to 4 inches.
Spinach, New Zealand	1 ounce		1 –1½	3 –3½	3 feet	18 inches.
Squash:						
Bush	½ ounce		1 –2	4 –5	4 to 5 feet	Drills, 15 to 18 inches; hills, 4 feet.
Vine	1 ounce		1 –2	8 –12	8 to 12 feet	Drills, 2 to 3 feet; hills, 4 feet.
Sweetpotato	5 pounds, bedroots	75	2 –3	3 –3½	3 to 3½ feet	12 to 14 inches.
Tomato	1 packet	35–50	½	3 –4	2 to 3 feet	1½ to 3 feet.
Turnip greens	1 packet		¼– ½	2 –2½	14 to 16 inches	2 to 3 inches.
Turnips and rutabagas	½ ounce		¼– ½	2 –2½	14 to 16 inches	2 to 3 inches.
Watermelon	1 ounce		1 –2	8 –10	8 to 10 feet	Drills, 2 to 3 feet; hills, 8 feet.

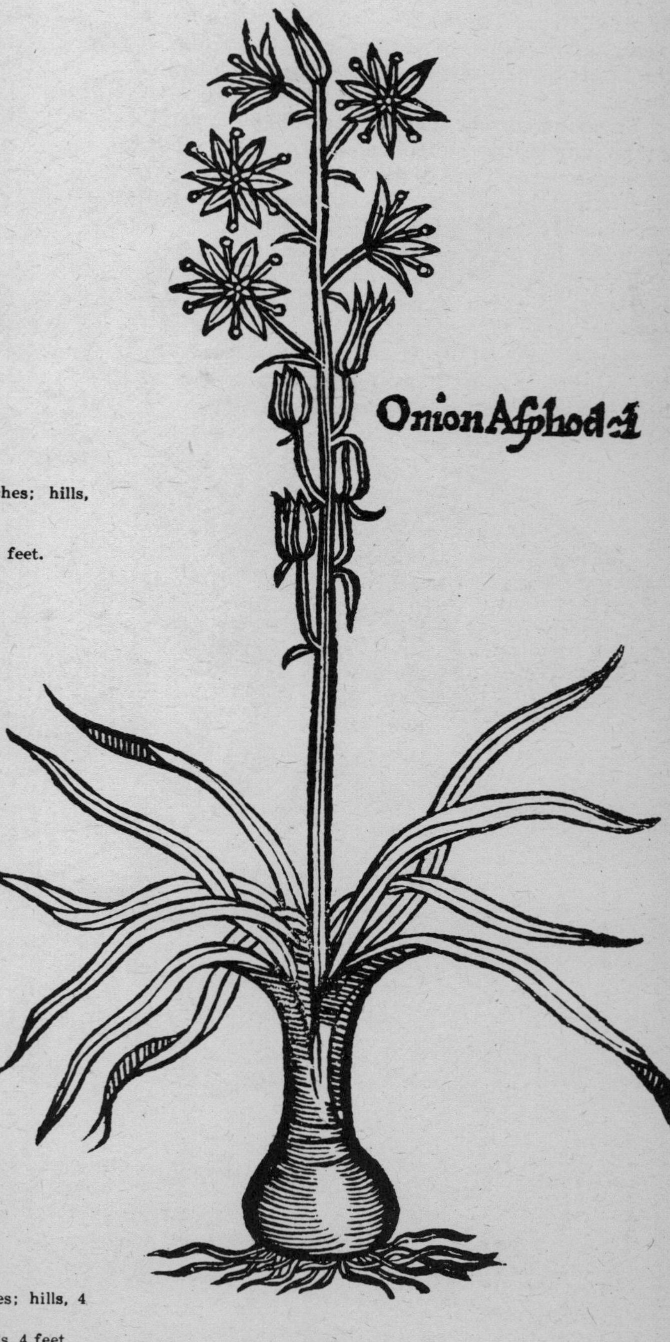

Onion Affhodel

EARLY
WHITE TURNIP.   SCARLET TURNIP.   WHITF TIPPED
                                                     SCARLET TURNIP.

starting annuals and vegetables from seed

IN THE HOME OR SMALL GREENHOUSE

Roy W. Judd, Jr., Extension Horticulturist
Richard A. Ashley, Extension Vegetable Specialist
Jay S. Koths, Extension Floriculturist

Garden Cucumbers.

Starting annuals and vegetables from seed can be rewarding or disastrous depending upon the outcome. Often times, people have a tendency to start seeds too early and then try to hold back the seedlings until they can be planted out-of-doors. This can either result in short, hard, yellow seedlings that grow very slowly or tall, spindly ones that topple over. Neither do well when planted out.

Seeds require certain conditions in order to germinate and grow properly. These include temperature, light and humidity. Also, sanitation practices must be followed in order to reduce disease problems.

Germination media: Soil mixes such as a 3-2-1 or 2-1- or even a 1-1-1 (soil, peat, sand) can be used to start seed . However, the mix must be treated to reduce disease problems.

On a large scale the soil may be steamed, 180°F for 30 minutes, or treated with chemicals — methyl bromide or Vapam according to manufacturer's directions. On smaller amounts, heating a 2-3 inch layer of mix in a preheated oven at 180°F for one hour   will pasteurize it.

To avoid the use of steam, chemicals or heat, use peat-lite mix. Many people have used it and found that it works very well. It is light, easy to handle and free from weed seed and pests.

	To prepare:	
	One Yard*	One Bu
Sphagnum peat moss (loose)	15 cu. ft. or 12 bu.	1/2 bu.
Horticultural Vermiculite	15 cu. ft. or 12 bu.	1/2 bu.
Ground limestone	10 lbs.	10 tbsp
Superphosphate (0-20-0)	4 lbs.	8 tbsp

*If plants are to remain in this mix for more than two week soluble fertilizers should be applied.

Containers: Anything that will hold about 2″ of the media and have drainage holes in the bottom can be used to start seeds. Fill the containers   with the moistened mix firm down lightly and mark rows

Seeds: Use only the best seeds. Old seeds or those that have not been stored properly may not germinate. If extra seeds are to be stored from one year to the next, keep them at 40-50°F in an airtight container. This could be a coffee can or other container with plastic cover. The humidity should also be kept below 50%. The average home refrigerator will provide these conditions.

Many people have a tendency to sow seeds too thick . Home gardeners should sow seeds about 1/4 inc apart and in rows. Cover larger seeds lightly with the soil mix washed sand or vermiculite. Leave small seeds uncovered. seeds are sown too thickly, tall spindly seedlings may result.

Some seeds are coated to form pellets while others ar attached to soluble tapes. This makes the seeds easier t handle. However, there is a tendency to cover these to deeply.

COOPERATIVE EXTENSION SERVICE
COLLEGE OF AGRICULTURE AND NATURAL RESOURCES, THE UNIVERSITY OF CONNECTICUT, STORRS

Larger seeds such as marigolds, zinnias, tomatoes, peppers, cucumbers, melons and pelletted seeds can be sown directly into small peat, clay or plastic pots filled with media. Specialized propagating units such as compressed peat-lite pellets (Jiffy-7's   ) or fiber blocks (BR-8, or Kys Kubes   ) can also be used for germinating seeds. These and peat pots would not have to be removed before planting . Be sure that these units are completely covered with soil when planted outside.

Water and humidity: After sowing and covering, water the seeds in. Do this with a fine mist   or sub-irrigation so that the seeds will not be washed around. After watering, try to keep the humidity at 80% or higher. This will reduce water loss from the germinating media.

Some growers cover the seed flats with wet burlap, clear plastic, or newspapers. Home gardeners may slip the seed flats into large clear plastic bags   . Place this in light but not in direct sunlight. Do not let the temperature in this plastic bag go above 85°F. Check the flats daily to make sure that the soil surface is moist. As soon as the seedlings emerge, remove the plastic bag.

CROSKILL'S PIG-TROUGH.

Temperature: This is one of the most critical factors in starting seeds. Temperatures too low or too high will reduce germination. See chart for proper germinating temperature (temperature of the mix, not the air). Bottom heat from electric cables, hot pipes, or radiators may assist in maintaining proper temperatures.

Light: Some annual and vegetable seeds require light to germinate. Place seed flats where some light is available. After seedlings emerge, provide full sunlight or, if not possible, use fluorescent lights and supply about 700-800 fc or 27 lamp watts per square foot. Containers with the seedlings should be placed 8 inches below the lamps. A 14-hour days should be provided, usually 8:00 a.m. to 10:00 p.m. Transplant the seedlings when the true leaves appear.

Hardening-off: About 7-10 days before planting outside, the plants may be hardened-off. This is done by lowering the temperature or withholding water. This may reduce the care in establishing plants in the garden but will reduce total growth. Do not harden-off cucumbers, melons or squash. During this period the plants should be in full sunlight.

Problems and causes:

Poor germination	Improper temperature
	Improper moisture
	Lack of light
	Damping-off (diseases)
	High soluble salts
	Non-viable seed
Poor seedling growth	Improper watering
	Lack of fertilizer
	Improper pH
	Insufficient light
Poor root growth	Lack of phosphorus or calcium
	Over-watering
Seedling rotting at soil line	Diseases (damping-off organisms)
Wilting of seedling	High soluble salts
	Improper watering (especially in peat-lite mixes)
Weak spindly growth	Low light intensities
	High temperatures
	Crowding

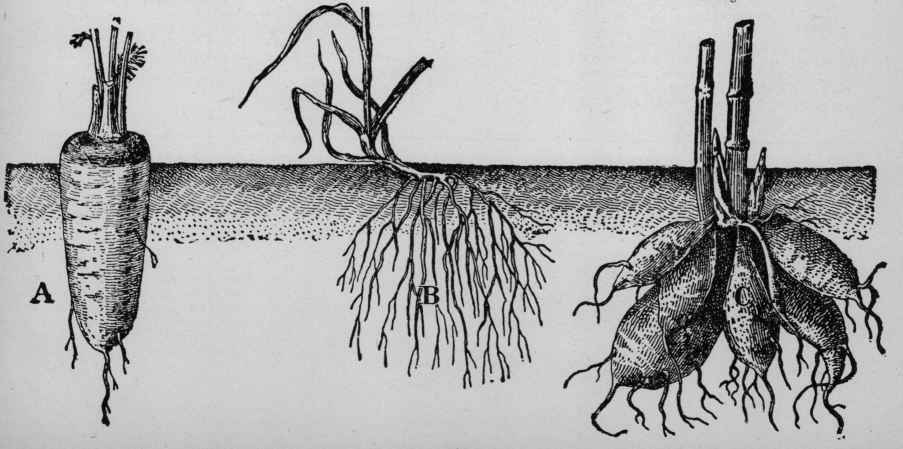

THINNING & TRANSPLANTING

YELLOW SUMMER TURNIP
RADISH.

ZEA MAYS (INDIAN CORN)

THINNING AND TRANSPLANTING VEGETABLES
E.L. Fullerton

WHICH KINDS TO LEAVE AND WHICH TO MOVE—
HOW FAR APART THEY SHOULD STAND—HOME-
MADE AND OTHER INEXPENSIVE DEVICES FOR
TRANSPLANTING VEGETABLES

It has been said that more good vegetables have
been ruined for want of being thinned at the proper
time than by any other cause. However, that may be,
one of the most puzzling things for the beginner is
to find out whether any particular vegetables should
be thinned or transplanted and how far apart the
plants should stand afterward. He will get some help
from the catalogues as to distances, but whether he
should transplant or thin is the kind of thing that is
not in the books.

There is a still greater difficulty. Even when a person knows how far apart the plants should stand, or
has good authority, it requires a good deal of nerve
to pull up and destroy the unnecessary seedlings—
more nerve than the average amateur possesses. While
it is possible to save some of the thinnings by eating
them or transplanting them, most of them are simply
in the way. They say that a person never becomes a
good gardener until he steels his nerves to this ruth-
less sacrifice. A vegetable must have plenty of room
to develop its best size and flavor. One can take no
pride in small or commonplace things. It is the quickly grown, finely flavored vegetables that are worth
working for and it is better to err on the side of giving
each plant too much space rather than too little. For
example, the seedsman says that endives must be
thinned to eight inches. I gave mine only six inches,
for it did not seem possible that those delicate seedlings could develop such magnificent heads of salad
leaves. Mine were good, but I soon realized that they
would have been better had I given them their allotted space. I would have had several heads less, but
one would have served the purpose of two.

"THE WORST WEED IN CORN IS CORN"

It is far more important to thin vegetables than to
thin flowers. In the former we want each plant to
develop to its fullest, whereas in flowers the evils of
overcrowding are not so apparent. We usually get a
sufficient wealth of bloom from the given area, although fewer plants would give better flowers.

Seeds are sown very thickly with the idea of having
plenty of young plants so as to provide against acci-
dents or less from insects. The thinnings of the following crops can be used in the kitchen: Celery, lettuce, carrots, beets, and spinach. The home gardener,
therefore, had better do the thinning of such crops
by degrees, not at one time, as is the rule with the
gardener for market.

White Dorkings

Thin out as necessity arises, but don't hesitate to
pull up and destroy the young plants before the row
gets too crowded and the plants become spindling.
When too many vegetables of one kind are allowed to
grow in the same row the great majority of them are
simply weeds. True it is that "The worst weed in corn
is corn."

THIN VEGETABLES TWICE

Seedlings that are allowed to remain where sown,
need to be thinned as carefully as possible. the first
time when they are about two inches high, in some
cases even sooner. The stockiest plants should be
allowed to remain, after thinning them to about one-
half the distance the plants are to stand from one
another. When these plantlets have a still sturdier
growth, they may be finally thinned to the distance
apart at which they are to remain. Firming the soil
each time in order that the roots of those that remain may not be left loose.

Reprinted from GARDEN MAGAZINE, 1905

THIN THESE

The figures show size the seedlings should be
when handled and the maximum distances apart
they should be after thinning.

Greens
Asparagus—3 inches high, 24 x 36.
Chard—3 inches high, 12 x 18.
New Zealand Spinach—2 inc. high, 12 x 24.
Orach—6 inches high, 24 x 26
Purslane—2 inches high, 4 x 12.
Spinach—1 inch high, 6 x 18.

Roots
Beets—4 inches high, 9 x 18.
Carrot—3 inches high, 6 x 18.
Parsnip—3 inches high, 6 x 18.
Rampion—2 inches high, 3 x 8.
Salsify—3 inches high, 4 x 18.

Scolymus—4 inches high, 6 x 18.
Scorzonera—3 inches high, 6 x 18.
Radish—2 inches high, 3 x 8.
Turnip—3 inches high, 4 x 18.

Salads
Chicory—4 inches high, 6 x 12.
Corn-salad—2 inches high, 6 x 6.
Cress—3 inches high, 3 x 6.
Dandelion—(2 weeks old), 6 x 6.
Endive—2 inches high, 12 x 12.
Lettuce—3 inches high, 8 x 12.

Seeds and Fruits
Beans (all sorts)—3 inches high, 12 x 24.
Corn—6 inches high, 12 x 36.
Cucumber—2 inches high, 36 x 36.
Martynia—4 inches high, 36 x 36.
Muskmelon—4 inches high, 60 x 60.

Okra—5 inches high, 18 x 24.
Pumpkin-4 inches high, 108 x 108.
Squash—4 inches high, 72 x 96.
Tomato—3 inches high, 36 x 48.

Sweet Herbs
Borage—2 inches in diameter, 10 x 10.
Catnip—6 inches high, 24 x 20.
Chervil—2 inches high, 4 x 12.
Fennel—4 inches high, 8 x 18.
Lavender—4 inches high, 12 x 24.
Marjoram, Sweet-4 inches high, 12 x 12.
Basil, Sweet-4 inches high, 8 x 8.
Parsley—2 inches high, 6 x 12.

Miscellaneous
Kohlrabi—4 inches high, 9 x 18
Leek-4 inches high, 5 x 12.
Onion—2 inches high, 12 x 20.

TRANSPLANTING

As a rule, transplanting, which is moving from the seed bed to the garden, results in injury to the plants. Celery, however, makes a strong tap root which is broken in transplanting, inducing a bunch of fibrous roots which is easy to transplant the second time. One result of transplanting is that the plants are set at a proper distance, and have room to develop to their very best.

TRANSPLANT ON A DULL DAY

Transplant on a dull day by preference or at dusk, and be careful not to let the roots of the young plants dry out. If they are taken up from a seedbed or cold-frame throw a little loose soil over the roots as they lie in the box or basket ready to be carried to the garden—and keep them covered until they are put into their new quarters.

For taking the young plants up from the seed-bed, a small hand fork is useful to loosen the soil. To set in the garden mark a straight line with a hoe, rake or stick using the garden line as a guide. It is very important to have the rows parallel and straight and it is economical of labor to have them regularly spaced so that the wheel hoe can be used up and down a large number without resetting the wheels.

TAKE ALL THE ROOTS

Digging those plants which have a well developed root at this time must be done carefully. Get all the

AMERICAN REAPING MACHINE.

roots. If the soil in its bed is very dry it must be watered so that the roots will not be broken in separating the young plants. If possible transplanting should be done in the late afternoon, so that the little plants will be able to take a hold in their new quarters before they are attacked by the heat of the day. The amateur can help them greatly by shading for a few days, by boards put edgewise along the sunny side of the row. Cabbage and tomato plants can be protected with paper cylinders made from old newspapers. Plants from pots are "knocked out" where they are planted and so suffer little check. The pot can be inverted over the young plant if the work is done on an unusually hot day, although it is not often necessary to shade pot grown plants. In the case of transplanting cabbage, leek, celery, cauliflower, etc., the same result is attained by reducing the top. About one third is twisted or cut off.

FIRM THE SOIL

Make the soil firm about thinned or transplanted seedlings. They should be made so firm, and the earth so closely packed, that the plants will not yield to a pretty firm pull. The drier the soil the harder and tighter it must be packed. Very wet soil must not be packed. Wait until it dries out and then go over the ground again.

Small plants are set in sufficiently well by firming the soil with the fingers, or the dibbler which is used for making the holes. Larger plants are best firmed by pressing with the ball of the foot. After watering, hoe at once, drawing a little fine dry earth about the plant to serve as a mulch.

FIBROUS ROOTS BETTER THAN TAP ROOTS FOR TRANSPLANTING

In transplanting the vital point is to have a good root growth. If a plant has a fine underground system, the above-ground, or leaf system, is nearly sure to be all right. If the roots are spread about, one plant tangled with another, they are certain to be broken when lifted to be separated and set elsewhere. If, however, they have been confined to a reasonably limited space, one plant separated from another, they are compact, and can be transported with a minimum check to their growth. If a plant's roots have been torn and mangled, they have to heal, and the plant must make new roots and become firm before any growth can take place above ground. On the other hand, if the roots have been confined to a small space, say that enclosed by a flower pot or a strawberry box, they can be set into the ground, where they will immediately expand without shock to their system, and the growth above ground will continue unchecked.

Reprinted from GARDEN MAGAZINE, 1905

BROAD-LEAVED ENDIVE.

TRANSPLANT THESE

The figures show size the seedlings should be when transplanted and the maximum distances apart to set them in the garden.

Greens
Beet—4 inches high, 9 x 18.
Brussels Sprouts—6 inches high, 12 x 18.
Cabbage—6 inches high, 24 x 36.
Celery—2 inches high, 3 x 48.
Kale—5 inches high, 12 x 18.
Pak-choi—3 inches high, 12 x 12
Pe-tsai—3 inches high, 12 x 120.

Roots
Beet—4 inches high, 9 x 18.
Sweet Potato (when frost is past)—18 x 24.

Salads
Cardoon—5 inches high, 24 x 36.
Celery (first)—2 inches high, 3 x 48; second) —6 inches high, 6 x 48.
Chicory—4 inches high, 6 x 12.
Endive—2 inches in diameter, 12 x 12.
Lettuce—4 inches high, 8 x 12.

Sweet Herbs
Borage—2 inches in diameter, 10 x 10.
Fennel—4 inches high, 8 x 18.

Seed Fruits
Bean, Lima—5 inches high, 36 x 36.
Eggplant—3 inches high, 36 x 36.
Martynia—4 inches high, 36 x 36.
Pepper—6 inches high, 18 x 24.
Tomato—6 inches high, 36 x 48.

Miscellaneous
Artichoke, Globe—6 inches high, 24 x 36.
Leek—8 inches high, 5 x 12.

ANNUAL FLOWER & VEGETABLE SEEDS

Annual Flower and Vegetable Seeds

Flower	Germinating Temperature	Sow Seeds About	Days to Germinate	Transplant About	Growing Temp.	Number of weeks from seed to planting
Ageratum	70	Mar. 20	5-10	Apr. 20	60	8-10
Alyssum	70	Mar. 10	5-10	Apr. 20	50	8-10
Amaranthus	70	Apr. 20	8-10	May 10	60	4-6
Aster	70	Apr. 20	7-10	May 10	60	6-8
Balsam	80	Apr. 10	7-10	May 5	60	6-8
Batchelor's Buttons	70	Mar. 5	7-14	Mar. 25	60	12-16
Begonia	70	Mar. 5	14-35	Apr. 5	60	10-16
Carnation	70	Mar. 5	14-21	Apr. 5	55	12-16
Cleome	70	Apr. 15	7-14	May 10	55	8-10
Celosia	70	Apr. 10	7-10	Apr. 25	65	4-6
Coleus	60	Apr. 5	10-14	Apr. 25	60	6-8
Cosmos	75	Apr. 25	5-10	May 10	70	6-8
Dahlia	70	Mar. 5	5-10	Mar. 25	55	10-12
Dusty Miller	65	Mar. 5	14-21	Apr. 5	50	10-12
Geraniums	75	Feb. 5	5-10	Mar. 5	60-65	18
Gomphrena	75	Apr. 15	12-14	May 10	70	8-12
Impatiens	70	Mar. 10	12-18	Apr. 5	60	9-12
Lobelia	70	Mar. 15	14-21	Apr. 15	60	9-12
Marigold	70	Apr. 10	5-7	Apr. 20	60	7-10
Morning glory	65	Apr. 15	5-7	May 5	60	6-8
Nasturtium	65	Apr. 15	6-8	May 5	60	6-8
Pansy	65	Jan. 5	10-20	Feb. 5	40-50	22-26
Petunia	70	Mar. 15	4-12	Apr. 15	50-55	10-12
Phlox	60	Apr. 10	7-14	Apr. 20	65	8-12
Portulaca	70	Apr. 5	10-18	Apr. 25	60	6-8
Salvia	70-75	Apr. 5	14-21	May 5	60-65	8-12
Scabiosa	70	Apr. 15	10-12	May 10	60	10-12
Nierembergia	70	Mar. 15	12-15	Apr. 5	60	12-15
Snapdragon	65-70	Mar. 10	7-14	Apr. 5	50	12-14
Strawflower						
Verbena	65	Mar. 10	14-28	Apr. 10	50-55	8-10
Zinnia	70	Apr. 25	5-10	May 10	60-65	4-6

b

Vegetable						
Broccoli	68-86	Mar. 5	3-10	Mar. 20	55-60	6-8
Brussel sprouts	68-86	Mar. 5	3-10	Mar. 20	55-60	6-8
Cabbage	68-86	Mar. 5	3-10	Mar. 20	55-60	6-8
Cantaloupe	68-86	May 5	4-10	———	60	3-4
Cauliflower	68-86	Mar. 5	3-10	Mar. 20	55-60	6-8
Celery	50-68	Mar. 5	10-21	Mar. 20	55-60	8-10
Cucumber	68-86	May 5	3-7	———	60	3-4
Eggplant	68-86	Apr. 20	7-14	Apr. 20	60	6-8
Lettuce	68	Mar. 15	7	Mar. 25	55-60	4-6
Onion	68	Apr. 5	6-10	Apr. 20	55	4-6
Parsley	75	Mar. 20	11-28	Apr. 20	55	6-8
Pepper	68-86	Apr. 10	6-14	Apr. 20	60	6-10
Squash	68-86	May 5	4-7	———	60	3-4
Tomato	68-86	Apr. 10	5-14	Apr. 20	60	6-10
Watermelon	68-86	May 5	4-14	———	60	3-4

DAMPING OFF & SEEDLING BLIGHTS

Stands of vegetable seedlings are frequently poor under humid conditions, particularly if the soil is cold and wet. Costly replanting or the production of weak, sickly plants is the result. The damage is usually caused by one or more soil-borne fungi that attack under conditions unfavorable for rapid seed germination and growth.

Seeds may rot and seedlings decay before emerging (preemergence damping-off). Young plants that do emerge may pale, curl, wilt, and collapse (postemergence damping-off) from a rot at the soil line and below. The base of the stem is generally water-soaked at first, then turns gray to brown or black, and rots. Seedlings of such plants as cabbage, cauliflower, tomato, and beans are girdled by brown or black sunken cankers. These plants may shrivel and become dark and woody (wirestem or collar rot), but they do not normally collapse. Transplants make slow growth or die.

CONTROL

1. Buy best-quality seed of recommended varieties.
2. Treat seed before planting as recommended elsewhere.
3. Plant in a light, well-drained, well-prepared, fertile seedbed at the time recommended for your area. If at all possible, sterilize the soil—preferably with heat—before planting.
4. Apply a soil insecticide, e. g., aldrin, dieldrin, chlordane, or heptachlor to the soil surface before planting, and immediately work into the top three to five inches of soil. Follow the manufacturer's directions printed on the package label. This treatment controls aphids, grubs, wireworms, ants, maggots, cutworms, and webworms which injure underground parts, allowing soil-borne organisms to enter and produce decay.
5. Avoid heavy soils, heavy seeding and overcrowding, poor air circulation, careless handling, too deep planting, and over-fertilizing (especially with nitrogen).
6. Keep the seedbed soil on the dry side after planting. Allow plenty of bright light.

(Adapted and condensed from material prepared by M. C. Shurtleff and B. J. Jacobsen of the Extension Service of the University of Illinois)

ASPARAGUS, Crown for Lifting.

—LARGE FLAG OR LONDON LEEK.

HOME GARDEN VEGETABLE PLANTING GUIDE

Vegetable	Suggested Varieties	Seed req'd for 100 ft. row	Reasonable yield 100 ft. row	Suggested field seeding or transplanting period (Southern Maritimes)	Time to harvest (days) from field seeding or transplanting	Storage period (weeks)	Remarks
Asparagus	Viking, Waltham Washington	1 oz. (65 plants)	30 lbs.	as early as possible	3 years	3-4	Harvest May 20-July 1.
Beans, green	Tendercrop, Tendergreen, Harvester, Contender, Provider, Sprite	1 lb.	50 lbs.	after danger of frost, until early July	60-70	1-2	Require warm location, full sun.
wax	Pure Gold Wax, Kinghorn Wax, Midas	1 lb.	50 lbs.	after danger of frost, until early July	60-70	1-2	Require warm location, full sun.
pole	Bluelake, Kentucky Wonder, Kentucky Wonder Wax	½ lb.	100 lbs.	after danger of frost, until early July.	70-90	1-2	Require staking.
Beets early	Little Egypt, Crosby Egyptian, Early Wonder	1 oz.	100 lbs.	From time soil can be worked.	60-80	2-3	Use thinned plants for greens.
maincrop	King Red, Ruby Queen, Detroit Dark Red, Mono-Germ	1 oz.	100 lbs.	From time soil can be worked until late June		3-10	Use thinned plants for greens.
Broccoli	Prime, Waltham 29	1 pkt.	50 lbs.	From time soil can be worked until early July.	70-90	1-2	4 to 6 weeks inside from seed for transplants.
Brussels Sprouts	Jade Cross	1 pkt.	50 lbs.	From time soil can be worked until mid June	80-100	3-4	4-6 weeks for transplants. Can be harvested until severe frost.
Cabbage early	Earliana, Early Greenball, Early Marvel, Golden Acre, Emerald Cross Hybird	¼ oz.	60 lbs.	From time soil can be worked	65-75	12-16	4-6 weeks from transplants. Small heads subject to splitting.
Cabbage mid-season	Bonanza, Copenhagen Market, Glory of Enkhuisen, Stonehead	¼ oz.	80 lbs.	May-June	75-85	12-16	Intermediate
late	Houston Evergreen, Storage Green, Danish Ballhead, Penn State Ballhead	¼ oz.	100 lbs.	May to early July	85-110	12-16	Heavy heads. H. Evergreen, and Storage Green retain green color in storage.
red	Red Acre, Mammoth Red Rock	¼ oz.	100 lbs.	May to early July	85-100	12-16	

47

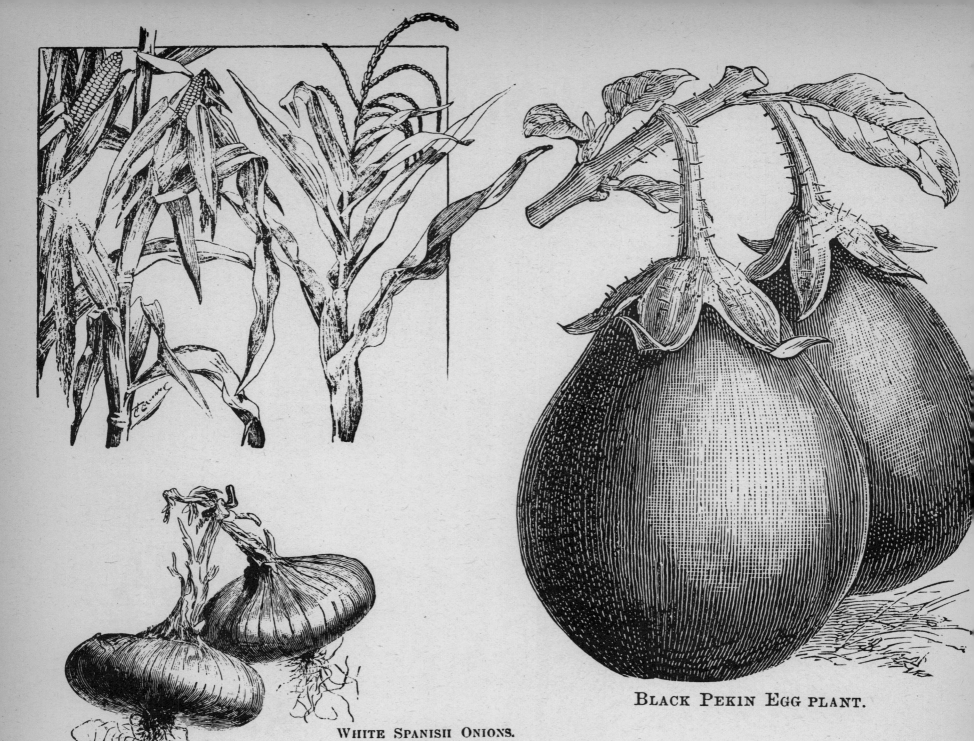

WHITE SPANISH ONIONS.

BLACK PEKIN EGG PLANT.

HOME GARDEN VEGETABLE PLANTING GUIDE

Prepared by
Atlantic Provinces Crop Protection and
Vegetable Committees

Information Canada

Vegetable	Suggested Varieties	Seed req'd for 100 ft. row	Reasonable yield 100 ft. row	Suggested field seeding or transplanting period (Southern Maritimes)	Time to harvest (days) from field seeding or transplanting	Storage period (weeks)	Remarks
Carrots cylindrical	Touchon, Special Long Type Nantes, Nantes 616	½ oz.	100 lbs.	May - June	80-100	16-20	Store where not too dry.
long	Hipak, Carousel, Imperator, Spartan Sweet						
Cauliflower early	Extra Early Snowball, Super Snowball	1 pkt.	60 heads	May - June	50-60	2-3	Tie leaves to blanch head.
late	Snowball Y, Snowball No. 84 Perfected Snowball, Snowball 57, Boomerang.	1 pkt.	60 heads	May - June	80-110	2-3	
Celery	Utah 52-70, Utah No. 15, Beacon, Spartan	1 pkt.	200 plants	late May - June	130-150	8-16	Seed must be sown inside, early. (March)
Citron	Colorado Preserving	½ oz.		after danger of frost	8-16	8-16	
Sweet Corn extra early	Polar Vee, Garden Treat	¼ lb.	100 ears	after danger of frost to Mid June	55-60	½-1	Loses flavor rapidly after harvest. Cool to 32°F. as soon as possible.
early	Market Beauty, Seneca Daybreak, Golden Rocket, North Star, Sunny Vee	¼ lb.	100 ears		60-75		
main season	Carmelcross, Summer Treat, Tasty Vee	¼ lb.	100 ears	After danger of frost to mid June	75-85	½-1	Loses flavor rapidly after harvest.
very late	Seneca Chief, Mellogold, Golden Jubilee	¼ lb.	100 ears	After danger of frost to mid June	85-110	½-1	Cool to 32°F. as soon as possible.
Cucumber slicing	Gemini 7, Highmark II, Marketmore, Tablegreen 65	½ oz.	600 fruits	After danger of frost to late June	55-75	1-2	Requires full sun, warm location
pickling	Northern Pickling, Pico, W.S.M.R. 12, Spartan Champion.	½ oz.			55-75	1-2	
Eggplant	Early Beauty Hybrid	1 pkt. (65 plants)		After danger of frost	90-110	1-2	Grow only in warmest area, from transplants.
Garlic	Giant Improved	400 cloves	60 lbs.	As early as possible	90-100	12-16	Tops can also be used.
Gourds	Mixed	½ oz.	500 fruits	After danger of frost	100		Transplant for increased maturity.

MAP-ZONES OF PLANT HARDINESS pp 58

HOME GARDEN VEGETABLE PLANTING GUIDE

Spanish Potatoes

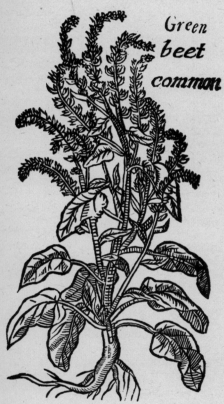

Green beet common

Indian. Millet.

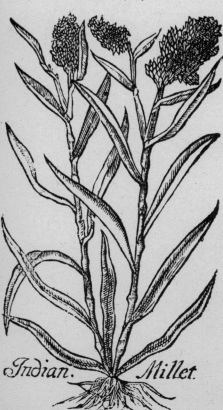

Vegetable	Suggested Varieties	Seed req'd for 100 ft. row	Reasonable yield 100 ft. row	Suggested field seeding or transplanting period (Southern Maritimes)	Time to harvest (days) from field seeding or transplanting	Storage period (weeks)	Remarks
Kohlrabi		½ oz.	100 lbs.	Early May to late June	50-60	2-4	Early turnip substitute
Lettuce leaf	Grand Rapids, Salad Bowl	¼ oz.	50 lbs.	Early May to mid July	45-50	2-3	Grows best in cool weather.
head	Premier G. L., Sunblest, Grest Lakes 659, Calmar	¼ oz.	100 heads	Early May to mid July	70-80	2-3	
Butter	Bibb, Buttercrunch Butter King	¼ oz.	100 heads	Early May to mid July	50-65	2-3	
Muskmelon (cantaloupe)	Mainerock, Burpee Hybrid, Sugar Salmon	½ oz.	100 fruits	After danger of frost.	80-90	2-4	Grow only in warmest areas. Should be transplanted.
Onions seeded yellow	Copper Gem, Autumn Spice, Earlibird, Early Harvest, Trapps No. 2.	½ oz.	100 lbs.	As early as possible. Late seeding results in small bulbs that do not mature properly.	100-110	12-32	Will tolerate some frost. Should be harvested when tops start to fall over, before wet fall weather.
red	Southport Red Globe, Ruby	½ oz.					
white	White Portugal	½ oz.					
transplants	Fiesta Sweet Spanish	¼ oz. (200 plants)			120-140		
sets	Stuttgarter, Ebenezer	2 lb.			50-70		
bunching	Stokes' Early Mild, South-port White Globe, Beltsville Bunching.	1 oz.			60-70	1-2	
Parsley	Champion Moss Curled	½ oz.	50 lbs.	Early May to early June	80-90	1-2	Will tolerate some shade.
Parsnips	Model, Hollow Crown, All American	½ oz.	100 lb.	May	130-140	8-16	Can be left in ground over winter.'
Peas bush	Laxton's Progress, Thomas Laxton, Little Marvel, Wando	1 lb.	40 lb.	As early as possible to early July.	60-70	1-2	Hardy, cool season crop.
pole	Tall Telephone	½ lb.			75-80		
freezing	Dark-skinned Perfection, Frostie, Sprite, Sparkle	1 lb.			60-70		
canning	Pride, Perfection, Nugget	1 lb.			60-70		
Pepper early sweet	Vindale, Canape	1 pkt. (75 plants)	50 lbs.	After danger of frost	70-80	4-6	Requires full sun, sheltered location. Must use transplants.
main-crop sweet	Bell Boy, Ace, Peter Piper		75 lbs.	After danger of frost	80-90	4-6	
hot	Long Thick Red		75 lbs.	After danger of frost	80-90	4-6	
Potato early	Sable, Fundy, Warba, Irish Cobbler	15 lbs.	250 lbs.	As early as possible to early June	80-90	12-24	An acid soil reduces potato scab. Cherokee and Netted Gem are scab resistant.
mid season	Keswick, Cherokee, Avon, Hunter	15 lbs.			90-110	12-24	
late	Kennebec, Netted Gem, Green Mountain	15 lbs.			110-120	12-24	
Pumpkin	Jack O'Lantern, Small Sugar	½ oz.	200 lbs.	after danger of frost	90-100	8-24	Harvest before frost.
Radish	Cherry Belle, Scarlet Globe, Red Boy, Champion	1 oz.	100 lbs.	as early as possible to late July	21-25	1-2	Many seedings may be made.
Rhubarb	Sunrise, MacDonald, Valentine, German Wine	(35 plants)	150 lbs.	May - June	2 years	2-3	Do not over-pick.
Rutabaga (winter turnip)	Laurentian, York	½ oz.	300 lbs.	May to early July	90-120	12-24	York is club root resistant.
Turnip	Purple Top White Globe, Golden Ball	½ oz.	100 lbs.	May - June	50-60	6-8	Golden Ball has yellow flesh.
Spinach spring	Long Standing Blooms-dale, Nores	1 oz.	50 lbs.	As early as possible	45-50	1-2	Cool season crop.
fall	Early Hybrid No. 7, Packer, Northland, Marathon	1 oz.	50 lb.	Mid July - August	45-50	1-2	Can be over-wintered with some protection.
Squash summer	Zuccini, Prolific Hybrid, Cocozelle	1 oz.		After danger of frost	50-70	1-2	Eat when small and tender.
winter	Bush Buttercup, Buttercup, Baby Hubbard, Sweet Keeper, Blue Hubbard, Butternut, Golden Nugget.	½ oz.	200 lb.	After danger of frost	75-110	8-24	Soil should be warm before planting.
Swiss Chard green	Lucullus, Fordhook Giant	1 oz.	25 lb.	May - June	60-65	1-2	Will tolerate some shade.
red	Rhubarb	1 oz.	25 lb.	May - June	60-65	1-2	Red stalks
Tomatoes early	Scotia, Fireball, New Yorker, Quebec 5, Springset	1 pkt. (50 plants)	300 lb.	Transplant outdoors after the danger of frost.	70-80	1-2	Requires warm, sunny location. Can be picked green, ripened 2-6 weeks at 55°F.
late	Harrow, Viscount, Longred				80-100	1-2	
Watermelon	Sugar Baby, New Hampshire, Midget	½ oz.	100 fruits	After danger of frost.	80-100	2-3	Grow only in warmest area. May be transplanted.

Ordinarie Garden Beane

MUSK-MELON.

THE MAKING OF A HOTBED

A Joyous Occupation for the Dullest Moment of the Year—a Practical Way to Hasten the Coming of Spring   H. Barry

The day dawned bright and balmy. The snow was disappearing at a remarkably rapid rate, and the first feeling of spring stirred in the blood. It was the New Year, and even though the shortest day of our northern year was scarcely at our backs, the sun seemed already to have gained in power and the days to have grown longer. One could not remain in the house. The garden called irresistibly. But what a blank disappointment confronted one as the feet met the unyielding and frozen ground! It forced upon the unwilling senses the fact that spring, real spring, was yet many weeks distant, and that snow, ice, storm and thaw were to follow each other many times before the buds and birds would come once more. Yet the senses refused to accept the inevitable. We felt that we MUST have growing things now! We must dabble in the soil and see seeds sprout. There was but one possibility—a hotbed. So a hotbed we resolved to have.

We knew nothing about it, but we felt sure that there would be several different ways and that one of them would be the best for us. There is always a better way of doing the common thing, and we always try to find it. There is no fun in doing the common thing in the common way. Our investigations usually start in books, but never end there. We prefer to see and examine the real thing, then discuss it with our friends and neighbors who we know have had experience. Then we evolve the new way. Don't follow literally either books or your neighbor's practice, but consult them both.

The fundamental principle of a hotbed is to make and maintain heat at a small cost. This may be a misleading statement, for it is not so important that the heat be made and maintained as that the cold be kept out. The cheapest way to supply heat is to use fresh manure, which gives off heat during fermentation. A hotbed may be made by running steam through pipes in the bottom of the bed, but this is never done unless special conditions give one the opportunity to do it economically.

Dig a pit three or four feet deep and the size of the frame or frames which are to cover it. Set into and around the edges of the pit a frame of wooden planks. Throw in two feet or more of fresh manure. Tramp it thoroughly to prevent too rapid fermentation or it will give up all its heat at once. Over this put four inches of fine rich soil, in which to sow the seed. Set glazed sash upon the frame and bank manure around the outside to prevent frost from penetrating from that quarter.

These are the main outlines of hotbed construction. The variations are innumerable, the chief factors in the cost being size, permanence, neatness and portability.

A permanent hotbed may be made of brick, heavy timber, or cement, while a movable frame of boards may be mortised, screwed, nailed, buttoned or pegged. If the garden space is small, a movable frame would certainly be the best, for even where there is ground to spare, many people will prefer to have the hotbeds out of sight in summer.

A wooden structure may be purchased complete—that is, planks for the sides and ends, and a glazed sash, or as many sashes as one desires to use. The regular size of a sash is 3 x 6 feet, and the cost about six dollars. As many of these units may be placed side by side as desired, or one or two large sashes can be made to order. These ready-made hotbeds are kept by all the leading seedsmen and may be shipped anywhere on short notice. You will find them in the catalogues.

There are two distinct methods of ventilating the plants—lifting and sliding the sash.

The planks are so placed that the sash, or sashes, either lie down on them, projecting a quarter of an inch, or slide in grooves which are made on the inside of the planking. Sliding sashes are better. Lifting is not only apt to bow the sash frame, but it is liable to blow shut, smashing the glass as it falls.

But to return to the frame. Suppose you are buying the material ready to set up. Place the planks so that the sash will be on a slant toward the front, i.e., the board at the back should be higher by a foot or more than the one at the front. This is done for two reasons: First, in order to shed water; second, to get as much sunlight as possible. For if the frame faces south (as it should always do, if possible), the southern sun of winter will reach it for the longest period. The planks may be made fast to corner posts, which should be placed firmly in the soil, or the ends may be mortised. These planks come with a groove on the inside, where the sash is to slide.

This information, gained from books and manufacturers, would not do for us, for we had some material which we wished to use. (It is a poor farmer or gardener that does not make use of every bit of stock-in-trade which he possesses.) So we visited a friend who has made some new hotbeds on his own plans.

This friend's frames are built of concrete, as neat and trim as can be. The walls are made of four inches of concrete, with an airspace of six inches, then four inches of concrete, and the whole fourteen inches are covered over with two or three inches of this compound. The beds are long, one admitting of seven 3 x 6-foot frames, while the other has eight of the same size. The covering—which all hotbeds must have to keep out the intense cold of night—consists of three thicknesses of burlap sewed together, a stick being run through one end just as a stick is run through the end of a window shade, except that this one projects a few inches at either end to form a handle. The other end of the burlap is fastened to one end of the hotbed frame. The burlap is rolled upon this stick when uncovering the frames. On the other end of the frame is a roll made on the same plan, but the material is waxed sheeting. This was made by spreading a low-grade melted paraffin on common sheeting with a calcimine brush. This raincoat is unrolled upon the burlap overcoat to protect the latter from snow and rain.

These hotbeds were just the thing for a country gentleman with a good-sized place, but for reasons connected with the bank and the children's education we decided to look further. There is a dear old-fashioned farm near us, with all the modern improvements money and ingenuity can provide. We made a pilgrimage thither and found a row of hotbeds watched over and tended by an old French soldier, long since turned gardener. These beds were covered with many strips of old floor-matting, and peeping from under these were straw mats. They looked as though the cold could not possibly penetrate, yet the raw north wind and fine sharp rain were penetrating to the marrow of our bones.

"Monsieur, can you grow things in them?" queried my wife (we were sure he could).

"Yes, madame, there is lettuce and radishes, spinach and violets in them. I will show."

The veteran uncovered the sash, and as he unrolled the floor-matting, we went into raptures over the straw mats made of golden rye straw, the heads with the grain threshed out, still upon them.

Reprinted from GARDEN MAGAZINE, 190

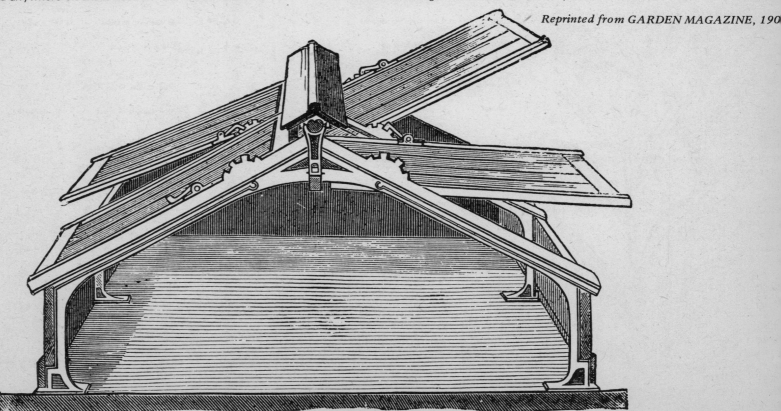

SPAN-ROOF FRAME.

"Oh, where did you buy them?"

"I make them myself. You cannot buy," he said. "You cannot buy thick like these. Of small use the ones you buy! The wind gets in and the cold. It kills everything."

"But how do you make them and where do you get the straw?"

"I will show you after. The straw—we raise it on the farm. Yes, they are fine, but the matting—it keeps off the rain from the straw, for the straw gets wet; the frost come; then my plants all freeze. It is much work, I tell you, much work. When it snows, then I must come out and sweep the mats, and shake them, then dry, for I cannot have wet mats!" And he shook his head. "Sometimes when its very cold I come out in the night."

What he did in the night he did not say. I doubt very much if he did anything. Probably it was like the mother who goes into the room and looks at a restless child. There is nothing to do, but she feels better when she has looked in.

Our Franco-Prussian friend now rolled back the thick straw mats and disclosed a still further protection, a time-honored one, known to all country dwellers as the best of chest-protectors, viz., old newspapers. These were laid all around the edge of the frame, while the glass rested at the upper end upon some more.

We laughed. The old soldier laughed, too, slapping his thigh and exclaiming, "The Frenchman, he have a good head!"

Then I took in some details of the construction of the frame itself. The slant was greater than any we had seen heretofore, and it seemed good. The front edge rested almost on the earth, while the entire frame was banked up with strawy manure. In fact, the glass rested upon the straw at the front. The back edge must have been raised nearly two feet, and, of course, the beds were protected by a high board fence on the north, while the slant of the frames was almost due south. The snow had been shoveled from around them, and they were set far enough from the fence for a person to work at the back of the frames. Our friend the gardener slid the sash upward, and I was surprised to find the plants so deep—a foot at least below the front edge. I did not ask any question. My common sense told me he had done this as an extra precaution against frost, for frost seldom penetrates the ground more than a foot, even in the open.

The earth was fine and rich and the heads of lettuce beautiful rosettes of green.

"Why, the walls of these beds are made of brick!" we exclaimed. "Tell us why you made them that way."

"I will tell you," replied the Frenchman. "First they were made of boards, but the mice and the rats they come in and eat my seeds when they just start and I can have nothing. So I say to myself, 'I fix you,' and then I build these. I dig out for my foundation three feet or more, then I put in one foot cement mixed with gravel and broken glass (the rat he not gnaw through that), then I build up my walls with brick and the rat he not get through that either. Then I put on my frames and have him all right."

"I notice the frames come very near the level in front," remarked my wife.

"Yes, madame, but I have them with straw banked, and the plants they are down deep. Come, I show you how to make the straw mats."

We followed, winding in and out among the quaint farm buildings (one of them is the grape house, which we hope to describe some day). Out in the

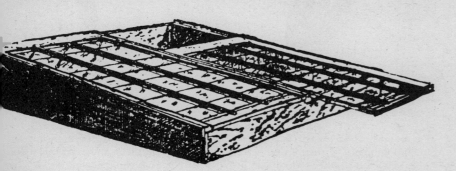

barn-yard he produced a wooden frame six feet square. At the top and bottom were holes at intervals. While we watched, the old soldier stretched cord, tarred cord or marlin twine from the top to the bottom, running the ends through the holes and making them fast. At the lower edge he left several inches of the cord, then took a handful of fresh straw, laid it against the strings, took the loose end of twine and bound it with a half-hitch. Six upright cords, and each one used on which to make a bind; two handfuls of straw make one row across and the heads are laid in the center. Handful after handful was laid on, one above the other, each row bound six times, until the frame was full. The ends were then well fastened, the twine cut from the frame, and a mat large enough to cover two sashes was completed. It was as pretty as a picture, and as easy to make as rolling off a log—when you know how.

We came home full of enthusiasm. "You can make the cement foundation and brick walls," said my wife, "but I will make the mats of golden straw. I shall feel like Ceres as I carry them in my arms."

Alas! those frames are but dreams of the future! For the present, some once-used plank and a large sash will suit us very well, for we have them ready to hand, and if the mice and rats don't disturb us it may answer several years.

However, these are the points we have gathered for practical use: The frame should be well sunk in the earth, for each year the earth and manure must be taken out and replaced. Therefore, unless the frame is well made and imbedded, it will collapse when this processs is gone through with. A proper slant is important. The front of the bed should be not more than four inches above the earth level, while the plants inside should be a foot below the level. The entire frame should be banked on the outside with hot manure to keep an even temperature. Air should be given only on warm (above freezing point) days. Water should be given when needed, and by keeping the frame tightly closed the rising moisture condenses on the glass, falling back again upon the plants.

One-light Frame.

Span-roofed Frame.

Hip-roofed Frame.

reprinted from GARDEN MAGAZINE, 1905

A BEGINNER'S EXPERIENCE WITH HOTBEDS

Early Vegetables from Two Strips of Land Measuring Twenty by a Hundred and Ten by Fifty

The way to get early vegetables is to have a hotbed and transplant young plants to the garden. Any vegetable can be transplanted provided its roots are not too much disturbed. This is best done by using the heavy, oiled-paper pots. If they are not available, use pasteboard boxes, paper-lined strawberry baskets or even boxes are ideal for partitions with strips of wood or pasteboard. Shredded-wheat biscuit boxes are ideal for large tomato plants and hills of melons, as the paper can be torn away without breaking a root. Tin cans can be slit down the side before filling with earth, thus making it possible to remove the growing plant without disturbing the roots.

SEVERAL CROPS ON THE SAME GROUND

In most gardens you will see a patch of yellow-looking corn (showing a lack of nitrogen), beets, onions, cabbage, etc., each kind by itself and not enough of any one. This year I found that the lettuce, cauliflower, beets and onions could be grown in the corn rows and do better there than by themselves, without shortening the corn crop. Thus, early in June, I started Hubbard squash between the corn rows, which took the place of the early vegetables, shading the ground between the corn and not giving the weeds a show. Each side of the row of muskmelons I put a row of early "Peep-o'-Day" corn, which was out of the way by the time the melons began to run. For melons, like all fruit-bearing, seed-ripening plants, must have sun, being unlike the plants of which we eat the foliage—i.e., lettuce, celery—which are improved by some shading. Between the hills of melons I grew bush Limas and radishes. On one piece of ground, ten by fifty, I put three rows of early potatoes, and on June 10th planted five hills of Hubbard squash between them, and on July 5th when I dug the potatoes I put in two rows of Stowell's Everygreen corn. The corn got above the squash just in time and bore a fair crop in October after the other corn was gone. The Hubbards produced twenty-two excellent squashes. Besides the manure plowed in and put in the squash hills, I used wood ashes and ground bone liberally.

White Leghorns

CORN ON JUNE 30TH

This year I had corn June 30th. When I told my neighbors about it they said nothing—they thought I lied. July 25th was the previous "record." Peep-o'-Day corn was what I used, planting it April 20th in boxes indoors. Under each hill I put a shovel of well-rotted manure, and on the surface of the ground worked in wood ashes liberally. Stowell's Evergreen was used for second plantings.

TOMATOES FROM JULY 8TH TILL FROST

Moore's King of the Earlies is the earliest tomato I know. I planted Chalk's Early Jewel on January 28th and had tomatoes from July 8th until frost. A dozen plants should supply a small family all summer and enable one to put up fifty cans. On my ten plants I tried experiments with soils and fertilizers, and though the one treated with muck and wood ashes ripened the first tomato, the vine that had no fertilizer did as well as any. Bordeaux mixture will prevent leaf blight on tomatoes.

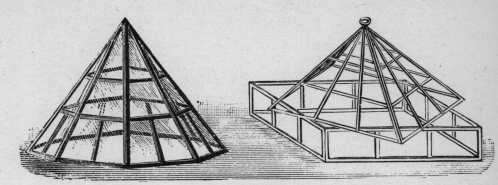

VARIOUS FORMS OF HAND LIGHTS.

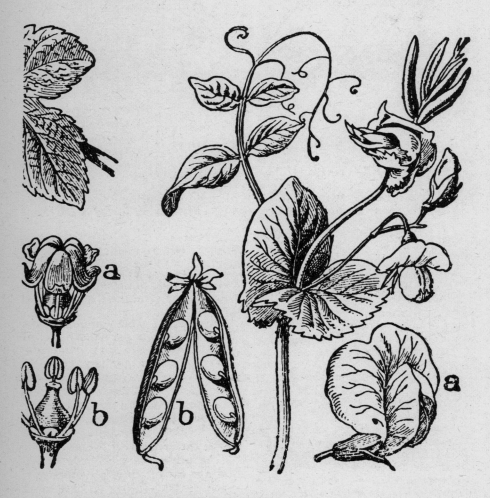

THE FIRST PEAS IN THE NEIGHBORHOOD

In the small garden I found that it is best to grow the high or brush peas, since it is more certain and saves space. Wire-netting two or three feet high can be used, and, though not as good as brush, saves labor. Peas want potash and lime. To have the first peas in the neighborhood, proceed as follows: In March, or as soon as the frost is out of the top of the ground, spade up a strip of ground, putting in a little lime, wood-ashes, and enough dry, sifted coal-ashes to make the soil dry and mealy. On each side of the wire-netting plant a row of peas, at the rate of a quart to ninety feet, using early seed, putting them on top of the ground and covering only half an inch deep. Then down each side run a piece of thin cheese-cloth, fastening it to the netting above and the ground below, making an "A" tent over the peas that will throw off snow and hard frosts. On warm and sunny days it should be let down, and only put up cold nights and during snow storms.

MUSKMELONS OF THE BEST QUALITY

Melons have a hard reputation for home planting, but I believe that even in heavy soil one can have melons in spite of drouth, blight and insects. In my garden the soil is heavy and clay, but from nine hills of Hackensack melons I had nearly a hundred cantaloups, some as large as small pumpkins and of such delicious flavor and sweetness that we jumped up and down and laughed when we ate them. Under each hill I put manure, muck and sifted coal ashes, and on the surface I worked in wood ashes, half a barrel to the nine hills, and some sand. Next year I shall plant the Emerald Gem and cover the ground with the darkest-colored sand I can get. The sand draws the sun and the heat develops the sugar in the melons. Early potatoes, lettuce, radishes, etc., can be grown between the hills, and a row of Peep-o'-Day corn each side of them, all of which will be out of the way by the time the vines begin to run. They must not be shaded, however. Melons require nitrogen and potash. Besides the manure, next year I shall put in a compost and dried blood, also ashes and sand on the surface. Liquid manure, diluted three times with water, is the best fertilizer of all. It should not, however, be allowed to touch the foliage. For blight use Bordeaux mixture, four pounds of copper sulphate and six of lump lime to fifty gallons of water, MIXED COLD. As this mixture settles rapidly, it should be stirred to the very bottom thoroughly every few minutes. Otherwise, one will burn the foliage. It can be put on with a broom, or one can obtain a brass pneumatic pump, which is invaluable for spraying beans, potatoes, rose bushes, grape vines, etc., as well as melons.

OUTWITTING THE ENEMIES OF VINES

The striped cucumber beetle is the worst enemy of the muskmelon. To fight him, first start the melons in the house or hotbed in pots or pasteboard boxes. This will not only give earlier melons, but also it will give them a start on the bugs. This year I started them on March 20th and had melons on August 10th. Second, dust the vines with tobacco dust, to prevent their eating them. Third, put air-slacked lime, mixed with turpentine, in and on the hill around the vines, or tobacco dust all around each vine where it comes out of the ground. This will prevent the beetle from going down and laying her eggs on the roots.

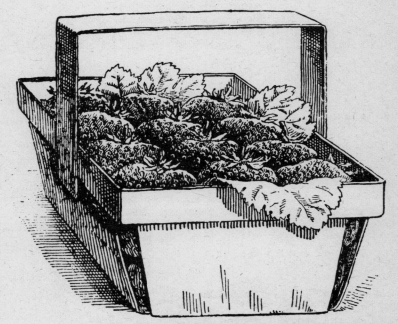

A CHIP BASKET OF STRAWBERRIES.

These eggs hatch into a grub that eats the vines off underground. Fourth, plant a "trap" vine of Hubbard squash nearby—this will call all the bugs away from the melons to the squash, where they can be destroyed with kerosene. Lime in the hill will help to keep away wireworms and cutworms, or they can be killed with kerosene emulsion or carbon bisulphide. The bugs can be caught on a tarred board or piece of fly-paper held on one side of the hill while they are fanned on it from the other.

The only effective way that man has yet been able to devise to fight the deadly squash vine borer, which is the larva of a night-flying, clear-winged moth, is to bury every joint of the running vines as they grow, thus letting them take root at many places. Then when a vine is seen wilting in the sun, examine the stalk and destroy every grub. Sometimes he can be removed without killing the vine by using the thin blade of a penknife and care. Other insects can be fought the same as for melons.

 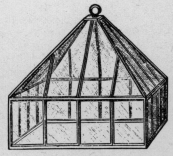

Copper Frame in one piece.   Iron Frame in one piece.

HAND-LIGHTS.

Electric heating of HOTBEDS

By James M. Stanley, Southern Region,
Agricultural Research Service

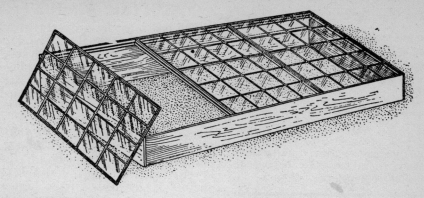

Electrically heated hotbeds are well suited for growing vegetable plants that are transplanted later to field or coldframe.

Such beds offer several advantages over manure- or fuel-heated beds. Less labor is required to operate the bed. More uniform and more positive control of temperature in the bed is possible. Therefore, more uniform plants of the desired quality usually can be produced.

An electrically heated bed may be more economical in the long run, provided it is properly built and electricity is available at reasonable cost.

BUILDING THE BED

Location

A good location is essential for satisfactory operation of the bed.

Select an area where the soil has good natural drainage that prevents excess moisture just beneath the hotbed. It should be close to a source of electricity and water. Buildings or other objects should not block sunlight from the bed.

The bed should have a southern exposure so that it receives the maximum amount of sunlight. If the area selected is on sloping land, a southern slope is preferable. Some form of windbreak on the north or windward side will help to reduce operating costs. A building makes an excellent windbreak, but it should not block the sunlight.

Size

Almost any size hotbed can be electrically heated. Beds 12 feet wide have been operated successfully, but a narrower bed is easier to work.

The size of the bed will depend on your planting requirements—kind of plants, number of plants, and spacing between plants and plant rows.

Table 1 contains information on planting various crops in a 6-by-3-foot bed.

A standard glass sash is 6 by 3 feet. If you plan to use this type of covering, a practical width for a bed is 5 feet 8 inches. The length would be a multiple of 3, such as 6, 9, 12, or 15 feet.

In determining the size of the bed, you should consider also the length of cable to be used.

Materials

Most beds are constructed with wood sidewalls. When electricity is used for heating, permanent-type beds are sometimes preferred. Concrete poured in place or masonry blocks are the best materials to use for the walls of a permanent bed. When properly constructed, the walls last longer and require less maintenance than wood walls. Concrete or masonry-block walls 6 inches thick will suffice if they are properly reinforced and supported on adequate footing. Use good mortar in laying masonry blocks. Poor joints permit air leakage and increase operating costs and maintenance.

If the walls are made of wood, use tongue-and-grooved dressed lumber 2 inches thick. If that type is not available, use 2-inch lumber, dressed on all sides, with weatherstripping on joints. Treat the wood with a 2-percent copper naphthenate solution to retard decay. *Do not use creosote or pentachlorphenol because they are harmful to plants.*

Ground Work

The bed area must be level. If sloping land is leveled, be sure that runoff water will not enter or stand around the bed.

It may be necessary to place cinders or gravel under the bed to insure proper drainage. Excavate the bed area to a depth of about 8 inches. After the walls are built, tamp cinders or gravel to a depth of 6 inches in the excavated space. Cover the cinders or gravel with burlap or some other material that will permit water to pass through yet prevent sand from sifting down.

Add a 2-inch layer of sand. The sand is important. It protects the heating cable, which is laid on it, from mechanical or chemical damage. Sharp stones may cut insulation or lead covering on heating cable. Cinders react chemically with the lead covering of cables and cause trouble.

Construction

Build the back, or north, wall 18 inches above the level at which the heating cable is placed. Side walls usually slope toward the front about 1 inch per foot of width. If the bed is 6 feet wide, the front wall will be 12 inches high. This will provide 6 inches of space between the soil and the sash along the front edge, which is ample room for plants.

If the bed area was excavated, extend the walls down to the bottom of the excavation. If the area was not excavated, extend the walls down to about 4 inches below the level at which the heating cable is placed.

The footing for concrete or masonry-block walls must be placed below the frostline. Otherwise, when the bed is not in use, trouble is likely to occur from freezing and thawing. The walls must be deep enough to prevent damage from freezing. The slope on the side walls is obtained by pouring concrete to the desired slope. With masonry-block walls, this is done by clamping forms to the walls after they are in place. Use a relatively dry concrete mixture.

Nail 1-by-4-inch boards to the outside top edge of the back and side walls. (The sashes extend over the edge of the front wall to shed water.) The boards serve as weatherstripping and reduce heat loss between walls and sashes. Bank soil against the outside of the walls to prevent air leakage.

---

[1] When the plants are transplanted to coldframes, allow a minimum of 4 square inches per plant. If the bed is used as a coldframe, the plants should be thinned to the same spacing. The bed will then accommodate about 600 plants. Sweet-potatoes are not transplanted to coldframes. They are transplanted directly to the field.

Covering

Glass sash is the best type of covering for hotbeds, but it is also the most expensive. Plastic films are cheaper and provide insulation equal to glass. Treated muslin is a satisfactory covering in warmer climates. The coverings must be adequately supported and secured.

Use removable sash supports between sashes. A 1-by-4-inch board, with a 1-by-2-inch board fastened on edge to its center, makes a good sash support, and also serves as weatherstripping.

HEATING CABLE

Selection

Various types of electric heating cable are available. Both lead-covered and plastic-covered give satisfactory results when used properly.

In selecting cable you must know how many watts per square foot of bed area are needed to provide adequate heat. In southern areas, 10 watts per square foot have proved adequate. In northern areas, where extremely low temperatures are anticipated during the period the bed will be used, as much as 16 watts per square foot may be needed.

The cables vary in length and wattage rating (heating capacity). Some are 60 feet long and are rated at 400 watts, or 6.7 watts per foot. Others are 120 feet long and are rated at 800 watts, also 6.7 watts per foot. Some are 60 feet long and are rated at 300 watts, or 5 watts per foot. Various other combinations in length and wattage rating are available.

Your power supplier or a qualified dealer can assist you in selecting heating cable.

TABLE 1.—*Seed required and plant capacity, 6- by 3-foot hotbed*

Plant	Amount of seed	Number of seedling plants [1]
Tomato	*Ounce* ½ to ¾	2,000 to 3,000.
Sweetpotato	*Bushels* 1½ to 2	3,000 to 4,000.
Cabbage	*Ounces* ¾	3,750.
Pepper	1½	2,000 to 2,500.
Eggplant	1½	3,000 to 4,000.
Lettuce	¼ to ½	2,500 to 4,000.

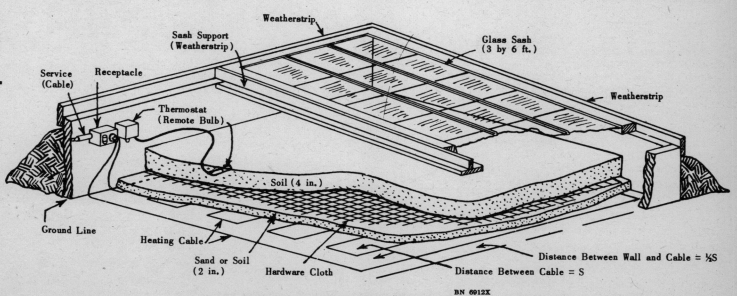

BN 6912X

Construction of an electrically heated hotbed.

Laying the Cable

Lay the cable on the soil at the bottom of the bed. Or, if the bed was excavated, lay it on the sand that was spread on the cinders or gravel.

NOTE.—In at least one section of the country, the practice is to embed the cable in concrete. Further information is available from your State Extension Agricultural Engineer.

The spacing between loops or sections of cable is important; it governs the number of watts per square foot of soil area. Uniform spacing is the method most commonly used. Determine the proper spacing as follows:

$$\text{Spacing (in inches)} = \frac{12 \times \dfrac{\text{watts}}{\text{per foot of cable}}}{\text{Wattage required per square foot of bed}}$$

Example: You have a 120-foot cable rated at 800 watts. You wish to supply 10 watts per square foot.

$$\text{Spacing} = \frac{12 \times (800 \div 120)}{10}$$

$$= \frac{12 \times 6.7}{10}$$

$$= \frac{80.4}{10}$$

$$= 8 \text{ inches}$$

The spacing between the outside cable and the wall is half the spacing between cables (or 4 inches in the example given).

After the cable is in position, cover it with a 2-inch layer of loose soil or sand. Then place a ½-inch-mesh hardware cloth on top of the soil or sand. The hardware cloth prevents possible damage to the cable when sharp instruments are used in working the bed.

Precautions

Observe these precautions when placing the cable:

Lay the cable in position carefully to avoid damaging the sheath or conductor. Kinks may damage or break the cable.

Do not cross one cable or section of cable over another.

Do not shorten the length of a cable. A shortened cable may become too hot and burn out.

ELECTRIC WIRING

The bed must be properly wired to operate satisfactorily. The wiring should conform to the National Electrical Code and to the requirements of the local power supplier. It should be installed by a qualified electrician.

Heating cables are designed to operate on either 120 or 240 volts. Small beds—4-sash size or less—can be operated satisfactorily on the lower voltage while it is desirable to operate larger beds on the higher voltage. The distance from point of electric service, amperage rating of thermostat to be used, and size bed to operate on a thermostat must be considered in determining proper voltage. Always connect the cable to a power supply of the specified voltage.

Install a weatherproof service switch, properly fused and grounded, on a pole adjacent to the bed. Select wire heavy enough to permit no more than a 2-percent voltage drop in its length. Use type U.F. service cable from the switch to the heating cable. *Make all connections to the heating cable watertight.*

THERMOSTAT

Installation

Connect a thermostat with an operating range of about 30° to 120° F. in the electric circuit to control the temperature in the bed. It can be a type that can be buried in the soil or one that has a remote-temperature bulb for that purpose. The type with a remote-temperature bulb is recommended for large beds. Thermostats that are buried in the soil work satisfactorily in small beds.

The thermostat must have sufficient current-carrying capacity to handle the electric load of the bed or section of bed that it controls. Large beds require a ther-

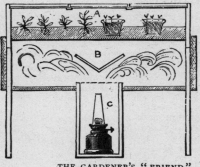

THE GARDENER'S "FRIEND"
PROPAGATOR.
Sectional View.

mostat for each section in which a different temperature is maintained, or for each electric circuit serving a cable or group of cables. Your power supplier's representative or an electrician can help you determine the size of thermostat required.

Place the temperature-sensing element (the thermostat or the remote-temperature bulb) one-third of the way across the width of the bed and at the same distance from the end wall. Some growers bury it about 1 inch in the soil. Others set it in a vertical position with the bottom half buried. In the latter position, it is affected by both soil and air temperatures. Do not place the thermostat or bulb directly above a heating cable or allow it to come in contact with a cable. For sweetpotatoes, place it among the seed potatoes.

Operation

To control the temperature in the bed satisfactorily, the thermostat

must have an "open" and "close" range of not more than 5°. Check its operation as follows:

Set the temperature indicator at the maximum temperature desired for the bed. Place the thermostat bulb in water. Heat the water to the maximum temperature desired for the bed. Use a reliable thermometer to determine the water temperature. A pilot lamp operated by the thermostat is handy to indicate thermostat operation. The thermostat should open—shut off the current—when the set temperature is reached. This is indicated by the pilot light going out. (A slight clicking noise also indicates that the thermostat opened.) If the thermostat did not open at the desired temperature, adjust it until it does.

Allow the water to cool 5°. The thermostat should close—turn on the current. This is indicated by the pilot lamp lighting. If the thermostat did not close, make the necessary adjustment if possible, or replace it with another one.

TWO-LIGHT FRAME.

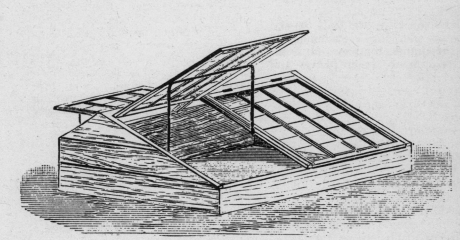

—THREE-QUARTER SPAN ROOF GARDEN FRAME.

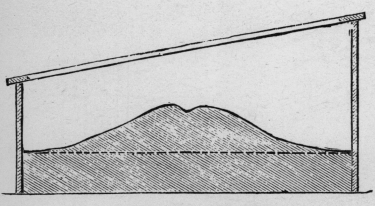

SECTION OF SIMPLE FRAME.

GILLINGHAM'S HEAT RADIATOR.

54

A TWO-LIGHT GARDEN FRAME IN ISOMETRICAL PERSPECTIVE.

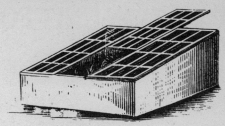

COLD-FRAME.

OPERATING THE BED

Soil for Plants

Place a 4-inch layer of good soil in the bed. Use soil that is free of weed seeds and disease. In many instances it is desirable to sterilize the soil with heat or chemicals to kill any weed seeds and to reduce the possibility of disease.

Your county agricultural agent can give you information about sterilization of the soil. He can also help you with testing the soil to determine what fertilization is needed.

AMATEUR'S HAND LIGHT.

GILBERT'S REGISTERED HAND GLASS.

temperature gets too high, ventilate the bed, but avoid exposing the plants to damage from wind, rain, or excessive cold. Some ventilation will probably be needed on all mild, sunny days.

Attention to watering is particularly important with electrically heated beds. Keep the bed moist at all times, but do not apply too much water. Apply water in the morning so that plant foliage will dry off before evening.

Conserving Heat

Good operating and maintenance practices conserve heat and reduce operating costs.

COLD FRAMES AND HOT BEDS—YOU NEED THEM

A greenhouse is not complete without its frames. They not only relieve the crowding of its benches but many things are better started or stored in frames and then removed to the greenhouse for further development, or the reverse.

For example, why crowd out roses for lettuce or spinach? Still you want both of them.

Why take up room you would devote to sweet peas, snap-dragons or stock for growing violets, when they actually do just as well in frames?

By all that is reasonable, if you have a greenhouse, you need frames.

Let us suggest that you have a heating pipe run to them from the greenhouse boiler and then you can use them in all weather without the bother of making hot-beds.

Let us further suggest that you add a little more to your investment and build them with masonry sides, cast-iron sills and steel T-bar rafters. Then you will have an equipment that will last as long as your greenhouse.

Regular 3 by 6 sash is used on these frames.

The masonry frames shown below are placed directly on the southern side of the greenhouse, leaving a passageway space of about three feet. This is a much better arrangement than joining them directly to the greenhouse, as the snow and ice from the roof are apt to slide down and break the glass in the sash.

Reprinted from The LORD & BURNHAM Archives.

Plant Growth

Plants grow rather rapidly in electrically heated beds. Therefore, do not seed the beds too early.

A soil temperature of 70° to 75° F. is ideal for planting most seed. After the seeds germinate, adjust the temperature to suit the particular plant. Cool-season crops, such as cabbage, cauliflower, and lettuce, require an air temperature during the day of 60° to 65°. Warm-season crops, such as eggplant, peppers, tomatoes, and melons, require an air temperature of 65° to 75°. For satisfactory results, night air temperatures might be 5° to 10° lower than day air temperatures.

To insure that the proper soil and air temperatures are maintained, use two thermometers—one for checking soil temperature and another for checking air temperature above the plants. Place the soil thermometer at the same depth in the soil as the thermostat or remote bulb.

Air temperature in the bed should not go above 85° F. If the

Be sure all joints are windtight. Keep soil banked around the outside of the walls. Replace broken or poorly fitting glass in glass sashes. Repair holes in glass-substitute material.

During extremely cold weather, cover sashes with straw or substitute material. This will protect plants and lower operating costs. But do not allow this additional covering to block out too much sunlight.

OPERATING COST

The cost of operating an electrically heated bed depends on the time of year, weather conditions, management, location, and construction.

Tests at various locations indicate that a 3-by-6-foot bed uses 1 to 2 kilowatt-hours of electricity per day.

Well-constructed beds cost less to operate than poorly constructed ones, and over a period of years the savings will pay for the additional building cost.

Glazing combined with Hollow Bricks or Tiles.

PROPAGATION UNIT FOR PLANTS

Plants that are germinated and grown to transplanting stage under artificial light get a headstart on plants that are started in the greenhouse or planted directly in the garden. This propagation unit is designed to use 1,500-milliampere fluorescent lamps. Some plants will do better with incandescent light added at a ratio of 1 watt incandescent light to 5 watts of fluorescent light.

The lamp bank in this unit consists of six two-lamp strip fixtures mounted to an angle iron framework. The lamp bank is suspended in an inverted V shape to distribute light uniformly over the 3-by 4-foot growing area. This area can be increased if 6- or 8-foot lamps are used. Two or more units can be mounted end-to-end to provide any desired growing area. The lamps can be left on continuously or controlled by a 24-hour timeclock to give any desired photoperiod.

For most plants, a 16-hour photoperiod should be adequate for satisfactory growth. Some plants will grow under continuous illumination, but others, such as tomato, require an alternating light and dark period.

The air temperature at the plant level will depend on the distance from the lamps. Normally, it will run at least 5 degrees to 10 degrees F. higher than room temperature during the day and will approximate room temperature during the night. If the temperature is too cold or too hot, the plants will be small and of poor quality. The temperature can be controlled with heaters and air conditioners in the surrounding room if it is too low or high. The temperature of the fluorescent lamps should be around 100 degrees F. on the glass surface near the center of the lamp. The light output goes down if the lamp is too hot or cold. The fan in this unit will keep the lamps and the plants at the correct temperature in a 70 degrees F. room.

The automatic watering system can be set to water the plants for one or more minutes for as many times as desired during the day. Some growers may want to substitute watering tubes for the needle-tube system. Watering assemblies can be purchased in units with 20 or more small tubes. Some tubes have a sliding shutoff valve at the end of each tube. Other growers may want to use spray nozzles, but care should be taken to keep the lamp unit dry.

Avoid placing this unit in a poorly ventilated or closed room because the plants will consume most of the available carbon dioxide. If the unit is in a closed room, use a small blower to bring fresh air into the growing area.

SEED BOXES.

NO. 1.—SHOWING SEED AS JUST SOWN IN SHALLOW BOXES (2 INCHES DEEP).

NO. 2.—SHOWS SEEDS, SUCH AS PANSIES, 3 OR 4 WEEKS AFTER SOWING.

NO. 3.—SHOWS THE PLANTS TRANSPLANTED, THE SAME SHALLOW BOXES BEING USED IN EACH CASE.

Under the propagation unit, seeds germinate and grow uniformly at an accelerated rate. Because the heat from the lamps dries the soil surface, the seed and young plants should be watered frequently.

The starting media should be sterile and should drain easily so that excess water will not stand on the soil surface. Use self-contained starting units, such as peat pellets or compressed paper blocks, for starting seedlings. You may also sow seed in a synthetic soil mix consisting of equal parts peat moss and vermiculite. These starting aids are available from most garden supply centers.

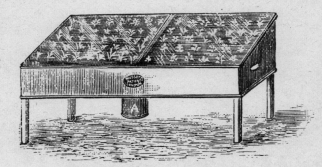

Mussett's Excelsior Propagator for Outdoor Use.

Begin fertilizing the plants with a water soluble fertilizer when they show their first true leaves. Start with 1 teaspoon of fertilizer per gallon of water, and double the amount of fertilizer as the plants become larger.

Many types of seedlings and cuttings have been grown successfully in this unit. At any time of the year you may grow herbs, radishes, lettuce, cherry tomatoes, and dwarf bedding plants.

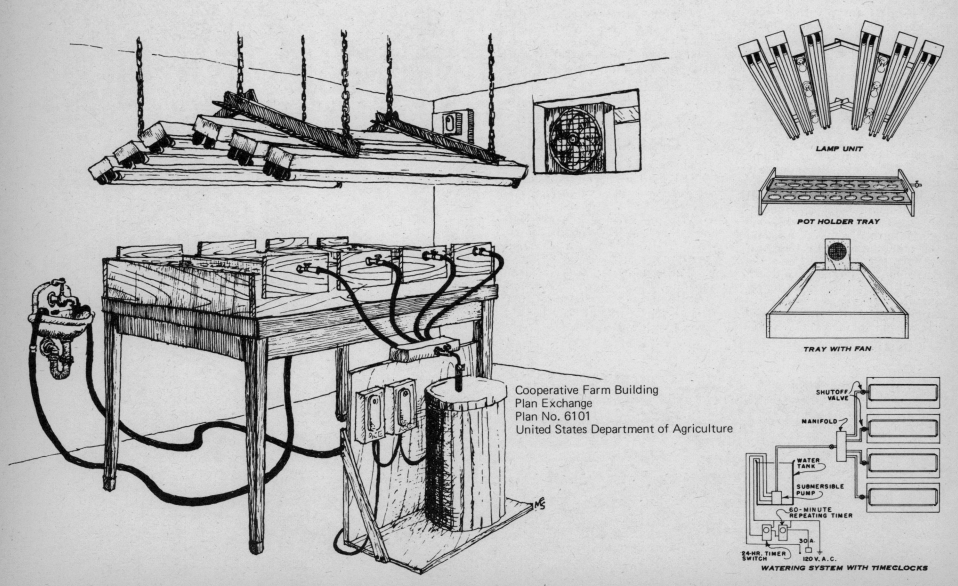

LAMP UNIT

POT HOLDER TRAY

TRAY WITH FAN

SHUTOFF VALVE

MANIFOLD

WATER TANK

SUBMERSIBLE PUMP

60-MINUTE REPEATING TIMER

24-HR. TIMER SWITCH

30 A.

120 V. A. C.

WATERING SYSTEM WITH TIMECLOCKS

Cooperative Farm Building
Plan Exchange
Plan No. 6101
United States Department of Agriculture

FOOD GARDENS

This portion of FOOD GARDENS is divided into various sections. The first section is a regional breakdown of vegetables and herbs that grow outdoors in various parts of the U.S. and Canada. It is outlined in the zone of hardiness map on page 58.

The second part is a guide to cultivation of specific vegetables including groupings of vegetables by families.

The third part describes pests and diseases, with special articles indicating the level of material available from the government and land grant colleges.

The last part of this section deals with bees, followed by two mushroom articles, one from the commercial area and the other a university booklet.

This material represents a high professional level of horticultural and agricultural writing. Credits follow each article and our Recommended Reading section on page **317** will allow you to follow up on this material.

1	Tree Fruit
2	Small Fruit
3	Herbs
4	Vine Vegatables
5	Root Vegetables
6	Green Vegetables
7	Espalier Fruit

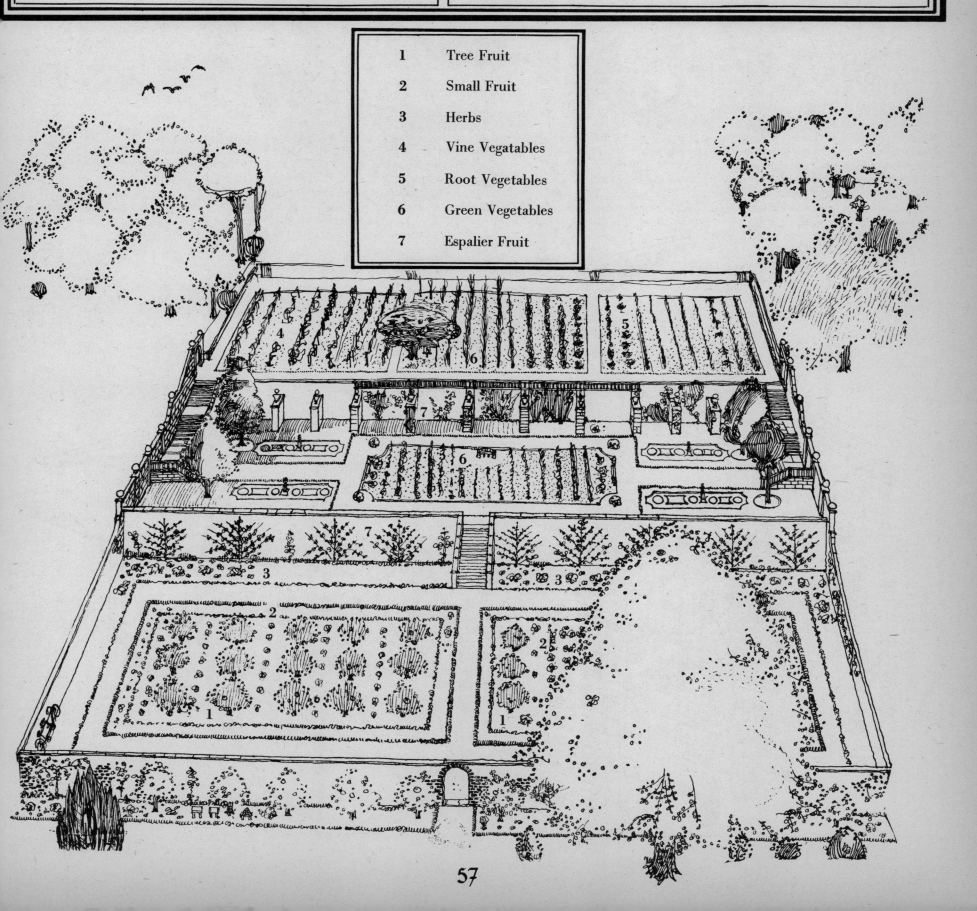

MAP-ZONES OF PLANT HARDINESS

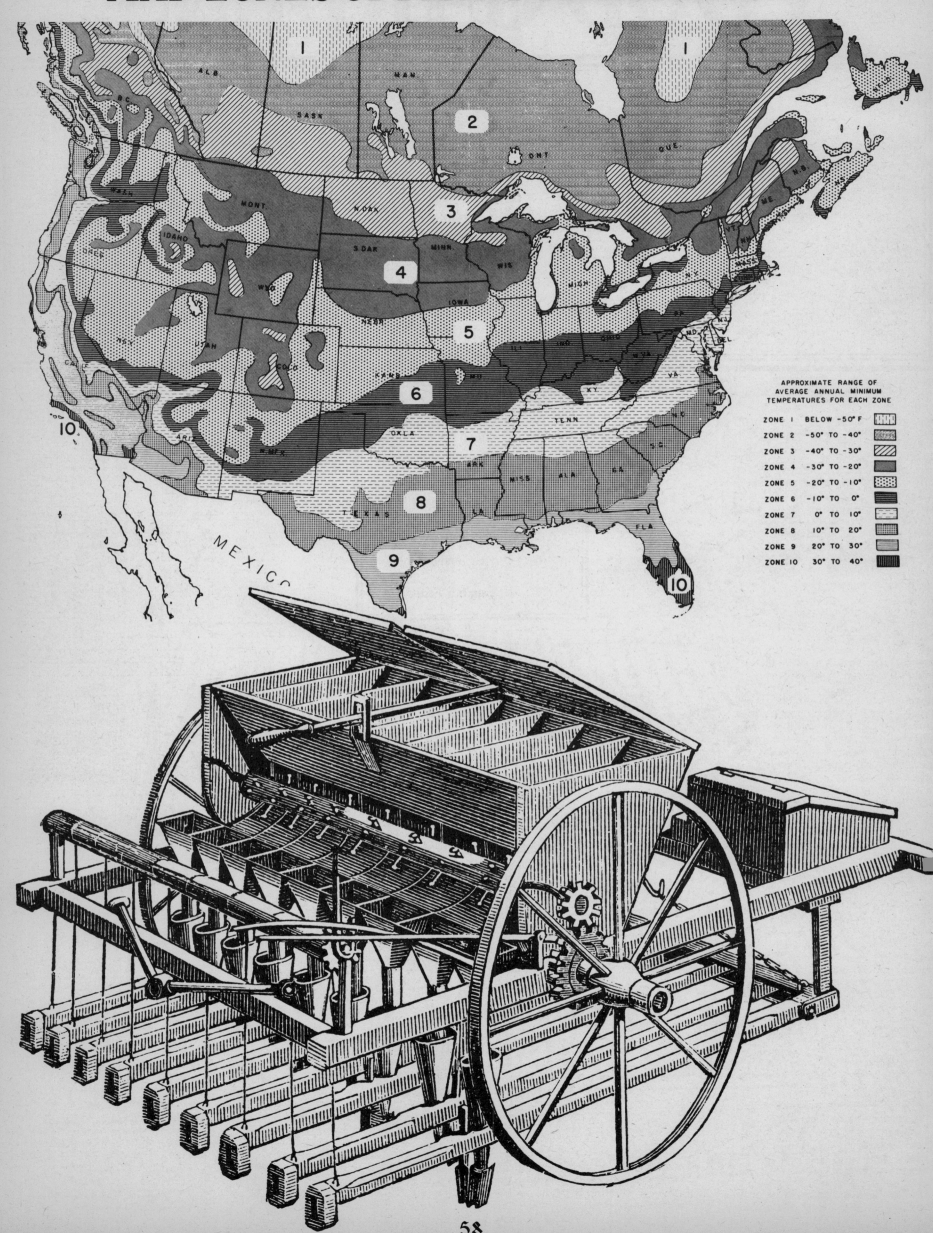

APPROXIMATE RANGE OF
AVERAGE ANNUAL MINIMUM
TEMPERATURES FOR EACH ZONE

ZONE 1   BELOW -50° F
ZONE 2   -50° TO -40°
ZONE 3   -40° TO -30°
ZONE 4   -30° TO -20°
ZONE 5   -20° TO -10°
ZONE 6   -10° TO 0°
ZONE 7   0° TO 10°
ZONE 8   10° TO 20°
ZONE 9   20° TO 30°
ZONE 10 30° TO 40°

McFAYDEN VEGETABLE GUIDE

McFAYDEN SEED CO. Ltd
P.O. Box 1600
Brandon, Manitoba

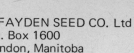

ZONE ③ ④ ⑤

Vegetable Gardening is "In" Again

W. ANDREW

CURLED OR DOUBLE CHERVIL.

The big farm vegetable garden; the vegetable patch on an urban or suburban lot; the vegetables grown on a rented plot; the vegetables in planters on a patio or apartment balcony, or even parsley, chives and radishes in a window box have become an "in" thing. Probably not since the "Victory Gardens" of the early forties have so many people grown so many vegetables. Housewives are seeking fresher more nutritious products than can sometimes be bought in the supermarkets, whole families are looking for "back to the land" projects, and inquisitive students and enthusiastic hobbyists are seeking the challenge and satisfaction accruing from the growing of vegetables.

In addition to providing nutritional, social and psychological benefits, a well planned and well maintained vegetable garden can considerably reduce the family food budget. Data available emphasizes the space allocated to a good vegetable garden is the most lucrative space on a general farm. Farm families who believe they cannot compete with the vegetable growing specialist at the price level the specialists receive, are forgetting that if they don't grow their own, they must purchase them at the retail price level, not at the level received at the farm by the market gardener or truck farmer. Certainly the cost of home grown vegetables is less than the price paid to bring them home from the store.

Should the foregoing comments appear to justify involvement in a vegetable garden, and you are a rank beginner, the awareness of a few basic principles may help. The first step is a plan.

Planning the Vegetable Garden. This, to many individuals, is the easiest and most pleasant part of growing a garden. It may even represent the total accomplishment of the less ambitious minority!

Plans can vary from a simple list of what kinds (species), to very detailed map-type presentations. We suggest that the beginner keep in mind:

A. The location or the site
1. As near the home as possible. Easily accessible for working at odd times and for harvest. Gardens on the back forty or on a lot several blocks away frequently do not get the attention that one in a more convenient location would get.
2. If there is any choice in slope or exposure keep in mind that a south

VEGETABLES	Seed Per 100 Feet of Row	Distance Between Rows	Apart in Rows After Thinning	Sowing Depth	INFORMATION	Days to Sprout Seed (approx.)	Days to Yield (approx.)
ASPARAGUS (R)	1 oz.	2-3 ft.	18-24 in.	½-1 in.	Sow seed early – transplant seedlings to permanent bed next spring.	15	3 years
BEANS, BUSH (C) (E) (F)	1 lb.	1½-2ft.	2-4 in.	1-2 in.	Do best on warm loam. For best quality gather just before using.	6	40-55
BEANS, BROAD (R)	2 lbs.	1½-2½ ft.	8-12 in.	1-2 in.	Plant earlier than other beans. Prefer cool growing season.	6	85
BEANS, POLE (C)	½ lb.	3 ft.	5-10 in.	1-2 in.	Train plants on fence or poles.	6	55-65
BEETS (R) (E) (M)	1 oz.	1½-2 ft.	2-4 in.	½-1 in.	Young beets have better quality. Use thinned plants for greens.	10	55-65
SWISS CHARD (R)	½ oz.	1½-2 ft.	8-12 in.	½-1 in.	Harvest outside stalks only. Stands hot weather.	10	55+
BROCCOLI, SPROUTING (A) (F)	½ oz.	2-2½ ft.	18-24 in.	¼ in.	Late sowing escapes summer heat at heading time.	10	60-80
BRUSSELS SPROUTS (A) (F)	½ oz.	1½-2 ft.	18-24 in.	¼-½ in.	Harvest lowest sprouts first and break off leaves below sprout.	10	75+
CABBAGE (A) (M)	½ oz.	2-2½ ft.	2 ft.	½ in.	Grow on rich land; plant closer for smaller heads. Start plants 4 to 5 weeks before setting out.	10	60-110
CANTALOUPE (D)	½ oz.	4-6 ft.	2-4 ft.	1-2 in.	Give warmest location in garden. Ripen on vine for flavour.	8	80-95
CARROT (R) (E) (M)	½ oz.	1½-2 ft.	1-3 in.	¼-½ in.	Young carrots have better quality. Thin at bunching stage.	12	70-85
CAULIFLOWER (A) (F)	¼ oz.	2-3 ft.	20-24 in.	¼ in.	Tie leaves over heads when nearing maturity.	8	70-100
CELERY (A)	½ oz.	2-3 ft.	6-8 in.	⅛-¼ in.	Do not sow late in districts with short growing seasons.	21	100-140
CITRON (D)	½ oz.	4 ft.	2-4 ft.	1 in.	Requires warm location in garden.	10	80-95
CORN, SWEET (C) (F)	¼ lb.	3 ft.	9-12 in.	1-2 in.	Keep rows side by side in block formation to help pollination. For best flavour pick ears just before using.	7	65-95
CRESS (R) (E)	½ oz.	1-1½ ft.	2-4 in.	¼ in.	Cut back plants for fresh crop of leaves.	14	25-40
CUCUMBER (D)	¾ oz.	3-6 ft.	1-2 ft.	½-¾ in.	Use white spine varieties for slicing. Use black spine varieties for pickles.	8	50-70
EGG PLANT (A)	⅛ oz.	2 ft.	18-24 in.	½ in.	Grow in rich warm soil.	10	80-100
ENDIVE (R) (C)	1 oz.	1½-2 ft.	8-10 in.	¼-½ in.	Grows best as a fall crop.	10	70+
HERB, DILL	1 oz.	2 ft.	8-12 in.	¼ in.	Easily grown annual.	8	65
SAGE	1 oz.	1½ ft.	6 in.	¼ in.	Hardy Perrenial.	7	75
SUMMER SAVORY	¼ oz.	1½ ft.	6 in.	¼ in.	Annual. Make successive sowings.	10	60
THYME	Pkt.	1½ ft.	6 in.	⅛ in.	Hardy Perennial.	10	85
KOHL RABI	½ oz.	1-2 ft.	4-6 in.	½ in.	Use when heads are smaller than tennis balls.	12	50+
LEEK (R)	½ oz.	1-2 ft.	4-6 in.	⅜ in.	Blanch stems by banking with earth.	10	130
LETTUCE, HEAD (R) (E)	¼ oz.	1½-2 ft.	12 in.	¼ in.	New kinds will head in hot weather.	7	75-90
LETTUCE, LEAF (R) (E)	½ oz.	1½ ft.	6 in.	¼ in.	Extra tender if not thinned.	7	40+
ONIONS, GREEN (R)	2 oz.	1-1½ ft.		½ in.	Early crop from sets, later from seed (except Perennial)	10	....
ONIONS, DRY (R)	½ oz.	1½-2 ft.	3-4 in.	½ in.	Late Spanish varieties usually started in cold frame.	10	95-130
PARSLEY (R)	½ oz.	1-1½ ft.	4-6 in.	¼ in.	Also grown in pots for winter use.	21	80+
PARSNIP (R)	½ oz.	1½-2 ft.	4 in.	½ in.	Fall frost improves the flavour.	18	100-110
PEAS (R) (E) (F)	1 lb.	2-3 ft.	1-3 in.	1-2 in.	Sow early, do best in cool weather.	8	60-80
PEPPER (A)	¼ oz.	1½-2 ft.	15-20 in.	¼ in.	Needs a protected site with rich warm soil. Use when green or red.	10	65-95
PUMPKIN (D)	1 oz.	8-10 ft.	2-4 ft.	1-2 in.	Manure under the seed bed helps.	8	100-110
RADISH (R) (E)	1 oz.	1-1½ ft.	1 in. (Spring) 3 in. (Sum'r)	½ in.	Use medium top varieties for early planting. Use short top varieties for summer planting.	5	25-40
RHUBARB	½ oz.	2-4 ft.	3 ft.	1 in.	Some variation in types grown from seed.	12	2 yrs.
SPINACH (R) (F)	1½ oz.	1-1½ ft.	3-6 in.	¾ in.	Does best under cool conditions and on rich loam.	8	40-55
VEGETABLE MARROW (D)	2 ozs.	3-4 ft.	2-3 ft.	1-2 in.	Requires rich, warm soil.	7	90-100
SUMMER SQUASH (D) (F)	2 ozs.	3-4 ft.	2-3 ft.	1-2 in.	Use when 5 or 6 days from blossom.	7	50-60
WINTER SQUASH (D)	1 oz.	6-8 ft.	3-4 ft.	1-2 in.	Manure under the seed bed helps.	9	80-120
TOMATO (A)	¼ oz.	2-4 ft.	2 ft. (Staked) 3 ft. (Unstkd)	¼-½ in.	Do not use too much Nitrogen; use 2-12-10 fertilizer.	10	60-90
SUMMER TURNIP (R)	½ oz.	1-2 ft.	3-4 in.	¼ in.	Best as a fall crop, use when young.	9	45-55
SWEDE TURNIP (M)	½ oz.	1½-2 ft.	6-8 in.	¾ in.	Grow on rich soil. Requires cool weather for quality turnips.	9	60-90
WATERMELON (D)	1 oz.	4-6 ft.	2-6 ft.	1-2 in.	Give warmest location in the garden.	8	70-95

Reference Notes

(A) Plants usually started indoors in early spring. Direct sowing in the garden requires more seed.
(C) Plant after ground is warm in spring.
(D) Plant after ground is warm or may be started indoors in pots providing roots are not disturbed in transplanting.
(E) Make several plantings for continued tender crops.
(F) Some varieties adapted for quick freeze storage.
(M) Make midsummer planting for winter storage.
(R) Rush first planting in the garden as soon as ground can be put in condition.

Testiculate Root (Orchis morio).

or southeast slope is usually ealier and warmer.
3. The area should be well drained. If it is not, open ditches, tile drains, raised beds or ridges should be considered.
4. Light is necessary for plant growth. The site chosen for a vegetable garden should get at least five hours of direct sunlight per day. Trees in close proximity shade the garden and compete for nutrients and moisture, but they also provide much needed shelter if they are not too close.
5. The garden should be close to a water supply. In almost any area of the Canadian prairie provinces the addition of supplementary water has proven beneficial.

B. Choosing the Crops
1. Consider the size of the garden. If it is small, concentrate on the highly perishable crops, e.g. peas, sweet corn, leaf lettuce, asparagus. They are much better fresh from the garden. Vegetables with trailing vines e.g. cucumber, squash occupy more space. Most root crops store fairly well and are generally available from outside sources.
2. Consider the preferences of the family. Allocate the major portion of the area to vegetables of proven popularity but try a new one now and then.
3. Consider the climate — In many areas of the so-called prairie provinces the growing season is somewhat short for such vegetables as melons, lima beans, eggplant and sweet potato.
4. Consider the ease of growing. Lettuce, snapbeans, carrots, tomatoes are fairly easy to grow. On the other hand, problems appear to arise more frequently in the

production of celery, escarole, limas, cucumbers.
5. Consider "Succession" cropping so that early maturing species might be followed by others in the same space e.g. radish followed by beans, or leaf lettuce followed by spinach.
6. Consider "Successive" cropping — by making use of cultivars (varieties) that mature at slightly different dates or plant the same cultivar at successive dates. A couple of heads of cabbage each week from the middle of July on is so much better than 30 heads in early or late August with nothing before or after.
7. Consider "Companion" cropping — Considered by many to be an even better use of space than successive or succession cropping. Grow rapidly maturing crops between rows or plants of slower growing crops. e.g. radish or green onions between tomatoes or late cabbage. The advantages of the extra production must be weighed

Vegetable Gardening is 'IN' Again

against the possibility of more difficult pest control, more difficulty in cultivating to control weeds, and the addition of higher levels of fertilizer and water than for a single crop.

C. The Layout

1. Group crops according to size. Small growing ones together, large growing ones together.
2. If rows run east and west, put the tall growing plants on the north side.
3. If there is a slope, run the rows across it or along the contour.
4. Plant sweet corn in several short rows rather than long single rows to promote pollination.
5. Put permanent plantings or perennials such as asparagus and rhubarb at one end or one side of the garden so it won't be necessary to work around the patch continually.
6. Adjust the spaces between the rows to the type of cultivation. e.g. close for hand cultivation and adapted to the equipment if mechanical cultivators are to be used.
7. Longer rows are usually easier to cultivate than short rows with fewer turns for the wheel hoe, garden tractor or big equipment.
8. It has been suggested that if you don't like weeds, plant the crops in alphabetical order. The weeds will then be close to the back row!

Once the planning has been done you are ready for action. Obtain a provincial or local list of recommended cultivators and purchase cultivars adapted to your needs (freezing, storing) and conditions.

Don't take gardening too seriously to begin with. It should be something to enjoy. Many vegetables will grow very well on their own simply as a consequence of seed being put into the ground. Don't be overawed by the experts. Don't be discouraged by mistakes. Everyone makes mistakes — even the experts. There will be many little ones and occasionally some big ones. Call or write your Department of Agriculture; the Departments of Plant Science and/or Horticulture at your University; Federal and Provincial Research Stations and, to some extent, parks departments (although they are usually better qualified in the fields of ornamental horticulture then they are in vegetable crops). Join a Horticultural Society or Garden Club or assist in the establishment of one if there isn't one in your community. Asking questions of neighbors with

NEW YORK STATE
Planting-Table for Vegetables–

reprinted from GARDEN MAGAZINE, 1905

A QUICK AND EASY GUIDE, SHOWING WHEN AND HOW TO PLANT SEVENTY-FOUR KINDS OF VEGETABLES, HOW TO CULTIVATE THEM, WHEN THEY ARE READY TO EAT, AND WHAT THEY ARE GOOD FOR—ADAPTED TO THE SMALL HOME GARDEN CULTIVATED BY HAND OR BY WHEEL-HOE

MARCH is the time to sow seeds in the hotbed, if you want to gain a month; sow in April and-you may gain a fortnight. Outdoors sow seeds of a few hardy vegetables, especially peas, and even corn, on March 15th, for if they are ruined by frost it is no matter in the home garden. Moreover the young plants can be covered on frosty nights by newspapers or boxes. What is folly for the truck gardener is good sense for the home gardener, because he has so little at stake. *Dates for Planting.*—These can never be exact, but there is no use in being hopelessly vague. Therefore, New York City is taken as a standard. In reckoning dates, allow six days difference for every hundred miles of latitude. North, later; South, earlier. The following dates are those of an average season

ALMANAC	THE SOIL	TREES AND WEATHER	TENDER VEGETABLES	HARDY VEGETABLES
March 1st	Too wet	Trees dormant	Sow indoors	Sow indoors
March 15th	Best land fit to work	Red maple in bloom	Sow indoors	Sow indoors—risk a few out
April 1st	Plowing season begins	Trees budding	Sow indoors	Sow all early crops outdoors
April 15th	Most of plowing done	Leaves out	Sow early crop outdoors	Sow main crop: transplant early
May 10th	Weeds humping	All danger of frost past	Sow main crop: transplant early	Sow last of main crop

Tender Vegetables.—The following are injured by even a slight frost and should, therefore, not be planted until all danger of frost is past, *i. e.*, about May 1st. Beans, corn, cucumber, egg-plant, melon, okra, pepper, pumpkin, squash, sweet potato, tomato.

Hardy Vegetables.—The following, if sown outdoors, or properly hardened before transplanting from hotbeds, will endure a frost. About April 15th is the time to sow the main crop; March 15th the early crops (outdoors). Asparagus, beet, borecole, broccoli, Brussels sprouts, cabbage, carrot, cauliflower, celery, corn-salad, cress, endive, horse-radish, kale, kohlrabi, leek, lettuce, onions, parsley, parsnip, pea, radish, rhubarb, salsify, sea-kale, spinach, turnip. (List from Bailey's "Horticulturist's Rule-Book.")

NAME OF VEGETABLE	WHEN TO PLANT — Early Crop	WHEN TO PLANT — Main Crop	DEPTH TO PLANT S=Seeds R=Roots (inches)	DISTANCE APART when thinned or transplanted (inches)	READY TO EAT (Figures mean days) Early Crop	READY TO EAT Main Crop	OTHER POINTS What the Vegetables are good for. Hints on Soil, Watering, Thinning, Transplanting, etc.
Artichoke, Globe	March indoors	April May	S. ½ R. deeper than before	24 x 36 24 x 36	Sept. to frost	Next summer	The green scales around the flower bud are boiled and eaten with mayonnaise. When done bearing for the year, the flowering stem may be cut back to ground and shoots blanched like celery. Plant shoots and suckers deeper than before.
Artichoke, Jerusalem		April May	S. ¼ R. 2	12 x 36		Aug. to frost	Tubers may be eaten raw or cooked in various ways. Blossom, a diminutive sunflower.
Asparagus		April	S. 1 R. 6	12 x 36 24 x 48	Third year	April June	Two-year-old roots may yield some the second year. Beds last twenty years or more. In the fall cut down all foliage and burn; then dress with salt and cover with one foot manure. Cut beds lightly the first yield. Sow radish with asparagus.
Basil, sweet		March	¼	8 x 8		June	Just before blooming cut back to three inches. Dry the leaves and bottle. Fragrance like cloves.
Beans, Lima (on poles)	Apr. 15 outdoors	May 1	2	Hills or drills 36 x 36		Aug. to frost	Plant seed with eye down. Manure should be used only to hold moisture; bone meal and wood ashes make a good fertilizer. Seeds may be started in frames, in pots, cans or sods, to secure an extra early crop.
Beans, snap and wax (dwarf)	May to Aug.		2	12 x 24	July	45	Plant one inch apart, eye down. Late varieties bear longer than early. A deeply dug rich soil is best. Do not use fresh manure. Three or four plantings enough for a small family. Sow every two weeks for succession.
Beets	Mar. 15 outdoors	Mar. 20 to Aug. 1	1½	9 x 18	May to June	50	Soak seeds over night in warm water; this hastens germination. The "thinnings" may be transplanted.
Borage		April May	¼	10 x 10		20	Young leaves used in flavoring beverages or boiled for greens. Flavor resembles cucumber. Blossom very pretty. Excellent food for bees.
Brussels sprouts		May June	½	12 x 18		150	Cultivate the same as a late cabbage. Young buds in angles of leaves are eaten. Should be touched with frost before picking.
Cabbage	Feb. Mar. indoors Apr. outdoors	May June	½	24 x 36	July	100	Ground should be very rich; liquid manure applied during August very beneficial. Late crop may be stored for winter use in cold cellars or pits.
Cardoon		May June	1	24 x 36 36 x 48		120	Roots perennial, need slight protection over winter. Leaves blanched; used like asparagus or served as a salad; bitter. When grown, the leaves must be blanched by tying, wrapping in matting or banking up. Blanching requires four weeks.

LARGE PARIS ARTICHOKE.

TUBERS OF JERUSALEM ARTICHOKE.

vegetable growing experience can flatter your neighbor — but don't make a nuisance of yourself.

As the garden begins to flourish, here are a few practical hints to consider.

To get white cauliflower curds, tie the leaves together at the top or bend some down toward the curd to shade it from the sun. Unshaded curds will be more creamy yellow than white.

To lessen splitting of cabbage heads when they have matured, give the heads a twist to break some of the small feeder roots.

Swiss Chard, as a greens crop, can be harvested from the outside in over a fairly long period. Because of its perishability it is generally not available from supermarkets. It is much better for summer growth than spinach.

Leaf lettuce will be ready to eat sooner and is more nutritious than the crisp head lettuce.

Regardless of how nicely you space out the seed of red beet or chard, some thinning may be necessary. The "seed" you sow is really a small dried "fruit" that usually contains more than one "seed".

The shape of carrots is generally influenced more by cultivar than by growing conditions. If you prefer long, slender slightly tapered carrots, don't buy and seed a short, fat cultivar.

Reduce the temperature of sweet corn immediately after harvest to retain the sweetness and do the harvesting in the cool of evening or morning rather than in the heat of the day.

Vegetable gardening is really a rewarding experience!

SIMPLE CONTRIVANCE FOR STRIKING CUTTINGS.

PLANTING TABLE FOR NEW YORK STATE

E. L. Fullerton

reprinted from GARDEN MAGAZINE, 1905

CELERIAC.

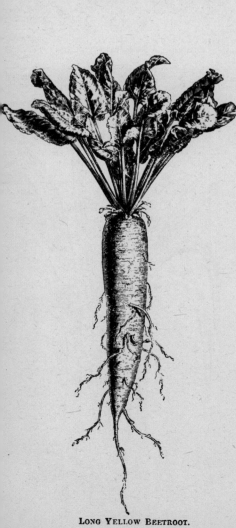

LONG YELLOW BEETROOT.

NAME OF VEGETABLE	WHEN TO PLANT		DEPTH TO PLANT S=Seeds R=Roots (inches)	DISTANCE APART when thinned or transplanted (inches)	READY TO EAT (Figures mean days)		OTHER POINTS What the Vegetables are good for. Hints on Soil, Watering, Thinning, Transplanting, etc.
	Early Crop	Main Crop			Early Crop	Main Crop	
Carrots	Apr.	June July	½	6 x 18	July	100	Sandy loam full of humus; dig deep. Early crop must be used as soon as large enough. Late crop may be stored in sand in cellars, or stored in pits.
Catnip		May Sept.	½	24 x 20		40	Young leaves used for seasoning herb. Whole plant may be dried when in blossom.
Celery and Celeriac	Feb. in hotbed	Apr. in seedbox June	Barely cover	6 x 48	As greens May	170	Two transplantings necessary from first to second seed beds, two inches apart, then into trenches in the garden where it is to be blanched. Rich soil; plenty of moisture. Celeriac a large rooted celery. Eat the root. Do not blanch.
Chards, Swiss Beet	April	May	½	12 x 18	June	60 to frost	A beet whose leaves instead of root are eaten. The whole leaf eaten like spinach, mixed with sorrel; or the midrib, which is white and fleshy, served like asparagus.
Chervil		Apr. June	Barely cover	4 x 12		45	Used like parsley, beautiful foliage; rather sweetish flavor. Chief ingredient of "fines herbes."
Chervil, turnip-rooted		Aug. to Sept.	½	4 x 12		Before frost	Root edible; treat like carrot; pull roots just before frost and store in a pit or root cellar. Cover with sand to exclude the air.
Chicory	Apr.	Apr. to June	½	6 x 12		100	Leaves boiled like spinach or blanched and used as salad. Roots ground, dried and used as substitute for coffee.
Chives		Apr.	R. as deep as before	12 x 12		May to Oct.	Leaves cut and used as flavoring; a delicate onion. Roots set as deep as before.
Corn, sweet	Apr. to May	June Aug. 1	1 early 1½ late	Hills 36 x 48 Drills 24 x 48, 9 x 36	July	55 to 90	Fairly rich soil, thorough cultivation, plenty of moisture at roots for best success. Tall varieties require more room than short.
Corn-salad	Aug. to Sept.	Apr. to May	¼	6 x 6	Next spring	60	In the fall when sown, protect with leaves or straw over winter. A good substitute for lettuce.
Cress, garden		Apr.	¼	3 x 6		40	Good substitute for water cress.
Cress, water		Apr. to June	S. or R. in shallow water	6 x 6	June	28	Excellent for brooks. Can be grown in garden.
Cucumber	Feb. to Mar. indoors	May to July	½	36 x 36 42 x 60		50 to 75	Plant several seeds in an inverted sod for early crop. In hills in the garden for late. Sow six seeds to hill endwise, thin to two best plants to a hill. Thin garden plants when striped beetle has disappeared.
Dandelion		Apr.	¼	6 x 6		Next March	Leaves boiled like spinach or blanched and used as salad.
Dock		Apr.	R. 2	10 x 10		90	Also propagated from seeds. The roots should be used like salsify and when young. Bitter. Used by Japanese. Set crown two inches deep.
Eggplant	Feb. indoors	Mar. indoors	½	36 x 36	July	80 to 160	Plenty of heat to start plants, then accustom them to cold before setting into garden. Rich soil and moisture needed.
Endive	Mar. indoors	Apr. to Sept.	¼	12 x 12	June	45	Fine appetizing salad, beautiful and delicious. When thirty days up tie with raffia and blanch the heart. Do this when dry—very susceptible to rot.
Fennel		Apr.	¼	8 x 18		20 to frost	Hardy perennial. Leaves used in salads and sauces. Sickish sweet flavor, beautiful foliage. Seed used for flavoring.
Garlic		Apr.	R. 1	6 x 12 12 x 12		Summer	Used for flavoring; very strong.
Horseradish		Sept. to May	R. 2 to 4	12 x 30		Mar. to Mar.	Roots grated and covered with vinegar, and tightly bottled. Best in rich, moist soil. Will grow anywhere.
Kale		Sept. to May	½	12 x 18		150	Do not sow in September, where winters are very severe. Old plants remain out all winter, freezing not injuring. Young leaves may be gathered from time to time or whole plant used at once. Heavy feeder.
Kohlrabi		May to June	½	6 x 12 12 x 24		115	Form of cabbage partaking of turnip's peculiarities. A large fleshy stem just above ground boiled and eaten like turnips. Cultivate like cabbage, but better not transplant.

Pisum sativum, dwarf form.

PLANTING TABLE FOR NEW YORK STATE

reprinted from *GARDEN MAGAZINE*, 1905

-Egyptian Onions.

Greater Leek-Garlick.

NAME OF VEGETABLE	WHEN TO PLANT		DEPTH TO PLANT S=Seeds R=Roots (inches)	DISTANCE APART when thinned or transplanted (inches	READY TO EAT (Figures mean days)		OTHER POINTS What the Vegetables are good for. Hints on Soil, Watering, Thinning, Transplanting etc.
	Early Crop	Main Crop			Early Crop	Main Crop	
Lavender		Apr. to May.	S. ¼ R. as deep as before	8 x 18 36 x 36		Before flowers fade	Set roots as deep as before. Used more as perfume than as flavoring. Flowers should be dried quickly in shade. Perennial. Cover in winter with six inches of litter.
Leeks		Apr. to May Sept.	1	5 x 12		110	Thin when four inches high to one and one-half inches; transplant when eight inches high to five inches. Transplant into trench with several inches of old manure. Set plants deep as possible without covering crown and below the surrounding surface. Fill in trench as plants grow, to blanch stalks.
Lettuce	Feb. to Mar. indoors	Apr. to Aug. 1	¼	8 x 12 12 x 24	Apr. May	21 to 65	Two distinct types; cabbage, close heading; cos, open and tall. Finely powdered rich soil necessary. Apply hen manure, or nitrate of soda when seedlings are several inches high. May be used green or dried for seasoning.
Marjoram, sweet		Apr. to May	¼	12 x 12		30 to 120	Perennial, grown as annual. Leaves and tips of shoots used for seasoning.
Martynia		Apr. to May	1	36 x 36		65	Will not germinate until ground is warm. Seed pods used for pickling in the same manner as cucumbers. Plant in hills or seed beds.
Mint, spear		Apr. to May	R. as deep as before	6 x 6		21	Delightful, refreshing herb, much used as a sauce to accompany lamb and mutton. Needs no protection over winter. Set roots as deep as before.
Mushrooms	Aug. outdoors	Sept. to Feb. indoors	Spawn 2	8 x 8	Nov.	Dec. to Feb.	Must be grown in hot manure in the dark. What looks like the whole plant is eaten.
Muskmelon	Apr. indoors	May to June	1	60 x 60	Aug.	100	Give plenty of well-rotted manure in hills at planting. Nitrate of soda in frequent minute quantities.
Mustard	Nov.	Apr. to May	¼			20	Sow in drills, or broadcast in a bed. Rake the bed or roll it so seed may be partly covered at least. Used in salads or boiled like spinach.
Okra	Mar. indoors	May	1½	18 x 24	July	100	Young seed pods stewed, also used in gumbo soup. Extra early crop by sowing in pots or cans in March or April in the house or coldframe. Plant seeds four inches apart at first.
Onion	Aug.	Apr.	S. ½ R. 2	12 x 20	May	100 to 160	May be raised from spring or fall sown seeds or sets. Chicken manure or nitrate of soda may be used.
Orach		Apr. to May	½	24 x 36		50	Used like spinach. Thin when six inches high and use thinnings. Coarser and ranker in flavor than spinach. Grows very tall when going to seed.
Parsley	Sept.	Apr.	½	6 x 12	May	50 to 75	Protect September-sown seed with leaves and branches over winter. Leaves used as garnish and for flavoring. Soak seeds over night in warm water.
Parsley, turnip-rooted		Apr. to Sept.	¼	5 x 12		120	Large turnip-like root with parsley flavor. Delightful addition to soups and stews. May be stored with carrots for winter. If sown in September may be wintered over with a covering of hay or straw.
Parsnip		Apr.	½	6 x 18		140	Seeds do not need very rich soil; should be dug fine and deep. Roots may be left out over winter or dug just before ground freezes and stored in sand (to exclude air) in a cool room or cellar.
Peanut	Mar. indoors	Apr.	1½	6 x 18		Oct.	Do not use manure in soil. Peanuts need lime, phosphoric acid and light sandy soil. The stems of the blossoms elongate, go into the ground and ripen the pods there.
Peas	Mar. outdoors	Apr. to June and in Oct.	3	6 x 24 18 x 36	May	36 to 80	Plant early kinds in double rows six to nine inches apart. Brush or wire make good supports. Use only very well rotted manure. Moisture very necessary. Plant in trench six inches deep, cover three inches and fill in as plants grow.
Peppers		Mar. indoors	½	15 x 24 18 x 30		140 to 150	Sweepings from a hen-house, or guano, the best fertilizer for peppers. Mix thoroughly with soil and apply again on top after plants have been set out three weeks.
Pe-tsai and Pak-choi		Apr. to May	½	12 x 12		40	Sometimes called Chinese Cabbage; used as salad in all ways lettuce is used. Extremely good, crisp and tender Pak-choi has a taller leaf and the midrib is used like chards and asparagus.

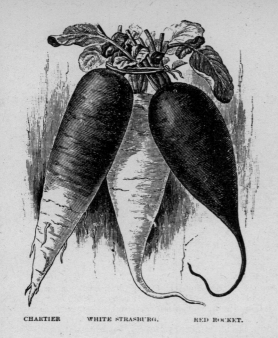

CHARTIER   WHITE STRASBURG.   RED ROCKET.

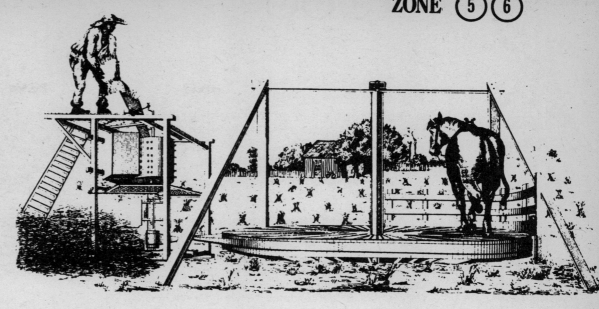

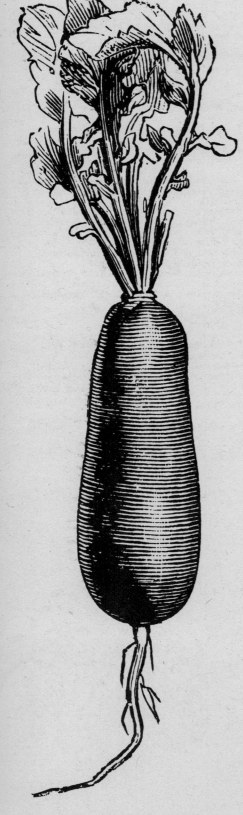

CHINA ROSE
RADISH.

PLANTING TABLE FOR NEW YORK STATE

reprinted from GARDEN MAGAZINE, 1905

NAME OF VEGETABLE	WHEN TO PLANT		DEPTH TO PLANT S=Seeds R=Roots (inches)	DISTANCE APART when thinned or transplanted (inches)	READY TO EAT (Figures mean days)		OTHER POINTS What the Vegetables are good for. Hints on Soil, Watering, Thinning, Transplanting, etc.
	Early Crop	Main Crop			Early Crop	Main Crop	
Potato	Apr. indoors	May to June	2 early 5 late	12 x 24 18 x 36	July	100 to 130	May be planted whole or cut to one, two or three eyes. Extra early crops may be secured by sprouting eyes in a warm, light room, or starting in a coldframe. Spray vines as soon as they appear, with Bordeaux and Paris green.
Pumpkin		May to June	1½	108 x 108		120	Be sure to plant as far away from melons and squashes as possible, as they will cross-fertilize. Make the hills very rich before sowing seed.
Purslane		Apr.	¼	4 x 12		90	Used by the French as a boiled green. Grows upright, unlike the common weed of our gardens.
Radish	Feb. to Mar. indoors	Apr. to Sept.	½	2 x 8 4 x 18	20 Apr.	30 to 45	Sow in seed boxes or hotbed for early crop and every ten days for succession. The same in the garden later. Sow winter radishes in fall. Don't use fresh manure. Growth must be rapid and soil loose and fine.
Rampion		May	Scatter	3 x 8		Oct. to Feb.	A poor sort of radish. Press the seed into the soil. This is about the smallest seed known.
Rhubarb		Sept. to Oct.	R 4	24 x 48 48 x 48		May to July	Set roots into very rich soil. Cover in winter with one foot of manure. Chicken-house sweepings particularly good. Dig under in spring. Break the stems, do not cut them.
Roquette		Apr. to May	¼	10 x 12		40	A most horrible odor as well as flavor. Copious watering modifies the strong taste. Flower white, not particularly striking.
Sage		May to Sept.	R. as deep	12 x 18			Set crown of plant just above surface. A flavoring herb. To dry, cut off branches, tie in bunches and hang in sun or warm room; powder and bottle immediately. Use the green leaves all summer. Ready to dry in September.
Salsify		Apr.	¼	4 x 18		Oct. through winter	Roots very long and straight. Sometimes called Oyster Plant. May be dug and stored for the winter like carrots, or left in the ground.
Scolymus		Apr.	½	6 x 18		170	Belongs to the thistle family. Leaves very prickly, variegated. Roots used like salsify.
Scorzonera	Sept.	Apr.	½	6 x 18		190	A delicate salsify; earth should be deeply dug and finely powdered, for the roots are long and straight.
Spinach		Mar. to May	1	6 x 12 6 x 18	Mar.	30	Protect slightly over winter. Will give two or three pickings. Sow often—say ten days—for succession.
Spinach, New Zealand		May	1	12 x 24		40	Not a true spinach, but a very good substitute, growing well through the hot, dry weather; an excellent midsummer green. Soak seed in hot water over night.
Squash	Mar. indoors	May to June	1	Bush 36 x 48 Late 72 x 96	60 to 65 July	125 Aug. to Sept.	Use plenty of manure, well rotted, and give ample space. Can be planted between rows of late corn, or in hills among other early and main crops, for vines to occupy ground later.
Sweet Potato	Mar. indoors		R. 3	18 x 24 24 x 36		120 to 150	A light, warm soil, long season and good seed. Whole potato must be sprouted under glass; sprouts cut off and transplanted.
Tarragon		Apr. to May	R. as deep	12 x 12		30 to 120	Young leaves a good addition to salads; may be dried and used as seasoning. Set plants same depth. Green leaves used in making tarragon vinegar.
Tomato	Feb. to Mar. indoors	Apr. seedbed	½	36 x 48 48 x 60	July	150	Have garden ground very rich and mellow. Do not keep seedlings too warm; they should be stocky and not too tall. Plant in hotbed, seedbox, pots or cans.
Turnip	Apr.	June to Aug.	½	4 x 18 8 x 30	June	70	Round or flat; white. May be stored over winter like carrots. Much more delicate than small rutabaga.
Udo		Mar. to Apr.	Broadcast	10 x 24		Second year Nov. to Dec.	When leaves turn brown in the fall, cut off and pile two feet of earth over the roots. In about forty days the shoots will appear and be ready to cut. Used like celery. The forcing variety can be blanched in a coldframe during the winter. Ready November and December of the second year.
Watermelon		May	1	96 x 96		100	Place plenty of well-rotted manure in the hills before sowing, or plant around a sunken half barrel. Pinch off ends of vines after fruit has set. Plant seeds edgewise, eyes down, ten in a hill.

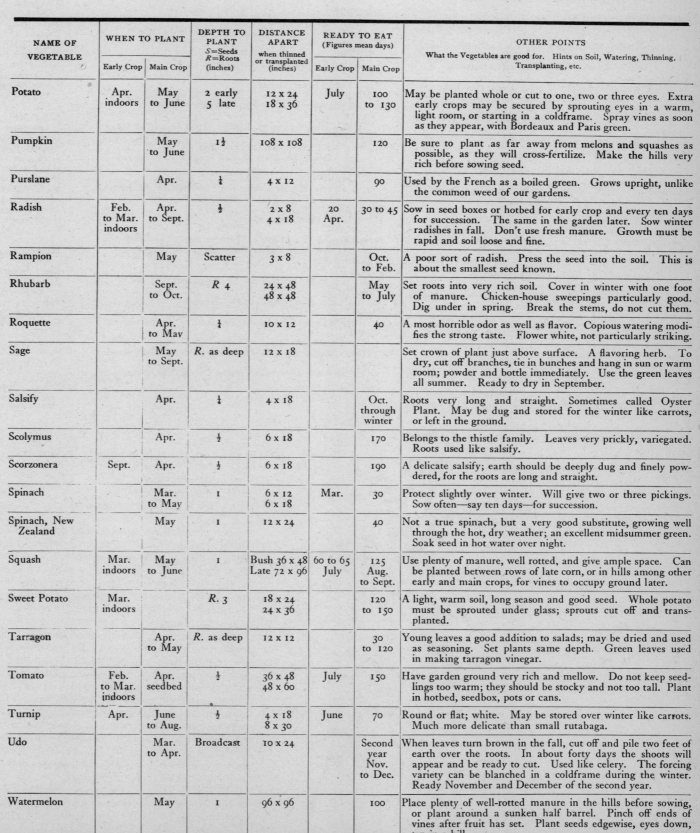

ZONE ④ ⑤ ⑥

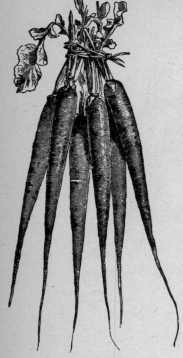

LONG SCARLET.

OLIVE SCARLET. OLIVE WHITE. FRENCH BREAKFAST.

SELECTED LIST OF VEGETABLE VARIETIES FOR HOME GARDEN USE IN NEW YORK STATE

P.A. Minges and L.D. Topoleski
Department of Vegetable Crops
N.Y. State College of Agriculture
Ithaca, New York 14853

Vegetable varieties for home garden use should be of relatively high quality, be dependable, embody disease resistance when possible, and have a fairly long harvest period. For many of the crops, it is recognized that other varieties not listed are satisfactory and that some might perform even better under certain conditions. Hybrid varieties often are available from only one seedsmen, so in some cases two similar hybrids are listed in order to provide more than one seed source.

Some of these varieties are widely adapted, others are best only for the Northeast.

ASPARAGUS
Mary Washington, Waltham Washington
BEANS
Green, bush — Tendercrop, Topcrop, Bush Blue Lake, Tendergreen
Wax, bush — Kinghorn Wax, Eastern Butterwax, Earliwax, Midas
Green, pole — Kentucky Wonder, Dade, Blue Lake
Lima — Fordhook 242, Thorogreen, King of the Garden (Pole)
Horticultural — Dwarf Horticultural, French's Horticultural
Edible Soy Beans — Prize, Verde, Kanrich (all rather late)
BEETS
Detroit Dark Red, Early Wonder, Ruby Queen
BROCCOLI
Green Comet (H), Waltham 29 (fall), Green Sprouting
BRUSSELS SPROUTS
Long Island Improved, Jade Cross (H)
CABBAGE
Early — Golden Acre—Yellows Resistant, Emerald Cross (H), Early Marvel, Sun-up, (H; YR)
Midseason — King Cole (H; YR), Market Prize (H), Savoy King (H), Red Acre, Ruby Ball (H)
Late — Danish Ball head, Chieftan Savoy
CARROTS
Nantes, Royal Chantenay, Danvers 126, Spartan Bonus (H), Baby Fingers
CAULIFLOWER
Snowball Imperial, Improved Super Snowball, Self-Blanche, Purple Head
CELERY
Summer Pascal, Utah 52-70
CHINESE CABBAGE
Michihli, Hybrid G, Crispy Choy (loose leaf)
CUCUMBERS
Slicing — Marketmore 70 (MR), Tablegreen 65 (MR), Sweet Slice (MR, H, non-bitter), Gemini (H; MR), Patio Pik (small vine)
Pickling — Wisconsin SMR 18, Pioneer (H;MR), Bravo (white spine, H, MR), Spartan Salad (MR; non-bitter)

EGGPLANT
Early — Early Beauty (H), Long Tom (H)
Main season — Black Magic (H), Jersey King (H), Black Beauty
ENDIVE
Salad King, Full Heart Batavian, Green Curled
KALE
Vates, Dwarf Green Curled
KOHLRABI
Early White Vienna, Early Purple Vienna
LETTUCE
Head — Ithaca, (spring), Fairton, Great Lakes 659 (fall), Big Boston
Bibb — Buttercrunch, Summer Bibb
Leaf — Prizehead, Black Seeded Simpson, Salad Bowl, Parris Island Cos
MUSKMELON
Burpee Hybrid, Harper Hybrid (F), Gold Star (H, F), Iroquois (F), Delicious 51 (F), Saticoy Hybrid (F; powdery mildew res.)
MUSTARD
Green Wave, Florida Broadleaf
ONIONS
Sweet Spanish (transplants), Ebenezer (sets), Downing Yellow Globe, Early Yellow Globe, Beltsville Bunching, White Bunching
PARSLEY
Perfection, Moss Curled, Plain Leaf, Banquet, Bravour
PARSNIPS
All American, Harris' Model, New No. 10
PEAS
Early — Greater Progress or Progress No. 9, Sparkle, Early Market
Midseason — Frosty
Late — Green Arrow, Perfected Freezer 60 (MR), Wando, Lincoln
Edible Pod — Dwarf Gray Sugar, Dwarf White Sugar

PEPPER
Ace (H), Green Boy (H), Canape (H), Early Calwonder, Staddon's Select (MR), Sweet Banana, Yolo Wonder (MR), Italian Sweet, Hungarian Wax (hot), Eastern Rocket (hot)
POP CORN
White Cloud (H), Peppy Hubrid, Eastern Sunburst
POTATOES
Katahdin, Sebago, Kennebec, Norland (early, red-skinned & scab res.)
PUMPKIN
Jack-O-Lantern, Spookie, Connecticut Field, Howden's Field, Youngs Beauty, Cinderella (bush)
RADISH
Champion, Cherry Belle, Scarlet Knight, Sparkler, Icicle, China Rose
RHUBARB
Canada Red, Ruby, Valentine, German Wine, Victoria
SWISS CHARD
Fordhook Giant, Rhubard, Lucullus
SPINACH
Spring — Long Standing Bloomsdale, America, Dark Green Bloomsdale
Fall — Virginia Blight Resistant Savoy, Savoy Hybrid
Summer — New Zealand
SQUASHES
Summer — Zucchini Hybrids, Burpee's Golden Zucchini, Seneca Prolific (H), Seneca Butterbar (H), White Bush Scallop, Patty Pan (H)
Winter — Waltham Butternut, Buttercup, Emerald (bush Buttercup), Golden Delicious, Bush Ebony, Table King (bush acorn), Table Queen, Gold Nugget
SWEET CORN: Yellow (all are hybrids)
Early — Earlivee, Royal Crest, Early Sungold, Golden Beauty, Sundance, Earlibelle, Yukon, Tastyvee
Main season — Jubilee, Seneca Chief, NK199, Stylepak, Gold Cup, Golden Cross Bantam, Illini Xtra Sweet
Bicolor — Sprite (early), Butter and Sugar, Harmoney (midseason), Sweet Sue (main season)
White — Silver Queen (late), Glacier (midseason), Silver Sweet (early, trial)
TOMATOES
Early — VF Gardener, Fireball VR, New Yorker (V), Springset (H;V;F), Presto (H; cherry)
Midseason — Supersonic (H;V;F), Better Boy (H;V;F), Jet Star (H;V;F), Sunray (yellow), Small Fry (H; cherry; V;F)
Late — Big Boy (H), Ramapo (H;V;F), Roma VF (pear)
TURNIPS
Purple Top White Globe, Amber Globe (F)
RUTABAHAS
American Purple Top, Laurentian
WATERMELON
Top Yield (H;F), Summer Festival (H), Sugar Baby, Crimson Sweet (F), Seedless Hybrid 313

H = Hybrid, but not used if indicated in name;
MR = Mosaic resistant;
F = Fusarium resistant;
YR = Yellows resistant;
V or VR = Verticillium resistant

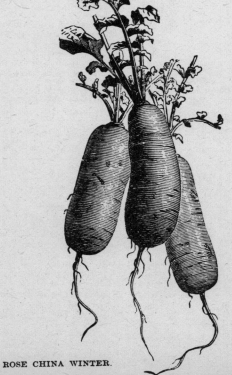

ROSE CHINA WINTER.

Seed of the above varieties may be available locally at garden supply stores or in packet display racks, or they may be ordered from seed houses. All of these varieties are listed by at least one of the seed firms located in New York or Pennsylvania who publish annual retail vegetable seed catalogs.

For crops normally transplanted, transplants usually are available locally at garden supply stores or nurseries, though all the desired varieties may not be in stock. Sometimes home gardeners will have to grow their own transplants in order to obtain the varieties of their choice. Crops normally transplanted in New York State include: tomatoes, peppers, eggplant, celery, Brussels sprouts, cauliflower, broccoli, cabbage, muskmelons and watermelons. Lettuce, cucumbers, and onions also can be transplanted, especially for early planting and harvest. It is best to use transplants for the Sweet Spanish type of onions, all early varieties, and for others when large bulbs are desired.

The supply of onion seed is very limited for the 1975 season so many varieties are unavailable. Some varieties of other crops are in short supply.

RAMPION.

64

Suggested Vegetable Varieties
IOWA-MIDWEST

Iowa State University
Cooperative Extension Service

ZONE ④ ⑤

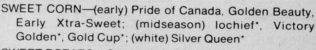

ASPARAGUS—Mary Washington*, Paradise*

BEAN, SNAP—Tendercrop*, Bush Blue Lake 274*, Spartan Arrow*, Topcrop*, (purple) Royalty*

BEAN, BUSH WAX—Kinghorn*, Goldcrop*, Cherokee*, Pencil Pod Black Wax*

BEAN, BUSH LIMA—Fordhook 242*, Henderson Bush*

BEAN, POLE—Kentucky Wonder*

BEET—Ruby Queen, Detroit Dark Red; (yellow) Burpee Golden

BROCCOLI—Premium Crop*, Green Comet*, Spartan Early*

BRUSSELS SPROUTS—Jade Cross*

CABBAGE—(early) Emerald Cross, Golden Acre Y. R.; (midseason) Copenhagen, Stonehead, Baby Head; (late) Wisconsin Hollander; (red—early) Ruby Ball; (red—midseason) Redhead

CARROT—Royal Chantenay, Danver's Half-Long, Nantes, Tender-Sweet

CAULIFLOWER—Early Snowball*, Snow Crown*, Purple Head*, Royal Purple*

CELERY—Golden Self-Blanching, Fordhook

CHINESE OR CELERY CABBAGE—Michihli

COLLARDS—Vates, Georgia

CUCUMBER—(slicing) Victory, Triumph, Spartan Valor, Sweet Slice; (pickling) Wisconsin S.M.R. 18, Ohio MR-17, Mariner

EGGPLANT—Jersey King, Royal Knight, Early Beauty, Black Beauty

ENDIVE—Green Curled, Salad King, Broad Leaved Batavian

KALE—Vates*, Dwarf Blue Scotch*

KOHLRABI—White Vienna, Purple Vienna

LEEK—American Flag

LETTUCE—Salad Bowl, Slobolt, Oak Leaf, Buttercrunch, Black Seeded Simpson, Ruby, Green Ice

MUSKMELON—Burpee Hybrid, Gold Star, Saticoy, Harper Hybrid, Supermarket

MUSTARD—Greenwave*, Tendergreen*

OKRA—Clemson Spineless*, Dwarf Green Long Pod*

ONION—Yellow Globe, Southport Red Globe, Sweet Spanish, White Bermuda, Yellow Bermuda, Ebenezer

PARSLEY—Paramount, Moss Curled

PARSNIP—All American, Hollow Crown

PEA—Little Marvel*, Freezonian*, Frosty*, Greater Progress*, Green Arrow*, Wando*; (edible podded or "snow" peas) Dwarf Gray Sugar*, Sweet Pod*

PEPPER—Canape, Bell Boy, Tokyo Bell, Vinedale, Early Bountiful; (yellow-fruited peppers) Golden Calwonder, Wonder Gold

POTATO—(red) Norland; (white) Superior, Kennebec, Norgold Russet, Irish Cobbler

PUMPKIN—Small Sugar, Jack-O-Lantern, Connecticut Field, Big Tom; (bush type) Cinderella; (for edible seeds) Lady Godiva

RADISH—Champion, Cherry Belle, Scarlet Knight, Comet, Sparkler, French Breakfast, White Icicle; (winter radish) Long Black Spanish, Round Black Spanish, China Rose

RHUBARB—McDonald*, Canada Red*, Honey-red*

RUTABAGA (OR SWEDE TURNIP)—American Purple Top, Macomber

SALSIFY—Mammoth Sandwich Island

SPINACH—America*, Bloomsdale*

SQUASH, SUMMER—Zucchini Hybrids* (Aristocrat, Ambassador, Elite, Chefini, Burpee Hybrid, etc.); Yellow Summer Crookneck*, Yellow Summer Straightneck*, Seneca Butterbar*, Patty Pan*

SQUASH, FALL and WINTER—Acorn, Table King (bush acorn), Waltham Butternut*, Gold Nugget* (bush), Kindred*, Buttercup*, Golden Delicious*, Hubbard*

SWEET CORN—(early) Pride of Canada, Golden Beauty, Early Xtra-Sweet; (midseason) Iochief*, Victory Golden*, Gold Cup*; (white) Silver Queen*

SWEET POTATO—Centennial, Goldrush, Nemagold

SWISS CHARD—Fordhook Giant*, Lucullus*

TOMATO—(early) Springset, Setmore, Spring Giant, Big Early Hybrid, Fantastic; (main crop) Cardinal, Surprise, Heinz 1350, Burpee VF, Supersonic, Jetstar, Avalanche, Big Boy; (container or garden types, medium-size fruits) Pixie, Patio; (container or garden types, cherry fruited) Small Fry, Red Cherry, Yellow Plum, Tiny Tim; (yellow fruit) Jubilee, Mandarin, Sunray

TURNIP—Just Right, Purple Top White Globe, Tokyo Cross

WATERMELON—Crimson Sweet, Dixie Queen, Petite Sweet, Sugar Baby, Seedless Hybrids

Other Plants Sometimes Grown In the Vegetable Garden

Black-eyed Peas, Celeriac, Chives, Citron, Dill, Edible Soybeans, Endive, Fava or Broad Beans, Flowering Cabbage, Flowering Kale, Garbanzo (Chick Pea), Garden Cress, Garden Huckleberry, Garlic, Gherkin Cucumber, Gourds, Guinea Bean, Herbs, Horseradish, Huck Tomato (Ground Cherry), Indian Ornamental Corn, Jerusalem Artichoke, Lemon Cucumber, Luffa Sponge Gourd, Mung Bean, New Zealand Spinach, Peppers (hot), Shallots, Strawberry Popcorn, Sunflower, Tampala, Turk's Turban Squash, Vegetable Gourd, Vegetable Spaghetti, Vine Peach, Witloof Endive (Chicory), Yard Long Bean.

MAP-ZONES OF PLANT HARDINESS pp 58

CONNECTICUT CORN HOUSE.

WISCONSIN

The Vegetable Garden
O.B. Combs and John A. Schoenemann
Cooperative Extension Program

MAP-ZONES OF PLANT HARDINESS pp 58

Vegetable	PLANTING TIME Indoors at Madison*	Outdoors at Madison*	SEEDS or PLANTS For 1 foot of row	For 100 feet of row	Depth Plant (Inches)	Between Rows (Inches)	SPACING Between Plants (Inches)	Amount for One Person	Days to First Harvest
ASPARAGUS		April 15	½ plant	50 plants	6 to 8	36 to 40	24	30 to 40 ft.	2 years
BEAN, bush lima		May 25	6 to 8	8 oz.	1 to 1½	24 to 30	3 to 4	30 to 40 ft.	70 to 80
BEAN, bush snap		May 10	6 to 8	8 oz.	1 to 1½	24 to 30	2 to 3	50 to 60 ft.	50 to 60
BEAN, pole snap		May 10	4 to 6	6 oz.	1 to 1½	30 to 36	4 to 6	20 to 30 ft.	60 to 65
BEET		April 15	10 to 15	1 to 1¼ oz.	¾ to 1	15 to 18	2 to 3	24 ft.	50 to 60
BROCCOLI	March 15	May 1 (plants)		40 to 50 plants	3 to 4	36 to 42	24 to 30	2 plants	60 to 70
BRUSSELS SPROUTS		May 15 (seeds)	2 to 4 seeds	1/8 oz.	¾ to 1	24 to 30	12 to 18	2 plants	90 to 100
CABBAGE, Early	March 15	May 1 (plants)		50 to 67 plants	3 to 4	24 to 30	12 to 18	5 plants	60 to 70
CABBAGE, Late		May 15 (seeds)		40 to 50 plants	3 to 4	30 to 36	18 to 24	12 plants	90 to 100
CARROT		April 15	30 to 40	¼ oz.	½ to ¾	15 to 18	1 to 2	48 ft.	60 to 70
CAULIFLOWER	March 15	May 1 (plants)		50 to 70 plants	3 to 4	24 to 30	12 to 18	4 to 6 plants	50 to 60
CELERY	March 15	May 20 (plants)	2 plants	200 plants	2 to 2½	36 to 42	4 to 6	5 to 6 plants	100 to 110
CHARD		April 15	10 to 15	1 to 1¼ oz.	¾ to 1	15 to 18	2 to 4	3 ft.	40 to 50
Chinese CABBAGE		June 20 (seeds)	15 to 20	1/8 oz.	¾ to 1	24 to 30	6 to 10	3 ft.	90 to 100
CUCUMBER		May 20	4 to 6	1/3 oz.	1 to 1½	42 to 48	4 to 6	12 ft.	50 to 60
EGGPLANT	March 15	June 1 (plants)		40 to 50 plants	3 to 4	36 to 42	24 to 30	2 to 3 plants	70 to 80
KOHLRABI		April 15	10 to 15	1/8 oz.	¾ to 1	15 to 18	3 to 4	5 to 6 ft.	50 to 60
LETTUCE, Head	March 15	May 1 (plants)	1 plant	100 plants	2 to 2½	18 to 24	8 to 10	3 to 4 plants	60 to 70
LETTUCE, Leaf		April 15	25 to 30	¼ oz.	¼ to ½	15 to 18	2 to 3	12 ft.	40 to 50
MUSKMELON	May 1	May 20 (plants)	4 to 6	1/3 oz.	¾ to 1	42 to 48	6 to 8	10 to 12 plants	80 to 90
ONION, Plants	Feb. 20	May 1	3 to 4 plants	300 to 400	2 to 2½	*15 to 18	2 to 3	12 ft.	110 to 120
ONION, Seeds		April 15	20 to 25	¼ oz.	½ to ¾	15 to 18	2 to 3	12 ft.	90 to 100
ONION, Sets		April 15	6 to 12 sets	3 to 4 lbs.	2 to 3	15 to 18	1 to 2	12 ft.	40 to 50
PARSLEY	March 15	May 1 (plants)	1 plant	100 plants	2 to 3	18 to 24	6 to 8	1 plant	30 to 40
PARSNIP		April 15	20 to 25	½ oz.	½ to ¾	24 to 30	2 to 3	12 ft.	100 to 120
PEA		April 15	12 to 15	1 lb.	1½ to 2	15 to 18	1 to 2	145 ft.	60 to 70
PEPPER	March 15	June 1 (plants)		50 to 70 plants	3 to 4	30 to 36	12 to 18	2 plants	60 to 70
POTATO, Early		April 15	1 piece	9 lbs.	3 to 4	30 to 36	12	100 ft.	80 to 100
POTATO, Late		April 15	1 piece	9 lbs.	4 to 6	36 to 42	12	300 ft.	130 to 140
PUMPKIN, Pie	May 1	May 20 (plants)	2 to 4	½ oz.	1 to 1½	48 to 60	15 to 18	4 ft.	90 to 110
PUMPKIN, Summer "Squash"		May 20	2 to 4 seeds	2 oz.	1 to 1½	48 to 60	15 to 18	2 plants	50 to 60
RADISH		April 15	20 to 25	1 oz.	½ to ¾	15 to 18	1	36 ft.	25 to 30
RHUBARB		April 15	1/3 plant	35 plants	6 to 8	48 to 54	36	2 plants	2 years
RUTABAGA		June 15	15 to 20	1/8 oz.	¾ to 1	24 to 30	6 to 8	12 ft.	100 to 110
SPINACH		April 15	20 to 25	1 oz.	½ to ¾	15 to 18	1 to 2	24 ft.	40 to 50
SQUASH, Winter	May 1	May 20 (plants)	2 to 4	2 oz.	1 to 1½	72 to 84	15 to 18	12 ft.	90 to 120
SWEET CORN		May 10	3 to 4	4 oz.	1 to 1½	30 to 36	8 to 10	84 ft.	65 to 90
TOMATO	March 15	May 20 (plants)		28 to 34 plants	3 to 4	36 to 42	24 to 36	12 plants	65 to 80
TURNIP		April 15	20 to 30	¼ oz.	½ to ¾	18 to 24	2 to 3	10 to 15 ft.	60 to 70

*Plant about one week later in central and about two weeks later in northern Wisconsin.

ILLINOIS VARIETIES

Crop	Amt. for 100 ft. of row	Variety recommended for use in Illinois	Days to harvest	Resistant to
Asparagus (plants)	75–100	Mary Washington	..	Rust
		Waltham Washington	..	Rust
		Tetra	..	....
beans (green)	¾ pound	**Bush, green**		
		Contender	53	Mosaic, powdery mildew
		Tendergreen, some types	53	Mosaic, rust, bacterial blight and wilt
		Harvester	54	Mosaic, rust
		Blue Lake	56	Mosaic
		Bush, yellow		
		Cherokee Wax	52	Rust, mosaic
		Gold Crop	54	Rust, mosaic
beans (lima)	½ pound	Henderson Bush	65	....
		Thorogreen	65	....
		Fordhook 242	75	....
		Thaxter	75	Downy mildew
Beets	1 ounce	Ruby Queen (main crop)	53	....
		Detroit Dark Red (main crop)	58	Boron deficiency
Broccoli	50–75 plants or 1 packet seed	Green Comet[a]	60	....
		Early Spartan	60	....
		Premium Crop[a]	60	Yellows
		Royal Purple Head	90	....
Brussels sprouts / Cabbage	1 packet / 75–100 plants or 1 packet seed	Jade Cross	83	
		Market Dawn[a]	63	Yellows
		Emerald Cross	63	....
		Resistant Golden Acre	64	Yellows
		Market Topper[a]	73	Yellows
		Market Prize[a]	76	Yellows
		Greenback	78	Yellows
		King Cole[a]	78	Yellows
		Resistant Danish	105	Yellows
		Vanguard II (Savoy)	72	Yellows
		Savoy King[a]	85	Yellows
		Red Danish (Red)	95	Yellows
		Red Ball[a]	70	Yellows
		Red Head[a]	75	Yellows
Carrots	¼ ounce	Nantes	70	....
		Gold Pak	75	....
		Waltham Hicolor	75	....
		Spartan Sweet[a]	75	....
Cauliflower (Ill. only)	50–75 plants or 1 packet seed	Early Snowball	54	Yellows
		Snow Crown[a]	60	....
Chard	1 ounce	Fordhook Giant	57	....
		Ruby	60	....
Chinese cabbage	1 packet	Michihili	70	....
Collards	1 packet	Green Glaze	75	....
Cucumbers	½ ounce	**Pickling**		
		Spartan Dawn[b]	51	Mosaic, scab
		SMR	53	Mosaic, scab
		Slicing		
		Burpee Hybrid[a]	60	Mosaic, downy mildew
		M & M Hybrid[a]	60	Mosaic, downy mildew
		Challenger[a]	65	Mosaic
		Saticoy[a]	65	Mosaic, downy mildew
		Poinsett	65	Downy mildew, leaf spot, anthracnose
Eggplant (plants)	50–75	Black Magic	72	....
		Black Beauty	80	....
		Burpee Hybrid[a]	80	....
		Long Tom[a] and Short Tom[a]	75	....
Kohlrabi	¼ ounce	Early White Vienna	55	....
Lettuce	1 packet	Grand Rapids	45	Multiple resistance
		Prize Head	45	....
		Simpson	45	....
		Salad Bowl	45	Multiple resistance
		Slobolt	45	Tipburn
		Summer Bibb (slow bolting)	62	Tipburn
		Ruby	47	Tipburn
		Buttercrunch	70	....
		Cos or Romaine	75	....
Muskmelons	½ ounce	Burpee Hybrid[a]	85	....
		Gold Star[a]	87	Fusarium wilt
		Harper Hybrid[a]	86	Alternaria blight, Fusarium wilt, mosaic
		Harvest Queen	90	Fusarium wilt
		Pride of Wisconsin	90	
		Samson (hybrid)	75	Powdery mildew, Fusarium wilt
		Supermarket[a]	88	Fusarium wilt, powdery mildew
Mustard	1 packet	Green Wave	45	....

Crop	Amt. for 100 ft. of row	Variety recommended for use in Illinois	Days to harvest	Resistant to
Okra	1 packet	Emerald	55	....
Onions	2–3 lb.	**Sets**		
		Ebenezer	90	....
		Golden Globe	90	
	¼ ounce	**Seed**		
		*Early Harvest (hybrid)	90	
		Early Yellow Globe	95	Fusarium rot, smudge
		*Empire	100	
		Downings Yellow Globe	110	Smudge
		Southport Red Globe	110	Fusarium rot, smudge
		Brown Beauty (hybrid sweet Spanish)	110	Pink root
		*Sweet Spanish	115	....
	300	**Seedlings (transplants)** *Starred items for seedlings		
	¼ ounce	**Bunching**		
		Evergreen	60	Smut, pink root
Parsley (seed)	1 packet	Moss Curled	70	
		Paramount	80	Septoria blight
		Plain or Italian	80	....
Parsnips (seed)	1 packet	Hollow Crown	125	....
		All American	125	....
		Model	125	Root canker
Peas	1 pound	**Early**		
		Wisconsin Early Sweet	60	Fusarium wilt, mosaic
		Little Marvel (W.R.)	62	Fusarium wilt, mosaic
		Thomas Laxton	63	Fusarium wilt
		Medium to late (for northern Ill. only)		
		Frosty	64	Fusarium wilt
		Pride	64	Fusarium wilt
		Early Perfection (W.R.)	67	Fusarium wilt, mosaic
		Sparkle	70	Fusarium wilt, mosaic
		Wando	71	Fusarium wilt, root rot
		Green Arrow	68	Downy mildew, Fusarium wilt
Peppers	50–75 plants or 1 packet seed	**Sweet Stuffing**		
		Tasty	70	....
		Bellringer	75	Mosaic
		Calwonder	72	
		Keystone Resistant Giant	76	Mosaic
		Yolo Wonder	76	Mosaic
		Sweet Banana	70	....
		Sweet Salad		
		Sunnybrook	73	Bacterial spot
		Hot		
		Hungarian Wax	70	....
		Long Red Cayenne	70	Bacterial spot
		Red Chili	84	Bacterial spot
		Cherry	75	....
Popcorn	1 ounce	Illinois Hulless (white)	95	
		White Cloud (white)	95	
		Purdue 216A (yellow)	105	
		South American Mushroom (yellow)[a]	105	
Potatoes (seed)	10–12 lb.	**Early**		
		Irish Cobbler	100	
		Medium to late (for northern Ill. only)		
		Norland	105	Scab
		Red Pontiac	110	
		Katahdin	120	Verticillium wilt
		Kennebec	120	Late blight
		Ontario	120	Late blight, scab, Verticillium wilt
		Sebago	120	Late blight
Pumpkins (seed)	1 ounce	Cinderella (bush)	100	
		Small Sugar	110	
		Spookie	110	
		Jack-o-Lantern	112	
		Connecticut Field	115	
Radishes (seed)	1 ounce	Early Scarlet Globe	22	
		Burpee White	23	
		Champion	23	
		Comet	23	
		Red Prince	23	Fusarium wilt
		Icicle	25	

[a] F₁ hybrids. [b] All female hybrid; 10 percent regular seed must be added for pollination.

A MISSOURI BARN.

ILLINOIS SUGGESTED VEGETABLE VARIETIES

Crop	Amt. for 100 ft. of row	Variety recommended for use in Illinois	Days to harvest	Resistant to
Rhubarb (plants)	30–50	Mac Donald	..	....
		Valentine	..	....
		Victoria	..	....
Spinach (seed)	1 ounce	**Spring**		
		Giant Nobel	43	....
		Bloomsdale Long Standing	44	....
		America	45	....
		Summer		
		New Zealand	65	....
		Fall		
		Early Hybrid 7	37	Blight, downy mildew
		Old Dominion	41	Blight
Squash (seed)	1 ounce	**Summer**		
		Butterbar	50	....
		Early Prolific Straightneck	50	....
		Zucchini	60	....
		Fall		
		Table King (Bush Acorn)	85	....
		Table Queen (Acorn)	90	Bacterial wilt
		Butternut	95	Bacterial wilt
		Buttercup	100	Bacterial wilt
		Winter		
		Kinred	100	....
		Delicious	100	Bacterial wilt
		Banana	105	....
		Hubbard	110	....
Sweet corn (seed)	1–2 ounces	**Early**		
		Early Sun Glow	68	....
		Golden Beauty	68	Bacterial wilt
		Spring Gold	68	....
		Earlibelle	68	....
		Main crop		
		Sprite	78	....
		F-M Cross (Bicolor)	78	Bacterial wilt
		Gold Cup	80	Helminthosporium
		Gold Winner	80	....
		Honey and Cream (Bicolor)	80	....
		Seneca Chief	80	Bacterial wilt
		N.K. 199	82	Bacterial wilt
		Golden Cross Bantam	82	Bacterial wilt, smut
		Stylepak	84	....
		White varieties		
		Silver Queen	85	Helminthosporium, bacterial wilt
		Country Gent., Ill. 13	90	Bacterial wilt, smut, rust
Sweet potatoes (plants)	100	Allgold	..	Wilt, internal cork, black rot, soil rot
		Centennial	..	Internal cork, wilt
		Goldrush	..	Wilt, white rust
		Nemagold	..	Root-knot, internal cork, wilt
		Porto Rico (Unit 1 strain)	..	....

Crop	Amt. for 100 ft. of row	Variety recommended for use in Illinois	Days to harvest	Resistant to
Tomatoes	35–75 plants or 1 packet seed	**Medium early**		
		Heinz 1350	75	Fusarium wilt, Verticillium wilt
		Cardinal	75	....
		Fantastic	76	Cracking
		Campbell 1327	75	Fusarium wilt, Verticillium wilt
		Jet Star[a]	72	Fusarium wilt, Verticillium wilt
		Main crop		
		Better Boy[a]	78	Fusarium wilt, Verticillium wilt, root knot
		Ramapo[a]	85	
		Supersonic[a]	79	Fusarium wilt, Verticillium wilt
		Manapal	82	Multiple resistance
		Manalucie	83	Multiple resistance
		Burpee VF	80	Fusarium wilt, Verticillium wilt
		Special purpose		
		Roma VF (paste)	76	Fusarium wilt, Verticillium wilt
		Red Cherry (large and small)	75	....
		Gardener's Delight (small fruit)	75	....
		Sugar Lump (small fruit)	75	....
		Jubilee (yellow)	80	....
		Golden Boy (yellow)	80	....
		Tiny Tim (dwarf)	68	....
		Patio[a], Pixie[a] (compact, medium fruit)	75	....
		Small Fry[a] (compact, small fruit)	72	Verticillium wilt, Fusarium wilt
		Delicious (extra large)	90	....
		Beefeater[a] (extra large)	90	....
Turnips	¼ ounce	Seven Top (for greens)	42	....
		Purple Top White Globe (main crop)(fall)	55	
Watermelons (seeded)	½ ounce	Sugar Baby	85	....
		Summer Festival[a]	85	....
		Charleston Gray	90	Fusarium wilt, anthracnose
		Crimson Sweet	90	Fusarium wilt, anthracnose
		Sweet Princess	96	Fusarium wilt, anthracnose
		Yellow Baby[a]	75	....
Watermelons (seedless)		Tri-X 313	90	Anthracnose
		Triple Sweet[a]	90	Anthracnose

[a] F_1 hybrids.

Illinois Extension Service

FLORIDA VEGETABLE VARIETIES

Crop	Varieties	Seed/Plants 100' of Row	Spacing in Inches Rows	Spacing in Inches Plants	Seed Depth Inches	Planting Dates in Florida (inclusive) North	Central	South	Plant Hardiness†	Pounds Yield 100'	Days to Harvest
Beans, Snap	Extender, Contender, Harvester, Wade, Cherokee (wax)	1 lb.	18-30	2-3	1½-2	Mar.-Apr. Aug.-Sept.	Feb.-Mar. Sept.	Sept.-Apr.	T	45	50-60
Beans, Pole	Dade, McCaslan, Kentucky Wonder 191 Blue Lake	1 lb.	40-48	15-18	1½-2	Mar.-June	Feb.-Apr.	Jan.-Feb.	T	80	60-65
Beans, Lima	Fordhook 242, Concentrated, Henderson, Jackson Wonder, Dixie Butterpea, Florida Butter (Pole)	1 lb.	26-48	12-15	1½-2	Mar.-June	Feb.-Apr.	Sept.-Apr.	T	50	65-75
Beets	Early Wonder, Detroit Dark Red	1 oz.	14-24	3-5	½-1	Sept.-Mar.	Oct.-Mar.	Oct.-Feb.	H	75	60-70
Broccoli	Early Green Sprouting, Waltham 29, Atlantic	60 plts. (¼ oz.)	30-36	16-22	½-1	Aug.-Feb.	Aug.-Jan.	Sept.-Jan.	H	50	60-70
Cabbage	Copenhagen Market, Marion Market, Badger Market, Glory of Enkhuizen, Red Acre, Chieftan Savoy	65 plts. (¼ oz.)	24-36	14-24	½	Sept.-Feb.	Sept.-Jan.	Sept.-Jan.	H	125	70-90
Carrots	Imperator, Gold Spike, Chantenay, Nantes	½ oz.	16-24	1-3	½	Sept.-Mar.	Oct.-Mar.	Oct.-Feb.	H	100	70-75
Cauliflower	Snowball Strains	55 plts. (¼ oz.)	24-30	20-24	½	Jan.-Feb. Aug.-Oct.	Oct.-Jan.	Oct.-Jan.	H	80	55-60
Celery	Utah 52-70, Florida Pascal	150 plts. (¼ oz.)	24-36	6-10	¼-½	Jan.-Mar.	Aug.-Feb.	Oct.-Jan.	H	150	115-125
Chinese, Cabbage	Michihli, Wong Bok	125 plts. (¼ oz.)	24-36	8-12	¼-½	Oct.-Jan.	Oct.-Jan.	Nov.-Jan.	H	100	75-85
Collards	Georgia, Vates	75 plts. (¼ oz.)	24-30	14-18	½	Feb.-Mar. Sept.-Nov.	Jan.-Apr. Sept.-Jan.	Sept.-Jan. Aug.-Nov.	H	150	50-55
Corn, Sweet	Silver Queen (white) Gold Cup Golden Security, Seneca Chief, many others	¼ lb.	34-42	12-18	½	Mar.-Apr.	Feb.-Mar.	Jan.-Feb.	T	15	80-85
Cantaloupes	Smith's Perfect, Seminole, Edisto 47, Gulfstream	1 oz.	70-80	48-60	¾	Mar.-Apr.	Feb.-Apr.	Feb.-Mar.	T	150	75-90
Cucumbers	Poinsett, Ashley (slicers), Wisconsin SMR 18, Pixie (picklers)	1 oz.	48-60	15-24	½-¾	Feb.-Mar.	Feb.-Mar. Sept.	Jan.-Feb.	T	100	50-55
Eggplant	Florida Market	30 plts. (¼ oz.)	36-42	36-48	½	Feb.-Mar. July	Jan.-Feb. Aug.-Sept.	Dec.-Feb.	T	200	80-85
Endive-Escarole	Deep Heart Fringed, Full Heart Batavian	1 oz.	18-24	8-12	¾	Feb.-Mar. Sept.	Jan.-Feb. Sept.	Sept.-Jan.	H	75	90-95
Kohlrabi	Early White Vienna	½ oz.	24-30	3-5	½	Mar.-Apr. Oct.-Nov.	Feb.-Mar. Oct.-Nov.	Nov.-Feb.	H	100	50-55
Lettuce (Crisp) (Butterhead) (Leaf) (Romaine)	Premier, Great Lakes types, Bibb, Matchless, Sweetheart, Prize Head, Ruby, Salad Bowl, Parris Island Cos, Dark Green Cos	½ oz.	12-18	12-18	¾	Feb.-Mar. Sept.	Jan.-Feb. Sept.	Sept.-Jan.	H	75	50-80
Mustard	Southern Giant Curled, Florida Broad Leaf	1 oz.	14-24	4-8	½	Jan.-Mar. Sept.-May	Jan.-Mar. Sept.-Nov.	Sept.-Mar.	H	100	40-45
Okra	Clemson Spineless, Perkins Long Green	2 oz.	24-40	18-24	1-2	Mar.-Apr. Aug.	Mar.-May Aug.	Feb.-Mar. Aug.-Sept.	T	70	50-55
Onions (Bulbing)	Excel, Texas Grano, Granex, White Granex, Tropicana Red	400 plts. or sets 1 oz. seed	12-24	3-4	¾	Jan.-Mar. Aug.-Nov.	Jan.-Mar. Aug.-Nov.	Jan.-Mar. Sept.-Nov.	H	100	100-130
(Green)	White Portugal or White types, Shallots (Multipliers)	800 plts. or sets 1½ lb. seed	12-24 18-24	1½-2 6-8	¾ ¾	Aug.-Mar. Aug.-Jan.	Aug.-Mar. Aug.-Jan.	Sept. Mar. Sept.-Dec.	H H	100 100	50-75 75-105
Parsley	Moss Curled, Perfection	1 oz.	12-20	8-12	¾	Feb.-Mar.	Dec.-Jan.	Sept.-Jan.	H	40	90-95
Peas	Little Marvel, Dark Skinned Perfection, Laxton's Progress	1½ lbs.	24-36	2-3	1-2	Jan.-Feb.	Sept.-Mar.	Sept.-Feb.	H	40	50-55
Peas, Southern	Blackeye, Brown Crowder, Bush Conch, Producer, Floricream, Snapea, Zipper Cream	1½ lbs.	30-36	2-3	1-2	Mar.-May	Mar.-May	Feb.-Apr.	T	80	70-80
Pepper (Sweet) (Hot)	Calif. Wonder, Yolo Wonder, World Beater Hungarian Wax, Anaheim Chili	60 plts. (¼ oz.)	20-36	18-24	½	Feb.-Apr.	Jan.-Mar.	Jan.-Feb. Aug.-Oct.	T	50	70-80
Potatoes	Sebago, Red Pontiac, Kennebec, Red LaSoda	15 lbs.	36-42	12-15	4-8	Jan.-Feb.	Jan.	Sept.-Jan.	SH	150	80-95
Potatoes, Sweet	U. S. No. 1, Porto Rico, Georgia Red, Goldrush, Nugget, Centennial	80 plts.	48-54	18-24	—	Mar.-June	Feb.-June	Feb.-June	T	75	120-140
Radish	Cherry Belle, Comet, Early Scarlet Globe, White Icicle, Sparkler (white tipped)	1 oz.	12-18	1-2	¾	Oct.-Mar.	Oct.-Mar.	Oct.-Mar.	H	40	20-25
Spinach	Virginia Savoy, Dixie Market, Hybrid 7	2 oz.	14-18	3-5	¾	Oct.-Nov.	Oct.-Nov.	Oct.-Jan.	H	40	40-45
Spinach, Summer	New Zealand	2 oz.	30-36	18-24	¾	Mar.-Apr.	Mar.-Apr.	Jan.-Apr.	T	40	55-65
Squash, (Summer)	Early Prolific Straightneck, Early Summer Crookneck, Cocozelle, Zucchini, Patty Pan	2 oz.	42-48	42-48	½	Mar.-Apr. Aug.	Feb.-Mar. Aug.	Jan.-Mar. Sept.-Oct.	T	150	45-60
(Winter)	Alagold, Table Queen, Butternut	2 oz.	90-120	48-72	2	Mar.	Feb.-Mar.	Feb.-Mar.	T	300	95-105
Strawberry	Florida 90, Tioga, Sequoia	100 plts.	36-40	10-14	—	Sept.-Oct.	Sept.-Oct.	Oct.-Nov.	H	50	90-110
Tomatoes (Large Fruited)	Manalucie,‡ Homestead-24, Indian River, Floradel,‡ Tropired, Big Boy‡ Walter,	35 plts. (¼ oz.)	40-60	36-40	½	Feb.-Apr. Aug.	Feb.-Mar. Sept.	Aug.-Mar.	T	125	75-85
(Small Fruited)	Large Cherry, Roma (Paste)	70 plts. (½ oz.)	36-48	18-24	½	Feb.-Apr. Aug.	Feb.-Mar. Sept.	Aug.-Mar.	T	200	75-85
Turnips	Japanese Foliage (Shogoin) Purple Top White Globe	1 oz.	12-20	4-6	½-¾	Jan.-Apr. Aug.-Oct.	Jan.-Mar. Sept.-Nov.	Oct.-Feb.	H	150	40-50
Water- (Large) melon (Seedless) (Small)	Charleston Gray, Congo, Jubilee, Crimson Sweet Tri-X 317 New Hampshire Midget, Sugar Baby	2 oz.	90-120	60-84	2	Mar.-Apr.	Jan.-Apr.	Feb.-Mar.	T	400	80-100

Other Vegetables for the Garden.—Jerusalem artichoke, Brussels sprouts, cassava, chayote, chives, dandelion, dasheen, dill, fennel, garbanzo bean, garlic, herbs, kale, leek, luffa gourd, honeydew melons, and rutabaga. Note — globe artichokes, asparagus, and rhubarb not well adapted to Florida.

† H—Hardy, can stand frost and usually some freezing (32°F) without injury.
SH—Slightly hardy, will not be injured by light frosts.
T—Tender, will be injured by light frost.
‡ Tomato varieties best adapted to staking.

J.M. Stephens in cooperation with workers of the Institute of Food and Agricultural Sciences. University of Florida, Gainesville

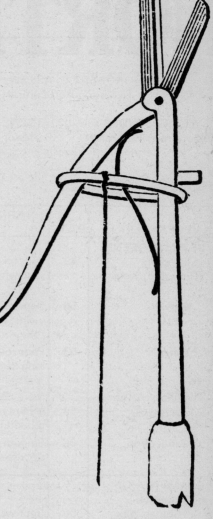

GRAPE GATHERER.

Common headed or set Leek.

ZONE ③ ④
NORTH DAKOTA

ROBERT G. ASKEW
Extension Horticulturist

EARL SCHOLZ
Associate Horticulturist

NEAL HOLLAND
Professor of Horticulture

Agricultural Experiment Station

RECOMMENDED VEGETABLES

VEGETABLE	DAYS	VARIETAL DESCRIPTION AND USE
BEANS (GREEN)*		
Topcrop *(Freezing, See p. 4)	49	Pods round, medium green, somewhat curved; use fresh, frozen.
Provider	50	Dependable, heavy early yields; pods straight and smooth, fully round.
Wade	53	Pods round, dark green, straight; long harvest season. Use fresh or frozen.
Improved Tendergreen	54	More productive than Tendergreen type. Pods set well off the ground.
Tendercrop	56	Smooth, meaty dark green, with slow seed development.
BEANS (WAX)*		
Topnotch Golden Wax	50	Improved Golden Wax, pods thick-flat, golden-yellow, stringless. Use fresh or frozen. Early.
Pencil Pod Black Wax	56	Popular for home freezing. Very productive.
Goldcrop	60	1974 AAS. Excellent variety for freezing or for eating freshly cooked.
BEANS (POLE)*		
Blue Lake	67	Good climber with pod set from base to top of plant. Excellent for freezing.
BEANS (LIMA)*		
Henderson Bush	65	Dependable. Very uniform growth. Table or freezing.

VEGETABLE	DAYS	VARIETAL DESCRIPTION AND USE
BEETS*		Beet greens are an excellent source of Vitamin A.
Ruby Queen	52	Round with smooth shoulders and crown. Small tap root.
Detroit Dark Red	58	Globe shaped, skin dark red, flesh deep blood red.
Sweetheart	60	Extra sweet, tender, solid red color, good for pickling.
BROCCOLI*		Plant transplants. Use while buds are small and tight; do not allow heads to flower.
Cleopatra	55	Hybrid, large, compact central head; vigorous side shoots. Long period of production.
Spartan Early	55	Dark green head, short stem; spring or fall planting.
BRUSSEL SPROUTS*		Requires aphid control. Plant transplants.
Jade Cross Hybrid	85	Plants tall; sprouts firm, medium size.
CABBAGE		Plant transplants. (Early varieties may be direct seeded.)
Stonehead	60	Extra early, extremely solid interior, very compact six inch heads 3½ lbs. Family size.
Golden Acre YR	63	Round, light green, small (3 lbs.) Family size.
Ruby Ball	68	For trial, Hybrid. Firm round heads of dark red color. Small core.
Market Topper	73	Good quality, uniform heads and has the ability to stand without bursting.

Barley Eares

WHITE LEAF BEETROOT.

LEEK.

North Dakota State University
Cooperative Extension Service Fargo, North Dakota /

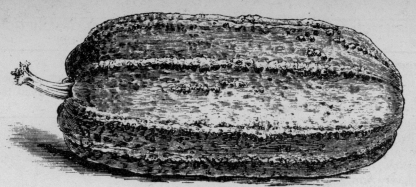

PATAGONIAN GOURD.

CELERIAC, or
TURNIP-ROOTED CELERY.

NORTH DAKOTA

VEGETABLE	DAYS	VARIETAL DESCRIPTION AND USE
CABBAGE (cont.)		
Market Prize	76	Vigorous, uniform hybrid. Blue-green color.
Savoy King	82	Hybrid Savoy. Large, uniform heads, flattened, globe-shaped. Good quality. Split resistant. For salads.
CARROTS*		Excellent source of Vitamin A.
Nantes (Coreless)	68	Narrow cylindrical shape; medium long with slight taper and blunt tip. Crisp and tender.
Red Cored Chantenay	68	Reddish-orange, uniform, tender and sweet. Core about same color as flesh. For storage, freezing and canning.
CAULIFLOWER*		Set out transplants about May 15-20. All must be tied as soon as curd is visible.
White Horse	55	Very uniform with deep mounded firm snow white heads.
Snowball Variety M.	59	Extra vigorous, large smooth white heads, well protected by inner fold leaves. Be certain to choose type M.
SWISS CHARD		
Lucullus	50	Leaves yellowish green, heavily crumpled with cream colored slender midrib.
SWEET CORN*		
Royal Crest	64	First early hybrid. Short shanked with very good taste qualities.
Earliking	66	Ears 7" long, 12 row and well filled. Excellent first crop.
Golden Rocket	67	Early market corn. Good quality.
Morning Sun	72	Sweet tender kernels, outstanding in maturity class.
Golden Beauty	73	Uniform ears, 6 to 7½ inches long. Does well in short season.
Yukon	75	For trial. 8 to 9 inch ears. Good quality, tender pericarp.
Golden Cross Bantam	84	Plant tall, good quality; standard hybrid sweet corn. Fresh or freeze.
NK 199	84	For trial, late. Widely used by processors, home and market gardeners. Excellent quality.
Early Xtra Sweet	85	Super sweetness. Corn retains sweetness over a reasonably long period. Keep isolated from other corns.

VEGETABLE	DAYS	VARIETAL DESCRIPTION AND USE
CUCUMBERS Pickling:		
Spartan Dawn	50	Gynoecious hybrid. Semi-blocky, slightly tapered toward blossom end, dark green, dark spines.
Improved Long Green	63	Desirable for ripe pickles. Home garden use.
CUCUMBERS Slicing:		
Spartan Valor	60	Gynoecious hybrid. Dark green, 8-9 inches long. Good producer.
Victory	60	1972 AAS. Disease resistant, gynoecious hybrid. Good yielder, excellent quality.
Marketer	66	Dark green, smooth. Good color, long, slim shape and firm flesh.
Marketmore	70	High yield, straight. Scab and cucumber mosaic tolerance.
LETTUCE (BUTTER-HEAD)		
Summer Bibb	62	Slow bolting; can be grown almost throughout the season.
Buttercrunch	64	Vigorous, very attractive, delicious leaves with tender ribs.
LETTUCE (HEAD)		
Pennlake	72	Head medium to small. Interior crisp and firm. Best variety.
LETTUCE (LEAF)		
Black Seeded Simpson	44	Large, upright, compact, leaves light green, broad and frilled. Good quality.
Grand Rapids	45	Popular loose leaf variety capable of continuous growth under adverse conditions.
MUSKMELON		Set out 20 day old transplants for early crop. For more earliness and higher yield, use clear plastic mulch.
Minnesota Midget	60	Early, small fruited (4 inch) short vine type.
Delicious 51 Seeds	90	Large oval to round fruits; coarsely netted. Orange flesh; quality good in warm seasons.
Transplants	78	
Gold Star Hybrid Seeds	94	Oval fruit, medium size, heavily netted with firm rind; flesh orange. High quality despite adverse weather.
Transplants	80	

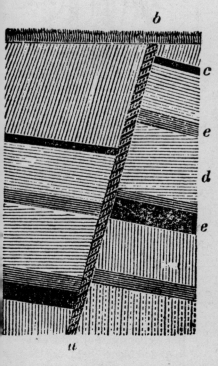

Although many strains and varieties of garden vegetables may be acceptable, some have consistently performed well under our conditions. Suggested vegetable varieties for North Dakota are listed in order of maturity (number of days required to produce a usable product) for each kind of vegetable. Seasonal weather conditions and growing location can influence the amount of time required to mature a given vegetable. We suggest selection of short season varieties for northern sections of the state. Vegetables starred (*) suitable for freezing; all varieties acceptable.

VEGETABLE	DAYS	VARIETAL DESCRIPTION AND USE
ONIONS		Direct seed or transplant for larger size.
Early Yellow Globe	98	Medium large, globe to flattened globe, skin tough, light yellow, flesh firm and white.
Ebenezer (sets)	105	Medium size thick-flattened, small neck. Skin yellow, flesh fine textured, mild, very firm.
Southport Red Globe	110	Medium large, deep globe shaped small neck, skin dark glossy red, flesh fine grained.
Southport White Globe	110	Medium size, globe shaped. Skin pure white, flesh ivory-white, fine grained, mild flavor.
PARSNIPS* Improved Hollow Crown	95	10 inches long by 3 inches thick at the shoulder. Vigorous, good quality.
PEAS* Little Marvel	62	Plants about 1½ feet tall; productive. 7-8 peas per pod.
Lincoln	66	Large vine, pod 3-3½ inches. 5-7 per pod. Long season harvest.
Wando	70	Large upright vine, peas medium large; good quality.
PEPPERS* Merrimack Wonder	63	Set out transplants. Very early. Yields under adverse conditions.
Lincoln Belle	65	Sets good quality fruit during cooler early summer season. Large, blocky, high quality.
PUMPKIN* Cinderella	95	Bush-type pumpkin, 10 inch, attractive.
Cheyenne Bush	100	Small, bright orange, flesh solid, deep golden yellow. Excellent for pies.
Sugar Pie	108	6-8 lbs., dark orange. Excellent for canning and pie.
RADISHES Cherry Belle	24	Globe to round, bright cherry-red; solid and crisp.
Champion	28	Large, remains crisp and firm to fairly large size.
White Icicle	30	Roots 4½-5 inches long, smooth, slender, tapering. White skin, mild.

VEGETABLE	DAYS	VARIETAL DESCRIPTION AND USE
SPINACH America	52	Leaves glossy, thick, dark green, rounded, heavily savoyed. Slow bolting type.
SQUASH* Summer: Aristocrat	48	1973 AAS. Bush plants. High quality, early.
Early Prolific Straightneck	51	Plants bush, fruits straight, tapered; skin fairly smooth, lemon yellow. Fresh or frozen.
Seneca Butterbar	51	Hybrid, long cylindrical shape. Bush plants. Yellow fruit, productive.
Winter (Storage): Gold Nugget	90	Bush type. Fruits small, flattened medium thick, golden yellow flesh. Hard orange skin. Bake whole.
Emerald	100	1973 NDSU introduction, bush type, very thick orange flesh of high quality.
Buttercup	100	Large vine-green skin with turban Excellent quality.
Kindred	100	Short vine, productive. Fruits red-orange; medium size.
TOMATOES Cherry-type: Droplet	65	Early, fruits solid, crack resistant Holds well on vine after ripening.
Small Fry	68	Hybrid cherry tomato. Color is bright, 1-inch fruit, marble round in shape.
Standard: Lark	59	Early, globe-shaped fruits, small to medium size. Good red interior color. NDSU 1973 Introduction.
New Yorker	59	Early, medium size fruits. Very susceptible to leaf diseases. Keep sprayed with fungicide.
Starfire	65	Early determinate variety - globe shaped fruits.
Sheyenne	66	Medium to large fruits, globular, smooth. Very productive-main crop tomato.
Firesteel	68	Scarlet, large, smooth flattened to deep globe, firm flesh.
Spring Giant	68	Hybrid, vigorous vines. Large, deep globular fruits.
Cannonball	71	1973 NDSU Introduction. Large, deep globe-shaped fruits. Excellent quality.

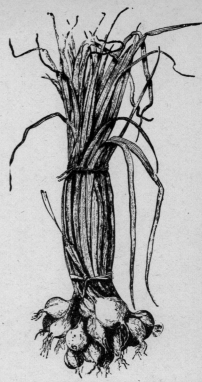

Bunch onions, grown from seed.

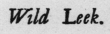

Wild Leek.

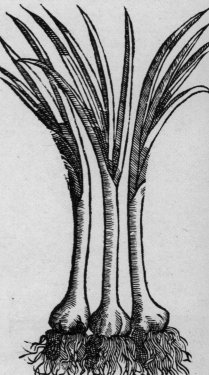

NORTH DAKOTA

BOARD RAFTER.

VEGETABLE	DAYS	VARIETAL DESCRIPTION AND USE	VEGETABLE	DAYS	VARIETAL DESCRIPTION AND USE
WATERMELON			F₁ Hybrid Top Yield for trial		Set out 20 day old transplants for early crop. For more earliness and higher yield, use clear plastic mulch.
New Hampshire Midget	80	Fruits small (2-4 lbs.) oval-round, skin medium green, darker green netting. Fair quality, seedy.	Seeds	90	Vigorous, disease resistant. Oval shaped, light-green skinned, about 20 lbs. Good quality. High yielding and early production when transplanted on clear plastic mulch.
Sugar Baby	88	Ice box variety, oval-round; skin black green with faint darker strips. Very attractive when cut.	Transplants	80	

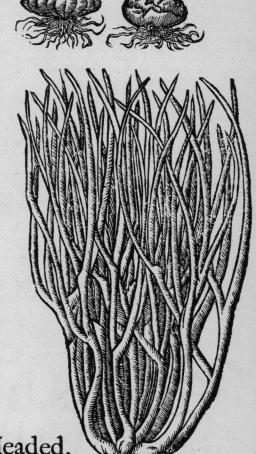

Scallion not Headed.

NORTH DAKOTA

Onion White flat or round.

USEFUL GARDEN INFORMATION

PLANT IN FIELD	VEGETABLE VARIETIES	SEED IN HOTBED	DISTANCE BETWEEN ROWS	DISTANCE BETWEEN PLANTS
HARDY VEGETABLES: Sow seed or transplant hardened plants as early as ground is ready to work well in spring (Average about April 20 for 2/3 of state)	Asparagus		4 ft.	24 in.
	Broccoli	Apr. 1	3 ft.	18 in.
	Cabbage (early)	Apr. 1	3 ft.	18 in.
	Cabbage (late)		3 ft.	18-24 in.
	Onions (seed)		1½ ft.	2 in.
	Onions (transplanting)	Apr. 1	1½ ft.	4 in.
	●Peas		2 ft.	2 in.
	Radishes		1½ ft.	1 in.
	Rhubarb		5 ft.	4 ft.
	Rutabaga		2 ft.	6 in.
	Spinach		2 ft.	4 in.
HALF-HARDY VEGE-TABLES: Sow seed or transplant hardened plants a week or two before average date of last killing frost in your area. (Average about May 10 for 2/3 of state)	Beets		2 ft.	2 in.
	Carrots		2 ft.	2 in.
	Cauliflower	Apr. 1	3 ft.	18 in.
	Lettuce (leaf)		2 ft.	8 in.
	Lettuce (head)	Mar. 15	2 ft.	15 in.
	Parsnips		2 ft.	4 in.
	Potatoes		3 ft.	12 in.
	Swiss Chard		2 ft.	6 in.
TENDER VEGETABLES Sow seed or transplant plants when soil is warm and after average date or danger of last killing frost in your area. (Average about May 25 for 2/3 of state)	Beans (wax and green)		2 ft.	4 in.
	Beans (dry and field)		2 ft.	4 in.
	Beans (lima)		2 ft.	4 in.
	●●Cucumbers		5 ft.	1 ft.
	●●Muskmelons		8 ft.	1 ft.
	Peppers	Apr. 1	3 ft.	18 in.
	Popcorn		3 ft.	12 in.
	Pumpkins		10 ft.	2 ft.
	Squash (summer)		3 ft.	2 ft.
	Squash (winter)		10 ft.	2 ft.
	Sweet Corn		3 ft.	12 in.
	Tomatoes	Apr. 20	5 ft.	4 in.
	●●Watermelons		8 ft.	1 ft.

●Plant peas in paired rows 6" - 12" apart with 2 foot aisles between double rows.
●●Vine crops, though commonly planted in hills, would be best grown in rows with plants spaced one to two feet apart.

Potato Onions.

CHICAGO ZONE ⑤

CHICAGO VEGETABLE VARIETIES

Richard DeLano
Garden Editor
CHICAGO DAILY NEWS
With Carl Dietz

For maximum production in your garden it is important that you grow the right varieties. Different vegetable varieties perform best in different areas. On the basis of years of experience we have found the following vegetable varieties are highly suited to Chicagolands unique climate. New introductions were tested in the horticulture gardens at Kishwaukee College in Malta, Illinois.

ASPARAGUS (Pick the first crop in 2 or 3 years); Plant roots or seed.
Mary Washington, Waltham Washington
BUSHBEANS—GREEN
Tendercrop, Spartan Arrow, Topcrop, Royalty (purple type), Tendergreen, Contender
BUSHBEANS—WAX (yellow)
Cherokee Wax, Top Notch Golden Wax, Goldcrop

POLE BEAN
Kentucky Wonder
LIMA BEANS
Fordhook 242, Thorogreen
POLE LIMA BEAN
King of the Garden (best pole lima for the Chicago area)
EDIBLE SOYBEANS
Kanrich, Early Green Bush
BEETS
Ruby Queen, Winter Keeper (does very well in Chicago soils), Detroit Dark Red, Burpee Golden (yellow), Difficult to germinate but worth the effort.
BROCCOLI
Premium crop, Green Comet, Spartan Early
BRUSSELS SPROUTS
Jade Cross
CABBAGE—EARLY
Golden Acre, Emerald Cross, Badger Market
CABBAGE—MIDSEASON
Marion Market, Glory, Stonehead, Red Acre
CABBAGE—LATE
Danish bladhead, Red Head, Wisconsin Hollander No.8, Savoy King (has crinkled foliage)
(for a continuous supply of cabbage for cole slaw, plant one variety from each group)
CAULIFLOWER (sow seed in mid-July for a Fall crop)
Early Snowball, Snow Crown

CARROTS
Nantes (good also for flowerbox or container growing), Spartan Sweet, Danvers Half Long, Gold Pak (best suited for sandy soils around the North Shore, South Holland, and Gary), Red Core Chantenay (Royal Chantenay another name)
CELERY (not suited for Chicago area home gardens)
CHARD, SWISS (an under-rated green for this area)
Should be planted more frequently in the Chicago area in place of Spinach.
Lucullus, Ruby, Broad White Rib
COLLARDS (grows very well in the Chicago area but needs protection from cabbage worm. Spray with Dipel. A product which is compatible with organic gardening.)
Vates, Georgia
CORN, SWEET—EARLY
Early Xtra Sweet (a very short variety), Early Sunglow (short variety)
CORN, SWEET—MEDIUM SEASON
Golden Beauty, Butter & Sugar, Golden Cross Bantam (this was the first hybrid sweetcorn variety and is still the standard by which all other varieties are compared.)
CORN, SWEET—LATE
Honey Cross, Iochief, Midway, Silver Queen (white), Tendermost
CUCUMBER, SLICING
Challenger, Ashley, Burpee Hybrid, Straight Eight, Spartan Valor

CUCUMBER, PICKLING
Spartan Dawn, Chicago Westerfield, Wisconsin SMR, Pixie (use for window boxes, urns or containers)

DILL
Long Island Mammoth (thrives in the Chicago area and you'll need it to go with your pickles)

EGGPLANT
Black Magic, Black Beauty, Blacknite

ENDIVE—Becomes quite bitter in the Chicago area but the best variety is: Full-Heart-Batavian (difficult as a spring crop. Seed in mid-July for fall use.)

KALE
Dwarf, Green Curled

KOHLRABI
Early White Vienna, Purple Vienna

LETTUCE
(Plant as soon as the ground thaws, which is mid-March in the Chicago area. Head types not suited to Chicago area gardens.)
Salad Bowl, Black Seeded Simpson, Buttercrunch, Grand Rapids, Bibb, Ruby (tastes good and will add color to the garden)

MUSKMELON (Cantaloupe)—start indoors or plant seed after the soil is 80 degrees F. at the two inch level at noon.
Burpee Hybrid, Pride of Wisconsin, Saticoy, Honey Rock, Samson

MUSTARD (must be harvested in cool weather or it can become fiery hot in the Chicago area.
Green Wave, Tendergreen

OKRA (a southern crop, but will grow here. Must be harvested when pods are four inches long.)
Emerald, Dwarf Green Early, Clemson Spineless

ONIONS, SETS
Ebenezer, Golden Globe

ONIONS, PLANTS
White Bermuda, Yellow Bermuda

ONIONS, SEED
Yellow Globe, Sweet Spanish, Southport Red Globe, White Sweet Spanish

PARSLEY (not a perennial in the Chicago area)
Paramount (plant as early as possible), Moss Curled (plant as early as possible), Hamburg (grown for the root which is harvested after frost the first year)

PARSNIP (plant mid-April)
All American, Harris Model

PEAS (plant in mid-March or as soon as the soil can be worked) Pick 80-90 days later.

EARLY PEAS
Wisconsin Early Sweet, Little Marvel, Laxton (don't confuse with Thomas Laxton which is not too suited for the Chicago area)

MAIN CROP PEAS
Green Arrow, Sweet Pod, Dwarf Grey Sugar (edible pods), Wando, Frosty

PEPPERS, SWEET
Bellringer, Bell Boy Hybrid, California Wonder, Yolo Wonder

PEPPERS, HOT
Hungarian Wax, Long Red Cayenne

POTATOES
(It is generally considered that it is more economical to purchase potatoes rather than produce them in a medium or small sized garden. Be sure to purchase special seed potatoes. Potatoes purchased at the produce department are usually treated so that they will not sprout.) Those with large gardens try:
Red: Norland
White: Superior, Kennebec, Katahdin

PUMPKIN
Big Max, Connecticut Field, Youngs Beauty, Cinderella, Small Sugar Pie, (Vines liberally produce 8-10" fruits).

RADISH, WHITE
Icicle, Burpee White, French Breakfast—red shoulder, white tip

RADISH, RED
Cherry Belle, Sparkler, Crimson Giant (will not get pithy if harvest is delayed a few days), Early Scarlet Globe, Scarlet Knight

RHUBARB (Plant Roots)
McDonald, Canada Red, Victoria, Ruby

RUTABAGA—Summers too hot in the Chicago area for this vegetable.

SALSIFY—risky in the Chicago area
Try— Mammoth Sandwich Island

SPINACH—Very difficult to get the seed to germinate in Chicago soils in Northern and Western Suburbs.
Sandy areas near Gary try: America Bloomsdale

SQUASH, SUMMER
Aristocrat, Elite, Yellow Summer Straightneck, Patty Pan, Caserta, Zucchini (all types good—Aristocrat, Chefini and Greyzini), Ambassador, Chefini, Seneca Butterbar, Cocozelle

ACORN SQUASH
Table King, Table Queen, DeMoines, Waltham Butternut, Kindred, Golden Delicious, Hubbard, blue and golden, Gold Nugget, Buttercup, Bannana

TOMATO—the more sun they receive, the more fruit they will produce.

MEDIUM EARLY
Spring Set, Heinz 1350 VF, Fantastic, Spring Giant VF, Cardinal, Terrific VFN

MAIN CROP
Burpees Big Boy, Wonder Boy VFN, Ramapo VF, Delicious (a good tasting giant brag tomato), Beefmaster (Beef-eater old name) VFN, Rutgers (this variety has been around for decades and still compares well with the new hybrids).

CHERRY TYPE
Cherry, Gardeners Delight, Sugar Lump
Cherry type for window boxes or containers, usually they produce fruit very early. Caution: fertilize container grown tomatoes sparingly. Too much fertilizer reduces fruit production.
Patio, Pixie, Presto, Tiny Tim VFN, Golden Boy (yellow fruit—low acid), Golden Jubilee (yellow fruit—low acid)
TURNIPS—Spring plantings usually result in small, bitter, and woody turnips. For best quality plant mid to late July for pulling after light frost.

GREENS
Seven Top, Shogoin

ROOTS
Just Right, Purple Top, White Globe, Tokyo Cross

WATERMELON—Ice box types are the best types for Chicago Suburban gardens.
New Hampshire Midget, Sugar Baby, Yellow Baby (yellow flesh)
Plant in larger gardens, in hills six by nine feet.

Some other unusual vegetables that can be grown in the Chicago area:
Artichoke (Jerusalem), Mangeliwurzel (type of white beet), Broccoli rapa (produces no heads), Chinese Cabbage, Cardoon, Celeriac, Witloof Chicory (use tender shoots), Chives (from seed), Popcorn, Corn salad, Cress (both upland and water), Dandelion (use new shoots in early spring), Leek, Cow peas, Rocket, Sorrel, Garlic (from cloves).

Special Notes:

VFN stands for verticillium, Fusarum, Nematode resistance. Nematodes are tiny almost microscopic worms that attack plant roots.

This year 1975, seedsmen have a normal supply of all varieties of vegetable seed on hand. However, an abnormally high demand is predicted. Therefore, order your seed as early as possible this year.

If your garden is quite shades—concentrate on leafy vegetables and greens.

CABBAGES.

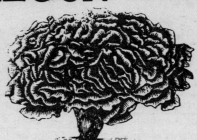

THESE recommendations are made by specialists in horticulture, botany, plant pathology, food technology, and home economics at Oregon State University in cooperation with seed companies. These recommendations are based on research, practical experience, and observation. It is a good idea to try new varieties on a small scale first. Cautious, reasonable testing of new varieties may pay big dividends. Very new varieties, while distinctly promising, may only be available in small packets on the year of release.

Most of these varieties are recommended for all of Oregon. Exceptions have been marked.

All varieties grown commercially are suitable for home gardeners, being well adapted to Oregon conditions. Home gardeners who are unable to find the recommended varieties at their seed store should shop from several catalogs.

Varieties in *italics* are suitable for processing.

ARTICHOKE (GLOBE)
French and Italian types (c), Green Globe

ASPARAGUS
Mary Washington, California 500, *Waltham Washington, UC 66, UC 72*

BEANS
(Many other snap bean varieties are suitable for home gardens.)

Bush type—green; Tendercrop, Gallatin 50, Tempo, Oregon 58, FM-14 (Romano)

Bush type—wax: Puregold, Earligold, Resistant Kinghorn

Pole type—green (Blue Lake types): FM-1K, FM-1L, Prime Pack, Asgrow 231
—green (other types): Columbia (E), Oregon Giant, Kentucky Wonder, Romano

Pole type—wax: Burpee Golden Wax

Bush lima—large seed: Fordhook 242, Concentrated Fordhook, Kingston
—small seed: Early Thorogreen, Clark's Bush, Henderson, Thaxter

Pole lima—King of the Garden

Dry—Seaway, Charlevoir, Pinto, Red Kidney

BEETS
Detroit Dark Red, Seneca Detroit, Green Top, *Burpee Golden*

BROCCOLI
Waltham 29, Northwest Waltham, Purple Head, *Crusader, Gem, Green Duke, El Centro, Green Comet*

BRUSSELS SPROUTS
Jade Cross, Jade E (F₁ hybrids), *Catskill, Green Gem*

CABBAGE
Spring planting: Early Jersey Wakefield, Golden Acre, Stonehead, Superette, Little Rock, Market Prize, Copenhagen, Bonanza, Marion Market, Danish Ballhead, Savoy King, Chieftan Savoy. Where yellows is a problem, use resistant strains.
Overwintered: Ferry's Round Dutch, Greenback, Red Head, Green Winter.

CABBAGE, CHINESE
Michihli, Wong Bok, Burpee Hybrid

CANTALOUPE
Spear, Oregon Delicious, Hales Best, Hearts of Gold, Crenshaw (E), Harper Hybrid, Gold Star, Supermarket, Saticoy Hybrid, Burpee Hybrid

CARROTS
Red Cored Chantenay, Royal Chantenay, Nantes, Imperator, Gold Spike, Gold Pak, Morse Bunching, *Spartan Sweet, Spartan Bonus*

OREGON

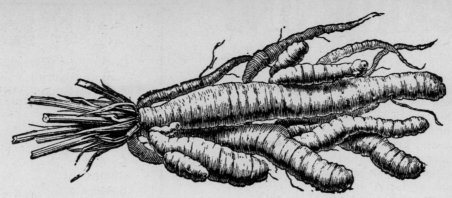

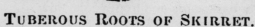

TUBEROUS ROOTS OF SKIRRET.

CAULIFLOWER
Main season: *Monarch 73m, Early Snowball, Snowdrift, Snowball X, Snowball Y, Self Blanche*

CELERY
Utah (many strains of this long, green petiole type available)

COLLARDS
Vates, Georgia

CORN, SWEET
North Star, Seneca Golden, Tokay Sugar (white), Sugar King, Golden Cross Bantam, NK-199, Jubilee, Silver Queen (white), Style Pak, Spring Gold, Northern Belle, Rapid Pak, Early Sunglow

CUCUMBERS
Pickling: SMR 18, SMR 58. For trial: Crusader, Explorer, Pioneer, *Spartan Advance, Ranger
Slicing: Burpee Hybrid, Surecrop Hybrid, Marketmore, Marketer, Straight Eight, Lemon Cucumber, other F₁ hybrids, Point set, Marketmore, Cherokee
Greenhouse: Burpee Hybrid, M&M Hybrid

EGGPLANT (in order of maturity)
Black Jack, Modern Midget (small), Black Magic, Black Beauty, New Hampshire (any F₁ hybrids)

ENDIVE
Green Curled, Batavian, Deep Heart

KALE
Dwarf Blue Curled Scotch, Dwarf Green Curled Scotch

KOHLRABI
White Vienna, Purple Vienna

LETTUCE
Heading: Pennlake, Premier, *Ithaca, Calmar
Leaf: Oak Leaf, Ruby, Bronze Leaf, Prizehead, Green Ice, Fordhook
Cos: Parris Island, Dark Green
Butterhead: Bibb, Buttercrunch, Summer Bibb, Mignonette

MUSTARD
Fordhook Fancy, Florida Broadleaf (smooth leaf), *Green Wave (long standing)

ONIONS
Western Oregon: Oregon Yellow Globe Danvers (for storing), Surprise, Fiesta
Eastern and southern Oregon: Sweet Spanish strains, El Capitan, Fiesta
Elevations 2,000 feet and over: Fiesta (A), Surprise
For pickling: Eclipse

PARSLEY
Triple Moss Curled, Paramount

PARSNIPS
Harris Model, All America, Hollow Crown

PEAS
Dark Green Perfection, Laxton 7, Jade, Alderman (tall growing), Miragreen, Midfreezer, Little Marvel, Perfected Freezer 60, Mohawk (enation mosaic resistant), Progress 9, Icer 95, Aurora, Oregon Sugar Pod
Edible pod types—Dwarf Gray Sugar, Sweetpod

PEPPER (in order of maturity)
Vinette Early Bountiful (small fruit), Early Calwonder 300, Pennwonder, Bellboy, Michigan Wonder, Yolo Wonder (mosaic resistant), Idabelle, Ruby King, Emerald Giant, Long Red Cayenne (hot), Midway, Jade, Bellringer, Keystone Resistant Giant, Park Wonder

PUMPKIN
Small Sugar, Connecticut Field, Dickinson, Jack O'Lantern, N.E. Pie, Big Max (novelty for exhibition), Lady Godiva (for edible seed only)

RADISH
Comet, Red Prince, Cherry Belle, Scarlet Knight, White Icicle, Burpee White, Stop Lite, Red Devil (Many other radish varieties are suitable for home gardens.)

RHUBARB
Crimson Wine, Canada Red, MacDonald, Riverside Giant
Hothouse forcing—Victoria, Crimson Wine, German Wine

OREGON STATE UNIVERSITY
**EXTENSION
SERVICE**

RUTABAGAS
American Purple Top

SPINACH
Fall planted: Early Hybrid 7 (Savoy), Dixie Market (Savoy), Viroflay (smooth leaf), Badger (Savoy)
Spring planted: American (Savoy), Bloomsdale Long Standing (Savoy), Viroflay (smooth leaf), Califlay (smooth leaf), Hybrid 424 (smooth leaf), Heavy Pack (smooth leaf), Pay Day
Overwintered: Old Dominion (Savoy)

SQUASH
Summer: yellow—Seneca Butterbar, Early Prolific Straightneck, Early Summer Crookneck, Goldbar, Goldneck green—Caserta, Cozella, Seneca Zucchini, Cocozelle, Burpee Hybrid, *Elite, Diplomat,* and other F₁ hybrid zucchinis
Winter: Golden Delicious, Hubbard (all types), Banana, Table Queen, Buttercup, Sweet Meat, Marblehead (E), Silver Bell, Quality, Butternut (several strains—Baby Butternut, Waltham Butternut, Hercules).

SWEET POTATO
Earligold, Jewell

TOMATO
Early Determinate (bush) (adapted to all parts of Oregon): Fireball, Willamette, *New Yorker,* Pixie, Presto
Early Indeterminate (vining): Valiant
Medium-Early Determinate (bush): Wasatch, Pritchand Early Pak 7 (E), *VF 145-21-4,* Springset, Spring Giant, Burpee Big Boy, Heinz 1350.
Medium-Early Indeterminate (vining): Moreton Hybrid, Big Boy Hybrid, Big Early Hybrid, Burpee Hybrid, Red Jacket, Burpee VF
Late Determinate (bush): Ace
Greenhouse: Michigan-Ohio Hybrid, Washington State Forcing, Moto Red
Cherry type: bush types: Small Fry, Tiny Tim, Patio
Yellow Indeterminate: Golden Boy

TURNIP
Purple Top, *Shogoin* (for greens and all white roots), *Just Right* (F₁ hybrid for greens and all white roots)

WATERMELONS
Klondike No. 11, Blue Ribbon Klondike (E), Crimson Sweet (E), Golden Midget, Charleston Gray, Shipper (E), New Hampshire Midget, and other small early hybrids

---

(*) New variety; recommended for small trial only.
(C) Oregon Coast.
(E) Eastern Oregon.
(W) Western Oregon only.
(A) Altitudes above 2,000 feet. Use early maturing varieties.

ONIONS.

SMALL PLOT GARDENING

John A. Wott

In these times of rising prices, more people than ever are returning to growing their own garden vegetables. There is no question that vegetables, harvested from the garden at their peak of quality are more nutritious and tasty than those often purchased in stores.

Many vegetables are easy to grow and furnish a good supply of energy, vitamins and minerals. Their greatest contribution is probably in vitamins A and C, but as a group they also furnish some vitamin B1 (thiamine), vitamin G (riboflavin), calcium, and iron.

Garden plots are springing up in back yards and front yards, and balconies, and in container-planters as well as rental plots in urban areas and sites surrounding factories. For successful small plot gardening, the gardener needs to follow only a few basic rules. Tackling too large an area or planting the more difficult vegetables may result in discouragement and failure, particularly for beginning gardeners.

Site selection

Try to select a site which has at least six hours of sunshine each day. Vegetables grown in shady locations usually have poorer quality. Often a space along a garage or house is useful. Rental plots, which have had a sod cover or grown in weeds for several years often are available.

In small yards, fences can often be used to support pole beans or cucumbers. Staking tomatoes and growing beans on chicken wire or wooden teepees will also conserve space.

Materials needed

Gather gardening materials early. Secure a spade or shovel, rake, hoe, garden hose or sprinkling can, string, stakes (both large and small), fertilizer and the desired seeds and plants.

Getting started

Decide which vegetables you want in your garden. Learn how much space they will need and how many seeds or plants are necessary. Then plan your garden on paper, so that when it is time to plant, you will know exactly what to do.

The amount of each vegetable to grow will also depend upon the needs of your family. Some suggested guidelines are:

Food Type	Daily serving per person	Pounds per year for a family of four
Potatoes and sweet potatoes	1-2	500
Tomatoes and citrus fruits	1	620
Leafy, green or yellow vegetables	1-2	660
Other vegetables and fruits	2 or more	640

Horticulture Department
Cooperative Extension Service
Purdue University

If possible, turn the soil in the fall. If not, then rototil, spade or plow the area to a depth of 6-8 inches as early in the spring as the soil is workable. Do not turn soil when it is wet because it will remain hard and lumpy all season. After it has dried, remove all sod clumps, sticks, stones and other debris and level with the rake.

Just before you level the soil for the last time, spread a general analysis fertilizer evenly over the garden area. Use 3-4 pounds per 100 square feet (10 ft. x 10 ft.) (generally 1 pound = 1 pint = 1 cup). Rake it in.

For best production, plant vegetables at the proper time, i.e. cool season crops early and warm season crops after the weather has warmed.

In small areas use one of these space saving techniques:

Interplanting — sow two fast-growing crops together in the row. Plant radishes, onions, spinach or lettuce between rows of cabbage, corn, Brussels sprouts and broccoli.

Intercropping — sow two types of seeds together, but use a fast and a slow growing type. For example, sow radishes and carrots together. When the radishes are harvested, then the carrots will be automatically thinned.

SEED COST

Cucumbers (Hybrid)	$ .50
Tomato (Hybrid)	.50
Zucchini Squash (Hybrid)	.50
Pepper (Hybrid	.50
Cabbage	.35
Lettuce	.35
Bush Beans	.35
Carrots	.35
Chard	.35
Beets	.35
Spinach	.35
Radish	.35
Parsley	.35
Green Onion (Sets)	1.00
Leeks	.35
Broccoli (Hybrid)	.75
Cauliflower (Hybrid)	.75
Brussels Sprouts (Hybrid)	.75
Peas	.35
TOTAL	$9.10

Succession planting — as soon as one crop is finished, plant another. When cool-season crops such as lettuce, spinach, radish, and peas are harvested, replant with beans, beets or turnips.

Short rows — Don't plant more than you will be able to use at one time, e.g. planting a long row of lettuce or two dozen cabbage plants which you can't possibly use at once. In small plot gardening, it is advisable to plant the exact amount needed.

Planting seeds

Mark out the area with stakes so that it is as even as possible. This not only looks better but it also helps maintenance.

For early spring sowing, mark out each row with twine tied tightly between the two end stakes. Open the furrow to the proper depth with a hoe and sow the seeds, trying to space properly. *Do not sow seeds too deeply!* Place carrots, radishes, and lettuce no deeper than ¼ inch. Large seeds such as peas, beans and cucumbers can be sown 1-1½ inches deep. Vine crops can be planted six seeds in a cluster or hill — then later thinned to four plants per hill.

Cover the seeds and lightly press the soil down with your hands or the rake. Be sure to label the rows.

Thin greens and root crops after the plants are 1-2 inches tall. Use the beet and lettuce thinnings for salads. Use scissors to thin so you won't disturb the other plants.

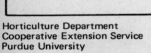

Planting plants

Secure sturdy transplants of recommended varieties from a reputable garden supplier. Plant at proper distances and set all plants slightly deeper than they were growing in the pot. Be sure to break down the edges and bottoms of peat pots. Tomatoes can be set deeper if they have tall spindly stems. Firm the soil and water in with a soluble plant food solution if possible. Set stakes or cages for tomatoes at planting time. Be sure to keep transplants well watered and protected from strong winds or bright sun until they are well established.

Summer care

Be sure to keep all weeds out. Weeds can be easily pulled when they are small. For larger weeds, use a hoe and use a shaving stroke so as not to dig more than ¼-½ inch deep. You do not have to loosen the soil if there are no weeds.

For low care maintenance and weed control, apply a 2-4 inch layer of an organic mulch over the row areas. This can then be turned into the soil in the fall. Vegetables need water. Apply at least one inch of water per week with a soaker hose to soak the soil 6-8 inches deep. Do not use light sprinklings.

YIELDS / SAVINGS

YIELDS	SAVINGS
60 Cucumbers @ 25¢ each	$ 15.00
100 lbs. Tomatoes @ $1.00 for 3 lbs	33.00
40 lbs. Zucchini @ 39¢ per lb.	15.60
40 lbs. Peppers @ 39¢ per lb.	15.60
24 heads Cabbage @ 39¢ head	9.36
48 heads Lettuce @ 59¢ head	23.52
25 lbs. Beans @ 39¢ lb.	9.75
48 lbs. Chard @ 59¢ lb.	28.32
36 lbs. Beets @ 29¢ lb.	10.44
36 lbs. Carrots @ 29¢ lb.	10.44
12 lbs. Spinach @ 59¢ lb.	7.08
24 bunches Radish @ 29¢ bunch	6.96
48 bunches Parsley @ 29¢ bunch	13.92
24 bunches Green Onions @ 25¢ bunch	6.00
28 bunches Leeks @ 59¢ bunch	16.52
24 heads Broccoli @ 49¢ head	11.76
12 heads Cauliflower @ 79¢ head	9.48
15 lbs. Peas @ 39¢ lb.	5.85
60 pts. Brussels Sprouts @ 59¢ pt.	35.40
TOTAL	$284.00

PARSNIP.   PIE PLANT

SPACING

15 ft. — 25 ft.

Cucumbers	2 ft.
Tomatoes	2 ft.
Zucchini Squash	2 ft.
Peppers	2 ft.
Cabbage	2 ft.
Lettuce	1½ ft.
Beans	2 ft.
Chard	1½ ft.
Beets	2 ft.
Carrots	1½ ft.
Spinach	1 ft.
Radish	1 ft.
Parsley	1 ft.
Green Onions	1 ft.
Broccoli/Cauliflower	2 ft.
Peas/Brussels Sprouts	2 ft.

SMALL PLOT GARDENING

CAULIFLOWER.

Certain vegetables are more prone to insect and disease attack than others. Vegetables growing properly usually are much less subject to attack. However, such vegetables as cucumbers, melons, and cabbage are also quite consistently pest-prone, so check with your local county extension office or garden supplier for recommended control measures. Checking vegetables daily will help you catch and remedy the problem promptly.

Harvesting

Vegetables should be harvested at the proper time, not necessarily always when the vegetable is at its largest stage. Learn what is the best harvest stage and then pick the vegetables and either eat fresh, can or freeze promptly for best garden freshness. Certain fall vegetables can also be stored for later winter use.

Related publications

HO-26 Tomatoes
HO-29 Vegetables for Salads
HO-66 The Fall Vegetable Garden
HO-67 Onions and Their Relatives
HO-101 Recommended Vegetable Varieties for the Home Garden
BP-8-6 Vegetable Disease Control
E-21 Vegetable Insect Control in the Home Garden

The information given herein is suppplied with the understanding that no discrimination is intended and no endorsement by the Indiana Cooperative Extension Service is implied.

Indiana residents may order single copies of up to 10 different publications free of charge. Quantities of any one publication are sold at cost of printing, and quotations will be furnished on request. All sales are subject to 4% Indiana sales tax. Residents of other states may order the publications for a charge of 20¢ per copy, or may request similar publications from their Land Grant University.

WHAT TO EXPECT FROM YOUR GARDEN

Vegetable	Approximate yield per 100 ft. of row	Approximate amount of fresh vegetable needed for 1 quart	
		Canned	Frozen
	lb.	lb.	
Asparagus	50	4	2-3
Beans, lima (pods)	20	4-5	4-5
Beans, snap	60	1½-2	1½-2
Beets	60	2½-3	2½-3
Broccoli	60	. . .	2
Cabbage	200	. . .	. . .
Carrots	75	2½-3	2½-3
Chard	50	. . .	3
Cucumbers	100	. . .	. . .
Eggplant	60	. . .	. . .
Lettuce, head	90 heads	. . .	. . .
Lettuce, leaf	50	. . .	. . .
Muskmelons	150		
Onions	100	. . .	. . .
Parsnips	100	. . .	. . .
Peas (pods)	30	4-5	4-5
Peppers	60	. . .	1½
Potatoes, early	60	. . .	. . .
Potatoes, late	75	. . .	. . .
Pumpkins	300	. . .	. . .
Radishes	100 bunches	. . .	. . .
Rhubarb	100	1	1½
Spinach	50	2-3	2-3
Squash, summer	160	2½-3	2-3
Squash, winter	400	2	3
Sweet corn, early	75 ears	4-5	4-5
Sweet corn, main-crop	85 ears	4-5	4-5
Sweet potatoes	80	2½-3	2-3
Tomatoes	500	3	. . .
Turnips	50	. . .	. . .
Watermelons	20 fruit	. . .	. . .

A 15' X 25' VEGETABLE GARDEN

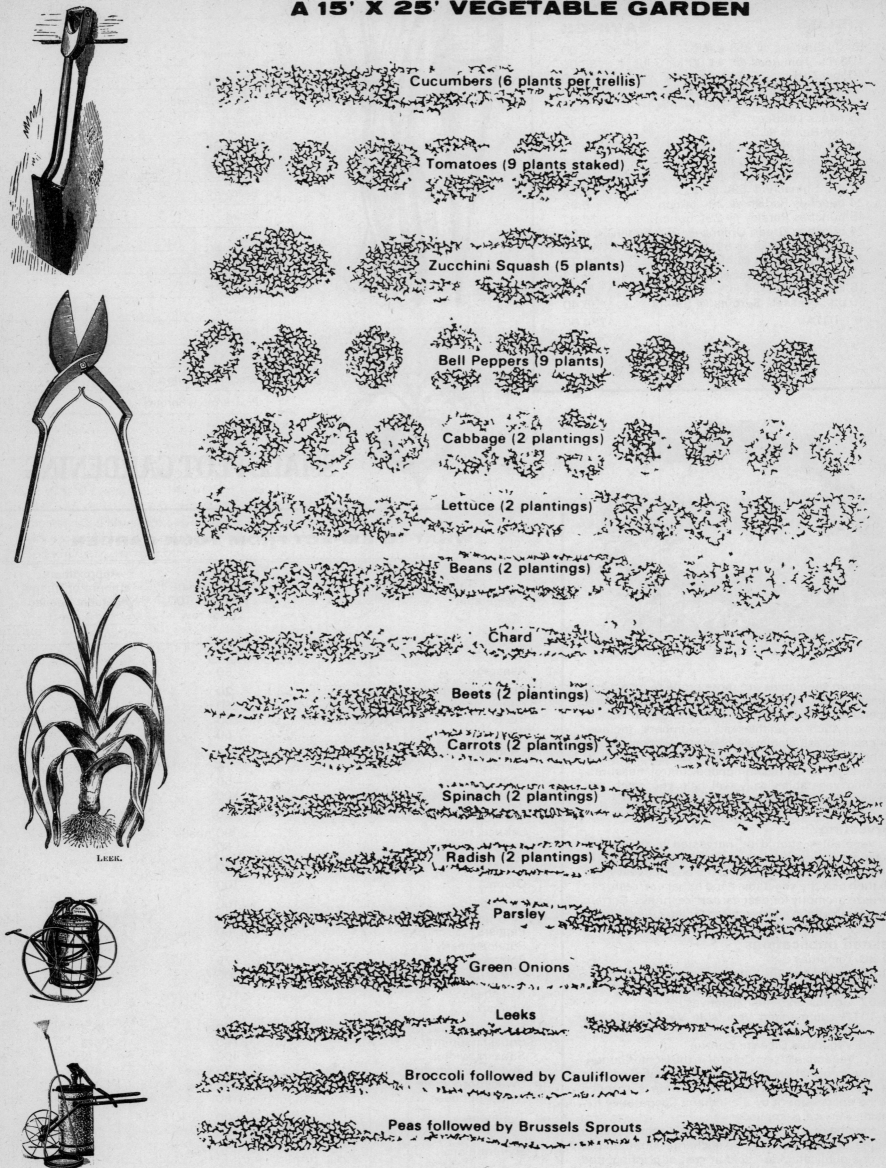

Cucumbers (6 plants per trellis)

Tomatoes (9 plants staked)

Zucchini Squash (5 plants)

Bell Peppers (9 plants)

Cabbage (2 plantings)

Lettuce (2 plantings)

Beans (2 plantings)

Chard

Beets (2 plantings)

Carrots (2 plantings)

Spinach (2 plantings)

Radish (2 plantings)

Parsley

Green Onions

Leeks

Broccoli followed by Cauliflower

Peas followed by Brussels Sprouts

LEEK.

25 ft

15 ft.

A 10' X 10' VEGETABLE GARDEN

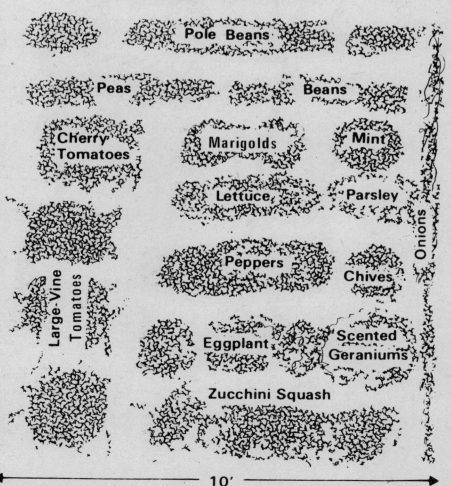

Staked Tomatoes | Peppers

Zucchini Squash | Cabbage

Onions | Beans

Spinach or Turnips | Peas

Radishes | Lettuce

10'

10'

A narrow matted row of strawberries.

A COMBINATION FLOWER-VEGETABLE GARDEN (10' X 10')

Pole Beans

Peas | Beans

Cherry Tomatoes | Marigolds | Mint

Lettuce | Parsley

Peppers | Chives

Large-Vine Tomatoes | Onions

Eggplant | Scented Geraniums

Zucchini Squash

10'

10'

SMALL AREA VEGETABLE GARDENS

SMALL AREA VEGETABLE GARDENS

From Nevada Gardener, Cooperative Extension Service, Horticulture Information Series

By Ronald H. Gustafson, County Extension Horticulturist

Space is no requirement for a productive vegetable garden and many new ideas have been developed to bring vegetables to the gardener who has little space.

PLANT IN FLOWER BEDS. Many good vegetables are planted in combination with flowers and around existing ornamental planting. This is especially good where only a limited or special kind of vegetable is wanted. A few tomatoes scattered around the yard do surprisingly well as do a few heads of lettuce, carrots, or other vegetables.

PLANT MORE IN A SMALLER AREA. Prepare the soil carefully, choose the right plants, and sow successive crops. Thin and weed mercilessly. Elaborate watering systems aren't necessary. You can even use a watering can. Choose vegetables that produce a lot—pole beans, beets, carrots, lettuce, radishes, tomatoes and zucchini squash. Avoid corn, melons and most viney crops, use fences or trellises to grow beans, tomatoes.

PLANT IN SUCCESSION. Plant one-half of the allotted space, wait until germinated, then plant the second half. Also plan on . . .

DOUBLE CROPPING. When one area is finished, replant again or choose another. Plant a lawn of carrots, etc., broadcasting the seed rather than in rows. Clue is thinning and weed control.

USE RAISED BEDS. When ground is too poor or shallow, use a raised bed. Hold soil with 1- or 2-inch boards and at least 12 inches high; 16 inches with a cap on top for sitting is more comfortable. For easy maintenance, it should be of 6 to 8 feet width if accessible from both sides, 3 to 4 feet if not. Soil mix should be high in organic matter and well-drained. Fertilize regularly. Raised beds can be protected easily from frost, pets, birds, they drain better, and are easy to maintain.

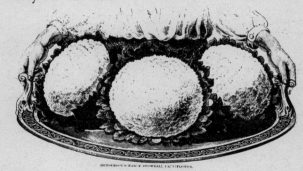

HENDERSON'S EARLY SNOWBALL CAULIFLOWER.

GROW IN CONTAINERS. Gardeners can create ideal growing areas in boxes, wire cages, baskets, pots, plastic bags or anything that is 8 to 10 inches deep. Use a good soil mix; such as 1/3 compost, 1/3 soil and 1/3 perlite or vermiculite. Avoid manures, due to salt buildup. Remember: drainage, watering and fertilization are critical.

Many vegetables can be grown in containers—viney ones can hang. Use many together to decorate the patio. Move inside when frost warnings appear. Build a rack to hold many containers. Watch drainage water so that it doesn't damage furniture or drip on neighbors in apartments below.

MIDGET VEGETABLES. Newly developed dwarf vegetables are available in varieties to help conserve space. Small tomatoes, cabbage, cantaloupe, cucumber, head lettuce, peas, corn and watermelon are all available.

HAND POLLINATION

From Nevada Gardener, Cooperative Extension
Service, Horticulture Information Series

Cucumbers, muskmelons, peppers, squash, watermelons
must be hand pollinated when insect activity is reduced
for any reason. These crops are pollinated when insects
visit the flowers and pollen sticking to them brushes off
onto the stigma.

VINE CROPS

Vine crops typically have two kinds of flowers on each
plant—numerous male flowers that appear first, and female
flowers with an obvious slightly swollen ovary just behind
the flower. When no insects are present, you should hand-
pollinate these female flowers. Use a small brush or piece
of cotton and wipe the yellow pollen from the anthers
of the male flower. Then dust it on the stigma of the female flower.

To pollinate peppers, you need only shake the whole
plant or tap the open flower clusters a few times a week,
preferably in the morning.

TOMATOES

Tomatoes are normally self-pollinating. But you will
have a better fruit set if you tap the open clusters of
flowers or shake the entire plant a few times a week, as
for peppers.

You can use commercial blossom set hormone solutions provided the nighttime temperature is below 60
degrees. But follow directions or you will have misshapen
fruits.

SWEET CORN

Corn must be planted in blocks where winds blow
across it as corn is pollinated by airborne pollen.

BEANS

Beans are typically self-pollinated, but to be sure, tap
the flowers as suggested for tomatoes and peppers.

EFFECT OF WATERING ON POLLINATION

If fruit does not set even after pollination, it could
be due to frequent, light watering.

Water your vegetable garden long enough to wet the
soil 18 to 24 inches deep, then wait until the surface
soil dries enough to crumble when run through your
fingers.

Vegetable Variety Recommendations for Commercial Plant Growers

J.W. Courter and J.S. Vandemark, Cooperative Extension Service, University of Illinois at Urbana-Champaign

ASPARAGUS

Mary Washington
Waltham Washington
Tetra

BROCCOLI

Spartan Early
Early Purple Head
Royal Purple Head
Green Comet*
Premium Crop

BRUSSELS SPROUT

Jade Cross*

CABBAGE

Emerald Cross*
King Cole*
Resistant Golden Acre (YR)
Greenback (YR)
Market Prize (YR)
Market Topper*
Market Dawn*
Resistant Danish (YR)

SPECIALTY CABBAGE

Savoy King*
Red Head (early)
Red Ball (early)
Red Danish (late)

CAULIFLOWER

Early Snowball
Snow Crown*

EGG PLANT

Black Magic*
Burpee Hybrid*

HERBS

Sage
Basil
Sweet Marjoram
Purple Basil
Summer Savory
Chives
Parsley (plain or curled)
Rosemary
Thyme

ONIONS

Sweet Spanish (yellow, white,
red), Ruby and Sweet Spanish Hybrid*

PEPPERS (mangoes)

Tasty*
Bellringer
California Wonder
Yolo Wonder
Keystone Resistant Giant

SPECIALTY PEPPERS

Sweet Banana
Hungarian Wax (hot)
Sunnybrook (Pimento)
Long Red Cayenne (hot)
Cherry (hot & sweet)

RHUBARB

Valentine
MacDonald
Victoria

SWEET POTATOES

Centennial
Goldrush
Puerto Rico (Unit 1 Strain)
Nemagold

TOMATOES

Medium Early
Cardinal*
Fantastic*
Campbell 1327
Jet Star*
Main Crop
Wonder Boy*
Big Boy*
Better Boy*
Manapal
Manalucie
Burpee VF*
Ramapo*
Supersonic*
Delicious (extra large)
Beefeater (extra large)

SPECIALTY TOMATOES

Red Cherry (large and small)
Gardener's Delight (small
fruit)
Sugar Lump (small fruit)
Jubilee (yellow)
Golden Boy (yellow)
Roma VF (paste)
Tiny Tim (dwarf)
Patio, Pixie (compact,
medium fruit)
Small Fry (compact, small
fruit)*

*Hybrids
YR, resistant to Yellows disease

Urbana, Illinois

A COMPLETE GARDEN FOR A FAMILY OF SIX

reprinted from GARDEN MAGAZINE 1905

Edited by Tom Riker

In the accompanying sketch (which is planned for 200 feet square, or almost one acre) we have endeavored to give as concise and complete a scheme as possible to supply a family of six grown persons with fruit, flowers and vegetables throughout the entire season, providing also for a well-filled fruit room and vegetable cellar all winter, and plenty of material for canning purposes.

The ideal conditions for a garden are these: The situation well sheltered from the north and northwest winds, and sloping gently toward the south. The warmth and protection will advance the season by at least two weeks, and there will be no need of artificial drainage.

Now grade off the ground at each side of the roads until a perfect level or even slope, as the case may be, is made. This done, it is an easy matter to grade the rest of your ground to them.

Having got the trades and levels, it is time to make the edging. There is room for individual fancy here. It may be a six- or eight-inch board one inch wide and fastened securely to 2 x 4-inch posts, driven firmly into the ground to within two inches of the top; fancy tile, or ordinary brick, set on end, leaving two inches above ground; long pointed stones, put down in the same manner; the evergreen boxwood may be planted; or sod cut from old-established pasture lots may be laid. Sod for this purpose should be twelve inches wide, and it must be perfectly straight on both edges. It is a cheap edging, and looks as well as any, but entails a good deal of work during the summer in keeping it cut.

Now for the road: Dig out the top soil to the depth of twelve or fifteen inches, carting it to fill any hollow places, or spread it evenly over the surface to increase the depth of the garden soil. Gather up all stones that are larger than hen's eggs and spread them evenly over the bottom of the road bed. It is unlikely that enough stones will be found to complete the bed, but coal ashes can be used instead. Fill up this to within an inch and a half of the top and finish off with gravel or pulverized blue stone, roll down thoroughly, and you will have a permanent road that will be both hard and dry.

If a hedge is planted on the east, north and west sides it will certainly add to the picturesque effect of the garden. Select Japan barberry. The barberry bushes should be planted fifteen inches apart, requiring 450 in all.

At the ends of the roads that lead to the north, east and west sides, and on a line with the hedge, are arches covered with climbing roses. Crimson Rambler will add considerably to the general effect.

Around the garden, but inside the hedge line, so as to shade the garden as little as possible, plant fruit trees. The apple trees, being the largest growing and requiring most room, should be planted at the north end. Eight trees will yield an abundance of fruit for summer and fall use, as well as plenty to store away for winter. When buying plums secure extra large trees; it pays. It is better to buy small peach trees. In a table further on in this article the seasons of harvesting the crops are indicated.

The fifty-foot-wide border on which these fruit trees are planted may be cultivated during the first few years, and small-growing, short-season vegetables, such as lettuce, radishes, etc., can be planted between the trees. It would add much to appearances, however, if lawn-grass mixture was sown here and the surface kept mown. Of course it would be necessary to cultivate a small space around each tree, and also a strip about one foot wide along the hedge.

to either of them damage is likely to result from the use of the lawn mower, and again there is the large question of whether there should be grass at all.

The plot marked No. 1 on the plan is devoted to small fruits and permanent roots, and has the lines running east and west. Twenty-five feet distant from the hedge (thus leaving ample room for the development of the apple trees) is a row of grapes. The twelve vines are planted six feet apart and are to be trained on a trellis. Six feet from the grapes plant one row of blackberries, allowing three feet between the plants. The next row, still six feet distant, is for raspberries, allowing two and a half feet between the plants. Next come red currants and gooseberries.

Rhubarb and horseradish are planted in the small-fruit section, because they are permanent plants and must not be moved every year. They occupy the next row, leaving room for five lines of asparagus (three feet between the lines and two feet between the plants in the lines).

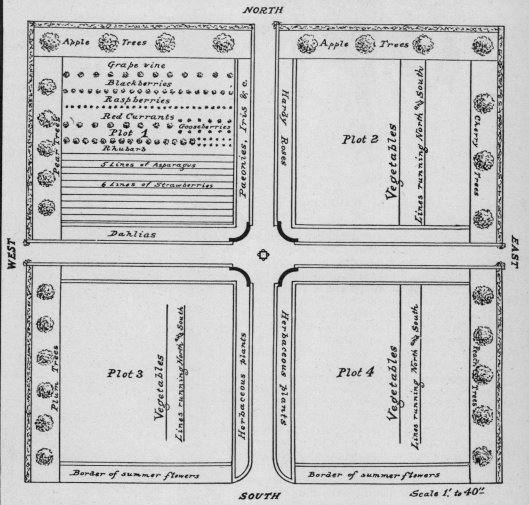

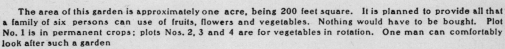

The area of this garden is approximately one acre, being 200 feet square. It is planned to provide all that a family of six persons can use of fruits, flowers and vegetables. Nothing would have to be bought. Plot No. 1 is in permanent crops; plots Nos. 2, 3 and 4 are for vegetables in rotation. One man can comfortably look after such a garden

Six lines of strawberries complete the fruit patch. Allow two and a half feet between the rows and eighteen inches between the plants in the rows. This is the only part of the plot in which rotation of crops is followed, potatoes and strawberries alternating.

Plots II., III. and IV. are devoted to vegetables and are to follow a sort of rotation. For instance, next year plant the various crops in the same relation to each other, but plot number III. becomes number II., plot number IV. becomes number III., and plot number II. becomes number IV. When the strawberry bed made on plot I. is to be renewed potatoes may be put in its place, the new strawberry patch taking the place of the potatoes in any of the vegetable plots. On the side of each plot and bordering the road is a five-foot border for flowers—a small pathway, one foot wide, is allowed at the back of each border. This will be found a great convenience for working the various plots. It should be used for all necessary traffic, and will prevent trampling and disfiguring the border by continual crossing and recrossing. This path should be properly made. Measure five feet from the path at each end of the plot, stretching the garden line from point to point, and with a spade or flat shovel dig a small trench three inches deep and twelve inches wide, scattering the soil evenly over the vegetable plot. By having the walk a little lower than the surrounding ground it will not be obtrusive, and there will be less likelihood of encroaching on either the flower border or the vegetable plot when you have occasion to use the path.

The tables given later indicate the best varieties to plant for a succession of crops in the order indicated.

Certainly they are not the most useful spots in the garden, but they are the prettiest, and merit as much care and planning as the more utilitarian divisions. We must have roses, and there is no other thing in the entire garden that will respond better to good treatment. If the soil is a light friable nature take away some of it, replacing by several inches of heavy turfy loam and well-decayed manure well mixed; old manure from the cow barn is preferred.

RAMPION.

There is room for one hundred and fifty plants in three rows, with the plants eighteen inches apart in the rows. Some people may think this is too little room, but since there are only three rows and the plants can be conveniently reached it will be ample. The border opposite the roses is recommended for peonies and iris. It seems a large space, but the variety of peonies and irises is so great and so beautiful, that it is our only excuse. The border will hold three rows, the peonies at the back. They should all be planted two feet apart in the rows.

Dahlias are becoming more and more popular for late summer and early fall flowers. Give them abundance of water and there will not be another spot in the whole garden during the autumn months that will give such pleasure. Three rows can also be planted in this border, but the plants must be four feet apart in the rows, the middle row alternating with the others. Altogether about five dozen plants can be accommodated.

The border opposite the dahlias may be devoted to gladioli, tuberoses, montbretias and various bulbs; also to stocks, asters, zinnias, marigolds, balsams, celosia, and such things as are raised from seed in the hotbed or in boxes in the window in early spring and planted outdoors about May 20th, when danger from frost is over. These subjects are all useful for cutting and come into flower after the peonies and irises are gone, and before the dahlias are ready to cut. The space allotted will accommodate four rows, the plants twelve inches apart in the rows.

There are two borders devoted to annuals. A row of pansies along the front of each, planted out before Easter, will brighten them until such time as the other occupants are large enough to make a display. Every thing else for the border can be sown there directly after May 1st, except sweet peas which can be sown in April in clumps along the back. Nearly all the best kinds can be bought for five cents a packet.

The variety of flowering plants from which a selection can be made to fill the herbaceous border is so great that an enumeration of the possibilities would be nearly a reproduction of a seed and plant catalogue. Of course there are certain principles that should be followed. It is better to sow thinly in irregular patches rather than in straight or in any evenly spaced design. The taller growing plants will be placed at the back, with a foreground of very low-growing kinds.

In the herbaceous borders there is a greater opportunity for individual taste and expression. There is a great deal to be said in favor of the herbaceous border as compared with the annual border, because once planted it is a permanent feature and becomes richer in its effect year by year. The soil should be well prepared and the space allotted will accommodate four rows of plants. Of course these are not to be set in rigid lines but grouped in masses, allowing about four or five plants, according to vigor of growth, from the front to the back of the border. Such plants as phloxes, asters, monk's-hood, larkspur and rudbeckia are desirable here. Next to the back row, one and a half feet from it, the plants alternating and also three feet apart, plant such things as Japanese anemones, chrysanthemums and lilies. Eighteen inches in front of this row, two feet apart in the line, plant phloxes, hybrids of maculata and paniculata. There are over fifty varieties of them in use, and they succeed one another in bloom all summer. You can also plant such things as Canterbury bells, coreopsis and foxglove.

In the front line, six inches from the edging and one foot between the plants, such early flowering bulbs should be used as snowdrops, crocuses, irises and tulips, and the low-growing phloxes.

On the border running along the southern end of the garden a display of bedding plants can be made, the two sides different.

In the center where the roads meet a sundial could be placed, or a barrel sunk to the level of the ground would furnish a water-lily garden.

1. REDUCTION BY ONE-EIGHTH.—Omit the fruit trees on the three sides and the border of summer flowering plants at the southern end. (This also means the doing away with the grass border that surrounds the garden.) The fruit trees might be massed in some other place, , and the flowering plants used in beds elsewhere.

2. THE ONE-HALF ACRE.—Cut the plan in two. Reduce the paths to six feet, and use only one-half the quantities enumerated. Peas and beans would be reduced to a minimum, so the potatoes, rhubarb and horseradish had better be dispensed with and their place given to peas and beans. Then use the quantities of these recommended for the one acre.

3. THE ONE-THIRD ACRE.—On a square lot, divide the space allowed for vegetables (say 120 x 120 feet) into three lots, do away with the cross-walks and have a two-foot path all around. The vegetables could then be grown in the same quantities as on the acre plot.

4. THE 60 X 60-FOOT GARDEN.—Reduce the quantities by half, do away with the potatoes as suggested under heading No. 2, and substitute peas and beans in the acre quantities.

In all these reduction schemes it is still assumed that the main idea in planning the garden is to maintain a full and constant quantity of vegetables all the year around for a family of six persons.

FRUIT TREES FOR THE QUARTER-ACRE PLOT, NO. 1

Seven Apples
Red Delicious (fall)
Yellow Delicious (fall)
McIntosh (fall)
Winesap (winter)
Yellow Transparent (summer)
Red Duchess (summer)
Jonathan (late fall)

3 Cherries
Montmorency (sour)
Black Tartarian (sweet)
Kansas Sweet (sweet)

5 Pear
2 Bartlett
2 Clapps Favorite
1 Duchess

Grapes
4 Niagara
2 Caco
4 Fredonia
2 Concord

Blackberry
24 Darrow

Raspberry totaling 30
Indian Summer red
Latham red
New Fall red
New Logan black
Morrison black
Cumberland black

8 White Currants

12 Gooseberries

200 Asparagus

300 Strawberry
Premier, Fairfax, Geneva, Ozark Beauty

6 Plum
2 Strawley
2 Burbank
2 Green Gage

12 Rhubarb

30 Horseradish

Peaches & Nectarines & Apricots
Elberta
Hale Haven
Golden Jubilee
Belle of Georgia
Manchu

Blueberries
Mammoth Cultivated

Boysenberry
New Thornless

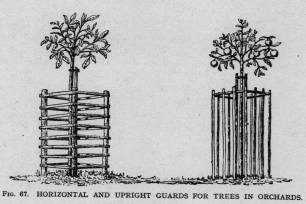

FIG. 67. HORIZONTAL AND UPRIGHT GUARDS FOR TREES IN ORCHARDS.

PLANTING LIST FOR PLOT NO. 2

No. of Rows	Space in feet
2 pole limas, 3½ feet apart	7
1 parsnips	2
1 salsify	2
½ eggplant	2
½ peppers	2
1 leeks	2
6 late potatoes, 3 feet apart	18
1 cucumbers	6
5 corn in succession, sown May 1st, 10th, 30th 4 feet apart (pumpkins and late squash to be sown between rows of corn)	20
1 early cabbage (cleared in time to sow one row corn June 20th, one June 30th)	3
1 early cauliflower (cleared in time to sow one row corn June 20th, one June 30th)	3
1 early turnips (cleared in time to sow one row corn June 20th, one June 30th)	2
2 late peas sown April 17th and May 1st (cleared in time to sow last two rows corn one July 8th, one July 16th)	8
Total for the 23 rows	77

PLANTING LIST FOR PLOT NO. 3, BEGINNING WEST SIDE

No. of Rows	Space in Feet
2 onion sets at two feet apart	4
1 beets	2
1 carrots	2
1 bush beans	3
1 kohlrabi	3
2 peas, 4 feet apart	8
First sowing of spinach to be between the rows of peas	
Total for the 8 rows	22
(This plot will be cleared by July 1st; to be sown in late carrots, rows 2 feet apart.)	
4 early potatoes, at 3 feet apart	12
1 spinach (second sowing)	2
1 beets	2
1 bush beans	3
1 carrots	2
1 turnips	3
1 kohlrabi	3
1 bush limas	3
Total for the 11 rows	30
(This plot will be cleared by July 20th, and will accommodate six rows of celery.)	
2 succession cabbage, 3 feet	6
1 dwarf Erfurt cauliflower	3
2 corn, Cory and Minnesota, at 4 feet apart	8
Total for the 5 rows	17
(Cleared August 1st, to be sown with rutabaga turnips.)	
1 row muskmelons (will be cleared about August 15th to be sown in winter beets)	6
The 25 rows for No. 3 will require	75

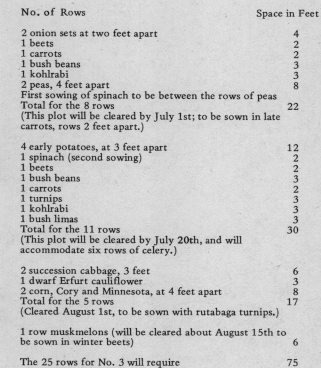

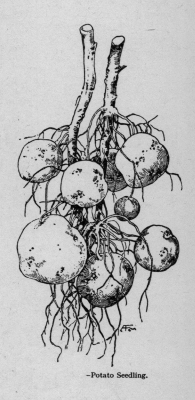

—Potato Seedling.

PLANTING LIST FOR PLOT NO. 4, BEGINNING EAST SIDE

No. of Rows	Space in Feet
2 tomatoes, 5 feet	10
1 okra	3
1 spinach	5
1 watermelons	5
1 summer squash	4
2 Brussels sprouts, 3 feet apart	6
6 onions, 18 inches apart (this onion ground will be cleared by August 20th, to be sown in Yellow Stone turnips for winter)	8
1 muskmelons (second sowing). (Will be cleared about August 20th, to be sown in winter spinach.)	8
The next twenty feet should be kept for making successional sowings of lettuce and radish, beginning about April 6th, and sowing at intervals of fifteen days, as the lettuce and radish are harvested. Three sowings of bush beans should be made from July 1 to August 1st, and two rows of endive sown about August 10th	21
1 cabbage, cauliflower, and Brussels sprouts (follow this by last sowing of lettuce)	2
1 parsley (sown one foot from border)	3
The 17 rows and 20 extra feed require	75

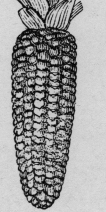

FIG. 386. LEEK.

—Chinese Artichoke (Stachys tuberifera).

USDA FROST TABLE

Crop	Planting dates for localities in which average date of last freeze is—						
	Jan. 30	Feb. 8	Feb. 18	Feb. 28	Mar. 10	Mar. 20	Mar. 30
Asparagus [1]					Jan. 1–Mar. 1	Feb. 1–Mar. 10	Feb. 15–Mar. 20.
Beans, lima	Feb. 1–Apr. 15	Feb. 10–May 1	Mar. 1–May 1	Mar. 15–June 1	Mar. 20–June 1	Apr. 1–June 15	Apr. 15–June 20.
Beans, snap	Feb. 1–Apr. 1	Feb. 1–May 1	Mar. 1–May 1	Mar. 10–May 15	Mar. 15–May 15	Mar. 15–May 25	Apr. 1–June 1.
Beet	Jan. 1–Mar. 15	Jan. 10–Mar. 15	Jan. 20–Apr. 1	Feb. 1–June 1	Feb. 15–June 1	Feb. 15–May 15	Mar. 1–June 1.
Broccoli, sprouting [1]	Jan. 1–30	Jan. 1–30	Jan. 15–Feb. 15	Feb. 1–Mar. 1	Feb. 15–Mar. 15	Feb. 15–Mar. 15	Mar. 1–20.
Brussels sprouts [1]	Jan. 1–30	Jan. 1–30	Jan. 15–Feb. 15	Feb. 1–Mar. 1	Feb. 15–Mar. 15	Feb. 15–Mar. 15	Mar. 1–20.
Cabbage [1]	Jan. 1–15	Jan. 1–Feb. 10	Jan. 1–Feb. 25	Jan. 15–Feb. 25	Jan. 25–Mar. 1	Feb. 1–Mar. 1	Feb. 15–Mar. 10.
Cabbage, Chinese	(2)	(2)	(2)	(2)	(2)	(2)	(2)
Carrot	Jan. 1–Mar. 1	Jan. 1–Mar. 1	Jan. 15–Mar. 1	Feb. 1–Mar. 1	Feb. 10–Mar. 15	Feb. 15–Mar. 20	Mar. 1–Apr. 10.
Cauliflower [1]	Jan. 1–Feb. 1	Jan. 1–Feb. 1	Jan. 10–Feb. 10	Jan. 20–Feb. 20	Feb. 1–Mar. 1	Feb. 10–Mar. 10	Feb. 20–Mar. 20.
Celery and celeriac	Jan. 1–Feb. 1	Jan. 10–Feb. 10	Jan. 20–Feb. 20		Feb. 20–Mar. 20	Feb. 20–Apr. 1	Mar. 15–Apr. 15.
Chard	Jan. 1–Apr. 1	Jan. 10–Apr. 1	Jan. 20–Apr. 15	Feb. 1–May 1	Feb. 15–May 15	Feb. 20–May 15	Mar. 1–May 25.
Chervil and chives	Jan. 1–Feb. 1	Jan. 1–Feb. 1	Jan. 1–Feb. 1	Jan. 15–Feb. 15	Feb. 1–Mar. 1	Feb. 10–Mar. 15	Feb. 15–Mar. 15.
Chicory, witloof					June 1–July 1	June 1–July 1	June 1–July 1
Collards [1]	Jan. 1–Feb. 15	Jan. 1–Feb. 15	Jan. 1–Mar. 15	Jan. 15–Mar. 15	Feb. 15–May 1	Feb. 15–May 1	Mar. 1–June 1.
Cornsalad	Jan. 1–Feb. 15	Jan. 1–Feb. 15	Jan. 1–Feb. 15	Jan. 1–Mar. 1	Jan. 1–Mar. 1	Jan. 1–Mar. 15	Jan. 15–Mar. 15.
Corn, sweet	Feb. 1–Mar. 15	Feb. 10–Apr. 1	Feb. 20–Apr. 15	Mar. 1–Apr. 15	Mar. 10–Apr. 15	Mar. 15–May 1	Mar. 25–May 15.
Cress, upland	Jan. 1–Feb. 15	Jan. 1–Feb. 15	Jan. 15–Feb. 15	Feb. 1–Mar. 1	Feb. 10–Mar. 15	Feb. 20–Mar. 15	Mar. 1–Apr. 1.
Cucumber	Feb. 15–Mar. 15	Feb. 15–Apr. 1	Feb. 15–Apr. 15	Mar. 1–Apr. 15	Mar. 15–Apr. 15	Apr. 1–May 1	Apr. 10–May 15.
Eggplant [1]	Feb. 1–Mar. 1	Feb. 10–Mar. 15	Feb. 20–Apr. 1	Mar. 10–Apr. 15	Mar. 15–Apr. 15	Apr. 1–May 1	Apr. 15–May 15.
Endive	Jan. 1–Mar. 1	Jan. 1–Mar. 1	Jan. 15–Mar. 1	Feb. 1–Mar. 1	Feb. 15–Mar. 15	Mar. 1–Apr. 1	Mar. 10–Apr. 1.
Fennel, Florence	Jan. 1–Mar. 1	Jan. 1–Mar. 1	Jan. 15–Mar. 1	Feb. 1–Mar. 1	Feb. 15–Mar. 15	Mar. 1–Apr. 1	Mar. 10–Apr. 1.
Garlic	(2)	(2)	(2)	(2)	(2)		
Horseradish [1]							Mar. 1–Apr. 1.
Kale	Jan. 1–Feb. 1	Jan. 10–Feb. 1	Jan. 20–Feb. 10	Feb. 1–20	Feb. 10–Mar. 1	Feb. 20–Mar. 10	Mar. 1–20.
Kohlrabi	Jan. 1–Feb. 1	Jan. 10–Feb. 1	Jan. 20–Feb. 10	Feb. 1–20	Feb. 10–Mar. 1	Feb. 20–Mar. 10	Mar. 1–Apr. 1.
Leek	Jan. 1–Feb. 1	Jan. 1–Feb. 1	Jan. 1–Feb. 15	Jan. 15–Feb. 15	Jan. 25–Mar. 1	Feb. 1–Mar. 1	Feb. 15–Mar. 15.
Lettuce, head [1]	Jan. 1–Feb. 1	Jan. 1–Feb. 1	Jan. 1–Feb. 1	Jan. 15–Feb. 15	Feb. 1–20	Feb. 15–Mar. 1	Mar. 1–20.
Lettuce, leaf	Jan. 1–Feb. 1	Jan. 1–Feb. 1	Jan. 1–Mar. 15	Jan. 1–Mar. 1	Jan. 15–Apr. 1	Feb. 1–Apr. 1	Feb. 15–Apr. 15.
Muskmelon	Feb. 15–Mar. 15	Feb. 15–Apr. 1	Feb. 15–Apr. 15	Mar. 1–Apr. 15	Mar. 15–Apr. 15	Apr. 1–May 1	Apr. 10–May 15.
Mustard	Jan. 1–Mar. 1	Jan. 1–Mar. 1	Feb. 15–Apr. 1	Feb. 1–Mar. 1	Feb. 10–Mar. 15	Feb. 20–Apr. 1	Mar. 1–Apr. 1.
Okra	Feb. 15–Apr. 1	Feb. 15–Apr. 15	Mar. 1–June 1	Mar. 10–June 1	Mar. 20–June 1	Apr. 1–June 15	Apr. 10–June 15.
Onion [1]	Jan. 1–15	Jan. 1–15	Jan. 1–15	Jan. 1–Feb. 1	Jan. 15–Feb. 15	Feb. 10–Mar. 10	Feb. 15–Mar. 15.
Onion, seed	Jan. 1–15	Jan. 1–15	Jan. 1–15	Jan. 15–Feb. 15	Feb. 1–Mar. 1	Feb. 10–Mar. 10	Feb. 15–Mar. 15.
Onion, sets	Jan. 1–15	Jan. 1–15	Jan. 1–15	Jan. 1–Mar. 1	Jan. 15–Mar. 1	Feb. 1–Mar. 20	Feb. 15–Mar. 20.
Parsley	Jan. 1–30	Jan. 1–30	Jan. 1–30	Jan. 15–Mar. 1	Feb. 1–Mar. 10	Feb. 15–Mar. 15	Mar. 1–Apr. 1.
Parsnip			Jan. 1–30	Jan. 15–Feb. 15	Jan. 15–Mar. 1	Feb. 15–Mar. 15	Mar. 1–Apr. 1.
Peas, garden	Jan. 1–Feb. 15	Jan. 1–Feb. 15	Jan. 1–Mar. 1	Jan. 15–Mar. 1	Jan. 15–Mar. 1	Feb. 1–Mar. 15	Feb. 10–Mar. 20.
Peas, black-eye	Feb. 1–May 1	Feb. 15–May 15	Mar. 1–June 15	Mar. 10–June 20	Mar. 15–July 1	Apr. 1–July 1	Apr. 15–July 1.
Pepper [1]	Feb. 1–Apr. 1	Feb. 15–Apr. 15	Mar. 1–May 1	Mar. 15–May 1	Apr. 1–June 1	Apr. 10–June 1	Apr. 15–June 1.
Potato	Jan. 1–Feb. 15	Jan. 1–Apr. 1	Jan. 15–Mar. 1	Jan. 15–Mar. 1	Feb. 1–Mar. 1	Feb. 20–Mar. 20	Mar. 1–Apr. 1.
Radish	Jan. 1–Apr. 1	Jan. 1–Apr. 1	Jan. 1–Apr. 1	Jan. 1–Apr. 1	Jan. 1–Apr. 15	Jan. 20–May 1	Feb. 15–May 1.
Rhubarb [1]							
Rutabaga				Jan. 1–Feb. 1	Jan. 15–Feb. 15	Jan. 15–Mar. 1	Feb. 1–Mar. 1.
Salsify	Jan. 1–Feb. 1	Jan. 10–Feb. 10	Jan. 15–Feb. 20	Jan. 15–Mar. 1	Feb. 1–Mar. 1	Feb. 15–Mar. 1	Mar. 1–15.
Shallot	Jan. 1–Feb. 1	Jan. 1–Feb. 10	Jan. 1–Feb. 20	Jan. 1–Mar. 1	Feb. 1–Mar. 1	Feb. 1–Mar. 10	Feb. 15–Mar. 15.
Sorrel	Jan. 1–Mar. 1	Jan. 1–Mar. 1	Jan. 15–Mar. 1	Feb. 1–Mar. 1	Feb. 10–Mar. 15	Feb. 20–Mar. 15	Feb. 20–Apr. 1.
Soybean	Mar. 1–June 30	Mar. 1–June 30	Mar. 10–June 30	Mar. 20–June 30	Apr. 10–June 30	Apr. 10–June 30	Apr. 20–June 30.
Spinach	Jan. 1–Feb. 15	Jan. 1–Feb. 15	Jan. 1–Mar. 1	Jan. 1–Mar. 1	Jan. 15–Mar. 10	Jan. 15–Mar. 15	Feb. 1–Mar. 20.
Spinach, New Zealand	Feb. 1–Apr. 15	Feb. 15–Apr. 15	Mar. 1–Apr. 15	Mar. 15–May 15	Mar. 20–June 1	Apr. 1–May 15	Apr. 10–June 1.
Squash, summer	Feb. 1–Apr. 15	Feb. 15–Apr. 15	Mar. 1–Apr. 15	Mar. 15–May 15	Mar. 15–May 1	Apr. 1–May 15	Apr. 10–June 1.
Sweetpotato	Feb. 15–May 15	Mar. 1–May 15	Mar. 20–June 1	Mar. 20–June 1	Apr. 1–June 1	Apr. 10–June 1	Apr. 20–June 1.
Tomato	Feb. 1–Apr. 1	Feb. 20–Apr. 10	Mar. 1–Apr. 20	Mar. 10–May 1	Mar. 20–May 10	Apr. 1–May 20	Apr. 10–June 1.
Turnip	Jan. 1–Mar. 1	Feb. 1–Mar. 1	Jan. 10–Mar. 1	Jan. 20–Mar. 1	Feb. 1–Mar. 1	Feb. 10–Mar. 10	Feb. 20–Mar. 20.
Watermelon	Feb. 15–Mar. 15	Feb. 15–Apr. 1	Feb. 15–Apr. 15	Mar. 1–Apr. 15	Mar. 15–Apr. 15	Apr. 1–May 1	Apr. 10–May 15.

[1] Plants.
[2] Generally fall-planted.

Earliest dates, and range of dates, for safe spring planting of vegetables in the open

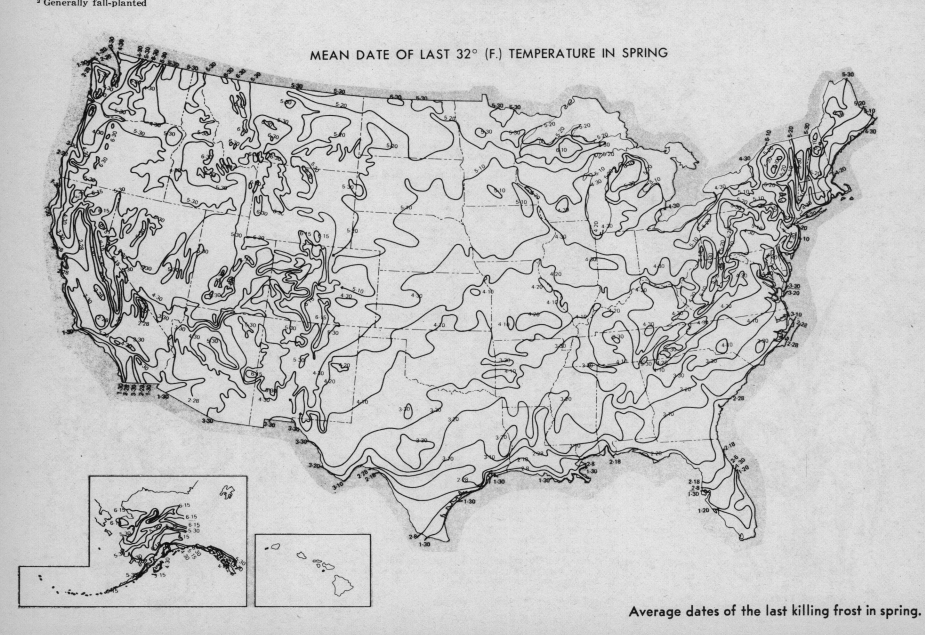

MEAN DATE OF LAST 32° (F.) TEMPERATURE IN SPRING

Average dates of the last killing frost in spring.

USDA FROST TABLE

Crop	\multicolumn{7}{c}{Planting dates for localities in which average date of last freeze is—}
	Apr. 10	Apr. 20	Apr. 30	May 10	May 20	May 30	June 10
Asparagus [1]	Mar. 10–Apr. 10	Mar. 15–Apr. 15	Mar. 20–Apr. 15	Mar. 10–Apr. 30	Apr. 20–May 15	May 1–June 1	May 15–June 1.
Beans, lima	Apr. 1–June 30	May 1–June 20	May 15–June 15	May 25–June 15			
Beans, snap	Apr. 10–June 30	Apr. 25–June 30	May 10–June 30	May 10–June 30	May 15–June 30	May 25–June 15	
Beet	Mar. 10–June 1	Mar. 20–June 1	Apr. 1–June 15	Apr. 15–June 15	May 1–June 15	May 1–June 15	May 15–June 15.
Broccoli, sprouting [1]	Mar. 15–Apr. 15	Mar. 25–Apr. 20	Apr. 1–May 1	Apr. 15–June 1	May 1–June 15	May 10–June 10	May 20–June 10.
Brussels sprouts [1]	Mar. 15–Apr. 15	Mar. 25–Apr. 20	Apr. 1–May 1	Apr. 15–June 1	May 1–June 15	May 10–June 10	May 20–June 10.
Cabbage [1]	Mar. 1–Apr. 1	Mar. 10–Apr. 1	Mar. 15–Apr. 10	Apr. 1–May 15	May 1–June 15	May 10–June 15	May 20–June 1.
Cabbage, Chinese	(2)	(2)	(2)	Apr. 1–May 15	May 1–June 15	May 10–June 15	May 20–June 1.
Carrot	Mar. 10–Apr. 20	Apr. 1–May 15	Apr. 10–June 1	Apr. 20–June 15	May 1–June 1	May 10–June 1	May 20–June 1.
Cauliflower [1]	Mar. 1–Mar. 20	Mar. 15–Apr. 20	Apr. 10–May 10	Apr. 15–May 15	May 10–June 15	June 1	
Celery and celeriac	Apr. 1–Apr. 20	Apr. 10–May 1	Apr. 15–May 1	Apr. 20–June 15	May 10–June 15	May 20–June 1	June 1–June 15.
Chard	Mar. 15–June 15	Apr. 1–June 15	Apr. 15–June 15	Apr. 20–June 15	May 10–June 15	May 20–June 1	June 1–June 15.
Chervil and chives	Mar. 1–Apr. 1	Mar. 10–Apr. 10	Mar. 20–Apr. 20	Apr. 1–May 1	Apr. 15–May 15	May 20–June 1	June 1–June 15.
Chicory, witloof	June 10–July 1	June 15–July 1	June 15–July 1	June 1–20	June 1–15	May 1–June 1	May 15–June 1.
Collards [1]	Mar. 1–June 1	Mar. 1–June 1	Apr. 1–June 1	June 1–20		June 1–15	June 1–15.
Cornsalad	Feb. 1–June 1	Feb. 15–Apr. 15	Mar. 1–May 1	Apr. 1–June 1	May 1–June 1	May 10–June 15	May 20–June 1.
Corn, sweet	Apr. 10–June 1	Apr. 25–June 15	May 10–June 15	May 10–June 1	May 15–June 1	May 15–June 15	May 15–June 15.
Cress, upland	Mar. 10–Apr. 15	Mar. 20–May 1	Apr. 10–May 10	Apr. 20–May 20	May 1–June 1	May 20–June 1	
Cucumber	Apr. 20–June 1	May 1–June 15	May 15–June 15	May 20–June 15	June 1–15	May 15–June 1	May 15–June 15.
Eggplant [1]	May 1–June 1	May 10–June 1	May 15–June 10	May 20–June 15	June 1–15		
Endive	Mar. 15–Apr. 15	Mar. 25–Apr. 15	Apr. 1–May 1	Apr. 15–May 15	May 1–30	May 1–30	May 15–June 1.
Fennel, Florence	Mar. 15–Apr. 15	Mar. 25–Apr. 15	Apr. 1–May 1	Apr. 15–May 15	May 1–30	May 1–30	May 15–June 1.
Garlic	Feb. 20–Mar. 20	Mar. 10–Apr. 1	Mar. 15–Apr. 15	Apr. 1–May 1	Apr. 15–May 15	May 1–30	May 15–June 1.
Horseradish [1]	Mar. 10–Apr. 10	Mar. 20–Apr. 20	Apr. 1–30	Apr. 15–May 15	Apr. 20–May 20	May 1–30	May 15–June 1.
Kale	Mar. 10–Apr. 10	Mar. 20–Apr. 10	Apr. 1–20	Apr. 10–May 1	Apr. 20–May 10	May 1–30	May 15–June 1.
Kohlrabi	Mar. 10–Apr. 10	Mar. 20–May 1	Apr. 1–May 10	Apr. 10–May 15	Apr. 20–May 20	May 1–30	May 15–June 1.
Leek	Mar. 1–Apr. 1	Mar. 15–Apr. 15	Apr. 1–May 1	Apr. 15–May 15	May 1–May 20	May 1–15	May 1–15.
Lettuce, head [1]	Mar. 10–Apr. 1	Mar. 20–Apr. 15	Apr. 1–May 1	Apr. 15–May 15	May 1–June 30	May 10–June 30	May 20–June 30.
Lettuce, leaf	Mar. 15–May 15	Mar. 20–May 15	Apr. 1–June 1	Apr. 15–June 15	May 1–June 30	May 10–June 30	May 20–June 30.
Muskmelon	Apr. 20–June 1	May 1–June 15	May 15–June 15	June 1–June 15			
Mustard	Mar. 10–Apr. 20	Mar. 20–May 1	Apr. 1–May 10	Apr. 15–June 1	May 1–June 30	May 10–June 30	May 20–June 30.
Okra	Apr. 20–June 15	May 1–June 1	May 10–June 1	May 20–June 10	June 1–20		
Onion [1]	Mar. 1–Apr. 1	Mar. 15–Apr. 10	Apr. 1–May 1	Apr. 10–May 1	Apr. 20–May 15	May 1–30	May 10–June 10.
Onion, seed	Mar. 1–Apr. 1	Mar. 15–Apr. 1	Mar. 15–Apr. 15	Apr. 1–May 1	Apr. 20–May 15	May 1–30	May 10–June 10.
Onion, sets	Mar. 1–Apr. 1	Mar. 10–Apr. 1	Apr. 1–May 1	Apr. 10–May 1	Apr. 20–May 15	May 1–30	May 10–June 10.
Parsley	Mar. 10–Apr. 10	Mar. 20–Apr. 20	Apr. 1–May 1	Apr. 15–May 15	May 1–20	May 1–June 1	May 20–June 10.
Parsnip	Mar. 10–Apr. 10	Mar. 10–Apr. 20	Apr. 1–May 1	Apr. 15–June 1	May 1–20	May 1–June 1	May 20–June 10.
Peas, garden	Feb. 20–Mar. 20	Mar. 10–Apr. 1	Mar. 20–May 1	Apr. 1–May 15	Apr. 15–June 1	May 1–June 15	May 10–June 15.
Peas, black-eye	May 1–July 1	May 10–June 15	May 15–June 1				
Pepper [1]	May 1–June 1	May 10–June 1	May 15–June 10	May 20–June 10	May 25–June 15	June 1–15	
Potato	Mar. 10–Apr. 1	Mar. 10–Apr. 15	Mar. 20–May 10	Apr. 1–June 1	Apr. 15–June 15	May 1–June 15	May 15–June 1.
Radish	Mar. 1–May 1	Mar. 10–May 10	Mar. 20–May 10	Apr. 1–June 1	Apr. 15–June 15	May 1–June 15	May 15–June 1.
Rhubarb [1]	Mar. 1–Apr. 1	Mar. 10–Apr. 10	Mar. 20–Apr. 15	Apr. 1–May 1	Apr. 15–May 10	May 1–20	May 15–June 1.
Rutabaga			May 1–June 1	May 1–June 1	May 1–20	May 10–20	May 20–June 1.
Salsify	Mar. 10–Apr. 15	Mar. 15–May 1	Apr. 1–May 15	Apr. 15–June 1	May 1–June 1	May 10–June 1	May 20–June 1.
Shallot	Mar. 1–Apr. 1	Mar. 15–May 15	Apr. 1–May 1	Apr. 10–May 1	Apr. 20–May 10	May 1–June 1	May 1–June 1.
Sorrel	Mar. 1–Apr. 15	Mar. 15–May 1	Apr. 1–May 15	Apr. 15–June 1	May 1–June 1	May 10–June 10	May 20–June 10.
Soybean	May 1–June 30	May 10–June 20	May 15–June 15	May 25–June 10			
Spinach	Feb. 15–Apr. 1	Mar. 1–Apr. 15	Mar. 20–Apr. 20	Apr. 1–June 15	Apr. 10–June 15	Apr. 20–June 15	May 1–June 15.
Spinach, New Zealand	Apr. 20–June 1	May 1–June 15	May 1–June 15	May 10–June 15	May 20–June 15	June 1–15	
Squash, summer	Apr. 20–June 1	May 1–June 1	May 1–30	May 10–June 10	May 20–June 15	June 1–20	June 10–20.
Sweetpotato	May 1–June 1	May 10–June 10	May 20–June 10				
Tomato	Apr. 20–June 1	May 5–June 10	May 10–June 15	May 15–June 10	May 25–June 15	June 5–20	June 15–30.
Turnip	Mar. 1–Apr. 1	Mar. 10–Apr. 1	Mar. 20–May 1	Apr. 1–June 1	Apr. 15–June 1	May 1–June 15	May 15–June 15.
Watermelon	Apr. 20–June 1	May 1–June 15	May 15–June 15	June 1–June 15	June 15–July 1	May 1–June 15	May 15–June 15.

[1] Plants.
[2] Generally fall-planted

Earliest dates, and range of dates, for safe spring planting of vegetables in the open—Continued

MEAN DATE OF FIRST 32° (F.) TEMPERATURE IN AUTUMN

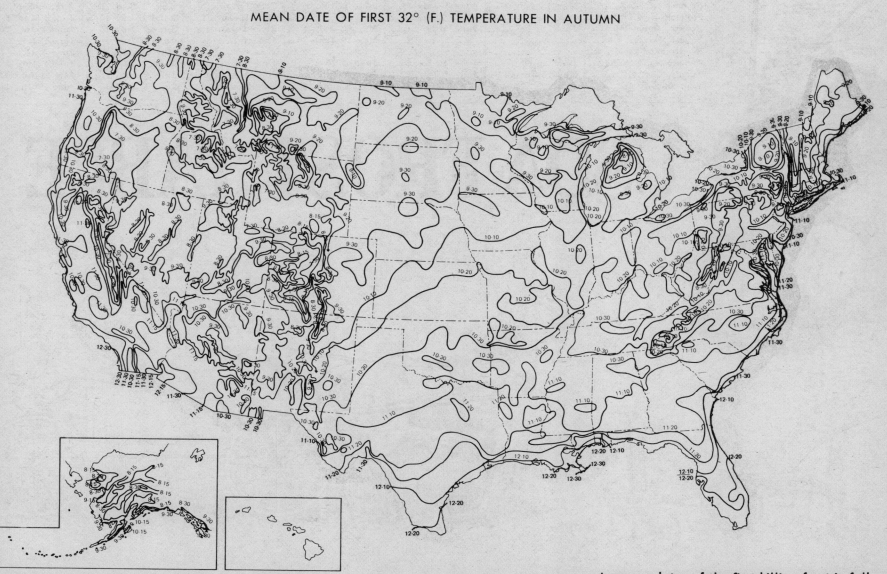

Average dates of the first killing frost in fall.

MINERAL OIL STOVE, WITH DOUBLE BURNERS.

Latest dates, and range of dates, for safe fall planting of vegetables in the open

Crop	Planting dates for localities in which average dates of first freeze is—					
	Aug. 30	Sept. 10	Sept. 20	Sept. 30	Oct. 10	Oct. 20
Asparagus[1]					Oct. 20–Nov. 15	Nov. 1–Dec. 15
Beans, lima				June 1–15	June 1–15	June 15–30.
Beans, snap		May 15–June 15	June 1–July 1	June 1–July 10	June 15–July 20	July 1–Aug. 1.
Beet	May 15–June 15	May 15–June 15	June 1–July 1	June 1–July 10	June 15–July 25	July 1–Aug. 5.
Broccoli, sprouting	May 1–June 1	May 1–June 1	May 1–June 15	June 1–30	June 15–July 15	July 1–Aug. 1.
Brussels sprouts	May 1–June 1	May 1–June 1	May 1–June 15	June 1–30	June 15–July 15	July 1–Aug. 1.
Cabbage[1]	May 1–June 1	May 1–June 1	May 1–June 15	June 1–July 10	June 1–July 15	July 1–20.
Cabbage, Chinese	May 15–June 15	May 15–June 15	June 1–July 1	June 1–July 15	June 15–Aug. 1	July 15–Aug. 15.
Carrot	May 15–June 15	May 15–June 15	June 1–July 1	June 1–July 10	June 1–July 20	June 15–Aug. 1.
Cauliflower[1]	May 1–June 1	May 1–July 1	May 1–July 1	May 10–July 15	June 1–July 25	July 1–Aug. 5.
Celery[1] and celeriac	May 1–June 1	May 15–June 15	May 15–July 1	June 1–July 5	June 1–July 15	June 1–Aug. 1.
Chard	May 15–June 15	May 15–July 1	June 1–July 1	June 1–July 5	June 1–July 20	June 1–Aug. 1.
Chervil and chives	May 10–June 10	May 1–June 15	May 15–June 15	(2)	(2)	(2)
Chicory, witloof	May 15–June 15	May 15–June 15	May 15–June 15	June 1–July 1	June 1–July 1	June 15–July 15.
Collards[1]	May 15–June 15	May 15–June 15	May 15–June 15	June 15–July 15	July 1–Aug. 1	July 15–Aug. 15.
Cornsalad	May 15–June 15	May 15–July 1	June 15–Aug. 1	July 15–Sept. 1	Aug. 15–Sept. 15	Sept. 1–Oct. 15.
Corn, sweet			June 1–July 1	June 1–July 1	June 1–July 10	June 1–July 20.
Cress, upland	May 15–June 15	May 15–July 1	June 15–Aug. 1	July 15–Sept. 1	Aug. 15–Sept. 15	Sept. 1–Oct. 15.
Cucumber			June 1–15	June 1–July 1	June 1–July 1	June 1–July 15.
Eggplant[1]				May 20–June 10	May 15–June 15	June 1–July 1.
Endive	June 1–July 1	June 1–July 1	June 15–July 15	June 15–Aug. 1	July 1–Aug. 15	July 15–Sept. 1.
Fennel, Florence	May 15–June 15	May 15–July 15	June 1–July 1	June 1–July 1	June 15–July 15	June 15–Aug. 1.
Garlic	(2)	(2)	(2)	(2)	(2)	(2)
Horseradish[1]	(2)	(2)	(2)	(2)	(2)	(2)
Kale	May 15–June 15	May 15–June 15	June 1–July 1	June 15–July 15	July 1–Aug. 1	July 15–Aug. 15.
Kohlrabi	May 15–June 15	June 1–July 1	June 1–July 15	June 15–July 15	July 1–Aug. 1	July 15–Aug. 15.
Leek	May 1–June 1	May 1–June 1	(2)	(2)	(2)	(2)
Lettuce, head[1]	May 15–July 1	May 15–July 1	June 1–July 15	June 15–Aug. 1	July 15–Aug. 15	Aug. 1–30.
Lettuce, leaf	May 15–July 15	May 15–July 15	June 1–Aug. 1	June 1–Aug. 1	July 15–Sept. 1	July 15–Sept. 1.
Muskmelon			May 1–June 15	May 15–June 1	June 1–June 15	June 15–July 20.
Mustard	May 15–July 15	May 15–July 15	June 1–Aug. 1	June 15–Aug. 1	July 15–Aug. 15	Aug. 1–Sept. 1.
Okra			June 1–20	June 1–July 1	June 1–July 15	June 1–Aug. 1.
Onion[1]	May 1–June 10	May 1–June 10	(2)	(2)	(2)	(2)
Onion, seed	May 1–June 1	May 1–June 10	(2)	(2)	(2)	(2)
Onion, sets	May 1–June 1	May 1–June 10	(2)	(2)	(2)	(2)
Parsley	May 15–June 15	May 1–June 15	June 1–July 1	June 1–July 15	June 15–Aug. 1	July 15–Aug. 15.
Parsnip	May 15–June 1	May 1–June 15	May 15–June 15	June 1–July 1	June 1–July 10	(2)
Peas, garden	May 10–June 15	May 1–July 1	June 1–July 15	June 1–Aug. 1	(2)	(2)
Peas, black-eye					June 1–July 1	June 1–July 1.
Pepper[1]			June 1–June 20	June 1–July 1	June 1–July 1	June 1–July 10.
Potato	May 15–June 1	May 15–June 15	May 1–June 15	May 1–June 15	May 15–June 15	June 15–July 15.
Radish	May 1–July 15	May 1–Aug. 1	June 1–Aug. 15	July 1–Sept. 1	July 15–Sept. 15	Aug. 1–Oct. 1.
Rhubarb[1]	Sept. 1–Oct. 1	Sept. 15–Oct. 15	Sept. 15–Nov. 1	Oct. 1–Nov. 1	Oct. 15–Nov. 15	Oct. 15–Dec. 1.
Rutabaga	May 15–June 15	May 1–June 15	June 1–July 1	June 1–July 1	June 15–July 15	July 10–20.
Salsify	May 15–June 1	May 10–June 10	May 20–June 20	June 1–20	June 1–July 1	June 1–July 1.
Shallot	(2)	(2)	(2)	(2)	(2)	(2)
Sorrel	May 15–June 15	May 15–June 15	June 1–July 1	June 1–July 15	July 1–Aug. 1	July 15–Aug. 15.
Soybean				May 25–June 10	June 1–25	June 1–July 5.
Spinach	May 15–July 1	June 1–July 15	June 1–Aug. 1	July 1–Aug. 15	Aug. 1–Sept. 1	Aug. 20–Sept. 10.
Spinach, New Zealand				May 15–July 1	June 1–July 15	June 1–Aug. 1.
Squash, summer	June 10–20	June 1–20	May 15–July 1	June 1–July 1	June 1–July 15	June 1–July 20.
Squash, winter			May 20–June 10	June 1–15	June 1–July 1	June 1–July 1.
Sweetpotato					May 20–June 10	June 1–15.
Tomato	June 20–30	June 10–20	June 1–20	June 1–20	June 1–20	June 1–July 1.
Turnip	May 15–June 15	June 1–July 1	June 1–July 15	June 1–Aug. 1	July 1–Aug. 1	July 15–Aug. 15.
Watermelon			May 1–June 15	May 15–June 1	June 1–June 15	June 15–July 20.

[1] Plants.
[2] Generally spring-planted

USDA FROST TABLE

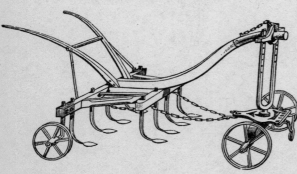

QUEEN ONIONS.

—Latest dates, and range of dates, for safe fall planting of vegetables in the open—

Crop	Planting dates for localities in which average date of first freeze is—					
	Oct. 30	Nov. 10	Nov. 20	Nov. 30	Dec. 10	Dec. 20
Asparagus [1]	Nov. 15–Jan. 1	Dec. 1–Jan. 1				
Beans, lima	July 1–Aug. 1	July 1–Aug. 15	July 15–Sept. 1	Aug. 1–Sept. 15	Sept. 1–30	Sept. 1–Oct. 1.
Beans, snap	July 1–Aug. 15	July 1–Sept. 1	July 1–Sept. 10	Aug. 15–Sept. 20	Sept. 1–30	Sept. 1–Nov. 1.
Beet	Aug. 1–Sept. 1	Aug. 1–Oct. 1	Sept. 1–Dec. 1	Sept. 1–Dec. 15	Sept. 1–Dec. 31	Sept. 1–Dec. 31.
Broccoli, sprouting	July 1–Aug. 15	Aug. 1–Sept. 1	Aug. 1–Sept. 15	Aug. 1–Oct. 1	Aug. 1–Nov. 1	Sept. 1–Dec. 31.
Brussels sprouts	July 1–Aug. 15	Aug. 1–Sept. 1	Aug. 1–Sept. 15	Aug. 1–Oct. 1	Aug. 1–Nov. 1	Sept. 1–Dec. 31.
Cabbage [1]	Aug. 1–Sept. 1	Sept. 1–15	Sept. 1–Dec. 1	Sept. 1–Dec. 31	Sept. 1–Dec. 31	Sept. 1–Dec. 31.
Cabbage, Chinese	Aug. 1–Sept. 15	Aug. 15–Oct. 1	Sept. 1–Oct. 15	Sept. 1–Nov. 1	Sept. 1–Nov. 15	Sept. 1–Dec. 1.
Carrot	July 1–Aug. 15	Aug. 1–Sept. 1	Sept. 1–Nov. 1	Sept. 15–Dec. 1	Sept. 15–Dec. 1	Sept. 15–Dec. 1.
Cauliflower [1]	July 15–Aug. 15	Aug. 1–Sept. 1	Aug. 1–Sept. 15	Aug. 15–Oct. 10	Sept. 1–Oct. 20	Sept. 15–Nov. 1.
Celery [1] and celeriac	June 15–Aug. 15	July 1–Aug. 15	July 15–Sept. 1	Aug. 1–Dec. 1	Sept. 1–Dec. 31	Oct. 1–Dec. 31.
Chard	June 1–Sept. 10	June 1–Sept. 15	June 1–Oct. 1	June 1–Nov. 1	June 1–Dec. 1	June 1–Dec. 31.
Chervil and chives	(2)	(2)	Nov. 1–Dec. 31	Nov. 1–Dec. 31	Nov. 1–Dec. 31	Nov. 1–Dec. 31.
Chicory, witloof	July 1–Aug. 10	July 10–Aug. 20	July 20–Sept. 1	Aug. 15–Sept. 30	Aug. 15–Oct. 15	Aug. 15–Oct. 15.
Collards [1]	Aug. 1–Sept. 15	Aug. 15–Oct. 1	Aug. 25–Nov. 1	Sept. 1–Dec. 1	Sept. 1–Dec. 31	Sept. 1–Dec. 31.
Cornsalad	Sept. 15–Nov. 1	Oct. 1–Dec. 1	Oct. 1–Dec. 1	Oct. 1–Dec. 31	Oct. 1–Dec. 31	Oct. 1–Dec. 31.
Corn, sweet	June 1–Aug. 1	June 1–Aug. 15	June 1–Sept. 1			
Cress, upland	Sept. 15–Nov. 1	Oct. 1–Dec. 1	Oct. 1–Dec. 1	Oct. 1–Dec. 31	Oct. 1–Dec. 31	Oct. 1–Dec. 31.
Cucumber	June 1–Aug. 1	June 1–Aug. 15	June 1–Aug. 15	July 15–Sept. 15	Aug. 15–Oct. 1	Aug. 15–Oct. 1.
Eggplant [1]	June 1–July 1	June 1–July 15	June 1–Aug. 1	July 1–Sept. 1	Aug. 1–Sept. 30	Aug. 1–Sept. 30.
Endive	July 15–Aug. 15	Aug. 1–Sept. 1	Sept. 1–Oct. 1	Sept. 1–Nov. 15	Sept. 1–Dec. 31	Sept. 1–Dec. 31.
Fennel, Florence	July 1–Aug. 1	July 15–Aug. 15	Aug. 15–Sept. 15	Sept. 1–Nov. 15	Sept. 1–Dec. 1	Sept. 1–Dec. 1.
Garlic	(2)	Aug. 1–Oct. 1	Aug. 15–Oct. 1	Sept. 1–Nov. 15	Sept. 15–Nov. 15	Sept. 15–Nov. 15.
Horseradish [1]	(2)	(2)	(2)	(2)	(2)	(2)
Kale	July 15–Sept. 1	Aug. 1–Sept. 15	Aug. 15–Oct. 15	Sept. 1–Dec. 1	Sept. 1–Dec. 31	Sept. 1–Dec. 31.
Kohlrabi	Aug. 1–Sept. 1	Aug. 15–Sept. 15	Sept. 1–Oct. 15	Sept. 1–Dec. 1	Sept. 15–Dec. 31	Sept. 1–Dec. 31.
Leek	(2)	(2)	Sept. 1–Nov. 1	Sept. 1–Nov. 1	Sept. 1–Nov. 1	Sept. 15–Nov. 1
Lettuce, head [1]	Aug. 1–Sept. 15	Aug. 15–Oct. 15	Sept. 1–Nov. 1	Sept. 1–Dec. 1	Sept. 15–Dec. 31	Sept. 15–Dec. 31.
Lettuce, leaf	Aug. 15–Oct. 1	Aug. 25–Oct. 1	Sept. 1–Nov. 1	Sept. 1–Dec. 1	Sept. 15–Dec. 31	Sept. 15–Dec. 31.
Muskmelon	July 1–July 15	July 15–July 30				
Mustard	Aug. 15–Oct. 15	Aug. 15–Nov. 1	Sept. 1–Dec. 1	Sept. 1–Dec. 1	Sept. 1–Dec. 1	Sept. 15–Dec. 1.
Okra	June 1–Aug. 10	June 1–Aug. 20	June 1–Sept. 10	June 1–Sept. 20	Aug. 1–Oct. 1	Aug. 1–Oct. 1.
Onion [1]		Sept. 1–Oct. 15	Oct. 1–Dec. 31	Oct. 1–Dec. 31	Oct. 1–Dec. 31	Oct. 1–Dec. 31.
Onion, seed			Sept. 1–Nov. 1	Sept. 1–Nov. 1	Sept. 1–Nov. 1	Sept. 15–Nov. 1.
Onion, sets		Oct. 1–Dec. 1	Nov. 1–Dec. 31	Nov. 1–Dec. 31	Nov. 1–Dec. 31	Nov. 1–Dec. 31.
Parsley	Aug. 1–Sept. 15	Sept. 1–Nov. 15	Sept. 1–Dec. 31	Sept. 1–Dec. 31	Sept. 1–Dec. 31	Sept. 1–Dec. 31.
Parsnip	(2)	(2)	Aug. 1–Sept. 1	Sept. 1–Nov. 15	Sept. 1–Dec. 1	Sept. 1–Dec. 1.
Peas, garden	Aug. 1–Sept. 15	Sept. 1–Nov. 1	Oct. 1–Dec. 1	Oct. 1–Dec. 31	Oct. 1–Dec. 31	Oct. 1–Dec. 31.
Peas, black-eye	June 1–Aug. 1	June 15–Aug. 15	July 1–Sept. 1	July 1–Sept. 10	July 1–Sept. 20	July 1–Sept. 20.
Pepper [1]	June 1–July 20	June 1–Aug. 1	June 1–Aug. 15	June 15–Sept. 1	Aug. 15–Oct. 1	Aug. 15–Oct. 1.
Potato	July 20–Aug. 10	July 25–Aug. 20	Aug. 10–Sept. 15	Aug. 1–Sept. 15	Aug. 1–Sept. 15	Aug. 1–Sept. 15.
Radish	Aug. 15–Oct. 15	Sept. 1–Nov. 15	Sept. 1–Dec. 1	Sept. 1–Dec. 31	Aug. 1–Sept. 15	Oct. 1–Dec. 31.
Rhubarb [1]	Nov. 1–Dec. 1					
Rutabaga	July 15–Aug. 1	July 15–Aug. 15	Aug. 1–Sept. 1	Sept. 1–Nov. 15	Oct. 1–Nov. 15	Oct. 15–Nov. 15.
Salsify	June 1–July 10	June 15–July 20	July 15–Aug. 15	Aug. 15–Sept. 30	Sept. 1–Oct. 15	Sept. 1–Oct. 31.
Shallot	(2)	Aug. 1–Oct. 1	Aug. 15–Oct. 1	Aug. 15–Oct. 15	Sept. 15–Nov. 1	Sept. 15–Nov. 1.
Sorrel	Aug. 1–Sept. 15	Aug. 15–Oct. 1	Aug. 15–Oct. 15	Sept. 1–Nov. 15	Sept. 1–Dec. 15	Sept. 1–Dec. 31.
Soybean	June 1–July 15	June 1–July 25	June 1–July 30	June 1–July 30	June 1–July 30	June 1–July 30.
Spinach	Sept. 1–Oct. 1	Sept. 15–Nov. 1	Oct. 1–Dec. 1	Oct. 1–Dec. 31	Oct. 1–Dec. 31	Oct. 1–Dec. 31.
Spinach, New Zealand	June 1–Aug. 1	June 1–Aug. 15	June 1–Aug. 15			
Squash, summer	June 1–Aug. 1	June 1–Aug. 10	June 1–Aug. 20	June 1–Sept. 1	June 1–Sept. 15	June 1–Oct. 1.
Squash, winter	June 10–July 10	June 20–July 20	July 1–Aug. 1	July 15–Aug. 15	Aug. 1–Sept. 1	Aug. 1–Sept. 1.
Sweetpotato	June 1–15	June 1–July 1	June 1–July 1	June 1–July 1	June 1–July 1	June 1–July 1.
Tomato	June 1–July 1	June 1–July 15	June 1–July 15	Aug. 1–Sept. 1	Aug. 15–Oct. 1	Sept. 1–Nov. 1.
Turnip	Aug. 1–Sept. 15	Sept. 1–Oct. 15	Sept. 1–Nov. 15	Sept. 1–Nov. 15	Oct. 1–Dec. 1	Oct. 1–Dec. 31.
Watermelon	July 1–July 15	July 15–July 30				

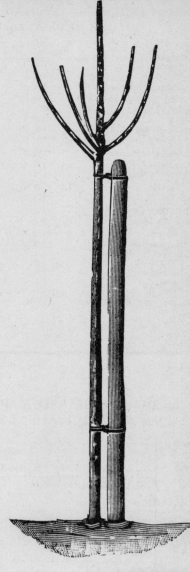

USDA FROST TABLE

[1] Plants.
[2] Generally spring-planted

To help you plan your Year 'Round Garden...

PHILADELPHIA AREA: Approximate Planting Distance and Time; Days to Harvest

COOL WEATHER VEGETABLES, Stand Light Frost

Variety	Space Between Rows	Plant Seeds Unless Noted	Days to Harvest
Beet, Burpee's Golden	1 ft.	Mid Apr. to Mid May; Mid July	55
Beet, Burpee's Red Ball	1 ft.	Mid Apr. to Mid May; Mid July	60
Broccoli, Burpee's Greenbud	1½ ft.	Mid Apr.*; Mid July	60**
Brussels Sprouts, Jadecross Hybrid	1½ ft.	Mid to Late June	80
Cabbage, Burpee's Copenhagen Market	1½ ft.	Mid Apr.*; Mid July	72**
Cabbage, Ruby Ball Hybrid	1½ ft.	Mid Apr.*; Mid July	68**
Carrot, Burpee's Goldinhart®	1 ft.	Mid Apr. to Mid May; Mid July	70
Cauliflower, Early Snowball A	1½ ft.	Mid Apr.*; Mid July	60**
Chard, Burpee's Fordhook	1 ft.	Mid Apr. to Mid July	60
Chard, Burpee's Rhubarb	1 ft.	Mid Apr. to Mid July	60
Collards, Georgia	1½ ft.	Mid Apr.; Mid July	80
Endive, Green Curled	1½ ft.	Mid Apr.; Mid July	90
Kale, Vates Blue Curled	1½ ft.	Late June to Mid July	60
Kohlrabi, Early White Vienna	2 ft.	Mid Apr. to Mid May; Mid July	55
Leek, Broad London	1½ ft.	Mid Apr. to Mid May	130
Lettuce, Burpee Bibb	1 ft.	Mid Apr.*; Late July	75**
Lettuce, Burpee's Green Ice (Cert. #7100001)	1 ft.	Mid Apr.*; Late July to Late Aug.	45
Lettuce, Burpee's Iceberg	1 ft.	Mid Apr.*; Mid July	85**
Lettuce, Ruby	1 ft.	Mid Apr.; Late July to Late Aug.	47
Lettuce, Salad Bowl	1 ft.	Mid Apr.; Late July to Late Aug.	45
Mustard, Southern Giant Curled	1½ ft.	Mid Apr.; Mid July	40

COOL WEATHER VEGETABLES, Stand Light Frost (Continued)

Variety	Space Between Rows	Plant Seeds Unless Noted	Days to Harvest
Onion, Southport Yellow Globe	1 ft.	Mid Apr.	115
Parsley, Extra Curled Dwarf	1 ft.	Mid Apr. to Mid May	85
Pea, Burpeeana Early	1 ft.***	Mid Mar. to Mid Apr.; Mid July	63
Pea, Oregon Sugar Pod	1 ft.***	Mid Mar. to Mid Apr.; Mid July	68
Radish, All Seasons White	1 ft.	Mid Apr. to Mid May; Aug.	45
Radish, Burpee White	1 ft.	Mid Apr. to Mid May; Aug.	25
Radish, Cherry Belle	1 ft.	Mid Apr. to Mid May; Aug.	22
Spinach, Bloomsdale, Long Standing	1 ft.	Mid Apr. to Mid May; Late July	48

*Start seeds indoors in March, set out plants.
**Time from when plants are set into garden.
***Peas can be planted in double rows 1 ft. apart, with about 2 ft. of space on either side of the double row

TENDER, HOT WEATHER VEGETABLES, Cannot Stand Frost

Variety	Space Between Rows	Plant Seeds Unless Noted	Days to Harvest
Bean, Bush Snap, Burpee's Tenderpod	1½ ft.	Mid May to Mid July	50
Bean, Bush Snap, Burpee's Greensleeves VP	1½ ft.	Mid May to Mid July	56
Bean, Bush Snap, Burpee's Brittle Wax	1½ ft.	Mid May to Mid July	52
Bean, Pole Snap, Romano	3 ft.	Mid May to Late June	60
Bean, Bush Lima, Burpee's Fordhook	1½ ft.	Late May to Mid June	75
Bean, Pole Lima, King of the Garden	3 ft.	Late May to Mid June	88
Cantaloupe, Burpee's Ambrosia Hybrid	3 ft.	Late May to Mid June	86

SMALL VEGETABLE GARDEN
For Maximum Harvest — 6 X 15 Feet

1 ft.	Tomato—Large Fruited—3 staked plants
2 ft.	Tomato, Pixie Hybrid — 5 staked plants
2 ft.	Zucchini Squash
2 ft.	Bush Snap Bean
1½ ft.	Bush Snap Bean — 2nd planting
1½ ft.	Carrots
1 ft.	Beets
1 ft.	Onions
1 ft.	Lettuce
1 ft.	Radishes

Cucumbers on netting or fence — 15 ft.

— 6 ft. —

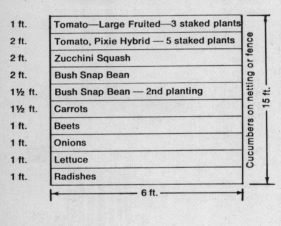

This garden in a sunny area yields an amazing amount of tasty, favorite vegetables. The tomatoes and cucumbers are grown on supports "in the air" to save space. Distance between rows is the closest possible for hand cultivation.

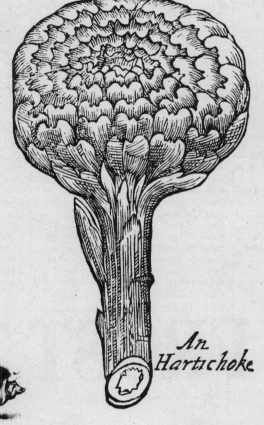

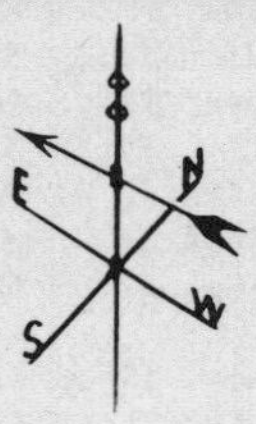

An Hartichoke

Bill-hook.

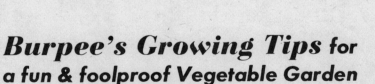

Burpee's Growing Tips for a fun & foolproof Vegetable Garden

Grow a Year 'Round Garden

with Burpee seeds and you can harvest delicious, money-saving vegetables nearly all year 'round.

- A little planning now will help you get the most from your garden, big or small, with the least effort.
- Consult the lists in this booklet for the closest possible spacing between rows, and the approximate planting and harvest dates for different vegetables.
- Notice that many varieties, for instance radishes, mature fast and that as soon as they're all harvested, you can plant another vegetable like bush beans in the same row. This succession planting keeps all of your garden space in continuous use and productive from spring to fall.
- Varieties such as beets, carrots, onions, squash and turnips can be stored for winter in a cool, frost-free place.
- Kale and Brussels Sprouts are so hardy they can stay right in the garden unprotected for winter use; carrots, parsnips, winter radishes, and salsify keep well in the ground under a straw covering (mulch) and are a fresh taste treat for winter menus.

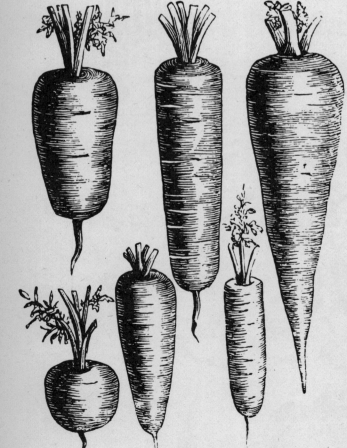

W. Atlee Burpee Co.

Clinton, Iowa 52732 • Warminster, Pa. 18974 • Riverside, Calif. 92502

88

GROWING VEGETABLES

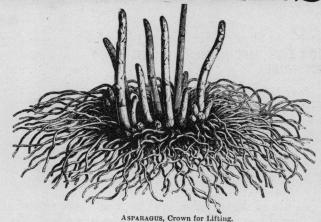

ASPARAGUS, Crown for Lifting.

Perennial Vegetables

The larger vegetables gardens need a number of perennials. Asparagus, horseradish, and rhubarb are the most important, but chives, bottom multiplier onions, and some of the flavoring and condiment plants, chiefly sage and mint, are also desirable. Unfortunately, asparagus, horseradish, and rhubarb are not adapted to conditions in the lower South.

All the perennial crops should be grouped together along one side of the garden, where they will not interfere with work on the annual crops.

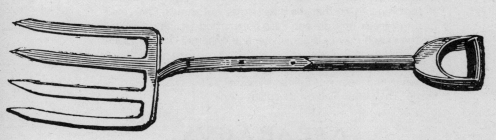

FLAT-TINED DIGGING-FORK.

Asparagus

Asparagus is among the earliest of spring vegetables. An area about 20 feet square, or a row 50 to 75 feet long, will supply plenty of fresh asparagus for a family of five or six persons, provided the soil is well enriched and the plants are given good attention. More must be planted if a supply is to be canned or frozen.

Asparagus does best where winters are cold enough to freeze the ground to a depth of a few inches at least. In many southern areas the plants make a weak growth, producing small shoots. Elevation has some effect, but, in general, the latitude of south-central Georgia is the southern limit of profitable culture.

The crop can be grown on almost any well-drained, fertile soil, and there is little possibility of having the soil too rich, especially through the use of manure. Loosen the soil far down, either by subsoil plowing or by deep spading before planting. Throw the topsoil aside and spade manure, leafmold, rotted leaves, or peat into the subsoil to a depth of 14 to 16 inches; then mix from 5 to 10 pounds of a complete fertilizer into each 75-foot row or 20-foot bed.

When the soil is ready for planting, the bottom of the trench should be about 6 inches below the natural level of the soil. After the crowns are set and covered to a depth of an inch or two, gradually work the soil into the trench around the plants during the first season. When set in beds, asparagus plants should be at least 1½ feet apart each way; when set in rows, they should be about 1½ feet apart with the rows from 4 to 5 feet apart.

Asparagus plants, or crowns, are grown from seed. The use of 1-year-old plants only is recommended. These should have a root spread of at least 15 inches, and larger ones are better. The home gardener will usually find it best to buy his plants from a grower who has a good strain of a recognized variety. Mary Washington and Waltham Washington are good varieties that have the added merit of being rust resistant. Waltham Washington is an improved strain of Mary Washington. It contains very little of the purple over-cast predominant in the Mary Washington, is a high yielder, and has good green color clear into the ground line. In procuring asparagus crowns, it is always well to be sure that they have not been allowed to dry out.

Clean cultivation encourages vigorous growth; it behooves the gardener to keep his asparagus clean from the start. In a large farm garden, with long rows, most of the work can be done with a horse-drawn cultivator or a garden tractor. In a small garden, where the rows are short or the asparagus is planted in beds, however, hand work is necessary.

For a 75-foot row, an application of manure and 6 to 8 pounds of a high-grade complete fertilizer, once each year, is recommended. Manure and fertilizer may be applied either before or after the cutting season.

Remove no shoots the year the plants are set in the permanent bed and keep the cutting period short the year after setting. Remove all shoots during the cutting season in subsequent years . Cease cutting about July 1 to 10 and let the tops grow. In the autumn, remove and burn the dead tops.

Asparagus rust and asparagus beetles are the chief enemies of the crop.

Robert E. Wester, horticulturist
Northeastern Region
Agricultural Research Service
United States Dept. of Agriculture

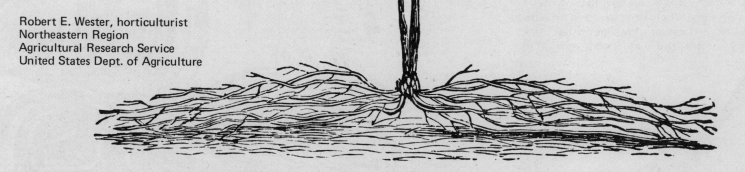

MANNER OF PLANTING ASPARAGUS.

ASPARAGUS

Reprinted from GARDEN MAGAZINE, 1905

ASPARAGUS FOR THE HOME GARDEN—
By FRANCIS HOPE

Asparagus is one of the best vegetables for the amateur's home garden. It is perfectly hardy, never fails to produce a crop, is one of the very first vegetables ready for spring and yields through June. It grows on any ordinary garden soil, but is surprisingly improved by high cultivation and heavy dressings of rich manure. The crop is earliest on sandy loam. It is not suited to land which is very wet.

There are two methods of starting a bed of asparagus, either from seed or from roots one or two years old. A good one-year-old root is very little different in appearance from a poor two-year-old one, but very different in productiveness; so don't look for bargain sales when buying.

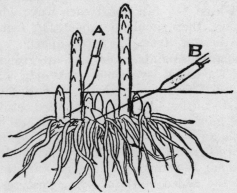

Good (*A*) and poor (*B*) modes of inserting the knife to cut asparagus. Some careful growers pull or break the shoots rather than cut them.

If you use the former method start with good seed, make the bed of the desired dimensions, fork it quite deep, work in a plentiful amount of fine, well-rotted manure, be sure the earth is made fine and friable, and, above all, see to it that it is well drained. Then sow the seed in rows fifteen inches apart, and bury them one inch and a half deep. Do not sow too thickly, for the plants must not stand, after thinning, closer together than three inches. It is a seed of slow germination, so it is well to plant radish seed in the same row—they will mark the row so that weeding can be done, break the surface of the soil to prevent baking, and give you a crop of radishes as a sort of extra dividend. Take good care of the young plants, keeping them free of weeds and the soil loose and mellow. In the fall, when the feathery leaves have turned yellow brown, cut the stalks off at the ground, dig up the bed to a depth of three inches, whiten the ground with salt, and put over the entire surface four to six inches of fresh, loose, stable refuse, filled with straw.

The following spring rake off the coarsest of this manure and dig the balance under. The young shoots appear early and if you have never seen them before, you will have to look closely for them. Asparagus may be forced, by lifting the roots carefully in the fall and placing them in a hotbed, or greenhouse. The roots should be covered, first lightly, then more heavily, until a depth of four to six inches has been obtained, using for this covering either well-rotted manure, or old tan bark.

Spring is by far the best time to make a new bed from roots. Do it any time from now until the end of June. They should be set in rows, the top of the stalks, or buds upon the roots, six inches below the surrounding level. It is wise to dig trenches for the roots, and to put in drainage, if the natural drainage is not good, then some well-rotted manure, a little bonemeal or complete fertilizer, and a layer of well-powdered loam. Mix all thoroughly, set the roots on this foundation, and fill the trench.

—SKELETON PLOW.

The cultivation of the roots is exactly the same as for seed-grown plants, only you do not need to sow radish seed, as the shoots are all ready to push up out of the ground.

The second year cut lightly. In the next, or second cutting season, cut every day up to June, allowing none to run up into stalk. The following year lengthen the cutting season, so that the harvest time may be a little longer, and increase each year until the season extends to eight weeks. After this period is reached, start over again, and the following year cut comparatively lightly, progressing in like proportion each succeeding year. This gives the roots a chance to recuperate. If you have two small beds, cut heavily in alternate years.

After you have ceased cutting, work over the ground a little and give the plants some food, for it is from this time and throughout the rest of the summer that the roots are storing strength for the coming season's crop. Liquid manure or nitrate of soda, one ounce in three gallons of water, is particularly beneficial during the cutting as well as during the growing season, and most satisfactory returns are certain.

Asparagus enemies are rust, root-rot and beetles. Rust comes on this plant as it does on beans. Brown specks appear and the leaf shrivels up and turns yellow. If rust appears, a fact you will soon remark, cut off all affected branches close to the ground and burn them at once. Early in the autumn do not fail to burn all the branches, so that the disease may not spread. Spraying with Bordeaux mixture and Paris green after cutting has ceased for the season may help somewhat and certainly cannot do any harm.

There are two beetles that feed upon this plant. One is known as the asparagus beetle, the other as the twelve-spotted beetle. They both feed on this plant alone.

ASPARAGVS:

HORSERADISH

Horseradish is adapted to the north-temperate regions of the United States, but not to the South, except possibly in the high altitudes.

Any good soil, except possibly the lightest sands and heaviest clays, will grow horseradish, but it does best on a deep, rich, moist loam that is well supplied with organic matter. Avoid shallow soil; it produces rough, prongy roots. Mix organic matter with the soil a few months before the plants or cuttings are set. Some fertilizer may be used at the time of planting and more during the subsequent seasons. A top dressing of organic matter each spring is advisable.

Horseradish is propagated either by crowns or by root cuttings. In propagating by crowns a portion of an old plant consisting of a piece of root and crown buds is merely lifted and planted in a new place. Root cuttings are pieces of older roots 6 to 8 inches long and of the thickness of a lead pencil. They may be saved when preparing the larger roots for grating, or they may be purchased from seedsmen. A trench 4 or 5 inches deep is opened with a hoe and the root cuttings are placed at an angle with their tops near the surface of the ground. Plants from these cuttings usually make good roots the first year. As a rule, the plants in the home garden are allowed to grow from year to year, and portions of the roots are removed as needed. Pieces of roots and crowns remaining in the soil are usually sufficient to reestablish the plants.

There is very little choice in the matter of varieties of horseradish. Be sure, however, to obtain good healthy planting stock of a strain that is giving good results in the area where it is being grown. New Bohemian is perhaps the best known sort sold by American seedsmen.

HORSERADISH GROWERS' GUIDE

Prepared by H. H. Thornberry
Department of Horticulture
University of Illinois
Urbana, Illinois
September 1953

Horseradish growers may improve their home-grown lines of plants by selecting desirable types of plants and roots and propagating these selections in a systematic procedure of harvesting, storing, and planting sets. A suggested procedure is as follows:

1. Search through the fields for desirable types of plants, and mark them for identification at harvest.

2. Label the selected plants in the field before digging. A label made of a piece of cloth or tag may be fastened to the root below the head with wire or string by partly lifting the roots.

3. Dig plants in the usual way.

4. When loading the roots in the field, put those with labels into a separate container.

5. Trim the roots from selected plants in the usual way. Keep all sets from one root together by putting a heavy rubber band (about size 64) around the bundle. The rubber band is easy to use, will not deteriorate during storage, and may be used the following season. Various bundles may be combined for storing.

6. Store and plant sets in the usual way. Plant sets from one bundle in a row at regular spacing; skip three spaces, and then start planting sets from another bundle. These extra spaces will be a means of identifying the group of plants from sets in one bundle or from one plant. The plants in groups will provide a means for more careful selection than is possible by observing a single plant. If no further selection is desired, use the sets in the usual way. If further selection is desirable, however, follow the remaining procedures.

7. In the second growing season before harvesting, again select desirable groups of plants and label them. Omit weak or undesirable plants.

8. In harvesting the selected plants, do the following
    (a) Keep sets from one plant in one bundle as in procedure five.
    (b) Keep the bundles of sets from one group of selected plants (between the three skipped spaces) together in one larger bundle for storage.

9. Plant sets in the usual way. Skip three spaces between sets from small bundles and six spaces between sets from large bundles.

10. In the third growing season, if further selection is desirable repeat the procedures.

11. If further selection is not desired, follow usual procedures in harvesting, storing, and planting.

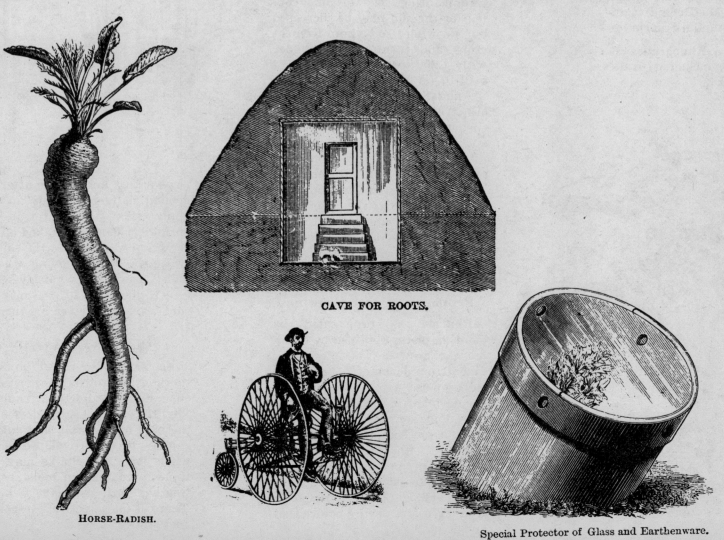

HORSE-RADISH.

CAVE FOR ROOTS.

Special Protector of Glass and Earthenware.

A good horseradish

RHUBARB

Rhubarb thrives best in regions having cool moist summers and winters cold enough to freeze the ground to a depth of several inches. It is not adapted to most parts of the South, but in certain areas of higher elevation it does fairly well. A few hills along the garden fence will supply all that a family can use.

Any deep, well-drained, fertile soil is suitable for rhubarb. Spade the soil or plow it to a depth of 12 to 16 inches and mix in rotted manure, leafmold, decayed hardwood leaves, sods, or other form of organic matter. The methods of soil preparation suggested for asparagus are suitable for rhubarb. As rhubarb is planted in hills 3 to 4 feet apart, however, it is usually sufficient to prepare each hill separately.

Rhubarb plants may be started from seed and transplanted, but seedlings vary from the parent plant. The usual method of starting the plants is to obtain pieces of crowns from established hills and set them in prepared hills. Top-dress the planting with a heavy application of organic matter in either early spring or late fall. Organic matter applied over the hills during early spring greatly hastens growth, or forces the plant.

A pound of complete commercial fertilizer high in nitrogen applied around each hill every year insures an abundant supply of plant food. The plants can be mulched with green grass or weeds.

Remove seedstalks as soon as they form. No leaf stems should be harvested before the second year and but few until the third. Moreover, the harvest season must be largely confined to early spring. The hills should be divided and reset every 7 or 8 years. Otherwise, they become too thick and produce only slender stems.

Crimson, Red Valentine, MacDonald, Canada Red, and Victoria are standard varieties.

Use only the leafstalk as a food. **Rhubarb leaves contain injurious substances, including oxalic acid. Never use them for food.**

ST. MARTIN'S RHUBARB.

Rhubarb is a cool-weather perennial plant. It does not thrive, and is rarely grown, in places where the summer mean temperature is much above 75° F. or where the winter mean is much above 40°. It grows best in the northern tier of States from Maine south to Illinois and west to Washington. The rhubarb plant needs a temperature below 50° to break dormancy. It is poorly adapted to most of the southern half of the United States. Some plantings survive only a few months in the lower South.

OUTDOOR PRODUCTION

Soils and Fertility

Rhubarb will thrive in almost any type of soil—peat, sand, or clay—if it is well drained and fertile. Rhubarb grows best, however, in deep, fertile loams that are well supplied with organic matter. The plant is tolerant of soil acidity and does best in a slightly to moderately acid soil. If the crop is to be grown for the early market, select a site that has a light sandy loam with a southern exposure.

Liberal quantities of fertilizer are needed to prepare land for planting. Broadcast 1,500 pounds of 10-10-10 fertilizer per acre before planting. The organic content of the soil may be increased by growing soil improvement crops and turning them under with 1,200 pounds per acre of 5-10-10 fertilizer.

Annual applications of fertilizers are usually needed. Before spring growth starts, broadcast about 400 pounds of ammonium nitrate and 200 pounds of muriate of potash and work into the soil.

An additional application of 60 pounds of nitrogen per acre may be applied in late June or early July. If followed by irrigation, the fertilizer will encourage growth for about another month.

Propagation and Planting

Rhubarb is propagated by planting pieces obtained by dividing the crowns. The pieces are taken from dormant 2- or 3-year-old crowns. After digging, split the dormant crowns between the large buds, or "eyes," to leave as large a piece of storage root as possible with each large bud. About four to eight pieces will be produced by each crown, depending on its size. Protect the pieces from excessive drying before they are planted.

In the northernmost regions, where severely cold weather strikes early after the growing season, the division of crowns and planting is best done in early spring. In regions of less severe winters and longer autumn seasons, the work may be done in autumn after the tops have been killed by the first freezes.

Propagation by seed is not recommended because rhubarb seedlings do not retain the characteristics of the parent plants.

Transplant crown pieces or sets 2 to 3 feet apart in furrows that are 4 to 5 feet apart, depending on the machinery that will be used later in the crop. Cover with 2 to 3 inches of soil. Press the soil firmly around the entire piece.

Varieties

Varieties for outdoor use that have red stalks are Crimson Wine, Valentine, McDonald, and Ruby. Crimson Wine produces larger stalks than the other three red stalk varieties. It also yields larger stalks than the forcing varieties that usually produce green stalks when grown outdoors.

Cultivation

To control weeds, shallow cultivation is required. Cover the

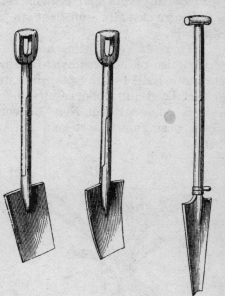

rows with a mulch soon after the ground is frozen. You can also apply strawy manure in the spring; it should be raked off the rows and worked into the soil between the rows. Leaving a heavy mulch over the rows delays early growth because it prevents the sun's rays from warming the soil.

Diseases and Insects

Foot rot, also called phytophthora crown rot, is the most serious disease affecting rhubarb. Slightly sunken lesions develop at the base of the stalk and enlarge rapidly to cause collapse of the whole leafstalk. Stalks may continue to collapse in moist, warm weather until the plant is killed. There is no effective control for foot rot.

One insect—the rhubarb curculio—may cause serious damage to rhubarb plants. This is a rusty snout beetle about three-fourths of an inch long. It bores into the stalks, crowns, and roots. It also attacks wild dock (coarse weeds).

This insect may be controlled by burning all infested plants; and by destroying wild dock growing in the area of the rhubarb patch. This should be done in July, after the beetles have laid their eggs.

In commercial forcing of rhubarb, leaf rots are a serious problem and can be controlled by—

• Sanitation—remove all broken pieces of roots and crowns from the forcing house.

• Ventilation—keep enough air circulating through the forcing house to keep the leaves dry.

• Chemical protection—spray captan at the rate of 2 pounds of 50-percent wettable powder in 100 gallons of water once a week during the forcing season.

Harvesting

The rhubarb harvest season is short, rarely extending more than 2 months. For field harvest, do not pull leafstalks from newly set plants during the first year, and pull only a few the second year.

Harvest only the largest and best stalks. The leafstalks separate readily from the crown and are easily harvested by grasping them near the base and pulling them slightly to one side in the direction in which the stalk grows.

Thin the smaller stalks to permit better development of those remaining. After harvesting, let the plants grow naturally, but remove the seedstalks. Cut off seedstalks as soon as they arise to conserve the energy of the plant for production of foliage and roots.

A heavy crop of rhubarb in any year depends on strong leaf growth the year before. Yields of 10 to 12 tons per acre per year are common. In the State of Washington, Crimson Wine yields up to 20 tons per acre per year.

INDOOR PRODUCTION

The term "forcing" of rhubarb means the winter growing of rhubarb stalks from large crowns that have been taken from the field into a house or other shelter

Credit is due Dr. Daniel R. Tompkins, Associate Professor, Horticultural Food Sciences, University of Arkansas, Fayetteville and Munns A. Caldwell, Extension Horticultural Agent, Macomb County, Michigan, for writing parts of the leaflet and for reviewing other sections.

that can be suitably heated. This method of production is referred to as hothouse production.

Varieties for indoor production or forcing are Victoria, German Wine, Sutton's Seedless, and Strawberry.

Field Production for Forcing

Crowns grown two full summers in the field under favorable conditions are large enough for forcing. Three-year-old crowns are not superior to 2-year-old crowns for this purpose if the cost of producing the crowns is considered.

Growth of crowns in the field largely indicates their potential value for forcing. Large crowns with a few large, strong buds are preferred to those with small or weak buds. Large fancy stalks cannot be developed from small, weak buds.

Those who force rhubarb year after year divide the crowns from part of their plantings to establish one new planting every year. This makes 2-year-old crowns each autumn. Crowns from fields that have been harvested for outdoor rhubarb are not recommended for forcing. They produce poor yields.

Structures for Forcing

Houses about 30 feet wide and 100 to 120 feet long are commonly used for forcing, but other sizes will also serve. These houses are usually of wood, with side walls about 4 to 6 feet high. A ridge 3 to 4 feet higher than the side walls is built through the middle. A row of purlin posts is placed on either side of the ridge, about halfway between the ridge and the side walls.

The end walls are removable, so that a vehicle can be driven through the house between the lines of posts when bringing in or taking out the roots. In some cases, however, the houses are not of sufficient height to permit driving through without removing the roof boards.

These roof boards rest on the side walls and ridgepole, they are covered with straw, manure, corn fodder, sod, or other material for the purpose of excluding light and conserving heat. Ordinarily, these boards are not placed in position until shortly before heat is to be applied. The floor is of soil.

Forcing structures may be heated by any convenient means. Small coal stoves were formerly in common use (1 stove for about 1,000 square feet of floor space), with long runs of stovepipe inside the house to help distribute the heat. Such installations, however, waste fuel and manpower. Hot-water furnaces with long runs of heat-radiating pipe are much

IRON WHEELBARROW.

more efficient and have displaced stoves to a considerable extent. Many growers also use forced-air gas heaters in the forcing house.

Crowns for the Forcing House

When top growth of rhubarb in the field stops in autumn, the buds on the crowns go into a rest period of many weeks. No satisfactory stalk production can be expected until the rest period is over.

Exposure of crowns in the field to temperatures below 50° F. for 7 to 9 weeks will bring them out of the rest period. They will grow when given the proper temperature in the forcing house.

Hard freezing in the field for a few days is not sufficient to bring crowns out of the rest. A field treatment of 28° F. for 6 weeks gave highest yields in experiments in Canada. Temperatures below 28° will reduce yields.

Crowns for forcing may be plowed out at any time that the soil can be worked after the tops

Cold Units

Soil temperature is measured in "cold units." A drop of one degree below 49° F. and above 28° is considered one cold unit.

A certain amount of chilling is required to bring the plants out of their rest period and to start growth in the forcing house. To do this, take soil temperature at a 4-inch depth between 8:30 and 9:30 a.m. in the fall. Any reading above 50° F. should be discontinued; the soil temperature must reach the base line of 49° before a reading is made.

Cold units should be recorded between early October and early December. If the temperature drops to 28° F. or below, do not count as cold units. Discard all cold units and start counting again, if the temperature drops below 24°.

CAUTION: Although the succulent leafstalks of rhubarb are excellent for sauces and pies, *the leaves of rhubarb must never be eaten.* The leaves contain amounts of oxalic acid and of oxalates sometimes great enough to cause fatal poisoning of those who eat them.

have died in autumn. Run a large plow deeply under the rows so the crowns will be turned out with a large mass of storage roots and with a minimum of injury.

The most common practice is to plow out the crowns soon after the tops are dead. The crowns are then left lying in the rough soil until it is convenient or necessary to put them into the forcing structure. They must, of course, be moved before extreme winter weather stops all field work.

Where weather permits, the plowed-out crowns are left exposed to low temperatures in the field for about 4 to 6 weeks. In western Washington where the winters are mild, however, the crowns are plowed-out just prior to forcing from mid-December through March. In some localities, the crowns are promptly placed in the cold-forcing structure, exactly as they are to stand during forcing.

The crowns are then kept cold, even frozen, until their rest period is over and it is time to start the heat. The "knock-down" type of structure (described in the section, Structures for Forcing), was developed to expose the bedded crowns to low temperature as well as to give protection and heat at the proper time.

Crowns bedded before chilling is completed and those bedded afterward are handled the same way. They are set on the earth floor of the house as close together as practicable. The spaces about them are filled with soil, and the soil is watered. Each crown re-

PRECAUTIONS

Pesticides used improperly can be injurious to man, animals, and plants. Follow the directions and heed all precautions on the labels.

Store pesticides in original containers under lock and key—out of the reach of children and animals—and away from food and feed.

Apply pesticides so that they do not endanger humans, livestock, crops, beneficial insects, fish, and wildlife. Do not apply pesticides when there is danger of drift, when honey bees or other pollinating insects are visiting plants, or in ways that may contaminate water or leave illegal residues.

Avoid prolonged inhalation of pesticide sprays or dusts; wear protective clothing and equipment if specified on the container.

If your hands become contaminated with a pesticide, do not eat or drink until you have washed. In case a pesticide is swallowed or gets in the eyes, follow the first aid treatment given on the label, and get prompt medical attention. If a pesticide is spilled on your skin or clothing, remove clothing immediately and wash skin thoroughly.

Do not clean spray equipment or dump excess spray material near ponds, streams, or wells. Because it is difficult to remove all traces of herbicides from equipment, do not use the same equipment for insecticides or fungicides that you use for herbicides.

Dispose of empty pesticide containers promptly. Have them buried at a sanitary land-fill dump, or crush and bury them in a level, isolated place.

NOTE. Some States have restrictions on the use of certain pesticides. Check your State and local regulations.

Guide for recording cold units

Soil temperature between 8:30 and 9:30 a.m. and (Degrees)	Cold Units (Degrees below 49° F.)	Accumulated Cold Units
Date		
1. 42°	7	7
2. 40°	9	16
3. 49°	0	16
4. 30°	19	35
5. 28°	20 (Maximum for one day)	55
6. 20°	0 (Discount below 24° F.)	55
7. 30°	19	74
8. 37°	12	86

Victoria and German Wine will require about 470 to 500 cold units to force successfully.

quires 1 to 2 square feet of bed space; the spacing depends on the geographical area in which they are grown.

Forcing Temperatures

When the bedded crowns have been chilled for a period of 6 to 8 weeks, the house may be closed and mild heat applied. If, however, it is planned to start forcing relatively late, then the crowns should be left unheated until forcing starts.

The best yields are obtained at a forcing temperature close to 56° F. Lower temperatures give more intense pink color in the stalks, which increases their attractiveness, but causes slower growth. At temperatures below 50°, stalk growth is very slow, which may result in lower yields.

Above 60° F., the stalk color becomes paler than at lower temperatures, the growth rate is faster, and yields begin to decline.

Above 65°, the growth rate is quite fast, the color is poor, and the total yields are much lower than at 55°.

Considering yield, color, and growth rate, a temperature of 56° F. is best. Regardless of temperature, the stalk color gradually becomes less intense toward the end of the forcing season as the crowns become exhausted.

Good results have been obtained experimentally with bottom heat supplied by electric hotbed heating cable at a house temperature of 50° F. and a bed temperature of 55°. Bed temperatures

of 65° or more will decrease yields and greatly increase power consumption. Humidity should be kept very high in the house.

Commercial growers in Washington and Michigan are now using gibberellic acid, a growth-regulating chemical, to increase production of forced rhubarb. Since gibberellic acid can replace all or part of the cold weather needed to break the rest period—rhubarb crowns can be forced earlier. Also, gibberellic acid increases the production and shortens the forcing season of crowns that have received sufficient chilling to break their rest period. (See the manufacturer's instructions for application rates and other details.)

Watering the Beds

Watering to keep the soil moderately moist (as in a good workable condition) helps to maintain good growth without impairing color or other quality of the stalks. Production falls off sharply in beds that become dry.

Harvesting and Preparing for Market

Harvesting normally is begun about a month to 6 weeks after the heat is applied. Duration of harvesting depends on such factors as variety, crown, vigor, and forcing temperature. The stalks are usually picked twice a week for a 2-to-3 month period. Many Washington growers double-crop their houses. Victoria is forced from about December 15 to March 1, followed by German Wine. After the roots are forced they should be discarded.

Stalks are picked when they are 12 to 20 inches long; the length depends on the variety and market requirements. Washington grown rhubarb is graded into two classes, fancy and extra fancy. Leaves are removed to within 1 inch of the top of the stalk. Boxes holding 15 pounds each are used for shipping.

Michigan rhubarb is sold in three grades: choice; small fancy; and fancy. Leaves are not removed from the stalks. The rhubarb is packed in cardboard cartons, each holding 5 pounds, and

are sent to market in "master" corrugated cardboard boxes containing 50 pounds net. A small amount, however, is packed in 15-pound boxes.

Home Forcing

The principles and methods described above can be adapted to the forcing of a few plants in a suitable home basement or cellar. A half dozen or so of good crowns produce enough rhubarb for the average family. Proper temperature will not be too difficult to provide, but the humidity of heated modern basements is likely to be too low.

PROTECT
Use Pesticides Safely
FOLLOW THE LABEL
U.S. DEPARTMENT OF AGRICULTURE

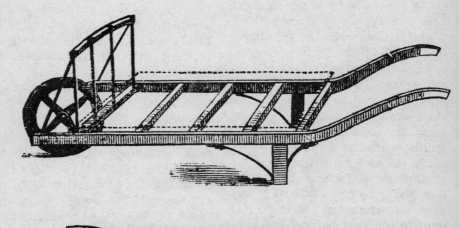

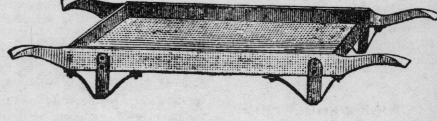

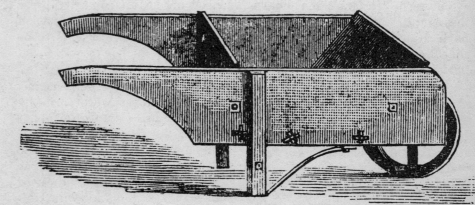

BARROWS, BASK

GREENS

CORN SALAD.

Greens are usually the leaves and leaf stems of immature plants, which in their green state are boiled for food. Young, tender branches of certain plants, New Zealand spinach, for example, are also used this way. All the plants treated here as greens except New Zealand spinach are hardy vegetables, most of them adapted to fall sowing and winter culture over the entire South and in the more temperate parts of the North. Their culture may be extended more widely in the North by growing them with some protection, such as mulching or frames.

Chard

Chard, or Swiss chard is a type of beet that has been developed for its tops instead of its roots. Crop after crop of the outer leaves may be harvested without injuring the plant. Only one planting is necessary, and a row 30 to 40 feet long will supply a family for the entire summer. Each seed cluster contains several seeds, and fairly wide spacing of the seeds facilitates thinning. The culture of chard is practically the same as that of beets, but the plants grow larger and need to be thinned to at least 6 inches apart in the row. Chard needs a rich, mellow soil, and it is sensitive to soil acidity.

Witloof Chicory

Witloof chicory, or French endive, is grown for both roots and tops. It is a hardy plant, not especially sensitive to heat or cold. It does, however, need a deep, rich, loamy soil without too much organic matter. The tops are sometimes harvested while young. The roots are lifted in

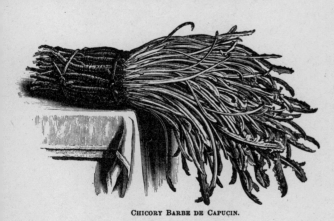

CHICORY BARBE DE CAPUCIN.

autumn and placed in a box or bed of moist soil in a warm cellar for forcing. They must be covered with a few inches of sand. Under this covering the leaves form in a solid head, known on the market as witloof.

The culture of chicory is simple. Sow the seeds in spring or early summer in drills about 18 inches apart. Later, thin the plants to 6 or 8 inches apart in the rows. If sown too early the plants shoot to seed and are worthless for forcing. The kind known as witloof is most generally used.

Collards

Collards are grown and used about like cabbage. They withstand heat better than other members of the cabbage group, and are well liked in the South for both summer and winter use. Collards do not form a true head, but a large rosette of leaves, which may be blanched by tying together.

Cornsalad

Cornsalad is also known as lamb's-lettuce and fetticus. Sow the seed in early spring in drills and cultivate the plants the same as lettuce or mustard. For an extra early crop, plant the seed in the autumn and cover the plants lightly through the winter. In the Southern States the covering is not necessary, and the plants are ready for use in February and March. The leaves are frequently used in their natural green state, but they may be blanched by covering the rows with anything that will exclude light.

Italian Corn Salad (*Valerianella eriocarpa*).

Chicory (*Cichorium Intybus*).

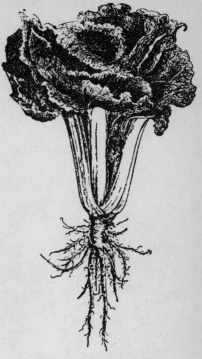

Swiss chard.

Witloof Chicory.

SEA KALE.

Kale

Kale, or borecole, is hardy and lives over winter in latitudes as far north as northern Maryland and southern Pennsylvania and in other areas where similar winter conditions prevail. It is also resistant to heat and may be grown in summer. Its real merit, however, is a cool-weather greens.

Kale is a member of the cabbage family. The best garden varieties are low-growing, spreading plants, with thick, more or less crinkled leaves. Vates Blue Curled, Dwarf Blue Scotch, and Siberian are well-known garden varieties.

No other plant is so well adapted to fall sowing throughout a wide area of both North and South or in areas characterized by winters of moderate severity. Kale may well follow some such early-season vegetable as green beans, potatoes, or peas.

In the autumn the seed may be broadcast very thinly and then lightly raked into the soil. Except for spring sowings, made when weeds are troublesome, sow kale in rows 18 to 24 inches apart and later thin the plants to about a foot apart.

Kale may be harvested either by cutting the entire plant or by taking the larger leaves while young. Old kale is tough and stringy.

GREENS

Mustard

Mustard grows well on almost any good soil. As the plants require but a short time to reach the proper stage for use, frequent sowings are recommended. Sow the seeds thickly in drills as early as possible in the spring or, for late use, in September or October. The forms of Indian mustard, the leaves of which are often curled and frilled, are generally used. Southern Curled and Green Wave are common sorts.

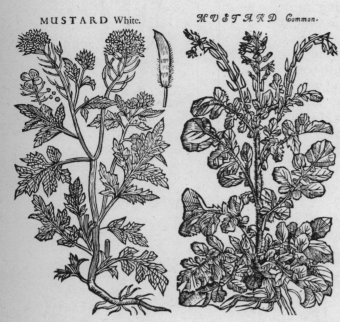

MUSTARD White.   MUSTARD Common.

Sorrel

Sorrel is a perennial that is usually started from seeds. It requires a rich, mellow, well-drained soil. Rows may be of any convenient distance apart. Thin the plants to about 8 inches apart in the rows. If the leaves alone are gathered and the plants are cultivated to prevent the growth of weeds, a planting should last 3 or 4 years. French Broad Leaf is a well-known variety.

Belleville Sorrel.

Spinach

Spinach is a hardy cool-weather plant that withstands winter conditions in the South. In most of the North, spinach is primarily an early-spring and late-fall crop, but in some areas, where summer temperatures are mild, it may be grown continuously from early spring until late fall. It should be emphasized that summer and winter culture of spinach is possible only where moderate temperatures prevail.

Spinach will grow on almost any well-drained, fertile soil where sufficient moisture is available. It is very sensitive to acid soil. If a soil test shows the need, apply lime to the part of the garden used for spinach, regardless of the treatment given the rest of the area.

The application of 100 pounds of rotted manure and 3 to 4 pounds of commercial fertilizer to each 100 square feet of land is suitable for spinach in the home garden. Broadcast both manure and fertilizer and work them in before sowing the seed.

Long Standing Bloomsdale is perhaps the most popular variety seeded in spring. It is attractive, grows quickly, is very productive, and will stand for a moderate length of time before going to seed. Virginia Savoy and Hybrid No. 7 are valuable varieties for fall planting, as they are resistant to yellows, or blight. Hybrid No. 7 is also resistant to downy mildew (blue mold). These two varieties are very cold-hardy but are not suitable for the spring crop, as they produce seedstalks too early. For horse or tractor cultivation, the rows of the garden should be not less than 24 inches apart; when land is plentiful they may be 30 inches apart. For wheel-hoe or hand work, the rows should be 14 to 16 inches apart. Spinach may be drilled by hand in furrows about 1 inch deep and covered with fine earth not more than $\frac{1}{2}$ inch deep, or it may be drilled with a seed drill, which distributes the seed more evenly than is ordinarily possible by hand. Thin the plants to 3 or 4 inches apart before they crowd in the row.

SORREL.

New Zealand Spinach

New Zealand spinach is not related to common spinach. It is a large plant, with thick, succulent leaves and stems, and grows with a branching, spreading habit to a height of 2 or more feet. It thrives in hot weather and is grown as a substitute in seasons when ordinary spinach cannot withstand the heat. New Zealand spinach thrives on soils suitable for common spinach. Because of their larger size, these plants must have more room. The rows should be at least 3 feet apart, with the plants about $1\frac{1}{2}$ feet apart in the rows. As prompt germination may be difficult, the seeds should be soaked for 1 or 2 hours in water at 120° F. before being planted. They may be sown, 1 to $1\frac{1}{2}$ inches deep, as soon as danger of frost is past. Successive harvests of the tips may be made from a single planting, as new leaves and branches are readily produced. Care must be taken not to remove too large a portion of the plant at one time.

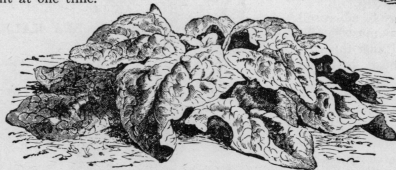

THICK-LEAVED SPINACH.

Turnip Greens

Varieties of turnips usually grown for the roots are also planted for the greens. Shogoin is a favorable variety for greens. It is resistant to aphid damage and produces fine-quality white roots if allowed to grow. Seven Top is a leafy sort that produces no edible root. As a rule, sow turnips to be used for greens thickly and then thin them, leaving all but the greens to develop as a root crop. Turnip greens are especially adapted to winter and early-spring culture in the South. The cultural methods employed are the same as those for turnip and rutabaga.

LONG STANDING SPINACH.

HENDERSON'S GOLDEN DWARF CELERY.

reprinted from GARDEN MAGAZINE ,1905

Celery can be grown in home gardens in most parts of the country at some time during the year. It is a cool-weather crop and adapted to winter culture in the lower South. In the upper South and in the North it may be grown either as an early-spring or as a late-fall crop. Farther north in certain favored locations it can be grown throughout the summer.

Rich, moist but well-drained, deeply prepared, mellow soil is essential for celery. Soil varying from sand to clay loam and to peat may be used as long as these requirements are met. Unless the ground is very fertile, plenty of organic material, supplemented by liberal applications of commercial fertilizer, is necessary. For a 100-foot row of celery, 5 pounds of a high-grade complete fertilizer thoroughly mixed with the soil are none too much. Prepare the celery row a week or two before setting the plants.

The most common mistake with celery is failure to allow enough time for growing the plants. About 10 weeks are needed to grow good celery plants. Celery seed is small and germinates slowly. A good method is to place the seeds in a muslin bag and soak them overnight, then mix them with dry sand, distribute them in shallow trenches in the seed flats or seedbed, and cover them with leafmold or similar material to a depth of not more than ½ inch. Keep the bed covered with moist burlap sacks. Celery plants are very delicate and must be kept free from weeds. They are made more stocky by being transplanted once before they are set in the garden, but this practice retards their growth. When they are to be transplanted before being set in the ground, the rows in the seed box or seedbed may be only a few inches apart. When they are to remain in the box until transplanted to the garden, however, the plants should be about 2 inches apart each way. In beds, the rows should be 10 to 12 inches apart, with seedlings 1 to 1½ inches apart in the row.

For hand culture celery plants are set in rows 18 to 24 inches apart; for tractor cultivation 30 to 36 inches apart. The plants are spaced about 6 inches in the row. Double rows are about a foot apart. Set celery on a cool or cloudy day, if possible; and if the soil is at all dry, water the plants thoroughly. If the plants are large, it is best to pinch off the outer leaves 3 or 4 inches from the base before setting. In bright weather it is well also to shade the plants for a day or two after they are set. Small branches bearing green leaves, stuck in the ground, protect the plants from intense sun without excluding air. As soon as the plants attain some size, gradually work the soil around them to keep them upright. Be careful to get no soil into the hearts of the plants. Early celery is blanched by excluding the light with boards, paper, drain tiles, or other devices. Late celery may be blanched also by banking with earth or by storing in the dark. Banking celery with soil in warm weather causes it to decay.

Late celery may be kept for early-winter use by banking with earth and covering the tops with leaves or straw to keep them from freezing, or it may be dug and stored in a cellar or a coldframe, with the roots well embedded in moist soil. While in storage it must be kept as cool as possible without freezing.

For the home garden Golden Detroit, Summer Pascal (Waltham Improved), and the Golden Plume are adapted for the early crop to be used during late summer, fall, and early winter. For storage and for use after the holiday season, it is desirable to plant some such variety as Green Light or Utah 52–70.

CELERY

By BARRY LORING

Why should anybody be afraid to grow celery? The reason why most amateurs fail with celery is that they plant it on a shallow, dry soil and do not give water often enough, or else they have ground wet to stagnation. While celery must have abundance of water, it demands good drainage. Therefore a deep soil is necessary and a wet place must be tile-drained. Soil for celery must be rich in nitrogen. Manure will provide the nitrogen for this purpose and increase the moisture holding capacity better than anything else. This is celery culture in a nut shell.

The early or August crop of celery is to be planted out in May, from seeds started indoors during February, and young plants need transplanting once indoors. The late or main crop is tended in the same way, but the seed is sown the last of March or April. If you have a well protected seed bed, or a coldframe, they can be started at once in either, and the improvised seed box is also fine for them. You may wonder why they have to be transplanted from the seed bed into another bed and thence into the garden, for it sounds like unnecessary work. You can trying sowing the seed in drills in a bed, thin out well and allow the plants to re-

WHITE PLUME CELERY, AS PUT UP FOR THE NEW YORK MARKET.

main there until it is time to set them out into the garden but this is what you will "go up against": Celery makes a long tap root, that is, a root which goes straight down into the earth with very few fine, side, or fibrous roots. When the tiny seedling is transplanted, the end of this tap root is usually broken, the fibrous roots are forced to start work, and they make a clump. Then when the second transplanting time comes, the root is not so long, but bunchy, and not nearly so liable to be badly injured. If the seedling is allowed to remain in the seed bed until setting out time comes, it has a root so long that it is almost invariably badly broken in lifting, and the shock being much greater the plant's progress is seriously retarded at the time when it needs to grow most quickly. Therefore, two transplantings are far ahead of one, and if one of these has been into an individual receptacle, that is better still.

When the seedlings appear, tend them carefully, turning the box each day that they may not be drawn in one direction toward the light. Keep them moist, but not wet, and not too warm, or they will be tall and spindly. If they are too thick, pull out a few weaklings and give the others a better chance. When the second leaf appears, and they are jostling and pushing elbows for room, transplant them into a second box, deeper than a flat, or into a coldframe, whence they can be planted into the garden.

Having filled a flat with finely sifted leaf mold, mixed with sand, scrape the earth off even with the top of the box, shake or press it down with the hand, and, if the soil is very dry, sprinkle it lightly with a rose sprayer and let it stand a little while before sowing the seed. There are two methods for doing this; one is to sow or sprinkle the seed over the entire surface; the other to mark shallow drills, one or two inches apart, and sow the seed thickly in these, barely covering it. I prefer the latter plan for in that way it is easier to lift the seedlings when the first transplanting time comes. Place the flat in a bright, moderately warm window, and water very gently when the surface shows a tendency to dry out. The seedlings appear in two or three weeks.

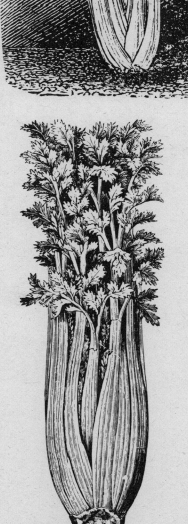

HENDERSON'S HALF DWARF CELERY.

CELERY

Celery loves light, rich soil, and the flavor of the plant is much finer from that kind of land, than when it is raised on a heavy clay, bog or peat soil. But it also demands plenty of water. Therefore a thorough preparation of the ground in dealing with the crop is more than usually profitable.

I reiterate, celery loves a very rich, light soil, well drained, and it craves plenty of water, often. Dig your trench, or bed, deep, put in some well-rotted manure, or, if you can possibly get hold of it, some hen droppings, and if the soot from the chimneys has not gone on the rose bed, add that too. A little bone-meal and wood-ashes will not do any harm, for celery is not subject to indigestion from over feeding.

Celery is an important crop for the home garden, as it occupies ground upon which some earlier crop has already matured. It can follow peas or spinach for instance. It likes nitrogen in abundance and so does particularly well as a second crop on the ground previously occupied by peas.

Have you decided which way to grow celery? If so let us set out the plants. The bed or row is made, raked fine, and the garden line run. Now make holes with the dibble, or, if your plants are too large, with a trowel, every six inches. Take up the plantlets carefully, having run a knife between them to separate the roots, and place them in a basket, box or pan, a few at a time. Set them one by one into the holes, firm the earth well around them, and at once protect each with a mulch. Proceed in this way to the end of the row. The mulch may be straw, leaves, hay, or cuttings from the grass—anything to conserve the moisture in the soil while the young plants get started. Water well after the mulch is on, and you ought to have celery fine enough to take a prize anywhere.

There are two diseases of celery, rust and blight. The former is shown by yellowish spots on the leaves, the latter first by watery spots, then by black dots. Good seed and healthy plants will probably escape both, but if forced to enter into combat with them use Bordeaux mixture.

There are several ways to blanch celery, so as to get the fine white stalks for table. One way is to make long rows, setting the plants six inches or a foot apart and as they grow drawing the earth up around them to form a bank on either side. One great precaution to be taken in doing this is to be very, very careful not to get any dirt at all into the heart of the plant. Careful "handling," as it is called, is of vital importance. Gather the leaves up tightly in one hand, holding the outer ones well around the heart or the young leaves in the center, and draw the earth up to the plant, firming it well. It is wise to have two people at this work, as it is difficult for one to manage alone. You can make double rows in this same way, setting the plants cris-cross, six inches apart, just as rails are laid for an old-fashioned Virginia fence.

A celery pit.

The plants may be set in single rows with enough earth drawn around them to hold them upright, and, when they are nearly grown, a board may be placed on either side, as close to the stems as possible, and almost to the top of the leaves. A strip or clamp is placed across the boards to keep them in position. A twelve-inch board would be wide enough, and the length in proportion to the length of the row to be blanched. To make sure that the leaves are well up, slide the boards in edgewise, raising the leaves as you make it perpendicular.

If you wish to use drain tile, set the plants a little further apart, according to the diameter of the tile used, five inches, inside measurement, being quite large enough. In order to place a tile over a plant, it is necessary to tie the leaves loosely together, with raffia, soft twine, or, better still, with a strip of soft paper twisted, for it will fall to pieces when damp, and the plant will again be free. Tile and boards are best for early celery, and they are both extremely useful for keeping the plant clean, while the tile has the further advantage of keeping it cool. Banking is better for late celery, as it can withstand frost better when protected by

CELERY AFTER "HANDLING."

earth, and the covering is more natural.

Beds four feet wide, and as long as you choose, may be made, and the celery plants set into them ten inches apart, with boards placed perpendicularly along the edges, to hold the plants in an upright position. I should not care for this method, since it would render weeding very difficult, though it would save land space. This celery would either have to be dug up and blanched by storing, or protected by earth or hay where it stood. I really think, for the amateur gardener, single rows are the best.

Blanching is done in three weeks if the plants are growing vigorously as in September; later as the weather gets colder it will take fully four weeks.

Keep some celery in the garden until after Christmas. If you are too busy to make a pit and the celery is already banked, throw some hay over the top of the bank, a little more when colder weather comes, and finally earth over that. If you can dig the roots and made a pit, it will be much easier to get at

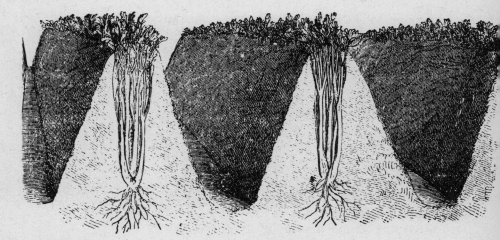

CELERY EARTHED UP.

when you want it. Dig a small trench about one foot deep, line the sides with hay (salt hay preferably), place the celery in the trench, roots down, and close together, seeing that the hay surrounds the plants entirely and then bank up the earth, to make a miniature mound. Work from north to the south, so that you can enter this aboriginal dwelling from the southern end. If frost gets through the earth, it can't get through the hay. Thus the celery is safe and happy.

CELERY STORED FOR WINTER.

-FINE CURLED GREEN WINTER ENDIVE.

Endive

Endive closely resembles lettuce in its requirements, except that it is less sensitive to heat. It may be substituted for lettuce when the culture of lettuce is impracticable. In the South, it is mainly a winter crop. In the North, it is grown in spring, summer, and autumn and is also forced in winter. Full Heart Batavian and Salad King are good varieties. Broadleaved endive is known on the markets as escarole.

Cultural details are the same as those for head lettuce. When the plants are large and well-formed, draw the leaves together and tie them so that the heart will blanch. For winter use, lift the plants with a ball of earth, place them in a cellar or coldframe where they will not freeze, and tie and blanch them as needed.

Lettuce

Lettuce can be grown in any home garden. It is a cool-weather crop, being as sensitive to

BLACK SEEDED SIMPSON LETTUCE.

heat as any vegetable grown. In the South, lettuce culture is confined to late fall, winter, and spring. In colder parts of the South, lettuce may not live through the winter. In the North, lettuce culture is particially limited to spring and autumn. In some favored locations, such as areas of high altitude or in far-northern latitudes, lettuce grows to perfection in summer. Planting at a wrong season is responsible for most of the failures with this crop.

Any rich soil is adapted to lettuce, although the plant is sensitive to acid soil. A commercial fertilizer with a heavy proportion of phosphorus is recommended.

Start spring lettuce indoors or in a hotbed and transplant it to the garden when the plants have four of five leaves. Gardeners need not wait for the end of light frosts, as lettuce is not usually harmed by a temperature as low as 28° F., if the plants have been properly hardened. Allow about 6 weeks for growing the plants. For the fall crop the seed may be sown directly in the row and thinned; there is no gain in transplanting.

For tractor cultivation, set lettuce plants 12 to 15 inches apart in rows 30 to 36 inches apart; for hand culture, about 14 to 16 inches apart each way. Where gardeners grow leaf lettuce or desire merely the leaves and not well-developed heads, the spacing in the rows may be much closer. In any case it is usually best to cut the entire plant instead of removing the leaves.

There are many excellent varieties of lettuce, all of which do well in the garden when conditions are right. Of the loose-leaf kinds, Black-Seeded Simpson, Grand Rapids, Slobolt, and Saladbowl are among the best. Saladbowl and Slobolt are heat resistant and very desirable for warm-weather culture. Of the heading sorts, Buttercrunch, White Boston, Fulton, and Great Lakes are among the best. The White Boston requires less time than the three others. Where warm weather comes early, it is seldom worth while to sow head lettuce seed in the open ground in the spring with the expectation of obtaining firm heads.

ENDIVES AND LETTUCE

── LOOSE-LEAF VARIETIES ──

541 SALAD BOWL. An Ideal Home Garden Variety. (M.T.)

48 days. A beauty in the garden and a delight on the table, Salad Bowl is the best loose-leaf home garden lettuce we know. Practically all season long, it stays in prime condition and it is so easily grown that everyone can raise all he needs from one or two plantings.

Each plant makes a decorative rosette of wavy, notched leaves, closely set on the short center stems. Always tender, sweet and delicious, Salad Bowl is a distinctive loose-leaf type of the highest quality, holding its flavor and fine texture despite summer heat. We think it is a perfect loose-leaf lettuce for home use.

542 SUMMER BIBB. Slow-Bolting Bibb—Top Quality.

62 days. This wonderful improvement on the famous Bibb lettuce was also developed by Dr. Raleigh. Together with Buttercrunch, it provides just about the finest eating lettuce you have ever tasted, and it can be grown all summer. Regular Bibb is delicious to eat but bolts to seed before it has really developed. Summer Bibb stands much longer and forms compact heads or dense clusters of leaves with the hearts blanching to creamy white. They have the same appearance and supreme quality as Bibb, and if you have never tried it, you have a real treat coming. Grow it for market and roadside stands too. Your customers will come back for more.

Joseph Harris Co., Inc. Rochester, N.Y.

PARSLEY

Parsley is hardy to cold but sensitive to heat. It thrives under much the same temperature

-EMERALD PARSLEY.

conditions as kale, lettuce, and spinach. If given a little protection it may be carried over winter through most of the North.

Parsley thrives on any good soil. As the plant is delicate during its early stages of growth, however, the land should be mellow.

Parsley seeds are small and germinate slowly. Soaking in water overnight hastens the germination. In the North, it is a good plan to sow the seeds indoors and transplant the plants to the garden, thereby getting a crop before hot weather. In the South, it is usually possible to sow the seed directly in drills. For the fall crop in the North, row seeding is also practiced. After seeding, it is well to lay a board over the row for a few days until the first seedlings appear. After its removal day-to-day watering will insure germination of as many seeds as possible. Parsley rows should be 14 to 16 inches apart, with the plants 4 to 6 inches apart in the rows. A few feet will supply the family, and a few plants transplanted to the coldframe in the autumn will give a supply during early spring.

Garden Cresses

-Fool's-Parsley (Æthusa Cynapium).

UPLAND CRESS

Upland cress, sometimes erroneously called peppergrass, is a hardy plant. It may be sown in all the milder parts of the country in autumn. In the colder sections it is sown in early spring as soon as the ground can be worked. The seeds are small and must not be covered deeply. After the plants are well established, thin them to 4 to 6 inches apart in the rows. This is a short-season crop that should be planted in quick succession to insure a steady supply.

ROOT VEGETABLES

Potatoes in the North and sweetpotatoes in the South are grown in almost every garden. Beets, carrots, and turnips are also widely grown in gardens. The vegetables in this group may be used throughout the growing season and also be kept for winter.

White   Beets.

BEETS

The beet is well adapted to all parts of the country. It is fairly tolerant of heat; it is also resistant to cold. However, it will not withstand severe freezing. In the Northern States, where winters are too severe, the beet is grown in spring, summer, and autumn.

Beets are sensitive to strongly acid soils, and it is wise to apply lime if a test shows the need for it. Good beet quality depends on quick growth; for this the land must be fertile, well-drained, and in good physical condition.

Midsummer heat and drought may interfere with seed germination. By covering the seeds with sandy soil, leafmold, or other material that will not bake and by keeping the soil damp until the plants are up, much of this trouble can be avoided. Make successive sowings at intervals of about 3 weeks in order to have a continuous supply of young, tender beets throughout the season.

Where cultivating is by hand, the rows may be about 16 inches apart; where it is by tractor, they must be wider. Beet seed as purchased consists of small balls, each containing several seeds. On most soils the seed should be covered to a depth of about an inch. After the plants are well established, thin them to stand 2 to 3 inches apart in the rows.

Early Wonder, Crosby Egyptian, and Detroit Dark Red are standard varieties suitable for early home-garden planting, while Long Season remains tender and edible over a long season.

GROWING BEETS

Prepared by
Plant Genetics and Germplasm Institute
Agricultural Research Service

Table, or garden, beets are grown in a wide range of soils and climates. Since beets produce their best color and quality in a cool climate, they are grown in the southern third of the United States as fall, winter, and spring crops; in the middle third as early summer or late fall crops; and in the northern third as summer and early fall crops.

SOILS

Table beets are grown in a variety of soils such as mucks, sands, sandy loams, and silt loams. It is generally difficult to get good stands on soils that have high clay content or those that pack or crust after a sprinkling or a rain. Early crops require sandy loam soils that warm up quickly in the spring. Heavier and more compact soils, as clay loams, are satisfactory for late spring or fall crops.

For best results, the soil should be deep, well-drained, friable, and adequately supplied with organic matter. Green manure crops, crop residues, animal manures, or composts—whichever is most practical—should be used to maintain soil fertility.

FERTILIZERS AND LIME

The land and amount of commercial fertilizer needed will depend on the soil type, natural fertility, and the amount of fertilizer applied to previous crops.

In general, truck gardens require up to 2,000 pounds per acre and home gardens require up to 4½ pounds per 100 square feet. The mixture of fertilizer normally recommended contains 10 percent of nitrogen, of phosphoric acid, and of potash. On soils low in potash, 8-16-16 or 5-10-30 may be used.

In large-scale plantings, broadcast muriate of potash (0-0-60) to correct potash deficiencies. On muck soils, use a high-potash, low-nitrogen fertilizer.

When a truck garden is about half grown, a topdressing of up to 150 pounds per acre of ammonium nitrate (or equivalent) may be used. For home gardens, use from ½ to 1 pound for each 100 feet of row. Internal blackspot of beets can be controlled by application of boron to the soil.

Beets grow best at a soil acidity from pH 6.0 to 6.8 but will tolerate neutral soils; and in some districts, alkaline soils.

Soil acidity should be determined by an accurate soil test. If necessary, use ground limestone to lower the acidity (raise pH value). Many States maintain soil testing services. Check with your county agricultural agent for instructions on how to take soil samples and where to send them for testing

VARIETIES

Beets are classified according to the shape of the root and the time of maturing. For example, Crosby's Egyptian, Green Top Bunching, Ruby Queen, and Early Wonder are flat or globular early maturing varieties. Detroit Dark Red, and Perfected Detroit are globular and medium early maturing varieties. Long Dark Blood, or Long Smooth Blood are late-maturing varieties.

The roots of most beets are dark red or purplish. However, when beets are grown in hot weather, the roots

WHITE OR SPANISH BEET.

may develop light-colored zones. In cool weather, these zones are less conspicuous. The light-colored zones tend to disappear when the beets are cooked. Sugar content in the root is highest when beets are grown in cool temperatures and good sunlight.

Crosby Egyptian and Early Wonder varieties are generally recommended when rapid growth to market-size is desired.

Both are slightly flattened and have alternate zones of purplish flesh in warm weather. Plantings that reach harvest stage in cool weather have darker flesh and less prominent differences in color zones.

For processing and where quick maturity is not important, Detroit Dark Red, Perfected Detroit, Ruby Queen, and Red Pak are most commonly grown. Certain varieties, such as Crosby Green Top, are grown for beet greens, but other varieties can be used if harvested at the proper time. Monogerm varieties with superior quality and uniformity have recently been developed. Examples of monogerm varieties are Pacemaker, Mono-King, Explorer, and Monogerm.

PLANTING AND CULTURE

Young beet seedlings are tender. To help them become established, work the soil into a friable condition free of trash, clods, and surface irregularities before planting.

Cover the seed 1 inch in sandy soils, about ¾ inch in sandy loams, and not deeper than ½ inch in finer textured soils. It is important that the cover depth is both uniform and correct to assure even germination.

For home gardens worked by hand, rows may be as close as 12 inches; for commercial plantings, they are normally 18 to 24 inches apart.

For drainage or irrigation purposes, plant beets on formed beds in paired rows that are 40 inches apart from center. Sow seeds at the rate of 5 to 6 per foot of row, 10 to 12 pounds per acre, or 1 ounce for 100 feet of row. If beets are grown for processing, increase seedling rate to 14 to 16 pounds of seed per acre.

When multigerm seed is used, remove excess plants to avoid crowding. Thin the seedlings when they are large enough to be handled but before they greatly exceed 2 inches in height. Later thinning may cause damage. Three to four plants per foot of row should be left upon final thinning.

To achieve uniform stands and an earlier crop, home gardeners should sow 4 or 5 seeds per inch in rows 3 inches apart. Transplant the seedlings 3 inches apart in the row when they are 2 to 3 inches high.

Beets may be planted from 3 to 4

For specific information on growing beets in your area, consult your county agricultural agent.

weeks before the average date of the last killing spring frost to 6 weeks before the average date of the first autumn frost except during very hot weather.

Beet seeds will germinate at soil temperatures from 40° to 85°F, with the optimum being 65° to 75°F.

WEEDS

Mechanical cultivation can control weeds between the beet rows, but herbicides are needed to control weeds in the rows.

Herbicides registered for use in planting table beets include cycloate and pyrazon. Cycloate is effective against annual grasses and should be applied before the beets and weeds emerge. Pyrazon will control many broadleaf weeds when used before emergence of beets and weeds.

State experiment station weed specialists can provide specific information on the herbicides to be used in their areas. Be sure to read and follow the label carefully.

Herbicides are not generally recommended for use in home gardens because of the difficulty in correctly treating small areas. Hand weeding and hoeing are usually adequate in small garden areas.

PEST CONTROL

The nature and severity of pests of table beets varies with growing areas. For this reason only general suggestions for pest control are made. Consult your county agricultural agent for more specific information. Read and follow the directions for use and the precautions indicated on the label of the pesticide to be used.

Leaf miners and aphids are the most common insect pests of beets; but webworms, flea beetles, and others may cause extensive damage to the crop.

Check frequently for insects and start control measures before damage occurs.

Aphids and leaf miners may be controlled with diazinon; flea beetles with carbaryl; and webworms with pyrethrins.

Cercospora leaf spot, the most common disease of beets, is identified by circular spots with reddish brown or purplish margins. The infected area later turns gray and drops out, giving the leaf a spothole appearance. Crop rotation, sanitation, and the use of fungicides, such as captan, control this disease.

Damping-off and seed rot can be reduced by seed treatment with captan or thiram.

211 CROSBY GREEN TOP. A Special Harris Selection.

60 days. Famous for its vigor and fine type, Crosby Green Top is a uniform, attractive strain of our own development. It is outstanding for quick growth and high quality in the home garden and for its clean bright green tops on the market. The roots are of flattened globe shape with fine tap roots, dark red inside and out, and the flesh is tender and delicious.

Crosby Green Top is ideal for bunching and its handsome roots and bright green tops command premium prices. Whether in spring, summer or fall, they retain their color and look as good as they taste.

Joseph Harris Co., Inc. Rochester, N.Y.

WHITE BEET.

BUILDING A ROOT HEAP.

GROWING BEETS, CARROTS, AND PARSNIPS

L. Williams and R. C. Herner

Department of Horticulture
Michigan State University

HARVESTING AND HANDLING

When grown for fresh market, beets are usually harvested when 1¾ to 2 inches in diameter.

Prepare beets for market immediately after they are pulled from the soil. If bunched, grade them by putting only beets of similar size and appearance together in a bunch. Remove dead or damaged leaves while bunching.

Put the bunches into field boxes and take them promptly to the packinghouse or shipping point. There, they can be washed thoroughly in clean water for shipment. Beets can also be topped and sold in perforated polyethylene bags.

STORAGE

Beets maturing in the late fall can be stored in cold, moist root cellars as long as 3 to 5 months. The plants will stand frost and mild freezing, but they must be removed from the field before hard freezing occurs.

For long storage, clip the tops close to the roots and sort out all diseased or decaying matter. Slatted crates or baskets are good containers; large bins are not.

The storage space should have a relative humidity of 95 to 98 percent to prevent excessive shrinkage. Keep the temperature as near to 32°F as possible; take care not to freeze the roots. Under these conditions, bunched beets with tops may be stored for 10 to 15 days. Higher temperatures shorten storage life and reduce quality.

Commercial storage at 32°F with a humidity of 95 percent is satisfactory.

Beets, carrots and parsnips are all root crops. They are among the easiest vegetable crops to grow and are attacked by very few insects and diseases. Although not as commonly grown as carrots and beets, parsnips are quite tasty and are excellent for flavoring soups and stews.

BOTANICAL INFORMATION AND HISTORY: Both carrots and parsnips are members of the same plant family, Umbelliferae, the parsley family, but belong to different genera. DAUCUS CAROTA is the scientific name given to the carrot and the parsnip is classified PASTINACA SATIVA. Beets, classified as BETA BULGARIS, belong to the goosefoot family, Chenopodiaceae. The carrot has been found growing wild on all continents except Australia, but the parsnip and beet were found only in Europe and Asia. The modern beet descended from the wild beet of southern Europe where the leaves alone were consumed as a potherb. Carrots, believed to have originated in the Near East, have been food plants since ancient times with the Greeks also using them as medicinals. Native to the Mediterranean region, wild parsnips were eaten in Greek and Roman times, but by the 16th century the parsnip became widely cultivated in northern Europe.

PLANTING SITE REQUIREMENTS: Although full sun is preferred, partial shade is acceptable for most root crops. The best soil type is a loam, but almost any soil is satisfactory if it is properly conditioned before planting. Prepare the soil by loosening it to a depth of at least 15" for parsnips and 10" for most carrots. For beets and short carrot varieties, the soil need only be worked to a depth of 8". Remove stones and other refuse in the row, since it will cause the roots to fork and become malformed. Working well rotted compost, manure or other organic material deeply into the soil will aid growth. Beets are quite sensitive to acid soils of pH less than 5.8 and soil of a very acid reaction should be limed before beets are planted.

PLANTING DIRECTIONS AND TIMING: Beets, carrots and parsnips are all quite cold tolerant and may be planted as soon in the spring as the ground can be worked, generally around April 1 in central Michigan. All three vegetables are grown from seed, and for carrots and beets, a succession of sowings is best to assure a continuous yield throughout the season. Plant beets every two weeks from late March through mid-April, since they do best in the cool temperatures of spring. Parsnips should be planted April 1. Carrots may be planted every two weeks from April until late June.

222 LONG SEASON Or "Winter Keeper". Superb Quality.

80 days. If you have never eaten Long Season, you are due for a pleasant surprise. They grow very large and rough-looking, but no matter how big they get, they are far more tender and sweet than any beet you have ever tasted. Thousands of our customers would not plant a garden without including plenty of Long Season.

It makes no difference whether the beets are young or old, small or large, they will remain tender all summer and fall and keep in fine condition all winter. The roots are a very deep red color throughout, and the large tops are light green. Long Season grows slowly but when the early-sown beets get tough and poor, it will be found to be of a matchless flavor that no other kind can approach.

Joseph Harris Co., Inc. Rochester, N.Y.

CARROTS

Sow the seeds of all three crops about ½" deep in rows 18" apart. The best seeds should be spaced 1" apart and the plants thinned to 3" apart when 6" high. Carrot and parsnip seeds should be sown about 25 seeds to the foot. Thin the carrots to 1" apart when 1" high and to 3" apart one month later. Parsnips should be thinned to a final spacing of 5" apart when 4" tall. Since carrot and parsnip seeds germinate slowly (2-3 weeks), it is essential to keep the seeded row moist and prevent crusting of the soil. A mixture of sand and soil or peat moss and soil covering the seeds will help keep the area moist. Sprinkle the row frequently to prevent drying.

FERTILIZING: Prior to seeding, a commercial fertilizer such as 5-10-10 or similar analysis may be worked into the row as it is being prepared. Three cups per 50' of row is adequate.

GENERAL GROWING INFORMATION: Rapid growth is essential to produce high quality root crops. Since water is often a limiting factor to growth, make sure the plants receive a good soaking each week if natural rainfall is low.

Weeding is another important practice. Pull weeds by hand or hoe shallowly when the crops are still small. After thinning, the plants should be mulched to a depth of 2" with compost, peat moss, straw or other organic material to keep in soil moisture and kill young weeds.

YIELD AND HARVEST INFORMATION: Beets and carrots are ready to eat in about 70 days, but parsnips require about 120 days. A 10' row of beets or carrots planted every other week is adequate for most families, and 10' of row per person of parsnips is about average. With carrots and parsnips, you may wish to make your last planting larger than the rest since the roots can be harvested throughout the winter months. Just mulch the row with 4" of straw, compost or leaves in the fall when the tops die down and the roots will keep quite well in the ground until ready for use. The mulch needs to be thicker for carrots.

Beets are ready for harvest when they are 1½-2" in diameter. The tops may be eaten also and are prepared in a similar way to spinach. Carrots should be pulled when the root tops are barely visible above the ground and are about 1" in diameter. Parsnips should be harvested when the roots are 2-3" in diameter.

PESTS: In general, the root crops have few insect and disease problems.

Carrots are usually grown in the fall, winter, and spring in the South, providing an almost continuous supply. In the North, carrots can be grown and used through the summer and the surplus stored for winter. Carrots will grow on almost any type of soil as long as it is moist, fertile, loose, and free from clods and stones, but sandy loams and peats are best. Use commercial fertilizer.

Because of their hardiness, carrots may be seeded as early in the spring as the ground can be worked. Succession plantings at intervals of 3 weeks will insure a continuous supply of tender carrots. Cover carrot seed about ½ inch on most soils; less, usually about ¼ inch, on heavy soils. With care in seeding, little thinning is necessary; carrots can stand some crowding, especially on loose soils. However, they should be no thicker than 10 to 15 plants per foot of row.

Chantenay, Nantes, and Imperator are standard sorts. Carrots should be stored before hard frosts occur, as the roots may be injured by cold.

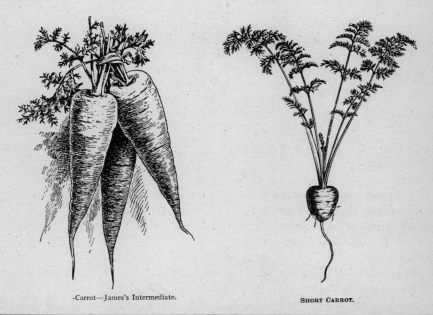

-Carrot—James's Intermediate.   SHORT CARROT.

318 PIONEER. Harris Hybrid of Finest Quality.

67 days. This Harris hybrid is the carrot our customers prefer ahead of all others. It resembles the popular Nantes types which have been garden favorites for many years, but it has many important advantages.

Hybrid vigor gives rapid emergence and quick growth, high uniformity and heavy yields. The roots are unusually smooth and richly colored inside and out. Best of all, their flavor, crispness and tenderness are second to none.

Many thousands of our customers call Pioneer the finest carrot they ever ate, and we sincerely regret that poor seed crops have resulted in a serious shortage. We can offer *packets only* of this great hybrid, but for customers who require larger quantities of seed, Scarlet Nantes, described at right, is a delicious and attractive carrot of this type. Where a longer hybrid can be grown, we recommend the new Trophy.

301 TROPHY. (New.) Longer Roots, Crisp and Sweet.

78 days. This is the latest introduction in the Harris plant breeders' trail-blazing work with hybrid carrots. Its roots are long, 7-9 in., and moderately tapered. On heavy clay soil, the longer carrots do not perform well, but on looser, deeply worked soils, Trophy will produce some of the smoothest, most uniform carrots you ever saw.

Their quality matches their appearance too. They're sweet and delicious with a brittle texture that is especially pleasing when you eat them raw. Their rich orange skin and interior color is particularly fine. Hybrid vigor gives quick growth and excellent yields of uniform and unusually handsome roots.

Joseph Harris Co., Inc. Rochester, N.Y.

RAISING BEDS RAISES CARROT QUALITY

Raised carrots may be the best carrots.

Research indicates that growing carrots on raised beds instead of conventional flat beds has several advantages. Experiments at the North Willamette Experiment Station, Aurora, show that carrots in raised beds are longer and have fewer defects.

Station horticulturalist W. A. Sheets also suspects that carrots will store longer in the ground when they are in raised beds. If this year's research supports Sheet's suspicions, it will have important implications for growers because carrots are the last crop processed during the harvest season. If quality can be maintained by leaving the carrots in the ground in raised beds, the practice would provide a cheap method of cold storage.

Storability in the ground without deterioration in carrot quality is also desirable for the fresh market trade. It offers fresh market producers an opportunity to extend availability of their produce.

Carrots in raised beds also are easier to harvest than those in flat beds when the soil is wet from fall rains.

The unusual cold spell of December 1972 limited that year's research to only two harvests and prevented any investigation of the long term effect of ground storage on carrot quality. However, yield and quality differences between carrots grown on raised beds and those grown on flat beds were significant.

On the first harvest date, the raised beds produced 10.7 tons of marketable carrots per acre compared to a marketable yield of 4.3 tons per acre from the flat beds. Carrots from raised beds also were 20 percent longer than those from flat beds.

On the second harvest date raised beds yielded 16.8 tons of marketable carrots per acre compared to 7.7 tons per acre from flat beds. Length advantage from raised beds dropped to six percent.

Although carrots from raised beds were larger, much of the increased yield was attributed to a better stand. Sheets is uncertain why there was an improved stand on the raised beds. They may have had higher soil temperatures that enhanced germination because sloping sides of the beds had better exposure to the sun's rays.

Number of unmarketable carrots was considerably less in raised beds. Cracked carrots dropped from 13 percent of those harvested in the flat beds to three percent of those harvested in raised beds. Number of crooked and double carrots dropped from 18 percent in flat beds to nine percent in raised beds.

Results that heavily favored raised beds in 1972 have failed to repeat so far with the 1973 crop. The first harvest actually gave a slight yield advantage to flat beds—12.9 tons of marketable carrots per acre compared to 12.3 tons. However, carrots from raised beds still were larger and more uniform in size.

Sheets is not discouraged by the 1973 results. Difference in results between the two years is probably due to a difference in bed preparation, he said. In both years raised beds were well worked from rototilling and shaping. In 1972, flat beds were given only shallow rototilling, but in 1973 they were rototilled eight inches deep, a process that would not usually be done commercially.

Bed shapers are readily available for commercial use. Most of the manufacturers are based in California where many row crops are grown on beds, said Sheets. Several of the machines, which cost around $2,500 if they have both rototilling and bed shaping capability, are already in use in the Salem and Stayton areas.

By adding accessories to the bed shaper, it is possible to till, shape, plant and spray all in the same trip over the field. In addition to the time and labor savings from fewer trips over the field, the current fuel shortage could make the practice even more lucrative this spring, said Sheets.

Beds used in the experiments at the North Willamette Experiment Station were raised six inches. Each bed was 22 inches across the top and beds were spaced 40 inches from center to center. Two rows of carrots with 14-inch spacing were planted on each bed.

Sheets said studies to determine the effect of raised beds on carrots will continue and will be expanded to include other root crops such as parsnips. Beds also may provide better drainage for fall and winter turnips, rutabagas and some of the over-wintering cole crops such as cabbage and cauliflower, he added.

(adapated and condensed from material supplied by the Agricultural Experiment Station of Oregon State University)

Garden Carrots

ROOT VEGETABLES

Celeriac

Celeriac, or turnip-rooted celery, has been developed for the root instead of the top. Its culture is the same as that of celery, and the enlarged roots can be used at any time after they are big enough. The late-summer crop of celeriac may be stored for winter use. In areas having mild winters the roots may be left in the ground and covered with a mulch of several inches of straw or leaves, or they may be lifted, packed in moist sand, and stored in a cool cellar.

Chervil

Chervil comes in two distinct types, salad chervil and turnip-rooted chervil. Salad chervil is grown about like parsley. The seeds must be bedded in damp sand for a few weeks before being sown; otherwise, their germination is very slow.

Turnip-rooted chervil thrives in practically all parts of the country where the soil is fertile and the moisture sufficient. In the South, the seeds are usually sown in the fall, but they may not germinate until spring. In the North, the seeds may be sown in the autumn to germinate in the spring; or the plants may be started indoors in later winter and transplanted to open ground later on. The spacing and culture of chervil are about the same as for beets and carrots.

Wild Chervil

Dasheen

The dasheen, a large-growing plant, is related to the ordinary elephant's-ear and looks like it. It is a long-season crop, adapted for culture only in the South, where there is normally a very warm frostless season of at least 7 months. It needs a rich loamy soil, an abundance of moisture with good drainage, and a fairly moist atmosphere. Small tubers—from 2 to 5 ounces in weight—are used for planting in much the same way as potatoes. Planting may be done 2 or 3 weeks before frosts are over, and the season may be lengthened by starting the plants indoors and setting them out after frost is past. Set the plants in 3½- to 4-foot rows, about 2 feet apart in the rows. Dasheen tubers may be dug and dried on the ground in much the same way as sweetpotatoes, and stored at 50° F. with ventilation.

DWARF APPLE-SHAPED CELERIC.

CELERIAC, or TURNIP-ROOTED CELERY.

Parsnip

The parsnip is adapted to culture over a wide portion of the United States. It must have warm soil and weather at planting time, but does not thrive in midsummer in the South.

In many parts of the South parsnips are grown and used during early summer. They should not reach maturity during midsummer, however. Furthermore, it is difficult to obtain good germination in the summer, which limits their culture during the autumn.

Any deep, fertile soil will grow parsnips, but light, friable soil, with no tendency to bake, is best. Stony or lumpy soils are objectionable; they may cause rough, prongy roots.

Parsnip seed must be fresh—not more than a year old–and it is well to sow rather thickly and thin to about 3 inches apart. Parsnips germinate slowly, but it is possible to hasten germination by covering the seed with leafmold, sand, a mixture of sifted coal ashes and soil, peat, or some similar material that will not bake. Rolling a light soil over the row or trampling it firmly after seeding usually hastens and improves germination. Hollow Crown and All American are suitable varieties.

Parsnips may be dug and stored in a cellar or pit or left in the ground until used. Roots placed in cold storage gain in quality faster than those left in the ground, and freezing in the ground in winter improves the quality.

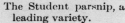

The Student parsnip, a leading variety.

PARSNIP.

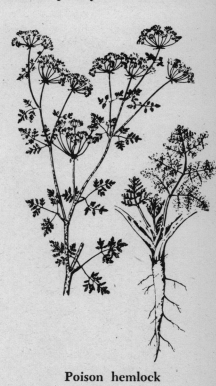

Poison hemlock

There is no basis for the belief that parsnips that remain in the ground over winter and start growth in the spring are poisonous. All reported cases of poisoning from eating so-called wild parsnips have been traced to water hemlock (*Cicuta*), which belongs to the same family and resembles the parsnip somewhat.

Be very careful in gathering wild plants that look like the parsnip.

Potato Fruits and Foliage.

Potato

Potatoes, when grown under favorable conditions, are one of the most productive of all vegetables in terms of food per unit area of land.

Potatoes are a cool-season crop; they do not thrive in midsummer in the southern half of the country. Any mellow, fertile, well-drained soil is suitable for potato production. Stiff, heavy clay soils often produce misshapen tubers. Potatoes respond to a generous use of commercial fertilizer, but if the soil is too heavily limed, the tubers may be scabby.

Commercial 5–8–5 or 5–8–7 mixtures applied at 1,000 to 2,000 pounds to the acre (approximately 7½ to 15 pounds to each 100-foot row) usually provide enough plant food for a heavy crop. The lower rate of application is sufficient for very fertile soils; the higher rate for less fertile ones. Commercial fertilizer can be applied at the time of planting, but it should be mixed with the soil in such a way that the seed pieces will not come in direct contact with it.

In the North, plant two types of potatoes—one to provide early potatoes for summer use, the other for storage and winter use. Early varieties include Irish Cobbler, Early Gem, Norland, Norgold Russet, and Superior. Best late varieties are Katahdin, Kennebec, Chippewa, Russet Burbank, Sebago, and the golden nemotode resistant Wanseon. Irish Cobbler is the most widely adapted of the early varieties and Katahdin of the late. In the Great Plains States, Pontiac and Red La Soda are preferred for summer use; the Katahdin and Russet Burbank for winter. In the Pacific Northwest, the Russet Burbank, White Rose, Kennebec, and Early Gem are used. In the Southern States, the Irish Cobbler, Red La Soda, Red Pontiac, and Pungo are widely

A Potato-plant.

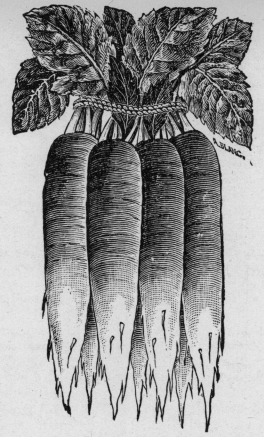

BECKERT'S CHARTIER RADISH.

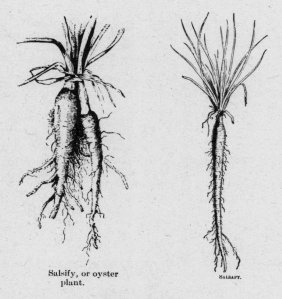

Salsify, or oyster plant. SALSIFY.

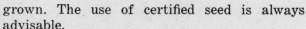

grown. The use of certified seed is always advisable.

In preparing seed potatoes for planting, cut them into blocky rather than wedge-shaped pieces. Each piece should be about 1½ ounces in weight and have at least one eye. Medium-sized tubers weighing 5 to 7 ounces are cut to best advantage.

Plant early potatoes as soon as weather and soil conditions permit. Fall preparation of the soil often makes it possible to plant the early crop without delay in late winter or early spring. Potatoes require 2 to 3 weeks to come up, depending on depth of planting and the temperature of the soil. In some sections the ground may freeze slightly, but this is seldom harmful unless the sprouts have emerged. Prolonged cold and wet weather after planting is likely to cause the seed pieces to rot. Hence, avoid too early planting. Young potato plants are often damaged by frost, but they usually renew their growth quickly from uninjured portions of the stems.

Do not dig potatoes intended for storage until the tops are mature. Careful handling to avoid skinning is desirable, and protection from long exposure to light is necessary to prevent their becoming green and unfit for table use. Store in a well-ventilated place where the temperature is low, 45° to 50° if possible, but where there is no danger of freezing.

Radish

Radishes are hardy to cold, but they cannot withstand heat. In the South, they do well in autumn, winter, and spring. In the North, they may be grown in spring and autumn, and in sections having mild winters they may be grown in coldframes at that season. In high altitudes and in northern locations with cool summers, radishes thrive from early spring to late autumn.

Radishes are not sensitive to the type of soil so long as it is rich, moist, and friable. Apply additional fertilizer when the seeds are sown; conditions must be favorable for quick growth. Radishes that grow slowly have a pungent flavor and are undesirable.

Radishes mature the quickest of our garden crops. They remain in prime condition only a few days, which makes small plantings at week

EARLY WHITE TURNIP. SCARLET TURNIP. WHITE TIPPED SCARLET TURNIP.

or 10-day intervals advisable. A few yards of row will supply all the radishes a family will consume during the time the radishes are at their best.

There are two types of radishes—the mild, small, quick-maturing sorts such as Scarlet Globe, French Breakfast, and Cherry Belle, all of which reach edible size in from 20 to 40 days; and the more pungent, large, winter radishes such as Long Black Spanish and China Rose, which require 75 days or more for growth. Plant winter radishes so they will reach a desirable size in the autumn. Gather and store them like other root crops.

CLARK'S NO. I POTATO.

Salsify

Salsify, or vegetable oyster, may be grown in practically all parts of the country. It is similar to parsnips in its requirements but needs a slightly longer growing season. For this reason it cannot be grown as far north as parsnips. Salsify, however, is somewhat more hardy and can be sown earlier in the spring.

Thoroughly prepare soil for salsify to a depth of at least a foot. Lighten heavy garden soil by adding sand or comparable material. Salsify must have plenty of plant food.

Sandwich Island is the best-known variety. A half ounce of seed will sow a 50-foot row, enough for most families. Always use fresh seed; salsify seed retains its vitality only 1 year.

Salsify may be left in the ground over winter or lifted and stored like parsnips or other root crops.

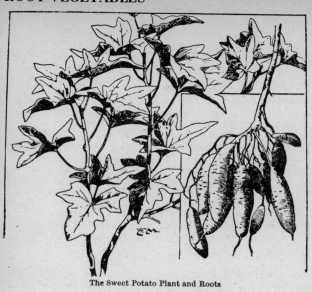

The Sweet Potato Plant and Roots

Sweetpotato

Sweetpotatoes succeed best in the South, but they are grown in home gardens as far north as southern New York and southern Michigan. They can be grown even farther north, in sections having especially mild climates, such as the Pacific Northwest. In general, sweetpotatoes may be grown wherever there is a frost-free period of about 150 days with relatively high temperature. Jersey Orange, Nugget, and Nemagold are the commonest dry-fleshed varieties; Centennial, Porto Rico, and Goldrush are three of the best of the moist type.

A well-drained, moderately deep sandy loam of medium fertility is best for sweetpotatoes.

Hamburg Parsley.

Heavy clays and very deep loose-textured soils encourage the formation of long stringy roots. For best results the soil should be moderately fertilized throughout. If applied under the rows, the fertilizer should be well mixed with the soil.

In most of the area over which sweetpotatoes are grown it is necessary to start the plants in a hotbed, because the season is too short to produce a good crop after the weather warms enough to start plants outdoors. Bed roots used for seed close together in a hotbed and cover them with about 2 inches of sand or fine soil, such as leafmold. It is not safe to set the plants in the open ground until the soil is warm and the weather settled. Toward the last, ventilate the hotbed freely to harden the plants.

The plants are usually set on top of ridges, 3½ to 4 feet apart, with the plants about 12 inches apart in the row. When the vines have covered the ground, no further cultivation is necessary, but some additional hand weeding may be required.

Dig sweetpotatoes a short time before frost, on a bright, drying day when the soil is not too wet to work easily. On a small scale they may be dug with a spading fork, great care being taken not to bruise or injure the roots. Let the roots lie exposed for 2 or 3 hours to dry thoroughly; then put them in containers and place them in a warm room to cure. The proper curing temperature is 85° F. Curing for about 10 days is followed by storage at 50° to 55°.

Turnip and Rutabaga

Turnips and rutabagas, similar cool-season vegetables, are among the most commonly grown and widely adapted root crops in the United States. They are grown in the South chiefly in the fall, winter, and spring; in the North, largely in the spring and autumn. Rutabagas do best in the more northerly areas; turnips are better for gardens south of the latitude of Indianapolis, Ind., or northern Virginia.

Turnips reach a good size in from 60 to 80 days, but rutabagas need about a month longer. Being susceptible to heat and hardy to cold, these crops should be planted as late as possible for fall use, allowing time for maturity before hard frost. In the South, turnips are very

Turnip—Early White Dutch.

popular in the winter and spring. In the North, however, July to August seeding, following early potatoes, peas, or spinach, is the common practice.

Land that has been in a heavily fertilized crop, such as early potatoes, usually gives a good crop without additional fertilizing. The soil need not be prepared deeply, but the surface should be fine and smooth. For spring culture, row planting similar to that described for beets is the best practice. The importance of planting turnips as early as possible for the spring crop is emphasized. When seeding in rows, cover the seeds lightly; when broadcasting, rake the seeds in lightly with a garden rake. A half ounce of seed will sow a 300-foot row or broadcast 300 square feet. Turnips may be thinned as they grow, and the tops used for greens.

Although there are both white-fleshed and yellow-fleshed varieties of turnips and rutabagas, most turnips are white-fleshed and most rutabagas are yellow-fleshed. Purple Top White Globe and Just Right are the most popular white-fleshed varieties; Golden Ball (Orange Jelly) is the most popular yellow-fleshed variety. American Purple Top is the commonly grown yellow-fleshed rutabaga; Sweet German (White Swede, Sweet Russian) is the most widely used white-fleshed variety. For turnip greens, the Seven Top variety is most suitable. This winter-hardy variety overwinters in a majority of locations in the United States.

Turnep Garden round.

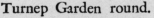

Turnip—Teltow.

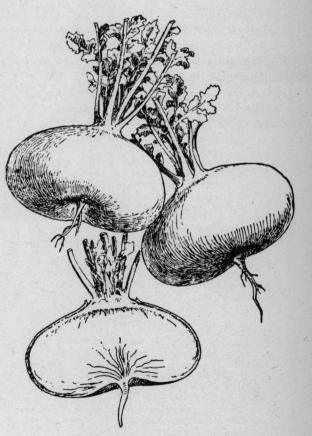

Turnip—Yellow Finland.

Turnip-Rooted Parsley

The root is the edible portion of turnip-rooted parsley. The flesh is whitish and dry, with much the same flavor as celeriac.

Turnip-rooted parsley requires the same climate, soil, and culture as parsley. It can withstand much cold, but is difficult to start in dry, hot weather. This vegetable may remain in the ground until after hard frosts. It may be lifted and stored like other root crops.

For the Long Haul — Plant Root Crops

Here are standard vegetables that will keep your family eating well from the beginning of the year to its end.

MAURICE FRANZ

Root vegetables are "must" planting this year.

The organic gardener — newcomer and oldtimer alike — knows that home vegetable production can be vital in 1975 — vital to the national economy, the family budget and its good health. Here are six basic root crops that should be raised this year for the following reasons:

1 — They give you all-winter eating when food supplies are low, but prices are high;
2 — Five of them — beets, carrots, parsnips, rutabagas and turnips — can give you two crops a year;
3 — Three of them — beets, rutabagas and turnips — give you vitamin-packed greens as well as nutritious roots;
4 — Yield, in relation to seeds sown, is prodigious, and should fill your bins, storage pits and cellars.

Now that you know why you should plant them, here is how it's done.

BEETS

Well-nourished red beets need a rich, mellow soil with at least eight inches of loamy textured topsoil that is free from stones. They thrive in slightly sandy soil that allows the roots to develop smoothly and will produce an earlier crop —provided plenty of organic matter has been worked into the soil to retain moisture and nourish the young plants.

Barbara Tripp has reported from eastern Pennsylvania that beets can be planted as early as the ground can be worked. She prepares the soil in March with goat manure generously laced with straw — covering the bed with this compost and then rotary tilling everything under as soon as the ground is dry enough to be worked.

Varieties that are recommended for good storage are DETROIT DARK RED and also WINTER KEEPER. Leanora Ashton of Wilmington, Delaware, has reported that she plants beet seeds in a trench, one inch deep with a layer of compost at the bottom. She spreads the seeds thinly to avoid crowding, and advises that if you are planting several rows they should be spaced about 16 inches apart.

Beets will grow satisfactorily in all parts of the country. In the Middle Atlantic states crops are generally raised in the spring, summer and fall — the final planting should be made about 8 weeks before frost. Plant the successive sowings through the three seasons at intervals of three weeks apart. This will give you a continuous supply of young, tender beets and fresh, new leaves.

CARROTS

Some gardeners and books advise that carrots can be planted as soon as the ground can be worked. However Ruth Tirrell, who does her planting in the Boston area, plants her peas about three weeks ahead of the carrots because she wants the soil to be dried out and crumbly to insure good growth. She feels that the soil should really be worked for carrots and that the earlier plantings should be made in light, sandy soil. Her first sowing in late April is followed by succession sowings until the big final one in midsummer.

Carrots should be sowed in shallower drills thinly in spring when germination is good, and thickly in hot, dry weather. In summer, watering may be needed until the seeds sprout. If the drill is covered with a little loose hay as a mulch, watering through it will keep the fine seeds from washing away. It also keeps the soil surface from crusting so that sprouting seeds can't break through. Seedlings should be thinned when one or two inches high, and again in a week or so. The plants that are meant to attain full size should stand two or three inches apart in the row. Preferred varieties include RED-CORD CHANTENAY and DANVERS HALF-LONG. Several pounds stored in a gunnysack in the garage will keep a family supplied with carrots after the ground gets too hard to dig in 20-below weather.

In general, root cellars and unheated basements are the best places in which to store carrots. They can also be stored between layers of soil and straw and a barrel half-buried out in the garden. Humidity of at least 90 percent is necessary to keep carrots firm and fresh. Temperatures are best around 30 to 40 degrees.

PARSNIPS

Parsnips like a deep, friable soil with a high humus content and plenty of moisture for maximum continuous growth. But don't try to grow them in an acid soil. Also avoid using fresh manures or fertilizer for parsnips, as this can cause the roots to split. The Lindemans of upper New York sow their seeds in the spring after the ground has been rotary-tilled, and a little compost and bone meal worked into the seeding row. Parsnips germinate slowly so they shouldn't be covered by more than a half inch of soil. Thinning is a must just as it is for carrots — otherwise your parsnips will be intertwined and stunted in size.

Parsnip seeds germinate slowly, not too well even when fresh, and should not be kept from year to year since they lose viability quickly. A packet of seed will sow 20 feet, an ounce 100 feet; yield from 100 feet is about two bushels.

Many old-timers will tell you that parsnips are a sweet vegetable which has to freeze to obtain its sweetness. So they may be left in the ground since they would stand freezing for convenience. They can be mulched over with hay, and dug when needed during the winter months. When handled properly, parnips are a crop that really extends from fall until spring.

RUTABAGAS

Sometimes called the swede turnip, rutabaga is a partial-season crop and fairly quick grower that should find a place in even the smallest garden. It offers the inducement of following early-season crops such as peas or lettuce to serve as a winter vegetable to feed your family. It is a hardy, cool-weather crop that will grow in any friable soil.

Rutabaga seeds are quite small and hard to handle. Mix with a little sand before sowing to keep them planted thinly. Sow in drills spaced at 22 inches apart — an ounce of seed will plant a 400-foot row. Cover with ¼ to one inch of soil, depending on how dry the weather is in your area in midsummer. If the soil is dried down to six inches, irrigate first and then sow as soon as it dries out enough to be worked. Next, cover the seed with ¾ of an inch of damp soil and firm lightly. Also planting rutabagas late in summer has them growing in the brisk cool nights that make them taste all the sweeter.

The best time to harvest your rutabaga is after there has a been a light frost, but before the ground freezes too hard. It is advisable to try and dig or pull up the crop when the ground is fairly dry. After pulling, cut the tops off an inch or so from the crown and layer the roots in crates or bushel baskets with straw, and put them in the barn, shed or garage for storage. They can be kept in a cellar storeroom in sand, but have a tendency to give off strong odors that may seep through the house. Maximum storage period is from three to four months.

According to tests run by Agricultural Experiment Stations, winter storage has no marked effect on the vitamin B or C content of this vegetable. Recommended varieties include MACOMBER, a white-fleshed rutabaga which is so sweet, mild-flavored and fine-textured that it may become the family favorite. If you like the yellow rutabaga, better try AMERICAN PURPLE TOP which has long been popular.

SALSIFY

Like most root vegetables, salsify is a long-season crop. Since it takes about 120 days to mature, seed must be planted as early in the spring as the ground can be worked. In areas where the soil cannot be turned early enough in the spring, the plot may be worked in the late fall, and the seed planted just before the ground freezes.

After the rains have settled in the soil for planting, stretch a line and make a shallow trench with a hoe, and then plant the seeds carefully. If your soil is heavy, cover the seed with about a half inch of soil. One ounce of seed will plant a 100-foot row; plant rows 15 to 30 inches apart, depending upon the method of cultivation.

Rows of salsify remain a crisp green long after the rest of the garden has been cut down by frost and cleaned up for the winter. Until the ground freezes, dig the roots as you need them, and bury the discarded leaves right in the rows as a soil-improving, green manure. With experience, you will find that by early winter almost half of your supply will have been used up. Before the hard freeze sets in, two-thirds of the remaining plants should be pulled out. Their tops should be cut back almost to the crown, and they should then be stored in an outdoor pit between layers of straw, covered with at least two feet of alternate layers of earth and straw. Once a week throughout the winter uncover the pit and remove as much salsify as needed.

The remaining third is left in the garden row until the spring thaw, after which these plants may be pulled and stored in the pit, where they will remain in good condition until well into the summer. Favorite varieties include MAMMOTH SANDWICH ISLAND which matures in 120 days, has whitish or slightly yellow roots, and reaches eight inches or more in length with the diameter of about 1¼ inches at the crown. This perhaps may be the best variety for the home garden.

TURNIP

Grown in good soil by organic methods, turnips have a definite but sweet and delicate taste, especially those which are not permitted to come to full size.

It's not necessary to limit yourself to a fall harvest. The first sowing of turnip seeds can be made early in the spring as the soil can be worked. All gardeners know that turnips do very well in cool weather, but the fact is that, like cabbage, beets, carrots and onions, they do equally well in the warm season. Gardener Tirrell prefers three varieties — the well-known PURPLE TOP WHITE GLOBE, GOLDEN BALL and NOIR LONGUE DE CALUIRE, a French turnip with black skin and light flesh, which reportedly is less susceptible to pests.

Turnips can be sown in the spring, and should be put in as early as the soil is workable so they can be harvested before the hot weather. Turnips started in midsummer and ready for harvest in fall don't have to be used up all at once. They will last for weeks in the ground, and should be dug up gradually as needed. Turnips, like rutabagas, may not be quite as hardy as carrots or parsnips, and should be mulched with hay or leaves, and later blanket-protected by snow so they will survive through the old year into the new. However, Ruth Tirrell feels it's better to dig the roots in the early winter, and store in a cool cellar or outdoor pit.

Out in Oklahoma, Ona Raney plants her fall turnips about the middle or end of September, selecting a plot where ground may not be plowed up for early spring plantings. She spreads compost over the plot, sows the seed broadcast, and then turns the sprinkler on them for a half hour each day — just enough to prevent the ground from drying out. In five days they are up and ready to grow, and a short time later are providing the family with young, tender greens. When the weather turns cold, the Raneys let the turnips take a couple of taste-improving, light frosts. Then they mulch with leaves from three oak trees in the backyard, while their neighbors use hay with equally good results. They weigh the leaves down with old boards, chicken wire or anything to hold them in place. As a result, these turnips can withstand temperatures down to 3 degrees Fahrenheit, plus several snows, sleets and blizzards.

Organic Gardening and Farming®

Vol. 22, No. 3
March, 1975

Better Gardening and Farming . . . Naturally

VINE CROPS

The vine crops, including cucumbers, musk-melons, pumpkins, squashes, watermelons, and citrons, are similar in their cultural requirements. In importance to the home gardener they do not compare with some other groups,

LATERAL GROWTH OF CUCUMBER.

especially the root crops and the greens, but there is a place in most gardens for at least bush squashes and a few hills of cucumbers. They all make rank growth and require much space. In large gardens, muskmelons and watermelons are often desirable.

Cucumber

Cucumbers are a warm-weather crop. They may be grown during the warmer months over a wide portion of the country, but are not adapted to winter growing in any but a few of the most southerly locations. Moreover, the extreme heat of midsummer in some places is too severe, and there cucumber culture is limited to spring and autumn.

The cucumber demands an exceedingly fertile, mellow soil high in decomposed organic matter from the compost pile. Also, an additional application of organic matter and commercial fertilizer is advisable under the rows or hills. Be sure the organic matter contains no remains of any vine crops; they might carry injurious diseases. Three or four wheelbarrow loads of well-rotted organic matter and 5 pounds of commercial fertilizer to a 50-foot drill or each 10 hills are enough. Mix the organic matter and fertilizer well with the top 8 to 10 inches of soil.

For an early crop, the seed may be started in berry boxes or pots, or on sods in a hotbed, and moved to the garden after danger of late frost is past. During the early growth and in cool periods, cucumbers may be covered with plant protectors made of panes of glass with a top of cheesecloth, parchment paper, or muslin. A few hills will supply the needs of a family.

When the seed is planted in drills, the rows should be 6 or 7 feet apart, with the plants thinned to 2 to 3 feet apart in the rows. In the hill method of planting, the hills should be at least 6 feet apart each way, with the plants thinned to 2 in each hill. It is always wise to plant 8 or 10 seeds in each hill, thinned to the desired stand. Cover the seeds to a depth of about ½ inch. If the soil is inclined to bake, cover them with loose earth, such as a mixture of soil and coarse sand, or other material that will not harden and keep the plants from coming through.

STANDARD SLICING CUCUMBERS

431 MARKETMORE 70. Disease Resistant Marketer Type.

67 days. This "70" Strain was developed by Dr. Henry Munger of Cornell from his original Marketmore and is among the finest slicers we offer for midseason crop. Its rich, glossy green color does not show stippling in hot weather, adapting it for midsummer growing in the North as well as for later-season use. It bears over a long period, yielding large picks of well-shaped, uniform fruit. Carrying resistance to scab and mosaic, it is a dependable producer, and when grown for fall crop, its disease tolerance makes it especially valuable. This is a cucumber of excellent quality and type, both for home and market, and we recommend it highly for the North.

Joseph Harris Co., Inc. Rochester, N.Y.

When cucumbers are grown primarily for pickling, plant one of the special small-size pickling varieties, such as Chicago Pickling or National Pickling; if they are grown for slicing, plant such varieties as White Spine or Straight Eight. It is usually desirable to plant a few hills of each type; both types can be used for either purpose.

Cucumbers require almost constant vigilance to prevent destructive attacks by cucumber beetles. These insects not only eat the foliage but also spread cucumber wilt and other serious diseases.

Success in growing cucumbers depends largely on the control of diseases and insect pests that attack the crop.

Removal of the fruits before any hard seeds form materially lengthens the life of the plants and increases the size of the crop.

Cucumbers and Melons for Summer Use—By E. L. Fullerton

HOW TO HAVE TENDER, DIGESTIBLE CUCUMBERS, AND SWEET, JUICY MELONS INSTEAD OF THE TOUGH, FLAVORLESS THINGS COMMONLY MET—VARIOUS WAYS OF SERVING AND OF PRESERVING FOR FUTURE USE

IN the full heat of the midsummer the watery, cool cucumber or the sugary melon is the most welcome "fruit" of our garden. It seems odd that the fleshy cucumber should be called a vegetable, when we always think of the same formation in the melon, its true cousin, as "fruit." The distinction after all is purely in flavor, and judging from some experiences we have had, the melons of some people do not deserve to be thus distinguished.

Both these groups are raised in exactly the same way, either in hills or around a sunken barrel. They may also be started in pots, cans, berry boxes, etc., or in a piece of sod in the coldframe, and transferred to the garden about the middle of May, by which means we cheat the season.

There are several distinct types of cucumber—long, short, smooth, spiny; trailing and climbing; white skinned and green skinned. Some varieties are raised for pickling; others to be sliced for table use. The pickling cucumbers or gherkins are gathered when quite young. For brine pickles a larger size is gathered. For ordinary pickling gather the young cucumbers when about one and one-half or two inches long, place them in a stone jar and cover with boiling hot brine strong enough to float an egg. Let them stand for twenty-four hours; then drain, wipe dry, place in a clean jar and cover with one quart of boiling vinegar, to which has been added one onion, twelve whole cloves, one ounce of mustard seed, and three blades of mace. In two weeks' time they are ready to use.

I know you will say just the same thing that I said when the cucumbers for pickling came in at the rate of three, four, or perhaps a dozen a day. "What, stop my work and pickle those few paltry things each day? Never! The game is not worth the candle." But try it and see. It is done a little at a time; thus it is hardly appreciated. Take a stone crock, cover the bottom with cucumbers and cover these with one-quarter of an inch of coarse salt; then put in another layer of cucumbers, another of salt, and so on until the cucumbers are used up. On top place a round board, just a trifle smaller

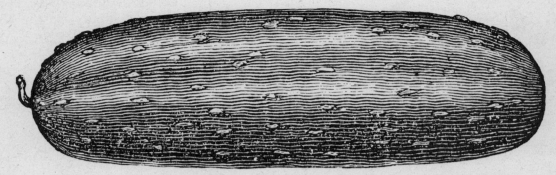

-IMPROVED WHITE SPINE CUCUMBER.

than the crock, and a good-sized stone to hold it down snugly. The next pickles that came to the house were added to the jar. By the time the crock was full a little water was poured in if the brine did not cover the cucumbers. A cloth was laid over the top, the board replaced with its weight and the cutfit stored away until a convenient time for pickling came. A few horseradish leaves placed under the cloth prevented molding, and the pickles would keep thus for months, even for years.

When the psychological moment arrives you may pickle all of your hoard of cucumbers, or only part of them, as you wish, proceeding thus: Remove the stone, the board and the cloth, wipe the scum from the surface of the brine and around the edges of the crock and wash the cloth and board. Remove such cucumbers as you wish to pickle, replace the coverings, and the rest will keep for another pickling bee.

Cover the subjects for execution with cold water; soak them three days, changing the water every day, and carefully wipe each one before dropping them into the preserving kettle, which contains enough vinegar to cover the cucumbers. Heat to the boiling point and turn occasionally. Do not cook the pickles, just heat them through, then remove from the vinegar, place in bottles and cover with fresh, cold vinegar, which may be spiced or not. Table cucumbers are usually served raw, although they may be cooked in divers ways. Always pick them in the early morning, and keep them in a cool, dark place. An hour before serving pare off the skin, slice as thin as possible and place in ice-cold water. Drain thoroughly when ready to carry to the table.

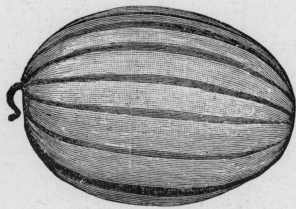

-ICING OR ICE RIND WATERMELON.

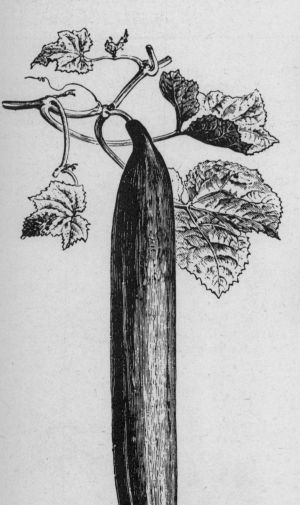

Fried cucumber can scarcely be distinguished from fried eggplant, and it is prepared in the same way, by paring the "seed pod," cutting it into slices about one-half an inch thick, dipping into egg which has been slightly beaten, then into cracker crumbs which have previously had a little salt and pepper mixed with them. Fry the slices in deep, hot fat, drain on paper, and they are ready to serve.

They may be stuffed with bread crumbs and chopped nuts highly seasoned, or with chopped raw meat in place of the bread. The cucumber is cut in half, the seeds scooped out and replaced by the selected mixture, the halves put together again and tied with string. They are then baked an hour and a half or until tender. Cucumbers may also be served boiled, covered with cream sauce, in which case the skin and seeds should be removed. They form in this way an excellent substitute for boiled onions.

"TELEGRAPH" CUCUMBER.

BROKEN FLOWER POT UTILIZED AS SHADE.

ALL KINDS OF SQUASHES AND PUMPKINS

Squash makes one of the most delightful and dainty of summer dishes, in our estimation. They are fleeting and delicate in flavor and texture, provided you secure the proper varieties. Crooknecks and yellow squashes are generally strong in flavor, while pattypans, vegetable marrow, and others of that type are extremely delicate.

Their culture is exactly the same as watermelon, even to the spacing of the hills; and their enemies are the same. An interesting

WATER MELON (CITRULLUS VULGARIS).

fact in regard to all these vine fruit-vegetables is that some flowers are male, while others on the same stem may be female. It is possible to have fine, healthy, strong vines which will not produce a single seed pod, if there have not been bees or insects near your vines to fertilize the flowers. The two blossoms are quite distinct, the female having a tiny bulb on the stem behind the calyx, while the male has not. If the pollen is carried from one to the other the bulb grows and develops, the flower in front of it falling off; but if

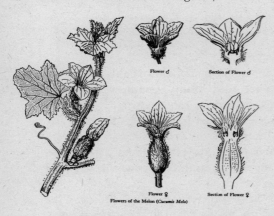

Flower ♂   Section of Flower ♂
Flower ♀   Section of Flower ♀
Flowers of the Melon (Cucumis Melo)

not fertilized the bulb as well as the blossom separates from the stem.

THE ENGLISHMAN'S FAVORITE

To me the finest of all the summer squashes are the pattypan and the vegetable marrow, the latter a favorite English variety, which is not generally appreciated in this country because we don't know when to eat it. We let it get too old.

Vegetable marrow squash may be peeled, cut into small pieces, the seed part removed

VAUGHAN'S XXX PICKLING CUCUMBER

and thrown away. Drop the prepared pieces into salt water, and cook until very tender. All should then be thoroughly drained and pressed through a colander. Returned to the pan in which it was boiled, it should be set on the back of the stove, uncovered, and allowed to steam. Add a teaspoonful of butter and a dash of pepper before serving. It will not suit an Englishman's palate unless it is served up piping hot. They may also be baked, fried, stewed with cream sauce, or prepared by any of the recipes for cucumbers. They are long and slender, rather greenish, and so extremely tender and tasty that they are becoming quite the rage.

The usual winter squashes include Hubbard, Marblehead, and Boston marrow. They grow to an enormous size, weighing more than a watermelon, and will keep in the cellar all winter, provided they are not subjected to a temperature lower than 50°.

Pumpkins are sisters to the summer squash. They are richer in flavor and are usually preferred for custards and pies, though they may be baked or boiled, prepared in the same way as any other vegetable. They can also be dried for winter use by being cut into thin strips and hung in the sun, then packed in tin boxes or glass jars. Soak these dried pieces in cold water over night and they will be ready to use.

RADISHES AS NURSES FOR MELONS

Muskmelons and watermelons are two of the most delicious "fruits" of the vegetable garden. They are both of goodly size, especially the latter, which sometimes weighs forty to fifty pounds when grown in the South. Muskmelons are more frequently raised in the home garden than watermelons, for the simple reason that they occupy less room. When the weather is warm and the leaves well out upon the trees—not before—make the melon beds, which should be three feet apart. Dig out a hole, four inches deep and twelve inches across, and place into it fine old manure full of humus, some bone meal and wood ashes, or hen manure, until level with the surrounding soil. Put three or four inches of soil over this and plant the seed, fifteen or twenty of them, together with some radish seed. Why? Because melons are slow of germination compared with radishes; the striped and the flea beetle love both, but if they can feast on radish leaves they will let the melons alone, so that the poor radishes can be used as cat's paws! When the melon seedlings are well up, thin so as to leave only the three finest plants in the hill. The striped beetle will now make a prolonged call unless made unhappy by Bordeaux. Invite him to move on, by means of this compound, and you will find that mildew also scarcely rings the bell.

The best fruit comes on the side branches, so we pinch off the ends of the runners to force side growth. Do not let the vines grow much more than two feet long without pinching. If allowed to run they will quickly cover an incredible space, but you won't get any more fruit, nor so good. Melons require plenty of water, as they are really a forced crop in this part of the country. If you

MELONS.

plant them in hills make a slight ditch around each and fill this with water every night or every other night. When the melon is ripe it parts from the stem with slight assistance, and the finest flavored fruit is that ripened on the vine. When the melons have set place a board under them.

WHEN A WATERMELON IS RIPE

Watermelons are raised in exactly the same way, by placing the hills four or six feet

COULOMMIER'S MELON.

apart, and allowing but one vine to remain to a hill. The best test for a ripe watermelon is to place the ear close to it, then press hard with the hand, and if the fruit is ripe it will yield slightly, and a cracking sound will be heard. Tap it with the fingers, and if the sound is hollow it is ripe.

There is but little waste to a watermelon, for the white part of the rind, pickled in sugar, vinegar and spices, makes a very acceptable dish to serve with meats.

CANTALOUP MELON (var. De Bellegarde).

Gourd

Gourds have the same general habit of growth as pumpkins and squashes and should have the same general cultural treatment, except that most species require some form of support or trellis to climb upon.

Gourds are used in making dippers, spoons, ladles, salt and sugar containers, and many other kinds of household utensils. They are also used for birdhouses and the manufacture of calabash pipes. But they are of interest chiefly because of their ornamental and decorative possibilities. The thin-shelled, or hard-drying, gourds are the most durable and are the ones that most commonly serve as decorations. The thick-fleshed gourds are more in the nature of pumpkins and squashes, and are almost as perishable.

The thin-shelled gourds of the Lagenaria group are gathered and cured at the time the shells begin to harden, the fruits become lighter in weight, and the tendrils on the vines near the gourds begin to shrivel and dry. For best results, give the gourds plenty of time to cure. Some kinds require 6 months or a year to cure.

The thick-shelled gourds of the Cucurbita group are more difficult to cure than the thin-shelled ones. Their beauty is of short duration; they usually begin to fade after 3 or 4 months.

All types of gourds should be handled carefully. Bruises discolor them and cause them to soften and decay.

ORNAMENTAL GOURDS

TURK'S CAP GOURD.

By Richard A. Ashley
Extension Horticulturist

Gourds are among the oldest known cultivated plants. From the earliest recorded history, gourds were used as ornaments, utensils, and storage containers.

Gourds are members of the family, *Cucurbitaceae*. Thus, they are related to the more familiar cucumber, melons, squash and pumpkins. Like their familiar cousins, gourds are warm climate plants thriving under the long, hot days of summer.

There are basically two types of gourds: those of the genus *Cucurbita* which are usually highly colored ornamental types, and those of the genus *Lagenaria* which are the more functional utensil gourds of historical importance.

Culture

Gourds are an easily grown annual vine. They adapt readily to training up a trellis, fence, or arbor. Such training results in fruits of exceptional quality and also provides an attractive landscape feature or temporary summer screen.

Gourds can be grown on a wide range of soil types. In Connecticut, a sandy soil or sandy loam soil is ideal as either will warm up earlier in the spring. In any case, the soil should be well drained.

The soil should be worked to a depth of about 8 inches and lime and fertilizer added as indicated by soil test results. An average fertilizer application would be 2½ to 3 lbs. of 5-10-10 per 100-square feet.

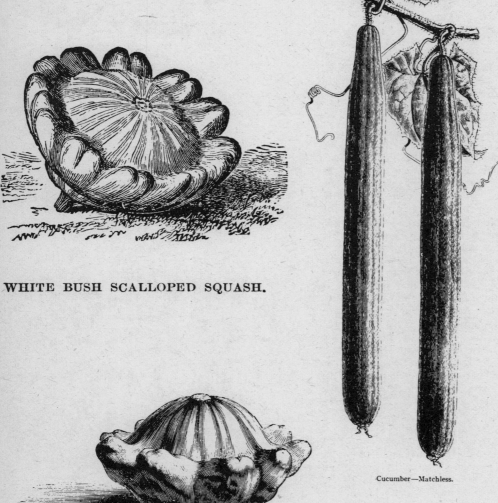

WHITE BUSH SCALLOPED SQUASH.

Cucumber—Matchless.

CROWN OR CUSTARD GOURD.

COOPERATIVE EXTENSION SERVICE
COLLEGE OF AGRICULTURE
AND NATURAL RESOURCES
THE UNIVERSITY OF CONNECTICUT, STORRS

Plant seed singly or in hills 2 feet apart in rows 5 to 9 feet apart. Since gourds require about 140 days to produce a full crop, additional yields can sometimes be obtained by starting plants indoors about 4 weeks before the date you intend to set them into the garden. If plants are started indoors, you must use individual containers for each plant, since gourds will not tolerate root disturbance during transplanting. Growing containers that can be pealed off or planted along with the plants are ideal but others can be used if care is taken not to disturb the root ball.

Gourds make very vigorous growth and frequently exhaust their supply of nutrients by mid-summer. A sidedressing of about 4 lbs. of 5-10-10 fertilizer per 100 feet of row will help maintain optimum growth.

Weeds must be controlled if good yields of high quality gourds are to be obtained. Chemical weed control has proven impractical with this crop; so weeds must be controlled by hand cultivation or the use of a mulch. Mulches have the added advantage of conserving soil moisture and keeping the fruit clean. If hand cultivation is used, care must be taken not to cultivate deeply as gourds are shallow rooted plants and can be seriously injured by deep cultivation.

Harvesting and Curing

Gourds are ready to harvest when the stems dry and turn brown. At this time, the rind should be hard but the skin is still quite tender and can be easily damaged. Care should be taken not to bruise or skin the gourds during harvesting as such injury increases the likelihood of decay during drying. The small decorative gourds should be harvested before the first frost. But, except for the first well-ripened fruits, it is best to leave gourds on the vine as long as possible or until frost actually threatens. The larger "utensil" gourds will tolerate light frost without injury.

Gourds are harvested by cutting the stems with a sharp knife or shears so as to leave a few inches of stem attached to the fruit. This stem may drop off during the drying process, but if it doesn't, it will add to the decorative effect.

After harvest, the gourds should be cleaned by wiping with a soft cloth dampened with rubbing alcohol. This will remove any decay organisms which may be adhering to the surface. If the fruit has garden soil adhering to it, it may be washed in warm, soapy water; then rinsed in clear water containing a household disinfectant. Gourds washed in water should be dried with a soft cloth.

Drying takes place in two stages: first, surface drying when the outer skin hardens and the surface color sets, then the final drying when much of the internal moisture is lost.

Surface drying takes about a week. It is accomplished by spreading the gourds in a single layer in slated trays, on newspaper, or on an open shelf in a well ventilated room, shed, porch, or garage. It is best that the gourds not touch each other. Each day turn the gourds and discard any fruit that is shriveling or developing soft spots. Also, if newspaper is used, replace it daily.

After surface drying is complete, an additional 3 to 4 weeks will be needed for final drying. For this process, store fruit in shallow containers in any warm, dry, airy location. Heat produces more rapid drying while the dryness discourages the development of decay organisms. Inspect the fruit every few days for signs of decay. Darkness is also an advantage during final drying as it prevents fading of colors.

Properly dried decorative gourds will retain their color for 3 to 4 months. This useful period can be extended by applying a protective coating of paste wax or shellac. Still the colors may become faded in 4 to 6 months.

Gourds with poor color may be used in certain situations by painting or guilding them. Gourds can be sprayed or brushed with flat or enamel paint by hanging them by the stem or suspending them on the rims of cans. A bright gild can likewise by applied by spraying or brushing. If a matte finish is desired, try painting the gourds with shellac. Then shake them in a bag with gold or silver powder while the shellac is still sticky.

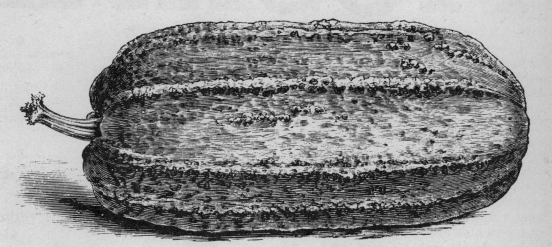

PATAGONIAN GOURD.

Muskmelon

The climatic, soil, and cultural requirements of muskmelons are about the same as for cucumbers, except that they are less tolerant of high humidity and rainy weather. They develop most perfectly on light-textured soils. The plants are vigorous growers, and need a somewhat wider spacing than cucumbers.

Hearts of Gold, Hale's Best, and Rocky Ford, the last-named a type not a variety, are usually grown in the home garden. Where powdery mildew is prevalent, resistant varieties such as Gulf Stream, Dulce, and Perlita are better adapted. Osage and Pride of Wisconsin (Queen of Colorado) are desirable home-garden sorts, particularly in the Northern States. Sweet Air (Knight) is a popular sort in the Maryland-Virginia area.

The Casaba and Honey Dew are well adapted only to the West, where they are grown under irrigation.

BALTIMORE MUSK MELON.

MUSKMELONS

MUSKMELONS are hot-weather plants. They grow best on well-drained sandy loam or silt loam soils in climates that are hot and dry.

Leaf diseases may cause severe damage in humid climates. However, muskmelon varieties are available that can be grown successfully on any good garden soil wherever the growing season is long enough—140 days or more without frost, and 85 days or more of warm weather. The length of growing season will depend on the variety of melon you choose.

For best results in growing muskmelons—

- Buy seed from a reputable source.
- Select varieties adapted to your area.
- Prepare the soil at least 30 days in advance of planting, if feasible.
- Plant after all damage of frost is past or use plant covers over early seeded hills.
- Keep the planting weed-free.
- Irrigate when needed.
- Protect the planting against diseases and insect pests.

LEAFLET NO. 509

This publication supersedes Farmers' Bulletin 1468, "Muskmelons."

VARIETIES

Choose muskmelon varieties that are adapted to your area. For best results, follow variety recommendations of your county agricultural agent or your State agricultural experiment station.

Some favorite muskmelon varieties—and the areas where they are grown—follow:

Southern States. — Edisto, Edisto 47, Delta Gold, and Perlita (resistant to downy and powdery mildews); Smith's Perfect (resistant to downy mildew); PMR 45 (resistant to powdery mildew); Hearts of Gold, Hale's Best, and Hale's Jumbo.

Northeastern and East North Central States.—Iroquois, Delicious 51, Honey Rock, Spartan Rock, and Harvest Queen (resistant to fusarium); Pennsweet, Pride of Wisconsin, and Rocky Ford.

Arizona and California.—PMR 5 and PMR 6 (highly resistant to powdery mildew); PMR 45 and PMR 450 (somewhat resistant to powdery mildew).

Irrigated areas of West and Southwest. — Casaba, Persian, Crenshaw, and Honey Dew melons are adapted primarily to long-season irrigated areas. They may be grown in other areas if the warm growing season is long enough—at least 120 days—but they are very susceptible to diseases aggravated by rain, and do not reach their best quality in rainy areas.

HACKENSACK MUSK MELON.

LIME AND FERTILIZER REQUIREMENTS

Needs for lime and fertilizer vary so widely, even over small areas, that specific recommendations cannot be given. Have your soil tested for lime and fertilizer needs before planting. For further information about soil testing, consult your county agricultural agent or your State agricultural experiment station.

Muskmelons will not grow well on strongly acid soils. These soils should be limed just enough to make them very slightly acid.

Commercial fertilizers are almost always needed for growing muskmelons successfully. A soil test will tell you how much fertilizer to apply. A good general garden fertilizer for your locality is usually satisfactory.

A typical program of fertilizer application is as follows:

- Apply ½ to 1 cup of mixed fertilizer (5–10–5, 5–10–10, or 4–8–8) to each hill three times during the growing season.
- Work the first application into the soil at planting time.
- Make the second application when runners are 12 to 18 inches long. Apply the fertilizer 6 to 8 inches away from the hill, along each side.
- Make the third application in bands, after the first melons set. Make bands 12 to 18 inches long and place them 6 to 8 inches away from the hill.

CULTURE

Preparing the Soil

Prepare the soil early enough for it to settle thoroughly by planting time. If you must turn under sod or other vegetation, do this in the fall to give the turned-under material time to decay. Do not follow this practice, however, if the soil is subject to erosion during the winter. If there is no vegetation to turn under, then plow, spade, or powertill the soil at least 1 month before planting.

Unless the muskmelon crop is to be grown on raised beds, the soil needs no further preparation until planting time. If the crop is to be grown on raised beds, form the beds about 1 month before planting.

Muskmelons usually are not grown on raised beds unless they are to be furrow irrigated. However, where soil is poorly drained and heavy rains occur frequently during the growing season, it is

U.S. DEPARTMENT OF AGRICULTURE

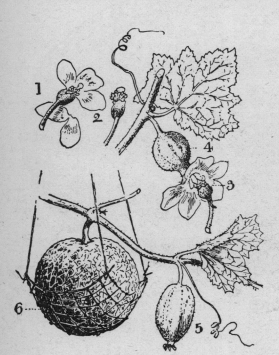

The Pollination of Melons

1. Male flower being denuded of its petals. 2. Male stigma with petals removed. 3. Pollination of female flower with male stigma. 4. Ovary. 5. Fruit swelling. 6. Melon net for supporting fruit.

GOLDEN NETTED GEM MUSK MELON.

FIGARI MELON.

QUEEN ANNE'S POCKET, OR DUDAIM, MELON.

MUSKMELONS

best to bed the soil before planting. Form the beds 5 to 7 feet from center to center and with drainage furrows between them.

Irrigated early-spring muskmelons usually are grown on beds that are laid out so they run east and west. Make these beds 5 to 7 feet from center to center and 2 to 2½ feet high from the peak to the bottom of the intervening furrow.

For irrigated summer crops, bed the soil only slightly.

Just before planting, till the soil lightly with a rotary tiller or smooth the surface with a rake.

Planting

If you are planting muskmelons in the open without covers, delay seeding until danger of frost is past. Your county agricultural agent or State agricultural experiment station can tell you the average frost-free date for your locality. If, to get an early start, you plan to use plant covers, seed no sooner than 1 month before the frost-free date.

You can buy plant covers made of glassine, paper, or plastic from your seed dealer. Put covers over seeded hills and leave them in place—except as ventilation may be necessary—until danger of frost is past.

When growing an early irrigated crop, space hills 18 to 24 inches apart, just above the irrigation waterline on the south side of the bed. Soil on the south side warms quickly and tender plants growing there are protected from cold winds.

For irrigated summer crops or nonirrigated crops, space hills 5 to 7 feet apart each way.

Using a spading fork or a hoe, pulverize a 1-foot area of soil in the center of each hill. Work fertilizer into the pulverized soil. Smooth the fertilized area and cover it lightly with field soil. Then place six or eight seeds in each hill. If you are seeding before the frost-free date, keep the seeds within an area that can be roofed with a plant cover.

Cover the seeds with about ½ inch of soil. Firm the soil over the seeds with the back of the hoe or with your hand.

Thinning

Thin the seedlings twice. When one or two true leaves have appeared between the seed leaves, thin plants to four per hill. One or two weeks later, thin again to two widely spaced plants per hill.

Cultivating

Cultivate lightly—only enough to control weeds and to break the soil crust after heavy rains. Cultivating too deep or moving muskmelon vines during cultivation can injure the shallow roots.

PREPARED BY PLANT AND GERMPLASM INSTITUTE, NORTHEASTERN REGION, AGRICULTURAL RESEARCH SERVICE

Irrigating

Do not irrigate muskmelons unless they need it. If you do irrigate, begin by soaking the soil thoroughly before planting. Plant as soon as the soil dries out enough.

Irrigate when plants first tend to wilt during the day, or when vigorous growth stops. Try to irrigate without wetting the foliage, because wet foliage is susceptible to leaf spot diseases. For best results, irrigate with a soaker hose or run water through the furrows between hills.

Though rainfall in the East usually supplies enough soil moisture for muskmelons, irrigation may be necessary during periods of drought. Then soak the soil thoroughly every 10 to 12 days.

HARVESTING

When muskmelons are ripe, their skins turn yellow and blossom ends yield slightly when pressed. With experience you can judge when melons are ready for picking.

If muskmelons are picked too soon, they do not develop their maximum sugar content. If they are allowed to stay on the vine too long, they lose sugar and become soft.

The first melons ripen slowly. As the season advances, ripening is more rapid. Pick every other day for the first week of harvest. During the second week, pick every day. Toward the end of the season, the oftener you can pick, the better.

Honey Dews, Crenshaws, Casabas, and Persians must be cut from the vines. When other kinds of muskmelons are ripe, they will separate easily from the vines if you press on the stems lightly or if you lift the melons slightly off the ground.

DISEASES AND INSECTS

Many diseases that damage muskmelons can be controlled by careful culture. You should:

- Select disease-resistant varieties.
- Buy high-quality, disease-free seed.
- Plant where muskmelons, watermelons, squashes, cucumbers, or pumpkins have not been grown for at least 3 years.
- Keep the planting free of weeds.
- Destroy all wilting or dying plants.

For more information on the control of diseases and insect pests of muskmelons, consult your county agricultural agent, your State agricultural experiment station, or your State agricultural college.

CANTALOUP MELON.

EMBROIDERED MARKET MELON.

PUMPKINS

Pumpkins are sensitive to both cold and heat. In the North, they cannot be planted until settled weather; in the South they do not thrive during midsummer.

The gardener is seldom jusified in devoting any part of a limited garden area to pumpkins, because many other vegetables give greater returns from the same space. However, in gardens where there is plenty of room and where they can follow an early crop like potatoes, pumpkins can often be grown to advantage.

The pumpkin is one of the few vegetables that thrives under partial shade. Therefore it may be grown among sweet corn or other tall plants. Small Sugar and Connecticut Field are well-known orange-yellow-skinned varieties. The Kentucky Field has a grayish-orange rind with salmon flesh. All are good-quality, productive varieties.

Hills of pumpkins, containing one to two plants, should be at least 10 feet apart each way. Pumpkin plants among corn, potato, or other plants usually should be spaced 8 to 10 feet apart in every third or fourth row.

Gather and store pumpkins before they are injured by hard frosts. They keep best in a well-ventilated place where the temperature is a little above 50° F.

688 CINDERELLA. A Bush Pumpkin!

95 days. For the first time you can now grow full-sized pumpkins in limited space. Developed by the Harris plant breeders and Dr. A. M. Rhodes of the Univ. of Illinois, Cinderella is a unique achievement, producing big, 10-inch Hallowe'en pumpkins on bush vines like summer squash. You can grow it at only 6 sq. ft. per plant! Remarkably uniform globe shape, smooth, bright orange skin, a most attractive pumpkin. Grow on well drained land and do not plant too early. Spraying with captan and maneb may be desirable.

Joseph Harris Co., Inc. Rochester, N.Y.

692 JACKPOT PUMPKIN

Hybrid Vigor, Bright, Round Fruit.

This Harris development is the first hybrid pumpkin and a fine one for home gardens. Its vines are more compact than standard pumpkins, only about ⅔ as large, saving garden space, but their hybrid vigor results in excellent yields. The pumpkins are medium-sized to fairly large with a uniformly round shape. The yellow-orange skin is smooth, hard and bright. They are ideal for Hallowe'en carving, and we have found their thick, dry flesh delicious in pies. A fine productive pumpkin to grow, especially where space is limited.

Joseph Harris Co., Inc. Rochester, N.Y.

BETTER PUMPKINS BY REVERSING EVOLUTION

By Ashby M. Rhodes

Man has cultivated pumpkin and squash for centuries. Cave dwellers of Mexico were using the fruits over 5,000 years ago. By the time of Columbus, pumpkin and squash were being grown for food over much of what is now the United States.

After many centuries of evolutionary process, the pumpkin family (genus Cucurbita) contains a large assortment of plant characters, which offer the possibility of new combinations for better varieties. As this genetic variability has developed, however, crossing the related plants of the pumpkin family has become more difficult.

Evolution can be compared with a game of cards in which Mother Nature has made the rules and dealt out the hands. The genes found in Cucurbita may be considered the deck of cards. Real cards are recognized by their suit and number or picture. Genes cannot be seen, but are recognized by their effects on individual characters, especially in the seed and peduncle (fruit stem).

Just as certain combinations of cards produce a winning hand, so certain combinations of genes survive as species. In the United States, the four annual cultivated species of Cucurbita are C. moschata, C. maxima, C. peopo, and C. mixta.

C. moschata, our oldest species, has a yellow to dark orange flesh with a fine to coarse grain. Typical varieties are the bell-shaped Butternut squash and the large-fruited Dickinson Field pumpkin. C. maxima has a yellow, fine-grained flesh and includes Blue Hubbard, Pink Banana, and the turban-shaped Buttercup varieties of squash. C. pepo has a coarse flesh, ranging in color from white to yellow-orange depending upon the variety. Connecticut Field, the traditional jack-o'-lantern pumpkin, and Royal Acorn squash are well-known fall varieties. Summer varieties include Yellow Crookneck and Zucchini squash. Also found in this species are the yellow-flowered gourds.

C. mixta varieties were considered as part of C. moschata until 1930, when specific characters were recognized as distinct enough to warrant a new name for this group. The flesh is coarse and is white to yellow. Varieties include the Green-striped Cushaw; Japanese Pie, in which the seed coat is split into oriental patterns, and White Cushaw, whose large fruits resemble the schmoos in "Li'l Abner."

Redeal

Rules of a card game prevent us from exchanging cards from one hand to another after the cards have been dealt. The exchange of genes by crossing species is prevented by sterility barriers that have arisen during the course of evolution.

But if we can't exchange cards, we can sometimes redeal them to get a new and possibly better hand. Before redealing, all hands are put back in the deck and reshuffled. Can we redeal genes to get a new species or perhaps improve an old one? In other words, can we reverse evolution in Cucurbita to a time before species evolved, and then reassemble the species into new or improved forms?

Fortunately, this idea of reversing evolution became a possibility when Whitaker of the U. S. Department of Agriculture discovered that C. lundelliana, a wild species from southern Mexico and Central America, was cross-compatible with our cultivated species. C. lundelliana is comparable to the remainder of the deck after all hands are dealt. Because it could be crossed with other species, the genes from several species could be reassembled into a common gene pool just as we might reassemble a deck of cards.

The gene pool was begun in 1956, when C. lundelliana was crossed with C. moschata and with C. maxima. These crosses were self-fertile and also cross-fertile with their parent species and with other species. By carefully intercrossing the different species, with C. lundelliana serving as a bridge, we have developed our gene pool

FRUIT OF CUCURBITA MAXIMA COURGERO.

or interbreeding population. Genes from one species, having been transferred to the pool, can now be retransferred to another species.

New bush pumpkins

Through the gene pool, the genes that control the bush form of growth in C. pepo are being transferred to the Dickinson Field variety in C. moschata. This variety is used by the Illinois canning industry, which processes about 60 percent of the nation's pumpkin.

The plant is a vining type. Fruits are set well away from the center of the row and must be wind-rowed before being mechanically loaded. If they were on a bush plant, they would be near the center of the row and would not have to be windrowed.

We began the transfer of genes by selecting several bush plants from the gene pool and crossing them with Dickinson Field. Since the bush plant character has a recessive type of inheritance it did not appear in full form in the first or F_1 generation after the cross. All plants of the F_1 generation contained both genes for vine growth and those for bush growth, but genes for vine growth partially dominated the others.

Both vine and bush plants appeared in the second or F_2 generation, since some of the plants did not carry the dominant genes for vining. The bushiest plants from the F_2 generation were crossed with Dickinson Field. The cycle, which is called backcrossing, will be repeated until the fruits of the bushy plants are like those of the vine plants. The only difference, then, between the old and the new Dickinson Field will be in form of growth.

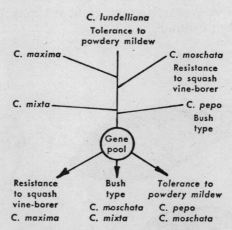

Schematic diagram of how a gene pool is formed and can be used to transfer genes from one species to another.

Other possibilities

As an extra bonus to our gene pool, C. lundelliana is tolerant to powdery mildew. This tolerance is being transferred to C. moschata and C. pepo. Tolerance to powdery mildew is inherited as a dominant character. Every generation in our backcross cycle will therefore have some disease-resistant plants, instead of every other generation as in our bush-transfer cycle.

By reversing evolution, we have made progress in improving Cucurbita varieties. This method of breeding could well be used to improve other crop plants in the future.

SQUASH AND WATERMELON

Squash

Squashes are among the most commonly grown garden plants. They do well in practically all parts of the United States where the soil is fertile and moisture sufficient. Although sensitive to frost, squashes are more hardy than melons and cucumbers. In the warmest parts of the South they may be grown in winter. The use of well-rotted composted material thoroughly mixed with the soil is recommended.

There are two classes of squash varieties, summer and winter. The summer class includes the Bush Scallop, known in some places as the Cymling, the Summer Crookneck, Straightneck, and Zucchini. It also includes the vegetable marrows, of which the best known sort is Italian Vegetable Marrow (Cocozelle). All the summer squashes and the marrows must be used while young and tender, when the rind

can be easily penetrated by the thumbnail. The winter squashes include varieties such as Hubbard, Delicious, Table Queen (Acorn), and Boston Marrow. They have hard rinds and are well adapted for storage.

Summer varieties, like yellow Straightneck , should be gathered before the seeds ripen or the rinds harden, but the winter sorts will not keep unless well-matured. They should be taken in before hard frosts and stored in a dry, moderately warm place, such as on shelves in a basement with a furnace. Under favorable conditions such varieties as Hubbard may be kept until midwinter.

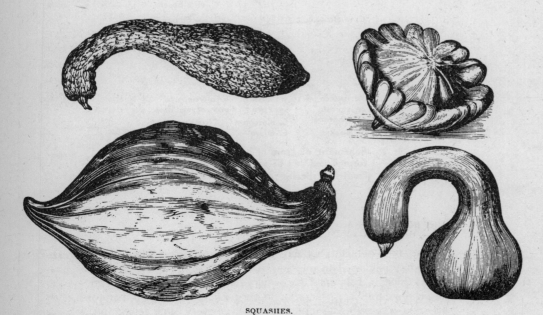

SQUASHES.

Watermelon

Only gardeners with a great deal of space can afford to grow watermelons. Moreover, they are rather particular in their soil requirements, a sand or sandy loam being best. Watermelon hills should be at least 8 feet apart. The plan of mixing a half wheelbarrow load of composted material with the soil in each hill is good, provided the compost is free from the

SCALY BARK WATERMELON.

WINTER MELON.

remains of cucurbit plants that might carry diseases. A half pound of commercial fertilizer also should be thoroughly mixed with the soil in the hill. It is a good plan to place several seeds in a ring about 1 foot in diameter in each hill. Later the plants should be thinned to two to each hill.

New Hampshire Midget, Rhode Island Red, and Charleston Gray are suitable varieties for the home garden. New Hampshire Midget and Sugar Baby are small, extra early, widely grown, very productive varieties. The oval fruits are about 5 inches in diameter; they have crisp, red flesh and dark seeds. Rhode Island Red is an early variety. The fruits are medium in size, striped, and oval; they have a firm rind and bright pink-red flesh of choice quality. Charleston Gray is a large, long, high-quality, gray-green watermelon with excellent keeping and shipping qualities. It is resistant to anthracnose and fusarium wilt and requires a long growing season.

The preserving type of watermelon—citron —is not edible when raw. Its culture is the same as that for watermelon.

LEGUMES

Beans and peas are among our oldest and most important garden plants. The popularity of both is enhanced by their wide climatic and soil adaptation.

Beans

Green beans, both snap and lima, are more important than dry beans to the home gardener. Snap beans cannot be planted until the ground is thoroughly warm, but succession plantings may be made every 2 weeks from that time until 7 or 8 weeks before frost. In the lower South and Southwest, green beans may be grown during the fall, winter, and spring, but they are not well adapted to midsummer. In the extreme South, beans are grown throughout the winter.

Green beans are adapted to a wide range of soils as long as the soils are well drained, reasonably fertile, and of such physical nature that they do not interfere with germination and emergence of the plants. Soil that has received a general application of manure and fertilizer should need no additional fertilization. When beans follow early crops that have been fertilized, the residue of this fertilizer is often sufficient for the beans.

On very heavy lands it is well to cover the planted row with sand, a mixture of sifted coal ashes and sand, peat, leafmold, or other material that will not bake. Bean seed should be covered not more than 1 inch in heavy soils and 1½ inches in sandy soils. When beans are planted in hills, they may be covered with plant protectors. These covers make it possible to plant somewhat earlier.

Tendercrop, Topcrop, Tenderette, Contender, Harvester, and Kinghorn Wax are good bush varieties of snap beans. Dwarf Horticultural is an outstanding green-shell bean. Brown-seeded or white-seeded Kentucky Wonders are the best pole varieties for snap pods. White Navy, or pea beans, white or red Kidney, and the horticultural types are excellent for dry-shell purposes.

Two types of lima beans, called butter beans in the South, are grown in home gardens. Most of the more northerly parts of the United States, including the northern New England States and the northern parts of other States along the Canadian border, are not adapted to the culture of lima beans. Lima beans need a growing season of about 4 months with relatively high temperature; they cannot be planted safely until somewhat later than snap beans. The small butter beans mature in a shorter period than the large-seeded lima beans. The use of plant protectors over the seeds is an aid in obtaining earliness.

Lima beans may be grown on almost any fertile, well-drained, mellow soil, but it is especially desirable that the soil be light-textured and not subject to baking, as the seedlings cannot force their way through a hard crust. Covering with some material that will not bake, as suggested for other beans, is a wise precaution when using heavy soils. Lima beans need a soil somewhat richer than is necessary for kidney beans, but the excessive use of fertilizer containing a high percentage of nitrogen should be avoided.

Both the small- and large-seeded lima beans are available in pole and bush varieties. In the South, the most commonly grown lima bean varieties are Jackson Wonder, Nemagreen, Henderson Bush, and Sieva pole; in the North, Thorogreen, Dixie Butterpea, and Thaxter are popular small-seeded bush varieties. Fordhook 242 is the most popular midseason large, thick-seeded bush lima bean. King of the Garden and Challenger are the most popular large-seeded pole lima bean varieties.

Pole beans of the kidney and lima types require some form of support, as they normally make vines several feet long. A 5-foot fence makes the best support for pole beans. A more complicated support can be prepared from 8-foot metal fence posts, spaced about 4 feet apart and connected horizontally and diagonally with coarse stout twine to make a trellis. Bean plants usually require some assistance to get started on these supports. Never cultivate or handle bean plants when they are wet; to do so is likely to spread disease.

CANADIAN FRENCH BEAN.

RUNNER OR CLIMBING KIDNEY BEAN
(PHASEOLUS MULTIFLORUS).

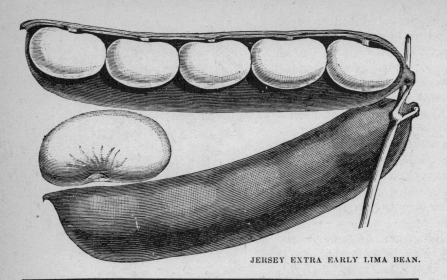

JERSEY EXTRA EARLY LIMA BEAN.

BEANS AND PEAS

L. Williams and R. C. Herner

Department of Horticulture
Michigan State University

Peas are one of the earliest spring vegetables. Both the regular garden peas and edible podded peas (called sugar or snow peas) can be grown in Michigan. Low growing varieties (bush types) which do not require staking are available as well as the vining (tall) types.

Beans are one of the easiest vegetables to grow, producing heavy yields with little care. Wax, snap, lima, pea, and kidney beans are all suitable for growing in Michigan. Snap and lima beans may be grown as either pole or bush varieties; all other bean types are exclusively bush type.

BOTANICAL INFORMATION AND HISTORY: Peas and beans are both classified as members of the Bean family, Leguminosae, characterized by plants which have pod-like fruit. Peas (Pisum sativum) are native to the Near East and North Africa. Beans (Phaseolus) belong to several different species. They are native to Central America and were widely cultivated by the time Columbus arrived.

PLANTING SITE REQUIREMENTS: Almost any soil is suitable for peas and beans. A sunny location is necessary, however. Extremely acid soils with pH less than 5.0 should be avoided.

PLANTING DIRECTIONS AND TIMING: PEAS: Peas may be planted in early spring as soon as the soil is workable, but before May 15 since the crop grows best at cooler temperatures. Any soil temperature above 40 degrees is satisfactory for seed germination. Sow the seeds 1" deep and 2-3 inches apart in rows 2' apart. BEANS: Bean seeds should not be planted until all danger of frost is past (about May 20 in central Michigan), and the soil has warmed to 60 degrees. Beans planted when the soil temperature is less than 60 degrees will rot and not germinate. To insure a continuous harvest, plant several 20' rows 10 days apart until about 8 weeks before frost is due. Fewer plantings of pole-type beans are necessary for a continuous supply since they have a longer bearing season than bush types. Beans should be planted 2" deep in lighter soils and 1" deep in heavier soils. For bush varieties, plant seeds 3-4" apart in rows 2' apart. If pole beans are used, 2-3 seeds at the base of each pole with 3' between poles in the row is satisfactory. If other training methods such as fences, trellises, or walls are used, seeds should be planted 6" apart.

FERTILIZATION: Peas and beans do not require as much fertilization as other garden vegetables, and the seeds are easily injured by direct contact with commercial fertilizers. However, if natural soil fertility is low, 1 cup of a commercial fertilizer (such as 5-10-10) per 50' of row may be mixed into the soil to a depth of 6" about 2 weeks before planting. The same rate of fertilizer sprinkled evenly near the row may be used during the summer if the plants have a yellowish appearance or are not growing well.

GENERAL GROWING INFORMATION: Adequate watering, especially during the period when pods are developing, is essential. Drought will cause pods to resemble "polywogs" in which only a few seeds develop and the rest of the pod shrivels to form a "tail".

24 EASTERN BUTTERWAX

Long, Tender, Flavorful Wax Beans.

Everyone who delights in the special flavor of wax or "butter beans" agrees that this is really something extra. The vines are large and strong-growing, bearing heavy picks of perfectly delicious, clear yellow pods. They are extra long, 6½ in. or more, oval-round, sometimes curved or uneven in shape but always delectable in quality, sweet and brittle. No wax bean quite matches the flavor of Eastern Butterwax picked fresh from your garden, and they are ideal for home **freezing** too.

83 TENDERCROP SNAP BEANS

Yield and Quality Combined.

Not only a great producer of handsome pods but of wonderful quality too, Tendercrop is a superb garden snap bean. Its 5½-in., round pods are plump, meaty and brittle, and our customers have given its rich flavor their highest praise. The pods hold their smooth, slender appearance for a long time on the vine and their color is a beautiful deep green. This is a leading example of the modern, high-quality, heavy-yielding snap beans, and we recommend it highly. Mottled purple seed

FRUITING PLANT OF DWARF OR FRENCH BEAN
(PHASEOLUS VULGARIS).

168 LINCOLN. (2½ ft.) The Sweetest and Tenderest.

67 days. For our own use, we still prefer Lincoln to any other main crop pea, and we always plant a few extra rows for ourselves. It has exceptional sweetness, tenderness and flavor, and is excellent to eat fresh or **frozen**. The pods are medium-sized (3–3½ in.), slender, curved and pointed, and they are tightly filled with small peas, up to 8 or 9 per pod. The vines are not large and are dependably productive in the garden. Lincoln has been most popular with our customers for over thirty years and is the best tasting pea we know.

Joseph Harris Co., Inc. Rochester, N.Y.

Several training systems can be used for climbing peas and beans. The pole system is the easiest, in which 8' poles are driven into the ground to a depth of 6" and 2 or 3 plants are allowed to grow up each pole. The teepee system utilizes 3 poles put together teepee shape and tied at the top with twine. Again, 2-3 plants are allowed to grow up each pole. A chicken wire trellis is also satisfactory.

YIELD AND HARVEST INFORMATION: GARDEN PEAS should be picked just before the peas have attained full size when the pods are firm and well filled. Shell and rinse the peas in cool water soon after picking and refrigerate for best flavor. Since the pods at the bottom of the plant mature first, picking should begin at the base of the plant and work upward. SUGAR PEAS should be picked when the pods reach full size, but before the seeds begin to develop. SNAP BEANS can be picked at any stage of development; however, they are more tender when picked young. For best quality, harvest before the pod begins to bulge. LIMA BEANS at the proper stage for picking should feel plump and somewhat firm. Both snap and lima beans should be harvested every 5 days. Harvest DRY BEANS (such as pea or kidney beans) as soon as the pods have fully matured and turned yellow but before they begin to break open.

Forty feet of row of lima beans per family member and 10' of snap or wax beans per person will meet the needs of most families. a 50' row of peas per person is about average.

Kidney Beans.

DISEASES: BEAN-RUST: Leaves of infected plants are covered with small, reddish brown spots, usually late in the season. Removing old vines after harvest will help decrease chances of infection the following season. Resistant varieties are also available. BACTERIAL BLIGHT: The disease appears as large, brown blotches on leaves. Spots may also develop on seeds. To control the disease, purchase seed certified as disease free. ROOT ROT: Occurs usually at cool temperatures when soils are wet. Plants may be stunted, yellowish, and may wilt. Control is only possible by planting in another uninfected area of the garden since the disease lives in the soil. Do not plant beans in the infected area again for 5 years. PEA-FUSARIUM: The lower leaves become yellow and the plants stunted. Control by the use of resistant varieties.

INSECTS: BEANS-MEXICAN BEAN BEETLE: An orange beetle with black spots which chews foliage from the underside. Hand picking or chemical control can be used. PEAS-PEA APHID: Small, pale green, soft-bodied insect found in large numbers on the growing tips of the plant. Sucks plant juices causing the plant to be weakened. Chemical control is required.

English Peas

English peas are a cool-weather crop and should be planted early. In the lower South they are grown at all seasons except summer; farther north, in spring and autumn. In the Northern States and at high altitudes, they may be grown from spring until autumn, although in many places summer heat is too severe and the season is practically limited to spring. A few succession plantings may be made at 10-day intervals. The later plantings rarely yield as well as the earlier ones. Planting may be resumed as the cool weather of autumn approaches, but the yield is seldom as satisfactory as that from the spring planting.

Alaska and other smooth-seeded varieties are frequently used for planting in the early spring because of the supposition that they can germinate well in cold, wet soil. Thomas Laxton, Greater Progress, Little Marvel, Freezonia, and Giant Stride are recommended as suitable early varieties with wrinkled seeds. Wando has considerable heat resistance. Alderman and Lincoln are approximately 2 weeks later than Greater Progress, but under favorable conditions yield heavily. Alderman is a desirable variety for growing on brush or a trellis. Peas grown on supports are less liable to destruction by birds.

SUGGESTED VARIETIES:

VARIETY	HABIT	TYPE	DAYS TO MATURITY
Tendercrop	Bush	Snap Bean (green)	53
Resistant Cherokee Wax	Bush	Snap Bean (wax or yellow)	52
Blue Lake	Pole	Snap Bean (green)	60
Thaxter	Bush	Lima Bean (small seeded)	74
King of the Garden	Pole	Lima Bean (large seeded)	88
Dwarf Gray Sugar	Dwarf	Edible Pod Pea	65
Greater Progress	Bush	Garden Pea	62
Green Arrow	Bush	Garden Pea	68

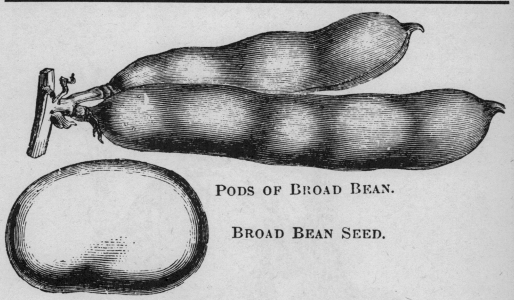

PODS OF BROAD BEAN.

BROAD BEAN SEED.

Sugar Peas

Sugar peas (edible podded peas) possess the tenderness and fleshy podded qualities of snap beans and the flavor and sweetness of fresh English peas. When young, the pods are cooked like snap beans; the peas are not shelled. At this stage, pods are stringless, brittle, succulent, and free of fiber or parchment. However, if the pods develop too fast, they are not good to use like snap beans, but the seeds may be eaten as shelled peas and are of the best flavor before they have reached full size. Dwarf Gray Sugar is the earliest and dwarfest sugar pea. It is ideal for home gardens, especially where space is limited and seasons are short. A larger and later variety, Mammoth Melting Sugar, is resistant to fusarium wilt and requires support to climb upon.

BEANS AND PEAS

Blackeye peas, also known as cowpeas or Southern table peas, are highly nutritious, tasty, and easily grown. Do not plant until danger of frost has passed because they are very susceptible to cold. Leading varieties are Dixilee, Brown Crowder, Lady, Conch, White Acre, Louisiana Purchase, Texas Purple Hull 49, Knuckle Purple Hull, and Monarch Blackeye. Dixilee is a later variety of southern pea. Quality is excellent and it yields considerably more than such old standbys as blackeyes and crowders. It is also quite resistant, or at least tolerant, to nematodes. This fact alone makes it a desirable variety wherever this pest is present. Monarch Blackeye is a fairly new variety of the blackeye type and much better adapted to southern conditions.

Heavy applications of nitrogen fertilizer should not be used for southern peas. Fertilize moderately with a low-nitrogen analysis such as 4–12–12.

For the effort necessary to grow them, few if any other vegetables will pay higher dividends than Southern table peas.

Soybeans

The soil and cultural requirements and methods of growing soybeans are essentially the same as for bush forms of common beans. Soybeans, however, are slower growing than most

GARDEN PEA.

garden beans, requiring 3 to 5 months for maturity, and warmer weather. They also are taller growing, the larger, later varieties requiring a greater distance between rows than dwarf snap beans. Small, early varieties may be planted in rows as close as 2 feet, but the larger, later ones require 3 feet between rows. The planting dates given in tables 4 and 5 are for midseason varieties (about 120 days), neither the earliest nor the latest kinds. Differences in time of development among varieties are so great that the gardener must choose the proper variety and know its time of maturity in making plans for planting in any particular locality. Kanrich and Giant Green are the most widely grown varieties.

In cooler sections the rate of development will be slower. Only the early varieties should be grown in the more northerly States, and the medium or late varieties in the South. Plantings should be made principally when tomatoes and other long-season, warm-weather crops are put in the garden.

For use as a green vegetable, soybean pods should be harvested when the seeds are fully grown but before the pods turn yellow. Most varieties produce beans in usable condition over a period of a week to 10 days. The green beans are difficult to remove from the pods unless the pods are boiled or steamed 4 to 5 minutes, after which they are easily shelled.

The yields per unit area of land are about the same as are usually obtained with peas and are thus less than can be obtained with many other vegetables. On this account, they appear of major interest only to gardeners having medium to large gardens.

CABBAGE GROUP

The cabbage, or cole, group of vegetables is noteworthy because of its adaptation to culture in most parts of the country having fertile soil and sufficient moisture and because of its hardiness to cold.

Broccoli

Heading broccoli is difficult to grow, therefore, only sprouting broccoli is discussed here. Sprouting broccoli forms a loose flower head (on a tall, green, fleshy, branching stalk) instead of a compact head or curd found on cauliflower or heading broccoli. It is one of the

EARLY WALCHEREN BROCCOLI.

newer vegetables in American gardens, but has been grown by Europeans for hundreds of years.

Sprouting broccoli is adapted to winter culture in areas suitable for winter cabbage. It is also tolerant of heat. Spring-set plants in the latitude of Washington, D.C., have yielded good crops of sprouts until midsummer and later under conditions that caused cauliflower to fail. In the latitude of Norfolk, Va., the plant has yielded good crops of sprouts from December until spring.

Sprouting broccoli is grown in the same way as cabbage. Plants grown indoors in the early spring and set in the open about April 1 begin to yield sprouts about 10 weeks later. The fall crop may be handled in the same way as late cabbage, except that the seed is sown later. The sprouts carrying flower buds are cut about 6 inches long, and other sprouts arise in the axils of the leaves, so that a continuous harvest may be obtained . Green Comet, Calabrese, and Waltham 29 are among the best known varieties.

BROCCOLI.

BRUSSELS SPROUTS

Brussels sprouts are somewhat more hardy than cabbage and will live outdoors over winter

BRUSSELS SPROUTS.

in all the milder sections of the country. They may be grown as a winter crop in the South and as early and late as cabbage in the North. The sprouts, or small heads, are formed in the axils (the angle between the leaf stem and the main stalk) of the leaves. As the heads begin to crowd, break the lower leaves from the stem of the plant to give them more room. Always leave the top leaves; the plant needs them to supply nourishment. For winter use in cold areas, take up the plants that are well laden with heads and set them close together in a pit, a cold-frame, or a cellar, with some soil tamped around the roots. Keep the stored plants as cool as possible without freezing. Jade Cross, a true F_1 hybrid, has a wide range of adaptability.

CAULIFLOWER, BROCCOLI, AND BRUSSELS SPROUTS

L. Williams and R. C. Herner

Department of Horticulture
Michigan State University

Colly flowers

Cauliflower, broccoli and Brussels sprouts are grouped under the term "cole crops." They do best in cold weather and have basically the same cultural requirements, diseases, and insect pests. These vegetables are good sources of vitamins A, B, C, niacin, iron, and calcium and are quite suitable for growing in Michigan gardens.

BOTANICAL INFORMATION AND HISTORY: Cauliflower, broccoli and Brussels sprouts are all members of the same plant family, Cruciferae, and of the same genus, BRASSICA. They are classified respectively as BRASSICA OLERACEA variety BOTRYTIS, BRASSICA OLERACEA variety ITALICA, and BRASSICA OLERACEA variety GEMMIFERA.

Cole crops originated centuries ago in Europe; in fact, Brussels sprouts were named for Brussels, Belgium.

PLANTING SITE REQUIREMENTS: Almost any soil is suitable for growing cole crops, provided it is well drained. Cauliflower is somewhat sensitive to acid soils, however, and will do best in a pH range of 5.5-6.6. A sunny or semi-sunny location is recommended.

PLANTING DIRECTIONS AND TIMING: Cole crops are generally grown from purchased transplants since few homes have conditions suitable for growing transplants from seed. Plants for summer harvest may be set out in late April and early May after the danger of hard frosts is past. They should be planted 20 inches apart with 2½ feet between rows to assure adequate growing room. A late fall crop of broccoli and cauliflower may be grown from seed sown 3/4" deep during June.

When transplants are used, it is often a wise precaution to place a cardboard or newspaper collar around each plant to prevent cutworm damage.

FERTILIZING: Before transplanting or sowing seeds, a complete fertilizer such as 5-10-10 or similar analysis should be mixed into the top 6 inches of the soil at a rate of 5 cups for every 50 feet of row to be planted. Sprinkle the fertilizer in a 1 foot wide band and mix in thoroughly with a hoe.

Fertilizer may be applied again 6 weeks after transplanting or sowing. Sprinkle the fertilizer at the same rate in a band on either side of the growing plants and water in.

GENERAL GROWING INFORMATION: One of the most important cultural practices necessary to grow good cole crops is proper watering during periods of drought. Failure to water during dry periods will reduce yields and quality. Always cultivate shallowly around cole crops when weeding since the roots are close to the soil surface and may be injured.

CAULIFLOWER: In order to produce a pure white head of cauliflower, the head must be shielded from sun by a process called blanching. Blanching consists of pulling the larger leaves of the plant over the developing heads when they are 2-3" in diameter and securing with twine or rubber bands to keep out sunlight. Failure to blanch will result in discolored heads having an odd flavor. Blanching may be avoided by planting a purple, green, or self-blanching variety.

BRUSSELS SPROUTS: As the Brussels sprout plant grows, you will notice the development of the small, round sprouts where the leaves of the plant join the main stem. At this time, the lower leaves should be removed by twisting them away from the stalk in order to allow sufficient room for the sprouts to develop. Leave the topmost leaves on the plant, removing only the bottom ones.

BROCCOLI: No special growing techniques are required.

YIELD AND HARVEST INFORMATION: Five plants per family member of each type of cole vegetable is usually adequate. Broccoli should be harvested before the buds open; cut the topmost stalk first and allow side stalks to develop for harvest later in the season. Cauliflower is best harvested when the heads are 6" in diameter, compact, and completely white in color. This will be 3-4 days after blanching if the weather is hot and 8-12 days if the weather is cold. Leaving the heads blanched too long will cause the covering leaves to rot and discolor the head. Brussels sprouts should be harvested first from the bottom of the plant, gradually working upward from the base as harvest continues. The sprouts should be at least 1" in diameter and should be picked before the plant leaves begin to yellow.

Broccoli, Early White.

VARIETIES FOR MICHIGAN: VEGETABLE	VARIETY	DAYS FROM TRANSPLANTING TO MATURITY
Broccoli	Green Comet	55
Broccoli	Spartan Early	55
Brussels Sprouts	Jade Cross	90
Spring Cauliflower	Snow King	55
Fall Cauliflower	Greenball (green colored head)	95
Fall Cauliflower	Self-Blanche	70
Fall Cauliflower	Royal Purple (purple colored head)	95
Fall Cauliflower	Snowball Imperial	58

Brussels sprouts.

Oxheart Cabbage.

DISEASES: Cole crops are generally subject to many root diseases which are caused by fungus contaminated soil. Examples of such diseases are clubroot, blackleg, and blackrot. Crop rotation and the use of treated seed are the best means of control.

INSECTS: CABBAGE MAGGOT: A small white worm which eats the roots of cole crops causing plants to wilt and die. Chemical control at the time of transplanting is required. IMPORTED CABBAGE WORM AND CABBAGE LOOPER: These small, green worms chew holes in the leaves of cole crops and may tunnel in developing buds. CABBAGE APHID: Small soft-bodied insects which injure cole crops by sucking plant juices and cause stunted growth and deformation.

Cauliflower

Cauliflower is a hardy vegetable but it will not withstand as much frost as cabbage. Too much warm weather keeps cauliflower from heading. In the South, its culture is limited to fall, winter, and spring; in the North, to spring and fall. However, in some areas of high altitude and when conditions are otherwise favorable, cauliflower culture is continuous throughout the summer.

Cauliflower is grown on all types of land from sands to clay and peats. Although the physical character is unimportant, the land must be fertile and well drained. Manure and commercial fertilizer are essential.

The time required for growing cauliflower plants is the same as for cabbage. In the North, the main cause of failure with cauliflower in the spring is delay in sowing the seed and setting the plants. The fall crop must be planted at such a time that it will come to the heading stage in cool weather. Snowball and Purple Head are standard varieties of cauliflower. Snow King is an extremely early variety with

CAULIFLOWER.

fair sized, compact heads of good quality; it has very short stems. Always take care to obtain a good strain of seed; poor cauliflower seed is most objectionable. The Purple Head variety, well adapted for the home garden, turns green when cooked.

A necessary precaution in cauliflower culture with all varieties, except Purple Head, is to tie the leaves together when the heads, or buttons, begin to form. This keeps the heads white. Cauliflower does not keep long after the heads form; 1 or 2 dozen heads are enough for the average garden in one season.

Kohlrabi

Kohlrabi is grown for its swollen stem. In the North, the early crop may be started like cabbage and transplanted to the garden, but usually it is sown in place. In the South, kohlrabi may be grown almost any time except midsummer. The seeds may be started indoors and the plants transplanted in the garden; or the seeds may be drilled in the garden rows and the plants thinned to the desired stand. Kohlrabi has about the same soil and cultural requirements as cabbage, principally a fertile soil and enough moisture. It should be harvested while young and tender. Standard varieties are Purple Vienna and White Vienna.

CABBAGE GROUP

HENDERSON'S EARLY SUMMER CABBAGE.

HENDERSON'S SELECTED EARLY JERSEY WAKEFIELD CABBAGE.

Cabbage

Cabbage ranks as one of the most important home-garden crops. In the lower South, it can be grown in all seasons except summer, and in latitudes as far north as Washington, D.C., it is frequently set in the autumn, as its extreme hardiness enables it to live over winter at relatively low temperatures and thus become one of the first spring garden crops. Farther north, it can be grown as an early summer crop and as a late fall crop for storage. Cabbage can be grown throughout practically the entire United States.

Cabbage is adapted to widely different soils as long as they are fertile, of good texture, and moist. It is a heavy feeder; no vegetable responds better to favorable growing conditions. Quality in cabbage is closely associated with quick growth. Both compost and commercial fertilizer should be liberally used. In addition to the applications made at planting time, a side dressing or two of nitrate of soda, sulfate of ammonia, or other quickly available nitrogenous fertilizer is advisable. These may be applied sparingly to the soil around the plants at intervals of 3 weeks, not more than 1 pound being used to each 200 square feet of space, or, in terms of single plants, 1/3 ounce to each plant. For late cabbage the supplemental feeding with nitrates may be omitted. Good seed is especially important. Only a few seed is needed for starting enough plants for the home garden, as 2 or 3 dozen heads of early cabbage are as many as the average family can use. Early

Cauliflower head with leaves trimmed off.

Jersey Wakefield and Golden Acre are standard early sorts. Copenhagen Market and Globe are excellent midseason kinds. Flat Dutch and Danish Ballhead are largely used for late planting.

Where cabbage yellows is a serious disease, resistant varieties should be used. The following are a few of the wilt-resistant varieties adapted to different seasons: Wisconsin Hollander, for late storage; Wisconsin All Seasons, a kraut cabbage, somewhat earlier; Marion Market and Globe, round-head cabbages, for midseason; and Stonehead for an early, small, round-head variety.

Cabbage plants for spring setting in the North may be grown in hotbeds or greenhouses from seeding made a month to 6 weeks before planting time, or may be purchased from southern growers who produce them outdoors in winter. The winter-grown, hardened plants, sometimes referred to as frostproof, are hardier than hotbed plants and may be set outdoors in most parts of the North as soon as the ground can be worked in the spring. Northern gardeners can have cabbage from their gardens much earlier by using healthy southern-grown plants or well-hardened, well-grown hotbed or greenhouse plants. Late cabbage, prized by northern gardeners for fall use and for storage, is grown from plants produced in open seedbeds from sowings made about a month ahead of planting. Late cabbage may well follow early potatoes, peas, beets, spinach, or other early crop. Many gardeners set cabbage plants between potato rows before the potatoes are ready to dig, thereby gaining time. In protected places, or when plant protectors are used, it is possible always to advance dates somewhat, especially if the plants are well hardened.

Chinese Cabbage

Chinese cabbage   is more closely related to mustard than to cabbage. It is variously called Crispy Choy, Chihili, Michili, and Wong Bok. Also, it is popularly known as celery cabbage, although it is unrelated to celery. The nonheading types deserve greater attention.

Chinese cabbage seems to do best as an autumn crop in the northern tier of States. When fullgrown, it is an attractive vegetable. It is not especially successful as a spring crop,

and gardeners are advised not to try to grow it at any season other than fall in the North or in winter in the South.

The plant demands a very rich, well-drained but moist soil. The seeds may be sown and the plants transplanted to the garden, or the seed may be drilled in the garden rows and the plants thinned to the desired stand.

A method of storing cabbages.

Cabage.

THE ONION GROUP

Practically all members of the onion group are adapted to a wide variety of soils. Some of them can be grown at one time of the year or another in any part of the country that has fertile soil and ample moisture. They require but little garden space to produce enough for a family's needs.

Chives

Chives are small onionlike plants that will grow in any place where onions do well. They are frequently planted as a border, but are equally well adapted to culture in rows. Being a perennial, chives should be planted where they can be left for more than one season.

Chives may be started from either seed or clumps of bulbs. Once established, some of the bulbs can be lifted and moved to a new spot. When left in the same place for several years the plants become too thick; occasionally dividing and resetting is desirable.

Garlic

Garlic is more exacting in its cultural requirements than are onions, but it may be grown with a fair degree of success in almost any home garden where good results are obtained with onions.

Garlic is propagated by planting the small cloves, or bulbs, which make up the large bulbs. Each large bulb contains about 10 small ones. Carefully separate the small bulbs and plant them singly.

The culture of garlic is practically the same as that of onions. When mature the bulbs are pulled, dried, and braided into strings or tied in bunches, which are hung in a cool, well-ventilated place.

In the South, where the crop matures early, care must be taken to keep the garlic in a cool, dry place; otherwise it spoils. In the North, where the crop matures later in the season, storage is not so difficult, but care must be taken to prevent freezing.

Leek

The leek resembles the onion in its adaptability and cultural requirements. Instead of forming a bulb it produces a thick, fleshy cylinder like a large green onion. Leeks are started from seeds, like onions. Usually the seeds are sown in a shallow trench, so that the plants can be more easily hilled up as growth proceeds. Leeks are ready for use any time after they reach the right size. Under favorable conditions they grow to 1½ inches or more in diameter, with white parts 6 to 8 inches long. They may be lifted in the autumn and stored like celery in a coldframe or a cellar.

LARGE FLAG OR LONDON LEEK.

Garlic.

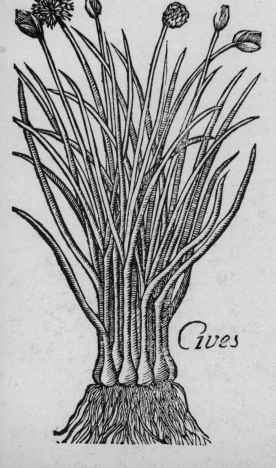

Chives

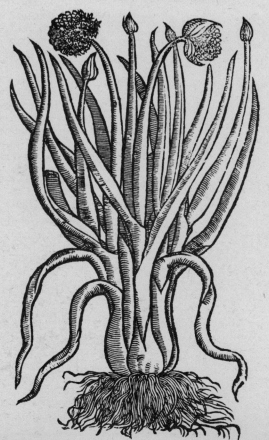

Scallion Headed.

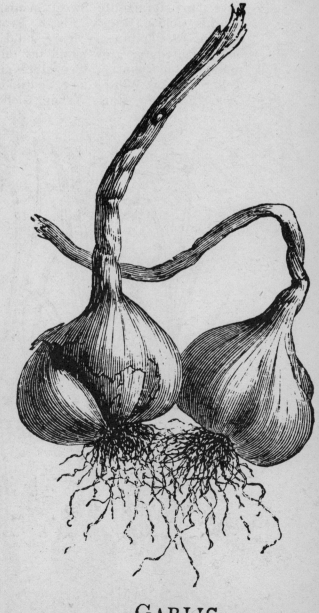

GARLIC.

Onion

Onions thrive under a wide variety of climatic and soil conditions, but do best with an abundance of moisture and a temperate climate, without extremes of heat or cold through the growing season. In the South, the onion thrives in the fall, winter, and spring. Farther north, winter temperatures may be too severe for certain types. In the North, onions are primarily a spring, summer, and fall crop.

Any type of soil will grow onions, but it must be fertile, moist, and in the highest state of tilth. Both compost and commercial fertilizer, especially one high in phosphorus and potash, should be applied to the onion plot. A pound of compost to each square foot of ground and 4 or 5 pounds of fertilizer to each 100 square feet are about right. The soil should be very fine and free from clods and foreign matter.

Onions may be started in the home garden by the use of sets, seedlings, or seed. Sets, or small dry onions grown the previous year—preferably not more than 3/4 inch in diameter—are usually employed by home gardeners. Small green plants grown in an outdoor seedbed in the South or in a hotbed or a greenhouse are also in general use. The home-garden culture of onions from seed is satisfactory in the North where the summers are comparatively cool.

Sets and seedlings cost about the same; seeds cost much less. In certainty of results the seedlings are best; practically none form seedstalks. Seed-sown onions are uncertain unless conditions are extremely favorable.

Several distinct types of onions may be grown. The Potato (Multiplier) and Top (Tree) onions are planted in the fall or early spring for use green. Yellow Bermuda, Granex, and White Granex are large, very mild, flat onions for spring harvest in the South; they have short storage life. Sweet Spanish and the hybrids Golden Beauty, Fiesta, Bronze, Perfection, El Capitan are large, mild, globular onions suited for growing in the middle latitudes of the country; they store moderately well. Southport White Globe, Southport Yellow Globe, Ebenezer, Early Yellow Globe, Yellow

Globe Danvers, and the hybrid Abundance are all firm-fleshed, long-storage onions for growing as a "main crop" in the Northeast and Midwest. Early Harvest is an early F_1 hybrid adapted to all northern regions of the United States. Varieties that produce bulbs may also be used green.

Shallot

The shallot is a small onion of the Multiplier type. Its bulbs have a more delicate flavor than most onions. Its growth requirements are about the same as those of most other onions. Shallots seldom form seed and are propagated by means of the small cloves or divisions, into which the plant splits during growth. The plant is hardy and may be left in the ground from year to year, but best results are had by lifting the clusters of bulbs at the end of the growing season and replanting the smaller ones at the desired time.

Red Great and Ronnd.

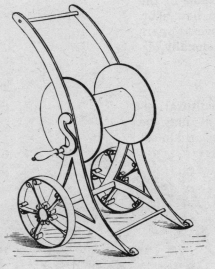

IRON HOSE REEL.

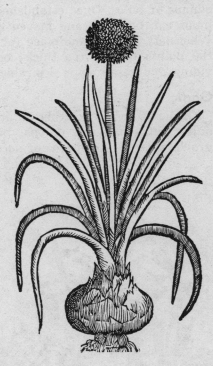

GARLIC

Garlic is a member of the onion family and garlic grows best under conditions that normally would support an onion crop. These are friable loam soils high in organic matter and good fertility.

The home gardener should find that his garlic crop will do well if he doubles the fertilizer maintenance level. Let us suppose that he elects to deal with a garlic crop on a plot as large as 1,000 square feet. This would mean the equivalent of 30 pounds of 10-10-10 fertilizer. A smaller plot would seem more likely and more desirable. Garlic (Allium satium) crops are of course of minor importance, but garlic seasoning is increasingly popular and a small plot set aside for garlic can be a desirable addition to many gardens.

Garlic is propagated by the planting of small cloves which are themselves divisions of the entire bulb. The full bulb will have a dozen or more of the cloves. The bulb is carefully separated and the cloves are planted one by one. The larger cloves are chosen, as the larger the clove, the larger the bulb is apt to be at harvest time. Gardeners should remember to pick seed bulbs that are big and smooth and free of disease.

Garlic must be planted relatively early. In many cases the gardener may find fall preparation of the soil of advantage if the soil can be fertilized and planted with a minimum necessity for tillage in the spring.

The rows should be spaced for distances of 18 to 30 inches, and the cloves are planted three to five inches apart—in an upright position to ensure a straight neck, with the cloves then covered to a depth of from one-half to one inch. Plants that are started too late may never bulb if the soil temperature remains higher than 68 degrees F.

The crop is usually harvested in August, or when the tops begin to fall over. After harvesting the garlic can be placed on trays with screens or with slatted bottoms. When the tops dry they can be removed and the bulbs then stored on trays or in mesh bags. The dried mature bulbs should be stored in dry areas, as garlic stored at humidities higher than 70% will tend to mold and roots will begin to sprout from the base of the bulb. For the gardener who chooses to grow only a few plants, he can braid the tops together with string and dry the bulbs in this fashion.

(Adapted and condensed from a publication of the University of Illinois College of Agriculture)

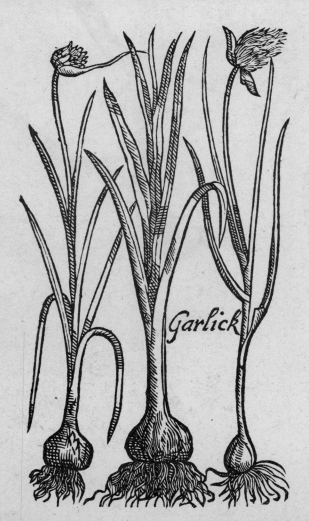

Garlick

FLESHY FRUITED VEGETABLES

The fleshy-fruited, warm-season vegetables, of which the tomato is the most important, are closely related and have about the same cultural requirements. All must have warm weather and fertile, well-drained soil for good results.

Eggplant

Eggplant is extremely sensitive to the conditions under which it is grown. A warm-weather plant, it demands a growing season of from 100 to 140 days with high average day and night temperatures. The soil, also, must be well warmed up before eggplant can safely be set outdoors.

In the South, eggplants are grown in spring and autumn; in the North, only in summer. The more northerly areas, where a short growing season and low summer temperatures prevail, are generally unsuitable for eggplants. In very fertile garden soil, which is best for eggplant, a few plants will yield a large number of fruits.

Sow eggplant seeds in a hotbed or greenhouse, or, in warm areas, outdoors about 8 weeks before the plants are to be transplanted. It is important that the plants be kept growing without check from low or drying temperatures

NEW YORK IMPROVED EGG PLANT.

BLACK PEKIN EGG PLANT.

or other causes. They may be transplanted like tomatoes. Good plants have stems that are not hard or woody; one with a woody stem rarely develops satisfactorily. Black Beauty Early Beauty Hybrid, and Jersey King Hybrid are good varieties.

Pepper

Peppers are more exacting than tomatoes in their requirements, but may be grown over a wide range in the United States. Being hot-weather plants, peppers cannot be planted in the North until the soil has warmed up and all danger of frost is over. In the South, planting dates vary with the location, fall planting being practiced in some locations. Start pepper plants 6 to 8 weeks before needed. The seeds and plants require a somewhat higher temperature than those of the tomato. Otherwise they are handled in exactly the same way.

Hot peppers are represented by such varieties as Red Chili and Long Red Cayenne; the mild-flavored by Penn Wonder, Ruby King, World-beater, California Wonder (fig. 29), and Yale Wonder, which mature in the order given.

One of the bell peppers.

RIBBED FRUITS OF TOMATO.

Tomato

Tomatoes grow under a wide variety of conditions and require only a relatively small space for a large production. Of tropical American origin, the tomato does not thrive in very cool weather. It will, however, grow in winter in home gardens in the extreme South. Over most of the upper South and the North, it is suited to spring, summer, and autumn culture. In the

more northern areas, the growing season is likely to be too short for heavy yields, and it is often desirable to increase earliness and the length of the growing season by starting the plants indoors. By adopting a few precautions, the home gardener can grow tomatoes practically everywhere, given fertile soil with sufficient moisture.

A liberal application of compost and commercial fertilizer in preparing the soil should be sufficient for tomatoes under most conditions. Heavy applications of fertilizer should be broadcast, not applied in the row; but small quantities may be mixed with the soil in the row in preparing for planting.

Start early tomato plants from 5 to 7 weeks before they are to be transplanted to the garden. Enough plants for the home garden may be started in a window box and transplanted to small pots, paper drinking cups with the bottoms removed, plant bands (round or square), or other soil containers. In boxes, the seedlings are spaced 2 to 3 inches apart. Tomato seeds germinate best at about 70° F., or ordinary house temperature. Growing tomato seedlings, after the first transplanting, at moderate temperatures, with plenty of ventilation, as in a coldframe, gives stocky, hardy growth. If desired, the plants may be transplanted again to larger containers, such as 4-inch clay pots or quart cans with holes in the bottom.

Tomato plants for all but the early spring crop are usually grown in outdoor seedbeds. Thin seeding and careful weed control will give strong, stocky plants for transplanting. A list of tomato varieties for home garden use in areas other than the Southwest is given in table 6.

In the Southwest, Pearson, Early Pack No. 7, VF 36, California 145, VF 13L, and Ace are grown.

Tomatoes are sensitive to cold. Never plant them until danger of frost is past. By using plant protectors during cool periods the home gardener can set tomato plants somewhat earlier than would otherwise be possible. Hot, dry weather, like mid-summer weather in the South is also unfavorable for planting tomatoes. Planting distances depend on the variety and on whether the plants are to be pruned and staked or not. If pruned to one stem, trained, and tied to stakes or a trellis, they may be set 18 inches apart in 3-foot rows ; if not, they may be planted 3 feet apart in rows 4 to 5

Table 6

Tomato varieties for areas other than the Southwest

Variety	Area
Ace	West
Atkinson	South
C17	East, Midwest
Fireball VF	East, North
Floradel	South
R1350	East, Midwest
Homestead-24	South
Manalucie	South
Marion	South
Morton Hybrid	North, East
Moscow VR	West
Small Fry	All areas
Spring Giant	East, Midwest
Supermarket	South
Supersonic	East, Midwest
Tropi-Gro	South
VFW-8	West

feet apart. Pruning and staking have many advantages for the home gardener. Cultivation is easier, and the fruits are always clean and easy to find. Staked and pruned tomatoes are, however, more subject to losses from blossom-end rot than those allowed to grow naturally.

GROWING TOMATOES IN THE HOME GARDEN

By Allen K. Stoner

Tomatoes are one of the most popular vegetables grown in home gardens. They grow under a wide variety of conditions with a minimum of effort, and they require relatively little space for a large production.

Of tropical American origin, tomatoes do not thrive in very cool weather. They are suited to spring, summer, and autumn culture over most of the North and upper South, and they will grow in winter in the extreme South.

Each tomato plant may be expected to yield 8 to 10 pounds of fruit. The number of plants needed will depend on the size of your family. To spread the tomato harvest over the growing season, stagger planting dates at 2- to 3-week intervals.

VARIETIES

Some tomato varieties are adapted to only certain areas of the country; others are more widely adapted. Choose a variety that is suitable to your part of the country and is resistant to fusarium and verticillium wilts. These diseases are likely to be a problem, and the only practical method of control is to grow resistant varieties.

A list of tomato varieties for home garden is given in the guide below.

PLANTING SITE

Tomatoes grow best in fertile, well-drained soil, but they will grow in almost any kind of soil.

Choose a site that receives direct sunrays all day.

SOIL PREPARATION

The time and method of preparing the soil for planting depend on the type of soil and the location of your garden.

In general, a cover crop should be grown in the garden during the winter to add organic matter to the soil. This is especially important with sandy soils that contain little organic matter.

Space the cover crop into the soil in early spring well in advance of planting.

Heavy clay soils in northern areas benefit from fall tilling and exposure to freezing and thawing during the winter. Also, gardens in dryland areas should be tilled in the fall and left rough so that the soil will absorb and retain moisture that falls during the winter.

Do not spade or work soil while it is wet unless the work will be followed by severe freezing weather. To test for moisture, squeeze a handful of soil. If it sticks together in a ball and does not readily crumble under slight pressure, it is too wet for working. Take the soil samples at both the surface and a few inches below. Sometime the surface is dry enough but the lower layers are too wet for working.

Moisture may also be tested by inserting a shovel into the soil. If soil sticks to the shovel, it is usually too wet to work.

**COOPERATIVE EXTENSION SERVICE
COLLEGE OF AGRICULTURE
AND NATURAL RESOURCES
THE UNIVERSITY OF CONNECTICUT
STORRS**

Fertilizing

Fertilizers applied during soil preparation will help tomato plants grow rapidly and produce well. The kind and amount of fertilizer you need depend on your locality and the natural fertility of your soil.

Generally, a 5-10-5 fertilizer (5 percent nitrogen, 10 percent phosphoric acid, and 5 percent potash) gives good results. Sometimes just manure or a nitrogen fertilizer is needed. Fertilizers that contain small amounts of iron, zinc, manganese, and other minor soil elements are necessary only if your soil is deficient in these elements.

Soil composition is best determined by a soil test. Contact your county agricultural agent or State experiment station for information on soil tests.

Fertilizer should be applied either a few days before planting or when the tomatoes are planted. A good practice is to spade the garden plot, spread the fertilizer by hand or with a fertilizer distributor, then go over the soil two or three times with a rake to get it in granular condition and to mix in the fertilizer. If the soil is left extremely rough, cultivate it once lightly before fertilizing.

Because of the small quantities of fertilizer required for some garden plots, it is easy to apply too much fertilizer. Chemical fertilizers should be weighed before application.

The table below shows how much fertilizer to use for each 100 to 2,000 square feet of garden area. For example, if your garden measures 500 square feet and soil testing indicates 400 pounds of a 5-10-5 fertilizer is needed for 1 acre, you find in the table that you should use 5 pounds.

Liming

Use lime only when a soil test shows it is needed. Do not apply lime in larger quantities than the test indicates. Most garden soils that are in a high state of fertility do not require additional lime.

If needed, however, any of the various forms of lime, such as hydrated and air-slacked lime, may be used; but the unburned, finely ground dolomitic limestone is best. Fifty-six pounds of burned lime or 74 pounds of hydrated lime is equivalent to 100 pounds of ground limestone. Finely ground oystershells and marl may be used as substitutes for limestone.

Sometimes tomato plants need the calcium provided by lime to help prevent blossom-end rot.

When using lime, spread it after plowing and mix it thoroughly into the topsoil. Although it can be applied in the fall or winter, it is best to apply lime in the spring because some of it may be washed from the soil during winter.

TOMATO

SEEDING OUTDOORS

In areas with a long growing season, tomatoes may be seeded directly into the garden.

Work the soil into a somewhat grandular condition. Sow the seeds in rows 4 to 5 feet apart. Keep the soil moist until the seeds germinate.

When the seedlings have 3 leaves, thin them out so they are spaced about one every 1½ to 3 feet.

SEEDING INDOORS

In the more northern areas, the growing season is likely to be too short for heavy tomato yields, and it is desirable to increase the length of the growing season by starting tomato plants indoors.

Sow the tomato seeds 5 to 7 weeks before the plants are to be transplanted into the garden. The seeds may be planted directly into small pots and growing containers, or you may sow them in flats and later transplant them individually into growing containers.

The first method involves less handling of the small plants, and there is less chance for the spread of tobacco mosaic virus. Also, seedlings develop more rapidly because the roots are not disturbed by transplanting.

However, seeding into flats and transplanting into pots is preferred by some gardeners, because less space is required initially and weak seedlings can be discarded leaving only the best plants for transplanting.

Loam or sandy soil, sand, shredded spagnum peat moss, vermiculite, and perlite may be used in various combinations to start seedlings.

Some of these combinations are:
1 part compost—1 part sand—2 parts topsoil;
1 peat moss—1 vermiculite;
1 peat moss—2 sand;
1 peat moss—1 perlite or sand—1 soil;
1 compost—1 vermiculite;
1 peat moss—1 vermiculite-1 perlite.

Various prepared mixtures for starting seeds are available commercially.

To insure good germination of tomato seed, the soil must be kept moist. Temperatures of 70 to 80 degrees F. are best during the germination period.

To help maintain proper temperature and moisture for germinating seeds, cover the flats or pots with panes of glass or sheets of plastic until the seedlings break through the soil surface . After germination, remove the cover and water the soil—but only as often as necessary to keep it moist to the touch.

Seeding into Flats

When seeding into flats, place seven to eight seeds per inch in rows and cover the seeds with ½ inch of starting mixture.

Transplant young seedlings into growing containers as soon as the stems have straightened and the leaves have opened—which is usually 10 to 14 days after sowing the seed. The earlier the seedlings are transplanted, the quicker they recover from the shock of being uprooted. Use 3-or 4-inch clay or peat pots or paper drinking cups with a hole punched in the bottom.

When transplanting young tomato seedlings, hold the plant by one of the leaves; even slight pressure on the stems can cause permanent injury. A rich topsoil with a very light addition of commercial garden fertilizer or one of the artificial soil preparations may be used to grow the transplants.

The best temperature for growing transplants are from 65 to 75 degrees F. during the day and 60 to 65 degrees at night. The young plants should be exposed to as much sunlight as possible. For best results, keep the plants in a hotbed or coldframe. If neither is available, keep them in front of a window with a western or southern exposure.

Seeding into Containers

When seeding in pots or some of the new plant-growing containers , fill the pots with starting mixture to within about ½ inch from the top of the pot. Plant one to three seeds 1/3 to 1/2 inch deep in the center of each pot. After germination, pots with more than one seedling should be thinned to a single plant.

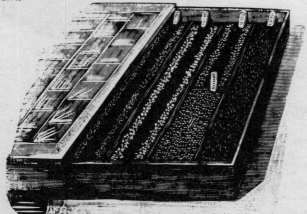

Transplanting to Garden

Plant tomato seedlings outside when the soil has warmed and there is little threat of frost. If there is danger of frost after the plants are put outside, protect them with paper or plastic coverings, newspapers, or boxes . Remove the covers during the day.

Set tomato plants into the garden at about the same depth as they were growing indoors . It isn't necessary to remove the containers if they are made of peat or paper. However, if clay containers were used, knock the plants out of the pots before transplanting.

After replanting, press the soil firmly around the plant so that a slight depression is formed to hold water. Then pour approximately 1 pint water (to which fertilizer has been added) around each plant to wash the soil down around the roots. Use 2 tablespoons of granular 5-10-5 fertilizer per gallon of water.

Distances between plants depend on the variety used and on whether the tomato plants are to be pruned and staked. If plants will be staked, plant them 18 inches apart in rows 3 feet apart. If plants will grow unstaked, plant them 3 feet apart in rows 4 to 5 feet apart.

Result of timely removal of all superfluous growth.

CARE

Watering

Tomatoes need about 1 inch of water per week. If rainfall is deficient, water plants thoroughly once a week. .

Heavy soakings at weekly intervals are better than many light sprinklings. Do not wet the foliage any more than is necessary while watering.

More frequent watering may be needed if the soil is sandy.

Fertilizing

Tomato plants benefit from fertilization while growing. When the first fruit is about the size of a half dollar, scatter uniformly around the plant a heaping teaspoon of 5-10-5 fertilizer 8 to 10 inches from the stem. Mix the fertilizer into the top ½ inch of soil and water thoroughly. Repeat once or twice a month.

If the soil is very low in fertility, more frequent fertilization may be necessary. Poor foliage color and stunted growth indicate a need for additional fertilizer.

Staking

Staking makes it easier to cultivate and harvest tomatoes, and helps prevent fruit rots. However, staked plants are more subject to losses from blossom-end rot than plants allowed to grow naturally.

If you plan to stake your tomatoes, insert the stakes soon after transplanting to prevent root damage.

Use wood stakes that are about 8 feet long and 1½ inches wide . Push the stakes into the soil about 2 feet. Tie soft twine or strips of rag tightly around the stake 2 to 3 inches above a leaf stem, then loop the twine loosely around the main stem not far below the base of the leaf stem and tie with a square knot. Or use plant ties, made of tape reinforced with wire, to fasten plants to stakes.

Wire fencing, about 6 feet high, may also be used to support a tomato plant. Form a circle around the plant with the fence.

Pruning

Prune tomatoes once a week. Remove the small shoots that appear at the point where the leaf stem joins the main stem Do not disturb the fruit buds, which appear just above or below the points where the leaves are attached to the leaf stem.

It is best to prune by hand. Grasp the shoot with your thumb and forefinger. Bend the shoot sharply to one side until it snaps; then pull it off in the opposite direction. Reversing the direction is necessary to prevent injury to the leaf axil or the main stem.

Controlling Weeds

Weeds compete with tomato plants for water, nutrients, and sunlight. Weeds also harbor insects and diseases and may be hosts for nematodes.

Cultivating.—The area around tomatoes should be kept free of weeds. Weeds can be removed by hand or with a hoe or cultivator. Loosen the soil with a hoe or cultivator so water can soak into the soil around the plant and reach the roots.

Soil fumigation.—Fumigating the soil with methyl bromide before planting is an excellent way to control practically all weeds and nematodes and many diseases in the tomato garden.

Plow to spade up the soil, then work it over with a harrow or rake. Place a plastic sheet over the area to be treated. Cover the edges of the sheet with soil to keep the methyl bromide from escaping; release the gas (in the quantity recommended by the manufacturer) under the plastic sheet. Keep cover in place 48 hours, then remove it. Cultivate the soil for aeration.

Tomatoes may be planted 72 hours after aeration. Precautions for the use of methyl bromide are given on the manufacturer's label and should be carefully followed.

Mulching.—Mulches help keep weeds down. They also reduce water loss from the soil and stabilize soil temperature.

Rolls of black polyethylene, paper and aluminum mulch are available in most garden stores   . Straw or leaves may also be used as mulch.

When using plastic, paper, or aluminum mulch, treat the soil with a broadcast application of fertilizer before applying the mulch. If you use organic mulch, it should be at least two inches deep on the soil to provide insulation, to hold water, and to control weeds.

Herbicides.—Many home gardeners have found herbicides a convenient and efficient means for controlling weeds in tomato plantings. Amiben or DCPA, applied to the soil immediately after transplanting, effectively controls weeds without injuring the plants. Follow directions on the manufacturer's label for use of these herbicides.

Carefully directed sprays of full strength stoddard solvent cleaning fluid will kill established weeds between mulched rows without damage to the tomato plants. Use this spray when there is no wind. Use a low pressure that gives a coarse spray. Thoroughly wet the weeds.

Bamboo Cane, with Tomato Plant turned out of 6-inch pot.

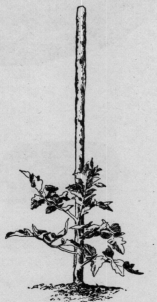

Stout end Stake, with Tomato Plant, showing type usually planted by market-growers.

BLOSSOM DROP

Home gardeners often find that blossoms drop off prematurely and the fruit fails to develop. Blossom drop is caused by (1) cold temperatures, (2) hot temperatures, or (3) excessive nitrogen fertilization. Nothing can be done to remedy the situation, and you can only wait for later flowers to produce fruit. Rarely does a plant continue to drop its flowers.

Tomato Leaf-Rust (*Cladosporium fulvum*).

HARVEST

To get the best flavor and color, harvest tomatoes after they are fully ripe. If tomatoes are picked green, they can be ripened at temperatures between 55 and 72 degrees F.

Light will increase the color of tomatoes somewhat but light is not essential to ripening. When tomatoes are placed in direct sunlight, the added heat often deteriorates their quality.

INSECT CONTROL

Several insect species damage tomatoes. Flea Beetles, tomato fruitworms, and hornworms may be controlled with carbaryl; aphids and leafminers with diazinon; and spider mites with dicofol. The insecticides can be obtained at a garden supply store. Follow the directions and heed all precautions on the label.

For further information on tomato insects, see U.S.D.A. Home and Garden Bulletin 46, "Insects and Diseases of Vegetables in the Home Garden." Single copies may be obtained from the Office of Information, U.S. Department of Agriculture, Washington D.C., 20250. Include ZIP Code in your return address.

DISEASE CONTROL

Two of the most common tomato diseases occurring in home gardens are fusarium and verticillium wilts. They are caused by fungi that live in the soil. Before the development of resistant varieties, gardeners were urged to plant in a different plot each year; this is still a good idea. The best control, however, is to grow one of the resistant varieties. Spraying or dusting is ineffective in controlling either of the wilt diseases.

Blossom-end rot is the most troublesome fruit rot for the home gardener. It is caused by a calcium deficiency and is aggravated by any kind of drought stress on the plants.

Calcium, in the form of finely ground dolomitic limestone, will help prevent blossom-end rot. It must be applied before tomatoes are planted.

Other fruit rots are caused by fungi. Usually these fruits rots are not a problem when plants are staked. Most fruit rots can be controlled either by (a) spraying with maneb or zineb fungicides at 10-day intervals, starting when the first cluster of fruit has formed, or (b) mulching with a suitable material such as black plastic.

In parts of the country where the leaves are frequently wet because of rain or dew, leaf spot diseases (such as early blight, late blight, and gray leaf spot) can be destructive. They can be controlled by applying maneb or zineb at intervals of 7 to 10 days. Be careful not to wet the foliage when watering the plants; use a soaker hose on the ground.

Virus diseases can cause a mottled discoloration and distortion of tomato foliage and sometimes can cause mottling of the fruit. Since tobacco mosaic virus is transmitted by direct contract, wash your hands and tools before touching the plants. Do not smoke while handling the plants.

Cucumber mosaic virus is transmitted by aphids that may be harbored in some perennial flowers or in nearby weeds. Cucumber mosaic can be controlled by eradicating perennial weeds like ground cherry, milk weed, catnip, and poke weed, and by spraying the tomato plants with an insecticide that controls aphids.

For additional information on tomato diseases, see Home and Garden Bulletin 46, "Insects and Diseases of Vegetables in the Home Garden" or Farmers Bulletin 2200, "Controlling Tomato Diseases." Single copies may be obtained from the Office of Information, U.S. Department of Agriculture, Washington, D.C. 20250. Include ZIP code in your return address.

TOMATOES

Love Apple

Tomato Plant, partially defoliated.

TOMATOES IN WIRE CAGES

Until the last few years the use of wire cages to hold tomato plants had been largely the province of the home gardener. The commercial growers had gone in for ground or staked plants almost exclusively—mainly because of the cost of the wire cages. But things have been changing, with the commercial growers now experimenting with caging because, chiefly, of the high cost of skilled labor needed to train, prune, tie, and stake tomatoes in ordinary commercial operations.

So the home gardeners who used cages for their tomato plants were on to something that is waxing in popularity, and other home gardeners should review the possibilities of caging. The main difficulty, as always, is the cost of the cages, both the material cost of the wire, and the considerable labor—paid or otherwise—needed to make the cages. As indicated earlier in this article, however, inherent virtues of the caging process are doing some things to offset the cost-and-trouble factors of the cages themselves. There is, however, no use denying or trying to minimize the money factor in caging. Cages run about 30 cents apiece, just for the wire. And you should assume 3,000 to 4,000 caged plants per acre.

Several years ago the Agricultural Experiment Station of the University of Illinois ran some experiments with caging, and following are some of the methods and findings.

The cages were made of 10-gauge 6 x 6-inch mesh concrete re-

MIKADO TOMATO.

inforcing wire. The wire was 5 feet wide, and cut into 4-foot lengths. Each length in turn was cut in half to make two sections 2½ feet by 4 feet. The center wire between the two sections was cut out. Then each section was bent to form a cylinder 2½ feet high and about 15 inches in diameter. The ends of the horizontal wires were bent into hooks to fasten the cages. The ends of the vertical wires were pushed into the soil to support the cage.

The experimenters put the cages in position over the plants within two weeks after planting—that is, before the plants were big enough to interfere with the positioning of the cages. The plants were spaced three feet apart in rows six feet apart. After the cages were in place the plants were not trained or pruned.

The Illinois experimenters report that early in the harvest period it did take more time to find and harvest the fruit inside the cages than with other types of tomato culture. This difference vanished as the season progressed, because the fruits were nearer the tops and outsides of the cages.

The most important finding was this: that the season yields of caged plants was equal to the yields of mulched plants and of tomatoes grown on cultivated soil. It should be emphasized that though the total yields for the season were the same for these several forms of cultivation, the proportions within the season were different. As already implied, early harvesting was delayed with the caged plants, with the losses made up later. To the commercial grower this is a major factor as early harvesting brings the highest prices. For the home gardener, usually, this factor would not be of any vital importance.

The experimenters say that the primary advantage of caging over staking appears to be from main season harvests. And an even greater advantage for caging was found when it was compared with ground culture. Caging significantly reduced culls and also reduced ground spotting—thus greatly increasing the amount of No. 1 fruits.

(Adapted and condensed from material by J. W. Courter and J. S. Vandemark of the University of Illinois Agricultural Experiment Station)

Trainers for Pot-Vines.

A tomato trellis.

-Common example of reckless defoliating.

POPCORN

POPCORN AND ITS MYSTERIES

Popcorn has been common in homes, and even more so in movie theaters, for half a century or more. It would seem unlikely that there would be anything particularly mysterious about those potentially explosive kernels of corn, so popular with almost everyone and hence worth consideration for his plot by the feed gardener. And yet there are two basic mysteries about popcorn. The first is that nobody knows why popcorn will pop and other types of corn kernels will not. And the second is that nobody knows, either, why some batches of apparently healthy popcorn do not pop well.

A few years ago Professor W. A. Huelsen of the University of Illinois ran a series of experiments on popcorn. While they did not solve the two mysteries just mentioned, the professor was able to determine that a number of possible causes for failure-to-pop can be eliminated. As an example, growers often will blame the failure to explode on frost damage. But in one experiment husked ears of popcorn were frozen for a day at temperatures as low as forty below and then thawed and dried at room temperature. The experimenters found no consistent failures that could be blamed on the freezing. In another test, popcorn was harvested weekly from early October to late December. And once again it was found impossible to find any consistent impairment that could be attributed to the temperature factor.

Professor Huelsen is quoted as saying that "six years of experimental work . . . eliminated a number of environmental factors which do not affect popping." But, he adds, "the reason why many normal-appearing lots fail to pop satisfactorily still remains elusive."

Tests over a number of years with many varieties of popcorn included an oven moisture test which lasts a week. Samples found to be too dry are watered to bring their moisture content up to 12.5 per cent. And if the sample is too moist it is dried to the proper moisture percentage. And in spite of all these precautions there were failures in attempts to pop some of the kernels.

Popcorn is an increasing interest to home gardeners. It is grown in the same way as field corn, but the grower should take certain precautions. If sweet corn and popcorn are grown too close together, they will cross. The sweet corn will pick up a starchy flavor, though the flavor is not unpleasant to most people. The popcorn potentiality for exploding expansion, however, will not necessarily be impaired by the crossing.

As for some expansion figures: when a popcorn kernel explodes it must expand 30 or more volumes to be accepted commercially. Many properly conditioned lots will expand up to 38 volumes.

Edited by Lars Skattebol

W.A. Huelsen
Illinois Research
University of Illinois Agricultural
Experiment Station

Miscellaneous Vegetables

Florence Fennel

Florence fennel is related to celery and celeriac. Its enlarged, flattened leafstalk is the portion used. For a summer crop, sow the seeds in the rows in spring; for an autumn and winter crop in the South, sow them toward the end of the summer. Thin the plants to stand about 6 inches apart. When the leafstalks have grown to about 2 inches in diameter the plants may be slightly mounded up and partially blanched. They should be harvested and used before they become tough and stringy.

ROLAND CHILLED PLOW.

Okra

Okra, or gumbo, has about the same degree of hardiness as cucumbers and tomatoes and may be grown under the same conditions. It thrives on any fertile, well-drained soil. An abundance of quickly available plant food will stimulate growth and insure a good yield of tender, high-quality pods.

As okra is a warm-weather vegetable, the seeds should not be sown until the soil is warm. The rows should be from 3 to 3½ feet apart, depending on whether the variety is dwarf or large growing. Sow the seeds every few inches and thin the plants to stand 18 inches to 2 feet apart in the rows. Clemson Spineless, Emerald, and Dwarf Green are good varieties. The pods should be picked young and tender, and none allowed to ripen. Old pods are unfit for use and soon exhaust the plant.

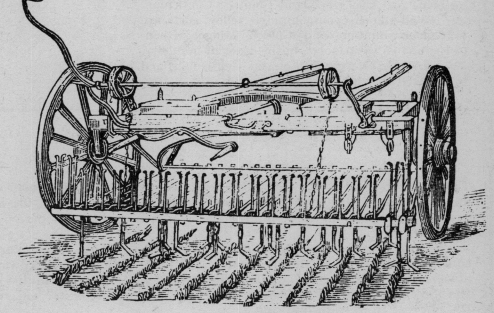

Garrett's Horse-hoe—End view.

Physalis

Physalis known also as groundcherry and husk tomato, is closely related to the tomato and can be grown wherever tomatoes do well. The kind ordinarily grown in gardens produces a yellow fruit about the size of a cherry. The seeds may be started indoors or sown in rows in the garden.

Sweet Corn

Sweet Corn

Sweet corn requires plenty of space and is adapted only to the larger gardens. Although a warm-weather plant, it may be grown in practically all parts of the United States. It needs a fertile, well-drained, moist soil. With these requirements met, the type of the soil does not seem to be especially important, but a clay loam is almost ideal for sweet corn.

In the South, sweet corn is planted from early spring until autumn, but the corn earworm, drought, and heat make it difficult to obtain worthwhile results in midsummer. The ears pass the edible stage very quickly, and succession plantings are necessary to insure a constant supply. In the North, sweet corn cannot be safely planted until the ground has thoroughly warmed up. Here, too, succession plan'ings need to be made to insure a steady supply. Sweet corn is frequently planted to good advantage after early potatoes, peas, beets, lettuce, or other early, short-season crops. Sometimes, to gain time, it may be planted before the early crop is removed.

Sweet corn may be grown in either hills or drills, in rows at least 3 feet apart. It is well to plant the seed rather thickly and thin to single stalks 14 to 16 inches apart or three plants to each 3-foot hill. Experiments have shown that in the eastern part of the country there is no advantage in removing suckers from sweet corn. Cultivation sufficient to control weeds is all that is needed.

Hybrid sweet corn varieties, both white and yellow, are usually more productive than the open-pollinated sorts. As a rule, they need a more fertile soil and heavier feeding. They should be fertilized with 5–10–5 fertilizer about every 3 weeks until they start to silk. Many are resistant to disease, particularly bacterial wilt. Never save seed from a hybrid crop for planting. Such seed does not come true to the form of the plants from which it was harvested.

Good yellow-grained hybrids, in the order of the time required to reach edible maturity, are Span-cross, Marcross, Golden Beauty, Golden Cross Bantam, and Ioana. White-grained hybrids are Evergreen and Country Gentleman.

Well-known open-pollinated yellow sorts are Golden Bantam and Golden Midget. Open-pollinated white sorts, in the order of maturity, are Early Evergreen, Country Gentleman, and Stowell Evergreen.

SWEET CORN

L. Williams and R. C. Herner
Department of Horticulture
Michigan State University

Fresh sweet corn is a favorite vegetable of many people. In addition to being rich in carbohydrates and sugars, sweet corn also contains vitamins A, B and C, minerals and protein. Many, but not all, sweet corn varieties preserve well by freezing and can be used later during the year.

BOTANICAL INFORMATION AND HISTORY. Sweet corn (scientific name Zea mays rugosa) belongs to the Gramineae, the same plant family as common lawn grasses. Corn (originally called maize) was the principle crop grown by many civilizations in the Americas. There it originated and is still used very widely as the main cereal crop in South and Central America. It was introduced to Europe in 1779 from America.

PLANTING SITE REQUIREMENTS: Sweet corn will grow in most soils, provided they are well drained and the area receives full sunlight. The quality of especially heavy clay soils or very sandy soils can be improved by the addition of organic matter such as leaves, compost, peat moss or grass clippings, before the corn is planted.

PLANTING DIRECTIONS AND TIMING: Since sweet corn is a warm season crop, the seeds cannot safely be planted until all danger of frost is past. However, many gardeners start planting about one month before the danger of frost is over since it takes a week or two for seeds to germinate. Also, the growing point of emerging corn seedlings remains below the soil for several days, which offers it some frost protection. Most gardeners are willing to gamble on losing a few seeds by planting them early, since they may be able to harvest some ears 2-3 weeks earlier than they would by waiting until all danger of frost is past before planting. Some home gardeners plant sweet corn in peat pots and transplant the whole pot into the garden when the seeds just begin to germinate or before the plants are 1" to 2" tall. By planting seeds of early, midseason, and late maturing varieties on the same day, one will be able to extend the harvest season to several weeks. Another method is to plant seeds of one variety at 2-week intervals so that the plants will mature and produce the crop in succession.

Seeds should be planted 2" deep and 10-12" apart, and 4 oz. of seed will plant a 100' row. It is advisable to plant several shorter rows 3' apart rather than one long row to insure adequate pollination of the ears. Proper spacing of the plants is important, since over-crowding causes fewer and poorer ears to be formed.

FERTILIZING: An application of fertilizer such as 12-12-12, 10-10-10 or similar analysis prior to planting will help the young corn plants become established rapidly. Spread fertilizer on the soil before planting in a band approximately 1' wide and at the rate of 1 cup for every 25' of row length. Mix it in the soil with a rake. Additional applications of high nitrogen fertilizer should be made when the corn is knee high and again when tassles appear. Applications at this time should be made as a side dressing, which consists of a light sprinkling of fertilizer in a 1' band on either side of the row, near the base of the stalks. One cup of fertilizer is sufficient to side dress 50' of corn row. Nitrogen deficiency is shown on corn plants by the rapid yellowing of the lower leaves, and a light green color on the younger leaves. If such symptoms occur, additional applications of a high nitrogen fertilizer should be made.

GENERAL GROWING INFORMATION: For best production, corn should be kept weed free. Mulching around the base of the young plants to a depth of 3" with leaves, grass clippings and other material will eliminate most weeds and conserve soil moisture. Shallow cultivation will eliminate the rest.

Watering during dry periods, especially from tassling until picking time, will also increase yield. Corn plants require at least 1" of water per week when temperatures are high and the plants are actively growing.

The growth of small shoots at the base of the plants (called suckering) is often found on garden sweet corn. Removal of these shoots is not necessary and may actually harm the plant.

Popcorn varieties should not be planted next to regular sweet corn varieties. The cross pollination between the two species will result in a mixture of the two types and cause them to be less edible.

YIELD AND HARVEST INFORMATION: A yield of 30 ears may be expected for every 25' of sweet corn planted, so that 3 rows each 25' long is ample for most families.

Sweet corn should be harvested as soon as kernels reach the milk stage; at this stage, the kernels pop readily when pushed with the thumbnail. Since sweet corn passes the prime edible stage in 7-10 days, it is important to check the garden every few days. The top ears on the stalk usually mature one or two days later than the bottom ears. Sweet corn loses quality very rapidly after harvest and should be eaten shortly after harvest or placed in the refrigerator.

SUGGESTED VARIETIES: In general, corn varieties which mature later in the season are of better quality. Also, several bi-color varieties having both white and yellow kernels are available, and are becoming increasingly popular.

SWEET CORN

VARIETY	COLOR	AVERAGE DAYS FROM PLANTING OR HARVEST
Butter vee	yellow	early - 58
Spring gold	yellow	early - 67
*Wonderful	yellow	midseason - 82
*Butter and sugar	bi-color	midseason - 78
*Silver queen	white	late - 92
*Golden queen	yellow	late - 94

*suitable for freezing and canning

PESTS: Smut: A disease causing misshapen abnormal gray growths on ears and stalks. Control by removing growths as soon as possible before they break open. Corn earworm: Feeds on kernels near the tip of maturing ears. Corn borer: Tunnels in the corn stalk causing its collapse. May also tunnel into ears of corn. Birds: Often eat the kernels at the tip of the ear. To control, place bags over the growing ears after the silks turn brown. Raccoons: May be a problem in rural areas. They eat mature ears at night, and may cause a substantial loss.

118 HARRIS' GOLD CUP. Small Kernels of Fine Flavor.

80 days. Another superb hybrid from Harris' plant breeders, Gold Cup is a real winner, especially for market and shipping. It is a tremendous yielder of trim, bright, small-grained ears of choice flavor and sweetness, holding their quality well and permitting a longer harvest period. Fine for **freezing.**

The kernels are refined-looking, closely placed, bright yellow and always appetizing in appearance. The uniform ears are not large, about 7½ in. long, but are filled to the tips with 14–16 rows of glossy kernels, well protected in smooth dark husks.

The plants are not tall, about 6½ ft., sturdy with few tillers, easy to spray and pick. Gold Cup can out-yield almost all other hybrids but needs high fertility, irrigation and adequate spacing. It makes a wonderful, delicious productive home garden corn.

134 SILVER QUEEN. Tenderest, Most Delicious White Corn.

94 days. Here is the corn we all look forward to—the supremely delicious Silver Queen, probably the best we have to eat. Its quality is really extraordinary, always tender and extra-sweet with a superb flavor all its own. It matures late, but it is a delightful treat in late summer and fall.

The ears are large and handsome, well-filled with 14–16 rows of glossy white kernels. They are delectable as soon as large enough but will hold on the stalk for a week or ten days with no sacrifice of quality, still just as wonderfully delicate with creamy texture, sweetness and rich flavor. Fine for **freezing** too. Vigorous plants, 7 ft. tall or more.

If you grow for roadside stands, be sure to plant plenty of Silver Queen, since it has created a whole new market for white corn and brings more repeat customers than any other. Tremendously popular. *Illustrated in color on inside front cover.*

Joseph Harris Co., Inc. Rochester, N.Y.

SUNFLOWERS

Himalayan Rabbit

L. L. Williams and R. C. Herner
Department of Horticulture
Michigan State University

Sunflowers are grown in home gardens for a variety of reasons. For some home gardeners, they are simply ornamental, providing a showy backdrop for the vegetable or flower garden. Others grow sunflowers to obtain the seeds which are quite tasty and contain appreciable amounts of phosphorus, calcium, iron and potassium plus several vitamins. The seeds are excellent winter food for birds and squirrels and are eaten by such bird species as cardinals, goldfinches and blue jays. Hamsters, gerbils and other house pets also enjoy them.

Commercially, sunflowers are raised for human food, bird feed or oil. Canada and Russia are large producers of sunflower seed with Minnesota and North Dakota ranking as the largest U. S. producers.

BOTANICAL INFORMATION AND HISTORY: The sunflower belongs to the Compositae family and is botanically classified Helianthus annuus. Native to America, it was grown extensively by the Indians for food. Spanish explorers in Central America brought the plant back to Spain in the mid-1500's where it is widely grown there to this day.

PLANTING SITE REQUIREMENTS: Sunflowers are extremely versatile and will grow well in most any soil type from sandy to clay. They are also very tolerant of very basic (alkaline) soils where other plants would not flourish. Fertilizer worked deep into the soil at the rate of 1 cup of commercial fertilizer (such as 5-10-10) per 50 feet of row will assure best growth and seed production.

PLANTING DIRECTIONS AND TIMING: Sunflowers may be planted several weeks before the date of the last killing frost, since the young plants are quite resistant to freezing and have survived temperatures into the 20's. With large sunflower varieties (10' tall), the seeds should be planted 6" apart in rows 18" apart and thinned to a final spacing of 18" apart in the row. If you are growing one of the smaller commercial varieties (5' tall), seeds can be planted 6" apart in rows 22" apart, and no thinning is necessary. In both cases, seeds should be planted 1" deep and watered in well if the soil is not moist.

GENERAL GROWING INFORMATION: Weeds are a frequent problem in sunflowers, but the problem can be largely eliminated by mulching the young plants with compost, grass clippings or similar material. Apply the mulch 3" deep covering the area around the base of each plant and between plants for best weed control. In addition to reducing weed problems, mulching also helps to hold in soil moisture and protects the soil from erosion.

Sunflowers are extremely drought resistant, but their greatest need for water is during the 3-week period from the time the flower begins to develop until the flower head is fully developed and expanded. If natural rainfall is lacking during this period, (late July to early August), supplemental water should be supplied.

Sun-Flower Greater.

Buff Leghorns

Sunflowers may be harvested as soon as the seeds begin to turn brown or the back of the heads turn yellow. Delaying the harvest can lead to a great percentage of the seeds beging lost to birds. Finish drying the seeds by hanging the heads upside down in a warm dry place for about 3 weeks. A garage usually works well for this purpose, and air circulation can be improved and the drying process hastened by the use of an electric fan.

To prepare sunflower seeds for eating, wait until they are fully dry, then soak overnight in a strong salt water solution. Drain the water, place the seeds on cookie sheets, and roast 3 hours at 200 degrees or until crisp. For use by birds and other animals, simply dry the seeds in the head as above, remove and store in a paper bag until ready to use

VARIETIES: The homeowner should decide for himself which of the many varieties he prefers to grow. Many unusual varieties such as red, striped and double types are available from seed catalogs. Gardeners raising sunflowers for seed should not raise double varieties, however, since these types do not produce seed.

PROBLEMS: Sunflowers are relatively free of insect, disease and similar problems. Among the few problems you may encounter are:

Empty seeds — usually this condition is due to a late season frost before pollination has been completed, and the sterile seeds will be arranged in a circle around the flower head.

Birds — birds are the main pest of sunflowers in many areas. Early harvesting may help, or the heads may be covered with perforated plastic bags.

Aphids — these small, soft bodied insects suck plant juices and in large numbers can cause stunting. Most all-purpose garden insecticides will kill aphids.

Leaf mottle — this disease is caused by a fungus which lives in the soil. Affected plants have dead areas along the veins in the leaves. Infected plants cannot be cured, but the condition can sometimes be prevented by planting the sunflowers in another area of the garden the following year.

ORNAMENTAL FOOD GARDENS

LONG WHITE VEGETABLE MARROW.

Have you ever considered growing food, beautiful food to replace or supplement ornamentals that are filling your garden with perfume and color but doing little for your belly?

These days, more and more gardeners are plowing up their lawns and flower beds to make room for food crops. But, this should not prevent them from enjoying the pleasures of ornamental gardening. All it takes is a little imagination, a lot of work, and thoughtful selection and placement of attractive, nourishing plant life.

Ambitious gardeners can do away with straight rows and plant formal designs and mazes that were popular in medieval France and England.

Imagine the delight of strolling along miniature paths, through well laid out patches of feathery carrot tops, high climbing pole beans, leafy lettuce and fragrant herbs.

Growing areas may be planted in stone-lined stars, circles, triangles, squares, pentagrams, hexagrams, any shape you like.

Paths may be kept free of weeds by laying in stone or mulch.

When you plan this type of garden, the size and growing time of mature plants must be considered, to avoid crowding and stunted growth. The information is usually available on seed packets.

Plan to use smaller plants such as radishes in pleasing geometric combination with mid-sized broccoli "bushes" and taller plants like tomatoes and corn.

Always leave access space to perform the daily work like weeding, fertilizing, and so forth.

Sweet scented herbs are healthful and nutritious additions to any ornamental food garden. Many are useful as companion plants to other food crops. Basil, borage and mint are a few herbs that keep particular garden pests away.

You cannot eat some flowers like marigolds but they should also be included in your ornamental food garden as natural pest controls. Other flowers should be included to attract bees for pollination. Climbing vine vegetables like peas and beans will form beautiful screens when trained to trellises. Corn and giant varieties of sun flowers also can be used as late summer screens.

Grapes have been trained to trellises for centuries to provide cool shady arbors where gardeners and guests may dally over drinks and conversation or spend some time in quiet comtemplation.

Squash and melons may be planted to dress up your fences with edibles.

If your fence is intended to keep intruders out in addition to being decorative, consider putting in rows of thorny berry canes and bramble fruit.

Privet hedges may be replaced with equally impenetrable, infinitely more beautiful Rosa Rugosa hedges—a source of rose hips extremely high in Vitamin C.

Fruit and nut trees come in all sizes and shapes. In season they will fill your garden with the sweet perfume of their blossoms, and yield harvests that please the palate. So, why choose trees that do less in your landscaping plans?

Certain varieties of vegetables are classified as ornamental vegetables. The list that follows was compiled by L. Williams and R. C. Herner from the Department of Horticulture at Michigan State University.

Utility and beauty may go hand in hand. Keep this in mind when you begin planning next year's garden. Try innovations of your own on the theme of food, beautiful food. Send some snap shots or suggestions our way if the results are pleasing.

ORNAMENTAL VEGETABLE GARDENS

L. Williams and R. C. Herner   Department of Horticulture
Michigan State University

Ornamental vegetables are vegetables which are raised not only to eat, but also for their attractive and unusual foliage, fruit or flowers. Ornamental vegetables make a handsome addition to both flower and vegetable gardens and can also be grown in containers to add decoration to patios or other outside areas.

Two of the varieties of beans which can be grown as ornamentals include 'Royalty' bush snapbean and 'Scarlet Runner' pole bean. 'Royalty' is a bush variety maturing in 51 days from seed to harvest and is grown for its deep purple colored pods. 'Scarlet Runner' is a climbing pole variety with bright red flowers and matures in 115-120 days. Seeds of 'Scarlet Runner' should be planted as soon as possible after the last frost date to assure an adequate growing season. Since it is a climbing plant, 'Scarlet Runner' may be supported with a string or wire trellis and can be used as a screen for a patio or porch area.

Many varieties of peppers are grown as ornamentals also. Several of the bell pepper varieties are 'Golden Calwonder,' which is golden yellow at maturity, and 'Bell Boy Hybrid' and 'Midway,' both of which are red at maturity. All three of these varieties mature in about 75 days from transplanting.

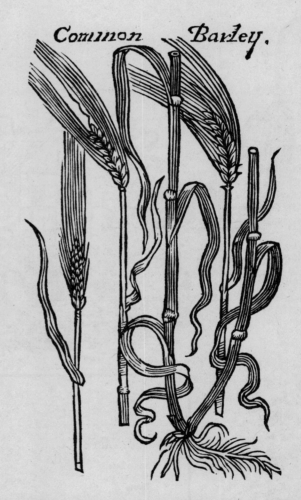

Common Barley.

Banana peppers are another ornamental pepper commonly grown. Fruits are about 7" long and ½" across changing from yellow to red when ripe. 'Hungarian Wax' maturing in 65 days from transplanting is a hot variety and 'Sweet Banana' (72 days) is its mild counterpart.

'Cherry Sweet' is a small variety of pepper with round fruits 1-1½" in diameter. It matures in 78 days to a red but mild pepper. 'Large Red Cherry' is a similar variety whose fruits are hot.

Three varieties of cauliflower with unusual head colors are sometimes grown for their ornamental value. 'Purple Head' and 'Royal Purple' have heads tinged with lavender when mature. 'Purple Head' is a 80-85 day variety from transplanting and 'Royal Purple' needs 95 days. Fanciers of the purple varieties say the flavor is somewhat like broccoli, but milder. Purple varieties are easier to grow than white ones and do not require the extra work of blanching. 'Greenball,' maturing in 95 days is another variety whose head is green in color.

Tomatoes need not always be round and red. 'Yellow Pear' produces small yellow fruits 1 3/4-2" long and 1" in diameter the shape of miniature pears. 'Yellow Plum' produces many plum size yellow fruits which are an interesting addition to any salad.

'Pixie' is an interesting patio tomato variety. Plants grow only 15" high and produce small cherry tomatoes. This variety can be grown in a flower pot or window box and be used to decorate a patio. Among the other midget varieties similar to 'Pixie,' are 'patio,' 'Small Fry,' and 'Tiny Tim.'

ORNAMENTAL VEGETABLES IN THE HOME GARDEN

Ornamental corn can be quite decorative. However, it can cross pollinate with sweet corn and leave the sweet corn less edible. One ornamental corn variety which produces standard size ears with yellow, red and white kernels is 'Rainbow' maturing in 110 days. If you wish to raise ornamental and sweet corn, plant a mid-season or early sweet corn variety such as 'Northern Belle,' 'Bravo' or 'Butter and Sugar,' planting both sweet corn and ornamental corn at the same time. The sweet corn will pollinate itself sooner than the ornamental corn and neither variety will be affected.

Strawberry popcorn is another interesting corn variety. The ears are about 3" long and covered with small maroon kernels. Strawberry corn matures in 105 days and the same procedure as outlined above for avoiding cross pollination will work for this variety.

Flowering cabbage and kale are similar in appearance and both mature in about 55 days from transplants. The leaves are tinged with red, pink and purple and are very showy.

Of the lettuce varieties, 'Ruby' and 'Red Salad Bowl' are two which are quite ornamental. They are red varieties of leaf lettuce and make attractive borders for vegetable and flower gardens. Both varieties are full size from seed in about 45 days.

Swiss chard is also grown as an ornamental, and in particular the variety 'Rhubarb' which has red stalks and leaf veins in dark green crinkly leaves. The plant grows 20-24" high and may be eaten either fresh in salads or cooked in a manner similar to spinach.

Red okra is a very unusual vegetable whose young pods are red on bushy red plants standing 5-6' high. The pods are red when young, turning dark green when mature and black in the fall if left on the plant.

FRUITS OF VEGETABLE MARROW.

FALL VEGETABLE GARDENING

L. Williams and R. C. Herner
Department of Horticulture
Michigan State University

Although spring is traditionally thought of as the time to start a vegetable garden, many vegetables can be planted in late June, July and August for harvest in September and October. Among the vegetables which can be grown for fall harvest are peas, cabbage, lettuce and other crops which do best in cooler temperatures. Many are frost tolerant and their flavor actually improves after a light frost. This type of gardening maximizes use of garden space, since new crops may be put in after early spring crops such as peas, leaf lettuce and radishes are harvested.

Vegetables to be grown for fall harvest can be seeded directly or transplanted in the garden. When buying seed for use in a fall vegetable garden, it is advisable to pick varieties which are well suited for growing in Michigan and which are quick maturing, so that the vegetables will be ready for harvest before the severe cold weather begins in November. Follow directions given on the seed packet for depth at which to plant the seed and spacing between plants and rows. Water in the seed to speed up germination. Fertilizer may not be necessary if the garden was fertilized well in the spring. However, if natural soil fertility is low, a commercial fertilizer such as 5-10-10 or similar analysis may be applied after the seedlings are rapidly growing at the rate of one cup per 25' of row length.

The following chart will enable you to plan which vegetables you would like to raise in your fall vegetable garden. Planting dates for seed are based on East Lansing and should be modified as necessary to suit your location.

Tall Scotch Kale.

VEGETABLE	SEEDING DATE	APPROXIMATE TIME OF HARVEST	SUGGESTED VARIETIES
Snap beans	June 30-July 15	August 20-Sept. 15	Provider Spartan arrow
Beets	July 1-15	September 1-October 1	Ruby queen Detroit dark red
Broccoli	June 20-30	Sept. 20-October 20	Green comet Spartan early
Brussels sprouts	June 20-30	October 15-November 1	Jade cross Long Island improved
Cabbage	June 20-30	October 1-October 30	Stonehead, Ruby ball (red), C-C cross
Cauliflower	June 20-30	October 1-October 30	Self-blanche Snowball imperial
Chinese cabbage	June 20-July 30	October 1-October 30	Early hybrid G Springtime
Kale	June 20-July 30	Aug. 15-Sept. 30	Dwarf blue curled Vates
Kohlrabi	June 20-30	October 1-15	Early white vienna
Lettuce (butterhead)	July 15-30	Sept. 15-October 15	Butter- crunch
Lettuce (leaf)	July 1-Aug. 15	Aug. 15-October 10	Salad bowl Grand Rapids
Peas	July 15-July 30	Sept. 15-Oct. 10	Freezonian, Greater progress Dwarf gray sugar (edible pod)
Radishes	Aug. 1-Sept. 1	Sept. 1-October 1	Cherry Belle Champion
Spinach	July 20-30	Sept. 1-20	America Viking
Turnips	July 1-Aug. 1	Aug. 15-October 1	Tokyo cross Just right

GROWING HERBS

Charles Marr
Kansas State Extension Horticulturist

Herbs are plants that are used as flavoring agents. The common herbs used in cooking are referred to as CULINARY herbs. Mild or savory herbs impart a delicate flavor to foods while the stronger or pungent herbs add zest to foods. A number of additional herbs are used for medicinal or ornamental purposes. This article, however, deals mainly with the culinary herbs which are used in cooking. These herbs are attractive and varied so their ornamental value is also important.

The leaves of most herbs are the part of the plant that is used although the seeds or roots of some herbs can also be used. They are needed in small quantities so usually only a few plants will be necessary to provide sufficient fresh and dried herbs for the entire season.

Herb gardening is becoming popular throughout Kansas. New enthusiasm in "natural" foods has heightened this interest. In addition, herbs add flavor and zest to creative cookery. Most food recipes can be accentuated and livened with proper use of culinary herbs.

LOCATION

The ornamental value of herbs enables them to be used in flower beds, borders, rock gardens, or corner plantings. Some herbs are annuals while others are perennial or come up year after year. You can locate annual herbs in your annual flower garden or vegetable garden. The perennial herbs should be located at the side of the garden where they won't interfere with next year's soil preparation.

Many gardeners establish a small herb garden near the home. Generally, a 6 to 10 foot square or rectangular area is sufficient. You can also use circular or free-form designs. Use the information contained in this publication for proper spacing and locate the tallest herbs to the back of the plot.

AS THE GARDEN GROWS

Care for the herb garden will be similar to your vegetable or flower garden. Select a sunny, well-drained location. Apply a balanced fertilizer but avoid excessive use of nitrogen fertilizers. Consult the guides available at your local extension office for soil preparation, fertilization, and other good garden cultural practices.

Water as necessary during dry periods. Generally, you will need about 1 inch of water per week, if not supplied by natural rainfall. A mulch will help conserve soil moisture and reduce weed growth as well. The mints prefer moist soil so they will require more frequent watering.

ESTABLISHING THE HERB GARDEN

Annual and biennial herbs can be established by planting the seed directly in the garden or starting seeds indoors for later transplanting to the garden. You can save seed produced by the herb plants for next year's crop or obtain seed from your local garden center or seed catalog.

To save your own seed, harvest the entire seed head after it has dried on the plant. The seeds should then be allowed to dry in a protected location that is cool and dry. After the seeds are thoroughly dry, thresh the seed from the seed heads and discard the trash. Store in labeled jars in a dark, cool, dry location.

Some herb seeds such as dill, anise, caraway, or corriander can be used for flavorings.

Perennial herbs can be propagated by cuttings or by division. Divide plants every 3 or 4 years in the early spring. The plants should be dug up and cut into several sections. You can also cut 4 to 6 inch sections of the stem and root these by placing the cuttings in moist sand in a shady area. In 4 to 8 weeks roots should form on these cuttings. Herbs such as sage, winter savory, and thyme can be propagated by cuttings. Chives, lovage, and tarragon can be propagated by division of the roots or crowns. Apple mint forms runners or stems that run along the ground so these can be easily propagated by covering a portion of the runner and allowing it to form roots.

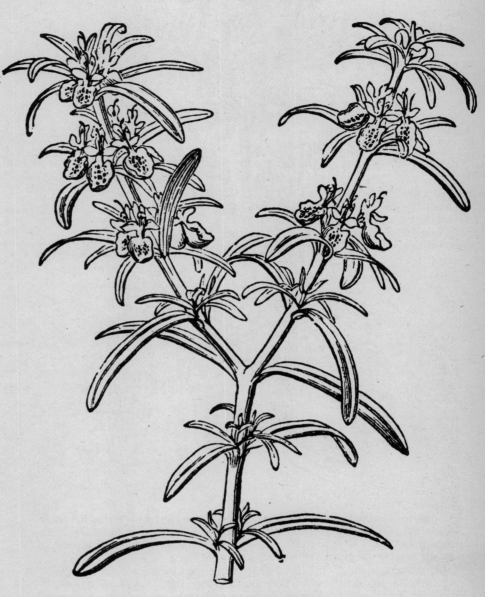

ROSEMARY.

PERENNIALS

PERENNIALS WILL GROW FROM SEED THE FIRST YEAR BUT WILL GROW YEAR AFTER YEAR. SOME CAN BE PROPAGATED BY SEVERAL OTHER MEANS AS WELL. A STRAW OR LEAF MULCH THROUGH THE WINTER MAY PROTECT THEM FROM WINTER DAMAGE.

CHIVES. Onion type leaves with blue round flower head. Can be grown in containers or outdoors in spring. Divide to increase. Space 5 in. Clip leaves as needed. Leaves—omelets, salads, soups, sauces, dips.

GARLIC CHIVES. Similar to chives. Same as chives. Substitute for garlic flavor.

PEPPERMINT. Vigorous bush-type plant with purple flowers. Prefers rich, moist soil. Space 8-10 in. Harvest young or mature leaves. Leaves—soups, sauces, tea, jelly. Sprigs—tea, sauce, summer drinks.

SPEARMINT. Pointed, crinkled leaves. Same as peppermint. Leaves—summer drinks, tea, mint sauce.

LEMON BALM. Crinkled, dull green leaves with white blossoms. Vigorous grower. Space 12 in. Prefers full sun. Harvest mature leaves. Leaves—soups, meat, tea, summer drinks.

LOVAGE. Grows quite tall. May start indoors & move to sunny location. Space 12-15 inches. Harvest mature leaves. Substitute for celery flavor.

OREGANO. Choose English strains. Produces pink flowers. Plant in rich soil. Space 8-10 in. Start in protected location and move to full sun. Harvest mature leaves. Leaves—soups, roasts, stews, salads.

ROSEMARY. Dark green foliage with small blue flowers. Start cuttings in early spring. Space 24 in. Harvest mature leaves. Leaves and sprigs—meats, sauces, soups. Dried leaves—as sachets to hang in closet with garments.

SAGE. Shrub-like plant with grey leaves & purple flowers. Plant in well drained location. Space 30 in. Harvest leaves before flowering. Leaves—meats, teas, fish, dressing, stews.

TARRAGON. Select French tarragon. Fine, dark green leaves. Prefers well drained soils. Space 12 in. Harvest mature leaves or sprigs. Leaves—salads, sauces, eggs, vegetables, salad vinegar.

THYME. Narrow, dark green leaves. Start seeds indoors. Prefers full sun & well drained soils. Space 10-12 in. Harvest leaves & flower clusters before first flowers open. Leaves—soups, salads, dressings, omelets, gravy, bread, vegetables.

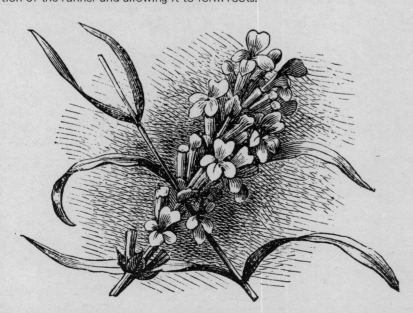

LAVENDER.

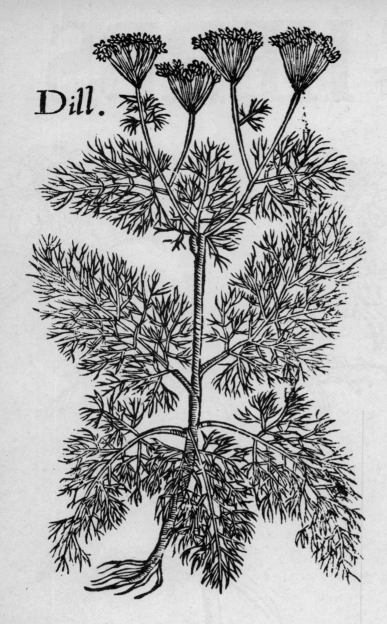

Dill.

ANNUALS GROW FROM SEED AND COMPLETE THEIR LIFE CYCLE IN ONE YEAR. THEY WILL BE KILLED BY FROST AND MUST BE STARTED FROM SEED EACH YEAR. BIENNIALS WILL OVERWINTER ONE SEASON AND PRODUCE SEED THE SECOND SEASON.

ANISE. Serrated leaves, small white flowers. Low spreading plant is a slow growing annual. Moderately rich soil. Likes full sun. Space 6-8 in. in rows & rows 12-14 in. apart. Harvest when seeds turn brown or use leaves while green as needed. Seed—pastries, candy, cookies, beverages, meat, soups. Leaves—salad or garnish.

BASIL. Leafy, light green foliage; flowers white or lavender. Fast growing annual. Start seed indoors in early April or seed in early spring. Space 12 in. Prefers protected sunny location. Harvest leaves when flowering begins. Cut plants 4-6 in. above ground. Leaves—soups, stews, omelets, salads, meats, sauces.

BORAGE. Coarse, rough hairy leaves. Produces light blue flowers in drooping clusters. Seed directly in early spring. Space 12 in. apart. Seeds may be slow to germinate. Harvest the young leaves & dry or cook fresh like spinach. Leaves—salads, greens, flowers and leaf tips—pickles, soups, stews.

CARAWAY. Carrot-like leaf with small creamy white flowers. Seed directly in spring & locate in full sun. Space 6 in. Harvest leaves when mature. Seeds will form midway through second season. Leaves—garnish. Seeds—breads, cakes, soups, sauces, salads.

CHERVIL. Similar to parsley, with light green lacy leaves. Flowers are small white clusters. Sow seed in moist, partially shaded location. Space 6 in. Harvest mature leaves & dry or use directly for garnishes. Leaves—salads, soup, meat, poultry, garnishes.

CORRIANDER. Large, coarse plant with white flowers. Sow seeds directly. Use full sun area and thin to 10 in. Harvest seeds when they begin to turn brown. Seeds are gen. used crushed. Seeds—patries, sauces, pickles, liquors.

DILL. Tall plant with feathery green leaves. Open umbrella shaped flower heads. Seed directly & thin to 12 in. If seeds mature & fall they will come up again next year. Harvest mature seed heads before seeds drop. May use small leaves as well. Sprigs of seed head—pickles, sauces, meats, salads, vinegar.

FENNEL. Fine, feathery leaves with broad bulb-like leaf base. Sow in early spring and thin to 12 in. Harvest either young sprigs & leaves or seeds. Sprigs—soups. Leaves—garnishes. Seeds—soups, breads.

PARSLEY. Curled or plain dark-green leaves. May be slow to germinate. Seed in early spring. Space 6-8 inches. Harvest mature leaves as needed. Leaves—garnishes.

SWEET MARJORAM. Fine textured plant with white flowers. Start seedlings in shade. Mature plants will grow in full sun. Space 8-10 inches. Harvest mature leaves. Leaves—salads, soups, dressings.

SUMMER SAVORY. Small gray-green leaves with purple and white flowers. A tender annual should be planted after danger of frost. Space 6-9 in. Harvest mature leaves. Leaves—salads, soups, dressings, poultry.

HARVESTING

Leaves of many herbs such as parsley and chives can be harvested for fresh seasonings. On these plants you can gradually remove some of the leaves as you need them. Don't remove all the foliage at one time. These plants will produce over a long period of time if they are well cared for.

On rosemary and thyme clip the tops when the plants are in full bloom. Usually, leaves and flowers are harvested together. Basil, fennel, mint, sage, summer savory, sweet marjoram, tarragon, and winter savory are harvested just before the plant starts to bloom.

Chervil and parsley leaves can be cut and dried anytime. Lovage leaves should be harvested early during the first flush of growth.

DRYING

After harvesting hang the herbs in loosely tied bundles in a well ventilated room. You can also spread the branches on a screen, cheese-cloth, or hardware cloth. For herbs where leaves only are needed, the leaves can be spread on flat trays. Keep dust off the herbs by a cloth or similar protective cover that will allow moisture to pass through.

It is generally best to dry naturally in a cool, dark room rather than use artificial heat. This can be done by experts but you may loose flavor and quality by attempting to use artificial heat.

STORAGE

When the herbs are thoroughly dry, they should be sealed in air-tight containers such as sealed fruit jars and stored in a cool, dark location. Any sign of moisture accumulating in the jars indicates that the herbs are not thoroughly dry. Flower stalks should be pulverized before putting them in the jars but the foliage herbs can be stored either pulverized or whole leaves depending on their intended use.

POTTED HERBS

Some herbs can be placed in pots and grown indoors during the winter months. They should be placed in a sunny, south window and cared for like houseplants. Herbs can either be dug up toward the end of the growing season and placed in pots or started from seed indoors.

Basil, chives, mint, parsley, sweet marjoram, and rosemary are best adapted to pot culture.

INFORMATION

Organized groups interested in herbs, their cultures, and uses are:

Herb Society of America
300 Massachusetts Avenue
Boston, Massachusetts 02115

National Herb Study Society
424 Perkins Street
Oakland, California 94610

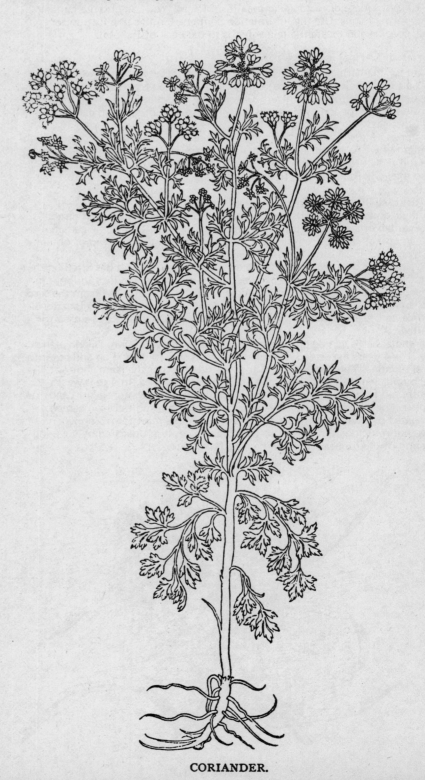

CORIANDER.

POTHERBS OR GREENS FOR THE MARITIMES

E. W. Chipman
Information Division
Canada Department of Agriculture
Ottawa, K1A OC7

WILD PLANTS

Many wild plants may be used for greens but most have a very limited use because they may be found only in certain places and even there they may or may not appeal to the human palate. At least four are quite widely used in the Maritimes. Since these plants grow wild, no cultural notes are given. As with the cultivated greens, the edible parts are best when they are young and tender.

Fiddlehead (Pteretis pensylvanica)

Fiddlehead is the name applied to the young emerging frond of the ostrich fern. The frond is smooth, angular, deeply chan- neled on the upper side, chaffy when young and flattened at the black base. Before emerging, the unfurled frond is covered with thin, papery, pale-brown scales. After the frond comes out of the ground this sheath breaks. This fern is found mainly in alluvial areas such as old river beds where flooding has occurred. It grows also in partial shade and is found in pure stands.

Lamb's-quarters (Chenopodium album)

Lamb's-quarters is one of the most common annual weeds of the Maritimes. The plants are erect and much branched, with stems that are smooth and more or less purple-striped. Leaves have a whitish mealy coating on the underside and toothed margins.

The early spring growth is desirable for greens. Plants in the fall, even though still young, are often short, and have hard tissue and flowers.

Purslane (Portulaca oleracea)

Purslane is also known as wild portulaca. Like lamb's-quarters, it is a common annual weed found, in the Maritimes, mainly in the warmer areas. This prostrate plant has many smooth reddish stems that form mats. The leaves are fleshy and smooth. Flowers are small and yellow, and open for only a short time in the morning. Because it grows best in hot weather, this plant makes a good summer green.

Seashore Plantain (Plantago oliganthos)

This plant is more commonly referred to as marsh green. It is found on the salt marshes and tidal flats, where it reproduces by both seeds and shoots. The leaves are long, narrow, pointed and borne in rosettes. The flowers are small and inconspicuous. It is used as a green when the plant is young and succulent.

CULINARY HERBS

By Arthur E. Hutchins, Orrin C. Turnquist, and Verna Mikesh

U.S.D.A.

Herbs are plants with aromatic and healing properties. Some herbs also have ornamental value. So herbs are classified according to their uses as medicinal, culinary, aromatic, or ornamental. Many herbs have several uses.

Culinary herbs had an important place in gardens of our ancestors. And they are now receiving increased attention and popularity. This article deals primarily with culinary or cooking herbs—their habits, uses, and culture. If you cannot care for a real herb garden, you can still plant some pleasing and attractive herbs in your flower and vegetable garden.

Herbs should play a more important part in American cookery. Their employment opens the way to preparation of many appetizing dishes. Herbs can make insipid foods appealing, can give a delightful cooling and stimulating flavor to drinks, can provide a new taste to warmed-over dishes. In many ways, herbs can help the homemaker banish monotony from her menus.

Owing to their pungent, distinctive flavors, herbs are used only in small quantities in a culinary product. So you need only a few plants.

Bitter=sweet

Borrage.

CARAWAY.

Small Coriander

KNOW YOUR HERB CULTURE

Fortunately for the gardener, most herbs are easy to grow. They care for themselves and survive under adverse conditions—almost like weeds. But they are most attractive and give finest results if properly planted and cared for.

Good Conditions—Good Growth

Herbs grow best in a sunny location, although partial shade may produce a more luxuriant growth. Sunshine is needed to make most herbs rich in the volatile oils responsible for odors and flavors. So a west, south, or southwest slope is preferable.

Any good garden soil is satisfactory for most herbs. Many herbs seem to prefer a rather meager, poor soil. If soil is too rich, their growth is often rank and the oils poor in quality.

Only a few herbs—particularly those frequently cut such as parsley, chives, and basil—require application of manure or other plant foods. Water-loving herbs such as mints, cress, lovage, pennyroyal, and angelica should have a fairly moist location. Most other herbs do best on a rather dry, well drained soil.

Prepare the soil before planting to aid in deep root penetration. Loosen soil to a depth of from 18 to 24 inches. If you plant herbs in your vegetable garden, you can obtain fair results with usual plowing. Break up all clods. Pulverize the surface very finely, especially if you use seeds instead of transplants.

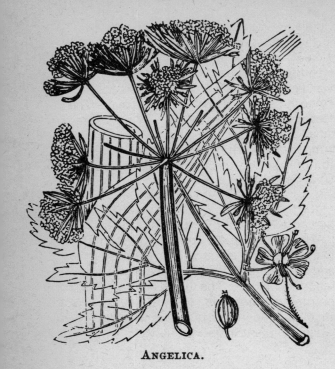

ANGELICA.

HERBS

The most popular herbs have a place in every garden. Many herbs have ornamental uses in borders, flower gardens, and as house plants. Try different varieties for many attractive effects.

Sweet Basil

Sweet basil, a branched annual, is extremely hardy. Bush basil is a dwarf form. Basil has a clovelike flavor. Leaves and tips of shoots are used in mock turtle soup, stews, dressings, white sauces, milk gravies, and for flavoring salads. When dried, they are used for spicing sausages and roasts.

Start basil early from seed and transplant 12 inches apart in rows 18 inches apart. A light, medium fertile, dry soil in a sunny location is best.

Borage

Borage is a coarse annual herb. It has clusters of pretty light-blue flowers which are candied, made into borage tea, and used for flavoring drinks. Young leaves and leafy tips are used in mixed salads, for garnishing, and in beverages.

Sow borage in the open in the spring about one-fourth inch deep. Thin it to stand about 12 to 15 inches apart. Borage does best on a poor, light, dry soil in a sunny location. It often reseeds itself.

Chive

The chive, a hardy perennial, is closely related to the common onion but is of much milder flavor. The green leaves are used for seasoning everything from soup to cheese, with the exception of pastries and desserts.

Chive plants are attractive with slender, pencil-shaped leaves and rose-purple flowers. They are well adapted as border or specimen plants in the perennial or rock garden and may be used as winter house plants.

Chives grow in any good garden soil. A sunny location is preferred, but they do fairly well in partial shade. Give chives light application of manure or commercial fertilizer if they are cut heavily. To propagate, divide old clumps and set out individual plants in fall or early spring.

Herbs require little attention after becoming established. Cultivate only often enough to kill weeds and provide a fine dust mulch. Except for moisture-loving herbs, watering is necessary only during severe drought. In general, herbs are remarkably free from insects and diseases. Only a few need fertilizing.

Methods of Propagating Vary

Tarragon, chives, pennyroyal, and the mints are always propagated by cuttings or divisions. Practically all other herbs may be propagated from seed. It is best to sow herbs early in flats or shallow boxes, transplant them into pots or flats when plants are small, and set them in the garden when outdoor growing conditions are favorable. This process provides a longer growing season.

Sow herbs shallow in the flats and cover them lightly with finely pulverized soil or sand. When herbs are seeded directly in the field, radishes are often sown with them to mark the row until herbs come up.

You can propagate most perennial herbs by cuttings of roots or tops. Top cuttings, a few inches long, usually root readily if placed in moist, shaded, light soil. As soon as they start growing, transplant them to the garden.

You may take up plants in fall and keep them in your house or greenhouse during the winter. Then make cuttings early enough in the spring so that they will be well rooted and ready for setting in the garden as soon as conditions are favorable. To be most successful, lift and transplant hardy perennial herbs every 3 or 4 years. If this cannot be done, a top dressing of rich soil each fall helps keep them healthy and vigorous.

Such herbs as sage, thyme, and savory are often propagated by layers. Lay selected branches, still connected with the plant, on the ground. Peg branches down and cover joints with an inch of soil. Under favorable growing conditions, roots form in 3 or 4 weeks. Then sever the layered branches from the plant and plant them whole or cut into as many pieces as there are rooted joints.

To divide mints thrust a sharp spade through the clump and transplant divided parts. If you divide other perennial herbs in the same manner, plants receive a severe check and are unsymmetrical. To divide chives pull plants apart from the clump and plant them individually. To divide garlic, plant the cloves into which bulbs are divided.

Britannica or Dark coloured-Water Dock

FENNEL.

Calaminta Americana.

Garden Cress

Garden cress is an annual cool-weather plant. Leaves are usually used in salads and also for garnishing.

Seed garden cress very early in rows 12 to 15 inches apart. A cool rich soil is desirable. Thin plants as needed for use. If leaves are removed without injuring the crown, the plant continues to bear.

Leaves are ready for use in 6 or 8 weeks after planting. Successive plants 10 days apart insure a continuous supply until hot weather—then plants quickly go to seed.

Dill

Dill is a hardy annual. Young leaves and stems of dill are often used for seasoning sauces and salads, for flavoring vinegar, and in pickles. Seeds are sometimes used in pastries, soups, and stews but most often in dill pickles.

Seed dill about one-fourth inch deep early in spring in a sunny location. If you want dill for use in dill pickles, plant it about 1 to 2 months before cucumbers will be ready.

Thin plants to stand 9 inches apart in rows 18 inches apart. Dill prefers sandy, medium fertile, well drained soil. Add water in dry periods.

Fennel

Fennel, a semihardy perennial, is cultivated as an annual. Two kinds are commonly grown in the garden—sweet fennel and Florence fennel. Sweet fennel is most popular and reaches a height of 3 to 4 feet. Florence fennel or Finocchio grows about 2 feet high and has thickened, overlapping leaf bases.

Fennel has a distinctive flavor that is attractive to many. Stems are often blanched and eaten like celery or endive. Carosella, a famous delicacy of Naples, is made from stems of sweet fennel cut before flowering and served with an oil or vinegar sauce.

Leaves are used for garnishing and in salads, soups, and puddings. They are especially good with fish dishes. Seeds are used in cakes, candies, and soups. The oil from seeds is used in liquors and soaps. Florence fennel is usually boiled and served with butter or cream sauce.

Fennel grows best on a sunny, poor to medium fertile, well drained soil that has plenty of lime. It is propagated from seed sown one-eighth to one-fourth inch deep in open ground in early spring. Thin sweet fennel plants to stand about 18 inches apart in rows 24 inches apart. If plants are to be used like endive or celery, cut and use flower stalks when they are about to bloom.

Space Florence fennel plants 6 to 12 inches apart in the row. When the thickened overlapping leaf bases form a swelling (called apple) about the size of an egg, heap a little earth halfway up the base. Cutting can usually begin 10 days later.

Great Burre Dock

Common Male Lavender.

Horseradish

Horseradish is a hardy perennial herb. It is used chiefly as an early spring relish or condiment for serving with meats. For this purpose, roots are ground and preserved in vinegar and may also be mixed with mustard.

Horseradish grows best in a cool, humid climate in a deep, rich, mellow, moist soil. Plant root cuttings, one-fourth to one-half inch across and 4 to 8 inches long, slightly slanting with the tops 3 to 4 inches below the soil surface. Plant cuttings as early as possible in the spring, 1 foot apart in rows 3 feet apart. Give the bed a heavy coating of well-rotted manure.

Mints

Mints are popular. Among the most commonly used perennial mints are: field, corn, or Japanese mint; peppermint; pennyroyal; bergamont or lemon mint; spearmint; and white woolly mint.

Leaves and young shoots are valuable in flavoring soups, stews, sauces, jellies, and beverages. Oils extracted from them are used in flavoring candy and gum, in scenting soaps and perfumes, and in preparation of medicine.

Mints propagate readily by cuttings or divisions. In general, they do best in a moist rich loam in partial shade. They are usually planted in beds.

In autumn, cut the old growth close to the ground. In spring, sift rich soil over plants to give runners a chance to root. Transplant beds every 3 or 4 years. Clumps may be forced during the winter in the hotbed, greenhouse, or boxes in the house.

Parsley

Parsley, a biennial, usually is cultivated as an annual. Leaves are used for flavoring, garnishing, and in salads.

Parsley seed is slow to germinate. Sow seed about one-eighth inch deep under glass and transplant plants to the garden 6 inches apart in rows 12 to 18 inches apart. If seeded outdoors, sow some quick germinating crop such as radishes with parsley to mark the row. Parsley does well in a sunny location on an average garden soil, moderately fertile and well drained but retentive of moisture. If you use outer leaves as needed, plants produce throughout the season.

In the fall you may dig up and pot plants. When potting, take a considerable part of the root system with the soil surrounding it. Reduce the foliage by removing a part of the outside leaves. Then handle the potted plant like any house plant.

At least a few herbs should be available for winter use. Most herbs are fairly easy to store and retain their aroma or flavor for a considerable time. Some kinds may be potted for winter and grown as house plants.

Cut foliage harvested for storage on a bright, dry day when plants are in full growth, vigorous, and full of sap, and just below flowering. Cut plants close to the ground, tie in bunches, and label. Hang them to dry in a cool, clean, dry, dustless, airy room such as an attic. Dry them as quickly as possible.

If desired, you may strip leaves off and dry them in trays. When dry enough to crumble, place leaves—whole or finely crumbled—in wide mouthed bottles or fruit jars. Then label and tightly cork or cover jars. Look at the jars daily for a few days. If any moisture is present, remove herbs and dry further.

Herbs must be thoroughly dry to keep well. Sweet basil, hoarhound, marjoram, sage, thyme, balm, savory, tarragon, lavender, parsley, celery, dill, fennel, and mint are most commonly dried.

Allow herbs grown for seed to ripen and then harvest them just before seeds start dropping. Place seeds with other attached parts on a paper or cloth to dry. When they are dry enough, thresh out and remove dirt and refuse. Then spread clean seeds in thin layers on a cloth of paper until they are thoroughly cured. Store them in glass jars.

Conditions for harvesting, curing, and storing should be the same as those necessary for preserving foliage. Among herbs whose seeds are commonly used are angelica, anise, celery, sweet cicely, coriander, cumin, dill, fennel, lovage, poppy (maw), and sesame (bene).

Herbs that you may take up in the fall, pot, and use as house plants include bush basil, chives, pot marigold, sweet annual marjoram, mints, parsley, rose geranium, rosemary, and lemon verbena.

CUT-LEAFED GERMANDER.

Sage

Sage, a perennial, is usually treated as an annual. Dried leaves are used chiefly for flavoring meat and poultry dressings, sausages, and cheeses. But the flavor is strong so use leaves sparingly.

With the exception of Holt's Mammoth variety which must be propagated by divisions or cuttings, sage is usually propagated by seed. Sow outdoors early in the spring about one-eighth inch deep. Thin plants to stand about 12 to 18 inches apart.

Sage prefers a rather spare, mellow, well drained garden loam.

Summer Savory

Summer savory is a small bushy annual with little pink or white flowers. Leaves, young shoots, and flowers are used in salads, meat and poultry dressings, meat sauces, croquettes, and stews, or are cooked with fresh peas and beans.

Sow seeds about one-fourth inch deep in a sunny location in the spring. Thin plants to stand about 6 to 18 inches apart. They grow well in an average garden soil that is poor in fertility and fairly dry. Cut foliage to be stored as soon as blossoms appear and dry it in the shade.

Winter Savory

Winter savory, a fairly hardy perennial, is a good ornamental plant. Although inferior in flavor to summer savory, its culinary uses and general cultural requirements are the same.

Winter savory may be propagated from seeds, cuttings, divisions, or layers. Since it does not transplant well, sow seeds where the plant is to remain.

Thymes

Thymes are small, fairly hardy perennials. They are often used for edgings and rockeries. Leaves are used for seasoning. The several cultivated forms are similar in culinary properties but vary in ornamental values. Leaves of young thyme shoots, green or dried, are used for seasoning soups, meat sauces, meat and poultry stuffings, sausages, cheeses, and gravies.

Common thyme is an erect bushy plant about 8 to 10 inches tall. It bears tiny, grayish leaves and lavender blossoms. Mother of thyme or creeping thyme makes a perfect mat of green in the rock garden. There are several varieties of lemon-scented thyme such as Silver, Golden, and Variegated which are useful as herbs or for the flower garden proper.

Thymes are easily propagated by cuttings, divisions, layers, or seeds. Seeds are small and are merely pressed gently into the surface of a well pulverized seedbed. They are usually sown indoors early in the spring. In early June, you may transplant plants to stand 6 to 12 inches apart in a sunny location. Soil should be medium fertile, light, and fairly dry.

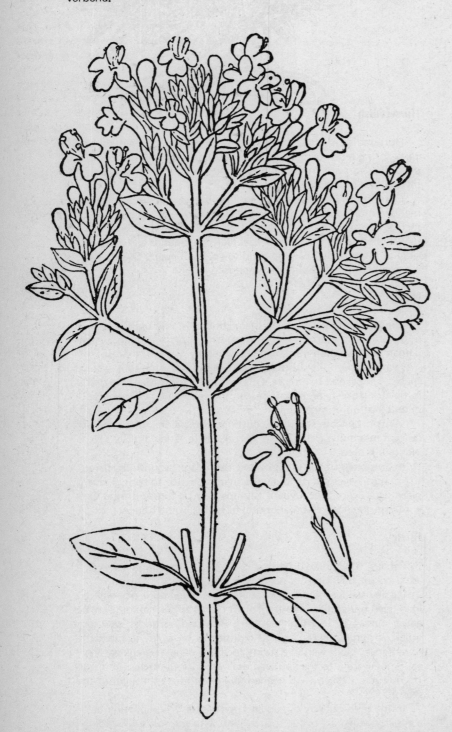

Common Marjoram (*Origanum vulgare*).

By LLEWELYN WILLIAMS, *Northeastern Region, Agricultural Research Service*

GINSENG

American ginseng[1] is a fleshy-rooted herb native to cool and shady hardwood forests from Quebec and Manitoba south to northern Florida, Alabama, Louisiana, and Arkansas. Wild ginseng has been harvested for many years and is cultivated commercially for its root, both in its natural range and in the Pacific Northwest.

American ginseng shows variations in characteristics, particularly in the roots. Western types usually have long, thin roots of undesirable qualities. Plants from the northern part of the country, particularly Wisconsin and New York, are the most desirable for export, furnishing roots of good size, weight, and shape, and are generally considered the best breeding stock. Cultivated roots usually are heavier and more uniform than wild roots, although they command a lower price in the market.

Ginseng is valued by some Chinese and Koreans, who believe the dried roots have stimulant properties.

[1] *Panax quinquefolius* L.

(There is, however, no scientific evidence to support that belief.) The market value of the cured root is based on color, maturity, size, and form.

DESCRIPTION

Ginseng grows about 1 foot tall. Leaves of mature plants usually consist of five ovate leaflets. It blooms in midsummer; the flowers are greenish yellow, borne in clusters. The fruit is a bright crimson berry, containing one to three wrinkled seeds the size of small peas. Mature root is spindle shaped, 2 to 4 inches long, and up to 1 inch thick. In plants upwards of 5 years old, the root is usually forked, with prominent circular wrinkles. Roots reach marketable size when 5 to 7 years old. They are dug, carefully washed to remove adhering soil, and dried. Only whole roots are acceptable in the trade.

Best quality root of proper age breaks with a somewhat soft and waxy fracture. Young or undersized roots dry hard and glassy and are less marketable.

PLANT MATERIALS

Ginseng is grown from seeds, seedlings, or roots. Plants free from blight or mildew and growing spontaneously in woodland may be transplanted to prepared beds.

Ginseng requires 5 to 7 years to mature from seed. By planting separate beds of seeds, 1-, 2-, and 3-year-old seedlings, and roots, the first crop can be scheduled in 3 or 4 years after planting. Each year after the first harvest, another crop will come to maturity.

Seeds

Plant seeds in the spring, as soon as the soil can be tilled. Only scarified or partially germinated seeds should be used for planting. They are planted 8 inches apart each way in permanent beds, or 2 by 6 inches apart in seedbeds. Cover seeds with 1 inch of forest soil, or well-rotted hickory or basswood sawdust; do not use pine or oak sawdust.

Seeds ripen in the fall, but generally do not germinate until the following fall. Do not allow ripe seeds to dry out. Store them in a cool, moist place. Use woodland soil, sand, loam, or sawdust as a storage medium.

Use of seeds instead of seedlings may prevent the introduction of disease to new plantations. Also, this is the least expensive way to start a plantation, but requires a longer period until harvest.

Some growers plant the seeds when they ripen in September, and cover the beds with leaf mold or mulch. They keep the beds covered until spring, when the seeds begin to sprout.

Seedlings

Ginseng seedlings are more expensive than seeds, but a crop

Rue (*Ruta graveolens*).

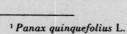
Spear Mint.

Sampire Rock Commom.

Basil.

COMMON CALAMINT.
CALAMINTHA OFFICINALIS, OR THYMUS CALAMINTHA.

The market for ginseng root is limited. It is estimated that 95 percent of the ginseng collected or grown in the United States is exported to the Orient. During the 3-year period, 1969 through 1971, such exports averaged only 158,980 pounds of dried root per year.

The prices paid for ginseng are high, and fluctuate greatly. During the same 3-year period, export price-per-pound averages were $38.12, $30.83, and $34.51.

High initial cost of planting stock, susceptibility to diseases, long maturing period, and a limited market indicate ginseng farming should be approached conservatively. Since yields of dried root average about 1 ton per acre, 100 to 200 acres of mature ginseng could easily supply the total market for 1 year.

Each year the U.S. Department of Agriculture receives thousands of requests for information on growing ginseng. In an effort to comply with these requests, the Department has prepared this Farmers' Bulletin.

grown from seedlings can be harvested 2 or 3 years sooner than a crop propagated from seeds. Several firms sell 1-, 2-, or 3-year-old seedlings. Three-year-old seedlings produce seed during the first fall after planting, which may be used for planting future crops. Set seedlings in permanent beds, 8 inches apart each way. Closer spacing tends to increase disease in the plantation.

Roots

Roots may be set any time from October to April, after soil has been tilled. Fall planting, however, is usually preferred. Plant roots 2 inches below the bed surface, and 8 inches apart each way. When roots are not available in woodland, beginners should purchase them from reputable growers. Roots grow more rapidly when not permitted to seed.

CULTURE

Ginseng may be grown directly in woodlots or in lath sheds with partial shade—an environment similar to the plant's natural habitat. Plants thrive best in loamy soil, such as found in oak and sugar maple forests in the North. Shade is essential.

Soil

Ginseng grows naturally on slopes of ravines and in well-drained sites where soil is formed from acid leaf mold of hardwood forests. The soil should be naturally dry and fairly light, and in condition to grow good vegetables without the addition of strong manure. By proper treatment almost any fairly good soil can be conditioned for ginseng growing. The addition of woodland soil gives best results. Very sandy soil tends to produce hard, flinty roots of inferior quality.

For seedbeds, break up soil to a depth of 6 to 8 inches, and remove all weeds, grasses, and roots. Mix 1-to-1 with fiber-free woodland soil. If the soil is inclined to be heavy, add enough sand so that mixture will not harden after heavy rain.

Beds

Selection of proper location, preparation of soil, and good drainage are important in planting ginseng. The best site for beds is a hardwood forest, with tall trees to provide reasonably dense shade, and with little undergrowth. Similar drainage and shade conditions should be maintained when growing ginseng in lath sheds.

Make beds 4 feet wide with walkways between them. For root planting, work the beds up to 12 inches deep. For seeds and seedlings, work the beds only 8 inches or so deep to prevent settling. Mound the center of permanent planting beds to provide space for more plants and, if located on flat ground, to facilitate good runoff of water.

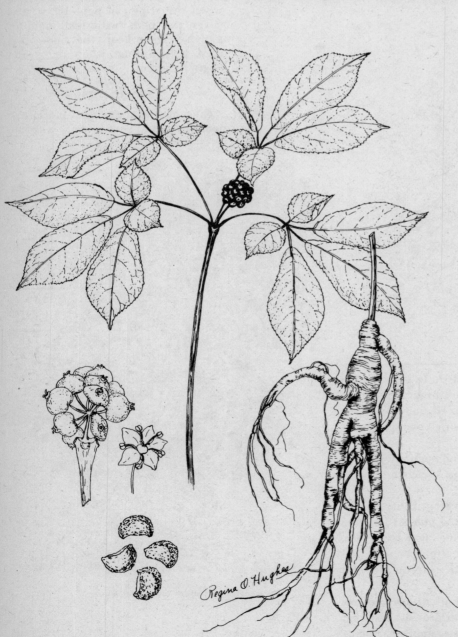

Branch, root, flower, berries, and seeds of American ginseng.

Slope the walkways so that they will drain water from the beds during heavy rains.

Shade

Ginseng needs three-fourths shade during the summer, and free circulation of air. The proper amount of shade can be provided in lath sheds or by trees in a forest planting. Others prefer woodland soil or rotted leaves 4 to 6 inches deep, spaded to a depth of about 8 inches, with fine raw bonemeal well worked in, and applied at the rate of 1 pound per square yard.

Protection

Fence beds to keep out animals and to discourage theft. Protect the beds from moles with boards or close mesh wire netting set 12 to 18 inches in the ground. Rodents may be controlled with traps.

HARVEST

A ginseng crop matures in 5 to 7 years. Generally the roots are dug in mid-October of the sixth or seventh year. Good roots are about 4 inches long, 1 inch thick below the crown, and average 1 ounce in the fresh state. Older roots possess the most substance and when properly cured bring the highest prices.

Digging

Dig the roots with their forks intact. Carefully free them of adhering soil so as to preserve their natural color and characteristic circular markings. Do not scrape or scrub them. The market value of the product is based, in part, on wholeness and appearance.

Some growers replant young and undersized roots, or heel them in until spring planting.

Drying

Dry the roots in a well-ventilated, heated room. Drying is usually started between 60° and 80° F., and after a few days the temperature is increased to 90°.

Another method, adopted by some growers, is to start drying between 100° and 110°, and when roots wilt lower the temperature to 90°.

Laths should run north to south to provide alternating sun and shade to the plants. Do not use burlap or muslin; they interfere with air circulation.

Cultivation

Ginseng requires relatively little cultivation. The beds should be kept free of grass and weeds, and the soil should be scratched with a light implement whenever it shows signs of caking. One active man can easily take care of about 2 acres of ginseng.

Mulching

A winter mulch over the crowns is essential to prevent heaving by frost. A 4- or 5-inch layer is ample in the most severe climate; less is needed in the South. Spread mulch when frost is imminent, and remove it in the spring before the first shoots appear. Light mulching to retain moisture during dry weather is also advisable.

Forest leaves or light brush, held in place with poultry netting, makes the best mulch. Cornstalks stripped of husks, bean vines, cowpea hay, and buckwheat straw are also suitable if they do not contain weeds, seeds, or other materials attractive to rodents.

Fertilizer

Many growers are opposed to excessive use of fertilizers. Heavy use of barnyard and chemical fertilizers lessens the resemblance of cultivated ginseng to the wild root. Overmanuring also forces growth and lowers the resistance of ginseng to the attacks of disease.

Some growers fertilize with leaves or old sawdust of hardwood trees, or with ground-up, rotted hardwood.

Spread the roots thinly on lattice or wire-netting shelves. Turn them frequently, but handle with care to avoid marring the surface or breaking the forks.

Roots more than 2 inches in diameter will need to be dried for about 6 weeks; smaller roots may be properly dried in less time.

Throughout the curing process, especially during damp weather, care should be taken to see that the root does not mold or sour. Do not overheat, as it tends to discolor the surface and spoil the texture of the root.

When well cured, the roots should be stored in a dry, airy, rodentproof place until ready for market.

Yield

The yield of cultivated ginseng depends on the condition under which the crop is grown, and the experience and skill of the grower. The estimated weight of dried 6-year-old root from a bed 4 by 16 feet is 10 pounds. Yields of dried roots from a well-managed planting should average about 1 ton per acre, although greater yields are often reported. Crops from forest plantings are reported to be about half those obtained in lath sheds, but production costs are also much less.

The value of the crop depends on the market at time of harvesting. There are several firms in the United States which buy ginseng.

VEGETABLE PESTS

Aphid. Tiny winged and wingless insects may be green, yellow, red, or black in color. Multiply very rapidly. Feed on radishes, cabbage, lettuce, peas, beans, tomatoes, cucumbers, cantaloupe, watermelons, spinach, turnips, and other plants.

Blister Beetles. Great numbers of blister beetles attack plants overnight. They may be brown, black, gray, or striped brown.

Cutworms. Soft bodied worms. They cut the transplanted plant at the ground surface.

Flea Beetles. Small beetles; jump quickly and cut holes in leaves early in the spring. They may feed on beets, cabbage, potatoes, radishes, spinach, strawberries, tomatoes, and turnips.

Grasshoppers. Small grasshoppers should be destroyed in fence rows outside the garden in May or June.

Stalk Borers. Slender borer, creamy white, with purple stripes lengthwise of the body. Brown or purple band behind the head.

Slugs. Wormlike, legless, shiny bodies usually found in damp protected places.

Spider Mites. Tiny webs on under side of leaf. Leaves turn brown. The use of sevin and thiodan on tomatoes, cucurbits, and beans may cause an increase of spider mites.

Pillbugs or Sowbugs. Many-legged gray animals that roll in a ball when disturbed. Found in protected areas where there is moisture and decaying organic matter.

Nematodes. Tiny worms; must be magnified to be seen. Galls on roots of stunted plants indicate nematodes.

Moles. Burrowing animals cut roots of plants as they search for insects.

White Grubs. Large C-shaped grubs destroy roots of plants. Some species may be in the soil 3 years before they emerge as June beetles.

Wireworms. Slender yellow hard shelled worms drill holes in roots and stems. Wireworms may be in the soil several years before they mature as click beetles.

Powdery Mildew. Faint, slightly discolored tiny specks, from which a white powdery mold develops and spreads over the leaves and other plant parts.

Chlorosis. In western and central Kansas perennial plants often become yellow and stunted if iron is not available for the plants. The leaves become yellow between the veins first. Well water often has enough mineral to tie up the iron, so this trouble often develops where such water is used for irrigation.

Vegetables and Their Pests

Pest and Damage

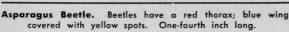

Asparagus Beetle. Beetles have a red thorax; blue wing covered with yellow spots. One-fourth inch long.

Asparagus Rust. Orange-red pustules on stems and foliage.

Beans

Pest and Damage

Bean Leaf Beetles. Red or yellow beetles with black spots. White larvae feed on roots of the plant.

Leafhoppers. Small green wedge-shaped flying insects. Suck juice from plant; nymphs run sidewise like crabs.

Tomato Fruitworm. Green or brown worms with light brown head and light stripe on side and beneath body.

Mexican Bean Beetle. Copper colored lady beetle with 16 black spots; yellow larvae have black spines.

Spider Mites.

Mosaic. Mottled (light and dark green) and curled leaves. Plants are stunted.

Bacterial Blights. Brown, dead areas on leaves. Water-soaked spots with reddish margins on pods. Reddish cankers on stems.

Rust. Powdery red and black pustules on leaves.

Beets

Pest and Damage

Flea Beetles.

Leafhopper.

Webworm. Slender active green worm with black spots and stripes, web the leaves together.

Poor Stand. Seeds decay in soil.

Cabbage, Cauliflower, Broccoli, Brussels Sprouts

Pest and Damage

Aphids.

Cabbage Worms. The imported cabbage worm and cabbage looper feed on leaves and bore into the head. The white butterfly seen in the garden is the adult of the imported cabbage worm.

Harlequin Bug. Black stink bug with bright yellow or red marks. The sucking insects may be found on horseradish, mustard, and other garden plants.

Damping-off. Young plants die in hotbed.

Yellows (wilt). May damage cabbage, kohlrabi, and kale. Yellowish green leaves; stunted plants, lower leaves drop. Disease first attacks one side of plant.

Black Rot and Blackleg. Black rot causes blackened veins and black ring in stem when cut across. Blackleg causes ashen-gray spots speckled with tiny black dots on leaves and stems.

Carrots

Pest and Damage

Celery Worm. Large green worm with black and yellow bands around the body.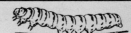

Carrot Weevil. Beetles lay eggs in carrot tops. When eggs hatch, white legless grub burrows in roots of carrots.

Black Rot. Fleshy roots are greenish black to jet black.

FOOD GARDENS' STATEMENT ON USE OF CHEMICALS

We have not recommended the use of chemical or commercial pesticides because of the many changes now taking place in government and industry concerning regulations and practices. Many of the well-known controls sold in garden centers have been taken off the shelves in the past few years and until industry and government decide on what is not harmful we reserve the right to watch and make a rational judgement when all the facts are in.

PESTS

Corn

Pest and Damage

Corn Earworm. Green or brown worms with light brown head and light stripe on sides and beneath body.

Stalk Borer.

Smut (fungus). Large white galls form on stalks, ears, and tassels. Galls burst, releasing masses of black fungus spores. Fungus survives in soil indefinitely.

Cucumber, Cantaloupe, Squash, Pumpkin, Gourd

Pest and Damage

Aphids.

Cucumber Beetles, Striped and Spotted Beetles. Destroy leaves when the plants come up, carry bacterial wilt disease. Larvae feed in roots of plants.

Squash Bugs. Large gray bugs suck sap from the plants.

Squash Vine Borer. White larvae feed in stem near base of runner.

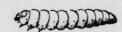

Lettuce Looper. Found on cabbage; may attack lettuce.

Damping-off. Young plants die in hotbed.

Bacterial Wilt. Plants wilt and die without apparent symptoms, except, occasionally, a white liquid can be squeezed from the cut stems. Brought to the plants each year by cucumber beetles.

Anthracnose and Alternaria. Reddish-brown or yellow circular spots on leaves. Elongated, tan canker on stems. Round, sunken spots with pinkish-tan centers (later turning dark) on fruits. Also attacks muskmelons and watermelons.

Mosaic. Mottled (green and yellow) and curled leaves; warty and spotted cucumber fruits. Also attacks muskmelon, squash, pepper, celery, and tomatoes.

Powdery Mildew. Gray growth over the leaves.

Eggplant

Pest and Damage

Fruit Rot and Leaf Spot. Brown and shrunken stems at soil line, spots on leaves, circular brown spots covered with blisters on fruits.

Damping-off. Young plants die in hotbed.

Onion

Pest and Damage

Onion Thrip. Tiny insects cause blotches on leaves.

Onion Plant Bug. Small green bugs suck juice from plant.

Neck Rot. Cooked, sunken appearance at top of bulb which may rot in field or storage.

Peas

Pest and Damage

Aphid.

Powdery Mildew.

Root Rots. Yellow and unthrifty plants with rotted roots.

Pepper

Pest and Damage

Fruit Rots. Bacterial and fungus spots and cankers. Carried on seed and lives in soil.

Blossom-End Rot. Dark and shriveled. Restricted to blossom-end of fruit.

Irish Potatoes

Pest and Damage

Colorado Potato Beetle. Adult beetles and pink larvae destroy leaves.

Blister Beetle.

White Grub.

Wireworm.

Potato Aphid.

Scab. Scabby spots on tubers. Fungus carried on seed and in soil.

Late and Early Blights. Disease spots on foliage.

Running-Out (viruses). Stunted plants and low yields. Leaves may be mottled, rolled, or curled.

Net Necrosis. Stringy black or brown in tubers due to high soil or storage temperatures.

Storage Rots. Tubers rot in storage.

Rhubarb

Pest and Damage

Rhubarb Curculio. Large-snout beetle; larvae feed in root of plant.

Crown and Root Rot. Brown sunken spots at base of leaf stalks; wilted leaves. Fungus is carried on roots and lives in soil.

Squash and Pumpkin

Pest and Damage

Bacterial Wilt.

Strawberry

Pest and Damage

Leaf Rollers. Worms web leaves together.

Strawberry Rootworms. Small grubs feed in the strawberry roots and leaves during the summer.

White Grubs.

Crown and Root Rot. Fungus lives in the soil.

Viruses. Symptoms are not easily detected; yields are reduced.

Leaf Spots. Purplish, brown, or white spots that have purplish borders.

Slime Mold. Gray or black frothy mass that spreads over plants and later turns into powder.

Dell E. Gates, Extension Entomologist
Claude L. King, Extension Plant Pathologist
Cooperative Extension Service
Kansas State University
Manhattan, Kansas

BOMBYX MORI, Known as Silk Worm

Sweetpotato

Pest and Damage

White Grubs and Wireworms.

Tortoise Beetles. Larvae feed on leaves.

Nematodes. Black spots where small roots join potato. Cracks in potatoes.

Stem Rot. Yellow and wilted plants. When cut across, stems have dark discolored ring toward the outside.

Tomato

Pest and Damage

Aphids.

Tomato Fruitworm.

Stalk Borers.

Blister Beetles.

Cutworms.

Stink Bugs. Cause white areas beneath skin of ripening Tomatoes.

Tomato Hornworm. Large green worm with a horn on its tail. Adult is the large hummingbird moth seen near flowers.

Damping-off. Young plants die in hotbed.

Fruit Rots. The many kinds are described in U. S. D. A. Agriculture Handbook No. 203, Tomato Diseases and Their Control. This can be purchased from Supt. of Documents, U. S. Government Printing Office, Washington, D. C. 20402. The price is 35 cents.

Septoria Leaf Spot. The disease yellows or kills the lower leaves first and then progresses upward. Small spots are on the dying leaves.

Virus (cucumber mosaic). Individual plants may appear as if affected by 2,4-D weed killer. Leaves are stringy and distorted. 2,4-D drift usually affects most of the plants in an area uniformly. A plant with cucumber mosaic is often beside a healthy plant.

Virus (curly top). Upward rolling and twisting of leaflets. Foliage leathery and plant is slightly yellowish. Branches and stems abnormally erect. Petioles of leaves curl downward. Often veins of leaves are purple.

Virus (tobacco mosaic). Light and dark green mottling of leaves. Plants somewhat stunted.

Fusarium Wilt. Cut into lower part of stem. If the ring of conducting tissues near the outside of stem is discolored tan or brown, Fusarium wilt is probably the cause.

Watermelon

Pest and Damage

Anthracnose. Dark spots on leaves and stems. At first, spots on fruits are small and raised. Later, they enlarge and become sunken and may have pinkish fungus growth in moist weather. Fungus also affects cucumbers and muskmelon. Carried on seed and lives in soil.

Damping-off. Young plants die in hotbed.

Wilt (fungus). Wilting starts at tips of runners and slowly spreads to entire vine. Plants eventually die. Fungus lives indefinitely in the ground.

CATERPILLAR OF LARGE CABBAGE BUTTERFLY.

Harti:choke:common.

APHIDS

ON LEAFY VEGETABLES
How To Control Them

BY W. J. REID, JR.,[1] AND F. P. CUTHBERT, JR., ENTOMOLOGISTS

Southern Region, Agricultural Research Service

Aphids, often called plant lice, are small, soft-bodied insects that suck juice from plants. They are present wherever crops are grown.

Aphids cause heavy losses to growers of leafy vegetables by—

● Reducing vigor and yield of plants.

● Contaminating edible parts.

● Transmitting destructive virus diseases of plants.

● Killing plants, if infestation is heavy.

Most species of aphids are about 1/16 inch long. Species differ in color. Some individuals of most species have wings; others do not.

Male aphids are rare. Females of all species give birth to living young in the summer. When cold weather approaches, females of most species mate and lay eggs. Females live about a month, and produce 80 to 100 young.

KINDS OF APHIDS

Several species of aphids attack leafy vegetables.

Green Peach Aphid

The green peach aphid,[2] known also as the spinach aphid and the tobacco aphid, is about the size of a cabbage seed. Both wingless and winged types are yellowish green or pinkish green; the winged type is darker.

This aphid feeds on many plants. It is most destructive to spinach, beets, celery, lettuce, and chard. It also causes some injury to cabbage and related cole crops, dandelion, endive, mustard greens, parsley, and turnip.

It spreads several virus diseases of plants, including beet mosaic, beet yellows (which also attacks spinach), and lettuce mosaic.

In the Southern States, in Arizona and California, and in extreme western Oregon and Washington, nearly all green peach aphids are females that deposit their young without mating. Reproduction takes place throughout the year. As many as 30 generations a year occur in the extreme South.

Continuous reproduction by unmated females, and overwintering of this form of the insect, occur as far north as warmer parts of New Jersey, Maryland, Virginia, Tennessee, Arkansas, and Oklahoma, and in at least one area in Washington.

In these and colder areas, males and egg-laying females also develop in the fall. This aphid generally survives the winter only in the egg

----

[1] *Retired.*

[2] *Myzus persicae.*

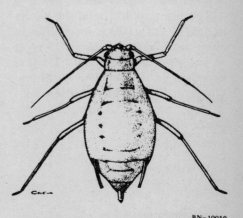

Green peach aphid, wingless form.

BN–10059

stage in areas where minimum temperatures drop to 0° F. or below. Eggs are laid mostly on peach, wild plum, and cherry trees. They hatch in the spring, and the young aphids feed where the eggs were laid. New broods develop and spread to vegetables and other host plants.

Cabbage Aphid

The cabbage aphid [3] is found throughout the United States. It is distinguished from other species by a powdery, waxy covering over its body. Color is grayish green.

This aphid feeds primarily on cabbage, cauliflower, collards, broccoli, kale, and other cole crops. It seldom damages mustard or turnips.

In the Southern States, 30 or more generations of females, both winged and wingless, are produced throughout the year. In colder climates, males and females occur in the fall; they mate and the females lay eggs that survive the winter. Eggs of this aphid usually are laid on the residues of host crops that have been left in the field.

Turnip Aphid

The turnip aphid [4] is also called the turnip louse and the false cabbage aphid.

This aphid resembles the cabbage aphid, but does not have a waxy body covering. It is pale green. The winged form has black spots, a black head, and transparent wings marked by black veins.

The turnip aphid is widely distributed in the United States and causes heavy losses to growers, especially in the South. It feeds chiefly on turnip, mustard, and radish plants. It also injures other crucifers, particularly in their seedling stage.

Full-grown females give birth to 50 to 100 young during their reproductive period of 20 to 30 days. In the Gulf Coast region as many as 46 generations have been observed in a year.

The habits of this insect are similar to those of the cabbage aphid, except that egg laying is rare.

Other Aphids

The bean aphid [5] ranges in color from dark olive-green to black. It has been found on beets in Arizona, and on beets and chard in other sections. It is not usually a serious pest of other leafy vegetables.

The bean aphid passes the winter in the North as eggs on species of euonymus, and to a limited extent on snowball and deutzia. Little is known of its life history in the South, but probably successive generations

---

[3] *Brevicoryne brassicae.*

[4] *Hyadaphis pseudobrassicae.*

[5] *Aphis fabae.*

[6] *Macrosiphum euphorbiae.*

---

of females are produced there throughout the year. A common weed, dock, is a favored host.

Macrosiphum ambrosiae is the scientific name of a large reddish aphid that damages lettuce in eastern Virginia, coastal South Carolina, and southern Texas. In eastern Virginia it feeds on endive plants.

An aphid known as *Macrosiphum barri* damages lettuce in Arizona, California, and some of the other western States.

The potato aphid,[6] which occurs in both green and pink colors, attacks spinach at times in the fall in Virginia.

NATURAL CONTROLS

Sometimes natural controls hold down the aphid population. Other insects that kill aphids are important natural controls. Fungus diseases and certain weather conditions also help destroy aphids.

Insects That Kill Aphids

Both parasitic and predatory insects help keep aphids in check.

Four-winged, wasplike insects parasitize aphids. The females lay eggs in the bodies of aphids; when the eggs hatch, the larvae feed on the aphids.

The parasites reproduce rapidly under favorable conditions. Usually they become abundant during spring and early summer.

The predatory insects that feed on aphids are lady beetles, soldier bugs, assassin bugs, and the larvae of lady beetles, syrphid flies, and green lacewings. They are most active during summer and fall.

If inspection shows that insect enemies are present, do not apply an insecticide unless the aphids begin to increase. Insecticides also kill the insects that kill aphids. Then, aphids that survive multiply rapidly, and repeated applications of insecticide become necessary.

Diseases

Fungus diseases sometimes kill aphids. However, this seldom happens before the aphids have become numerous and caused considerable damage.

Aphids killed by a fungus change shape and turn tan or light brown. Sometimes the fungus attaches them to the plant.

Weather

Aphids are sensitive to weather conditions. Hard, driving rains kill large numbers of some species. Damp weather favors the development of diseases that kill aphids.

Aphids reproduce most rapidly at moderate temperatures. High temperatures are unfavorable to the kinds of aphids that attack leafy vegetables.

CONTROL MEASURES

You can control aphids by following cultural practices that keep the insects in check, and by applying insecticide.

Cultural Practices

These cultural practices insure better crops, and help keep aphids under control:

• Start with a well-prepared, fertile seedbed.

• Do not plant on land from which a similar aphid-infested crop has been recently removed.

• Do not plant near a growing crop of aphid-infested vegetables.

• Clear the field and surrounding area of aphid host plants.

• Plant seed in drills, to facilitate cultivation and application of insecticide.

• Apply a nitrogenous fertilizer (20 to 30 pounds of nitrogen per

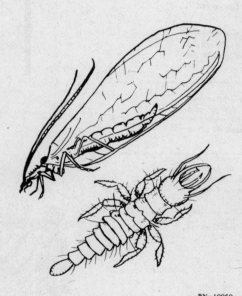

BN–10060

Adult and larva of green lacewing.

acre) soon after plants come up. Fertilize plants adequately throughout their growth.

• Irrigate during dry weather, if possible.

• Harvest the crop as soon as it is ready. Dispose of crop residue immediately.

STRIKING CUTTINGS.

BIO-CONTROL COMPANION PLANTS
NICHOLS GARDEN NURSERY
1190 North Pacific Hwy.
Albany, Oregon 97321

REPELLENTS FOR:

ANTS — Mulch, sprinkle bone meal; APHIDS — Mulch, garlic, wood ashes, lady bugs; BEETLE — (Mexican)-Cosmos, aster, chrysanthemum; EARWIGS — Hang strips of rags on stakes, in trees. Drown. Or cans filled with water in vegetable row; FLIES — Tansy, Basil; NEMATOES — Marigold planted for two to three years throughout garden; SLUG & CUT WORMS — Wood ashes; RABBITS — Dust plants with talcum powder or gallon glass jug half filled with water; SNAILS & SLUGS — Fill pie pan with 1½" beer and bury to ground level. The slugs & snails will drown in the beer; SPIDER MITES — To 5 gallons of water add 6 tbspns. buttermilk, and 4 cups wheat flour, mix and douse.

REPELLENTS FOR VEGETABLES

ASPARAGUS — Plant near tomato; BEANS: Green beans — Plant near potatoes, Lima-Nasturtium, garlic, savory, Pole — Marigold, savory, Peas — Compost in furrow, wood ashes, Snap — Garlic; BROCCOLI — Sage, mint; CABBAGE — Mustard, sage, tar paper squares, mint; CAULIFLOWER — Sage, mint; CUCUMBER — Radish, nasturtium; EGGPLANT — Mulch, basil, hot pepper; KOHLRABI — Marigold, sage, mint; LETTUCE — Garlic, mulch; MELON — Radish, nasturtium, brew made with garlic, onion, hot pepper, peppercorns, etc., mixed with one cup detergent to 1 gallon water. Let stand and brew. Use ½ cup of this brew to one quart water and douse plants; SEEDLINGS — Same brew as above; TOMATOES — Basil, dill, plant near asparagus; TURNIP — Tar paper squares; Other useful flowers and herbs — Aster, anise, artemisias, dahlias, feverfew, hyssop, horse-radish, marigold (French) lavender, savory, tansy, tarragon, yarrow.

Bulbous-rooted Chervil (*Chærophyllum bulbosum*).

Scientists are now discovering that many plants produce actual plant medicines which are natural bactericides and fungicides. For instance, a few drops of an extract from cauliflower seeds has been found to inactivate the bacteria causing black rot, and radish seeds also contain an antibacterial substance. In Helsinki, Professor A. I. Virtanen, testing nearly 1,300 plants, found that 305 of them contained antibiotic substances which were especially high in the cruciferae (mustard family).

Folklore has credited garlic and onions with medicinal properties which are now being established experimentally. Researchers, using garlic juice or commercial liquid and powdered extracts, and disguising the odor with a deodorizing agent, found it to contain a powerful antibacterial agent. It is an effective destroyer of diseases that damage stone fruits, cucumbers, radishes, spinach, beans, tomatoes, and nuts.

T. A. Tovstoles, a Russian biologist, experimented with a water solution of onion skin. Used as a spray three times daily at five-day intervals, the solution gave an almost complete kill of hemiptera, a parasite which attacks more than a hundred different species of plants.

Onion spray will also serve as a nontoxic fumigant.

PESTICIDES

United States Department of Agriculture

in the Home
in the Garden

You can control pests in your home and garden—with Safety—if you use pesticides properly.

Before buying a pesticide, check the label. Make sure it lists the name of the pest you want to control.

Read the label

If not handled and applied properly, many pesticides can injure (some can even kill) wildlife, fish, honey bees, domestic animals or humans. The first rule of safety in using any pesticide is to read and follow the directions and precautions on the container label. Do this each time you use a pesticide; don't depend on your memory. Many pesticide manufacturers include leaflets of instructions with their products. Carefully read these also.

Store Pesticides Safely

Store pesticides in closed, well-labeled containers, where children or pets cannot reach them. Do not place them near food or feed. Do not store them under the sink, in the pantry, or in the medicine cabinet.

Always leave pesticides in their original containers. Be sure the labels remain on them. If a pesticide is marked "Poison," it will have an antidote statement on the label. Be sure to read it. In case of accident, take container with you when seeking medical assistance.

Do not save or reuse empty containers. Rinse glass or metal containers with water and dispose of them properly.

Apply Pesticides Safely

Read the label first. Determine the right amount of the right pesticide to use. Over dosage is wasteful; it won't kill more insects; it may be injurious to plants, and may leave a harmful residue on fruits and vegetables.

Be careful not to get pesticides on food, dishes, or cooking utensils.

Remove pets and their food and water pans before applying pesticides.

Keep people, particularly children, away from areas where you are mixing or applying pesticides.

Dilute or mix sprays outdoors or in a well ventilated place.

When the label warns against it, be sure to avoid breathing pesticidal dusts or mists. Keep your face away from, and to one side of, the cap when opening a container.

Handle liquid concentrates and oil-base sprays as though they were flammable.

Place poison bait out of reach of children and pets. (Baits for rats, ants, and roaches account for a high percentage of the cases of accidental swallowing of pesticides by children under 12 years of age.)

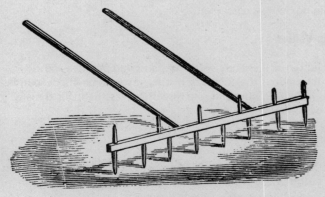

DOUBLE MARKER.

Do not use a pesticide in the home if the label says a gas mask is required in its application.

In handling any pesticide, avoid contact with the skin. Use protective equipment if the label recommends it. Avoid excessive contamination of clothing when spraying or dusting.

Do not use your mouth to blow out clogged lines, nozzle tips, or other equipment parts, or to siphon a pesticide from a container.

When spraying or dusting pets, be sure pesticide is labeled for such use.

Do not smoke while handling pesticides.

Protect Wildlife, Fish, Honey Bees

When pesticides are applied to extensive land areas, every precaution should be taken to avoid contamination of streams, lakes, or ponds in order to protect fish and wildlife.

When pesticides are applied on the home grounds, avoid contaminating fish ponds.

Do not apply pesticides (particularly insecticides) to fish-bearing water unless the label specifically recommends the material for such uses) then apply it only at the specified rates.

Do not apply pesticides to or near home aquariums or fish bowls. Remove these from the room before spraying.

Bees and other pollinating insects have definite times for visiting plants. To prevent loss of these beneficial insects, do not apply pesticides during those times.

Avoid drift of pesticides. Don't spray or dust in the garden if the day is windy.

Protect Crops, Plants, Drinking Water

Apply pesticides only to the plants listed on the label.

Be sure to read the label before applying pesticides to growing vegetables or fruits. They may leave unsafe residues if applied at improper times and rates. Observe specified safe intervals between the last pesticide application and harvest.

Do not allow pesticide spray or dust to drift. When applying weed killer, keep it from coming in contact with your flowers, shrubs and other valuable plants.

Do not apply pesticides near dug wells were they might contaminate the drinking water. Do not apply them on areas from which they may be carried by runoff onto other areas.

Follow These Safety Measures

Wash with soap and water and change clothing immediately if you spill a pesticide concentrate on skin or clothing.

If you get a concentrate in your eyes, flush them with plenty of water for 15 minutes and get medical attention.

If you accidentally swallow some pesticide, or if you feel ill effects after using it, call your physician at once. Read the label to him, naming the active chemical ingredient. Observe any antidote instructions on the label.

BENEFICIAL INSECTS

Utah State University
Extension Services
Logan, Utah

By Reed S. Roberts

Introduction

Every kind of insect, no matter how abundant or how rare, is a part of nature and as such is important. Man may arbitrarily classify an insect as to its importance, but ecologically speaking there are no unimportant insects.

There are approximately 1,000,000 different species of insects living on this globe we call our world. The majority of these are beneficial, or at least not directly detrimental to man's welfare. It is believed by some entomologists that the good done by the beneficial insects outweighs the harm done by the injurious ones.

The list of beneficial insects which follows is both selective and relative. For example, some of the predators and parasites prey upon both injurious and beneficial insects. Many of the insects which pollinate valuable seed crops also pollinate weeds and other undesirable plants. Some insects are beneficial in one stage of their life cycle and injurious in another. We haven't even tried to list the hundreds of insects which feed on weeds.

Predators and Parasites

In general, an insect predator is larger than the insect upon which it preys and it may attack and kill several different insects over a period of time. In contrast, an insect parasite is usually smaller than its host and it often completes most of its life cycle in or on one individual insect.

Some common examples of insect predators and parasites are as follows: dragonflies, damselflies, mantids, minute pirate bugs, three-legged bugs, damsel bugs, stink bugs, aquatic bugs which feed on mosquito larvae, snake flies, lacewings, antlions, tiger beetles, ground beetles, rove beetles, checkered beetles, sandalids, ladybird beetles, blister beetles, stiletto flies, tangle-veined flies, bee flies, dance flies, long-legged flies, humpbacked flies, big headed flies, marsh flies, flesh flies, tachinid flies, braconid wasps, ichneumonid wasps, chalcids, cuckoo wasps, and many other families of wasps.

Insect Pollinators of Plants

Insect pollinators of plants are among the most valuable of all insects and their importance to the welfare of mankind can hardly be overestimated. It should be noted however, that a given insect pollinator may pollinate both beneficial and unwanted plants. Many pollinate weeds. An insect may pollinate a valuable seed plant in one stage of its life cycle and yet be a harmful insect in another stage.

Insect pollinators are found in many insect orders, the following being the most important:
Diptera—Many species of flower visiting flies
Lepidoptera—Many species of flower visiting butterflies and moths
Hymenoptera—Many species of flower visiting bees and wasps
Within the order Hymenoptera we find the fig wasp which is so essential to the pollination of figs. The wild bees, such as the leaf-cutting bees, alkali bees and bumble bees are especially important as pollinators.

Scavengers

These are the insects which feed upon the tissues of dead plants and animals breaking down the organic matter and making it available to other organisms. One only need ponder the problem which would accrue if the bodies of dead plants and animals remained intact, to appreciate the tremendous importance of these insects.

There are many insect scavengers, but probably the best known are the carrion and burying beetles.

Most dung feeders and some of the wood feeders and soil insects also play an important role in breaking down organic matter.

Insect Products

There are some insect products and by-products which are useful to man. A select few are listed as follows:
1. Honey, beeswax and royal jelly from honey bees
2. Shellac and varnish from the secretions of the lac insect
3. Dyes from various insect galls and the cochineal insect
4. Tannic acid for inks from the galls of cynipid wasps
5. Candles from the wax produced by the Chinese wax scale
6. Silk from the well known silkworm

Shows the method of securing the production of roots from branches, so as to enable the cultivator to reduce the size of a plant.

As Food For Other Organisms

Many insects serve as a major source of food for birds, reptiles, amphibians, fish and other animals. In some countries there are insects which are used as food by man. A few examples of these are as follows:
1. Mayflies and caddisflies serve as an important source of food for many kinds of fresh water fish.
2. Many small flies, gnats and mosquitoes serve as a major source of food for birds.
3. In many countries there are people who eat such insects as locusts, ants, termites, beetle grubs, caterpillars and grasshoppers.

Biological Control

Hundreds of insects have been tested for use in controlling noxious weeds and injurious insects. Some have proven successful, many have not.

The use of ladybird beetles to control certain species of aphids is well known.

Probably less known are the moth larvae and beetles that feed on certain noxious weeds.

Aesthetic Values

Colorful butterflies and beetles have inspired painters and jewelers throughout the course of history. Even some insect sounds and ways have been put to music. Insects are fascinating and many people have enjoyed studying them.

Scientific Studies

Some very significant scientific advances have been made through research with insects. We need only mention the progress made in genetics through the study of the little vinegar fly, Drosophila.

Insect populations are often used as an index of ecological conditions, such as pollution.

PRAYING MANTIS AND LADYBUGS

NOTES ON THE CHINESE PRAYING MANTIS
(Tenodera Aridifolia Sinensis)

Praying mantis egg cases are available from about Dec. 1st to early June depending on demand. Hatching period is in the spring months, as late as June in northern U.S. and earlier accordingly in the warmer southern states. The eggs hatch out when the weather becomes warm and their insect prey also becomes available at that time. The warmer the weather the shorter the hatching time. After hatching the baby Mantises (nymphs) emerge from the case and float to the ground. They resemble a large mosquito when young and are very difficult to see as they blend easily with plant life. After hatching the egg cases appear the same—no change in any way. Thru spring and summer they shed their skin many times. They vary in color, gray, green, pinkish; usually darken with age. Their color is natural camouflage—fools even other insects.

They have an enormous appetite—never seem to get enough to eat. In their young stages they eat aphids, flies, small caterpillars and other soft-bodied insects. As they grow they start to eat larger insects and later in season eating such large insects as grasshoppers, large beetles and of course smaller insects. With plenty to eat these Chinese species and especially the female sometimes grow to the enormous size of 5 inches long. In size and appetite they are giants compared to the smaller native Mantises. The female usually eats the smaller male after mating. They do not eat vegetation—are carnivorous or "meat-eaters".

The Mantises vary from Ladybugs in that they lay in wait for their prey and when close enough snap it up with a lightning movement of their strong forelegs, whereas Ladybugs are constantly on the prowl searching for food. Mantises seldom eat Ladybugs due to bitter taste—go well together. However, when hungry enough they eat even each other.

Mantises are poor at flying and walk slowly. If they have plenty to eat they usually stay close to where they were born. With plenty to eat the female sometimes lays eggs in the fall, cases well enough to stand severe winter climates; thus possibility of new hatch for following year. If she deems she may fly to a more suitable place to lay her eggs.

Mantises are very ferocious looking creatures but harmless to humans. If handled properly they do not bite. Do not pick them up behind forelegs. The dark-colored fluid from their mouths is harmless. They can become tame enough to be pets—will sometimes eat raw meat and insects from your fingers. The Mantis is the only known insect that can turn its head to look over its shoulder. Nature placed the strong forelegs in a position to remind one of praying; from this they derived their name.

INSTRUCTIONS: Attach or hang the egg case to a bush, hedge, limb or anything two or more feet above ground. A needle with white thread may be run throu outer surface of case—not too deep to damage the eggs; then hung easily where desired. This hanging and/or swinging helps keep birds and other predators away from the case. By oiling the upper part of the string would help keep ants away. High air pollution may have adverse effects on hatching and survival. These egg cases can be stored in home refrigerator just above freezing: slight dampness ideal. Some tests indicate 75 to 90% hatch out. About 200 eggs per case.

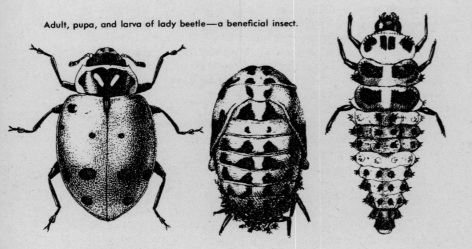

Adult, pupa, and larva of lady beetle—a beneficial insect.

Bio-Control Co., 10180 Ladybird Dr., Auburn, Calif., 95603

THE LADYBIRD BEETLE
(HIPPODAMIA CONVERGENS)

Out in the valleys of the far west, particularly in California, there is born in the spring during April and May, a tiny white form of life almost invisible to the naked eye. Immediately it starts to eat; tiny organisms, eggs and insects fall victim to its voracious appetite. It grows until it is a half inch in length, looking like a small alligator, a darkish gray color with orange spots here and there. This is called the larvae, which when attaining its growth goes into a moulting condition, clinging to weeds, grass stems, etc. A few days of this and the back splits open and an adult Ladybird is born. Generally speaking, the life span is one year.

Whenever they are where there is food they eat. Forty to fifty aphids per day is not unusual, this being their favorite food. Running out of aphids does not stop them, however, as they will also eat a variety of other insects, eggs, larvae, etc. Among those which the Ladybird destroys are the fruit scales, the mealy bugs, bollworm, leaf worm, leafhoppers, fleahoppers and corn ear worm. On some of these they destroy only the eggs and larvae as the adults are too large for them to handle. The Ladybug is carnivorous, a meat eater, and does not harm vegetation. When the Ladies run out of food they hibernate in beds in the hills where they can be gathered up and taken to places where there is food for them. The plant-destroying insects are their favorite food.

During the past several years a great many experiments have been conducted for the control of harmful insects which threaten our food supplies. Many new and devastating poisons have been invented and used, some with rather disappointing results.

The main trouble with the new poisons is that they destroy the balance which nature intended; that is, the poisons make no distinction between the harmful insects and the beneficial ones which keep them under control. However, we realize something must be done when things get out of hand; a favorable balance must be maintained if we are to raise our food crops with any degree of success. Natural methods are recognized as the best whenever and wherever it is possible to achieve them.

The U. S. Dept. of Agriculture has caused any number of predatory and parasitic insects and beetles to be imported from foreign countries in an effort to do this. One of the main troubles with these foreign imports is that they fail to survive in this country; climatic conditions, harvesting methods and the saturation with poisonous sprays are all factors contributing to failure. Not all are failures. Once in a while they come up with something that is a great success and poison is no longer needed.

The ladybug, being native to this country, will survive anywhere unless killed off with poisons, in which case they may be replaced at cost muchless than that of poisonous sprays. In using biological control methods the beneficial insects are left to survive and multiply, eventually gaining the control or balance which nature intended.

When left to themselves, the process is as a rule too slow to save a crop from damage, but by giving them a little help, control can be achieved in a relatively short time. In severe cases the arsenate of lead and nicotine sprays and dusts may be used with very little damage to the insect population, thus keeping the cost of control down to a point considerably below that of depending on poison alone.

Contact poisons such as Parathion, Malathion, DDT and others are very injurious to the soil as well as killing the beneficial insects: the bees which pollinate and make the trees and vegetation fertile being particularly affected. DDT kills the bacteria in the soil which makes it productive. Earthworms have been found to be almost non-existent where this and other poisons of this type have been used extensively.

The Convergent Ladybird is one predatory beetle which can be gathered in its natural habitat at a cost much cheaper than poison sprays and/or other types of pest predators. In the control of aphids which suck the life out of plants of all kinds, there is probably no better method of control. A little study and experimentation in this method of pest control can be very beneficial to any farm, ranch or garden.

The spotted or yellow alfalfa aphid discovered in New Mexico in 1954 has since spread over most of Arizona and California as well as other parts of the country and can be appreciably controlled by use of these little beetles. Poisonous sprays are almost useless in many respects. Cattle became sick and died during efforts to control this new pest. The milk from cows became contaminated with some of the poison. Some experiments performed showed a 75% control was achieved with the use of Ladybugs, enough to save the crop.

One thing about the use of Ladybugs is that rain or irrigation will not wash them off as in the case of poisons. A gallon for ten acres at about time of last frost is normally enough for the first release. After each cutting a gallon for 15 acres is usually sufficient.

Many gardeners and flower growers use the Ladybugs in the control of aphids and other pestiferous insects. Thousands of gallons are used by farmers and growers in Texas, Oklahoma, Ohio, Nebraska, Kansas, Colorado, Florida, Idaho, Arizona, New Mexico, California and many other states every year. Some foreign countries, and especially Mexico, are importing large quantities yearly for more economical and better control on various crops.

In the application and general use of the Ladybug it has been found that late evening after sundown is the best time of day to release them. When put out during the heat of the day they are much more apt to fly and scatter. When released while it is cool, or after dark, they have a better chance to forget their fright of being handled. They will not fly at night and by morning will have settled down ready to go to work.

About June 1st when young Ladybugs become available they may be kept in an ordinary refrigerator for several days or even weeks if placed where they will not freeze. This keeps them in a dormant condition and they do not require food. They may be removed from the package and placed in a small cloth bag, preferably made of light cotton, tied tightly at the top, put in the refrigerator and then released as needed.

In March, April and especially in May, it is wise to release Ladybugs on evening of same day as received to avoid mortality. It is at this time of year they are starting to come to the end of their life cycle and they die not only of this natural cause but also from hunger since their stored fat is becoming more and more depleted. Orders should be placed so arrival would be when there is some immediate feeding. A good tentative date for receiving and releasing Ladybugs is about the time of the last frost.

PLANT DISEASES

DOWNY MILDEW OF VINE CROPS

By M. C. Shurtleff and B. J. Jacobsen
Department of Plant Pathology, University of Illinois at Urbana-Champaign

Downy mildew, caused by the fungus Pseudoperonospora cubensis, is primarily a disease of cucumber, muskmelon, cantaloupe, squash, pumpkin, gourds, and West Indian gherkin. Watermelon, citron, calabash, cassaba, and vegetable-marrow are not commonly attacked, while wild cucumber and other related weed hosts normally escape infection. Only members of the cucumber family (cucurbits) become infected. The disease is confined mostly to the leaves, although fruit may be of poor quality owing to loss of foliage. Downy mildew is more common and destructive in the humid Atlantic and Gulf Coast States.

Primary infections in the field generally come from (1) fungus spores produced on greenhouse-grown cucumbers or (2) spores produced on southern crops and carried progressively northward on moist air currents during the spring and summer. The spores are disseminated locally from plant to plant and from field to field by splashing rains, moist air currents, insects, and men working among infected plants. Heavy dews, fogs, frequent rains, and high humidity favor infection and rapid multiplication of the causal fungus. Temperature is not as critical as it is with many other vegetable diseases. Infection may occur over the relatively wide temperature range of 50 degrees to 86 degrees F., the optimum being 61 degrees to 72 degrees F. Periods of hot, dry weather tend to check the spread of the fungus. The downy mildew fungus does not overwinter in plant debris, and apparently is not seed-borne.

SYMPTOMS

The first symptom is usually the appearance of indistinct, pale-green areas separated by dark-green areas on the upper leaf surface. In this stage, the disease resembles a mosaic mottling. The pale-green areas soon become yellow, angular to irregular spots bounded by the leaf veins. On some cucurbits the upper surface of the spot is first yellow and then reddish-brown to almost black. A downy, pale-purplish to grayish-purple mildew—containing tremendous numbers of spores—grows from the undersurface to these spots when dew or rain is present. The mildew may range from white to almost black. Diseased leaves soon wither, cup upward, and turn brown. Downy mildew usually first infects the older leaves nearest to the center of the hill about the time vines are beginning to set fruit. In rainy, humid weather the disease progresses outward from the center of the vine until the entire vine is killed or only the youngest leaves at the runner tips remain alive. Downy mildew may spread so rapidly that affected vines appear to be frosted. Fruit formed during disease attacks commonly remain dwarfed and poor in flavor.

CONTROL

1. Plant varieties resistant to downy mildew. Cucumber varieties should have resistance to scab and mosaic; cantaloupe and muskmelon, to fusarium wilt; whenever possible. These diseases also limit production of these crops.

These muskmelon and cantaloupe varieties are resistant to downy mildew: Dolee, Edisto, Edisto 47, Floridew, Florigold, Forisom, Georgia 47, Golden Perfection, Gulf Stream, Home Garden, Perlita, Planters Jumbo, Rio Sweet, Saticoy Hybrid, Seminole, Smith Perfect, Supermarket, Texas Resistant No. 1, and Topmark.

These are the downy-mildew-resistant cucumber varieties: Ashe, Ashley, Ashley F_1 Hybrid, Barclay, Bounty, Bravo, Burpee Hybrid, Challenger, Cherokee 7, Chipper, Dixie, Early Marketer, Early Surecrop, Explorer, Fletcher, Frontier, Galaxy, Gemini, Highmark II, Hiyield, M & M Burpee, Magnolia, Mariner, P-51 D.M.R., Palmetto, Palomar, Patio Pik, Pickmore, Pioneer, Pixie, Poinsett, Polaris, P.R. 10, P.R. 27, P.R. 39, Premier, Princess, Ranger, Selander, Sably, Santez, Satiny Hybrid, Smoothie, Southern Cross, Stono, Sweet Slice, Tec Long, Total Market Hybrid, Triple Purpose, Triumph, and Victory.

No resistant varieties of squash or pumpkin are available.

2. Fungicidal applications may be necessary on susceptible varieties during warm, humid weather (61 degrees to 72 degrees F.). It is especially important to get good coverage of the lower leaf surface, since infections commonly occur on the undersides of leaves. Spraying is more effective than dusting, since more thorough coverage is obtained. The use of a spreader-sticker is suggested. Fixed or neutral copper fungicides may cause some burning of foliage, stunting, and reduction in yields. The copper fungicides do NOT provide control of the anthracnose fungus, which is active during the same weather conditions as the downy mildew fungus; however, the copper fungicides do provide some control of the angular leaf spot bacterium.

Mixtures of the fungicides and fixed or organic copper fungicides may be of use where angular leaf spot control is desired. When mixed with copper fungicides, folpet, difolatan, Polyram, maneb, zineb, and zinc ion maneb may decompose while standing. Therefore, mix only the amount to be used for each day's application. Bordeaux mixture is incompatible with many of the above fungicides.

3. Long rotations with crops outside the cucumber family, seed treatment, plowing under or burning of crop debris, not handling plants when they are wet, and control of cucurbit weeds are recommended. Using these practices will help check other diseases, such as angular leaf spot, Alternaria leaf spot, anthracnose, and scab.

FRUITING PLANT OF DWARF OR FRENCH BEAN (PHASEOLUS VULGARIS).

ROOT AND STEM ROTS OF GARDEN BEANS

By Malcolm C. Shurtleff and M. B. Linn

Three common root and stem rots may damage garden beans when conditions do not favor the best growth of the plants. These rots are caused by common soil-inhabiting fungi that attack bean plants at any stage of growth. Infection usually occurs early in the growing season when the weather is cool and the soil moisture content high. The causal fungi may live for several years in the soil in the absence of beans or other cultivated crops. The fungi causing these diseases are spread from plant to plant and from field to field by surface-drainage water, farm equipment, or other means whereby infested soil is moved from one location to another. Losses are greatest where little or no rotation is practiced.

1. Fusarium Dry Root Rot and Stem Rot (Fusarium solani f. phaseoli)

A slight reddish discoloration of the taproot appears a week or more after the seedling emerges. The discoloration gradually becomes brick-red as the diseased area enlarges to cover most of the taproot, or reddish streaks develop on the taproot below the soil surface. The taproot later turns brown and lengthwise cracks generally develop. The small lateral roots and the end of the taproot usually shrivel and die. Affected plants are somewhat stunted and grow more slowly than healthy plants. Later a cluster of fibrous roots may form just under the soil surface and above the stem decay. These roots frequently keep the plant alive—but in a weakened state—until harvest. Unless soil moisture is deficient, an almost normal crop may be produced. If extended dry weather occurs, the leaves turn yellow and drop prematurely, and pods are few and poorly filled. In severe attacks, many plants are killed, reducing the number of plants in the row.

This strain of Fusarium fungus attacks only beans. It lives between seasons in bean straw and manure. Once it is introduced it may live indefinitely in the soil even though the land is not planted to beans.

2. Rhizoctonia (Pellicularia) Root Rot and Stem Canker, Damping-off (Rhizoctonia solani — Pellicularia filamentosa)

Young bean seedlings wilt and collapse (damp-off) from a water-soaked rotting of the stem near the soil line, or they may be twisted and stunted. Adjoining plants may later become affected. Stem cankers are reddish-brown to brick-red, are slightly sunken, and extend lengthwise on the stem. The stem-pith of diseased plants may also turn brick-red. Affected plants are often stunted, and their leaves turn yellow.

Rhizoctonia is found in practically all agricultural soils. This fungus is capable of attacking several hundred different kinds of plants, including all known vegetables.

3. Pythium Root Rots, Damping-off (Pythium spp.)

Seedlings wilt quickly and die (damp-off) from a watery rot that is colorless to dark brown. The slimy outer tissue of the stem slips easily from the central core. When half-mature plants become infected, they may survive for a week or more, but eventually they wilt and die. In hot, moist weather, they may wilt and die rapidly from a soft rot of the stem at the soil line.

A number of species of this common soil-borne fungus attack beans and a wide variety of other plants, especially in the seedling stage.

CONTROL

1. Practice a four- or five-year—or preferably longer—rotation between bean crops. Where feasible, include grasses, cereals, and green manure crops in the rotation.
2. Cut all cover crops and let them dry completely. Plow six to eight weeks before planting.
3. Plant certified, disease-free seed as shallow as soil moisture will permit.
4. Plant only in warm, well-prepared, well-drained, and well-fertilized soil capable of supporting excellent vine growth. Fertilize on basis of soil test.
5. Avoid deep and close cultivation, which shears off fibrous roots and provides wounds through which the causal fungi may enter.
6. Do not feed infected bean straw and refuse to livestock or use it for bedding.
7. In the fall, cleanly plow down all diseased bean refuse left on the field.
8. In the future this disease complex will probably be controlled by applying a broad-spectrum soil fungicide in the furrow at planting time. At present no fungicide recommendations can be made, as results to date have been somewhat erratic. No current fungicide controls all root and stem rots of beans. In many tests, spraying or dusting a 50-50 mixture of PCNB (Terraclor) and captan into the furrow at seeding time has given good control of Rhizoctonia (Pellicularia) root and stem rot. Improved standards have often resulted. Do not expect protection for more than a week or two after the bean seed germinates. Use 1-to-1 mixtures of PCNB and captan according to the manufacturer's directions.

COMMON CORN SMUT

By Malcolm C. Shurtleff and A. L. Hooker
Department of Plant Pathology, University of Illinois at Urbana-Champaign

Common corn smut, caused by the fungus Ustilago maydis, is a disease well known to most corn growers. The smut fungus attacks only corn—field (dent and flint), Indian or ornamental, popcorn, and sweet—and the closely rated teosinte (Zea Mexicana). Common corn smut is most destructive to sweet corn. It is most prevalent on plants that have been injured by detasseling, hail, insects, or cultivation or spraying equipment.

Losses from smut are variable and rather difficult to measure, ranging from a trace up to 6 percent or more in localized areas. In rare cases the loss in an individual field of sweet corn may reach 100 percent. The number, size, and location of the smut galls or "boils" on a plant affect the amount of yield loss. Reduction is greatest when large galls are located on or above the ear. Smut also increases barrenness or sterility in diseased plants. Galls resulting from detasseling are usually small and generally cause little damage.

Heaviest smut infection generally occurs when rainfall is light during early stages of growth, followed by moderate rainfall. Vigorous plants are most susceptible but may escape the more serious effects of smut because of their rapid growth. Corn grown on soil that is particularly high in nitrogen and organic matter frequently shows more smut than corn grown on soil that is well balanced in fertility.

Smut galls are not poisonous to animals except as they increase the dust content of dry fodder.

SYMPTOMS

Common corn smut is easily recognized and is probably the best known disease of corn. All actively growing or embryonic corn tissue above ground is susceptible. Galls are commonly found on the tassels, husks, ears and kernels, stalks, leaves, axillary buds, and rarely the aerial roots. As the smut galls enlarge, they are covered with a glistening, greenish-to-silvery-white membrane. Later the inner tissue darkens as a result of spore formation. Mature galls are five inches or more in diameter and are filled with millions of microscopic, black, greasy to powdery spores. These teliospores (chalmydospores) are released when the white outer membrane of the gall ruptures at maturity. The spores, easily blown long distances by the wind, perpetuate the smut fungus overwinter.

When animals eat "smutty" stalks, leaves, and ears, the spores may remain alive in passing through the animal's alimentary canal and be carried in the manure. When infested manure is spread on crop land, sporidia produced by the germinating teliospores may be blown or washed to the surface of a corn plant, germinate, and cause infection. The time interval between infection and the formation of mature galls varies from one to three weeks or more. Spores formed in the first smut galls may germinate and infect the same or other corn plants. Galls form and spores disseminate more or less continuously through the summer growing period.

Smut spores are killed by the acids in silage.

Control

1. Avoid mechanical injuries to the plant when cultivating or spraying.
2. Corn hybrids differ in apparent resistance. Choosing the best-adapted resistant hybrids and varieties available is the most feasible means of controlling smut. These types possess substantial resistance to many biotypes of the corn-smut fungus. In general, corn breeders should avoid using very smut-susceptible inbreds and their hybrids or varieties in their breeding programs. The difference in apparent resistance between corn lines is often based on protection given by the sheath and husks.
3. Maintain a well-balanced soil fertility program based on a soil test.
4. Protection against corn insects, e.g., corn earworm and European corn borer, by timely DDT or sevin sprays, often decreases the incidence of smut in sweet corn.
5. In home gardens, cut out and destroy galls before the smut "boils" rupture and spores are released.
6. Seed treatment is not effective.

TIPBURN

TIPBURN OF LETTUCE AND ENDIVE

By M.C. Shurtleff, J.W. Courter, and B.J. Jacobsen
Department of Plant Pathology, University of Illinois at Urbana-Champaign

Tipburn is a non-infectious disease that may occur suddenly and destructively wherever lettuce, endive, and escarole mature during warm to hot (70 degrees F. or above), cloudy, humid weather followed by bright, sunny days. It is common in home gardens and greenhouses in Illinois.

Tipburn develops on leaf lettuce only under unusual conditions, and commonly not on crisphead varieties until the plants begin to develop a solid head. It usually appears just before the plants are ready to harvest. It detracts from the appearance of lettuce and related salad crops, and when it is severe they are unsalable. Injury seldom occurs in young plants or in the young leaves of older plants.

Environment conditions that promote rapid succulent growth and the accumulation of toxic soluble salts in the guttation water on the edges of the leaves predispose plants to tipburn. The most important of these conditions are high soil fertility (especially high nitrogen), inadequate ventilation, high soil moisture or a fluctuating soil moisture, night temperatures above 65 degrees F., high relative humidity, and low temperatures during early development followed by relatively high temperatures at maturity. The interrelations of soil and air are still not fully understood.

When conditions favor rapid absorption of water by the plant and transpiration (loss of water vapor from the leaves) is reduced, droplets of guttation water form along the edges of the leaves. These droplets contain significant amounts of salts and organic acids. Tipburn occurs when these soluble salts become concentrated along the leaf margins.

Symptoms

The first symptom is the appearance of translucent or water-soaked specks between the larger veins and about ¼ inch from the edge of the leaf. These specks soon turn into small, dead, brown to black spots that may increase in number and size until the entire leaf margin wilts and turns brown to black and leathery. Ordinarily only a few leaves of the head are affected. In leaf and Bibb types, tipburn may appear on any of the leaves. In tight-headed varieties, it is usually most severe on the outer leaves. It may also appear later on the inner leaves as a browning of the leaf margins and veins. Damage is not apparent until the head is cut open or the outer leaves are removed. Under prolonged favorable conditions for tipburn, most of the leaves in the head are affected. When conditions are favorable for only short periods, the new leaves may develop normally, though the damaged leaves do not recover.

Various rot-producing bacteria and fungi may enter the killed marginal tissues—especially on the inner leaves—in warm, moist weather and produce a wet rot or slime. Rotting may progress until the entire head is destroyed.

Most types of lettuce are susceptible to tipburn, although partly resistant varieties and strains of crisphead and leaf lettuce have been developed. Butterhead and Cos or Romaine varieties are generally very susceptible. Under favorable conditions for the development of tipburn, even the most resistant varieties show typical symptoms.

CONTROL

1. Where possible, sow lettuce varieties and strains that are tolerant or resistant to tipburn. Although many varieties of head lettuce have resistance, they are not well adapted to Illinois.
2. In the home garden, grow lettuce during the cool spring and fall.
3. In greenhouses, grow leaf lettuce at night temperatures of 45 to 50 degrees F. and Bibb lettuce at 50 to 55 degrees F. When possible, maintain day temperatures of 60 to 70 degrees F.
4. Grow lettuce in soils that do not favor excessively rapid succulent growth. Plant in deep, well-drained, well-tilled, mellow soil. Avoid soils having high levels of soluble salts.
5. Space and thin plants for good aeration. In greenhouses, ventilate to maintain proper temperature and, equally important, to maintain adequate levels of carbon dioxide. Maximum ventilation is desirable.
6. Avoid excessive fertilization, especially with materials containing large amounts of quickly available nitrogen, e.g., ammonium nitrate, sodium nitrate, urea, and ammonium sulfate. In greenhouses, keep the soluble salt content of the soil as low as possible.
7. Water sparingly as lettuce, endive, and escarole approach maturity, especially during cloudy, humid, warm weather.

BEES

How To Move Bees

Elbert R. Jaycox

Elbert R. Jaycox, Extension Apiculturist, Department of Horticulture, University of Illinois, Urbana-Champaign Campus

Moving bees is a relatively easy job if you know the right way to do it. This job usually requires some hard work if you have to lift heavy hives by hand, but you can quickly learn to keep the bees under control.

Bees can be moved most easily at night, any time after they have quit flying. Cool, rainy days with temperatures low enough to keep the bees in the hive are also suitable for short moves. At night, there is time enough to get the job done before the bees want to fly again. You do not have that advantage if you move bees in the early morning while it is cool, but it is sometimes easier and more convenient to do it then.

If there are only a few hives to move, you may want to cleat, staple, or band them to hold the hive parts together. Since whatever method you use will disturb the colony, do it well in advance of moving so that the bees will have time to calm down. Use liberal quantities of cool smoke at the entrance and at any other openings in the hive when you do the job. The hive can be closed with a folded piece of wire screening pushed into the entrance. The screen is easy to remove later—an advantage when you reach your destination. Close any other openings with grass, rags, or masking tape. It is easier and less work to move a large number of hives with their entrances open and without any special preparation. When doing so, you must use your smoker to keep the bees under control.

The proper use of smoke is the most important part of the moving job. Use it liberally. Keep the smoker well filled and tamped down, so the smoke stays cool. Obviously, you can dispense with smoke on screened colonies until you are ready to remove the screens. When you are ready to screen the hives, or to lead unscreened ones into a vehicle, smoke all the entrances heavily. Wait two or three minutes for it to take effect. Be sure that no bees remain outside the hives entrances. Insert the screens if you are using them. As you put open hives into the vehicle, smoke them again after they are in place. Do not hesitate to smoke a hive any time you see bees coming out of it. The car or truck should have the lights off and the motor running while you are loading. The engine vibration helps quiet the bees.

Place the hives as close together as possible in the vehicle. This keeps them from moving around enroute to the new location. They should be tied down to hold them in place and to keep the lids on. When you tie, be careful that you do not split the hives open. Smoke the entire load before tying it. Face the hive entrances forward if you are moving more than three or four colonies.

When you reach your destination, leave the engine running, turn off the lights, and relight the smoker. Do not slam the doors. Smoke the hives liberally, untie them, and unload them from the vehicle. Colonies in open hives may have clustered outside the entrances. If so, smoke them and wait long enough for the bees to go back into their hives. A fine spray of water will also help get them back inside the hives. In extremely hot weather or after a long, rough ride, the bees may be so heavily clustered that it would be best to wait until early morning to unload them.

Arrange the hives in an irregular pattern as you unload them. This helps reduce any drifting of bees between hives. Remove any screens, using smoke, before leaving the apiary.

Bees become familiar with the area around their hives. If the hive is moved only a short distance, many will return somewhat "mechanically" to the old location. Move your hives at least two miles, if you can, to prevent this. Otherwise, move them as far as you can; if necessary, kill any bees that become a nuisance at the old site.

Additional information about moving bees, and about beekeeping in general, is available in Circular 1000, BEEKEEPING IN ILLINOIS, Cooperative Extension Service, University of Illinois at Urbana-Champaign, 1969. Copies of this 132-page book are available for $1 from your county Extension adviser or from the Office of Agricultural Publications, 123 Mumford Hall, University of Illinois at Urbana-Champaign, Urbana, Illinois 61801.

PESTICIDES
and
HONEY BEES

By Elbert R. Jaycox
University of Illinois at Urbana-Champaign
College of Agriculture
Cooperative Extension Service

Many PESTICIDES that are necessary in crop production are highly toxic to honey bees. Properly used, the materials benefit beekeepers as well as farmers by providing greater acreages of plants capable of producing food for bees, livestock, and people, instead of being damaged or eaten by pests. Bee losses from pesticides cannot be entirely avoided but they can be minimized by the cooperative efforts of spray operators, beekeepers, and farmers.

Where to start

Proper dosages of pesticides and adherence to the recommendations on the label are the first considerations in preventing losses of bees as well as avoiding injury to people and farm animals. In any case, highly toxic materials should not be applied to any flowering plants on which honey bees are working. If an application must be made, consider whether the bee colonies can be moved or other, less toxic materials and better timing can be used. These measures may control the insect pest with less danger to bees.

Methods of application

Ground application of pesticides is generally safer for bees than air application. The hazard from air application may be somewhat reduced by not turning the aircraft over blooming crops or transporting materials across them. Applications of pesticides to large areas, as in the control of grasshoppers, mosquitoes, armyworms, and cereal leaf beetles, and repeated applications to limited areas, increase the hazard to honey bees.

COLLEGE OF AGRICULTURE
DEPARTMENT OF HORTICULTURE

CONSTRUCTION DETAILS
10-FRAME BEE HIVE
(¾-inch-thick lumber)

Detail of cover construction

A — Saw kerf with tin or roofing paper strip set in before nailing and gluing.

COVER 19⅞" 16¼" 1 x 4 cleat

SHALLOW HIVE BODY 5¾" 19⅞" 16¼"

SHALLOW FRAME — As below but 5-3/8" deep.

DADANT OR ILLINOIS DEPTH HIVE BODY 6⅝" 19⅞" 16¼"

DADANT DEPTH FRAME

DEEP HIVE BODY 9⅝" 19⅞" 16¼"

1 x 2 cleat optional in place of handhold

Inside dimensions
L - 18-3/8"
W - 14-3/4"
D - 9-5/8"

DEEP FRAME

BOTTOM (Should be treated with wood preservative such as pentachlorophenol.) ¾" ⅜" 19⅞" 21¾" 16¼" 1 x 4 or 2 x 2 cleat

Detail of frame rest
Rabbeted corners, not dovetailed.

Selection of materials

The formulation of the material plays an important role in its toxicity to bees. In general, sprays are safer than dusts, and emulsifiable concentrates are less toxic than wettable powders. Granular materials usually are not hazardous to bees. At present there are no safe, effective repellents that can be used to keep bees away from treated areas.

Fungicides, acaricides (miticides), herbicides, and blossom thinners are relatively nontoxic. These materials and the insecticides can be placed in three groups in relation to their effects on bees.

Highly toxic. This group includes materials that kill bees on contact during application and for one or more days after treatment. Bees should be moved from the area if highly toxic materials are used on plants the bees are visiting. This group includes:

aldrin	heptachlor
arsenicals	Imidan
azinphosethyl	lindane
(Ethyl Guthion)	malathion, conventional
azinphosmethyl (Guthion)	malathion, low volume
Azodrin	Matacil
BHC	Metacide
Bidrin	methomyl (Lannate)
Bomyl	methyl parathion
carbaryl (Sevin)	Methyl Trithion
chlordane	mevinphos (Phosdrin)[a]
diazinon	Mobam
dichlorvos (DDVP, Vapona)[a]	naled (Dibrom)[a]
dieldrin	parathion
dimethoate	phosphamidon
EPN	tepp[a]
fenthion (Baytex)	Zectran
Gardona	Zinophos

[a] Short residual activity. Can usually be applied safely when bees are not in flight. Do not apply over hives.

Moderately toxic. These materials can be used with limited damage to bees if not applied over bees in the field or at the hives. Correct dosage, timing, and method of application are essential. This group includes:

carbophenothion (Trithion)	mirex
DDT	oxydemetonmethyl
demeton (Systox)	(Meta Systox R)
disulfoton (Di-Syston)	Perthane
endosulfan (Thiodan)	phorate
endrin	tartar emetic
Galecron (Fundal)	TDE
methyl demeton	
(Meta Systox)	

Relatively nontoxic. Materials in this group can be used around bees with few precautions and a minimum of injury to bees. The greatest number of materials are in this group which includes:

allethrin	dinocap (Karathane)
Aramite	dioxathion (Delnav)
Bacillus thuringiensis	dodine (Cyprex)
binapacryl (Morocide)	Dyrene
Bordeaux mixture	ethion
captan	fenson
chlorbenside	ferbam (Fermate)
chlorobenzilate	folpet (Phaltan)
chloropropylate	Genite 923
copper compounds	glyodin
cryolite	maneb
Dessin	methoxychlor
dicofol (Kelthane)	Morestan
Dimite (DMC)	nabam
dinitrocyclohexylphenol	nicotine
(DNOCHP)	Omite

-Dewhurst's hive.

ovex	sulfur
Pentac	tetradifon (Tedion)
Polyram	toxaphene
pyrethrum	trichlorfon (Dylox)
rotenone	zineb
sabadilla[a]	ziram
Strobane	

[a] Twenty-percent dust may cause bee losses.

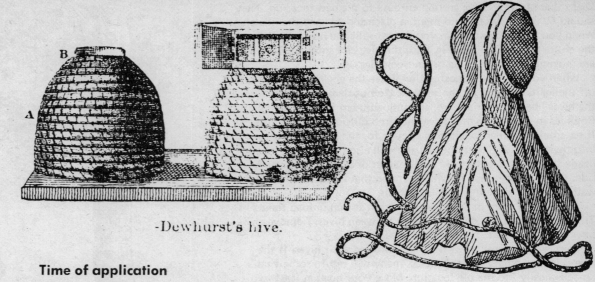

-Dewhurst's hive.

Time of application

The proper timing of applications allows the use of the moderately toxic materials on crops visited by bees. Applications can be made between 7 p.m. and 7 a.m. when bees are not foraging. Evening applications are safer than early morning applications except when they are made over or near apiaries on hot nights when bees may be clustered on the fronts of the hives. Adjustments in timing may also be necessary on warm mornings when bees are flying earlier than usual. Some crops, such as sweet corn and cucurbits (melons, squash), shed pollen early in the day. By 4 p.m. they are unattractive and are no longer visited by bees.

Oblique piece to elevate a village hive.

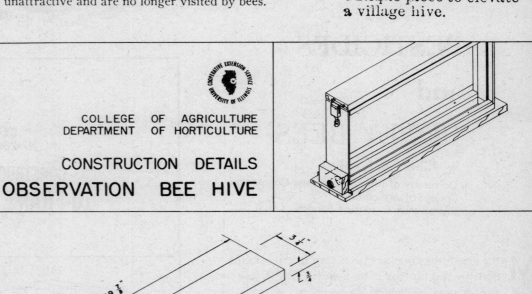

COLLEGE OF AGRICULTURE
DEPARTMENT OF HORTICULTURE

CONSTRUCTION DETAILS
OBSERVATION BEE HIVE

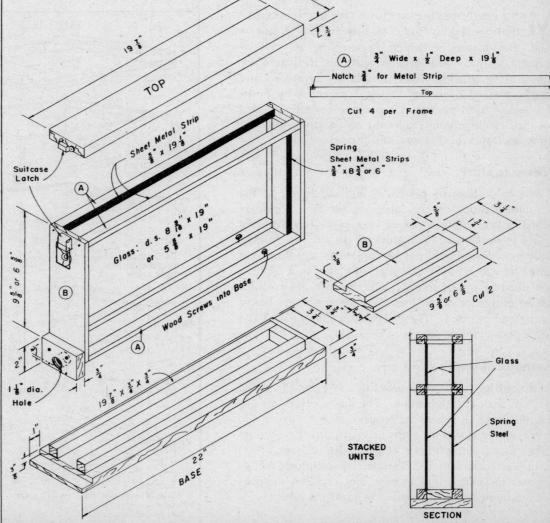

Plants that may present problems

Treatments that include any of the following crops and wild plants may create bee poisoning problems.

— Legume seed crops in bloom (sweetclover, red clover, lespedeza).

— Cucurbits in bloom (squash, cucumber, cantaloupe, watermelon).

— Vegetable seed crops in bloom (onion, carrot, asparagus).

— Cut-flower and flower seed crops in bloom.

— Cover crops in bloom beneath orchard trees (white clover, chicory, dandelion).

— Weeds in bloom in grain fields (mustard).

— Sorghum and corn, especially sweet corn, when shedding pollen.

— Soybeans in bloom after July 15.

— Cotton throughout the season (blooms and extrafloral nectaries).

Other hazards to bees

Although most bee losses result from their visits to treated blossoms, they may also occur when bees collect water or honeydew (sweet insect secretions) from

foliage or other objects in the treated area. Drift of pesticides over apiaries or onto blooming nontarget crops may be just as lethal as direct application.

Exchange of information

The prevention of bee losses is the joint responsibility of the spray operator, the farmer, and the beekeeper. It is fostered by mutual understanding and cooperation which includes the exchange of information before pesticides damaging to bees are used. Prior notice to the beekeeper is essential to allow him to arrange for protection or movement of his colonies. In many cases the bees cannot be moved because of wet ground, the weight of individual colonies, or the lack of alternative apiary sites.

The beekeeper's obligation

The beekeeper's responsibility for preventing pesticide damage to his bees begins when he establishes an apiary, either permanently or for crop pollination. He should familiarize himself with the cropping practices in the area and the pest-control methods in use. In some cases he can *expect* damage to his bees and, if so, he must weigh the risk against the anticipated returns from honey or pollination fees. Pest-control operations in orchards and on cotton, lima beans, and sweet corn have made many areas off-limits to bees. Bees for fruit pollination should be held in locations away from the orchards until prebloom spraying is completed and trees are 10 to 25 percent in bloom. Bees should be moved out of the orchard after three or four days of good pollinating weather, thereby avoiding the calyx sprays.

In emergency situations bees can be confined to their hives for short periods. This is practical only for applications of materials with short residual toxicity that must be applied to a blooming crop with bee hives in the field or nearby. Loose-fitting covers are placed over the hives during the night or early morning when the bees are not flying. They are removed two or three hours after the application or at least by midmorning. Black polyethylene sheeting is most commonly used but burlap is better if the colonies are not directly exposed to the spray. Confinement for longer periods — a day or more — is possible by keeping the burlap covers damp.

Beekeepers should always provide their name, address, and telephone number to owners of land on which their apiaries are located for notification of farm operations affecting their bees. All apiaries should be identified by a placard bearing the owner's name, address, and telephone number in letters legible at a distance of 50 feet or more. Such signs often deter vandalism and are valuable when people wish to contact the apiary owner.

The growing complexity of farming places additional responsibility on the beekeeper. He should be familiar with commonly used pesticides and their toxicity to bees. He should also know as much as possible about the relations of his bees to the nectar and pollen plants in his territory. For example, the beekeeper must be aware that bees collect pollen on corn and melons primarily in the morning. He should also expect to find bees visiting soybean blossoms in late July and early August when other legumes become less attractive. Only with such information can he take an active part in minimizing losses of bees from pesticides.

Additional sources of information

County extension advisers and extension specialists in apiculture and entomology can provide additional information about honey bees and pesticides. The following publications, as well as others by the same authors, are valuable sources of information about the toxicity of specific compounds.

L. D. Anderson and E. L. Atkins, Jr. Toxicity of pesticides and other agricultural chemicals to honey bees. California Agricultural Extension Service AXT-251. 1967.

Entomology Research Division, U.S. Department of Agriculture. Protecting honey bees from pesticides. Leaflet 544. 1968.

Carl Johansen and A. H. Retan. Insecticide toxicity to honey bees. Washington Cooperative Extension Service E.M. 2805. 1967.

HOW TO FEED BEES

-Bee Louse,
seen from above.

-Bee-Louse,
seen from below.

By William P. Nye, George F. Knowlton and Reed S. Roberts

Every beekeeper has to feed his bees at some time. He may feed them to keep them from starving or to stimulate them to rear brood. Stimulation of brood rearing is practical only in areas where the honey flow comes very early.

The best way to feed bees is to leave combs containing 50 to 60 pounds or more of honey with them when the honey crop is harvested. If this is done, rarely will it be necessary to feed them during the following spring. Occasionally, a poor season will not permit the bees to store enough honey, even for winter. On the other hand, the beekeeper sometimes takes away more honey than he realizes or an unusual winter causes the bees to consume more honey than usual. In either case, feeding becomes necessary. If extra combs of disease-free sealed honey are not available, the bees should be fed sugar syrup.

Feed the Bees Sugar Syrup

Fall feeding of the bees in preparation for winter requires a thick syrup, made by mixing and stirring two parts of sugar with one part of hot water until the mixture is completely dissolved. The syrup fed in the spring is usually thinner, the proportions being equal parts of sugar and water. An even thinner solution is used for stimulative feeding in the spring by mixing two parts of water with one part of sugar.

Kinds of Bee Feeders

A large number of different bee feeders have been devised. The simpler ones are the best and most commonly used. The Boardman Entrance Feeder is a block that can be inserted into the entrance of a hive. It holds an inverted canning jar which has several small holes punched in the lid, allowing the syrup to escape only as fast as the bees can consume it. The syrup is held in place by atmospheric pressure just as in poultry waterers. This feeder can be examined and refilled without disturbing the bees. Its main disadvantage is that in cool weather the bees will not go down to the entrance to get the syrup. Boardman Feeders can be purchased from bee supply firms.

Another feeder in common use, which also utilizes the atmospheric pressure principle, is made from a friction-top can, such as a 5 or 10 pound honey pail. Holes are punched in the lid with a 3-penny nail. For slow stimulative feeding of thin syrup, two or three small holes will do. If the beekeeper wants the bees to take substantial quantities of heavy syrup as fast as possible, 30 or 40 holes about 1/16 inch in diameter are necessary. When the can is filled with warm syrup, it should be inverted over the frames and wrapped in a burlap sack to conserve the heat.

Then, an empty hive body should be placed over the can(s) with the hive cover on top. To feed a colony for winter, the bees can be given two or three cans at once. Some commercial beekeepers merely have a 3/4 inch hole in the cover and invert the can of syrup over it with a stone on top to hold it down when empty.

Another type of feeder used by some beekeepers is the division board feeder. This consists of a water-tight box the size and shape of a frame which hangs in a hive in place of a frame. It is usually left in place all year. When feeding is necessary, the hives are open and syrup is poured into the feeders. A stick floating on the surface of the syrup prevents the bees from drowning.

FEEDING BEES DRY SUGAR

Under some conditions bees can be fed dry sugar with safety. This is one of the easiest ways to feed them. The procedure is as follows. Spread a sheet of newspaper over the frames and punch a hole or two in it with a pencil. Pour about 3 to 5 pounds of dry, granulated sugar on the newspaper and spread it evenly. Since the cover probably won't fit down over the sugar, it may be necessary to put a wooden frame or shallow super under the cover.

The best time to use dry sugar is early in the spring. The bees must be able to get water in order to utilize the sugar. If there isn't sufficient water in the hive from condensation, they must be able to fly every day and get it. Under these conditions, feeding dry sugar works well and avoids excitement.

HAND-LIGHT WASP TRAP.

DESTROYING
BEES and WASPS

By Elbert R. Jaycox
University of Illinois at Urbana-Champaign
College of Agriculture
Cooperative Extension Service

-Debeauvoy's bee-box, with sloping roof and shelves.

-Vertical frame of box

-Feburier's bee-box, with vertical division and sloping roof.

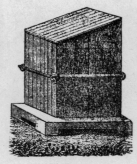
-Huber's experimental leaf-hive.

Bees and wasps are two of the insects most beneficial to man. Bees produce honey and wax, and serve as important pollinators; wasps attack and destroy many kinds of harmful insects including flies and caterpillars. In spite of their value, several kinds of bees and wasps are unwelcome in and around buildings because of their ability to sting and their tendency to defend their nests. Wasps are rather similar to bees in appearance, and honey bees are often blamed for the misdeeds of some of the social wasps such as the hornets and yellow jackets. Wasps can sting repeatedly while the honey bee stings only once and leaves a stinger at the site of the sting.

Both wasps and bees can be readily controlled with insecticides. Honey bees present more serious removal problems because of the larger size of their colonies and their tendency to nest within the walls of buildings.

Honey bee swarms

In spring and early summer, honey bee colonies divide by swarming. Half or more of the worker bees leave their home to begin a new colony, usually with their old queen. They cluster temporarily on some object such as a tree branch for a period of a few hours to several days, and then enter a new home such as a hollow tree or the wall of a building.

Swarms are not usually a problem unless they land in an inconvenient spot or if they are molested. They are best left alone until they leave. Otherwise, contact the local police department or other agencies for the names of beekeepers willing to collect swarms. The low value of the bees themselves and other problems of collecting swarms have forced many beekeepers to charge for the service. An alternative is to have the bees killed by a pest-control operator who will also

Insecticide sprays and dusts

Spray formulation	*Amount / gallon water*
Carbaryl (Sevin)	
50-percent wettable powder	2 tablespoons
Chlordane	
45-percent emulsifiable concentrate	2 tablespoons
72-percent emulsifiable concentrate	1 tablespoon
40-percent wettable powder	2 tablespoons
Lindane	
25-percent wettable powder	2 tablespoons
Malathion	
50- to 57-percent emulsifiable concentrate	2 teaspoons
25-percent wettable powder	1 tablespoon

Dust formulations
Carbaryl (Sevin) — 5-percent
Chlordane — 5-percent
Lindane — 1-percent
Malathion — 4- or 5-percent

Precautions

The insecticides listed here may be injurious to man and other animals if used improperly. Use them only when needed, and handle and store them with care. Bees and wasps are highly beneficial insects. Kill only those that may be a hazard to people around your home, farm, or place of business.

Other bees

Bumble bees are occasionally a problem when they nest in and around buildings or near walks. They like to nest in old mattresses, car cushions, and other places such as mouse nests. The colonies vary widely in disposition and size, with rarely more than a few hundred bees. They can be killed by insecticide dust or spray applied to the nest at night. Use the same compounds suggested for use on honey bees.

Carpenter bees are large metallic-colored bees similar in size and general appearance to bumble bees. They are solitary bees that rarely sting, but often frighten people when they bore holes and nest in redwood or other soft woods around a home. They can be killed by injecting insecticide dust, spray, or aerosol into their individual nest holes. Use the materials suggested for honey bees.

Wasps

Hornets, yellow jackets, and paper wasps are social wasps that build gray-colored paper nests in the open or under ground. They often sting people who approach nests located under eaves, in shrubbery, or in underground cavities near buildings or walks. Solitary wasps, even the very large cicada-killer wasp that nests in the ground, rarely sting unless they are handled or get caught in your clothing. They have no instinct to protect their nests as the social species do.

Nests above ground should be sprayed at night with chlordane or lindane. Mix the spray from emulsifiable concentrate or wettable powder. Aerosol spray cans are not suitable for this purpose. Underground nests can be treated by spraying or dusting the same materials into the entrance at night. Cover the entrance with a shovelful of moist soil after treatment.

charge for doing the job. If one person agrees to come for the bees, do not contact other people about doing the same job.

Honey bees in buildings

When a swarm enters a building, it begins to build combs of wax in which to rear young bees and store honey. Only at this time, when the bees first enter, can they be killed without having to open the wall and remove large quantities of dead bees, wax, and honey. If the colony has been in place as long as a month, it must be removed after it is killed, to prevent problems from the odors of decaying bees, other insect pests entering the wall, and honey released within the wall as combs melt or are destroyed by other insects or mice.

Insecticides are the safest and most satisfactory materials for killing bees in buildings. Do not use fumigants or other poisonous or flammable compounds. Carbaryl (Sevin), chlordane, lindane, and malathion are most suitable. *All of them are toxic to humans and must be used with care according to the directions on the container label.*

Before applying an insecticide, you must know the location of the colony in the wall, especially in relation to the flight entrance. In many cases, the colony's nest is far enough away from the entrance that insecticides applied at the entrance will not reach the bees. The bees' nest should be located by tapping on the wall at night and listening for the area of loudest buzzing sounds. The bees keep the nest center at about 95° F., a temperature high enough to warm the wall beside it so that you may be able to feel as well as hear the nest location.

Either dust or spray formulations can be used within walls or other cavities, but dusts generally disperse better within them. Apply the insecticide at night through the entrance hole if the colony is fairly close to it in the wall. Otherwise, drill a hole in the wall above the colony and apply the dust or spray through it. Afterwards, seal the hole and all other holes through which bees might enter or leave the wall. An extremely large colony may require an additional treatment after about 10 days to kill emerging young bees.

After all sound and flight activity have ceased, or at least within 2 weeks, open the wall and remove all dead bees, combs, and honey. These must be burned or buried because they are attractive to other bees and are toxic to both bees and people. Do not expose the honey and wax where other bees can reach it or you may damage valuable honey bee colonies nearby. The location within the wall will be attractive to other swarms unless it is sealed tightly to keep them out. An additional application of lindane or chlordane spray will also help to prevent the entry of another swarm.

There is an element of risk, or at least uncertainty, in dealing with bees, and you may prefer to have the job done either by a competent pest-control operator or an experienced beekeeper. No matter who does the job, it may pose problems and considerable expense, at least in man-hours of labor. Systems of trapping the bees or removing them alive from the wall usually are not satisfactory and are not recommended.

When bees or wasps enter a room or an automobile, they rarely sting and usually fly to a window. In a room they can be killed with an aerosol spray containing one of the insecticides mentioned above. If a bee enters your car, remain calm, stop the car, and open the windows to let it out. A bee or wasp on the windshield or rear window may have to be "herded" out with a map or newspaper, or crushed quickly with a handkerchief or wad of paper.

MUSHROOM CULTURE

Compiled by L. V. Busch
Department of Environmental Biology
University of Guelph

This guide on mushroom culture has been prepared for the amateur grower. Its purpose is to present to the prospective producer the basic techniques of mushroom culture which have been used successfully, and to assist him in starting in an economical way.

Careful consideration must be given to the following if a good crop is expected: (a) location of mushroom beds; (b) manure or compost in which the mushrooms are grown; (c) spawn; and (d) temperature. Casual attention to any one of these essentials means failure.

LOCATION OF MUSHROOM BEDS

For the amateur the best location is the cellar, basement of a barn, or any tight, light-proof, well-ventilated building. The following conditions must be met to assure a reasonably good yield.

1. Easy ventilation of the room is necessary because a steady supply of fresh air is required for good growth.

2. Direct sunlight must not fall on the bed.

3. An air temperature not above 68 degrees F. nor below freezing is required after casing the beds. Insulated walls will prevent rapid fluctuations in temperature.

4. Atmosphere must not be too humid, a relative humidity of 70% being recommended.

PREPARING THE COMPOST

Originally only horse manure was used for the growing of mushrooms. However, due to the difficulty of obtaining this product, other materials have lately been used with considerable success. Both methods are given below.

1. Horse Manure Compost

Horse manure containing a moderate amount of straw is the best material in which to grow mushrooms. Too much straw in the manure must be avoided since this tends to dry out and cool off the compost during fermentation.

The amount of manure required will depend upon the kind of manure, the length of time it has been composted and the depth of the beds. A ton of fresh manure composted about four weeks will fill about 100 sq ft of bed 6 inches deep. If composted for 2 to 3 weeks, a ton of fresh manure will fill about 120 to 150 sq ft of bed 6 inches deep.

MUSHROOMS.

To prepare the compost, the manure is piled neatly and carefully outside, preferably under shelter, with the edges of the pile square and the top level. The size of the pile will depend on the amount of compost desired; however, it is well to remember that too small a pile will not cure properly. Be sure the pile is firm, but do not pack too tightly. Let the pile stand about a week, at which time the temperature at the center should be about 150 to 170 degrees F. The pile is now ready for turning; make sure that all lumps are broken up and that the manure on the outside of the pile is placed in the center of the new pile. The manure should feel moist to the hand but not wet; squeeze a handful—if it moistens the palm but no drops ooze out between the fingers, the moisture content is correct. When the compost is too dry a careful watering of the drier areas will prove beneficial, but one must avoid over-wetting. At each turning, the pile should be constructed as above. The manure is turned every 5 to 7 days until sufficiently fermented to be placed in the beds; the number of turnings usually varies between 3 to 5 times. At this time the following points may be noted.

A. The compost should be brown in color.

B. Lumps, when twisted in the hands, break apart, and the straw is no longer tough and fibrous.

C. The compost should not have an objectionable, sour or rancid odor.

VIEW OF A MUSHROOM BED

2. Synthetic Compost

By synthetic compost is meant the making of compost other than horse manure. Since it is a substitute, mushroom production must equal that obtainable from horse manure, the cost must be no greater, and the compost must be reproducible from one mix to the next. This is possible by using the following method developed by the Department of Botany and Plant Pathology of the Pennsylvania State University.

The basic ingredients are loosely crushed corncobs and a hay mixture, preferably one containing some clover. The hay is not chopped, and should be cut and cured at the best stage for feeding. The amount of hay and corncobs may vary between 2/3 hay and 1/3 cobs to 1/3 hay and 2/3 cobs.

A ton of dry hay-corncob mixture will fill approximately 300 sq ft of bed 6 inches deep. Again the length of time of composting will have considerable influence on the amount of bed space actually filled. The longer the material is composted, the less bulk there is left to place in the beds.

Procedure

The hay is wetted thoroughly and piled in as large a pile as possible. It is tightly packed, and the cobs, which also have been soaked, are placed on top. The pile is first turned at the end of 2 or 3 days, and completely soaked, again packing the pile. After another 2 to 3 days the pile is given its second turning, and for each ton of dry cob-hay mixture the following are added:

1. 25 lb. potassium chloride
2. 30 lb. calcium cyanamid OR urea OR 25 lb. ammonium nitrate
3. 50 lb. gypsum
4. a maximum of 75 lb. dry brewer's grain OR 300 lb. chicken manure.

The amount of brewer's grain or chicken manure is varied, depending upon the amount of clover which was present in the original hay; the more clover, the less grain or chicken manure required (e.g. no clover, use the full amount of grain or chicken manure; 100% clover, use no grain or chicken manure). The new pile should not be packed except in very cold weather or when using very coarse hay. In 3 or 4 days after all the ingredients have been added, turn the pile for the third time. It should be very hot at this time, frequently above 175 degrees F., and have a distinct ammonia smell. The hay does not become very soft, but does darken; the cobs turn quite soft and are almost black in color. After another 2 or 3 days the compost is ready to put into the beds or trays. At this time the compost should contain all the water it will hold. The total time from the start until the beds are filled varies from 8 to 12 days. (Before filling the beds see the section on cleaning and fumigating the house.)

After the beds are filled, try to hold the temperature of the compost at 140 degrees F. until all odor of ammonia has disappeared. This is sometimes difficult to do, and much more fresh air will be required than with manure. The beds should be ready for spawning 3 to 7 days after filling, at which time the temperature is dropped by ventilating the room until 70 to 80 degrees F. is reached. Remember that a high moisture content is essential for good results with synthetic compost. Once the beds are ready for spawning, the procedures are exactly the same as those used for manure compost.

Recently a method for producing mushrooms using sawdust has been developed by the University of Florida. If interested, write for "The Production of Mushrooms from Sawdust", Florida Engineering and Industrial Experiment Station, College of Education, University of Florida, Gainesville, Florida.

Straw may be used for synthetic compost if desired. The following formula has been supplied by the Mushroom Growers Association, Agriculture House, Knightsbridge, London, S.W. 1., England.

To each ton of straw add the following:

Activator 1 at the first turning and Activator 2 at the final turning. The rest of the procedure for the production of straw compost is the same as that given for the synthetic compost using hay and corncobs.

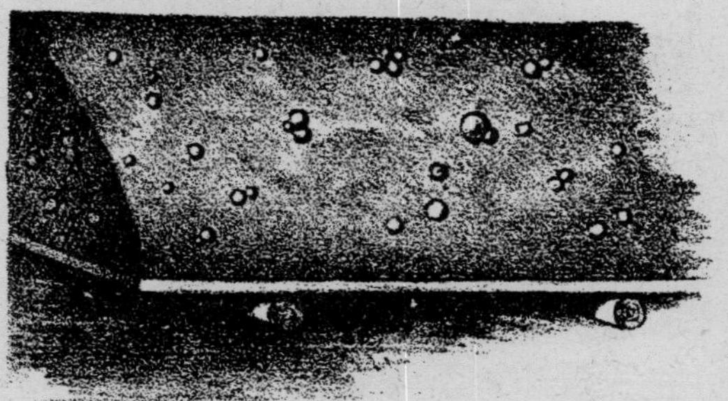

Activator 1	cwt	lb	oz
Dried blood (12% N)	3	0	0
Superphosphate		14	0
Gypsum		35	0
Sulfate of potash		14	0
Carbonate of lime		50	0
Manganese sulfate			12
Iron sulfate			12
Copper sulfate			2½
Aluminum sulfate			2½
Zinc sulfate			1¼
Ammonium molybdate			1¼
Boric acid			1¼
Chromium sulfate			½

Activator 2			
Superphosphate		14	0
Gypsum		70	0
Potassium bromide			¼
Potassium iodide			¼

These quantities are to be used with one ton of dry wheat straw.

Embossed

CLEANING AND FUMIGATING THE HOUSE

The first consideration in mushroom culture is to maintain cleanliness within the mushroom house. The beds should be cleaned immediately after the crop is finished, and the old compost taken away. The boards should be scraped and cleaned thoroughly, and then washed off with a hose, using as much pressure as possible. If the boards can be placed out in the sun for a short time, so much the better. Prior to filling the house, the floors, walls, and particularly the boards used in the beds, should be sprayed very thoroughly with a suitable disinfectant.

MUSHROOM BED ON RUDE SHELF AGAINST WALL OF CELLAR.

An alternative method of handling tobacco spawn is to crumble it into a clean container and plant a teaspoonful in each location. Grain spawn is handled similarly and is probably the best generally used spawn at present.

CARE OF THE BED AFTER PLANTING

Insect Control

For the control of mites, phorids and sciarids on mushrooms, use malathion 50% EC at the rate of approximately 1 tbsp. of malathion EC per 100 sq. ft. of bed. Use enough water to give good coverage.

Make thorough applications as soon after picking as possible. Repeat treatments as necessary, usually twice a week.

Make no applications within 48 hours of harvest.

Temperature and Moisture Control of the Beds

At no time after planting should the temperature of the beds exceed 85 degrees F. The following schedule is recommended:

1st week — 72 to 75 degrees F.

2nd week —68 to 70 degrees F. The temperature may be lowered by adjusting the ventilation.

The above schedule must be maintained without undue chilling or drying out of the manure during ventilation. A light watering (avoid excess) will help prevent drying out of the beds.

Mushroom Cave in Paris.

Several good fungicides are available, a few of which are mentioned below:
   a. Bordeaux 4-4-40 made by dissolving 4 lb. bluestone in 40 gal. water and then adding 4 lb. of hydrated lime.
   b. Lime sulfur—12½ lb. dry lime sulfur to 40 gal. water—a very dependable and safe fungicide. (Note: Lime sulfur is toxic to the skin.
   c. Formaldehyde—3 pt. to 40 gal. water. (A special gas mask should be used when applying this spray.)

A number of new fungicides are on the market; manufacturer's directions must be followed in their application. One of the more promising new materials is Elgetol; use a dilution of 1 or 2 parts to 100 parts of water and thoroughly spray walls, ceilings, floors and both sides of bed boards. This spray will stain clothing and has a yellow color but is not harmful to skin or lungs at the dilution noted.

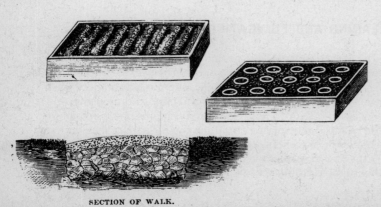

SECTION OF WALK.

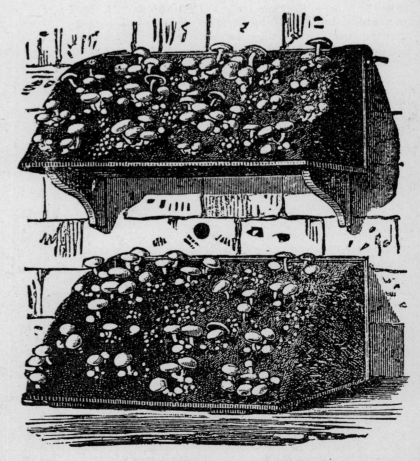

MUSHROOM (AGARICUS CAMPESTRIS.)

PREPARING THE BEDS FOR MANURE COMPOST

After the manure is properly fermented, it is placed in the beds and packed firmly with the back of the fork; do not tramp. Each bed should contain a full 6 inches of manure filled in at a uniform depth. Long manure should be packed more tightly when wet or short manure. Place an accurate thermometer in each bed and check the temperature every morning. The temperature, after a slow, steady rise, should reach 130 to 140 degrees F. by the fourth day. Be careful that the bed does not exceed 145 degrees F. Too high temperatures can be prevented through careful ventilation of the house. The ventilators should be opened every day for a 10-minute period to supply fresh air.

After the fifth day the temperature should start to drop slowly. Try to maintain an even drop by adjustment of ventilation until a temperature of 80 degrees F. has been reached. By this time the beds must be moist but no drops of water should appear between the fingers when a handful of compost is squeezed. The beds are now ready for spawning.

MUSHROOMS ON SHELVES.

SPAWNING

Three general types of spawn are on the market today; brick or bottle manure spawn, tobacco stem spawn, and grain spawn. The spawn should be on hand well in advance of being required. One bottle of manure or tobacco spawn will seed about 30 to 40 sq. ft of bed space.

Tobacco spawn is broken into pieces the size of a golf ball and placed on the bed approximately where it is to be planted. The rows are generally from 8 to 10 inches apart both ways, and should be no closer than 4 to 5 inches to the sides of the bed. The manure is lifted to a depth of about 2 inches and the piece of spawn crumbled in the bottom of the hole. The crumbled spawn should cover about 2 square inches in the bottom of this hole. The manure is replaced and patted into place. If the manure is wetter than normal, plant the spawn nearer the surface; if drier, plant slightly deeper. Manure spawn is handled in the same way except that it should not be crumbled.

MUSHROOM - BEDS IN MARKET-GARDENS, KENSINGTON, ENGLAND.

Casing

The mushroom organism grows and obtains its nourishment from the compost by means of thread-like filaments termed mycelium. A good growth of mycelium will appear blue-gray in color and be abundant. Inspect the beds at regular intervals and when the mycelium appears against the sides of the bed (raise the board up slightly to ascertain this) or the mycelial growth between individual pieces of spawn has almost met, it is time to put on the casing soil.

Type of soil. The best soil for casing is a medium loam containing a small amount of clay and without too much organic matter. The soil should not be acid; a pH between 7.0 and 7.5 is recommended.

Method of Application. The casing soil is spread over the top of the bed to a depth of 1¼ inches. Be very careful that the layer of casing soil is level and that you do not apply too much. For best results this casing soil should be slightly moist when applied.

Treatment After Casing

The temperature of the beds after casing should be between 52 and 56 degrees F. When small "pin heads" (very small mushrooms) appear on the surface it is time to water the casing soil. Previous to this, if the soil appears dry, a light watering will prove beneficial. Use a fine "rose" when watering. Two or three waterings may be required before the "button" stage is reached. Do not over-water. It is bad practice to apply water to the beds after the button stage is developed. Wait until the current "flush" or "break" is finished before applying more water. In other words, water during the interval between or just preceding each successive crop of mushrooms.

PICKING

Mushrooms are picked before the veil breaks. They should not be pulled out from the beds; instead, the cap is grasped lightly and twisted until the stalk comes free. When picking one mushroom in a group, care must be taken not to break off the entire cluster. When all mushrooms from a cluster have been picked, the old butt from which they have been growing, and other dead tissue on the surface of the bed, should be removed and destroyed. Before the mushrooms are sent to market the bottom portion of the stem is cut off and disposed of with the trash mentioned above.

Removal of the mushroom butt leaves a hole in the casing soil which should be filled in with fresh soil to which about 5% lime has been added. Make sure that the surface of the bed is left level.

In conclusion, the very exacting nature of mushroom growing should be stressed. This does not mean that the rules are followed blindly, but with understanding. The following publications are suggested as sources of additional information on mushroom culture.

1. "Mushroom Growing in the United States", U.S.D.A. Farmer's Bulletin No. 1875, from Supt. of Documents, Government Printing Office, Washington 25, D.C. 15 cents. Revised, 1955.

2. Mushroom Growing To-day by F.C. Atkins, 1961. Faber & Faber Co., 24 Russell Sq., London, England.

3. Mushroom Growing for Everyone by Roy Genders. 1969. Faber & Faber Co., 24 Russell Sq., London, England.

4. Sources of Information on Mushroom Research and Production—Vegetable crop series 97, University of California, Davis, California.

Grain spawn is the type normally used and may be obtained from Canadian Spawn Supply Co., P. O. Box 385, Richmond Hill, Ontario.

MUSHROOMS IN BEDS.

HOW TO IDENTIFY MUSHROOMS

By N. F. Oebker and D. P. Rogers   University of Illinois, Urbana

Hunting mushrooms is a favorite pastime for many people. It is not only a source of food, but a means of recreation as well. It is fun to find and identify the many types of mushrooms. To distinguish those that are good to eat from those that are not requires both knowledge and experience. But with the proper information the different varieties can be distinguished quite easily.

There are no simple rules or general principles for telling the difference between poisonous and edible mushroom. Color or shape is no indication. It is not true that mushrooms are poisonous if a silver spoon tarnishes when put into the pan in which the mushrooms are cooking—or that they are edible if the spoon does not tarnish. Neither is it true that those that peel easily are edible. And soaking or boiling poisonous mushrooms in salt water will not make them harmless. Many other such tests have been suggested, but all of them are unreliable. A species of mushroom can be identified only after one considers all of its characteristics.

If you have any doubt about the edibility of a mushroom, do not use it until you have identified it beyond all doubt. For a beginner, the safest plan is to learn to identify one or two good species, and eat only them, and then gradually add others. Knowing a few species thoroughly is a good deal better than following vague general rules for identification.

To identify mushrooms, consult someone who is trained in this field. When collecting and preparing mushrooms for identification, follow these suggestions:

1. Carefully dig up the mushroom, including the entire stem, with a knife. Take special care not to leave any part of it, as all parts are needed for proper identification.

MUSHROOMS (AGARICUS CAMPESTRIS), in the "Button" stage of development, and one older.

2. Collect several specimens in various stages of development because no single feature of any mushroom is sufficient to determine its identity or edibility. Five to ten specimens will usually be enough.
3. Do not select specimens that are old, decaying, or infested with insects. Also remove bits of soil or other plants that may cling to the specimens you wish to keep.
4. Record the color, odor, and size of the fresh mushroom and tell where it was growing (tree stump, dead or living tree, lawn, etc.).
5. As soon as possible after finding the mushroom, identify the species or send it to someone who can identify it. In the field, wrap specimens carefully in soft paper or large green leaves so that they will stay as fresh as possible until they can be examined. Many species decay quickly.
6. A spore print is helpful in identification. Make one by placing the cap of the mushroom on dark paper under a bowl or tumbler.
7. Preserve mushroom specimens by drying them in a warm air current. Place them on a metal mesh screen or a piece of paper, and suspend near a heat outlet in the house or above the furnace. Take care to avoid too much heat. On warm summer days you can lay them on a paper in the sun to dry. Turn them over from time to time. During these operations, be sure to keep your identification notes with the specimen.
8. Keep dried mushroom specimens in small cardboard boxes to which are glued labels with the following information: name, habitat, date, place of collecting, and name of the person(s) who found and identified the specimen. Keep specimens in a dry place, and if necessary put a few moth flakes in each box to keep insects out.

MUSHROOM GROWING AND THE MUSHROOM INDUSTRY

By Aron Kinrus
Agronomist
American Mushroom Institute
Box 373
Kennett Square, Pa. 19348

MUSHROOMS GROWN IN BOTTOM OF OLD CASK

This article is prepared for people interested in learning how mushrooms grow, but not how to grow mushrooms. Individuals seeking information on mushroom growing are frequently misled into believing that it is an occupation offering unusual opportunities for profit with little effort, little experience and a small capital investment required. Often a beginner spends a considerable part of his savings on a mushroom growing venture before realizing that he is entering a well established and competitive field with a modest margin of profit. The beginner will almost certainly be disappointed if he expects to make easy profits during the years he is learning to grow mushrooms. Considerable physical labor is required for the preparation of mushroom beds or trays, perhaps more than in any horticultural venture.

To obtain profitable yields the grower must have adequate facilities, a thorough knowledge of the principles of mushroom growing, and a skill that can be developed only through long experience. The minimum size of a mushroom growing establishment required to make a livelihood for a family is one with at least 20,000 square feet of harvesting area. The cost of building and equipping a plant of this size is approximately $50,000. Additional working capital of about $10,000 is required to pay for the compost, spawn and other expenses.

Of the many species of edible fungi which have been identified by botanists, only one, AGARICUS BISPORUS, has been developed as a cultivated mushroom in the United States.

A fundamental difference between mushrooms and green plants is that the plants can manufacture their own food, whereas mushrooms cannot. Fungi, because of the absence of chlorophyll, cannot carry on photosynthesis and must depend upon organic matter for nutrition.

The "seed" of the mushroom are the spores which are of minute size and infinitesimal weight. You can get an idea of the size when you know that one mushroom, permitted to mature, will produce sixteen billion spores. However, it is estimated that in nature only one out of a billion grows. Given a favorable environment, the spores produce a threadlike mass called mycelium which, under the proper conditions, develop edible mushrooms.

Spawn is produced in a laboratory under sterile conditions. When a satisfactory strain has been developed, it can be maintained in the laboratory year after year by periodically transferring portions of mycelium to fresh growing media. There are over a dozen spawn laboratories in the United States that produce pure cultures of mycelium on special media which is then called spawn.

The spawn is grown on prepared compost which undergoes a two phase preparation—Phase I (outdoor composting) and Phase II (indoor/pasteurization). The main task of Phase I is to make the compost uniform and well watered and supplemented. Compost can be prepared from "synthetic" ingredients—horse manure, or a blend of part horse manure and part synthetic.

VIEW OF UNHEATED MUSHROOM - HOUSE.

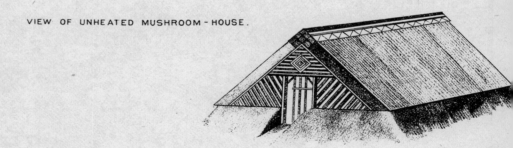

Compost ingredients harbor a great number of microorganisms (microbes). They grow and reproduce as water is added and the pile is built. Microbes require suitable temperature, adequate moisture, sufficient oxygen and available food. Their growth also causes the temperature of the pile to increase.

During this phase of composting the microbes convert the ingredients. Once the temperature reaches 140 degrees F, carmelization—a drastic chemical change—takes place. The pile temperature must get high enough to cause direct chemical reactions which push it to 175 degrees F. As long as microbes have access to water, balanced nutrition, and oxygen in sufficient quantities, the pile will continue to heat. The first phase is complete as soon as the composting material becomes pliable, has a moisture content of 70-75%, the odor of ammonia is sharp and has a dark brown color indicating carmelization has occurred.

Phase II is only successful if Phase I has been carried out properly to promote physical, chemical and biological breakdown—and only then to the right degree. Pasteurization is necessary to free the compost of undesirable microbes and insects. Through the proper manipulation of temperature and ventilation Phase II can be successful.

As the temperature increases, thermophilic (heat-loving) microbes are favored. This group of organisms is very efficient in using the ammonia present in the compost as a growth factor. By so doing the ammonia is incorporated into microbial cells and ultimately is available to the mushroom. The increasing temperature causes pasteurization. This process requires an air and compost temperature of 140 degrees F., by either steam being introduced into the house, or the house being partially closed to allow the compost to heat the air. Either procedure can produce the same result—140 degrees F. for four hours in both the compost and air.

Pasteurization implies the eradication of harmful insects, mites, nematodes, fungi and bacteria, but it does not include the elimination of all fungi and bacteria. If the compost and all other exposed surfaces are not subjected to this temperature regime, pasteurization will not be completed leaving some harmful organisms to reproduce and grow.

These subsequently can cause difficulty in the mushroom crop. The peak temperature of compost must, therefore, reach 140 degrees F. for at least four hours if adequate pasteurization is to be accomplished.

GROWING CYCLE

Composts vary as do mushroom houses. Handling of Phase I and II should be guided by the conditions of the compost and growing houses. If everything has been performed correctly and the compost temperature in the growing house comes down to 70-75 degrees F., and the compost is free of ammonia, the compost is ready for spawn planting. This procedure is called, in grower's language, "spawning". The most recommended procedure is the through-spawning method, mixing the spawn with the compost at the rate of 1 quart per 15 sq. ft. of compost.

The spawn is allowed to grow in the compost for about 7 days while the temperature is held at approximately 70 degrees F. The bed temperature is then lowered to between 65 degrees and 70 degrees while the spawn continues to grow for an additional week or two. At the end of this period the cottony growth of mushroom spawn will have permeated most of the compost. Some ventilation is provided during the growth of the spawn and the surface layer of manure is watered lightly to retain an appropriate moisture content of about 65 percent throughout all of the compost in the bed.

After the spawn has "run" in the compost 2 or 3 weeks, a layer of about an inch of "casing" soil or peat is spread over the surface of the bed. The soil should be a loam that is neither too sandy in texture nor too high in clay, and neutral in reaction. If the soil to be used for casing is acid, it is usually neutralized by adding ground limestone. This soil is kept moist with very light watering until the mushrooms begin to form. The first mushrooms will appear all over the surface of the bed about 3 weeks after casing.

At the time mushrooms appear, the temperature is lowered to a chosen point between 55 degrees and 65 degrees F. If a slowly developing crop with a long harvest season is desired, the temperature is held at about 55 degrees. If more rapid development with a short harvest season is desired, the temperature is held at about sixty-two degrees. Mushrooms will continue to develop for 2 or 3 months, depending on the temperature. They usually appear in sudden outbreaks at intervals of about 10 days. These outbreaks are called "flushes" or "breaks" and are followed by periods with only a few mushrooms appearing on the bed. As the harvest period lengthens the number of mushrooms forming gradually decreases. Usually additional water is applied to the surface of the bed at the time each break is appearing. The soil moisture must be maintained at a rather high level to obtain maximum crops.

During the growth of the mushrooms the humidity of the air in the mushroom house must be maintained above 80 percent to prevent drying out of the mushroom caps. At the same time considerable ventilation must be supplied to assure maximum yields. Usually it is advisable to give as much ventilation as possible without interfering with temperature and humidity control, or causing a cracking of the surface of the mushrooms.

The mushroom spawn apparently wants absolute peace when casing has taken place and does not want to be disturbed by water applied on the surface. The spawn must—immediately after casing—make its entrance in the casing material from the "warm" compost pillow under optimum humidity conditions, in order to be able to build up a strong and dense growth, especially just in the passage between compost and casing material. If a casing material containing too much moisture is put on, the water will leak down on the compost, and this for various reasons is very undesirable. On the other hand, a too dry material means a long and thin growth, which never will get any peace for development, because one automatically tries to raise the humidity by repeated waterings. If, however, the casing has the optimal humidity, only very light waterings are needed to replace the daily evaporation, and the spawn will not get shocked or disturbed in any other way.

When the first mushrooms are formed, and especially at the time of the 2nd flush, the problem during the rest of the crop seems only to be a matter of keeping the temperature constant at about 60 degrees F., adding the necessary amounts of water to the casing material without silting and at the same time making sure that sufficient ventilation keeps the carbon dioxide concentration at a level below 0.1-0.2% where the mushrooms are formed.

The extra yield which can be obtained by careful treatment of the beds during the rest of the cropping period—if a normal good growing technique is used—is small compared with what can be reached by using the right growing technique in the period between casing and first mushrooms.

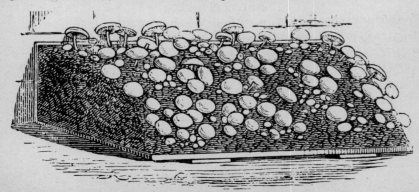

HARVESTING AND MARKETING

Mushrooms are "picked" just before the cap expands to expose the "gills". In this stage of growth they may range from 1 inch to 3 inches in diameter. After the mushroom or clump of mushrooms has been picked, the remaining fleshy mushroom tissue is carefully removed from the soil and the hole filled with fresh soil. Large numbers of young "button" mushrooms from one-eighth to three-eighths inch in diameter die off after the larger mushrooms are removed, even on normal beds, presumably because harvesting the large mushrooms breaks many of the strands connecting the young mushrooms with their supply of nutrients in the compost. With a little practice these dead or damaged mushrooms are easily distinguished from healthy buttons and are removed from the bed to prevent spread of decay. This job must be done thoroughly at frequent intervals in order to assure maximum crops.

When the mushrooms are to be sold on the fresh market the stumps are usually cut off at the time of picking and the mushrooms are sorted according to size, freedom from blemishes, and certain other requirements. They are packed in 7-ounce or 1-pound cartons, or in 3-pound baskets. In most large cities they are sold by fruit and vegetable produce dealers. These merchants receive the mushrooms on consignment, set the wholesale price in accordance with supply and demand, and charge the grower a 10-percent commission for their services. The daily wholesale price of fresh mushrooms is usually quoted in the local newspapers.

In some localities the grower may have a choice between sending his mushrooms to produce dealers, to canneries, or to soup makers. The demand for canned mushrooms has increased in recent years until, at the present time, most of the mushroom crop is sold in cans. One-third is marketed as fresh mushrooms, one-third as canned mushrooms, and the remainder is processed in soup. The sale of both canned mushrooms and mushroom soup has played a very important part in the nationwide acceptance of mushrooms as an everyday food product. National advertising of mushroom soup has once and for all dispelled from the mind of the average housewife the unfounded fear of mushroom poisoning. This product quickly won popularity since it is a relatively inexpensive item of good quality. The processing industries also serve as important and indispensable factors for stabilizing the price of mushrooms in large production centers.

COSTS AND RETURNS

Mushroom growers encounter most of the economic difficulties that confront producers of other perishable crops. The profit depends on the success of the crop and the prices received from the market. Because yields are highly variable, the cost of producing a pound of mushrooms is difficult to estimate but frequently is 25-35 cents per pound.

The most important items of cost are:

Interest on the investment, depreciation, compost, soil, spawn, pest control, labor for composting, filling, spawning, casing, picking and packing for market, and emptying the beds.

The price differs from one locality to another and from one season to another. It is usually beyond the grower's control. Because his product is highly perishable, he must send it to market on the day it is harvested or provide expensive refrigeration. Warm spells in the early fall and late spring may greatly increase the supply of mushrooms for several days at a time by raising the temperature in mushroom houses. The temperature rise is reflected in an increased rate of growth of the mushrooms and in the production of a larger proportion of small mushrooms. In congested centers of mushroom growing, this usually occurs in hundreds of mushroom houses at the same time, and the grower often finds himself in the untenable position of producing the most mushrooms when the price is below the cost of production.

PERSPECTIVE ELEVATION OF MR. DAVID LYMAN'S BARN—FROM THE NORTH WEST.

WHEN TO HARVEST YOUR VEGETABLES

HARVESTING

From Nevada Gardener, Cooperative Extension Service, Horticulture Information Series

ASPARAGUS	Wait 2 years before harvesting first crop after planting. Snap off spears when 6-8 inches high.
BEANS	Pick before large seeds develop; when young and succulent.
LIMA BEANS	Pick when pods are full and green, before they turn white.
BEETS	Dig when desired size—greens best when very young.
BROCCOLI	Harvest flower heads before the flowers open.
BRUSSELS SPROUTS	Pick sprouts when hard and outer leaves have slightly yellow appearance.
CABBAGE	Harvest when heads are solid.
CHINESE CABBAGE	Harvest when heads are firm.
CARROTS	Harvest when roots are long but still tender.
CAULIFLOWER	Harvest when head is good sized but compact.
CELERIAC	Harvest when tuberous base is 2-3" in diameter.
CELERY	Harvest when stalk clump is 2-3" in diameter.
CHARD, SWISS	Cut leaves from outside of plant; the younger the better.
COLLARD	Harvest whole young plants when about one-fourth grown.
CORN	Ready when you poke your finger into a plump kernel and milk pops out.
COWPEA	Harvest when seeds can be easily removed from pods but before the pods dry out.
CUCUMBER	Harvest before color changes and seeds begin to harden.
EGGPLANT	Give fruit the thumb-press test, if flesh springs back, green— if not, harvest.
ENDIVE	When plants reach 12" in diameter, tie leaves together at top. Harvest when well-blanched.
GARLIC	Harvest when tops begin to die.
JERUSALEM ARTICHOKE	Dig tubers anytime after bloom.
KALE	Pick tender smaller leaves. Light frost improves flavor.
KOHLRABI	Harvest when a globe portion of stem reaches 2" in diameter.
LEEK	Start blanching when plant is 6" high. Harvest entire plant when well-blanched.
MELONS	Cantaloupe—harvest at full slip— when they can be pulled cleanly from stem leaving a smooth cavity. Crenshaw, honeydew, casaba—harvest when they soften and turn yellow.
NEW ZEALAND SPINACH	Cut off 4 to 6" of the tips of the branches.
OKRA	Harvest pods when about 4 days old.
ONION	Harvest when tops change color and fall over. Dig and allow tops to completely dry.
PARSNIP	Dig during winter for best flavor.
PEAS	Harvest when pods filled but before peas harden.
PEPPER	Pick when large and firm but before color change. Hot peppers, left until colored.
POTATO, SWEET	Dig when vine turns yellow. If frosted before this, dig at once. Warm storage improves flavor.
POTATO	Dig when tubers are large enough for use. Those to be stored should be left in ground until vines partially die.
PUMPKIN	Harvest when skin is definitely hard to penetrate with thumbnail.
RADISH	Harvest when at edible size, usually at 3-4 weeks after planting.
RHUBARB	Pull off leaf stocks but no more than 1/3 at a time. Wait until new growth matures before next harvest. Cut off seed stocks when they appear.
SHALLOTS	Dig in fall.
SPINACH	Cut only large leaves, early spring crop in Nevada.
SUMMER (BUSH) SQUASH	Cut off fruit when immature, 3-6" long.
VINING or WINTER SQUASH	Harvest when shells are hard.
TOMATO	Harvest when red ripe.
TURNIPS	Dig when good table size—about 2". For greens, use young leaves.
WATERMELON	When thumped in the early morning, they should sound dull not metallic. Also the ground spot will turn slightly yellow.

DOLLAR HARVEST

HARVEY S. ROTTENBERG

Here are several suggestions for home gardeners who want to turn green thumbs into greenbacks.

SEEDLINGS

Many localities are without a source of started annual vegetable, herb and ornamental seedlings. If you live in such an area there is an opportunity to earn some money in the spring.

Start seeds indoors in flats or peat pots. If you are more energetic, construct simple greenhouses or frames for your crop and expand as your market grows.

GARDEN MAINTENANCE

Many beginning gardeners start in business mowing lawns, cleaning beds, raking leaves, pruning trees and planting flowers for other people. Try to innovate. New ideas are worth money. Offer to turn lawns into food gardens. See if you can turn all those leaves you normally haul to the dump into a dollar harvest by selling the rich leaf mold to organic gardeners and ornamental fanciers.

SPECIALIZED GROWERS

Become an expert in one area of indoor or outdoor ornamental horticulture. Raise roses, flowering bulbs, African violets, cacti and succulents, or any other marketable variety that holds your fancy.

"PICK YOUR OWN" PLANTATIONS

If you are fortunate enough to own a field next to a well traveled road, you can go into the "pick your own" business. Plant large crops of several varieties. Hang out a sign inviting bargain hunting motorists to pick their own strawberries, corn, tomatoes, beans, peas and so on. Leave enough space between your rows to accommodate the clumsiest customer or you will see lots of profits trodden into the ground.

HERBS

There is always a market for tasty, sweet scented herbs, fresh cut, dried or potted. Some gardeners bottle herb vinegars to broaden their line. Others sell the herbs packaged as sachets and teas.

GOURDS

Ornamental gourds may be sold as they are plucked from the vine or you may turn these decorative beauties into ingenious gift items like bowls, cups or birdhouses. Let your imagination run free. But, remember to consider the cost of your labor in the selling price.

CHRISTMAS

If you are the patient type put in a crop of evergreens for Christmas trees. Then sit back for about ten years while your investment matures. White spruce, Balsam, Douglas fir, Scotch pine and Austrian pine may be grown for this purpose. But, before you get involved, check with your County agent and someone already in the business. There isn't a trade that doesn't have its tricks.

GARDEN SCHOOLS

This enterprise requires both gardening skills and teaching skills. If you have the combination and own or rent a piece of land, there are many folks who would like to garden but lack both the skills and the land. Let your students practice your teachings on small plots so they may try different methods and compare results. If you experiment with food gardening, successful students get to eat their diplomas!

ORNAMENTAL TRUCK GARDENS

Buy or grow ornamental cuttings. Load them on your wagon and head for a crowded street corner. Check local peddling laws to avoid encounters with law officers who may not sympathize with your ecologically improving enterprise.

Remember, ornamentals draw a better price if they are displayed in attractive, unusual containers. Consider a merger with a potter.

PLANT DOCTORS

A plague of self-appointed plant doctors has sprung up in several cities. I suppose as long as some people are too lazy to read a few books and learn how to care for their plants other people are entitled to soak them for twenty-five dollars per house call, plus extras.

CO-OP PRODUCE MARKETS

Band together with your friends and neighbors to offer your produce in co-op marketplaces on the weekend. A vacant lot, unused parking lot or drive-in theatre is all the space you need. Add a flea market to draw more customers. A country fair atmosphere and bargain prices will bring people more miles than you imagine.

PROCESSED PRODUCE

Old timey jams, jellies, fruit butters, pickles and preserves are always appealing to folks who haven't got the time to make them.

But, before you turn your kitchen into a processing plant, check with local health authorities for regulations. And, please be ever so careful. Botulism and food poisoning are killers.

MONEY GARDENS

HOW TO GET INTO THE GARDENING BUSINESS

Every year as the summer wanes and harvest time approaches, thousands of tiny roadside stands appear through the country.

While the enterprising youngsters and families who man these ramshackle outposts of free enterprise may not think of it in quite this way, they are part of a multi-billion dollar industry servicing more Americans than most people realize.

There are over thirty-three million gardeners in the United States. According to industry sources, they spend over $3 billion a year on nursery stock alone. This figure does not include the billions of additional dollars that gardeners spend on their lawns, tools, greenhouses, birdbaths, books, and so on.

"Well," you may think to yourself, "here's a business that sounds interesting. There certainly are enough potential customers, and they are spending. Besides, it would be nice to work with the ecology, plants, puttering around in the soil, simple things like that."

Well the truth is that it's not all that simple, as many folks trying to capitalize on the green plant boom found out.

It's all work, work, work and it requires training and knowledge. Cover the petunias with polyethylene.

Unload a ton of fertilizer. Spray the semi-tropicals. Pray that it doesn't rain on the four weekends in Spring when you're going to do more than one quarter of your business for the year. And, answer the same questions over, and over, and over again for your customers.

If not discouraged at this point you may have the stuff to make it in the gardening business. But, how should you start?

First, familiarize yourself with the industry. The best way is to seek information from professionals and their trade organizations.

The American Association of Nurserymen issues "Something Worth Doing", the bulletin for high school students, (on page 172). Its suggestions apply to anyone considering a career in The Nursery Industry. The association membership lists and source guides are invaluable to beginners.

There are also regional and state trade organizations that can be very helpful and should be consulted, since they are in touch with the special conditions which apply in your locality.

HARVEY S. ROTTENBERG

A list of professional, semi-professional and trade organizations you ought to be familiar with appears on page 90 of the first GARDENER'S CATALOGUE.

The Four-H Clubs, The Future Farmers of America and your state extension services are also good sources of information. They are listed on pages 287-289 of the first GARDENER'S CATALOGUE. Of course, check into the programs that local horticultural schools and botanical gardens offer.

Continued on page 172

GARDEN CAREERS

for your career
CONSIDER SOMETHING WORTH DOING

Working toward a more livable world . . . toward a cleaner and more beautiful environment. These are some of the rewards from careers in the nursery and landscape industry that offer diverse opportunities for challenge and achievement . . . for responsibility and satisfaction . . . for personal growth and financial reward.

Doing something worthwhile to help save our world from ecological abuse has been the goal of men and women in the nursery and landscape industry for generations. By providing leadership and technical ability they help prevent and correct the visual pollution that surrounds us, purify our air, clarify our waters, stabilize our precious soils, help abate the din of noise . . . contributing in many ways to make the quality of our lives a little better.

If you are seeking such a career, you will find the nursery and landscape industry draws from all educational levels, from many disciplines, and caters to myriad interests. Agricultural Sciences . . . Business Administration . . . Biological Sciences . . . Agronomy . . . Marketing . . . Horticulture . . . Sales . . . Soil Management . . . Retailing . . . Landscape Design . . . Education . . . Traffic Management . . . Advertising . . . Research . . . Packaging . . . all these are a part of this fulfilling industry.

These and the many other areas of endeavor in the industry offer the enterprising young person a challenge to learn and grow . . . they really represent *something worth doing.*

THE INDUSTRY

The nursery and landscape industry consists of several basic types of operations:

- *Wholesale Growers* — those whose basic concern is the original growth, care and production of plants for sale to retail nurseries of landscaping firms who may grow them to "Finished" size.
- *Landscaping Firms* — those who are concerned with the preparation and execution of landscape designs for the beautification of specific areas. Designs for larger areas are generally created by professional landscape architects. Smaller design plans and homeowner landscape plans are often prepared by a landscape firm's own design specialists. Such a specialist usually does his own estimating, selling, supervising, planting and execution of the design.
- *Garden Centers* — those retail firms specializing in selling plants, lawn care items, garden materials — fertilizers, pesticides, lawn mowers, lawn and deck furniture, and a variety of other products relating to garden living, home landscaping. If the firm only retails nursery plants the display and sales area is often called a "sales yard."
- *Mail Order Firms* — those firms whose primary business is to advertise and sell plant materials through the mails. Some mail order firms specialize in producing, packaging and shipping plants to fill orders secured by other firms.
- *Agency Operations* — these are of two types: the *wholesale broker,* who acts as the sales agent for one or more wholesale growers; and the *independent sales agent,* who sells directly to homeowners or others, generally in connection with planning sketches and recommendations for plantings.

Most nursery firms are a combination of two or more of these basic types of businesses and, therefore, offer the prospective employee a wide variety of career opportunities.

The history and practices of the industry attest to the great potential for an individual to experience personal and career growth.

EDUCATION, SCHOOLS & CURRICULA

In addition to the formal educational opportunities discussed below, the industry offers a great chance to learn on the job and progress upward through the ranks. Many have started as landscape helpers, grounds personnel or in other jobs and have moved up as their knowledge and skills grew.

Regardless of the specific interest you may have in some aspect of the nursery and landscape industry for long-range career plans, a good basic knowledge of the growing sciences will be important to your success.

An increasing number of secondary schools are offering vocational courses which give the student a broad perspective of the careers in horticulture and its related fields.

Two-year vocational courses are offered at a number of colleges or community colleges which are generally very practical, relatively inexpensive, and offer a wide enough variety of electives to give the student a reasonable choice of courses. Some of these provide valuable field training or working experience.

Full four-year courses leading to a bachelor's degree, and advanced study leading to a master's or doctorate in one of the many disciplines are offered at a large number of universities and colleges. Many allow students to begin specializing after the second year — pointing to a career in production or production services, business management, marketing, research, teaching, design, sales, or a host of related activities.

If you have an interest in landscape architecture or landscape

---

Rewarding career opportunities . . . in caring for Nature's gifts. A chance to have a hand in building and protecting a better environment . . . through your future in the nursery and landscape industry.

design, you will find a wide choice of universities, colleges and established recognized correspondence schools offering this specialized training.

If possible, it is always valuable for the student, in any field, to gain ground floor experience in his chosen career. The industry does offer part-time and summer opportunities which provide rich experience and pleasure, as well as income to the student.

TYPICAL JOBS

Some of the typical jobs you would find in various nursery industry companies are listed below to give you an idea of the variety. These were selected from actual nursery operations.

Agronomist — concerned with soil management and land use; responsible for field drainage, rotation, fertilization, irrigation, weed control, cover crops, soil structure, etc. *Spray Specialist* (in some nurseries called entomologist or plant pathologist) — concerned with spraying for insect, plant disease and weed control. *Division Manager* — responsible for growing, pruning and managing one of the major divisions of a large wholesale growing operation. *Assembler* — responsible for assembling orders; full knowledge of plant material necessary. *Foreman of various crews* — responsible for managing and supervising the work of canning, pruning, staking and other crews, generally quite skilled. *Truck Driver and Equipment Handler* — operator of various fork lifts, semi-trucks, front end loaders, soil shredders, and other machinery. *Maintenance Supervisor* — responsible for maintenance of equipment, buildings and grounds. *Production Controller* — responsible for seeing that all production is kept up to pre-established quotas. *Sprayer and Pruner* — concerned with these plant care areas. *Traffic Manager* and *Assistant* — responsible for all shipping. *Packing Superintendent* — works with traffic to handle all protection and packing of plant materials for shipment. *Propagation Foreman* — supervises the rooting of cuttings, germination of seeds, grafting and budding of plants in greenhouses, cold frames and outdoor seed beds. *Quality Control* — responsible for selection and field tagging of orders; must have knowledge of kinds of nursery stock and industry standards.

In other operations, typical jobs include *Grounds Keeper, Landscape Superintendent, Landscape Helper, Landscape Crew Foreman,* and others concerned with the day-to-day growing of plants and the execution of landscaping plans.

On the business side, you would find need for general managers and assistants, department managers, marketing managers, advertising managers, direct mail specialists, salesmen and general office help.

This is not an inclusive list, but it is intended to give the prospective nurseryman or landscape specialist a view of the diversity of the industry.

The industry offers a chance in business and the growing sciences in a profession whose major goal is always to improve and protect nature's gifts for a better environment.

MONEY GARDENS —continued from page 171

Once you've studied the possibilities the gardening industry has to offer, the best advice we can offer is to earn while you learn. Take some courses, pick your spot, try to find a job.

If you always wanted to open a little plant shop, first try working as a clerk in someone else's shop. There you can learn the intricacies of seasonal ordering and keeping stock alive. Remember, plants are a perishable commodity and spoilage shows heavily on the bottom line. So, until you learn the business, let someone else pay for your mistakes.

If you are the type of person who has always dreamed of starting a giant mail order empire in your basement or garage, gardening items offer great possibilities since some of them carry as much as 700% mark-ups.

While Burpee Seed Company grossed over $100 million dollars in one year, you ought to start small, perhaps with only one item. First, study all the items and advertising techniques successful mail order houses use to attract customers. Then do exactly the same thing. It may not be an original idea, but you know it works. You can tell if a company—large or small—is successful in a given market when you see their ads constantly reappearing in the same place.

FOR MORE INFORMATION

If you have an interest in the nursery and landscape industry, it would be wise to visit local nurseries, landscape firms, or garden centers to get first-hand information of job opportunities, salary potential, and type of training necessary.

Your guidance counselor can help you find universities and colleges that offer courses of study in your field of interest. Write them, or write to

American Association of Nurserymen
230 Southern Building
Washington, D.C. 20005

THE RICE-PAPER TREE.

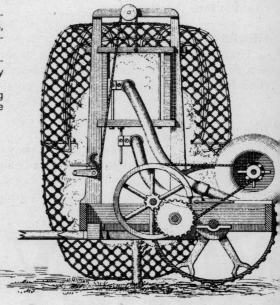

Business people only repeat ads in media that produce for them. If it produces for them, maybe the market is big enough to support a new competitor. And, maybe, just maybe, you are that competitor.

The "earn while you learn" philosophy should also apply to future growers and landscapers. The best place to learn is in the fields and greenhouses. Take any job for starters. Perhaps one day you will have acres of your own under glass.

But, whatever segment of the gardening industry you choose, always remember we are talking about business.

No matter how green your thumb is, good business practice is essential to success unless you are one of those fortunate individuals blessed by pure dumb luck.

Old rules like "buy cheap and sell dear" apply as strongly in this business as in any other. Accounting skills are as valuable as fertilizer. The greatest profits are achieved by the sharpest traders and in the gardening industry competition is fierce.

Good luck and remember to let us know if you start any gardening enterprise. Maybe you'll find it on a GARDENER'S CATALOGUE source list someday.

GROWING FRUIT OUTDOORS

Reprinted from

The American Fruit Culturist

By John J. Thomas

1855

Orchard Standard Tree.

The climate and soil of our country afford unequalled facilities for the cultivation of fruit. A rich treasure lies within the reach of its inhabitants, in the profusion of delicious kinds, which successive months may be made to supply. Yet, a small portion have availed themselves fully of these advantages. Even the existence of most of the finer varieties, are but partially known. The rapid increase of fruit culture within the past few years, has but thinly spread its bounties over a widely expanded and thickly peopled territory.

In traversing the country, neat cottages and comfortable farm-houses are seen everywhere interspersed, and plenty is indicated by loaded orchards and abundant harvests. But how many of the prosperous owners are aware of the rare delicacies their fertile lands are capable of yielding? How many of them, for instance, are familiar with that perfumed, golden, midsummer fruit, the apricot? What portion cultivate enough of the best peaches to obtain "from the loaded bough the mellow shower," for ten successive weeks? What number know that plums, rich, juicy, and bloom-dusted, may be had fresh from the tree, from early wheat harvest till the ground freezes in autumn? Who among them partake of the twenty best melting pears, out of the thousand varieties which have borne fruit in this country? And especially, who practically knows, that a whole yearly circle of fruits is within his reach, beginning with the most refreshing strawberries, raspberries, and cherries, for early summer; including the richest plums, apricots, peaches, and nectarines, for summer and autumn; and closing with high-flavored pears and apples, extending their season of ripening through all autumn and winter, and far into the succeeding year? Happily, the number of cultivators is rapidly increasing, who may place upon their tables many delicious sorts, on almost any day of the entire year.

The cultivation of fruit has been retarded by a mistaken estimate of the time required for young trees to come into bearing. But this error is fast disappearing before skillful culture. It is become well known, that he who plants trees, plants for himself, as well as for his children. Bad treatment may long retard the growth and bearing of a tree. Enveloped in weeds and grass, what young plant could flourish? What farmer would think a moment of raising good corn in the thick and tall grass of a meadow? No wonder, then, that a young tree, similarly treated, lingers in feebleness and disease. But give it for a few years a mellow, clean, and fertile soil, and vigorous shoots, and expanding branches, will soon bend under copious loads of fruit. To adduce instances,--in a single garden, apple trees, the fifth year from setting out, yielded a bushel each; peach trees, the third summer, bore three pecks; and a Bartlett pear, two years from transplanting, gave a peck of superb fruit; none of them were an inch in diameter when transplanted, nor was their treatment better than that which every good farmer gives his carrots and potatoes.

It can be hardly necessary, with our present rapidly increasing commerce in fruit, to point out the pecuniary profits resulting from its culture. But those who have only raised the more common, or second-rate sorts, can hardly appreciate the heavy returns from the

FRUIT CULTURE, 1855

finest, under the best culture. To such, a few examples may be interesting.

C. A. Cable, of Cleveland, Ohio, obtained in 1845, from an orchard of one hundred cherry trees, twenty years old, more than one thousand dollars. The trees were twenty-five feet apart, and no other crop occupied the ground, which was enriched and kept well cultivated.

Hill Pennell, of Darby, Pa., sold in 1846, two hundred and twenty-five dollars worth of early apples, from half an acre.

A farmer near Fishkill, N.Y. sold fifteen hundred dollars worth of plums in a single season. Richard I. Hand of Mendon, Monroe county, N.Y., sold in 1845, four hundred and forty dollars worth of Roxbury Russet and Northern Spy apples from one acre of orchard.

James Laws, of Philadelphia, sold three hundred dollars worth of Isabella and Catawba grapes, the fourth year from planting, from three-eighths of an acre, or at the rate of eight hundred dollars per acre.

Hugh Hatch, of Camden, N.J., obtained from four trees of the Tewksbury Blush, one hundred and forty bushels of apples, or thirty-five from each tree; of these ninety baskets (of about three pecks each) sold late in the following spring for one dollar per basket.

Examples almost beyond number may be given where single trees have yielded from five to ten dollars a year in fruit and many instances where twenty or thirty dollars have been obtained. An acre of such would be equal to any of the preceding instances. If one tree of the Rhode Island Greening will afford forty bushels of fruit, at a quarter of a dollar per bushel, which has often occurred, forty such trees on an acre would yield a crop worth four hundred dollars. But taking but one quarter of this amount as a low average for all seasons and with imperfect cultivation, one hundred dollars would still be equal to the interest on fifteen hundred per acre. Now, this estimate is based upon the price of good winter apples for the past thirty years, in our most productive districts; let a similar calculation be made with fruits rarer and of a more delicious character. Apricots, and the finer varieties of the plum, are often sold for three to six dollars per bushel; the best early peaches from one to three dollars; and pears, from hardy and productive trees, for an equal amount. Of the three former kinds, two to five bushels per tree, with good management is a frequent crop; and on large pear trees five times this quantity. An acquaintance received eight dollars for a crop grown on two fine young cherry trees, and twenty-four dollars from four young peach trees, of only six years growth from the bud. In western New York, single trees of the Doyenne or Virgalieu pear have often afforded a return of twenty dollars or more, after being sent hundreds of miles to market. An acre of such trees, well managed, would far exceed in profits a fine hundred-acre farm.

But the anxious inquiry is suggested, "Will not our markets be surfeited with fruit?" This will depend upon the judgment and discretion of cultivators. With the exception of the peaches of Philadelphia, and the strawberries of Cincinnati, a great deficiency is still felt in all our large cities. Of these two fruits, large plantations are brought rapidly into full bearing. The fruit, when ripe, quickly perishes, and cannot be kept a week; yet thousands of acres in peach trees, bending under their heavy crops, are needed for the consumption of one city, and broad fifty-acre fields, reddened with enormous products, send many hundred bushels of strawberries daily into the other. If, instead of keeping but three days, sorts were now added which would keep three months, many times the amount would be needed. But the market would not be confined to large cities. Railroads and steamboats would open new channels of distribution throughout the country, for increased supplies. Nor would the business stop here. Large portions of the eastern continent would gladly become purchasers, as soon as sufficient quantities should create facilities for a reasonable supply. Our best apples are already eagerly bought in London and Liverpool, where nine dollars per barrel is not an unusual price for the best Newtown pippins. And by packing in ice, Doyenne pears, gathered early in autumn in New York, have been sold at mid-winter in Calcutta--peaches have been safely sent to Jamaica--and strawberries to Barbadoes. The Baldwin apple has been furnished in good condition in the East Indies, two months after it is entirely gone at Boston.

Good winter apples always command a market. For the past thirty years such fine varieties as the Swaar, Rhode Island Greening, and Esopus Spitzenburgh, have scarcely varied from twenty-five cents a bushel in some of the most productive portions of the country, remote from market. Late keepers are sold early in the summer for more than triple that sum. An acre of forty trees, with good culture, will average through all seasons not less than

two hundred bushels, or fifty dollars a year. Instances are frequent of thrice this amount. The farmer, then, who sets out twenty acres of good apple orchard, and takes care of it, may expect at no remote period a yearly return of five to fifteen hundred dollars a year, and even more, if a considerable portion is occupied with late keepers. This is, it is true, much more than the majority obtain; but the majority wholly neglect cultivating and enriching the soils of their orchards.

Mayfarth's Apple Parer, Corer, and Slicer.

It is not, however, merely as a source of income, that the cultivation of the finer kinds become profitable. The family which is at all times supplied with delicious and refreshing fruit from its own gardens, has within its reach not only a very important means of economy, but of real domestic comfort. An influence is thus introduced of an exalted character; a tendency is directly exerted towards the improvement of the manners of the people. Every addition to the attractions of home, has a salutary bearing on a rising family of children. The difference between a dwelling with well planted grounds, and well furnished with every rural enjoyment, and another where scarcely a single fruit tree softens the face of bleakness and desolation, may, in many instances , and to many a young man just approaching active life, serve as the guiding influence between a useful life on the one hand, or a roving and unprofitable one on the other-- between a life of virtue and refinement from early and favorable influences, or one of dissipation and ruin from the over-balancing effects of a repulsive home. Nor can any man, even in the noon or approaching evening of life, scarcely fail to enjoy a higher happiness, with at least an occasional intercourse with the blossoming and loaded trees which his own hand has planted and pruned, than in the noise of the crowd and tumult of the busy world.

FRUITING BRANCH OF KUMQUAT (CITRUS JAPONICA).

THE ORANGE FAMILY

Citrus, L. Aurantiaceae, of botanists

The Orange family includes the common orange, (Citrus aurantium;) the Lemon, (C. limonum;) the Lime, (C. limetta;) the Shaddock, (C. decumana;) and the Citron, (C. Medica;) all different species, with the same general habit.

The Orange, a native of Asia, is the most attractive and beautiful of fruit trees, with its rich, dark evergreen foliage, and its golden fruit; and it may well therefore enjoy the reputation of being the golden apple of the Hesperides. When to these charms we add the delicious fragrance of the blossoms, surpassing that of any other fruit tree, it must be conceded that, though the orange must yield in flavour to some other fruit, yet, on the whole, nothing surpasses an orange grove, or orchard, in its combination of attractions—rich verdure, the delicious aroma of its flowers, and the great beauty of its fruit.

The south of Europe, China, and the West Indies, furnish the largest supplies of this fruit. But it has, for a considerable time, been cultivated pretty largely in Florida, and the orange groves of St. Augustine yield large and profitable crops. Indeed, the cultivation may be extended over a considerable portion of that part of the Union bordering on the Gulf of Mexico; and the southern part of Louisiana, and part of Texas, are highly favorable to orange plantations. The bitter orange has become quite naturalized in parts of Florida, the so-called wild orange seedlings furnishing a stock much more hardy than those produced by sowing the imported seeds. By continually sowing the seed of these wild oranges, they will furnish stocks suited to almost all the Southern States, which will in time render the better kinds grafted upon them, comparatively hardy.

North of the latitude, where, in this country, the orange can be grown in groves, or orchards, it may still be profitably cultivated with partial protection. The injury the trees suffer from severe winters, arises not from their freezing--for they will bear, without injury, severe frost--but from the rupture of sap-vessels by the sudden thawing. A mere shed, or covering of boards, will guard against all this mischief. Accordingly, towards the south of Europe, where the climate is pretty severe, the orange is grown in rows against stone walls, or banks, in terraced gardens, or trained loosely against a sheltered trellis; and at the approach of winter they are covered with a slight moveable shed or frame of boards. In mild weather, the sliding doors are opened and air is

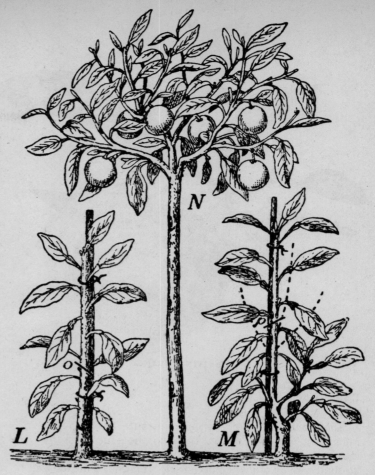

FORMS OF ORANGE TREES.

References : L, Orange tree one year from the bud : *o*, point of pruning to form a conical or pyramidal tree. M, conical tree in second year : *p*, point of shortening ; dotted lines indicate growths the result of pruning the leader. N, standard in third year after heading.

admitted freely—if very severe, a few pots of charcoal are placed within the enclosure. This covering remains over them four or five months, and in this way the orange may be grown as far north as Baltimore.

Soil and Culture.—The best soil for the orange is a deep rich loam. In propagating them, sow, early in the spring, the seeds of the naturalized or wild bitter orange of Florida, which gives much the hardiest stock. They may be budded in the nursery row the same season, or the next, and for this purpose the earliest time at which the operation can be performed (the wood of the buds being sufficiently firm), the greater the success. Whip, or splice grafting, may also be resorted to early in the spring. Only the hardiest sorts should be chosen for orchards or groves, the more delicate ones can be grown easily with slight covering in winter. Fifty feet is the maximum height of the orange in its native country, but it rarely forms in Florida more than a compact low tree of twenty feet. It is better therefore to plant them so near as partially to shade the surface of the ground.

Varieties.—From among the great number of names that figure in the European catalogues, we select a few of those really deserving attention in each class of this fruit.

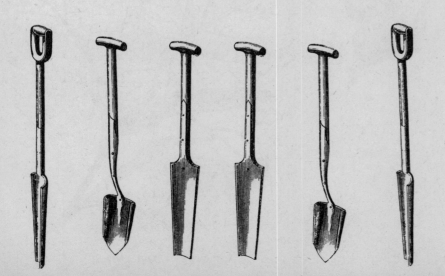

Orange Tree against a Wall in the Open Air at Osborne

FRUITING BRANCH OF ORANGE.

THE ORANGE

The Orange (Oranger, French; Pomeranze, German; Arancio, Italian; and Naranja, Spanish) is on the whole the finest tree of the genus. Its dark green leaves have winged foot-stalks, its fruit is round with an orange coloured skin. It is one of the longest lived fruit trees, as an instance of which we may quote the celebrated tree at Versailles, called "the Grand Bourgon," which was sown in 1421, and is at the present time in existence, one of the largest and finest trees in France.

The fruit of the orange is universally esteemed in its ripe state. The bitter orange is used for marmalades; the green fruits, even when as small as peas, are preserved, and used in various ways in confectionary; the rind and pulp are used in cooking; and the orange flowers distilled, give the orange flower water, so highly esteemed as a perfume and in cookery.

Besides the common sweet orange, the most esteemed sorts are the Maltese, and the blood-red, both of excellent flavour with red pulp. The Mandarin Orange is a small, flattened fruit, with a thin rind separating very easily from the pulp, frequently parting from it of itself, and leaving a partially hollow space. It comes from China, and is called there the Mandarin, or noble orange, from its excellent quality. The flesh is dark orange coloured, juicy and very rich.

The St. Michael's orange is a small fruit, the skin pale yellow, the rind thin, the pulp often seedless, juicy, and lusciously sweet. It is considered the most delicious of all oranges, and the tree is a most abundant bearer.

The Seville, or bitter orange, is the hardiest of all the varieties, enduring very hard frosts without injury. It has the largest and most fragrant flowers: the pulp, however, is bitter and sharp, and is valued chiefly for marmalades. The Double Bigarde is a French variety, of this species, with fine double blossoms.

The Bergamot orange has small flowers, and pear-shaped fruit. The leaves, flowers, and fruit, being peculiarly fragrant, it is highly esteemed by the perfumer, and yields the bergamot essences. "The rind, first dried and then moistened, is pressed in moulds into small boxes for holding sweetmeats, to which it communicates a bergamot flavour."

Besides the above, the Fingered, Sweet-skinned, Pear-shaped, and Ribbed oranges, are the most striking sorts, all chiefly cultivated by curious amateurs.

FRUITING BRANCH OF MANDARIN ORANGE.

The Lemon (Limonier, of the French and German; Limone, Italian; Limon, Spanish) has longer paler leaves than the orange, the footstalks of which are naked or wingless; the flowers tinged with red externally, and the fruit is oblong, pale yellow, with a swollen point, and usually an acid pulp. Its principal use is in making lemonade, punch, and other cooling acid drinks.

Besides the common Lemon, there is an Italian variety, called the Sweet Lemon, the pulp of which is sweet and good.

FRUITING BRANCH OF LEMON (C. acida).

THE LIME

The Lime (Limettier, of the French) differs from the Lemon by its smaller, entirely white flowers, and small, roundish, pale yellow fruit, with a slight protuberance at the end. The acid, though sharp, is scarcely so rich and high as that of the lemon, and is used for the same purposes. The green fruit is more esteemed than any other for preserving. The Italians cultivate a curiously marked variety called Pomo d'Adamo, in which Adam is said to have left the marks of his teeth.

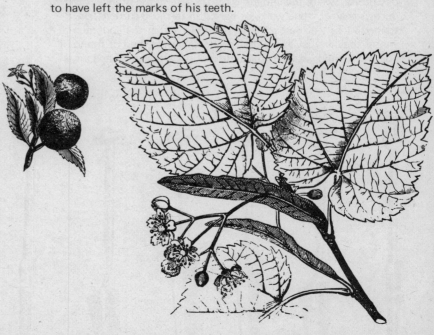

FLOWER OF THE LIME.

Shaddock Tree (Citrus decumana).

THE SHADDOCK

The Shaddock (Pampelmous, French; Arancio massimo, Italian) may be considered a monstrous orange, with a comparatively tasteless pulp. It is a native of China and Japan, and has its name from Dr. Shaddock, who first carried it to the West Indies. The leaves are winged, like those of the orange, the flowers white, and the fruit globular. Its size is very large, as it often weighs six or eight pounds. The pulp is sweetish, or subacid, and the juice is rather refreshing. It is, however, more showy than useful, and certainly makes a magnificent appearance in a collection of tropical fruits.

THE CITRON

The Citron (Cidratier of the French; Citronier, German; Cedrato, Italian) is one of the finest growing trees of this family, with large, oblong, wingless leaves, and flowers tinged with purple externally. The fruit, shaped like that of the lemon, is much larger, of a yellow colour, warted and furrowed externally. The rind is very fragrant, and very thick, the pulp is subacid, and is used in the same way as that of the lemon. It is chiefly valued however for the rich sweetmeat or preserve, called citron, made from the rind.

The Madras citron is considered the largest and best variety.

THE OLIVE

Olea Europea, L.; Oleinae, of botanists; Olivier, of the French; Oehlbaum, German; Ulivo, Italian; Olivo, Spanish.

The Olive, which, as Loudon justly remarks, furnishes, in its invaluable oil, the cream and butter of Spain and Italy, will undoubtedly one day be largely cultivated in our Southern States. Already small plantations of it have been formed by a few spirited gentlemen in Georgia and Mississippi, and its adaptation to the Southern parts of the Union near the sea-coast, tested. The apathy of Southern planters generally, respecting all products but cotton and rice, is the only reason for the tardy manner in which this and other valuabale trees are introduced into cultivation there.

The uses and value of the olive-oil are still comparatively unknown in this country. In the South of Europe it is more valuable than bread, as, to say nothing of its wholesomeness, it enters into every kind of cookery, and renders so large a quantity of vegetable food fit for use. A few olive trees will serve for the support of an entire family, who would starve on what could otherwise be raised on the same surface of soil; and dry crevices of rocks, and almost otherwise barren soils in the deserts, when planted with this tree, become flourishing and valuable places of habitation.

The olive is a native of the temperate sea-coast ridges of Asia and Africa; but it has, time out of mind, been cultivated in the South of Europe. It is a low evergreen tree, scarcely twenty feet high, its head spreading, and clothed with stiff, narrow, bluish green leaves. Its dark green or black fruit is oval, the hard fleshy pulp enclosing a stone. In a pickled state the fruit is highly esteemed. The pickles are made by steeping the unripe olives in ley water, after which they are washed and bottled in salt and water, to which is often added fennel, or some kind of spice. The oil is made by crushing the fruit to a paste, pressing it through a coarse hempen bag, into hot water, from the surface of which the oil is skimmed off. The best oil is made from the pulp alone: when the stone also is crushed, it is inferiour.

Propagation and Culture.—A very common mode of propagating the olive in Italy, is by means of the uovoli (little eggs). These are knots or tumours, which form in considerable numbers on the bark of the trunk, and are easily detached by girdling them with a penknife, the mother plant suffering no injury. They are planted in the soil like bulbs, an inch or so deep, when they take root and form new trees. It is also propagated by cuttings and seeds. The seedlings form the strongest and thriftiest trees; they are frequently some months in vegetating, and should therefore be buried an inch deep in the soil as soon as ripe.

The wild American olive (Olea Americana, L.) or Devil-wood, a tree that grows more or less abundantly as far North as Virginia, will undoubtedly prove a good stock, on which to engraft the European olive. It is of a hardier habit, and though worthless itself, may become valuable in this way.

The olive tree commences bearing five or six years after being planted. Its ordinary crop is fifteen or twenty pounds of oil per annum, and the regularity of its crop, as well as the great age to which it lives, renders an olive plantation one of the most valuable in the world.

THE POMEGRANATE

Punica granatum, L.; Granatacea, of botanists; Grenadier, of the French; Granatenbaum, German; Melagrano, Italian; Granado, Spanish.

This unique fruit, the most singularly beautiful one that ever appears at the dessert, is a native of China and the South of Europe. It grows and bears very readily in this country, as far North as Maryland and the Ohio river, though the fruit does not always mature well north of Carolina, except in sheltered places. It is even hardy enough to stand the winter here, and will bear very good fruit, if trained as an espalier, and protected in winter.

The fruit is as large as an apple. Its skin is hard and leathery, of a yellowish orange colour, with a rich red cheek. It is crowned in a peculiar manner with the large calyx, which remains and increases in size after the flower has fallen. There is a pretty big bit of mythological history told by Rapin, the French poet, respecting this fruit. Bacchus once beguiled a lovely Scythian girl, whose head had been previously turned by the diviners having prophesied that she would some day wear a crown, and who therefore lent a willing ear to his suit. The fickle god, however, not long after abandoned her, when she soon died of grief. Touched at last, he metamorphosed her into a pomegranate tree, and placed on the summit of its fruit, the crown (calyx), which he had denied to his mistress while living.

The fruit of the common pomegranate is acid, but the cultivated variety bears fruit of very agreeable sweet flavour. The interior of the fruit consists of seeds enveloped in pulp much like those of the gooseberry, but arranged in compartments, and of the size and colour of red currants. Medicinally it is cooling and much esteemed, like the orange, in fevers and inflammatory disorders.

The tree is of low growth, from twelve to twenty feet, with numerous slender twiggy branches, and is very ornamental in garden scenery, either when clad with its fine scarlet flowers or decked with fruit, which hangs and grows all summer, and does not ripen till pretty late in the season. It is well worthy of a choice sheltered place at the north, on a wall or espalier rail, where it can be slightly protected with mats or straw in winter; and it deserves to be much more popular than it now is in every southern garden. If raised in large quantities there, it would become a valuable fruit for sending to the northern cities, as it is now constantly sent from the south of Europe to Paris and London. Hedges are very often made of it near Genoa and Nice.

Propagation and Culture.—This tree is readily propagated by cuttings, layers, suckers or seeds. When by seeds, they should be sown directly after they ripen, otherwise they seldom vegetate. Any good rich garden soil answers well for the Pomegranate—and, as it produces little excess of wood, it needs little more in the way of pruning, than an occasional thinning out of any old or decaying branches.

FRUITING BRANCHLET OF POMEGRANATE.

Varieties.—There are several varieties. The finest, viz.:
1. The Sweet-fruited Pomegranate (Grenadier a Fruit Doux), with sweet and juicy pulp.
2. The Sub-acid Fruited Pomegranate; the most common variety cultivated in gardens.
3. The Wild, or Acid-Fruited Pomegranate, with a sharp acid flavour; which makes an excellent syrup.

Besides these, there are several double-flowering varieties of the Pomegranate which are very beautiful, but bear no fruit. They are also rather more tender than the fruit-bearing ones. The finest are the Double Red Pomegranate, with large and very splendid scarlet blossoms, and the Double White Pomegranate, with flowers nearly white. There are also the rarer varieties, the Yellow-Flowered and the Variegated Flowered Pomegranate—seldom seen here except in choice green-house collections.

FRUIT CULTURE , 1855

MAKING APPLE CIDER

By Leslie Hudson

from GARDEN MAGAZINE, 1905

Cider making offers a good opportunity of saving the surplus apples from the home fruit garden, after the best have been put into the cellar for winter use, thus making valuable apples that otherwise would be thrown away. A bruise which would render an apple unfit for storage does not impair it as a source of cider.

The best cider is not made from sweet apples, or from apples that have little juice, such as Ben Davis, but from good, juicy, sour kinds, such as Northern Spy, Baldwin and the like. It is often advisable to mix a few sweet apples in with the sour ones to soften the taste of the cider, but this is a matter of taste.

If good specimen of Northern Spy are used, the cider will prove an expensive luxury. Therefore, any undersized apples and any that become bruised in handling may be used.

For the man who intends making only a small amount of cider each year—enough for consumption in his own household during the winter—a mill worked by hand and pressing the pomace of only two or three bushels of apples is the most practical. A mill of this sort will cost anywhere from $10 up, according to the size. The usual amount of cider that can be pressed from a bushel of crushed apples is four gallons. This amount varies, so that while some bushels give five gallons others only produce two gallons. The introduction of steel knives to cut the apples, and modern methods of pressing out the juice from the pomace, has made old farmers shake their heads. They declare that the old wooden crushers produce the finest cider and can never be equaled.

The old-fashioned method of preparing pomace for pressing is the best. Upon a layer of rye straw is placed a layer of pomace. Then more straw and more pomace until the press is filled. After this "cheese," as it is called, is pressed the first time, the pressure may be relieved and the cheese stirred up with a crowbar. Then the pressure should be applied again.

After the cider has been all squeezed out it may be placed in casks, with bunghole uncorked, and left for several weeks to "work." Then the bungs can be put in place and the cider is ready for use.

After the cider is drawn off for the first time it can be clarified by breaking and dropping twelve or more eggs in the barrel. This is especially good practice if it is intended to bottle the cider.

Cider, if kept perfectly air tight from the time it is made, will usually keep sweet all winter if placed in new casks, but will become harder all the time. Various preservatives are used to keep it sweet and yet non-alcoholic, but they rob the cider of its flavor.

Good vinegar can be obtained by leaving the bung out of the barrel, not only until the cider stops working but until it gets sour. For the first few days the cider is left to stand to make vinegar it should be stirred up by means of a stick inserted through the bunghole.

GRAFTING is the art of combining a twig or bud of one plant with a branch or root of another so that a union forms and growth continues.

Grafting is used mainly to propagate trees, to change varieties for pollination or other purposes, to develop trees on hardy, disease resistant, or dwarfing stocks, and to repair trees damaged by rodents or equipment.

Of the many methods of grafting, only cleft grafting, whip grafting, bridge grafting, and shield budding are described here.

Grafting in the orchard is done in spring from the time growth starts until full bloom. Root grafting (bench grafting) for the propagation of trees may be done anytime during the dormant season. Shield budding is done from mid-July to early September. Stone fruits are propagated in the nursery by budding--other methods are not satisfactory. Apples, pears and quince may be propagated by budding or whip grafting.

To better understand these descriptions, you need to know some common terms used in grafting. These terms will be used often:

Scion--The twig or bud which will become the top of the new plant.

Stock--The root or rooted part of the plant upon which the scion is grafted. A stock may be a young seedling plant or a large tree.

Cambium--A thin layer of cells between the bark and the wood which unite the scion and stock. As the tree grows, cambium cells divide to produce bark on the outside and wood on the inside.

Graft union--The place where the scion and stock grow together. For a graft union to form, there must be contact between the cambium layers of the stock and the scion.

GRAFTING

--George Klingbeil & Malcolm Dana

University of Wisconsin EXTENSION SERVICE
COLLEGE OF AGRICULTURE, MADISON

THE CLEFT GRAFT

Select one year old water sprouts (suckers)

1.

Cut these sprouts for scions in February or March when trees are dormant. Store in a cool moist place.

The cleft graft is used to topwork old trees.

PREPARING THE STOCK

• Select branches that will provide for a well-balanced tree. They should be about 2 inches or less in diameter and near the trunk or on main scaffold limbs.

• Select a knot-free, straight section on the stock branch. To avoid tearing the bark, saw off the limb about a foot above the selected point. Make the final cut at the upper part of the smooth section at right angles to the grain. Smooth the cut surface with a sharp knife.

2.

First saw off a branch not over 2" in diameter.

3.

Next smooth top and edges of cut end.

• With the grafting tool and mallet, split the stock through the center. It is not necessary to drive the grafting tool more than 2 inches into the stock. Cut any slivers within the cleft.

• With the wedge of the grafting tool, open the cleft wide enough to insert the scions.

4. Then split stub with grafting tool.

Preparing the Scion

• Shape the lower end of the scion into a wedge about 1½ inches long. The lower end of the wedge may be left blunt.

• Make the inner side of the wedge thinner than the outside (see illustration). The lowest bud on the scion should be slightly above the bevels of the wedge and on the outside (thick side) of the scion.

• Shorten the scion to 3 buds. Cut the top of the scion with a sloping cut ¼ inch above the upper bud.

• Do not let the scions dry. It is best to prepare them when they are to be used.

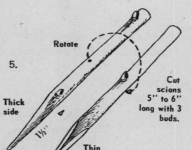

5.

Rotate

Thick side

Thin side

Cut scions 5" to 6" long with 3 buds.

Making the Graft

• Insert the scions with the thick side facing the outside of the stock and with the cambium of the scions in contact with the cambium of the stock. Do not insert the scions at an angle. Since the bark of the stock is thicker than that of the scions, set the scions in from the outer bark of

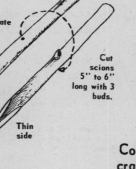

Open cleft with screwdriver. Insert scions with thick edge of cut on scion to the outer edge of stub.

6.

the stock so the two cambium layers can meet. Be sure the top of the bevel cuts are even with the stock.

• Remove the wedge and seal the stub, cracks, and tip of the scions with grafting compound to prevent the graft from drying out.

• Let the scions grow undisturbed the first season. The following spring, cut back the poorest growing scion to a few buds and let the stronger scion continue growth. Leave both scions until the graft is completely healed and then remove the weaker one.

Coat cut end and cracks of stub and tips of scion with grafting compound.

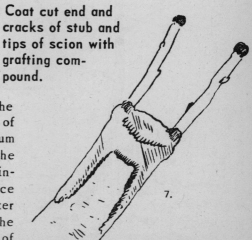

7.

THE WHIP GRAFT

Young apple and pear trees may be topworked by whip grafting and propagated by root grafting. The stock and scion should be the same diameter where they are grafted. Use one-year old scion wood that is ¼ to ⅜ inch in diameter.

- Select a stock that is smooth and straight. With root grafts, some side roots may be trimmed off where the graft is to be made.

- Make a smooth, sloping cut through the stock about 1½ inches long. On the surface of this cut, about one-third of the way from the tip, make a slit or tongue about ½ inch long. Slant this slit slightly toward the base or heel of the first cut.

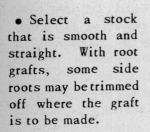

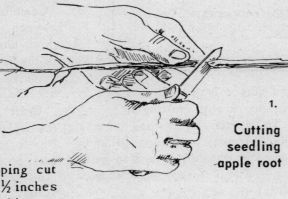

Cutting seedling apple root

1.

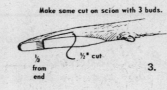

Make same cut on scion with 3 buds.

⅓ from end   ½" cut   3.

- The scion should be about 4 inches long (3 buds) and prepared in the same manner as the stock with the tongue at the base of the scion.

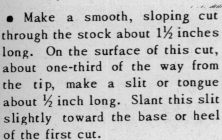

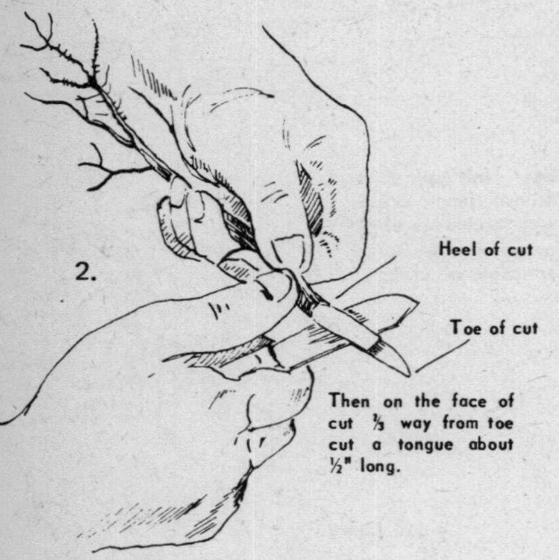

2.

Heel of cut
Toe of cut

Then on the face of cut ⅓ way from toe cut a tongue about ½" long.

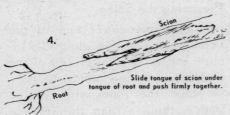

4.

Scion

Slide tongue of scion under tongue of root and push firmly together.

Root

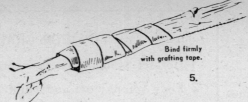

Bind firmly with grafting tape.

5.

- Fit the cut surfaces of the scion and stock firmly together, slipping the tongue of the scion under the tongue of the stock. The cambium layers should match on one or both sides. If the toe of either scion or stock extends beyond the heel of the other, cut it off evenly.

- Wrap the stock and scion firmly with grafting tape or rubber tape. It is best to seal the grafting tape with grafting compound.

- When the scion starts to grow, cut the grafting tape to prevent girdling. Rubber tape need not be removed as it will weather away by itself.

- Shoots growing on the stock should be cut back the first year and kept cut off completely from the second year on.

6.

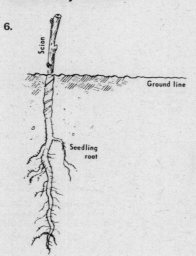

Scion

Ground line

Seedling root

GRAFTING

TOP WORKING WITH GRAFTING

The hibernal variety to be used as a stock, usually 2 to 3 years old.

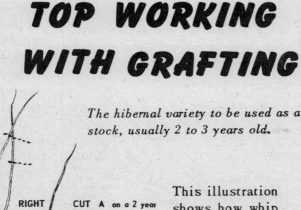

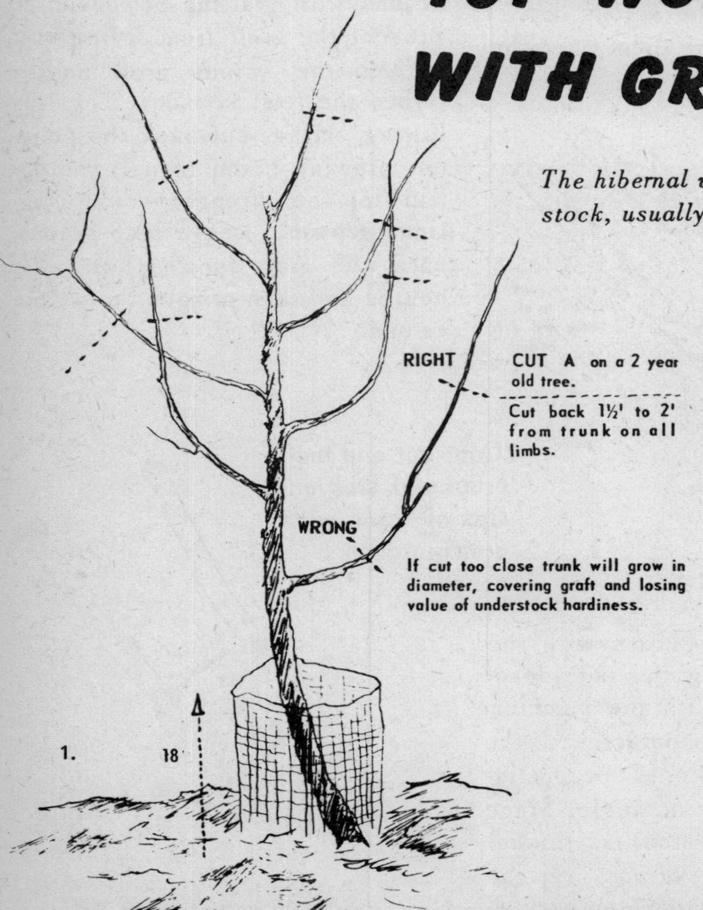

RIGHT

CUT A on a 2 year old tree.

Cut back 1½' to 2' from trunk on all limbs.

WRONG

If cut too close trunk will grow in diameter, covering graft and losing value of understock hardiness.

This illustration shows how whip grafting is used to produce trees with hardy understocks.

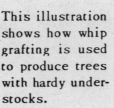

1.   18'

Cut 1½" bevel

2.

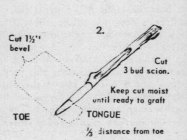

Cut 3 bud scion.

Keep cut moist until ready to graft

TOE   TONGUE

⅓ distance from toe

3.

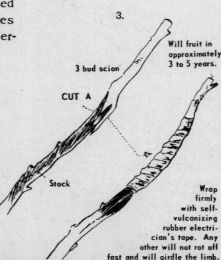

3 bud scion

Will fruit in approximately 3 to 5 years.

CUT A

Stock

Wrap firmly with self-vulcanizing rubber electrician's tape. Any other will not rot off fast and will girdle the limb.

TOOLS AND MATERIALS

Certain tools and materials are needed to do a good job of grafting.

Cleft Grafting
- A sharp knife
- A grafting tool (a suitable substitute is a sturdy butcher knife and a screw driver)
- A hammer or mallet
- A fine-toothed saw
- Grafting compound and a brush to apply it.

Whip Grafting
- A sharp knife
- Grafting compound
- Grafting tape

(Rubber electrician's tape may be substituted for the grafting compound and tape.)

Budding
- A sharp knife
- Rubber budding strips (raffia, cotton twine, rubber bands may be substituted for the budding strips)

Bridge Grafting
- A sharp knife
- Flat-headed wire nails ¾ inch long
- A hammer
- Grafting compound and a brush to apply it.

GRAFTING COMPOUNDS

The most commonly used grafting compounds are the water emulsions of asphalt. They are readily available, can be applied cold, hold well, and are inexpensive. Do not use roofing asphalt or tar--they contain materials injurious to trees. You can buy ready-made grafting waxes. However you can make a good brush wax from: 5 pounds of rosin, one pound of beeswax, ½ pound of powdered charcoal and ½ cup of raw linseed oil. Melt the rosin over heat, add beeswax and melt. Add the linseed oil, remove from heat and slowly add the charcoal, stirring constantly. It is best to pour the mixture into shallow pans and allow it to harden. The wax must be melted for use. Do not apply extremely hot wax to the tree.

Do not use improvised, unproven materials to protect grafts.

SCION WOOD

Scion wood for grafting should be collected from trees when they are dormant. Select well-hardened and mature water sprouts or one-year-old terminal growth about ¼ to ⅜ inch in diameter. To keep the scions in a dormant condition until needed, store them in moist moss or sawdust in a cold place.

SHIELD BUDDING

Budding is usually done from mid-July to early September. It is used to propagate stone fruits and may be used to propagate apples, pears, and ornamentals.

- Select bud sticks from vigorous present season's growth. Clip off the leaves leaving about ½ inch of leaf stem for a bud handle. Do not use immature buds that are located near the tips of new growth. Keep the bud sticks from drying out.
- Select a stock ¼ to ½ inch in diameter, usually current season's growth. Make a T-shaped cut through the bark of the stock. The base of the T should be toward

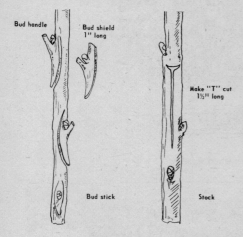

Bud handle
Bud shield 1" long
Make "T" cut 1½" long
Bud stick
Stock

the base of the stock. Carefully loosen the corners of the bark.

- Cut the bud shield (scion) with a sharp knife, starting about ½ inch below the bud and cutting upward to ½ inch above the bud. Cut into the wood below the bud about twice as deep as the bark. Then make a cross cut about ½ inch above the bud going only through the bark. Lift off the bud leaving the wood sliver on the bud stick.

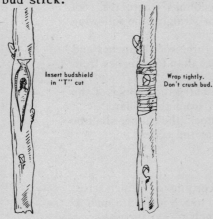

Insert budshield in "T" cut
Wrap tightly. Don't crush bud.

- Place the tip of the bud shield into the opening at the top of the T on the stock and slide the shield into the T cut.
- When the bud is in position, wrap it with rubber budding strips, twine, or raffia. Start with a self-binding loop slightly below the base of the T, continue wrapping to above the T using a self-binding loop at the top to prevent unwrapping. Do not cover the bud.

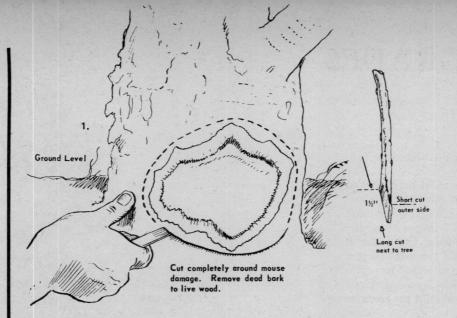

1.
Ground Level
Cut completely around mouse damage. Remove dead bark to live wood.

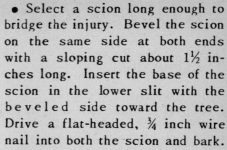

1½"
Short cut outer side
Long cut next to tree

THE BRIDGE GRAFT

This graft is used to bridge over an injured area on the trunk of a tree. Select scions for bridge grafting from hardy varieties.

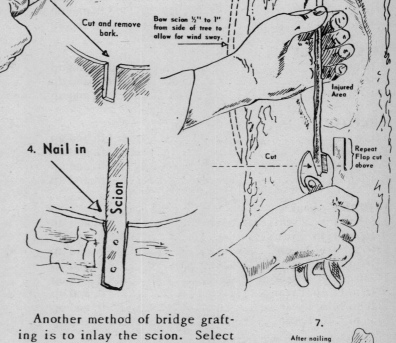

2.
Injury
Mark for scion cut along side scion
Cut and remove bark.

6.
Cut scion to fit snugly under flap.
Cut approximately 1½" long by diameter of scion wide.
Bow scion ½" to 1" from side of tree to allow for wind sway.
Injured Area
Cut
Repeat Flap cut above

3. Cut scion to fit.

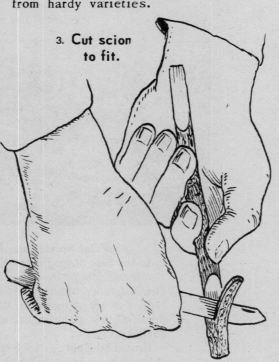

4. Nail in
Scion

- Clean the injured part of the stock of all dead bark and cut back the irregular edges of the bark at the upper and lower part of the injury evenly to live wood.
- Below the injury cut a vertical slit about 2 inches long in the live bark. Lift the edges of the bark with a dull, smooth wedge having a diameter similar to the scion.
- Make a second slit at the upper side of the injury directly above the lower slit.

5.
Cover graft with compound.
2"

Another method of bridge grafting is to inlay the scion. Select a curved scion, make it long enough to extend about 1½ inches beyond the injured area at each end. Cut the scion as directed above, but remove the point or toe (see figure). Tack the scion lightly to the bark where it is to be placed. Mark around each end of the scion to get the exact size, remove the scion and cut out the bark. Fit the scion into the channels in the bark and carefully nail it down. Seal with grafting compound.

- Select a scion long enough to bridge the injury. Bevel the scion on the same side at both ends with a sloping cut about 1½ inches long. Insert the base of the scion in the lower slit with the beveled side toward the tree. Drive a flat-headed, ¾ inch wire nail into both the scion and bark.
- Follow the same method with the top of the scion, making certain to get a "bow" in the scion to allow for tree sway.
- Place scions at 2-inch intervals around the injured part of the tree. When the scions are all in place, carefully seal the graft unions and the injured area with grafting compound. Keep all shoots removed from scions.

7.
After nailing apply grafting compound over graft and injured area.

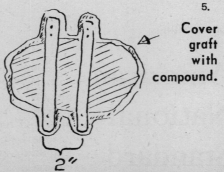

8.
Nail through flap and scion solidly into tree.
No. 18 Wire nails

In cases where bridge spans are impractical, approach grafts or inarching may be used. Plant seedlings or rooted whips near the injured trunk and graft the whip to the tree above the injured area.

FRUIT TREE GRADES

DECIDUOUS

GENERAL

All trees should have reasonably straight bodies according to habit of growth.

All grades five-sixteenths and larger should be branched except one year Sweet Cherry, and well rooted. The nine-sixteenths and eleven-sixteenths should have three or more side branches. Caliper should be taken two inches above the collar or bud. Height shall be taken from the collar if grafted or from the union of the bud and stock if budded.

The caliper shall govern, height being intended to represent average height of most varieties. Slow growing kinds may fall short of height specified. Age should be given as one year, two years, etc.

Caliper (in inches)	Minimum Heights

APPLE—Standard, CHERRY—Sweet, PEACH, PEAR—Standard & PLUM (1 and 2 years)

11/16 and up	4½ ft. and up
9/16 to 11/16	4 ft. and up
7/16 to 9/16	3 ft. and up
5/16 to 7/16	2 ft. and up

PEAR—Dwarf & QUINCE

9/16 and up	3½ ft. and up
7/16 to 9/16	3 ft. and up
5/16 to 7/16	2 ft. and up

APPLE—Dwarf

9/16 and up	3½ ft. and up
7/16 to 9/16	2½ ft. and up
5/16 to 7/16	2 ft. and up

APRICOT

11/16 and up	4 ft. and up
9/16 to 11/16	3 ft. and up
7/16 to 9/16	2½ ft. and up
5/16 to 7/16	2 ft. and up

CHERRY—Sour

11/16 to 1 in., 2 years	4 ft. and up
9/16 to 11/16, 2 years	3½ ft. and up
7/16 to 9/16, 2 years	3 ft. and up
5/16 to 7/16, 2 years	2 ft. and up
11/16 and up, 1 year	3½ ft. and up
9/16 to 11/16, 1 year	3 ft. and up
7/16 to 9/16, 1 year	2½ ft. and up
5/16 to 7/16, 1 year	2 ft. and up

ONE YEAR STANDARD

It is accepted practice in the three West Coast states, Washington, Oregon and California, to grade one year old standard fruit tree stock (apples, pears, cherries, plums, peaches, nectarines, apricot and quince) in intervals of 1/8 inch as follows:

1 yr. 3/4 inch and up
1 yr. 5/8 inch and up
1 yr. 1/2 inch to 5/8 inch
1 yr. 3/8 inch to 1/2 inch
1 yr. 1/4 inch to 3/8 inch

SEEDLINGS

Caliper Measurement

Caliper shall be taken at the collar or ground line and grade shall correspond to the following caliper:

3/8 in. — 3/8 in. to 7/16 in.
1/4 in. — 1/4 in. to 3/8 in.
No. 1 — 3/16 in. to 1/4 in.
No. 2 — 1/8 in. to 3/16 in.
No. 3 — 1½/16 in. to 2/16 in.
No. 4 — 1/16 in. to 1½/16 in.
Exception: Grade No. 1 "Straight" of Apple Seedlings shall be graded from 3/16" to 5/16" caliper.

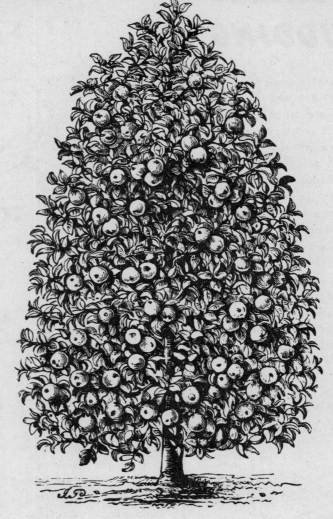

Pyramidal Tree in a finished state.

Special Specifications:

In the case of seedlings with limbs there shall be at least two inches above the collar free of limbs for one-half the circumference of the seedling.

In case of Apple and Pear Seedlings where the root description is given as branched or straight, the following shall apply:

Branched Root — Not less than three root branches and point of branching shall be not more than four inches from the collar.

Straight Root — The root shall carry the caliper of the grade for not less than six inches from the collar.

In the case of "cutting" grown stock, the caliper shall be taken on the original "cutting," at the collar.

CITRUS

Citrus stocks are to be graded according to 1/8 inch series as follows: 3/8 to 1/2 inch; 1/2 inch to 5/8 inch; 5/8 inch to 3/4 inch; 3/4 inch to 1 inch; 1 inch to 1¼ inches.

Age in years is to be given; that is one or two years. Caliper is to be taken 1/2 inch above the bud union. Minimum size to be 3/8 inch except that tangerine, mandarin or lime trees may be sold in 5/16 to 3/8 inch caliper.

American Association of Nurserymen, Inc.
230 Southern Building, Washington, D.C.

American National Standard

An American National Standard implies a consensus of those substantially concerned with its scope and provisions. An American National Standard is intended as a guide to aid the manufacturer, the consumer, and the general public. The existence of an American National Standard does not in any respect preclude anyone, whether he has approved the standard or not, from manufacturing, marketing, purchasing, or using products, processes, or procedures not conforming to the standard. American National Standards are subject to periodic review and users are cautioned to obtain the latest editions.

SMALL FRUITS

All small fruit plants must be well rooted. No injured, dwarfed or odd shape plants shall be included in any grade.

RUBUS (RASPBERRY, THE HANSELL).

RASPBERRIES

8.1.1 SUCKER AND ROOT CUTTING PLANTS

GRADE NO. 1
Sucker and root cutting plants, also tip plants, should be graded 3/16 inch and up in caliper at collar; sucker plants should have 10 inches or more of live top; tip plants, 8 inches or more live tops; and well rooted.

GRADE NO. 2
Sucker and root cutting plants, also tip plants, 1/8 inch and up in caliper at collar; sucker and root cutting plants to have 8 inches or more of live top; tip plants, 6 inches or more of live tops, and all proportionately well rooted.

TRANSPLANTED RASPBERRIES

GRADE NO. 1
All transplanted raspberries should caliper 1/4 inch and up at collar and have 15 inches or more of live top, and be well rooted.

GRADE NO. 2
Number two must caliper 3/16 inch and up with 12 inches or more of live top, and be well rooted.

RUBUS (DEWBERRY, LUCRETIA).

FRUITING BRANCH OF RED CURRANT.

DEWBERRIES, BLACKBERRIES, BOYSENBERRIES, YOUNGBERRIES

ROOT CUTTINGS

GRADE NO. 1
Root cuttings should caliper 1/8 inch and sucker plants should caliper 3/16 inch and up at collar and have 12 inches or more of live top, and be well rooted.

GRADE NO. 2
Root cuttings should caliper 3/32 inch and up and sucker plants should caliper 1/8 inch and up at collar and have 8 inches or more of live top, and be proportionately well rooted.

TRANSPLANTED BLACKBERRIES

GRADE NO. 1
Should caliper 1/4 inch and up at collar and have 12 inches or more of live top, and be well rooted.

CURRANTS

GRADE 2 YR. NO. 1
Shall measure 12 inches and up in height, with two or more branches, and be well rooted.

GRADE 1 YR. NO. 1
Shall measure 9 inches and up in height; if single cane plants, to be 12 inches high, and be well rooted.

GRADE 2 YR. NO. 2
Same specifications as 1 Yr. No. 1.

BLUEBERRIES
All measurements to indicate overall height of plant from crown to tip of plants. All well rooted and well branched in proportion to height.

Low training of blackberries.

Lucretia dewberry.

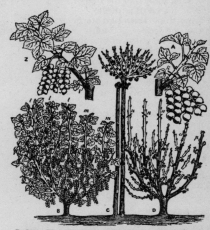

FIG. 268. CHARACTERISTIC GROWTHS AND FORMS OF RED CURRANT BUSHES. SUMMER AND WINTER PRUNING.

References: Z, unpruned side branch; l, pruning mark too low—no basal buds (compare with A). A, pruned side branch: i, summer growth pinched at the bar; f, second growth; h, point of winter pruning (compare with Z). B, bush in summer: l, three branches with side growths unpinched; m, two branches with summer shoots pinched. C, standard. D, bush in winter: n, three unpinched branches marked for pruning at the bars; c, branch with detached shoots, indicating winter pruning; p, pruned branch. N.B.—The bush has nine branches, four at the back not being shown.

1 year Rooted Cuttings	3-6 in.
2 year No. 1	9-12 in.
2 year No. 2	6-9 in.
3 year No. 1	12-18 in.
4 year No. 1	18-24 in.

GOOSEBERRIES

GRADE 2 YR. NO. 1
Shall measure 12 inches and up in height, with three or more canes, or equivalent side branches, and be well rooted.

GRADE 1 YR. NO. 1
Shall measure 8 inches and up in height, with two or more branches, or equivalent side branches, and be well rooted.

GRADE 2 YR. NO. 2
Same specifications as 1 Yr. No. 1.

GRAPE VINES
Grading of Grape Vines is based mainly on root system.

GRADE 2 YR. NO. 1
The lightest growing varieties should have 12 inches or more of live top; stronger growing varieties should be proportionately larger and all well rooted.

GRADE 1 YR. NO. 1
Lightest growers should have 6 inches or more of live top; stronger growers should be proportionately larger and all well rooted.

GRADE 2 YR. NO. 2
Same specifications as 1 Yr. No. 1.

STRAWBERRY PLANTS

MINIMUM GRADE
There shall be at least ten (10) main roots, not less than three (3) inches long, and a minimum crown diameter of 5/16 in. measured at the base.

PRUNING THE HOME ORCHARD

By S.W. Fletcher

"I reckon I had better go out and trim up my fruit trees today. I haven't trimmed them for three years, and they are getting all choked up with wood." So remarked my neighbor from his porch one gusty March morning, surveying the half-dozen trees in his yards with the pride of ownership. I saw him start out with saw and ladder, and with the evident determination of atoning for past neglect by doing a good job. A few hours later I was called out to view his handiwork. He had certainly "trimmed up" the trees literally; and he had done a "good job" without doubt. A third of the top of each tree was on the ground. All the lower limbs had been removed. I expostulated. "You have pruned too heavily. Next year you will have a big crop of suckers and less fruit." But my neighbor was satisfied with his job. He had trimmed up the trees. Did not the pile of brush bear witness to the thoroughness of his work?

My neighbor's pruning is like that of many other home orchardists—well meant, but misguided. It is not so much that people do not prune enough, as that their pruning is not wisely directed. Butcher pruning ruins as many trees as the neglect of pruning.

No two trees can be pruned exactly alike, if they are pruned correctly. Pruning is a matter of judgment, not of rule. No man can tell you how you should prune your trees without seeing them; that lies between your own judgment and the condition of the trees. Nevertheless, there are a few principles of pruning which apply everywhere. The home fruit grower, no matter where he lives, who keeps these principles in mind, will not go far astray in his pruning.

The first rule is: Prune regularly and lightly. The average home orchard is neglected for two to four years; then it is pruned too heavily.

The reason why the trees, after severe pruning, make a very vigorous growth of wood and clothe the naked limbs with suckers, is that Nature is trying to restore the balance which the pruner upset. There is normally a balance between the top of the tree and its roots. There is only as much top as there are roots to support it; the top is the expression of the roots. If, then, a tree loses a third of its top by an ice storm or by cut-throat pruning, the roots immediately endeavor to restore the equilibrium by pushing out more top. Hence suckers and watersprouts.

The important point about this to the home fruit-grower is the fact that when the tree is making such a strenuous effort to regain its normal complement of top, it is likely to be seriously reduced in fruit bearing. Trees which "run to wood" are not usually fruitful. Many a backyard fruit tree is unproductive for no reason other than spasmodic and very heavy pruning. The practical method, then, is to prune regularly and lightly—a little every year, not a great deal every three or four years. Do not let your desire to do a "good job" turn you into a tree barber. If your trees seem to be growing too fast, the very worst thing you could do is to cut out a lot of wood every winter—that only aggravates the trouble, and the trees will grow faster than ever. In these cases the excessive growth must be checked by such means as withholding fertilizers, ceasing tillage, summer pruning, and—as a last resort—girdling. But fruit trees do not often grow too fast in the home garden.

FORMING THE HEAD

Let us begin with a tree set last spring. It was cut back severely when planted, to equalize the loss of roots from transplanting. Now this tree, with one season's growth, has seven to twelve lusty branches started. Select four or five of the strongest to form the framework of the tree. They are the scaffold limbs. No two of these should be nearly opposite each other, as this makes a bad crotch which will be likely to split under stress of winds or a heavy crop of fruit or ice. Be very careful about this "forming the head." Head back the framework limbs one-third to one-half and cut out all others close. Head back the branches to make the tree stocky.

THE SECOND, THIRD AND AFTER YEARS

At the end of the second season's growth it will be found that two or three shoots have arisen from near the end of each of the scaffold limbs. Save one or two of the best of these, avoiding crotches; head them back and cut out the rest.

After the second or third year it is usually best, in my judgment, to cease heading-in, except as a special treatment for shoots growing out of bounds. Thereafter the tree should be allowed to take its natural form, except when it becomes straggling, or lopsided; and the pruning should consist of thinning out entirely, not of heading-in. In some sections peaches and apricots are often, and plums sometimes, headed back annually to advantage. Annual heading-in keeps the peach, which is naturally a straggling grower, in more compact shape; and it also thins the fruit, which is borne only on the new wood. Weak, unthrifty trees may often be rejuvenated by a severe heading-back. With these possible exceptions, I believe that heading-in should usually cease after the trees are three to four years set.

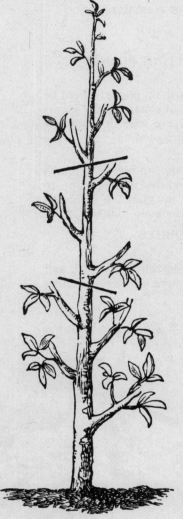

Pyramidal
Pruning.

THE PRUNING OF BEARING TREES

How should bearing trees be pruned? First cut out all dead limbs. They are a menace to the living parts as long as they remain on the tree, breeding rots and often parasitic diseases. Never allow dead branches or stubs to stay on a fruit-tree at any time. Second, where branches crowd, cross and interlace, making in summer a dense mass of foliage which the sun cannot penetrate, do a little thinning. Large, highly colored and fine-flavored fruit cannot be produced in a tangle of branches and beneath a curtain of leaves. This is just where the fruit is covered with fungus, also; the germs which cause it cannot grow without moisture, and if the sun has a chance to dry off the foliage and fruit there is sure to be less scabby and rotten fruit. Thin out, but be careful! The most desirable quality in a man who prunes is conservatism. Think twice before taking off any limb. See if you cannot save it by taking off another smaller limb which interferes with it. If a tree is pruned carefully from the time it is set there should be no necessity for cutting off very large limbs when it is old. A careful man goes over his trees, young and old, several times during the growing months, rubbing off and checking shoots which he sees will make trouble later. Husband the energies of your trees by preventing, instead of curing, overcrowding in the top.

In regions where there is liability of serious injury to fruit trees from sunscalding, the tops are not thinned as much as in more humid sections. It is necessary to keep the fruit trees of the western plains, as Nebraska and of California, much thicker topped than the trees of the Atlantic States.

WHEN TREES ARE PLANTED TOO CLOSELY

The all-too-common mistake of "trimming-up" fruit trees usually arises from the fact that they were planted too closely. Some home orchards look as though they were planted for timber instead of fruit. It is bad enough to have the trees cramped at the roots and jostled at the top, resulting in a poor yield and a poorer quality; but when the tops begin to crowd many people augment the difficulty by trimming off the lower branches. Just why they do this I could never understand. The result can be seen everywhere—orchards of "leggy" trees, their bearing surface reduced to a mere tuft of branches thirty feet from the ground. The owner trimmed them up, so they would have more room! The very best style of pruning for such orchards, if the trees are not more than twenty to twenty-five years old and are still healthy, is to cut out at least every other tree. This will give the remainder a chance to spread. There is more surface for bearing fruit on one symmetrical, well-rounded-out tree, shaped like an inverted bushel basket, than on three trees of the telegraph pole kind which one sees in many home orchards. Don't squeeze trees in the orchard like pines in a forest. Give them a chance to spread out, root and branch, and so do their best.

A peach tree, without pruning, as commonly seen.

A peach tree, pruned by the shortening-in mode.

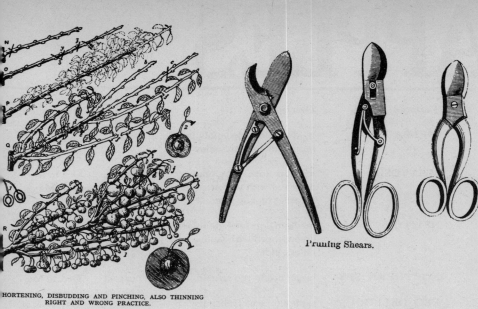

SHORTENING, DISBUDDING AND PINCHING, ALSO THINNING
RIGHT AND WRONG PRACTICE.

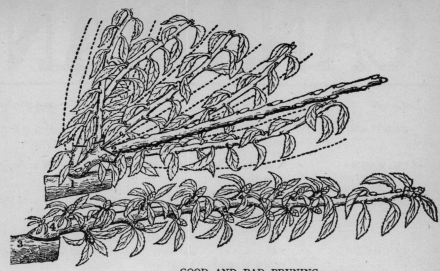

GOOD AND BAD PRUNING.

Top : barren wood ; *bottom :* fruitful wood. (For references see text.)

THE TIME OF YEAR TO PRUNE

What time of the year shall I prune? Again I should be glad to take refuge in generalities. Of course, there is no one best time for pruning. The old saw, "Prune when your knife is sharp," is good advice so far as it goes, provided the man only cuts out suckers and wayward or super-fluous shoots as they appear. The man who takes pride in the appearance of his fruit garden will nip here and check there all the growing season. But the main pruning should be done when the tree is dormant. Pruning is amputation. No matter how con-siderately done, it is always a shock to the tree. The shock is much less, generally, if the operation is performed when the vital energies of the tree are quiescent. Pruning can be done at any time between the fall of the leaves and the bursting of the buds, but it is usually best to wait until early spring—February or March, in most sections—because then the wound soon begins to heal. If pruning is done in early winter, the remain-ing limbs are more likely to winter-kill, especially with peaches and plums; and, moreover, the cut sur-faces evaporate much moisture from the tree, reducing its vitality and making it more liable to winter in-jury. Just before the sap rises is the ideal time to prune in most cases.

Fig. 283. SPUR PRUNING

References: H, vine in the first year of spur pruning: m, lowest wire of trellis; n, bearing shoot spurred to two buds; o, bearing shoot spurred to one bud; p, cane shortened so as to originate four bearing shoots (inclined) and a leader; q, laterals cut off close to the cane; r, buds taken out. I, vine in the second year of spur pruning: s, leader cane; t, bearing shoots pruned to two buds; u, bearing shoots pruned to one bud; the dotted lines indicate the direction of shoots from the buds left; v, good system of bearing when pruned to two buds; w, shoot not allowed to bear fruit; x, bad plan of bearing in pruning to two buds. J, spur pruning with two buds: y, bearing shoot cut away after fruiting; z, untrueed shoot shortened to two buds; the dotted lines indicate third year's growth: a, shoot allowed to bear, and cut away afterwards to c; b, shoot uncropped and shortened to two buds.

WHERE SUMMER PRUNING IS ALLOWABLE

Summer pruning is advantageous only when trees are growing over-vigorous-ly, to the detriment of their fruitful-ness. Summer pruning is one of the best ways of checking this undue growth if the cessation of tillage and withholding of fertilizers fail to do it. Young trees on very rich soil, which are late in coming into bearing, may sometimes be thrown into bear-ing by summer pruning. Keeping in mind the principle, "Checking growth induces fruitfulness," and remembering that summer pruning does check growth severely, since it removes a large number of those plant kitchens—the leaves. The home orchardist can decide if his trees need this special treatment. Summer pruning is a special treatment for special cases. Spring pruning is generally best for the majority of trees, which have not made an un-usually heavy growth.

DON'T LEAVE LONG STUBS

Be careful—be very careful how you make the cuts. A few weeks ago I examined twenty-eight small home orchards from fifteen to twenty-five years old. Of the 940 trees which were originally set in these orchards, 328 are now gone, and twenty-eight more are blown down, split open—rotten-hearted. This loss of 30 per cent is not greater, I believe, than the average loss in home orchards of that age the country over. What is the cause? Carelessness.

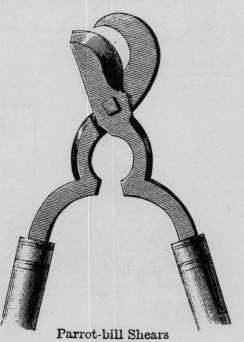

Parrot-bill Shears

Some of those missing trees the borers fattened in; some the mice girdled; some the plow barked; but I am con-vinced from my examination of the remainder that two-thirds of them died from the effects of careless pruning. Where limbs had been removed in past years, I found stubs from three to twelve inches long. The idea was to keep the rot, which would start at the cut end, away from the tree! Then the long stubs make such convenient places for hanging baskets and climbing around the tree! The results may be seen in thousands of orchards the country over. The wounds do not heal and the rot does get in, and work down into the trunk. Some windy day the own-er finds one of his trees blown down—rotten-hearted!

HOW TO MAKE A WOUND HEAL

Long stubs never heal well. They are out of the way of the flow of sap which contains the healing material. Nothing can draw this up to the wound except leaves, and the stubs have no leaves, unless suckers appear. Saw close. We want to cover that wound with healing tissue—the "callus"—just as soon as possible. As long as it remains open it is a menace to the tree. We can help Nature by using a sharp saw—ragged wounds heal slowly; and by covering the wound with some aseptic material while it is healing. Shellac, coal tar and grafting wax are sometimes used, but

paint is best. White lead is much better than ochre for this purpose. Make it thick, so it will not run, and brush it thoroughly into the wood. The paint does not help the wound to heal directly, but it keeps the wood sound while the wound is healing, and prevents the evapora-tion of moisture from the tree. All wounds more than an inch and a half wide should be painted—you cannot afford to neglect it. Old wounds not yet completely healed over should be repainted. All body wounds, as wintersplits, borer in-juries and team injuries, should be treated the same way.

BURN THE PRUNINGS

All prunings should be burned at once and the ashes returned to the orchard soil. Do not let them ac-cumulate from year to year in some corner. They may harbor pests.

IS PRUNING UNNATURAL?

After a man has done a conscientious job of pruning, it is more than likely that his neighbor, who does not prune and whose fruit shows it, will lean over the fence and remark, "Don't you know that pruning is unnatural? Nature doesn't prune, why should man? We can't improve on Nature. Her way is always best."

If you care to retort, ask him if he is satisfied with Nature's apples, pears, plums—the sour, seedy and dimin-utive fruits of the thickets. Tell him that Nature is after as many seeds as she can get, to reproduce the species. She is not concerned so much about the size, juiciness and flavor of the pulp surrounding these seeds. But man is; and since he seeks for a product that is unnatural in one sense, and since this can be done only by unnatural methods, it will pay him to prune. How skilful some men are at inventing excuses for their laziness!

Buy a pair of pruning shears! You will find that pruning is one of the most fascinating operations in hor-ticulture, because it brings the man into the closest touch and sympathy with his plants. Nothing can ex-ceed the delight of finding plants plastic in your hands, and fashioning them at will.

COMMON-SENSE RULES

The fist of my advice, then, is this: Prune regularly, not spasmodically. Study your trees—each one is a new problem in pruning. Head-in young trees, thin out old trees. Prune in early spring. Prune close; don't leave stubs. Paint all large wounds.

CANADIAN APPLES

Variety	Description	Use	Availability*
CORTLAND	large, flat globular; bright red striped	all purpose	Oct. to Feb.
CRIMSON BEAUTY	medium, roundish; deep red striped	cooking	Aug., Sept.
DELICIOUS	elongated, narrowing to 5-point base; bright red striped	dessert	Nov. to Feb.
DUCHESS	medium or small, globular; yellow-green with red stripes	cooking	Aug., Sept.
FAMEUSE (SNOW)	medium, globular; bright solid red	dessert	Oct. to Dec.
GOLDEN DELICIOUS	same shape as Delicious; bright gold color	all purpose	Nov. to Mar.
GOLDEN RUSSET	medium or small, globular; golden brown, with roughened skin due to russeting	dessert	Dec. to Mar.
GRAVENSTEIN	medium, globular; red striped on yellow	all purpose	Sept. to Nov.
GREENING	large, lopsided globular; bright green, turning yellow	cooking	Nov. to Feb.
JONATHAN	small to medium; deep red with greenish-yellow patches	all purpose	Oct. to Jan.
LOBO	large, lopsided globular; deep red with white pin dots	dessert	Sept. to Nov.
MELBA	medium, lopsided globular; red streaked with yellow	all purpose	Aug., Sept.
McINTOSH	medium, lopsided globular; deep red with yellow splashes on one side	all purpose	Oct. to April or May
NEWTON	medium, lopsided globular; green tinged with yellow on one side	all purpose	Jan. to May
NORTHERN SPY	large; bright red striped	all purpose	Dec. to Mar.
RED DELICIOUS	same shape as Delicious; but brighter red striped	dessert	Nov. to Mar.
ROME BEAUTY	large, round; red striped with pin dots	all purpose	Dec. to Mar.
SPARTAN	medium to large, globular; solid red with white pin dots	all purpose	Oct. to May
WEALTHY	medium, bright red striped, yellow splashes on one side	all purpose	Sept. to Dec.
WINESAP	medium, globular; bright red with yellow splashes and white pin dots	all purpose	Dec. to May
YELLOW TRANSPARENT	small to medium, round; greenish yellow	all purpose	August

*Controlled atmosphere storage has made it possible to extend the storage of some varieties beyond the times specified.

reproduced by permission of INFORMATION CANADA

Dwarf or Low Standard Tree on Paradise Stock.

AWARDED BY THE NEW YORK STATE Agricultural Society.

CERES

To Mrs. S. G. Andrews
For 2 Infants' Hoods
At State Fair Rochester

State Agricultural Rooms.
Albany, September 1851.
V. B. M. Munson, Secretary.

RECOMMENDED FRUIT AND NUT VARIETIES FOR SOUTHERN FRUIT GARDENERS
(check with local growers first)

James J. Anding
Southern Fruit Council

APPLES
Scarlet Pimpernel, Lodi, Late Red June, Champion, Pumpkin Sweet, St. Edmunds Pippin, Roxbury Russet, Lamb Abbey Pearmain, Yates Mother, Early Strawberry, Laxton's Fortune and Smokehouse. For south of Baton Rouge to Gulf—Anna, Ein Shemer, Meshki and Live Oak.

PEACHES
Andigold, Southland, July Elberta, Hiland, Keystone, Sam Houston Erly-red-free, Cherokee nectarine, Peacharine, Indian Free and Indian cling. For south of Baton Rouge—Tejon, Bonita, Red Ceylon, Indian Cling.

PEARS
Douglas, Orient, Kieffer, Seckle, Winter Nelis, Monterrey, Le Conte, Baldwin, Dabney, Yates, Magness, Moonglo, Mericourt. South of Baton Rouge—Pineapple.

PLUMS
Gold, Methley, Munson, Friar, Burbank Plumcot, Satsuma, Apricot Plum, Mexican Plum, Wildgoose, Santa Rosa. South of Baton Rouge—Methley, Gold, Munson.

GRAPES
All varieties of muscadines from New Orleans northward. Bunch Grapes, Black King, Delaware, Champanel, Extra, Lenoir Carmen, Ellen Scott, and Marguerite.

BLUEBERRIES
All varieties of Rabbiteye parentage such as Sunblue, Tifblue, Coastal, Homebell, Woodard.

DEWBERRIES
New Orleans and northward, Lucretia.

CITRUS
Sunny Hill Lemon, Owri satsuma, Major Tiawanica Lemon. South of Baton Rouge—Owri satsuma, Meyer Lemon, Kumquat New Orleans and south, Hamblin Orange, Louisiana Sweet Orange, Navel Orange, Clementine Tangerine.

Do not plant south of Jackson, Miss.—Sweet and sour Cherries, Apricots, Raspberries, and Rhubarb.

[F]RUIT, NUT, AND GRAPE [V]ARIETIES FOR THE [H]OME ORCHARD

[S]outhern California
[C]oast and Valley Areas South of
[th]e Tehachapi Mountains

[?]D. Rizzi and James A. Beutel,
[Ex]tension Pomologists, Davis;
[?]G. Platt, Extension Subtropical
[Ho]rticulturist, Riverside; and A.N.
[Ka]simatis, Extension Viticulturist,
[Da]vis.

[Th]e following is a selection of var-
[ie]ties of fruits, nuts, and grapes that
[ha]ve been successfully used in south-
[er]n California for home planting.
[W]here a number of varieties are
[av]ailable, they are listed in the order
[of] their ripening. Pollination require-
[m]ents are also given when production
[of] normal yields requires more than
[on]e variety. The appropriate variety
[in] an adjoining yard could provide
[po]llination.

[A]LMOND
[No]npareil, Ne Plus Ultra. Two
[va]rieties are necessary for proper
[po]llination.
[A]PPLE
[Be]verly Hills, Winter Banana, White
[W]armain. Plant more than one
[va]riety to help pollination. Apples
[wi]th higher chilling requirements
[ar]e not advised for coastal and inter-
[me]diate areas.
[A]PRICOT
[Ro]yal Blenheim.
[A]VOCADO
[Zu]tano, Fuerte, Bacon, Rincon,
[Ha]ss, Anaheim. Hass, Anaheim and
[Ri]ncon in warm locations only.
[Ba]con and Zutano will stand colder
[lo]cations; Fuerte moderately cold.
[B]LACKBERRY
[Yo]ung, Boysen, Nectar, Ollalie.
[Ol]lalie best suited to warm coastal
[ar]eas.
[C]HERIMOYA
[Bo]oth, Bays, Chaffey, Ott, Ryerson.
[C]HERRY
[M]ontmorency (a red pie-cherry).
[Sw]eet cherries not adapted.
[F]EIJOA
[Co]olidge, Superba, Choiceana.
[Su]perba and Choiceana require
[cr]oss-pollination.
[F]IG
[Mi]ssion, Brown Turkey and Osborne—
[all] areas. Kadota—interior areas only.
[Wh]ite Genoa—for coastal areas only.
[G]RAPE
[In]terior Areas: Perlette, Cardinal,
[Re]d Malaga, Thompson Seedless,
[Is]abell and Scarlet—American grape
[ty]pe for jelly and juice; Tokay,
[Ri]bier, Muscat of Alexandria.
[Co]astal Areas: Pierce and Niagara—
[Am]erican grape type for jelly and
[ju]ice.
[G]RAPEFRUIT
[Ma]rsh, Red Blush. Red Blush—
[de]sert areas and hot interior valleys.
[G]UAVA
[Ca]ttley. This selection is more tol-
[er]ant to cold than other selected
[va]rieties of guava.
[L]EMON
[Eu]reka, Lisbon. Lisbon—better
[sui]ted for extremely hot and cold
[ar]eas.
[L]IME
[Ta]rss (warm locations only).
[L]OQUAT
[Ch]ampagne, Gold Nugget.
[M]ANDARIN ORANGE
[Sa]tsuma, Clementine(Algerian),
[Na]ncy, Kinnow, Kara. Clementine—
[ne]eds pollinator such as Dancy.
[N]ECTARINE
[Si]ver Lode (white flesh), Goldmine,
[Pa]namint, Pioneer (yellow flesh).
[O]LIVE
[Ma]nzanillo, Sevillano.
[O]RANGE
[Wa]shington Navel, Valencia.
[P]EACH
[Co]astal Areas: Tejon, Desertgold,
[Ve]ntura, Sundar.
[In]land Areas: Springtime, Meadow-
[lar]k, Golden Blush, Saturn, Babcock,
[Ea]rly Elberta (satisfactory in some
[ye]ars), Bonita, and Saturn. Varieites
[for] coastal areas can also be grown.
[Mo]untain Areas: Redhaven, July
[El]berta, Redglobe, Elberta, Fay
[El]berta, Rio Oso Gem.
[PE]CAN
[Ba]rton, Success, Mahan, Burkett,
[Se]lect. Suggested for hot interior
[ar]eas only. Barton provides pollen
[for] itself and other varieties.

PERSIMMON
Hachiya, Fuyu.
PLUM
Santa Rosa, Mariposa, Satsuma, Late
Santa Rosa. Satsuma requires one
other variety for pollination.
POMEGRANATE
Wonderful—interior valleys.
QUINCE
Smyrna, Pineapple.
RASPBERRY
Willamette. Not recommended for
hot dry areas.
SAPOTE (White)
Pike, Coleman.
STRAWBERRY
Fresno, Tioga, Torrey, Salinas
WALNUT
Placentia, Payne. Not suggested for
hot dry areas.

Jùglans règia.
The *common*, or Royal, Walnut.

Full-grown winter tree at Studley, 82 ft. high; diam. of the head, 96 ft.

FRUITING BRANCH OF THE COMMON WALNUT.

(*Juglans Regia.*)

SHOWING CLUSTER OF FRUIT AND FOLIAGE.

Cooperative Extension Programs
University of Wisconsin—Extension
University of Wisconsin—Madison

Northern Grown Nuts
By G. C. Klingbeil

Native Nuts

Unlike introduced nuts, native nuts are cold tolerant, but to varying degrees. In descending order, their relative hardiness is butternut, hazelnut, American chestnut, hickory, and black walnut. Butternuts, the most hardy, are found statewide. Hickories are most common in the Fox River Valley and in southern Wisconsin. Black walnuts are most common in south-western Wisconsin, with scattered groves and trees throughout the state.

American chestnuts, which are fairly cold tolerant, are survivors on the fringe of the region where chestnut blight once killed most of this species. The trees are self-sterile and single trees will not produce nuts. A few small groves in Wisconsin do produce nuts.

Native hazelnuts are dying out because of the disappearance of open pastures. They are unable to live in the low-light conditions of reforested and wooded areas.

Varieties of most native nuts can be purchased from larger nurseries.

Non-Native Nuts

Pecans, Persian (English) walnuts, filberts, peanuts, and heartnuts are generally not grown in Wisconsin because they are not adapted to the cold climate.

The Persian (English) walnuts found in Wisconsin are descendants of relatively hardy trees grown in the Carpathian Mountain region of the Ukraine and Poland. These Carpathian walnuts were distributed throughout the Midwest by the Wisconsin State Horticultural Society. However, they are not recommended for Wisconsin because they are seriously injured and often killed when early winter temperatures drop to minus 20 degrees Fahrenheit. A few trees have reached maturity here and produce nuts.

Filberts or hazelnuts can grow in Wisconsin, but only in limited areas. The most common in the northern Midwest is the American hazelnut, from which several improved strains and varieties have been selected. The Rush and Winkler varieties are examples. The Winkler is most hardy, but both will grow in southern Wisconsin in areas suited to them. Filberts should be cross-pollinated with another filbert

Table 1 — Food Value of Nuts*

Nut	Water %	Protein %	Fat %	Carbohy-drates %	Calories per ounce	Crackout %
Almond	5	21	55	14	190	55
Beechnut	4	22	57	13	200	60
Black Walnut	3	30	58	6	195	26
Butternut	4	28	61	6	215	15
Chinese Chestnut, dry	6	11	8	70	115	77
Chinese Chestnut, fresh	43	6	6	41	70	85
Filbert	6	13	64	5	215	62
Hickory Nut	4	15	67	11	220	38
Pecan	3	12	71	8	225	50
Persian Walnut	3	18	61	14	205	42

* Reprinted from "The Nut Jar — a Cookbook" by permission of the Michigan Nut Growers Association.

variety or with a wild, native hazelnut.

Peanuts are not a true nut but are a legume related to beans and peas. Commercially they are not grown north of a line from Washington, D. C. to southern Illinois. They require a long growing season of at least 150 frost-free days. When planted outside their normal range, yields are low, pods do not fill properly, and the seeds (peanuts) are of low quality.

To harvest peanuts, dig up the entire plant—tops, roots, and pods. Wash the soil from roots and pods. Cure for several weeks by drying the entire plant in a cool, rodent-free place. Then remove the pods and store the peanuts in a rodent-proof container.

For suggestions on roasting and other recipes, write the National Peanut Council, DuPont Circle Building, Washington, D.C. 20036.

Pests

Squirrels and chipmunks probably cause the greatest loss of nuts, but insects and diseases are also pests of nut trees and their fruit. Control is not commonly practiced on a regular schedule.

In black walnuts, walnut husk maggot larvae may infect nut husks. Anthracnose, a serious fungus disease, causes early loss of leaves. Army worms, in periodic outbreaks, may eat all foliage on some branches or on an entire tree. Two or three years of early defoliation by these pests weakens and sometimes causes death of black walnut trees.

In butternut, a fungus causes dieback. It infects the limbs of weak trees. The limbs die progressively from the twigs to the larger branches.

Hickories are not seriously affected by insects or disease.

Hazelnuts are often destroyed by a fruit worm.

Fertilization

Periodic application of fertilizer improves nut tree growth. Use a complete fertilizer such as 12-12-12 or one with similar analysis. Apply one pound per inch of trunk diameter (breast high) in spring every three to five years. Spread the fertilizer on the soil surface under the tree or put it into holes punched into the soil under the drip area of the tree. The holes can be made with a crow bar or similar tool and should be 15 to 18 inches deep.

NUT TREE INFORMATION

	BLACK WALNUT	BUTTERNUT	CHINESE CHESTNUT	HAZELS AND FILBERTS	HEARTNUT	HICKORIES	PERSIAN WALNUT
Climatic Region	Well adapted to southern Michigan.	Extremely hardy.	Chestnuts are about as hardy as peaches. Planting should be confined to areas where peaches are winter hardy.	The American hazel is fully hardy, but the European hazel or filbert isn't. Hybrids between these two species vary in hardiness.	Extremely hardy.	Shagbark hickories do well throughout lower Michigan, except in extremely dry or wet areas.	Early maturing varieties are s isfactory as far north as M in Michigan and perhaps fart along the lake where the gr ing season is 150 days or mo
Soil	Does best in deep, fertile, moist, drained soils.	Does best in deep fertile, moist soils.	Well-drained gravelly type of soil, suitable for peaches, is ideal. Soil should be slightly acid. Avoid heavy, strongly alkaline and poorly-drained soils.	Good water drainage is essential.	Will grow on infertile sandy soils, but does better on deep, fertile soils.	Prefer light, well drained, loamy soils.	Needs deep, fertile soil wh retains moisture in summ Swampy, poorly-drained ar and droughty, eroded hillsi are not suitable.
Air Drainage	Avoid frost pockets.	Will do better in frost pockets than black walnuts.	Good air drainage required. Late spring freezes may kill new shoots and tender leaves if planted in a frost pocket.	Good air drainage is essential.	Avoid frost pockets.	Avoid frost pockets.	A fair amount of air drainage desirable. Trees in frost pock may have blossoms and r leaves killed by late spring fr
Site	Yards, fence rows, on northern or eastern slopes, permanent pastures, large lawns.	Yards, fence rows, permanent pastures, large lawns, low hillsides, river banks.	Does best on slopes and hilltops where there is good air drainage.	Do well on moist sites if soil drainage is adequate. Low areas that form frost pockets should be avoided because of both winter cold and spring frost.	Yards, fence rows, large lawns.	Low hillsides and river banks.	Does well in pastures and o grassy areas if sufficient moisture and nutrients are a able. Level or gently-slop land is best.
Varieties for Michigan	Adams, Allen, Beck, Elmer Myers, Grundy, Snyder, Sparrow, Stambaugh, Thomas.	Crackezy, Lingle, Love, Sherwood, White.	Abundance, Crane, Kuling, Meiling, Nanking.	Bixby, Buchanan (both American hazels); Italian Red, Latson, Potomac, Reed, Rush, Winkler.	Fodermaier, Mitchell, Walters, Wright.	Abscoda, Glover, Kirtland, Lingenfelter, Romig, Wescheke.	Broadview, Colby, Fickes, stenmaier, Gratiot, Greenha Hansen, Lake, Merkel, Metca McDermid, McIntyre, McKins Neyer No. 1, Somers, Winchel
Culture	Weed control is necessary for newly planted and small trees. Mulching with straw or wood shavings is beneficial, particularly during dry periods in the summer. Trees need little or no pruning. An occasional limb may be shortened or removed to maintain symmetry. Black walnuts are usually pollinated naturally.	Usually pollinated naturally or self pollinated.	Weed control is important, especially with young trees. Mulching should help. Keep sod clipped (4 to 5 times/year.) Extremely low crotches should be avoided by removing limbs to a height of 2 to 4 feet above ground. Scaffold branches may then be selected 18 to 24 feet apart to form a modified leader type of tree. Subsequent pruning will be very light. Need more than one variety (at least 2 or 3) for pollination.	Weed control is necessary for newly planted and small trees. Mulching with straw or wood shavings is beneficial, particularly during dry periods in the summer. Trees need little or no pruning. An occasional limb may be shortened or removed to maintain the symmetry of form. Need more than one variety (at least 2 or 3) for pollination.	Usually pollinated naturally or self pollinated.		Pollen shedding and stigma ceptivity usually occur at di ent times. Therefore, 3 or m different varieties should planted to insure proper change of pollen.
Time of Bearing	Seedling trees come into production in 8 to 12 years. Grafted trees will start to bear earlier.	Named varieties usually begin bearing 2 to 4 years after planting.	Seedling trees come into bearing at about 7 years of age. Grafted trees start to bear about a year after planting.	Named varieties should start bearing the third year after transplanting, if properly cared for.	Named varieties usually begin bearing 2 to 4 years after planting.	Named varieties usually bear in 10 to 20 years.	Seeding trees come into proc tion in 6 to 10 years. Gra trees bear earlier.
Yield	Variable. Tend to have alternate bearing habits. One to three bushels of hulled nuts per mature tree.	One to several bushels of hulled nuts per mature tree.	Yields vary, but usually average about 20 to 50 pounds of hulled nuts per mature tree.	One to 6 quarts of hulled nuts per mature bush.	One to 6 bushels of hulled nuts per mature tree.	One half to 1½ bushels of hulled nuts per mature tree.	Mature trees have been kn to yield 200 lbs. of hulled n per tree (about 6 bushels). G care is necessary to prod good yields. Average yields 50 to 125 lbs. can be expec

Pollination

Most nut trees have staminate (male) and pistillate (female) flowers on the same tree and depend upon wind for the transfer of pollen from male to female flowers. Some nuts, particularly hickories, are mostly self-sterile and the pollen must come from another tree.

Moderately warm breezy weather during bloom, which occurs when the foliage is nearly full grown, aids in fruit set. Cold rainy weather during bloom may cause failure in pollination and result in poor fruit set.

Collecting and Curing Nuts

Collect nuts as soon as they drop from their trees.

Immediately remove hulls from hickories and walnuts to get a lighter colored, better flavored nutmeat. Wear waterproof gloves when handling black walnuts—their stain doe not come off easily. Remove any remaining pulp from black walnuts by washing with agi tation.

Allow hazelnut clusters to wilt for a day o two. This makes their husks easier to remove

After removing the hulls of walnuts, hickories, and hazelnuts, spread the nuts thinly in a dry, airy location to cure for four to six weeks.

For best quality nutmeats, crack nuts soo after curing.

Nuts can be successfully cracked using thi method:

1. Soak hickory nuts in boiling water for 15 to 20 minutes to make them easier to crack and the nutmeats easier to remove.
2. Use a sturdy hammer and a solid cracking block (anvil, iron or hardwood block).
3. Hold the nut firmly in position on the block as shown here.
4. Strike the nut with the hammer so that the shell shatters.
5. Collect the cracked nuts in a container and separate the nutmeats from the shells later in comfort and under good light conditions.
6. Dry the nutmeats thoroughly before storage and then put them in an airtight container in a refrigerator or freezer.

Poorly filled or dried-up nutmeats usually result from too cold or too short a growing season, or from early loss of leaves caused by insects or disease.

Black walnuts produce a toxin which can kill some plants when they are planted near walnut tree roots. Apples, tomatoes, potatoe and alfalfa are particularly sensitive.

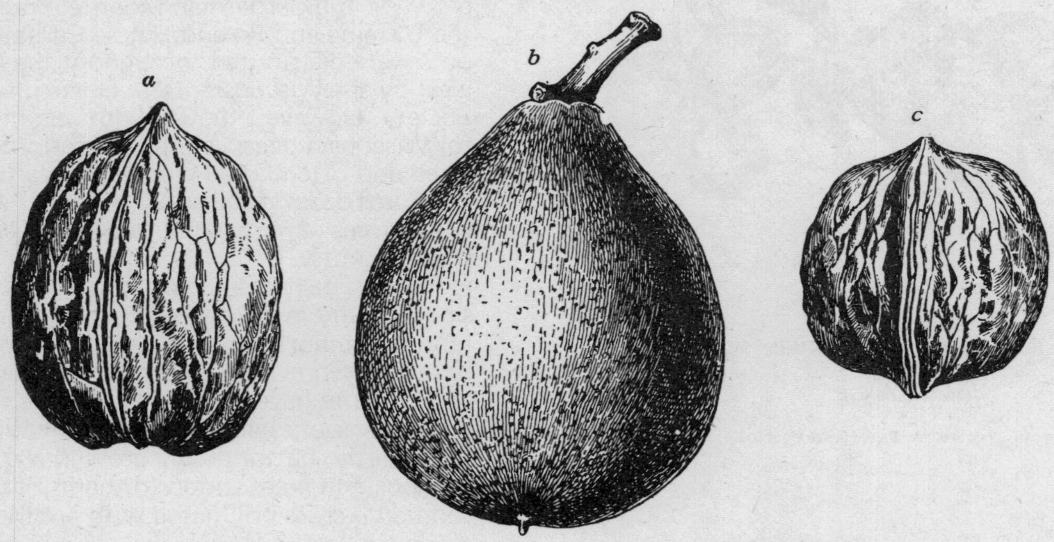

Walnuts. *a*, Parisienne. *b*, Pear-shaped (fruit). *c*, Noix Saint-Jean

Table 2 — Spacings for Various Nut Species

Nut Species	Hedgerow Planting			On the Square	
	Between trees (feet)	Between rows (feet)	Number of trees per acre	Distance each way (feet)	Number of trees per acre
Black Walnuts	40 to 50	70	12 to 16	60	12 to 13
Butternuts	35 to 40	60	18 to 21	50	17 to 18
Chinese Chestnuts	35 to 40	55	19 to 23	40	27 to 28
Hazels and Filberts	12 to 15	15	193 to 242	15	193 to 194
Heartnuts	40 to 45	65	14 to 17	50	17 to 18
Persian Walnuts	30 to 35	60	20 to 25	50	17 to 18

Table 3 — Recommended Fertilizer Rates for Nut Trees*

Age of Tree	Pounds of Actual Nitrogen			Pounds of 12-12-12		
	Per Acre	Per Tree		Per Acre	Per Tree	
		20 Trees/A	200 Trees/A		20 Trees/A	200 Trees/A
2 years	2 to 4	.1 to .2	.01 to .02	20 to 30	1 to 1½	⅛
5 years	9 to 15	½ to ¾	.05 to .08	80 to 120	4 to 6	½
10 years	21 to 33	1 to 1½	.1 to .15	180 to 270	9 to 13½	1 to 1½
15 years	34 to 50	1½ to 2½	.2 to .25	280 to 420	14 to 21	1½ to 2

* Based on the rate of 50 pounds of actual nitrogen/acre/year for mature orchards. Recommended rates for mature orchards are 50 to 100 pou of actual nitrogen/acre/year.

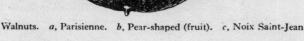

How peanuts are grown.

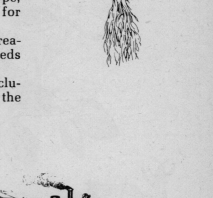

Astor Perry, Peanut Specialist
North Carolina State University

Four types of peanuts are grown in the United States. In North Carolina and Virginia, the entire production is of the large Virginia-type, used for making cocktail peanuts. The biggest, brightest pods are used for roasting in the hull.

Two major types are grown in the Georgia-Florida-Alabama area—the small seeded runner and the Spanish. Both have small pods and seeds and are excellent for making peanut butter and peanut candy.

In Texas and Oklahoma the Spanish type is grown almost exclusively, because it does better under dry conditions. New Mexico grows the Valencia-type, excellent for roasting in the hull.

Each peanut flower is complete, containing both male (anther) and female (stigma) for reproduction. Because both parts are enclosed in the flower, self-fertilization generally occurs rather than cross-fertilization. When fertilized, the ovary begins to enlarge and extend to form a "peg" which gravity pulls towards the soil. The peg carries the newly-formed embryo at its tip, penetrates the soil and turns horizontal. The pod then begins to form.

Peanuts are planted about 2 inches deep in rows 24-36 inches apart with seeds dropped every 4-6 inches in the row. The soil is packed down firmly for good contact.

Given warmth, moisture and some air, a complex set of growth-control enzymes take place within the embryo. Cells begin to enlarge and the seed swells.

When the soil temperature is between 65-70° the seed germinates. About 2 days after planting, the tip of the primary root breaks through the seed coat and starts downward. Five days after planting the primary root is already some 6 inches long and lateral roots have appeared.

Meanwhile, a peculiar white structure (hypocotyl), located just above the true roots, begins to enlarge, pushing the two halves of the seed coat (cotyledons) upward and cracking the soil surface about 8 days after planting.

In about 14 days, the first "square" of 4 leaves unfolds. Each leaf consists of a slender stem (petiole) bearing 4 leaflets. At the crown of the plant you can see a cluster of leaflets, still folded, from which new shoot growth emerges. Just above the attachment of each cotyledon lateral branches begin developing. These lower laterals are the primary origin of later flowering branches. Care must be taken in early cultivation to avoid injuring or burying them.

Easy Way

Hard Way

ANUT EXTENSION AND RESEARCH

bama

M.D. Bond
ension Peanut Specialist
ourn University
ourn, AL 36830

Luther Farrar
ension Plant Pathologist
om 108, Extension Hall
ourn University
ourn, AL 36830

rida

Ben Whitty
ension Agronomy Specialist
Newell Hall
versity of Florida
nesville, FL 32601

Allen Norden
onomy-IFAS
versity of Florida
nesville, FL 32601

orgia

Frank McGill
ension Agronomy
. Box 48
versity of Georgia
on, GA 31794

Sam Thompson
ension Plant Pathology
. Box 48
versity of Georgia
on, GA 31794

rth Carolina

Astor Perry
ension Agronomy Specialist
x 5155
Williams Hall
C. State University
eigh, NC 27607

J.C. Wells
ension Plant Pathology
x 5397
C. State University
eigh, NC 27607

lahoma

Roy Sturgeon, Jr.
ension Plant Pathologist
Life Science East
lahoma State University
lwater, OK 74074

Leland Tripp
ension Crop Specialist
x 1008
lahoma State University
lwater, OK 74074

uth Carolina

Fred Smith
pt. of Plant Pathology
om 307, Long Hall
mson University
mson, SC 29631

xas

Phil Hammond
tension Entomologist
xas A & M University
llege Station, TX 77843

Wendell Horne
tension Plant Pathologist
xas A & M University
llege Station, TX 77843

Ben Spears
tension Agronomist
xas A & M University
llege Station, TX 77843

rginia

Al Allison
tension Specialist
. Box 217
P.I.
lland, VA 23391

Preston Reid
rector
dewater Research Center
P.I.
lland, VA 23391

W. Wyatt Osborne
ept. of Plant Pathology
P.I.
acksburg, VA 24061

PEANUTS, MAMMOTH VIRGINIA

How the young plants mature and are harvested.

During the next 6-8 weeks, the plants undergo a rapid vegetative growth investing their energy in developing a hat-sized canopy of leaves for maximum light interception and a strong subway system of roots for taking in nutrition and moisture from the soil. They even go into partnership with neighboring bacterial organisms which attach themselves to the plant's roots forming clusters of nodules which produce nitrogen.

At about 6 weeks, certain enzymes within the plant suddenly shift emphasis from vegetative growth to reproductive growth. We do not know what tells these enzymes to shift. An accumulation of plant sugar is thought to be at least one trigger. At any rate, flower buds develop and the familiar stalk bearing attractive yellow petals appears.

Flowering continues for some 8 weeks although less than 10% of the flowers actually produce mature peanuts. The developing pods require a high concentration of calcium and, since calcium does not move readily from roots to pods, this must be applied directly to the fruiting area. Landplaster is generally applied in a wide band over the plants when flowering first begins. The first flowers on the plant are usually the ones that end up as mature fruit at harvest.

Healthy plants require soil slightly on the acid side with a pH of 5.8-6.2 for best growth. Being a legume, nitrogen is not required in well-inoculated soil since the plants make their own. Phosphorous, potassium, calcium, magnesium, sulfur, boron, manganese, copper and molybdenum are required, the proper amounts being determined by soil test. Fertilizer is applied broadcast and turned under during the late winter or early spring.

By the end of 8-12 weeks the pegs that will develop into mature pods have entered the soil and are beginning to enlarge. The yield and quality of the kernels in the pods determine profit. As the season progresses, the plant continues to grow and flower eventually producing 40 or more mature pods. As maturity approaches, the plants begin to lose some of their green color because the kernels use the plant's food supply for growth. Finally, a point is reached where the fully-mature pods just barely make up for the shedding of the overmature pods. Then it is time for harvesting.

ARACHIS HYPOGÆA (PEANUT).

Dormouse

Earthnut (*Arachis hypogœa*)

Harvesting...

begins early in some sections. Before the summer is half gone, digging starts in Georgia and South Texas, where they are able to plant early. Many growers in these areas plant the Spanish peanut which matures in 120 days. As fall approaches, digging expands to other sections of the peanut belt, although it's not in full swing until October in the Virginia-Carolina and Oklahoma areas. By the last of October, digging is virtually complete in all sections.

Fruit Growing In The North

P. J. PETERS

Fruit growing in Western Canada is a risky business. The farther north you go, the greater the risks. The greater he risks, the greater the determination of growers and hobbyists to prove that fruit can be grown. In the absence of the necessary research the information gained through experience by these hobbyists, if shared with others, can be a boon to those who are interested in this phase of work.

Wind shelter becomes very important as you go farther north. A well-protected area has a micro-climate of its own. This means that fruit trees should be planted in the most protected spot of the garden. Another major consideration is soil. Most fruit trees and tender fruit varieties must have good internal drainage. They do not tolerate wet feet, yet need frequent watering. Most fruit varieties are susceptible to high salt content.

There are few varieties of fruit that are completely hardy for northern conditions. The trick in fruit growing is to plant the hardier varieties in the right locations and to use all the tricks of the trade to help these varieties to grow and fruit. Low level fruit growing could be a title for this paper. The suggestions presented are for people

FRUITING BRANCHLET OF PEAR.

who have the inclination, the time, the ability, and the perseverance that is needed to grow fruit in the north.

Is there any way in which fruit can be grown more successfully? What about better varieties? We believe that "espalier" is the answer. Russia is doing some successful work in this area. Let's take a quick look at "espalier".

Espalier is a French word derived from the Italian "spalliera", something to rest the spalla (shoulder) against. "Espalier" may describe any plant trained flat in one plane — a two-dimensional tree or shrub as it were, with height and width, but almost no depth.

This is not new. The Romans espaliered fruit trees against their walls. France, Spain and England have espaliered fruit trees, flowering trees and shrubs for beautification for centuries. Russia is using this method for fruit production on orchards. Our interest in this method stems from an interest in overwintering more none-hardy material.

Anything that becomes covered with snow will usually overwinter. To grow fruit trees in the north, espalier them as low as possible against a south wall or against an evergreen or dense herbaceous hedge.

The simplest espalier pattern is that of the horizontal cordon, either single or double as illustrated. The single

Fruit tree	Years from planting to bearing	Useful life in years	Estimated production per tree at		
			3 years	6 years	10 years
Apples					
Dwarf	2 to 4	10 to 15	0 to 2 pecks	1 to 2 bushels	3 to 5 bushels
Semidwarf	3 to 4	15 to 20	0 to 2 pecks	1 to 3 bushels	4 to 10 bushels
Spur type	3 to 4	15 to 20	0 to 2 pecks	1 to 3 bushels	4 to 10 bushels
Standard	4 to 6	15 to 20	none	0 to 2 bushels	5 to 15 bushels
Apricot					
Standard	3 to 5	15 to 20	0 to 1 peck	1 to 2 bushels	2 to 4 bushels
Nectarine					
Standard	2 to 3	10 to 15	1 to 2 pecks	1 to 3 bushels	3 to 5 bushels
Peach					
Dwarf	2 to 3	5 to 10	1 to 2 pecks	1 to 2 bushels	1 to 2 bushels
Standard	2 to 3	10 to 15	1 to 2 pecks	1 to 3 bushels	3 to 5 bushels
Pear					
Dwarf	3 to 4	10 to 15	0 to 2 pecks	1 to 2 bushels	1 to 3 bushels
Plum					
Standard	3 to 5	15 to 20	0 to 2 pecks	1 to 2 bushels	3 to 5 bushels
Sour cherries					
Meteor, North Star, and Suda Hardy	2 to 3	10 to 15	0 to 1 peck	1 to 2 pecks	2 to 3 pecks
Standard	3 to 5	15 to 20	0 to 1 peck	2 to 4 pecks	8 to 12 pecks
Sweet cherry					
Standard	4 to 7	15 to 20	none	0 to 3 pecks	8 to 16 pecks

Basic Pruning Steps For Espalier

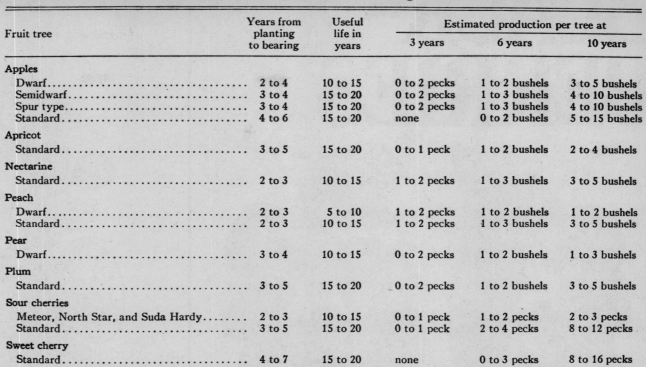

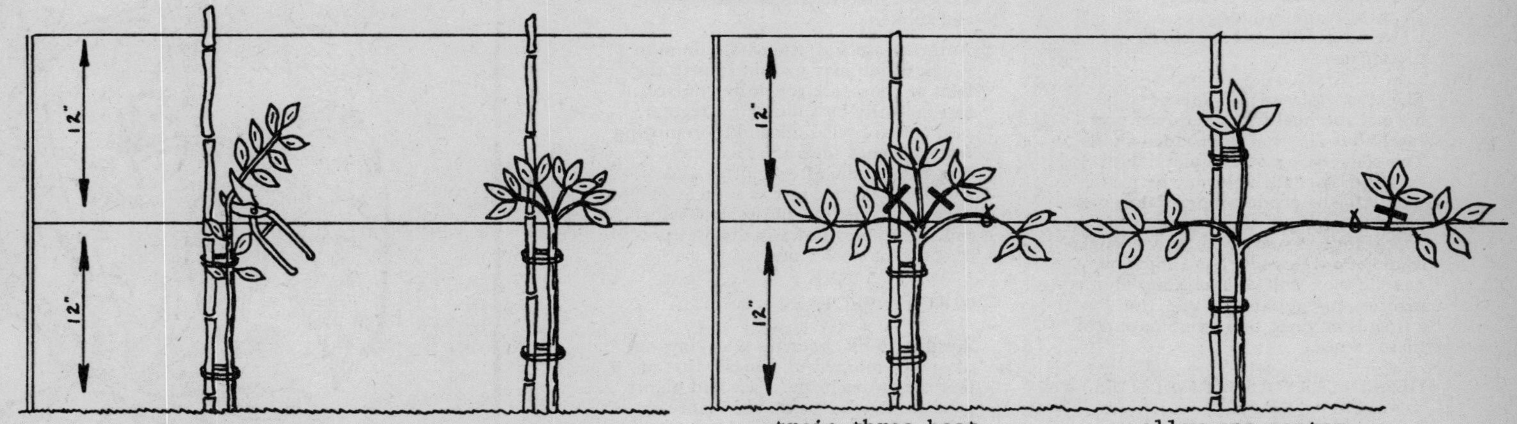

cut to height of first cordon

wait for new shoots

train three best shoots on bottom cordon; prune excess

allow one center shoot to continue; pinch offshoots on horizontals

SPACING, BEARING AGE, AND PRODUCTION OF SMALL FRUITS

Fruit[a]	Planting distance[b]		Interval from planting to fruiting	Life of plants	Height of mature plant	Estimated annual yield per plant[e]	Suggested number of plants for family of 5
	Between rows	Between plants					
	feet	feet	years	years	feet		
Strawberries (matted row)	4	2	1	3–4	1	½–1 qt. per foot of row	100
Currants	6–8	4	2	12–15	3–4	3–4 quarts	4–6
Gooseberries	6–8	4	2	12–15	3–4	4–5 quarts	4–6
Raspberries							
Red	6–8	3–4	1	8–10	4–5	1½ quarts	20–25
Black	6–8	3–4	1	8–10	4–5	1 quart	20–25
Purple	6–8	3–4	1	8–10	4–5	1 quart	20–25
Blackberries							
Erect	6–8	4–5	1	10–12	3–5	1 quart	15–20
Trailing or semi-trailing	6–8	6–10	1	8–10	6–8 (staked or trellis)	4–10 quarts	8–10
Blueberries	8–10	6–8	2	20+	6–10	3–4 quarts	8–10
Grapes	8–10	8–10	3	20+	6 (trellised)	¼–½ bushel	5–10
Everbearing strawberries (hills)	1–1½	1–1½	½	2–3	1	½ quart	100
Everbearing raspberries	8	3	½	8–10	4–5	1 quart—spring ½ quart—fall	15–20 15–20

a Listed in approximate order of ripening from early spring to fall.
b Minimum suggested spacings. See discussion of plant spacings in text.
e At full bearing age, with good care.

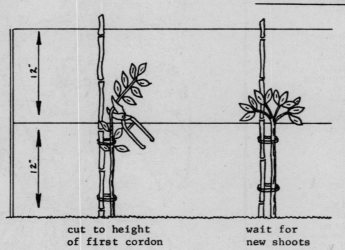

cordon is best for overwintering, as it is easy to throw up a foot or two of snow to cover the cordon.

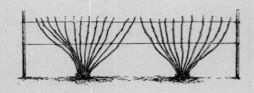

We suggest that Manitoba growers try and espalier a stembuilder tree, known as "Nertchinsk". After the cordons begin to establish, the tender variety is budded onto the "Nertchinsk". We use the "Nertchinsk" to incorporate stem hardiness to our espaliered cordons. Study "Stembuilders for Prairie Orchards" (Publication No. 460, Manitoba Department of Agriculture).

We further suggest that interested parties obtain the book by Harold O. Perkins called "Espaliers and Vines for the Home Gardener". This is published by D. Van Norstrand Company (Canada) Ltd., 25 Hollinger Road, Toronto 16, Canada.

Espalier work offers the opportunity for poetic expression through the use of ornamental plants. It can become an absorbing hobby.

BLACK-BERRIES

STERILITY IN BLACKBERRIES
C.C. Zych and M.C. Shurtleff
Dept. of Plant Pathology
University of Illinois at Urbana--Champaign

Blackberry plants that appear to be normal and healthy may flower profusely but may fail to produce fruit. This failure may be complete, with no fruit set at all; or it may be partial, with the production of misshapen berries, ranging from nearly normal in appearance to some with only a single drupelet developed. The condition may be the result of hereditary abnormalities, insect damage, infection by a fungus or virus, or a combination of these causes.

HEREDITARY ABNORMALITIES

Poor fruit set may be the result of gene or chromosome combinations that do not permit effective self-pollution. Plants and flowers appear normal but the pollen produced will not bring about fertilization of the ovules, which is necessary for normal fruit development. McDonald (a semi-trailing variety) and Advance (a trailing variety) are unfruitful when planted alone. Other commercially important varieties are generally self-fruitful, and may be planted alone in large blocks without concern about this type of sterility.

Sometimes, plantings in which a few too many plants produce little or no marketable fruit are simply mixtures of wild blackberries. Such plants should be dug out and destroyed as soon as they are identified, since they are usually more vigorous than the productive plants and tend to replace them.

INSECT DAMAGE

Mites, thrips, tarnished plant bugs, and adult beetles of the raspberry fruit worm may sometimes account for some of the fruit malformations. These insects feed on the flower buds, stamens, or pistils. Extensive damage from these insects is uncommon. Special sprays to control them are generally not warranted, especially when a regular pest-control schedule is followed. Illinois Extension Circular 935, Growing Small Fruits in the Home Garden, gives the latest information on pest control in home gardens. Commercial growers should write directly to one of the authors for the latest pest-control recommendations.

FUNGUS INFECTION

Anthracnose is the most common fungus disease that may affect fruit development. It is seldom severe on the fruit of erect blackberries, but that of trailing blackberries is often badly infected. When immature drupelets are infected, this prevents normal ripening—causing the fruit to be small, brown, dry, and woody.

Drupelets that are attacked when they are more mature will become brown and sunken.

Anthracnose and other less-common fungi, which may be injurious to the fruit at times, are generally controlled satisfactorily by following a regular, pest-control schedule and by removing fruiting canes soon after harvest. These canes die after fruiting and should be pruned-out as soon after harvest as possible, in order to minimize the spread of any diseases present on the new canes.

VIRUS INFECTION

Sterility in blackberries is a symptom of one or more virus diseases that affect the entire plant. Affected plants produce new canes that are more vigorous, with rounder and glossier leaflets than normal. The leaves also develop a brilliant, premature fall reddening. The flowers appear to be normal, but only a few drupelets will develop on each receptacle. The production of fruit buds for the next season is also reduced. The virus will spread in a planting, but its means of spreading (other than by root suckers) is still undetermined.

There are no chemicals that may be applied to control virus-induced blackberry sterility. The following measures are recommended:

1. Grub-out unfruitful plants that fail to set fruit, removing as much of the root system as possible. Destroy them at once.

2. Do not use root suckers to propagate plants from fields where the sterility virus has previously been found.

3. Always remove old canes after harvest.

4. Destroy neglected planting and wild bramble patches that are near new plantings.

5. Purchase virus-free plants from nurserymen who will certify that their plants were produced from fruitful stock.

WISCONSIN RASPBERRIES

G. C. Klingbeil, E. K. Wade and C. F. Koval

Gerarde's picture of the raspberry, 1597.

The Plant

The root and crown of a raspberry plant are perennial, but an individual cane lives only two years (figure 1). Each spring the plant produces new canes (primocanes) to replace those that die. Red raspberries produce primocanes from crown buds and from sucker shoots on underground lateral stems called "turions". These suckers come up at random and result in a thick bramble patch if they are not controlled. Black and purple raspberries produce primocanes only from the crown buds on the original plant and so remain where you first plant them.

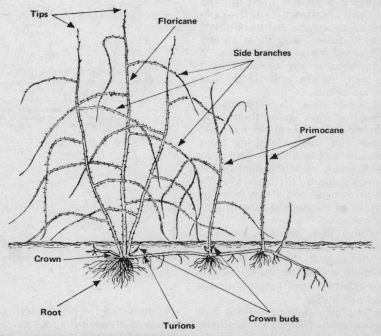

Figure 1. First and second year raspberry canes.

Summer Varieties

Most raspberries are summer bearing. They produce fruit on the side branches of second year canes (floricanes) between mid-July and early August. The canes produce no fruit the first year.

Raspberry—Arched training

Fall Varieties

Some red raspberries are everbearing or fall bearing. They are recommended for only the southern third of the state, where the growing season is the longest. These varieties produce fruit on the primocane tips in the fall of the first year. The second year they produce on the side branches of the floricanes between mid-July and early August. In Wisconsin it is better to eliminate this summer crop completely in order to maximize the fall crop (see fall bearing varieties page 10).

Soil

Raspberries grow best in full sunlight, on an airy site sheltered from direct winds. Areas where water stands after a rain are not desirable. To decrease desease and insect problems, isolate raspberries from wild varieties, and plant them in fields not previously occupied by wild raspberries. The fruit generally ripens earlier on a southern slope than on a nothern exposure, which is usually cooler and wetter.

Raspberries perform well on most soils that are moderately fertile, well drained and easily worked, but a deep sandy loam, high in organic matter, is ideal. Avoid light sandy soil unless water for irrigation is available. Do not plant raspberries on heavy clay soils unless no other location is available. Raspberries do best in soils that are slightly acid, with a pH of 6.0 to 6.8.

Varieties

Hardiness is a plant's ability to withstand cold temperatures. Select a hardy variety adapted to Wisconsin conditions and use virus-free plants when available.

Red raspberries are most common in Wisconsin, with the largest number of adapted varieties available. They originated from the American red raspberry and from hybrids of this species and the European red raspberry. Yellow raspberries are the same, except the fruit is amber in color.

You can grow many red varieties but the following have been the most successful:

JUNE. This is a summer bearing variety that ripens very early. Berries are bright red, medium-sized, round, attractive, moderately firm and of fair quality. They are easy to pick but must be handled carefully. Plants are moderately vigorous, productive and fairly hardy, but they are susceptible to mosaic and often produce few new shoots. Fruit ripens about 10 days before Latham berries.

LATHAM. This summer bearing variety yields attractive, light red fruit that turns dark when over-ripe. The large, round, moderately firm, mild-flavored berries are of fair to good quality, but they tend to crumble. Plants are vigorous, upright, productive and hardy. They are subject to mosaic but resist other diseases fairly well.

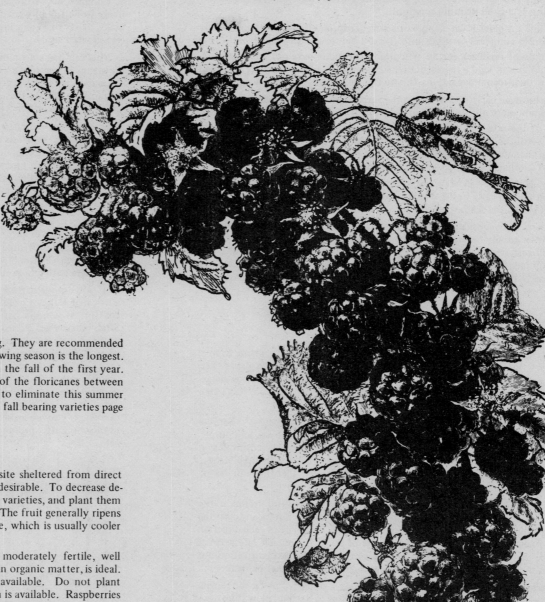

Raspberry—Belle de Fontenay, an autumn-fruiting kind

BOYNE. This summer bearing variety is excellent for home gardens. The tender, glossy, dark red, medium-sized fruit is good for processing and freezing. Its flavor is superior to Latham's. Canes are moderately vigorous, sturdy, winter hardy and very productive.

FALL RED. This is a vigorous, fall bearing variety that reproduces suckers readily. Fruit is fairly large and good quality, but the fruit stems are brittle and break easily.

Other suggested summer varieties are: Viking, a large fruited variety originated in Ontario, Canada, that ripens just before Latham; Taylor, a medium-large fruited variety that ripens with Latham but is quite subject to mosaic; Newburgh, a large-fruited variety that ripens just ahead of Latham, but lacks Latham's hardiness.

Hilton and Heritage are suggested for trial. Hilton, a summer variety, has the largest fruit of any raspberry but lacks quality and cane sturdiness. Heritage, a fall variety, has very high quality, medium-sized fruit. Neither have been grown extensively in Wisconsin.

Black and purple raspberries thrive in southern and eastern Wisconsin in favorable locations. Black raspberries originated from the American black raspberry. They are generally not as hardy as red raspberries, but if properly managed they will produce more fruit per acre than reds. The berries have a distinctive flavor, but they are seedy. Purple raspberries are hybrids of red and black varieties. They grow similar to blacks but are more vigorous and slightly hardier. The berries are large and good quality, but less attractive then red berries. They are good fresh and excellent for freezing. If you follow proper cultural practices, purple raspberries will substantially out-produce red and black types.

Black varieties adapted to our conditions are Blackhawk and Cumberland. Blackhawk is fairly resistant to anthracnose and produces well.

Recommended purple varieties include Sodus, Clyde and Marion. Sodus is most commonly grown but Marion is equally productive and fairly hardy. Clyde is equal to Marion in hardiness and is more vigorous and productive. Amethyst, a recent introduction from Iowa, is suggested for trial. It has exceptional quality but its hardiness in Wisconsin conditions is not fully known.

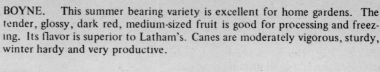

A rooting tip of the black raspberry.

Fertility Program

Well-fertilized, healthy plants have tall, thick new canes, dark green leaves and higher quality fruit. To make the soil more fertile, plow under a cover crop, such as clover or soybeans, or a good application of stable manure or compost. Fall plowing, 8 to 10 inches deep, is preferred. Early in the spring, cultivate the soil until it is in a good planting condition.

If you did not plow down manure or a cover crop, and if the soil is not already fertile, work a complete fertilizer into the soil before planting. The best types and amounts of fertilizer for all Wisconsin conditions have not been fully determined. You can send a representative soil sample to a laboratory for analysis[*] and follow their recommendations, or you can follow these general suggestions.

Apply nitrogen early each spring in the form of sulfate of ammonia, nitrate of soda, or ammonium nitrate. Ammonium nitrate (30-0-0) is most commonly used. Apply it at the rate of 2 to 3 pounds per 100 feet of row, or ¼ cup per hill. Or apply a fertilizer such as 10-10-10, which contains nitrogen, phosphorus and potash, at the rate of 4 to 5 pounds per 100 feet of row, or ½ cup per hill. Stable manure is another good fertilizer that you can apply liberally.

Apply all fertilizer in very early spring, before growth starts, to encourage maximum growth early in the season. Late fertilization keeps canes growing and succulent late in the season, making them more susceptible to winter damage.

Raspberries are considered to be "hardened off" if they stop growing and lose their leaves naturally before killing frosts occur. Canes hardened off before severe frosts will suffer less winter injury. Sowing an annual plant, such as oats, for a cover crop late in summer helps harden the canes because the crop will use some of the excess nitrogen and moisture in the soil.

Planting

Planting is usually done in the spring. Buy certified raspberry plants from a reliable nurseryman to be sure you are getting pest-free, true-to-name plants. Set the plants slightly deeper than they were growing, in a hole or furrow large enough to accommodate the roots. Pack the soil firmly around the roots and water them well.

The favored planting system in Wisconsin is the "narrow hedgerow". Set red raspberries every 2 to 3 feet in rows at least 6 feet apart. Set black and purple raspberries every 4 feet in rows at least 6 feet apart. Allow new red raspberry shoots to spread along the row but do not let them spread wider than 18 inches. Wider stands are hard to weed and prune and invite diseases that thrive in damp, slow drying conditions.

Red raspberries can also be grown in the "hill" system. "Hill" refers to the cluster of canes that develops around a single plant. It does not mean to set the plant in a mound of soil. Set the plants in holes 5 to 6 feet apart in each direction and allow new shoots to spread to a diameter of about 1 foot. Tie all the canes to a stake in the center of each hill. This system allows cross cultivation but yields less than the hedgerow system because there are fewer canes per acre.

With proper care and normal weather conditions, a raspberry patch can remain productive for 15 to 18 years. When the patch begins to decline, plow it up.

Propagation

You can expand your original plantings the following spring with home grown plants. To propagate red raspberries, select the strongest canes or sucker shoots that grow beside the established row. Dig them to include a good root system and cut the tops back 8 to 10 inches before planting. Do this in either the spring or fall.

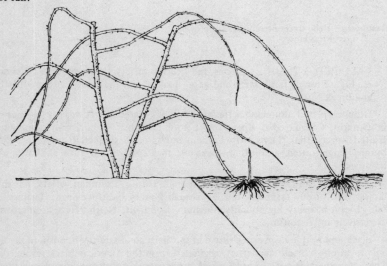

Figure 2. Producing new black and purple raspberry plants by tip layering.

Black and purple raspberries do not send up suckers. They propagate from the tips. In late summer, when the side branches are long enough to reach the ground, cover the tips with 4 to 6 inches of soil (figure 2). By cold weather the tips should have good root systems. The following spring, dig the rooted tips, cut away the parent laterals to a height of a few inches, and set the new plants in their permanent place.

---

*Soil and Plant Analysis Laboratory, 806 South Park Street, Madison, Wisconsin 53715, or Soil Testing Laboratory, Marshfield Experimental Farm, Marshfield, Wisconsin 54449. For detailed information on soil sampling see Extension Circular 644, "Sampling Soils For Testing", available from county University Extension offices in Wisconsin.

Mulching

In Wisconsin a mulch is desirable. It increases the soil's moisture holding capacity and suppresses weeds. If mulch material is expensive or scarce, use it only in the rows around the hills, and cultivate the area between the rows.

Chopped hay, straw and strawy stable manure make good mulch but they are likely to be full of weed seeds. It is better to use old silage, leaves and lawn clippings, or sawdust, shavings and wood chips, because these materials are usually free of weed seeds.

You can make a simple temporary trellis with stakes and binder twine. Set the stakes in the row at 15-to 20 foot intervals. Tie the binder twine to the end stake and then fasten it to each stake down the row. Repeat on the opposite side of the row. If the canes are very heavy, tie the two lines of twine together at intervals.

Stable manure used as a mulch also adds nutrients, so avoid late applications that may keep the plants growing too late in the fall. Apply other mulches when ever they are available, but avoid smothering young suckers in the spring. Apply additional nitrogen along with sawdust and wood shavings to speed mulch decomposition and to protect against plant nitrogen deficiency.

Training

Training makes picking easier. If you use the hill system, set a permanent stake — metal or treated wood — in the center of each hill. Tie the canes loosely to stakes with a heavy twine after you have pruned them. Don't tie young shoots or suckers until late summer or fall.

If you use the narrow hedgerow system, trellis to hold canes upright is strongly advocated but not absolutely necessary. The trellis aids in picking and in pest control. If you use permanent supports, space them at intervals along the row. Stretch heavy gauge, rustproof wire between the posts, using either one wire, two wires at different heights, or two wires at the same height. If you string two wires at the same height, place them 3 to 4 feet above ground level. Place the canes between the wires to eliminate tying (figure 3). If the wires spread, hold them together with a hook of wire. Fasten one end of the hook loosely, but permanently to one wire and bend the other end to hook over the remaining wire. You can move these hooks easily along the wire where they are most needed. If you use a single wire or one wire above the other, tie the canes loosely to the wires after pruning.

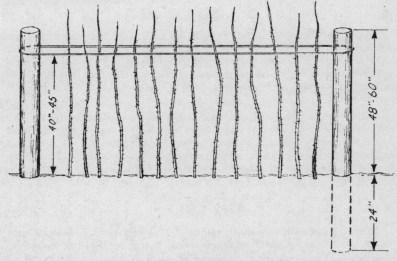

Figure 3. A permanent trellis. Cedar posts (4 to 6 inches in diameter) are spaced about 20 feet apart. Set posts at least 24 inches into the ground.

Pruning

Red Raspberries

SUMMER PRUNING. Immediately after the last harvest, cut out at ground level and burn all canes that have borne fruit (figure 4). This eliminates a disease source and allows new shoots more freedom to grow. Thin new shoots at this time, leaving three to four of the sturdiest canes per foot of row (or six to eight canes per hill in the hill system). Do not cut back the cane tips until the following spring when die-back and winter damage can be determined.

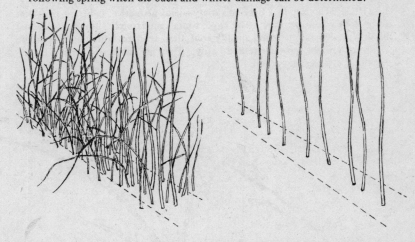

Figure 4. Red raspberries before and after summer pruning. These canes are planted in a narrow hedgerow.

DORMANT PRUNING. This pruning is done in the spring after all danger of winter injury is past. If you haven't already pruned out the old canes and thinned the new shoots, do it at this time.

Cut back slightly any side branches on the remaining fruiting canes. Also cut back the tips of the fruiting canes slightly. This is called "heading back" and prevents the canes from becoming top heavy. Severe heading back greatly reduces the crop, so never cut off more than one-fourth the total length of the cane (figure 5). Some tips commonly die back in winter and should be cut off at this time, too.

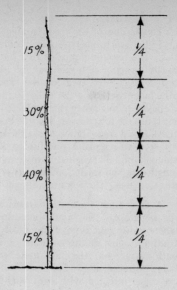

Figure 5. "Heading back" a red raspberry cane. Here you see the average percentage of total production by each quarter of the cane. Never cut off more than the top quarter.

Black Raspberries

SUMMER PRUNING. When new shoots are 24 inches high, pinch out the tip of each shoot so that each cane will produce several side branches (figure 6). This makes the fruit easier to pick and keeps the berries cleaner.

Immediately after harvest, cut out at ground level and burn all the canes that have borne fruit.

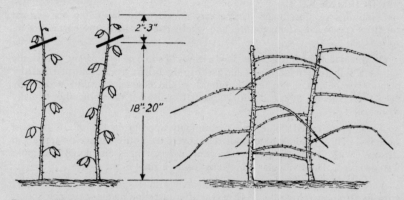

Figure 6. Tipping or summer pruning. Both black and purple raspberries are "tipped". Purple raspberries are more vigorous than the blacks, so let them grow to 30 inches before tipping.

DORMANT PRUNING. Before growth starts in the spring, cut all side branches back to about 12 inches (figure 7). Select four or five of the sturdiest new canes per plant and remove and burn all others. Remove all fruiting canes at this time, if you didn't do it the previous summer.

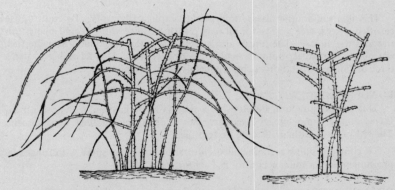

Figure 7. Black raspberries before and after dormant pruning. Purple raspberries are pruned the same way, except the side branches are cut back to 24 inches.

Purple Raspberries

SUMMER PRUNING. Pinch out the tips of new shoots when they are about 30 inches tall. The canes will then form side branches. After harvest, cut out at ground level and burn all canes that have borne fruit.

DORMANT PRUNING. Before growth starts in the spring, select four or five sturdy canes per plant and remove and burn all others. Cut all the side branches on the remaining canes back to 2 feet. Secure the canes to a trellis or stake. Remove old fruiting canes at this time, if you didn't do it the previous summer.

Fall Bearing Varieties

Everbearing or fall bearing red raspberries produce the fall crop on primocane tips. To increase the number of primocanes, and thus increase the fall crop, cut off all canes at or slightly below the soil surface late each fall. Use a sharp tool to prevent damage to the crown.

The following spring, new shoots (primocanes) will begin to grow. These canes will produce fruit on the tips (and side branches, if any) early in the fall. Fruit will continue to ripen until cold weather sets in.

By removing all the canes each fall, you eliminate the summer crop completely, because there are never any second year canes (floricanes)— —the canes on which the summer crop is produced. If you want a summer crop, plant a summer variety in addition to the fall variety. By doing this you will have berries ripening continuously from mid-July until late fall.

Insect Control

Using the good cultural practices outlined in this circular will usually keep insect problems at a minimum. But some pests occasionally become too abundant despite the cultural practices, and you will need temporary chemical control measures. Certain insect pests will always be troublesome if there are many wild host plants near the patch.

If emergency control measures or a preventive control program are necessary, consult Fact Sheet 38.

RASPBERRY CANE MAGGOT
This insect causes the cane tips to wilt or break off in late spring or early summer. The base of the wilted portions turns purple and the broken ends look like they were cut with a knife. The adult cane maggot is a small grayish fly about two-thirds as large as a housefly. Flies appear shortly after growth begins in the spring and lay their eggs in new buds or in the tips of new shoots. The maggots or worms, feed around the inside of the stem and completely girdle it. Maggots work downward in the stem below the break point and remain there all winter.

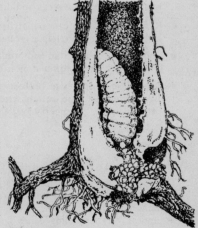

Figure 8. Adult cane maggot and larvae damage.

To control, carefully examine the patch each May and June. If you see dropping cane tips, cut them off several inches below the girdle point and burn. Remove injured canes missed in the early season examination during late fall or winter. You probably won't need chemical control as the insects rarely attack more than a few shoots in a planting.

RED-NECKED CANE BORER
This adult red-necked cane borer is a bluish-black beetle about ¼-inch long. It appears on the canes in late May or June. The beetle's "neck" is a distinctive coppery-red color. It lays its eggs in the cane bark and the larvae bore beneath the bark. The boring causes the stem to swell ½-to-1½ inches in diameter, several inches along the cane. By late fall the swellings contain creamy white-colored grubs up to ½-inch long.

To control, cut out and burn all canes with abnormal swellings during the fall and winter. If the problem persists, you may need to apply a pre-bloom insecticide to the canes.

RASPBERRY CROWN BORER
This insect causes the leaves to turn red prematurely and the cane to wilt in late summer. The borer is about 1-inch long with a white body and brown head. It feeds in the larger roots, in the crown or at the base of canes. The adult moth looks like a yellow jacket wasp and appears in late summer or early fall. It lays its eggs on the foliage, and the larvae crawl to the crown. They winter under the bark just below the soil surface. In the spring the larvae attack new cane buds and finally move downward toward the crown. It takes them two years to develop completely.

To control, dig and remove infested plants completely when possible. You may need an insecticide in problem patches. Apply the insecticide as a drench around the base of each plant in early May. Repeat the treatment for at least two years.

Figure 9. Raspberry Crown Borer and damage to the crown.

RASPBERRY CANE BORER
When this insect lays its eggs, it makes a double row of punctures around the stem tip, causing the cane tips to wilt. The adult female is a slender, black and yellow striped beetle about ½-inch long with very long antennae. Grubs bore down the cane a few inches and hibernate for the winter. The following season grubs bore downward within the cane, causing it to die.

To control, remove wilted cane tips 5 to 6 inches below the punctured area. Burn the prunings to destroy the insects inside.

RASPBERRY SAWFLY
This insect is probably Wisconsin's most common raspberry foliage pest. The spiny, pale worms attack first when leaves are about three-fourths grown. They feed along the leaf edge, eating irregular holes until only the leaf veins remain. Characteristically, the worms raise their head and tail when disturbed. The adult is a black wasp with yellow and reddish markings.
To control, apply an insecticide just before the first blossoms open.

MITES
Occasionally, spider mites become troublesome, particularly during prolonged hot dry weather. The minute creatures feed on the undersurface of leaves causing the foliage to become spotted with white or brownish flecks. If there are too many, leaves will begin to fall and fruit will dry up.

To control, use a dormant spray if mites are a persistent problem. To check the population during the growing season use a miticide.

RASPBERRY FRUIT WORM
The grub is slender, whitish and about ¼-inch long. It feeds inside buds or in developing fruit, usually causing the fruit to drop or decay before harvest. Full-grown larvae drop to the ground, pupate and emerge as beetles the following

season. Beetles are light brown, hairy and about 1/8-inch long. They feed on the tender foliage. Adult beetles will partially skeletonize the leaves. They lay their eggs on or near buds and green fruit.

To control, cultivate soil thoroughly in late summer to break up the pupal cases. If chemical control is necessary, apply the insecticides just before the first blossoms open and again after the blossom period.

Figure 11. Adult Raspberry Fruit Worm.

PICNIC BEETLES
Also called sap beetles, these small black insects with reddish-yellow spots on their backs become a severe nuisance soon after berries begin to ripen. The beetles are attracted to over-ripe fruit. They may become abundant if excessive food sources are available outside the patch.

To control, remove all damaged or diseased fruit in the patch if possible. Frequent picking will help reduce the amount of over-ripe fruit and decrease the area's attractiveness to the beetles. If the beetles become extremely abundant, you may need an insecticide treatment to salvage the fruit. Insecticides are available that you can use during the harvest period with only brief interruptions in harvest.

Weed Control

Cultivate raspberries to control weeds. Use hand tools, tractor drawn cultivators or disks. Begin soon after you set the plants out and repeat often enough to control weeds. Stop cultivating just before harvest to avoid damaging ripened fruit and to encourage canes to mature (harden) early. Never cultivate deeper than 2 or 3 inches.

Consider using herbicides as an alternative to or in combination with cultivation. Herbicides will control annual weeds and perennial quackgrass. For chemical weed control suggestions, see the latest edition (revised annually) of Wisconsin Special Circular 38, "1970 Chemical Weed Control Recommendations for Fruit Crops".*

Disease Control

Follow these recommended cultural practices to reduce the disease problems that cut your yields and lower fruit quality.

- Plant only disease-free nursery stock. This generally means buying certified plants from reliable plant growers and nurseries.
- Destroy wild or abandoned bramble patches near garden and commercial plantings. Weed out weak and diseased plants in established plantings.
- Remove and burn canes that have fruited, as well as weak and badly diseased canes immediately after harvest.
- Control weeds and thin and prune plants properly to insure good air circulation. High and continued moisture conditions favor disease development.
- Use fungicide sprays to protect plantings against certain diseases. Follow a recommended application schedule. For specific information refer to Fact Sheet 38, "Raspberry Pest Control for Home Gardeners."*

ANTHRACNOSE
This fungus disease can attack all raspberries, but black and purple varieties are more susceptible than most red varieties. Small purplish spots appear on the young canes and spurs. They enlarge and become somewhat oval-shaped and slightly sunken, with buff-colored centers and purple borders. As heavily infected canes mature, they dry out and crack lengthwise. Berries on these canes are small, dry and seedy. With late season infections the spots are generally larger, more buff or gray than purple and so much more numerous that they join together and produce a condition known as "gray-bark". These late season spots are more superficial than the early infections and do not have sunken centers. Dark-colored fruiting bodies develop in a radial pattern on the gray infected area.

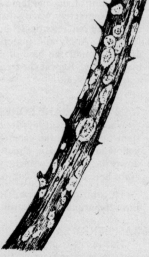

Figure 11. Anthracnose

To control, follow recommended cultural practices and use the fungicide spray schedule recommended for anthracnose in Fact Sheet 38. Plant black varieties in a different place than red raspberries.

*Available from your county University Extension offices in Wisconsin.

SPUR BLIGHT
This is one of the most troublesome fungus diseases attacking red raspberries, but it seldom affect other varities. The infection appears first on the new green canes in late spring or early summer. Bluish-brown or purplish-brown discolored areas on the canes, usually at a leaf attachment. The areas enlarge and lengthen up to 2 inches or more. When these infected canes become fruiting canes the next season, the side branches growing from the diseased areas are weak and the leaves yellowish. The affected area remains purplish to dark brown until late summer or fall, when it turns grayish. The bark splits lengthwise and small "pimples" (pycnidia) appear on the diseased area. These contain fungus spores.

A short time later numerous black pustules appear on the same area. These are immature bodies (perithecia) where a different type of spore (ascospore) resemble the fruiting bodies of the anthracnose fungus in its "gray-bark" stage, but they are more scattered rather than being arranged in a radial or concentric pattern. Berries on canes infected with spur blight are dry, small and seedy.

Figure 12. Spur Blight

To control, follow recommended cultural practices, and be especially sure to remove the old fruiting canes at the end of the fruiting period, thin out the rows and keep the planting weed free. Fungicide sprays help control this disease.

VERTICILLIUM WILT
Symptoms of this fungus disease vary considerably depending on seasonal conditions, especially temperature, and whether red or black raspberries are involved.

On infected black raspberries, lower leaves of some of the current year's cane will be a dull green in late spring, rather than the bright green of normal, healthy plants. As the disease progresses up the stem, the older leaves yellow and finally drop off. The tip of the shoot will start to wilt, and the entire shoot finally withers and dies.

A symptom called "blue stem" commonly appears on the shoots of most varieties. This is a dark blue color that covers the entire surface or appears as streaks. With severe wilt, the plant's vascular system is discolored and looks water-soaked. These vascular symptoms appear mainly in the roots.

Verticillium wilt may affect only one or two shoots of a half-dozen or more growing from one crown. The first year after infection many of the new shoots survive. They will be the fruiting canes the second year, but if they were infected the previous year, they will either be dead or show poorly developed buds.

Sometimes the buds on seemingly healthy canes open normally only to have the leaves turn yellow and stop growing. These leaves eventually wither, together with the branches to which they are attached. If berries do develop, they remain small and of poor quality.

Wilt symptoms on red raspberries are about the same as on the black varieties, but because the new canes are produced at a distance from the parent plant, they are often disease free even if the parent plant is infected.

This is a soil-bourne disease that infects through the roots. To control, use certified disease-free plants for all new plantings, since wilt-infected plants can transmit the disease. The fungus also infects other plants, including strawberries, egg plants, tomatoes, potatoes and coniferous species. It is advisable to use a three or four year rotation, including mainly grain crops.

POWDERY MILDEW
This fungus infection develops as a grayish-white coating or deposit on the leaves during damp, muggy weather. Heavy dews favor mildew development. The red variety, Latham, is quite susceptible.

To control, follow recommended cultural practices and spray with fungicides recommended for mildew control in Fact Sheet 38.

ORANGE RUST
This fungus disease attacks only black and purple raspberries. Blister-like reddish-orange pustules, containing spore masses, develop on the underside of the leaves in the spring. Canes or shoots bearing the rust-infected leaves often look weak and spindly. The disease eventually invades the entire plant, including the root.

To control, dig and burn all plants showing rust on the leaves. Start any new plantings from rust-free stock. (Orange rust can also originate from wild brambles growing nearby, especially blackberries.)

YELLOW LEAF RUST
This fungus disease appears mainly on red varieties, causing small, yellow blisters on the leaves. Leaves, especially lower ones, turn yellow and drop. Black or brown spots appear in autumn on the underside of the leaves. You easily can mistake yellow leaf rust for orange rust.

To control, follow recommended cultural practices and remove and burn old fruiting canes immediately after harvest.

LATE RASPBERRY RUST
This fungus disease appears in July or August and may cause premature defoliation. Small, golden yellow rust blisters develop on the underside of the leaves. It may also infect canes.

To control, follow the procedures suggested for yellow leaf rust.

MOSAIC

This is the most common of several virus diseases that attack raspberries. It is transmitted by one or more species of aphids and can be mild to severe. It may cause a very light leaf mottling early in the season with no visible injury. Or it may cause a rough, blistered mottling, stunt growth and decay plant tissue. Infected foliage may turn yellow. If the leaves are only mottled, the plants may grow fairly normally for several years, although fruit yield and quality will decline each year. Warm weather sometimes hides leaf mottle symptoms.

To control, prune out plants as soon as they show symptoms of virus infection. This practice is not practical or effective if over 20 percent of the plants are infected in a planting. When establishing a new planting try to obtain plants that have been certified as "essentially virus free." Such plants are usually available only from certain nurseries and plant growers in the eastern United States, and possibly from one or two sources in Wisconsin. Isolate virus-free plantings from all wild brambles and from any old raspberry plantings.

Figure 13. Mosaic

LEAF CURL

At least two distinct virus diseases of the leaf curl type are transmitted by apparently only one type of aphid. The main symptoms are a downward curling of the leaves and shortened internodes. Certain varieties such as the Cuthbert red raspberry and the Cumberland blackcap are quite susceptible.

To control, follow the procedures suggested for mosaic.

STREAK

The main symptom of this virus disease is a purple streaking of the canes. The infected canes also tend to curve downward by midsummer. During the first season of infection the symptoms are mild and infected canes may not show the purple streaking. Apparently only black raspberries are affected.

To control, follow the procedures suggested for mosaic.

CROWN GALL

This bacterial disease causes irregular, warty swellings or growths often an inch or more in size at the ground line or on the stubs of lateral roots that you have broken or cut during planting or cultivating. Crown gall on black raspberries can appear at the root crown where canes have broken off.

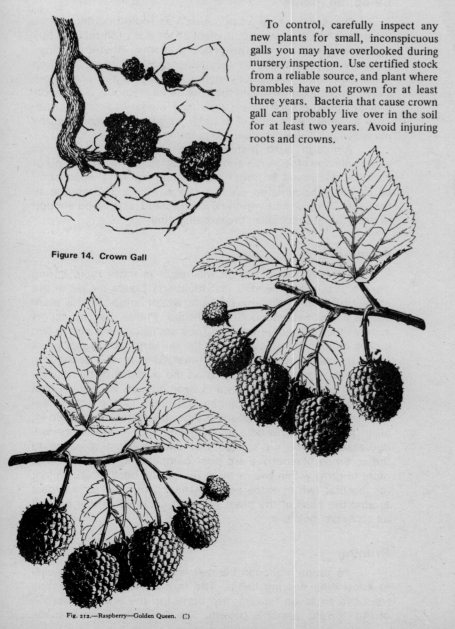

To control, carefully inspect any new plants for small, inconspicuous galls you may have overlooked during nursery inspection. Use certified stock from a reliable source, and plant where brambles have not grown for at least three years. Bacteria that cause crown gall can probably live over in the soil for at least two years. Avoid injuring roots and crowns.

Figure 14. Crown Gall

Fig. 212.—Raspberry—Golden Queen. (°)

FRUITING BRANCHLET OF RASPBERRY.

THE WINEBERRY,
AN AMATEUR'S FRUIT

By Ida M. Angell

After ten years' experience we still feel that the wineberry is one of the best small fruits for the amateur. Our garden is small, but if we had to give up something it would not be wineberries. They are delightful as fresh fruit for hot weather, on account of their pleasant flavor; with plenty of sugar we prefer them to raspberries. They make one of the best of jellies, very like currant jelly both in taste and looks. They are also good for jams, preserves and canning. The bushes and the size and form of the fruit are similar to raspberries, but the fruit is dark, transparent red, like a currant, and the flavor is like a combination of the two.

Our bushes yield every year, and have given us enough to eat fresh and to preserve for winter. They are worth raising for the jelly alone. Unripe berries should be used. If left on the vines till dead ripe they will make a darker, guava-like jelly that has a very good taste but is harder to make and may require gelatin to thicken it.

Put the unripe berries in the inner section of a double boiler without water. In the outer section put cold water and set on the stove until the berries are heated until soft. Mash and strain and boil the juice twenty minutes, adding an equal bulk of heated sugar stirred until dissolved. Bring the mixture to a boil quickly, and pour at once into hot jelly glasses. It is the quickest of all jellies to thicken; put in a cold place, it is hard and solid in an hour.

We also make a good hot-weather drink from the wineberries. They are just covered with water and heated till soft, then strained. One-third the bulk of sugar is added and it is boiled up and bottled for present use, to mix with an equal amount of cold water.

Our experience is that the plants are hardy, easily cultivated, bear transplanting well in fall or spring, and easily adapt themselves to climate and soil. But, on the other hand, many people report failures with them—the plants seem to winter kill in one garden and to thrive in another one close by.

Quite independently of the plant as a fruit, it is very valuable as an ornamental shrub. The under sides of the leaves are silvery white, and in a wind the waving of the silver and green colors is very charming. The calyx forms a bur, like a moss rosebud, which provides a covering from before the blossoming season, after which it closes and protects the berry until it is ready to ripen. As the fruit turns red the bur opens again. This and the slight honey-like stickiness on both bur and berry seem to protect against all insects. But the stickiness is no disadvantage, for they are the cleanest of berries to pick and to handle. Each bunch contains berries in all stages, from the small, hard burs to dead-ripe fruit, ready to fall to the ground. The canes are also covered with a reddish, hairlike growth.

Sprouting habit of red raspberry.

Our patch was started from about a dozen plants bought two or three years after their introduction. The plants were set in a rough spot, next to a stone wall, but the place evidently agreed with them. They have flourished and taken possession, rooting (like blackberries) from the tips of their canes until there was a growth which we had to clear out, transplanting some last summer (which grew abundantly and bore well this season).

If left alone they make a thicket. We do not understand where the report originated that they winter kill. One authority recommends cultivating until the second year as the fruit is setting, claiming that later culture injures the setting of fruit and encourages a continuation of wood growth that may winter kill. According to that, lack of cultivation is no drawback. In spite of stony ground and the ignorant culture, pruning and transplanting by an uninformed laborer, our plants have run riot and claim more room than we can spare. Those under the trees, in partial shade, have larger berries and more of them and are the stronger-looking vines.

The new canes that grow this year are the bearers of next year. Those that have borne this year can be cut off after the bearing season or left until March. If the plants are cut at a convenient height they send out side shoots that bear the following season.

Reprinted from GARDEN MAGAZINE, 1905

HIGHBUSH BLUEBERRIES

Robert E. Gough
and Vladimir G. Shutak

University of Rhode Island
Cooperative Extension Service

Bulletin 143
1973 edition

Figure 2. Vigorous 'Earliblue' blueberry bush after one season in the field. Left, before pruning; right, after pruning.

Introduction

Blueberries are native to New England. For years they have grown wild on small hummocks in swamps and on higher ground. Early selection from the wild, so universal with other fruit plants, did not occur in the case of the highbush blueberry until 1906, when Dr. Frederick V. Coville of the United States Department of Agriculture initiated a breeding, selection, and cultural management program for this fruit. A rapidly growing industry has since developed in the United States, with commercial highbush blueberry plantings estimated at 30,000 acres in 1973.

Rhode Island is ideally situated for the production of cultivated highbush blueberries. Not only is the soil nearly ideal for this fruit, but the market is superb, with very little or no competition within the state at this time.

This bulletin outlines the essentials for the successful culture of the cultivated highbush blueberry by homeowners and commercial growers.

Soil Conditions

The highbush blueberry requires moist and acidic soil. Most satisfactory plant growth results where the soil pH reaction is between 4.2 and 5.2. Too high a pH reaction may result in difficulties due either to iron deficiency, resulting in a chlorotic condition of the plant characterized by yellowing of the leaves, or to the lack of the ammonia form of nitrogen most easily assimilated by the plant.

In cases where the pH reaction of the soil is too low, ground magnesium limestone may be applied to raise the soil pH to about 4.2. Where the pH is as high or higher than 5.2, very finely ground sulfur or ammonium sulfate may be used to increase acidity. The addition of sulfur to soils with a relatively high pH will allow both iron and ammonia to become naturally available. These soil treatments should be based on soil test results.

Peatmoss, sawdust, leaf mould, and other types of peaty organic matter should constitute a high percentage of any blueberry soil. Not only is organic matter beneficial to soil organisms, but it also helps improve soil aeration and water-holding capacity. Maple leaves should not, however, be used in soil conditioning.

The fine fibrous roots of the blueberry plant develop best in moist, but well aerated soil. Blueberries should never be planted in extremely wet soil. These plants are very sensitive to a high water table during their growing season. To prevent water injury to the plant the water table should be at least 20 inches below the surface. Blueberries may be planted in peaty swamp areas only if drainage ditches are provided, or if the plants are situated on mounds as they are often found naturally.

Climatic Requirements

Although the highbush blueberry plant is quite hardy, it is not advisable to plant it in any location where winter temperatures are likely to fall below −20°F, unless the snow drifts deeply there. The snow cover in this case would act as insulation from the extreme cold.

Planting sites surrounded by hills or dense stands of trees have poor air drainage. This may increase both frost damage and the incidence of fungus diseases by increasing the humidity of the area.

Areas free from prolonged drought and in full sunlight should be selected for planting.

Preparation of the Soil

When possible, the soil should be prepared at least one season ahead of planting in order to incorporate thoroughly fertilizer and organic materials, and bring weeds, especially quackgrass, under control. A cover crop of buckwheat may be planted and incorporated into the soil in the early fall previous to planting. This should be followed by a cover crop of winter rye. A complete fertilizer such as 10-10-10-2 or 10-10-10 in sufficient quantity to produce a heavy cover crop growth, and enough lime, if needed, to bring the soil reaction to a pH of about 4.2, should be added before planting the cover crops. Both of these applications should be based on soil tests. The winter rye should be plowed under in early spring and the soil brought to a fine texture by thorough harrowing or rototilling. If, in addition to the cover crops, peatmoss or sawdust is needed to lighten the heavy soils, additional fertilizer should be used. Soil preparation should preferably be completed ten days to two weeks before planting.

In addition to, or in place of, complete soil preparation, individual planting holes may be dug and prepared as early in the spring as possible. It is best, when preparing the hole for planting, to use a mixture of one-third loam, one-third sand, and one-third organic matter such as peatmoss, leaf mould, or sawdust. A handful of complete fertilizer, such as 10-10-10, will provide sufficient nutrients for initial plant growth. Thorough mixing of all these materials will prevent root injury. The additions of sand and/or organic matter are especially desirable on both very heavy and very light soils to improve soil structure.

Selecting Plants

Blueberries may be purchased as rooted cuttings or as plants one to five years old. In most cases it is preferable to buy vigorous, disease free, two-year-old plants. Rooted cuttings or one-year plants may be less expensive, but must be given great care and will unduly delay harvest. Older plants are usually more expensive and may not be as vigorous. It is important to obtain plants from a reputable nursery to assure trueness to name. As a rule, it is safer to get plants from nearby nurseries, thus avoiding delay in planting.

Although most plantings will produce suitable crops when only one blueberry variety is included, pollination by other varieties will result in larger fruit, earlier ripening when compared to self-pollinated plants, and a higher percentage of fruit set. Three or four varieties, interplanted, should be enough to adequately accomplish cross-pollination.

Planting

Although fall plantings will result in more rapid spring growth, it is recommended that blueberry plants be set in the early spring to avoid any possible winter injury to the plant before it has become well established. Plants may be set as soon as the soil can be worked. They are usually set one to two inches deeper than they were in the nursery, four to eight feet apart, in rows spaced eight to ten feet. Spacing will depend on the type of equipment used and on the purpose of the plantation. Dig holes deep enough and wide enough so that no root crowding will occur. After setting the plant, fill the hole three-quarters full with soil and flood it. After the water has soaked in, fill in the rest of the hole and tamp firmly. This practice will decrease the soil air spaces that allow certain diseases to thrive. Since blueberries are poor competitors, allow no other plant to grow within two or three feet of the base of each plant for the first two or three years. A mulch of straw or sawdust around the base of the plant will help accomplish this as well as conserve moisture.

Pruning

To prune highbush blueberries correctly, it is essential to know their bearing habits. The fruit buds, each containing from five to seven flowers, are borne on the terminal portion of the current season's growth. The buds are formed in the

Figure 3. Vigorous 'Coville' blueberry bush after two years in the field. Left, before pruning; right, after pruning.

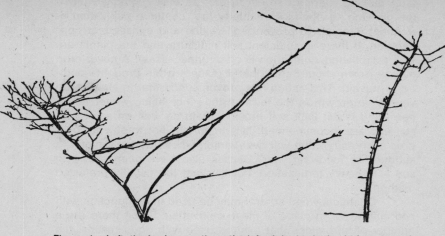

Figure 4. Left, the bushy growth on the left of the bush should be removed during pruning. Right, the short lateral side shoots of this bush will produce inferior berries and should be removed during pruning.

axils of leaves during the late summer and early fall and remain dormant during the winter. They bloom and produce fruit the following summer (Fig. 1).

Pruning should start immediately after planting and be continued each year in March or early April, just before the buds begin to swell. All weak, spindly growth should be removed from newly set plants, and their large flower buds should be removed to prevent fruiting. This procedure will encourage strong healthy bushes. Early fruiting will delay the vegetative growth necessary for large-sized bushes and a profitable plantation. It is most important to remember that since the crop is borne on wood produced the preceding year, the first consideration should be to develop a strong, vigorously growing bush.

After one growing season in the field, the more vigorous bushes may be allowed to bear a very small crop, not in excess of one pint per bush. The number of fruit buds should be reduced to a favorable balance with the vegetative growth by removing any weak or unthrifty wood. If enough buds have not been removed, thin out or head back the remaining bearing shoots. On smaller, less vigorous plants, weak growth and all fruit buds should be removed (Fig. 2).

After two seasons in the plantation, most bushes may be allowed to bear a small crop of one to two pints per bush. The emphasis, however, should still be on establishing a good healthy, vigorous bush — not on fruit production. Again, remove all unthrifty growth and try to allow the crop to be borne on the strong canes. If this procedure is followed, good growth of the bush is assured. Heavy fruit production at this time may result in dwarfed plants (Fig. 3).

If well grown bushes were started as healthy two-year-old plants, they may be considered mature bushes after four or five growing seasons in the field.

There are three points to consider in pruning a mature bush; (1) prune lightly enough to ensure a heavy crop for the current year; (2) prune severely enough to secure large-sized berries, and (3) prune enough to balance crop and bush vigor and thus assure sufficient new fruit wood for continuous bearing. Certain relatively simple procedures will accomplish these goals.

After the removal of all diseased or dead wood, old or unthrifty canes should be cut level to the ground, to a two-or three-inch stub, or to a low, vigorous side shoot. Soft, basal autumn growth should be removed entirely, as this type of growth often winter-kills and is very susceptible to fungus disease. Such growth is not stiff and springy, but limber and often irregularly flat-sided instead of round. Since profitable production decreases after about five years, all canes five years old or older should be removed. This can be accomplished by removing the oldest one-fifth of the canes each year. Absence of new shoots frequently indicates that the bush is overcrowded with old canes and/or underfertilized. Prune these bushes severely enough to promote the growth of three to five new shoots from the base of each plant each year. After the first two steps are completed, the bush should be thinned. This is accomplished by removing twiggy or bushy growth clusters and weak lateral shoots (Fig. 4). Erect growing varieties should be thinned out more in the center, while spreading varieties usually require more pruning of the lower, drooping branches. Since blueberries will sometimes tend to overbear, some flower-bud thinning may be beneficial. This may be accomplished by heading back some of the bearing shoots, which serves to thin

the crop and improve berry size. In pruning, always remove less vigorous, thin growth and leave thicker, more vigorous wood. Experiments have shown that buds borne on thick wood open later in the spring. Thus, they are less susceptible to frost damage. This type of wood also produces larger berries. Unpruned bushes may degenerate rapidly into a thick, twiggy mass of unfruitful wood (Fig. 5).

Fertilization

Since growing plants remove a certain amount of nutrients from the soil, an additional supply should be added to keep the plant in good growth. Most experts agree on a 1-1-1 ratio of mixed fertilizer such as 10-10-10 or 15-15-15. If possible, at least half of the nitrogen should be in slowly available organic form. The fertilizer should also contain two percent magnesium oxide which will be represented in the analysis by a fourth number such as 10-10-10-2. There are normally two periods of top growth, referred to as flushes. The first flush starts in early spring and continues for several weeks. After a short interval, a second flush starts in late June. Newly set plants should not be fertilized after planting until the secondary growth period begins. If the first application of fertilizer is applied too soon, it may result in reddened foliage and a several weeks' delay in the starting of new growth. A small handful of fertilizer should be spread over the root area at least four inches away from the crowns of the plants. A second application may be made in late July. The fertilizer application should be increased each year until mature bushes are receiving about one pound per plant two-thirds applied in late April and the other third in June.

If mature bushes show low vigor, an additional application of one-half pound of fertilizer per bush in November will build up food reserves in the plant and allow a quick spurt of growth in the spring. It is important that this practice be avoided on healthy bushes, however, as under this condition it will promote excessive soft growth that is highly susceptible to disease.

The type of soil and its fertility will influence fertilization practice. On sandy soil, where leaching is a problem, more fertilizer may be required, but there is also a greater danger of root injury from high concentrations at one time. As a corrective measure for poor growth on this type of soil, bury up to three bushels of peatmoss per plant in the soil around the bush beneath the ends of the branches. The plant's root system will develop into the peatmoss. The larger plant that results from this procedure is better able to use the available fertilizer and moisture. If for some reason a bush does not bear a crop, fertilization must still be continued. The idea that if there is no crop the bush needs no fertilizer, is false. Adjust the amount of fertilizer by observing two plant signs: (1) pale green or yellowish leaves and lack of vigor that may be caused by a lack of nitrogen; and (2) a browning of the tips and margins of the leaves that may be caused by too much fertilizer. The injury from over-fertilization may be lessened by heavy watering to reduce the soil solution concentration and encourage leaching. Such injury usually occurs when fertilizer is applied too near the crown of the plant, dropped in clumps, or applied in dry weather.

Soil Management

Blueberries are very poor competitors for water and nutrients and require especially good soil aeration. Shallow, clean cultivation practiced frequently enough during the growing season will aerate the soil and keep heavy weed growth down. To avoid knocking ripe berries off the bush, cultivate after picking. Unripe berries are not as easily knocked off. If the growing season is particularly dry, continue cultivation at frequent intervals to prevent soil-caking and consequent poor aeration. If there is sufficient soil moisture and the plants are well established, cultivation is often unnecessary. A cover crop may be sown about September 1 (except when drought conditions prevail). This action has proven successful in slowing up vegetative growth in the fall and thus increasing winter hardiness, and it will limit soil erosion. Oats do well on such acid soil and are recommended. It is important not to sow a cover crop such as rye that will over-winter, since it is too difficult to subdue the following year. Berries also have been grown in sod with heavy fertilization, but it is not the usually preferred method.

Chemical weed control may be used in conjunction with sod culture, or in place of clean cultivation. Since there are a number of herbicides that may be used with good results, the grower should consult his state Agricultural Experiment Station for the latest recommendations.

In the Northeast, mulching is perhaps the wisest soil management practice and is highly recommended for small home plantings. At least four to six inches of mulching material is required. Straw, wood chips, or sawdust may be used. Of these three, sawdust is perhaps the best. Experiments conducted at the University of Rhode Island Agricultural Experiment Station have shown substantially higher crop yields when sawdust mulch was used, as well as a reduction in maintenance labor great enough to at least partially compensate for the cost of the material. Soft- and hardwood sawdust show equally good results. Preliminary tests with wood chips indicate that this material may be substituted for sawdust.

Under sawdust, the soil acidity remains nearly constant. Soil temperatures are higher in the winter and lower in the summer and remain relatively constant from day to day. Soil moisture content is higher under sawdust than under clean cultivation. When this material is used, it should be spread evenly over the whole area if possible. In any event, slanting it away from the plant should be avoided since this may result in rainwater running off and the plant suffering from shortage of moisture. Some researchers advise not using fresh sawdust.

As well as keeping soil moisture levels high and reducing weed growth, sawdust mulch adds valuable organic matter to the soil. As the under layers of sawdust decay, additional sawdust must be added every two or three years to maintain the proper depth. If the plants show a nitrogen deficiency as previously described, add additional fertilizer at the regular time to correct it, because, under mulching conditions, the soil microorganisms use some of the available nitrogen to break down the mulch.

Propagation

Propagating media may be horticultural peatmoss or, better, a mixture of peat and sand, half and half by volume. Coarse peat is not satisfactory and very fine peat may become too wet and poorly aerated. The rooting medium should be placed in the tray or bed about a week ahead of time and thoroughly soaked. Dry peat is very difficult to wet and hot water may be necessary. Never add fertilizer to the medium at this time.

Propagating beds for both hardwood and softwood cuttings may be made of convenient size with six-to-eight-inch sides (Fig. 6). Copper or galvanized screening is placed on the bottom to exclude grubs, moles, and mice and to provide

thorough drainage and aeration. The tray may be set on coarse gravel or cinders or may be placed on cedar logs to keep the bottom a few inches off the ground. Cuttings in trays should be protected from direct sunlight and excessive drying by placing them in a lath house or under a shade of cheesecloth, tobacco cloth, or fly screening, varnished to further reduce light penetration. An arch of concrete reinforcing wire covered with polyethylene and Saran cloth (45 percent shade), or burlap may also be placed over the bed. Miniature beds for use indoors may be constructed in a similar manner using arched coat-hangers and clear plastic sandwich wrap (Fig. 7).

As soon as most of the cuttings have rooted, the polyethylene should be removed but the shade left on until about mid-September. More even temperature and light conditions will be found on the north side of buildings. On the larger frames, cuttings may be kept moist with an automatic mist control system. By using automatic mist, good results are obtained without any additional shading or coverage. On smaller frames, hand watering may be in order. No watering should ever be done in the heat of the day or in the evening. A fan may also be installed to promote air circulation. Modern commercial propagation is done either in large lath houses or in standard open propagating beds.

The most common method of propagation is by hardwood cuttings. However, blueberries can also be propagated by softwood cuttings, mounding, and layering. The propagation procedure is not difficult, but requires more than ordinary attention to details.

Hardwood cuttings are made from dormant, healthy, well-matured shoots of the previous season's growth. Poorly hardened or thin shoots should be avoided. If the shoot pith is brown, the shoot is of poor quality and should be discarded. Always take cuttings at least 50 feet from the nearest virus-infected plant. Shoots from which cuttings are taken are usually 10 to 30 inches in length and are referred to as "whips." Only that portion bearing leaf buds is selected.

Wood for cuttings may be taken in the fall and stored in a cool, (35° to 40°F) moist, but not wet, ventilated place, and packed in damp sphagnum moss, sawdust, or similar material, or may be taken in the spring just before bud growth begins (early April).

Cuttings are usually three to four inches long and about one-quarter inch in diameter. Thicker or thinner wood does not do well. The cut should be clean with no crushed tissues. Make basal cuts just below a bud. The top cut should be made about one-quarter inch above a bud. Cuttings are usually placed vertically in a rooting medium one inch apart, with two inches between rows and with only the topmost bud protruding. Treatment of hardwood cuttings with a root-promoting chemical has not been generally successful. After setting the cuttings, thorough watering settles the material around them. Leaves will develop very soon and high humidity is necessary until the roots form (two to three months) following the first flush of the top growth period.

When the second flush of top growth begins, roots have formed and fertilization is recommended. A liquid fertilizer, commonly a 16-32-16 analysis, is used at the rate of three pounds in 50 gallons of water or two level tablespoonfuls per gallon. One gallon should be enough for about 25 square feet of bench surface. All foliage should be rinsed with water immediately after application. Weekly applications are made until mid-August.

Rooted cuttings are usually left in the propagating bed for the winter and protected from alternate freezing and thawing by a straw mulch, although they may be transplanted to the nursery in September. Where plants are retained in propagating beds through the winter, the soil should be mounded

Figure 5. Left, young, bearing 'Earliblue' blueberry bush before pruning. Right, the same bush after pruning.

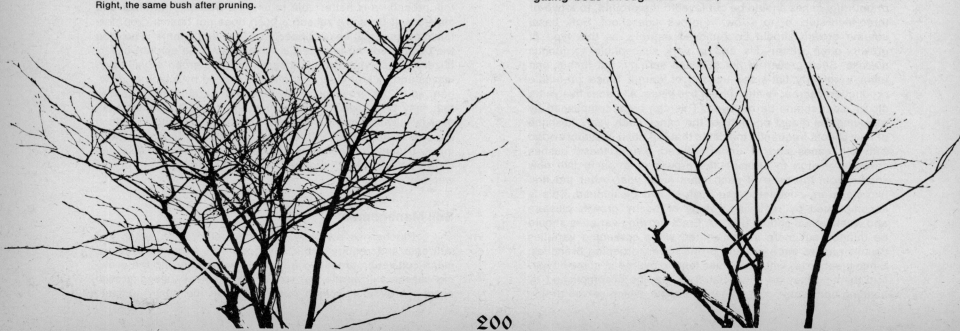

around the sides of the frame to reduce the amount of bottom ventilation and freezing. In most cases, transplanting later than September does not permit root development substantial enough to prevent winter heaving. Cuttings are set in the nursery one foot apart in rows spaced 18 inches apart. If the soil is fertile, no fertilizer is needed the first year.

Softwood cuttings, unlike hardwood cuttings, are taken while the plant is actively growing. The best time to take these cuttings is just after the first flush has hardened sufficiently to be handled, and just before the second flush of growth starts.

Cuttings should be four inches in length with all of the leaves except the upper two removed to avoid excessive transpiration. When mist is used, remove only the leaves on the lower half. Softwood cuttings may be dipped in a rooting compound such as indole butyric acid to promote rooting. Straight cuttings will root nearly as well as heel or mallet cuttings. The straight cuttings consist only of the shoot, while heel cuttings have a segment of older bark and wood attached to them, and mallet cuttings have a complete section of older wood at the bottom.

Relatively easy varieties to root from cuttings are: 'Earliblue', 'Blueray', 'Collins', 'Coville', 'Berkeley', and 'Herbert', while 'Jersey' is less easily rooted, and 'Bluecrop' is quite difficult to root.

Harvesting

In harvesting blueberries, pickers should be instructed to handle fruit carefully and to avoid tearing and bruising. Since cultivated highbush blueberries do not ripen evenly in the cluster, ripe berries should be rolled from the cluster into the palm of the hand with the thumb. This method may prevent immature berries from becoming detached.

It is preferable that the berries be picked directly into the boxes in which they will be sold. Where possible, a shoulder or belt fastening should be provided for the container so that both hands are free for picking.

Berries continue to grow and enlarge for some time after they appear ripe (blue). Too early harvesting results in reduced yield. By allowing berries to become fully ripe (three to six days after turning fully blue), the flavor is improved and the size and sweetness increased. Although unripe berries will turn blue after harvesting, sugar content and volume is noticeably lower than in berries allowed to ripen completely on the bush. Since overripe berries shrivel and may drop badly, the entire plantation should be picked about once a week.

Most cultivated blueberries are placed in pint baskets for sale. It is important that there be a minimum amount of handling since it may destroy the berry's attractive whitish waxy surface cover or bloom.

Many commercial growers cover the baskets with sheets of cellophane with gummed labels attached and the cellophane held in place by a rubber band. Such a covering reduces water loss, protects from dust, and improves appearance. Depending upon the local demand, it may pay to do some sizing.

In recent years, the problems of harvesting and marketing have been circumvented by letting the customer do the harvesting. At a fixed price per quart or per pound the grower may do his business through "pick-your-own" sales. Under these circumstances the grower often ropes off portions of his field for easier control of the public. Signposts with a set of rules for each section, often keep the public within the control of the grower or his supervisors. Guest books may be on hand for the customer to sign. They will not only provide a list of the potential customers of a particular grower, but will also supply an estimate of the future needs of the grower by recording the approximate number of pickers in any one season.

Recent developments in mechanical harvesters make it possible to use this method for harvesting blueberries. We will not discuss here the many different types and merits of mechanical harvesters. Suffice it to say that all of these types have one thing in common — they harvest, at one time, all of the berries which will fall off at a particular force. There will be berries which are fully mature and should be harvested, but, invariably, there will also be some berries which are not fully mature. This method necessitates further sorting to remove green berries.

Variety Selection

Because blueberries require cross-pollination for maximum crops, at least three varieties should be planted. To provide a long picking season, early, mid-season, and late varieties should be selected. Many of the varieties recommended in earlier bulletins have been superseded. While existing plantings of some of the older varieties, such as 'Concord,' 'Dixi,' 'Pioneer,' and 'Scammell' may be maintained, none of these varieties is recommended for new plantings in this area. Varieties considered promising for this area are listed below in order of ripening.

Earliblue

The bush is hardy, vigorous, upright, spreading, and fairly productive. The cluster is medium-sized and loose. The berry is large, aromatic, light blue, firm, of good dessert quality, resistant to cracking, has medium scar, and does not drop readily.

Bluetta

The bush is short, compact-spreading, medium vigorous, and consistently productive. The berry is medium-sized, light blue, firm and has a broad scar.

Collins

The bush is erect, vigorous, and fairly productive. Fruit cluster is medium-sized and rather tight. The berry is large, light blue, firm, highly flavored, and does not drop or crack readily.

Blueray

The bush is hardy, productive, vigorous, upright, and spreading. The clusters are small and tight. The berry is very large, light blue, firm, aromatic, of high dessert quality, with medium scar, and is resistant to cracking.

Bluecrop

The bush is hardy, productive, upright, drought-resistant and vigorous. The clusters are large and medium-loose. The berry is large, very light blue, firm, slightly aromatic, of medium dessert quality, has a small scar, and is resistant to cracking.

Berkeley

The bush is upright, vigorous, productive, open-spreading and easy to prune and propagate. The clusters are loose. The berry is very large, light blue, firm, mild flavored, slightly aromatic, of medium dessert quality, with a large dry scar. It is well liked for its beautiful color, firmness, productiveness, and large size.

Herbert

The bush is vigorous, open-spreading, and productive. The cluster is medium-loose. The berry is very large, medium blue, aromatic, tender, of very high dessert quality, has a medium scar, and is resistant to cracking.

Darrow

The bush is vigorous, upright, and consistently productive. The cluster is medium-loose. The berry is large, light blue, firm, aromatic, tart when not fully ripe, resistant to cracking, and has a good scar.

Coville

The bush is vigorous, upright, spreading and very productive. The cluster is loose. The berry is very large, medium blue, firm, highly aromatic, tart when not fully ripe, attractive, of very good dessert quality, resistant to cracking, and has a good scar. It does not drop and is excellent for processing.

Lateblue

The bush is erect, vigorous, and consistently productive. The berry is large, firm, light blue, aromatic, tart when not fully ripe, and has a good scar.

QUINCE

Meech Quince (Meech's Prolific).

QUALITY QUINCES in the BACK YARD
By S. W. Fletcher

Because quinces cannot be eaten out of hand they are almost universally neglected in the home fruit garden. Nine times out of ten—and I am tempted to say ninety-nine times out of a hundred—the man who tills, fertilizes and sprays his apples, pears, peaches and plums will relegate his quince bushes to a dishonorable place by the sink drain, where they have to fight for an existence with wet soil, blight, curculio and burdocks. The popular notion that quinces do best when planted in some wet and weedy spot where no other fruit will thrive has been brought about by the general inclination to let them shift for themselves. The fact is, however, that a quince appreciates a well-drained site and good culture fully as much as its more popular relatives, the apple and the pear.

No one who has ever seen a well-groomed quince bush hanging full of beautiful yellow fruit—the golden apples of the Hesperides—will ever be satisfied with the indifferent crop of knotty, wormy, blight-spotted fruit that a majority of back yard quince bushes produce. Do not be misled by the popular notion, born of indifference, that quinces thrive under neglect. Sometimes they thrive in spite of neglect, but never because of it. Even though one has only a half dozen bushes—enough to make many jars of delicious marmalade—it will pay to give these six plants a chance to do their best.

WELL—DRAINED SOIL BEST

Without doubt quinces do best, in general, on a heavy clay loam, one that is heavier and that holds more moisture than would be best for apples, pears or plums, but this does not mean that the soil should be wet. It must be well drained, naturally or artificially, for best results. Quinces will often grow well on light soils, but they are not apt to be as long lived or as productive.

Quinces should be planted from ten to fifteen feet apart each way, depending upon the strength of the soil. The common distance—six to eight feet—is not enough. Plants that are three years old are usually preferred for planting. It is a very simple matter to grow them at home. At any time between November and February take hardwood cuttings from the best quince bush that you can find anywhere. The cuttings may be from eight to fifteen inches long, and should be made only of wood of the last season's growth. Tie the cuttings in bunches, butt ends together, and bury them in moist sand or moss in the cellar. In the spring set them out of doors, twelve inches apart. At the end of two or three years they are ready for planting.

Another simple way of multiplying quinces is by mounding. Cut back an old bush so that it will send up many shoots from the roots. Heap soil around the base of these, six or more inches high. In a year roots will have been thrown out from the lower end of each shoot, then it may be separated from the mother plant and set out. The ends of quince branches may be bent down, covered with soil in the spring, and will be rooted by fall. Thrifty three-year-old quince plants should cost not over twenty cents each at a nursery. They usually begin to bear somewhat the second year after planting, and are in full bearing six to eight years later. If cared for properly quince bushes should bear well at least two score years.

HOW TO TRAIN AND PRUNE

At the time of planting the grower must decide whether it is better to train his quinces into trees or bushes. If he desires trees he will cut off the stem from ten to eighteen inches high, keeping all other shoots removed. Quinces may be headed higher, if necessary, even as high as three feet, but this gives trees that are too high for easy spraying, pruning and picking. Low heading is better, particularly because of convenience in spraying, for in most parts of the country a good crop of really first-class quinces cannot be raised without one or more sprayings.

If bush quinces are desired, several of the strongest of the many shoots that naturally spring from the roots are permitted to remain and to fruit, the weaker shoots being cut out. Bush quinces have one great advantage over tree quinces. If a borer ruins one of the stems, that one may be cut out and there will still be other stems to bear; but if borers girdle the stem of a tree quince the whole plant is ruined. On the other hand, it is my observation that low-tree quinces usually bear better fruit, if well cared for, than bush quinces. The borers must be persecuted anyway, so, in my opinion, the home fruit-grower had better grow quinces in the form of a low-headed tree.

The pruning of quinces should consist mainly of thinning out dead, diseased and crowding branches, doing this each year if necessary, and always in winter or very early spring. Some people find it advantageous to head back the strongest shoots also, especially if the quinces are making a very vigorous growth, say of fourteen to twenty-four inches yearly. A third to a half of the last year's growth is cut off, as is often practised on peaches. This thins the fruit, since quinces are borne on the ends of the growth of the previous season. But annual heading-in tends to make the trees run to wood, and it may, if persisted in, defeat the very end for which it is practised. A safe rule is to head back occasionally, especially the strongest shoots that are growing out of bounds, but to confine the pruning mostly to the taking out of dead, blighted and crowding branches. If, however, the quinces have been neglected and are ragged and full of useless wood, or have been making an unsatisfactory growth, a sharp heading-in, coupled with fertilizing and tillage, may be just the sort of stimulus they need. Saw the larger limbs close; paint all wounds over one-half inch wide, especially if they are in crotches.

FRUIT AND LEAVES OF PORTUGAL QUINCE.

TILLAGE SHOULD NOT BE NEGLECTED

I do not suppose that one quince in a thousand planted in this country has ever been tickled with a cultivator. There are very few commercial quince orchards of any size, and these, almost without exception, are as carefully tilled as an apple orchard should be. They would not be profitable otherwise. But very rare indeed is the quince tree in a home orchard that is not obliged to struggle with grass roots for a drink. Now and then hens make a dust bed beneath them, or hogs uproot the turf in search of hog dainties, but this is a make-shift sort of tillage. I do not know that I have ever seen a dozen quinces mulched. For the most part they fight for an existence with sod, weeds, and perhaps the roots of an over-shadowing fruit tree. Stir the ground around the old quince bushes and see if they do not respond right joyously. The way they will grow and bear under careful tillage is a revelation to anyone who is familiar only with the sod-sick bushes in the back yard. Of course there are cases where quinces should be left in sod, as when the soil is very wet and when they are making a very thrifty growth in spite of the sod. But for the most part it will pay to till them. Till quinces as you would plums or apples, and for the same reasons. Remember, however, that quinces are shallow-rooted, and do not till them deeply. Plow shallow, and do not use a deep-working cultivator.

The fertilizing of quinces does not differ from the fertilizing of the other trees in the fruit garden. Good tillage will help wonderfully to keep the trees well fed. Supplement this with occasional dressings of muriate of potash and South Carolina rock or bone, or other standard fertilizers rich in potash and phosphoric acid. Old, unthrifty quinces, especially those in sod, may be rejuvenated with liberal dressings of barnyard manure. The guide in fertilizing, in every case, should be the condition of the trees and of the crop. Stunted, sickly trees need a tonic. Nitrogen is a plant tonic; it may be fed to best advantage in the form of barnyard manure, if that can be had; failing this, in a leguminous cover crop, and in nitrade of soda, dried blood, or other commercial fertilizers containing this plant food.

Reprinted from GARDEN MAGAZINE, 1905

GRAPES PACKED IN A BASKET AND PLACED
IN A "FLAT."

NIAGARA.

VINE ON THE EXTENSION SYSTEM (AFTER WETMORE).

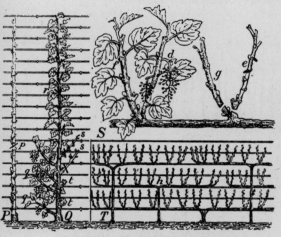

TRAINING AND PRUNING VINES ON OUT-
DOOR WALLS.

References: P, single stem upright vine in autumn after planting;
p, point of winter pruning. Q, single stem upright vine in the
second year, showing: q, bearing shoots pinched; r, point of
shortening the cane at the winter pruning; s, leafless bearing shoots
to be pruned to two buds as shown at the bars; t, bearing shoots or
spurs after pruning. S, d, bearing shoot to be cut away at the winter
pruning (see e); f, successional shoot to be shortened to two buds (see
g). T, h, horizontals extending equally on both sides of the stem.

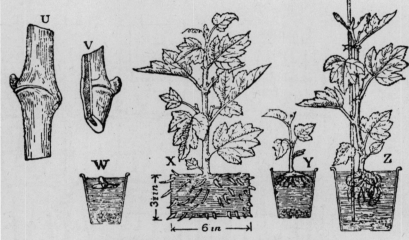

RAISING GRAPE VINES FROM "EYES."

References: U, part of a cane with a bud. V, eye prepared for
insertion. W, eye inserted in a 3-in. pot. X, growth from the eye or
bud in turf. Y, cane from an eye inserted in a pan or bed, then
potted off. Z, cane transferred from a 3-in. to a 5-in. pot.

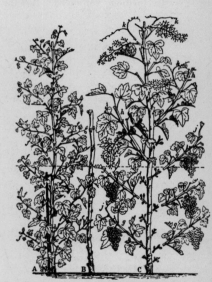

TRAINING A YOUNG VINE FROM A CUT-BACK TO FRUIT IN A POT, AS A
"SUPERNUMERARY" AND AS A PERMANENT VINE.

References: A, vine in first growth from cut-back; a, disbudded shoot; b, laterals and sub-laterals
stopped at one leaf; c, point of removing laterals in autumn or when the foliage is ripening; d, point
of heading cane in autumn; e, extension of growth and laterals from header; f, sub-laterals extended.
B, pruned cane. C, second year's growth; the detached shoots show disbudding up to the trellis;
g, h, and i, laterals if allowed to grow for fruiting; k, side or bearing shoots; i, leader or main stem
—all the detached growths are not wanted on young permanent vines; j, laterals pinched to one
leaf; k, tendrils.

The Training and Pruning of Grapes—By John Craig

ONE of the earliest recollections of the writer on grape-training matters was associated with a whitewashed board fence, covered or nearly covered with a luxuriant vine-growth thickly interspersed with huge clusters of black grapes. These grapes were in the garden of one of the residents of the little town of Niagara-on-the-Lake. The variety was Black Hamburg. It was the wonderment of the community and the delight of the owner, Mr. Pafford, who was then mayor of this somewhat ancient, over-grown Canadian village. Think of growing and ripening Black Hamburg, a hothouse grape, in even the most favorable portion of Ontario! Mr. Pafford selected a warm place and made it warmer by cutting off the north winds with a board wall. He concentrated that still more by whitewashing this tight, high board fence on the south side. His grapes were carefully pruned so that each vine should have just so many fruit-bearing buds, the fruit so thinned that each cane should have just so many bunches, and the berries thinned in the bunch so that all could develop fully. Hamburg was not the only European grape which Mr. Pafford grew. Golden Chasselas and Black Muscats also decorated his boundary line. Nor did he stop with these. Figs in variety were grown in this wonderful garden. Exhibits of these and of the grapes were made at the World's Fair in 1893 and caused people to open their eyes and ask questions. Mr.

Pafford's Hamburg grapes will live in the history of that part of the country.

Of course, it goes without saying that the grapes and figs were taken from the trellis in winter, laid on the ground and well "happed" up with soil, forest leaves and other mulching material.

The amateur can often take advantage of walls upon which to train grapes; he can also use grapes for covering unsightly objects. They are exceedingly tractable and plastic by nature, and accommodate themselves to apparently difficult situations. The training of grapes is one thing. This means the adopting or choosing of a certain method of growing them. Whether the grower shall lead out two arms at right angles, and in opposite directions from the upright stem, and from these direct parallel upright canes; or whether he shall lead out in radiating fashion several canes from the base; or whether he shall lead long canes up over an arbor for the purpose of completely enshrouding it, are matters of training.

The pruning of grape-vines consists in cutting back the right amount of the current season's growth—the amount which experience says a grape of a certain habit of growth and certain amount of individual vigor should respond to properly. The pruning of grapes is a simple matter when their habit of growth is understood. We prune either to check or stimulate vigor, to

encourage fruit production, or, on the other hand, to discourage it.

The fruit of all varieties we deal with in the North and East is borne on the wood produced during the current year's growth, and this wood springs from buds produced by last year's shoots. Each bud of last year—except those which come from suckers or base shoots—is a promise of a fruit-bearing shoot, and each shoot is a promise of from two to five bunches of grapes. These promises are not all fulfilled, but they are realized in proportion as the grape is healthy and the season favorable. It is, then, not difficult on a five- or six-year-old grape-vine to estimate with a fair degree of accuracy how many bunches of fruit we may have if we prune to leave fifteen or twenty fruit-bearing buds. With this general proposition in mind, the pruning of the grape is not difficult.

The purposes of training, on the other hand, are to dispose the grape suitably so that it may ripen its fruit evenly and well. The amateur can afford to train as his fancy dictates. The commercial grower must train to suit his climate, soil, varieties, and the kind of labor which he is obliged to employ. In either case, the object is to produce the approximate number of fruit-bearing shoots the vigor of the variety suggests that it should carry for the best results.

The "fan system" is used most freely where vines are protected in the autumn by laying them down and covering them with soil. The canes are carried up from the ground in a divergent manner, in the form of a fan. The old canes are cut out and removed from time to time as they grow too rigid to allow of easy bending. At the close of the growing season, after the leaves have fallen, the greater number of the canes are cut back to the last bud. A few of the strongest are left, in order to carry the fruit to a greater height upon the trellis.

There is a tendency on the part of the grower who prunes after this fashion to allow too much wood to remain on the plant in the autumn, especially when it is young. The vine should not be allowed to bear the second year after setting out, and only a small crop the third year. I realize that instructions of this kind are much easier given than understood and carried out. A heavy crop of fruit borne by young vines the third year after planting will sometimes ruin the yield for two or three succeeding years, and occasionally destroy the vines. The prospective crop may be more or less accurately estimated by multiplying the number of buds by two; this kind of estimate may be used as a guide in pruning. The fan system aims at starting the canes near the ground, giving the vine practically several main stems.

The "high renewal" system, or modifications of it, is probably more generally adopted throughout commercial grape sections than any other. It aims at starting the head about two feet from the ground, so that the main branches are tied to the lower

Reprinted from GARDEN MAGAZINE, 1905

wire. The vine is usually started the second year with two canes striking out in Y-shaped fashion. In the fall of the same year all side shoots are cut back closely and the main canes cut back to four or five buds each. The third season, three or four of

CHARACTERISTIC GROWTHS OF GOOSEBERRY. SUMMER AND WINTER PRUNING.

References: Erect spreading bush. Right side: summer condition. Left side: winter condition. Back branches not shown: *p*, worn-out primary branch in summer; *q*, point of cutting it out after gathering the fruit; *r*, subsidiary branches in fruit; *s*, side shoots shortened; *t*, terminal shoots topped; *u*, successional base growths to supplant worn-out branches *v*, branches with side growths shortened; *w*, branch with all summer shoots; *x*, branch with all summer shoots in winter, showing waste—a crop of twigs; *y*, point of winter pruning side shoots; *z*, branch (summer pruned) in winter, showing small parts (detached) needing removal; *a*, worn-out branch in winter —to be cut out at *g*; *b*, dead spurs; *c*, subsidiary branch left entire to supplant *a*; *d*, subsidiary branch winter pruned ; *e*, side shoots spurred in ; *f*, spurs.

the strongest shoots springing from the center of the head are allowed to grow. In the autumn these replace the outer arms, and are in turn replaced by them the following season. The aim is, then, to renew the fruiting canes from different parts of the old wood every year. The number of buds to be left will depend upon the strength of the variety and the individual plant. Concord, Niagara and Worden will carry with safety more wood than Moore's Early or Delaware, and this is true without reference to the method employed. As the

canes grow they are tied to the wires of the trellis, distributing the foliage as much as possible. It is usually found necessary to go over the vineyard two, three and occasionally four times during the summer.

The "horizontal two-arm system" is especially adapted to sections of the country where it is advisable to give the vines winter protection. Two strong canes are trained in opposite directions. The laterals springing from these are trained perpendicularly. In the autumn the laterals are cut back to short one-eye spurs. When the spurs become weak they are renewed, as is an entire arm occasionally. This system calls for a four-wired trellis, in order to properly tie the strong upright growths. Well adapted to wall or high garden trellis, the three methods of training described thus far are all on the upright plan; in those which follow the vines hang down.

The "four-cane Kniffin" is essentially a commercial system and exclusively adopted in field culture in certain parts of New York State. In this system the trellis consists of two wires. The main cane is carried to the top wire and from it an arm is trained each way on the two wires. The side canes are tied to the wires and the lower ends allowed to hang free. Several modifications of this system are in use.

We now come to over-head or arbor systems. In one of these systems (and there are many which may be modified to suit the needs of the amateur) the vines are carried up seven-foot posts and allowed to rest on cross wires, forming in this way a kind of arbor. One plan is to nail a cross-piece to each post at right angles to the pole. This

FRUITING POT VINE.

extends three feet on each side. Three wires are stretched on these, one at each end, the other in the middle to the posts. The trellis is thus a horizontal one and six feet above the ground. An unbranched trunk is carried up to the middle wire and the canes spread either side from this point. A T-shaped head is considered the ideal form. Another over-head system is known as the "cross-wire Kniffin." In this a small post six or seven feet high is set for each vine. The tops of the posts are connected by cross wires. The vines are trained up the posts, and on reaching the top four arms are trained outward, one on each wire. In the autumn the arms are cut back to six or eight buds each. The amateur

may start two canes from the ground, spreading as they rise, and may depend upon laterals to cover his arbor.

"Post training" is only satisfactory where there is plenty of heat to ripen the grapes, and gives fullest satisfaction with weak-growing varieties. Four- or five-foot stakes may be used. Two or three canes are trained up each year from the ground. It is strictly a renewal plan. Much summer pruning and pinching are required to regulate growth. But on the other hand, the vines may be tucked in four by four feet apart. Delaware, Golden Drop, and Campbell's Early can be grown on posts with some satisfaction.

Pruning of the annual kind may be done after the leaves are killed by frost or the wood is thoroughly ripened. When the vines are taken off the trellis, as in 30-degree-below-zero sections, the pruning is done just before laying the canes down in autumn. Where the vines do not need winter protection, the pruning may be done any convenient time during late fall or winter. It should not be deferred till the sap flows in spring, as vines pruned at this time are often weakened by excessive bleeding.

It is always desirable to remove the shoots that spring from or near the base of the vine, except when they are required for a special end. These shoots are quickly broken out, or nipped off when soft and succulent. A certain amount of shortening back is also desirable. This should not be done too early in the season. If pinched early in the growing season, a great mass of laterals is produced and the amount of work very much augmented.

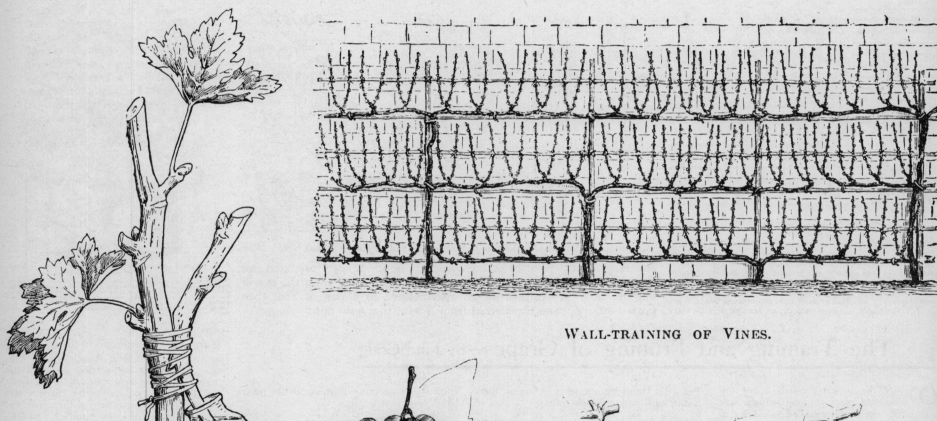

WALL-TRAINING OF VINES.

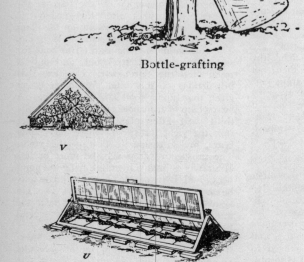

Bottle-grafting

GROUND VINERIES.

References : U, vinery on one height of bricks. V, larger vinery on two heights of bricks: *i*, slates or tiles ; *j*, bricks on which the vine rods can rest.

Royal Muscadine Grapes

Black Monukka Grapes

Gros Coleman Grapes

currants and gooseberries

by G. C. Klingbeil
Extension Horticulturist*

*With the assistance of E.K. Wade, Extension Plant Pathologist and J.L. Libby, Extension Entomologist.

Currants, prized for making jellies, jams, pies and juice, and gooseberries, for good jam and other culinary purposes, are well suited to home fruit gardens. Sufficiently hardy to be grown in all parts of Wisconsin, both crops prefer good soil, moisture and cool climate. They do well in partially shaded areas where most other bush fruits do not thrive.

Climbing currant.

Cool Sites Preferred

Currants and gooseberries prefer a cool, moist location. Areas that are shaded or partially shaded are satisfactory. They should have good air circulation around them. These fruits can be grown in areas not well adapted to other fruits, such as grapes and raspberries.

A moist but well-drained soil high in organic matter is best. A very liberal application of well-rotted stable manure or shredded peat moss worked into the soil before planting is desirable. All perennial weeds should be eliminated before planting.

Spring Planting Best

Plants purchased from nurseries are usually one year old, the most desirable age. Older plants are slower to start and frequently are plants that were unsalable the previous season. Plants may be set in either fall or spring, but spring planting is preferred in this area.

Plant currants and gooseberries about three feet apart in a permanent location. With average care, they should be productive for a minimum of ten years. Before planting, remove broken and excessively long roots. Set the plants in a hole deep enough so that the lowest branches will be below the surface of the soil. Pack soil firmly around the roots.

Currants and gooseberries are self-fruited, so no special provision for cross-pollination needs to be provided.

Starting Plants

It is probably best to purchase plants from a reliable nurseryman. However, these plants are propagated quite readily from cuttings or by layering if you wish to start your own plants.

Currants are generally propagated from hardwood cuttings. Select cuttings 6 to 10 inches long from matured last season's growth. Collect them in the winter or very early spring and store in moist peat moss, sawdust or sand in a location cold enough to prevent growth. Do not store in a food freezer.

Early in the spring, plant cuttings six to eight inches apart in a row with the top end two to three inches above the soil. Press soil firmly around each cutting. Rooted cuttings are usually ready to transplant in one or two years.

Gooseberries may be propagated by cuttings, but layering is usually more successful. Select several canes or branches and, while still attached to the plant, bend the branches down and cover with 2 - 3 inches of soil. Base and tips of branches should be exposed. A weight on the branches or a forked stick driven into the ground over the branches will hold them securely.

Plants layered in spring are usually rooted by fall and those layered in fall usually by spring. When well rooted, cut the young plants from the parent and move to the new location.

Avoid Weed Competition

It is essential to keep weeds controlled around the plants. Both currants and gooseberries are shallow rooted and are poor competitors with quack grass and bluegrass. Shallow cultivations are necessary after the plants are established.

Weeds can be reduced and the condition of the soil improved by the use of a good mulch. Lawn rakings, well-rotted manure, crushed corncobs, sawdust, peat moss and other materials make a suitable mulch. The mulch should be a minimum of four inches deep and should be replenished periodically to maintain the proper depth.

Fertilize Annually

Any form of animal or poultry manure can be used to provide fertility for the plant. Apply annually early in the spring. If such fertilizers are not readily available, use a complete fertilizer of a 1-1-1 ratio. If a 10-10-10 analysis is used, about one-half pound (1 cupful) per plant is usually sufficient. If a mulch of sawdust or corn cobs is used, twice that amount may be necessary the year mulch is applied. Spread fertilizer evenly around the plant very early each spring.

Pruning for Production

The fruiting habits of red and white currants and gooseberries are similar, so pruning practices are the same. Fruit is borne on spurs from wood two or more years old. Prune during the dormant period, usually early in spring before growth starts.

After the first season's growth, select up to six well-distributed, sturdy shoots. Cut out those remaining at ground level. After the second season's growth, save the two-year-old canes. Select four to six one-year-old canes and remove all others. After the third season, save the two- and three-year-old canes. Select up to six one-year-old canes and remove all others. After the plants are four years old, remove all four-year-old canes. Continue the selection of six one-year-old canes.

A mature bush is maintained by the removal of all four-year-old wood and any one-year-old canes in excess of the six selected.

To properly prune an old and neglected plant, cut out older canes and thin out newer-bearing canes to encourage new cane development. A properly pruned producing plant should have 8 to 12 bearing canes and four to six one-year-old shoots.

It may be necessary to provide a means of support for fruit-laden canes on strong growing plants.

FRUITING BRANCH OF RIBES GROSSULARIA.   One of the English-American gooseberries.

Currant Varieties

Red Lake (red) - One of the best. Vigorous, hardy and productive. Fruit is large and of good quality. Considered a late-ripening variety. (Originated by the University of Minnesota.)

Wilder (red) - A vigorous, moderately hardy and productive variety. Fruit is large, mild and of good quality. Ripens slightly earlier than Red Lake. Fruit does not readily drop or shatter.

Cascade (red) - An excellent early-ripening variety. Fruit is generally larger and ripens at least a week earlier than Red Lake. One of the mildest-flavored varieties and considered by many to be one of the finest in quality.

White Grape (amber) - The most common white currant variety. Berries are large, light amber in color and have a delightful mild flavor.

There are many other varieties of currants. These listed are the most commonly grown and most readily obtainable from nurseries. Since only a limited number of nurseries propagate currants, plants of all varieties may not be grown by all nurseries.

Gooseberry Varieties

Downing (green) - Most commonly grown variety. Vigorous, hardy and productive. Fruit is somewhat small, pale green in color, but of good quality.

Poorman (red) - Moderately productive, hardy and vigorous. Does quite well on heavy soils. Fruit is medium in size and of good quality. Plants are less thorny than most varieties.

Chautauqua (green) - A European type. Bush is moderately vigorous and reasonably hardy. Fruit is large and light green in color. The European types are not commonly grown, so it may be difficult to obtain plants readily.

Pixwell (red) - Hardy productive variety. Canes have limited thorns. Fruit is medium in size, pink when ripe and often borne in clusters.

Common Pests

The most common insect pests found damaging currants and gooseberries a r e imported currant worm, currant aphid and currant borer. Less common insect pests are currant fruit fly, San Jose scale and red spiders.

Insects

Imported Currant Worm. The mature worm is about three-fourths of an inch long, green in color, y e l l o w i s h at both ends, with a black head. The young worms are covered with black spots. The insect usually appears in early spring when currant leaves are nearly full grown. The worms are chewing insects with enormous appetites and can, if uncontrolled, strip the foliage in a few days. Feeds on white and red currant and gooseberry foliage.

Currant Aphid. Often referred to as a p l a n t l o u s e, the aphid is green in color. They appear early in spring just as t h e foliage begins to grow. They feed on the under side of the foliage, sucking juice from the leaf cells which causes t h e leaves to be curled and puckered. The upper surface between the veins appears raised or blistered and is usually reddish o r reddish-brown in color. These pests prefer red currants to white currants and will attack gooseberries.

Currant Borer. The adult is a wasp-like, clear-winged moth about one-half inch long with a b l a c k body with several yellow bands. They usually are found in e a r l y June in southern Wisconsin, laying eggs on currants. The larvae or worm that hatches bores into the larger branches where it eats out the pith. The worm is creamy white in color and about one-half inch long at m a t u r i t y in fall. They overwinter i n the branch as larvae, pupate in the spring, and emerge as an adult moth in late May. They prefer currants, but often are found in gooseberries.

Common Diseases

The more common diseases found on currants and gooseberries are: anthracnose, leaf spot, and powdery m i l d e w. Other diseases of less importance are cane blight or wilt, Botrytis dieback and gray mold berry rot, White pine blister rust, cluster cup rust, and virus infections. The most common virus disease is currant mosaic.

Anthracnose. This is a fungus infection appearing first as numerous dark brown to black dots scattered at random over one or both surfaces of the leaf. The infection may a p p e a r at any time during the growing season. The spots enlarge, become more angular in outline and sometimes have a purplish margin. Affected leaves s o o n turn yellow, followed by leaf drop. This weakens the plant, reducing vigor and productivity, resulting in smaller fruit of lower quality.

Leaf Spot. Quite commonly called "Septoria leaf spot," the name of the parasitic s t a g e of the fungus causing the infection. This leaf spot can be told from that caused by anthracnose by noting these differences: The spots normally appear on the foliage in June. At this time they resemble anthracnose somewhat. But, they soon enlarge and the central area becomes light in color with a brown border. Sooner or later, tiny black specks will be seen scattered over the surface of each spot. These are bodies containing the spores of the organism. This does not occur on anthracnose leaf spots. The diseased leaves, especially on currants, turn yellow and drop.

Powdery Mildew. Two t y p e s of p o w d e r y mildew attack R i b e s plants -- "American" and "European." We are concerned only with the American type. Mildew i s most important as a disease on gooseberry but d o e s occur in a mild form on currant. White, powdery patches of the fungus a p p e a r first on the lower parts of the bush, attacking the leaves, shoots, and berries. As the infection progresses, the e n t i r e surface of the leaves, etc., becomes covered w i t h the growth. Older infections form a thin, felt-like coating t a n to reddish-brown in color. Black dots called perithecia, which contain spores of the fungus, appear in the "mycelial mats" covering the affected areas. Heavy mildew deposits will cause stunting and premature drying of the foliage, affecting fruit production and weakening the plants.

Diseases of Minor Importance

Caneblight or wilt. A fungus organism that causes a sudden wilting and dying of scattered canes or whole bushes, most evident just before the fruit ripens.

Botrytis. The infection produces a dark colored dieback of the tips of the branches a n d a gray mold rot of the berries. May occur during wet, humid weather where plantings are in low areas with poor air circulation.

White pine blister rust. U r e d i a l s t a g e appears in the spring as small yellow spots on the underside of the leaf. By late summer, yellow to brown threadlike growths develop on or near these infection spots on the leaf. They contain "t e l i o s p o r e s" which germinate a n d produce "sporidia" that i n f e c t the white pine in the fall. European black currants and wild gooseberries are t h e main hosts of b l i s t e r rust when white pines are growing in the vicinity.

Cluster cup rust. May p r o d u c e striking symptoms on species of wild gooseberries or in neglected h o m e garden plantings, b u t causes slight damage. The rust affects leaves, stems and fruit but is commonly found on the leaves and leaf petioles. The leaf is thickened where the cluster cup later appears. The spots have a reddish appearance. The sedge plant is the alternate host of this rust.

Currant mosaic. A p p e a r s as a chlorotic pattern (light a n d dark areas) on the leaves. The lighter-green areas gradually turn white.

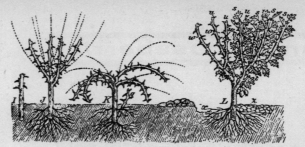

TRAINING ERECT AND PENDULOUS GOOSEBERRY BUSHES.

References: I, a cutting prepared and inserted in the ground; J, an erect-growing bush in the autumn of the first year from the cutting, showing bars for pruning to outside buds; the dotted lines represent growths of the year following. K, a pendulous bush, one year from the cutting: shortening to upper buds (see bars); the dotted lines indicate the growths in the second year; q, sucker properly detached from the socket. L, erect bush in the second year: s, branches in growth; t, side shoot pinched, to be cut closely back in winter; u, branches in autumn; w, point of pruning branches to outside buds; x, soil removed from the roots; y, rich compost or manure placed in the opening; z, fresh soil placed on winter dressing.

State Regulations

All s p e c i e s of currant and gooseberry bushes are alternate host plants of the disease called white pine blister rust. According to the Wisconsin State Department of Agriculture Regulations, Administrative Code 25, W h i t e Pine Blister Rust control areas have been designated by the Wisconsin State Department of Agriculture.

Excerpts from this code say that these plants may not be grown within 1,500 feet o f any white pine nursery or within 900 feet o f a designated W h i t e Pine Blister Rust control area. In addition, movement of currant or gooseberry plants both interstate and intrastate requires a permit w h i c h can be obtained from the State Department of Agriculture.

For more detailed information about permits and regulations, write: P l a n t Industry Division, Wisconsin State Department o f Agriculture, Hill Farm State Office Building, Madison, Wisconsin.

Houghton's Seedling.

Fruiting Shoot of Spineless Gooseberry

CAPE GOOSEBERRY (PHYSALIS PERUVIANA EDULIS) IN FLOWER AND FRUIT.

References: 1, fruit half natural size in section; 2, inflated calyx

STRAWBERRY BARRELS

John A. Wott & R. A. Hayden

Want to grow strawberries? Cramped for space? Then try a strawberry barrel. A strawberry barrel clothed in green leaves and draped with fringes of red berries is ornamental as well as useful.

Use a wooden barrel or any solid material which has been thoroughly washed to remove all materials injurious to strawberry plants. The size may range from a nail keg to 55-gallon whiskey barrels (Figure 2). Do not use vinegar, dill pickles, brine or paint barrels, since these may contain toxic materials.

HORTICULTURE DEPARTMENT COOPERATIVE EXTENSION SERVICE PURDUE UNIVERSITY LAFAYETTE, INDIANA 47907

Barrel preparation

Bore several holes (1-1½ inches in diameter) in the bottom of the barrel for drainage. For large barrels, six holes spaced midway from the center to the outside of the barrel are sufficient. Ideally the barrel should also be placed on a wooden platform with casters so that it may be turned and all plants can receive sunlight. A base of bricks or 2 x 4's would be an acceptable alternative base. In either case, there must be holes in the platform, so the drainage holes in the barrel are not closed.

Then, beginning at the top just under the hoops, chalk spots around the sides of the barrel, for two-inch holes from which the plants will grow. These holes should be evenly spaced, preferably 6-8 inches apart. Ideally, the rows should be six inches apart. The second row should then be placed six inches below the first row with the holes staggered between those in the first. The third row will have its holes directly under the holes of the first row and six inches below the second row, etc. However, barrel size and hoop arrangement may vary. A spacing of 8 x 8" or 10 x 6" would be ideal.

The largest, sturdiest barrel may have 2-3 rim hoops at the top and bottom, along with one hoop below and one above the center or one at the center. Such a barrel will take four rows of holes or 30 to 40 holes for plants. In addition, there will be room on the top for eight to ten more plants. Thus for a 55-gallon barrel, 50 total plants would be needed.

An expansion bit and brace will be needed to bore these wide 2-inch holes.

Filling the barrel

First, place a layer of pebbles or pieces of broken flower pots over the holes in the bottom of the barrel. This will prevent too rapid drainage and loss of soil from the drainage holes. If your barrel is one of the largest, place a four-inch flower pot with the bottom knocked out in the center of the barrel over the drainage layer. A smaller barrel or keg will take a smaller pot.

A drainage core must be constructed from either a 4-inch tile or a rolled newspaper or hardware cloth. Roll a newspaper into a 3-4" wide tube, long enough to fit into the pot and to extend up to the top rim of the barrel. You will need an assistant to hold this tube in the center of the barrel while you pour porous drainage material such as coarse sand, gravel, perlite or bits of broken flower pots into it. Fill the tube up to the level of the bottom row of holes. Then fill in around this drainage core with the soil mixture up to the first row of holes. Water in each layer of soil before placing plants.

ART. XXII.   *A Plan for a Strawberry Wall.*
By ROBERT BYERS, Esq.

Sir,

As it has been proved, beyond a doubt, that the finest strawberries have been produced from one year old plants, and as their culture deserves our greatest attention, the fruit being, perhaps, one of the most wholesome in the world, the following plan for their culture may be valuable to your readers as possessing more advantages than the ordinary methods.

Suppose a bed 20 ft. long by 3 ft. 6 in. wide, place round this bed, stones or bricks about 6 in. high, and as nearly level as you can with convenience, fill the within space, and about an inch above it, with compost in which there is a fourth gravel or small stones.   Around the whole bed place your plants 6 in. apart (it will require about 94 plants for the first tier). Again, place another course of stones of the same size, beveling inwards on all sides at angle of 45° (*fig.* 94.); this fill with

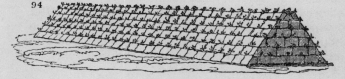

94

the same compost, and plant as for the first row of plants. Proceed thus, stratum super stratum, until you have raised your bed about 3 ft. high, which will give you six rows of plants around your bed and one row at the top.   The advantages of this bed are as follows : — A much larger quantity of plants is grown on a given quantity of ground.   You obtain a succession crop, by placing your bed north and south.   You can water them with facility from the top, in which a trench should be left for that purpose.   The fruit can be gathered with more ease and convenience, and the last and most important advantage which I shall name, is, that your fruit is free from sand and earth; should heavy rains occur during the period of its ripening.

I am, Sir, &c.

Mount Pleasant, near Swansea,   R. W. BYERS.
July, 1829.

If tile are used, they can be easily chipped with a wrench to the correct length. Do not fill the field tile with drainage material.

Soil mixture

Strawberries will grow in soil of almost any texture, providing it does not stay wet for long periods, yet has enough organic matter to hold water during dry spells. A fairly sandy mixture assures good drainage. Sand and peat moss, half and half, added to loamy soil in the same quantity as the sand-peat mixture is ideal. This makes a mixture of ¼ sand, ¼ peat and ½ soil. Fertilizer consisting of ¼ pint complete commercial fertilizer or two quarts of dried manure or leaf mold plus a half pint of bone meal should be added to each bushel of the sand-soil-peat mixture.

Varieties

Everbearing varieties will provide berries as well as color all season. Ozark Beauty is a recommended everbearing variety.

Planting

Push a plant through each hole in the bottom row, letting the top of the plant hang outside with its crown even with the surface of the barrel . Spread the roots out well and cover with soil. Pack the soil rather firmly to prevent excessive settling when watered.

Pour more drainage mixture into the newspaper core up to the next row of holes. Then add soil around it and water, being careful not to wet your newspaper above its filling .

Continue in this manner by row until the soil is near the top of pot . Set another inverted bottomless flower pot over the top of the newspaper tube with the edge of the pot an inch or two higher than the rim of the barrel. Fill this center pot with the drainage material, burying the top of the newspaper tube. The newspaper will soon rot away .

Set additional plants about eight inches apart in the leveled soil surrounding the pot on the top of the barrel. Set them with their crowns level with the soil surface .

Care

The plants can be watered by running a hose into the drainage tube and filling with water. Do this often enough to provide ample moisture, but do not water-log the soil. The top row can be irrigated by applying water onto the soil surface.

During the growing season, the plants can be fertilized every month with a dilute solution of a complete fertilizer. Discontinue fertilizer applications about September 1.

Pinch off any flowers for the first month. This will enable the plants to more rapidly establish themselves. Well-established plants will fruit satisfactorily for two or three years in succession. After midsummer, the plants will form runners, which should be clipped off, causing the original plants to form multiple crowns and mat in the holes.

Winter protection

Protect the plants from hard freezing and also alternate freezing and thawing by moving the barrel into a building or covering with several inches of straw.

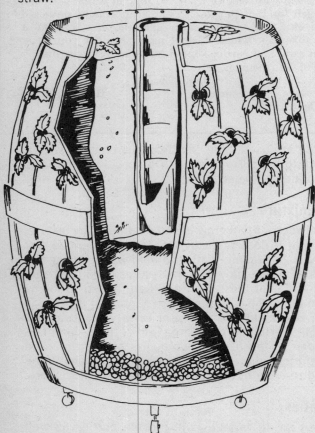

Completed strawberry barrel.

Fruit Varieties for North Dakota

Robert G. Askew
Extension Horticulturist

Neal Holland
Associate Horticulturist
Agricultural Experiment Station

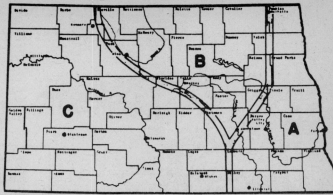

Hardiness Zone Map of North Dakota

MANY VARIETIES OF FRUITS are available from nurseries, but not all are adapted to North Dakota conditions. You should select varieties that will mature their crops in the somewhat shorter season in this area. The varieties you choose must be hardy enough to withstand our winters.

New varieties are introduced frequently, and they need to be grown for a number of years before any definite recommendations can be made about them. Many older varieties are still among the best, while a few are not as good as more recent introductions.

POLLINATION

Many tree fruit varieties cannot set fruit with their own pollen, so you must select and plant two different varieties to insure proper pollination (that is, two varieties of apples or plums, etc.)

HARDINESS

For planting in North Dakota, always select fruit tree varieties that are known to be hardy and that will produce good quality fruit.

Hardiness is especially important in new fruit tree plantings. After some experience, you may wish to try some semi-hardy varieties, but beginners should start with a few trees that are not only hardy but practical. The Dolgo crab-apple, Haralson apple, and Opata sandcherry are examples.

Soil conditions, available moisture, and both winter and summer temperatures strongly influence growth of woody plants in North Dakota.

Under natural conditions, soil and moisture seem to influence the growth of woody plants more than do temperature differences within the limits of the state. The map is based largely upon observed growth response of woody plants. Zone A is considered as the most favorable and Zone C the least favorable. Many variations occur within each zone and a poor site in Zone A, for example, may be less favorable for a given tree than a good site in Zone C. Consider these zones as general selection and planting guides, not as hard and fast rules.

SANDCHERRY - PLUM HYBRIDS

VARIETY	HARDINESS ZONE			DESCRIPTION
	A	B	C	
Hiawatha*	T	T	T	Large size. Purple skin, dark red flesh. Fairly sweet, juicy, firm. Very good quality. Mid-August.
Sacagawea*	T	T	T	Medium to large size. Purple skin, dark red flesh. Fairly sweet, juicy. Mid-August.
Deep Purple	T	T	T	Large size. Dark purple skin, dark purple flesh. Nearly freestone. Sweet, juicy, firm. Good quality. Late August.
Opata	R	R	R	Small to medium size. Reddish-purple skin, green flesh. Sweet, juicy. Good quality. Late August.
Dura	R	R	R	Medium size. Purple skin, red flesh. Sweet, juicy. Fruit keeps in good condition on tree. Late August.
Sapalta	R	T	T	Medium size. Purple skin, red flesh. Sweet, juicy. Excellent quality. Late August.
Compass	R	R	R	Small size. Dark red skin, yellowish flesh. Tart, juicy. Use for canning. Good pollinizer. Early September.

Be sure to plant at least two varieties to insure pollination. Some varieties are noted as good pollinizer varieties.

CHERRY.

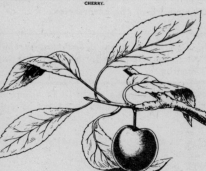

Prunus communis

May Bigarreau.   Knight's Early Black.

Early Purple Guigne.   Black Tartarian.   Black Eagle.

THE DOWNER CHERRY.

Sour or pie cherries.

CHERRIES

	A	B	C	
North Star (Sour)	T	T	T	Medium size. Dark red skin, yellowish flesh. Juicy. Good quality. Early July.
Meteor (Sour)	T	T	T	Bright red skin, bright yellow flesh. Juicy. Good quality. Mid-July.
Nanking Cherry Orient Drilea	R	R	R	1/2-inch diameter. Bright red skin, yellow flesh. Sweet, juicy with pleasant flavor. Excellent for fresh use or jelly. Early July.
Korean Cherry	R	T	T	Up to 3/4-inch diameter. Red skin, yellowish flesh. Sweet, juicy. Excellent for fresh use or jelly. Late August to early September.

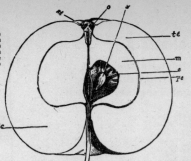

Slice lengthwise through an Apple, showing the globular fleshy receptacle (pome) in which the carpels are embedded. At *c* and at *s* are the withered remnants of the calyx and of the stamens respectively; *tc* shows the fleshy part of the receptacle; *p* is the rind of the receptacle; *m*, the fleshy portion; *e*, the core or true seed-vessel; *s*, the seed.

The Jonathan.

APPLE VARIETIES

Maturity dates given vary from year to year due to season and location. Home storage conditions affect keeping quality of the fruit. R - Recommended for general planting; T -- Recommended for trial; G - Graft on branches of hardy tree (Dolgo Crab).

VARIETY	HARDINESS ZONE			REACTION TO FIRE BLIGHT	DESCRIPTION
	A	B	C		
Mantet	R	R	R	Susceptible	Yellow, striped and blushed with red. Medium size. Excellent quality. Hardy and productive. Fresh and sauce. Mature August 20. 1 week storage.
Oriole	R	T	T	Moderately Susceptible	Greenish yellow with red. Vigorous, hardy. Fresh and cooking. Mature August 25. 2 week storage.
Red Duchess	R	R	R	Moderately Resistant	Red. Medium size. Reliable, hardy. Pie, sauce, jelly. Mature August 25. 2 week storage.
Beacon.	T	T	T	Susceptible	Red. Medium size. Fair quality. Fresh and cooking. Mature September 1. 2 weeks storage.
Garrison*	T	T	T	Moderately Resistant	Red. Medium size. Very good quality. Fresh and cooking. Mature September 10. 4 weeks storage.
Mandan*	T	T	T	Moderately Resistant	Medium red. Medium size, productive, hardy. Fresh and cooking. Mature September 10. 2 month storage.
Dakota*	T	T	T	Moderately Resistant	Deep red over yellow. Medium size, productive, hardy. Fresh and cooking. Mature September 15. 6 weeks storage.
Wealthy	RT	GT	G	Susceptible	Yellowish, striped and blushed with red. Medium size. Good quality. Fresh and cooking. Mature September 15. 4 weeks storage.
Killand*	T	T	T	Moderately Resistant	Red color. Medium size. Good storage apple of good quality. Fresh and cooking. Mature September 20. Stores 3-4 months.
Lakeland	T	T	T	Susceptible	Medium size; red color. Very good quality. Cooking and dessert. Mature September 20. 6 weeks storage.
Minjon	G	G	G	Moderately Susceptible	Red. Small to medium size. Questionable hardiness. Fresh and cooking. Mature September 20. 6 weeks storage.
Peace Garden*	T	T	T	Moderately Susceptible	Red. Medium size. Good storage apple of good quality. Fresh and cooking. Mature September 25. Stores 4-6 months.
Thorberg*	T	T	T	Moderately Resistant	Red. Medium to large size. Very good quality. Fresh and cooking. Mature September 20. Storage 2 months.
Haralson	R	R	R	Moderately Resistant	Red. Medium size. Fair to good quality. Stores well. Proven variety. Matures October 1. Stores 4-6 months.
Redwell	R	T	T	Moderately Susceptible	Bright red. Late maturing. Slow to come into bearing. Fresh and cooking. Mature October 1. Stores 3 months.
Fireside	G	G	G	Moderately Susceptible	Red. Large size. Excellent quality. Late maturing. Questionable for general planting. Matures October 10. Stores 3 months.
Connell Red	G	G	G	Moderately Susceptible	Red sport of Fireside. Should have some characteristics.
Prairie Spy	G	G	G	Susceptible	Yellow with bright red blush. Medium to large. Good storage apple. Excellent quality. Late maturing, questionable for general planting. Mature October 10. Stores 3 months.

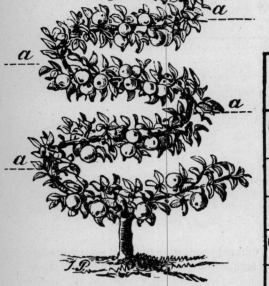

Zig-zag Cordon for a Wall.

Siberian Crab (*Pyrus baccata*).

* Recent introductions from the Great Plains Field Station, Mandan, North Dakota. Some of these North Dakota developed fruits may prove to be our most useful varieties. They were grown and observed at Mandan for many years, but have been slow in reaching nursery trade.

Peace Garden and Garrison are available at a number of nurseries. Mandan and Dakota are being propagated with limited availability. Killand and Thorberg are not generally available in nursery trade.

CRABAPPLE VARIETIES

VARIETY	HARDINESS ZONE			REACTION TO FIRE BLIGHT	DESCRIPTION
	A	B	C		
Dolgo	R	R	R	Resistant	Bright red. Small size. Jelly crab. Pickling. Hardy tree for grafting tender varieties (top-working). Mature September 1.
Centennial	R	T	T	Moderately Resistant	Medium to bright red. Medium to large size. Productive. Fresh, canning, sauce and jelly. Mature September 15.
Chestnut	R	R	R	Moderately Susceptible	Greenish-yellow with a few red strips. Large size. Very good quality. Fresh and cooking. Matures September 20. Stores 1 month.
Red River	R	R	R	Moderately Resistant	Red. Large-sized crab. Good quality. Stores well. Hardy. Fresh and cooking. Matures October 1. Stores 2 months.

Crab Apple (*Pyrus Malus*).

HARDY PLUM VARIETIES

VARIETY	HARDINESS ZONE A	B	C	DESCRIPTION
Tecumseh	R	R	R	Medium size. Red skin, yellow flesh. Juicy, sweet. Good quality. Fresh and cooking. Mid-August.
Underwood	R	R	R	Large size. Medium dark red. Juicy, sweet. Very good quality. Fresh and cooking. Mid-late August.
Redcoat	R	R	R	Medium size. Dark red, yellow flesh. Freestone. Quality fair for fresh use, good for cooking. Productive. Late August.
LaCrescent	T	T	T	Medium size. Yellow skin, yellow flesh. Juicy, tender. Delicious flavor. Excellent quality. Late August.
Gracious*	T	T	T	Large size. Red skin, yellow flesh. Freestone. Sweet, juicy. Very good quality. Late August.
Chinook*	T	T	T	Medium size. Red skin, yellow flesh. Sweet, juicy. Very good quality. Use as pollinizer. Late August.
Waneta	R	R	R	Very large size. Yellow overlain with dark red. Yellow flesh. Sweet, juicy. Good quality. Early September.
South Dakota	R	R	R	Medium size. Red skin, yellow flesh. Very sweet, juicy. Quality good for fresh use and jelly (not jams). Pollinizer. Early September.
Pipestone	T	T	T	Large size. Red skin, yellow flesh. Sweet, juicy. Very good quality. Early September.
Superior	T	T	T	Large size. Heart-shaped. Red skin, yellow flesh. Sweet, juicy, firm. Excellent quality. Less hardy. Early September.
Fiebing	T	T	T	Large size. Dark red skin, yellow flesh. Sweet, juicy. Very good quality. Early September.
Kaga	T	T	T	Medium size. Flattened, round shape. Dark red skin, yellow flesh. Sweet with distinctive flavor. Mid-September.
Toka	T	T	T	Very similar to Kaga. Both are good quality. Use both as pollinizers. Mid-September.

Be sure to plant at least two varieties to insure pollination. Some varieties are noted as good pollinizer varieties.

FRUITING BRANCH OF GREEN GAGE PLUM.

COOPERATIVE EXTENSION SERVICE
NORTH DAKOTA STATE UNIVERSITY
FARGO, NORTH DAKOTA 58102

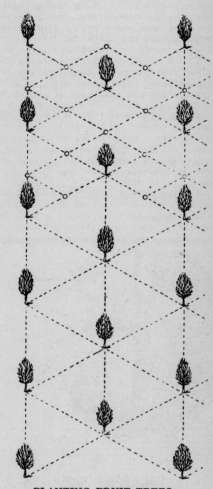
PLANTING FRUIT TREES.
Equilateral triangle planting; the circles show positions for temporary trees.

Roman Apricot.

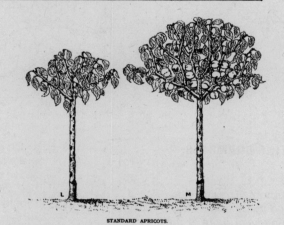
STANDARD APRICOTS.

HARDY APRICOTS

	T	T	T	
Scout	T	T	T	Large size. Golden yellow, blushed red. Flesh is deep yellow, not juicy. Fair quality. Late July.
Moongold	T	T	T	Large size. Yellow skin and flesh. Sweet sprightly flavor. Freestone. Good quality. Late July.
Sungold	T	T	T	Large size. Golden orange skin. Sweet mild flavor. Freestone. Good quality. Late July.
Mantoy*	T	T	T	Large size. Golden yellow skin. Sweet, juicy. Freestone. Good quality. Early August.

Plant two varieties to insure pollination. Apricots bloom early and frequently are frozen by spring frosts. This usually limits fruiting to about three years out of five. Plant only in a well protected and well-drained site.

PEARS

Bantam	T	T	T	Small fruited. Good quality. Does not have any grit cells. Some resistance to fireblight. Early September.
Golden Spice (Minn. #4)	T	T	T	Small to medium size. Yellow with red blush. Fair quality. Some resistance to fireblight. Mid-September.
Parker	T	T	T	Large size for hardy pears. Medium yellow. Borderline hardiness. Susceptible to fireblight. Mid-September.
Tait Dropmore	R	R	R	Medium size. Fair quality. One of the hardiest pears. Fresh, cooking. Mid-September.
Pioneer	T	T	T	Medium to large. Fair quality. Fresh, cooking. Late September.

Pears lack winter hardiness and should be tried only in well protected sites. Due to their susceptibility to fireblight, they should be planted apart from apples and crabapples.

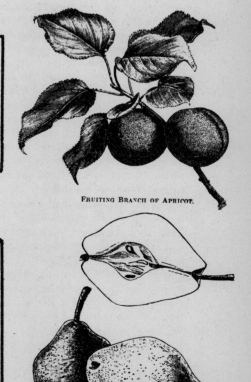
FRUITING BRANCH OF APRICOT.

Kieffer Pear (after Bailey).

For fruit tree culture, see Circular 327 TREE FRUIT CULTURE FOR NORTH DAKOTA

Common Fruit Insects

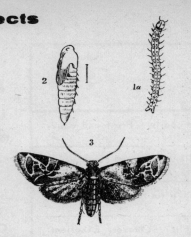

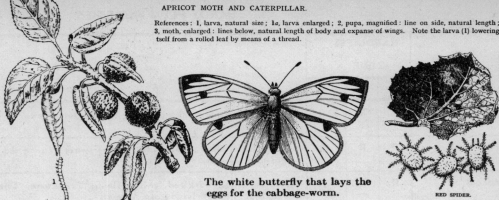

APRICOT MOTH AND CATERPILLAR.

References : 1, larva, natural size ; 1a, larva enlarged ; 2, pupa, magnified : line on side, natural length ; 3, moth, enlarged : lines below, natural length of body and expanse of wings. Note the larva (1) lowering tself from a rolled leaf by means of a thread.

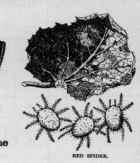

CODLIN MOTH (CARPOCAPSA POMONELLA).

References—*Top* : Moth enlarged ; line, natural expanse of wings. *Centre* : grub enlarged on Apple twig. *Bottom* : larva in Apple, showing entrance by the eye, channel to and destruction of pips, channel to rind, serving as outlet for dirt.

The white butterfly that lays the eggs for the cabbage-worm.

RED SPIDER.

Codling moths (1) destroy apples in poorly cared for individual trees or orchards. Larvae developing in fruit cause "wormy apples." "Sting" occurs when first instar larvae are prevented from entering the fruit. Young worms enter through the calyx cup at the blossom end in early June. A second generation attacks in late July or early August, entering the side of the fruit. Larvae overwinter in thick silken cocoons under loose trunk bark, in protected sites around the tree base or ground nearby.

Apple maggots (2) attack home orchards and threaten commercial orchards. Severe fruit injury occurs near neglected or poorly sprayed trees. Called "railroad worms," they leave brown winding bacterial trails just under the skin of some varieties. For further details see Circular 619.

Red-banded leaf rollers (3) feed primarily on foliage; larvae will feed on the fruit surface, producing shallow, irregular scars. The first generation attacks foliage and some immature fruit in June; the second feeds on mature fruit causing heaviest damage in August. They overwinter in the pupal stage in rolled leaves on the ground.

Green fruitworms (4) feed on new foliage of backyard trees in the spring and then on developing apples for several weeks after fruit set. They eat large, irregular cavities in the sides and stem end of the fruit. Larvae rest on twigs or branches nearby damaged fruit.

Apple aphids (5) feed on fruiting clusters early in the season causing stunted, misshapen, hard, knotty apples. Later feeding causes severe russeting or black markings from honeydew and sooty mold fungus. Feeding on growing terminals causes curls, stunts and distortions. Of numerous species in Wisconsin, the green-colored apple aphid is most troublesome.

San Jose scales (6), most severe in eastern Wisconsin, attach to twigs, branches, trunks, leaves and fruit. They cause circular, gray or brownish-gray spots about 1/16-inch wide with a slightly raised, yellow center. Red circles surrounding individual scales are characteristics.

Cherry fruit flies (7) have only recently troubled Wisconsin's sour cherry producing area. They are not a problem on individual trees in other state areas.

Plum curculios (8) severely affect apples, cherries, plums and other Wisconsin tree fruits. Firest, they feed on developing buds and flower petals. As fruit forms, the female cuts a half-moon shaped slit through the skin, eats a small cavity and deposits an egg. After larvae feed for a time, the fruit usually drops to the ground. Fruit which does not drop develops knots, depressions or fan-shaped scars.

Two-spotted mites (9) usually cause problems in late summer. European red mites cause early season injury. Mites are about 1/50 inch long, and vary in color. Feeding on lower leaf surfaces, they remove plant sap through their needle-like mouthparts. A fine webbing may appear on the underside of leaves, which turn bronze as feeding continues.

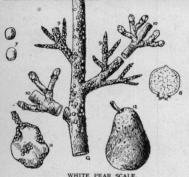

WHITE PEAR SCALE.

References: 7, female, enlarged, showing form ; 8, female, under side, greatly magnified ; G, infested Pear branch ; 9, 9, spurs enfeebled, wood buds forming instead of blossom buds ; 10, 10, clean growths with blossom buds ; 11, deformed Pear caused by scale ; 12, clean Pear.

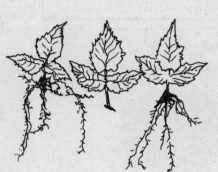

Laying-down trellis-grown blackberries.

THE LEAF-BUD METHOD OF PROPAGATING BRAMBLES

Brambles can be propagated by several methods. They include suckering, layering, root cuttings, division, and the tip method. Generally a variety can be propagated easily in one or more of these ways. However, some varieties, such as the Purple Autumn raspberry, rarely produce any suckers and usually bear fruit at the tips of the canes during autumn. Thus the use of the tip method is limited. Fortunately, this variety can easily be propagated by leaf-bud cuttings. These are cuttings composed of a leaf with an axillary bud and a small portion of stem tissue attached. Well-rooted cuttings may be obtained in two weeks.

CUTTING BED. Best results have been obtained in propagating frames covered with standard hotbed sash provided with bottom heating. A temperature ranging from 70 degrees to 80 degrees F. maintained by a thermostatically controlled electric heating cable is desirable. But if it is not available, bottom heat may be supplied by decaying stable manure in the bottom of the frame. Unheated coldframes may also be used, but rooting will take longer and a lower percentage of rooted cuttings will be obtained. Clean, sharp sand or a mixture of three parts sand to one part peat moss makes a satisfactory rooting medium.

SOURCE OF CUTTINGS. Cuttings may be taken from well-grown plants from mid-July to mid-September in Illinois. Plants grown in a dry field with leaves heavily coated with dust will give a lower percentage of rooted cuttings. One or two current-season shoots may be removed from each plant, depending on the total number of shoots and the vigor of the parent plant. Leaf-bud cuttings from the lateral shoots of one-year canes should not be used, since they usually flower and do not grow shoots.

PREPARING THE CUTTINGS. It is best to use only the mid-portion of the cane, discarding the old leaves on the basal portion and the small unexpanded ones on the upper end. The cuttings are made in about the same way that shield buds are taken for budding purposes.

To prepare the cuttings, hold the shoot by the lower end and make a shallow cut below the leaf. Make a second cut beginning above the leaf and passing under the bud to meet the first cut. The heel should not be much over one-half inch long, and the second cut should not penetrate the pith but should pass parallel with the surface through the solid wood cylinder that surrounds the pith. Let the cuttings fall into a suitable receptacle containing a damp cloth, paper, or moss, to prevent drying out before setting in the frame.

SETTING THE CUTTINGS. Plant the cuttings as soon as possible. Place them about two inches apart in rows spaced five inches apart, with the base of the leaf petiole about one inch deep. Tamp them in firmly, water thoroughly and, when the frame is full, cover with sash and shade them to prevent the tops from wilting. Water occasionally after setting, but not too much or the cuttings will rot.

AFTER-CARE. Rooting should take place within ten days to two weeks, or four weeks at most for the slower rooting types. Then pot the rooted cuttings and put them back in a covered, shaded frame. Gradually harden them off by increasing light and ventilation. Cuttings taken from mid-July to mid-August may be transplanted to the open field in the autumn. Cuttings taken later in the season should be gradually hardened off in the frames and allowed to remain in the frames until the following spring, when they should be set out in the open field.

This system of propagating is not successful with every type of bramble. Usually the varieties that propagate themselves naturally by rooting at the tips or that are immediate offspring of tip-rooting crossed with suckering varieties will root from leaf-bud cuttings.

The advantage of this method is that a large number of plants can be obtained quite rapidly from a small number of mother plants. At the same time, cutting out canes for leaf-bud cuttings should not be so severe as to impair fruit production by the parent plants.

(Adapted and condensed from material by C. C. Zych of the Extension Service of the University of Illinois)

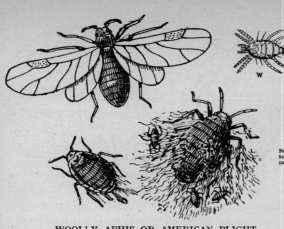

COMMON FRUIT INSECTS

WHY FRUIT TREES FAIL TO BEAR

J. Hull and D. M. Jones
Department of Horticulture
Michigan State University

WOOLLY APHIS OR AMERICAN BLIGHT.

References: *Upper figure*, winged female; *lower left-hand figure*, wingless female; *lower right-hand figure*, viviparous female and young in wool.

Grape berry moth larvae (10) web the fruit together. Grapes turn dark purple and drop from stems when about pea size. A second generation eats holes in nearly ripened fruit.

Oriental fruit moths (11) cause injury similar to codling moths. They are not a problem in Wisconsin.

Peach tree borers (12) affect cherry and plum trees. Larvae feed just beneath the bark, destroying living tissue and sometimes girdling the trunk and main roots. Gum masses often exude from the feeding area. A more serious pest in Wisconsin is the lesser peach tree borer.

For additional information consult: Bulletin 548, Wisconsin Apple Insects; and Bulletin 555, Cherry Insects and Diseases in Wisconsin.

These comments were prepared by C. F. Koval, assistant professor of entomology, Madison.

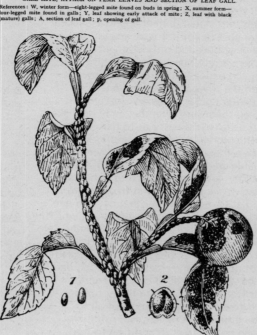

GALL MITE, ATTACK ON PEAR LEAVES AND SECTION OF LEAF GALL.
References: W, winter form—eight-legged mite found on buds in spring; X, summer form—four-legged mite found in galls; Y, leaf showing early attack of mite; Z, leaf with black (mature) galls; A, section of leaf gall; p, opening of gall.

SOFT SCALE ON ORANGE SPRAY.
References: 1, female, natural size; 2, female, magnified.

HOW TO KEEP OLIVES FROM FRUITING

Olive (*Olea Europæa.*)

Evergreen olives, excellent hardy ornamental trees for So. Nevada, begin to fruit at an early age unless treated to prevent this.

When fruit falls and is crushed underfoot the stains are carried into the house. To many homeowners, this is its biggest fault as a tree.

Spray with Naphthelene Acetic Acid (NAA)

Do this when trees are in full bloom. Since not all blooms open at the same time, repeat in 10 days. This is the same growth regulator sold in local garden shops and nurseries for rooting cuttings, inducing flowering in pineapples, thinning olives, etc.

You can use any good sprayer, but be sure to achieve thorough over-all fogging to eliminate fruiting. Skimpy coverage will permit many flowers to be pollinated and go on to produce the messy crop of fruit.

Water Treatment

Spraying the tree several times with a good force of water from the garden hose during its blooming period will also help discourage olive fruit set.

Pruning European Olives

Little if any pruning is necessary to shape this tree. When pruning is necessary, thin out the center of the tree removing all dead branches and weak growth. Keep all suckers removed from the base of the tree.

If additional trunks are desired, one or two of these suckers may be left. Multi-trunk olive trees are the best specimen trees and carry the highest price. Keep all foliage removed from the trunk area of the tree to give it a better appearance.

Young fruit trees will begin to bear fruit after they have become old enough to blossom freely. The health of the tree and its environment, its fruiting habits, adequate pollination, variety, rootstock and the cultural practices used, influence its ability to flower and produce fruit. If just one of these conditions is unfavorable, yields may be reduced.

BEARING AGE. The length of time from planting to fruit bearing varies with the type of fruit. Trees that grow at a moderate rate generally bear fruit sooner than fast-or-slow-growing varieties. Rootstocks also influence earliness of bearing. Following are the ages, from planting, at which trees may begin to bear fruit:

VARIETY	TIME IN YEARS	VARIETY	TIME IN YEARS
Apple	3-5	Peach	2-3
Apricot	2-4	Pear	4-6
Cherry, sour	3-5	Plum	4-6
Cherry, sweet	5-7	Quince	5-6

Dwarf apple and dwarf pear trees may begin to bear 1 to 2 years earlier than standard size trees.

TREE HEALTH. Maintain healthy trees free from insects and diseases. Most diseases and insects can be controlled through the periodic application of an "All-Purpose Fruit Spray". These sprays are mixtures of fungicides and insecticides, which are effective against most fruit tree pests.

CLIMATE AND WEATHER. Extreme cold during winter dormancy may kill the flower buds and occasionally the branches. Winter weather rarely threatens hardy apple, pear, plum and sour cherry varieties. Sweet cherries are relatively sensitive to cold until they become dormant. Peace trees are very vulnerable to cold weather. Their buds can be killed by mid-winter temperatures near 10 degrees F. below zero. As flower buds grow and open, they become more susceptible to injury from frost. The exposed buds can usually withstand temperatures near 24 degrees F. However, the open blossoms of practically all fruit trees will be killed at temperatures below 27 degrees to 28 degrees F.

When a heavy frost is expected, covering the tree will sometimes prevent bud or blossom injury, provided temperatures do not fall too low and cold weather is of short duration. Polyethylene sheets or plastic bags are usually effective but cheesecloth and even old bed sheets may be used.

POLLINATION. Fruit trees require pollination for fruit formation. Without sufficient pollination, trees may blossom abundantly, but will not bear fruit.

Some species of fruit trees have perfect flowers. Both anthers, which contain the pollen, and the pistils, which develop into fruit, are located in the same blossom. If they bear fruit as a result of pollination from their own anthers, these trees are called "self-fruitful". However, many types of fruit trees with perfect flowers cannot produce fruit from their own pollen. These require pollen from another variety and are called "self unfruitful".

Some species of fruit trees do not fit conveniently into either category. These species have male trees that produce pollen and female trees that produce fruit. To grow them successfully, it is necessary to plant at least one tree of each gender near each other.

Examples of self-fruitful types include: sour cherry, apricot (except Perfection and Riland), most peach (except J. H. Hale and several others), European type plums, such as the Stanley, Green Gage and Italian Prune and quince.

"Self-unfruitful" types include: many apple, pear, and sweet cherry, and Japanese and American plum trees. To pollinate adequately, plant two or more varieties near each other.

The following planting practices are recommended:

APPLE. Plant at least two varieties for pollination. Do not plant poor pollen-producing varieties such as Baldwin, Gravenstein, Staymen, Winesap, and Rhode Island Greening, or plant at least two other varieties with these to insure adequate pollination.

SWEET CHERRY. Big, Lambert and Napoleon (Royal Ann) cherry trees do not pollinate one another. Plant a pollinating variety such as Black Tartarian, Republican, Van or Windsor, or a sour cherry such as Montmorency nearby.

PEAR. Many varieties of pears are completely or partially self-unfruitful. For adequate pollination, plant at least two varieties together. Bartlett and Seckel pears will not pollinate each other, and Magness cannot be used as a pollinator.

PLUM. Since many varieties of Japanese and American plums are self-unfruitful, plant two or more varieties together.

BIENNIAL BEARING. Some fruit trees, especially some apple varieties, produce abundant crops one year and sparsely the next. This 'biennial bearing' of fruit trees can be modified to obtain annual production by early and heavy fruit thinning during years of heavy fruit set.

CULTURAL PRACTICES. Fruit trees need full sunlight for best production. Avoid placing trees where they are shaded by buildings or other trees. To reduce competition from weeds or grass, cultivate, mulch or apply a weed killer. Prune trees to develop at desirable form and remove excessive growth and dead or diseased branches. Protect developing fruit and foliage from insect and disease damage throughout the season.

GATHERING FRUIT

S.W. Fletcher

Reprinted from Garden Magazine, 1905

Many people lose a large part of the product of the home orchard because they do not pick and store the fruit properly. Only last winter I saw a man throwing apples into his cellar with a coal shovel. He had shaken off all that could not be picked easily from the ground, dumped them into a springless farm wagon and jolted them across a rocky pasture to the house cellar, there to be shoveled out like so many potatoes. I asked the man if he did not think it would pay him to give his fruit a little better care. "What's the use?" he replied. "My fruit does not keep well any way. It's all gone by Christmas. I lay it to the poor soil on which it is grown." I did not tell him what I laid it to.

APPLES IN A BUSHEL SIEVE.
Bad—fruit too loose and hay used.

By permission of the British Basket Co. Ltd.

THE BONNET.

Most people have more respect for the tenderness of fruit; but there is still a woeful lack of appreciation of the extreme susceptibility of fruit to injury from careless handling. Commercial growers, as a rule, are more careful with their fruit than amateurs, because the returns from a single shipment of bruised fruit are a convincing argument against carelessness. It is a shame for a man to raise good fruit only to lose, because of improper handling, a part of what it might be worth to him.

The time of picking makes a great difference in the quality and the keeping of fruits. The various kinds, and sometimes different varieties of the same kind, require different treatment in this respect. Experience is the best guide, because the ripening changes of fruit vary with soil, climate, variety, season and a dozen other factors.

In general, the greener the fruit when picked the longer it will keep, and also the poorer it will be in quality. All our common orchard fruits, with the exception of many varieties of pears, reach their highest quality only when they are allowed to ripen in the natural way—on the trees. The sooner they are picked before this time the more likely they are to be sour, astringent, dry, stringy, mealy, insipid, and everything else that is inexcusable in a dessert fruit. The home fruit grower can let his fruit ripen on the trees, and secure all the high colors, flavors and aromas that develop during the final stages of ripening. He gets infinitely more satisfaction from his fruit than those who are forced to buy in the general market fruit that was taken from the tree while yet more or less immature, and before the exquisite flavor of a fresh, tree-ripened fruit have developed. The peaches, pears, plums and apricots that come to Eastern markets from the Pacific coast are often picked two weeks before they would be mature if allowed to remain on the trees. No wonder they are not always as of high quality when they reach us as our own tree-ripened fruit. Usually the home orchardist will let his fruit ripen on the trees, except, of course, winter varieties of apples and pears. In some cases early picking may be advantageous, especially for the purpose of prolonging the season of a certain variety or saving it from biped or insect enemies, even though it may be at the expense of quality.

APPLES — Some summer and fall varieties of apples ripen well on the trees, but most of them should be picked when they are well colored and have reached full size, but are not yet soft; i.e., they may be mature but not ripe. Summer apples especially are likely to water-core or rot if not picked before fully ripe. In the neighborhood of Boston, growers of Williams, a summer variety unexcelled for home use, spread a straw mulch beneath the tree and allow the apples to ripen on the trees and drop upon it. The time of picking winter apples varies considerably. If it is desired to keep them very late, they may be picked a little green, but usually it is best not to harvest them until mature—well colored, of full size, and usually with brown seeds, although the color of the seeds is not always a reliable guide to maturity. Some winter varieties, such as Spy, are often allowed to hang upon the trees for a few weeks after the first frost. From the home orchardist's point of view—that of good eating—the chief desideratum is complete maturity, which brings quality; and the signs of maturity are readily distinguished by an observing person.

PEARS — Most varieties of pears should be picked when mature, but not ripe, and ripened in a cool, dark place. This applies with especial force to the early sorts, as Summer Doyenne, which are likely to be dry and stringy if tree ripened: and most of all to Clapps, which, nine times out of ten, will rot at the core if left to ripen on the tree. In addition to the usual signs of approaching maturity—heightening color, full size, and darkening seeds—the snapping of the fruit stem from the spur is an especially reliable guide. Experienced growers take the fruit in the hollow of the hand and bend it straight upward from the spur. If the stem snaps off easily and smoothly at its attachment to the spur, the fruit is mature and the whole crop may be picked with safety, though none of the fruits may be at all soft. If, however, the stem breaks off below its attachment to the spur, the fruit is probably not yet ready for the basket.

PLUMS are more commonly picked when nearly or quite ready for eating than any other orchard fruit; but, if necessary, as in commercial growing, they may be picked some time before ripe. The Japanese varieties, as Abundance and Red June, can be gathered when quite green, and will color and ripen well if stored properly. The common varieties of the European class, as Bradshaw and Lombard, may be picked while still hard; but when grown for home

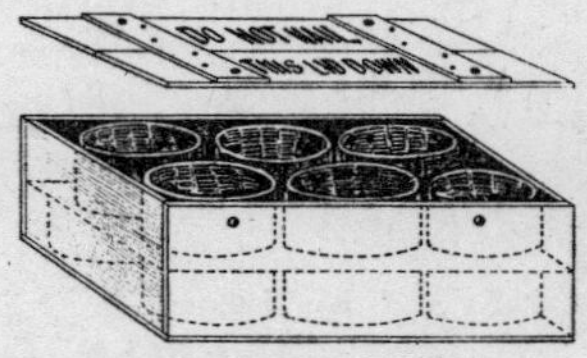

Strawberry Box (Glover & Co., Ltd.)

A BOX OF GREENGAGE PLUMS.

use plums should always be allowed to hang on the tree as long as possible. If there is difficulty with rot, the fruit may be gathered early to save it, although the rot is often quite as serious in the storage room as on the trees. Certain varieties of native plums, as Wildgoose, are likely to burst open some seasons if allowed to ripen on the tree and drop to the ground in their natural way. Early harvesting remedies this trouble. With these exceptions the home grower should let his plums hang till their delicate aroma and juicy plumpness assure him that they are ready to grace the center of his table.

CHERRIES are usually picked when they are ready to be eaten. For marketing they are commonly picked just before they ripen. If there is difficulty with birds, boys or rot, it will pay the home grower also to pick his cherries before they are fully ripe. This is the only way to handle rot if it starts at that time. Many a man has had a crop of cherries rot in one night, just when the fruit was ready to be eaten. In wet seasons especially one must forestall this disease by early picking, as spraying does not usually control it. For the birds, plant a tree or two of mulberries near the cherries; the fruit ripens about the same time, and birds prefer the mulberries. I have no advice to offer on handling the boys, except to give them a pocketful occasionally.

PEACHES AND APRICOTS should be picked when fully ripe, for the best quality; but, if necessary, as soon as they show the first signs of ripening. If the fruit is of good size and well colored it may be tested for maturity by pressing it gently with the ball of the thumb. If it feels springy, or gives at all, it may

By permission of the British Basket Co. Ltd.

PATENT WOOD COVER FOR A CHIP BASKET.

be picked safely and ripened in storage, though these fruits cannot be expected to have quite the sweetness and aroma of tree-ripened fruit. The earliest varieties, as Amsden and Alexander, which are more liable to rot than later sorts, may often be saved to some extent by early picking.

Care in picking is not an unimportant point. One can pick fruit either carefully or carelessly—handle it like eggs or like potatoes. The delicate and perishable nature of fruit ought to be apparent to everybody; yet I have seen, I suppose, more than a hundred different men shake off, or knock off, with poles, apples and pears that they expected to put in the cellar. Every jam, knock, jolt, fall, rub, that injures the skin or bruises any of the pulp, usually becomes a rotten place sooner or later.

I used to work for an old farmer who preferred "specked" apples to any other. In fact, he would not eat any that were not specked; he said the pulp was of better quality next to the speck. Most of us, however, have not such a refined taste; we like sound fruit.

The only way to have sound fruit is to pick it and handle it with care. No shaking can be allowed, except of fruit that cannot be reached even by the most agile boy. No knocking fruit off with poles. These may do when the fruit is wanted for drying or for cider—though I doubt it—but never when it is destined for the table. Hand picking, and the most scrupulously careful hand picking, must be insisted on in the home orchard. The various picking devices, designed to break or twist off fruit into wire fingers or pass it down through canvas bags, are all impracticable on any large scale. They take too much time. Stick to hand picking, if your trees are so shaped as to admit of it.

It makes a difference how the fruit is separated from the branch. An apple should be separated by slightly twisting the fruit and bending it upward. If it is pulled off, the stem is likely to be broken or pulled off, in either case the fruit is not likely to keep as well as fruit with stems on; neither does it look as well. Pears are picked in the same way, and always with stems on. In gathering plums and cherries, do not grasp the fruit itself, but the stem, which should always be left on unbroken. The bloom of plums should be preserved, not only because it adds to the attractiveness of the fruit, but also because it prevents the evaporation of the fruit juices. Peaches and apricots are pulled off with a slight twist.

Conveniences for gathering form an important problem to the commercial grower, but the man who grows a small amount of fruit for home use is not troubled by it; he uses whatever ladders, baskets, etc., are handy. For peaches, apricots, plums and pears and Morello cherries, there is nothing better than a ten-foot step-ladder. Get one having a one-legged brace; on sloping ground it stands up better than one with two legs. For apples and sweet cherries and other tall trees, light rung ladders are best. If the ladder is brought into a point at the top, like an inverted V, it can be pushed more easily between the branches. A cheap and effective picking ladder can be made at home by nailing rungs on a stout pole of the right length. Climbing around the trees should be avoided as much as possible. There is almost sure to be more or less abrasion of the bark by boots, and these places make ugly wounds.

For a picking receptacle, any box or basket will do if the fruit is handled carefully enough. A half-bushel splint basket which has been padded with burlaps and provided with an S wire hook is excellent for apples. A still better arrangement, in the opinion of many, is a grain sack slung over the shoulders, with one corner of the mouth caught to one corner of the bottom. If the mouth is held open with a hoop the bag can be filled more easily. Excepting the sack, whatever is used to pick into should be padded. In emptying baskets or sacks do not pour the fruit out roughly. With one hand keep the rolling fruit from bruising and gently sidle it into the receptacle. If fruit has to be carried any distance on a wagon, by all means let it be a spring wagon if possible. These little points mean much in the keeping of fruit, especially apples and pears that are to be stored for winter use.

GREENHOUSES

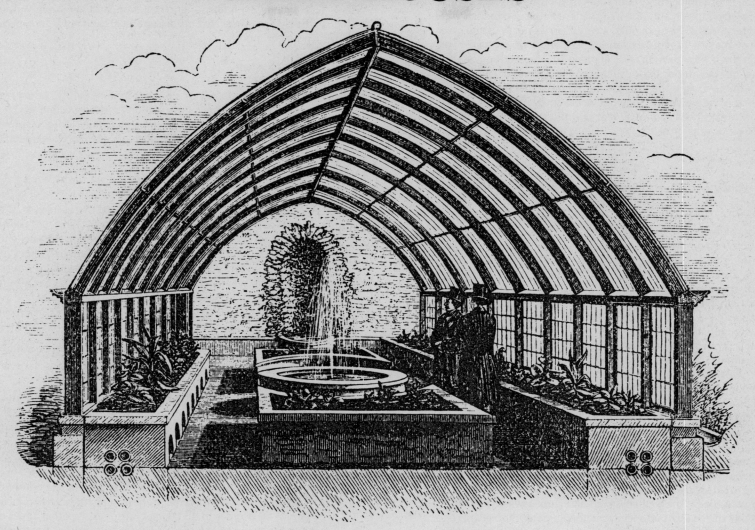

GREENHOUSE LOCATION AND ORIENTATION

By J. N. Walker and G. A. Duncan

University of Kentucky
College of Agriculture
Cooperative Extension Service

Most greenhouses are erected to produce plants during the off-season; therefore, they must provide a desirable plant environment. Correct location and orientation of the house are of paramount importance in providing ideal environmental conditions. Since location can also influence the heating cost, labor utilization, and disease factors, economic success may also depend on the site selection.

Recommendations for locating and orientating your greenhouse are given in this publication. The following specifications are the ideal ones; however, some builders may not be able to follow each suggestion given, depending on individual limitations of their houses. For example, houses used for display and sales purposes are often connected to existing buildings; therefore, they may have to sacrifice some of those factors described for production-type greenhouses. Bench culture or similar production practices may also justify deviation from some of the standard requirements. To provide optimum plant response and teaching effectiveness, however, the authors believe recommendations should be followed as nearly as possible in building all houses used for educational purposes.

LOCATION OF THE GREENHOUSE

Sunlight

Sunlight provides energy for plant growth, and is generally the limiting factor in greenhouses. When planning the construction, give primary consideration to obtaining maximum sunlight exposure during those "short" days of mid-winter when the sun is lowest in the sky. Maximum sun altitude (angle of sun above earth's horizon) occurs at noon and varies from a high on June 21 to a low on December 21. Solar altitudes for selected latitudes (distance measured in degrees north and south from the equator) and times of day are given in Table 1. The latitude of 42 degrees would correspond to Detroit, Michigan; 38 degrees to Lexington, Kentucky; 34 degrees to Little Rock, Arkansas; and 30 degrees to New Orleans, Louisiana. At solar noon, the sun is located due south. This means that the building site should preferably have an open southern exposure. If the land slopes, it should ideally slope to the south.

Do not build near large trees, buildings, or other obstructions which will shade the building. Figure 1 gives the ratio of shadow length and height obstructions for selected solar altitudes. To determine how far away an obstruction must be to prevent a shadow

on the greenhouse, multiply these ratios by the obstruction height. As a general rule, the greenhouse should be located at least 2.5 times the height of the object away from it, in either the east, west, or south direction. Even objects this tall will cast long shadows in the early morning when the sun is particularly low in the sky.

Soil

When plants are to be grown in the soil covered by the greenhouse, select a site where a deep, good draining, fertile soil is available. A sandy loam or silt loam type soil is preferred. Avoid top soil below which a tight hardpan is present. Although organic matter and artificial types of conditioners can be added, problems are reduced if a site with good natural soil is selected. Grading often produces uneven soil conditions within the greenhouse. Careful soil analysis and preparation are necessary if even plant growth is to be achieved. Before any organic matter or additives are mixed with the soil, make a complete soil analysis and carefully follow the resulting recommendations.

Avoid areas where chemical residues which would injure greenhouse crops may persist, including places heavily sprayed with damaging weed killers and herbicides. If you question the degree of danger, grow selected plants in samples of the soil to determine if any detectable injury occurs. Noxious weed seeds can also be a problem, but generally proper sterilization methods will kill most weed seeds.

Where a good soil is not available for the location of the greenhouse, consider cultural techniques using artificial media such as peat and vermiculite.

Drainage

Select a site that is level and well drained to reduce problems with salt build-up and insufficient soil aeration. A high water table may result in saturation of the soil and prohibit effective use of the greenhouse. Ground water which flows into the house may carry soil diseases. If necessary, tile drain the area enclosed by the greenhouse. Tile lines within the greenhouse can also be used for steam sterilization if properly placed in the soil.

Ground beds should be nearly level. If they slope in any direction, water will tend to concentrate in the low areas, accentuating any problems of poor drainage. Slopes within the greenhouse also allow hot air to rise and cold air to settle, creating added problems for the environmental system to overcome. A greenhouse in a low, damp area could be subject to higher humidities and dampness which accentuate leaf mold, diseases, etc.

Sheltered Area

Although obtaining maximum sunlight should have first consideration, placing the greenhouse in a sheltered area will reduce wind-induced heat losses. For example, a wind barrier north of the greenhouse may materially reduce heating costs; yet it would have little effect on the light received. Trees are helpful in preventing winter heat loss, but deciduous trees which lose their leaves in the winter are not effective when the heat loss potential is greatest.

In areas of heavy winter snowfall where snowdrifts occur, wind and snow breaks need to be 100 feet or more away from the greenhouse to reduce major drifts.

Utilities

A greenhouse requires a number of utilities, notably electricity, water, and an energy source for heat.

Electricity: The electric service for ventilation alone will require approximately 4 to 6 kilowatts for a ¼-acre range. For a small hobby-sized house, connected loads of up to 1 to 2 kilowatts are not unusual. If lights are used for photoperiod control or supplemental lighting, the electric load will increase significantly. Normally the electric power companies will willingly supply the necessary service; however, the grower should attempt to anticipate his intended electric usage and provide sufficient entrance capacity to allow for full electric utilization.

Water: A reliable supply of clean water is mandatory. A water requirement of up to 1/3 gallon per square foot per day may be needed. Depending upon the soil type, up to 1 gallon of water per square foot may be put on the soil at one time. Water from ponds has the disadvantage of being cold during the winter. If this water is used directly for irrigation, plant roots may chill, causing a detrimental effect. Pump water from such sources into a large storage tank within a heated portion of the greenhouse or headhouse so that its temperature will approach that of the plants. Also, with ponds, the possibility of chemical pollution exists unless the surrounding drainage area is carefully controlled.

Energy Source: The availability of an inexpensive energy source is often one of the most important factors in determining where to build a greenhouse range. Natural gas is a widely preferred fuel because of its clean performance, low maintenance, and relatively low cost. Not only is it one of the lower cost fuels, but gas heating equipment is generally among the least expensive for initial cost, annual maintenance, and operating costs. LP Gas, fuel oil, and coal are alternate sources of fuel and can be transported to greenhouse locations that are not close to gas lines.

Electric energy is becoming more competitive in many areas for greenhouse heating where the above fuels are in short supply or rapidly rising in costs. Hot-air resistance heating units can be used in hobby or individual houses. Central hot-water furnaces could be more suitable for larger combined houses of ¼ acre or more. Since heating costs can be as much as two-thirds of the production cost for some crops, select a location and energy source carefully for future availability and economy.

Emergency Power

Standby emergency power equipment sized for electrical support of heating equipment, air circulation, and minimum ventilation is vital when winter storms disrupt local service for long periods (2 hours or more).

Alarm System

The consequences of a heating system failure during freezing temperatures can be catastrophic. An alarm system which is independent of the electrical service should, therefore, be provided. Place the alarm bell in a residence or location where people are normally present.

Convenience

Locate the greenhouse near your place of residence, if possible, or where a caretaker can be housed nearby. This will prove convenient for security and will facilitate care during weekends or holiday periods. If the ventilation and watering systems are not fully automatic, operator care will also be mandatory during sunny periods. Should a heating failure occur, corrective action must be prompt.

ORIENTATION OF THE GREENHOUSE

Light Availability and Shading Effects

Orientation of the greenhouse for maximum light availability is also an important consideration. Manbeck and Aldrich ("Analytical Determination of Direct Visible Solar Energy Transmitted by Rigid Plastic Greenhouses," "Trans. of ASAE, 1967) report that an east-west orientation (i.e., the ridge of the house running east and west) is preferable in the winter for northern locations (above 40 degrees to 45 degrees latitude). At other times of the year for the northern regions and at all times for the southern regions, a north-south orientation of the ridge is preferable. Since light is most critical during mid-winter, growers in the northern latitudes (i.e., 40 degrees N or greater) should use the east-west orientation for single-width houses if possible. With east-west orientation, however, a problem is encountered with ridge and furrow houses. A definite shadow line develops within the houses due to the north sloping roof sections and the gutter between sections of the house. This shadow effect is usually sufficient to result in reduced plant growth in the region of the house affected. Depending upon the width of span, the shadow area can be 10 percent or more of the house space. Although shadows occur within north-south oriented ridge and furrow houses, the shadows move across the floor of the house as the day progresses and noticeable reduction in growth in one region of the greenhouse is not normally apparent.

A circular span-roof conservatory glazed with flat glass

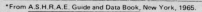

Table 1.—Solar Altitudes for Selected Latitudes and Time*

Latitude	Date	Solar Altitudes at Specified Times, Degrees (Angle β of Figure 1)		
		8:00 a.m. and 4:00 p.m.	10:00 a.m. and 2:00 p.m.	12:00 (noon)
42°	Dec 21	4°	19°	25°
	Mar 21 & Sept 21	22	40	48
	June 21	37	59	72
38°	Dec 21	7°	22°	29°
	Mar 21 & Sept 21	23	43	52
	June 21	37	60	76
34°	Dec 21	9°	26°	33°
	Mar 21 & Sept 21	24	46	56
	June 21	37	62	80
30°	Dec 21	11°	29°	37°
	Mar 21 & Sept 21	26	49	60
	June 21	37	63	84

*From A.S.H.R.A.E. Guide and Data Book, New York, 1965.

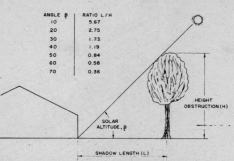

ANGLE β	RATIO L/H
10	5.67
20	2.75
30	1.73
40	1.19
50	0.84
60	0.58
70	0.36

Figure 1. Ratio of shadow length and obstruction height for selected solar altitudes.

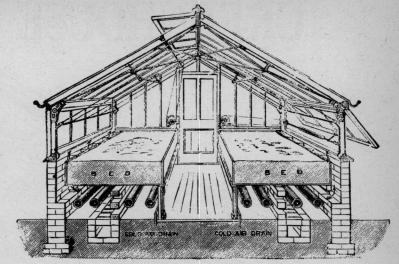

INTERIOR VIEW OF SPAN-ROOF PLANT HOUSE, ETC.

Environmental Equipment

Ventilation, cooling and heating systems are noticeably affected by the way the greenhouse is oriented and the equipment installed.

Ventilation: Ventilation air should not have to move more than 120 to 150 feet across the house between entrance and exit. Design and install fan ventilation systems so that air moves with (in the direction of) prevailing summer winds rather than against them. This procedure will eliminate opposing air forces which decrease the air flow rate by 10 percent or more. Usually, you should install exhaust fans in the leeward end of the greenhouse and fresh air inlet shutters in the windward end. However, sometimes a sidewall fan location in the leeward side and fresh air inlets on each end are best for certain houses.

Cooling System: When pad cooling is used, locate pads on the north wall (end or side) of the greenhouse(s) to prevent shading. For best cooling effectiveness, air should not travel over 100 feet between pads and the exhaust fans. For long houses, over 100 feet in length, locate the bank of pads in a widewall at the center of the house with fans in each end. (NOTE: A water supply of approximately 1 to 2 gallons per minute per 100 square feet of pads is generally required. Also, 100 square feet of pad areas per 1,200 to 1,500 square feet of greenhouse floor area is typical. Obtain more detailed information on pad cooling before making a decision to purchase.)

Heating System: The greenhouse heating system should provide adequate heat supply and distribution throughout the house for environmental uniformity. Consistent heat supply is especially important toward the northwest portion of glass houses or those with sizeable cold air leakage and infiltration.

SITE LAYOUT

Grade and Fill

Prior to erecting the greenhouse, grade and fill those areas where changes are needed to level the site, establish drainage, roads, parking, etc. If you plan to practice soil culture, remember that poor existing soil must be removed and replaced by 12 inches or more of good topsoil. Grade and fill the sub-soil material to requirements, then replace the top soil without compaction. Any subsurface tiling or utility lines can be placed during these operations.

Transportation and Parking

When selecting the site, try to locate near a good road so that materials can be conveniently moved to and from the greenhouse. Sufficient room for turning and parking vehicles is desirable for greenhouses of commercial size, especially when bedding plants and flowers are sold on the premises. Allow 18 feet for head-in parking spaces and 26-30 feet clearance for back-out and turning. Make any curves or turns with 18-20 feet inside radius.

Headhouses

Place headhouses on the north side of the greenhouse to avoid shading a portion of the house. Attachment to the greenhouse or a connecting passageway makes work, handling, and greenhouse operations more convenient but complicates construction techniques to attach without leaks and other maintenance problems. Processing facilities, cold storage rooms, and other such facilities should be adequately incorporated into the ultimate layout.

Expansion

When building, always keep future expansion in mind. Most successful ranges are expanded several times after the first house or small range area is constructed.

SUMMARY

Important points to remember are:

Orient and locate the house for maximum sunlight. In southern latitudes, the ridge should run north-south, and in northern latitudes, east-west.

Avoid placing the house near objects east, west, or south which will shade the house.

Place in an area sheltered from northerly and north-westerly high winds if possible.

Locate on a deep good soil which is well drained and where surface water does not run into the house.

Avoid sloping beds or floors in the greenhouse. Locate the greenhouse near adequate and reliable sources of utilities--electricity, water and gas.

Provide good access roads, parking, and turnaround area.

Position headhouses or supporting facilities on the north side.

Arrange initial construction so that the range can be expanded.

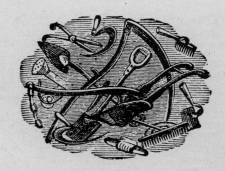

GREENHOUSE STRUCTURES

By J. N. Walker and G. A. Duncan

Deparment of Agricultural Engineering
University of Kentucky
College of Agriculture
Cooperative Extension Service

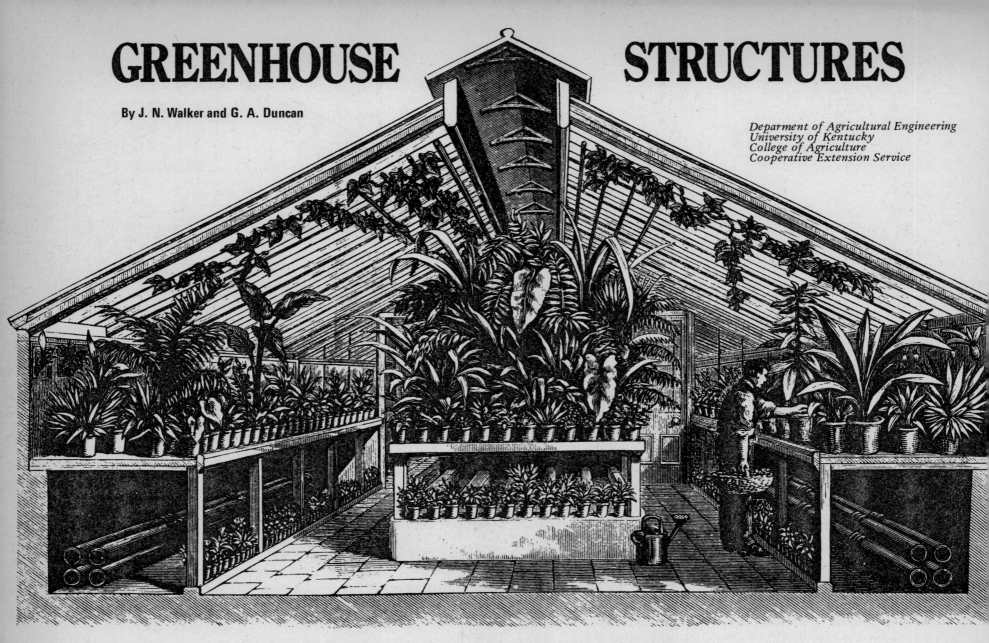

LARGE TROPICAL PLANT AND ORCHID HOUSE, WITH OPEN HEATED TANK IN CENTRE.

Greenhouses vary from small hobby types, some as small as window-box units, to ranges which cover several acres in one enclosure. All of them have one thing in common, they are built to permit the off-season production of plants. The basic purpose of the greenhouse structure is to provide a reliable enclosure within which an environment favorable to plant growth can be created.

In terms of use, greenhouses could be classed as: (1) commercial, (2) Part-time, (3) educational, or (4) hobby. Commercial houses are those in which production is a year-around enterprise. Normally, the labor requirement is at least one full-time man. However, with family-owned greenhouses, commercial production may be carried out with less than a full-time man equivalent using family help. In commercial greenhouses, operations are generally permanent and long depreciation schedules are acceptable. Annual cost is generally more important than the initial cost; however, if capital is limited, the initial cost may still govern the type of construction used. In determining the annual costs, depreciation, interest, maintenance, insurance, taxes and operating costs must all be considered.

Part-time greenhouses are operated for only part of the year or for supplemental income. Examples include houses used for only bedding plant production, for single flower crops like poinsettias, for expansion areas when seasonal production exceeds average year-around space needs, and for nursery rooting or over-wintering. The permanent type houses can be used for such production, but the annual costs of permanent type houses generally require year-around use to justify them economically. Some type of low-cost construction is therefore used. Depending upon the crop, the environmental control equipment may also be less than that used in the more permanent type houses. For instance, houses for over-wintering nursery stock may have little or no heat and only minimal ventilation. For other crops the environmental control equipment may need to be comparable to that in the best permanent greenhouses.

Educational greenhouses are those associated with schools or training establishments. Permanent construction is generally used. Due to the high potential for accidental breakage or vandalism in many areas, good quality, rigid plastic or double-strength glass often proves the most desirable house covering. Within educational greenhouses, maximum flexibility is desired. Usually a portion of the house is for ground beds and a portion is arranged with benches. Clear span construction affords the maximum flexibility and is recommended.

Hobby houses are generally small units where a variety of home or garden plants can be grown. In most hobby greenhouses, a highly uniform environment is not as necessary as with other types of production houses. A variation in environment is often desirable since some plants need warmer and drier conditions than others. The ability to control the environment automatically in such houses is very important since there will always be periods when the greenhouse operator will not be present and unusual variations in conditions could ruin all plants within the house.

FUNCTIONAL FEATURES

Regardless of its use, every greenhouse must meet certain functional requirements. For those planning to build, an understanding of these requirements will help in selecting a design. In the discussion that follows, the remarks are largely directed towards commercial, educational, and part-time greenhouses, but will also be generally applicable to the hobby types as well.

Strength

Every greenhouse must be designed to withstand the loads which will be imposed upon it without failure or significant deformation. The primary loads which must be considered are wind and snow. In addition, if a crop such as tomatoes is also to be supported from the structure, this must be considered in the design.

Wind Loads

For most sections of the United States, the major load which must be considered is wind. The wind speeds used in design of acrop production buildings should be the winds as given by ASAE[1] for a 25-year recurrence interval. This means that you would expect winds of the given intensity to occur once every 25 years. For the majority of the United States, except for the two regions shown in Figure 1, the maximum expected wind speed would be 80 mph. In the two shaded regions, special consideration should be given to design, and the advice of engineers who are aware of the local wind conditions should be sought.

A wind blowing at 80 mph develops a maximum possible pressure of 16.4 lbs. per sq. ft. on a flat surface perpendicular to the wind. This is equivalent to approximately 30 inches of snow! However, the actual wind loads on buildings are not this severe because of a height adjustment factor.

Wind speeds are measured and reported by the U. S. Weather Bureau for a height of 30 feet above the ground. The wind velocity reduction from 30 feet above ground to the ground surface is shown in Figure 2. The pressure developed by the wind is related to the square of the wind velocity. Therefore, the wind pressure reduces more rapidly than the wind velocity as the ground surface is approached. As shown in Figure 2, the pressure and wind velocity at 15 feet height are approximately 85% and 90%, respectively, of that at 30 feet. At 10 feet the values are 73% and 85% respectively. The height of the building will, therefore, affect the wind load.

The effective height of a building is defined as the distance above the ground at which the wind force acts.

For many buildings, it is the eave height (H). However, for wide buildings or steep-roofed buildings where the height from the eaves to the peak is greater than the eave height, the effective height is the distance from the ground to midroof (H plus E/2). The eave plus mid-roof distance can become fairly large and result in large effective wind pressures that are important in building designs. For example, if an 80 mph wind speed, as reported by the U.S. Weather Bureau, occurs and the effective building height is 8 feet, the maximum potential wind pressure would be reduced by a factor of .68 which results in the wind pressure being reduced from 16.4 to 11.1 lbs. per sq. ft. For a building 100 ft. long, the forces against the building could possibly total 8,880 lbs. However, one more factor in wind forces must be considered.

The full wind pressure is not normally developed on the surface of the buildings because of shape and orientation. The wind generally hits the surfaces at some angle, depending upon the building profile, and an aerodynamic effect develops. This is similar to the forces which are created over the surface of an airplane wing. Due to the aerodynamic action, an uplifting or suction force develops on many building surfaces. To describe the forces, wind force coefficients are used. These coefficients are multiplied by the wind pressure to determine the design wind forces. A negative coefficient represents a suction or uplifting force and a positive coefficient, a pressure or inward acting force. Typical coefficients are shown in Figure 4. For each roof shape, the windward roof section coefficient varies considerably with the height to width ratio and roof slope. The other coefficients are affected only slightly by changes in these values. For

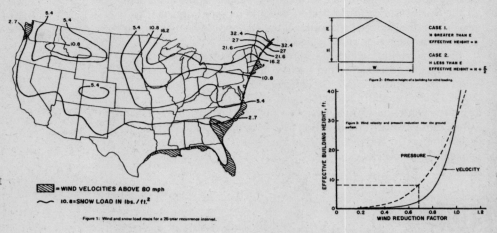

WIND VELOCITIES ABOVE 80 mph
10.8 = SNOW LOAD IN lbs./ft.²

Figure 1: Wind and snow load maps for a 25-year recurrence interval.

the upper roof sections and for the roof and wall sections on the side away from the wind, uplift or suction occurs, the magnitude of uplift being 0.50 to 1.0 of the potential wind pressure force. For example, for a semicircular greenhouse with an effective height of 8 feet and E/w equal to 0.4 (Figure 4), the lower ¼ roof section on the windward side would have an inward acting pressure of 5.4 lbs. per sq. ft. (11.1 lbs./sq. ft. times 0.49) For the same greenhouse, an uplift of 7.8 lbs. per sq. ft. would occur in the center section; and on the downwind side, an outward acting force of 6.4 lbs. per sq. ft. would be expected. Interestingly, the uplift force is the largest force and is of a magnitude comparable to snow loads in most areas of the United States. This means that anchorage of the building and covering to prevent wind uplift and overturning of the building is just as important as providing adequate supports for snow loading!

The problem can become even more critical if a large door is left open on the windward side of the building during high winds. If this happens, a positive pressure builds up inside the greenhouse so that not only is there an uplift suction force due to the aerodynamic effect, there is also a pressure on the inside equal in magnitude to about 0.7 of the potential wind force acting in the same direction. These two combined forces, when they occur, are generally greater than the full potential wind force!

DESIGN FOR RIDGE-AND-FURROW ROOF CONSERVATORY.

Snow Loads

Snow is a different problem in that it acts downward. In heated greenhouses, it is seldom a major problem. The heat tends to melt the snow and, if the greenhouses are properly designed, the snow slides off and snow loading will not cause failure. If the houses are unheated and melting does not occur, or if the greenhouses are of the connected ridge and valley type, then the potential for high snow loads significantly increases.

The snow loads which can be expected on a typical unheated greenhouse on a 25-year recurrence interval are also shown in Figure 1. As can be seen, the majority of the United States would have an expected snow load of less than 10.8 lbs. per sq. ft. even when the houses were unheated. It is, therefore, recommended that greenhouses be designed for downward acting loads of 10 to 12 lbs. per sq. ft. This is a commonly used design load in the greenhouse industry. For houses which are located in the higher snow loads area of the Northeastern United States, it would be very important to use heavier design loads and/or keep the greenhouse heated during the periods when high snow loads could occur.

Since high winds would result in snow being blown from the roofs, designs normally do not need to consider both snow and wind loads simultaneously. Greenhouses which are designed for a 10 to 12 lbs. per sq. ft. snow load and which are well anchored to resist the wind uplift forces have generally proven satisfactory. Since winds cause an overturning action as well as uplift, lateral bracing is also important and must be included. This is of particular importance in long houses.

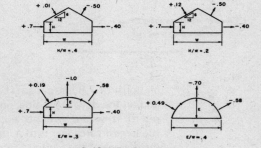

Crop Loads

If the greenhouse roof frame is also to support a crop load, such as tomatoes, additional strength may be required. Tomatoes with a heavy crop load which are tied with string to the greenhouse frame can add as much as 4 lbs. per sq. ft. to the roof load. For a spring tomato crop, this magnitude of load would occur during late spring or early summer when snow loads were not a problem. A fall tomato crop, however, would have its maximum fruit weight in the late fall when it would be possible to have heavy snow. This would be particularly true in the heavy snowfall areas.

Foundations

For both snow and wind conditions, the loads imposed upon the structure must be carried to the ground by the foundation and footings. The foundation and footings, must, therefore, resist uplift, overturning, and downward acting loads. The downward load includes not only snow and possibly the crop weight, but also the dead weight of the structure itself.

Though the size of foundations and footings would depend upon the size and type of the greenhouse and the loads which occur, all foundations for permanent greenhouses should be of a durable material and should extend below the frost line or to a minimum depth of 18 inches, whichever is greater. Little support can be expected from the loose topsoil and earth within the top 6 to 12 inches. If post construction is used, where the main sidewall members are set directly into the ground and where the soil around the post is intended to prevent overturning, depths deeper than 18 inches are required. The most common failure of greenhouses constructed in this manner is the tipping of sidewalls with a subsequent dropping of the ridge line and a weakening of the rafter-to-eave plate joint. Though the filling of post holes with concrete is helpful this is not a substitute for placing the posts to an adequate depth. The horizontal load which a circular pier can safely withstand in a typical silt-loam type soil is given in Table 1[6]. As can be seen from the data, pier depth is the most important factor. Increasing the depth of embedment from 1'6" to 3'6" increased the safe load 5 to 8 times. The height of the load was also important with an increase from 0'6" to 6'6" reducing the allowable load by a factor of 3 to 5. The allowable load was linearly related to the diameter of the pier with a doubling of the allowable load with a doubling of the pier diameter. The most critical condition

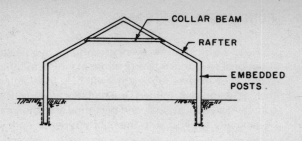

Table 1: Safe Horizontal Loads in Pounds on Circular Piers in A Silt-Loam Soil.

Pier Diameter	Height of Load above ground surface	Horizontal loads, lbs. Pier Depth		
		1'6"	2'6"	3'6"
8"	6"	190	559	992
	3'6"	68	245	488
	6'6"	42	157	333
12"	6"	286	839	1488
	3'6"	102	367	747
	6'6"	62	235	499
16"	6"	380	1118	1984
	3'6"	136	489	996
	6'6"	83	313	665

obviously is a shallow, small diameter footing loaded at eave height.

For permanent greenhouses, concrete is the most suitable foundation material. A 2,500 PSI or better mix should be ordered if ready-mix concrete is used. If a continuous foundation is used along the full length of the house, it is recommended that 3/8" diameter reinforcing rods be placed horizontally in the foundation approximately 1 ½" from the bottom and top and 1 ½" from the edges of the foundation. This is particularly desirable in areas where high soil moisture exists, where rock outcroppings occur, or where some fill has been used and the foundation is near the surface of the original soil. Where fill has been used, the foundation or footings should always be placed sufficiently deep so that they bear on the undisturbed soil on which the fill was placed.

Special precaution must be taken with foundations if rigid-frame construction is used. As snow or other loads occur on rigid frames, there is a tendency for the base legs of the frame to spread and horizontal forces as large as the vertical loads can be developed. This spreading tendency must be resisted if the frames are to carry the loads without failure. This means that foundations such as masonry block, which have low resistance to horizontal loads, should not be used for supporting rigid-frames untill proper reinforcement is done.[3]

Maximum Light Transmission

In most greenhouses light becomes the limiting factor in growth during much of the off-season production period. Consequently, everything which can be done to obtain maximum light intensity within the greenhouse should be accomplished. Orientation is important and is discussed in another article[7]. As a general rule, the greenhouse ridge should run north and south in the southern parts of the United States and east and west in the northern areas with plant rows running north-south. The roof slope should also be about 28 degrees (6:12 slope) or more whenever possible.

The most important features in obtaining maximum light transmission are to minimize the number and size of structural members in the roof area and to use a highly transparent glazing material. It is for these reasons that wide span glass and certain plastics are used. The use of stronger, wide-span covering material reduces the number of supporting members required, and thereby reduces shading. Wooden truss houses, though providing clear span unobstructed interiors, have the disadvantage that there are more members to cause interference with light and thus are not recommended. Only properly designed and fabricated steel or aluminum trusses should be used. Overhead heating, irrigating, and electrical lines should also be kept to a minimum to prevent light blockage.

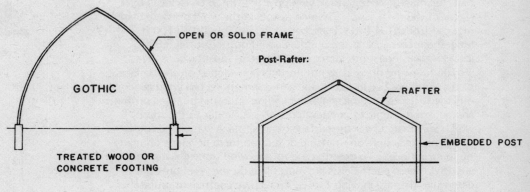

-Simplest construction, but requires more wood or metal than some other designs.

Structural Influence on Heating and Ventilation

The final success of a greenhouse will generally depend upon the ability of the operator to control the environmental conditions within the greenhouse. Though any shape structure can be successfully heated or ventilated, some designs greatly increase the difficulty or cost in providing an adequate system. In these cases, a less than optimum system is often installed, which then creates problems in management.

In greenhouses used the year around, the solar intensity during the winter will often become sufficiently intense to require ventilation even when outside temperatures are near freezing. If this air is brought into the house and directed on the crop without first intermixing with the air within the greenhouse, growth will be hurt. Similarly, if hot air from heating units is allowed to come in direct contact with the plants, rapid drying and poor growth will also occur. In most greenhouses, attempts are made to mix ventilation or heating air with the greenhouse air in the greenhouse space above the crop. In bedding plant, lettuce and other low crop production, adequate space exists within even low profile houses to effectively achieve this mixing above the crop. However, with tall crops such as tomatoes, or mum production on benches, adequate space may not be available. This is particularly true in narrow houses where the rise from the eaves to the peak is small. Some growers argue that they want low houses to minimize the volume of air they must heat, but this volume is not a truly important factor. The important factor in the cost of heating is the amount of exposed wall or ceiling area, since any heat added to a greenhouse remains in the house until it passes through the covering material. Though an increase in height does increase the wall area, this is usually a very small increase in the total amount of exposed area. As a general rule, at least 1/3 of the total house volume should be unoccupied if it is intended to use this space for the introduction and intermixing of ventilation or heating air with the greenhouse air.

Ventilation and evaporative cooling both require the introduction of large quantities of outside air during bright warm days. A common method of doing this is to place fans in one sidewall or end and introduce the air through baffles, pads, or louvers in the opposite wall or end. When this is done, the air picks up the solar heat in the house as it moves across the house, resulting in the air gradually increasing in temperature as it nears the fan. If this temperature rise and air velocity are to be kept within reasonable limits, the distance across the house from the fans to the air inlet openings should not be more than 100 to 120 feet. The house length or width in the other direction can be any desired dimension depending on the size of greenhouse range desired.

Further information and details on greenhouse heating and ventilation systems are available in other publications of this greenhouse series which can be obtained from the Agricultural Engineering Department, University of Kentucky.

Working Height

The height of the house in the walk areas should never be less than 6'6''. This allows a working man to move conveniently through the house. For tall crops such as tomatoes, 6 feet should also be the minimum height at the eaves, and 7 feet is commonly considered as being the minimum desirable height. For low crops, the eave height can be as low as 4 feet, as long as greenhouse workers do not have to regularly move back and forth in this area of the house. Some quonset type houses severely restrict plant growth around the outer walls due to the low curvature.

Roof Slope

One other important factor is the roof slope of the greenhouse. The roof slope affects the run-off of condensed water from the ceiling. Slopes of 28 degrees (6:12 slope) are generally considered as minimal if run-off without severe dripping is to occur. With lower slopes, run-off is restricted, and dripping is a serious problem. With some of the plastic covering materials where drops occur more readily than they do on glass, even greater slopes would be desirable.

Access

In most greenhouses it is necessary on occasion to remove large amounts of vines or plants which are to be discarded, and in some instances, to remove the soil or rooting media. On these occasions, large doors in the end of the greenhouse will prove useful. This permits the use of tractors or large wheeled carts or wagons. Such doors also facilitate the use of large equipment for tillage operations within the greenhouse. If walking tractors are to be used, 4-foot wide doors are adequate, but 6 to 8 foot doors are desirable if standard-size, four wheel tractors and wagons are to be used within the greenhouse.

TYPES OF GREENHOUSE STRUCTURES

Greenhouse structures come in a variety of shapes and styles. All are acceptable if properly designed and erected. The features discussed in the previous section should be considered in selecting a specific type of greenhouse. In addition, cost, aesthetic appearance, flexibility and availability should be considered.

The various common shapes and advantages or special features of each type are listed below:

Quonset

Simple and efficient construction using thin-wall electrical conduit for houses up to 10 to 12 feet wide (build yourself) or galvanized steel pipe commercially formed for wider houses up to 36 or 40 feet.

Primarily used with plastic covering which is applied externally. Strong fastening at the ends and edges (and ridge sometimes) is very important. Various types of extruded metal bars with rod inserts and screw-down clamps are available. Wider spans with larger curvatures bendable can be used with the rigid-plastic panels.

Internal layer of plastic is difficult to apply and therefore external double-layer with the air inflation technique is recommended.

Provides clear-span interior with minimum shading but has some side-wall height restriction on tall crops unless higher foundation supports are used. Higher foundations increase significantly the strength required and the potential for wind damage.

Not suited for ridge and furrow designs. Each house should be separate from another.

Usually have to use extra wooden construction for ends, doors, fan-shutter-louver framing, etc. End-wall covering may be the same as rest of structure. Sometimes solid material is used on a north end-wall.

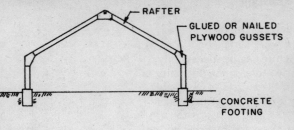

RAFTER

GLUED OR NAILED PLYWOOD GUSSETS

CONCRETE FOOTING

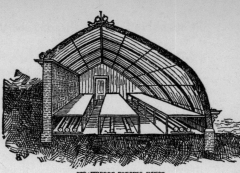

STRAWBERRY FORCING HOUSE.

A Semi-attached Domed Conservatory.

Gothic

Fabricated by bending pipe or laminating wood strips in a gothic shape.

Has pleasing aesthetic appearance.

Construction and covering features similar to quonset above.

Good height near side-walls but has greater exposed-surface-to-ground-area-ratio which allows more heat loss than other designs. Good air circulation is required to prevent air and heat stratification in the gable. The extra volume allows adequate space for mixing ventilation or heated air with the greenhouse air.

Usually built of wood from blueprints. Commercial pre-fab packages are limited in availability.

Post-Rafter

Simplest construction, but requires more wood or metal than some other designs:

Clear-span interior, but limited in width to approximately 20 or 24 feet with wood due to rafter size and strength. Wider houses can be built with steel or aluminum, depending on design.

Wood construction is primarily used with low-cost film plastic coverings.

Requires strong widewall posts and deep post embedment to withstand outward rafter forces and wind pressures.

Smooth interior and exterior for easy covering.

A-Frame

Comparable to the wooden post-rafter construction above except the collar beam strengthens the rafter construction for wider houses but hinders placement of an inner liner.

Rigid-Frame

Provides high strength per unit of wood used and is suitable for self construction with proper materials and blueprints in widths of 10 to 40 feet.

Used in many commercial designs of steel or aluminum structures and especially glass covered houses.

Unobstructed clear-span interior.

Smooth interior and exterior for ease of covering with film or rigid plastic materials for most build-your-own designs.

Excellent strength permits a relatively small number and size of wood or metal members to be used, resulting in minimum shading.

Proper foundation piers or concrete wall required for adequate support of large lateral loads developed with such frames.

Suitable for ridge and furrow type construction.

Post-Truss

Wood trusses not recommended due to excessive shading. Use only steel or aluminum designs having adequate strength and minimum shading.

Clean-span floor area, but truss members obstruct gable space.

Commercial designs available in widths up to 60 feet or more.

Well suited to covering with rigid plastic panels or glass panes, depending on sash bars used. Not often covered with film plastics.

Sidewalls must resist lateral wind loads which require strong posts and adequate embedment, and, normally, concrete back-fill around posts.

Suitable for ridge-and-furrow type construction.

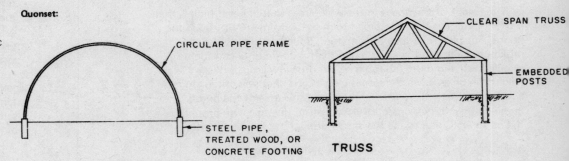

Quonset:

CIRCULAR PIPE FRAME

STEEL PIPE, TREATED WOOD, OR CONCRETE FOOTING

CLEAR SPAN TRUSS

EMBEDDED POSTS

TRUSS

SEED-TESTING GREENHOUSE.

STRUCTURAL MATERIALS

The most common structural materials are wood, galvanzed steel, and aluminum.

Wood

The most commonly used material with home or local contractor-constructed greenhouses is wood. It is also used to a limited extent by some commercial greenhouse manufacturers for the gothic shaped structure and for glass supporting bars. Regardless of where wood is to be used in a greenhouse, the high moisture environment which exists within a greenhouse makes it mandatory that only the most decay resistant wood species or treated lumber be used if reasonably long life is desired. The subject of decay resistance and preservative treatment is covered in detail in another publication in this series.[2]

The most decay resistant species in order of their decay resistance are: 1. Black locust, 2. Osage-orange, 3. Red cedar, 4. Redwood, 5. White oak, and 6. Cypress.

With the exception of the first two listed, none of the untreated wood species are as durable as preservative treated lumber. For greenhouse use, the treatment should be with one of the water-borne salt-type preservatives such as Chromated Copper Arsenate ("Osmose K-33", or "Greensalts"), Ammonical Copper Arsenite ("Chemonite"), or Fluor Chrome Arsenate Phenol ("Tanalith", "Wolman", or "Osmosalts"). When properly treated, such material will last for 20-30 years or more in greenhouse use. (Note: Some of the above treatments are not rated for "ground contact" use.)

When wood is used for the main structural frame, care should be taken to use only high grade wood. Many of the designs are based upon select structural quality, which is the highest grade normally used in construction. Some of the designs further specify that any defects in the lumber be placed out of the high stress areas. With the rigid-frame designs, this high stress area is the stud and rafter closest to the eave joint.

When plywood is used for gussets with trusses or rigid-frames, it would be exterior grade, and one of the faces should be a smooth face at least "C" grade or better. Also, the plywood should be preservative treated for long life comparable to the treated wood. The edges of plywood should be well painted to prevent moisture from entering into the edges and causing delamination.

Glue

Gluing of wooden joints is frequently specified and used because of the superior strength obtained per unit of wood used. Though casein or "white" glue is commonly used for structural gluing, the high moisture condition in greenhouses requires an adhesive highly resistant to moisture. Thus, the casein or "white" glues should never be used for greenhouse construction. The adhesive which has the moisture resistance capabilities desired and which can yet be used under normal conditions is resorcinol resin. This adhesive will cure at temperatures at 70 degrees F or above and is marine-rated for use in "humid" environments. It is a reasonably good gap filler and is tolerant of some minor surface irregularities. This adhesive is actually stronger and more durable than wood. Resorcinol adhesive is not available in all localities; but, due to its exception performance regardless of the exposure condition and its ease of use, no other adhesive should be substituted without an engineer's approval. Tests on the gluing of plywood to treated lumber[5] indicate that adequate joint strength can be obtained with resorcinol adhesive with pentachlorophenol or the salt-type preservative treated lumber if visible oil and preservative crystals are removed by sanding or wire brushing prior to gluing. Step-by-step procedures for glue-nail construction of wooden rigid-frames is available in another publication of this greenhouse series.[3]

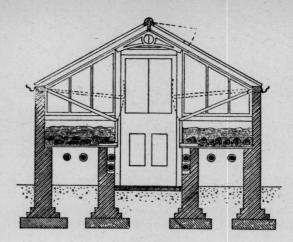

-Section of Propagating Pit

Steel

Steel is commonly used for commercially manufactured houses. Occasionally growers bend steel pipe to form small quonset or gothic shaped houses. The high moisture within a greenhouse can result in excessive rust. All steel should be painted or galvanized. If galvanizing is done, it should preferably be done after all cutting and welding has been performed. Those areas where bare metal is exposed by cutting or welding should be painted. If steel is kept painted, it is a highly durable material and should last indefinitely. Care must be taken when cleaning dirty glass with acid, due to the corrosiveness of the acid on galvanized coatings and paint. Acid should be kept away from the steel as much as possible. After completion of the cleaning, the metal affected should be repainted.

Aluminum

Aluminum is being used more extensively by commercial manufacturers due to its light weight and excellent durability. Aluminum generally requires no maintenance and is very attractive. Its high strength makes it possible to use small roof support members, minimizing shading problems. Aluminum has not yet been used to any extent in owner-fabricated, build-your-own type greenhouses.

COVERINGS

The type of structure used must be compatible with the covering desired. All the quonset and wooden structures can utilize film plastic; some can use corrugated fiberglass. Most all the commercial steel and aluminum designs use fiberglass or glass materials for covering. A separate publication of this greenhouse series discusses the characteristics and selection of various greenhouse coverings in detail.[4]

PLANS FOR GREENHOUSES

Blueprint plans for building your own greenhouse are available from most County Extension Offices or from the Plan Service, Department of Agricultural Engineering, University of Kentucky, Lexington, Kentucky, 40506. Most of the plans are for wooden construction and range in size from small hobby houses to 30 and 40-foot wide rigid-frame designs, or a multiple width ridge-and-furrow design.

Many commercial companies now have pre-fab "packages" for erecting your own quonset or similar type houses. Also, several companies provide complete planning design, sale and erection of greenhouse facilities. These are mostly the larger fiberglass and glass covered educational or commercial type structures.

RANGE OF ORCHARD HOUSES.

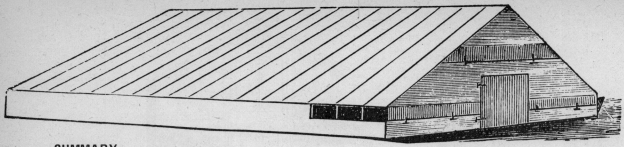

SUMMARY

The type of greenhouse one builds should depend upon its use, location, size, and the grower's preference. The grower should consider both the initial and annual costs. If capital is limited, initial cost is very important. Possibly one of the designs which would permit and initial covering with low cost film but a later covering with a rigid plastic would be preferable. As a general rule, the increased durability of well constructed glass houses and the reduced annual maintenance costs due to the elimination of recovering results in glass greenhouses and many of the plastic greenhouses having comparable annual costs. In determining what type of greenhouse to build, a grower will need to consider these factors:

Initial cost—Is capital limiting or is the long term future unclear?

Annual cost—How much are the actual annual costs which must be borne by the production income?

Insurance—can the house be insured against fire, and is the insurance high? Some of the plastic houses cannot be insured for fire and the poorer plastic house designs cannot be insured for structural failure.

Taxes—Are plastic houses not taxed or taxed at a low rate as temporary structures in the community in which the house is to be built?

Heating costs—the use of a double layer of film can reduce heating costs by 30 to 40%. Double covering reduces light and requires some extra labor for annual or every-other-year installation.

Environmental control—Does the design lend itself to easy installation of heating and ventilating equipment and provide an environment suitable for the crop being grown?

Flexibility—Can the crop being grown be changed if the economic picture changes and can the structure be easily expanded for a larger range?

Structural strength—Is hail a problem in the area in which the house is to be built? Are there other physical hazards or unusual circumstances?

Labor simplification—Does the design permit the use of mechanical equipment? Will it allow future installation of mechanization?

There are not simple, clear-cut answers to the above questions, and the grower must select the type of house he feels will best meet his needs. Still, he should select a sound design which can withstand the wind and snow loads in the area in which the house will be built. The failure of a greenhouse structure can have catastropic consequences, and a poorly-designed house will almost always end up being the most expensive.

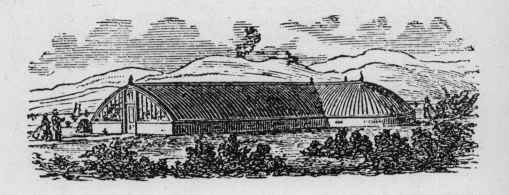

References

[1] American Society of Agricultural Engineering, "Yearbook 1972." American Society of Agricultural Engineering, St. Joseph, Michigan.

[2] Duncan, G. A. and J. N. Walker. 1971. "Preservative Treatment of Greenhouse Wood." Kentucky Cooperative Extension Service, AEN—6, University of Kentucky, Lexington, Kentucky, 40506.

[3] Duncan, G. A. and J. N. Walker. "Rigid-Frame Greenhouse Construction." Kentucky Cooperative Extension Service, AEN—15, University of Kentucky, Lexington, Kentucky, 40506.

[4] Duncan, G. A. and J. N. Walker. "Greenhouse Coverings." Kentucky Cooperative Extension Service, AEN—10, University of Kentucky, Lexington, Kentucky, 40506.

[5] Walker, N. N. 1966. "Gluing of Plywood to Treated Lumber." Transactions of ASAE, 9 (5): 669-670, 674.

[6] Walker, J. N. and E. H. Cox. 1966. "Design of Pier Foundations for Lateral Loads." Transactions of ASAE, 9 (3): 417-420.

[7] Walker, J. N. and G. A. Duncan. 1971. "Greenhouse Location and Orientation." Kentucky Cooperative Extension Service, Misc. 397. University of Kentucky, Lexington, Kentucky, 40506.

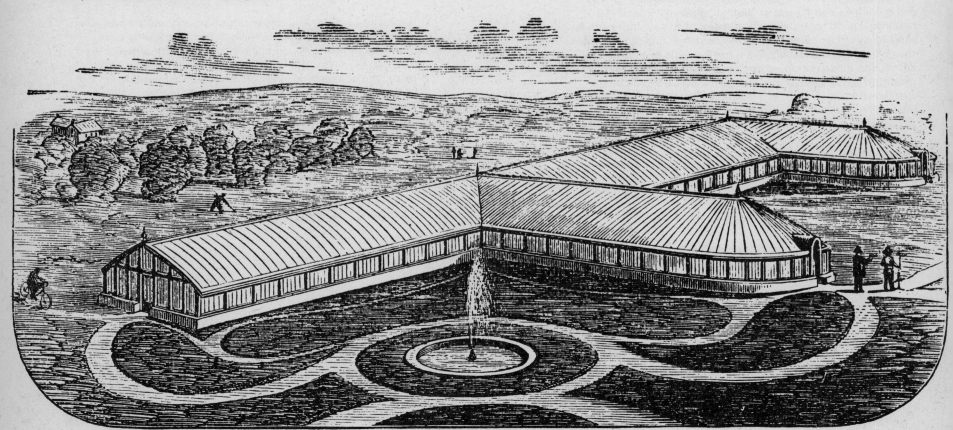

BUYING A GREENHOUSE

By William A. Roberts, P. E.

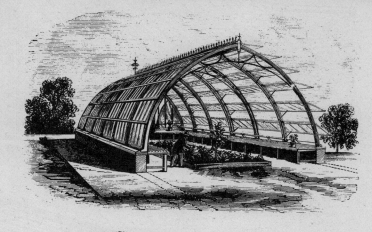

William A. Roberts is chief engineer for Lord & Burnam, a post he has held since 1954. He is a civil engineering graduate of Rennselaer Polytechnic Institute and is a registered professional engineer in six states.

Every greenhouse owner is subject to tremendous risks inherent in the ownership of a glass or plastic-covered structure—complete and competent insurance coverage notwithstanding.

Greenhouses naturally can become the victims of such weather-induced perils as severe wind and sandstorms, tornados, cyclonic thunderstorms—and snow storms plus accumulation of unusual snow loads.

While none of these hazards is necessarily common in their severest form in every locality, a prudent greenhouse owner will want, nevertheless, to be assured that he owns a structure in which design and engineering has taken all such hazards into consideration and is built, therefore, to withstand them.

To overlook the vital factor of good design is to court disaster at a time when one can least afford it.

Even if the worst were to happen and a greenhouse structure were to fail under extreme weather conditions where insurance completely covered the loss, an owner must still think of the adverse effects on the business itself with possible loss of crops as well as the losses sustained in trying to get back into operation.

Yes, it is better to be safe than sorry, and the wisest growers will protect their total business investments and operation by specifying and insisting upon the best possible structure available on the market at the time of purchase.

In some areas of the United States, this past winter proved to be an unusually severe one with snow loads causing considerable damage in some instances.

Could these damages have been avoided?

The answer depends upon the original specifications of the structures involved and whether the construction actually carried out such specifications faithfully. This is a point where a buyer must be wary for his own protection. If he understands construction, then it is suggested that he make a thorough inspection of the new structure before he makes final payments on his contract. Lacking that skill, he would be advised to invite the assistance of an independent professional to be sure that his structure meets fully the specifications originally laid down.

Such construction and design details are often perplexing and uninteresting to a layman. Nevertheless, a greenhouse owner is well advised to acquaint himself with some of the basics of these matters for his own protection and that of his business.

How then can a greenhouse be evaluated in advance to determine the load limits it is capable of holding? And, when buying a greenhouse, what can the purchaser do to guard against a potential failure of the structure at any time in the future as a result of a weather-created peril?

Southern Florist and Nurseryman, April 18, 1969

Pteris serrulata cristata.

DESIGN FOR ORNAMENTAL CONSERVATORY.

Actually, there are a few essential steps that a buyer can take up to reduce such risks to the utmost minimum. The following five considerations are the most critical:

(a) Loading—when considering a particular style or model of greenhouse, have the manufacturer explain what loading the structure is capable of carrying. This factor is usually expressed in pounds per square foot of ground covered.

Armed with this figure, a buyer can determine the suitability of the model in question for his particular locality based upon the recommendations of the National Greenhouse Manufacturers Association as well as those of consulting architects or engineers in that area.

The maximum load imposed upon any greenhouse will probably consist of snow accumulations. If one figures approximately eight pounds per square foot of snow, one can estimate the strength needed in the structure based upon the amount of snow that usually builds up on the greenhouse roof.

(2) Bay spacings—be extremely wary of spacings between trusses that are unusual and non-standard in the industry. Most greenhouse manufacturers employ either 8-feet, 7-3/4 inches, or 10-feet 3-3/4 inches spacings in their designs. These spacings are based upon loads that are representative for given areas.

Where spacings are indicated in excess of these figures, the framework of the structure cannot be the same as for the standard spacings noted above and a strategic reinforcement is required to strengthen the key parts. Lacking such precautions, the allowable loads will, of necessity, be reduced significantly.

In the case of the 10-feet, 3-3/4 inch bays, which consist of five lites of 24-inch glass between trusses, should one extra lite be added making the spacing 12 feet, 4-1/2 inches, the live loading alone is increased 20 per cent. In such instance, if the structural frame is not designed to absorb this increased live load, the allowable load per square foot will be reduced accordingly.

One buying a greenhouse with the large bay spacings should be aware of the potential increase in risk of sub-standard loading capability under severe weather conditions.

(3) Truss-eave plate—greenhouse buyers should be cautioned to pay attention to the type of connection joining the truss to the side post of the eave junction. Be extremely wary of designs which specify castings other than malleable iron to make such structural connections.

Absolute reliability of non-malleable castings is questionable owing to imperfections and flaws in their interior which are not visible to the naked eye. Disastrous results, including complete failure of the greenhouse structure, can occur where an imperfect casting might break up under undue stress.

The safest type of connecting plate used by most manufacturers today is a heavy, extruded aluminum unit whose design has been proved by the test of time since first introduced to the market about 15 years ago.

(4) Sufficient bolting—at junctions or points where components of the greenhouse structure meet, all parts should be attached with a positive connection such as a bolt through or into each part. Where one member merely lies on another and depends upon a notch or slot to hold it in place, there is always the danger of such member moving in the direction of the notch under extra heavy loading. Under such conditions, the two members may separate, resulting in either localized or complete failure.

(5) Pioneering can be costly—it cannot be reiterated too strongly that a grower should positively know what he is buying. Human nature being what it is, for instance, it is understandable that most children—given the chance—will jump at the opportunity of being the first in their neighborhood with a new toy.

Sometimes these new toys turn out to be very exciting and perform wonderfully well, but if this attitude of being first is "your thing," then you must also be ready for some rough disappointments.

This advice applies directly to greenhouses, particularly with reference to the latest design gimmick that may hit the market. A far safer approach to greenhouse buying is to examine other houses in the general region and discuss their performance under adverse conditions with their owners.

In this manner, it is possible to learn what type of greenhouse holds up best in one's own locality. If, after all this reconnoitering and checking, you still feel that something new and untried is the thing you want, you should still seek the advice and assistance of experienced greenhouse designers who can try to merge your desires and ideas with their experience gained from other installations in the past.

One final words of advice. The NGM has formulated and established minimum standards and criteria of greenhouse construction to which all members are committed and which were specifically intended for the protection of growers and greenhouse buyers all over America.

These standards include recommendations for proper wind and snow loadings depending upon the various geographical localities throughout the United States, ventilation and cooling and minimum heat loss criteria.

Thus, a grower is assured of getting a quality greenhouse design when he purchases a house from any member of the association. In dealing with any member of the association, he will be gaining full advantage of these standards and will be providing himself with the best kind of greenhouse design insurance.

-LEAN-TO HOUSE.

SECTION OF IMPROVED LEAN-TO ORCHARD HOUSE.

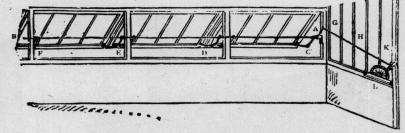

-LEVER TACKLE APPLIED TO FRONT LIGHTS OR SIDE LIGHTS OF HOUSE.

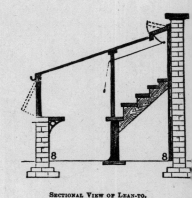

SECTIONAL VIEW OF LEAN-TO.

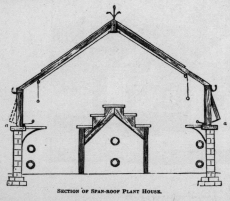

SECTION OF SPAN-ROOF PLANT HOUSE.

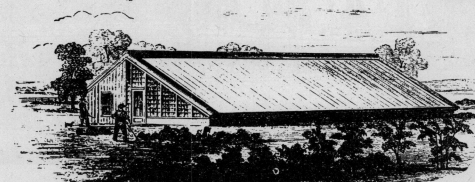

HELPFUL HINTS

Location The most important consideration in selecting a site for your greenhouse is the availability of light from November through February. The sun is at its lowest and weakest point during these months and your greenhouse should receive at least three to four hours of sunlight daily. A free-standing model can be placed in any direction that blends well with its surroundings—your yard and home. Lean-to or attached greenhouses should have a southern, southeastern or southwestern exposure—in that order. Other considerations are accessability and the availability of water and power.

Heating A good guide as to what type of fuel you should use is that which is in adequate supply at a reasonable price. Check local sources of natural and bottled gas, fuel oil and electricity for rates and a cost estimate of a winter heating season.

To determine the B.T.U. requirements of your Turner Greenhouse you must first determine the degree differential—the difference in degrees between the temperature you wish to maintain inside the greenhouse and the lowest expected outside temperature—then multiply the degree differential and the B.T.U. factor which is listed with each model in the catalog.

Example: You intend to purchase a Turner Model 1418 and you want to maintain an inside temperature of 60 degrees. You expect a low outside temperature of 10 degrees. Therefore, you have a differential of 5. Multiply 5 x 7,200 (B.T.U. factor for Model 1418) = 36,000 B.T.U. requirement.

If you cannot find a heater with the exact B.T.U. capacity, choose one with a greater rating. You will have a safety margin and it may provide the extra heat needed should you decide to enlarge your greenhouse.

Greenhouse floor and base Perhaps the best and least expensive floor is dirt covered with gravel or rock which will hold humidity and help prevent 'drying-out'. Flagstone, brick or patio blocks can be used in the aisles.

Turner Greenhouses require no expensive masonry or concrete walls. A simple concrete footing or mudsill is all that is required. Do not build your base until plans have been received from Turner Greenhouses.

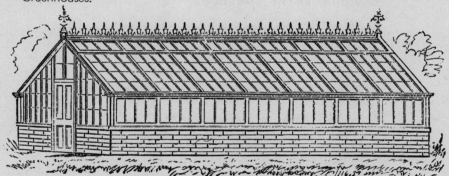

Ventilation Proper ventilation in a greenhouse is critical for several reasons: to control temperatures; to permit an intake of fresh air; and to aid in controlling humidity. Ridge ventilators are widely used and can be automatically controlled. Automatic fans are becoming increasingly popular and are easily adapted to Turner Greenhouses. Our system employs a shutter-mounted exhaust fan in one end of the greenhouse and a motorized inlet shutter in the other. Both components are controlled by a common thermostat. On a temperature rise the thermostat activates the fan and inlet shutter, expelling stale air and drawing in fresh air. Another feature of the system is ventilating in very cold weather. The fan can be unplugged and only the inlet shutter will open which will prevent a rush of cold air into the greenhouse.

Automatic exhaust fans or ridge ventilators are not capable of cooling your greenhouse during summer months, therefore other devices must be used. The most effective device is an evaporative cooler or a cooling pad/fan system. Water is circulated through a fiber pad. As air is pulled into the greenhouse through the pad, it is cooled. Cooling pads are not adaptable to Turner Greenhouses but evaporative coolers are. We shall be happy to assist you in the selection of a cooler for your greenhouse.

Humidity The amount of moisture in the air plays an important role in the growth of plants. The variety of plants in the greenhouse will determine the correct level of humidity—probably between 50 and 70%. A hygrometer within the greenhouse will give you the exact reading at all times. The introduction of humidity or moisture will also have a cooling effect.

Simple methods of raising humidity are 'wetting-down' floors and benches or syringing the foliage of plants. Automatic humidifiers controlled by a humidistat can be set at the desired level and the moisture will be restored as needed.

TURNER GREENHOUSE

P.O. BOX 1260
Highway 117 South
Goldsboro, N.C. 27530

Shading There are numerous means and devices to shade your greenhouse. Shading compounds are usually inexpensive but more time and effort is required. Slats of aluminum, redwood and bamboo are available. We have found saran covers to be excellent for many reasons. It is a lightweight material easily installed and removed and it will not rot, rust or mildew. We offer a standard medium shade of 63%. Other shades, lighter or darker, are available upon request. Turner Greenhouses has saran covers in stock that are proven performers.

Maintenance Neglecting your greenhouse can be expensive in terms of replacing equipment and plants. A clean greenhouse reduces the threat of diseases and pests. Cuttings, leaves and other debris should be removed from the benches and the floor. During winter months the surface of the greenhouse should be clean to allow maximum light penetration. Always immediately repair or mend breaks or tears in the covering. Follow the manufacturers' suggested policies for care and maintenance, periodically check all equipment; heaters, fans, vent apparatus and control. Check wiring for wear and outlets for proper service.

If you are interested in an item not illustrated in our catalog, please contact our office. We offer additional greenhouse equipment and supplies and would be most happy to help you in your selection of same.

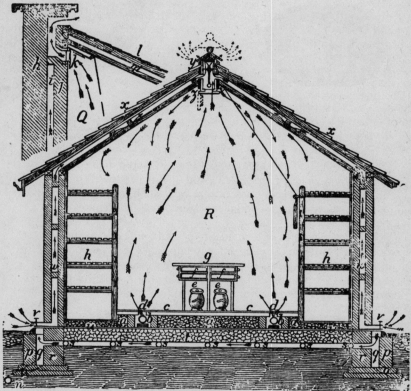

FRUIT ROOM SHOWN IN SECTION.

References: Q, part section of lean-to against north wall, showing insulation of fruit room and top ventilation; h, north wall; i, 4½-in. air cavity; j, 9-in. wall built in cement; k, ventilator—arrow showing direction of air; l, roof, double ceiled; m, air cavity in roof. R, section through ground plan; n, land drains; o, rubble drains taking water from outside area; p, 9-in. earth retaining wall; q, outside air cavity; r, 14-in. solid wall; s, 3-in. air-drains; t, rubble; u, damp course; v, 2-in. iron pipe with valve; w, hollow wall, showing projecting bricks across cavity—arrows indicate air entering 2-in. pipe, ascent of cavity and exit by roof ventilator; x, roof, showing projecting eaves, guttering, double ceiling and air cavity; y, cover of ventilator closed —dotted outline raised; z, inside shutter closed—dotted outline shows it open with pulley, line and weight attached; a, concrete; b, 4-in. hot-water pipe; c, path, ornamental tiles laid in cement; d, heated flue grating; e, closet for jars; f, drawers for choice fruit; g, table top. Arrows indicate direction of air when expelling damp; h, fruit shelves.

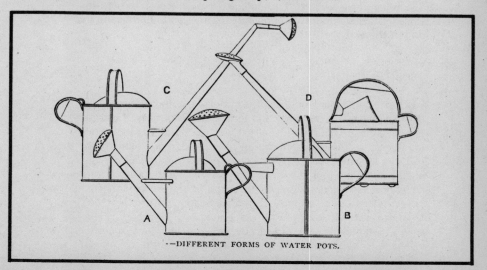

--DIFFERENT FORMS OF WATER POTS.

GREENHOUSE VEGETABLE PRODUCTION

The author is Hunter Johnson, Jr., Extension Vegetable Specialist, Riverside.

AGRICULTURAL EXTENSION

UNIVERSITY OF CALIFORNIA

Producing greenhouse-grown vegetables can be profitable, but it is a difficult and complex enterprise. To be successful, you must carefully plan and execute both culture and marketing. You should aim for high yields of consistently top quality produce. This requires good management practices as well as the technical knowledge necessary to grow good plants. Almost all failures are due to poor management.

While good yields of high quality produce are basic to success, good marketing practices are equally important. Even though quality fruits or vegetables usually sell easily, do not leave the marketing to chance. For maximum returns, develop your marketing plans and arrangements before harvest.

LOCATION

An ideal location for a greenhouse is where the light intensity is high, winter air temperatures are moderate, and atmospheric humidity is low. While such locations are difficult to find, they provide the best environment for crop growth and minimize the fuel and power costs for cooling and heating the greenhouse.

High desert areas provide excellent light intensity, but the winters are cold and the summers hot. Low desert areas are hot in the summer with frequent periods of high humidity, but the winters are mild. Coastal areas have mild winter temperatures, but the humidity is often high and the light intensity reduced by overcast skies or fog. Some locations are also subject to long periods of winter fogs and overcast. Avoid metropolitan areas because of air pollution.

Construct greenhouses on level, well-drained soil. Sandy loam soils 4 to 5 feet deep are best if you plan to grow the crop in field soil. Locate the greenhouse far enough from trees and buildings so they do not shade it.

CONSTRUCTION

When designing a greenhouse, it is important to provide maximum light and adequate humidity and temperature controls. Clear polyethylene plastic sheeting (usually 4 mils thick) is a practical covering for wood-frame greenhouses in terms of cost and light transmission. However, polyethylene deteriorates due to weathering and sunlight and must be replaced every year. Various other plastic coverings, such as polyvinyl chloride and fiberglass, last longer than polyethylene but cost more. To reduce heating costs in very cold locations, use two layers of film separated by a 1½ to 2-inch air space. Metal-frame greenhouses covered with fiberglass or glass are available for more permanent installations, but these cost considerably more than do wood-frame greenhouses.

ENVIRONMENTAL CONTROL

Humidity control is important for preventing fungus diseases of plant foliage. Keep the humidity below 85 percent by using a combination of heat, fans, and ventilation. Temperature control is important for plant growth and fruit set. Maintain optimum temperatures to obtain the best growth and yield. Suggested temperatures for various crops are as follows.

Tomatoes: day 75 degrees to 80 degrees F.; night, not below 60 degrees F. High daytime temperatures (85 degrees to 90 degrees F. and above) can cause fruit set failure and prevent red color development in the maturing fruit.

Cucumbers: day, 80 degrees to 85 degrees F.; night, 65 degrees to 70 degrees F. Lower temperatures delay plant growth and fruit development.

Lettuce: day, 65 degrees to 70 degrees F.; night, 50 degrees to 55 degrees F. Higher temperatures induce seed stalks in some varieties.

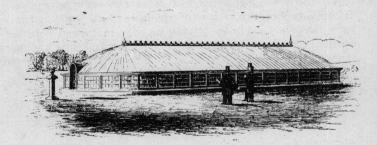

WHAT TO GROW

Tomatoes are the most commonly grown crop. Yields depend on the length of the harvest period. In general, you can expect 6 to 10 pounds of fruit per plant during a 2- to 3-month fall harvest period; 15 to 18 pounds of fruit per plant from spring crops harvested over a 4- to 5-month period. High average yields require a combination of experience, knowledge, and good management. Varieties frequently grown are Tropic, Michigan-Ohio Hybrid, Floradel, and Manapal.

Cucumbers can also be a successful greenhouse crop. They grow more rapidly than tomatoes, produce earlier, and yield more fruit per plant. European, Holland, or forcing varieties are recommended because they are seedless, have better flavor, and require no bees for pollination. Good management can lead to yields of 20 to 30 pounds of fruit per plant during a 3- to 4-month harvest period. Many varieties are available, but Toska 70 and Fertila are very widely grown.

Lettuce is an important eastern greenhouse crop. In the west, however, field-grown lettuce competes heavily, making the greenhouse product more difficult to market. Butterhead and loose-leaf varieties need less time to mature and so are the best choices.

Try other crops, such as beans, peppers, or eggplant, on a very limited scale until you know the crop's greenhouse adaptability and the extent of the market.

Both Florida and Mexico produce large quantities of field-grown vegetables during the winter. Greenhouse growers in the western United States should consider this because you can only realize premium prices on a well-supplied market if the greenhouse produce is of superior quality.

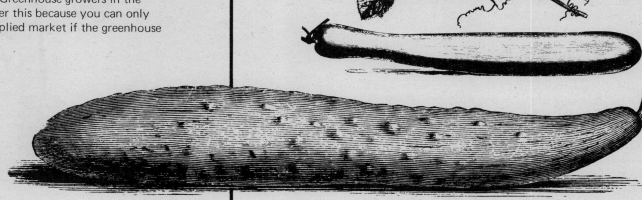

CULTURE

Space greenhouse tomatoes to allow 3 to 4 square feet per plant. Train the plants to single stems supported by strings hanging from overhead wires. You can also train cucumbers to single stems, using a spacing of 3 square feet per plant. If you train plants by the lateral branching system, you should use a wider spacing—6 to 8 square feet per plant.

Use furrow irrigation or drip irrigation systems if you grow plants in soil beds. Sprinklers are less practical because of structural and plant interference and because wet foliage increases disease problems.

Fertilization programs vary with the crop, the soil, and the type of cultural system used, but it is essential to supply the plant's nutritional needs. A plant tissue and soil analysis program helps avoid both excesses and deficiencies. Beware of indiscriminate insurance-type fertilization programs. Consult your local farm advisor for assistance in planning your fertilizer program.

SOILLESS CULTURE

Gravel, sand, or artificial soil mixes are often used for greenhouse vegetable production. While soilless systems cost more because of the additional equipment and materials involved, they are practical if native soils have poor structure or drainage or contain soil-borne diseases. However, soilless culture offers no special advantage in yield or quality over a good, pathogen-free agricultural soil.

DISEASE AND INSECT PROBLEMS

Without proper control, plant diseases and insect pests can severely damage or ruin your crop. Fungicides and insecticides are often required, but it is essential to use them with caution and only on the recommendation of a competent authority.

FINAL WORD

Large-scale greenhouse vegetable production is costly and exacting and only those with suitable knowledge should try it. You can acquire experience at a minimum expense by beginning on a small scale, by discussions with your farm advisor and successful growers, and by studying all available publications on the subject.

IN-DOOR CONSERVATORY AGAINST A WINDOW.

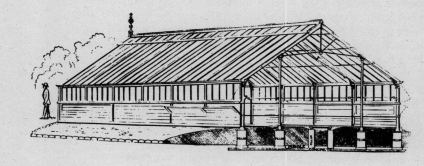

GREENHOUSE CUCUMBER PRODUCTION

By Hunter Johnson, Jr., Extension Vegetable Specialist, Riverside, California

The cucumber varieties grown in European greenhouses are different in both appearance and flavor from the field-grown salad cucumbers familiar to most American consumers. European greenhouse cucumbers (also known as Holland, or forcing) are typically elongated, straight to slightly curved, and somewhat ribbed. They are dark-green and seedless with a thin tender skin that doesn't require peeling. The fruits usually weight about 1 pound and are 12 to 16 inches long. They have a milk flavor without any bitterness. The unique appearance and excellent quality of this cucumber make it especially suitable for production in certain greenhouses.

CULTURAL PRACTICES

Greenhouse cucumbers grow rapidly under optimum environmental conditions, with fruit production beginning 60 to 70 days after seeding. Temperatures ranging from 80 degrees to 85 degrees F. are desirable during the day. While peak daytime temperatures of 90 degrees to 95 degrees F. are tolerable, prolonged periods of high temperatures may affect fruit quality. At night, maintain temperatures no lower than 65 degrees F.; temperatures in the 50 degree to 60 degree F. range will slow growth considerably.

You can successfully grow cucumbers in either soil beds or artificial growing media as long as you use suitable management techniques. Soils for cucumber production should be well drained, low in soluble salts, and free of plant pathogens. Light sandy soils are preferable.

If greenhouse soils do not meet these criteria and cannot be improved, there are several artificial rooting media that have proven successful. These are peat-lite (a mixture of sphagnum peat and horticultural vermiculite), straw bales (usually wheat straw), sand culture, or gravel hydroponics. While it is more expensive to grow crops in any artificial media than in soil, this method should be considered as an economically sound alternative when native soils are unsuitable.

There are two types of European greenhouse cucumber varieties with respect to flowering characteristics. The monoecious type has both male and female flowers; the gynoecious type has only female flowers. Gynoecious varities differ in their degree of femaleness, which is both genetically and environmentally controlled. Low light intensity plays an important part in the appearance of male flowers on some "female" varieties. Plant growth and fruit appearance are similar in both monoecious and gynoecious types, and all fruit develops parthenocarpically (without the need of pollination).

It is not desirable to pollinate European greenhouse cucumber varieties because the resulting seed development causes fruit distortion, which reduces quality and market appearance. With the monoecious varieties, remove the male blossoms before they open to prevent chance pollination. With both types, screen all vents and doors to exclude bees that may be carrying pollen from outside plantings.

Gynoecious varieties are preferred because yields are generally better and there is no need to remove male blossoms. Some good gynoecious varieties used successfully are Fertila, Factum, Femfrance, Femspot, and Toska 70.

Since seed is expensive, always grow the crop from transplants. Grow the transplants in 3- or 4-inch pots. Smaller containers do not allow enough space to avoid crowding. Peat-lite is the recommended growing medium, but a mixture of peat and sand or a light sandy loam may also grow good plants. Fertilizers for the potting soil are described in the publication on peat-lite, or in U.C. Type Soil Mixes for Container-Grown Plants.

Plant the seeds 1/2 to 3/4 inch deep using one seed per pot. This is less expensive than planting extra seed and thinning. Thoroughly irrigate the pots and then cover them with a thin sheet of clear polyethylene plastic to maintain moisture for germination. Keep the greenhouse temperature between 70 degrees to 85 degrees F. Remove the sheet of plastic as soon as the first seedlings begin to emerge. Irrigate tne pots frequently enough to keep the soil moist but not tco wet. Set the transplants in the greenhouse beds about 3 weeks after seeding, or when two true leaves have fully developed.

It is standard to grow greenhouse cucumbers in single rows, allowing 6 to 8 square feet per plant. You can do this if you have 4-foot-wide aisleways and 1½ to 2 feet between plants in the row. The effects of closer spacing are being investigated and, to date, a spacing of 5 square feet per plant has not reduced yields or fruit size under high light conditions.

Support cucumber plants by tying them to strings that are suspended from a horizontal wire. Attach the wire to the top of the wall at each end of the house and run it in the direction of the plant row. Place the wire about 6½ to 7 feet high so that you can easily reach the tops of the plants from the ground. Use heavy sisal or polyethylene twine for the supporting string. Loosely attach the supporting string around the main stem at the base of the plant with a nonslip knot. Do this a week or so after transplanting when vertical growth is beginning. As the plants grow, loosely wind the main stems around the string, or attach the stems to it with special plastic clips. Do this frequently enough to prevent any sagging or stem bending.

FRUITING MELONS ON LATERALS ON THE EXTENSION SYSTEM.
References: *i*, fruit set; *j*, fruit not set; *k*, flower after fertilisation; *l*, point of stopping if space is limited; *m*, point of stopping where space admits of extension.

You can use various pruning and trimming systems to avoid excessive growth and maintain fruit production. On gynoecious types, female flowers and lateral branches are produced in every leaf axil throughout the plant. The goal of pruning is to leave the maximum amount of leaf surface and developing fruit that the plant can support, but not so much that it interferes with air circulation or seriously reduces the supply of light. A basic practice in all pruning systems is to remove all lateral branches and main stem fruit from the first several (five to seven) leaf nodes. If not removed, the fruit on these lower nodes will touch the bed surface during development and become second-grade fruit due to curvature, or unmarketable due to decay at the tip.

You can use various systems for pruning the rest of the plant. In one common system, the next five laterals are stopped at one leaf (and one fruit). Subsequent laterals may be stopped at two leaves, but allow the top two or three laterals (near the overhead support wire) to grow. Train the laterals across the aisleway, along the horizontal wire, or allow them to hang down over the wire. Remove main stem fruit up to 4 feet to force lateral fruit development.

If left unpruned, main stem fruit always mature considerably earlier than the fruit on the lateral branches. For this reason, it may be possible to obtain high yields from more dense stands of plants pruned to a single main stem. This system is currently being investigated, but growers may wish to test the idea in their own greenhouses.

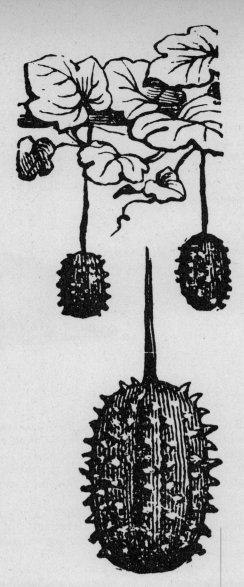

WEST INDIAN GHERKIN OR BURR CUCUMBER.

Greenhouse cucumbers are fast-growing plants; never allow them to suffer from lack of water or nutrients. If grown in soil beds, apply all the phosphorus and potassium needed and a small amount of nitrogen before planting. You can use animal manure to supply part of the nutrients and some organic matter. Mix the fertilizer thoroughly into the top few inches of soil. Reasonable amounts of pre-plant fertilizer to apply per acre are: 100 pounds of phosphorus, 50 pounds of potassium, and 50 pounds of nitrogen. You can also apply zinc at 10 to 20 pounds per acre, but this and other minor elements are usually adequately supplied by field soils. Feed the crop with nitrogen in the irrigation water in small increments of 15 to 30 pounds per acre per week.

If growing cucumbers in peat-lite, follow the directions in the peat-lite publication, and supplement this with nitrogen at 15 to 30 pounds per acre per week in the irrigation water. If grown by gravel hydroponics or sand culture, feed four to six times daily with a complete nutrient solution.

Slight fruit curvature can be tolerated in first-grade fruit, but excessive curving or crooking affects market appearance and reduces market value. Curvature in the fruit begins at or shortly after blossoming and is caused by the expansion of the young fruit against a nearby leaf, petiole, or stem. Occasionally, severe curvature develops when a flower petal becomes stuck on the spines of the young ovary. You can reduce the fruit cuvature problem by moving leaves or petioles that are in the path of developing fruit, and by pruning lateral branches while they are short.

Harvest the fruit after it has reached sufficient size, but before any yellowing begins at the blossom end. Fruit of proper market size weigh about 3/4 to 1 pound and are 12 to 16 inches long, the dimensions differing with the variety. You can expect 25 to 35 fruits per plant in a 90- to 120-day harvest period with proper environment and management.

After harvest, the thin-skinned fruit is highly susceptible to softening through moisture loss. As soon as possible after harvest, package greenhouse cucumbers and place them under conditions that will prolong the storage life. If packaging and storage must be temporarily delayed, keep the fruit in covered containers away from direct sunlight. To prevent moisture loss and maintain quality, package the fruits individually in shrink-wrap plastic sleeves. The best storage conditions are at 55 degrees F. and a high relative humidity (90 to 95 percent). Maintain the temperature at 55 degrees F. or above to prevent chilling injury.

DISEASE AND INSECT PESTS

Virus diseases (cucumber mosaic and watermelon mosaic) can create serious problems in greenhouse cucumber production. None of the varieties presently available are resistant to these diseases. Since mosaic viruses are carried and transmitted by aphids from host plants (other susceptible crops and weeds) outside the greenhouse, the physical barrier of the greenhouse structure offers some assistance in preventing entry of aphids and other insects, if the vents are adequately screened.

Powdery mildew is more prevalent and currently a greater hazard than virus diseases. Present varieties of greenhouse cucumbers have no resistance to this disease. If you do not control powdery mildew, it can seriously affect plant growth and fruit quality.

Gray mold (Botrytis cinerea) can be a serious problem if the humidity is not properly controlled. Fortunately, you can completely prevent this disease by providing adequate air circulation and a greenhouse climate to prevent the collection of condensed moisture on plant surfaces.

White fly, serpentine leaf miner, and two-spotted mites are three insects that are known to be very damaging to cucumbers. Control measures for these and other insect pests are being investigated, but at present no specific recommendations can be made.

Insecticides and fungicides labeled for use on field-grown cucumbers are not necessarily safe to use in the greenhouse. Those who choose to try these materials should be cautious. Efforts are being made to clear materials for greenhouse pest control, but no published recommendations are available at this time.

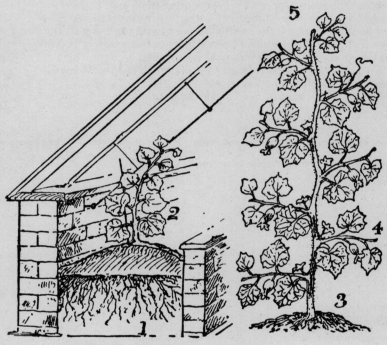

Stopping and Training Melons

1. Hotbed. 2. Plant reaching trellis. 3. A cordon-trained plant. 4. Side shoots stopped. 5. Main stem stopped.

REFERENCES

1. Matkin, O.A. and Philip A. Chandler. 1957. U.C. TYPE SOIL MIXES FOR CONTAINER-GROWN PLANTS. Berkeley: U.C. Agricultural Experiment Station, Leaflet 89.
2. Johnson, Hunter, Jr. 1971. PEAT-LITE: AN ARTIFICIAL SOIL MIX. Riverside: U.C. Agricultural Extension (mimeo).
3. Johnson, Hunter, Jr. 1971. STRAW BALE CULTURE OF GREENHOUSE VEGETABLES. Riverside: U.C. Agricultural Extension (mimeo).
4. Johnson, Hunter, Jr. 1971. USEFUL REFERENCES FOR GREENHOUSE VEGETABLE PRODUCTION. Riverside: U.C. Agricultural Extension (mimeo).
5. Jensen, Merle H. 1971. THE HOUSE OF POLYETHYLENE BARRIERS BETWEEN SOIL AND GROWING MEDIUM IN GREENHOUSE VEGETABLE PRODUCTION. (Sand culture). Proceedings, Tenth National Agricultural Plastics Conference, November 1971.
6. Loughton, Arthur. 1971. GROWING LONG SEEDLESS CUCUMBERS IN PLANT-RAISING GREENHOUSES. Toronto: Ontario Department of Agriculture and Food, Parliament Buildings, Canada, July 1971.
7. Berry, Wade L. and Hunter Johnson, Jr. 1971. PREPARATION METHOD FOR NUTRIENT SOLUTION. Riverside: U.C. Agricultural Extension (mimeo).
8. 1972 GREENHOUSE VEGETABLE PRODUCTION RECOMMENDATIONS. Publication 365. Toronto: Ontario Department of Agriculture and Food, Parliament Buildings, Canada.

RING CULTURE

By Raymond Sheldrake, Jr. and Stewart Dallyn, Dept. of Vegetable Crops, Cornell University, Ithaca, New York

INTRODUCTION

Tomatoes are normally produced in soil which serves as the floor of the greenhouse. This soil is highly modified with organic matter to improve its physical structure. Also, it is a well known fact that sterilization of this soil is essential at least once a year and steam has been the best method with chemicals providing a poor second. Actually, ground beds can never be completely decontaminated.

In recent years, many have wanted to produce the so-called "hothouse" tomato and for one reason or another have found the handling of particular soils troublesome or they were not equipped to perform a satisfactory job of sterilization. Many soils have poor drainage characteristics or are thoroughly infested with pathogenic organisms and new growers particularly experience serious problems.

It is for these reasons that the authors explored the possibilities of other types of culture beginning about six years ago. The methods reported herein have particular merit and many growers have found them useful.

What is Ring Culture?

Ring culture is a system of growing tomatoes developed originally in England in which the tomato plant is set into a round (8-10 inch diameter) ring of plastic film or tar paper. The rings have no top or bottom, and are spaced out on a bed of lightweight aggregate 4-6 inches deep.

What is Trough Culture?

Trough Culture is a system of growing tomatoes in a long, narrow, plastic lined bed containing an artificial lightweight media. It is very similar to ring culture but without the use of the rings. In both cases, the trough must be impermeable to roots.

Why Ring or Trough Culture?

The most common cause of poor yield of greenhouse tomatoes is the presence of soil-borne, disease-producing organisms (Fusarium sp., Verticillium sp., nematodes, etc.) In most commercial greenhouses, soils are disinfested by steaming, but many new growers do not have the equipment for steam sterilization and it is practically impossible to completely decontaminate soils throughout the entire root zone. The authors, therefore, have attempted to utilize and modify the

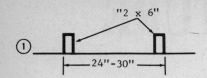

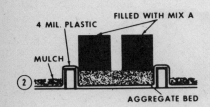

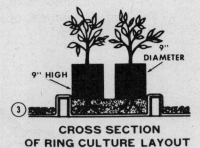

CROSS SECTION
OF RING CULTURE LAYOUT

original English technique of ring culture to produce a method whereby excellent yields of tomatoes can be produced in glass or plastic greenhouses without the need of sterilization. Basically, the technique employed is to install a barrier of plastic sheeting under the troughs containing the rooting aggregate which prevents the roots from penetrating into the infested soil beneath. It has also been demonstrated in our work during recent years that Tomato Mosaic Virus (TMV) is present in greenhouse soil and even steaming does not go deep enough to deactivate the virus. Work in England has shown that chemical fumigants actually increase the incidence of infection with TMV.

For several years, experiments have been carried on with ring culture. Since this technique was successful the authors attempted to find out if the rings were necessary. Various experiments have been conducted in England and Europe and especially on the Isle of Guernsey and these "newer ideas" appear to have merit; especially for smaller growers in the U.S.A. The basic difference between "ring" and "trough" culture is that in the trough method, the plants are simply set in a long, narrow trough filled with a growing medium.

Both methods have worked satisfactorily and the difference in yield has generally been slightly in favor of ring culture, but either will work and produce a good crop. In very early plantings during the cold and cloudy periods of February and March, the ring culture seems to have quite an advantage in that the growing medium in the rings is able to warm up much more readily and the plants do begin growth faster due to the higher temperature around the roots. Also, the taller "soil" column will provide for better root aeration.

The How of Ring Culture and Trough Culture

Step 1. - Prepare the house.

Clean everything out of the house and smooth the floor area. A slight slope or grade from one end of the trough to the other was originally suggested. However, it now seems more practical to use a level area and cut a few drainage holes in the edge of the plastic of the trough.

Step 2. - Plan the bed layout.

Efficiency of production is important in realizing a profit from tomatoes. The rows may run lengthwise of the house or across the width.

The inside of the trough for two rows of tomatoes should be 24-32 inches in width. A wider trough will give more rooting area. Probably the best way to determine the width of the trough is to allow 30-36 inch aisles for walking and divide the rest of the area into troughs. This does not mean that the plants will be set to the edge of the trough which would certainly crowd the worker in the aisle. The plants should be set 6-8 inches from the edge of the trough giving at least 4-5 feet been plants across the aisle. Narrower troughs can be used to accomodate single row culture.

The plants in a twin row set-up should be 18-20 inches apart in each row and the rows should be about 12 inches apart depending upon the trough width. In a single row trough system the troughs should be 15-18 inches wide but it does seem more economical to use the twin row system. In a single row system the plants are set 12-14 inches apart in a straight line.

Tomato plants require about 4 square feet per plant for proper development and management. Therefore, on an acre basis, approximately 10,500 plants would be needed. Closer spacing increases disease problems and reduces fruit size.

Step 3. - Building the Troughs or Aggregate Beds.

With 2 by 6 inch lumber or rough 1 by 6 lumber standing on edge it is a fairly simple task to construct the bed with parallel sides. The lumber is butted together. The butt joints are tied together by nailing on a piece of 1 by 6 lumber about 24 inches long. To maintain the parallel sides, another piece of 1" by 4" wood as wide as the bed can be nailed to the bottom sides of the bed about every 10 feet or pipe stakes can be driven into the ground to hold the sides parallel.

In earlier work with ring culture, beds have been constructed with 2 by 4 lumber and after these beds are filled and the rings are set on top of them sufficient material is available for rooting. At this writing, it does seem more practical to use 6 inch wide lumber and end up with a 6 inch deep bed for either system.

Step 4. - Line beds with plastic film.

The inside of the aggregate bed is lined with 2 or 4 mil plastic. The film should extend up and over the side boards and into the aisle for 6 inches or more. This film could be any color and some advantage has been reported in using a snow white film which would reflect light to the undersides of the plants.

The beds cannot be left in a watertight condition. Some drainage is necessary. On short beds (up to 30 feet), drainage may be from the ends. However, on longer beds, holes should be cut in the plastic on the side wall about 1-2 inches from the bottom. One inch holes every 10 feet on each side should be adequate.

Some growers have utilized 1 or 2 inches of peanut hulls, shredded sugar-cane, or straw, applied to the aisles to facilitate walking and for absorption of any excess moisture. This organic material will also supply carbon dioxide to plants. It is the authors' opinion that this technique is questionable and should only be used in cases where the aisles are muddy. Bringing in organic material of this nature can be a source of many fungi and often insects and nematodes can be brought in. Some of the best operations have been set up on concrete floors. Wide sheets of polyethylene can be used to line the floor of the greenhouse before the troughs are put in. This will give wall to wall ground coverage and provide absolute weed control. This will also reduce evaporation from the soil and thus reduce the absolute humidity within the greenhouse which will make relative humidity easier to regulate. Holes for drainage can be punched in the middle of the aisles.

Step 5. - Fill the bed.

The plastic lined bed is now ready for filling. A lightweight and sterile material has obvious advantages. In the earlier work with ring culture two different media were used: one for the trough and one for the rings. Many organic type growing media could be used and whether ring culture or trough culture is used it seems feasible at this time to recommend that the same material be used in the troughs as in the rings. If the rings are not used the plants are simply planted right in the mix that is used to fill the troughs. The best mixture to date has been Cornell Peatlite Mix which is a 50-50 mixture of sphagnum peat moss and vermiculite.

Two variations of the formula for the Cornell Peatlite Mix are given below in order of preference.

For one cubic yard of mix for tomato production:

Two variations of the formula for the Cornell Peatlite Mix are given below in order of preference.

For one cubic yard of mix for tomato production:

Mix I

Shredded sphagnum peat moss	11 bushels
Horticultural Vermiculite	11 bushels
Limestone	10 pounds
Superphosphate (20 percent)	2 pounds
Calcium or Potassium Nitrate	1½ pounds
Iron (Chelated) such as NaFe, 138, or 330	1 ounce (about 2 level tablespoonfuls)
Borax	½ ounce (tablespoonful)

Mix II

Shredded sphagnum peat moss	11 bushels
Horticultural Vermiculite	11 bushels
Limestone	10 pounds
5-10-10 premium grade fertilizer*	6 pounds
Iron (Chelated) such as NaFe, 138, or 330	1 ounce (about 2 level tablespoonfuls)

* Other similar analyses could be used. Premium grade is suggested because such grades contain minor elements (especially boron). If premium grade is not available use 1 tablespoon of Borax per cubic yard. Fritted Trace Elements (FTE 503 or 504) can be used in place of the Boron at 2 ounces per cubic yard.

The plastic-lined troughs should be filled level with the Mix. It is desirable when making this Mix to add some water while mixing and this will facilitate future wetting at the time of planting.

Step 6. - Prepare rings.

If ring culture will be used, one of the simplest ways to prepare rings is to cut 9-inch lengths from "layflat" polyethylene tubing of 2 or 4 mil thickness (a mil is .001 inch). If tubing of 14-inch "layflat" width is used, a 9-inch diameter ring will be produced when opened. This tubing can be either clear or black. The advantage of using polyethylene tubing on early-set tomatoes is the fact that this 9-inch column of Mix which extends above the trough will warm up much easier than the trough and early root growth is stimulated. Also, rolled roofing paper (about 40 pound grade and usually 36 inch width) can be cut into 9-inch strips and formed around a cylinder such as a stovepipe and the edges of the paper stapled to form the ring.

Step 7. - Filling the rings.

Since the major purpose of ring culture or trough culture is to produce tomatoes without the hazard of soil-borne organisms, it is imperative to use extreme care in preparing the growing medium. The Cornell Mix mentioned above should be mixed in a clean mixer or on a thoroughly clean concrete or black-top area. The area or mixer can be thoroughly washed and can be disinfected with a simple solution of 1 part of Clorox and 10 parts of water. Care should be taken that all tools and equipment are clean and that the Mix is not contaminated. When using Cornell Peatlite Mix it is not necessary to sterilize it. Neither the sphagnum peat moss nor the vermiculite have been found to carry any serious disease organisms and the Mix can be used immediately after mixing.

If polyethylene tubing is used for rings, a funnel device is needed, such as a length of stovepipe (8 inch diameter), and a small grain scoop to handle the Mix. If tarpaper rings are used no funnel is needed. The rings are filled about two-thirds full if potted plants are to be set. They can be filled to within 1 inch of the top after setting the plants.

Step 8. - Growing the plants.

The plants that will be used in this system should be grown in the same Mix. If by chance the plants are purchased from another grower, make absolutely certain that the soil or other media used to grow the plants was steam sterilized. All efforts in this system of production will be wasted if one would bring in plants that already contained a fungous disease or were infested with nematode or virus.

A good tomato plant has a thick stem, good dark green color, and is about as wide as it is high. The plants for this crop should be grown in a 4-5 inch plastic or clay pot. They can be grown pot to pot for the first 2-3 weeks but must be spaced out so the plant stems are 7-8 inches apart each way. They need plenty of light and air circulation and temperatures must be carefully controlled. Day temperatures might run 70 on bright days and 65 on cloudy days.

Night temperatures should run 58-60 degrees. A good liquid feed once a week is essential but do not keep the mix on the wet side. In summary these plants need plenty of light, good air circulation, adequate nutrition, and actually to be grown on the dry side. These plants can be set into the rings about an inch deeper than they were in the growing container. When the plant has been set the ring is filled to within 1 inch from the top and the medium is firmed lightly. If the plants are being set in the trough culture method, follow the same techniques and firm the Mix around each plant. A starter fertilizer in solution is recommended at this time. Use at least 1 pint around the base of each plant which will firm the Mix.

Step 9. - Fungicide drench.

Immediately after setting and applying starter solution a stem drench of Captan (50 percent) and Terraclor (PCNB 75 percent) should be applied with a small sprayer using very little pressure. Apply in such a way that the stem area at the soil surface is thoroughly wetted. Use 16 ounces of Captan (50 w.p.) and 4 ounces of Terraclor (75 w.p.) per 100 gallons. This amounts to 5 level tablespoonfuls of Captan and 1½ tablespoonfuls of Terraclor in 5 gallons. This may also be applied with a small cup or dipper. This treatment will reduce loss of plants from organisms which produce a collar rot or stem rot.

Step 10. - Pollination.

The flower clusters must be vibrated to cause pollination. Therefore, just as soon as any flowers open in the first cluster, the cluster should be vibrated to shake the pollen from the male parts of the flower to the female part where fertilization and fruit set can occur. It is important to get fruit set on the early clusters and since the weather is usually poor during this period of the spring crop, vibration should be done daily. The cluster can be vibrated with an electric or battery operated vibrator for best results. Hitting the wires with a stick will shake the twine and the plant but is usually not as effective. In later clusters after the weather improves, vibration every other day may be adequate. We generally suggest vibration after 10:00 a.m. in the morning when hopefully, the relative humidity will be less and the pollen will shed more easily.

Step 11. - Support the plant.

To support the plants, plastic twine is tied to a top wire and to the base of the stem. The top wire can be No. 9, stretched tightly over the center of each row. Some growers use one wire for the double-row system, but two are preferred. The loop that is tied around the base of the plant should be such that it does not slip and a good technique is to leave about 15 inches of extra twine at the top. This extra twine is used later on to let the plants down when they reach the top of the wire and when the lower clusters have been picked. The plants must be tied soon after planting. Do not let them get tall and fall over before tying.

Step 12. — Pruning.

Tomatoes are usually pruned to a single stem. This requires frequent removal of "suckers" or side shoots. One such sucker will arise from the point of attachment of the leaf to the stem. Plants must be pruned every 5 to 7 days. The side shoots should be removed before they get 3 inches long. When pruning, the twine is twisted or spiraled around the stem to support the plant. Lower leaves can be removed up to the cluster being harvested and continued as harvesting proceeds.

Neglected Plant—side-shoots not removed.   Result of timely removal of all superfluous growth.

Step 13. — Disease control.

The fungous diseases that can cause serious trouble are gray mold (Botrytis cineria) and leaf mold (Cladosporium fulvum). Both of these problems are generally the result of improper heating and ventilation practices resulting in a situation of high relative humidity. Heating and circulation within the greenhouse are of utmost importance. In fact, some ventilation while heating is the only way to remove moisture. Fungicide sprays for the two pathogens mentioned are fairly ineffective. Some heat should be used even when outside temperatures are at or above the desired minimum. This will reduce humidity and assist in prevention of leaf mold.

Blossom-end rot is really a physiological disorder and is not caused by a pathogen. It is usually attributed to a moisture stress and will become obvious following any wilting of the plant when young fruit are present. Technically, it is associated with low calcium levels in the young fruit and moisture stress very likely affects the mobility of calcium into the fruit. A water-logged bed will reduce root oxygen and water uptake and produce the same disorder. Therefore, good drainage and adequate calcium in the nutrition program are important.

Step 14. — Insect control.

The most common insects that trouble the tomato crop are aphids, spider mites, and whitefly. Any or all of these can become serious pests and a regular weekly systematic program is the best answer. Each state has recommendations for insect control and it is difficult to suggest what should be used. The main point is to use compounds that will kill these insects and not allow them to build up nor leave a toxic residue. Many of the compounds will do an effective job on aphids and whitefly. (Malathion, Phosdrin, Thiodan and others.) Spider mites require other compounds but proper use of Naled (Dibrom) appears to do a good job and will also get aphids and whitefly.

All of these compounds are very poisonous and extreme care needs to be employed in their use. Read the label carefully and also obtain the best recommendation from your state university.

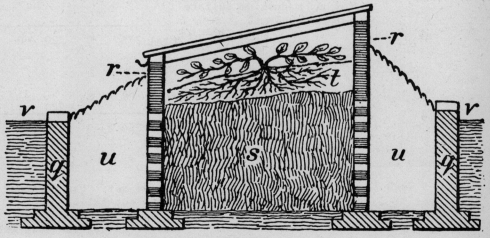

A MANURE-HEATED PIT FOR MELONS.
(Scale, ⅕ in.=1 ft.)

References : q, 9-in. retaining walls ; r, 4½-in. walls, built in cement, pigeon-holed to the height of the retaining walls ; s, bed of fermenting material ; t, 10 in. to 12 in. of soil ; u, space for linings ; v, ground level.

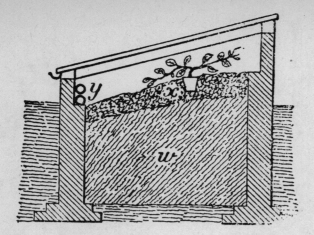

A LEAN-TO PIT FOR MELONS WITH MANURE FOR BOTTOM HEAT AND PIPES FOR TOP HEAT. (Scale, ⅛ in.=1 ft.)

References: *w*, fermenting material for bottom heat; *x*, soil; *y*, hot-water pipes for top heat.

Step 15. — Watering and feeding.

If the directions are followed for the Mix in this publication the subsequent feeding of the crop is simplified. The Mix will provide good physical properties for water retention as well as good aeration. The pH is in the proper range and substantial quantities of most elements are present while the soluble salts level is much below the range of excess. However, it is necessary to add more nutrients as the crop progresses.

Care in watering is very important especially at first. If very vigorous plants are set in the Mix during dark cloudy weather in late winter, liquid applications should be sparse and temperatures should be lowered to 56-58 degrees F (nights) and 60-65 degrees F (days). If plants are run wet and warm during such periods, vegetative growth will be excessive and quite frequently no fruit will be set on early trusses. After the first fruit is set, more liquid can be applied and the temperatures increased 4 degrees at night and greater during sunny days (60-62 F night and 70-75 days.)

Several approaches have been taken to satisfy the need for additional nutrients. It often depends upon the type of equipment available and especially upon whether fertilizer proportioning equipment is used. A few possibilities are given below.

Schedule I - This schedule utilizes commercially available fertilizer salts and is designed as a constant liquid feed program.

MATERIALS

Feed A

20-20-20 soluble commercial fertilizer at 2 pounds per 100 gallons of water.

Feed B

	ppm in solution				
	N	P	K	Ca	Mg
0.5 pound potassium Nitrate	78		220		
0.5 pound ammonium Nitrate	200				
0.5 pound magnesium sulfate					57
1.0 ounce chelated Iron					
Total	278	0	220	0	57

Feed C

	N	P	K	Ca	
1.0 pound calcium Nitrate	186			250	
0.5 pound potassium Nitrate	78		220		
Total	264	0	220	250	0

Schedule I for Spring Crop

Week 1. Feed A starting when plants are set. Use at least 1 quart per plant to settle mix around pot ball.

Week 2. Feed A when moisture is needed. Do not run beds wet; keep on the dry side.

3.	Feed B	10.	Feed A	17.	Feed C
4.	B	11.	B	18.	B
5.	B	12.	C	19.	C
6.	B	13.	B	20.	B
7.	C	14.	C	21.	C
8.	B	15.	A	22.	B
9.	C	16.	B	23.	C
				24.	B

		ppm in solution			
		N	P	K	Mg
Week 1	(set plants) 20-20-20 at 2 pounds per 100 gallons. Use 1 quart per plant	474	206	394	
Week 2	20-20-20 at 1 pound per 100 gallons	237	103	197	
Week 3	20-20-20 at 1 pound per 100 gallons	237	103	197	
Week 4	25-5-20 at 1 pound per 100 gallons	296	25	197	
Week 5	25-5-20 at 1 pound per 100 gallons	296	25	197	
Week 6	25-5-20 at 1 pound per 100 gallons	296	25	197	
Week 7	25-5-20 at 1 pound per 100 gallons	296	25	197	
Week 8	25-5-20 at 1 pound per 100 gallons	296	25	197	
Week 9	25-5-20 at 1 pound per 100 gallons	296	25	197	
Week 10	25-5-20 plus Magnesium Sulphate at 1 pound/100 gallons	296	25	197	114
Week 11	25-5-20 at 1 pound per 100 gallons	296	25	197	
Week 12	25-5-20 at 1 pound per 100 gallons	296	25	197	
Week 13	25-5-20 at 1 pound per 100 gallons	296	25	197	
Week 14	25-5-20 plus Magnesium Sulphate at 1 pound/100 gallons	296	25	197	114
Week 15	25-5-20 at 1 pound per 100 gallons	296	25	197	
Week 16	25-5-20 at 1 pound per 100 gallons	296	25	197	
Week 17	25-5-20 at 1 pound per 100 gallons	296	25	197	
Week 18	25-5-20 plus Magnesium Sulphate at 1 pound/100 gallons	296	25	197	114
Week 19	25-5-20 at 1 pound per 100 gallons	296	25	197	
Week 20	25-5-20 at 1 pound per 100 gallons	296	25	197	
Week 21	25-5-20 at 1 pound per 100 gallons	296	25	197	
Week 22	25-5-20 at 1 pound per 100 gallons	296	25	197	
Week 23	25-5-20 at 1 pound per 100 gallons	296	25	197	
Week 24	25-5-20 at 1 pound per 100 gallons	296	25	197	

Schedule II is set up to provide the proper levels of nutrients throughout the Spring greenhouse tomato crop. Each time the crop is watered, it should be watered with this solution.

Schedule III - (A one-feed method)

20-20-20 commercial soluble fertilizer (preferably with minor elements included).

1. Use 3 pounds per 100 gallons of water and apply one quart per plant when the plants are set.
2. Apply this amount once each week until the 10th week and then apply this amount twice per week from then on.
3. Plants will require moisture in between feedings and clear water should be used.
4. The high phosphorous in this feed may induce iron chlorosis (yellowing of the new growth). If this appears, spray the tops of the plants with chelated iron (8-12 percent iron) at ½ teaspoonful per gallon or add one ounce with 100 gallons of liquid applied.

Schedule IV - (For Fall Crop)

1. Use 20-20-20 at 3 pounds per 100 gallons at 1 quart per plant for first 2 weeks.
2. Constant feed from then on with: 1.0 pound Calcium Nitrate per 100 gallons. 0.7 pound Potassium Nitrate per 100 gallons.

This feed program will provide 290 ppm of Nitrogen (N) and 305 ppm of potassium (K). The vermiculite should supply the additional potassium usually applied to a Fall crop.

Feeding the Crop - General.

A tomato crop demands fairly large amounts of nutrients. The most logical way to supply these nutrients in this type of culture appears to be with constant liquid feed of the proper strength. Schedule I or II would best achieve this purpose. These solutions could be made up in barrels or tanks and pumped out onto the crop. A better approach would be to use a good fertilizer injection system right in the water line. An injector may have a ratio of 1:100 or some other value.

All water and feed solutions should be applied through some type of irrigation system. The thin capillary tube systems work very well and one tube is generally placed at each plant in the trough culture or in each ring if the ring culture system is used.

One of the latest ideas on automatic watering is to use the Chapin Drip-Hose which uniformly distributes liquid through pores spaced every 8 inches.

Moisture management is extremely important. When plants are first set, the entire trough need not be wet but as the plants grow and roots spread into the Mix from the trough is squeezed by hand, free water should run out.

Bilabiate Corolla

234

THE GRAPE UNDER GLASS

I. L. Powell, edited by Tom Riker

Reprinted from Garden Magazine, 1905

VINE IN A POT FOR THE TABLE.

There is a mistaken notion that fruit growing under glass and plastic is necessarily a very expensive indulgence. But if the house is there it is just as easy to grow good fruit as it is to produce good roses or carnations, and to many people there will be a good deal more satisfaction in luscious hothouse grapes or peaches than in the flowers. Fruits do not require a great heat unless forcing is contemplated, which is not likely.

Good soil is of the first importance. Good, or at least reasonably good, plants may be grown from poor beginnings if good soil is given them, but poor soil will invariably mean poor plants and poor fruit.

By a good soil I mean one that does not reach any of the extremes of soil consistency. Not sand, clay, muck or humus; but a friable loam containing a fair percentage of all these elements. If your soil is not of such consistency it must be made so. Heavy clay loam and humus, added to a light sandy soil, will improve it, and vice versa. Soil from a pasture or grass field is preferable, with the sod included, if it is possible to obtain it. To this add about one-quarter or one-fifth bulk of animal manure, prepared at least six weeks beforehand. Mix thoroughly by turning together at least three times. About one-half peck of good bone meal should be added to each cubic yard of compost.

With such a soil either peaches, nectarines, strawberries, grapes or figs can be grown in pots, tubs or boxes. For borders, if the trees or vines are to be planted out, use less manure, say about one-sixth to one-eighth, according to quality. Cow manure is preferred.

The next important thing is careful attention to watering. The soil in the box or pot must be neither constantly saturated nor allowed to get so dry that it is dusty. Other points are: as free circulation of air at all times as is consistent with the required temperature; houses that are not shaded by any other objects, and the plants themselves so placed that they will receive the full benefit of the sun's rays; a free use of the hose and nozzle, with a good pressure of water (not less than twenty-five pounds to the square inch) on the under side of leaves to control the red spider; a good heating system, and eternal vigilance in all respects. This looks like a lot of bother, but it is no more after all than good gardening always calls for.

One word of caution in reference to watering and syringing, and that is that syringing should be done only when the sun is shining brightly, and generally as early in the morning as possible; watering must be carefully done during periods of dull, cloudy weather if the house contains plants in flower or ripening fruits.

The most commonly glass-grown fruit is the European grape, and by having several sections of the houses started into growth at various times a succession of ripened grapes may be had from the middle of May or the first of June until the first of the following March. The roots must have drainage, and a naturally well-drained location should be secured if possible. If the situation is at all low or wet, a somewhat elaborate drainage system is necessary. First, a coating of cement two or three inches thick is to be put in the bottom of the border before putting in the drainage. The cement bottom should be given a slope in the same direction as the surface of the surrounding ground and drained at the lower end. The bottom should then be covered to a depth of at least six inches with small stones, broken bricks, etc., over which should first be placed a covering of long straw or other coarse material, and over this one layer of good sod, turned upside down, after which the border may be filled with the compost. If some larger broken pieces of bone are mixed through the compost it may prove beneficial, and the depth of the border should be sufficient to allow at least two feet of compost, and three feet would be better.

If the grapes are to be ripened from the middle of May to the first of August, the structure should face the south. A lean-to or shed roof is preferable, but for the sake of appearance a three-quarter-span house is generally used.

For early ripening it is probably better to have the border entirely inside the house, or, if extended outside the house, it should be enclosed by a wall, covered with sash, and have at least one line of heating pipe run through it. Grapevines for planting out should be strong one-or two-year-old vines that have been grown in pots, and if for early ripening should be started into growth before being planted in the borders.

In December the early vinery must be started into growth, and for early grapes a temperature for the first three or four weeks, or until the flower bunches are well developed, will be required at night, 45 to 50 degrees; day, with bright sun, 55 to 65 degrees. After the flower bunches are developed the temperature may be raised still another five degrees both night and day, and when the flowers are opening it may be raised still another five degrees. During the flowering period keep the house somewhat drier than before. Often the amateur fails to get grapes because he does not see to the fertilization of the flower. Give the vine a sharp knock during the driest and warmest period of the day, while the flowers are open. The pollen will be distributed sufficiently. The crop will be removed by July 1st, when the borders must be kept dry, especially in October and November.

To have good-flavored grapes at whatever time they may be ripened requires a warm and dry atmosphere. During this period a temperature of 75 to 85 degrees may be maintained during bright days.

In growing an "intermediate" crop give the same treatment as

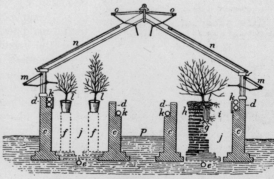

SPAN-ROOF FIG HOUSE FOR EARLY FORCING. (Scale, ⅛ in.=1 ft.)

References: *c*, 9-in. walls; *d*, 4½-in. walls built in cement; *a*, drains; *f*, 9-in. loose brick pillars to stand pots on; *g*, brick pedestal, against which turf *h* is built, and the roots of the tree laid-in on one side; *i*, side without turf wall, showing roots; *f*, pits for fermenting materials; *h*, 4-in. hot-water pipes; *l*, Fig trees in pots; *m*, side-lights open; *n*, roof-lights movable; *o*, top-lights open; *p*, pathway.

for the early, except that the drying is not necessary, and that instead of starting it into growth in December wait until the middle of February or even the first of March.

The late vinery should be retarded as long as possible. This is done by tying down the vines near the soil, leaving the side vents wide open (except in severe freezing weather) and placing a boxing over the top and by the side of the vines, thus shutting them off from the heat of the house and leaving them in this position until the growth has started.

The one drawback to grapes under glass or plastic is the long wait after planting. The first year's growth should be allowed to extend about half way up to the top of the house to the ventilator, at which point they should be stopped, i.e., pinched back. The second year the vines may be allowed to extend nearly to the ventilator, and the portion of the previous year's growth will produce side growths or "laterals." No fruit can be carried until the third year, when, if all has gone well, from three to five bunches may be allowed to develop on each vine.

NOTCHING VINE ROOTS.

References: *a*, roots notched to cause the emission of fibres; *b*, result of notching vine roots; *c*, adventitious roots from the collar; *d*, mulching; *e*, border; *f*, drainage; *g*, drain.

Just a glimpse of half the grapery. When you consider that the other half is equally loaded with fruit, you appreciate how over a ton and a half were picked from it.

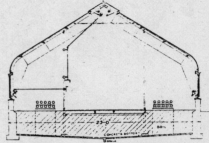

Grapery Section.
From this section of an even span grapery you can see how the roof is wired to support the vines, and the method of confining the roots by making a concrete bottom about three feet below the ground line. Such an arrangement gives a perfect control over the amount of moisture and nourishment that reach the roots.

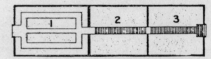

This plan shows a house divided into compartments for an early and late grapery; and one for chrysanthemums. If all three compartments were devoted to grapes, giving you a crop to come in between the early and late; you could have fruit 275 days of the year.

GRAPERIES

Graperies or vineries, as many call them, may be either cool or heated.

What is known as a cold grapery depends entirely on the protection of the glass and the conservation of the sun's heat to bring the fruit along. A full month can be gained this way, over outdoor grown fruit. In sections of the country where the season is so short that the frost nips the fruit before ripening, they are particularly valuable. Usually a grapery with artificial heat gives the greatest satisfaction.

If you want a continual supply from May day to New Year, then three separate compartments will do it for you. One each for early fruit, medium and late. Even if you have an abundance of outdoor grapes and do not care especially to have them out of season, still the superiority in flavor, the meaty juiciness of the fruit and the size and beauty of the bunches of those grown under glass is an abundant reward for the investment of a grapery.

The amateur often exclaims upon seeing a house of grapes with the floor space entirely unoccupied: "What a waste of space!" It is not so. The overhead area is filled with vines and every square foot is producing, whereas, in the flower-growing houses a part of the area covered by glass is unavailable, it being devoted to the essential walks. Vines can also be grown in pots, but because of the restricted root growth cannot be maintained in vigorous fruitful condition for many years. The interior view above can hardly fail to make you envious.

LORD & BURNHAM'S ARCHIVES

THREE-QUARTERS SPAN-ROOF VINERY.

References: *a*, ground level; *b*, outlet land drain; *c*, longitudinal border drains; *d*, rubble; *e*, outside border; *g*, rain-water tank; *h*, path; *i*, 4-in. hot-water pipes; *j*, 1½-in. hot-water pipes; *k*, side lights; *l*, south top lights; *m*, north top lights. The angle of the roof is 35°.

STRAWBERRY GRAPES.

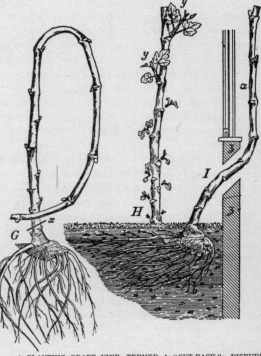

A PLANTING GRAPE VINE, TERMED A "CUT-BACK"; DISBUDDING; PLANTING IN OUTSIDE BORDER.

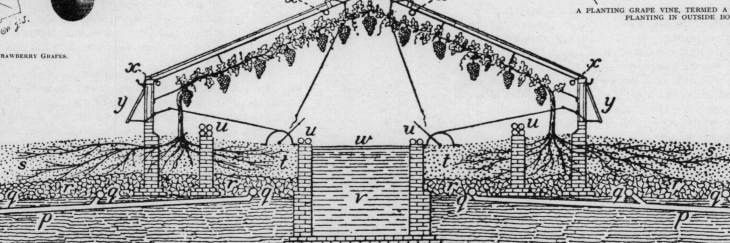

SPAN-ROOFED VINERY.

References: *p*, outlet drains; *q*, drains lengthwise of borders; *r*, rubble drainage; *s*, outside borders; *t*, inside borders; *u*, 4 in. hot-water pipes; *v*, rain-water tank; *w*, path; *x*, 1½ in. hot-water pipes; *y*, side lights; *z*, top lights.

COLD GRAPERIES

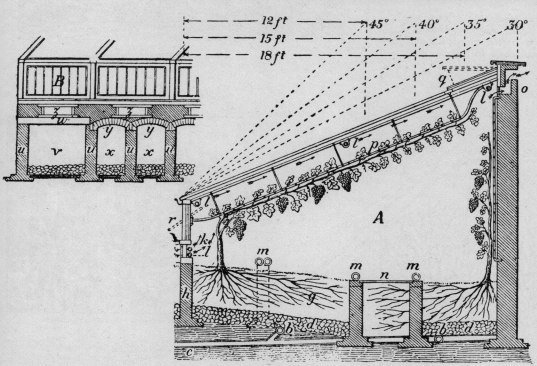

A LEAN-TO VINERY. (Scale: ⅛ in.=1 ft.)

References: A, lean-to vinery: b border drains; c, main border drain; d, rubble drainage, 1 ft. deep; g, inside border (outside border present, but not shown); h, front wall, 9-in. pillars with stone head; k, arrows showing ingress of air from ventilators in the front wall; l, 1½-in. galvanised wrought-iron hot-water pipes; m, 4-in. hot-water pipes; n, pathway, iron grating; o, back-wall ventilators; p, trellis, 2 ft. from the glass; q, top lights; r, front lights. B, part elevation of front wall: u, 9-in. pillars; v, large opening covered with stone head, w; x, small openings with skew-back arches, y; z, wall ventilators.

COOL GRAPERY

LORD & BURNHAM'S ARCHIVES

While speaking of vineries, we must not lose sight of the cool one, which has on its side the advantage of not requiring any heat, thus entirely eliminating the heating bill. Of course, the number of varieties that you can grow without artificial heat is somewhat limited, but there is a goodly list. You will get at least six weeks' start over those grown in the open.

In sections where the season is too short to ripen fruit outdoors, the cold grapery is admirable. We have built several for that purpose in the Green Mountains of Vermont.

The Leanto house makes an admirable one. If you have a wall or building with a southern exposure against which it can be built, so much the better, as the cost will be considerably less.

We have in mind a man living at Bennington, Vermont, who each season raises over half a ton of grapes from a Leanto house only 16 feet wide and 50 feet long. In addition to the grapes, he also grows countless bedding and vegetable plants as well, for early setting out. All of this is accomplished without burning a pound of coal or any other fuel.

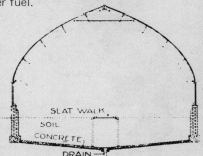

This section of the curvi-linear vinery shows what is known as a "border" of masonry wall and floor, for confining the roots and furnishing perfect drainage.

-LEAN-TO VINERY, IN SECTION.

GROUND VINERY.

BANANA HOUSE. (Scale, ¼ in.=1 ft.)

References: *a*, narrow borders for plants; *b*, narrow border at 9-ft. intervals for Monstera; *c*, narrow border at ends only for Granadilla; *d*, paths; *e*, dividing wall up centre of bed; *f*, drainage; *g*, drains; *h*, cold pit; *i*, hot-water pipes; *j*, ventilators.   The detached plan shows: *k*, restricted root-space at planting; *l*, temporary 4½-in. walls; *m*, space given to each plant after it has occupied *k* with roots; *n*, roots in full space; *o*, corner for standing young plants.

THE BANANA-TREE.

BANANAS

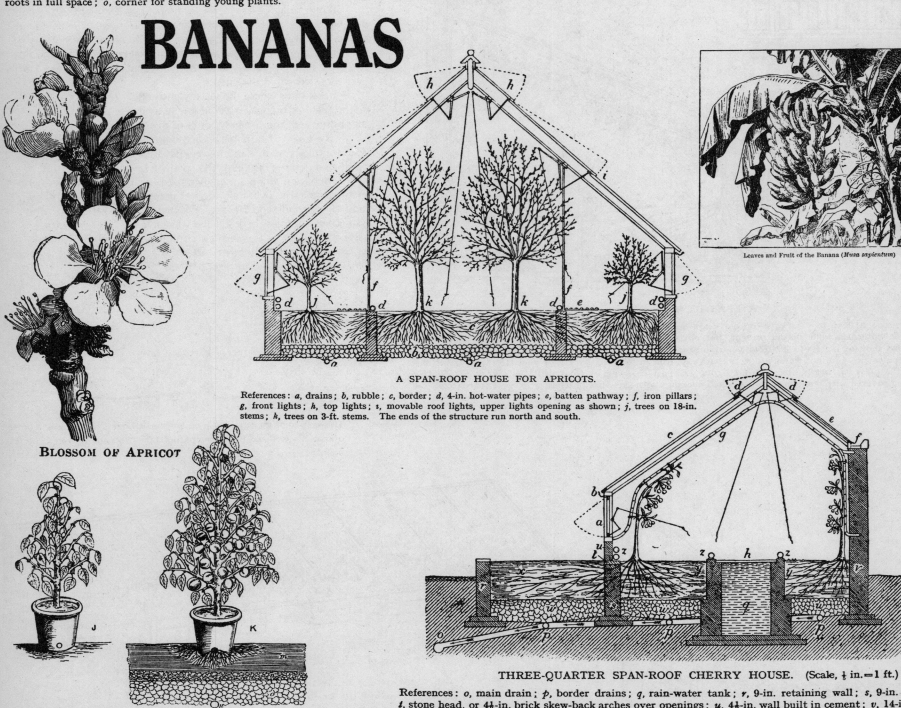

Leaves and Fruit of the Banana (*Musa sapientum*)

A SPAN-ROOF HOUSE FOR APRICOTS.

References: *a*, drains; *b*, rubble; *c*, border; *d*, 4-in. hot-water pipes; *e*, batten pathway; *f*, iron pillars; *g*, front lights; *h*, top lights; *i*, movable roof lights, upper lights opening as shown; *j*, trees on 18-in. stems; *k*, trees on 3-ft. stems.   The ends of the structure run north and south.

BLOSSOM OF APRICOT

PYRAMID APRICOT TREES IN POTS.

References: J, one-year pyramid; K, fruiting pyramid; *m*, 6 in. of rich compost, in which the pot is placed 1 in. over the side holes; *n*, 3 in. of old mortar rubbish; *o*, 6 in. of rubble; *p*, drain.

THREE-QUARTER SPAN-ROOF CHERRY HOUSE. (Scale, ¼ in.=1 ft.)

References: *o*, main drain; *p*, border drains; *q*, rain-water tank; *r*, 9-in. retaining wall; *s*, 9-in. pillars; *t*, stone head, or 4½-in. brick skew-back arches over openings; *u*, 4½-in. wall built in cement; *v*, 14-in. back wall; *w*, rubble drainage; *x*, outside border; *y*, inside border; *z*, 4-in. hot-water pipes; *a*, front lights; *b*, spout; *c*, movable front roof-lights; *d*, top lights; *e*, movable back lights; *f*, gutter; *g*, trellis; *h*, pathway.

PEACHES AND NECTARINES

There are two distinct ways of growing peaches and nectarines under glass; dwarf trees in pots, and the ordinary size trees planted directly in the soil of the house. Of the latter there are two methods, one, to plant the trees along the sides and train them on trellises along the roof; the other, to plant them away from the sides and train them on cross trellising. This last is considered by far the best, as the light can reach all sides of the trees equally, ripening and coloring the fruit more evenly. More trees can also be planted in the same space. For instance, in a 33-foot house six trees are all that could be planted on the sides, allowing the necessary room for future expansion. With cross trellising, like in the same house twelve trees could be grown successfully, or with No. 1, six larger trees could be grown. In addition to the number of trees so gained, there is also the great advantage of being able to readily spray them on both sides. Peaches and nectarines grown in either of these ways have exquisite delicacy of flavor. The skins are thin and take on unthought of beauty of colorings. The meat also has a variable color beauty of its own, is free from shreds and always juicy. *LORD & BURNHAM'S ARCHIVES*

LEAN-TO PEACH HOUSE. (Scale, $\frac{1}{16}$ in.=1 ft.)

References: *m*, 3-in. border drains; *n*, rubble drainage; *o*, border; *p*, batten paths; *q*, 4-in. hot-water pipes; *r*, back wall trees; *s*, curvilinear trellis trees; *t*, shelf for potted Strawberry plants; *u*, movable roof lights. The house might be used with another arrangement as follows: *v*, front trellis; *w*, trees with roots passing through openings in the front wall to the outside border (*x*); *y*, batten pathway. The paths (*p*), shelf (*t*), and trellis (*s*) are omitted in this arrangement. The arrows show the rays of light reaching the base of the back wall trees.

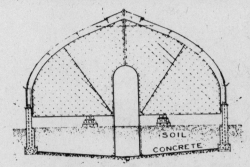

Number 1 —Section of a curvilinear fruit house showing cross trellis arranged for two trees, one on either side of the walk.

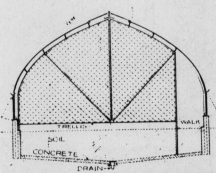

Number 2 —Section of curvilinear house showing cross trellis with side walk for supporting spread of one tree only.

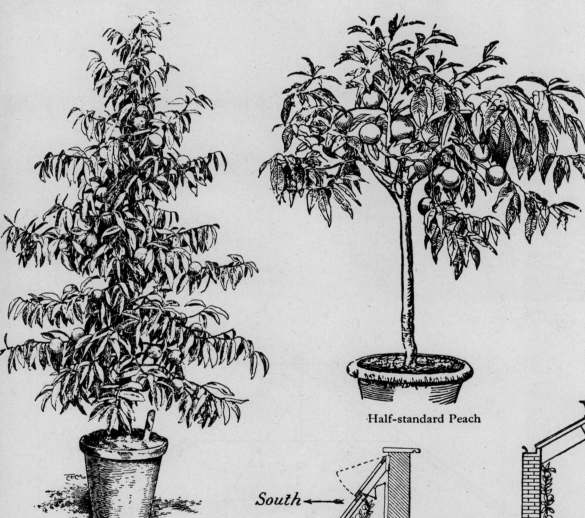

Peach—Crimson Galande
Tree sixteen years old.

Half-standard Peach

References: 1, 3-in. drain; 2, drainage; 3, border; 4, 9-in. brick pillars; 5, batten pathway; 6, 4-in. hot-water pipes; 7, 1½-in. hot-water pipes; 8, oak sill; 9, wood ventilator opening the whole length of the house; 0, movable roof lights.

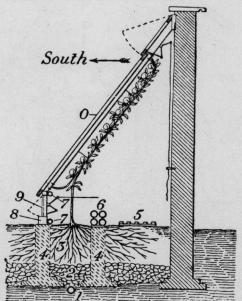

LEAN-TO PEACH HOUSE FOR EARLY FORCING. (Scale, $\frac{1}{8}$ in.=1 ft.)

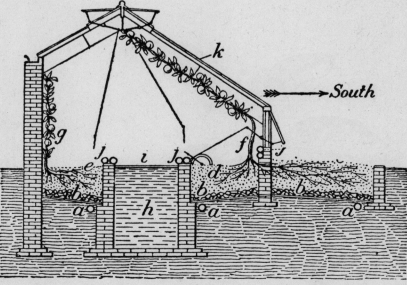

A THREE-QUARTER SPAN-ROOF PEACH HOUSE FOR FORCING. (Scale, $\frac{1}{8}$ in.=1 ft.)

References: *a*, 3-in. tile-drains; *b*, rubble for drainage; *c*, outside border; *d*, inside border; *e*, back border; *f*, permanent trees; *g*, temporary trees; *h*, rain-water tank; *i*, path; *j*, 4-in. hot-water pipes; *k*, movable roof lights.

239

ORANGERIES

FRUITING BRANCH OF COMMON ORANGE.

FRUITING BRANCH OF MANDARIN ORANGE.

When you consider that oranges were the first fruit known to be grown under glass, several centuries ago, it is rather strange that it should have been pursued only in recent years in this country.

The very first record of a glass enclosed house for growing purposes of any kind, history states as being for ripening oranges to a perfection "fit for a king of France."

If you have never happened to be in one of the modern orangeries when in bloom, you, indeed, have a treat in store.

The waxy leaved trees are festively decked in their creamy blossoms, while the air is laden with sweetness.

The fruit so grown has a rare delicacy of flavor—a height of ripened perfection hardly possible even in their native sunny climes.   *LORD & BURNHAM'S ARCHIVES*

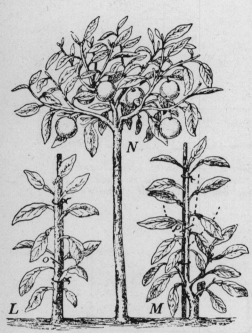

FORMS OF ORANGE TREES.

References : L, Orange tree one year from the bud : o, point of pruning to form a conical or pyramidal tree. M, conical tree in second year : p, point of shortening ; dotted lines indicate growths the result of pruning the leader. N, standard in third year after heading.

A newly started grove

FLOWERING BRANCHLET OF COMMON ORANGE.

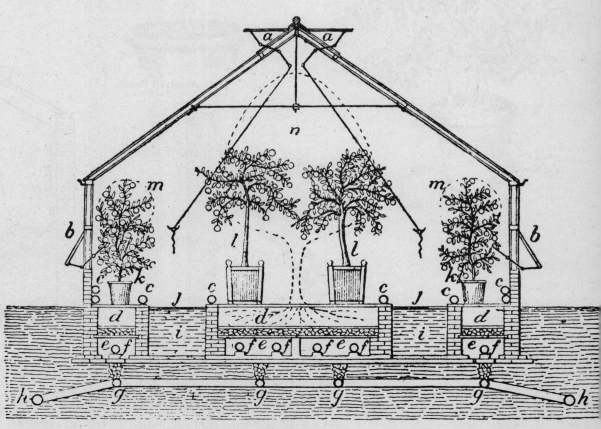

ORANGERY.

FRUITING BRANCH OF FIG.

FIGS

Figs are another thing that ought to be grown more generally. They are not difficult to handle, do splendidly in a small house and yield two crops each year—what more could one ask?

LORD & BURNHAM'S ARCHIVES

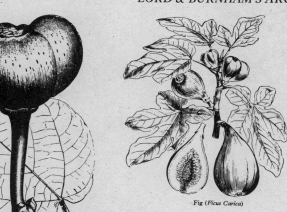

FRUIT AND LEAF OF FICUS ROXBURGHII.

Fig (*Ficus Carica*)

Fig—Osborn's Prolific

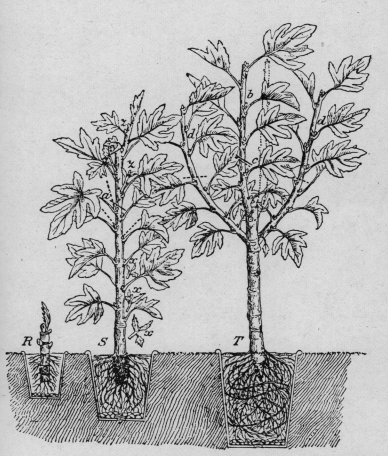

ORIGINATING ROUND-HEADED AND FAN-SHAPED FIG TREES.

References: R, a Fig cutting striking. S, the young tree shifted into a larger pot and grown with a single stem: *x*, disbudded shoots; *y*, point of stopping; *z*, laterals; *a*, point of winter pruning. T, tree in the second year, showing formation of head: *b*, leader; *c*, point of shortening it in winter; *d*, side shoots unpruned. The dotted bars indicate points of stopping to form a bush.

Standard Fig in pot—St. John's

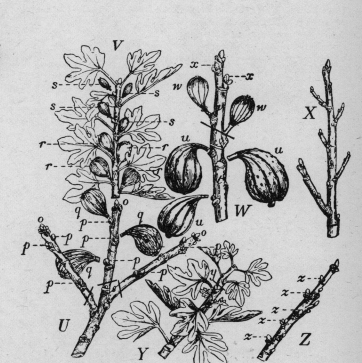

CHARACTERISTIC GROWTHS AND FRUIT PRODUCTION IN THE FIG.

References: U, indoor branch (for details of cultivation under glass see further on): *o*, previous season's terminal growths; *p*, embryo Figs in bud; *q*, first-crop Figs—the two lowest ripe. V, current year's growth: *r*, second-crop Figs; *s*, third-crop Figs from trees started early and kept growing until late; otherwise this will be the first crop in succeeding year. W, outdoor branch: *t*, previous year's wood; *u*, first-crop Figs ripe (August or September); *v*, current year's growth; *w*, second-crop Figs — generally worthless; *x*, embryo Figs—first crop of the following year. X, weak, sappy, crowded shoot of last season, destitute of embryonic Figs. Y, similar shoot to X, but grown under full exposure to sun, and pinched at *y*. Z, result of growing thinly and pinching: *z*, embryo Figs—the first crop of the succeeding season.

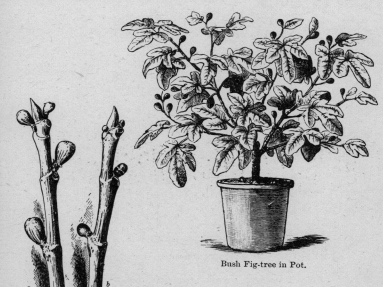

Bush Fig-tree in Pot.

a, Fruit-buds too large to winter; *b* fruit-buds of right size to winter.

Fig-shoots

PRUNING A YOUNG FIG TREE, AND SUMMER PINCHING.

References: G, shortening branches to form bush and pyramid trees: *x*, points of pruning back to form a bush; *y*, points of shortening to form a pyramid, also *x*, except *a* I. H, tree in foliage showing pinching: *z*, first stopping; *a*, second pinching; *b*, extent of growth removed shown by detached points.

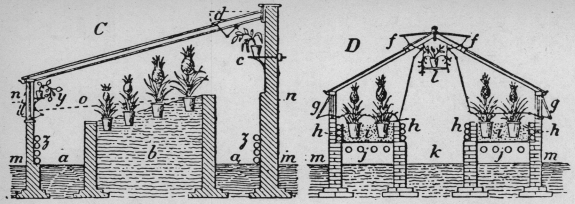

LEAN-TO HOUSE AND SPAN-ROOF HOUSE SUITABLE FOR PINE APPLES. (Scale, $\frac{1}{8}$ in. = 1 ft.)

References: C, lean-to house: *y*, shelf; *z*, 4-in. hot-water pipes; *a*, paths; *b*, pit for leaves or tan; *c*, shelf; *d*, top lights; *l*, front lights. D, span-roofed house: *f*, top lights; *g*, side lights; *h*, 4-in. hot-water pipes; *i*, plunging beds; *j*, hot-air chambers with 4-in. hot-water pipes; *k*, path; *l*, shelves; *m*, ground levels. If there is no front path in C: *n*, ground level; *o*, bed level outline.

PINE APPLE (SMOOTH-LEAVED CAYENNE).

Pine-apple—Charlotte Rothschild

Pine-apples (Jamaica)

PINEAPPLES

Pineapples grown under glass are quite a novelty in this country, but if people only knew how choice the "pines" then are in their succulent meatiness, how free from woodiness and indigestibleness, they would certainly be grown in every greenhouse of any considerable size.

LORD & BURNHAM'S ARCHIVES

HOUSE SUITABLE FOR PINERY, IN SECTION.

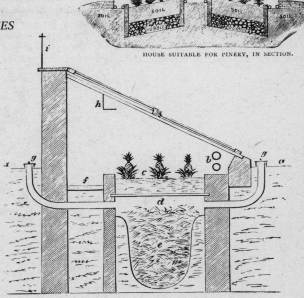

Meudon Pine-house

a a Ground-line. *b*, Hot-water pipes for top-heat. *c*, Bed of peat soil in which the Pine-apples are planted. *d*, One of the iron bars for supporting the boarded flooring on which the bed of soil rests. *e*, Vault filled with stable-dung and leaves. *f*, Foot-path. *g g*, Air-holes. *h*, Shelf for Strawberries. *i*, Iron rail over which the straw mats are hung when the house is uncovered

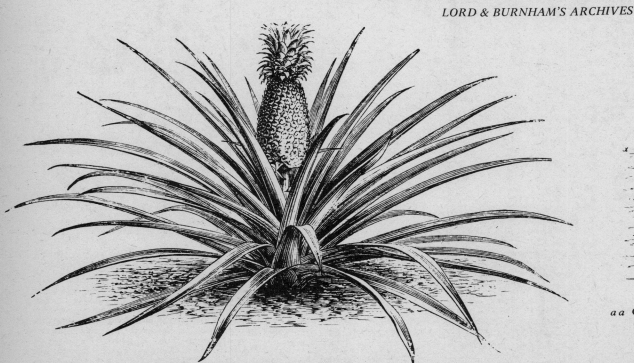

SMOOTH-LEAVED CAYENNE PINE-APPLE.

POT GRAPE VINE IN FRUIT
COILED ROUND STAKES.

Old Jack Frost had dragged the mercury down to 5 below the day we took
this picture at Newport, R. I. The center bench was filled with potted fruit,
while the side ones were growing good, lusty vines laden with cucumbers.

TRELLIS FRUITS

If you want to devote one or more compartments entirely to the growing of peaches or nectarines, with the idea of getting the very height of results, then plant your trees directly in the soil and train your trees up fan-shaped over trellises running across the house. When the ridge of such a compartment or house runs north and south at right angles to the trellises, then the sun in its daily travels will reach each side of the trees equally, causing a uniform ripening and coloring of the fruit. A peach or nectarine picked at exactly the right time is so lusciously ripe and tender that even the pressure of the finger will bruise it. A glass shelter is absolutely necessary to obtain such heights of perfection.

LORD & BURNHAM'S ARCHIVES

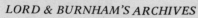

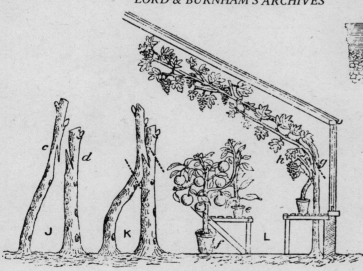

INARCHING.

POTTED FRUIT

Quite the most interesting way to grow fruit under glass is in pots. There are many points in its favor. In the first place it is cheaper, as the orchard house is filled with the dwarf trees in pots for only five or six months of the year, and the rest of the time the house is available for other uses, chrysanthemums, for instance.

With potted fruit, you can easily have a greater variety, and do not stop at peaches and nectarines, but add apples, pears, plums and cherries as well.

Each tree takes up but little space and it is surprising the quantity of fruit a dwarf tree will yield.

This is a great point for the man with the small house as he can have all the fun of an orchard with many varieties of fruit.

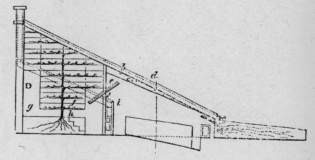

When anyone mentions growing peaches, nectarines, cherries, and the like under glass, you at once erroneously picture in your mind extensive houses and large expenditures.

Truth to tell, potted fruit takes no more room than a compartment of roses or carnations: in fact, much less, because they are only in the house from January till about August. All the rest of the time the space can be used for other things.

Often you find such a fruit compartment filled in the Fall with vegetables, or a glorious wealth of chrysanthemum blooms.

There are very few things grown under glass that take any less heat, unless perhaps it's violets. So, you see, the coal cost is surpassingly low.

The potted trees are brought in from an unheated storage room in January and gradually a few degrees of heat increased each day; quite as Nature does in her heralding of Spring's arrival. Through February the maximum of artificial heat requirements will be reached. After that, so much of the sun's heat will be attracted and conserved by the glass, that every day lessens the coal or other fuel to be burned.

And as for the fruit itself—no outdoors grown can approach it for meaty succulence or delicious delicacy of flavor.

You have fruit at its highest perfection, as a result of being able to control and supply ideal growing conditions.

It does seem to us you are decidedly missing something by not having at least one potted fruit compartment.

LORD & BURNHAM'S ARCHIEVES

ORNAMENTALS UNDER GLASS

LORD & BURNHAM
Irvington on Hudson

GERANIUM ARGENTEUM.

STEM, BRANCHES, AND FLOWER OF CEREUS PROCUMBENS.

OPTIMUM NIGHTTIME GROWING TEMPERATURES NEEDED BY GREENHOUSE PLANTS

It is important to make use of the "micro-climates" present in every home greenhouse.

The Tables following have been compiled to pinpoint OPTIMUM NIGHTTIME GROWING TEMPERATURES for all the plants discussed in this handbook. Here you will find six groupings of plants, assembled by 5-degree changes in temperature. These are MINIMUM NIGHT GROWING TEMPERATURES FOR OPTIMUM RESULTS. Day temperatures can and should be about 10 degrees higher. There is no need to limit your growing to plants that require the exact same temperatures—take advantage of those micro-climates.

We believe that the best plants are grown when the OPTIMUM NIGHT GROWING TEMPERATURES are provided. However, almost all plants cultivated in home greenhouses are tolerant of considerable variation. For example, many plants that can be grown at 55 degrees can also be grown at 50 degrees. They will be firmer in growth, may mature later and flowers will tend to last longer. The same plants may also be grown at 60 degrees, but these will be softer, probably taller, and flower petals will fade more rapidly.

GREENHOUSE PLANTS THAT NEED A MINIMUM TEMPERATURE OF 45 DEGREES

AGAPANTHUS (Lily-of-the-Nile)
CALCEOLARIA (Pocketbook Plant)
CAMPANULA ISOPHYLLA (Bellflower, Bluebell, Star of Bethlehem)
CHOISYA (Mexican Orange)
CHRYSANTHEMUM CARINATUM (Annual)
CYMBIDIUM ORCHID (Some, but not all at this temperature)
CYTISUS (Broom) ("Canariensis Genista" of florists) (force)
FREESIA
LACHENALIA (Cape Cowslip)
LOBELIA
MATHIOLA INCANA (Stock)
NEMESIA
ODONTOGLOSSUM ORCHID (Some, but not all at this temperature)
PRIMULA OBCONICA (Primrose)
PRIMULA SINENSIS (Chinese Primrose)
RANUNCULUS (Buttercup, Crowfoot)
SENECIO CRUENTUS (Cineraria)
SPARMANNIA
SWAINSONA (Winter Sweet Pea)
VIOLA TRICOLOR (Pansy or Heart's-ease)

GREENHOUSE PLANTS THAT NEED A MINIMUM TEMPERATURE OF 40 DEGREES

ACACIA
ANEMONE
CALENDULA OFFICINALIS (Pot Marigold)
CAMELLIA
DELPHINIUM AJACIS (Larkspur)
ERICA (Heath or Scotch "Heather")
IRIS, DUTCH (force)
PIQUERIA TRINERVIA (Stevia)

GREENHOUSE PLANTS FOR SPRING FLOWERS

Abutilon
Acacia
Acalypha hispida
Achimenes
Aeschynanthus (Trichosporum)
Agapanthus
Ageratum
Alyssum maritimum
Amaryllis
Anthurium
Antirrhinum
Astilbe japonica
Azalea
Begonia, fibrous rooted
Beloperone
Bessera elegans
Boston Daisy
Bougainvillea
Brunsvigia
Cacti, and other Succulents
Calceolaria
Calendula officinalis
Callistephus chinensis
Camellia
Capsicum
Centaurea cyanus
Chrysanthemum carinatum
Citrus
Clarkia elegans
Clematis
Clerodendrum
Clivia
Columnea
Crossandra
Crocus
Cyclamen

Cytisus canariensis
Daphne cneorum
Delphinium ajacis
Dianthus caryophyllus
Episcia
Erica
Eucharis grandiflora
Eucomis
Exacum
Felicia amelloides
Fuchsia
Gardenia
Gazania
Geranium
Gerbera jamesoni
Gladiolus
Gloriosa
Godetia
Haemanthus
Heliotrope
Hibiscus
Hyacinthus
Hydrangea, Blue
Hydrangea, Pink
Iberis
Impatiens
Iris, Dutch
Ixia
Ixora
Jacobinia
Jasminum
Lachenalia
Lantana
Lathyrus odoratus
Lilium
Lobelia

Mathiola incana
Narcissus
Nemesia
Nicotiana
Nierembergia frutescens
Orchids
Ornithogalum
Osmanthus fragrans
Oxalis
Passiflora
Pentas
Petunia
Primula malacoides
Primula obconica
Rechsteineria
Roses
Saintpaulia
Salpiglossis
Schizanthus
Senecio cruentus
Spathiphyllum
Strelitzia
Stephanotis floribunda
Swainsona
Tagetes erecta
Trachymene caerulea
Tropaeolum
Tulip
Veltheimia
Viola tricolor
Zantedeschia
Zinnia elegans
Zygocactus

GREENHOUSE PLANTS THAT NEED A MINIMUM TEMPERATURE OF 50 DEGREES

LORD & BURNHAM
Irvington on Hudson

AGERATUM (Floss Flower)
ANTIRRHINUM (Snapdragon)
ASTILBE JAPONICA (Spirea)
BOSTON DAISY (Chrysanthemum frutescens, Marguerite)
BUDDLEJA or BUDDLEIA (Butterfly Bush)
CALLISTEPHUS CHINENSIS (China Aster)
CAPSICUM (Christmas Pepper)
CHRYSANTHEMUM FRUTESCENS (Marguerite, Paris or Boston Daisy)
CHRYSANTHEMUM PARTHENIUM (Feverfew)
CITRUS (Calamondin, Citron, Lemon, Orange)
CROCUS (force)
CYCLAMEN
DAPHNE CNEORUM
DIANTHUS CARYOPHYLLUS (Carnation)
EXACUM
FELICIA AMELLOIDES (Agathea, Blue Daisy)
GODETIA (Satinflower)
HAEMANTHUS (Blood Lily)
IBERIS AMARA and UMBELLATA (Candytuft)
IMPATIENS (Sultana or Patience Plant)
IXIA
KALANCHOE
LATHYRUS ODORATUS (Sweet Pea)
MILLA BIFLORA (Mexican Star)
MYOSOTIS (Forget-me-not)
NEPHROLEPIS BOSTONIENSIS (Boston Fern)
NERINE
NERIUM OLEANDER
NICOTIANA (Flowering Tobacco)
NIEREMBERGIA FRUTESCENS (Cup-flower)
ONCIDIUM ORCHID (Some, but not all at this temperature)
ORNITHOGALUM
OSMANTHUS FRAGRANS (Sweet Olive)
OXALIS
PASSIFLORA (Passion Flower)
PENTAS (Egyptian Star-cluster)
PLUMBAGO (Leadwort)
PRIMULA MALACOIDES (Baby Primrose, Fairy Primrose)
SCHIZANTHUS (Butterfly Flower, Poor Man's Orchid)
TROPAEOLUM (Nasturtium)
VALLOTA (Scarborough Lily)
VELTHEIMIA

GREENHOUSE PLANTS THAT NEED A MINIMUM TEMPERATURE OF 55 DEGREES

ALYSSUM MARITIMUM (Sweet Alyssum)
AMARCRINUM
APHELANDRA
AZALEA
BELOPERONE (Shrimp Plant)
BOUGAINVILLEA
BRASSAVOLA ORCHID
CATTLEYA ORCHID
CENTAUREA CYANUS (Cornflower or Bachelor's-button)
CLEMATIS
CLIVIA
CROSSANDRA
EPIDENDRUM ORCHIDS (Some, but not all at this temperature)
GERANIUM (Pelargonium species and varieties)
GERBERA JAMESONI (Transvaal Daisy)
HYDRANGEA, BLUE and PINK
IXORA
JACOBINIA (King's Crown)
JASMINUM (Jasmine or Jessamine)
LANTANA
NARCISSUS (Daffodil) (force)
PAPHIOPEDILUM ORCHID (Some, but not all at this temperature)
PETUNIA
REINWARDTIA
ROSES (pot)
SALPIGLOSSIS (Painted Tongue)
SEDUM
SMITHIANTHA (Naegelia or Temple Bells)
STRELITZIA (Bird of Paradise)
TAGETES ERECTA (African Marigold)
TECOMARIA CAPENSIS (Cape Honeysuckle)
ZANTEDESCHIA (Calla-Lily)
ZYGOCACTUS (Thanksgiving, Christmas or Easter Cactus)

EPIPREMNUM MIRABILE

GREENHOUSE PLANTS FOR SUMMER FLOWERS

Abutilon	Crossandra	Lantana
Achimenes	Dianthus caryophyllus	Lilium
Aeschynanthus (Trichosporum)	Episcia	Lobelia
Agapanthus	Eucharis grandiflora	Nierembergia frutescens
Ageratum	Eucomis	Orchids
Allamanda	Fuchsia	Passiflora
Alyssum maritimum	Gardenia	Petunia
Amarcrinum	Gazania	Plumbago
Anthurium	Geranium	Saintpaulia
Begonia, fibrous rooted	Gloriosa	Salpiglossis
Begonia, tuberous	Gloxinia	Smithiantha
Beloperone	Gypsophila	Sinningia speciosa
Boston Daisy	Haemanthus	Sparmannia
Cacti, and other Succulents	Heliotrope	Spathiphyllum
Caladium	Hibiscus	Strelitzia
Callistephus chinensis	Hoya carnosa	Stephanotis floribunda
Campanula isophylla	Hydrangea, Pink	Swainsona
Centaurea cyanus	Impatiens	Tropaeolum
Chrysanthemum parthenium	Incarvillea	Zantedeschia
Citrus	Ixora	Zephyranthes
Clematis	Jacobinia	Zinnia elegans
Cleodendrum	Jasminum	
Columnea	Kaempferia	

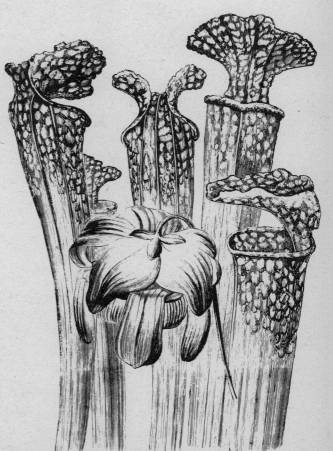

UPPER PORTION OF PITCHERS AND FLOWER OF SARRACENIA DRUMMONDII.

GREENHOUSE PLANTS THAT NEED A MINIMUM TEMPERATURE OF 65 DEGREES

AECHMEA (Bromeliad)
AESCHYNANTHUS (Trichosporum, Lipstick Vine)
AMARYLLIS
ANANAS (Bromeliad)
ANTHURIUM
BEGONIA, FIBROUS-ROOTED (Eax Begonia, B. semperflorens)
BEGONIA, TUBEROUS
BILLBERGIA (Bromeliad)
BROMELIADS
BROWALLIA
CRASSULA (Jade Plant)
CRYPTANTHUS (Bromeliad)
EPISCIA
EUCHARIS GRANDIFLORA (Amazon Lily)
EUCOMIS (Pineapple Flower)
GARDENIA
GLADIOLUS
GLORIOSA (Climbing Lily, Glory Lily)
GUZMANIA (Bromeliad)
HIBISCUS ROSA—SINENSIS (Chinese Hibiscus)
NEOREGELIA (Bromeliad)
PHALAENOPSIS ORCHIDS
PHILODENDRON
SAINTPAULIA (Africa Violet)
SINNINGIA SPECIOSA (Gloxinia)
SPATHIPHYLLUM
STEPHANOTIS FLORIBUNDA (Madagascar Jasmine)
STREPTOSOLEN JAMESONI (Orange "Browallia")
TILLANDSIA (Bromeliad)
VRIESEA (Bromeliad)
ZEPHYRANTHES (Zephyr-Flower, Fairy or Rain-Lily)

GREENHOUSE PLANTS THAT NEED A MINIMUM TEMPERATURE OF 60 DEGREES

ABUTILON (Flowering Maple)
ACALYPHA HISPIDA (Red-hot Cat-tail or Chenille Plant)
ACHIMENES (Nut Orchid or Hot-water Plant)
ALLAMANDA
ARDISIA CRISPA (Coralberry)
ASPARAGUS FERN (A. sprengeri and A. plumosus)
BEGONIA, SEMI-TUBEROUS (Christmas Begonia)
BESSERA ELEGANS (Mexican Coral Drops)
BOUVARDIA
BRUNSVIGIA (Cape Belladonna or Belladonna Lily)
CACTI AND OTHER SUCCULENTS
CALADIUM
CENTROPOGON
CHRYSANTHEMUM MORIFOLIUM (fall)
CLARKIA ELEGANS
CLERODENDRUM
CODIAEUM (Croton)
COLEUS
COLUMNEA
EUPATORIUM (Mist-flower)
EUPHORBIA FULGENS (Scarlet Plume)
EUPHORBIA PULCHERRIMA (Poinsettia)
FUCHSIA
GAZANIA
GYPSOPHILA (Annual Baby's-breath)
HELIOTROPE
HOYA CARNOSA (Wax Plant)
HYACINTH, DUTCH (force)
INCARVILLEA ("Hardy Gloxinia")
KAEMPFERIA
LILIUM (Lily) (force)
RECHSTEINERIA (Gesneria cardinalis)
SOLANUM (Christmas Cherry)
TRACHYMENE CAERULEA (Didiscus, Blue Lace Flower)
TULIP (force)
ZINNIA ELEGANS (Common Zinnia)

LORD & BURNHAM
Irvington on Hudson

GREENHOUSE PLANTS FOR FALL FLOWERS

Abutilon	Gypsophila
Acalypha hispida	Haemanthus
Achimenes	Heliotrope
Aeschynanthus (Trichosporum)	Hibiscus
Ageratum	Impatiens
Alyssum maritimum	Ixora
Amarcrinum	Jacobinia
Anthurium	Kalanchoe
Aphelandra	Lantana
Begonia, fibrous rooted	Nerine
Begonia, tuberous	Nierembergia frutescens
Beloperone	Orchids
Boston Daisy	Pentas
Bougainvillea	Petunia
Bouvardia	Primula sinensis
Cacti, and other Succulents	Reinwardtia
Callistephus chinensis	Saintpaulia
Centaurea cyanus	Smithiantha
Chrysanthemum morifolium	Sinningia speciosa
Citrus	Solanum
Columnea	Spathiphyllum
Crossandra	Strelitzia
Cyclamen	Stephanotis floribunda
Dianthus caryophyllus	Swainsona
Episcia	Tecomaria capensis
Eucharis grandiflora	Vallota
Eupatorium	Zinnia elegans
Geranium	Zygocactus
Gloxinia	

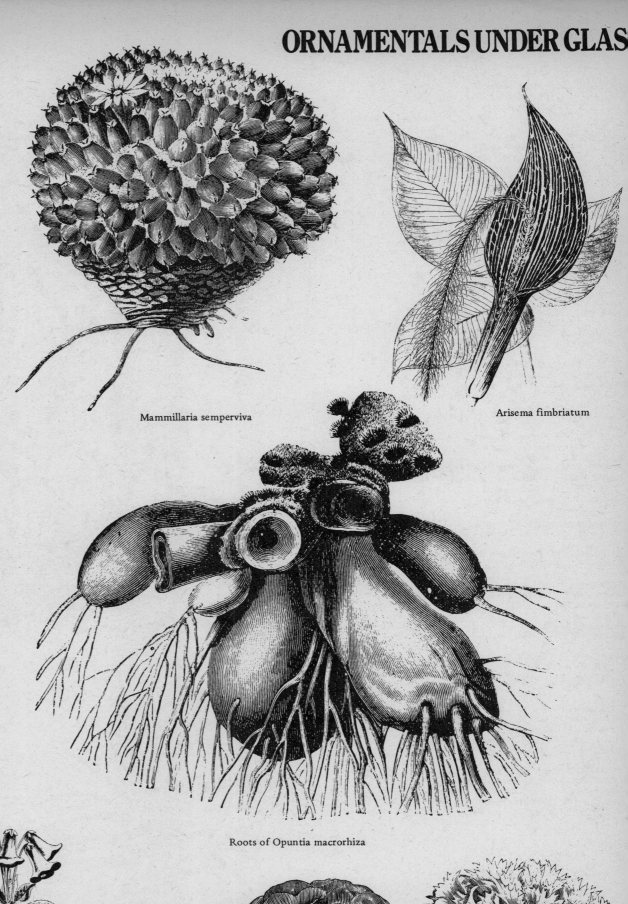

Mammillaria semperviva

Arisema fimbriatum

Roots of Opuntia macrorhiza

DROOPING-FLOWERED GLOXINIA.

SINGLE DAHLIAS (1) BEACON AND (2) UTILITY—VARIETIES ILLUSTRATING FLOWERS SLIGHTLY REFLEXED.

A. Allegatière.   Laura.
TREE CARNATIONS.

Selections For a Warm Fernery

Adiantum amabile.
  Bausei.
  cardiochlaena
  concinnum.
  concinnum latum.
  cuneatum.
  cuneatum grandiceps.
  Farleyense.
  macrophyllum.
  Pacotti.
  Seemanni.
  tenerum.
  trapeziforme.
  Williamsi.

Alsophila australis.
  excelsa.
Aspidium macrophyllum.
  viviparum.
Asplenium Belangeri.
  cicutarum.
  formosum.
  longissimum.
Asplenium nobile.
  viviparum.

Blechnum brasiliense.
  corcovadense.
  occidentale.

Cheilanthes farinosa.
  hirta Ellisiana.
Cibotium Barometz.
  princeps.

Davillia bullata.
  dissecta.
  fijiensis.
  Mooreana.
  tenuifolia Veitchi.
Goniophlebium appendiculatum.
  subauriculatum.
Gymnogramma chrysophylla Laucheana.
  ochracea.
  peruvianum argyrophylla.
Hemionitis palmata.
Lastrea Richardsi multifida.
Lomaria discolor bipinnatifida.
  gibba.
Lygodium palmatum.
  scandens (japonicum).
Microlepia hirta cristata.
Nephrodium molle.
Nephrolepis davallioides furcans.
  Duffi.
  pectinata.
  tuberosa.
Nothochlaena chrysophylla.
  nivea.
Phlebodium aureum.
Platycerium alcicorne majus.
Platyloma flexuosa.
Polypodium diversifolium.
Polystichum triangulare laxum.
Pteris Bausei.
  longifolia Mariesi.
  ludens.
  serrulata Mayi.
  tricolor.

Selections For A Cool House

Adiantum affine.
  assimile.
  capillus-Veneris (in variety).
  cuneatum.
  decorum.
  formosum.
  pubescens.
  venustum.
Angiopteris evecta.
Aspidium mucronatum.
Asplenium bulbiferum.
  Colensoi.
  flaccidum.
  palmatum.
  Veitchianum
Blechnum gracile.
  latifolium.
Cheilanthes Bergeana.
  elegans.
Cibotium regale.
  spectabile.

Cyathea dealbata.
  medullaris.
Davallia canariense.
  tenuifolia Burkei.
Dicksonia antarctica.
  squarrosa.
Doodia aspera multifida.
Gleichenia dichotoma.
  rupestris.
Gleichenia Speluncae
Goniophlebium sepultum.
Hymenophyllum caudiculatum.
Hypolepis millefolium.
Lastrea atrata.
  aristata variegata.
  fragrans.
Leucostegia immersa.
Litobrochia robusta.
Lomaria blechnoides.
  ciliata.
Lygodium scandens (japonicum).
Microlepia anthriscifolia.
Moheria thurifraga.
Nephrodium molle corymbiferum.

VIEW OF UNDERGROUND FERNERY.

ASPLENIUM CETERACH.

WINTER CHERRY.

PHALÆNOPSIS AMABILIS.

LORD & BURNHAM
Irvington on Hudson

FERNS

GREENHOUSE PLANTS FOR WINTER FLOWERS

Acalypha hispida
Ageratum
Alyssum maritimum
Amaryllis
Anemone
Anthurium
Antirrhinum
Azalea
Begonia, fibrous rooted
Begonia, semi-tuberous
Beloperone
Boston Daisy
Bougainvillea
Bouvardia
Browallia
Brunsvigia
Buddleja or Buddleia

Cacti, and other Succulents
Calendula officinalis
Callistephus chinensis
Camellia
Centaurea cyanus
Citrus
Clivia
Columnea
Crossandra
Crocus
Cyclamen
Dianthus caryophyllus
Erica
Eucharis grandiflora
Eupatorium
Eurphorbia fulgens
Euphorbia pulcherrima

Exacum
Felicia amelloides
Freesia
Geranium
Gerbera jamesoni
Godetia
Heliotrope
Hibiscus
Hyacinthus
Impatiens
Iris, Dutch
Ixia
Ixora
Jacobinia
Kalanchoe
Lachenalia
Lantana

Lathyrus odoratus
Lilium
Mathiola incana
Myosotis
Narcissus
Nemesia
Nerine
Nicotiana
Nierembergia frutescens
Orchids
Osmanthus fragrans
Oxalis
Pentas
Petunia
Piqueria trinervia
Plumbago
Primula malacoides

Primula sinensis
Ranunculus
Rechsteineria
Reinwardtia
Roses
Santpaulia
Smithiantha
Senecio cruentus
Solanum
Sparmannia
Swainsona
Tecomaria capensis
Trachymene caerulea
Tropaeolum
Tulip
Viola tricolor
Zantedeschia
Zygocactus

ROOFTOP GARDENS

ROOF TOP GARDENS

You have no doubt heard about the New York millionaire who fulfilled his dream of being just an ordinary "dirt farmer" by constructing a $2 million roof garden.

He had corn, eggplants, tomatoes, chickens—the whole works—until the city stepped in and asked him to remove them.

It seems the local bureaucrats all were against little old dirt farms cluttering up their skyline.

-Peach in a Perforated Pot

CITY TERRACE FRUIT CASES

FRUIT TREES IN CASES FOR CITY TERRACES
By Tom Riker

During the many years I worked as a designer of city terraces in New York City, I continually tried to incorporate fruit trees into the basic design. The customers were sold on the idea that small ornamental trees (such as dogwood, cherry, flowering crabs and the like), would produce much more beauty. But, I was able, on many occasions, to sell and install apples, pears, peaches, figs and had the pleasure of having gardeners tell me that they actually produced fruit on the terrace. The problems of growing fruit trees on terraces are winter winds in the North and pollination in season. Many of the terrace owners found the task of self-pollinating too much work, so they had small trees without fruit. The foliage of the various fruit trees did expand the texture of the design. But, they could have had fruit with a little more work. To solve the problem of winter wind the following technology from the past has come to light. I suggest you try building glass or plastic cases against the walls and grow espaliered fruit, both for the ornamental value and pleasure of recreating a part of the gardening past.

I have found many graphic and written examples of the training and cultivation of fruit trees for restricted areas in books on horticulture from the turn of the century and earlier. The training concerns itself with the art of espaliered deciduous fruit trees and vines usually found in glass houses designed strictly for the propagation and cultivation of these plants. Many of us seem to be awed by the possibility of growing peaches, grapes, figs and cherries inside, but you can grow fruit in simple cases, easily constructed on the terrace, or in your yard, that will bear fruit in the "off season" and give you gardening pleasure during the slow gardening months.

I do not want to over-simplify the technology of controlled fruit growing under such conditions but merely to state that the gardener with a working knowledge of fruit culture and ornamental practices in training and grafting can indeed accomplish the above with some work.

The type of "cases" I am referring to would function as an "upright cold frame". To consider the heating of such cases for northern gardens especially on the wind-swept terraces of the cities is a technical problem that can be solved but would present certain engineering difficulties. I was thinking more of a forcing frame or case rather than an upright greenhouse. This frame would give you a significant jump on the season.

1. Basic construction of the frames should follow the same procedure as building cold frames. Remember that the heat and rays of the sun are very important in development of early fruit so be sure to face the frames south or east when possible. White wall may act as reflectors on other exposures.

2. To protect container grown fruit trees during the winter months to prevent freezing, cover tubs or barrels with straw or leaves then cover the mulching material with burlap.

3. The cases will solve the problem of early frost thus providing the plant with a jump on the season. When you have only space for a few trees or vines this method will insure a harvest.

Many of the "older" gardening books and magazines have really covered the subject in every detail. Fruit culture books from England —1900 and back to about 1875—can be found in some city libraries or horticultural libraries. The material lists may differ but the general rules still prevail.

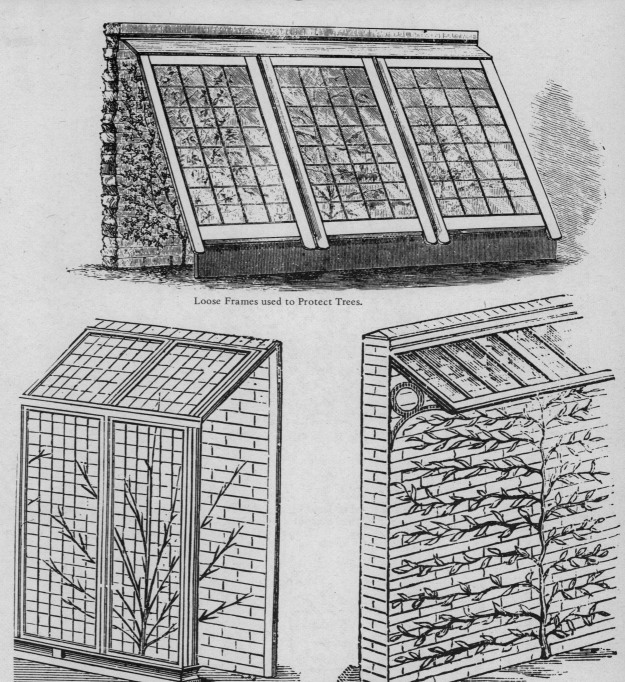

Loose Frames used to Protect Trees.

Wall Case

Glass Coping for Walls.

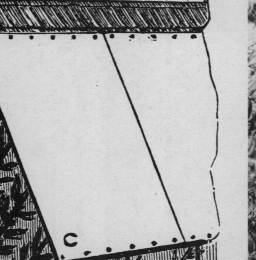

French Shelter of Canvas for Fruit Trees.

From "The Terrace Gardener's Handbook"
by Linda Yang
Doubleday & Company, Garden City, N.Y.

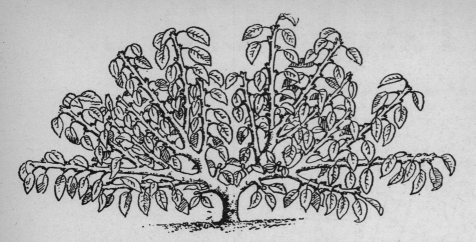

ESPALIERED FRUIT TREES

Training Fan-shaped Apricot Trees; Result of Three Prunings.

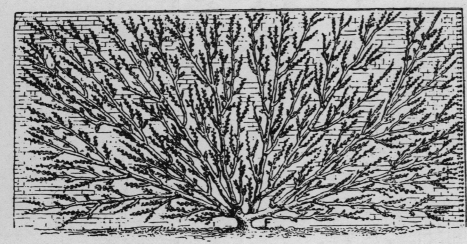

Established Full-sized Fan-shaped Apricot Tree on a Wall.

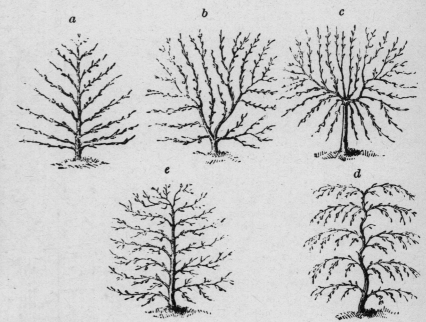

Below left: Pear as
Double Vertical Cordon.

VARIOUS MODES OF TRAINING.

a, the herring-bone fan ; *b*, the irregular fan ; *c*, the stellate fan ; *d*, the drooping fan ; *e*, the wavy fan ;
f, the horizontal ; *g*, the horizontal with screw stem ; *h*, the horizontal with double stem ;
i, the vertical with screw shoots ; *k*, the vertical with upright shoots.

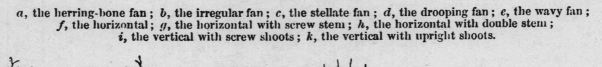

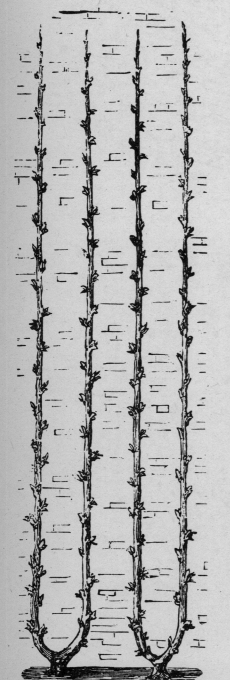

Glazed Cover for Fruit Walls with Upright Front.

STORING VEGETABLES AND FRUIT

COVERING HEAP WITH EARTH.

Agricultural Marketing Research Institute
Agricultural Research Service

STORING VEGETABLES AND FRUITS IN BASEMENTS, CELLARS, OUTBUILDINGS, AND PITS

You can store vegetables and fruits without refrigeration in basements, cellars, outbuildings, and pits, but you need cool outdoor air to cool the stored products.

STORAGE FACILITIES

The kind of storage facility that you will need depends largely on the climate in your area. Storage facilities described in this publication are not practical unless you live in an area where outdoor temperatures during winter average 30 degrees F. or lower.

HOUSE BASEMENT

A well-ventilated basement under a house with central heating may be used for ripening tomatoes and for short-term storage of potatoes, sweet-potatoes, and onions.

But to store vegetables and fruits over winter (long-term storage) in a basement that has a furnace, you will need to partition off a room and insulate it.

Build the room on the north or east side of the basement, if practicable, and do not have heating ducts or pipes running through it.

You need at least one window for cooling and ventilating the room. Two or more windows are desirable, particularly if the room is divided for separate storage of fruits and vegetables. Shade the windows in a way that will prevent light from entering the room.

Equip the room with shelves and removable slatted flooring. These keep vegetable and fruit containers off the floor and help circulation of air. The flooring also lets you use water or wet materials (such as dampened sawdust) on the floor to raise the humidity in the room.

Store vegetables and fruits in wood crates or boxes rather than in bins.

CELLAR UNDER HOUSE WITHOUT CENTRAL HEAT

Cellars under houses without central heat have long been used successfully for winter storage of fruits and vegetables in colder parts of the United States.

These cellars usually have an outside entrance and a dirt floor. The door is a means of ventilating the cellar and regulating the temperature. Some cellars have no windows. If there is a window, it aids in ventilating and in temperature control.

You need at least one window, if the cellar has separate compartments for vegetables and fruits. Shade the windows in a way that will prevent light from entering the cellar. Light causes potatoes to turn green and become bitter. Insulate the ceiling so cold air will not chill the house.

OUTDOOR STORAGE CELLARS

Outdoor storage cellars can be constructed partly or entirely below ground. Cellars constructed below ground are better because they maintain a desirable temperature longer and more uniformly than cellars that are above ground.

Outdoor storage cellars may be attached to your house or located in your yard or under an outbuilding. They should be convenient to your kitchen.

UNDERGROUND CELLARS

The walls and roof of an underground cellar must be strong to support the weight of earth over the roof. Stone and masonry block in combination with concrete can be used, but a cellar made of reinforced concrete is better.

Figure 1 shows an underground cellar. The whole structure, except the door, is covered with soil. Wire screen over the outside ends of air intakes and ventilators keeps out birds and small animals. This structure can also serve as a storm cellar or a protective shelter against radioactive fallout. (For further information, see your local civil defense organization.)

The cellar plan shown in figure 1 is identified as "Plan 5948." Working drawings of this plan may be obtained through your county agricultural agent or from your State Extension Service at your State agricultural college. Give the plan number when you order. There is usually a small charge.

If working drawings of this plan are not available in your State, write to the Cooperative Farm Building Plan Exchange and Rural Housing, Building 228, ARC-East, Agricultural Research Service, U. S. Department of Agriculture, Beltsville, Md. 20705. Include your ZIP Code in your return address. The U. S. Department of Agriculture does not distribute drawings, but will direct you to a State that does distribute them.

PARTLY UNDERGROUND CELLARS

One type of cellar that can be used in colder parts of the country has walls of masonry that are partly under ground. Soil is banked around three walls, and one wall is left exposed for an insulated double door. If you have more than one storage compartment, an air inlet and a ventilator are needed for each one. Ventilators are indicated in figure 1.

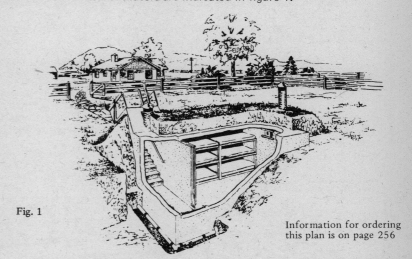

Fig. 1

Information for ordering this plan is on page 256

Plan 5948

Underground cellar that can also serve as a storm and fallout shelter.

OUTBUILDINGS

Storing vegetables and fruits in aboveground storage buildings is practical only where the climate is consistently cold, but only if the average temperature is not below freezing. Even in these climates temperatures may drop to zero or below, and supplemental heat may be needed on very cold nights. Thermostatically controlled heat may be used if electricity is available. Only a small amount of heat is necessary to prevent subfreezing temperature in a building. Storage temperature should be watched closely when low temperatures are predicted.

Aboveground storage buildings can be built of masonry or lumber, but they must be well insulated. Hollow-block walls, regardless of thickness, have little insulating value. Put vermiculite, or some other dry granular material, in the channels of hollow blocks as each layer of block is laid. If you use cinder blocks, scrub them on both sides with cement grout to make them less porous. Then paint them on the inside with aluminum paint; the paint serves as a moisture barrier. Lay tar paper between the ceiling and joists as a moisture barrier, and spread at least 12 inches of dry sawdust or other granular material in the attic above the ceiling.

A frame building can be built of 2-by 4-inch studding and rafters. Make walls tight by sheathing the inside and outside of the frame with matched lumber. Insulate the space between the walls with loose fill or mineral wool blanket. Put laminated kraft paper (with asphalt between layers), aluminum foil, or polyethylene between the insulation and inside walls as a moisture barrier. Put building paper over the outside sheathing before you lay shingles or siding to make the building tight. Paint the inside of the building with aluminum paint or whitewash.

To ventilate aboveground storage buildings, you need intake and exhaust vents.

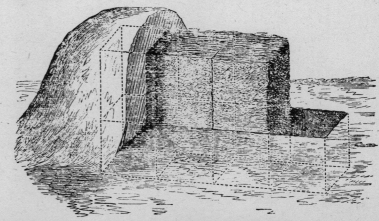

PIT OF SOUR FODDER.

PITS

Cone-shaped outdoor pits are often used for storing potatoes, carrots, beets, turnips, salsify, parsnips, and cabbage. They are sometimes used for storing winter apples and pears. The pit may be built on the ground, or in a hole 6 to 8 inches deep in a well-drained location. Build the pit as follows:

Spread a layer of straw, leaves, or other bedding material on the ground.

Stack the vegetables or fruits on the bedding in a cone-shaped pile. Do not store vegetables and fruits in the same pile.

Cover the vegetables or fruits with more bedding.

Cover the entire pile with 3 or 4 inches of soil.

Firm the soil with the back of a shovel to make the pit waterproof.

Dig a shallow drainage ditch around the pit.

Small pits containing only a few bushels of vegetables or fruits will get sufficient ventilation if you let the bedding material over the vegetables extend through the soil at the top of the pile. Cover the top of the pile with a board or piece of sheet metal to protect the stored products from rain; a stone will hold the cover in place.

To ventilate large pits, place two or three boards or stakes up through the center of the pile of vegetables or fruits to form a flue. Cap the flue with two pieces of board nailed together at right angles.

It is difficult to remove vegetables and fruits from cone-shaped pits in cold weather. And once a pit is opened its entire contents should be removed. For these reasons it is better to construct several small pits rather than one large one. Put a small quantity of different vegetables in each pit. This makes it necessary to open only one pit to get a variety of vegetables. When several vegetables are stored in the same pit, separate them with straw or leaves. Do not store apples and pears in vegetable pits.

Another type of pit is made simply of a barrel covered with several layers of straw and earth.

Pits should be made in a different place every year. Leftovers in used pits usually are contaminated.

KEEPING THE STORAGE SPACE CLEAN

Keep storage facilities for vegetables and fruits clean. Get rid of vegetables and fruits that show signs of decay. At least once a year, remove all containers from your storeroom. Then clean them and air them in the sun. Wash and whitewash the walls and ceiling of your storeroom before you put the containers back into storage.

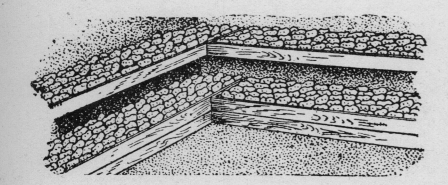

REGULATING THE TEMPERATURE

You will need at least two reliable thermometers (preferably of a kind that records minimum and maximum temperatures) to carefully regulate storage temperature. Place one thermometer in the coldest location of the basement, cellar, or outbuilding, and place the other thermometer outdoors.

Regulate storage temperature by opening and closing doors, windows, or other openings used as ventilators.

Outdoor temperatures well below 32 degrees F. are necessary to cool storage air to 32 degrees and to maintain that temperature. Once cooled to 32 degrees the temperature will rise again if ventilators are closed, even though outdoor temperature is about 25 degrees. Close ventilators tightly whenever the outdoor temperature is higher than the storage temperature. Watch indoor and outdoor temperatures closely. In most regions, daily adjustment of ventilators usually is necessary to maintain desired storage temperatures.

The danger of overventilating during subfreezing weather is that stored products will freeze if you are not careful. For example, in an insulated storage cellar partly above ground at Beltsville, Md., it was found that full ventilation both day and night was necessary to maintain a temperature of 32 degrees F. if outdoor temperatures ranged between 18 degrees and 30 degrees during the day and dipped to 10 degrees at night. If minimum temperature at night, under conditions of normal air movement, was 8 degrees for 5 or 6 hours, the storage temperature dropped to 30 degrees. During a night of high wind, however, a minimum of 12 degrees cooled the cellar to 30 degrees.

Temperature requirements of stored crops and points at which they freeze are given in table 1.

MAINTAINING PROPER MOISTURE

Without proper moisture, stored vegetables and fruits shrivel, lose quality, and eventually become unfit to eat. Humidity requirements for vegetables and fruits are discussed below and are summarized in table 1.

Two ways of maintaining proper humidity are (1) the use of water to raise the humidity of the storage air, and (2) the use of ventilated polyethylene bags and box liners. Moisture can be added to storage air by sprinkling the floor frequently, by placing large pans of water under fresh-air intake vents, by covering the floor with wet materials such as straw or odorless sawdust, or by a combination of these. However, these methods will not prevent shriveling of root crops.

The easiest and most effective way to control moisture loss in root crops and in certain other crops is to put them in polyethylene bags or box liners. Cut a few 1/4- to 3/8-inch holes in the sides of the bags or liners to permit ventilation. Tie the bags and fold over the tops of box liners, but do not seal them.

HANDLING VEGETABLES AND FRUITS

Vegetables and fruits that are to be stored should be handled carefully to prevent damage. Give special attention to containers that you use for harvesting and storing. Use containers that have smooth inner surfaces. Protruding wire staples in baskets and hampers are particularly damaging.

Lightweight tub buckets and plastic-coated stave baskets (egg baskets) are good containers for harvesting. If the soil is sandy, rinse the containers frequently to reduce skin breaks.

Standard apple boxes and lug boxes used for shipping tomatoes, grapes, and nectarines are good storage containers. Slatted crates can be made easily from melon crates.

TABLE 1.—*Freezing points, recommended storage conditions, and length of storage period of vegetables and fruits.*

Commodity	Freezing point	Place to store	Storage conditions Temperature	Storage conditions Humidity	Length of storage period
	° F.		° F.		
Vegetables:					
Dry beans and peas		Any cool, dry place	32° to 40°	Dry	As long as desired.
Late cabbage	30.4	Pit, trench, or outdoor cellar	Near 32° as possible	Moderately moist.	Through late fall and winter.
Cauliflower	30.3	Storage cellar	...do...	...do...	6 to 8 weeks.
Late celery	31.6	Pit or trench; roots in soil in storage cellar.	...do...	...do...	Through late fall and winter.
Endive	31.9	Roots in soil in storage cellar	...do...	...do...	2 to 3 months.
Onions	30.6	Any cool, dry place	...do...	Dry	Through fall and winter.
Parsnips	30.4	Where they grew, or in storage cellar.	...do...	Moist	Do.
Peppers	30.7	Unheated basement or room	45° to 50°	Moderately moist.	2 to 3 weeks.
Potatoes	30.9	Pit or in storage cellar	35° to 40°	...do...	Through fall and winter.
Pumpkins and squashes	30.5	Home cellar or basement	55°	Moderately dry.	Do.
Root crops (miscellaneous).		Pit or in storage cellar	Near 32° as possible	Moist	Do.
Sweetpotatoes	29.7	Home cellar or basement	55° to 60°	Moderately dry.	Do.
Tomatoes (mature green).	31.0	...do...	55° to 70°	...do...	4 to 6 weeks.
Fruits:					
Apples	29.0	Fruit storage cellar	Near 32° as possible	Moderately moist.	Through fall and winter.
Grapefruit	29.8	...do...	...do...	...do...	4 to 6 weeks.
Grapes	28.1	...do...	...do...	...do...	1 to 2 months.
Oranges	30.5	...do...	...do...	...do...	4 to 6 weeks.
Pears	29.2	...do...	...do...	...do...	See text.

Remove all crushed, cut, or decaying vegetables and fruits from those that are to be stored. If damaged or infected garden products are placed in storage, serious losses from decay are likely to occur.

See that vegetables and fruits have as little field heat as possible when you put them in storage. Harvest in early morning, or let the crops cool outdoors overnight before storing them.

Waxing vegetables for home storage is not recommended, although wax has been used for several years on certain fresh vegetables and fruits to improve their sales appearance and to reduce moisture loss.

STORING VEGETABLES

More kinds of vegetables than fruits can be stored at home. Storage requirements of vegetables vary greatly, but certain ones can be stored together (see table 1).

To store vegetables successfully you must provide each vegetable with the temperature, humidity, and ventilation needed to control moisture loss, maintain flavor, and hold decay to a minimum.

Conditions under which vegetables keep best are discussed in this section.

DRY BEANS AND PEAS

All kinds of dry beans and peas, including lima beans and soybeans, may be kept for home use. You can dry beans and peas in two ways:

1. Pick the pods as soon as they are mature and spread them in a warm, dry place until they are thoroughly dry; or—

2. Pull and dry the bean plants like hay after most of the pods are ripe.

After drying the beans, shell them and give them one of the following treatments to protect them from destruction by moths and weevils:

1. Refrigerate them at 0 degrees F. or below for 3 or 4 days.

2. Heat them in an oven at 180 degrees F. for 15 minutes. As an added precaution, leave the beans in the oven for an hour after you turn off the heat.

LATE CABBAGE

Cabbage may be stored in outdoor storage cellars, in cone-shaped pits, or in long pits (fig. 5). The advantage of long pits over cone-shaped pits is that you can remove a few heads of cabbage from a long pit without disturbing the rest of the pit.

To store cabbages in a long pit, pull the plants out by the roots, place them head down in the pit, and cover them with soil.

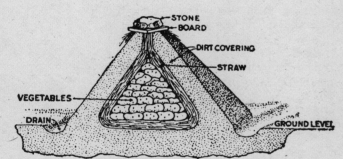

Fig. 5—Irish potatoes in an outdoor mound. This mound must be in a well-drained location. After removing 2 or 3 inches of earth, pile the potatoes on a 2 or 3-inch layer of dry straw, leaves or hay. Cover the vegetables with 2 or 3 inches of straw, leaves or hay, and cover this with 3 or 4 inches of earth. Increase the thickness of the earth layer as severe weather approaches, making it as much as 12 inches in extremely cold climates. Manure or corn stalks should be piled over the mound. The straw, coming to the top, will afford ventilation. The opening should be covered for protection from rain.

Fig. 7—This shows cabbage, pulled with roots, stored in a shallow trench, with roots down. The roots are covered with earth. The stakes, projecting 2 feet above the surface of the earth, serve as supports for boards or poles which make an enclosure. This frame should be banked with dirt (b). Across the top place poles or plank and cover with straw, hay or corn fodder (a). Make the trench as long as necessary and any width up to 8 feet.

You can also store cabbage in a shallow trench that is framed with stakes or poles and covered with straw (Fig. 7) To store cabbage this way, pull the plants out by the roots and set the plants side by side with their roots in the trench. After you put the plants in the trench, pack soil around the roots. Then build a frame about 2 feet high around the trench. The frame may be made of boards or poles or of stakes driven into the ground. Next, bank soil around the frame. Finally, place poles across the top of the frame to hold a covering of straw, hay, or corn fodder.

Heads of cabbage may be stored on shelves in an outdoor storage cellar. Do not keep them in your basement, because cabbage odor is likely to spread through the house.

LATE CELERY

Celery plants of late-maturing varieties may be stored for 1 or 2 months in the garden. To store celery this way, bank a few inches of soil around the base of the plants at the end of the growing season; build the bank up to the top of the plants before severe freezing occurs. As the weather becomes colder, cover the banking with straw or corn fodder held in place with boards.

Another way to store celery is to dig a trench 10 to 12 inches wide, about 24 inches deep, and any desired length

Dig the plants when they are fully grown. Take a clump of soil with the roots. Then pack the plants in the trench. Water the plants as you put them in the trench, and leave the trench open long enough for plant tops to dry off. Unless the soil is very dry at the time of storing or extended warm weather follows it, you do not have to water again.

Make a sloping roof for the trench by setting a 12-inch board on edge beside the trench; bank soil against the board. Then put boards, poles, or cornstalks (from which the tops have been removed) across the trench with one end resting on the upright board and the other end on the ground.

Spread a light covering of straw or other material that will pack closely over the roof. As the weather becomes colder, add more covering. Celery stored this way will keep until late winter.

You can also store celery in a hotbed   . First remove surplus soil from the hotbed and substitute a covering of boards for the sash. Then pack the celery in the hotbed in the same way that is described for storing celery in a trench.

Celery may be stored on the floor of a basement storage room or in an outdoor storage cellar. For this kind of storage, take celery plants from the garden just before freezing occurs. Dig up the roots in a clump of soil. Then set the plants on the floor (roots down) and pack them tightly. If moderately moist, the celery will keep well for 1 to 2 months.

Do not store celery in a cellar with turnips or cabbages; they taint the flavor of celery.

ENDIVE

Endive kept in a storage cellar under conditions described for cellar storage of celery will keep for 2 or 3 months. When storing endive in a cellar, tie the leaves together to help blanching.

ONIONS

Onions must be mature and thoroughly dry to keep well in storage. Damaged onions and onions that have thick necks will not keep.

Store onions in a dry, well-ventilated place, such as an attic or unheated room. Keep them in well-ventilated containers such as slatted crates or open-mesh bags. Fill the bags half full and hang them on overhead hooks. Fill the crates half full and stack them on crossbars. Do not store onions in cellars. Slight freezing will not harm onions, if they are not handled while frozen.

Onions grown from sets are hard to keep. However, one way to store them is to place them in a single layer, necks down, on poultry netting that is suspended in a cold but nonfreezing place.

Fig. 8—A barrel can be made into a good storage pit for cabbage, turnips, potatoes etc. Barrel is placed on its side and covered with straw and dirt.

HOW TO USE USDA GRADES IN BUYING FOOD

It's hard to judge the quality of many foods you buy in the grocery store. But USDA (U.S. Department of Agriculture) grades for food can help you.

The grades are measures of quality. If a food has been graded by a Government grader, it may carry the official grade mark, shaped like a shield. This folder shows the official shield-shaped grade marks used on different foods and tells what they mean.

Grading of food is voluntary, paid for by the packer or processor who requests it.

This is the grade mark used on canned, frozen, and dried fruits and vegetables. It is also used on a few related products like honey, jam and jelly.

There are three grades: U.S. Grade A (Fancy); U.S. Grade B (Choice or Extra Standard); and U.S. Grade C (Standard)

Not many of these products carry the U.S. grade mark on their labels. The ones you are most likely to see are frozen vegetables, frozen orange juice, jam, and jelly.

However, if the label has one of the grade names on it, without the U.S. in front of the name, then it must measure up to that quality even though it has not been officially graded. An example would be a label with the word "Fancy" or "Grade A" on it.

Most are at least Grade B quality—and this is quite good. Grade A, of course, is excellent—use it for desserts or salads where looks and texture are important. Grade B fruits and vegetables are not required to be as uniform in size and color as Grade A products, nor quite as tender or free from blemishes.

Grade C products are fairly good quality, just as wholesome and nutritious as the higher grades—and they sell for less.

This grade mark may be used on fresh fruits and vegetables. When you see it, it means good quality produce. And it means that the product was packed under the supervision of an official Governement grader.

Although most fresh fruits and vegetables are sold at wholesale on the basis of U.S. grades, not many are marked with the grade when they are sold in the grocery store.

The typical range of grades for fresh fruits and vegetables is U.S. Fancy, U.S. No. 1, and U.S. No. 2. For some products, there are grades above and below that range. For instance, grades for apples are U.S. Extra Fancy, U.S. Fancy, U.S. No. 1, and U.S. Utility.

The grades are based on the product's color, size, shape, maturity, and number of defects. The lower grades are just as nutritious as the higher grades. The difference is mainly in appearance, waste, and preference.

This is the grade mark used on canned, frozen, and dried fruits and vegetables. It is also used on a few related products like honey, jam and jelly.

This grade mark may be used on fresh fruits and vegetables. When you see it, it means good quality produce. And it means that the product was packed under the supervision of an official Government grader.

-Interior of Bunyard's Fruit-room

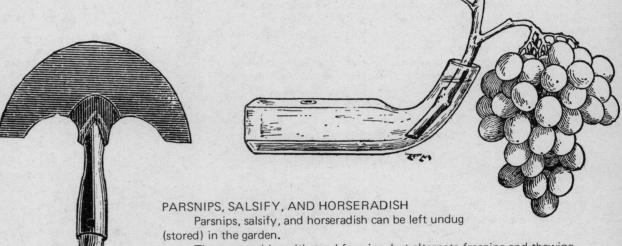

PARSNIPS, SALSIFY, AND HORSERADISH

Parsnips, salsify, and horseradish can be left undug (stored) in the garden.

These vegetables withstand freezing, but alternate freezing and thawing damages them. If you store them in the ground, mulch them lightly at the end of the growing season. Keep them covered until outdoor temperatures are consistently low. Then remove the mulch to permit thorough freezing. After they have frozen, mulch them deep enough to keep them frozen. These vegetables may also be stored like other root crops.

PEPPERS

Mature-green bell peppers can be kept in home storage for 2 or 3 weeks if they are properly handled. Firm, dark-green peppers are best for storage.

Pick peppers just before frost. Then wash them and sort them according to maturity and firmness.

Close control of moisture and temperature conditions is needed for successful storage of peppers. A polyethylene liner with twelve to fifteen ¼-inch holes placed in a container such as a lug box is a good way to maintain high humidity. The temperature should be between 45 degrees and 50 degrees F. Serious decay can occur at 40 degrees or lower in 3 weeks.

Hot varieties of peppers are easiest to store after they are dry. You can dry them in two ways:

1. Pull the plants and hang them up; or—
2. Pick the peppers from the plants and string the peppers up on a line.

Store dry peppers in a cool, dry place such as an attic or unheated room. Do not store them in cellars.

POTATOES

Potatoes that are to be stored require special handling at harvest time. Dig potatoes carefully and remove them promptly from the garden to prevent sun and wind damage. If late blight is present, delay digging until potato vines are dead and dry.

Store only sound potatoes free of serious cuts and bruises.

EARLY POTATOES

Because outdoor temperatures usually are high when early-crop potatoes are harvested, cool storage conditions are difficult to maintain. However, you can hold the temperature of early potatoes down near 70 degrees F. at harvest time by digging them in early morning.

After harvest, cure early potatoes by holding them in moist air for 1 to 2 weeks at 60 degrees to 75 degrees F. The curing heals skinned areas and small cracks, and thus helps to prevent decay.

Do not spread freshly harvested potatoes in windy or sunny locations to cure them. If you do, wounds will not heal and damaged tissues will dry out and become discolored. Coating potatoes with hydrated lime is not recommended.

Decay of early potatoes is not likely to be a problem if you store them at 70 to 75 degrees F. Losses become serious, however, at 80 degrees or above. A storage temperature of 60 degrees, if obtainable, would be ideal for keeping early potatoes 4 to 6 weeks.

In areas that have mild temperatures in summer, early-crop potatoes can be left in the ground until fall and dug as needed. If you keep potatoes in the ground, bank (or ridge) soil around the plants when you cultivate in late summer. This will protect the potatoes from light, which causes them to turn green, and will allow good drainage. Do not keep potatoes undug in the garden if you live in an area that has high temperatures and heavy rainfall.

LATE POTATOES

Late-crop potatoes are better than early-crop potatoes for long-term storage. Since outdoor temperatures usually are low when late-crop potatoes are harvested, cool storage conditions are easy to maintain.

After harvest, cure late potatoes by holding them in moist air for 1 to 2 weeks at 60 degrees to 75 degrees F. Wounds do not heal at 50 degrees or below. After curing, and as soon as outdoor temperatures permit, lower storage temperatures to about 35 degrees to 40 degrees for winter storage.

Late potatoes keep well for several months in basement storage rooms, in cellars, or in cone-shaped pits. The potatoes keep best in moderately moist air. Store potatoes in the dark to prevent them from turning green.

Potatoes stored at about 35 degrees F. for several months tend to become sweet. This condition usually can be corrected by holding the potatoes at about 70 degrees for a week or two before you use them.

PUMPKINS AND SQUASHES

With proper care, hard-rind varieties of winter pumpkins and squashes will keep for several months. Harvest them before frost, and leave a piece of stem on them when you cut them from the plants. Store only well-matured fruits that are free of insect and mechanical injuries.

Pumpkins and squashes for long-term storage keep better if they are cured for 10 days at 80 degrees to 85 degrees. If these temperatures are impracticable, put the pumpkins and squashes near your furnace to cure them. Curing hardens the rinds and heals surface cuts. Bruised areas and pickle-worm injuries, however, cannot be healed.

After curing the pumpkins and squashes, store them in a dry place at 55 degrees to 60 degrees F. If stored at 50 degrees or below, pumpkins and squashes are subject to damage by chilling. At temperatures above sixty degrees, they gradually lose moisture and become stringy.

Acorn squashes will keep well in a dry place at 45 degrees to 50 degrees F. for 35 to 40 days. Do not cure acorn squashes before storing them. They turn orange, lose moisture, and become stringy if cured for 10 days at 80 degrees to 85 degrees or if stored at 55 degrees or above for more than 6 to 8 weeks.

A dark-green rind at harvest is an indication of succulence and good quality.

Do not store pumpkins and squashes in outdoor cellars or pits.

ROOT CROPS (MISCELLANEOUS)

Root crops such as beets, carrots, celeriac, kohlrabi, rutabagas, turnips, and winter radishes should not be put in storage until late fall. These crops

Naples Gourd. Fruit large, sometimes 1½ft. long; rind a deep green, turning yellow when thoroughly ripe, smooth;

TRAP FOR WASPS AND FLIES IN GREENHOUSES.

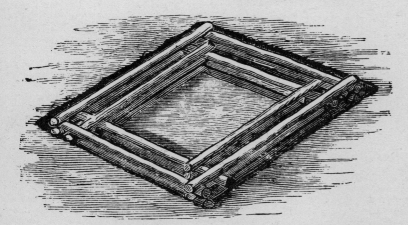

EXCAVATION AND BASE OF ROOT HOUSE.

withstand autumn frosts and are better off in the garden until nights are cold enough to permit proper storage temperatures.

Dig root crops when the soil is dry, and immediately prepare them for storage. Cut the plant tops about one-half inch above the crown. You may wash the roots if you let them dry off before storing them. Do not expose them to drying winds; and see that they are cool when you put them in storage.

PRAIRIE ROOT CELLAR.

Root crops keep best between 32 degrees and 40 degrees F. They require high humidity to prevent shriveling. Continued storage at 45 degrees causes them to sprout new tops and to become woody.

Turnips and rutabagas give off odors; do not store them in your basement or home cellar. You may store them with other root crops and vegetables in an outdoor cellar or pit. Turnips may be left in the garden longer than most other crops. They withstand hard frosts, but are damaged by alternate freezing and thawing.

All other root crops can be stored together in your basement storage room or home cellar. Root crops keep their crispness longer when bedded in layers of moist sand, peat, or sphagnum moss. However, polyethylene bags and box liners with about four ¼-inch holes are easier to use than bedding. Root crops can be stored in crates or boxes in moist air, but they gradually lose moisture and quality unless polyethylene liners are used.

A cone-shaped pit is a good storage place for root crops; but only in areas where the root crops can be protected from freezing.

SHUTTER FOR PIT.

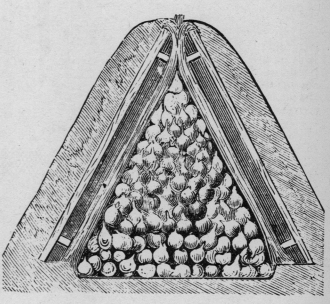

SECTION OF FINISHED PIT.

SWEETPOTATOES

Sweetpotatoes that are well matured, carefully handled, and properly cured can be kept until April or May at 55 degrees to 60 degrees F.

Sweetpotatoes are easily bruised and cut. Handle them carefully and as little as possible. Put them directly in storage containers at harvest. Cure freshly dug sweetpotatoes by holding them for about 10 days under moist conditions at 80 degrees to 85 degrees F. In the absence of better facilities, sweetpotatoes can be cured near your furnace. To maintain a high humidity during curing, stack storage crates and cover them with paper or heavy cloth. If the temperature near your furnace is between 65 degrees and 75 degrees, the curing period should last 2 or 3 weeks. At the end of the curing period, move the crates to a cooler part of your basement or house where a temperature about 55 degrees to 60 degrees can be maintained.

In houses without central heating, sweetpotatoes can be kept behind a cookstove or around a warm chimney. If you keep sweetpotatoes this way, wrap them in fireproof paper (to slow down temperature changes) and store them in boxes or barrels.

Sweetpotatoes are subject to damage by chilling. Do not store them at 50 degrees F. or below.

Outdoor pits are not recommended for storage of sweetpotatoes, because the dampness of outdoor pits encourages decay.

TOMATOES

With special care, tomatoes can be stored in fall for about 4 to 6 weeks. Tomatoes taken from nearly spent vines usually are not as good as tomatoes from vigorous vines and are more subject to decay. Therefore, plant tomatoes late in the planting season so vines will be vigorous when you are ready to harvest.

Harvest tomatoes just before the first killing frost. If an unexpected frost occurs, tomatoes not damaged by freezing can be salvaged and ripened. If you live in an area where outdoor temperatures are likely to range between 32 degrees and 50 degrees F., harvest tomatoes within 4 to 5 days after such temperatures occur to prevent damage by chilling.

Pick tomatoes from the plants. Remove the stems to prevent them from puncturing tomatoes.

After harvesting tomatoes, wash them and let them dry off before you store them. Wiping the soil from tomatoes is not recommended because it causes sand scarring, which may lead to decay.

Store tomatoes that show red in separate containers from green tomatoes. This reduces bruising and separates tomatoes that can be used first. Pack green tomatoes one or two layers deep in shallow boxes or trays for ripening.

Mature green tomatoes reach an eating-ripe stage at 65 degrees to 70 degrees F. in about 14 days. Ripening can be slowed down by holding the tomatoes at 55 degrees. Do not hold tomatoes at 50 degrees or below for more than a few days. At 55 degrees mature-green tomatoes need about 25 to 28 days to ripen. Less mature green tomatoes need more time to ripen.

An airy cellar or outbuilding where temperature can be maintained at about 55 degrees to 58 degrees is satisfactory for holding tomatoes. A room with moderately moist air is best. Too much dampness encourages decay. If the room is too dry, the tomatoes—especially the more immature ones—will shrivel before they ripen. Wrapping tomatoes helps to slow down moisture loss, but is not completely effective in a dry room. Polyethylene-film bags and box liners, if perforated, help prevent shrivelling, but they may increase decay.

Stored tomatoes should be sorted at 7- to 10- day intervals. Separate tomatoes that show red from those that are still green. Remove tomatoes that show decay.

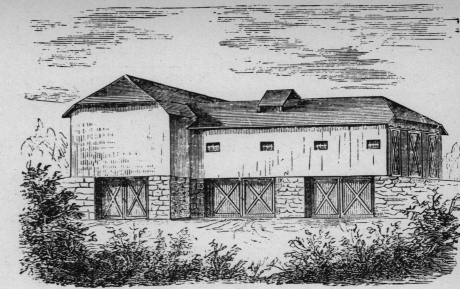

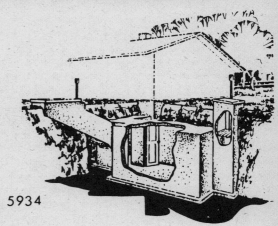

5934

5860

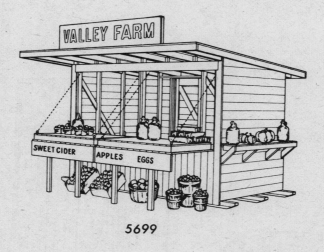

5699

HOW AND WHERE TO SECURE PLANS

OBTAINING PLANS

Plans listed herein may be obtained through your local Cooperative Extension Agent. You are encouraged to secure plans from him so that you can compare them with other plans that he may have and recommend.

Plans also may be obtained from Agricultural Engineering Extension, Riley-Robb Hall, Cornell University, Ithaca, New York 14850. Please order by plan number and enclose your remittance, making it payable to Cornell University. Plans cannot be sent until your check or purchase order is received. Orders from individuals and orders for less than $1.00 cannot be accepted unless accompanied by payment in advance. The following discounts apply to orders of $10.00 or more.

$ 10. 00 to $ 49. 99   10%
$ 50. 00 or more   20%

ADDITIONAL PLAN LISTS

In addition to this plan list, several others describing agricultural structures and fixed equipment are available from your Cooperative Extension Agent, or from Agricultural Engineering Extension, Riley-Robb Hall, Cornell University, Ithaca, N.Y. 14850. These lists describe the information presented on the drawings to aid in your selection of an appropriate plan and are collected for specific topics (such as beef, cattle equipment, dairy, grain, livestock, machinery, poultry, storages, and trussed rafters).

Requests for House plans should be directed to the Department of Design and Environmental Analysis, New York State College of Human Ecology, Martha Van Rensselaer Hall, Ithaca, New York 14850.

5934   **$0. 50**

Underground reinforced concrete combination Farm Fallout Shelter and Storage features a main shelter area 8' x 12'. The length can be increased to anything required or desired to fit personal needs. All construction details, including steel reinforcing, entrance layout, emergency exit, loading chute, and ventilation piping are shown. The layout illustrated shows the structure attached to the basement of a house. Check local requirements where building codes are in force if the design is to be used primarily as a fallout shelter. (1 sheet)

5866   **$0. 50**

Reinforced concrete Storm and Storage Cellar (shown attached to basement of house) 9' - 4" x 11' - 4" — not including length of loading chute for produce or entrance. Door, ventilation, and complete construction details included. (1 sheet)

5176   **$0. 50**

Two different designs illustrated for flat-roofed and dome-roofed (semicircular) reinforced concrete below-ground Vegetable Cellars. Complete details shown for storages 8' x 12', 10' x 12', and 12' x 12' for 280 to 500 bu. capacity. Door, stair, ventilation details included as well as a bill of materials for the flat-roofed storage. (1 sheet)

5860
MP805   **$1. 50**

A 10' x 18' - 11" insulated Forced Air Fruit Cooler 11' - 2" high. Holds about 250 bushels of fruit at one time. Four fans circulate air from an ice bunker through lugs in the cooling tunnel. Total fan delivery should be about 6500 cfm. at ¾ inch static pressure. Six plywood fruit cars, each holding two stacks of lugs, can be moved into the cooling tunnel on fixed roller skate type wheels. The lugs can be stacked about 7 ft. high. (3 sheets)

6027   **$1. 50**
MP1131

This plan shows a 30' x 60' Roadside Market of concrete masonry construction and clear-span trusses. Over half the area is for display and sales with the remaining area utilized by a 6' x 12' utility room, 8' x 8' office, 10' x 14' refrigerated room and a receiving and storage area. Open front may be closed at night or off-season by five overhead doors. Construction details shown. (3 sheets)

5983   **$1. 00**
MP1032

This Roadside Stand 8' x 16' and designed to display fresh produce. Four shelf units are hinged to permit variation in width, height and number of display surfaces. The shelves are protected by a long roof projection on the front of the shed. A durable stand built on pressure-treated posts embedded in concrete. (2 sheets)

5982   **$0. 50**

Two Display Stands for Produce each having three semicircular shelves cut from one 4' x 8' sheet of plywood. Type I has wood framed shelf supports and type II has four supports cut from one sheet of plywood. Both are easily disassembled for moving or storage. Construction details and materials list shown. (1 sheet)

5699   **$0. 50**

A Movable Roadside Stand, 6' x 12' mounted on skids. Hinged front panels drop down to provide a counter display area. The enclosed structure is of all wood construction and has a shed-type roof. (1 sheet)

STORING FRUITS

Only fruits that mature late in fall or that can be purchased on the market during winter can be considered for home storage. Most fruits that can be stored keep best at 31 degrees F.

If you store a large quantity of fruit each year, special storage facilities should be provided.

Apples, pears, grapes, and other fruits absorb odors from potatoes and certain other vegetables. Storing fruits and vegetables together, therefore, is not recommended.

APPLES

The length of time that apples can be stored depends on variety, maturity and soundness at harvest, and storage temperature. For long-term storage, the temperature should be as close to 32 degrees F. as possible. The rate of ripening or softening of apples at a given temperature after harvest depends on the variety. In general, apples ripen about four times as fast at 50 degrees as at 32 degrees. They become overripe rapidly at 70 degrees or above.

Apples can be stored successfully at home if the weather turns cold soon after harvest. In many sections, however, temperatures remain moderate for a month or more after the normal harvest date of many varieties. Varieties that mature in September—for example, Grimes Golden and Jonathan—cannot be kept long. Golden Delicious, Delicious, and Stayman will become overripe in 3 to 4 weeks if temperatures are not below 50 degrees F. Late-maturing varieties such as Yellow Newtown (Albermarle Pippin), Winesap, Arkansas (Mammoth Black Twig), and York Imperial are best for storage in the home.

Apples keep best in cellars that can be cooled by frosty night air in fall and can be maintained at a low temperature (about 31 degrees F.) until early spring.

Apples can be stored in many ways, but they must be protected from Freezing (28 degrees to 30 degrees F.) and shriveling. For example, when days and nights are cold, apples can be stored in insulated boxes in outbuildings, in hay in a barn, in straw-lined pits, or in soil- and straw-covered barrels. These methods of storage, however, will not protect apples against freezing if outdoor temperatures remain below 10 degrees F. If you store apples in a pit, cover them with straw and then paper to keep them dry.

Pick apples when they are mature but still hard. Red apples should be well colored at harvest.

See that apples you store are free from insect and mechanical injuries.

Do not store apples that have glassy spots in the flesh, known as "water core."

Stored apples need moderate moisture to prevent shriveling. Perforated polyethylene bags and box liners are useful to prevent shriveling of all varieties of apples, particularly Grimes Golden and Golden Delicious. Do not seal or tie bags or liners; and see that they have about ten to twelve ¼-inch holes to permit ventilation and to maintain a desirable humidity. Decay is encouraged if the humidity is too high, especially if the temperature is much above 32 degrees F.

For best results, each variety should be ripened and eaten at its peak of quality. Do not store apples too long.

CITRUS FRUITS

Citrus fruits can often be purchased to advantage at wholesale prices and, therefore, may be desirable for storing in the home.

Citrus fruits may be stored in a fruit cellar for short periods, if the storage temperature is kept as close to 32 degrees F. as possible, but not freezing.

GRAPES

In northern sections of the country where grapes mature as outside temperatures approach 32 degrees F., it is possible to keep grapes for a month or two, if the grapes are fully ripe and free of decay at harvesttime.

Store grapes in a cold, moderately moist place. Because grapes absorb odors from other vegetables and fruits, they should be stored alone or in a fruit cellar. Among grape varieties produced in the Northeast, Catawbas have the best keeping quality, but other varieties can be kept satisfactorily.

PEARS

For proper flavor and texture, pears must be ripened after harvest. Pick pears when they are fully mature, but still hard and green. Pears are ready for picking when they change from deep green to pale green.

Bartlett and Kieffer pears are usually ripened immediately after harvest at 60 degrees to 65 degrees F. and are canned or preserved. Kieffer pears require 2 to 3 weeks to ripen. Bartlett pears ripen faster than Kieffer pears.

Store pears with apples or under similar conditions. See that pears are cool and free of defects when you put them in storage.

If pears are stored too long or at too high a temperature or if the temperature for ripening is too high (75 degrees F. or above), they break down without ripening.

VIEW OF COMBINED WAGON AND TOOL HOUSE.

—PERSPECTIVE VIEW OF MR. KYLE'S BARN.

OTHER PLAN LISTS

Revised by: H.A. Longhouse and W.W. Irish

—FRONT VIEW OF PIGPEN, ETC.

5983

HOME CANNING

Consumer and Food Economics Institute
Agricultural Research Service
United States Department of Agriculture

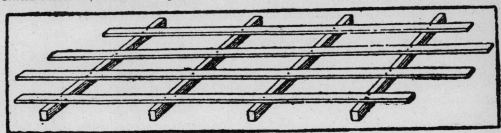

FIG. 1. Home-made rack for wash-boiler.

Organisms that cause food spoilage—molds, yeasts, and bacteria—are always present in the air, water, and soil. Enzymes that may cause undesirable changes in flavor, color, and texture are present in raw fruits and vegetables.

When you can fruits and vegetables you heat them hot enough and long enough to destroy spoilage organisms. This heating (or processing) also stops the action of enzymes. Processing is done in either a boiling-water-bath canner or a steam-pressure canner. The kind of canner that should be used depends on the kind of food being canned.

Right Canner for Each Food

For fruits, tomatoes, and pickled vegetables, use a boiling-water-bath canner. You can process these acid foods safely in boiling water.

For all common vegetables except tomatoes, use a steam-pressure canner. To process these low-acid foods safely in a reasonable length of time takes a temperature higher than that of boiling water.

A pressure saucepan equipped with an accurate indicator or gage for controlling pressure at 10 pounds (240° F.) may be used as a steam-pressure canner for vegetables in pint jars or No. 2 tin cans. If you use a pressure saucepan, add 20 minutes to the processing times given in this publication for each vegetable.

Getting Your Equipment Ready

Steam-Pressure Canner

For safe operation of your canner, clean petcock and safety-valve openings by drawing a string or narrow strip of cloth through them. Do this at beginning of canning season and often during the season.

Check pressure gage.—An accurate pressure gage is necessary to get the processing temperatures needed to make food keep.

A weighted gage needs to be thoroughly clean.

A dial gage, old or new, should be checked before the canning season, and also during the season if you use the canner often. Ask your county home demonstration agent, dealer, or manufacturer about checking it.

If your gage is off 5 pounds or more, you'd better get a new one. But if the gage is not more than 4 pounds off, you can correct for it as shown below. As a reminder, tie on the canner a tag stating the reading to use to get the correct pressure.

The food is to be processed at 10 pounds steam pressure; so—

If the gage reads high—	If the gage reads low—
1 pound high—process at 11 pounds.	1 pound low—process at 9 pounds.
2 pounds high—process at 12 pounds.	2 pounds low—process at 8 pounds.
3 pounds high—process at 13 pounds.	3 pounds low—process at 7 pounds.
4 pounds high—process at 14 pounds.	4 pounds low—process at 6 pounds.

Have canner thoroughly clean.—Wash canner kettle well if you have not used it for some time. Don't put cover in water—wipe it with a soapy cloth, then with a damp, clean cloth. Dry well.

Water-Bath Canner

Water-bath canners are available on the market. Any big metal container may be used as a boiling-water-bath canner if it is deep enough so that the water is well over tops of jars and has space to boil freely. Allow 2 to 4 inches above jar tops for brisk boiling (see sketch). The canner must have a tight-fitting cover and a wire or wooden rack. If the rack has dividers, jars will not touch each other or fall against the sides of the canner during processing.

If a steam-pressure canner is deep enough, you can use it for a water bath. Cover, but do not fasten. Leave petcock wide open, so that steam escapes and pressure does not build up inside the canner.

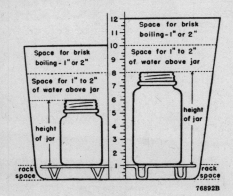

76892B

Glass Jars

Be sure all jars and closures are perfect. Discard any with cracks, chips, dents, or rust; defects prevent airtight seals.

Select the size of closure—widemouth or regular—that fits your jars.

Wash glass jars in hot, soapy water and rinse well. Wash and rinse all lids and bands. Metal lids with sealing compound may need boiling or holding in boiling water for a few minutes—follow the manufacturer's directions.

If you use rubber rings, have clean, new rings of the right size for the jars. Don't test by stretching. Wash rings in hot, soapy water. Rinse well.

Tin Cans

Select desired type and size.—Three types of tin cans are used in home canning—plain tin, C-enamel (corn enamel), and R-enamel (sanitary or standard enamel). For most products plain tin cans are satisfactory. Enameled cans are recommended for certain fruits and vegetables to prevent discoloration of food, but they are not necessary for a wholesome product.

The types of cans and the foods for which they are recommended are:

Type of can	Recommended for—
C-enamel	Corn, hominy.
R-enamel	Beets, red berries, red or black cherries, plums, pumpkin, rhubarb, winter squash.
Plain	All other fruits and vegetables for which canning directions are given in this bulletin.

In this bulletin, directions are given for canning most fruits and vegetables in No. 2 and No. 2½ tin cans. A No. 2 can holds about 2½ cups, and a No. 2½ can about 3½ cups.

Use only cans in good condition.—See that cans, lids, and gaskets are perfect. Discard badly bent, dented, or rusted cans, and lids with damaged gaskets. Keep lids in paper packing until ready to use. The paper protects the lids from dirt and moisture.

Wash cans.—Just before use, wash cans in clean water; drain upside down. Do not wash lids; washing may damage the gaskets. If lids are dusty or dirty, rinse with clean water or wipe with a damp cloth just before you put them on the cans.

Check the sealer.—Make sure the sealer you use is properly adjusted. To test, put a little water into a can, seal it, then submerge can in boiling water for a few seconds. If air bubbles rise from around the can, the seam is not tight. Adjust sealer, following manufacturer's directions.

FIG. 3. A type of commercial canner for hot-water bath, using wood, coal, charcoal, chips, cobs, or brush.

General Canning Procedure

Selecting Fruits and Vegetables for Canning

Choose fresh, firm fruits and young, tender vegetables. Can them before they lose their freshness. If you must hold them, keep them in a cool, airy place. If you buy fruits and vegetables to can, try to get them from a nearby garden or orchard.

For best quality in the canned product, use only perfect fruits and vegetables. Sort them for size and ripeness; they cook more evenly that way.

Washing

Wash all fruits and vegetables thoroughly, whether or not they are to be pared. Dirt contains some of the bacteria hardest to kill. Wash small lots at a time, under running water or through several changes of water. Lift the food out of the water each time so dirt that has been washed off won't go back on the food. Rinse pan thoroughly between washings. Don't let fruits or vegetables soak; they may lose flavor and food value. Handle them gently to avoid bruising.

Filling Containers

Raw pack or hot pack.—Fruits and vegetables may be packed raw into glass jars or tin cans or preheated and packed hot. In this publication directions for both raw and hot packs are given for most of the foods.

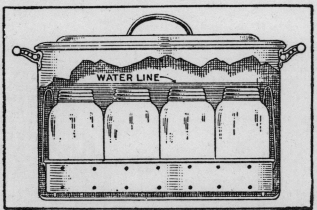

FIG. 2. Wash-boiler with rack for jars.

Most raw fruits and vegetables should be packed tightly into the container because they shrink during processing; a few—like corn, lima beans, and peas—should be packed loosely because they expand.

Hot food should be packed fairly loosely. It should be at or near boiling temperature when it is packed.

There should be enough sirup, water, or juice to fill in around the solid food in the container and to cover the food. Food at the top of the container tends to darken if not covered with liquid. It takes from ½ to 1½ cups of liquid for a quart glass jar or a No. 2½ tin can.

Head space.—With only a few exceptions, some space should be left between the packed food and the closure. The amount of space to allow at the top of the jar or can is given in the detailed directions for canning each food.

Closing Glass Jars

Closures for glass jars are of two main types:

Metal screwband and flat metal lid with sealing compound. To use this type, wipe jar rim clean after produce is packed. Put lid on, with sealing compound next to glass. Screw metal band down tight by hand. When band is tight, this lid has enough give to let air escape during processing. Do not tighten screw band further after taking jar from canner.

Screw bands that are in good condition may be reused. You may remove bands as soon as jars are cool. Metal lids with sealing compound may be used only once.

Porcelain-lined zinc cap with shoulder rubber ring. Fit wet rubber ring down on jar shoulder, but don't stretch unnecessarily. Fill jar; wipe rubber ring and jar rim clean. Then screw cap down firmly and turn it back ¼ inch. As soon as you take jar from canner, screw cap down tight, to complete seal.

Porcelain-lined zinc caps may be reused as long as they are in good condition. Rubber rings should not be reused.

Exhausting and Sealing Tin Cans

Tin cans are sealed before processing. The temperature of the food in the cans must be 170° F. or higher when the cans are sealed. Food is heated to this temperature to drive out air so that there will be a good vacuum in the can after

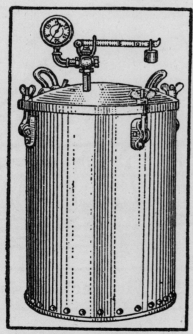

FIG. 4. Steam pressure canner; home and community canning.

processing and cooling. Removal of air also helps prevent discoloring of canned food and change in flavor.

Food packed raw must be heated in the cans (exhausted) before the cans are sealed. Food packed hot may be sealed without further heating if you are sure the temperature of the food has not dropped below 170° F. To make sure, test with a thermometer, placing the bulb at the center of the can. If the thermometer registers lower than 170°, or if you do not make this test, exhaust the cans.

To exhaust, place open, filled cans on a rack in a kettle in which there is enough boiling water to come to about 2 inches below the tops of the cans. Cover the kettle. Bring water back to boiling. Boil until a thermometer inserted at the center of the can registers 170° F.—or for the length of time given in the directions for the fruit or vegetable you are canning.

Remove cans from the water one at a time, and add boiling packing liquid or water if necessary to bring head space back to the level specified for each product. Place clean lid on filled can. Seal at once.

Processing

Process fruits, tomatoes, and pickled vegetables in a boiling-water-bath canner according to the directions on page 10. Process vegetables in a steam-pressure canner according to the directions on page 16.

Cooling Canned Food

Glass jars.—As you take jars from the canner, complete seals at once if necessary. If liquid boiled out in processing, do not open jar to add more. Seal the jar just as it is.

Cool jars top side up. Give each jar enough room to let air get at all sides. Never set a hot jar on a cold surface; instead set the jars on a rack or on a folded cloth. Keep hot jars away from drafts, but don't slow cooling by covering them.

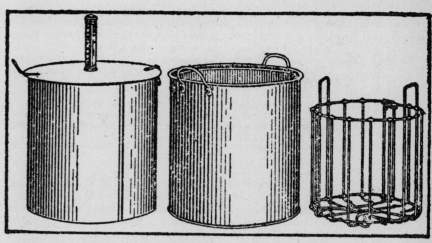

FIG. 5. Water-seal outfit. On the left is shown the cover, with thermometer. In the center is the double walled vat or holder. On the right is a crate for jars.

Tin cans.—Put tin cans in cold, clean water to cool them; change water as needed to cool cans quickly. Take cans out of the water while they are still warm so they will dry in the air. If you stack cans, stagger them so that air can get around them.

Day-After-Canning Jobs

Test the seal on glass jars with porcelain-lined caps by turning each jar partly over in your hands. To test a jar that has a flat metal lid, press center of lid; if lid is down and will not move, jar is sealed. Or tap the center of the lid with a spoon. A clear, ringing sound means a good seal. A dull note does not always mean a poor seal; store jars without leaks and check for spoilage before use.

If you find a leaky jar, use unspoiled food right away. Or can it again; empty the jar, and pack and process food as if it were fresh. Before using jar or lid again check for defects.

When jars are thoroughly cool, take off the screw bands carefully. If a band sticks, covering for a moment with a hot, damp cloth may help loosen it.

Before storing canned food, wipe containers clean. Label to show contents, date, and lot number—if you canned more than one lot in a day.

Wash bands; store them in a dry place.

FIG. 6. Aluminum pressure canner.

Storing Canned Food

Properly canned food stored in a cool, dry place will retain good eating quality for a year. Canned food stored in a warm place near hot pipes, a range, or a furnace, or in direct sunlight may lose some of its eating quality in a few weeks or months, depending on the temperature.

Dampness may corrode cans or metal lids and cause leakage so the food will spoil.

Freezing does not cause food spoilage unless the seal is damaged or the jar is broken. However, frozen canned food may be less palatable than properly stored canned food. In an unheated storage place it is well to protect canned food by wrapping the jars in paper or covering them with a blanket.

On Guard Against Spoilage

Don't use canned food that shows any sign of spoilage. Look closely at each container before opening it. Bulging can ends, jar lids, or rings, or a leak—these may mean the seal has broken and the food has spoiled. When you open a container look for other signs—spurting liquid, an off odor, or mold.

It's possible for canned vegetables to contain the poison causing botulism—a serious food poisoning—without showing signs of spoilage. To avoid any risk of botulism, it is essential that the pressure canner be in perfect order and that every canning recommendation be followed exactly. Unless you're absolutely sure of your gage and canning methods, boil home-canned vegetables before tasting. Heating usually makes any odor of spoilage more evident. Bring vegetables to a rolling boil; then cover and boil for at least 10 minutes. Boil spinach and corn 20 minutes. If the food looks spoiled, foams, or has an off odor during heating, destroy it.

Burn spoiled vegetables, or dispose of the food so that it will not be eaten by humans or animals.

How To Can Fruits, Tomatoes, Pickled Vegetables

Points on Packing

Raw pack.—Put cold, raw fruits into container and cover with boiling-hot sirup, juice, or water. Press tomatoes down in the containers so they are covered with their own juice; add no liquid.

Hot pack.—Heat fruits in sirup, in water or steam, or in extracted juice before packing. Juicy fruits and tomatoes may be preheated without added liquid and packed in the juice that cooks out.

Sweetening Fruit

Sugar helps canned fruit hold its shape, color, and flavor. Directions for canning most fruits call for sweetening to be added in the form of sugar sirup. For very juicy fruit packed hot, use sugar without added liquid.

To make sugar sirup.—Mix sugar with water or with juice extracted from some of the fruit. Use a thin, medium, or heavy sirup to suit the sweetness of the fruit and your taste. To make sirup, combine—

4 cups of water or juice.....	2 cups sugar.....	For 5 cups THIN sirup.
	3 cups sugar.....	For 5½ cups MEDIUM sirup.
	4¾ cups sugar...	For 6½ cups HEAVY sirup.

Heat sugar and water or juice together until sugar is dissolved. Skim if necessary.

To extract juice.—Crush thoroughly ripe, sound juicy fruit. Heat to simmering (185° to 210° F.) over low heat. Strain through jelly bag or other cloth.

To add sugar direct to fruit.—For juicy fruit to be packed hot, add about ½ cup sugar to each quart of raw, prepared fruit. Heat to simmering (185° to 210° F.) over low heat. Pack fruit in the juice that cooks out.

To add sweetening other than sugar.—You can use light corn sirup or mild-flavored honey to replace as much as half the sugar called for in canning fruit. Do not use brown sugar, or molasses, sorghum, or other strong-flavored sirups; their flavor overpowers the fruit flavor and they may darken the fruit.

Canning Unsweetened Fruit

You may can fruit without sweetening—in its own juice, in extracted juice, or in water. Sugar is not needed to prevent spoilage; processing is the same for unsweetened fruit as for sweetened.

Processing in Boiling-Water Bath

Directions.—Put filled glass jars or tin cans into canner containing hot or boiling water. For raw pack in glass jars have water in canner hot but not boiling; for all other packs have water boiling.

Add boiling water if needed to bring water an inch or two over tops of containers; don't pour boiling water directly on glass jars. Put cover on canner.

When water in canner comes to a rolling boil, start to count processing time. Boil gently and steadily for time recommended for the food you are canning. Add boiling water during processing if needed to keep containers covered.

Remove containers from the canner immediately when processing time is up.

Processing times.—Follow times carefully. The times given apply only when a specific food is prepared according to detailed directions.

If you live at an altitude of 1,000 feet or more, you have to add to these processing times in canning directions, as follows:

| Altitude | Increase in processing time if the time called for is— | |
	20 minutes or less	More than 20 minutes
1,000 feet	1 minute	2 minutes.
2,000 feet	2 minutes	4 minutes.
3,000 feet	3 minutes	6 minutes.
4,000 feet	4 minutes	8 minutes.
5,000 feet	5 minutes	10 minutes.
6,000 feet	6 minutes	12 minutes.
7,000 feet	7 minutes	14 minutes.
8,000 feet	8 minutes	16 minutes.
9,000 feet	9 minutes	18 minutes.
10,000 feet	10 minutes	20 minutes.

To Figure Yield of Canned Fruit From Fresh

The number of quarts of canned food you can get from a given quantity of fresh fruit depends upon the quality, variety, maturity, and size of the fruit, whether it is whole, in halves, or in slices, and whether it is packed raw or hot.

Generally, the following amounts of fresh fruit or tomatoes (as purchased or picked) make 1 quart of canned food:

	Pounds
Apples	2½ to 3
Berries, except strawberries	1½ to 3 (1 to 2 quart boxes)
Cherries (canned unpitted)	2 to 2½
Peaches	2 to 3
Pears	2 to 3
Plums	1½ to 2½
Tomatoes	2½ to 3½

In 1 pound there are about 3 medium apples and pears; 4 medium peaches or tomatoes; 8 medium plums.

Directions for Fruits, Tomatoes, Pickled Vegetables

Apples

Pare and core apples; cut in pieces. To keep fruit from darkening, drop pieces into water containing 2 tablespoons each of salt and vinegar per gallon. Drain, then boil 5 minutes in thin sirup or water.

In glass jars.—Pack hot fruit to ½ inch of top. Cover with hot sirup or water, leaving ½-inch space at top of jar. Adjust jar lids. Process in boiling-water bath (212° F.)—

Pint jars _____ 15 minutes
Quart jars _____ 20 minutes

As soon as you remove jars from canner, complete seals if necessary.

In tin cans.—Pack hot fruit to ¼ inch of top. Fill to top with hot sirup or water. Exhaust to 170° F. (about 10 minutes) and seal cans. Process in boiling-water bath (212° F.)—

No. 2 cans _____ 10 minutes
No. 2½ cans _____ 10 minutes

FIG. 7. Home canner and steam cooker holding 14 quart jars. Requires same time as hot-water bath.

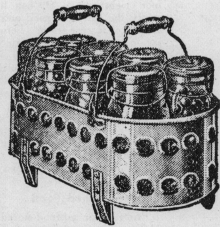

FIG. 8. Rack for jars.

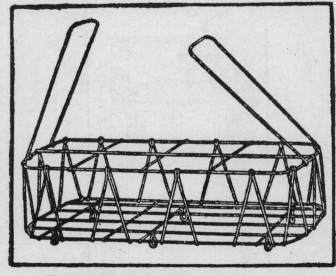

FIG. 9. Wire rack for jars.

BOTULISM

Delores Bonander
Home Economist
Fresno County
Co-operative extension work in agriculture and home economics,
U. S. Department of Agriculture and University of California cooperating.

So many of you have questions about canning, it seems to me we need to be reminded of the hazards of botulism. Therefore, we are preparing these questions and answers on botulism.

WHAT IS BOTULISM?

Botulism is the poisoning caused by the toxin produced by botulinus bacteria as they grow in food. The bacteria themselves are not poisonous, actually, we eat them every day. Only the toxin they produce as they grow in the ABSENCE OF AIR in LOW ACID FOODS is poisonous. However, there is no need to be alarmed about botulism, if proper home canning methods are followed.

HOW CAN BOTULISM BE PREVENTED?

Always can only fresh, firm fruits and vegetables that have been thoroughly cleaned; and meats, fish and poultry in sound condition. Use a PRESSURE CANNER with a tested gauge for canning low-acid vegetables or meats, fish and poultry. Process foods according to a reliable timetable. NEVER process for less than the prescribed time.

Applesauce

Make applesauce, sweetened or unsweetened. Heat to simmering (185°–210° F.); stir to keep it from sticking.

In glass jars.—Pack hot applesauce to ¼ inch of top. Adjust lids. Process in boiling-water bath (212° F.)—

Pint jars_____ 10 minutes
Quart jars_____ 10 minutes

As soon as you remove jars from canner, complete seals if necessary.

In tin cans.—Pack hot applesauce to top. Exhaust to 170° F. (about 10 minutes) and seal cans. Process in boiling-water bath (212° F.)—

No. 2 cans_____ 10 minutes
No. 2½ cans_____ 10 minutes

Apricots

Follow method for peaches. Peeling may be omitted.

Beets, Pickled

Cut off beet tops, leaving 1 inch of stem. Also leave root. Wash beets, cover with boiling water, and cook until tender. Remove skins and slice beets. For pickling sirup, use 2 cups vinegar (or 1½ cups vinegar and ½ cup water) to 2 cups sugar. Heat to boiling.

Pack beets in glass jars to ½ inch of top. Add ½ teaspoon salt to pints, 1 teaspoon to quarts. Cover with boiling sirup, leaving ½-inch space at top of jar. Adjust jar lids. Process in boiling-water bath (212° F.)—

Pint jars_____ 30 minutes
Quart jars_____ 30 minutes

As soon as you remove jars from canner, complete seals if necessary.

Berries, Except Strawberries

● Raw Pack.—Wash berries; drain.

In glass jars.—Fill jars to ½ inch of top. For a full pack, shake berries down while filling jars. Cover with boiling sirup, leaving ½-inch space at top. Adjust lids. Process in boiling-water bath (212° F.)—

Pint jars_____ 10 minutes
Quart jars_____ 15 minutes

As soon as you remove jars from canner, complete seals if necessary.

In tin cans.—Fill cans to ¼ inch of top. For a full pack, shake berries down while filling cans. Fill to top with boiling sirup. Exhaust to 170° F. (10 minutes); seal cans. Process in boiling-water bath (212° F.)—

No. 2 cans_____ 15 minutes
No. 2½ cans_____ 20 minutes

● Hot Pack.—(For firm berries)—Wash berries and drain well. Add ½ cup sugar to each quart fruit. Cover pan and bring to boil; shake pan to keep berries from sticking.

In glass jars.—Pack hot berries to ½ inch of top. Adjust jar lids. Process in boiling-water bath (212° F.)—

Pint jars_____ 10 minutes
Quart jars_____ 15 minutes

As soon as you remove jars from canner, complete seals if necessary.

In tin cans.—Pack hot berries to top. Exhaust to 170° F. (about 10 minutes) and seal cans. Process in boiling-water bath (212° F.)—

No. 2 cans_____ 15 minutes
No. 2½ cans_____ 20 minutes

Cherries

● Raw Pack.—Wash cherries; remove pits, if desired.

In glass jars.—Fill jars to ½ inch of top. For a full pack, shake cherries down while filling jars. Cover with boiling sirup, leaving ½-inch space at top. Adjust lids. Process in boiling-water bath (212° F.)—

Pint jars_____ 20 minutes
Quart jars_____ 25 minutes

As soon as you remove jars from canner, complete seals if necessary.

In tin cans.—Fill cans to ¼ inch of top. For a full pack, shake cherries down while filling cans. Fill to top with boiling sirup. Exhaust to 170° F. (about 10 minutes) and seal cans. Process in boiling-water bath (212° F.)—

No. 2 cans_____ 20 minutes
No. 2½ cans_____ 25 minutes

● Hot Pack.—Wash cherries; remove pits, if desired. Add ½ cup sugar to each quart of fruit. Add a little water to unpitted cherries to keep them from sticking while heating. Cover pan and bring to a boil.

In glass jars.—Pack hot to ½ inch of top. Adjust jar lids. Process in boiling-water bath (212° F.)—

Pint jars_____ 10 minutes
Quart jars_____ 15 minutes

As soon as you remove jars from canner, complete seals if necessary.

In tin cans.—Pack hot to top of cans. Exhaust to 170° F. (about 10 minutes) and seal cans. Process in boiling-water bath (212° F.)—

No. 2 cans_____ 15 minutes
No. 2½ cans_____ 20 minutes

Fruit Juices

Wash; remove pits, if desired, and crush fruit. Heat to simmering (185°–210° F.). Strain through cloth bag. Add sugar, if desired—about 1 cup to 1 gallon juice. Reheat to simmering.

In glass jars.—Fill jars to ½ inch of top with hot juice. Adjust lids. Process in boiling-water bath (212° F.)—

Pint jars_____ 5 minutes
Quart jars_____ 5 minutes

As soon as you remove jars from canner, complete seals if necessary.

In tin cans.—Fill cans to top with hot juice. Seal at once. Process in boiling-water bath (212° F.)—

No. 2 cans_____ 5 minutes
No. 2½ cans_____ 5 minutes

Fruit Purees

Use sound, ripe fruit. Wash; remove pits, if desired. Cut large fruit in pieces. Simmer until soft; add a little water if needed to keep fruit from sticking. Put through a strainer or food mill. Add sugar to taste. Heat again to simmering (185°–210° F.).

In glass jars.—Pack hot to ½ inch of top. Adjust lids. Process in boiling-water bath (212° F.)—

Pint jars_____ 10 minutes
Quart jars_____ 10 minutes

As soon as you remove jars from canner, complete seals if necessary.

In tin cans.—Pack hot to top. Exhaust to 170° F. (about 10 minutes), and seal cans. Process in boiling-water bath (212° F.)—

No. 2 cans_____ 10 minutes
No. 2½ cans_____ 10 minutes

Peaches

Wash peaches and remove skins. Dipping the fruit in boiling water, then quickly in cold water makes peeling easier. Cut peaches in halves; remove pits. Slice if desired. To prevent fruit from darkening during preparation, drop it into water containing 2 tablespoons each of salt and vinegar per gallon. Drain just before heating or packing raw.

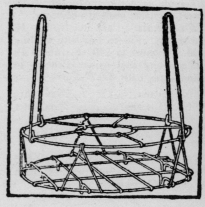

FIG. 11. Wire rack for jars.

● Raw Pack.—Prepare peaches as directed above.

(Continued on next page)

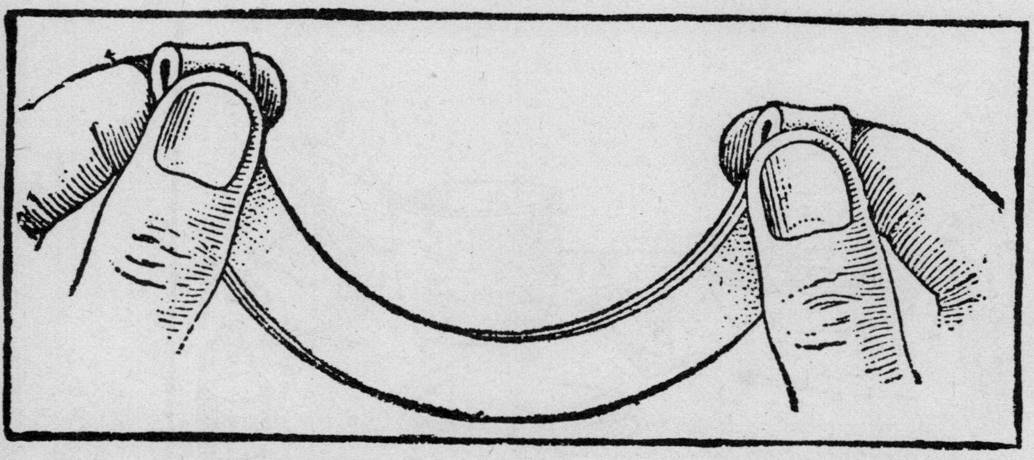

FIG. 10. Simple test for rubbers. A perfect rubber will show no crease or break after being folded tightly several times.

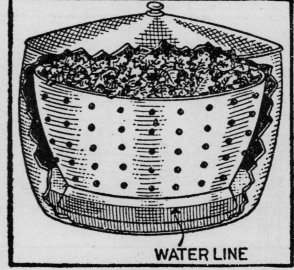

WATER LINE

FIG. 12. Use of a colander to blanch greens in steam.

HOW CAN I KNOW WHETHER OR NOT A JAR OF FOOD IS CONTAMINATED?

It is not always possible to tell if the food is capable of causing botulism by looking at it or smelling it. Contaminated food does not always have a disagreeable odor or show pressure in the can, jar, or bottle. For this reason, always boil home canned vegetables or meats at least 10 minutes before tasting. Begin counting the time when the food reaches a rolling boil and stir frequently to be sure that all of the food is thoroughly heated. (Greens and home canned corn should be boiled for 20 minutes.)

IS BOTULINUS TOXIN EVER PRESENT IN ACID FOODS?

No, not as long as the food remains sufficiently high in acid. However, if acid foods such as fruits, tomatoes, rhubarb and pickles become low acid through the growth of mold and yeast, they may become contaminated. So any jar or can of fruit that shows appreciable mold and yeast growth should be destroyed.

IS IT SAFE TO USE JAM OR JELLY THAT IS MOLDY ON THE SURFACE?

A thick, solid jam or jelly with a small amount of mold on the surface is safe to eat. The high-solid and high sugar content of the jam or jelly prevents the growth of botulinus bacteria even if the mold has neutralized a little of the acid. Exceptions are fig, pear, or persimmon jam which are very low in acid. If any mold shows on these, the jam should be destroyed.

CAN YOU GET BOTULISM FROM HOME CANNED PICKLES?

Properly prepared pickles contain a sufficient amount of acid to prevent the growth of botulinus bacteria. Use only tested recipes. Do not alter the proportions given in these recipes. Do not use homemade vinegar. Use good clear standard vinegar, free from sediment, with 5% acetic acid. Avoid long boiling of the vinegar solution to prevent loss of the acetic acid which is important in the keeping quality of pickles.

In glass jars.—Pack raw fruit to ½ inch of top. Cover with boiling sirup, leaving ½-inch space at top of jar. Adjust jar lids. Process in boiling-water bath (212° F.)—

Pint jars_____ 25 minutes
Quart jars_____ 30 minutes

As soon as you remove jars from canner, complete seals if necessary.

In tin cans.—Pack raw fruit to ¼ inch of top. Fill to top with boiling sirup. Exhaust to 170° F. (about 10 minutes) and seal cans. Process in boiling-water bath (212° F.)—

No. 2 cans_____ 30 minutes
No. 2 ½ cans_____ 35 minutes

● **Hot Pack.**—Prepare peaches as directed above. Heat peaches through in hot sirup. If fruit is very juicy you may heat it with sugar, adding no liquid.

In glass jars.—Pack hot fruit to ½ inch of top. Cover with boiling liquid, leaving ½-inch space at top of jar. Adjust jar lids. Process in boiling-water bath (212° F.)—

Pint jars_____ 20 minutes
Quart jars_____ 25 minutes

As soon as you remove jars from canner, complete seals if necessary.

In tin cans.—Pack hot fruit to ¼ inch of top. Fill to top with boiling liquid. Exhaust to 170° F. (about 10 minutes) and seal cans. Process in boiling-water bath (212° F.)—

No. 2 cans_____ 25 minutes
No. 2½ cans_____ 30 minutes

Pears

Wash pears. Peel, cut in halves, and core. Continue as with peaches, either raw pack or hot pack.

Plums

Wash plums. To can whole, prick skins. Freestone varieties may be halved and pitted.

● **Raw Pack.**—Prepare plums as directed above.

In glass jars.—Pack raw fruit to ½ inch of top. Cover with boiling sirup, leaving ½-inch space at top of jar. Adjust jar lids. Process in boiling-water bath (212° F.)—

Pint jars_____ 20 minutes
Quart jars_____ 25 minutes

As soon as you remove jars from canner, complete seals if necessary.

In tin cans.—Pack raw fruit to ¼ inch of top. Fill to top with boiling sirup. Exhaust to 170° F. (about 10 minutes) and seal cans. Process in boiling-water bath (212° F.)—

No. 2 cans_____ 15 minutes
No. 2½ cans_____ 20 minutes

● **Hot Pack.**—Prepare plums as directed above. Heat to boiling in sirup or juice. If fruit is very juicy you may heat it with sugar, adding no liquid.

In glass jars.—Pack hot fruit to ½ inch of top. Cover with boiling liquid, leaving ½-inch space at top of jar. Adjust jar lids. Process in boiling-water bath (212° F.)—

Pint jars_____ 20 minutes
Quart jars_____ 25 minutes

As soon as you remove jars from canner, complete seals if necessary.

In tin cans.—Pack hot fruit to ¼ inch of top. Fill to top with boiling liquid. Exhaust to 170° F. (about 10 minutes) and seal cans. Process in boiling-water bath (212° F.)—

No. 2 cans_____ 15 minutes
No. 2½ cans_____ 20 minutes

Rhubarb

Wash rhubarb and cut into ½-inch pieces. Add ½ cup sugar to each quart rhubarb and let stand to draw out juice. Bring to boiling.

In glass jars.—Pack hot to ½ inch of top. Adjust lids. Process in boiling-water bath (212° F.)—

Pint jars_____ 10 minutes
Quart jars_____ 10 minutes

As soon as you remove jars from canner, complete seals if necessary.

In tin cans.—Pack hot to top of cans. Exhaust to 170° F. (about 10 minutes) and seal cans. Process in boiling-water bath (212° F.)—

No. 2 cans_____ 10 minutes
No. 2½ cans_____ 10 minutes

Tomatoes

Use only firm, ripe tomatoes. To loosen skins, dip into boiling water for about ½ minute; then dip quickly into cold water. Cut out stem ends and peel tomatoes.

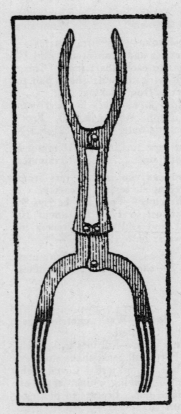

FIG. 13. A jar-lifter is useful.

● **Raw Pack.**—Leave tomatoes whole or cut in halves or quarters.

In glass jars.—Pack tomatoes to ½ inch of top, pressing gently to fill spaces. Add no water. Add ½ teaspoon salt to pints; 1 teaspoon to quarts. Adjust lids. Process in boiling-water bath (212° F.)—

Pint jars_____ 35 minutes
Quart jars_____ 45 minutes

As soon as you remove jars from canner, complete seals if necessary.

In tin cans.—Pack tomatoes to top of cans, pressing gently to fill spaces. Add no water. Add ½ teaspoon salt to No. 2 cans; 1 teaspoon to No. 2½ cans. Exhaust to 170° F., (about 15 minutes) and seal cans. Process in boiling-water bath (212° F.)—

No. 2 cans_____ 45 minutes
No. 2½ cans_____ 55 minutes

● **Hot Pack.**—Quarter peeled tomatoes. Bring to boil; stir to keep tomatoes from sticking.

In glass jars.—Pack boiling-hot tomatoes to ½ inch of top. Add ½ teaspoon salt to pints; 1 teaspoon to quarts. Adjust jar lids. Process in boiling-water bath (212° F.)—

Pint jars_____ 10 minutes
Quart jars_____ 10 minutes

As soon as you remove jars from canner, complete seals if necessary.

In tin cans.—Pack boiling-hot tomatoes to ¼ inch of top. Add no water. Add ½ teaspoon salt to No. 2 cans; 1 teaspoon to No. 2½ cans. Exhaust to 170° F. (about 10 minutes) and seal cans. Process in boiling-water bath (212° F.)—

No. 2 cans_____ 10 minutes
No. 2½ cans_____ 10 minutes

Tomato Juice

Use ripe, juicy tomatoes. Wash, remove stem ends, cut into pieces. Simmer until softened, stirring often. Put through strainer. Add 1 teaspoon salt to each quart juice. Reheat at once just to boiling.

In glass jars.—Fill jars with boiling-hot juice to ½ inch of top. Adjust

(Continued on next page)

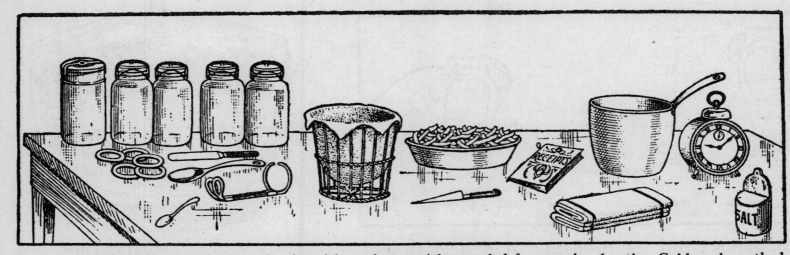

FIG. 14. Table arranged conveniently with various articles needed for canning by the Cold-pack method. The picture shows jars, rubbers, knife for removing air bubbles in containers, spoons, jar lifter, wire basket for blanching, knife for paring and coring, book of directions, towels, pan for cold-dipping, alarm clock and salt.

BOTULISM

WHAT FOODS MUST BE CANNED IN A PRESSURE COOKER?

All non-acid vegetables, meats, fish and poultry must be canned in a pressure canner because they require a temperature higher than that of boiling water. You must use steam under pressure to obtain these high temperatures.

WHAT FOODS MAY BE CANNED SAFELY IN A WATER BATH?

Acid fruits, tomatoes, rhubarb and vegetables pickled or canned in an acid solution may be processed in boiling water. Today's newer varieties of tomatoes are less acid than those grown formerly, so it is now necessary to add three teaspoons of vinegar or two teaspoons of lemon juice to each quart of tomatoes.

WHAT FOODS MAY BE CANNED BY THE OPEN KETTLE METHOD?

This method is suitable only for some fruit juices of thin consistency and only when tested procedures are followed exactly. The open kettle method is not recommended for most foods because spoilage organisms may enter the jars when food is transferred from kettle to jar. Never use this method for non-acid vegetables.

MY MOTHER USED THE OVEN METHOD FOR CANNING FRUITS. IS IT SAFE?

No, the oven method is not recommended for any food. Because of the uneven distribution of heat within the oven, the interior of the jars may never reach a sufficiently high temperature to destroy spoilage organisms. In addition, the jars may explode and damage the interior of the oven or cause harm to the individual.

jar lids. Process in boiling-water bath (212° F.)—

Pint jars_____ 10 minutes
Quart jars_____ 10 minutes

As soon as you remove jars from canner, complete seals if necessary.

In tin cans.—Fill cans to top with boiling-hot juice. Seal cans at once. Process in boiling-water bath (212° F.)—

No. 2 cans_____ 15 minutes
No. 2½ cans_____ 15 minutes

How To Can Vegetables

Can vegetables according to general directions on pages 5 to 8, the detailed directions for each vegetable on pages 18 to 28, and special directions below that apply only to vegetables.

Points on Packing

Raw pack.—Pack cold raw vegetables (except corn, lima beans, and peas) tightly into container and cover with boiling water.

Hot pack.—Preheat vegetables in water or steam. Cover with cooking liquid or boiling water. Cooking liquid is recommended for packing most vegetables because it may contain minerals and vitamins dissolved out of the food. Boiling water is recommended when cooking liquid is dark, gritty, or strong-flavored, and when there isn't enough cooking liquid.

Processing in a Pressure Canner

Use a steam-pressure canner for processing all vegetables except tomatoes and pickled vegetables. A pressure saucepan may be used for pint jars and No. 2 cans (see p. 3).

Directions.—Follow the manufacturer's directions for the canner you are using. Here are a few pointers on the use of any steam-pressure canner:

● Put 2 or 3 inches of boiling water in the bottom of the canner; the amount of water to use depends on the size and shape of the canner.

● Set filled glass jars or tin cans on rack in canner so that steam can flow around each container. If two layers of cans or jars are put in, stagger the second layer. Use a rack between layers of glass jars.

● Fasten canner cover securely so that no steam can escape except through vent (petcock or weighted-gage opening).

● Watch until steam pours steadily from vent. Let it escape for 10 minutes or more to drive all air from the canner. Then close petcock or put on weighted gage.

● Let pressure rise to 10 pounds (240° F.). The moment this pressure is reached start counting processing time. Keep pressure constant by regulating heat under the canner. Do not lower pressure by opening petcock. Keep drafts from blowing on canner.

● When processing time is up, remove canner from heat immediately.

With glass jars, let canner stand until pressure is zero. Never try to rush the cooling by pouring cold water over the canner. When pressure registers zero, wait a minute or two, then slowly open petcock or take off weighted gage. Unfasten cover and tilt the far side up so steam escapes away from you. Take jars from canner.

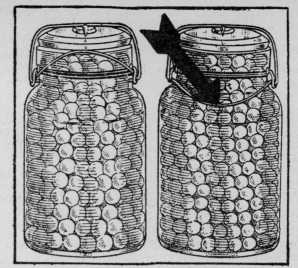

FIG. 15. To the left is a bail-top jar partially sealed and ready for sterilization. The top bail is snapped into place and the lower bail left free. To the right is shown the way to complete the seal.

With tin cans, release steam in canner as soon as canner is removed from heat by opening petcock or taking off weighted gage. Then take off canner cover and remove cans.

Processing times.—Follow processing times carefully. The times given apply only when a specific food is prepared according to detailed directions.

If you live at an altitude of less than 2,000 feet above sea level, process vegetables at 10 pounds pressure for the times given.

At altitudes above sea level, it takes more than 10 pounds pressure to reach 240° F. If you live at an altitude of 2,000 feet, process vegetables at 11 pounds pressure. At 4,000 feet, use 12 pounds pressure; at 6,000 feet, 13 pounds pressure; at 8,000 feet, 14 pounds pressure; at 10,000 feet, 15 pounds pressure.

A weighted gage may need to be corrected for altitude by the manufacturer.

To Figure Yield of Canned Vegetables From Fresh

The number of quarts of canned food you can get from a given amount of fresh vegetables depends on quality, condition, maturity, and variety of the vegetable, size of pieces, and on the way the vegetable is packed—raw or hot pack.

Generally, the following amounts of fresh vegetables (as purchased or picked) make 1 quart of canned food:

	Pounds		Pounds
Asparagus	2½ to 4½	Okra	1½
Beans, lima, in pods	3 to 5	Peas, green, in pods	3 to 6
Beans, snap	1½ to 2½	Pumpkin or winter squash	1½ to 3
Beets, without tops	2 to 3½	Spinach and other greens	2 to 6
Carrots, without tops	2 to 3	Squash, summer	2 to 4
Corn, sweet, in husks	3 to 6	Sweetpotatoes	2 to 3

FIG. 16   FIG. 17   FIG. 18

In the pictures on this and the next page are shown successive steps in canning by the Single Period Cold-pack Method. FIG. 16 shows paring and coring with sharp knife. FIG. 17 shows blanching with wire basket. FIG. 18 shows blanching with cheesecloth.

IS IT SAFE TO USE OLD MAYONNAISE OR OTHER SIMILAR JARS FOR CANNING?

No, use only standard canning jars that are free from cracks or nicks. Plain glass jars are not strong enough to withstand the high temperature of canning, so are not safe to use.

IS IT SAFE TO REUSE METAL LIDS?

No, be sure that you use new lids each time you can and that the lids are from "fresh stock." In order to secure a good seal, the sealing compound on the lid must be softened so that it will adhere to the jar. When lids have been on hand for several years, the sealing compound may harden and not soften sufficiently to obtain an adequate seal.

BOTULISM

HOW TIGHT SHOULD THE METAL BAND BE SCREWED DOWN OVER THE LID?

The band should be screwed down firmly enough to hold the lid in place and prevent the contents of the jar from spilling out into the canner during the processing. The band SHOULD NOT be tightened with a wrench or screwed down so firmly that venting cannot occur. During the processing the air and the food in the jars expand, air escapes from the jar by venting through the jar can. As the contents of the jar cool, a vacuum forms which pulls the lid down to make an airtight contact between the lid and the jar. An airtight seal is essential to prevent food spoilage.

HOW CAN I TEST FOR A GOOD SEAL?

After the jars are cool, you may test the seal. Do not attempt to do so while the jars are still warm. To test the seal, notice the top of the jar. A concave lid indicates a good seal, or tap on the lid with a spoon. A clear ring indicates a good seal. Or press on the lid with a finger; the lid should not give. Or lift the jar by the lid after the screw band is removed (if improperly sealed, the lid will come off.)

Directions for Vegetables

Asparagus

● **Raw Pack.**—Wash asparagus; trim off scales and tough ends and wash again. Cut into 1-inch pieces.

In glass jars.—Pack asparagus as tightly as possible without crushing to ½ inch of top. Add ½ teaspoon salt to pints; 1 teaspoon to quarts. Cover with boiling water, leaving ½-inch space at top of jar. Adjust jar lids. Process in pressure canner at 10 pounds pressure (240° F.)—

Pint jars_____ 25 minutes
Quart jars_____ 30 minutes

As soon as you remove jars from canner, complete seals if necessary.

In tin cans.—Pack asparagus as tightly as possible without crushing to ¼ inch of top. Add ½ teaspoon salt to No. 2 cans; 1 teaspoon to No. 2½ cans. Fill to top with boiling water. Exhaust to 170° F. (about 10 minutes) and seal cans. Process in pressure canner at 10 pounds pressure (240° F.)—

No. 2 cans_____ 20 minutes
No. 2½ cans_____ 20 minutes

● **Hot Pack.**—Wash asparagus; trim off scales and tough ends and wash again. Cut in 1-inch pieces; cover with boiling water. Boil 2 or 3 minutes.

In glass jars.—Pack hot asparagus loosely to ½ inch of top. Add ½ teaspoon salt to pints; 1 teaspoon to quarts. Cover with boiling-hot cooking liquid, or if liquid contains grit use boiling water. Leave ½-inch space at top of jar. Adjust jar lids. Process in pressure canner at 10 pounds pressure (240° F.)—

Pint jars_____ 25 minutes
Quart jars_____ 30 minutes

As soon as you remove jars from canner, complete seals if necessary.

In tin cans.—Pack hot asparagus loosely to ¼ inch of top. Add ½ teaspoon salt to No. 2 cans; 1 teaspoon to No. 2½ cans. Fill to top with boiling-hot cooking liquid, or if liquid contains grit use boiling water. Exhaust to 170° F. (about 10 minutes) and seal cans. Process in pressure canner at 10 pounds pressure (240° F.)—

No. 2 cans_____ 20 minutes
No. 2½ cans_____ 20 minutes

Beans, Dry, With Tomato or Molasses Sauce

Sort and wash dry beans (kidney, navy, or yellow eye). Cover with boiling water; boil 2 minutes, remove from heat and let soak 1 hour. Heat to boiling, drain, and save liquid for making sauce.

In glass jars.—Fill jars three-fourths full with hot beans. Add a small piece of salt pork, ham, or bacon. Fill to 1 inch of top with hot sauce (see recipes below). Adjust jar lids. Process in pressure canner at 10 pounds pressure (240° F.)—

Pint jars_____ 65 minutes
Quart jars_____ 75 minutes

As soon as you remove jars from canner, complete seals if necessary.

In tin cans.—Fill cans three-fourths full with hot beans. Add a small piece of salt pork, ham, or bacon. Fill to ¼ inch of top with hot sauce (see recipes below). Exhaust to 170° F. (about 20 minutes) and seal cans. Process in pressure canner at 10 pounds pressure (240° F.)—

No. 2 cans_____ 65 minutes
No. 2½ cans_____ 75 minutes

Tomato sauce.—Mix 1 quart tomato juice, 3 tablespoons sugar, 2 teaspoons salt, 1 tablespoon chopped onion, and ¼ teaspoon mixture of ground cloves, allspice, mace, and cayenne. Heat to boiling.

Or mix 1 cup tomato catsup with 3 cups of water or soaking liquid from beans and heat to boiling.

Molasses sauce.—Mix 1 quart water or soaking liquid from beans, 3 tablespoons dark molasses, 1 tablespoon vinegar, 2 teaspoons salt, and ¾ teaspoon powdered dry mustard. Heat to boiling.

Beans, Dry, Baked

Soak and boil beans according to directions for beans with sauce.

Place small pieces of salt pork, ham, or bacon in earthenware crock or a pan.

Add beans. Add enough molasses sauce to cover beans. Cover crock and bake 4 to 5 hours at 350° F. (moderate oven). Add water as needed—about every hour.

In glass jars.—Pack hot beans to 1 inch of top. Adjust jar lids. Process in pressure canner at 10 pounds pressure (240° F.)—

Pint jars_____ 80 minutes
Quart jars_____ 100 minutes

As soon as you remove jars from canner, complete seals if necessary.

In tin cans.—Pack hot beans to ¼ inch of top. Exhaust to 170° F. (about 15 minutes) and seal cans. Process in pressure canner at 10 pounds pressure (240° F.)—

No. 2 cans_____ 95 minutes
No. 2½ cans_____ 115 minutes

Beans, Fresh Lima

Can only young, tender beans.

● **Raw Pack.**—Shell and wash beans.

In glass jars.—Pack raw beans into clean jars. For small-type beans, fill to 1 inch of top of jar for pints and 1½ inches for quarts; for large beans, fill to ¾ inch of top for pints and 1¼ inches for quarts. Beans should not be pressed or shaken down. Add ½ teaspoon salt to pints; 1 teaspoon to quarts. Fill jar to ½ inch of top with boiling water. Adjust jar lids. Process in pressure canner at 10 pounds pressure (240° F.)—

Pint jars_____ 40 minutes
Quart jars_____ 50 minutes

As soon as you remove jars from canner, complete seals if necessary.

In tin cans.—Pack raw beans to ¾ inch of top; do not shake or press beans down. Add ½ teaspoon salt to No. 2 cans; 1 teaspoon to No. 2½ cans. Fill cans to top with boiling water. Exhaust to 170° F. (about 10 minutes) and seal cans. Process in pressure canner at 10 pounds pressure (240° F.)—

No. 2 cans_____ 40 minutes
No. 2½ cans_____ 40 minutes

● **Hot Pack.**—Shell the beans, cover with boiling water, and bring to boil.

In glass jars.—Pack hot beans loosely to 1 inch of top. Add ½ teaspoon salt to pints; 1 teaspoon to quarts. Cover with boiling water, leaving 1-inch space at top of jar. Adjust jar lids. Process in pressure canner at 10 pounds pressure (240° F.)—

Pint jars_____ 40 minutes
Quart jars_____ 50 minutes

As soon as you remove jars from canner, complete seals if necessary.

In tin cans.—Pack hot beans loosely to ½ inch of top. Add ½ teaspoon salt to No. 2 cans; 1 teaspoon to No. 2½ cans. Fill to top with boiling water. Exhaust to 170° F. (about 10 minutes) and seal cans. Process in pressure canner at 10 pounds pressure (240° F.)—

No. 2 cans_____ 40 minutes
No. 2½ cans_____ 40 minutes

Beans, Snap

● **Raw Pack.**—Wash beans. Trim ends; cut into 1-inch pieces.

In glass jars.—Pack raw beans tightly to ½ inch of top. Add ½ teaspoon salt to pints; 1 teaspoon to quarts. Cover with boiling water, leaving ½-inch space at top of jar. Adjust jar lids. Process in pressure canner at 10 pounds pressure (240° F.)—

Pint jars_____ 20 minutes
Quart jars_____ 25 minutes

As soon as you remove jars from canner, complete seals if necessary.

In tin cans.—Pack raw beans tightly to ¼ inch of top. Add ½ tea-

(Continued on next page)

FIG. 19   FIG. 20   FIG. 21

After blanching, as shown in FIGS. 17 and 18, vegetables and fruits are cold-dipped, as shown in FIG. 19. In FIG. 20 is shown the process of filling jar, by use of funnel. FIG. 21 shows the partial sealing of jar. With bail-top jar adjust top bail only; with screw top jar screw top on lightly. (Continued at bottom of opposite page.)

— BOTULISM continued

HOW DO I KNOW MY PRESSURE CANNER GAUGE IS OPERATING CORRECTLY?

Have the gauge or pressure indicator tested with a master gauge or maximum thermometer. If the indicator is not accurate, adjust it or buy a new one. With a toothpick or pipe cleaner keep the opening clean in the stem of the gauge. Never immerse the gauge in water. Check the gauge before each canning season and at any time the indicator fails to return to zero, or when something unusual happens, like dropping it.

WHAT IS THE BEST WAY TO PREPARE FRUITS AND VEGETABLES FOR CANNING?

Choose sound fruits, fresh, firm and ripe but not overripe or soft. Use fresh garden vegetables. Sort and pick out any that are spoiled or green. Wash in water to which a small amount of chlorine bleach has been added (4 teaspoons chlorine bleach to each gallon of water). A small amount of chlorine bleach added to the wash water will not cause an off flavor and will help to sanitize fruits and vegetables.

BOTULISM

HOW LONG CAN I KEEP CANNED GOODS?

Canned goods stored in a cool, dry place (50-60 degrees), may be kept 12 months or longer. If the food is stored on a top shelf where the temperature is from 90-105 degrees F., it will darken within six months or less. If food must be stored in a garage, the storage area should be insulated. The extreme temperatures of some summers will cause canned food stored in a hot garage (110-120 degrees) to deteriorate within 1 to 3 months.

DO BLACK SPOTS ON THE LID OF CANNED FOODS MEAN THAT THE FOOD HAS SPOILED?

No, the black spots are caused by natural compounds in the food which may be released from the food during the canning process. It is harmless.

spoon salt to No. 2 cans; 1 teaspoon to No. 2½ cans. Fill to top with boiling water. Exhaust to 170° F. (about 10 minutes) and seal cans. Process in pressure canner at 10 pounds pressure (240° F.)—

No. 2 cans_____ 25 minutes
No. 2½ cans_____ 30 minutes

● **Hot Pack.**—Wash beans. Trim ends; cut into 1-inch pieces. Cover with boiling water; boil 5 minutes.

In glass jars.—Pack hot beans loosely to ½ inch of top. Add ½ teaspoon salt to pints; 1 teaspoon to quarts. Cover with boiling-hot cook-

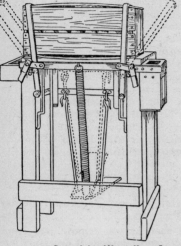

By permission of Messrs. Haynes Bros.
THE "BOXER" PRESS FOR APPLE BOXES.

ing liquid, leaving ½-inch space at top of jar. Adjust jar lids. Process in pressure canner at 10 pounds pressure (240° F.)—

Pint jars_____ 20 minutes
Quart jars_____ 25 minutes

As soon as you remove jars from canner, complete seals if necessary.

In tin cans.—Pack hot beans loosely to ¼ inch of top. Add ½ teaspoon salt to No. 2 cans; 1 teaspoon to No. 2½ cans. Fill to top with boiling-hot cooking liquid. Exhaust to 170° F. (about 10 minutes) and seal cans. Process in pressure canner at 10 pounds pressure (240° F.)—

No. 2 cans_____ 25 minutes
No. 2½ cans_____ 30 minutes

Beets

Sort beets for size. Cut off tops, leaving an inch of stem. Also leave root. Wash beets. Cover with boiling water and boil until skins slip easily— 15 to 25 minutes, depending on size. Skin and trim. Leave baby beets whole. Cut medium or large beets in ½-inch cubes or slices; halve or quarter very large slices.

In glass jars.—Pack hot beets to ½ inch of top. Add ½ teaspoon salt to pints; 1 teaspoon to quarts. Cover with boiling water, leaving ½-inch space at top of jar. Adjust jar lids. Process in pressure canner at 10 pounds pressure (240° F.)—

Pint jars_____ 30 minutes
Quart jars_____ 35 minutes

As soon as you remove jars from canner, complete seals if necessary.

In tin cans.—Pack hot beets to ¼ inch of top. Add ½ teaspoon salt to No. 2 cans; 1 teaspoon to No. 2½ cans. Fill to top with boiling water. Exhaust to 170° F. (about 10 minutes) and seal cans. Process in pressure canner at 10 pounds pressure (240° F.)—

No. 2 cans_____ 30 minutes
No. 2½ cans_____ 30 minutes

Beets, Pickled

See page 12.

Carrots

● **Raw Pack.**—Wash and scrape carrots. Slice or dice.

In glass jars.—Pack raw carrots tightly into clean jars, to 1 inch of top of jar. Add ½ teaspoon salt to pints; 1 teaspoon to quarts. Fill jar to ½ inch of top with boiling water. Adjust jar lids. Process in pressure canner at 10 pounds pressure (240° F.)—

Pint jars_____ 25 minutes
Quart jars_____ 30 minutes

As soon as you remove jars from canner, complete seals if necessary.

In tin cans.—Pack raw carrots tightly into cans to ½ inch of top. Add ½ teaspoon salt to No. 2 cans; 1 teaspoon to No. 2½ cans. Fill cans to top with boiling water. Exhaust to 170° F. (about 10 minutes) and seal cans. Process in pressure canner at 10 pounds pressure (240° F.)—

No. 2 cans_____ 25 minutes
No. 2½ cans_____ 30 minutes

● **Hot Pack.**—Wash and scrape carrots. Slice or dice. Cover with boiling water and bring to boil.

In glass jars.—Pack hot carrots to ½ inch of top. Add ½ teaspoon salt to pints; 1 teaspoon to quarts. Cover with boiling-hot cooking liquid, leaving ½-inch space at top of jar. Adjust jar lids. Process in pressure canner at 10 pounds pressure (240° F.)—

Pint jars_____ 25 minutes
Quart jars_____ 30 minutes

As soon as you remove jars from canner, complete seals if necessary.

In tin cans.—Pack hot carrots to ¼ inch of top. Add ½ teaspoon salt to No. 2 cans; 1 teaspoon to No. 2½ cans. Fill with boiling-hot cooking liquid. Exhaust to 170° F. (about 10 minutes) and seal cans. Process in pressure canner at 10 pounds pressure (240° F.)—

No. 2 cans_____ 20 minutes
No. 2½ cans_____ 25 minutes

Corn, Cream-Style

● **Raw Pack.**—Husk corn and remove silk. Wash. Cut corn from cob at about center of kernel and scrape cobs.

In glass jars.—Use pint jars only. Pack corn to 1½ inches of top; do not shake or press down. Add ½ teaspoon salt to each jar. Fill to ½ inch of top with boiling water. Adjust jar lids. Process in pressure canner at 10 pounds pressure (240° F.)—

Pint jars_____ 95 minutes

As soon as you remove jars from canner, complete seals if necessary.

In tin cans.—Use No. 2 cans only. Pack corn to ½ inch of top; do not shake or press down. Add ½ teaspoon salt to each can. Fill cans to top with boiling water. Exhaust to 170° F. (about 25 minutes) and seal cans. Process in pressure canner at 10 pounds pressure (240° F.)—

No. 2 cans_____ 105 minutes

● **Hot Pack.**—Husk corn and remove silk. Wash. Cut corn from cob at about center of kernel and scrape cob. To each quart of corn add 1 pint boiling water. Heat to boiling.

In glass jars.—Use pint jars only. Pack hot corn to 1 inch of top. Add ½ teaspoon salt to each jar. Adjust jar lids. Process in pressure canner at 10 pounds pressure (240° F.)—

Pint jars_____ 85 minutes

As soon as you remove jars from canner, complete seals if necessary.

In tin cans.—Use No. 2 cans only. Pack hot corn to top. Add ½ teaspoon salt to each can. Exhaust to 170° F. (about 10 minutes) and seal cans. Process in pressure canner at 10 pounds pressure (240° F.)—

No. 2 cans_____ 105 minutes

Corn, Whole-Kernel

● **Raw Pack.**—Husk corn and remove silk. Wash. Cut from cob at about two-thirds the depth of kernel.

In glass jars.—Pack corn to 1 inch of top; do not shake or press down.

(*Continued on next page*)

FIG. 22    FIG. 23   FIG. 24

After partially sealing jars, place them in hot-water bath. FIG. 22 shows jar being placed in ordinary household wash-boiler for sterilizing. FIG. 23 shows the adjustment of cover, with cloth to give tighter fit and make it hold the steam. FIG. 24 shows jars being removed. (Continued at bottom of next page.)

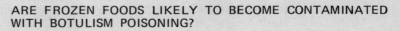

BOTULISM

ARE FROZEN FOODS LIKELY TO BECOME CONTAMINATED WITH BOTULISM POISONING?

No, the low temperature of the freezer retards the growth of spoilage organisms. The bacteria cannot function at very low temperatures.

IF I SUSPECT THAT A JAR OF FOOD IS CONTAMINATED HOW SHOULD I DISPOSE OF IT?

Boil the food at least 10 minutes then flush down the toilet, if it is liquid enough. This will prevent contamination of the water supply. Boil the jar, the lid and the ring in strong soap and detergent a half hour. Break the jar, dispose of the jar, the ring and the lid.

DO NOT DISCARD FOOD WHERE IT MAY BE EATEN BY ANIMALS. DO NOT BURY IT IN THE GROUND. BOTULISM SPORES LIVE IN THE GROUND. DO NOT THROW THE JAR IN THE TRASH WITHOUT BREAKING IT. SOMEONE ELSE MIGHT USE IT.

Apple Peeling and Coring Machine

Double Copper Preserving-pans, with water space, for home use

Add ½ teaspoon salt to pints; 1 teaspoon to quarts. Fill to ½ inch of top with boiling water. Adjust jar lids. Process in pressure canner at 10 pounds pressure (240° F.)—

Pint jars_____ 55 minutes
Quart jars_____ 85 minutes

As soon as you remove jars from canner, complete seals if necessary.

In tin cans.—Pack corn to ½ inch of top; do not shake or press down. Add ½ teaspoon salt to No. 2 cans; 1 teaspoon to No. 2½ cans. Fill to top with boiling water. Exhaust to 170° F. (about 10 minutes) and seal cans. Process in pressure canner at 10 pounds pressure (240° F.)—

No. 2 cans_____ 60 minutes
No. 2½ cans_____ 60 minutes

● **Hot Pack.**—Husk corn and remove silk. Wash. Cut from cob at about two-thirds the depth of kernel. To each quart of corn add 1 pint boiling water. Heat to boiling.

In glass jars.—Pack hot corn to 1 inch of top and cover with boiling-hot cooking liquid, leaving 1-inch space at top of jar. Or fill to 1 inch of top with mixture of corn and liquid. Add ½ teaspoon salt to pints; 1 teaspoon to quarts. Adjust jar lids. Process in pressure canner at 10 pounds pressure (240° F.)—

Pint jars_____ 55 minutes
Quart jars_____ 85 minutes

As soon as you remove jars from canner, complete seals if necessary.

In tin cans.—Pack hot corn to ½ inch of top and fill to top with boiling-hot cooking liquid. Or fill to top with mixture of corn and liquid. Add ½ teaspoon salt to No. 2 cans; 1 teaspoon to No. 2½ cans. Exhaust to 170° F. (about 10 minutes) and seal cans. Process in pressure canner at 10 pounds pressure (240° F.)—

No. 2 cans_____ 60 minutes
No. 2½ cans_____ 60 minutes

Hominy

Place 2 quarts of dry field corn in an enameled pan; add 8 quarts of water and 2 ounces of lye. Boil vigorously ½ hour, then allow to stand for 20 minutes. Rinse off the lye with several hot water rinses. Follow with cold water rinses to cool for handling.

Work hominy with the hands until dark tips of kernels are removed (about 5 minutes). Separate the tips from the corn by floating them off in water or by placing the corn in a coarse sieve and washing thoroughly. Add sufficient water to cover hominy about 1 inch, and boil 5 minutes; change water. Repeat 4 times. Then cook until kernels are soft (½ to ¾ hour) and drain. This will make about 6 quarts of hominy.

In glass jars.—Pack hot hominy to ½ inch of top. Add ½ teaspoon salt to pints; 1 teaspoon to quarts. Cover with boiling water, leaving ½-inch space at top of jar. Adjust jar

lids. Process in pressure canner at 10 pounds pressure (240° F.)—

Pint jars_____ 60 minutes
Quart jars_____ 70 minutes

As soon as you remove jars from canner, complete seals if necessary.

In tin cans.—Pack hot hominy to ¼ inch of top. Add ½ teaspoon salt to No. 2 cans; 1 teaspoon to No. 2½ cans. Fill to top with boiling water. Exhaust to 170° F. (about 10 minutes) and seal cans. Process in pressure canner at 10 pounds pressure (240° F.)—

No. 2 cans_____ 60 minutes
No. 2½ cans_____ 70 minutes

Mushrooms

Trim stems and discolored parts of mushrooms. Soak mushrooms in cold water for 10 minutes to remove adhering soil. Wash in clean water. Leave small mushrooms whole; cut larger ones in halves or quarters. Steam 4 minutes or heat gently for 15 minutes without added liquid in a covered saucepan.

In glass jars.—Pack hot mushrooms to ½ inch of top. Add ¼ teaspoon salt to half pints; ½ teaspoon to pints. For better color, add crystalline ascorbic acid—$\frac{1}{16}$ teaspoon to half-pints; $\frac{1}{8}$ teaspoon to pints. Add boiling-hot cooking liquid or boiling water to cover mushrooms, leaving ½-inch space at top of jar. Adjust jar lids. Process in pressure canner at 10 pounds pressure (240° F.)—

Half-pint jars_____ 30 minutes
Pint jars_____ 30 minutes

As soon as you remove jars from canner, complete seals if necessary.

In tin cans.—Pack hot mushrooms to ¼ inch of top of cans. Add ½ teaspoon salt to No. 2 cans. For better color, add ⅛ teaspoon of crystalline ascorbic acid to No. 2 cans. Then fill to top with boiling-hot cooking liquid or boiling water. Exhaust to 170° F. (about 10 minutes) and seal cans. Process in pressure canner at 10 pounds pressure (240° F.)—

No. 2 cans_____ 30 minutes

FIG. 25

FIG. 26

FIG. 27

After removal from hot-water bath jars are inverted to test for leakage (FIG. 25) and left inverted until cooled. They should be cooled rapidly, but protected from draft. FIG. 26 shows wrapping jar in brown paper to exclude light. FIG. 27 shows storage on shelves. If shelves are exposed to light, do not neglect wrapping.

TIN CAN RECOMMENDATIONS

If you insist on preserving in tin cans the following recommendations apply:

BEST SIZE FOR HOME USE

No. 2 cans will hold 19 ounces fluid content, about 2½ cups.
No. 2½ cans will hold 28 ounces fluid content, about 3½ cups.

USE

PLAIN TIN for apples, apricots, asparagus, green beans, white cherries, okra, peaches, pears, peas, spinach, tomatoes.
C-ENAMEL corn, carrots, lima beans.
R-ENAMEL beets, berries, red cherries, fruit juice, plums, pumpkin, rhubarb, sauerkraut, squash, sweet potato.

The best bet is to let your supplier know what produce you intend to process and follow their recommendations.

Okra

Can only tender pods. Wash; trim. Cook for 1 minute in boiling water. Cut into 1-inch lengths or leave pods whole.

In glass jars.—Pack hot okra to ½ inch of top. Add ½ teaspoon salt to pints; 1 teaspoon to quarts. Cover with boiling water, leaving ½-inch space at top of jar. Adjust jar lids. Process in pressure canner at 10 pounds pressure (240° F.)—

Pint jars_____ 25 minutes
Quart jars_____ 40 minutes

As soon as you remove jars from canner, complete seals if necessary.

In tin cans.—Pack hot okra to ¼ inch of top. Add ½ teaspoon salt to No. 2 cans; 1 teaspoon to No. 2½ cans. Fill to top with boiling water. Exhaust to 170° F. (about 10 minutes) and seal cans. Process in pressure canner at 10 pounds pressure (240° F.)—

No. 2 cans_____ 25 minutes
No. 2½ cans_____ 35 minutes

Peas, Fresh Blackeye (Cowpeas, Blackeye Beans)

● **Raw Pack.**—Shell and wash blackeye peas.

In glass jars.—Pack raw blackeye peas to 1½ inches of top of pint jars and 2 inches of top of quart jars; do not shake or press peas down. Add ½ teaspoon salt to pints; 1 teaspoon to quarts. Cover with boiling water, leaving ½-inch space at top of jars. Adjust jar lids. Process in pressure canner at 10 pounds pressure (240° F.)—

Pint jars_____ 35 minutes
Quart jars_____ 40 minutes

As soon as you remove jars from canner, complete seals if necessary.

In tin cans.—Pack raw blackeye peas to ¾ inch of top; do not shake or press down. Add ½ teaspoon salt to No. 2 cans; 1 teaspoon to No. 2½ cans. Cover with boiling water, leaving ¼-inch space at top of cans. Exhaust to 170° F. (about 10 minutes)

and seal cans. Process in pressure canner at 10 pounds pressure (240° F.)—

No. 2 cans_____ 35 minutes
No. 2½ cans_____ 40 minutes

● **Hot Pack.**—Shell and wash blackeye peas, cover with boiling water, and bring to a rolling boil. Drain.

In glass jars.—Pack hot blackeye peas to 1¼ inches of top of pint jars and 1½ inches of top of quart jars; do not shake or press peas down. Add ½ teaspoon salt to pints; 1 teaspoon to quarts. Cover with boiling water, leaving ½-inch space at top of jar. Adjust jar lids. Process in pressure canner at 10 pounds pressure (240° F.)—

Pint jars_____ 35 minutes
Quart jars_____ 40 minutes

As soon as you remove jars from canner, complete seals if necessary.

In tin cans.—Pack hot blackeye peas to ½ inch of top; do not shake or press peas down. Add ½ teaspoon salt to No. 2 cans; 1 teaspoon to No. 2½ cans. Cover with boiling water, leaving ¼-inch space at top of cans. Exhaust to 170° F. (about 10 minutes) and seal cans. Process in pressure canner at 10 pounds pressure (240° F.)—

No. 2 cans_____ 30 minutes
No. 2½ cans_____ 35 minutes

Peas, Fresh Green

● **Raw Pack.**—Shell and wash peas.

In glass jars.—Pack peas to 1 inch of top; do not shake or press down. Add ½ teaspoon salt to pints; 1 teaspoon to quarts. Cover with boiling water, leaving 1½ inches of space at top of jar. Adjust jar lids. Process in pressure canner at 10 pounds pressure (240° F.)—

Pint jars_____ 40 minutes
Quart jars_____ 40 minutes

As soon as you remove jars from canner, complete seals if necessary.

In tin cans.—Pack peas to ¼ inch of top; do not shake or press down. Add ½ teaspoon salt to No. 2 cans; 1 teaspoon to No. 2½ cans. Fill to top with boiling water. Exhaust to 170° F. (about 10 minutes) and seal cans. Process at 10 pounds pressure (240° F.)—

No. 2 cans_____ 30 minutes
No. 2½ cans_____ 35 minutes

● **Hot Pack.**—Shell and wash peas. Cover with boiling water. Bring to boil.

In glass jars.—Pack hot peas loosely to 1 inch of top. Add ½ teaspoon salt to pints; 1 teaspoon to quarts. Cover with boiling water, leaving 1-inch space at top of jar. Adjust jar lids. Process in pressure canner at 10 pounds pressure (240° F.)—

Pint jars_____ 40 minutes
Quart jars_____ 40 minutes

As soon as you remove jars from canner, complete seals if necessary.

In tin cans.—Pack hot peas loosely to ¼ inch of top. Add ½ teaspoon salt to No. 2 cans; 1 teaspoon to No. 2½ cans. Fill to top with boiling water. Exhaust to 170° F. (about 10 minutes) and seal cans. Process at 10 pounds pressure (240° F.)—

No. 2 cans_____ 30 minutes
No. 2½ cans_____ 35 minutes

Potatoes, Cubed

Wash, pare, and cut potatoes into ½-inch cubes. Dip cubes in brine (1 teaspoon salt to 1 quart water) to prevent darkening. Drain. Cook for 2 minutes in boiling water, drain.

In glass jars.—Pack hot potatoes to ½ inch of top. Add ½ teaspoon salt to pints; 1 teaspoon to quarts. Cover with boiling water, leaving ½-inch space at top of jar. Adjust jar lids. Process in pressure canner at 10 pounds pressure (240° F.)—

Pint jars_____ 35 minutes
Quart jars_____ 40 minutes

As soon as you remove jars from canner, complete seals if necessary.

In tin cans.—Pack hot potatoes to ¼ inch of top. Add ½ teaspoon salt to No. 2 cans; 1 teaspoon to No. 2½ cans. Fill to top with boiling water. Process in pressure canner at 10 pounds pressure (240° F.)—

No. 2 cans_____ 35 minutes
No. 2½ cans_____ 40 minutes

Potatoes, Whole

Use potatoes 1 to 2½ inches in diameter. Wash, pare, and cook in boiling water for 10 minutes. Drain.

In glass jars.—Pack hot potatoes to ½ inch of top. Add ½ teaspoon salt to pints; 1 teaspoon to quarts. Cover with boiling water, leaving ½-inch space at top of jar. Adjust jar lids. Process in pressure canner at 10 pounds pressure (240° F.)—

Pint jars_____ 30 minutes
Quart jars_____ 40 minutes

As soon as you remove jars from canner, complete seals if necessary.

In tin cans.—Pack hot potatoes to ¼ inch of top. Add ½ teaspoon salt to No. 2 cans; 1 teaspoon to No. 2½ cans. Fill to top with boiling water. Exhaust to 170° F. (about 10 minutes) and seal cans. Process in pressure canner at 10 pounds pressure (240° F.)—

No. 2 cans_____ 35 minutes
No. 2½ cans_____ 40 minutes

Pumpkin, Cubed

Wash pumpkin, remove seeds, and pare. Cut into 1-inch cubes. Add just enough water to cover; bring to boil.

In glass jars.—Pack hot cubes to ½ inch of top. Add ½ teaspoon salt to pints; 1 teaspoon to quarts. Cover with hot cooking liquid, leaving ½-inch space at top of jar. Adjust jar lids. Process in pressure canner at 10 pounds pressure (240° F.)—

Pint jars_____ 55 minutes
Quart jars_____ 90 minutes

(Continued on next page)

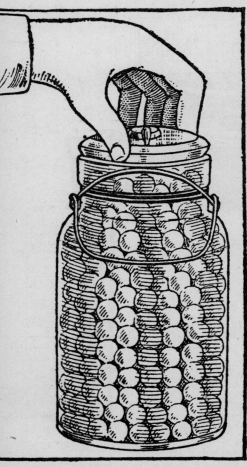

FIG. 28. A simple test for proper sealing of bail-top jars is to loosen top bail and lift jar by taking hold of top with the fingers.

CANNING IN TIN. FIG. 29. Wiping juice and syrup from groove. FIG. 30. Applying cap and wiping groove with brush dipped in soldering fluid. FIG. 31. Placing clean hot capping steel on can and melting solder into groove.

CANNING IN TIN, continued. FIG. 32. Turning steel to distribute solder. Fig. 33. Raising steel to allow solder to harden after pressing down on center rod. FIG. 34. Sealing with drop of solder after exhausting can and wiping vent hole.

As soon as you remove jars from canner, complete seals if necessary.

In tin cans.—Pack hot cubes to ¼ inch of top. Add ½ teaspoon salt to No. 2 cans; 1 teaspoon to No. 2½ cans. Fill to top with hot cooking liquid. Exhaust to 170° F. (about 10 minutes) and seal cans. Process in pressure canner at 10 pounds pressure (240° F.)—

No. 2 cans _____ 50 minutes
No. 2½ cans _____ 75 minutes

Pumpkin, Strained

Wash pumpkin, remove seeds, and pare. Cut into 1-inch cubes. Steam until tender, about 25 minutes. Put through food mill or strainer. Simmer until heated through; stir to keep pumpkin from sticking to pan.

In glass jars.—Pack hot to ½ inch of top. Add no liquid or salt. Adjust jar lids. Process at 10 pounds pressure (240° F.)—

Pint jars _____ 65 minutes
Quart jars _____ 80 minutes

As soon as you remove jars from canner, complete seals if necessary.

In tin cans.—Pack hot to ⅛ inch of top. Add no liquid or salt. Exhaust to 170° F. (about 10 minutes) and seal cans. Process in pressure canner at 10 pounds pressure (240° F.)—

No. 2 cans _____ 75 minutes
No. 2½ cans _____ 90 minutes

Spinach (and Other Greens)

Can only freshly picked, tender spinach. Pick over and wash thoroughly. Cut out tough stems and midribs. Place about 2½ pounds of spinach in a cheesecloth bag and steam about 10 minutes or until well wilted.

In glass jars.—Pack hot spinach loosely to ½ inch of top. Add ¼ teaspoon salt to pints; ½ teaspoon to quarts. Cover with boiling water, leaving ½-inch space at top of jar. Adjust jar lids. Process in pressure canner at 10 pounds pressure (240° F.)—

Pint jars _____ 70 minutes
Quart jars _____ 90 minutes

As soon as you remove jars from canner, complete seals if necessary.

In tin cans.—Pack hot spinach loosely to ¼ inch of top. Add ¼ teaspoon salt to No. 2 cans; ½ teaspoon to No. 2½ cans. Fill to top with boiling water. Exhaust to 170° F. (about 10 minutes) and seal cans. Process in pressure canner at 10 pounds pressure (240° F.)—

No. 2 cans _____ 65 minutes
No. 2½ cans _____ 75 minutes

Copper Jam-pan (steam)

Squash, Summer

● **Raw Pack.**—Wash but do not pare squash. Trim ends. Cut squash into ½-inch slices; halve or quarter to make pieces of uniform size.

In glass jars.—Pack raw squash tightly into clean jars to 1 inch of top of jar. Add ½ teaspoon salt to pints; 1 teaspoon to quarts. Fill jar to ½

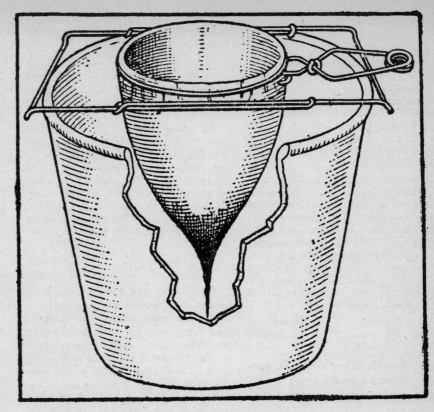

FIG. 35. Straining fruit juice.

inch of top with boiling water. Adjust jar lids. Process in pressure canner at 10 pounds pressure (240° F.)—

Pint jars _____ 25 minutes
Quart jars _____ 30 minutes

As soon as you remove jars from canner, complete seals if necessary.

In tin cans.—Pack raw squash tightly into cans to ½ inch of top. Add ½ teaspoon salt to No. 2 cans; 1 teaspoon to No. 2½ cans. Fill cans to top with boiling water. Exhaust to 170° F. (about 10 minutes) and seal cans. Process in pressure canner at 10 pounds pressure (240° F.)—

No. 2 cans _____ 20 minutes
No. 2½ cans _____ 20 minutes

● **Hot Pack.**—Wash squash and trim ends; do not pare. Cut squash into ½-inch slices; halve or quarter to make pieces of uniform size. Add just enough water to cover. Bring to boil.

In glass jars.—Pack hot squash loosely to ½ inch of top. Add ½ teaspoon salt to pints; 1 teaspoon to quarts. Cover with boiling-hot cooking liquid, leaving ½-inch space at top of jar. Adjust jar lids. Process in pressure canner at 10 pounds pressure (240° F.)—

Pint jars _____ 30 minutes
Quart jars _____ 40 minutes

As soon as you remove jars from canner, complete seals if necessary.

(Continued on next page)

Couple of Copper Preserving-pans with Steam-jackets and Tilting-frames

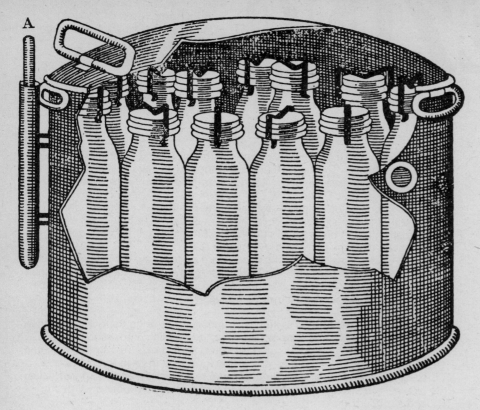

Lee's Patent Fruit-bottling Apparatus, showing thermometer (A) at side, and bottles placed in boiler ready for heating

In tin cans.—Pack hot squash loosely to ¼ inch of top. Add ½ teaspoon salt to No. 2 cans; 1 teaspoon to No. 2½ cans. Fill to top with boiling-hot cooking liquid. Exhaust to 170° F. (about 10 minutes) and seal cans. Process in pressure canner at 10 pounds pressure (240° F.)—

No. 2 cans _____ 20 minutes
No. 2½ cans _____ 20 minutes

Squash, Winter

Follow method for pumpkin.

Sweetpotatoes, Dry Pack

Wash sweetpotatoes. Sort for size. Boil or steam until partially soft (20 to 30 minutes). Skin. Cut in pieces if large.

In glass jars.—Pack hot sweetpotatoes tightly to 1 inch of top, pressing gently to fill spaces. Add no salt or liquid. Adjust jar lids. Process in pressure canner at 10 pounds pressure (240° F.)—

Pint jars _____ 65 minutes
Quart jars _____ 95 minutes

As soon as you remove jars from canner, complete seals if necessary.

In tin cans.—Pack hot sweetpotatoes tightly to top of can, pressing gently to fill spaces. Add no salt or liquid. Exhaust to 170° F. (about 10 minutes) and seal cans. Process in pressure canner at 10 pounds pressure (240° F.)—

No. 2 cans _____ 80 minutes
No. 2½ cans _____ 95 minutes

Sweetpotatoes, Wet Pack

Wash sweetpotatoes. Sort for size. Boil or steam just until skins slip easily. Skin and cut in pieces.

In glass jars.—Pack hot sweetpotatoes to 1 inch of top. Add ½ teaspoon salt to pints; 1 teaspoon to quarts. Cover with boiling water or medium sirup, leaving 1-inch space at top of jar. Adjust jar lids. Process in pressure canner at 10 pounds pressure (240° F.)—

Pint jars _____ 55 minutes
Quart jars _____ 90 minutes

As soon as you remove jars from canner, complete seals if necessary.

In tin cans.—Pack hot sweetpotatoes to ¼ inch of top. Add ½ teaspoon salt to No. 2 cans; 1 teaspoon to No. 2½ cans. Fill to top with boiling water or medium sirup. Exhaust to 170° F. (about 10 minutes) and seal cans. Process in pressure canner at 10 pounds pressure (240° F.)—

No. 2 cans _____ 70 minutes
No. 2½ cans _____ 90 minutes

Questions and Answers

Q. Is it safe to process foods in the oven?

A. No, oven canning is dangerous. Jars may explode. The temperature of the food in jars during oven processing does not get high enough to insure destruction of spoilage bacteria in vegetables.

Q. Why is open-kettle canning not recommended for fruits and vegetables?

A. In open-kettle canning, food is cooked in an ordinary kettle, then packed into hot jars and sealed without processing. For vegetables, the temperatures obtained in open-kettle canning are not high enough to destroy all the spoilage organisms that may be in the food. Spoilage bacteria may get in when the food is transferred from kettle to jar.

Q. May a pressure canner be used for processing fruits and tomatoes?

A. Yes. If it is deep enough it may be used as a water-bath canner (p. 4). Or you may use a pressure canner to process fruits and tomatoes at 0 to 1 pound pressure without having the containers of food completely covered with water. Put water in the canner to the shoulders of the jars; fasten cover. When live steam pours steadily from the open vent, start counting time. Leave vent open and process for the same times given for the boiling-water bath.

Q. Must glass jars and lids be sterilized by boiling before canning?

A. No, not when boiling-water bath or pressure-canner method is used. The containers as well as the food are sterilized during processing. But be sure jars and lids are clean.

Q. Why is liquid sometimes lost from glass jars during processing?

A. Loss of liquid may be due to packing jars too full, fluctuating pressure in a pressure canner, or lowering pressure too suddenly.

Q. Should liquid lost during processing be replaced?

A. No, never open a jar and refill with liquid—this would let in bacteria and you would need to process again. Loss of liquid does not cause food to spoil, though the food above the liquid may darken.

Q. Is it safe to use home canned food if liquid is cloudy?

A. Cloudy liquid may be a sign of spoilage. But it may be caused by the minerals in hard water, or by starch from overripe vegetables. If liquid is cloudy, boil the food. Do not taste or use any food that foams during heating or has an off odor.

Q. Why does canned fruit sometimes float in jars?

A. Fruit may float because pack is too loose or sirup too heavy; or because some air remains in tissues of the fruit after heating and processing.

Q. Is it safe to can foods without salt?

A. Yes. Salt is used for flavor only and is not necessary for safe processing.

Q. What makes canned foods change color?

A. Darkening of foods at the tops of jars may be caused by oxidation due to air in the jars or by too little heating or processing to destroy enzymes. Overprocessing may cause discoloration of foods throughout the containers. Pink and blue colors sometimes seen in canned pears, apples, and peaches are caused by chemical changes in the coloring matter of the fruit. Iron and copper from cooking utensils or from water in some localities may cause brown, black, and gray colors in some foods. When canned corn turns brown, the discoloring may be due to the variety of corn, to stage of ripeness, to overprocessing, or to copper or iron pans. Packing liquid may dissolve coloring materials from the foods. The use of plain tin cans will cause some foods to lose color (p. 4).

Q. Is it safe to eat discolored canned foods?

A. The color changes noted above do not mean the food is unsafe to eat. However, spoilage may also cause color changes. Any canned food that has an unusual color should be examined carefully before use (p. 8).

Q. Does ascorbic acid help keep fruits and vegetables from darkening?

A. Yes. The addition of ¼ teaspoon of crystalline ascorbic acid (vitamin C) to a quart of fruit or vegetable before it is processed retards oxidation, which is one cause of darkening of canned foods. One teaspoon of crystalline ascorbic acid weighs about 3 grams (or 3,000 milligrams).

Q. Is it all right to use preservatives in home canning?

A. No. Some canning powders or other chemical preservatives may be harmful.

Q. Why do the undersides of metal lids sometimes discolor?

A. Natural compounds in some foods corrode the metal and make a brown or black deposit on the underside of the lid. This deposit is harmless.

Q. When canned or frozen fruits are bought in large containers, is it possible to can them in smaller containers?

A. Any canned or frozen fruit may be heated through, packed, and processed the same length of time as recommended for hot packs. This canned food may be of lower quality than if fruit had been canned when fresh.

Q. Is it safe to leave food in tin cans after opening?

A. Yes. Food in tin cans needs only to be covered and refrigerated.

Q. Is the processing time the same no matter what kind of range is used?

A. Processing times and temperatures in this bulletin are for canning in a pressure canner or boiling-water bath with any type of range.

Q. Can fruits and vegetables be canned without heating if aspirin is used?

A. No. Aspirin cannot be relied on to prevent spoilage or to give satisfactory products. Adequate heat treatment is the only safe procedure.

FREEZING

Consumer and Food Economics Institute
Agricultural Research Service
United States Department of Agriculture

HOME FREEZING OF FRUITS AND VEGETABLES

There is no "out of season" for products of your garden and orchard—if you have a home freezer or space in a neighborhood locker plant.

Freezing is one of the simplest and least time-consuming ways to preserve foods at home. It keeps well the natural color, fresh flavor, and nutritive values of most fruits and vegetables. Frozen fruits and vegetables are ready to serve on short notice because most of the preparation they need for the table is done before freezing.

Directions are given in this bulletin for freezing many fruits and vegetables that give satisfactory products when frozen at home or in the locker plant. It is important that the directions be followed carefully, because the quality of product can vary with freshness of produce used, method of preparation and packaging, and conditions of freezing.

GENERAL FREEZING PROCEDURES

WHAT TO FREEZE

Freezing is not necessarily recommended as the preferred way for preserving all products listed in this bulletin. What to freeze must be decided on the basis of family needs and desires, on freezer space and cost of freezer storage, and on other storage facilities available.

It may be more economical, for instance, to store some fruits and vegetables in a vegetable cellar than to freeze them. But to you freezing may be worth the extra cost because of the convenience of having the products prepared so they can be readied quickly for serving.

Costs of owning and operating a home freezer vary with the rate of turnover of foods, electricity used, costs of packaging materials, repairs, and the original price of the freezer.

Some varieties of all fruits and vegetables freeze better than others. Because growing conditions differ widely throughout the country and different varieties of fruits and vegetables are available in different localities, it is not practical to specify in this publication the varieties suitable for freezing. Write to your State extension service, experiment station, or college of agriculture for information on local varieties that give highest quality when frozen.

If you have doubts as to how well a fruit or vegetable will freeze, it would be well to test it before freezing large quantities. To test, freeze three or four packages and sample the food after freezing. This shows the effect of freezing only, not the effect of storage.

Some fruits and vegetables do not make satisfactory products when frozen. They include green onions, lettuce and other salad greens, radishes, tomatoes (except as juice or cooked). Research may provide directions later for preparing good frozen products from some of these foods.

CONTAINERS FOR FREEZING

The prime purpose of packaging is to keep food from drying out and to preserve food value, flavor, color, and pleasing texture.

All containers should be easy to seal and waterproof so they will not leak. Packaging materials must be durable and must not become so brittle at low temperatures that they crack.

To retain highest quality in frozen food, packaging materials should be moisture-vapor-proof, to prevent evaporation. Many of the packaging materials on the market for frozen food are not moisture-vapor-proof, but are sufficiently moisture-vapor-resistant to retain satisfactory quality of fruits and vegetables during storage. Glass, metal, and rigid plastic are examples of moisture-vapor-proof packaging materials. Most bags, wrapping materials, and waxed cartons made especially for freezing are moisture-vapor-resistant. Not sufficiently moisture-vapor-resistant to be suitable for packaging foods to be frozen are ordinary waxed papers, and paper cartons from cottage cheese, ice cream, and milk.

RIGID CONTAINERS. Rigid containers made of aluminum, glass, plastic, tin, or heavily waxed cardboard are suitable for all packs, and expecially good for liquid packs. Glass canning jars may be used for freezing most fruits and vegetables except those packed in water. Plain tin or R-enamel cans may be used for all foods, but some foods may be better packed in cans with special enamel linings: C-enamel for foods containing considerable sulfur—corn, lima beans, carrots; R-enamel for highly colored foods—beets, berries, red cherries, fruit juices, plums, pumpkin, rhubarb, squash, sweetpotatoes.

NONRIGID CONTAINERS. Bags and sheets of moisture-vapor-resistant cellophane, heavy aluminum foil, pliofilm, polyethylene, or laminated papers and duplex bags consisting of various combinations of paper, metal foil, glassine, cellophane, and rubber latex are suitable for dry-packed vegetables and fruits. Bags also can be used for liquid packs.

Bags and sheets are used with or without outer cardboard cartons to protect against tearing. Bags without a protective carton are difficult to stack. The sheets may be used for wrapping such foods as corn-on-the-cob or asparagus. Some of the sheets may be heat-sealed to make a bag of the size you need. Sheets that are heat-sealing on both sides may be used as outer wraps for folding paperboard cartons.

SIZE. Select a size that will hold only enough of a fruit or vegetable for one meal for your family.

SHAPE. Rigid containers that are flat on both top and bottom stack well in a freezer. Round containers and those with flared sides or raised bottoms waste freezer space. Nonrigid containers that bulge waste freezer space.

Food can be removed easily, before it is thawed, from containers with sides that are straight from bottom to top or that flare out. Food must be partially thawed before it can be removed from containers with openings narrower than the body of the container.

Bags, sheets, and folding paperboard cartons take up little room when not in use. Rigid containers with flared sides will stack one inside the other and save space in your cupboard when not in use. Those with straight sides or narrow top openings cannot be nested.

SEALING. Care in sealing is as important as using the right container. Rigid containers usually are sealed either by pressing on or screwing on the lid. Tin cans such as are used in home canning require a sealing machine or special lids. Some rigid cardboard cartons need to have freezer tape or special wax applied after sealing to make them airtight and leakproof. Glass jars must be sealed with a lid containing composition rubber or with a lid and a rubber ring.

Most bags used for packaging can be heat-sealed or sealed by twisting and folding back the top of the bag and securing with a string, a good quality rubber or plastic band, or other sealing device available on the market. Some duplex bags are sealed by folding over a metal strip attached to the top of the bag.

Special equipment for heat-sealing bags or sheets for freezing is available on the market, or a household iron may be used. To heat-seal polyethylene or pliofilm bags or sheets used as overwraps, first place a piece of paper or heat-resistant material made especially for the purpose over the edges to be sealed. Then press with a warm iron. Regulate heat of the iron carefully—too much heat melts or crinkles the materials and prevents sealing.

As manufacturers are constantly making improvements and developing new containers it is a good idea, when you buy, to note how containers are to be sealed.

REUSE. Tin cans (with slip-top closures), glass, rigid plastic, and aluminum containers can be reused indefinitely. It is difficult to reuse aluminum foil boxes, because edges of lids and containers are folded over in sealing. Tin cans that require a sealer must be reflanged with a special attachment to a sealer before they are reused. A tin can or lid that is dented should not be used if it cannot be sealed.

Reuse of rigid cardboard cartons, unless plastic-lined, is not generally advisable because cleaning is difficult. Folding paperboard cartons used to protect an inner bag can be reused.

COST. When you compare prices of the containers that are available in your locality, consider whether they will be reusable or not. If containers are reusable, a higher initial cost may be a saving in the long run.

CARE OF PACKAGING MATERIALS. Protect packaging materials from dust and insects. Keep bags and rolls of wrapping materials that may become brittle, such as cellophane, in a place that is cool and not too dry.

FREEZING ACCESSORIES. Check on other items that help make packaging easier. Some containers are easier to fill if you use a stand and funnel. Special sealing irons available on the market or a regular household iron may be used for heat-sealing bags, wrappers, and some types of paper cartons. With some sealing irons, a small wooden block or box makes sealing of bags easier and quicker.

PACKING

Pack food and sirup cold into containers. Having materials cold speeds up freezing and helps retain natural color, flavor, and texture of food.

Pack foods tightly to cut down on the amount of air in the package.

When food is packed in bags, press air out of unfilled part of bag. Press firmly to prevent air from getting back in. Seal immediately, allowing the head space recommended for the product.

Allow ample head space. With only a few exceptions, allowance for head space is needed between packed food and closure because food expands as it freezes.

Keep sealing edges free from moisture or food so that a good closure can be made. Seal carefully.

Label packages plainly. Include name of food, date it was packed, and type of pack if food is packed in more than one form. Gummed labels, colored tape, crayons, pens, and stamps are made especially for labeling frozen food packages.

LOADING THE FREEZER

Freeze fruits and vegetables soon after they are packed. Put them in the freezer a few packages at a time as you have them ready, or keep packages in the refrigerator until all you are doing at one time are ready. Then transfer them to the home freezer or carry them in an insulated box or bag to the locker plant. Freeze at zero degrees F. or below.

Put no more unfrozen food into a home freezer than will freeze within 24 hours. Usually this will be about 2 or 3 pounds of food to each cubic foot of its capacity. Overloading slows down the rate of freezing, and foods that freeze too slowly may lose quality or spoil. For quickest freezing, place packages against freezing plates or coils and leave a little space between packages so air can circulate freely.

After freezing, packages may be stored close together. Store them at zero degrees F. or below. At higher temperatures foods lose quality much faster. Most fruits and vegetables maintain high quality for 8 to 12 months at zero degrees or below; citrus fruits and citrus juices, for 4 to 6 months. Unsweetened fruits lose quality faster than those packed in sugar or sirup. Longer storage will not make foods unfit for use, but may impair quality.

It's a good idea to post a list of frozen foods near the freezer and keep it up to date. List foods as you put them in freezer, with date; check foods off list as you remove them.

IN CASE OF EMERGENCY

If power is interrupted or the freezer fails to refrigerate properly, do not open the cabinet unnecessarily. Food in a loaded cabinet usually will stay frozen for 2 days, even in summer. In a cabinet with less than half a load, food may not stay frozen more than a day.

DRY ICE TO PREVENT THAWING. If the power is not to be resumed within 1 or 2 days, or if the freezer may not be back to normal operation in that time, use dry ice to keep the temperature below freezing and to prevent deterioration or spoilage of frozen food.

Twenty-five pounds of dry ice in a 10-cubic-foot cabinet should hold the temperature below freezing for 2 to 3 days in a cabinet with less than half a load and 3 to 4 days in a loaded cabinet, if dry ice is obtained quickly following interruption of power. Move any food stored in a freezing compartment of a freezer to the storage compartment. Place dry ice on boards or heavy cardboard on top of packages. Open freezer only when necessary. Don't handle dry ice with bare hands; it can cause burns. When using dry ice, room should be ventilated. If you can't get dry ice, try to locate a locker plant and move food there in insulated boxes.

REFREEZING

Occasionally, frozen foods are partially or completely thawed before it is discovered that the freezer is not operating.

The basis for safety in refreezing foods is the temperature at which thawed foods have been held and the length of time they were held after thawing.

You may safely refreeze frozen foods that have thawed if they still contain ice crystals or if they are still cold—about 40 degrees F.—and have been held no longer than 1 or 2 days at refrigerator temperature after thawing. In general, if a food is safe to eat, it is safe to refreeze.

Even partial thawing and refreezing reduce quality of fruits and vegetables. Foods that have been frozen and thawed require the same care as foods that have never been frozen. Use refrozen foods as soon as possible to save as much of their eating quality as you can.

POINTS ON FREEZING FRUITS

Most fruits can be frozen satisfactorily, but the quality of the frozen product will vary with the kind of fruit, stage of maturity, and type of pack. Pointers on selecting fruit properly are given in the directions and must be followed carefully to be sure of a good frozen product.

Generally, flavor is well retained by freezing preservation. Texture may be somewhat softer than that of fresh fruit. Some fruits require special treatment when packed to make them more pleasing in color, texture, or flavor after thawing. Most fruits are best frozen soon after harvesting. Some, such as peaches and pears, may need to be held a short time to ripen.

BEFORE PACKING

All fruits need to be washed in cold water. Wash a small quantity at a time to save undue handling, which may bruise delicate fruits such as berries. A perforated or wire basket is useful. Lift washed fruits out of the water and drain thoroughly. Don't let the fruit stand in the water—some lose food value and flavor that way and some get water-soaked.

In general, fruit is prepared for freezing in about the same way as for serving. Large fruits generally make a better product if cut in pieces or crushed before freezing. Many fruits can be frozen successfully in several forms. Good parts of less perfect fruit are suitable for crushed or pureed packs.

Peel, trim, pit, and slice fruit following the directions later in this article. It is best to prepare enough fruit for only a few containers at one time, especially those fruits that darken rapidly. Two or three quarts is a good quantity to work with.

If directions call for fruit to be crushed, suit the method of crushing to the fruit. For soft fruits, a wire potato masher, pastry fork, or slotted spoon may be used; if fruits are firm they may be crushed more easily with a food chopper. For making purees a colander, food press, or strainer is useful.

Use equipment of aluminum, earthenware, enameled ware, glass, nickel, stainless steel, or good-quality tinware. Do not use galvanized ware in direct contact with fruit or fruit juices because the acid in fruit dissolves zinc, which is poisonous.

Metallic off-flavors may result from the use of iron utensils, chipped enameled ware, or tinware that is not well tinned.

WAYS TO PACK

Most fruits have better texture and flavor if packed in sugar or sirup. Some may be packed without sweetening.

In the directions for freezing, three ways of packing are given for fruits whole or in pieces—sirup pack, sugar pack, and unsweetened pack. Directions are also given for packing crushed fruits, purees, and fruit juices.

Your selection of the way to pack the fruit will depend on the intended use. Fruits packed in a sirup are generally best for dessert use; those packed in dry sugar or unsweetened are best for most cooking purposes because there is less liquid in the product.

Even though unsweetened packs generally yield a lower quality product than packs with sugar, directions in this publication include unsweetened packs whenever they are satisfactory, because they are often needed for

special diets. Some fruits, such as gooseberries, currants, cranberries, rhubarb, and figs, give as good quality packs without as with sugar.

SIRUP PACK. A 40-percent sirup is recommended for most fruits. For some mild-flavored fruits lighter sirups are desirable to prevent masking of flavor. Heavier sirups may be needed for very sour fruits.

In the directions for each fruit, sirups are called for according to the percentage of sugar in the sirup. Below is a master recipe from which any of the sirups can be made. It takes one-half to two-thirds cup of sirup for each pint package of fruit.

SIRUPS FOR USE IN FREEZING FRUITS

Type of sirup	Sugar[1] Cups	Water Cups	Yield of sirup Cups
30-percent sirup	2	4	5
35-percent sirup	2-1/2	4	5-1/3
40-percent sirup	3	4	5-1/2
50-percent sirup	4-3/4	4	6-1/2
60-percent sirup	7	4	7-3/4
65-percent sirup	8-3/4	4	8-2/3

[1]In general, up to one-fourth of the sugar may be replaced by corn sirup. A larger proportion of corn sirup may be used if a very bland, light-colored type is selected.

Dissolve sugar in cold or hot water. If hot water is used, cool sirup before using. Sirup may be made up the day before and kept cold in the refrigerator.

When packing fruit into containers be sure the sirup covers the fruit, so that the top pieces will not change in color and flavor. To keep the fruit under the sirup, place a small piece of crumpled parchment paper or other water-resistant wrapping material on top and press fruit down into sirup before closing and sealing the container.

SUGAR PACK. Cut fruit into a bowl or shallow pan. Sprinkle the sugar (quantity needed given in the directions for each fruit) over the fruit. To mix, use a large spoon or pancake turner. Mix gently until juice is drawn out and sugar is dissolved.

Put fruit and juice into containers. Place a small piece of crumpled parchment paper or other water-resistant wrapping material on top to hold fruit down in juice. Close and seal the container.

UNSWEETENED PACK. Pack prepared fruit into containers, without added liquid or sweetening, or cover with water containing ascorbic acid. Or pack crushed or sliced fruit in its own juice without sweetening. Press fruit down into juice or water with a small piece of crumpled parchment paper as for sirup and sugar pack. Close and seal containers.

TO KEEP FRUIT FROM DARKENING

Some fruits darken during freezing if not treated to retard darkening. Directions for such fruits list antidarkening treatment as part of the freezing preparation. Several types of antidarkening treatments are used because all fruits are not protected equally well by all treatments.

ASCORBIC ACID. For most of the fruits that need antidarkening treatments, ascorbic acid (vitamin C) may be used. This is very effective in preserving color and flavor of fruit and adds nutritive value.

Ascorbic acid in crystalline form is available at drug stores and at some locker plants, in various sized containers from 25 to 1,000 grams. (Crystalline ascorbic acid may be obtained also in powdered form.) One teaspoon weighs about 3 grams; thus there are approximately 8 teaspoons of ascorbic acid in a 25-gram container. In the recipes, amounts of crystalline ascorbic acid are given in teaspoons.

Ascorbic acid tablets can be used but are more expensive and more difficult to dissolve than the crystalline form. Also filler in the tablets may make the sirup cloudy. The amount of ascorbic acid in tablets is usually expressed in milligrams.

To use, dissolve ascorbic acid in a little cold water. If using tablets, crush them so they will dissolve more easily.

A VIEW OF AN ICE HOUSE IN A BARN.

IN SIRUP PACK. Add the dissolved ascorbic acid to the cold sirup shortly before using. Stir it in gently so you won't stir in air. Solutions of ascorbic acid should be made up as needed. Keep sirup in refrigerator until used.

IN SUGAR PACK. Sprinkle the dissolved ascorbic acid over the fruit just before adding sugar.

IN UNSWEETENED PACK. Sprinkle the dissolved ascorbic acid over the fruit and mix thoroughly just before packing. If fruit is packed in water, dissolve the ascorbic acid in the water.

IN FRUIT JUICES. Add ascorbic acid directly to the juice. Stir only enough to dissolve ascorbic acid.

IN CRUSHED FRUITS AND FRUIT PUREES. Add dissolved ascorbic acid to the fruit preparation and mix.

ASCORBIC ACID MIXTURES. There are on the market special antidarkening preparations—usually made of ascorbic acid mixed with sugar or with sugar and citric acid. If you use one of these, follow the manufacturer's directions. In these mixtures ascorbic acid is usually the important active ingredient. Because of its dilution with other materials, ascorbic acid purchased in these forms may be more expensive than the pure ascorbic acid.

CITRIC ACID, LEMON JUICE. For a few fruits citric acid or lemon juice (which contains both citric acid and ascorbic acid) makes a suitable antidarkening agent. However, neither is as effective as ascorbic acid. Citric acid or lemon juice in the large quantities needed in some cases would mask the natural fruit flavors or make the fruits too sour.

Citric acid in crystalline or powdered form is available at drugstores and some locker plants. When using citric acid, dissolve it in a little cold water before adding to the fruit according to directions for that fruit.

STEAM. For some fruits steaming for a few minutes before packing is enough to control darkening.

TABLE OF FRUIT YIELDS

The following table will help you figure how much frozen fruit you can get from a given quantity of fresh fruit and will help in making cost comparisons.

The number of pints of frozen food you can get depends upon the quality, variety, maturity, and size of the fruit—and whether it is frozen whole or in halves, in slices, in cubes, or in balls.

FRUIT	FRESH, AS PUR- CHASED OR PICKED	FROZEN
Apples	1 bu. (48 lb.) 1 box (44 lb.) 1-1/4 to 1-1/2 lb.	32 to 40 pt. 29 to 35 pt. 1 pt.
Apricots	1 bu. (48 lb.) 1 crate (22 lb.) 2/3 to 4/5 lb.	60 to 72 pt. 28 to 33 pt. 1 pt.
Berries[1]	1 crate (24 qt.) 1-1/3 to 1-1/2 pt.	32 to 36 pt. 1 pt.
Cantaloups	1 dozen (28 lb.) 1 to 1-1/4 lb.	22 pt. 1 pt.
Cherries, sweet or sour	1 bu. (56 lb.) 1-1/4 to 1-1/2 lb.	36 to 44 pt. 1 pt.
Cranberries	1 box (25 lb.) 1 peck (8 lb.) 1/2 lb.	50 pt. 16 pt. 1 pt.
Currants	2 qt. (3 lb.) 3/4 lb.	4 pt. 1 pt.
Peaches	1 bu. (48 lb.) 1 lug box (20 lb.) 1 to 1-1/2 lb.	32 to 48 pt. 13 to 20 pt. 1 pt.
Pears	1 bu. (50 lb.) 1 western box (46 lb.) 1 to 1-1/4 lb.	40 to 50 pt. 37 to 46 pt. 1 pt.
Pineapple	5 lb.	4 pt.
Plums and prunes	1 bu. (56 lb.) 1 crate (20 lb.) 1 to 1-1/2 lb.	38 to 56 pt. 13 to 20 pt. 1 pt.
Raspberries	1 crate (24 pt.) 1 pt.	24 pt. 1 pt.
Rhubarb	15 lb. 2/3 to 1 lb.	15 to 22 pt. 1 pt.
Strawberries	1 crate (24 qt.) 2/3 qt.	38 pt. 1 pt.

[1]Includes blackberries, blueberries, boysenberries, dewberries, elderberries, gooseberries, huckleberries, loganberries, and youngberries.

Best for freezing are fresh, tender vegetables right from the garden. The fresher the vegetables when frozen the more satisfactory will be your product.

FIRST STEPS

Washing is the first step in the preparation of most vegetables for freezing. However, lima beans, green peas, and other vegetables that are protected by pods may not need to be washed.

Wash vegetables thoroughly in cold water. Lift them out of the water as grit settles to the bottom of the pan.

Sort vegetables according to size for heating and packing unless they are to be cut into pieces of uniform size.

Peel, trim, and cut into pieces, as directed for each vegetable below.

HEATING BEFORE PACKING

An important step in preparing vegetables for freezing is heating or "blanching" before packing. Practically every vegetable, except green pepper, maintains better quality in frozen storage if heated before packing.

The reason for heating vegetables before freezing is that it slows or stops the action of enzymes. Up until the time vegetables are ready to be picked, enzymes help them grow and mature. After that they cause loss of flavor and color. If vegetables are not heated enough the enzymes continue to be active during frozen storage. Then the vegetables may develop off-flavors, discolor, or toughen so that they may be unappetizing in a few weeks.

Heating also wilts or softens vegetables and makes them easier to pack. Heating time varies with the vegetable and size of pieces.

TO HEAT IN BOILING WATER. For home freezing, the most satisfactory way to heat practically all vegetables is in boiling water. Use a blancher which has a blanching basket and cover. Or fit a wire basket into a large kettle, and add the cover.

For each pound of prepared vegetable use at least 1 gallon of boiling water in the blancher or kettle. Put vegetables in blanching basket or wire basket and lower into the boiling water. A wire cover for the basket can be used to keep the vegetables down in the boiling water.

Put lid on blancher or kettle and start counting time immediately. Keep heat high for time given in directions for vegetable you are freezing. Heat 1 minute longer than the time specified if you live 5,000 feet or more above sea level.

TO HEAT IN STEAM. In this publication, heating in steam is recommended for a few vegetables. For broccoli, pumpkin, sweetpotatoes, and winter squash both steaming and boiling are satisfactory methods.

To steam, use a kettle with a tight lid and a rack that holds a steaming basket at least 3 inches above the bottom of the kettle. Put an inch or two of water in the kettle and bring the water to a boil.

Put vegetables in the basket in a single layer so that steam reaches all parts quickly. Cover the kettle and keep heat high. Start counting the steaming time as soon as the lid is on. Steam 1 minute longer than the time specified in directions if you live 5,000 feet or more above sea level.

OTHER WAYS TO HEAT. Pumpkin, sweetpotatoes, and winter squash may be heated in a pressure cooker or in the oven before freezing. Mushrooms may be heated in fat in a fry pan. Tomatoes for juice may be simmered.

COOLING

After vegetables are heated they should be cooled quickly and thoroughly to stop the cooking.

To cool vegetables heated in boiling water or steam, plunge the basket of vegetables immediately into a large quantity of cold water—60 degrees F. or below. Change water frequently or use cold running water or iced water. If ice is used, you'll need about 1 pound of ice for each pound of vegetable. It will take about as long to cool the food as it does to heat it. When the vegetable is cool, remove it from the water and drain thoroughly.

To cool vegetables heated in the oven, a pressure cooker, or a fry pan—set pan of food in water and change water to speed cooling.

DRY PACK MORE PRACTICAL

Either dry or brine pack may be used for most vegetables to be frozen. However, in this publication the dry pack is recommended for all vegetables, because preparation for freezing and serving is easier.

TABLE OF VEGETABLE YIELDS

The table below will help you figure the amount of frozen food you can get from a given amount of a fresh vegetable. The number of pints of frozen vegetables you get depends on the quality, condition, maturity, and variety—and on the way the vegetable is trimmed and cut.

APPROXIMATE YIELD OF FROZEN VEGETABLES FROM FRESH

VEGETABLE	FRESH, AS PURCHASED OR PICKED	FROZEN
Asparagus	1 crate (12 2-lb. bunches) 1 to 1-1/2 lb.	15 to 22 pt. 1 pt.
Beans, lima (in pods)	1 bu. (32 lb.) 2 to 2-1/2 lb.	12 to 16 pt. 1 pt.
Beans, snap, green, and wax	1 bu. (30 lb.) 2/3 to 1 lb.	30 to 45 pt. 1 pt.
Beet greens	15 lb. 1 to 1-1/2 lb.	10 to 15 pt. 1 pt.
Beets (without tops)	1 bu. (52 lb.) 1-1/4 to 1-1/2 lb.	35 to 42 pt. 1 pt.
Broccoli	1 crate (25 lb.) 1 lb.	24 pt. 1 pt.
Brussels sprouts	4 quart boxes 1 lb.	6 pt. 1 pt.
Carrots (without tops)	1 bu. (50 lbs.) 1-1/4 to 1-1/2 lb.	32 to 40 pt. 1 pt.
Cauliflower	2 medium heads 1-1/3 lb.	3 pt. 1 pt.
Chard	1 bu. (12 lb) 1 to 1-1/2 lb.	8 to 12 pt. 1 pt.
Collards	1 bu. (12 lbs.) 1 to 1-1/2 lb.	8 to 12 pt. 1 pt.
Corn, sweet (in husks)	1 bu. (35 lb.) 2 to 2-1/2 lb.	14 to 17 pt. 1 pt.
Kale	1 bu. (18 lb.) 1 to 1-1/2 lb.	12 to 18 pt. 1 pt.
Mustard greens	1 bu. (12 lb.) 1 to 1-1/2 lb.	8 to 12 pt. 1 pt.
Peas	1 bu. (30 lb.) 2 to 2-1/2 lb.	12 to 15 pt. 1 pt.
Peppers, sweet	2/3 lb. (3 peppers)	1 pt.
Pumpkin	3 lb.	2 pt.
Spinach	1 bu. (18 lb.) 1 to 1-1/2 lb.	12 to 18 pt. 1 pt.
Squash, summer	1 bu. (40 lb.) 1 to 1-1/4 lb.	32 to 40 pt. 1 pt.
Squash, winter	3 lb.	2 pt.
Sweetpotatoes	2/3 lb.	1 pt.

AN ICE STACK AGAINST A BANK.

FREEZING

Dick's cast-iron Cheese-press.

VEGETABLE	Time to allow after water returns to boil Minutes [2]
Asparagus	5-10
Beans, lima:	
Large type	6-10
Baby type	15-20
Beans, snap, green, or wax:	
1-inch pieces	12-18
Julienne	5-10
Beans, soybeans, green	10-20
Beet greens	6-12
Broccoli	5-8
Brussels sprouts	4-9
Carrots	5-10
Cauliflower	5-8
Chard	8-10
Corn:	
Whole-kernel	3-5
On-the-cob	3-4
Kale	8-12
Kohlrabi	8-10
Mustard greens	8-15
Peas, green	5-10
Spinach	4-6
Squash, summer	10-12
Turnip greens	15-20
Turnips	8-12

[1] Use ½ cup of lightly salted water for each pint of vegetable with these exceptions: Limba beans, 1 cup; corn-on-the-cob, water to cover.
[2] Time required at sea level; slightly longer time is required at higher altitudes.

HOW TO USE FROZEN FRUITS AND VEGETABLES

Fruits

Serving uncooked. Frozen fruits need only to be thawed, if they are to be served raw.

For best color and flavor, leave fruit in the sealed container to thaw. Serve as soon as thawed; a few ice crystals in the fruit improve the texture for eating raw.

Frozen fruit in the package may be thawed in the refrigerator, at room temperature, or in a pan of cool water. Turn package several times for more even thawing.

Allow 6 to 8 hours on a refrigerator shelf for thawing a 1-pound package of fruit packed in sirup. Allow 2 to 4 hours for thawing a package of the same size at room temperature—½ to 1 hour for thawing in a pan of cool water.

Fruit packed with dry sugar thaws slightly faster than that packed in sirup. Both sugar and sirup packs thaw faster than unsweetened packs.

Thaw only as much as you need at one time. If you have leftover thawed fruit it will keep better if you cook it. Cooked fruit will keep in the refrigerator for a few days.

COOKING. First thaw fruits until pieces can be loosened. Then cook as you would cook fresh fruit. If there is not enough juice to prevent scorching, add water as needed. If the recipe calls for sugar, allow for any sweetening that was added before freezing.

Frozen fruits often have more juice than called for in recipes for baked products using fresh fruits. In that case use only part of the juice, or add more thickening for the extra juice.

USING CRUSHED FRUIT AND PUREES. Serve crushed fruit as raw fruit—after it is partially or completely thawed. Or use it after thawing as a topping for ice cream or cakes, as a filling for sweet rolls, or for jam.

Use thawed purees in puddings, ice cream, sherbets, jams, pies, ripple cakes, fruit-filled coffee cake, and rolls.

SERVING JUICE. Serve frozen fruit juice as a beverage—after it is thawed but while it is still cold. Some juices, such as sour cherry, plum, grape, and berry juices, may be diluted 1/3 to 1/2 with water or a bland juice.

Vegetables

The secret of cooking frozen vegetables successfully is to cook the vegetable until just tender. That way you save vitamins, bright color, and fresh flavor.

Frozen vegetables may be cooked in a small amount of water or in a pressure saucepan, or by baking or panfrying.

COOKING IN A SMALL AMOUNT OF WATER. You should cook most frozen vegetables without thawing them first. Leafy vegetables, such as spinach, cook more evenly if thawed just enough to separate the leaves before cooking. Corn-on-the-cob should be partially thawed before cooking, so that the cob will be heated through by the time the corn is cooked. Holding corn after thawing or cooking causes sogginess.

Bring water to a boil in a covered saucepan. The amount of water to use depends on the vegetable and the size of the package. For most vegetables one-half cup of water is enough for a pint package. The frost in the packages furnishes some additional moisture.

Put the frozen vegetable in the boiling water, cover the pan, and bring the water quickly back to a boil. To insure uniform cooking, it may be necessary to separate pieces carefully with a fork. When the water is boiling throughout the pan, reduce the heat and start counting time. Be sure pan is covered to keep in the steam, which aids in cooking. Cook gently until vegetables are just tender.

Add seasonings as desired and serve immediately.

The following timetable shows about how long it takes to cook tender one pint of various frozen vegetables—and how much water to use. Use the table only as a general guide. Cooking times vary among varieties and with the maturing of the vegetable when it is frozen.

The time required for cooking vegetables is slightly longer at high than at low altitudes because the temperature of boiling water decreases about 2 degrees F. with each 1,000 feet above sea level.

COOKING IN A PRESSURE SAUCEPAN. Follow directions and cooking times specified by the manufacturer of your saucepan.

BAKING. Many frozen vegetables may be baked in a covered casserole. Partially defrost vegetable to separate pieces.

Put vegetable in a greased casserole; add seasonings as desired. Cover and bake until just tender.

The time it takes to bake a vegetable varies with size of pieces and how much you thaw them before baking.

Approximate time for baking most thawed vegetables is 45 minutes at 350 degrees F. (moderate oven). Slightly more time may be required if other foods are being baked at the same time.

To bake corn-on-the-cob, partially thaw the ears first. Brush with melted butter or margarine, salt, and roast at 400 degrees F. (hot oven) about 20 minutes.

PAN FRYING. Use a heavy fry pan with cover. Place about 1 tablespoon fat in pan. Add 1 pint frozen vegetable, which has been thawed enough to separate pieces. Cook covered over moderate heat. Stir occasionally. Cook until just tender. Season to taste, and serve immediately.

Peas, asparagus, and broccoli will cook tender in a fry pan in about 10 minutes. Mushrooms will be done in 10 to 15 minutes and snap beans in 15 to 20 minutes.

OTHER WAYS TO PREPARE FROZEN VEGETABLES. Vegetables that are cooked until tender before freezing need only to be seasoned and heated before serving. Cooked frozen vegetables can be used in many dishes in the same ways as cooked fresh vegetables. They may be creamed or scalloped, served au gratin, or added to souffles, cream soups, or salads.

Pumpkin, winter squash, and sweetpotatoes may be thawed and used as the main ingredient in pie fillings.

DRYING

Consumer and Food Economics Institute
Agricultural Research Service
United States Department of Agriculture

Authors: Jack Cooper, Martin Miller, Frank Winter, and George York

INTRODUCTION

Drying, one of the oldest methods of food preservation, is primarily the process of removing moisture from a food material to a point at which microorganisms are inhibited from growing. The water content of properly dried vegetables is usually 5% or less. Prior to modern times, vegetables were dried by the sun, but now dehydrators are more practical. The steps involved in vegetable drying are preparation, blanching, drying, packaging, and storage.

PREPARATION

Select your vegetables carefully. If they are not fresh and in prime condition for cooking, they are not suitable for drying. The vegetables should be washed and prepared as described in Appendix 1 on the same day they are harvested.

BLANCHING

Blanching is the process of heating vegetables sufficiently to inactivate enzymes. If the enzymes are not inactivated, they will cause deteriorative changes during the drying process and storage. Compared to blanched vegetables, unblanched vegetables will have poorer flavor and color after they have been dried. Blanching may be done in hot water or in steam. While water blanching usually results in more leaching of vegetable solids, it takes less time under kitchen conditions than steam blanching.

DIRECTIONS FOR STEAM BLANCHING

Equipment. Needed are a kettle with a tight fitting lid to use as a steaming container, and a colander, wire basket, or sieve that will fit in the steaming kettle.

Procedure. Add 1½ to 2 inches of water to the steamer and heat to boiling. Place the colander or basket containing loosely packed vegetables into the steamer and leave until they are heated through and wilted. See Appendix 1 for recommended blanching times. Test by cutting through the center of a blanched particle. It should appear cooked (translucent) nearly to the center.

DIRECTIONS FOR WATER BLANCHING

Use only enough water to cover the product. Bring the water to a boil and gradually stir in the product, following the directions in Appendix 1. Re-use the same water for additional lots when blanching the same vegetable and adding new water as necessary. Keep the lid on the kettle while blanching.

DRYING

The recommended procedure is by dehydration, however, sun drying may be used. Dehydrator Drying. One of the most simple dehydrators available for home drying is the kitchen oven. With it are needed drying trays, an appropriate thermometer, and a small fan.

DIRECTIONS FOR CONSTRUCTION OF TRAYS FOR OVEN DRYING

1) Use wood that is clean, dry, and free from pitch and odors such as Douglas fir. Do not use yellow pine or other resinous or odorous woods.

2) Outside dimensions must be at least 1½ inches smaller than the inside width of the oven.

3) When loaded with prepared vegetables and stacked in the oven, there must be at least 2½ inches between the trays and 3 inches of free space at the top and bottom of the oven.

4) The tray bottoms may be constructed of ¼ inch wide wooden slats that are ½ inch apart, or from stainless steel hardware cloth. Do not use galvanized screen as the zinc coating may dissolve and contaminate the food, making it unfit for human consumption.

5) To prevent sticking during drying, a "spray-on" vegetable oil may be sparingly applied to the wood.

6) Cheese cloth may be spread over the slats for drying of smaller pieces. Remember drying shrinks the vegetable pieces so they may fall between slats when dried.

DIRECTIONS FOR OVEN DRYING

1) Load two to four trays with no more than four to six pounds of prepared vegetables distributed between them. The vegetables should be in a single piece layer. Do not dry more than one kind of vegetable at the same time unless drying times (see Appendix) are the same. Odorous vegetables should be dried separately.

2) Place an accurate and easily read thermometer on the top tray toward the back.

3) Preheat the oven to 160 degrees F (71 degrees C) and then add the loaded trays. Prop the door open at least four inches.

4) Place a fan outside the oven so that air is directed through the opening and across the oven. This will aid in circulation. Change the fan from one side to the other and from the top to medium height during drying to vary air circulation.

5) Maintain the temperature during drying at 140 degrees F (60 degrees C). It takes less heat to maintain the temperature at 140 degrees F during the latter drying stage. Watch the temperature carefully toward the end of the drying period to prevent scorching.

6) Examine the vegetables often and turn the trays frequently to prevent scorching. At the start of the drying process, there is little danger of scorching, but when nearly dry, they may scorch easily.

7) The time for drying varies according to the type of vegetable, the size of the pieces, and the load on the tray. The time at 140 degrees F varies from 6 to 16 hours.

8) To determine when the vegetables are sufficiently dry, use the recommended test found in Appendix 1. Be sure to cool before testing.

HOME DRYING IN A SPECIALLY CONSTRUCTED DEHYDRATOR

Plans for the home-built dehydrator described below are available from Fresno County Farm and Home Advisors Office, 1720 South Maple Avenue, Fresno, California 93702.

DIRECTIONS FOR USE OF A SPECIALLY CONSTRUCTED HOME DEHYDRATOR

1) The dehydrator will hold a total of from 7 to 9 pounds of prepared leafy vegetables or about 14 pounds of other prepared vegetables. Distribute the prepared vegetables on the trays in a single piece layer. Cheesecloth may be spread over the slats for drying smaller pieces. Different kinds of vegetables may be dried at the same time but do not mix them on the same tray unless they are properly separated. Odorous vegetables should be dried separately.

2) Preheat dehydrator to 160 degrees F.

3) Place the trays of prepared vegetables in the dehydrator with the top tray nearly touching the door, the second tray nearly touching the rear wall, and alternate in a similar way. This arrangement forms the air channel which forces the air evenly over all the trays. From 1 to 7 trays may be used.

4) Place an accurate, easily read thermometer on the bottom tray.

Appendix 1 appears on page 277.

"Gnom" Fruit and Vegetable Drier for gardens and farms

GRAPES STAGED FOR EXHIBITION.

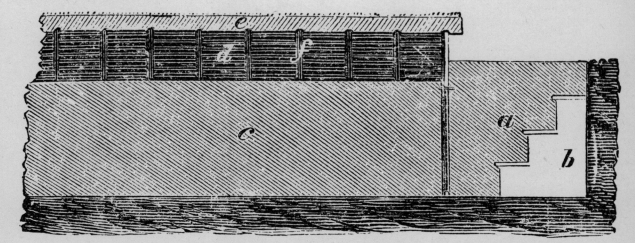

LENGTHWISE SECTION OF ROOT CELLAR.

In selecting corn to be saved for seed, choose the most perfect ears.

DRYING

5) After placing the trays in the dehydrator, the temperature will drop. Bring the temperature up to 140 degrees F during the latter stage of drying.

6) Examine the vegetables from time to time (½ to 2 hour intervals, depending on the vegetable). To get uniform drying rotate the trays and, if necessary, turn the product.

7) At the start of the drying process, there is little danger of scorching, but when nearly dry, they scorch easily. Even slight scorching destroys the flavor and may lower the nutritive value, so be careful to not allow the temperature to rise above 140 degrees F, especially during the latter stage of drying.

8) Be sure to place the dehydrator in a well ventilated room so that the evaporated water will be carried away.

9) The time for drying varies according to the type of vegetable, the size of the pieces, and the load on the tray; usually, the time at 140 degrees F varies from 6 to 16 hours.

10) Check Appendix 1 for the test to determine when your vegetables are dry. Be sure to cool the material before testing.

SUN DRYING

Drying in sun is unpredictable unless temperatures are over 100 degrees F and the relative humidity is low. If temperature is too low, humidity too high, or both, spoilage (souring or molding) will occur before drying is achieved.

Place the prepared vegetables on clean trays, as for dehydrator drying; trays can be covered carefully with cheesecloth to guard against insects. Raise cheesecloth above the product so that it does not contact the product and be sure to protect the sides against insects. Such a cover will slow up the drying process.

Turn the product once a day. If the temperature at night is more than 20 degrees F lower than the daytime temperature, place the trays in the house.

It will probably take three to four days to complete drying, depending upon size and air temperature. It is advisable to chop vegetables to small sizes no larger than ½ inch cubes.

PACKAGING

Dehydrated vegetables are free from infestation when removed from the dehydrator or oven but are immediately susceptible to contamination. They should be packaged as soon as they are cool. Use dry, scalded, insect-proof containers. Suitable containers are jars with well-fitting lids, such as home canning jars. Coffee cans may be used if the dried vegetables are first placed in a plastic bag. The dried vegetables should be packed into the container as tightly as possible without crushing. In spite of precautions, sun dried vegetables may be contaminated by insects. To kill any possible insects or their eggs, the packaged dried vegetables should be placed in the home freezer for 48 hours.

STORAGE

Store the containers of dried vegetables in a dry, cool, and dark place. If they are not stored in the dark, wrap all clear containers with a paper or foil to prevent the penetration of light. Lower storage temperatures extend the shelf life of the dried product.

All dried vegetables deteriorate to some extent during storage, losing vitamins, flavor, color, and aroma. For this reason, they will not retain their appeal indefinitely. Carrots, onions, and cabbage deteriorate at more rapid rates than other vegetables and will generally have a shelf life of only six months. Some vegetables, however, will be good after a year's storage. As a general rule, plan on using within six to ten months.

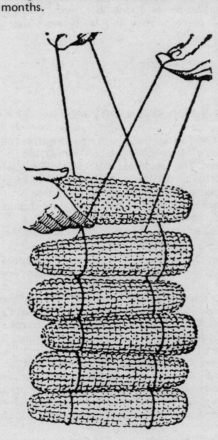

A good way of hanging seed corn to dry.

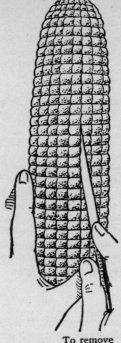
To remove kernels when preparing to plant or to test seed, insert knife between rows and pry sideways.

NUTRITIONAL CHANGES IN VEGETABLES DURING DRYING

Fresh vegetables provide man with bulk, energy, minerals, and vitamins. Bulk is provided by the indigestible fiber and energy is provided by the starch or sugar. Neither the bulk nor the energy yielding properties of vegetables are affected by the drying process.

During blanching, a portion of the minerals and vitamins will be lost by leaching. The amount of leaching depends upon the care exercised in blanching. To keep leaching to a minimum, blanch only as long as required. Do not underblanch, however, because the enzymes will not be inactivated and the dried vegetables will be of inferior quality.

Some nutrient losses during drying are unavoidable. By following the directions carefully, however, a tasty as well as wholesome product can be prepared. Remember, it is important that proper directions for blanching, drying, and storage be followed, and that the dried vegetables be consumed as early as possible to keep the nutritional losses to a minimum.

The Family Apple Parer and Slicer

COOKING OF DRIED VEGETABLES

Dried foods are not as easily prepared as fresh, frozen, or canned foods. The removed water must be added back, either by soaking, cooking, or a combination of both.

Many vegetables lose their fresh flavor during drying. For this reason, flavorings such as basil, garlic, onions, and chili sauce may be added during cooking to improve flavor.

One pound of dried vegetables is the equivalent of eight to twelve pounds of fresh vegetables.

Root, stem, and seed vegetables should be soaked for ½ to 2 hours in sufficient cold water to keep them covered. After soaking, simmer until tender, allowing excess water to evaporate.

Greens, cabbage, and tomatoes do not need to be soaked. Simply add sufficient water to keep them covered and simmer until tender.

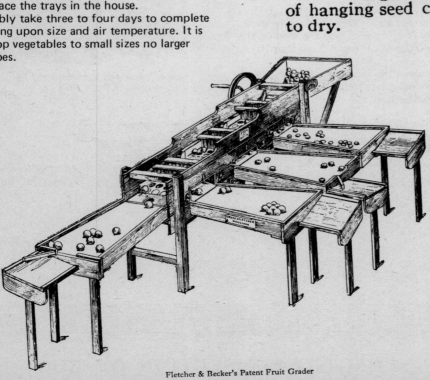
Fletcher & Becker's Patent Fruit Grader

DRYING

Important: Drying temperature should be no more than 140 degrees F.

Cool the test piece before testing for dryness.

Appendix 1

Artichoke, Globe. Only tender hearts are suitable. Cut hearts into 1/8 inch strips. Heat in boiling solution of 3/4 cup water & 1 T. lemon juice. 6-8 minutes depending on size. Brittle.

Asparagus. Only tender tips should be dried. Wash thoroughly & halve large tips. Steam 4-5 minutes. Water 3½-4½ minutes. Leathery to brittle.

Beans, Green. Use only tender stringless varieties. Wash thoroughly. Cut in short pieces or lengthwise. Steam 3½-4 minutes. Water 3 minutes. Very dry, brittle.

Beets. Use only small, tender beets. Cook as usual. Cool; peel. Cut into shoe-string strips 1/8 inch thick. Already cooked. No further blanching required. Tough, leathery.

Broccoli. Use young, fresh stalks. Trim and cut as for serving. Wash thoroughly. Quarter stalks lengthwise. Steam 5 minutes. Preferred Method is Water 4½ minutes. Brittle.

Brussel Sprouts. Use small, tight, fresh sprouts. Cut in half, lengthwise through stem. Steam 6-7 minutes. Water 4½-5½ minutes. Very dry to brittle.

Cabbage. Copenhagen Market, Danish Ball Head, Golden Acre, Savoy Winningstradt. Remove outer leaves, quarter & core. Cut into strips 1/8 inch thick. Steam 2½-3 minutes or until wilted. Water 1½-2 minutes or until wilted. Tough to brittle.

Carrots. Danvers Half Long, Imperator, Morse, Bunching, Nantes, (Chantennay not recommended). Use only crisp, tender carrots. Wash thoroughly. Cut off roots & tops; preferably peel, cut in slices or strips 1/8 inch thick. Steam 6-7 minutes. Water 5-6 minutes. Tough, leathery.

Cauliflower. Use small, fresh buttons. Prepare as for serving. Steam 4-5 minutes. Preferred Method is Water 3-4 minutes. Tough to brittle.

Celery. Both leaves & stalks may be dried. Use only crisp, tender stalks relatively free from "strings" & small, green, leaves. Trim stalks. Wash stalks and leaves thoroughly. Slice stalks. Steam 3-4 minutes. Water 2-3 minutes. Brittle.

Corn on the Cob. Stowells Evergreen, Country Gentlemen, Golden Bantam. Ears should be young, tender & in milk stage. Husk, trim. Steam until milk does not exude from kernel when cut, usually 5-6 minutes. Water 4-5 minutes. Dry, brittle.

Corn, cut. Use same varieties and prepare same as corn on the cob, except cut the corn from the cob after blanching.

Egg Plant. Use same directions as for squash, summer.

Horseradish. Wash; remove all small rootlets & stubs. Peel or scrape roots. Grate. No blanching. Very dry and powdery.

Mushrooms. Young, medium sized, freshly gathered, "Gills" pink, free of insects or any blackening. Scrub thoroughly. Discard any tough woody stalks. Cut tender stalks into short sections. Do not peel small mushrooms or "buttons". Peel large mushrooms & slice. Steam 3-4 minutes. Water 3 minutes. Very dry and leathery.

Okra. Wash, trim & slice crosswise in 1/4-1/8 inch strips. Steam 4-5 minutes. Water 3-4 minutes. Tough to brittle.

Onions. Creole varieties, Ebenezer, Southport Globes, Sweet Spanish, White Portugal. (Only onions with strong aroma and flavor should be dried). Wash & remove outer "paper shells". Remove tops and root ends & slice 1/8-1/4 inch thick. No blanching. Brittle.

Parsley. Wash thoroughly. Separate clusters. Discard long or tough stems. No blanching. Brittle, flakey.

Peas. Use young, tender peas of a sweet variety. (Mature peas become tough and mealy.) Shell. Steam 3 minutes. Water 2 minutes. Crisp, wrinkled.

Peppers and Pimentos. Ripe or Green: California Wonder, Merimack Wonder, Oakview Wonder. Ripe: Fordhook, Rocky Ford, Wonder Giant. Wash, stem, core. Remove "partitions". Cut into dices about 3/8 by 3/8 inch. No blanching needed. Brittle.

Potatoes. Russett Burbank, White Rose. Wash, peel. Cut into shoe-string strips 1/4 inch in cross section, or cut in slices 1/8 inch thick. Steam 6-8 minutes. Water 5-6 minutes. Brittle.

Spinach and other greens (Kale, parsley, chard, mustard). Use only young, tender leaves. Trim, wash very thoroughly. Steam 2-3 minutes or until thoroughly wilted. Water 2 minutes. Brittle.

Squash. Banana. Wash, peel, slice in strips about 1/4 inch thick. Steam 3 minutes. Water 2 minutes. Tough to brittle.

Squash, Hubbard. Cut or break into pieces. Remove seeds & seed cavity pulp. Cut into 1 inch wide strips. Peel rind. Cut strips crosswise into pieces about 1/8 inch thick. Steam until tender. Tough to brittle.

Squash, Summer. Crookneck, Scallop (Patty-pan), zucchini. Wash, trim, cut into 1/4 inch slices. Steam 4 minutes. Water 3 minutes. Brittle.

Tomatoes for stewing. Firm-ripe tomatoes with good color, no green spots. Steam or dip in boiling water to loosen skins. Chill in cold water. Peel. Cut into sections about 3/4 inch wide, or slice. Cut small pear or plum tomatoes in half. Steam 2-3 minutes or until soft. Water 1-2 minutes or until soft. Slightly leathery.

Appendix 1

HOME DRYING OF FRUITS
Follow directions in this publication—using table below for specific fruits.

FRUIT	PREPARATION	TREAT BEFORE DRYING Choose one of the following 3 methods.			TEST FOR DRYNESS (cool before testing)
		Sulfur (preferred)	Steam blanch	Water blanch	
Apples	Peel and core, cut into slices or rings about ⅛ inch thick.	45 minutes	Steam 5 minutes, depending on texture	—	Soft, pliable, no moist area in center when cut in half
Apricots	Pit and halve for steam blanch or sulfuring. For water blanch, leave whole and pit and halve after blanch.	2 hours	Steam, 3–4 minutes	4–5 minutes	Same as apples
Figs	Preferable to partly dry on tree. Normally drop from tree when ⅔ dry. Leave whole.	No treatment necessary.			Flesh pliable, slightly sticky but not wet
Grapes	Leave whole. Grapes dry in less time if dipped in lye 10 seconds.				Raisinlike texture, no moist center
Nectarines and peaches	When sulfuring, pit and halve. If desired, remove skins.	2–3 hours	Steam 5 minutes if halved, 8 minutes if whole. Skin can be removed after blanching.	8 minutes; skin can be removed after blanching	Same as apples
Pears	Cut in half and core. Peeling preferred.	5 hours	Steam 6 minutes (peeled, will be soft)		Same as apples
Persimmons	Use firm fruit as ripe is too difficult to handle. Using stainless steel knife, peel, slice.	No treatment necessary.			Light to medium brown, tender but not sticky
Prunes	For sun-drying, dip in boiling lye solution to check skins. For oven-drying, rinse in hot tapwater. Leave whole.				Leathery; pit should not slip when squeezed

HOME STORAGE OF NUTS, CEREALS, DRIED FRUITS, AND OTHER DRIED PRODUCTS

Prepared by Jean Roth, Home Economist, Emeritus, assisted by Christine Groppe, Extension Nutritionist, Berkeley, and George York, Extension Food Technologist, Davis.

The off-flavors that develop in nuts and cereals are caused largely by chemical changes in fat. These changes can be slowed by protecting the products from air and warm temperatures. Mold is not usually a problem unless there are changes in temperature that cause moisture to condense. To prevent mold, follow the procedure recommended for prevention of rancidity.

CONTAINERS

Glass jars, metal cans, and rigid plastic containers are best. Soft plastic does not guarantee protection against insects, and therefore should be used only when storing in the refrigerator or freezer or when the plastic wrapped nuts are placed in one of the recommended containers.

NUTS

The shells protect the nutmeats against staleness, but homemakers often prefer to store shelled nuts. Nuts can turn rancid in 6 weeks or less, or they can keep their fresh flavor for as long as 2 years if stored at low temperatures in recommended containers.

Fill containers with nuts, to exclude all air possible, since air causes deterioration. Whole nutmeats keep better than smaller pieces, since less surface is exposed to the air. High temperatures and added fats and salt hasten rancidity. For this reason, it is best to wait until just before using the nutmeats to heat them or add butter, oil, or salt.

CEREALS

Cereals will keep well for some time if stored in a cool place in containers that keep out air, moisture, and insects.

DRIED FRUITS

Store all dried fruits at a low temperature in a recommended container that will keep out air, moisture, and insects. This slows darkening of the fruit and unpleasant changes in flavor and prevents loss of moisture.

PANTRY INSECTS

The best protection against insects is to be sure there is no food available to them. The eggs or larvae of insects may be present in almost any dried food, even though they cannot be seen. Store all foods in glass, metal, or rigid

Water boils 212° | 220, 200 — Kills in approximately 1 minute
Oven — 180
160 — Kills in 5 minutes to 1 1/2 hours
140
120 — Kills in approximately 2 hours
With a gas oven, pilot light alone might suffice | 100 — Kills in approximately 2 days
80
Room temperatures | 60 — Insects live and grow
Refrigerator — 40 — Retards activity. Kills in 1 to 6 months
Water freezes 32° — 20
0 — Kills in 2 days to 1 month
Freezer — -20
Temp. °F

EFFECTS OF HEAT AND COLD ON ALL STAGES OF COMMON PANTRY INSECTS

plastic containers. Then, if insects develop, they will be confined in the container and cannot spread to other areas.

Pantry insects in any stage of development can be destroyed by high or low temperatures.

At 0° F insect life is destroyed in 2 days to 1 month. At 20° to 50° F, the insects stop feeding and die of starvation in 1 to 6 months. The containers then can be removed from freezer or refrigerator and stored in a cool place.

To kill insects in dried foods by heat, place the material in an oven at 120° to 130° F for 2 hours. Spread the material thinly so the heat will penetrate all areas.

Caution: Since heat speeds rancidity in nuts, we recommend that they be used soon after being given heat treatment.

Dried fruits may be plunged in boiling water to kill insect life. Before storing fruits treated with hot water, blot the surface water from the fruit with towels, or place the fruit in an oven at a low temperature until the surface water has evaporated.

Dry ice sometimes is used to kill insects. As the dry ice disappears, it leaves carbon dioxide gas in place of air, and the insects die. For instructions in the use of this method, see Agricultural Extension Service publication AXT 107 "Common Pantry Pests." This publication also gives directions for use of insecticides for serious infestations of insects.

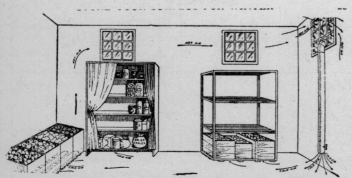

This suggests an arrangement for storage in a cool cellar. An earth floor is best, as it gives off some moisture. If the floor is of concrete it should be covered with 2 or 3 inches of sand and this should be sprinkled with water occasionally. In the drawing a pane in the upper part of one window is shown to be missing. This is to allow the escape of heated air. In severely cold weather close these openings. The stove pipe fitted into the place for one of the lower panes admits cold air. Instead of a stove pipe a wooden flue, made of old boards or parts of boxes, may be used. Bins and boxes should be placed on slats to lift them from the floor and allow circulation. For this same purpose bins and boxes should be at least one or two inches from the wall. Air holes bored in sides and bottom of bins and boxes help circulation. Protect glass jars from light.

Shallow bins or shelves with board sides, for storing root crops in cool cellar. The air of the room must not be allowed to become too dry, as this will cause the vegetables to shrivel. Potatoes must be protected from light.

INDOOR GARDENING

Plant a farm in flower pots this Spring, and cultivate your window sills. If you can grow ornamental house plants, why not grow some you can eat? It's easy. Vegetables will certainly decorate your window; they may even make a dent in your grocery bill. If you can expand your growing area to a fire escape or a terrace or a rooftop, you're really in business.

First, appraise your assets. Five to six hours of sun on a rooftop, terrace or fire-escape rates AAA. There's nothing you can't grow, including eggplant, green peppers and strawberries. An unobstructed south window may be almost as good. East or west unobstructed windows will give you fine leafy vegetables and root vegetables. "Garden Cress" will grow even in your north window.

Seek the Unusual

In choosing your crops, search out the unusual variety—"Buttercrunch" or red-edged "Prizehead" for your lettuce, West Indian "Gherkin" cucumbers, and rugola. Since your farm is measured in inches, not acres, choose small varieties of tomatoes, carrots, and eggplants. Try your favorite herbs—any with shallow instead of tap roots will grow in a container. Parsley, chives and mint prefer partial shade; basil, dill, marjoram, dwarf rosemary and thyme require full sun.

With that bit of an introduction, let's plan a hypothetical window, 3 feet wide by 6 feet high with a 10 inch sill, and an ideal southern exposure. On the sill there is space for one "Tiny Tim" tomato plant in a 10 inch pot, another 10 inch pot with two or three "Patio-Nik" cucumber plants, and a 10 inch square flat with 100 lettuce and/or radish seedlings every month of the growing season. Depending on the size and plant selection, six to ten hanging plants will fit suspended in the window itself. Cherry tomatoes, spinach, other lettuce varieties, peppers, "Tiny Sweet" carrots, and sun-loving herbs can all be suspended with various lengths of cord from hooks or from a "chinning bar" installed at the top of the window.

Every Seed is a Plant

Our West Side plant stores have already begun to stock tempting vegetable seedlings and pre-planted starter kits, as well as seeds. If you can use only one or two plants of a variety, it's best to buy the seedling. For larger plantings, start from scratch, and certainly use seeds for fast germinating "mass" plantings of radishes and leaf lettuce. Read the directions on each packet of seeds carefully. Notice the "ready" date—25 days for radishes, 45 days for Spartan Red tomatoes, 52 days for Gherkin cucumbers, etc.

When should you start? Right now, if you can guarantee 65 to 70 degrees for a box of soil and air temperatures of 70 to 75 degrees. Choose a container at least 2 inches deep to use as a seed-germinator. If you want to compete with supermarket vegetable prices, use recycled containers, such as tin cans,

HOW TO GROW VEGETABLES IN YOUR APARTMENT

Nadine C. Zamichow
Landscape Designer, New York, N.Y.
reprinted from
Wisdoms Child

plastic boxes, styrofoam cups and waxed milk cartons laid lengthwise with one side removed. Punch drainage holes at 2 inch intervals in the bottom and on the sides ¼ inch up from the bottom. Fill the container with a sterile growing medium, such as vermiculite. Dampen thoroughly with warm water and tamp down. Press small seeds into the dampened medium; cover larger seeds with a thin layer of the same medium. Put a whole container into a large plastic bag to retain the moisture. You can germinate more than a thousand seeds in a 3 by 10 inch area, but DON'T! Every seed is a plant; each one will be healthier with space to breathe.

A good germinating container can also be made by filling a plastic bag with the dampened vermiculite. Tie it closed and punch holes in the bottom for drainage. Put the bag in a water-tight container lined with gravel to catch the drippings, and plant the seeds in holes poked into the top surface. The plastic bag has the advantage that it can be shaped to fit inside any other decorative container.

Whichever germinating container you choose, keep it moist, covered with plastic in a warm place, out of the sun until the seeds germinate.

After the Sprout

As soon as you see the first sign of a sprouted seed, move the container into sunlight and take off the plastic to let in the air. Mist the seedlings daily to replace the moisture that transpires. The first two leaves that appear are the cotyledons. Wait until the next pair—the "true" leaves—appear. Then prick out the plant and move it into its permanent site. Take care when transplanting to loosen under the whole plant with a flat handle. Scoop under all the roots, while supporting the plant by one leaf, not the stem—if the stem breaks, you lose the plant; if the leaf breaks, it will grow back. Seedlings grown in vermiculite lift out very easily with all their roots intact. Leave whatever vermiculite clings to the roots.

Seedlings should be transplanted into containers that will allow for their mature growth. Lettuce and radishes, however, can be planted an inch apart and thinned directly into the salad bowl as they grow too close together.

NAPLES GOURD

Cauliflower head with leaves trimmed
off.

Of Soil and Fertilizer

I recommend a soil-less mix like Jiffy-Mix
for "potting-on" because it is lightweight, drains
well and is free of soil-born diseases. (Die-hard
dirt farmers will want to mix sterilized potting
soil with equal parts of perlite and sand and
milled sphagnum moss.) Jiffy-Mix also comes
in Jiffy-7 peat pellets that swell seven times
their size when watered to a total height of
2 1/8 by 1 3/4 inches wide. Seeds may be sown
directly into them, eliminating the germinating
tray. If too many seeds germinate, you can
cut the extras off at the soil line; if none develop, you can transplant from another more
flourishing unit. The Jiffy-7's are encased in
a plastic net that allows the roots to penetrate.
Thus the whole unit can be transplanted undisturbed into a larger pot when necessary.
They cost about a dollar a dozen, less in larger
quantities. Six pounds (one-half bushel) of
Jiffy-Mix is a little more than $4.00. Both con-
tain artificial nutrients, but should be fertilized
once a week when growth begins.

-GREEN GLOBE ARTICHOKE.

Fertilizers have three numbers on their packages (e.g., 12-31-14 or 20-20-20) which refer
to the nitrogen, phosphorous, and potassium
content, listed always in that order. The numbers indicate the percentage of these three
elements in the formula. A high middle number
(phosphorous) is recommended for vegetables.

Salad Time

Keep the seedlings compact and bushy, pinching the tops off, if necessary. Spindly growth
is usually a sign of too little light. Add a lamp,
or flourescent tube six to eight inches above
the seedling if you can. The plants will grow
toward the light, so keep turning them (another reason for using the lighter soil-less mix).
If you plan to move the seedlings outside,
give them six to eight weeks indoors, and
"harden them off" by exposing them outside
gradually. Seedlings of the cabbage family and
lettuce are tough and can be set outside to
brave the cold in mid-April. Keep the tender
vegetables, tomatoes, eggplant, peppers, indoors until mid to late May.
Recommended varieties were selected from
the Burpee, Stokes, Guerney or Suttons Seeds
catalogs. If your garden is successful this year,
you'll want to join the enthralled group of
gardeners who fantasize over the seed catalogs
all winter long. But for your first garden rely
on the choice of your favorite west side plant
store and invite me for a salad at harvest time.

-OLDEN TIME SIDE-WINGS.

SAVOY CABBAGE.

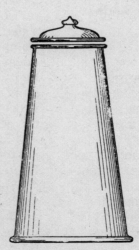

-Rhubarb Pot.   -Sea-kale Pot, high lid.

280

HOUSE PLANT CARE

John A. Wott

Horticulture Department
Cooperative Extension Service
Purdue University

House plants can help create a pleasant home environment. Small plants can add color and scenery to windows or tables, while larger ones can soften and blend with groups of furniture. An important part of the 'indoor landscape,' plants can create a feeling of spaciousness and cool even in the warmest weather.

If you have often been puzzled as to why some house plants thrive, while others refuse to flourish, even with tenderest care, this publication is for you. Most house plant problems can be easily corrected, and even more easily prevented.

First, realize that most of the foliage plants known as house plants are really native to tropical forests. Therefore, it is necessary to create an environment that meets the basic requirements of a very tropical creature. This is why, for instance, most house plants prefer a humid atmosphere and indirect light. Of course, there are exceptions, and these are discussed also. Keep in mind that good, sound cultural methods, preventive care, and careful attention are the best substitutes for a green thumb.

Light

Plants vary considerably in their light requirements. For example, plants such as the Croton need direct sunlight, while Philodendron will grow under low light intensities. If plants are grown in insufficient light their leaves turn yellow and die.

In this publication is a partial guide to the light requirements of some common houseplants. Use it as a guide for the selection and placement of your house plants.

If window sill space is in short supply, hang basket planters, make glass shelves, or build a "bay window greenhouse" by extending the window and adding shelves for plants requiring higher light intensities. Light from reading lamps is also beneficial, but the new "broad spectrum" fluorescent lights are

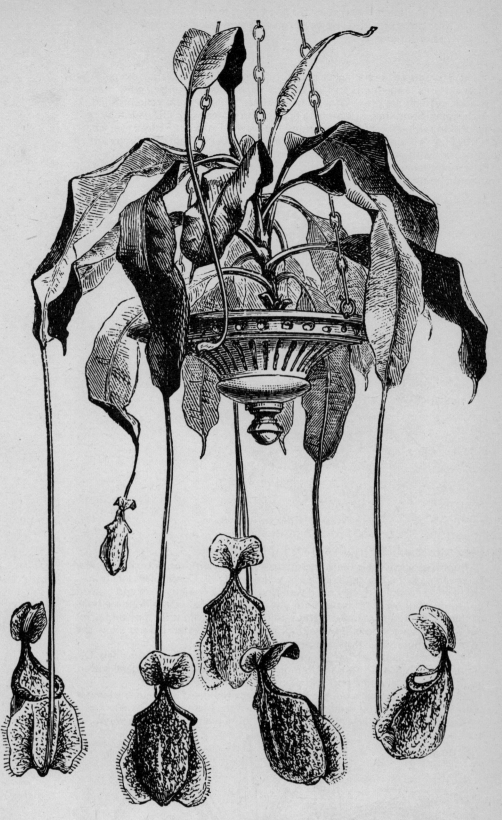

NEPENTHES RAFFLESIANA.

DANDELION (TARAXACUM OFFICINALE).

usually better. Generally, artificial fluorescent light 10 to 14 inches above the plants will provide sufficient light for plants requiring medium light intensity, such as the African Violet. A combination of ½ warm white to ½ cool white light is best. If they appear spindly, plants need more light or should be closer to artificial light. For even growth, turn the plants once a week so they receive uniform light on all sides.

Temperature and ventilation

Most house plants grow well between 60 and 75 degrees F. They may be spindly if kept warmer. Always keep them away from hot or cold drafts, warm appliances and heat registers. Flowering plants will retain blossoms longer if lower temperatures are provided. Temperatures above 75 degrees F. hasten the death of flowers and make plants more spindly as well as less resistant to disease and insect attack.

Some plants will thrive in hot and dry conditions, often managing to go without watering for a week or more. The following are examples:

Plants which will grow in hot and dry conditions

Common Name	Scientific name
Aeonium	Aeonium arboreum
Tiger Aloe	Aloe varigata
Zebra Plant	Cryptanthus zonatus var. zebrinus
Echeveria	Echeveria gigantea
Mother of Thousands	Kalanchoe daigremontiana
Air Plants	Kalanchoe pinnata
Lamb's Ear Kalanchoe	Kalanchoe tomentosa
Sedum	Sedum sp.

-Shelves for Plants.

Proper ventilation is necessary for good plant growth. In most homes, ample fresh air is provided. However, guard against escaping gases from gas appliances or furnaces.

Humidity

Most plants require a higher humidity than that of the average home. Any means of increasing humidity will be beneficial to your plants. Today many heating systems are provided with humidifiers, which should be kept filled with water. Sprinkling or syringing plants with water on bright days may be helpful in raising the humidity around the leaves. Fittonia (Fittonia verschaffelti), Baby's Tears (Helxine soleiroli), and Strawberry Plant (Saxifraga sarmentosa) will tolerate high humidity conditions. Growing plants together or setting them on a tray of gravel with moisture in the tray is also helpful in raising humidity.

SAXIFRAGA SARMENTOSA TRICOLOR.

Watering

Improper watering is the cause of most house plant problems. Both under- and over-watering can cause leaves to yellow and fall. Check plants daily to establish a schedule. If they need watering (soil dry ¼ inch down and tapped pot sounds hollow), add water until moisture drips out of the drainage hole of the pot. Wait a few minutes and water the plant again until moisture drips out of the drainage hole. Be sure to discard drainage water. Do not allow the bottom portion of the pots or plants to stand in water.

With small plants, weight is a good indicator of when water is needed. Dryer plants feel lighter than those with moist soil. Some dedicated gardeners even go so far as to weigh the pots and plants on a small scale.

If you prefer, water from the bottom. Place the plant in a saucer of water until the top of the soil is moist. Then remove the plant and let excess moisture drain away. Never keep ordinary house plants standing in water continuously.

PANDANUS CANDELABRUM VARIEGATUS.

Fertilizing

Water your house plants with a dilute fertilizer solution, especially during the rapid summer growing season. Prepare a solution by mixing one teaspoon of soluble fertilizer in 1 gallon of water. Such analyses as 20-20-20, 5-10-5, 4-12-4, or 7-7-7 may be used. Apply once a month during the growing season. Often a grower will purchase a commercially-prepared soluble fertilizer. He should then use it according to the directions on the container.

The new slow release fertilizers, such as Osmocote, save fertilization time. Apply 1-2 teaspoons to each six-inch pot every three months and larger amounts to larger pots, and incorporate into the soil. Each time you water, some fertilizer is released.

Repotting

It is best to purchase a prepared soil mixture free of weeds, insects and disease organisms. If you mix your own, sterilize the soil for 20-30 minutes in a 180 degree F oven.

In the spring when new growth starts, turn each of your plants upside down, tap the edge of the pot and remove the plant. If the roots are in a solid mass, remove part of the old soil and shift the plant to a pot (with a drainage hole) 1 or 2 inches larger in diameter. Fast-growing plants may need an even larger pot. Add new soil. For most plants, use 1/3 sphagnum peat moss, 1/3 garden soil (loam) and 1/3 sand. For cactus, use ½ quartz sand and ½ garden soil. After adding soil, water as usual. You may need to check and repot fast-growing plants more often than once a year. Usually you will not need to water so often for a few months after repotting.

When a house plant has reached a desirable size, then do not repot it. Instead, remove some of the soil at the top of the pot at least once a year and replace with fresh soil.

Additional care

Most plants, except those with hairy leaves, respond to an occasional bath. Syringing the plants weekly with a fine spray of clean water removes accumulated dust and keeps the stomates (pores) open. For small plants, place in the sink or shower. During warm, summer rains house plants can be placed out-of-doors.

ECHITES NUTANS.

SHORT COURSE ON BROMELIAD GROWING UNDER LIGHTS

Dr. George Milstein

DURO-LITE LAMPS, INC.
17-10 Willow Street, Fair Lawn, New Jersey
Home Lighting Division of Duro-Test Corp.

WHAT IS A BROMELIAD?

"Let us play the old guessing game of 'Twenty Questions', only we shall not need that many answers to locate the Bromeliaceae. First, it is a plant, a member of the vegetable kingdom. Second, it is a seed plant and not one reproducing by spores. Third, it is an Angio-sperm, or plant with seeds enclosed in an ovary, and not a Conifer. Fourth, it is a Monocotyledon with one leaf on the sprout, like corn, instead of a pair like the bean. With this goes a character that is much easier to see, namely leaves with parallel veins like those of grass. Fifth, it has showy flowers with real petals, and not a lot of dry scales, like grass. Sixth, its petals are all alike as in a lily, but there are only three of them, while there appear to be six in a lily.

"Finally, flowers are scarcely necessary (for identification), for if you see parallel-veined leaves with scales on them somewhere, there is little else the plant can be but a bromeliad. However, within these limits, you can find such tremendous diversity as that between the pineapple and the Spanish moss."

Lyman B. Smith, Ph.D.
Senior Botanist, Smithsonian Institution

Just as a prophet is rarely recognized in his own country, so the beauty of bromeliads and their value as houseplants is relatively unknown in American horticulture. This is all the more amazing since many species of bromeliads have become increasingly popular in most western European countries for the past 50 years. Even many American retail florists know little about this exotic plant family. The mystery deepens when one learns that the entire family of the Bromeliaceae is indigenous to the Western Hemisphere, ranging from Virginia to middle Argentina. The most common and wide-spread species, Tillandsia usneoides, or "Spanish moss," is found from Florida to northern Argentina.

Bromeliads grow in nature in three ways: (1) epiphytic (on trees); (2) terrestrial (on the ground); and (3) saxicolis (on rocky surfaces). As is seen in the sketch of a schematic bromeliad, the plant is made up of the following parts:

LEAVES: These range in character from hard and stiff to soft, thin and delicate. The surfaces of the leaves range from shiny smoothness to a woolly fuzzy scurf. This scurf is made up of modified scale cells (see Fig. I) which help the plant to absorb water from its surroundings. In most cases, the leaves are arranged in a rosette with the bases overlapping to form a tank or reservoir that can hold a comparatively large amount of water. These leaf bases also are rich in scale cells which enable the plant to absorb water and dissolved food material from the tanks.

Leaves of bromeliads usually display brilliant patterns and colors. Very often, they are of "discolor" variety, which means that one surface, usually the upper, is green, while the other, the lower, is red or maroon. The patterns, as a rule, are made up of an arrangement of scales in mottled designs, spots and horizontal or vertical stripes or bars. Often a condition occurs that causes "variegation" or striping along the length of the leaf. This is thought to be caused by a harmless virus. The stripes are usually alternately green with white or ivory. Frequently, under the proper lighting conditions, the white or ivory turns a bright pink or red, producing what is called a "tricolor" variety. Generally, this tricolor variation is not

283

passed on to future generations by means of seed but only through the asexual or offset method of bromeliad reproduction.

(Bromeliads reproduce both sexually, by means of seeds, and asexually, through the production of offsets. These latter usually arise at the bases of the plant but also, frequently, from leaf axils. There can be great variations in plants produced from the seeds of a single plant but, except if a sport develops, all offsets are exact duplicates of the mother plant.)

STEMS: Bromeliads are true shrubs and while they all possess stems these are often so short as to be almost imperceptible. However, there are some species, especially in the genus Tillandsia, where a stem is formed and this may be rather long.

ROOTS: Since the majority of bromeliads is epiphytic, two different types of roots are developed. One, which becomes very tough and almost as strong as steel, is developed to attach and hold the plant to a tree trunk or branch, or the surface of a stone cliff. The other type is much softer and serves in food and moisture absorbtion. Since most bromeliads feed almost entirely through the scales on their leaves, many thrive with few or no roots. In fact, in some species, the plants have evolved to such a high state that roots are no longer necessary for food intake or support purposes. This may be seen in species of Tillandsia, such as Spanish moss (T. usneoides) where the plant is held on to trees by a sort of tangled drapery, and T. purpurea, which is tumbled about by the wind on a stony ground. Both these plants feed entirely through scale cells.

INFLORESCENCE

The parts of the plant described above are those usually visible to the grower most of the time. However, when the plant reaches maturity and when all growing conditions have been favorable and in proper balance, the plant will finally flower and create seeds to be scattered to develop new plantlets in other locations.

Bromeliads produce an enormous variety of inflorescences or flower clusters. It is the inflorescence that laymen think of as the "flower" in many genera. Often the inflorescence is extremely long-lasting and may even retain its color for weeks or months. However, the flowers themselves actually only last from a few hours to two days. In some species, the inflorescence is so simple as to consist of a single flower. In other cases it may consist of a single stalk or peduncle. In yet others, it may be a multi-branched complex structure bearing tens of thousands of flowers. In still others, no peduncle is visible.

As seen in the illustration, the inflorescence consists of the following parts:

PEDUNCLE OR STALK: In some cases, as in the genus Neoregelia (see Fig. XI), the inflorescence is sunk deep in the cup of the leaf rosette and, while there is a peduncle, it is so short that the bracts and the berries of the inflorescence conceal it completely. In other species, the stalk is long and

erect and may be single or multi-branched. There are bromeliads which have limp, pendant inflorescences. In the case of Aechmea filicaulis, the inflorescence can hang down as much as six feet. There are also inflorescences that begin as hanging stalks and then recurve and grow upwards at a 45° angle to the ground.

BRACTS: Most peduncles have bracts growing along their entire lengths. Bracts are protective sheaths from which the branches may emerge; flowers are produced on the branches. The bracts are usually brilliantly colored, and these may stay long after the flowers have faded.

FLOWERS: In some genera, the beginning of the flower is berry-like in appearance. This is seen in the subfamily Bromelioideae. In the subfamily, Tillandsia, the flowers emerge from bracts that are often arranged in a feather or spear shape.

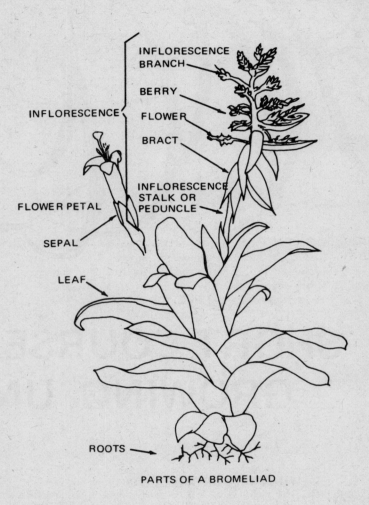

PARTS OF A BROMELIAD

BERRIES: After the Bromelioideae flowers are pollinated, the ovaries with attached calyxes develop into beautifully-colored berries. It is these berries that are usually seen and remain on the inflorescence for a very long time. In many species, the leaves in the center of the plant that surround the inflorescence turn a dazzling red. It is the bright color which attracts insects and birds to aid in pollination. It is the same brilliantly-colored leaves, bracts and berries that attract the attention of birds and animals to use the berries as food.

In the berries, the seeds are covered by a hard indigestible husk and are enveloped by a sticky jelly-like substance that is the "meat" of the berry. After the berry is ingested, the seeds pass through the alimentary canal of the animal or bird without being digested. They are then deposited by the creature in the droppings either on the ground or the branches of trees. A fascinating bit of information about berries, particularly those formed by the Aechmeas, is that those berries which become fertile (develop viable seed) change color, usually a very bright blue or yellow, while those that are sterile never put on color. This another method whereby nature ensures that animals and birds are only attracted to eat the fertile berries to insure live seed distribution.

SEED CAPSULES: Those bromeliads which do not develop berries as described above bear their seed in capsules. These capsules are not brightly colored since it is not necessary for them to be spread by living creatures. When the seeds ripen, the capsules split open into three sections and the seeds, which are plumed like dandelions, are expelled and are carried by the wind to new areas where they germinate.

The botanical name for the family of bromeliads is Bromeliaceae. The family is divided into three subfamilies.

1. PITCAIRNIOIDEAE: In this subfamily are found the most primitive members of the family. They are mainly terrestrial plants with heavy spines on their leaf edges. As a rule, they can tolerate extremely dry conditions and so are frequently mistaken for succulents, and so are often erroneously included in cacti and succulent collections. They have very beautiful inflorescences. The seeds of this subfamily have two or three wings attached to their surfaces. The leaves are very fibrous. The genera belonging to this subfamily often found in indoor horticulture, are Dyckia, Hechtia and Pitcairnia.

2. TILLANDSIOIDEAE: Members of this group all have smooth or entire leaf edges and are almost entirely epiphytic. This is by far the biggest subfamily. These are highly evolved plants and have been able to adapt themselves to many varieties of environment over a greater area than all the rest of the family. They have developed bizarre foliage markings and colors. Their inflorescences are beautiful in form and color and some of the species have a lovely fragrance to attract insects. The seeds are borne in capsules and are plumed. The genera belonging to this subfamily often found in indoor horticulture are Guzmania, Tillandsia and Vriesea.

3. BROMELIOIDEAE: Most of the bromeliads grown indoors and as windowsill plants are members of this subfamily and are mostly epiphytic, though there are many terrestrial members. The leaf edges are almost all spiny. The leaves are usually arranged in rosettes which may be cup-shaped or tall and tubular or vase-shaped. These plants have foliage with the most attractive markings and patterns in many striking colors.

"Discolors" are often seen as are "variegations" and "barrings." The inflorescences show a greater variation in form, size, color and arrangement of flowers than the other two subfamilies. In this group the flowers develop into berries filled with a sweet sticky jelly which surrounds the seed. The bracts on the inflorescences are also brilliantly colored as are the peduncles and are often long-lasting. The genera of this subfamily usually found in indoor horticulture are: Aechmea, Billbergia, Cryptanthus, Neoregelia and Nidularium.

It may be well to give brief descriptions of the eight most popular genera that may be grown indoors. After each generic description is a brief listing of those species and hybrids which are adaptable to conditions found in the average metropolitan home or apartment.

GENERA OF THE BROMELIACEAE

AECHMEA (see Fig. III): Probably the most popular of all bromeliads. The plants have foliage so attractive that growers are content to raise them for this alone though the shapes and colorings of the inflorescences are spectacular. The leaf edges are spined. Most of the species are epiphytic, and most have deep cups to hold water. Desirable species and hybrids: (1) Zebra-like chocolate markings against a pale green background - Ae. orlandiana, Ae. fosteriana and their hybrid offspring, Ae. X 'Bert'; (2) Discolor foliage with blue flowers on red berries carried on long-lasting inflorescences - Ae. miniata var. discolor, Ae. fulgens var. discolor and their hybrid offspring Ae. X 'Maginalli'; (3) Dark, almost black, bars on a pale green or white background - Ae. fasciata, the most popular bromeliad in the world, and Ae. chantimi; (4) Plants that turn a brilliant red in their center leaves before and during flowering - Ae. recurvata var. benrathii and Ae. recurvata var. ortgiesii; (5) Plants with hanging inflorescences - Ae. racinae, Ae. victoriana and their hybrid offspring Ae. X 'Foster's Favorite,' the first bromeliad granted a U.S. patent.

BILLBERGIA (see Fig. VII): These plants are usually tall and tubular or urn-shaped. They are usually epiphytic with spiny-edged leaves. The foliage of some is among the most gorgeous in the entire bromeliad family. These plants are easily hybridized. The one so-called short-coming of this genus is their short-lived inflorescences. But, when they do bloom with fantastic color combinations, the effect is well worth waiting for. In a single inflorescence, it is not uncommon to see reds, yellows, oranges, greens, blues, purples and even other colors. Usually the inflorescences arch over gracefully, although a few have upright peduncles. Most Billbergias mature in a short time and some species may flower more than once a year. Desirable specis and hybrids: B. nutans (easiest of all bromeliads to grow and flower); B. pyramid-alis; B. venezuelana; B. amoena; B. horrida; B. X 'Fantasia'; B. X 'Santa Barbara'; B. X 'Catherine Wilson'; B. X 'Muriel Waterman'; and B. saundersii hybrids.

CRYPTANTHUS (see Fig. XII): The plants of this genus are commonly called "Earth Stars", and when one sees them this is easy to understand. They are terrestrial and, because their usual habitat is the floor of the jungle, the require less light than most other genera. Their leaves are hard and stiff, and usually the edges are waved with a "pie-crust" effect and spined. The patterns and markings of the foliage are strange; the leaves of some species resemble an exotic snake-skin.

The leaves are flat and grow low and paralell to the ground in a many-pointed star shape. They are grown mainly as foliage plants but their pretty white flowers, emerging low in the cups, add to the attraction of this plant. Desirable species and hybrids: C. fosterianus; C. bivittatus; C. beuckerii; C. bromelioides var. tricolor; C. X 'It'; C. X 'Racinae'.

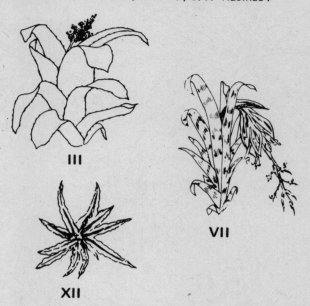

III

VII

XII

GUZMANIA (see Fig. XVI): This genus is characterized by thin, strap-like, smooth-edged leaves often patterned and figured. Frequently, a delicate tracery of thin red "pencil marks" run in parallel lines along the length of the leaves. The inflorescences are generally upright with red, white or yellow flowers peeping out in clusters from behind orange, yellow or red bracts which are sometimes striped. Often these bracts are arranged in a tulip or lily shape at the end of the peduncle. Desirable species and hybrids: G. lingulata (all varieties); G. zahnii; and G. X 'Magnifica.'

NEOREGELIA (see Fig. XI): There are two lovely phenomena associated with this genus. One is that some of the species develop brilliant red leaf tips, earning the nickname of "Painted Ladies' Fingernail." Also, in many species, the central portion of the leaves surrounding the inflorescence turn a dazzling crimson. The spiny-edged leaves may also have red spots and markings. The plants are epiphytic and since the inflorescences are developed so low in the cups, they are usually overlooked. The flowers are blue or white. This genus is easily adapted to indoor horticulture. Desirable species and hybrids: N. carolinae; N. carolinae var. tricolor, N. spectabilis hybrids; N. tristis; N. marmorata hybrids; N. ampullaceae.

NIDULARIUM (see Fig. VIII): These plants are products of the tropical rain forests. Like the Neoregelias, which they resemble superficially, they are also epiphytic and have spiny edges on their leaves. A simple way to differentiate Neoregelias from Nidulariums is to examine their inflorescences. The Nidularium inflorescence shows the bracts rather distinctly while the inflorescence rises above the cup. The foliage of many of the species is purplish, and in some species stripes run along the length of the leaves. Desirable species and hybrids: N. innocentii; N. innocentii var. lineatum; N. procera; N. fulgens.

TILLANDSIA (see Fig. IV): More bromeliads belong to this genus than any other. It includes species that have adapted themselves to varying conditions and in so doing have managed to take on an amazing number of forms. Some of the tiniest bromeliads are included, as well as species with the most spectacular flowers, even more beautiful than orchids. The leaves show a great variation; some are tough and string-like; others soft, thin and strap-like; while in still others the lower part of the leaf is of a spoon-like shape which gives the plant a pseudo-bulbous appearance. In many cases the leaves are covered with a gray fuzz of scales. Desirable species: T. lindenii, T. cyanea, T. ionantha.

VRIESEA (see Fig. XV): This genus includes members that seldom fail to evoke comments from viewers. Both the foliage and inflorescences are spectacular. The leaves are smooth and complete. Like the Tillandsias, most Vrieseas are epiphytic. The leaves are generally heavy and may be covered with spots, bars, irregular patterns or odd-shaped markings. The inflorescences, usually brilliant and of one or more colors, may be upright like a sword or spear, or pendulous or even curved. The colorful bracts are large and may be triangular or boat-shaped. These plants are usually quite sensitive to cold. Desirable species and hybrids: V. splendens (after Ae. fasciatea the second most popular bromeliad); V. X 'Mariae'; V. carinata; V. hieroglyphica.

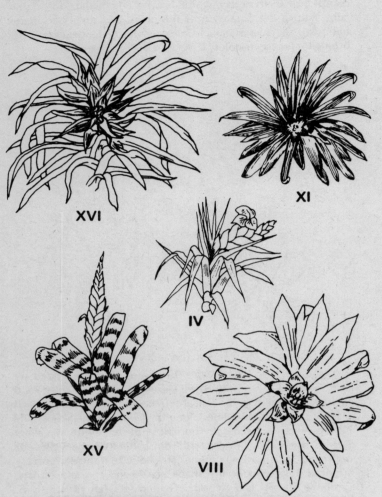

XVI

XI

IV

XV

VIII

BROMELIADS AS HOUSEPLANTS

The following basic factors must be observed in growing bromeliads successfully in the house: Light, Moisture (this includes water and humidity), Temperature, Ventilation, Nutrients, and Growing Media. Naturally, for optimum results, all must be in near perfect balance to ensure healthy blooming plants.

LIGHT

Light has been the factor which, up to now, has been the most difficult to achieve in the home growing of bromeliads or any other houseplants. In the temperate climate zone, those who could afford to do so have built greenhouses in which to grow the beautiful exotics from the tropics. Persons with lesser means had to depend on their windowsills for sufficient light to grow their plants, only to discover that smog and air pollutants diminished the quality and quantity of light received by the plants. Even the panes of windowglass soon become coated with an oily sooty deposit which actually deletes as much as 50% of the light passing through them.

To overcome these handicaps, many indoor horticulturists have been forced to depend upon various types of incandescent and fluorescent lights. Unfortunately, even the so-called "daylite" fluorescent tubes have given only a fraction of true life-giving light to the plant surfaces. This good light is necessary for most houseplants and expecially bromeliads to develop their full potential of bloom.

How fortunate, therefore, are we that certain industrial concerns have expended great effort to produce a light which could give off a true natural light. The most successful of these has been Duro-Lite Lamps, Inc., Fair Lawn, New Jersey, whose research has developed the "Vita-Lite" and "Naturescent" fluorescent tubes.

These bulbs emanate rays that are 91% true daylight, by actual test. I have been using these tubes since their introduction and

have found them superior to all others. Vita-Lite and Naturescent have produced fantastic results for me. In many cases, the plants grown indoors under these lights have developed in an even better fashion than many similar species seen growing out-of-doors in tropical areas.

It is best to mount the fluorescent lights in fixtures that contain a minimum of 4 parallel tubes. These fixtures should be so situated that bromeliads may be placed from 6 to 24 inches from the light source. Shorter plants can be set upon upside-down flower pots to raise them closer to the light. Aechmeas, Billbergias and Neoregelias should be grown nearest to the fixture, Cryptanthus, Nidulariums and some Guzmanias placed furthest away and Tillandsias, Vrieseas and the majority of Guzmanias set at a medium distance.

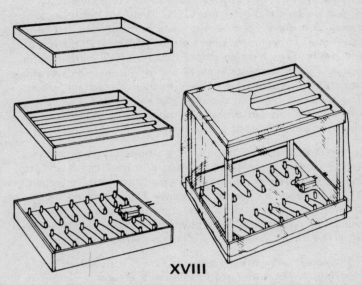

XVIII

For optimum results, the fixtures should be connected to an automatic timing device that can control the lights so that they function for 15-hour periods each day.

It has been my experience that once the all-important factor of lighting is solved, everything else in indoor horticulture is simple. It is then possible to have your Bromeliads reach their fullest potential of gorgeous, exotic beauty.

MOISTURE

In considering the effects of moisture, one should remember how the plants grow in nature. All Bromeliads feed either entirely or partially through their modified stomata, the scales. Since so many of them are epiphytic, the roots are specialized either for support or for feeding.

Many Bromeilads grow in locales where they receive a heavy bath of dew at night. Because of the heating conditions in homes, the air quickly becomes dry and dehumidified. This may be rectified in two ways. (Examine Figs. XVIII and XIX). A simple device can be constructed of four pieces of scrap lumber (boards 1" x 3" to 1" x 6" may be used). The dimensions depend upon the size of the windowsill or the area to be covered. Cover the frame with a piece of heavy plastic large enough to overlap in all directions. Push the plastic down to fit inside the frame, and fill the trough-like plastic depression with coarse builder's sand, vermiculite, perlite, pebbles or very coarse crushed stone or gravel. Tack the plastic to the top of all sides of the frame, and tuck all the excess plastic under the edges of the frame to conceal the crude lumber.

When water is poured into this tray of filling material for ¾ths of the height, the natural evaporation of water will supply humidity to plants.

Another helpful and important adjunct is a cold mist humidifier. If this is used nightly, the resultant raising of the moisture content of the air will not only benefit the plants, but the family of the horticulturist and its possessions as well! Besides this humidifying it is necessary to keep the plant cups filled with water. The potting mixture needs to be watered only when dry. Too frequent watering of the planting media may cause bromeliads to rot and spoil. One of the great benefits of growing bromeliads is that they are almost self-watering and may safely be left for two or three weeks as long as their natural reservoirs are filled to capacity. For those who wish to grow their plants epiphytically (methods given below) it is very necessary to spray these plants once or twice daily so that they may thrive in a natural manner.

TEMPERATURE

Since most bromeliads come from tropical and sub-tropical regions, they will not thrive under cold conditions in the home, even though many of them will not be damaged too severely by short freezing spells in their natural habitat. Most seem to thrive under the same house conditions as their owners. In fact, too high a temperature over a long period will cause severe damage due to excessive transpiration from the leaves. A maximum of 70° during the day and between 55° and 65° at night is the best temperature range. If the plants are grown on windowsills, it would be wise to seal the edges of the window to prevent chilling drafts.

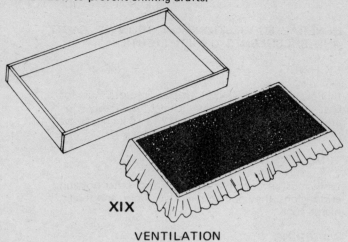

XIX

VENTILATION

Most growers ignore this most important factor in indoor horticulture. They forget that plants, like all growing things, must breathe in order to live. Plants require a constant supply of carbon dioxide to survive, and when windows are kept shut or sealed all winter, circulation of air is not possible, and no fresh supply of gases is available. This condition may be corrected in many ways. The simplest is to open a window in another room on days that are not too frigid. Another is to keep a slow-moving electric fan going most of the day. This induces air circulation. If one uses the cold mist humidifier mentioned in the section on moisture, the fan that sprays the mist into the air will also circulate it.

NUTRIENTS

It is not necessary to feed Bromeliads very often. A weak solution of an all-purpose fertilizer may be used every two or three weeks if all other growing factors are favorable. It is wise to ensure that the fertilizer does not precipitate and leave a residue in the cups of the plants, as this can accumulate and eventually clog the feeding scale cells of the leaves. It is not necessary to feed the roots as frequently as the cups; probably every other time is sufficient.

Freesia refracta alba.

GROWING MEDIA

Writings about the horticultural requirements of other plant families place a great deal of stress on the proper formulae, with exact measurements to make up a correct potting mixture. Bromeliads are demanding in one factor alone. They must be grown in media that permit quick drainage of water and sufficient circulation of air around the roots. Since we are dealing with plants that are largely epiphytic, it must be remembered that in nature the roots are fastened to tree bark that is quite acid. This gives us a hint as to the type and consistency of the growing medium. It should be made up of non-alkaline materials that supply moisture without getting too soggy. It should be porous enough to enable the water to drain off readily while allowing air to reach the roots

As a rule, pure soil gets too muddy and prevents efficient air circulation. A good mix is based on coarse German peat moss.

To this is added leaf mold, humus, perlite, bark chips, lava rocks and/or chopped osmunda or tree fern fiber. The peat moss should make up at least ½ of the mixture, while any one or a few of the other ingredients may be added to make up the balance. The mixture should be placed loosely around the roots without packing.

For those who wish to grow their plants epiphytically, two methods are suggested. The plants may be fastened to pieces of driftwood in attractive displays, or they may be tied to slabs of tree ferns. The haapu or Hawaaiian tree fern is preferable to the Mexican variety. Plants that are grown epiphytically dry out very quickly and they should have at least one or two daily sprayings with a fine mist atomizer. In nature, even though the epiphytic roots are always exposed to air, they never dry out due to their nightly dew bath.

FORCED BLOOM STIMULATION IN BROMELIADS

A unique phenomenon associated with the Bromeliaceae is that it is the only family that can be induced to bloom out of season by chemical means. Many years ago it was discovered that if ethylene comes into contact with mature or nearly mature bromeliads it causes them to flower at almost any scheduled time. Ethylene is a product of burning wood or leaves, and it is also emitted by ripening fruit.

Acetylene gas, a product of dissolving calcium carbide in water, has an effect similar to ethylene. So does "Omaflora," a fairly new compound for controlling the fruiting of pineapples in the field. The active ingredient in "Omaflora" is hydrazine which, incidentally, is an active ingredient in rocket fuel.

Since most of the above materials may be dangerous if used in the home, the following harmless method for inducing flowering is recommended. A healthy, mature bromeliad with an excellent root system has all the water drained from the cup and is then placed inside a transparent air-tight plastic bag together with a large fragrant ripe apple. After four or five days the plant is removed from the bag, water replaced in the cup, and the still good apple may be eaten! Depending on the genus involved, the plant will start its inflorescence from six to fourteen weeks.

Yucca Treculeana.

CACTUS & SUCCULENTS

BLOOMING CACTUS AND SUCCULENTS AS
HOUSEPLANTS UNDER FULL-SPECTRUM LIGHT

DURO-LITE LAMPS, INC.
17-10 Willow Street, Fair Lawn, New Jersey
Home Lighting Division of Duro-Test Corp.

by Dr. George Milstein

Long popular as houseplants because of their
unusual growth habits, colorations and general
form, cacti and succulents have not been known
to bloom indoors. Yet outdoors they produce
some of the loveliest blossoms in the plant kingdom. In order to blossom, these two plant
groups need the full spectrum of sunlight, including the ultraviolet. And even the sunniest
of windows will filter out the ultraviolet from
the incoming daylight.

Now, in experiments conducted at the Brooklyn
Botanic Garden under the supervision of chief
taxonomist George Kalmbacher, world-wide
authority on cacti and succulents, it has been
shown that many dozens of varieties thrive—and
flower beautifully—under Vita-Lite full-spectrum
fluorescent light.

Developed by Duro-Lite Lamps, Inc., of Fair
Lawn, N.J., Vita-Lite is a remarkable simulation of natural sunlight in appearance and spec-
tral composition of the light as well as in beneficial ultraviolet emission. No previously-de-
veloped fluorescent has ever been effective in
growing cacti and succulents. In addition, etio-
lation (spindly, elongated growth) which occurs
with other types of light was not noticed under
Vita-Lite.

This means that for the first time, many cacti
and succulents can now be grown indoors at
anytime of the year. The report of this phenomenon, as observed by Mr. Kalmbacher, appears
in the reprint nearby.

GENERAL SUGGESTIONS ON GROWING CACTI AND SUCCULENTS UNDER LIGHTS

LIGHTING

In almost each case, Vita-Lite is an absolute must for
best results since it simulates sunlight so closely. Operate lights 14 to 16 hours daily, 12 to 16 inches above
the plants.

TEMPERATURE

While most of these plants come from rather hot and
arid regions, they do like their days warm and their
nights cool.

WATERING

Succulents require more frequent waterings than most
cacti, but both groups will need additional quantities
of moisture in their growing seasons, usually the spring.

POTTING MEDIA

Porous material is a must. Mix together some good
garden soil with coarse builder's (not beach or salty)
sand. To this, add small amounts of leaf mold, bone
meal, rotted manure and a very small portion of agricultural lime. Plants such as Christmas or Orchid
Cactus, which are normally air-plants, can use more
leaf mold and humus in the mix and a substitution
of perlite and bark chips or osmunda fiber instead of
the builder's sand.

FEEDING

Generally speaking, these plants will appreciate weak
solutions of fertilizer low in nitrogen but high in
phosphorus and potassium. Feeding should be supplied
in the active growing season and discontinued during
the dormant seasons, which in many cases is the fall
and winter.

PEST CONTROL

Most pests such as mealy bugs and scale can be controlled by mild sprays containing weak malathion
solutions.

CEREUS PLEIOGONUS.

MAMMILLARIA SULCOLANATA.

CEREUS CTENOIDES.

ECHINOCACTUS HAYNII.

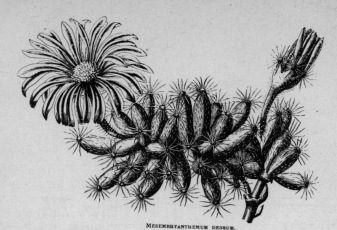

WINDOW BOXES

CACTUS AND SUCCULENT JOURNAL

All those who grow plants under lights will be interested in the letter of George Kalmbacher in the International Miniatures Robin. He wrote, "There have been a number of fluorescent tubes offered in the past, but none could effect growth of cactus and many succulents. Now, however, a company called Duro-Test has developed a tube that includes the part of the sun's spectrum that causes tanning of human skin, the ultraviolet that is invisible, and harmless. It is, it seems to me, this band that is so important to cacti and other succulents, that has been missing in the past. We have three fixtures of four tubes each of 40 inch length, and have a number of succulents and cacti to get a quick idea of how useful they might be in promoting good, normal growth. We keep the lights on 16 hours. It is two months since we started, as a project of mine. During this time the cacti have been doing fine, apparently. Growth of nearly all plants has been pronounced and obvious. Euphorbias seem to do amazingly well. Echeverias, known not to do well under other lights, do very well, as do related genera. We have them growing in a laboratory that is kept warm at all times for other reasons. I would prefer to have the laboratory cold at night, but anyway, our results show that for one's pleasure or profit, cacti and other succulents can be grown in winter, as if it were summer . . . Trichocaulon cactiforme has developed numerous flower buds since it was put under these lights, which, by the way, are called Vita-Lite. Crassula tecta var. fragilis has become a real beauty and is flowering. Other crassulas also doing excellent."

Mesembranthemum minimum

NOTE

One of the most frequent questions asked of the writer is how to bring Christmas Cacti and Crown of Thorns (Euphorbia splendens) to bloom each year, since these plants are usually dormant during our (North Temperate) summer months.

About the middle of June, decrease the amount of light and water, and stop feeding. About the end of September, increase the watering and step up the amount of light so that by mid-October the plants are receiving no more than 10 to 11 hours of light. They can be shielded from more light each night by covering them with an opaque bag. By Christmas time, they should burst into beautiful bloom.

MESEMBRYANTHEMUM TESTICULATUM.

AUTOMATIC WATERING OF POT PLANTS AND WINDOW BOXES

By W. E. Larmie   University of Rhode Island

House plants and window boxes are the pride and joy of many people, yet sometimes they can be a terrific burden. Plants require care, and without this, they will become sick and eventually die.

One of the most burdensome chores in having plants in the home is the watering that must be done. In most instances, this is a daily chore; although with some plants you can let them go without water for a few days, providing other conditions are not too unfavorable.

However, if one plans to go on a vacation for a few days, something must be done to keep the plants watered. This sometimes involves standing them in the bathtub, or imposing on a neighbor to take care of them. Either of these might not be too desirable.

If one depends only on showers during the summer to keep the window boxes wet, he is probably in for a big disappointment. Watering both house plants and window boxes by the use of wicks can be the answer. In most instances when wick culture is used, it is necessary to add water only once every two or three weeks. A reservoir is used, and the water is supplied gradually to the bottom of the pot or box. It is then distributed throughout the soil by capillarity. When water is added, it is usually put directly in the reservoir. An occasional overhead watering of the plants will prevent an accumulation of salts near the soil surface. Also, when fertilizer is added, it should be watered in from the top.

One might compare this system to a public water system in that there is a reservoir, and lines running from the reservoir to points where the water is needed. In wick culture, the wicks can be compared to the pipe lines.

Potted Plants

For potted plants, little material is needed for wick culture. A container is necessary to act as a reservoir. This can be of any type. A glass baking dish, or a rectangular cake pan can be used.

Next some kind of a stand must be built over the reservoir to hold the plants. A relatively simple stand can be made by nailing two laths together with small strips of wood and laying this directly on top of the pan holding water. Separate the laths by 1/2 inch to allow room for the wick to go through into the water.

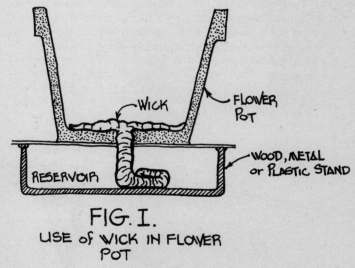

FIG. I.
USE of WICK IN FLOWER POT

The wick can be of many materials such as burlap, oil lamp wick or cheesecloth, but fiberglass wick material seems to be superior. This can be purchased at most of the leading seed stores. For pot plants, a wick 4" to 6" long is usually sufficient. This depends upon the height of the plant above the reservoir. The wick should be pushed through the hole in the pot leaving about two inches inside. This should be unraveled and spread uniformly in the bottom of the pot. For plants that require little water, the glass wicks can be pulled apart, and only two or three strands of the material used. Sometimes a little sand is placed on top of the wick but this is not necessary. The plant is then potted in the normal manner. After potting, put the wick through the hole in the stand and into the reservoir. Add water to the reservoir when necessary.

Window Box

The window boxes should be a little deeper than the ordinary window box to allow for the reservoir of water in the bottom.

One-inch boards about eight inches wide may be used for the window box. The box can be of any desired length, but the width should be about eight inches at the top and six inches at the bottom (inside measurements). One-half inch material may be used for the false bottom.

Fiberglass wicking is probably the best material to use for wicks. However, burlap, or any other material that will conduct water, will serve. The disadvantage of using burlap or cloth is that it rots readily and can be used only for a short time.

To make the bottom section of the box watertight, use a good caulking compound. Horticultural asphalt should be painted over the entire inside. This not only helps to make the box watertight, but also preserves the wood.

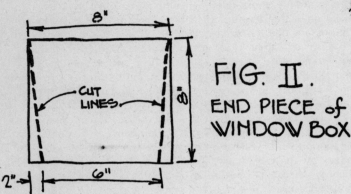

FIG. II.
END PIECE of WINDOW BOX

Construction

Cut two 8-inch boards to the desired length of the box. Then take two 8" x 8" pieces of the same material and cut out the ends as indicated in Figure II.

Next attach the front and back boards to the ends securely with galvanized screws. It will then be necessary to plane the bottom edge of the two side boards to provide a flat surface to which a bottom board of the same material can be screwed.

At this point it is best to waterproof the box. Use a good grade of caulking compound and paint the entire inside with horticultural asphalt. It will probably be necessary to let the box dry for a few days before doing further work on it.

The false bottom should be about two inches above the bottom of the box held in place by small strips nailed along the sides. Holes about 1/2" to 5/8" in diameter should be drilled every 8" to 10" along the centerline. It is through these that the wicks are inserted. One relatively large hole should be made near one end to hold the pipe through which water is poured into the reservoir.

The false bottom should fit quite tightly to prevent sand and soil from seeping into the reservoir. Again it will probably be necessary to use a plane to get the proper angle so a good fit is made. To insure longer life, a coat of asphalt should be applied.

Wick material should be cut into 5" lengths and placed through the holes to the bottom of the reservoir. Unravel the top of the wick and spread it uniformly along the bottom.

The pipe through which water is poured into the reservoir should be at least 3/4" in diameter and 8" long. The bottom should be cut in such a way that water will flow into the reservoir without hindrance. (See Fig. III) You may use plastic

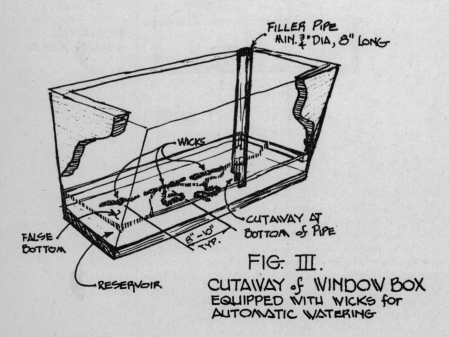

FIG. III.
CUTAWAY of WINDOW BOX
EQUIPPED WITH WICKS for
AUTOMATIC WATERING

or rubber garden hose or galvanized pipe.

Filling Box

Now that the box is completed you are ready to fill it. First place a layer of sand 1/2" to 3/4" deep over the false bottom and wicks. Then fill the box with good soil to within 1" to 1-1/2" of the top.

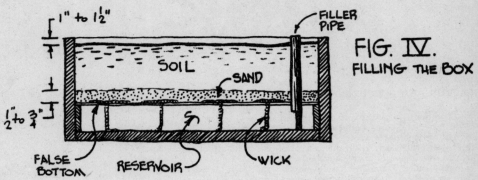

FIG. IV.
FILLING THE BOX

This completes the box except for the actual planting. You will find that most plants will do well in this box. Geraniums, vinca, and ageratum are some of the more common plants that do very well when watered this way.

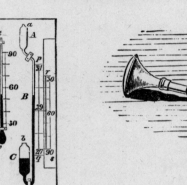

Garden Hose

DURO-LITE LAMPS, INC.
17-10 Willow Street, Fair Lawn, New Jers
Home Lighting Division of Duro-Test Cor

INDOOR GARDENING WITH ARTIFICIAL LIGHT
DURO-LITE HORTICULTURAL BULLETIN

How Does Light Make Plants Grow?

PHYTO-ILLUMINATION is the art of gardening by artificial illumination. Although a relatively new process, it represents one of the most important horticultural achievements of this century. With our mounting ecological problems it might well be our century's salvation, since plants provide needed oxygen and moisture to the atmosphere.

Plants depend on good light for good growth, but relying on sunlight coming through a window a small part of the day is not enough. Clouds, haze, smog, and dirty, sooty windows all further prevent the proper and sufficient light from reaching plants. Fortunately, healthy plants and flowers can be grown and kept vital without any natural sunlight at all; full-spectrum artificial light provides an excellent substitute and has the advantage of permitting plants to flourish on bookshelves, in stairwells and corridors, and other windowless areas.

PHOTOSYNTHESIS is the growth process basic to plants. Carbon dioxide in the air combines with water and minerals in the soil to form carbohydrates. This happens because of the action of light on chlorophyll, a substance found in all green plants.

PHOTOPERIOD — Light and dark periods and their relative lengths have an effect on plant maturity. Actually, recent investigations have proven that it is not the length of day which affects growth, but the duration of the dark period which follows. The dark period of each day affects flowering and seeding of most plants. Although many plants can grow under continuous light, nearly all plants prefer a dark period each day for normal growth. All plants need some darkness periodically to grow well or to trigger flowering. The ideal photoperiods of plants vary, some preferring long days and short nights; others the reverse; and some equal day-night periods.

PHYTOCHROME is a chemical pigment found in plants. Discovered only three or four years ago, this pigment, when acted upon by light, triggers growth changes from seed to fruit throughout the life of the plant. Red light energy activates this pigment, encouraging fast plant growth.

LIGHT IS MEASURED IN WAVELENGTHS. As a matter of brief basic background, it is important to consider the nature of light and its effect on plant growth. White (or natural) light is composed of red, orange, yellow, green, blue, violet and ultra-violet energy.

Red energy, in addition to triggering growth, promotes maturity and flowering. Generally, however, too much red light causes plants to become tall and "leggy". Blue light used alone causes short, stocky growth with fewer blossoms or no flowering at all. Much of the yellow and green light is reflected by green foliage, but the trace energy absorbed is very important in producing healthy, normal plants.

FULL-SPECTRUM LIGHT is white light in its proper balance of energies. Sunlight is full-spectrum light; it cannot be improved upon. Under sunlight, virtually all plant and animal life evolved and flourished. And under sunlight all things are seen as they really are—in their true colors. The best artificial lights for indoor light gardening are those that most closely match sunlight.

FLUORESCENT LIGHT GARDENING

The first attempts at indoor light gardening with fluorescent lamps involved combining lamps of different colors or mixing the fluorescents with incandescents. This was necessary to obtain the better balance of light energy which plants require for good growth. Although some success was realized, these systems left much to be desired.

In time, "plant growth" fluorescents were developed, but these had exaggerated red and blue characteristics. Plants not only looked unnatural under them, but usually failed to fulfill their promise. (Often it was even difficult to recognize whether a plant was healthy or not.) It became apparent that while plants may respond to various colors of light, they need a "naturally balanced" combination to grow normally and with the proper shape and color.

Research at Duro-Lite a few years ago exceeded all previous accomplishments and led to the production of the first full-spectrum fluorescent lamp. Called "Natur-escent", this lamp simulates the visible spectrum of natural sunlight to a remarkably close degree.

Subsequently, Duro-Lite developed "Vita-Lite", a fluorescent lamp duplicating all the visual characteristics of Natur-escent and also emitting a controlled amount of ultra-violet for an even more accurate simulation of sunlight.

Like sunlight, Natur-escent and Vita-Lite are full-spectrum light sources.

Prize-winning plants can now be grown indoors under Vita-Lite or Natur-escent during any season of the year, thus greatly enhancing the rewards of indoor gardening. African Violets, Begonias, Bromeliads, Cacti, Chrysanthemums, Geraniums, Gloxinias, Orchids, Roses, and many other exotic plants, both trocial and subtropical, can be grown well in indoor light gardens.

From a more practical point of view, many kinds of seeds, cuttings and leaves can be started indoors for later planting outdoors when weather conditions are favorable. Vegetables such as tomatoes can be three or four weeks ahead of schedule for spring outdoor transplanting and will yield fruit much earlier.

Since both Vita-Lite and Natur-escent closely simulate the energy produced by sunlight, they provide the indoor horticulturist with a most efficient tool. Plants often suffer shock when moved from sun to incomplete artificial light or from indoors to outdoors. This problem can be avoided with use of full-spectrum artificial light.

Based on wattage consumption (the electrical power you pay for) fluorescent lamps are about three times more efficient than incandescent bulbs in converting electrical energy into visible light energy. Vita-Lite and Natur-escent are considerably more efficient in converting electrical energy into the light energy utilized by plants. Unlike common fluorescent lamps, Vita-Lite and Natur-escent emit a high degree of red energy and thus are excellent for phytochrome activation.

Euphorbia meloformis

To determine how much light a plant will require, consider where and how it grows best in its natural environment. Most vegetables, for instance, grow in full sunlight, which means as much light as possible must be supplied indoors. Such foliage plants as Philodendron grow in full shade and therefore can grow normally with relatively little artificial light. Exotic plants, such as Bromeliads, grow in varying conditions depending on the species; some grow in deep shade in the jungle, while others grow in bright sunlight.

High-intensity light is provided by a four-lamp 40-watt fluorescent fixture located 8 to 12 inches above the plants. This illuminates a plant area of 2' x 5'.

Medium-intensity light is provided in the system above with lamps 16 to 30 inches above the plants, or with a two-lamp 40-watt fixture located 8 to 12 inches above the plants. This effectively illuminates an area of 1¼' x 5'.

PLANTS TO GROW UNDER VITA-LITE: African violets, Amaryllis family, Annual plants, Bromeliads, Cacti, Fuschias, Geraniums, Indoor flowering bulbs, Lily bulb family, Narcissus, Orchids, Succulents and Tulips

PLANTS TO GROW UNDER NATUR-ESCENT: African violets, Amaryllis family, Balloon-type plants, Begonias, Cinerea, Droxineas, Exotic blooming plants, Ferns, Fuschias, Geraniums, Gesneriads, Lily bulb family, Primrose and most foliage plants.

INCANDESCENT LIGHT GARDENING

Although fluorescent lamps have become the most popular source for growing plants, incandescent bulbs can be effectively utilized in combination with fluorescents, and in many instances where it is not possible or practical to use fluorescents.

For visual purposes, incandescent light is high in red, moderate in blue and green, and good in the other colors. Since it is important that the light source approach sunlight as closely as possible, Duro-Lite developed the incandescent "Plant Lite". A unique light-blue tint in the glass helps correct inherent incandescent color deficiency to provide the "natural" light energy plants need.

PORTION OF PLANT, WITH FLOWER, OF CEREUS BERLANDIERI.

It has been common practice to use footcandles or illumination level as a guide to the effectiveness of the light being used for plant growth. This is not a sound basis for judgment because the human eye (and the footcandle meter) is most sensitive to yellow and green light, while the light energy most effective for plant growth is in the red and blue area. Lamp-watts per square foot of growing area provide a better basis for measurement.

To root cuttings or to germinate seeds, 10 to 14 watts per square foot of growing area is recommended. With the light source 8 to 12 inches above the soil or cuttings, a light period of 14 to 16 hours will produce good results. Proper control of temperature, humidity, ventilation, fertilization, and soil acidity, as recommended for specific plants, must also be followed.

When growing plants with incandescent lamps it is advantageous to use reflector (R) types. Duro-Lite R-30 Plant Lite Reflector Bulb (4130) and R-40 Plant Lite Reflector Flood (4147), both with regular medium bases, have been the object of intensive testing to prove their successful application for indoor light gardening. The sealed-in reflector stays brighter longer since it cannot get dirty. The smooth underside, through which light is emitted, is resistant to dirt. These bulbs provide correct color and uniform illumination on plants.

TEMPERATURE, HUMIDITY & VENTILATION

With rare exceptions, most plants prefer daytime temperatures of 68 degrees F to 85 degrees F and night temperature of 55 degrees F to 73 degrees F. Indoor winter heating conditions often cause drying-out. Humidity must be provided by humidifiers or by keeping the plant pots on gravel or bark beds which are kept moist at all times. Periodic, careful fertilization is also necessary. Ventilation or air movement is beneficial to plants. The important thing to remember is that plants need all the natural conditions for normal culture, including good balanced light.

Under full-spectrum lighting, plants appear as they do outdoors. This makes possible correct evaluation of the plants' need for nutrition, medication, insect control, heat and carbon dioxide as well as their responses to treatment.

PLANT LIGHTS

DURO-LITE LAMPS, INC.
17-10 Willow Street, Fair Lawn, New Jersey
Home Lighting Division of Duro-Test Corp.

Starting seedlings indoors now under horticultural lights gives the gardener a head start on warm weather planting of his "victory" garden to help defeat the high cost of vegetables next summer.

It also could mean that his family is eating vine-ripened tomatoes and beans long before his neighbors are.

The techniques for starting both vegetables and flowers from seeds under lights are a specialty of John K. Michel, horticultural consultant to the Duro-Lite Home Lighting Institute. For those who have never experienced the accomplishment this type of gardening provides he has the following hints:

The first thing to do is find a place for your garden. Almost any area in the house, small or large, can be used including attics, basements, closets and shelf areas. An important consideration is easy access to water and electricity.

Having decided on the area, you should use suitable fluorescent lighting fixtures and lamps. The most practical fixtures are bare-bulb two-lamp 20-watt and two- and four-lamp 40-watt channel strip models available in lighting, hardware and department stores. The number of fixtures/lamps of course depends on the size of the area. For a good lighting level you should have 15 to 20 watts of fluorescent light per square foot of growing area. This means that a. . .

- two-foot, two-lamp 20-watt unit will light a 18" x 24" area,
- two-foot, four-lamp 20-watt unit will light a 24" x 30" area (higher intensity),
- four-foot, two-lamp 40-watt until will light a 24" x 50" area and
- four-foot, four-lamp 40-watt unit will light a 30" x 56" area (higher intensity).

While industrial strips are the most practical and economical, you may prefer to buy a portable adjustable unit on legs or even a tiered unit.

The most important consideration is the type of fluorescent lamp you choose. All plants grow outdoors naturally, in natural light which radiates all the wavelengths of the complete light spectrum from ultraviolet through violet, indigo, blue, green, yellow, orange and red. Plants respond best to a balance of all these and don't do as well or suffer when the light is deficient or missing this balance.

The need for full-spectrum light was fulfilled by the scientists and engineers at the Duro-Lite Corporation a few years ago when they developed a combination of fluorescent phosphors that supplies the full-spectrum of natural sunlight including the beneficial portion of ultraviolet in a fluorescent tube. The lamp is called Vita-Lite full-spectrum fluorescent. This patented Vita-Lite lamp supplies the complete "indoor sunshine" essential to the life support of vegetables and many types of exotic vegetation. An earlier development called Natur-escent is also an excellent plant growth full-spectrum lamp but does not include the ultraviolet.

Incidentally, these lamps provide the sunlight spectrum and also look like outdoor natural daylight. They not only grow vegetables, flowers and other plants well but render their colors naturally. They do not have the eerie color of some of the earlier growth lamps.

To control the lights effectively and get the best usage you may wish to invest in an automatic timer which will turn your system on and off automatically. For growing vegetables a 10- to 14-hour light period followed by a 10- to 14-hour dark period is important.

After you have installed or placed your lighting units in your planting area, the next step is to set up your trays, pots or flats. Plastic trays 12"x12" to 12"x18" are easiest to handle. These are available in garden shops, nurseries and variety stores in many sizes to accommodate your area.

Next, get your growing media into the trays. The bottom layer about ½" deep should be pebbles, gravel or broken crockery. Fill the trays with a good growing mixture. Don't use regular garden soil for this. Your best bet and least troublesome would be a commercially packaged mixture. There are many favorite recipes of soil mixtures which can be found in any horticultural or gardening book. Any good nursery will recommend or even make a mixture for you. The soil mixture should be watered down (not muddy) and then you are ready to plant your seeds. Many flowers and vegetables germinate rapidly indoors under lights. Among them are tomatoes, miniature tomatoes, eggplant, radishes, peppers, asparagus, beets, broccoli, cauliflower,

celelry, cucumbers, marigolds, zinnias, petunias and coleus.

Seeds can be obtained from grocery supermarkets, nurseries and seed companies, which have beautifully illustrated catalogs. It is best to follow the package directions for planting your seeds. A good rule of thumb is to plant any seed to a depth of two or three times the seed's size. The seed trays should be kept three to five inches from the lights. When the plants germinate, try to keep the tops of plants three to six inches from the lights. It is important to maintain the other elements for good vegetable growth to insure complete success. In addition to the above elements, you should also be concerned with humidity, temperature, fertilizer, watering, ventilation and insect and disease prevention.

FLUORESCENT LIGHTS HELP GARDENER START SEEDS NOW, PARE BILLS LATER

SMILAX ORNATA.

HUMIDITY can be provided by keeping your flats or trays on a layer of pebbles, gravel or pine bark or chips in a waterproofed tray filled to the top of the layer with water. An easier method is to operate a cold mist humidifier. A sheet of plastic or Visqueen over the whole area (above the lights) will provide a sort of greenhouse and retain humidity.

TEMPERATURE — most vegetables prefer 70-75 degrees during the light cycle and 55-65 degrees during the dark cycle. But one doesn't have to be fanatical about this. Temperatures above 78 to 80 degrees should be avoided.

FERTILIZER is necessary but should be used sparingly. About one-half the strength recommended in the directions should be applied about once each week or 10 days. An all-purpose liquid is easiest to handle.

WATERING is frequently over-done. The soil should be dry to the touch before watering. Frequency will vary with the conditions in your house and with how it retains humidity. Plants should be watered well when they need it and then allowed to dry between waterings.

Plants breathe in order to survive, but reverse the respiratory process of animals and people. They absorb carbon dioxide and produce or exhale oxygen. This is nature's way of maintaining a balance between vegetables, plants and animals.

VENTILATION or air exchange is necessary to provide a fresh supply of gases. A slow-moving fan or ventilation from another room will take care of this.

INSECTS AND DISEASE are best prevented by starting with and maintaining clean sanitary environmental systems. Then vigilance to determine any problem is important. Any plant infestations should be removed. Much information can be obtained from nurseries or horticultural books regarding the treatment of specific problems.

A little care and common sense in observing all the elements will assure good results and good vegetable and flower seedlings for transplanting into your outdoor garden.

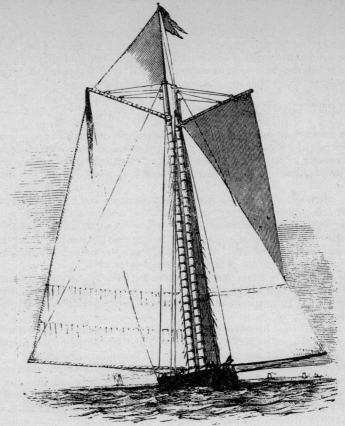

GROWING FRESH FOOD HYDROPONICALLY ON SMALL BOATS

From the moment the first sailors ventured further than their own horizon, man at sea contended with the elements of his own survival. Never is the challenge so great as when the immense, boundless ocean tests his ingenuity and courage. The isolation is such a humbling experience that it makes man seek meaning in what usually is taken for granted.

All long distance ships always took fresh fruit and vegetables before leaving port. But, on voyages lasting years, the fresh food became nothing but a memory. Large ships under sail are now a thing of the past. But, they have been replaced with the smaller vessels, and smaller crews.

Many of the long distance sailors, such as Sir Francis Chichester and Erik Hiscock (both circumnavigators of the globe) kept to a meatless diet. Among their stores were grain, nuts, herbs, and honey to supplement their diets. Only recently has the possibility of growing fresh food on board been a reality.

Two forms of growing on board are now available to the vagabond sailors whose diet is basically vegetarian.

Water Cresses round leavd

Common Basil

The first is growing sprouts. One can grow bean sprouts in plastic jugs as one grows them at home. This will provide an added ingredient for salads and is one form of fresh food.

The second is small hydroponic growers. Although the U. S. Navy has installed these growers on submarines, the general public is completely unaware of their existence. With a compact soilless system, one could supplement the canned food diet with fresh food indefinitely.

There are basic limitations one should be aware of. Most important is to realize that space is crucial in a savage sea. The diagrams below suggest two possible stowage areas available; one for artificial light, the other for direct sunlight.

The grower below should be put in an easily accessible stowage locker that is deep and narrow. I suggest those spaces between the hull and bulkhead that are often too narrow for usual stowage. Remember, most plants need light and air venilation should be installed above the plants and connected to an adequate, rechargeable power source. An extra

battery, wind-generated or solar energy cell may be necessary. The air flow should be great enough to provide sufficient CO_2 to your plants.

The grower on deck should consist of a hinged, plastic skylight hatch with the hydroponic units resting inside a deep box that will contain the complete grower. Openings for the switch below should be added. Ventilation may be provided from tubes cross-fed to air scuppers on deck. For both growers the nutrients should be changed accordingly. In certain northern climates, heating coils may be necessary to keep environmental conditions constant.

A wooden, gimbaled frame should be built to hold each hydroponic grower balanced to the rocking sea. Large plants with fruit (tomatoes for example) can be brought aboard thus eliminating the pollination problem. Most of the "crop" will be green.

We suggest you experiment with the possibility and let us know your failures and successes.

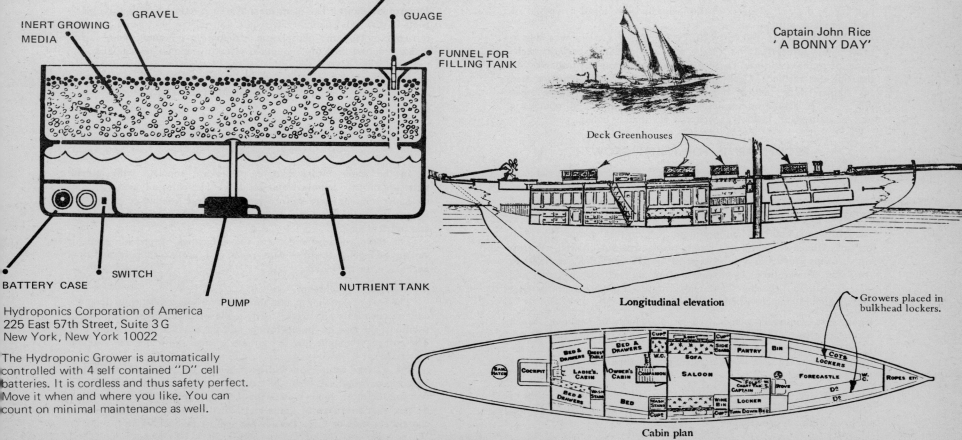

INERT GROWING MEDIA

GRAVEL

GROWING AREA

GUAGE

FUNNEL FOR FILLING TANK

BATTERY CASE

SWITCH

PUMP

NUTRIENT TANK

Captain John Rice 'A BONNY DAY'

Deck Greenhouses

Longitudinal elevation

Growers placed in bulkhead lockers.

Cabin plan

Hydroponics Corporation of America
225 East 57th Street, Suite 3 G
New York, New York 10022

The Hydroponic Grower is automatically controlled with 4 self contained "D" cell batteries. It is cordless and thus safety perfect. Move it when and where you like. You can count on minimal maintenance as well.

HYDROPONICS

J.D. Butler and N.F. Oebker

—Experiments in Water-culture (by Dr. Nobbe) at the Experimental Station in Tharandt, Saxony.

During the past several decades, many amateur and commercial gardeners have become interested in growing plants with their roots in an artificial medium instead of soil. This method of growing plants is commonly known as "hydroponics." It is also sometimes referred to as nutrient-solution culture, soilless culture, water culture, gravel culture, and nutriculture.

Soilless culture of plants is not new. One of the first experiments in water culture was made by Woodward in England in 1699. He was trying to determine whether water or the solid portion of the soil was responsible for plant growth. By the mid-nineteenth century, Sachs and Knop, the real pioneers in this field, had developed a method of growing plants without soil.

In the late 1920's and early 1930's, Dr. W. F. Gericke was able to grow plants successfully on a large scale through the laboratory technique of solution culture. Dr. Gericke used the term "hydroponics" to describe this method of growing plants. Today, hydroponics is used in commercial production, but it is employed mostly in those areas where soil is lacking or unsuitable for plant growth. Hydroponics is also a tool in plant research as well as a fascinating hobby.

REQUIREMENTS FOR PLANT GROWTH

The requirements for plant growth in soil culture and nutriculture are the same. The only fundamental difference between the two methods is the manner in which the inorganic nutrients required for growth are supplied to the roots.

Temperature. There is an optimum temperature range for plant growth. Above or below this range, plants will not do well. Warm-season crops usually do well between 60° and 75° or 80° F., with 60° F. the night temperature. Cool-season crops do well between 50° and 70° F., with 50° F. the night temperature. Temperatures for best growth should be maintained whenever possible.

Light. Most cultivated plants need large amounts of sunlight. When plants are grown indoors, additional artificial light is sometimes needed. If plants are grown entirely under artificial light, the intensity of the light must be very high without causing the temperature to rise above the optimum range.

Water. Water should be available in adequate amounts in the soil or in soilless culture for proper growth. Too little or too much water will not give optimum growth.

Oxygen. In soil that is not waterlogged, adequate oxygen should be available. In hydroponic systems for growing plants, there may not be sufficient oxygen in the nutrient medium. To provide enough oxygen, it is often necessary to bubble air through the solution surrounding the roots.

Carbon Dioxide. Carbon dioxide, a gas, is taken up through the surface of the leaf and furnishes carbon and oxygen. These elements are required, along with hydrogen, in the manufacture of carbohydrates. Carbohydrates are used by the plants as food.

Mineral Nutrients. The plant must absorb certain minerals through its roots to survive. The minerals required in relatively large amounts are nitrogen, potassium, phosphorus, calcium, magnesium, and sulfur. Those required in small amounts are iron, manganese, boron, zinc, and copper. Molybdenum and chlorine are also useful to plants, but the quantities required are so minute that they are usually supplied in the water or along with the other mineral nutrients as impurities.

SYSTEMS OF SOILLESS CULTURE

Water Culture

In the water-culture method, plants are supplied with mineral nutrients directly from a water solution. The chief advantage of this method over aggregate culture is that a large volume of solution is always in contact with the root system, providing an adequate water and nutrient supply.

The major disadvantages are the difficulties of providing an air supply (oxygen) for the plant roots and proper support and root anchorage for the plants.

Materials and Equipment

The cost of growing plants through hydroponics depends upon the cost of chemicals and water used in the preparation of the nutrient solutions, the size of the operation, and the amount of mechanization. The cost may be quite low if you have a small setup and use available materials.

For a large setup, you will need a tank or trough constructed of concrete or wood. A depth of 6 to 18 inches and a width of 2 to 3 feet are the most common sizes for the larger tanks. If you use wood, be sure that it is free of knots and sealed with asphalt that does not contain creosote or tars. Do not use asphalt that leaves an oil film on the surface of the water. If the system is small, you can use glass jars, earthenware crocks, or metal containers. Metal containers should be well painted on the inside with an asphalt-base paint. Glass jars must be painted on the outside with dark paint to keep out light. A narrow strip should be left unpainted so that the level of the solution can be seen in the glass container.

The seedbed or plant bed should be 3 or more inches deep and large enough to completely cover the trough or tank. To support the litter, cover the bottom of the bed with chicken wire or ½-inch-mesh hardware cloth painted with an asphalt-base paint. Fill the bed with litter. The litter may be of wood shavings, excelsior, sphagnum moss, peat, or some other organic material fairly resistant to decay. Germinate the seed in sand or vermiculite and transplant to the water-culture bed. Keep the bed moist until the plants get their roots down into the nutrient solution.

Germinating Peas, growing in Water, one deprived of its Cotyledons.

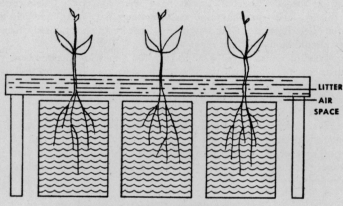

Cross-section of a simple water-culture system.

Aeration

The water-culture method often fails because of inadequate aeration of the solution. The space between the seed bed and the nutrient solution may provide enough air for the roots of certain plants. But you must make special provision to allow an exchange of air between this space and the air outside. Prop up the seed bed a fraction of an inch or drill holes in the container or tank just above the highest solution level.

If you have trouble aerating the roots, use an aquarium air pump. Do not stir the solution too vigorously. You may damage the tender roots and cause poor plant growth. Pumping the air through an air stone, a perforated pipe, a porous glass tube, or a hose covered with a fine screen will reduce root damage by breaking down the air bubbles.

Water Supply

An adequate supply of pure water is essential for this system of hydroponics. The mineral content of water varies from place to place. In some areas, water is softened by replacing the calcium and magnesium with sodium. Sodium is toxic to certain plants when present at high levels. Boron and copper may be toxic at very low levels in the water, even though these elements are required in minute quantities for plant growth. Usually the minerals in water are not detrimental to plant growth. Calcium and magnesium, which are often present in water, are beneficial to plants.

Applying Nutrient Solution

Nutrient solution may be added by hand, by means of a gravity-feed system, or mechanically.

In a small setup, the nutrient solution can be mixed in small containers and added by hand as needed.

In a large setup, the gravity-feed system can be used effectively. The nutrient solution is mixed in a vat and tapped from the vat as needed. A large earthen jar or barrel will serve as the vat. If you use a metal barrel or container, paint the inside with an asphalt-base paint.

A pump can be used to transfer the material from the mixing vats to the growing tanks. Use a special non-rusting pump, or wash the pump carefully after each use. This precaution is necessary because the chemicals used in the nutrient solution will corrode metal.

The time to add nutrient solution depends upon the temperature and the growth of the plants. When the plants are young, the space between the seedbed and the nutrient solution may be quite small (sometimes one-half inch is sufficient). As the plant roots grow, lower the nutrient level slowly, keeping the level of the solution as constant as possible.

When the temperature is high and evaporation rapid, the plants may need additional solution every day. *Keep the roots at the correct level in the water.* The roots will die if allowed to dry out.

The container or tank should be drained completely every two weeks and the nutrient solution renewed from the mixing vats. This operation should be arranged so that it can be accomplished in a short time. If more than a few minutes elapse between the time of draining the tanks and refilling them, the roots will dry out. To delay the drying of the roots, change the solutions on a cloudy day or after the sun has gone down.

Transplanting seedlings or seeding directly into the seedbed will get the plants growing under the solution-culture system. The litter must be kept moist until the roots become established in the nutrient solution.

Transplant seedlings carefully. Work the roots through the support netting into the nutrient solution; then build up the litter around the plant to support it.

Aggregate Culture

This method is often referred to as "sand culture" or "gravel culture." Aggregates are used much as soil is used in conventional plantings — to provide anchorage and support for the plants.

The aggregate in the tank or container is flooded with a nutrient solution as required. The advantages of this system of hydroponics over the water-culture method are lack of trouble in aerating the roots, ease of transplanting seedlings into the gravel or other aggregate medium, and less expense.

Materials and Equipment

The tank or container should be *watertight* to conserve the nutrient solution. Construction materials will depend upon the size of tank or container. Large tanks can be built of wood, asphalt paper, concrete, or metal. The wood should be free of knots, and cracks should be sealed against leakage with asphalt. Asphalt paper can be used with wood framing to make a workable tank. A metal tank should be painted on the inside with an asphalt-base paint.

Metal, earthen, and glass containers can be used quite successfully for a small-scale operation. Ground beds, flower pots, baskets, and even bean hampers have been used in aggregate culture. Since they are not watertight, however, some of the solution is lost. Metal containers should be painted on the inside with an asphalt paint, and glass containers should be painted on the outside with a dark-colored paint.

The aggregate material may differ greatly in composition. Well-washed silica sand makes one of the better materials. But any sand,

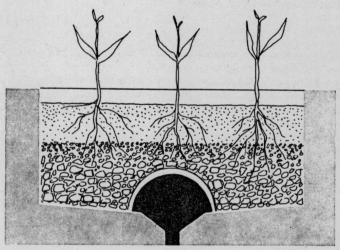

Cross-section of plants growing in aggregate culture.

preferably of coarse texture, that does not contain lime may be used. Sand is a desirable medium because of its ability to hold moisture, and because plants may be easily transplanted to it.

A mixture of sand and gravel makes a very good medium if the sand or gravel does not contain much lime. Well-washed cinders may be used, provided that they are not high in toxic materials. Other materials such as peat moss, vermiculite, wood shavings, etc. are also satisfactory. You can obtain aggregate materials from local lumber yards, garden centers, or garden-supply houses.

Aeration

Aeration is much easier in aggregate culture than in the water-culture system. Draining and refilling the tank with nutrient solution causes air to move in and out of the aggregate material, thus supplying adequate oxygen to the roots.

Water Supply

Water requirements for this system are the same as those for the solution-culture methods. The mineral nutrients and the minerals present in the water as impurities accumulate in the aggregate materials as a result of evaporation. To overcome this accumulation of minerals, flood the aggregate material with water every two weeks. Drain off the water to wash out the minerals.

Applying Nutrient Solution

The "slop" or surface method is the simplest for adding the nutrient solution. In this method, the solution is poured over the aggregates by hand. A manual gravity-feed system with buckets or other vats and small growing containers may be used. The vat is attached to the bottom of the tank or container with a flexible hose, and is raised to flood the tank and lowered to drain it. The vat may be lowered and raised by hand or by means of a mechanical device. The vat should be covered to prevent evaporation and filled with new nutrient solution at least once every two weeks.

The gravity drip-feed system also works satisfactorily, and reduces the amount of labor. The vat is higher than the tank in this system, and the solution drips from the vat just fast enough to keep the aggregate moist.

A manual gravity-feed system.

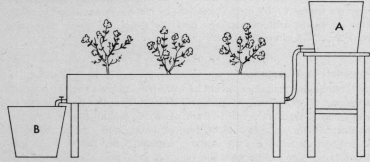

A simple gravity-feed system. The solution flows from vat A into the aggregate material in the growing bed. When the growing bed is flooded, the solution is drained into vat B and then returned to vat A.

A pump can be used to raise the solution to the desired depth for sub-irrigation. Sub-irrigation is a system of supplying the nutrients by raising and lowering the solution level from the bottom. The solution must be raised to a higher level for younger plants than for older plants. A timer may be arranged on the pumping system so that the nutrient solution can be added whenever necessary. If the pump is not a non-rusting pump, it should be washed carefully after each

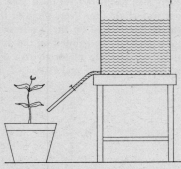

A gravity drip-feed system.

use to prevent rusting. This mechanical system for adding the nutrient solution is practical only for a large setup.

The nutrient material must be added and drained or raised and lowered in the tanks once or twice a day. When the weather is especially hot and dry, the aggregate material may need more than two drenchings. Examine the aggregate material frequently to be sure that it has not dried out around the roots. After a few examinations, you will know about when the nutrient solution should be added. Remember — frequent drenchings will cause little harm, and permanent injury may result if the plant roots dry out.

Do not use the nutrient solution more than two weeks. If the solution is used for longer periods, it will probably build up salts or fertilizer residues that will damage the plants.

Seedlings or rooted cuttings may be used in this system. The aggregate material should be flooded and the solution drained off before planting. This will leave a well-packed, moist seedbed.

Seeds may be planted directly in the aggregate material. Do not plant too deep. Flood or sprinkle the tank with water frequently to prevent the aggregate material from drying out at the surface. If this happens, small seedlings may die. A few days after the seedlings have germinated, start using nutrient solution.

The safest way to get the plants established is by transplanting the seedlings from a germination bed. The seed should be germinated in a medium that is free of soil. Soil on the roots may cause them to rot, and may also cause trouble by getting into the nutrient solution.

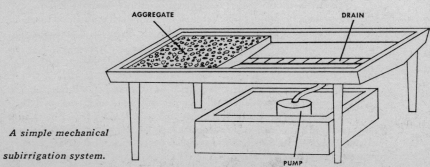

A simple mechanical subirrigation system.

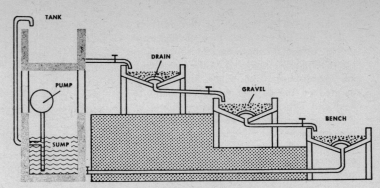

Cross-section of a mechanical gravity-feed system.

PREPARING THE NUTRIENT SOLUTION

For proper growth, plants must be supplied with nitrogen, phosphorus, potassium, calcium, magnesium, sulfur, iron, manganese, boron, zinc, copper, molybdenum, and chlorine. Within certain limits of composition and total concentrations, there can be a rather wide range in the nutrient solutions suitable for plant growth. Usually the small amount of minerals in the water supply can be ignored. When nutrients are deficient or present in excess in the solution, however, the plants will suffer. For this reason, you must be careful in selecting and adding the minerals that go into the nutrient solution.

Purity of the nutrient materials or chemicals is important in preparing a solution. In some cases, the fertilizer grade of a chemical may be used, and in other cases, a technical-grade or food-grade chemical may be needed. The best grades have few impurities; the lower or fertilizer grades may have more. Sometimes the plants may use the impurities. Because of the low price of the fertilizer-grade chemicals, they should be used whenever possible.

Many formulas have been devised for supplying the nutrient requirements for plant growth. Most of these recommendations will give satisfactory results, but they often require less than one gram of chemicals that are not easy to obtain.

Paint the storage vats and containers used for the nutrient solution to prevent exposure to light, and close the vats and containers to prevent contact with the air. Evaporation of the solution, whether through the atmosphere or through plants, reduces the amount of water and increases the proportion of salt in the solution. Too much salt may be detrimental to the plants.

Pre-Mixed Chemicals

The chemicals needed for hydroponic plant growth are now being mixed in the correct proportions. These mixtures may be obtained through catalogs, or from garden-supply stores and reputable fertilizer suppliers. They are relatively inexpensive, and small quantities will go a long way in growing plants. Follow the directions on the container.

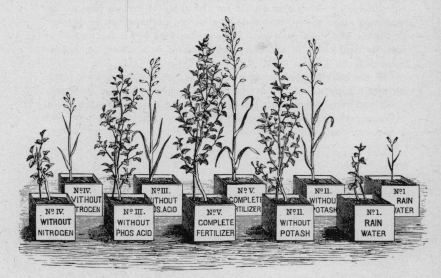

BUCKWHEAT AND OATS GROWN IN PURE SAND, AND SUPPLIED WITH DIFFERENT FERTILISING INGREDIENTS.

Self-Mixed Chemicals

You may want to prepare your own nutrient solution. The nutrient solution given below was worked out by the late Dr. D. R. Hoagland of the University of California. This solution supplies the major elements required for plant growth. It is easy to prepare, and usually gives satisfactory results.

Salt	Grade	Nutrients	Amount for 25 gallons of solutions	
			ounces	level tablespoons
Potassium phosphate (monobasic)	Technical	Potassium Phosphorus	½	1
Potassium nitrate	Fertilizer	Potassium Nitrogen	2	4 (of powdered salt)
Calcium nitrate	Fertilizer	Calcium Nitrogen	3	7
Magnesium sulfate	Technical	Magnesium Sulfur	1½	4

The table below can be used as a guide for adding nutrients required in very small amounts. You can obtain the chemicals listed from a garden-supply store or drug store. When you buy manganese chloride, zinc sulfate, or copper sulfate, be sure that the formulas for these salts are the same as those shown in the table. The amounts of solution given may be more than you will need. The amounts of chemical salts and water needed may be reduced by one-half or even more.

. . . .

Salt (all chemical grade)	Nutrients	Amount of water to add to 1 tsp. of salt	Amount to use for 25 gallons of solution
Boric acid, powdered	Boron	½ gallon	½ pint
Manganese chloride ($MnCl_2 \cdot 4H_2O$)	Manganese Chlorine	1½ gallons	½ pint
Zinc sulfate ($ZnSO_4 \cdot 7H_2O$)	Zinc Sulfur	2½ quarts	½ teaspoon
Copper sulfate ($CuSO_4 \cdot 5H_2O$)	Copper Sulfur	1 gallon	⅛ teaspoon
Iron tartrate	Iron	1 quart	½ cup

. . . .

Zinc sulfate and copper sulfate usually do not need to be added because of their presence as impurities in the water and in the other chemical compounds used in making up a nutrient solution. If you use the water-culture method of growing plants, it may be necessary to add the iron solution once or twice a week. You may want to use the chelated form of iron, since this form will not readily precipitate out of the solution. Mix 1½ ounces of NaFe EEDTA 13 percent Fe_2O_3 in 5 quarts of water. Use ¼ pint of this solution in 25 gallons of water.

Other sources of nutrients may be substituted for those in the tables as long as they furnish the mineral nutrients needed by the plants. The toxic effects of some chemicals upon plant growth must always be considered when making substitutions.

After all of the chemicals have been mixed into the solution, check the pH (acidity or alkalinity) of the solution on a pH scale. The pH scale runs from 0 to 14. Any solution below 7.0 is acid, and any solution above 7.0 is basic or alkaline. A pH of 7.0 is neutral.

Plants that do well at a low pH (between 4.5 and 5.5) include azaleas, buttercups, gardenias, and roses. Plants that will grow at a pH level between 7.0 and 7.5 include potatoes, zinnias, pumpkins, and myrtle. Usually plants will not grow with any success in solutions below a pH of 4.0 or above a pH of 8.0. For most plants, the solution should be slightly acid within a range of 5.5 to 6.5.

Use an indicator or pH tester to determine the pH of the solution. Indicator papers register pH within different ranges. When dipped into the solution, the paper will change color at different pH levels. There are other devices for determining pH, and testing kits may be obtained from scientific and chemical supply houses.

If the pH is above the desired range, it can be brought down by adding dilute sulfuric acid. Add the acid in very small quantities, stirring the solution at the same time. An eye dropper is useful for this purpose. Count the drops. After a few drops have been added, retest the solution. Continue adding acid and retesting until the solution reaches the desired pH range. If you count the drops of acid, you can put the same number of drops into the solution each time the solution is made up. You will not need to make further pH tests as long as the water and chemicals of the solution remain unchanged.

SYMPTOMS OF PLANT-NUTRIENT DEFICIENCIES

Plants will usually display definite deficiencies if the nutrients are not present in adequate amounts. The following symptoms may occur if the level of one mineral nutrient is not high enough to be within the range needed for best plant growth. There may be several reasons other than a nutrient deficiency why a plant will display a definite symptom. But if one of the deficiency symptoms occurs, a lack of the proper nutrient may be suspected, and the amount of that nutrient increased.

Deficient nutrient	Symptoms
Nitrogen	Leaves are small and light green; lower leaves lighter than upper ones; not much leaf drop; weak stalks.
Phosphorus	Dark-green foliage; lower leaves sometimes yellow between veins; purplish color on leaves or petioles.
Potassium	Lower leaves may be mottled; dead areas near tips and margins of leaves; yellowing at leaf margins continuing toward center.
Calcium	Tip of the shoot dies; tips of young leaves die; tips of leaves are hook-shaped.
Magnesium	Lower leaves are yellow between veins (veins remain green); leaf margins may curl up or down or leaves may pucker; leaves die in later stages.
Sulfur	Tip of the shoot stays alive; light-green upper leaves; leaf veins lighter than surrounding areas.
Iron	Tip of the shoot stays alive; new upper leaves turn yellow between veins (large veins remain green); edges and tips of leaves may die.
Manganese	Tip of the shoot stays alive; new upper leaves have dead spots over surface; leaf may appear netted because of small veins remaining green.
Boron	Tip of the shoot dies; stems and petioles are brittle.

EXPERIMENTS FOR YOU TO TRY

Many interesting experiments can be performed with soilless culture. Two experiments, the first dealing with pH levels, and the second with nutrient materials, are outlined below. You may want to work out variations of these experiments or try others of your own.

Experiment 1: pH Levels

Use the nutrient solution shown in the tables on pages 12 and 13, or a solution prepared from commercial pre-mixed nutrients. Adjust the pH of the solution to between 5.5 and 6.5.

Pour the solution into three containers. Do not change the pH of the solution in the first container. This solution is the "check" or "control." Lower the pH of the solution in the second container to below 4.0 by adding dilute sulfuric acid. Raise the pH of the solution in the third container to 8.0 or above by adding a dilute sodium hydroxide (NaOH) solution. Test the pH of the solutions with an indicator.

The following plants do well at a pH range between 5.5 and 7.0: carrot, coleus, cucumber, geranium, orange, pepper, petunia, strawberry, turnip, and violet. Grow a plant from this list in each of the three solutions. Choose only *one kind* of plant (pepper, for example), and be sure the plants are about the same size. If you use seeds, plant them all at the same time.

Notice the differences in growth between the plants in the three solutions. You may want to set up various pH ranges to find the best pH in which to grow a particular plant.

Experiment 2: Nutrient Levels

You will need to prepare three nutrient solutions for this experiment. The first solution is a pre-mixed nutrient solution or the "stand-

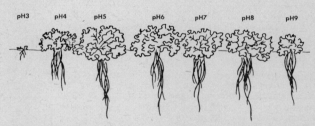

pH3   pH4   pH5   pH6   pH7   pH8   pH9

Effect of various pH levels on the growth of lettuce (from D. I. Arnon and C. M. Johnson).

ard" solution listed in the tables on pages 12 and 13. Use *twice* the recommended amounts of nutrients in the second solution. For the third solution, use *one-half* the recommended amounts of nutrients. You will probably not want to prepare 25 gallons of each solution. The amounts of salts and water may be reduced by one-half, one-fourth, or even more, as long as you mix the proper proportion of ingredients for each of the three solutions.

Be sure to grow the *same kind* of plant in each container so that you can compare results between the plants. If you transplant into these containers, choose plants that are uniform in size. By varying the nutrient and pH levels and observing the effects of these changes upon the plants, you can determine the proper pH and nutrient levels for a particular plant.

Effect of various nutrient levels on plant growth.

This circular was prepared by J. D. Butler and N. F. Oebker, former staff members of the Department of Horticulture, University of Illinois. Plant hobbyists may also be interested in Circular 817, "Plant Breeding as a Hobby," and Circular 886, "Plant Regulators." A copy of these publications can be obtained by writing the Publications Office, College of Agriculture, Urbana, Illinois.

FOR FURTHER INFORMATION

The Complete Guide to Soilless Gardening, W. F. Gericke, Prentice Hall, New York, 1940. (Available in libraries.)

Growing Ornamental Greenhouse Crops in Gravel Culture, D. C. Kiplinger, Ohio Agricultural Experiment Station Special Circular 92, Wooster, 1956. 37 pages.

Hunger Signs in Crops, The American Society of Agronomy and The National Fertilizer Association, Washington, D. C., 1951. (Available in libraries.)

Hydroponics — The Science of Growing Crops Without Soil, Joseph P. Biebel, Florida Department of Agriculture Bulletin 180, Tallahassee, 1960. 51 pages.

Methods of Growing Plants in Solution and Sand Cultures, J. W. Shive and W. R. Robbins, New Jersey Agricultural Experiment Station Bulletin 636, New Brunswick, 1937. 24 pages.

Nutriculture, Robert B. and Alice P. Withrow, Purdue University, Agricultural Experiment Station Circular 328, Lafayette, Indiana, 1948. 60 pages.

Successful Gardening Without Soil, C. E. Ticquet, Chemical Publishing Company, New York, 1956.

The Water-Culture Method for Growing Plants Without Soil, D. R. Hoagland and D. I. Arnon, California Agricultural Experiment Station Circular 347, Berkeley, 1950. 32 pages.

Planting-Table for Flowers—By Leonard Barron

FOR the purpose of reckoning dates, New York City is generally taken as a standard. Allow six days' difference for every hundred miles of latitude.

DATES FOR PLANTING

January 15th.—Sow indoors tender annuals and biennials which are to be treated as annuals.

February 15th.—Successional sowing of biennials and annuals indoors.

March 1st.—Sow all kinds indoors.

March 15th.—Sow sweet peas outdoors.

April 1st.—If ground is free from frost, sow hardy annuals in the garden.

April 15th.—Sow all hardy seeds outdoors.

May 1st.—Sow more seed of hardy annuals in the garden. Risk first tender annuals.

May 15th.—Sow all tender annuals outdoors. Plant out from indoors and complete the garden.

June 1st.—Plant out bedding stock, cannas, and other subtropical plants.

September 15th.—Sow sweat peas and other hardy annuals outdoors.

How to Make a Flower Bed.—Dig the soil a foot deep at least. Use plenty of well-rotted manure. If the soil is very wet, dig out two feet deep and put in a layer of stones, clinkers or broken crockery. Annuals want all the sun they can get.

How to Get Early Flowers.—You may gain a month by starting flowers indoors in boxes. The March number of THE GARDEN MAGAZINE has a lot of pictures that show just how to do it.

Small Seeds.—Rake the surface perfectly smooth. Use the back of the rake. Sow the seed; don't cover it, tread it in, or press it with a board.

How to Water Plants.—Soak them thoroughly. Don't dribble. Water at night. Next morning rake the ground. Don't let a crust form.

Tender Annuals.—These will not endure early frost in spring; balsam, castor oil, gourds, morning glory, nasturtium, petunia, cosmos, portulaca.

NAME OF FLOWER	WHEN TO SOW		DEPTH TO PLANT (inches)	HOW FAR APART when thinned or transplanted (inches)	WHEN THEY FLOWER		NUMBER OF WEEKS IN BLOOM	COLOR OF FLOWERS	HEIGHT (feet)	OTHER POINTS Hints on Soil, Watering, Transplanting, etc.
	Indoors	Outdoors			Early Crop	Main Crop				
Alyssum, sweet	Mar.	Apr. Sept.	½	6	July	Aug. to Sept.	20	white	½	Sept. sown will bloom May. Keep flowers cut and they bloom six months.
Aster, China	Feb. Apr.	May	½	18	July to Aug.	Sept. to Oct.	6	blue, red, white	1	Don't overfeed or plants will get disease. Try wood ashes to control disease.
Balsam	Mar.	May	½	12	May	July	8	red, white, pink	2	For largest flowers cut off side shoots and grow to single stem. Likes water.
Calendula, Pot Marigold	Mar. Apr.	Apr.	½	8	June	July to Oct.	12	orange-yellow	1	Impossible to fail. Self sows. Flower heads used in soups. Can sow Sept.
Carnation (Margaret)	Feb.	Apr.	¼	6	July	Sept.	2	pink, red, white, var.	¾	Florists' carnations, survive one winter. Margarets best for garden.
Candytuft		Apr. July	¼	6		June to Sept.	4	red, white	½	Excellent for limestone soils. Don't transplant. Best low annual for rocks.
Castor oil	Mar. May	June	2	36 x 72				insignificant	2 to 8	Grown for tropical foliage effect. Don't disturb roots in transplanting.
Coreopsis	Mar.	May	¼	10	June	Aug. to Nov.	12	brown, yellow	1 to 2	(*Calliopsis elegans*) Includes best brown flowers in cultivation. Self sows.
Cornflower		Apr. May	¼	4 x 6		June to Sept.	8	deep blue	1	Cut flowers young; they grow larger in water. Best of dwarf blue annuals.
Cosmos	Feb. Apr.	May	¼	18 x 24	Aug.	Oct. to Nov.	8	pink, white, yellow	4 to 10	Get early varieties, start indoors. Plant out deeply. Tie to chicken wire.

reprinted from GARDEN MAGAZINE, 1905

CARNATION, DAN GODFREY.

PANSY (*Viola tricolor—large-flowering garden variety*).

GERANIUM—"MRS. POLLOCK."

VICTORIA ASTER.

THE CINERARIA.

NAME OF FLOWER	WHEN TO SOW		DEPTH TO PLANT (inches)	HOW FAR APART when thinned or transplanted (inches)	WHEN THEY FLOWER		NUMBER OF WEEKS IN BLOOM	COLOR OF FLOWERS	HEIGHT (feet)	OTHER POINTS Hints on Soil, Watering, Transplanting, etc.
	Indoors	Outdoors			Early Crop	Main Crop				
Evening Primrose (Lam'k)	Jan.	Sept.	¼	18 x 24	Aug.	June, next yr.	6	pale yellow	1	(*Œnothera Lamarckiana*) Opens at dusk. Fragrant. Flowers 4 to 5 inches.
Forget-me-not		Apr. May	¼	4	Next May	June to Aug.	8	pale blue, white	½	Naturalize along brooks. Will grow in gardens. Water and partial shade.
Four o'clock	Feb. Mar.		¼	36	Aug.	Aug. to Oct.	12	white, yellow, carmine, var.	2 to 3	Shrubby, but grown as annual. Sometimes self sows. Roots kept in cellar.
Foxglove	Jan.	May	don't cover	18	Aug.	July next yr.	4 to 8	pink, white	2 to 4	Best results by sowing gloxinia-flowered strain in fall in a frame.
Gourds	Mar.	May	¼	6				fruits: green, yellow, white	10 to 30	Grown for curious fruits. Train on trellis or arbor. Treat like squash.
Hollyhock	Feb.	June	1½	12	Aug.	July, next yr.	12	rose, maroon, yellow, white	4 to 7	Cut main growth after flowering. Ever-blooming strain flowers first year.
Larkspur (annual)	Feb.	Apr. Sept.	⅛	6 x 18	June	July to Oct.	16	red, blue, wh., pink, yel.	½ to 2	Keep flowers cut. Slow to sprout; better sow in fall.
Lavatera	Jan.	Apr.	⅛	18	July	Aug. to Oct.	6	white	3	(*L. trimestris*) Mallow family. Flowers four inches across.
Lobelia cardinalis	Aug.	Apr.	¼	4	Next July	Aug.	4	carmine	¾	Cardinal flower. Best in deep, moist well-drained soil; e. g., brook side.
Lobelia Erinus	Feb.	Apr.	¼	6	June	Aug.	8 to 12	white, blue	½	Best blue-flowered, low-edging plant. Common in parks. Will stand manure.
Love-in-a-Mist	Feb.	Mar. Apr.	⅛	6	May	July to Sept.	16	white, yellow, blue, brown	1 to 2	Profuse, finely cut foliage, good to mix with other cut flowers. Self sows.
Lupine	Jan.	Mar.	½	3 x 6	June	July	4	white, blue, yellow	½ to 5	Lime hater. Great range colors. Pea-like flowers in clusters like wistaria.
Marigold	Feb. Mar.	Apr. May	¼	12	June	Aug.	8	light yellow, orange, brown	½ to 2	Early plants which flower in pots before planting never stop till frost.
Mignonette	Feb. Mar.	Apr. Aug.	¼	6	May to July	July to Oct.	3 to 4	greenish	1	Make sowings for succession. Does not transplant well. Last sowing for winter.
Morning-glory	Feb. Apr.	May	1	4	July	Aug. to Oct.	10	blue, red, white, var.	15 to 30	Best vine for trellis. Soak seed in warm water. Self sows. First frost kills.
Nasturtium	Mar. Apr.	May	1	10 x 12 12 x 36	June	July to Oct.	8 to 10	scarlet, yellow, maroon	1 to 5	Thin dwarf kinds best on thin soil. Dies at first frost. Leaves as salad.
Nicotiana	Feb.	Apr.	⅛	12	July	Sept.	6	white, red	4 to 6	N. *affinis* white; new hybrids, red to violet. N. *sylvestris* very bold. Good.

GARDEN MAGAZINE, 1905

HAND-BOUQUET.

GROUP OF PANSIES.

POMPONE CHRYSANTHEMUM.

PRIMULA SPECTABILIS WULFENIANA.

CHRYSANTHEMUM SEGETUM GRANDIFLORUM.

NAME OF FLOWER	WHEN TO SOW		DEPTH TO PLANT (inches)	HOW FAR APART when thinned or transplanted (inches)	WHEN THEY FLOWER		NUMBER OF WEEKS IN BLOOM	COLOR OF FLOWERS	HEIGHT (feet)	OTHER POINTS Hints on Soil, Watering, Transplanting, etc.
	Indoors	Outdoors			Early Crop	Main Crop				
Pansy	Jan. Feb.	June July	$\frac{1}{8}$	6 x 12	May to June	Sept. to Oct.	6 to 8	purple, blue, white, yellow	$\frac{1}{2}$ to 1	Aug. sown flowers May. Protect slightly for winter. Best early bedding plants.
Petunia	Mar. Apr.	May	don't cover	12 x 12	May	Sept.	10	magenta, white	1 to 2	Ordinary type flowers profusely all summer. Thrives anywhere. Self sows.
Phlox, annual	Feb.	Mar. May	$\frac{1}{8}$	4 x 6	May	July to Aug.	4 to 12	white, red, yel., maroon	$\frac{1}{2}$ to 1	Best dwarf plant, for general purposes. Self sows. Makes good pot plant.
Pink, China " Japan	Feb. Feb.	Mar. Apr.	1–16	6 x 12	May	Aug.	4 to 6	white, rose, maroon	1	Showy; 3 inches across with curious mixture of colors. Stands cold, not wet.
Poppy " California		Mar. May	$\frac{1}{8}$	8	June to July	Aug. to Sept.	3 to 4	pink, scarlet	$\frac{1}{2}$ to 1	Delicate colors in Shirley strain. Don't transplant. Most brilliant red annual.
Poppy, Iceland	Jan.	Apr.	$\frac{1}{8}$	8	June	Aug.	3	yellow, white, orange	1	Sept. sown flowers May. Small flowers. Good for greenhouse in March.
Poppy, oriental	Sept.	Apr. May	$\frac{1}{8}$	36	July	Sept.	12	scarlet	3	Bold perennial. Divide plants May or Sept. Flowers 8 to 10 inches across.
Portulaca		June	don't cover	66		July	12	white, red, magenta	$\frac{1}{2}$	Germinates in hot weather. No use to sow early. Can transplant in flower.
Rocket	Aug.	Apr.	1–16	12	May	Aug. to Sept.	6	white, flesh, purple, red	1 to 3	(*Hesperis matronalis*) Grows in old brickwork. Can sow seed as gathered.
Salpiglossis	Feb.	Apr.	1–16	6	June	July to Sept.	10	variously colored	2	Always in flower. Curiously mixed and striped colors. Grow alone in beds.
Salvia splendens	Feb. Mar.	June	$\frac{1}{4}$	18 x 36	June	Aug. to Oct.	12	scarlet	3	Get early and dwarf strains. Sunshine or shade. Plant with green backgr'nd.
Scabiosa	Jan. Feb.	Apr.	1–16	4		July to Aug.	4	lt. rose, crim., blue, pur., wh.	1	Sow every month outdoors. Good for cutflowers.
Schizanthus	Jan.	Apr.	$\frac{1}{4}$	6	May	June to Oct.	6 to 8	violet or lilac and yellow	2	Sept. sown makes good pot plants for flower. Don't crowd. Use wood ashes.
Snapdragon	Feb. Mar.	Apr. May	$\frac{1}{4}$		May	July to Aug.		red, white, yellow	$1\frac{1}{2}$	Wants rich, well-drained soil. Sept. sown seed, protected, flowers in May.
Stock, ten-weeks	Mar.	May	$\frac{1}{4}$	12 x 12	June	July	10	pink	$1\frac{1}{2}$	Don't transplant. Very fragrant at evening. Pinch out leading shoot.
Sunflower	Apr.	May	$\frac{1}{2}$	24 x 48	July	Aug. to Oct.	6	yellow	2 to 10	Tallest growing annuals. Seeds good for chicken feed.
Sweet pea		Apr. June	3	4 x 24		July to Oct.	4 to 8	white, scarlet, blue, yellow	4 to 6	Sow early and cut flowers. Sept. sowing gives strong vine. Trench deeply.
Sweet William	Mar.	Mar. April	1–16	6 x 6	June	July to Oct.	3	maroon, blue, white, pink	$\frac{1}{2}$ to 1	"Cluster-flowered pink." Very fragrant. Likes moist, rich soil.
Verbena	Feb. Apr.	Mar.	$\frac{1}{4}$	10 x 15	May	June to Sept.	8	red, blue	1	Grand for pegging down in beds. Always in flower. Often frag. from seed.
Zinnia	Mar.	Apr. May	$\frac{1}{2}$	6	June	July to Nov.	12 to 15	red, scarlet, yellow, mag.	$1\frac{1}{2}$ to 2	Gorgeous, bushy; always in flower. Get selected strains for pure colors.

GARDEN MAGAZINE, 1905

Fancy Pansy

PHLOX DRUMMONDII.

PRIMULA VULGARIS FLORE-PLENO, showing Habit and detached Flower.

FLOWERING BRANCHES OF PHLOX SUBULATA NIVALE

THE PATENT "MULTUM-IN-PARVO" LAWN MOWER.
Right Side, without Grass Box.

THE "WORLD" LAWN MOWER.

THE PATENT "SILENS MESSOR" MACHINE.

Nevada Gardener

THE PATENT "EXCELSIOR" LAWN MOWER.

LAWNS

THE "EXCELSIOR JUNIOR" LAWN MOWER.

HOW TO WATER YOUR LAWN

Lawnowners typically make two mistakes: (1) Water too often and not long enough. (2) Apply water too fast, waste more water in runoff than soaks into the soil.

ROOTS CAN'T SEEK OUT WATER

Roots develop only where there is water. If you water only long enough to wet just the top inch or two of the soil, the roots won't be found much deeper. When your lawn has such a shallow root system, you are forced to water often—even daily instead of weekly.

TOO-FREQUENT WATERING LEADS TO WEEDS AND DISEASES

Keeping the surface wet encourages weed seeds to sprout, and fungus diseases to flourish. Stretching the interval between waterings results in a deep rooting that can go much longer between waterings.

MANY SOILS ABSORB WATER SLOWLY!

Lawn sprinkler systems apply as much as 3" of water per hour—but the typical lawn soil absorbs less than ¼" per hour! Unless your sprinkler is ON for 5 minutes, then OFF for 5-20 minutes or whatever time is needed for the water to soak in, you not only waste enormous amounts of water but this runoff damages the soil.

Safe rule of thumb: DON'T water unless a 3" depth needs to be re-wet, or you have not watered for 10 days.

Plain

Wire-armoured

WATER LONG ENOUGH TO RE-WET THE SOIL 6" DEEP

Poke a screwdriver into the soil; if it goes down only 3" before meeting much resistance, i.e. dry soil, start watering. You will need to have 3/4" of water to actually soak into the soil to re-wet it. If your soil absorbs water at the typical ¼" per hour rate, count on 3 hours of ON/OFF watering.

START WATERING EARLY IN SPRING

Drying starts early in the spring. Use the screwdriver test; start watering when it goes in easily only 3" deep.

WATER ONLY WHEN REALLY NEEDED

Once you start watering for the year, hold off watering again until grass shows signs that it will wilt if not watered. Look for a slight color change, to a blue-black, or when foot-prints make a lasting impression.

Even in midsummer your lawn should not need watering more than once or twice a week. CAUTION: This assumes you have been watering deeply each time—long enough to wet 6" deep—so that roots are deep. If you have been watering every other day or so, your lawn will be so shallow rooted that you cannot make the switch to the once-a-week schedule this year without risking losing your lawn.

EARLY MORNING BEST TIME TO WATER—LATE AFTERNOON WORST

You want your grass dry when the sun goes down. Otherwise you risk serious fungus diseases damage, especially if the night temperature stays above 70 degrees.

Mid-day watering is fine—will not burn the leaf blades.

DEFINITELY AVOID THE EVERY-OTHER-DAY KIND OF WATERING!!

THE PATENT "MONARCH" LAWN MOWER.

THE PATENT GRASS EDGE CLIPPER.

THE "EASY" LAWN MOWER.

RANSOME'S "NEW" AUTOMATON LAWN MOWER.

Lawn-sprinkler

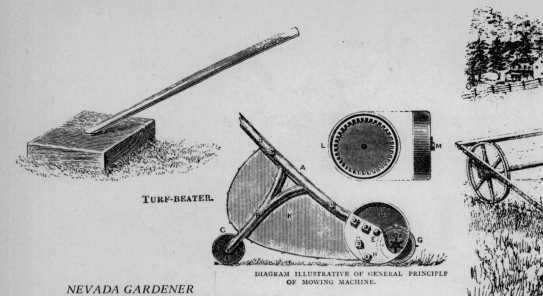

TURF-BEATER.

DIAGRAM ILLUSTRATIVE OF GENERAL PRINCIPLE
OF MOWING MACHINE.

NEVADA GARDENER
COOPERATIVE EXTENSION SERVICE
HORTICULTURE INFORMATION SERIES

REMOVING THATCH; WHAT IS THATCH?

Thatch is made up of grass clippings, dead roots, decaying tree leaves, and other materials that have collected at the soil surface. It forms a barrier under the grass which can shed irrigation water and reduce the effectiveness of fertilizers. This causes shallow rooting thus weakening the grass, making it easier for weeds, disease and insects to invade. Thatch makes ideal environment for lawn pests and makes control more difficult.

Thatch forms under all turf, but bermuda grass and bent grass produce the most.

HOW DO YOU CHECK FOR THATCH?

Take your knife and cut a 1 inch plug of sod three inches deep. All that stuff between the soil and the green is thatch you need to eliminate.

HOW TO GET RID OF THATCH

Rent a power rake with a flail reel that you can adjust down into the thatch about a half an inch depth. Repeat every few months until the thatch is removed.

Don't be afraid of the enormous pile of thatch the power rake leaves in its path; it all needs to be removed.

Do de-thatch only when the grass is dry. Do turn slowly and carefully to avoid unnecessary tearing. Do remove all the debris promptly.

WHEN IS THE BEST TIME TO DE-THATCH?

Early spring, although mid-autumn is OK. Avoid hot weather; recovery of the grass will be too slow and weeds will take over.

Hot weather is also a bad time because you must fertilize immediately after de-thatching and hot weather and fertilizer don't mix! Spring de-thatching, followed by fertilizing, leaves a torn and beaten appearance for only a few weeks as new growth soon masks the frayed grass blades.

CAN I DE-THATCH TOO OFTEN?

YES, de-thatching is a "MAJOR SURGERY". Use it sparingly, and as corrective action, not routine maintenance. Thatch builds up because of our dry hot summers and the soil bacteria do not have the right environment to work actively on it. Bermuda grass and bent grass should be mowed at a half inch to keep thatch at a minimum. Catch the clippings with all grasses. Mow at a height of two inches on common lawn grasses in northern Nevada.

Once thatch is under control, de-thatching may be needed only every other year.

SHANKS' PATENT LAWN MOWER.

THE "INVINCIBLE" LAWN MOWER.

THE "COVENTRY LAWN MOWER.

THE "EXCELSIOR" HORSE LAWN MOWER.

The Hardy Water-Lilies Worth Growing—By Henry S. Conard

NUMBER VI OF THE "LITTLE MONOGRAPHS" OF GARDEN GENERA—A SERIES OF ARTICLES SUPPOSED TO BE JUICIER AND RATHER MORE ACCURATE THAN THE OLD-STYLE BLOODLESS BOTANY

A POND of water-lilies is a possibility for anyone who can give *two square feet* of water surface in a sunny spot.

If you do make a water garden have it near at hand so you can see the flowers when at their best, and with all hardy water-lilies we must count on enjoying them in the morning or early afternoon. The flowers close at specific times for each kind, varying from noon to four or, at least, five o'clock.

A GARDEN IN A TUB

Water-lilies in tubs are better than nothing at all. A kerosene barrel sawed in half will furnish two tubs, each big enough for one plant. The tubs should be well washed out and soaked for some time in water, in order to remove as much as possible of the oil and the glue which is put on to render the vessel tight. Three or four days to a week will suffice for this.

It will be better, though not essential, to have the tub sunk about half its depth in the earth, so as to keep the roots cool. For though the leaves and flowers love sunshine, the black ooze in which the roots naturally live is always cool.

MAKING THE COMPOST

Fill the tub half or two-thirds with a mixture of equal parts good garden soil and well-rotted cow manure. When setting out the plant spread out the roots well, and after filling in the soil cover with an inch of sand Fill up the tub with water and our little water-lily pond is complete. The addition of a little water every day or two, to replace what is lost by evaporation, is all the further attention that will be needed until winter sets in.

If old cow manure is not available use ground bone—a small double handful is enough for such a tub as is described. The sand for covering is not a necessity, but it serves to keep in place the earth and manure.

One caution—do not use mud or swamp muck in the water garden.

If I am to choose one water-lily only for such a small effort, I will take the little

growth, but the flower is bright yellow and the leaves are very heavily blotched with distinct reddish-brown patches. It gets these characteristics from the native Mexican water-lily (*N. Mexicana*), which is found in Florida, Texas and Mexico. This is a very peculiar species, scarcely hardy as far north as Philadelphia, and certainly cannot be classed as a hardy *garden* plant. For, though it will *exist* in water of a depth of three feet, it will not bloom if left continuously out of doors. It is a shy bloomer even at its best.

For those who prefer pink there is the Laydeker's pink pigmy (*Nymphæa Laydekeri*, var. *rosea*), another hybrid of the Chinese water-lily. It resembles its Chinese parent in size, habit and character of leaf. The flowers, however, which are produced in great numbers, are more cup-shaped. When the flower first opens the petals are of a delicate shell pink. On subsequent days the inner petals change to rose, and finally to a deep carmine rose color, with two or three flowers of different ages open at once.

These three pigmy varieties are neat enough in all surety, but will only be chosen for a small tank or a Japanese garden, where everything is done on a miniature scale.

FOR GARDENS OF FOUR FEET SQUARE

In the next sized garden, where four feet square or perhaps more can be given to a plant, a very wide choice presents itself. We may now have white, yellow, pink, orange or deep-red flowers, and, whereas the very small gardens we have to be content with flowers about two inchcs, we will now be able to grow some six or eight inches across. And we can use the half barrels, sunk bodily in the tank or pond, for tubs in which to set the plants. Still better will it be to have tubs three to six feet in diameter for the plants, and set three stocks of a kind in each tub. This insures a continuity of bloom.

For the smaller spaces, of say two to four feet square, Marliac's yellow (*Nymphæa Marliacea*, var. *chromatella*), the *N. Laydekeri*

AQUATICS

NELUMBIUM LUTEUM.

LEAVES OF SOLDANELLA IN AUTUMN, FAT WITH FUEL, SEEN FROM ABOVE.

Chinese pigmy water-lily, *Nymphæa tetragona*. It is the most satisfactory, because it will quickly cover the water with its small horseshoe-shaped leaves. These are dark green, with faint and picturesque brown blotches on the upper surface, dull red beneath, and the combination is rich in color. Then again, it is a good plant for flowering—a good specimen will keep up a continuous succession of its little star-like flowers throughout the season, from June to September. Often two or three flowers will be open at once. The eight or ten snowy petals surround a group of stout golden stamens, and in the centre is a broad, yellow, basin-shaped stigma. The flower opens each day about noon and closes again at five in the afternoon, repeating this on three or four successive days. It exhales a delicate fragrance, like that of a tea rose.

If a change from the pure white is wanted we may choose one of the smaller hybrids of the pigmy water-lily. For bright yellow take the yellow pigmy (*Nymphæa tetragona*, var. *helvola*), similar in size and in habit of

BUD BEGINNING TO MELT ITS WAY UP THROUGH ICE IN A DOME-SHAPED HOLLOW.

BUD, SOMEWHAT LATER, ENCLOSED IN A GLOBE OF AIR WITHIN THE ICE-SHEET.

varieties and *N. exquisita* will do well. But the great majority will not do their best on a water surface less than four feet square.

The first named (*chromatella*) is decidedly the hardiest and most satisfactory of all the garden water-lilies. It is also one of the oldest, dating from about 1888. The flower is bright yellow, and on its first day sits like a golden cup on the water. It has other very decided claims to favor: A single stock will give a continuous bloom from the first of June until frost, and often there will be two flowers open at once. The leaves usually float on the water, and are beautifully mottled with reddish brown. But in shallow water, or when crowded, both leaves and flowers rise several inches into the free air and grow with a look of rank luxuriance. The plant increases rapidly in favorable circumstances, so that the possessor of a single shoot will soon be able to supply his neighbors. It is perfectly hardy, even in water so shallow that it must certainly freeze to the bottom. The fragrant yellow water-lily (*N. odorata*, var. *sulphurea*) is more delicate, and is easily distinguished when out of flower because the blotched leaves are always floating. The flower is composed of slender spreading petals. Its chief interest lies in the fact that it is the offspring of two native species (*N. odorata* and *N. Mexicana*).

SOME REALLY GOOD WHITE HYBRIDS

Among whites none of the wild species is sufficiently free-flowering to win a place in a small collection. We have, however, some superb varieties. I think *N. Gladstoniana* is the best of these. It is thoroughly hardy and a stronger grower. The leaves are of a rich green color, and may reach ten or twelve inches across. Of the flower what shall I say? Its many snowy petals stand out in all directions, making an airy sphere of glistening whiteness six or eight inches in diameter. The flower opens early in the morning and does not close until two or three o'clock in the afternoon, and often reappears on four successive days. The plant will give a goodly number also from a single shoot in a season, though there must be three or four shoots to insure continuous bloom. The only quality that this water-lily lacks is a sweet scent.

Similar to this in its flower is the white Marliac lily (*N. Marliacea*, var. *albida*), a very rank grower, which often raises its dark-green leaves and flowers well above the water.

A GROUP OF REDS AND ROSES

There are two red-flower Marliac lilies of identical habit with the preceding, but one (*N. M.*, var *carnea*) has light, pearly, pink flowers, the other (*N. M.*, var. *rosea*) is deep rose. None of the three can be said to bloom freely. *N. Wm. Doogue* resembles *N. M.*, var. *carnea*, but has larger flowers, sometimes six inches across, and rather more of them. It is of American origin, while all the *Marliacea* and *Laydekeri* varieties are French and take their group names from their raisers.

The flowers have the slender, graceful petals of the common white pond-lily and the delicious scent of that species, but are of a beautiful rose pink color. As in the type species the flowers open about six A. M. or earlier and close about noon, but this variety has the peculiarity of keeping its sepals continuously open. The closed flower therefore forms an ovate mass of pink, standing on a four-rayed star of dull white. It is a shy bloomer, and must be raised in considerable numbers to give a good effect. It is impatient of the summer heat of Philadelphia, but does well in its chief habitat, Cape Cod. One of the Marliac group, called *N. exquisita*, is a more vigorous and more floriferous variety.

THE DEEP RED WATER-LILIES

The flowers of the deep red varieties are more or less cup-shaped, i. e., the petals are erect and concave. From a pale pink on the outermost petals the color deepens toward the centre of the flower to a deep crimson. The stamens are crimson or deep orange red on the outer face, with bright orange or yellow anther cells. In full sunshine the effect is rich and striking. The plants are strong growers for the most part, but slow to propagate. They produce a fine circle of large round leaves and a goodly number of their magnificent blooms, which often reach five or six inches across. The splendid coloring of this group is derived from the Swedish water-lily (*N. alba*, var. *rubra*), which is very hard to tame. It has been grown with tolerable success in northern New York and in Massachusetts, but is not to be recommended. *N. sanguinea* has flowers of rosy, purple-spotted carmine; *Laydekeri purpurata* is rosy crimson with orange-red stamens; *Wm. Falconer*, bright garnet and as much as seven inches across, perhaps the most gorgeous of the lot; *James Gurney*, smaller and dark rose, and *James Brydon* are among the best known of these.

A distinct and beautiful series of varieties in which red and yellow are blended has been produced by combining the Swedish water-lily with our native yellow water-lily (*N. Mexicana*). The effect of the deep red in the centre of the flower with pale yellow on the outer petals is extremely striking. The brown blotching of the leaves which is seen in most of these red-yellow water-lilies is inherited from the American parent. For small gardens or where one does not want to get off with a minimum of labor these are ideal plants. They do not spread rapidly but maintain a single strong shoot, from which an ample supply of leaves and flowers arises. *N. Robinsoni* and *N. Seignoreti* are the oldest and best known of this group. The former bears a peculiar "ear-mark," by which it may always be recognized. As in all the nymphæas, the leaf is round, and attached to the petiole near the centre. On the basal side a deep cleft divides the leaf from the margin, nearly or quite to the petiole. The borders of this cleft are very constantly smooth

VICTORIA REGIA AND OTHER AQUATICS AT THE JARDIN DES PLANTES, PARIS.

NYMPHÆA ALBA.

FLOWER REACHING THE SUR-FACE OF THE ICE AND OPENING IN A CUP-SHAPED DEPRESSION.

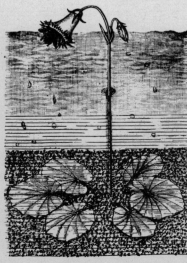

FLOWER VISITED BY A BEE, WHICH FERTILISES IT.

GROUP OF FLOWERS IN DIFFERENT STAGES PROTRUDING THROUGH THE ICE-SHEET.

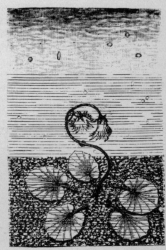

PAIR OF FLOWERS WHICH HAVE FAILED TO REACH THE SURFACE, OPEN-ING IN A SPHERE-SHAPED HOLLOW.

and entire. But in *N. Robinsoni* there is a peculiar crimped notch on each side, midway of the cleft; it also has floating flowers, where-as those of its companion stand six inches above the water. The bright combination of yellow, orange and red which, characterizes the flowers of this group is suggested by the name of one of the most recent members, *N. Aurora*, the flowers of which, opening with a yellowish color, get redder and redder as they age.

➤ If you have a large pond there will be room for the less floriferous varieties. The common pond-lily (*N. odorata*), unequalled for sweetness, may be planted. Words cannot picture a large bed of this in full bloom. It is one of those things that one must see to know its beauty and charm. The northern *N. tuberosa* is a more rampant grower, and indeed it will take complete possession of the pond if not opposed. Its flowers are large, pure white, but scentless and few in number. Ample space will also make it well worth while to plant *N. odorata*, var. *rosea*, the pink Cape Cod variety. The fact that it makes few flowers to a shoot is lost sight of in a large bed. In the shallows *N. odorata*, var. *minor* will do well. It is a diminutive odorata, which can get on fairly well even if the water completely dries away from around it.

TWO EXCELLENT KINDS FOR DEEP WATER

Those hitherto mentioned will as a rule give best results in water having a depth of from one to two feet above the root-stocks. *N. odorata* and *N. tuberosa* it is true will stand three or four feet. But for depths of two to five feet *N. alba*, var. *candidissima* is to be recommended. Large plants of this will make a wide spread of 10-inch leaves, and will produce splendid white flowers from the first of June until frost. This is one of the earliest bloomers in spring. It is exceedingly strong and hardy.

For depths of water up to eight or ten feet the giant Southern pond-lily (*N. odorata*, var. *gigantea*) is best. It is little more than a large odorata. The leaves reach a foot or more in diameter, the flowers four or five inches.

HANDLING CUT FLOWERS

Water-lilies do well as cut flowers if they are properly handled. The flower selected for cutting must be newly opened. In nature the life of each bloom is limited to three or four days, but in the house it may keep a day or two longer. Occasionally death seems

Floating and Submerged Leaves of Ranunculus aquatilis.

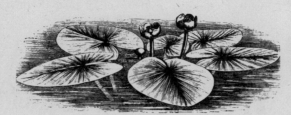

NUPHAR LUTEUM.

to overtake the motor centres while the flower is still open, and then it remains several days before the petals wither. The new flower may be recognized by these features: (1) The stamens spread apart at the centre of the flower, leaving a free passage down to the stigma; (2) the anthers are plump and round and have not yet begun to shed any pollen; (3) the basin-like stigma is filled with liquid excreted from its surface.

The flower stalk is scarcely able to supply the petals with water; the cut flower should be floated in a dish or, if placed in a vase, the vase should be full to the brim with water, the flower projecting as little as possible. When carried from the sunny garden into the house the flower is likely to close, on account of the diminished light, but it will open again next morning as well as if it were outside.

More than sixty named varieties of nymphæa have been placed on the market. Many of them are so much alike that only the professional can distinguish them, and even he must often depend on the label for certainty. The following table will aid in identifying any of the hardy kinds.

GARDEN MAGAZINE, 1905

Victoria Regia

THE WINTER STORAGE OF TENDER BULBS, TUBERS AND CORMS

H. F. HARP

THE PRAIRIE GARDEN, 1975

The large variety of bulbs, tubers and corms used during the summer as bedding plants often presents a storage problem when winter comes. The tuberous begonias, dahlias, gladiolus, cannas, and the others, all highly susceptible to frost damage, must be lifted and given frost-proof storage if they are to be grown successfully the following year.

TUBEROUS BEGONIAS

Where these showy plants are used in window boxes and sheltered beds they can be protected from light frosts by covering with newspapers or other material. When this is no longer possible carefully dig the plants with the soil adhering to the roots, pot or replant them in deep boxes and place them on the basement floor in plenty of light. The successful storage of tuberous begonias depends to a large extent on the proper ripening of the bulbs. To ensure this, water the plants sparingly while in the basement cutting off the supply when the leaves turn yellow. When the tops of the plant separate from the bulbs at the slightest touch they are ripened and may be removed from the soil. Store them at 50°F. in boxes of dry peat, Vermiculite or Perloam.

CANNAS

The plants are lifted soon after the first killing frost removing excess soil from the roots and cutting off the tops to leave stubs three inches long. Lay out the roots on newspaper in the basement; leave them for a week or so then pack them away. Use slightly moistened peat or a half mixture of peat and sand in boxes deep enough to hold the roots with an inch of the storage media over them. Cannas will likely rot if stored too wet and too cool; it stored too hot and dry, the roots will shrivel. Inspect them every two or three weeks dampening the peat if required. Once during the period of storage the roots should be examined for disease; cutting out bad portions then treating the wounds with dusting sulphur before returning them to storage. Recommended storage temperature is 50°F.

DAHLIAS

After the stalks are killed by frost they should be cut off three inches above the ground. Dig the roots a week later. Dahlia roots are easily damaged so dig and handle them carefully. From the 'neck' portion of the fleshy roots next year's growth buds are initiated. Roots with ruptured necks are useless.

Set the newly dug plants in the sun for a few hours and then on the basement floor for a week or two before packing them for winter. Dahlias store best in boxes of dry sawdust, peat or Perloam; plastic bags are used for storing root divisions. Roots which have been divided into planting-size pieces are dusted with sulphur then placed in plastic bags and packed in boxes of sawdust.

Periodic inspections are made to check humidity, dampening the storage media if the roots are shrivelling. The recommended storage temperature is 45°F. with medium humidity.

TUBEROSE BULB WITH SETS.

GLADIOLUS

Gladiolus corms (bulbs) are dug in late September or early October, preferably on a warm, sunny day. Dry the corms in the sun for a few hours then cut the tops off leaving a stub an inch in length. The best ripening conditions are provided by high temperature (80, 85°F.) and a free circulation of air around the corms.

Small quantities of corms can be ripened and stored in shallow trays stacking them one above the other to save space. The bottoms of the trays should be made of lath or fine chicken wire to ensure good air circulation. Place pieces of 1 x 2 inch lumber between each tray when stored one above the other. When the corms are dry, clean off the remains of last year's corms and other debris then dust with 'Captan'. The recommended storage temperature is 40-50°F. with the relative humidity 50 to 75 per cent. Monthly examinations should be made from December until May for shrivelling caused by excessively dry air or premature shoot growth caused by dampness.

MISCELLANEOUS TENDER BULBS AND ROOTS

Anemones (St. Brigid)

The fleshy roots are dug in late August or early September, gradually dried off and stored in the manner recommended for dahlias.

Caladiums

Used as porch plants or as bedding plants in shady areas caladiums are tender to the lightest frost. They are taken indoors when the first frost

threatens. Dig the plants with soil attached to the roots setting them in boxes on the basement floor. The fleshy roots are dried in the same way as the tuberous begonias then stored in boxes of dry peat in a warm cupboard where the temperature is maintained at 60-65°F.

Calla Lilies

There are several kinds of calla lilies used either as potted plants or for summer bedding. The ripening process is the same as recommended for tuberous begonias except that the storage temperature is a little higher (55°F.). Potted callas can be stored in their pots after they have been gradually dried out. Store the pots on their sides on the basement floor. Callas used as bedding plants are dug up after the first light frost, replanted in boxes of peat then stored in the basement.

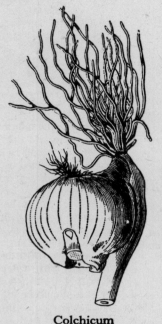

Colchicum —Corm

Tigridia (Shell Flower)

The tigridias, being more tender than the gladiolus are planted a bit later and harvested a bit earlier, otherwise they require the same treatment. The best storage temperature is 50°F. Cool, damp storage will cause the corms to rot.

Tuberose (Polianthes tuberosa)

These sweet-scented, late-blooming bulbs are dug up and potted or boxed after the first light frost. The bulbs are stored in dry peat when the top growth has died down. The recommended storage temperature is 40-50°F.

Ranunculus — various forms of R. asiaticas (The Persian Buttercup)

These have tender fleshy roots which are stored over winter in the manner recommended for dahlias. They are harvested in late August or early September and stored in dry peat kept at 45°F.

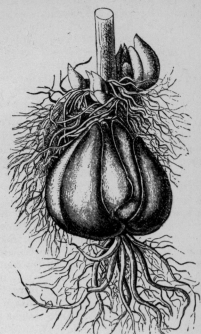

LILY BULB WITH BULBLETS.

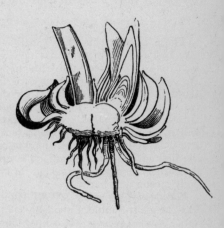

Lily—Scaly Bulb

Vallota (Scarborough Lily) and Sprekelia (Jacobean Lily)

These are used as porch plants flowering in late summer. The bulbs are ripened by gradually withholding the water supply. When the leaves are yellow store the bulbs in their pots where the temperature can be maintained at 45-50°F.

Zephranthes (Zephyr Flower)

Small bulbs, used as pot plants and rock garden subjects. Plants in the open ground are potted in September following the first frost. By restricting the water supply the leaves turn yellow and the bulbs ripen. Store them in soil kept barely moist at 40-45°F.

Canada Department of Agriculture, Research Branch
Experimental Farm, Morden, Manitoba
(Reprinted — courtesy Manitoba Department of Agriculture)

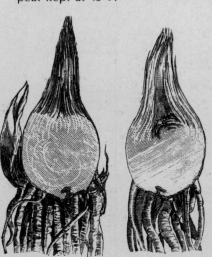

—SOUND BULB.   —BULB DECAYED AT CENTER.

Hyacinth Bulb with Offsets

PINUS CEMBRA.

THUYA GIGANTEA.

TAXUS BACCATA DOVASTONI.

PICEA SMITHIANA.

Evergreens for Every Place and Purpose

LISTS OF THE BEST KINDS RECOMMENDED FOR DIFFERENT PURPOSES IN ALL PARTS OF THE COUNTRY BY LEADING AMATEURS, BOTANISTS, NURSERYMEN, PARK SUPERINTENDENTS AND OTHERS INTERESTED IN CONIFERS

While the Standard Latin names used throughout these lists present a formidable appearance, they are the only ones which it is safe to use in ordering what you want. The common names vary so much that nurserymen do not use them.

reprinted from GARDEN MAGAZINE, 1905

For the English equivalents of these Latin names see page 308

RAPID GROWING

LARGE TREES: *Pinus Strobus. Abies Nordmanniana. Picea excelsa. Pinus resinosa* and *sylvestris.* For the South: *Cedrus Deodara, Libocedrus decurrens.*

SMALL TREES: *Thuya occidentalis, orientalis* and var. *pyramidalis. Pinus rigida, densiflora. Picea pungens. Abies balsamea.*

SLOW GROWING

TREES: *Picea pungens* and *orientalis. Cedrus Atlantica. Taxus baccata.*

SHRUBS: *Juniperus Virginiana, Cephalotaxus Fortunei, Juniperus communis, Taxus Canadensis,* the *Chamæcyparis* family (*Retinosporas*).

SHORT LIVED

TREES: *Picea excelsa. Pinus sylvestris. Abies balsamea.*

ORNAMENTAL: *Juniperus communis,* var. *Hibernica. Cupressus macrocarpa. Chamæcyparis pisifera,* var. *squarrosa. Pinus Austriaca.*

THE HARDIEST

TALL: *Picea pungens. Pinus ponderosa, Strobus, sylvestris. Abies concolor. Pseudotsuga Douglasii. Picea Engelmanni.*

DWARF: *Pinus montana,* var. *Mughus. Chamæcyparis* (*Retinospora*) in variety. *Picea nigra,* var. *Doumettii.*

FOR GIVING SHADE

GOOD: *Picea Canadensis* and *excelsa. Pinus sylvestris, Strobus* and *resinosa.*

BAD: *Thuya orientalis* and *occidentalis. Juniperus Virginiana.* All *Chamæcyparis.*

FOR SEASIDE GARDENS

TALL: *Pinus sylvestris, Austriaca, Strobus, Bungeana* and *rigida.*

DWARF: *Pinus montana,* var. *Mughus. Juniperus communis* and *Sabina.*

COAL-SMOKE RESISTERS

[Evergreen plants do not endure soft coal smoke. In cities such as Chicago and Pittsburg the conifers grow only in favored spots.]

Pinus Austriaca, montana, var. *Mughus,* and *sylvestris. Picea pungens. Taxus Canadensis.*

FOR HOUSE DECORATION

IN TUBS: *Chamæcyparis* (*Retinospora*) *pisifera, plumosa, aurea,* and *squarrosa. Pinus Strobus,* var. *brevifolia, Juniperus communis* and *Chinensis. Araucaria excelsa* (tender). *Thuya occidentalis* and *orientalis* in varieties.

IN WINDOW BOXES: *Thuya orientalis aurea. Chamæcyparis plumosa aurea. Juniperus* in variety.

FOR HEDGES

SHEAR SEVERELY: *Taxus cuspidata* and *baccata. Picea excelsa, Canadensis,* and *nigra.*

SHEAR LIGHTLY: *Thuya occidentalis. Chamæcyparis plumosa.*

BEST GLOBULAR

Thuya occidentalis globosa and vars. *Reidi, compacta, Hudsonica,* and *Hoveyi. Thuya orientalis compacta, Rosedale hybrid. Pinus montana,* var. *Mughus.*

DWARF, FOR EDGING

GOLDEN: *Chamæcyparis pisifera* var. *plumosa aurea* (when young). *Thuya orientalis,* var. *compacta aurea. Juniperus communis,* var. *Douglas Golden.*

GREEN: *Juniperus recurva,* var. *squamata, prostrata* and *Sabina. Chamæcyparis pisifera,* var. *plumosa,* var. *obtusa nana. Thuya orientalis,* var. *compacta.*

WOODLAND PLANTING ON LARGE SCALE

[Conifers in general should be planted as close as 5 x 5 feet each way]: *Pinus Strobus* and *resinosa. Tsuga Canadensis. Juniperus Canadensis* (in dry situations). *Picea excelsa.* In the South: *Pinus Thunbergi. Cryptomeria Japonica.*

ACCORDING TO SOIL

DRY: *Juniperus Virginiana. Chamæcyparis* (*Retinospora*) *obtusa. Pinus Strobus* and var. *brevifolia, montana,* var. *Mughus, divaricata, rigida, sylvestris, ponderosa, Banksiana* (under extreme conditions). *Juniperus Sabina, communis Alpina. Picea pungens.*

SWAMP AND MARSH: *Chamæcyparis thuyoides. Taxodium distichum. Juniperus Virginiana,* var. *Barbadensis. Larix laricina. Thuya occidentalis. Picea nigra.* The spruces grow in moist soils, though not exactly in swamps.

HEAVY: *Tsuga Canadensis. Picea excelsa, pungens, alba. Abies Nordmanniana, balsamea. Pinus Strobus.*

LIGHT: *Juniperus Virginiana. Pinus Strobus, rigida, ponderosa, Cembra, resinosa. Chamæcyparis sphæroidea.*

SHALLOW: *Tsuga Canadensis. Juniperus Virginiana. Pinus Austriaca, sylvestris, divaricata, rigida, Banksiana. Thuya occidentalis. Picea excelsa, rubra.*

FOR EDGING IN FORMAL GARDENS

[The really good conifers are either not sufficiently dwarf, or they will not withstand severe clipping.]

GREEN FOLIAGE: *Thuya occidentalis,* var. *Little Gem, Tom Thumb* and *ericoides. Juniperus Japonica. Taxus tardiva. Chamæcyparis pisifera,* and vars. *plumosa, squarrosa.*

MONŒCIOUS BRANCHLET OF TAXUS BACCATA, showing—*m,* Clusters of Male Flowers ; *f,* Fruits almost fully grown, with the arillus almost concealing the seed ; *f',* a Young Fruit, in which the arillus only half conceals the seed ; *g,* Gall of Yew Gall-midge (*Cecidomyia Taxi*), consisting of the swollen terminal bud, resembling a cone of green leaves, among which the larvæ live.

CYPRESS.

GOLDEN FOLIAGE: *Chamæcyparis pisifera, var. plumosa aurea. Juniperus Canadensis, var. aurea.*

BEST DWARFS TWO TO SIX FEET HIGH

GREEN: *Juniperus communis, Japonica* and *Sabina. Thuya occidentalis* and vars. *Little Gem* and *compacta.*

VARIEGATED: *Juniperus Japonica, var. alba spica, communis, var. Douglas's Golden. Taxus baccata aurea,* and other varieties.

BEST PROSTRATE

FOR ROCKERY OR GARDENS: *Juniperus Sabina, var. tamariscæfolia, communis, var. alpina, communis prostrata, recurva, var. squarrosa,* and *Chinensis prostrata. Taxus Canadensis.*

SHRUBS AND SMALL TREES

FOR GARDEN SPECIMENS: *Picea orientalis, pungens, var. glauca, Englemanni,* and *Omorika. Juniperus Virginiana, var. glauca. Sciadopitys verticillata.*

FOR MASSING AT ENTRANCES

Pinus montana, var. Mughus. Tsuga Canadensis macrophylla. Juniperus communis and var. *aurea,* and others of prostrate habit. *Thuya occidentalis* in varieties—*Chamæcyparis* and *Taxus* of sorts, green and golden. *Picea excelsa,* and *pungens, var. glauca. Pinus Strobus.*

UPLAND AS OPPOSED TO MEADOW

TREES: *Pinus Strobus* and *rigida,* very good; *Austriaca,* and *sylvestris,* fair. *Picea nigra* and *alba. Juniperus Virginiana* (best). *Larix decidua. Abies concolor.*

SHRUBS: *Taxus baccata, cuspidata* (partial shade), *Canadensis. Chamæcyparis pisifera. Pinus montana, var. Mughus. Thuya occidentalis* and *Juniperus communis* and *Sabino.*

WIND-SWEPT TRACTS

TREES: *Juniperus Virginiana. Pinus rigida, Austriaca, Strobus. Picea excelsa.*

SHRUBS: *Chamæcyparis pisifera, var. obtusa nana. Picea alba. Pinus montana, var. Mughus*

WEEPING OR PENDULOUS

Tsuga Canadensis, var. pendula Sargenti. Taxodium distichum, var. pendula, Juniperus communis, var. oblonga, var. pendula, Picea excelsa, var. inverta, Chamæcyparis pisifera, var. obtusa pendula.

COLUMNAR HABIT

Thuya occidentalis, var. pyramidalis. Juniperus Virginiana (when young). *Thuya gigantea, var. Lobbi. Taxus communis, var. Hibernica. Chamæcyparis Lawsoniana, var. erecta viridis. Cupressus sempervirens fastigiata* (for the South).

GARDEN MAGAZINE, 1905

Transplanting Carriage

English Names of Some Common Conifers

Abies balsamea	Balsam fir	Pinus Strobus	White pine
Abies concolor	White fir	Pinus Strobus, var. brevifolia	Dwarf white pine
Abies Nordmanniana	Nordmann's fir	Pinus sylvestris	Scotch pine
Araucaria excelsa	Norfolk Island pine	Pinus Thunbergi	Japanese black pine
Cedrus Atlantica	Mt. Atlas cedar	Pseudotsuga Douglasii	Douglas spruce
Cedrus Deodara	Deodar	Sciadopitys virticillata	Umbrella pine
Cephalotaxus Fortunei	Fortune's cluster-flowered yew	Taxodium distichum	Bald cypress
Chamaecyparis pisifera	Retinospora	Taxodium distichum, var. pendula	Weeping bald cypress
Chamaecyparis Lawsoniana, var. erecta viridis	Dense Lawson's cypress	Taxus baccata	Yew
Chamaecyparis sphaeroidea	White Cedar	Taxus baccata, var. aurea	Golden yew
Chamaecyparis thuyoides	Japan cedar	Taxus Canadensis	Trailing yew
Cryptomeria Japonica	Japan cedar	Taxus cuspidata	Japanese yew
Cupressus macrocarpa	Monterey cypress	Taxus tardiva	Dwarf yew
Cupressus sempervirens, var. fastigiata	Erect Roman cypress	Thuya gigantea, var. Lobbi	Yellow cypress
Juniperus Canadensis	Canadian juniper	Thuya occidentalis	Arborvitae
Juniperus Canadensis, var. aurea	Golden Canadian juniper	Thuya occidentalis, var. globosa compacta	Compact arborvitae
Juniperus Chinensis	Chinese juniper	Thuya occidentalis, var. globosa Hoveyi	Hovey's arborvitae
Juniperus Chinensis, var. prostrata	Prostrate Chinese juniper	Thuya occidentalis, var. globosa Hudsonica	Hudson's dwarf arborvitae
Juniperus communis	Common juniper	Thuya occidentalis, var. globosa Reidi	Dwarf green arborvitae
Juniperus communis, var. aurea	Golden juniper	Thuya occidentalis, var. pyramidalis	Tall arborvitae
Juniperus communis, var. alba spica	White-tipped juniper	Thuya orientalis	Chinese arborvitae
Juniperus communis, var. Douglas Golden	Douglas's golden juniper	Thuya orientalis, var. aurea	Golden Chinese arborvitae
Juniperus communis, var. Hibernica	Irish juniper	Thuya orientalis, Var. Compacta aurea	Dwarf golden Chinese arborvitae
Juniperus communis, var. prostrata	Dwarf juniper	Thuya orientalis, var. Rosedale hybrid	Rosedale hybrid arborvitae
Juniperus communis, var. recurva squarrosa	Drooping juniper	Thuya occidentalis, var. pyramidalis	Tall Chinese arborvitae
Juniperus Japonica	Japan juniper	Tsuga Canadensis	Hemlock
Juniperus prostrata	Carpet juniper	Tsuga Canadensis, var. microphylla	Dense growing hemlock
Juniperus recurva, var. squamata	Hardy drooping Indian juniper	Tsuga Canadensis, var. pendula Sargenti	Sargent's weeping hemlock
Juniperus Sabina	Savin		
Juniperus Sabina, var. tamariscaefolia	Tamarisk-leaved juniper		
Juniperus Virginiana	Red cedar		
Juniperus Virginiana, var. Barbadensis	Barbadoes cedar		
Juniperus Virginiana, var. glauca	Glaucous red cedar		
Larix decidua	European larch		
Larix laricina	Tamarack		
Librocedrus decurrens	Incense cedar		
Picea alba	White spruce		
Picea Canadensis	White spruce		
Picea Engelmanni	Engelmann's spruce		
Picea excelsa	Norway spruce		
Picea excelsa, var. inverta	Weeping Norway spruce		
Picea nigra	Black spruce		
Picea nigra, var. Doumettii	Dense black spruce		
Picea Omorika	Servian spruce		
Picea orientalis	Oriental spruce		
Picea pungens	Rocky Mountain spruce		
Picea pungens, var. glauca	Colorado blue spruce		
Picea rubra	Red spruce		
Pinus Austriaca	Austrian pine		
Pinus Banksiana	Gray pine		
Pinus Bungeana	Lace-bark pine		
Pinus Cembra	Swiss stone pine		
Pinus densiflora	Japanese red pine		
Pinus divaricata	Gray pine		
Pinus montana	Swiss mountain pine		
Pinus montana, var. Mughus	Mugho pine		
Pinus ponderosa	Yellow pine		
Pinus resinosa	Red pine		
Pinus rigida	Pitch pine		

Cupréssus sempervirens.
The evergreen, or *common* Cypress.

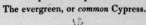

15 ft. high, 3 in. diam.

Pinus sylvéstris.
The wood, or common Scotch, Pine.

Full-grown tree at Thompson's Villa, Richmond, 25 ft. high; diam. of the head, 40 ft.

ROSES

Hand Sprayer

HOW TO PLANT A ROSE

WHAT'S THE BEST SPOT IN THE YARD?

Roses grow best where they have full sunshine all day. They will grow reasonably well if they have at least 6 hours of sun a day. Morning sun is preferable.

Any soil that will grow weeds will grow roses, but planting and watering will be easier for you if you first loosen a really heavy, sticky clay soil by spading or rototilling into it a 4" layer of peat or compost.

WHAT'S THE BEST TIME OF YEAR TO PLANT ROSES?

Spring in Northern Nevada—unless you are planting container-grown roses—they can be planted any time of year.

WHAT PRE-PLANTING CARE IS NEEDED?

Bare-root roses should be soaked overnight in a bucket of water. If bare-root plants have started to sprout new leaves, examine carefully. By the time you trim off dead and broken shoots, and prune the tops back to 8-10" as you should do for any rose bush before planting it, the plant may not be worth buying—neither are the heavily waxed plants.

WHAT'S THE BEST SPACING FOR ROSE BUSHES?

Hybrid teas	2-2½ feet
Floribunda	2-2½ feet
Grandiflora	2½-3 feet
Climbers	5-6 feet

DIGGING THE HOLE

1. Make it deep enough—about 12 inches, and wide enough—about 20 inches. You want to be able to spread the roots out. If they are crowded, twisted, or swirled around, they will remain that way and never grow out into the surrounding soil.
2. Build up a small cone of soil in the center of the hole. The main rose roots grow almost straight down. You can slide them down this cone until the bud union "joint" is at ground level. (In Northern Nevada this union needs to be exposed to the sun each spring to stimulate new growth from the union.)
3. Carefully work conditioned soil around the roots. Press firmly to be sure there are no air pockets left to dry out the roots.
4. Fill to within 1" of the ground level. Water thoroughly. Wait for the water to be absorbed. Finish filling with soil.
5. Water once a week. Check to see that you have wet the soil 8-10" deep. Roses use lots of water, but they do not like to stand in water.

ROSA NOISETTIANA.

CAUTION

Roses planted before the frost season is over—and all fall-planted roses if you decide this risk—should have the soil mounded up around them 4-6" deep. After all danger of frost, gradually remove the extra soil.

CONTAINER GROWN ROSES

Roses planted from containers are simply removed from the container and placed in a hole 6 inches wider on all sides.

Soil is conditioned as suggested for planting bare root roses. Be sure the depth allowed the bud union to be at ground level.

NEVADA GARDENER
COOPERATIVE EXTENSION SERVICE
HORTICULTURE INFORMATION SERIES

Branch of *Rosa Gallica*, showing prickly stem, stipules, pinnate leaves, definite inflorescence, flower-buds, and expanded corolla, as described in the text.

POWDERY MILDEW ON ROSES

WHAT DOES IT LOOK LIKE?

You can see a white, powdery coating on young leaves, shoots, and buds, as if someone very evenly dusted them with a white powder. When the infection is severe the young growth becomes distorted and stunted.

CAN IT BE CONTROLLED?

Yes. Since the fungus overwinters on infected buds, leaves, and shoots, the first approach is to clean up and burn any dead plant material lying around. Spring pruning will also remove any infected areas still on the plant.

Powdery mildew is not too difficult to control with any one of a number of rose sprays or dusts for mildew control. Look on the label of ingredients for benomyl, folpet, ferbam, dnocap, or wettable sulfur. A product containing any one of these will do a fine job of checking the disease. Be sure to follow the directions explicitly.

NEVADA GARDENER
COOPERATIVE EXTENSION SERVICE
HORTICULTURE INFORMATION SERIES

SWING WATER BARROW.

GARDEN ENGINE.

THE GRAND NEW HYBRID TEA ROSE, PRINCESS OF NAPLES.

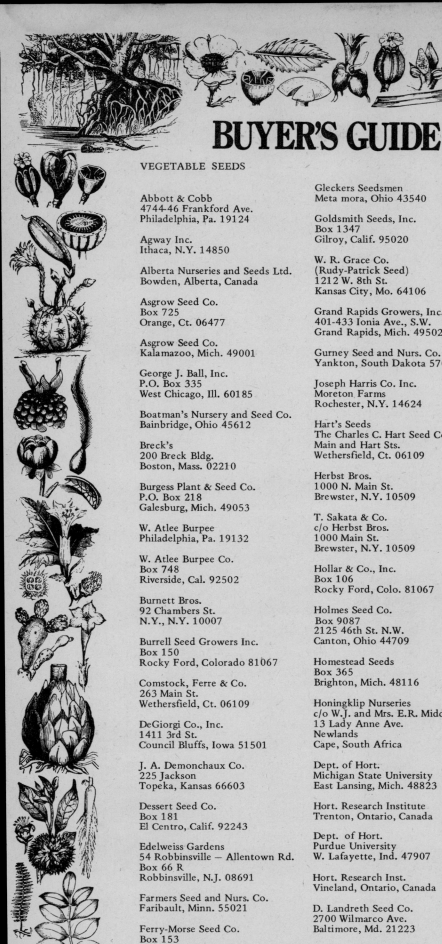

BUYER'S GUIDE

VEGETABLE SEEDS

Abbott & Cobb
4744-46 Frankford Ave.
Philadelphia, Pa. 19124

Agway Inc.
Ithaca, N.Y. 14850

Alberta Nurseries and Seeds Ltd.
Bowden, Alberta, Canada

Asgrow Seed Co.
Box 725
Orange, Ct. 06477

Asgrow Seed Co.
Kalamazoo, Mich. 49001

George J. Ball, Inc.
P.O. Box 335
West Chicago, Ill. 60185

Boatman's Nursery and Seed Co.
Bainbridge, Ohio 45612

Breck's
200 Breck Bldg.
Boston, Mass. 02210

Burgess Plant & Seed Co.
P.O. Box 218
Galesburg, Mich. 49053

W. Atlee Burpee
Philadelphia, Pa. 19132

W. Atlee Burpee Co.
Box 748
Riverside, Cal. 92502

Burnett Bros.
92 Chambers St.
N.Y., N.Y. 10007

Burrell Seed Growers Inc.
Box 150
Rocky Ford, Colorado 81067

Comstock, Ferre & Co.
263 Main St.
Wethersfield, Ct. 06109

DeGiorgi Co., Inc.
1411 3rd St.
Council Bluffs, Iowa 51501

J. A. Demonchaux Co.
225 Jackson
Topeka, Kansas 66603

Dessert Seed Co.
Box 181
El Centro, Calif. 92243

Edelweiss Gardens
54 Robbinsville — Allentown Rd.
Box 66 R
Robbinsville, N.J. 08691

Farmers Seed and Nurs. Co.
Faribault, Minn. 55021

Ferry-Morse Seed Co.
Box 153
Buffalo, N.Y. 14225

Ferry-Morse Company
Box 100
Mountain View, Calif. 94040

Henry Field Seed and Nurs. Co.
Shenandoah, Iowa 51601

H. G. German Seed Co.
Smethport, Pa. 16749

Germania Seed Co.
5952 N. Milwaukee Ave.
Chicago, Ill. 60646

Gleckers Seedsmen
Meta mora, Ohio 43540

Goldsmith Seeds, Inc.
Box 1347
Gilroy, Calif. 95020

W. R. Grace Co.
(Rudy-Patrick Seed)
1212 W. 8th St.
Kansas City, Mo. 64106

Grand Rapids Growers, Inc.
401-433 Ionia Ave., S.W.
Grand Rapids, Mich. 49502

Gurney Seed and Nurs. Co.
Yankton, South Dakota 57078

Joseph Harris Co. Inc.
Moreton Farms
Rochester, N.Y. 14624

Hart's Seeds
The Charles C. Hart Seed Co.
Main and Hart Sts.
Wethersfield, Ct. 06109

Herbst Bros.
1000 N. Main St.
Brewster, N.Y. 10509

T. Sakata & Co.
c/o Herbst Bros.
1000 Main St.
Brewster, N.Y. 10509

Hollar & Co., Inc.
Box 106
Rocky Ford, Colo. 81067

Holmes Seed Co.
Box 9087
2125 46th St. N.W.
Canton, Ohio 44709

Homestead Seeds
Box 365
Brighton, Mich. 48116

Honingklip Nurseries
c/o W.J. and Mrs. E.R. Middlemann & Son
13 Lady Anne Ave.
Newlands
Cape, South Africa

Dept. of Hort.
Michigan State University
East Lansing, Mich. 48823

Hort. Research Institute
Trenton, Ontario, Canada

Dept. of Hort.
Purdue University
W. Lafayette, Ind. 47907

Hort. Research Inst.
Vineland, Ontario, Canada

D. Landreth Seed Co.
2700 Wilmarco Ave.
Baltimore, Md. 21223

Le Jardin du Gourmet
West Danville, Vt. 05873

A. H. Hummert Seed Co.
2746 Chouteau Ave.
St. Louis, Mo. 63103

Johnny's Selected Seeds
N. Dixmont, Me. 04932

J. W. Jung Seed Co.
Randolph, Wis. 53956

Keystone Seed
101 Chateau Ave.
St. Louis, Mo. 63123

Keystone
Box 1438
Hollister, Ca. 95023

Letherman Seed Co.
505 McKinley Ave. N.W.
Canton, Ohio 44704

Mark Martin
Irrigation Exp. Station
Prosser, Wash. 99350

Earl May Seed and Nurs. Co.
Shenandoah, Iowa 51601

A. E. McKenzie Co.
Box 1060
Brandon, Manitoba, Canada
R7A 6E1

Merrimack Farmer's Exchange
Concord, N.H. 03301

Mail Box Seeds
Shirley Morgan
2042 Encinal Ave.
Alameda, Ca. 94501

Natural Development Co.
Box 215
Bainbridge, Pa. 17502

Niagara Seeds
Box 2508
El Macero, Ca. 95618

Niagara Seeds
Niagara Chemical Div.
FMC Corp.
Middleport, N.Y. 14105

Northrup King & Co.
1500 Jackson St. N.E.
Minneapolis, Minn. 55413

Northrup King & Co.
Box 959
Minneapolis, Minn. 55440

L. L. Olds Seed Co.
Box 1069
2901 Packers Ave.
Madison, Wis. 53701

George W. Park Seed Co.
Box 31
Greenwood, S.C. 29646

W. H. Perron & Co.
515 Labelle Blvd.
Chomeday, Port Quebec, Canada

Peto Seed Co.
Box 138
Saticoy, Ca. 93003

Clair Phillips
Grand Rapids, Mich. 55744

Pieters-Wheeler Seed Co.
Box 217
Gilroy, Ca. 95020

Leonard Pike
Texas A & M Univ.
College Station, Texas 77843

Plant Intro. Station
Experiment, Georgia 30212

Porter & Son
Stephenville, Texas 76401

Reed Bros.
Cortland, N.Y. 13045

Martin Rispens & Sons Seed Store
3332 Ridge Rd.
Lansing, Ill. 60438

Seedway Inc.
Robson Quality Seeds Inc.
Hall, N.Y. 14463

P. L. Rohrer & Bros. Inc. Seedsmen
Lancaster County
Smoketown, Pa. 17576

Rogers Bros. Seed Co.
Box 2188
Idaho Falls, Idaho 83401

Harry E. Saier
Dimondale, Mich. 48821

R. H. Shumway
Box 777
628 Cedar St.
Rockford, Ill. 61101

Royal Sluis
Box 22
Enkhaizen, Holland

Sluis and Groot
c/o Peter Sluis
Box 580
Menlo Park, Ca. 94025

Spring Hill Farm
36 Spring Hill Rd.
East Sandwich, Mass. 02537

Standard Seed Co.
Kansas City, Mo. 64120

Fred's Plant Farm
Fred Stoker
Box 107, R. 1
Dresden, Tenn. 38225

Stokes Seeds
737 Main St.
Box 548
Buffalo, N.Y. 14240

Suttons Seeds
The Royal Seed Establishment
Reading, England
RG6 1AB

George Taits & Sons, Inc.
900 Tidewater Drive
Norfolk, Va. 23516

Takii & Co., Ltd.
Box 7
Kyoto Central
Kyoto, Japan

Tenn. Nurs. & Seed Co.
Tenn. Nurs. Rd.
Cleaveland, Tenn. 37311

Otis S. Twilley Seed Co.
Box 1817
Salisbury, Md. 21801

U. of California
Dept. of Veg. Crops
Davis, Ca. 95616

Willhite Melon Seed Farms
Box 85
Weatherford, Texas 76086

Woodside Seed Growers
(Northrup-King)
200 S. Main St.
Box C
Rocky Ford, Colo. 81067

HERBS

Aphrodisia
28 Carmine St.
New York, N.Y. 10014

Apothecary
Altman's Dept. Store
34th St. & Fifth Ave.
Manhattan, N.Y.

Bolgiano Seed Co.
411 N.Y. Ave. N.E.
Washington, D.C. 20002

Borchelt Herb Gardens
474 Carriage Shop Rd.
East Falmouth, Mass. 02536

W. Atlee Burpee Co.
Philadelphia, Pa. 19132

Casa Yerba
Star Route 2, Box 21
Day's Creek, Oregon 97429

Caswell-Massey Co. Ltd.
320 W. 13th St.
N.Y., N.Y. 10014

China Herb Company
428 Soledad
Salinas, Ca. 93901

Comstock, Ferre Co.
263 Main St.
Wethersfield, Ct. 06109

Cottage Herb Farm Shop
311 State St.
Albany, N.Y. 12210

Cottage Herb Farm
Marlboro, N.H. 03455

The Cottage Herb Gardens
Washington Cathedral Mt. St.
Albans, Washington, D.C. 20022

Farmer's Seed & Nurs. Co.
Faribault, Minn. 55021

Forbes Garden Center
Hanover, N.J. 07936

Gilbertie
Sylvan Ave.
Westport, Ct. 06880

Greene Herb Gardens, Inc.
Greene, R. I. 02827

Gurney Seed & Nursery Co.
Yankton, S. D. 57078

Joseph Harris Seed Co.
Rochester, N.Y. 14600

Charles Hart Seed Co.
Hart and Main Sts.
Wethersfield, Ct. 06109

Haussmann's Pharmacy
534-536 W. Girard Ave.
Philadelphia, Pa. 19123

Hav'alook Garden
10045 W. Grand River Ave.
Fowlerville, Mich. 48836

Heise's Wausau Farms
Route 3
Wausau, Wis. 54401

Hemlock Hill Farm
Litchfield, Ct. 06759

Herbarium
Route 2, Box 620
Kenosha, Wis. 53140

Hickory Hollow
Route 1, Box 52
Petertown, W. Va. 24963

Hilltop Herb Farm
Box 866
Cleveland, Texas 77327

Holmes Seed Co.
Canton, Ohio 44700

Indiana Botanic Gardens, Inc.
Box 5
Hammond, Indiana 46325

Kiel Pharmacy, Inc.
109 Third Ave.
New York, N.Y. 10003

Mail Box Seeds
Shirley Morgan
2042 Encinal Ave.
Alameda, Ca. 94501

Meadowbrook Herb Garden
Wyoming, Rhode Island 02898

Dr. Michael's Herb Center
1223 North Milwaukee Ave.
Chicago, Ill. 60622

Nature's Herb Co.
281 Ellis St.
San Francisco, Ca. 94102

Nichols Garden Nursery
1190 North Pacific Hwy.
Albany, Ore. 97321

L. L. Olds Seed Co.
P.O. Box 1069
2901 Packer's Ave.
Madison, Wis. 53701

Penn Herb Co.
603 North Second St.
Philadelphia, Pa. 19123

George Park Seed Co.
Greenwood, S. C. 29646

Pine Hills Herb Farms
P. O. Box 144
Roswell, Ga. 30075

Plantation Gardens
Rustburg, Va. 24588

The Potters of Baraboo
Rt. 4
Baraboo, Wis. 53813

Roger's Herb Farm
Holbrook St.
Norfolk, Mass. 01056

State Seed & Nursery
Helena, Mt. 59601

Snow-Line Farm
11846 Fremont
Yucaipa, Ca. 92399

Taylors Garden
2649 Stingle Ave.
South San Gabriel, Ca. 91770

The Tool Shed Herb Nursery
Salem Center, Turkey Hill Rd.
Purdys Station, N.Y. 10578

Well Sweep Herb Farm
317 Mt. Bethel Rd.
Port Murray, N.J. 07865

HEALTH FOODS
AND HERBAL REMEDIES

Indiana Botanic Garden
Hammond, Ind. 46325

Arrowhead Mills
Box 866
Hereford, Texas 79045

Walnut Acres
Penns Creek, Pa. 17862

FRUITS, NUTS, BERRIES

Ahrens and Son Nursery
Huntingburg, Ind. 47542

Alberta Nurseries & Seeds Ltd.
Bouden, Alberta, Canada

J. Herbert Alexander
Middleboro, Maine 02346

W. F. Allen Co.
Salisbury, Md. 21801

George J. Ball, Inc.
West Chicago, Illinois 60185

Baums Nursery
Rt. 2
New Fairfield, Ct. 06810

Boatman's Nursery & Seed Co.
Bainbridge, Ohio 45612

Bountiful Ridge Nurseries
Princess Anne, Md. 21853

Brittingham Plant Farms
2538 Ocean City Rd.
Salisbury, Md. 21801

Bunting's Berries
Selbyville, Del. 19975

Burnett Bros. Inc.
92 CHambers St.
New York, N.Y. 10007

W. Atlee Burpee Co.
Philadelphia, Pa. 19132

Cobles Nut Tree Nursery
Rt. 1
Aspers, Pa. 17304

Common Fields Nursery
Town Farm Rd.
Ipswich, Maine 01938

Comstock, Ferre & Co.
263 Main St.
Wethersfield, Ct. 06109

The Common Co.
Box 534
Augusta, Arizona 72006

E. C. Cooke
Visalia, Calif. 93277

Decorah Nursery
Box 125
Harpers Ferry, Iowa 52146

The Denholm Seed Co.
222 North A St.
Lompoc, Calif. 93436

Farmer Seed & Nursery Co.
Fairbault, Minn. 55021

Fruit Haven Nursery
Rt. 1
Kaleva, Mich. 49645

Galletta Bros.
Hammonton, N. J.

H. G. German Seeds, Inc.
Smethport Pa. 16749

Gleckers Seedmen
Metamora, Ohio 43540

Goldsmith Seeds
Box 1347
Gilroy, Calif. 95020

Gurney Seed & Nursery Co.
Yankton, S. Dakota 57078

J. Harris Seed Co., Inc.
Moreton Farm
Rochester, N. Y. 14624

Charles C. Hart Seed Co.
Main & Hart Streets
Wethersfield, Ct. 06109

Herbst Brothers Seedmen, Inc.
1000 N. Main St.
Brewster, N. Y. 10509

Hilltop Orchards
Hartford, Mich. 49057

Homestead Seeds
Box 365
Brighton, Mich. 48116

A. H. Hummert Seed Co.
2746 Chouteau Ave.
St. Louis, Mo. 63103

James W. Humphreys
431 5th Ave.
Huntington, W. Va. 25701

Interstate Nurseries
Hamburg, Iowa 51644

Henry Leuthardt Nursery
Montauk Hwy.
East Moriches, N. Y. 11940

Malielski's Berry Farm
7130 Platt Rd.
Ypsilanti, Mich. 48197

Mayo Nursery
Rt. 14
Lyon, N. Y. 14489

J. E. Miller Nurseries
Canandaigua, N. Y. 14424

Walter K. Morss And Son
Rt. 3
Bradford, Maine 02830

Natural Development Co.
Box 215
Bainbridge, Pa. 17502

Nourse Farms
Box 485, R.F.D.
South Deerfield, Maine 01373

L. L. Olds Seed Co.
P. O. Box 1069
Madison, Wisconsin 53701

Pan American Seed Co.
Box 438
West Chicago, Ill. 60185

George Park Seed Co.
Greenwood, S. C. 29646

Clair Phillips
Grand Rapids, Mich. 55744

Robson Quality Seeds
Hall, N. Y. 14463

P. L. Rohrer & Bro. Inc., Seedsmen
Lancaster County
Smoketown, Pa. 17576

Harry E. Saier
Dimondale, Michigan 48821

R. H. Shumway
Box 777
628 Cedar St.
Rockford, Ill. 61101

Stark Bros. Nursery
Louisiana, Mo. 63353

Stokes Seeds
737 Main St.
Box 548
Buffalo, N. Y. 14240

Sutton's Seeds
The Royal Seed Est.
Reading, England
RG6 1AB

Tenn. Nursery & Seed Co.
Tenn. Nursery Road
Cleaveland, Tenn. 37311

Otis S. Twilley Seed Co.
Salisbury, Md. 21801

Vaughan's Seed Co.
Chimney Rock Road
Bound Brook, N. J. 08805

Wayside Gardens
Mentor, Ohio 44060

Zilke Bros. Nursery
Baroda, Mich. 49101

GRAPES

Boordy Vineyard
Riderwood, Maryland 21139

Chalet Du Lac Vineyards and Nursery
Route 1, Box 9F
Altus, Arkansas 72821

Foster Nursery Co., Inc.
Fredonia, New York, 14063

Johnston Vineyards
4320 N. Barnes
Oklahoma City, Oklahoma 73112

Southeast Nurseries
Box 321-A
Raleigh, North Carolina 27609

Southmeadow Fruit Gardens
Birmingham, Michigan 48009

CURRANTS AND GOOSEBERRIES

Foster Nursery Co., Inc.
Fredonia, New York 14063

Southmeadow Fruit Gardens
Birmingham, Michigan 48009

STRAWBERRIES

Ahrens Strawberry Nursery
R. R. 1 box 721
Huntingburg, Indiana 47542

W. F. Allen Co.
Salisbury, Maryland 21801

James W. Brittingham
2538 Ocean City Blvd.
Salisbury, Maryland 21801

E. J. Bryan
Washburn, Wisconsin 54891

Buntings' Nurseries, Inc.
Selbyville, Delaware 19975

Chapman Berry Farm
E. Leroy, Michigan 49655

The Conner Co., Inc.
P.O. Box 534
Augusta, Arkansas 72006

Fruit Haven Nursery, Inc.
Kaleva, Michigan 49645

Lewis Strawberry Nursery
Rocky Point, N.C. 28457

Mullins Plant Farms
Chattanooga, Tenn. 37411

New Jersey Small Fruits Council, Inc.
P.O. Box 185
Hammonton, New Jersey 08037

Rayner Bros., Inc.
Salisbury, Maryland 21801

Romines Plant Farm
Dayton, Tenn. 39321

J. H. Shivers Plant Farm
Allen, Maryland 21810

Smith Berry Gardens
Ooltewah, Tennessee 37363

Vites Strawberry Farm
Box 552
Niles, Michigan 49120

Zollar-Greening
Benton Harbor, Michigan 49023

BLUEBERRIES

A. G. Ammon
Box 488
Chatsworth, New Jersey 08019

D. A. Byrd
Locota, Michigan 49063

Finch's Blueberry Nursery
Bailey, North Carolina 27807

Galleta Bros. Blueberry Farms
Hammonton, New Jersey 08037

Hartman's Blueberry Plantation
Grand Junction, Michigan 49056

Alexander J. Herbert
Middleboro, Mass. 02346

Keefe Blueberry Plantation
Grand Junction, Michigan 49056

River View Nursery
McMinnville, Tenn. 37110

H. B. Scammell and Son
Toms River, New Jersey 08753

BLACKBERRIES AND RASPBERRIES

Dale Basham Nursery
Alma, Arkansas 72921

Bountiful Ridge Nurseries
Princess Anna, Maryland 21853

E. J. Bryan
Washburn, Wisconsin 54891

Fruit Haven Nursery, Inc.
Kaleva, Michigan 49645

New York State Fruit
    Testing Cooperative Assoc.
Geneva, New York 14456

Rayner Bros. Inc.
Salisbury, Maryland 21801

Phil Robers Nursery
Lake Geneva, Wisconsin 53147

Theodore Stegmaier Nursery
Route No. 4
Cumberland, Maryland 21501

ELDERBERRIES

New York State Fruit Testing
    Cooperative Assoc.
Geneva, New York 14456

SMALL FRUIT PLANTS

Ackerman Nurseries
Bridgman, Michigan 49106

Boatman's Nursery and Seed Co.
Bainbridge, Ohio 45612

Bountiful Ridge Nurseries
Princess Anne, Maryland 21853

Burgess Seed and Plant Co.
Galesburg, Michigan 49053

Cumberland Valley Nurseries, Inc.
McMinnville, Tenn. 37110

Emlong Nurseries, Inc.
Stevensivlle, Michigan 49127

Farmer Seed and Nursery Co.
Faribault, Minn. 55021

Earl Ferris Nursery
Hampton, Iowa 50441

Henry Field Seed and Nursery Co.
Shenandoah, Iowa 51601

French Nursery Co.
Clyde, Ohio 43410

Gurney Seed and Nursery Co.
Yankton, South Dakota 57078

Hillemeyer Nurseries
Lexington, Kentucky 40500

Ideal Fruit Farm and Nursery
Stilwell, Okla. 74960

Inter-State Nurseries, Inc.
Hamburg, Iowa 51640

Kelly Bros. Nurseries
Dansville, New York 14437

Krider Nurseries, Inc.
Middlebury, Ind. 46540

Lafayette Home Nursery, Inc.
LaFayette, Ill. 61449

J. E. Miller Nurseries
Canandaigua, New York 14424

Monroe Nursery Co.
Monroe, Michigan 48161

Neosho Nurseries
Neosho, Missouri 64850

New York State Fruit Testing
  Cooperative Association
Geneva, New York 14456

Ozark Nursery
Tahlequah, Oklahoma 74464

Scarff's Nursery, Inc.
New Carlisle, Ohio 45344

R. H. Shumway
Rockford, Illinois 61100

Spring Hill Nurseries Co.
Tipp City, Ohio 45371

Stark Bros. Nurseries and Orchards Co.
Louisiana, Missouri 63353

Stern's Nurseries
Geneva, New York 14456

Tennessee Nursery Co., Inc.
Cleveland, Tennessee 37311

COMMERCIAL SOURCES OF LIVING INSECTS

Beneficial Insect Company
383 Waverly St.
Menlo Park, CA 94025

Bio-Control Company
10180 Ladybird Drive
Auburn, CA 95603

The Butterfly Breeding Farm
275 Colwick Road
Rochester, N.Y. 14624

Turtox / Cambosco
(Macmillan Science Co.)
8200 South Hoyne Ave.
Chicago, Ill.

Gothard, Inc.
P.O. Box 370
Canutillo, TX 79835

Hazard's Insecticide Laboratory
R.R. No. 5, Box No. 195
Wilmington, OH 45177

Insect Control and Research, Inc.
1330 Dillon Heights Ave.
Baltimore, MD 21228

Miller Tropical Emporium
3702 Jennifer St, N.W.
Washington, D. C.

NASCO
Fort Atkinson, WI 53538

Pyramid Nursery & Flower Shop
P.O. Box 5274
Reno, NV 89503

Rainbow Mealworms
126 E. Spruce St.
Compton, CA 90220

Robert Robbins
424 N. Courtland
East Stroudsburg, PA 18301

Fountain's Sierra Bug Co.
P.O. box 114
Rough and Ready, CA 95975

Selph's Cricket Ranch, Inc.
Box 2123, DeSoto Station
Memphis, TN 38102

Western Biological Control Labs
P.O. Box 1045
Tacoma, WA 98401

APIARIES

Miriam Alper
Rt. 1, Box 1122
Avon Park, Fla. 33825

Johnnie Arnouville
Box 106
Hamburg, La. 71339

R. W. Bayer
19090 W. 4th Ave.
Stevinson, Calif. 95374

Beemaster Inc.
311 W. 28th Ave.
Bellevue, Nebraska 68005

Bee Industries Service
P. O. Box 9
Atwater, Calif. 95301

The Beekeepers
Rt. 1, Box 268
Lincoln, Calif. 95648

Bolling Bee Co.
Rt. No. 4
Greenville, Ala. 36037

E. J. Bordelon Apiaries
P. O. Box 33
Moreauville, La. 71355

Richard Bordin
Rt. 3, Box 99
Chico, Calif. 95926

Bovee Apiaries
Courtney V. Bovee
Rt. 1, Box 594
Red Bluffs, Calif.

Alan Buckley
3108 Buckingham Ct.
Modesto, Calif. 95350

Callahan & Sons Bee Farm
Eugene Callahan
Box 31 F
Theriot, La. 70397

Calvert Apiaries
Calvert, Ala. 36513

C. E. M. Apiaries
P. O. Box 303
Grass Valley, Calif. 95945

Chenevert & Son Apiaries
Rt. 1, Box 618
Cottonport, La. 71327

Colston Apiaries
Rt. 1, Box 17 A
Taylorsville, Ga. 30178

Geo. E. Curtis & Sons, Inc.
LaBelle, Fla. 33935

Daigrepont Apiaries
Rt. 1, Box 17
Hessmer, La. 71341

Dickman Apiaries
Rt. 2, Box 284-C
Bay Minette, Ala. 36507

Jack E. Egeland
Cedar Lane, Texas 77415

Eisele Apiaries
Box 1146
Avon Park, Fla. 33825

Floyd's Apiaries
112 Fairbrook St.
Pineville, La. 71360

Howard Forrester Apiaries
R. R. 3
Cumming, Ga. 30130

John D. Fuhrer
Rt. 1, Box 535
Esparto, Calif. 95627

Merk Gaspard
P. O. Box 131
Marksville, La. 71351

Gaspard Apiaries
Rt. 1, Box 374-B
Mansura, La. 71350

Guillot Bee Farm
Hessmer, La. 71341

Harper Apiaries
New Brockton, Ala. 36351

Lennie Harris
P. O. Box 161
Ayden, N. C. 28513

Ronald Hazard
Rt. 2
Poynette, Wis. 53955

Donald Hodges, Sr.
3066 Odle Drive
Anderson, Calif. 96007

Holcombe Apiaries
P. O. Box 303
Shelbyville, Tenn. 37160

Holder Homan Apiaries
Shannon, Miss. 38868

Honey Farms
7340 River Rd.
Oakdale, Calif. 95361

Jackson Apiaries
P. O. Box 56
Funston, Ga. 31753

Kane Apiaries
Rt. 1, Box 192
Hallettsville, Texas 77964

The Walter T. Kelley Co.
Clarkson, Ky. 42726

Kidney's Bee Ranch
P. O. Box 161
Loomis, Calif. 95650

C. F. Koehnen & Sons
Route 1, Box 240
Glenn, Calif. 95943

McCary Apiaries
Buckatunna, Miss. 39322

Mitchell's Apiaries
Bunkie, La. 71322

Normand Bee Farm
General Delivery
Hessmer, La. 71341

J. L. O'Ferrell & Sons, Inc.
Box 221
LaBelle, Fla. 33935

Ray Olivarez Apiaries
Rt. 3, Box 221
Orland, Calif. 95963

C. L. Paul
Apiaries
Vick, La. 71372

Pelican State Apiaries
P. O. Box 2904
Baton Rouge, La. 70821

Penner Apiaries
Rt. 3, Box 3886
Red Bluff, Calif. 96080

Perrin's Apiary
Rt. 1, Box 240
Ponchatouia, La. 70454

Phylor Farms
P. O' Box 160
Sheridan, Calif. 95681

Alfred Reason
P. O. Box 27
Hamburg, La. 71339

James W. Richards
1411 CHampagnolle
El Dorado, Ark. 71730

Rossman Apiaries, Inc.
P. O. Box 905
Moultrie, Ga. 31768

W. E. Shackelford
Rt. 1, Box 210 A
Rio Oso, Calif. 95674

Shumans Bee Company
407 Jefferson St.
Hazlehurst, Ga. 31539

Spade Apiaries
1981 Clear Creek Rd.
Redding, Calif. 96001

Ben A. Spade
Happy Valley Apiaries
17132 Lassen Ave.
Anderson, Calif. 96007

Stover Apiaries, Inc.
Mayhew, Miss. 39753

Strachan Apiaries
2522 Tierra Buena Rd.
Yuba City, Calif. 95991

Ron Swickard
Buzzy Bee Apiaries
P. O. Box 1153
Loomis, Calif. 95650

Trent Valley Apiaries
P. O. box 27
Harrells, N. C. 28444

Turner Apiaries
Rt. 2, Box 19-A
Bukie, La. 71322

J. C. Walker
Rogers, Texas 76569

Walton C. Walker
4901 Foothill Blvd.
Oroville, Calif. 95965

Weaver Apiaries
Rt. 1, Box 111
Navasota, Texas 77868

C. G. Wenner & Son
Rt. 1, Box 283
Glenn, Calif. 95943

Whitley's Apiaries
1247 Salisbury Ave.
Albemarie, N.C. 28001

The Wilbanks Apiaries
Claxton, Ga. 30417

Williams' Apiaries
Rt. 1, Box 6-B
Macon, Miss. 39341

York Bee Company
P. O. Box 307-412
Orange St.
Jesup, Ga. 31545

SOUTHERN GROWN

VEGETABLE PLANTS

Ace Growers, Inc.
Box 96
Cairo, Georgia 31728

Brown's-Omaha Plant Farms
787 Plant House
Omaha, Texas 75571

Butt's Plant Farms
Thorndale, Texas 76577

Carolina Plant Farms
Bethel, North Carolina 27812

The Conner Company
Augusta, Arkansas 72006

J. P. Councill Co.
Franklin, Virginia 72006

Cupp Plant Farms, Route 1
Cullman, Alabama 35055

Dixie Plant Co.
P.O. box 327
Franklin, Virginia 23851

Evans Plant Co.
Dept. 8
Ty Ty, Georgia 31795

Farrier-Omaha Plant Farms
Box 787
Omaha, Texas 75571

J. P. Fields
Gibsland, Louisana 71028

P. D. Fulwood
Tifton, Ga. 31794

Irrigated Plant Farms
Thorndale, Texas 76577

Joyner's Plant Farm
Route 2, Sedley Road
Franklin, Virginia 23851

Piedmont Plant Co.
Albany, Georgia 31701

Schroer Plant Farms
Valdosta, Georgia 31601

Service Plant Co.
Omega, Georgia 31775

Speedling, Inc.
P.O. Box 7098
Sun City, Florida 33586

Steel Plant Co.
Gleason, Tenn. 38229

Sunsweet Plant Farms
Chula, Georgia 31733

Lewis Taylor Farms
Route 1
Tifton, Georgia 31794

Texas Plant Farms
Jacksonville, Texas 75766

R. P. Thomas
Gibsland, La. 71028

B. Thornill
Wisner, Louisiana 71378

GREENHOUSES

Aluminum Greenhouses Inc.
14615 Lorain Ave.
Cleveland, OH 44111

George Ball Corp.
East Chicago, Ill.

Environmental Dynamics
Box 996 MN
Sunnymead, CA 92388

Gothic Arch Greenhouses
Dept. 1-2, Box 1564
Mobile, AL 36601

Growers Supply Co.
Dept. 1132H
Ann Arbor, MI 48103

Indoor Gardening Supplies
Box 40551H
Detroit, MI 48240

James R. Waite, Inc.
Box 78-N4
Manhasset, NY 11030

Lord & Burnham
Irvington-on-Hudson
Irvington, NY 10533
Maco
Box 109D
Scio OR 97374

McGregor Greenhouses
Box 36-2H
Santa Cruz, CA 95063

National Greenhouse Co.
Dept. 25, Box 5961
Kansas City, MO 64111

Peter Reimuller
The Greenhouseman
Box 2666-F2
Santa Cruz, CA 95063

Sturdi-Built Manufacturing Co.
Dept. H, 11304 SW Boones Ferry Rd.
Portland, OR 97219

The Green House
95-15 Flower St.
Bellflower, CA 90706

Tube Craft, Inc.
1311 W. 80th St.
Cleveland, OH 44102

Turner Greenhouses
Route 117 S
Goldsboro, NC 27530

Vegetable Factory Greenhouses
Box 2235, Dept. H-2
Grand Central Station
New YOrk, NY 10017

Janco Greenhouses
J. A. Neari ng Co., Inc.
Box 348
10788 Tucker St., Dept. H-2
Beltsville, MD 20705

GREENHOUSE PLANTS, BULBS, SEEDS AND SUPPLIES

Abbots Nursery
Route 4, Box 482
Mobile, Ala. 36609

Alberts & Merkel Bros.
P.O. box 537
Boynton Beach, Fla. 33435

Antonelli Bros. 2545 Capitola Rd.
Santa Cruz, Calif. 95010

Ashcroft Orchids
19062 Ballinger Way NE
Seattle 55, Washington

Bart's Nursery
522 Fifth St.
Fullerton, Whitehall, Penn. 18052

Beahm Gardens
2686 E. Paloma St.
Pasadena, Calif. 91107

Better Plastics, Inc.
P.O. Box 820
Kissimmee, Fla.

Buell, Albert H.
Eastford, Connecticut 06242

Burgess Seed and Plant Co.
Galesburg, Michigan 49053

Burnett Bros., Inc.
92 Chambers St.
New York, N'Y' 10007

Burpee, W. Atlee, Co.
Philadelphi a, Penn. 19132

Buynak's
3871 W. 133rd St.
Cleveland, Ohio 44111

Cactus Pete's
5454 Valley Boulevard
Los Angeles 32, Calif.

California Jungle Gardens
11977 San Vicente Blvd.
Los Angeles, Calif 90049

Clarelen Orchids
Fox Bluff on Lake Mendotta
Waunakee, Wisconsin

Cook's Geranium Nursery
712 North Grand
Lyons, Kansas 67554

DeGiorgi Co., Inc.
Council Bluffs, Iowa 51504

De Japer, P. and Sons, Inc.
188 Asbury St.
South Hamilton, Mass 01982

Dolbow, Dorothy J.
149 W. Main St.
Penns Grove, New Jersey

Dos Pueblos Orchid Company
P.O. box 158
Goleta, Calif. 93017

Farmer Seed and Nursery Co.
Faribault, Minn. 55021

Fennell Orchid Co.
The Orchid Jungle
26715 Southwest 157th Ave.
Homestead, Fla. 33030

Field, Henry
Seed and Nursery Co.
Shenandoah, Iowa 51601

Floralite Co.
4124 E. Oakwood Rd.
Oak Creek, Wisc. 53154

French, J. Howard
Baltimore Pike
Lima, Penn. 19060

Fuch's Orchids
Box 113
Naranja, Florida

Girard Nurseries
Geneva, Ohio 44041

Goedert, Robert D.
P.O. box 6534
Jacksonville, Fla. 32205

Green Acres Nursery
14451 Northeast Second St.
North Miami, Fla. 35161

Hausermann's Orchids
Box 363
Elmhurst, Ill. 60128

Hilltop Farm
Rt. 3 Box 216
Cleveland, Texas

House Plant Corner, The
P.O. box 810
Oxford, Maryland 21654

Howard, S. M., Orchid Species
11802 Huston St.
North Hollywood, Calif. 91607

Hoyt, Gordon M.
Orchids
Seattle Heights, Wash. 98063

Ilgenfritz, Margaret
Orchids
Monroe, Mich.

Jones and Scully, Inc.
2200 Northwest 33rd Ave.
Miami, Fla. 33142

Joyner's
P.O. box 12642
St. Petersburg, Fla

Kartuz, Michael J.
92 Chestnut St.
Wilmington, Mass. 91887

Kellar, Fœne V.
827 Main
Harrisonburg, Va. 22801

Krogman's Violetry
1325 Parkway Dr.
Brookfield, Wisconsin 53005

Lager and Hurrell Orchids
426 Morris Ave.
Summit, New Jersey 07901

McLellan, Rod, Co.
1450 El Camino Real
South San Francisco, Calif. 94080

Merry Gardens
Camden, Maine 04843

Moore Miniature Roses
2519 E. Noble Ave.
Visalia, Calif. 93277

Nies Nursery
5710 Southwest 37th St.
West Hollywood, Fla. 33023

Nuccio's Nurseries
3555 Chaney Trail
Altadena, Calif. 91002

Pearce Seed Co.
Moorestown, New Jersey 08057

Reasoner's Tropical Nurseries, Inc.
P.O. box 1881
Bradenton, Fla,

Rivermont Orchids
P.O. Box 67
Signal Mountain, Tenn.

Roehrs, Julius, Co.
East Rutherford, New Jersey 07073

Harry E. Saier
Dimondale, Michigan 48821

Select Violet House
2023 Belmont
Youngstown, Ohio 44501

Smith Potting Soil Co.
2513 E. 19th St.
Tulsa, Okla.
Siputz African Violet Greenhouses
34304 Moravian Dr.
Fraser, Michigan

Stern's Nurseries, Inc.
Geneva, New York 14456

Stewart, Fred A., Inc.
1212 E. Las Tunas Dr.
San Garbiel, Calif.

Terrace View Gardens
Greencastle, Indiana 46135

Tinari Greenhouses
Bethayres, Penn. 19006

Tube Craft, Inc.
1311 W. 80th St.
Cleveland, Ohio 44102

Violets by Elizabeth
3131 Montrose Ave.
Rockford, Ill.

Volkmann Bros. Greenhouses
2714 Minert St.
Dallas, Texas 75129

Wilson Bros.
Roachdale, Indiana 46172

Yoho and Hooker
Box 1165
Youngstown, Ohio 44501

Yoshimura Bonsai Co., Inc.
200 Benedict Ave.
Tarrytown, New York 10591

Young, Dorothy
2937 Rutland
Des Moines, Iowa 50311

Rudolph Ziesenhenne
1130 North Milpas St.
Santa Barbara, Calif. 93103

SOURCES FOR CHEMICALS & SUPPLIES FOR HYDROPONICS

Burwell Geoponics
Box 125-DH
Rancho Santa Fe, Calif. 92067

Hydroculture, Inc.
10016 W. Glendale Ave.
Glendale, Ariz. 85301

Hydrokist, Inc.
7252 Osbun Road
San Bernardino, Calif. 92404

Hydroponic Specialties
Box 1013
Carlsbad, Calif. 92008

Pan American Hydroponics
Box 470
Grapevine, Texas 76051

Royal Garden Farms
Hurricane, Utah 84737

Techni-Culture, Inc.
7335 E. 6th Ave.
Scottdale, Arizona 85252

Pot-grown Clematis—Princess of Wales

WILDFLOWERS

Allgrove
Box 459 H
Wilmington, Mass. 01887

Applewood Seed Co.
Route 3, Box 84
Golden, Colo. 80401

Arthur Eames Allgrove
No. Wilmington, Mass. 01887

Alpenglow Gardens
13328 Trans-Canada Hwy.
North Surrey P.O.
New Westminster, B.C.
Canada

Baldwin Seed Co. of Alaska
Box 1003
Seward, Alaska 99664

Claude A. Barr
Prairie Gem Ranch
Smithwick, So. Dakota 57782

Conley's Garden Center
Boothbay Harbor, Maine 04538

Ferndale Nursery and Greenhouse
Askov, Minn. 55704

Gardens of the Blue Ridge
Ashford, No. Carolina 28603

Griffey Nursery
Rt. 3, Box 17 A
Marshall, No. Carolina 28753

Jamieson Valley Gardens
Rt. 3B
Spokane, Wash. 99203

Laura's Collectors Garden
513 S. Raymond St.
Seattle, Wash. 98118

Leslie's Wildflower Nursery
30 Sumner St.
Methuen, Mass. 01844

Lousenberry Gardens
P.O. Box 135
Oakford, Ill. 62673

Mellinger's Inc.
2310 W. South Range Rd.
North Lima, Ohio 44952

Midwest Wildflowers
Box 64B
Rockton, Ill. 61072

Mincemoyers
R.D. 5, Box 397 H
Jackson, N.J. 08527

Ruth Mooney
Seligman, Mo. 65745

Radford Palmer
R.D. No. 1
Durham, N. H. 03824

Clair Phillips
Grand Rapids, Minn. 55744

Putney Nurseries
Putney, Vt. 05346

The Rock Garden
R.F.D. 2
Litchville, Maine 04350

Clyde Robin
Box 2091
Castro Valley, Calif. 99546

Savage Garden
P.O. Box 163
McMinnville, Tenn. 37110

Siskyou Rate Plant Nurs.
522 Franquette St.
Medford, Ore. 97501

Sky Cleft Gardens
Camp St. Ext.
Barre, Vt. 05641

The Three Laurels
Marshall, No. Carolina 28753

Vick's Wildflower Gardens
Box 115
Gladwyne, Pa. 19035

The Wild Garden
8243 N.E. 119th St.
Kirkland, Wash. 98033

Woodlands Acre Nursery
Marie Sperka
Rt. 2
Crivitz, Wis. 54114

FOOD DEHYDRATER OVEN
P.O. Box 37366
2237 Losantville Ave.
Cincinnati, Ohio 45222
$55.00 with operator's manual included

FOOD AND HERB DRYER
Hickory Hollow
Route One Box 52
Peterstown, W. Va. 24963
$30.00

DRYER PLANS
Hickory Hollow
Route One Box 52
Peterstown, W. Va. 24963

GLASS CANNING JARS

Ball Corporation
1509 S. Macedonia Ave.
Muncie, Indiana 47302
various jars and lids, rubber liners
information from Consumer Division

J. G. Durrand International
Millville, N.J. 08332
Luminarc Canning & Storing Jars

H. E. Lauffer Company, Inc.
Belmont Drive
Somerset, N. J. 08873
"Le Parfait" French Preserving Jars

Kerr Glass Mfg. Corp.
Box 97
Sand Springs, Okla. 74063
various jars and lids, rubber liners
information from Consumer Division

TIN CANS AND HAND-OPERATED SEALERS

Freund Can Company
193 West 84th St.
Chicago, Illinois 60620
312-224-4230

Dixie Canner Equipment Company
P.O. Box 1348
Athens, Georgia 30601
Sheller, Pressure cooker. A few other home canning needs.

FREEZER RECOMMENDATIONS

Because of inadequate space and budget we were unable to test home freezer units ourselves. However, Consumer Reports, produced annually by the Consumers Union, rates these units regularly. Write to Consumer Reports, 256 Washington Street, Mount Vernon, New York, 10550, for the most up-to-date ratings

FREEZING CONTAINERS

Ball Corporation
1509 S. Macedonia Ave.
Muncie, Indiana 47302
Plastic freezer bags and boxes.

CANNING AND PRESERVING EQUIPMENT

More jars and lids, cold-pack canners, pressure canners, pressure cookers, blanchers, stock pots, lifters, holders, wrenchers, choppers, grinders, shredders, crushers, presses, scales, colanders and the like.

Cumberland General Store
Route 3 Box 479
Crossville, Tennessee 38555

Mother's General Store
Box 506
Flat Rock, North Carolina 28731

J. C. Penny Co., Inc.
(Catalogue Address)
Circulation Department
11800 Burleigh Street
Milwaukee, Wisconsin 53201

Montgomery Ward
618 West Chicago Avenue
Chicago, Ill. 60607

REVIEWS

By Tom Riker

THE AUTUMN OF THE EAGLE, George Laycock
A well written, powerful tale of the American eagle. The historical background of the naturalists and the struggle to save the eagle is well worth the price of the book. A look at the vanishing wilderness and the space needed for wild birds and animals.

A VOICE FOR WILDLIFE, Victor B. Scheffer
This book is a plea for sanity in dealing with our wildlife and wild places. Victor Scheffer is a leader in the "new conservation" teaching systems. A must for teachers.

RODALE BOOKS
Year after year this organization turns out good gardening books that everyone interested in food gardening should have in his or her library. We list most of the books under organic reading. As far as we can see this group has done more for American food gardeners than any other publishing house.

THE GREENGROCER, Joe Carcione and Bob Lucas
A must for the shopper. A complete guide to buying fresh fruit and vegetables. Written by a produce man who knows the business. A one-book guide to better buying with an understanding of what you are buying.

THE TERRACE GARDENER'S HANDBOOK, Linda Yang
As a terrace designer and horticulturist I suggest that everyone with a terrace or backyard read and reread this long-overdue book on city gardening. Linda Yang's new book is completely updated and current and packed with answers to all those questions I have been asked for years as a designer and a garden store owner.

By Susan Olshan

THE COMPLETE BOOK OF HOME PRESERVING, Ann Seranne
This book is written by a professional food consultant and has a gourmet interest in good tasting, good looking food. Ms. Seranne surveys the history of food preservation and gives comprehensive directions and helpful hints for canning, jelly-making, pickling, brining, smoking, curing, drying and freezing.

THE COMPLETE BOOK OF PICKLES & RELISHES, Leonard Louis Levinson
A cookbook of more than 500 recipes for pickles and relishes collected from kitchens all over the world. From the opening chapter on commercial pickling to the closing hints for developing prize-winning pickle displays, this book covers it all.

STOCKING UP, How to Preserve the Food You Grow, Naturally, by the Editors of "Organic Gardening and Farming" Rodale Press, Inc.

THE COMPLETE BOOK OF FREEZER COOKERY, Ann Seranne
The largest and most comprehensive on the subject is by food professional Ann Seranne. This book contains directions for freezing fruits, vegetables, herbs, meats, fish, poultry and dairy products. An entire chapter is dedicated to the freezer itself: what kind to buy, where to place it, how to care for it, how to package food for the freezer, and how to arrange stored food.

COOKING FOR YOUR FREEZER, Audrey Ellis
Another freezer cookbook, COOKING FOR YOUR FREEZER, contains a good, though somewhat condensed, introduction on home freezers and how they work, information on how to prepare foods for freezing and many recipes.

VEGETABLE GARDENING

Abraham, George. The Green Thumb Book of Fruit and Vegetable Gardening, Prentice-Hall Inc., Englewood Cliffs, N.J.
Brooklyn Botanic Garden. 1972. The Home Vegetable Garden. Handbook No. 69, Brooklyn Botanic Garden, Brooklyn, N.Y.
Carcione, Joe. The Greengrocer. Chronicle Books, San Francisco, Calif.
Crockett, James U. 1972. Vegetables and Fruits. (Encyclopedia of Gardening Ser.) Time-Life Books, N.Y.
Faust, Joan Lee. Book of Vegetable Growing, N.Y. Times.
Harrison, S.G. 1969. Oxford Book of Food Plants. Oxford Univ. Press, Inc., Fairlawn, N.J.
Hollander, Susan A. and Timothy K. Burrage on Vegetables. Houghton-Mifflin Company.
Knott, J.E. 1962. Handbook for Vegetable Growers, John Wiley & Sons, N.Y.
Herner, Robert C. and J. Lee Taylor. 1974. Home Vegetable Garden Variety Recommendations. Coop. Ext. Ser., Bull. E-760 (a), Michigan State Univ.
Taylor, J. Lee. 1973. Home Vegetable Garden. Coop. Ext. Ser., E-529, Farm Sci., Michigan State Univ.
Thompson, Homer C. and W. C. Kelley, 1957. Vegetable Crops. 5th Ed. McGraw-Hill, Hightstown, N.J.

USDA BULLETINS:
HM-27 Growing asparagus in the home garden
HM-28 Growing beans and peas in the home garden
HM-29 Growing beets, carrots and parsnips in the home garden
HM-30 Growing cabbage and Chinese cabbage in the home garden
HM-31 Growing cauliflower, broccoli and Brussels sprouts in the home garden
HM-32 Growing lettuce in the home garden
HM-33 Growing muskmelons and watermelons in the home garden
HM-34 Growing onions and related plants in the home garden
HM-35 Growing potatoes in the home garden
HM-37 Growing pumpkins and squash in the home garden
HM-38 Growing radishes, turnips and rutabagas in the home garden
HM-39 Growing rhubarb in the home garden
HM-40 Growing sweet corn in the home garden
HM-41 Growing tomatoes in the home garden
HM-42 Tomato cages for the home garden
HM-43 Fall vegetable gardening
HM-44 Ornamental vegetables for the home garden

DOVER PUBLICATIONS

Allen, H. Warner. The Romance of Wine. Dover Publications, Inc. 1971.
Appleyard, Alex. Make Your Own Wine. Dover Publications, Inc. 1972.
Clark, Rosetta E. Herb and Savory Seeds. Dover, 1972.
Coulter, Francis C. A Manual of Home Vegetable Gardening. Dover, 1973.
Fox, Helen Morgenthau. Gardening With Herbs For Flavor and Fragrance. Dover, 1970.
Graham, Verne Ovid. Mushrooms of the Great Lakes Region. Dover, 1970.
Grieve, M., F.R.H.S. Culinary Herb & Condiments. Dover, 1971.
Hedrick, U. P. Fruits For the Home Garden. Dover, 1973.
Kamm, Minnie Watson. Old-Time Herbs For Northern Gardens. Dover, 1971.
Kauffman, C. H. The Gilled Mushrooms (Agaricaceae) of Michigan and the Great Lakes Region, Vol. I & II. Dover, 1971.
Krieger, Louis C. The Mushroom Handbook. Dover, 1967.
McIlvaine, Charles and Robert K. Macadam. One Thousand American Fungi. Dover, 1973.
Northcote, Lady Rosalind. The Book of Herb Lore. Dover, 1971.
Peterson, Maude Gridley. How To Know Wild Fruits. Dover, 1973.
Robbins, Ann Roe. Twenty-five Vegetables Anyone Can Grow. Dover, 1974.
Rohde, Eleanour Sinclair. A Garden of Herbs. Dover, 1969.
Simon, Andre L. How To Make Wines and Cordials From Old English Recipe Books. Dover, 1972.
U.S.D.A. Complete Guide To Home Canning, Preserving and Freezing. Dover, 1973.

FREEZING, CANNING, STORAGE, EXHIBITING

Anonymous. 1970. Storing Vegetables and Fruits in Basements, Cellars, Outbuildings and Pits. Home and Garden Bull. 119, USDA, US Govt. Printing Office, Washington, D.C.
Department of Horticulture. 1972. Storing Garden Vegetables in Michigan. Dept. of Hort. Mimeo, Michigan State Univ., E. Lansing.
Dragonwagon, Crescent. Putting Up Stuff for the Cold Time. Workman Publishing Co.
Ellis, Audrey. Cooking For Your Freezer. Transatlantic Arts.
Forsyth, F. R., C. L. Lockhart and C. A. Eaves. 1972. Home Storage Room for Fruits and Vegetables. Publ. 1478, Canada Dept. of Agr., Ottawa, Ontario.
Franklin, Everett W. 1971. Home Storage of Vegetables. Publ. 268, Ontario Dept. of Agr. and Food, Parliament Bldgs., Toronto.
Gould-Marks, Beryl. Preserves, How to Make and Use Them. Transatlantic Arts, Inc.
Hardin, Carl N. 1968. Selecting and Exhibiting Fruits and Vegetables. Coop. Ext. Serv. Misc. Publc. 386, West Virginia Univ., Morgantown.
Hertzberg, Ruth, Beatrice Vaughan and Janet Greene. Putting Food By. Stephen Greene Press, Brattleboro, Vt.
Levinson, Leonard Louis. The Complete Book of Pickles & Relishes. Garden Way Publishers.
Loveday, Evelyn V. Complete Book of Home Storage of Vegetables and Fruits. Garden Way Publishers.
Lutz, J.M. and R.E. Hardenburg. 1968. The Commercial Storage of Fruits, Vegetables and Florist and Nursery Stocks. rev. Agri. Handbook No. 66, USDA, US Govt. Printing Office, Washington, D.C.
Organic Gardening and Farming Editors. Stocking Up, How to Preserve the Foods You Grow, Naturally. Rodale Press.
Plagemann, Catherine. Fine Preserving. Simon and Schuster, N.Y.
Seranne, Ann. The Complete Book of Home Preserving. Doubleday & Company, Inc.
Seranne, Ann. The Complete Book of Freezer Cookery. Doubleday & Company, Inc.
Taylor, J. Lee. 1973. How to Select Vegetables for Exhibit. 4-H Bull. 397, 4-H Youth Programs, Coop. Ext. Ser. Michigan State Univ., E. Lansing.
Troop, E.W. 1969. Judging Standards for Horticultural Shows. Publc. 1395, Canada Dept. of Agr., Ottawa, Ontario.
Turner, Mary and James Turner. Making Your Own Baby Food. Workman Publishing Co.
Turnquist, Orrin C. 1964. Harvesting and Storing Garden Vegetables. Coop. Ext. Ser. Folder 172, Univ. of Minnesota, St. Paul.
U.S.D.A. Complete Guide to Home Canning, Preserving and Freezing. Dover Publications.
Wejman, Jacqueline. Essays by Charles St. Peter. James & Jellies. 101 Productions.

RECOMMENDED READING

HERBS

Anderson, Frederic. How to Grow Herbs for Gourmet Cooking, Hawthorne Books, Inc. N.Y.
Atkins, F. C. Mushroom Growing Today. Macmillan, N.Y.
Bardswell, Francis A. The Herb Garden, Adam and Charles Black, London.
Brooklyn Botanic Garden Record. Handbook on Herbs, Brooklyn, N.Y.
Brownlow, Margaret. Herbs and the Fragrant Garden, Dacton, Longman, and Todd, London.
Charles, V. K. Some Common Mushrooms and How to Know Them. U.S.D.A. Circular 143. Supt. of Documents, Govt. Print. Office, Washington 25, D. C. 1953.
Christensen, C. M. Common Fleshy Fungi. Burgess, Minneapolis, Minn. 2955.
Clairborne, Craig. Herb and Spice Cook Book, Cooking With Herbs and Spices (new title) Harper-Row, N.Y.
Clarkson, Mrs. Rosetta E. Herbs, Their Culture and Uses, Macmillan, N.Y.
Culpeper, Nicholas. Culpeper's Complete Herbal, London, N.Y. and Foulsham.
Eifert, Virginia S. Exploring for Mushrooms. Dept. of Registration and Education, Ill. State Museum, Springfield, Ill.
Murrill, W. A. Edible and Poisonous Mushrooms. Text and chart. Author, N.Y., 1916. The N.Y. Botanical Garden, N.Y. 58, N.Y.
Pomerleau, R. Mushrooms of Eastern Canada and the U.S. Editions Chantecler, 8125 Blvd. St. Laurent, Montreal 4, Canada, 1951.
Sanecki, Kay N. The Complete Book of Herbs, Macmillan & Company, N.Y.
Smith, A. H. Mushrooms in Their Natural Habitats. Sawyer's Inc., Portland, Oregon, 1949. 1 vol. text, 1 vol. stereokodachrome illustrations, viewer.
Smith, A. H. The Mushroom Hunter's Field Guide. Univ. of Michigan Press, Ann Arbor, Michigan, 1958.
Thomas. W. C. Field Book of Common Mushrooms. Putnam's, N.Y. 1948.
Wakefield, E. M. and Dennis, R. W. G. Common British Fungi. Gawthorn, London, England, 1950.

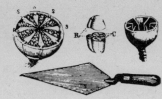

ORGANIC GARDENING REFERENCES

Alkire, Lura Jim and Stanley Schuler. Home Freezing for Everyone, M. Murrows, New York.

Barrett, Thomas. Harnessing the Earthworm, Wedgewood Press.

Beaumont, Arthur. Artificial Manures: The Conservation and Use of Organic Matter for Soil Improvement.

Bowers, Warner and Lucile. Common Sense Organic Gardening. Stackpole Books.

Concan Over, Joseph A. Weeds, Guardians of the Soil, Devin-Adair Co., Old Greenwich, Ct.

Foster, Catharine Osgood. 1972. The Organic Gardener. Vintage Books, Random House, N.Y.

Free, Montague. 1957. Plant Propagation in Pictures. Doubleday and Company, N.Y.

Gillespie, Janet. Peacock Manure and Marigolds, A "No Poison" Guide to a Beautiful Garden. Ballantine Books, N.Y.

Howard, Sir Albert. 1940. An Agricultural Testament, Oxford University Press, N.Y. pp. 253.

Hunter, Beatrice. 1971. Gardening Without Poison, Houghton-Mifflin Co., Boston, Mass.

Hunter, Beatrice. 1971. The Natural Foods Cookbook. Pyramid Publications Inc., N.Y.

Jenks, Joran. Stuff We're Made Of. Devin-Adair Co., Old Greenwich, Ct.

Kervran, C. Louis. 1972. Biological Transmutations. Swan House Publishing, Binghamton, N.Y.

Kohn, Bernice. 1972. The Organic Living Book. Illustrations. The Viking Press, Inc., N.Y.

Kraft, Ken. Fruits For the Home Garden, Monroe, N.Y.

Kraft, Ken. Garden to Order. Doubleday, Garden City, N.Y.

Langer, Richard W. 1972. Grow It! Saturday Review Press, New York.

Lappe, Francis M. 1971. Diet For a Small Planet. Ballantine Book, Inc. N.Y. pp. 300.

Loveday, Evelyn V. 1972. Complete Book of Home Storage of Vegetables and Fruits. Garden Way Publishing Co., Charlotte, Vt. pp. 152.

Ogden, Samuel. 1971. Step-by-Step to Organic Vegetable Growing. Rodale Press, Inc. Emmaus, Pa. pp. 182.

Organic Gardening and Farming Magazine. Rodale Press, Emmaus, Pa.

Organic Gardening and Farming Magazine staff. Guide to Organic Foods Shopping & Organic Living, Rodale Press, Emmaus, Pa.

OG & F staff. 101 Questions Answered About the Wonderful Organic Method of Gardening, Rodale Press, Emmaus, Pa.

OG & F staff. Best Ideas For Organic Vegetable Growing, Rodale Press, Emmaus, Pa.

OG & F staff. All About Mulch, Rodale Press, Emmaus, Pa.

OG & F staff. Best Methods for Growing Fruits and Berries, Rodale Press, Emmaus, Pa.

OG & F staff. Best Ways to Improve Your Soil. Rodale Press, Emmaus, Pa.

OG & F staff. Compost and Mulch Gardening, Rodale Press, Emmaus, Pa.

OG & F staff. Control Garden Pests, Rodale Press, Emmaus, Pa.

OG & F staff. How Organic Methods Bring You Garden Success, Rodale Press, Emmaus, Pa.

OG & F staff. Make Compost In 14 Days, Rodale Press, Emmaus, Pa.

OG & F staff. Organic Fertilizing—The Secret of Garden Experts, Rodale Press, Emmaus, Pa.

OG & F staff. Organic Guide to Planting and Care of Trees and Shrubs, Rodale Press, Emmaus, Pa.

OG & F staff. Sunflower Seed, The Miracle Food, Rodale Press, Emmaus, Pa.

OG & F staff. The Organic Way to Plant Protection, Rodale Press, Emmaus, Pa.

OG & F staff. You Can Grow Beautiful Roses, Rodale Press, Emmaus, Pa.

Philbrick, Helen and Richard Gregg, 1966. Companion Plants—and how to use them. Devin-Adair Company, Old Greenwich, Ct. pp. 111.

Philbrick, John and Helen. 1971. Gardening For Health: The Organic Way. Steiner, Rudolf Publications. Blauret, N.Y. pp. 93.

Picton, Lionel J. 1949. Nutrition and The Soil, Devin-Adair Co., Old Greenwich,

Portala Institute. 1971. The Last Whole Earth Catalog. Distributed by Random House, N.Y. pp. 447.

Prendergast, Chuck, Introduction to Organic Gardening, North Qualith paperback.

Rabb, R. L. and F. E. Gutherie. Concepts of Pest Management. North Carolina University Press, Raleigh, N.C.

Rodale Press, J. I. Rodale. Ed and Staff, Emmaus, Pa.

Rodale Press. 1945. Pay Dirt. pp. 245.

Rodale Press. 1966. The Organic Way to Plant Protection. pp. 355.

Rodale Press. 1969. Best Ideas For Organic Vegetable Growing. pp. 197.

Rodale Press. 1970. Lawn Beauty the Organic Way. pp. 411.

Rodale Press. 1971. How to Grow Vegetables and Fruit by the Organic Method. pp. 926.

Rodale Press. 1971. The Complete Book of Composting. pp. 1007.

Rodale Press. 1971. The Organic Directory. pp. 168.

Rodale Press. 1971. The Organic Way to Mulching. pp. 192.

Rodale, Jerome. Encyclopedia of Common Diseases, Rodale Press, Emmaus, Pa.

Rodale, Jerome. How to Landscape Your Own Home, Rodale Press, Emmaus, Pa.

Rodale, Robert, The Best Gardening Ideas I Know, Rodale Press, Emmaus, Pa.

Rodale, Robert. 1971. The Basic Book of Organic Gardening, Ballantine Books, Inc., N.Y. pp. 377.

Rossi, Barbara. 1971. Everyday Organic Gardening, Universal Publishing and Distributing Corp., N.Y.

Schuler, Stanley. Gardening From the Ground Up, Macmillan, New York.

Schuler, Stanley. Gardening With Ease, Macmillan, New York.

Schuler, Stanley. How To Grow Almost Everything. M. Evans, Philadelphia, Pa.

Seeling, R. A. 1971. Science, Fairy Tales and "Organic" Food. United Fresh Fruit and Vegetable Association Yearbook. Washington, D. C. pp. 51-59.

Stephenson, W. A. Seaweed in Agriculture and Horticulture.

Stout, Ruth and Richard Clemence. 1971. The Ruth Stout No-Work Garden Book. Rodale Press, Emmaus, Pa. pp. 218.

Swan, L. A. 1964. Beneficial Insects, Harper and Row Publications, N.Y.

The Organic Morning Glory Message Magazine. San Francisco, Calif.

Tyler, Hamilton. Organic Gardening Without Poisons. Van Nostrand-Reinhold, N.Y.

Wickenden, Leonard. 1972. Gardening With Nature. Fawcett Publications, N.Y.

Wittrock, Gustave L. 1971. The Pruning Book. Rodale Press, Inc. Emmaus, Pa. pp. 176.

FRUITS

Abraham, George. 1970. The Green Thumb Book of Fruit and Vegetable Gardening. Prentice-Hall Inc., Englewood Cliffs, N.J.

Childers, Norman F. 1973. Modern Fruit Science 5th ed. Rutgers Univ. Press, New Brunswick, N.J.

Davidson, R.H. and L.M. Peairs. 1966. Insect Pests of Farm, Garden and Orchard. 6th ed. John Wiley & Sons, Inc. N.Y.

Darrow, George M. The Strawberry. Holt, Rinehart and Winston, Inc., N.Y.

Eck, Paul and N.F. Childers eds. 1967. Blueberry Culture. Rutgers Univ. Press, New Brunswick, N.J.

Kraft, Ken and Pat Kraft. 1968. Fruits for the Home Garden. William Morrow and Co., Inc. N.Y.

Logsdon, Gene. Successful Berry Growing. Rodale Press, Emmaus, Pa.

Shoemaker, James S. 1975. Small Fruit Culture. 4th ed. Ari Publishing Co., Inc. Westport, Ct.

Teskey, Benjamin J. and J.S. Shoemaker. 1972. Tree Fruit Production. 2nd ed. Ari Publishing Co., Inc., Westport, Ct.

Tukey, Harold B. 1964. Dwarfed Fruit Trees. The Macmillan Co., N.Y.

Winkler, A. J., et. al. General Viticulture. University of Calif. Press.

USDA Publications. Copies of the following bulletins can be obtained from the Publications Division, Office of Communication, U.S. Department of Agriculture, Washington, D.C. 20250. The bulletin code number is needed with your order.

Bridge Grafting and Inarching Damaged Fruit Trees. L-508.

Why Fruit Trees Fail to Bear. L-172.

Insects on Deciduous Fruits and Free Nuts. G-190.

Establishing and Managing Young Apple Orchards. F-1897.

Growing Apricots for Home Use. G-204.

Growing Blackberries. F-2160.

Thornless Blackberries for the Home Garden. G-207.

Growing North American Bunch Grapes. F-2123.

Control of Grape Diseases and Insects in the Eastern U.S. F-1893.

Growing Raspberries. F-2165.

Controlling Diseases of Raspberries and Blackberries. F-2208.

Strawberry Culture: Eastern United States. F-2028.

DISEASES AND INSECTS, BEES

Chupp, C. and Sherf, A.F. 1960. Vegetable Diseases and Their Control. Ronald Press Co., N.Y.

Cress, Donald C. and Potter, H.S. 1974. Home Vegetable Garden Disease, Insect Control. Coop. Ext. Ser. Bull. E-760(b), Michigan State Univ.

Mitchell, Theodore B. Bees of the Eastern United States. The North Carolina Agricultural Experiment Station.

Morse, Roger A. Bees & Beekeeping. Cornell University Press.

Reed, L.B. and Raymon E. Webb. 1971. Insects and Diseases of Vegetables in the Home Garden. rev. Home and Garden Bull. 46, USDA, U.S. Govt. Printing Office, Washington, D.C.

Walker, John C. 1952. Diseases of Vegetable Crops. McGraw-Hill Book Co., Princeton, N.J.

Westcott, Cynthia. 1964. Gardener's Bug Book. 3rd ed. Doubleday & Co., Inc. Garden City, N.Y.

Westcott, Cynthia. 1971. Plant Disease Handbook. 3rd ed. Doubleday & Co., Inc., Van Nostrand Reinhold Co., N.Y.

ORNAMENTALS

Bryan, John E. and Coralie Castle. The Edible Ornamental Garden. 101 Productions, San Francisco, Cal.

Carpenter, Philip L., et. al. Plants in the Landscape. W. H. Freeman & Co., San Francisco, Cal.

Cherry, Elaine C. Fluorescent Light Gardening. Van Nostrand Reinhold Company, N.Y.

Cruso, Thalassa. Making Things Grow. Alfred A. Knopf, N.Y.

Douglas, James Sholto. Beginner's Guide to Hydroponics. Drake Publishers, Inc., N.Y.

Eaton, Jerome A. Gardening Under Glass. Macmillan, New York.

Elbert, George A. The Indoor Light Gardening Book. Crown Publications, N.Y.

Elbert, George A. and Virginia F. Elbert. Growing Herbs Indoors. Crown, N.Y.

Schery, Robert W. A Perfect Lawn. Macmillan, New York.

Yang, Linda. The Terrace Gardener's Handbook. Doubleday & Co., N.Y.

Zion, Robert L. Trees for Architecture and the Landscape. Van Nostrand Reinhold, N.Y.

BOOKLETS—USDA

HM-51 Petunias for color in the home landscape
HM-52 Growing the daylily and lily-of-the-valley
HM-53 The care and handling of lilies
HM-54 Why peonies fail to bloom
HM-55 Wildflower protection in Michigan
HM-56 The culture of ferns
HM-58 Proper care of houseplants
HM-59 Growing avocados in the home
HM-60 Air layering of house plants
HM-61 Home forcing of spring flowering bulbs
HM-62 Foliage plants
HM-63 Tree Geraniums
HM-64 Dish gardens
HM-65 Terrariums
HM-66 Suggested plants for terrariums or dish gardens
HM-67 Pot culture of the Norfolk Island Pine
HM-68 Jerusalem cherries
HM-69 Proper Care of Christmas Flowering Plants
HM-70 Cookbook of annuals in the home garden
HM-71 Making compost for the home garden
HM-72 Growing sunflowers for seed and ornamental value
HM-73 Weed control in the home vegetable garden
HM-74 Weed control in landscape and flower plantings
HM-75 Growing grapes in the home garden
HM-76 Working with wet areas in the landscape
HM-77 Why plants fail to bloom

Laplander's Sledge,

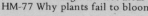

USEFUL REFERENCES FOR GREENHOUSE VEGETABLE PRODUCTION

Compiled by Hunter Johnson, Jr.
Extension Vegetable Specialist
University of California, Riverside

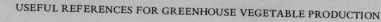

TOMATOES:

Greenhouse Tomatoes. Guidelines for Successful Production. Wittwer, S. H. and Shegemi Honma. Michigan State University Press, East Lansing. 1972.

Commercial Production of Greenhouse Tomatoes. Stoner, Allan K. USDA Agriculture Handbook No. 382. 1971. Order from U. S. Government Printing Office, Washington, D. C.

Profitability of Tomato Production under Plastic Greenhouses. Dhillon, P. S. and P. J. Kirschling. A. F. 335. College of Agriculture and Environmental Science, Rutgers University, New Brunswick, New Jersey. 1971.

Growing Tomatoes in Plastic Greenhouses. Larsen, J. E. Texas Agricultural Extension Service, Texas A & M University, College Station, Texas. 1970.

Growing Greenhouse Tomatoes in a Peat-Vermiculite Media. Veg Crops Offset Series No. 33. Taylor, G.A. and R.L. Flannery. College of Agriculture and Environmental Science, Rutgers University, New Brunswick, New Jersey. 1970. (revised)

Growing Greenhouse Tomatoes in Ohio. Brooks, William M. Publication SB-19. Ohio State University Cooperative Extension Service, Columbus. 1969.

Production of Greenhouse Tomatoes in Ring Culture or in Trough Culture. Sheldrake, Raymond,Jr., and Stewart Dallyn. Cornell Veg Crops Mimeo No. 149. Cornell University, Ithaca, New York, 1969.

Tomato Production in Plastic Greenhouses. Schales, F. D. and P. H. Massey, Jr. Publication 154. Extension Division, Virginia Polytechnic Institute, Blacksburg. 1968.

Greenhouse Tomatoes: Structures, Production, Marketing. Corgan, J. N., et al. Circular 387. Cooperative Extension Service, New Mexico State University, University Park, 1967.

Growing Tomatoes in Greenhouses. Vincent, C. L. Station Circular 276. Washington State University Agricultural Experiment Station, Pullman. 1961. (revised)

Tomato Growing by Prescription. Dorey, Ruben, Blanford Press, Ltd. London, England. 1960. (out of print)

A New Approach to Fertilizing Greenhouse Tomatoes. Larsen, J. E., C. D. Welch, and C. Gray. Dept. Information Rep. No. 16. Texas Agricultural Extension Service, Texas A & M University, College Station, Texas.

CUCUMBERS:

Greenhouse Cucumber Production, Johnson, Hunter, Jr. AXT-n79. Agricultural Extension Service, University of California, Riverside. 1972.

Growing Long Seedless Cucumbers in Plant-Raising Greenhouses. Loughton, Arthur, Factsheet AGDEX 292/20. Ontario Department of Agriculture and Food, Horticultural Research Institute, Vineland Station, Ontario, Canada. 1971.

Manual of Cucumber Production. Ministry of Agriculture, Fisheries and Food. Bulletin 205. Published by Her Majesty's Stationery Office, London, England. 1969.

GENERAL

Controlled Environment Agriculture: A Global Review of Greenhouse Food Production. Dalrymple, Dana G. Foreign Agricultural Economic Report No. 89. USDA Foreign Development Division, Economic Research Service. Order from U. S. Government Printing Office, Washington, D. C. 1973.

Greenhouse Vegetable Production. Johnson, Hunter, Jr. OSA No. 249. Agricultural Extension Service, University of California, Riverside. 1972. (revised)

Greenhouse Vegetable Production in Ontario. Wiebe, John. Publication 526. Dept. of Agriculture & Food, Parliament Bldgs., Toronto, Ontario, Canada. 1971.

Proceedings Third Annual Southwest Greenhouse Vegetable Conference, Las Vegas, Nevada, 1971. Published by the Max C. Fleischman College of Agriculture, University of Nevada, Reno.

Greenhouse Vegetable Research. Researfch Summaries. Published annually in April by Ohio Agricultural Experiment Station, Wooster.

INSECT & DISEASE CONTROL:

Greenhouse Tomatoes — Disease Control. Partyka, Robert E. and Leonard J. Alexander. SB-16. Ohio State University Cooperative Extension Service. Columbus. 1972.

Greenhouse Vegetable Production Recommendations. Publication 365. Ontario Dept. of Agriculture & Food, Parliament Bldgs., Toronto, Ontario, Canada. 1974.

Insect Control on Greenhouse Vegetables. Bulletin 517. Prepared by the Greenhouse Insect Control Recommendation Committee, Cooperative Extension Service, Ohio State University, Ohio Agricultural Research & Development Center, Wooster. 1974.

The Glasshouse Environment in Relation to Diseases and Insects. Baker, Kenneth. Department of Plant Pathology, University of California, Berkeley. 1965.

CONSTRUCTION, HEATING AND VENTILATION:

Greenhouse Location and Orientation. Walker, J. N. and G. A. Duncan. Misc. 397. Cooperative Extension Service, University of Kentucky, Lexington. 1971.

Preservative Treatment of Greenhouse Wood. Duncan, G. A. and J. N. Walker. Misc. 396. Cooperative Extension Service, University of Kentucky, Lexington. 1971.

Design and Operation of Greenhouse Cooling System. Allen, W. S. AENG 1. Agricultural Engineering Dept., Texas A & M University, College Station. 1971.

Air Makes the Difference. Sheldrake, Raymond, Jr. American Vegetable Grower. January 1971

Small Plastic Greenhouses. Parsons, Robert A. AXT-328. Agricultural Extension Service, University of California, Davis. 1971. (revised)

Plastic Greenhouse. Parsons, Robert A. MA-22. Agricultural Extension Service, University of California, Davis. 1970.

Heating and Ventilating Greenhouses.Roberts, W. J. Rutgers University, New Brunswick, New Jersey. 1969.

The Greenhouse Climate Control Handbook. Acme Engineering & Manufacturing Company, Muskogee, Oklahoma. 1969.

Double Covering a Film Greenhouse Using Air to Separate the Layers. Roberts, William J., Associate Extension Specialist in Agricultural Engineering, Rutgers University, New Brunswick, New Jersey. Paper presented at Eighth Annual National Agricultural Plastics Conference, San Diego, California, 1968.

Developments in Air-Supported Plastic Greenhouses. Rodda, E. D., R. M. Perkins, and A. H. Holland. Transactions of the American Society of Agricultural Engineers, St. Joseph, Michigan. 1967.

Planning, Constructing, and Operating Plastic Covered Greenhouses. Sheldrake, Raymond, Jr. Cornell Miscellaneous Bulletin 72, Cornell University, Ithaca, New York. 1966.

Temperature Patterns in a Poly-Tube Ventilated Greenhouse. Parvin, P. E., R. H. Sciaroni, and R. G. Curley. California Agriculture. University of California, Berkeley. November 1966.

V.P.I. Gothic Greenhouse. Gray, R. W. II, McNeil Marshall, and P. H. Massey, Jr. Circular 760B. Virginia Cooperative Extension Service, Virginia Polytechnic Institute, Blacksburg. 1966.

Building Hobby Greenhouses. USDA Agriculture Information Bulletin No. 357. 1973. For sale by Superintendent of Documents, U.S. Government Printing Office, Washington, D.C. 20402.

SOILLESS CULTURE, HYDROPONICS, AND SAND CULTURE:

Beginners Guide to Hydroponics. Douglas, James Sholto. Drake Publishers, Inc., New York. 1972.

The Use of Polyethylene Barriers Between Soil and Growing Medium in Greenhouse Vegetable Production. Jensen, Merle H. Environmental Research Laboratory, University of Arizona, Tucson. 1971.

A Peat-Vermiculite Mix for Growing Transplants and Vegetables in Trough Culture. Larsen, John E. Texas A & M University, College Station. 1971.

Soilless Culture of Commercial Greenhouse Tomatoes. Maas, E. F. and R. M. Adamson. Information Division, Canada Department of Agriculture, Ottawa, Ontario, Canada. 1971.

Growing Greenhouse Tomatoes in a Peat-Vermiculite Media. Veg Crops Offset Series No. 33. Taylor, G. A. and R. L. Flannery. College of Agriculture and Environmental Science, Rutgers University, New Brunswick, New Jersey. 1970. (revised)

Nutriculture — A Guide to the Soilless Culture of Plants. Maynard, D. N. and A. V. Barker. Pub. No. 41. University of Massachusetts, Amherst. 1970.

Hydroponics, the Bengal System. Douglas, J. S. Oxford University Press. 1970.

Hydroponics as a Hobby — Growing Plants Without Soil. Leaflet 423. Butler, J. D. and N. F. Oebker. College of Agriculture and Environmental Science, Rutgers University, New Brunswick, New Jersey. 1970. (revised)

Production of Greenhouse Tomatoes in Ring Culture or in Trough Culture. Sheldrake, Raymond, Jr., and Stewart Dallyn. Cornell Veg Crops Mimeo No. 149. Cornell University, Ithaca, New York. 1969.

Soilless Cultivation and its Application to Commercial Horticultural Crop Production. Stoughton, R. H. Food & Agriculture Organization, Rome, Italy. 1969. Can be purchased at $1 per copy from: Administrative Unit, Distribution & Sales Section, Food & Agriculture Organization of the United Nations, Via delle Terme di Caracalla, Rome, 00100, Italy. When ordering, also mention the symbol of this document: MI/95768.

Guide to Commercial Hydroponics. Schwarz, Meir. Israel Universities Press, P.O. Box 7145, Jerusalem, Israel. 1968.

Sand and Water Culture Methods Used in the Study of Plant Nutrition. Hewitt, E. J. Commonwealth Bureau of Horticultural and Plantation Crops. Technical Bulletin No. 22. Second Edition. 1966.

Growing Plants in Solution Culture. Epstein, Emanuel and B. A. Krantz. AXT-196. University of California Agricultural Extension Service, Berkeley. 1965.

Cornell Peat-Lite Mixes for Commercial Plant Growing. Boodley, James W. and Raymond Sheldrake, Jr. Information Bulletin 43. Cornell University, Ithaca, New York. 1973.

Profitable Growing Without Soil. Hollis, H. F. The English Universities Press, Ltd. London, England. 1964.

Commercial Hydroponics, Facs and Figures. Bentley, Maxwell. First South African Edition. Benton Books, Johannesburg, South Africa. 1959.

The U. C. System for Producing Healthy Container-Grown Plants. Baker, Kenneth F., et al. Manual 23. University of California Agricultural Experiment Station, New Brunswick, New Jersey. 1956.

The Water-Culture Method for Growing Plants Without Soil. Hoagland, D. R. and D. I. Arnon. Circular 347. University of California Agricultural Experiment Station, Berkeley. 1950. (out of print)

Soilless Growth of Plants. Ellis, Carleton and M.W. Swaney. Second Edition, Reinhold Publishing Company, New York. 1947.

The Complete Guide to Soilless Gardening. Gericke, W. F. Prentice Hall, New York. 1940.

Automatically Operated San Culture Equipment. Eaton, Frank M. Jour. Agric. Res. 53(6):433-443. 1936.

CHILDREN'S BOOKS

Casey, Lydian. Outdoor Gardening. Lerner Publications Co., 1975.

Cooper, Elizabeth K. and Padraic Cooper. Sweet and Delicious Fruits of Tree, Bush and Vine. Children's Press, Chicago, Ill. 1973.

Dickson, Naida. The Biography of a Honeybee. Lerner Publications Co., 1974.

Fenten, D. X. Indoor Gardening. Franklin Watts, Inc. 1974.

Jones, Claire, et. al. Pollution: The Food We Eat. Lerner Publications Co. 1974.

Scheib, Ida. The First Book of Food. Revised by Carol E. Welker. Franklin Watts, Inc. 1974.

Skelsey, Alice and Gloria Huckaby. Growing Up Green, Parents and Children Gardening Together. Workman Publishing Co. 1973.

Sweningson, Sally. Indoor Gardening. Lerner Publications Co. 1975.

WILDFLOWERS

Courtenay, Booth and James H. Zimmerman. Wildflowers and Weeds. Van Nostrand Reinhold Company.

Fernald, Merritt Lyndon and Alfred Charles Kinsey; Revised by Reed C. Rollins. Edible Wild Plants of Eastern North America. Harper and Row Publishers, N.Y.

Klimas, John E. and James A. Cunningham. Wildflowers of Eastern America. Alfred A. Knopf.

Orr, Robert T. and Margaret C. Orr. Wildflowers of Western America. Alfred A. Knopf.

GENERAL ECOLOGY

Commoner, Barry. The Closing Circle. Alfred A. Knopf, N.Y.

Huxley, Julian. Man in the Modern World.

Laycock, Autumn of the Eagle. Charles Scribners Sons, N.Y.

Scheffer, Victor B. A Voice for Wildlife. Charles Scribners Sons, N.Y.

POISONOUS PLANTS

The Case for the Guilty Garden

by Robert F. Lederer

Executive Vice President

The American Association of Nurserymen

I've been reading a number of books, magazine articles, and press releases with some really great titles—if you're a mystery story fan. Look at these:

"Deadly Harvest"
"The Sinsister Garden"
"Poison in the Backyard"
"The Deadly Dozen"

Pretty scarey, aren't they! These days when mass hysteria seems almost a way of life, it takes a pretty bloodcurdling title to attract attention.

And that would be alright, perhaps, except that THESE books and articles and newspaper columns aren't mystery-suspense stories. They all deal with the same subject: some plant life that grows contains substances harmful to humans under certain conditions.

That has been true, of course, since the beginning of the world—and it is a fact which everyone of us must learn at about the same time we learn to live with matches, electricity, water, strange dogs and cats, traffic in the street, medicine cabinets, table salt, and any number of other elements in our environment.

But that's not the way the subject is being approached these days. The approach taken by most of the materials presented to readers makes a very strong impression that mother nature is lurking in every dark corner waiting to pounce with her green, growing weapons of death. And, unfortunately, a normally responsible news media has let its guard down and appears more than anxious to print such damaging and false claims.

INVESTIGATING THE "CRIME"

So let's investigate this "crime" . . . take a look at some of the facts . . . try to put them into a proper perspective . . . and see if we don't come up with a solution to the case.

First—let's look at the weapon: poison.

A booklet written by a physician carries this statement: In 1967, 2,890 poisonings by plants occurred; 2,884 of these involved children under five years of age." Think of it, 2,884 little children poisoned by plants in a single year!

The problem with this kind of statement is that it is misleading. In fact, knowing that it was written for laymen, a case can be made accusing the doctor of making a FALSE statement. The fact is, the word POISON is usually interpreted by the average reader to mean DEATH. What DOES it mean?

"The term 'poisonous plant' designates many kinds of plants as well as a wide range of poisoning effects. The effects may generally be classified as: allergies; dermatitis or skin irritation; internal poisoning caused by eating plant parts; and mechanical injury from sharp prickles, spines or thorns." That's the definition in one of the better authoritative books on the subject, written by a botanist and a pediatrician, James Hardin and Jay Arena.

So that's the weapon we're talking about. Plant poisons. They can make you sneeze, itch, scratch you, and some, taken in the wrong dosage, can make you sick or even kill you.

THE SOURCE OF THE "CLUES"

But we need more facts, and there seems to be just one source of information on reported cases of POISONING from plants. That's the National Clearinghouse for Poison Control Centers in Washington, D. C. The statistical information in the books and magazine articles and newspaper releases on the subject all comes from that Clearinghouse. It was established in 1958 as the Poison Control Division of the Food and Drug Administration's office of Product Safety to collect the experiences of the hundreds of Poison Control Centers in cities all across the country—and to distribute information to them.

It's interesting to see what can happen with the kind of statistics the Clearinghouse publishes.

Look at this headline from a supposedly reputable magazine: "Poisonous Plants Grow Everywhere—Even In Your Own House. And a Surprising Number of People Have Died from Eating Them."

Or this statement from a magazine article: "Of the 13,000 victims stricken by plant poisoning last year, some fatally, 12,000 were children."

Those are very frightening statements. But let's check them against the Clearinghouse report from which the writers got their information.

53 people were hospitalized that year for suspected ingestion of harmful plants. One person died—from eating a quantity of rhubarb leaves.

So . . . the writer who used the phrase "some of them fatally" was writing about one person. And the other writer's "surprising number of people" also turned out to be that same individual. This kind of journalism is, of course, readily accepted by the reader but in fact serves no one's best interests.

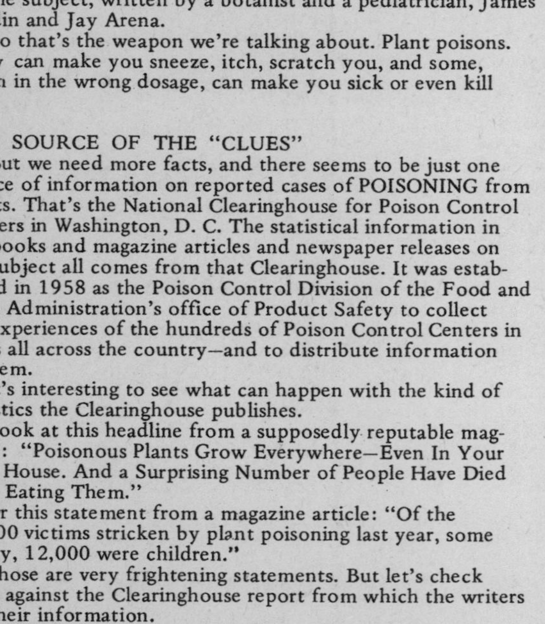

So let's look even more closely at the data that is available from the National Clearinghouse for Poison Control Centers.

Although the Control Centers were originally established to serve the medical profession, last year 86% of the calls dealing with plants came from non-medical people. Instead of answering questions from medical professionals, the greatest number of cases were enquiries by concerned parents calling for information when their child had eaten some form of plant. This is a valuable service the Control Centers provide, and the first thing a parent should do is call a physician or the Poison Control Center at the slightest suspicion that a child has eaten something "off limits."

But look what happens then. When the report of an inquiry is sent into the National Clearinghouse it goes into the computer as a reported case of ingestion—and a writer who is careless . . . either accidentally or intentionally . . . can translate that as a case of plant poisoning.

Here's an actual example. Somewhere in this country last year someone called a Poison Control Center and said, "My child has just eaten some wild blackberries! Is he in danger?" The people at the Poison Control Center probably looked in their records and said, "No danger. They're perfectly safe." (I'm quoting the blackberry information from the Hardin and Arena book I mentioned earlier, by the way.)

So far, so good. But that call about blackberries . . . and two others like it . . . are listed in the Clearinghouse report for 1970—as cases of ingestion—and blackberries are listed in their run-down of "Types of Poisoning." That's preposterous!

You think that's an isolated example? Not at all. A quick count shows at least 26 titles which don't belong on the list. "Beans" for instance. Just plain "beans!" Mulberries. Spices. That's right . . . a category identified as "spices." Wild strawberries. Catnip. Nutmeg is on the list . . . and that's not even commonly available except as a processed food.

When that kind of list is used to make a case about plant dangers, the whole business is blown out of proportion . . . with the result that plants in general are suspected of being poisonous.

The National Clearinghouse reports a total of 4,308 cases of plant ingestion in 1970—and one-third of those were in reference to the kind of plants or products I've talked about which don't belong on a list of dangerous plants.

As I said, there were 4,308 cases reported by the Clearinghouse. 381 of them required treatment of one kind or another. That's 9% of the total, and that means 91% of the cases did not have treatment described in the report. 90 persons went to the hospital—35 of them under five years old.

Two deaths were reported from the ingestion of plants. One of those was from an overdose of Peyote—an hallucinogenic drug that grows wild in the southwest. The other death was attributed to crabapple. Now, the medical authorities agree that crabapples, raw, in jelly, or in pies are perfectly safe and rather delicious . . . so we questioned the Clearinghouse on that one. Here's what they told us: "The 1970 death listed to crabapple was in error and due to a punching error." In other words, it was a clerical mistake. No death occurred. But just wait: soon you' ll be reading lurid newspaper stories about the deadly crabapple which is striking down innocent victims! And when that happens, please remember—it just ain't so.

PAUSE FOR A MID-POINT SUMMARY

I've tried to make two points so far.

One . . . there are a number of reckless writers publishing frightening but false information based largely on what must be concluded to be an intentional misuse of statistics collected by the National Clearinghouse for Poison Control Centers.

Two . . . it's fairly easy to misuse those statistics if you want to, because the way they're put together needs some serious overhauling. I'm happy to report that, partly as a result of our investigations, the Clearinghouse is taking steps in that direction, particularly in the proper labeling of some of their charts and tables. For example, they have written to us saying, "Type of Poisoning' on page 9 of the September-October 1971 Bulletin would be more accurately worded 'Type of product reported to be ingested.'" That's good progress.

A THIRD POINT

Now there's a third point to make. It is possible (and probably more profitable) to write half-truths or folklore stories for the sake of drama. Here's a sample.

One writer said, "Rhododendron contains a poison that has shown up in honey made by bees that visited the plant." He's right as far as he went. But what he didn't say is that the honey had such a vile taste no one could accidentally eat the large quantity needed to be harmful.

Another one wrote: "Many people have died merely from eating steaks that have been speared on oleander twigs and roasted over a fire." The leaves and wood of the oleander are not suitable for human consumption, and people have been made ill from using their branches as skewers. Avoid doing that. But we have not been able to find any record of anyone having been fatally poisoned in this way. Our conclusion—and that of the medical authorities we have researched—is that this is an old wives' tale. It makes a spine-tingling story for a certain type of writer—but there aren't facts to back it up.

THE POINSETTIA STORY

And one of the most persistent old wives' tales of them all is finally being put to rest, I think. Two scientists at the Ohio State University have published the findings from an elaborate research study they made with poinsettias. You've heard or read about poinsettias. "Take a bite of a poinsettia leaf and you'll die."

Well, Robert Stone and W. J. Collins mixed batches of homogenized poinsettia parts and force-fed the mixture in large doses to 160 laboratory rats. (They had to force-feed the stuff because poinsettias really taste awful.)

What happened? Nothing. None of the rats threw up, or stopped eating, or got unromantic . . . or died.

In other words, their results coincided with those of other scientific investigators who have analyzed the whole plant and found the extracts to contain common plant sterols or triterpenes—none considered commonly toxic. And they are unable to find any authenticated record of a person dying from eating poinsettias.

With the new research report in his hands, the Director of the Division of Hazardous Substances and Poison Control at the Food and Drug Administration's Bureau of Product Safety has said: "We concur with the investigators that large doses of homogenate of the poinsettia plant are not toxic to the rat." And he said, " . . . to our knowledge the ingestion of small amounts of the poinsettia plant has not presented a serious health hazard."

John M. Kingsbury, perhaps the foremost writer on the subject, has informed Stone and Collins that he is modifying his public statements in accord with their findings about poinsettias.

And perhaps those popular writers who have a field day every Christmas season with their dire warnings about the prettiest holiday plant of them all will take a cue from the FDA and Dr. Kingsbury. I suppose it will take awhile.

POSITIVE ACTION

What am I saying—that we should be unconcerned about poisoning from plants . . . or that the general public should not be informed on the subject? Not at all.

There are plants which are hazardous if they are used improperly. Some cause allergies. Some skin rashes. Some can cause death.

Some are found in the home environment—and everyone should know them. Most are found in the wilderness, and anyone going on an outing should be able to identify them.

THE SOLUTION

What is needed is accurate, reasonable and factual information, free of flaming words and alarmist phrases that some seeking recognition seem to enjoy using.

In a minute I want to suggest five steps which I think must be taken as protection against the danger which exists from those plants which are harmful. But first I want to say a word about a couple of ideas which have been encouraged by the sensational literature on the subject . . . ideas that deserve to be rejected.

TWO COURSES TO BE REJECTED

Now-and-then someone will propose that all plants identified as poisonous be outlawed and destroyed. This is just plain impractical. There is no way to eliminate all plant life which could be harmful if it were eaten in the strong quantity or in the wrong way.

Because potato shoots or leaves can cause indigestion doesn't mean that we stop eating potatoes. The one death from plant poisoning recorded in 1969 was from eating rhubarb leaves—but that doesn't mean we should make rhubarb pie illegal.

Another suggestion has been that all plants with harmful potential be LABELED with some kind of warning. In most cases, plants involved in reports of adverse effects are native plants which people come in contact with in the wild, and the task of labeling them is pretty ludicrous.

Even if a label were required to indicate that a plant may be hazardous, there is no assurance the label would be kept on a plant once it is added to the home landscape. The underground stems of the beautiful iris, for example, cause a digestive upset if they are eaten. It is unlikely that a label on an iris bulb would be kept on display after planting.

Another point. 73% of the reports of cases involving plants going through the National Clearinghouse in 1970 involved children under five years of age. That's an age when written instructions have very little value. It's an age when children are taught to stay out of the medicine cabinet, out of the street, out of electric sockets . . . and away from a long list of threatening things.

And that brings me to the positive steps I think are so important.

FIVE PROTECTIVE STEPS

First . . . and this is the best rule of all. The effective way to deal with the problem of hazardous substances—ANY suspicious substances—is to avoid them. Just never eat anything that is unknown to you. And, as part of that rule, be sure every child in the family learns the same lesson.

Second: become familiar with all the plant-life in your area, yard and home. Know them by name. Your retail nursery center or florist can help you identify those which could cause an adverse reaction under certain circumstances . . . and it will be good to have the scientific name for them.

The third point: If your children use any kind of seeds or fruits or stems as playthings or as skewers for meat or marshmallows, be sure you know what they are. If you're not sure, substitute them with something you recognize.

Fourth: avoid smoke from any burning substance—including plant material—unless you know exactly what it is and that it is harmless.

And the fifth point I want to make is this: in any case of suspected ingestion of an unknown substance call your doctor or the Poison Control Center. Be prepared, if at all possible, to give the name of the substance involved, and save any evidence which might help identify it.

IN CONCLUSION

So there you have another perspective on the "case for the guilty garden."

Some 700 plants have been identified as "poisonous" . . . but that means anything from a mild allergy to a severe indigestion or, in isolated cases, death if the wrong part of the wrong plant is eaten in the wrong way. Hysterical shouts and impetuous, ill-advised action are not the answer. Accurate information—given to the public in a properly prepared program of education—is.

The men and women of the nursery and florist industries want every individual to be informed, so everyone can enjoy nature's bountiful growing gifts—in safety, without fear.

INDEX continued on page 320

FEEDBACK FEEDBACK FEEDBACK FEEDBACK FEEDBACK FEEDBACK FEEDBACK FEEDBACK FEEDBACK FEEDBACK FEEDBACK FEEDBACK FEEDBACK FEEDBACK FEEDBACK

Dear Sir:
I just received my copy—wow! What a delightfully pleasant, extraordinary surprise! Thank you, for a difficult job, beautifully done. The source lists are indeed valuable and so gratefully appreciated. As you said, the iceberg has just been barely delineated. Hopefully, our technology that put a man on the moon, will also discover some things about the vegetable kingdom that may make that moon step seem ordinary. A book was published a couple years ago entitled THE SECRET LIFE OF PLANTS by Peter Thompkins & Christopher Bird that was fascinating, though-provoking reading and begged for further study. I tried without avail to obtain further info from the bibliography via the local library and Wyoming University. If you haven't read the book please do. Perhaps you and your firm would have a better chance at locating a lending source for further study than small me. If you do—boy! would I appreciate hearing about it. Wyoming is a great place to live and a true gardener's challenge, however, it is in the middle of no where as far as education and source tradewinds blow. Again, my very best wishes for further successes with the Catalogue. And thank you again.

Mrs. Nanette Galloway
Lander, Wyoming

When we contacted the publishers of the book you mention, we were informed that it is classified as an occult book rather than a gardening book. Perhaps that is why you had difficulties following up in your search for more information. The book is one of many that we believe tends to remystify the study of plant life rather than demystify it. Until people like Thompkins and Bird come up with better evidence to support their case, we will rely on the solid, useful type of information we offer for your consideration in GARDENER'S CATALOGUE books. Perhaps the tale that follows will explain why. A number of years ago, we had the occasion to visit Clive Baxter, one of the leading exponents of plant perception theories in the country. At the time he was also one of the leading proponents of lie detector technology and was conducting experiments with polygraphs and plants. He claimed his work showed plants responded to emotions in their environment. We waited as he hooked a polygraph machine to a philodendron plant. The demonstration that followed was not particularly conclusive. Finally, one of us leaped suddenly from his chair shouting, "You die, filthy philodendron" and ground a hot cigarette out on one of the leaves. The polygraph registered no response at all. Baxter claimed the plant was too exhausted to emote at that point. We were not convinced. What do you think about it?

Gentlemen:
Congratulations on a unique publication and More by all means.
You may be interested to know about The Terrarium Association and publication: "Terrarium Topics." Although only nine months old we have a national membership (with queries coming from abroad). Perhaps you may care to elaborate further with a paragraph or two—how to plant a cider jug or similar gallon sized bottle? There are photographs to illustrate the process as well as some vintage drawings of terraria.

Robert C. Baun
The Terrarium Association
57 Wolfpit Ave.
Norwalk, Ct. 06851

P.S. The Post Office returned this material stamped Addressee Unknown. It was mailed to the box No. given in The Gardener's Catalogue.

You have produced a nice publication. We will have more on terrariums in other editions of THE GARDENER'S CATALOGUE. Your first letter was returned because of a typo which appeared in the first printing. The correct post office box is No. 3302, not 3202. The post office people have been very helpful in forwarding mail to us. But, some letters and cards got through their net and were returned.

MORE FEEDBACK ON PAGES 4 &5

INDEX

FRUITING BRANCHLET OF PEAR.

HE GARDENER'S "FRIEND" PROPAGATOR.
Isometrical Perspective View.

CODLIN MOTH AND GRUB (CARPOCAPSA POMONANA).

FEEDBACK

Dear fellow gardener,

The Gardener's Catalogue is really enlightening and delightful! I have some tidbits of information to pass along that I have gleaned from various publicized sources and experience that I think might interest you. The first tidbit concerns the soil. A good book on organic gardening is Gardening Without Poisons by Beatrice Trum Hunter. (Berkeley Pub., 200 Madison Ave., N. Y. 10016) Another author, the late Jethro Kloss who wrote Back to Eden (Lifeline Books, Box 1552, Riverside, Cal. 92502) talks about a fast organic method of revitalizing the soil and growing earlier and more crops every year with a revolutionized system of crop rotation and plowing. This next tidbit I ran across in The Herbalist Almanac (put out by Indiana Botanic Gardens, which they borrowed from The Domestic Encyclopedia, by Dr. A. F. Willich: Dr. Willich said that Seawrack, if properly applied, could fertilize soil up to 8 years, while manure or dung has to be replaced every 2 or 3 years. There is a company which advertised a product (similar to the Jiffy products) in the January issue of Southern Living (published by the Progressive Farmer Co., Birmingham, Ala.) called Sea-gro seed starter cubes that have liquid seaweed as fertilizer. The company claims that the liquid also speeds up germination. The company is Sudbury Laboratory Inc., Sudbury, Mass. (Minimum order is 6 dozen for less than $3.00.) Another tidbit that I found out about through experience is that freshly picked and shredded purple or green sweet basil repels snails. I often used the under-developed flower stalks, which I snipped to encourage bushy growth, to form a solid ring around the base of the stem, after transplanting because the shock made the plants more vulnerable to pests. Renew every week as needed, be sure to do this before sundown because snails come out at night. I do not think that cutworms like it either, because they did not touch any of the basil when I set it out. I do not know this as fact, but I had a lot of basil growing close to the chives, parsley and carraway; while our "neighborhood night-stalking" rabbit ate the monkey grass and other goodies it did not touch the basil or anything in the proximity of it. In your list of Botanical outlets, you left out Clarks Natural Herbs, Chafee, N. Y. 14020. They grow many of their own herbs, and sell them by the pound, half pound and box. Their price list is free.

I hope my information has been helpful to you and I hope that I have aroused your curiosity—curiosity is the initiating drive or force behind investigation and experimentation. I am looking forward to your next catalogue.

Could you please inform me about the buyer's co-operative that you spoke of in the introduction? I think that an article about the laws and regulations concerning standards of quality in seeds, plant stock and supplies would be a great aid to consumers.

Yours truly,
Jane Southerland
Trussville, Alabama

We don't know about Jethro Kloss' ability as a gardener. But, we do know that many of the concoctions he suggests elsewhere in the book are very out dated and may be dangerous. As we noted earlier in the book, the future of the buyer's co-op is still in question. Truth in seed labeling and a discussion of USDA grades appears in this volume. More on the subject should be included in our future books.

SKELETON PLOW.

The Catalogue is surely a big undertaking and I welcome its invitation to make a contribution. Dr. Ben Clark's introductory article on germination and seed testing belongs at the beginning of the book where you have put it. It mentions that State Seed Laboratories conduct seed tests for residents. A directory of these Laboratories may be obtained from the Secretary of the Association of Official Seed Analysts: R. H. Hoffman, New Jersey State Seed Lab., P. O. Box 1888, Trenton, N. J. 18625. This list includes commercial seed laboratories which do service testing. After I retired from the seed industry, I edited a booklet describing contributions, which the Society of Commercial Seed Technologists have made to the science of seed testing since it was formed in 1922. You are welcome to use any information contained in enclosed copy of the book. The Society publishes a quarterly News Letter obtainable from its editor: Jane Barris, Jacob Hartz Seed Co., Box 946, Stuttgart, Arkansas, 72160.

Your list of Botanical Gardens on page 296 does not include some of Boerner Botanical Gardens which is Milwaukee County's large and popular establishment. A description of it is enclosed. You do mention some of its collections on pages 83 and 198.

I visited the Honeywell Gardens at Wabash, Ind. this summer and found its 110 acres of planting to be outstanding. Trust of interest -

Yours truly,
Wells Oppel
Wauwatosa, Wis.

MORE FEEDBACK ON PAGES 4 & 5

INDEX INDEX INDEX INDEX INDEX INDEX INDEX INDEX INDEX INDEX FEEDBACK FEEDBACK FEEDBACK FEEDBACK FEEDBACK FEEDBACK FEEDBAC
INDEX INDEX INDEX INDEX INDEX INDEX INDEX INDEX INDEX INDEX FEEDBACK FEEDBACK FEEDBACK FEEDBACK FEEDBACK FEEDBACK FEEDBAC

320

INDEX

MUSTARD Common.

FRUITING BRANCHLET OF PEAR.

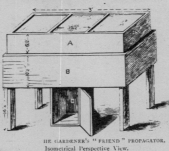

THE GARDENER'S "FRIEND" PROPAGATOR.
Isometrical Perspective View.

CODLIN MOTH AND GRUB (CARPOCAPSA POMONANA).

FEEDBACK

Dear fellow gardener,

The Gardener's Catalogue is really enlightening and delightful! I have some tidbits of information to pass along that I have gleaned from various publicized sources and experience that I think might interest you. The first tidbit concerns the soil. A good book on organic gardening is Gardening Without Poisons by Beatrice Trum Hunter. (Berkeley Pub., 200 Madison Ave., N. Y. 10016) Another author, the late Jethro Kloss who wrote Back to Eden (Lifeline Books, Box 1552, Riverside, Cal. 92502) talks about a fast organic method of revitalizing the soil and growing earlier and more crops every year with a revolutionized system of crop rotation and plowing. This next tidbit I ran across in The Herbalist Almanac (put out by Indiana Botanic Gardens, which they borrowed from The Domestic Encyclopedia, by Dr. A. F. Willich: Dr. Willich said that Seawrack, if properly applied, could fertilize soil up to 8 years, while manure or dung has to be replaced every 2 or 3 years. There is a company which advertised a product (similar to the Jiffy products) in the January issue of Southern Living (published by the Progressive Farmer Co., Birmingham, Ala.) called Sea-gro seed starter cubes that have liquid seaweed as fertilizer. The company claims that the liquid also speeds up germination. The company is Sudbury Laboratory Inc., Sudbury, Mass. (Minimum order is 6 dozen for less than $3.00.) Another tidbit that I found out about through experience is that freshly picked and shredded purple or green sweet basil repels snails. I often used the under-developed flower stalks, which I snipped to encourage bushy growth, to form a solid ring around the base of the stem, after transplanting because the shock made the plants more vulnerable to pests. Renew every week as needed, be sure to do this before sundown because snails come out at night. I do not think that cutworms like it either, because they did not touch any of the basil when I set it out. I do not know this as fact, but I had a lot of basil growing close to the chives, parsley and carraway; while our "neighborhood night-stalking" rabbit ate the monkey grass and other goodies it did not touch the basil or anything in the proximity of it. In your list of Botanical outlets, you left out Clarks Natural Herbs, Chafee, N. Y. 14020. They grow many of their own herbs, and sell them by the pound, half pound and box. Their price list is free.

I hope my information has been helpful to you and I hope that I have aroused your curiosity—curiosity is the initiating drive or force behind investigation and experimentation. I am looking forward to your next catalogue.

Could you please inform me about the buyer's co-operative that you spoke of in the introduction? I think that an article about the laws and regulations concerning standards of quality in seeds, plant stock and supplies would be a great aid to consumers.

Yours truly,
Jane Southerland
Trussville, Alabama

We don't know about Jethro Kloss' ability as a gardener. But, we do know that many of the concoctions he suggests elsewhere in the book are very out dated and may be dangerous. As we noted earlier in the book, the future of the buyer's co-op is still in question. Truth in seed labeling and a discussion of USDA grades appears in this volume. More on the subject should be included in our future books.

SKELETON PLOW.

The Catalogue is surely a big undertaking and I welcome its invitation to make a contribution. Dr. Ben Clark's introductory article on germination and seed testing belongs at the beginning of the book where you have put it. It mentions that State Seed Laboratories conduct seed tests for residents. A directory of these Laboratories may be obtained from the Secretary of the Association of Official Seed Analysts: R. H. Hoffman, New Jersey State Seed Lab., P. O. Box 1888, Trenton, N. J. 18625. This list includes commercial seed laboratories which do service testing. After I retired from the seed industry, I edited a booklet describing contributions, which the Society of Commercial Seed Technologists have made to the science of seed testing since it was formed in 1922. You are welcome to use any information contained in enclosed copy of the book. The Society publishes a quarterly News Letter obtainable from its editor: Jane Barris, Jacob Hartz Seed Co., Box 946, Stuttgart, Arkansas, 72160.

Your list of Botanical Gardens on page 296 does not include the name of Boerner Botanical Gardens which is Milwaukee County's large and popular establishment. A description of it is enclosed. You do mention some of its collections on pages 83 and 198.

I visited the Honeywell Gardens at Wabash, Ind. this summer and found its 110 acres of planting to be outstanding. Trust of interest -

Yours truly,
Wells Oppel
Wauwatosa, Wis.

MORE FEEDBACK ON PAGES 4 & 5

INDEX INDEX INDEX INDEX INDEX INDEX INDEX INDEX INDEX INDEX INDEX FEEDBACK FEEDBACK FEEDBACK FEEDBACK FEEDBACK FEEDBACK FEEDBACK
INDEX INDEX INDEX INDEX INDEX INDEX INDEX INDEX INDEX INDEX FEEDBACK FEEDBACK FEEDBACK FEEDBACK FEEDBACK FEEDBACK FEEDBACK

320

INDEX continued on page 320

FEEDBACK FEEDBACK FEEDBACK FEEDBACK FEEDBACK FEEDBACK FEEDBACK FEEDBACK FEEDBACK FEEDBACK FEEDBACK FEEDBACK FEEDBACK FEEDBACK FEEDBACK

Dear Sir:
I just received my copy—wow! What a delightfully pleasant, extraordinary surprise! Thank you, for a difficult job, beautifully done. The source lists are indeed valuable and so gratefully appreciated. As you said, the iceberg has just been barely delineated. Hopefully, our technology that put a man on the moon, will also discover some things about the vegetable kingdom that may make that moon step seem ordinary. A book was published a couple years ago entitled THE SECRET LIFE OF PLANTS by Peter Thompkins & Christopher Bird that was fascinating, though-provoking reading and begged for further study. I tried without avail to obtain further info from the bibliography via the local library and Wyoming University. If you haven't read the book please do. Perhaps you and your firm would have a better chance at locating a lending source for further study than small me. If you do—boy! would I appreciate hearing about it. Wyoming is a great place to live and a true gardener's challenge, however, it is in the middle of no where as far as education and source tradewinds blow. Again, my very best wishes for further successes with the Catalogue. And thank you again.
Mrs. Nanette Galloway
Lander, Wyoming

When we contacted the publishers of the book you mention, we were informed that it is classified as an occult book rather than a gardening book. Perhaps that is why you had difficulties following up in your search for more information. The book is one of many that we believe tends to remystify the study of plant life rather than demystify it. Until people like Thompkins and Bird come up with better evidence to support their case, we will rely on the solid, useful type of information we offer for your consideration in GARDENER'S CATALOGUE books. Perhaps the tale that follows will explain why. A number of years ago, we had the occasion to visit Clive Baxter, one of the leading exponents of plant perception theories in the country. At the time he was also one of the leading proponents of lie detector technology and was conducting experiments with polygraphs and plants. He claimed his work showed plants responded to emotions in their environment. We waited as he hooked a polygraph machine to a philodendron plant. The demonstration that followed was not particularly conclusive. Finally, one of us leaped suddenly from his chair shouting, "You die, filthy philodendron" and ground a hot cigarette out on one of the leaves. The polygraph registered no response at all. Baxter claimed the plant was too exhausted to emote at that point. We were not convinced. What do you think about it?

Gentlemen:
Congratulations on a unique publication and More by all means.
You may be interested to know about The Terrarium Association and publication: "Terrarium Topics." Although only nine months old we have a national membership (with queries coming from abroad). Perhaps you may care to elaborate further with a paragraph or two—how to plant a cider jug or similar gallon sized bottle? There are photographs to illustrate the process as well as some vintage drawings of terraria.
Robert C. Baun
The Terrarium Association
57 Wolfpit Ave.
Norwalk, Ct. 06851

P.S. The Post Office returned this material stamped Addressee Unknown. It was mailed to the box No. given in The Gardener's Catalogue.

You have produced a nice publication. We will have more on terrariums in other editions of THE GARDENER'S CATALOGUE. Your first letter was returned because of a typo which appeared in the first printing. The correct post office box is No. 3302, not 3202. The post office people have been very helpful in forwarding mail to us. But, some letters and cards got through their net and were returned.

MORE FEEDBACK ON PAGES 4 &5